12th Edition

ARCHITECTURE

Residential Drafting and Design

by

Clois E. Kicklighter

W. Scott Thomas, M. Ed., MCCTE
Instructor, Architectural Design Drafting
Shadow Ridge High School
Surprise, AZ

Joan C. Kicklighter, CFCS
Coauthor of *Residential Housing and Interiors* and *Upholstery Fundamentals*
Terre Haute, IN

Publisher
The Goodheart-Willcox Company, Inc.
Tinley Park, Illinois
www.g-w.com

Manufactured in the United States of America.

Library of Congress Catalog Card Number 2015037831

ISBN 978-1-63126-315-6

3 4 5 6 7 8 9 – 18 – 21 20 19 18

Cover image: ShortPhotos/Shutterstock.com
Back cover image: Alita Bobrov/Shutterstock.com

Library of Congress Cataloging-in-Publication Data

Names: Kicklighter, Clois E., author. | Thomas, W. Scott, author.
Title: Architecture residential drafting and design / by Clois E. Kicklighter, W. Scott Thomas.
Description: 12th edition. | Tinley Park, IL : Goodheart-Willcox Company, Inc., [2018] | Includes index.
Identifiers: LCCN 2015037831 | ISBN 9781631263156
Subjects: LCSH: Architecture, Domestic—Designs and plans. | Architectural design.
Classification: LCC NA7115 .K46 2017 | DDC 728--dc23 LC record available at http://lccn.loc.gov/2015037831

Preface

Amy Walters/Shutterstock.com

Architecture: Residential Drafting and Design provides the basic information necessary for planning various types of dwellings. It presents basic instruction in preparing architectural working drawings using traditional (manual) as well as computer-based methods. Further, the text was developed to serve as a reference for design and construction principles and methods. It is intended to help build the necessary technical skills to communicate architectural ideas in an understandable, efficient, and accurate manner.

Architecture: Residential Drafting and Design is organized so that the content is presented in the logical order of use. The functional organization and layout of the text, the step-by-step procedures, and the easy-to-understand discussions make it easy for learners to learn and for teachers to teach.

Architecture: Residential Drafting and Design covers all phases of architectural drafting and design. The text is highly illustrated with both traditional and modern products and building techniques. The colorful layout includes numerous features to expand on chapter topics and promote interest. In addition to providing information on architectural drafting, design, and construction, the text includes excellent coverage of computer-aided drafting and design (CADD), architectural CADD applications, parametric modeling applications, and building information modeling (BIM). The text includes detailed coverage on creating architectural plan drawings, sections, details, elevations, and presentation drawings. It covers architectural styles, room planning, materials and construction methods, building systems, green building technology, and career opportunities. The text presents construction methods and products such as steel framing, engineered wood products (EWPs), concrete block, exterior insulation finish systems (EIFS), insulated concrete forms (ICFs), structural insulated panels, geothermal heat pumps, in-house water treatment devices, and green building products. The text also contains an extensive reference section. Features appearing throughout the text address topics such as employability skills, entrepreneurship, workplace ethics, designing for health and safety, and sustainable building practices.

Topics that address issues related to handicapped access are covered throughout the text. These topics address allowing for clear space, providing lower countertops, planning extra light, and so on.

Many of the end-of-chapter activities are designed to be completed using a CADD system. While these activities are intended to be completed with CADD, most can be completed using traditional drafting methods for those who do not have access to a CADD system.

The parametric modeling procedures presented in this text address 3D modeling tools and processes used in parametric modeling software. These procedures cover methods and techniques for creating a 3D parametric model of a building, also known as a building information model (BIM). An introduction to BIM processes is presented in Chapter 12, *Building Information Modeling.*

This text is intended for architectural drafting and design classes in high schools, vocational and technical schools, community colleges, universities, adult learner curriculum, and apprenticeship programs. A complete learning package for diverse classes in architectural design is available. The package includes a comprehensive workbook that is designed for use with the text. Also included are drawing files for completing drafting and design problems with CADD software. This is a *complete* teaching/learning package. This text will also serve as a valuable reference for builders, carpentry classes, skilled tradeworkers, interior designers, appraisers, and building departments.

About the Authors

During his career, Dr. Clois E. Kicklighter was a nationally known educator and the author of several books in the fields of architecture, drafting, and construction technology. He held a variety of industrial, teaching, and administrative positions and retired as dean and professor at the School of Technology at Indiana State University. He held the highest leadership positions in the National Association of Industrial Technology (NAIT). Dr. Kicklighter was awarded the respected Charles Keith Medal for exceptional leadership in the technology profession.

Dr. Kicklighter's published textbooks include *Drafting & Design: Engineering Drawing Using Manual and CAD Techniques*; *Modern Masonry: Brick, Block, Stone*; *Residential Housing and Interiors*; *Upholstery Fundamentals*; and *Modern Woodworking*.

W. Scott Thomas is an instructor of architectural design drafting for the Signature Architecture Program at Shadow Ridge High School, Dysart Unified School District, in Surprise, Arizona. Scott teaches residential and commercial architectural design, structural steel detailing/modeling, civil drafting, and GIS technology.

Scott has been a secondary and postsecondary educator for 25 years and is the owner and principal building designer of Thomas Design Associates, LLC. Scott also does extensive work with the Arizona Department of Education's CTE Division as a member of numerous architectural design drafting curriculum development and guidelines committees. During his teaching career, Scott has had national champions in architectural drafting competitions at the SkillsUSA National Leadership and Skills Conference in 2012 and 2014 (with Shadow Ridge High School) and in 2005 (with Northwest Education Center in Phoenix, Arizona). In 2015, the Signature Architecture Program at Shadow Ridge High School was named the Outstanding Technical Education Program by the Association for Career and Technical Education (ACTE). In 2016, the International Technology and Engineering Educators Association (ITEEA) awarded Scott with the Teacher Excellence award and the Signature Architecture Program with the Program Excellence award.

Scott's educational background includes a master's degree in career and technical education and a bachelor's degree in education from Northern Arizona University. He is a master certified career and technical educator (MCCTE) with the Association for Skilled and Technical Sciences (ASTS) and is a Director Emeritus of the American Design Drafting Association (ADDA).

Joan C. Kicklighter is the coauthor of *Residential Housing and Interiors*, *Upholstery Fundamentals*, and instructional materials in family and consumer sciences. She has taught classes in business and family and consumer sciences at the high school and adult levels. Mrs. Kicklighter's educational background includes a baccalaureate degree from Indiana State University and graduate work at Eastern Michigan University. She is certified in Family and Consumer Sciences.

ADDA Approved Publication

ADDA

The content of this text is considered a fundamental component to the design drafting profession by ADDA International. This publication covers topics and related material, as stated in the ADDA Curriculum Certification Standards and the ADDA Professional Certification Examination Review Guides. Although this publication is not conclusive, with respect to ADDA standards, it should be considered a key reference tool in pursuit of a professional career.

Reviewers

The authors and publisher wish to thank the following industry and teaching professionals for their valuable input into the development of **Architecture: Residential Drafting and Design**.

Brian Aranguena
Drafting Instructor
ADDA Deputy Director
Lake Havasu High School
Lake Havasu City, AZ

Mike Coler
Instructor
South Plains College
Levelland, TX

Brian Emerson
Engineering and Robotics Lab Instructor
Center for Advanced Research and Technology
Clovis, CA

Leon Kassler
Technology Faculty Professor
York County Community College
Wells, ME

Alex Kyser
Skilled and Technical Sciences Education Programs Professional
Nevada Department of Education
Carson City, NV

Justin Miley
ACE Coordinator, Architecture Instructor
MacArthur High School
Irving, TX

Andrew Ray
Program Chair—AS Construction Programs
Valencia College
Orlando, FL

Jack Reece
Drafting Instructor
Wheeler High School
Marietta, GA

Sheryl Sutphen
Instructor
Plano West Senior High School
Plano, TX

Dr. Steve Sweigart
Engineering/Architecture Instructor
Johns Creek High School
Johns Creek, GA

Harold Weston
Drafting/Technical Design Instructor
George Jenkins High School
Lakeland, FL

Kenneth C. Zamora, Architect
Architecture Instructor
Applied Technology Division
Fresno City College
Fresno, CA

Acknowledgments

The authors and publisher would like to thank the following individuals and companies for their assistance and contributions.

AFM Corporation
Melvin Denny Ako
Alpine Structures
Alvin & Company
American Forest & Paper Association
American Institute of Steel Construction
American Institute of Timber Construction
Amwood Homes Inc.
Andersen Windows Inc.
APA—The Engineered Wood Association
Appel Design Group Architects
ARBA Studios
Archaus Architects Limited
Arcways, Incorporated
Meritxell Arjalaguer
Arthur Rutenberg Homes, Inc.
The Atrium Door and Window Corporation
Eric K. Augspurger
Autodesk, Inc.
Marcin Balcerzak
BELL Architects
BluPrint Design + Build
Boise Cascade Corporation
Boral Roofing
Broan-NuTone LLC
David Brownlee
Caradco
Carrier Corporation
CertainTeed Corporation
ConForm Global
Cor-A-Vent, Inc.
Costello Builders Inc.
Crane Co.
David Wright House, LLC
Department of Veterans Affairs
DesignGroup
Dennis Dixon
Donley Brothers Company
Dryvit Systems, Inc.
Environmental Protection Agency
FEMA
First Alert
Darlana Fowler
The Garlinghouse Company
Helmuth A. Geiser, Member AIBD
General Electric Company
Genesis Studios, Inc.
Georgia-Pacific Corporation
Josh Gibson
Goodys Home Design
Graphisoft
Hans Construction
Heatilator, Inc.
Hewlett-Packard
Anice Hoachlander
International Code Council
James Hardie Siding Products
K & S Testing and Engineering, Inc.
Brad L. Kicklighter
Kohler Co.
K.Taylor Architectural Renderings
Lizz Layman
Lennox Industries, Inc.
Leviton Manufacturing Co., Inc.
Lite-Form, Inc.
Martin Drafting and Design, Inc.
Marvin Windows and Doors
Eilis Maynard
Morgan Products, Ltd.
The National Audubon Society
Network Rail and Jacobs
NOEM - noem.com
Norandex/Reynolds Building Products
Osmose Wood Products
The Panel Clip Company
Anthony J. Panozzo
Thomas Paradis, Northern Arizona University
Peachtree Doors, Inc.
Pella Windows and Doors
Potlatch Forests, Inc.
Rob Potts
Pozzi Wood Windows
Radiant Heat Inc.; Uecker, E.
Andrew Ray
Reward Wall Systems, Inc.
Sater Design Collection, Inc.
SHoP Architects
SoftPlan Systems, Inc.
SpaceJoist/Alpine
Square D Company
Staedtler Mars GmbH & Co.
Superior Fireplaces
Tiffany N. Thomas, Ph.D.
Trus Joist
TrusWal Systems, Inc.
UDA Technologies
US Department of Commerce Weather Bureau
US Department of Energy
US Geological Survey
US Green Building Council
Vanguard Plastics Inc.
Vermont Castings
Ryan Verpooten
Viridian Reclaimed Wood
WCI Communities, Inc.
Weather Shield Mfg., Inc.
The Williamson Company
Woodfold Manufacturing

G-W Integrated Learning Solution

Together, We Build Careers

At Goodheart-Willcox, we take our mission seriously. Since 1921, G-W has been serving the career and technical education (CTE) community. Our employee-owners are driven to deliver exceptional learning solutions to CTE students to help prepare them for careers. Our authors and subject matter experts have years of experience in the classroom and industry. We combine their wisdom with our expertise to create content and tools to help students achieve success. Our products start with theory and applied content based upon a strong foundation of accepted standards and curriculum. To that base, we add features and tools designed to help promote effective and efficient teaching and learning. G-W recognizes the crucial role instructors play in preparing students for careers. We support educators' efforts by providing time-saving tools that help them plan, present, and assess with traditional and digital activities and assets. We provide an entire program of learning in a variety of print, digital, and online formats, including economic bundles, allowing educators to select the right mix for their classroom.

Student-Focused Curated Content

Goodheart-Willcox believes that student-focused content should be built from standards and accepted curriculum coverage. Standards from Precision Exams were used as a development reference in this text. **Architecture: Residential Drafting and Design** also uses a building block approach with attention devoted to a logical teaching progression that helps students build upon their learning. We call on industry experts and teachers from across the country to review and comment on our content, presentation, and pedagogy. Finally, in our refinement of curated content, our editors are immersed in content checking, securing figures that convey key information, and revising language and pedagogy.

Precision Exams Certification

Goodheart-Willcox is pleased to partner with Precision Exams by correlating **Architecture: Residential Drafting and Design** to the Architectural Design I Standards. Precision Exams Standards and Career Skills Exams were created in concert with industry and subject matter experts to match real-world job skills and marketplace demands. Students that pass the exam and performance portion of the exam can earn a Career Skills Certification™. Precision Exams provides:

- Access to over 140 Career Skills Exams™ with pretest exams and posttest exams for national Career Clusters.
- Instant reporting suite access to measure student academic growth.
- Easy-to-use, 100% online exam delivery system.

To see how **Architecture: Residential Drafting and Design** correlates to the Precision Exams Standards, please visit www.g-w.com/architecture-2018 and click on the Correlations tab. For more information on Precision Exams, including a complete listing of Career Skills Exams™ and Certificates, please visit https://www.precisionexams.com.

Flashon Studio/Shutterstock.com

Text Features

Objectives.
List providing an overview of the chapter content. The objectives explain what should be understood on completion of the chapter.

Key Terms.
List of important terms introduced in the chapter. The terms in this list are displayed in ***bold italic type*** when they first appear in the chapter text.

Green Architecture.
Features addressing green building technology with a focus on materials and construction methods used in residential construction.

Employability.
Features addressing preparing for employment and facing challenges encountered on the job.

Chapter 11

Designing for Sustainability

Objectives

After completing this chapter, you will be able to:

- Explain the difference between sustainability and green building.
- List seven major sustainable design concepts and explain how they apply to residential design.
- Explain the concept of building information modeling.
- Identify national certification programs for green building.

Key Terms

building information modeling (BIM)
daylighting
dioxins
ecosystem
fly ash
geothermal energy
gray water
green building
greenwashing
net zero energy building
nonrenewable energy source
persistent bioaccumulative toxicants (PBTs)
reclaiming
recycling
renewable energy source
semi-volatile organic compounds (SVOCs)
solar energy
solar harvesting
sustainability
sustainable building
volatile organic compounds (VOCs)
weatherization
xeriscaping

"Sustainability," "green building," "going green"—you have almost certainly heard these terms. Surprisingly, many people do not have a clear understanding of their meanings. Most of us are aware that our current lifestyles have had unintended negative consequences on the environment. We are beginning to realize that practices that harm the environment, along with the depletion of natural resources, will have a long-term effect on our ability to survive on this planet. Sustainability is a positive response to this problem. It involves people who are looking for ways to reduce our "footprint," or impact on the environment, and help preserve the Earth and its resources for future generations. See **Figure 11-1**. This chapter explains the concepts of sustainability and green building as they apply to residential architecture and construction.

Sustainability vs. Green Building

Many people use the terms *sustainability* and *green building* to mean exactly the same thing. In fact, they are different. Strictly speaking, the concept of ***sustainability*** includes meeting the needs of humans for food, housing, and other needs and wants, without using up resources that cannot be replaced, and without affecting the environment negatively. By extension, a ***sustainable building*** is one that can be built, used for a long time, and then reused or recycled, all without using up resources and impacting the environment negatively. Achieving true

255

Chapter 2 Basic House Designs 39

Green Architecture
Container Housing

One efficient type of green housing is the *container house*, which is made from a shipping container, also known as an *Intermodal Steel Building Unit (ISBU)*. See **Figure A**. ISBU construction is a good option for affordable housing, emergency housing, and storage. The trend started from a "grass roots" movement to re-use salvaged or surplus metal shipping containers from land and sea transportation of goods. There is no longer a surplus, however, and most container housing today uses new material.

The containers are made of non-corrosive *Corten steel*, a durable metal designed to withstand the elements by making its own protective layer of rust. Although each container is structurally independent, the ISBUs fit together to form "building blocks" for house construction. They can be stacked and connected in various geometric shapes and sizes to provide the framework of the house. See **Figure B**. Openings cut into the containers accommodate doors, windows, and walls.

By leaving the metal exposed, the designer can give the house an industrial look. For a more traditional look, the exterior can be covered with siding, masonry, or stucco. The interior can be finished with the same materials used in traditional construction.

A container house qualifies as "green" because it is made of sustainable and reusable materials. Converting a container into a house uses less energy than recycling the steel. A container has a life span of about 100 years. In addition, a container house can be designed and built for energy efficiency.

A Hansenn/Shutterstock.com

B Martin Bilek/Shutterstock.com

Figure A—These student apartments were made from recycled steel shipping containers.
Figure B—Windows and doors are cut into the ISBUs, often before they are set in place. In this design, two sides have also been removed to increase the size of the living area to span two or more containers.

The one-and-one-half story house has some additional building costs that are not incurred with a one-story house. Stairs, dormers, and complicated roofs are the principal sources of additional costs. Other disadvantages include less mobility (stairs), low ceilings and limited window space on the second level, and more difficult maintenance due to the added height.

The one-and-one-half-story design is versatile. It can be adapted to various styles such as the Saltbox, Tudor Revival, and Craftsman. The most recognizable is the traditional Cape Cod. See **Figure 2-10**. It can be built as a small two-bedroom, one-bath house with the attic unfinished. The attic can be finished later, deferring the costs of expansion until additional space is needed.

Chapter 14 Floor Plans 335

the opening, rather than a centerline. In concrete masonry unit construction, some drafters prefer to dimension the window and door openings to their centers rather than to the rough openings.

Interior walls are commonly dimensioned to the faces of stud walls. Refer to **Figure 14-11A**. One method is to give the dimensions to the same side of the walls throughout the drawing. Depending on school or office practice, dimensions may also be given to both sides of interior walls. Another practice is to dimension interior walls to their centers. In this case, a short line is drawn down the middle of the wall at the termination point of the dimension to show that the center is indicated.

Overall dimensions are necessary to provide the total length and width of the structure. Always verify the dimensions by adding all the partial dimensions together. Their sum should equal the overall dimension. For example, in **Figure 14-11A**, 4′ + 11′ + 5′ equals 20′, which matches the overall 20′ dimension. One of the most frequent errors in dimensioning is that partial dimensions do not add up to equal the total distance.

The overall length and width of major wall segments should be lengths that are multiples of 4′. Building material sizes are keyed to this dimension and much unnecessary waste will result if this rule is not applied.

Frequently, notes are required to present information that cannot be represented by a conventional dimension or symbol. These notes

Employability
Creating a Portfolio

When you interview for an architectural job, your interviewer will expect you to present samples of your work to showcase your qualifications. A *portfolio* is a selection of work that you collect and organize to show your qualifications, skills, and talents.

Some people prefer a print portfolio that contains actual drawings and other items they have created. Others choose to create an e-portfolio, or digital portfolio. Both types have advantages and disadvantages. For example, an e-portfolio is much easier to transport than a print portfolio—all you need is a USB drive. However, a print portfolio may have more impact because it is easier for the interviewer to see the quality of the actual drawings you have made by hand (in manual drafting) or the neatness and appropriateness of the prints you have made (in CADD).

Now is a good time to think about which type of portfolio you want to create and to actually start it. You do not need a lot of finished drawings to begin your portfolio. In fact, a portfolio is a "living" tool. In other words, you will constantly add to it, and occasionally remove items from it.

What should you include in your portfolio? In general, you should include items that show your technical skills and level of accomplishment. For example, for an architectural job, you would almost certainly include examples of architectural working drawings, including at least one floor plan.

Activity

After completing this chapter, use the Internet to search for *print portfolio* and *e-portfolio*. Read articles about each type of portfolio and locate examples of portfolio work created by others. Determine which type of portfolio you will create and review the floor plans you have created. Choose one that you consider to be your best work so far and place it in your portfolio. If you are building a print portfolio, print the drawing on good-quality paper or vellum and place it in a folder or envelope that is large enough to hold the drawing without folding it. Some companies make professional portfolio cases; you may want to consider one of these at some point. For now, a large envelope may meet your needs just as well.

If you are building an e-portfolio, obtain a USB drive that you can dedicate entirely to your portfolio. Do not use the drive for anything else. Label it carefully so that you do not accidentally overwrite or delete the contents. If you created your floor plan drawing using CADD, copy the drawing to the USB drive. If you created the drawing using manual techniques, you can scan the drawing using a scanner and save the resulting file on your USB drive. In most cases, however, CADD drawings work better with e-portfolios.

Internet Resources. List of companies and organizations in architecture and construction relating to the chapter content.

Suggested Activities. Assignments providing opportunities to apply drawing skills and solve problems.

Problem Solving Case Study. Features presenting challenges that occur in working with clients or coworkers, requiring a design solution or course of action.

Summary. Breakdown of key concepts providing an additional review tool for the student.

542 Section 4 Construction Systems and Supplemental Drawings

Summary

- Windows and doors should be planned carefully to ensure maximum contribution to the overall design and function of the structure.
- Doors are classified as either interior or exterior doors and can be further grouped according to their construction, uses, function, or location.
- Each door identified in a set of drawings should appear in a door schedule with its specifications.
- Windows of the same general type may vary from manufacturer to manufacturer, so it is very important to obtain window specifications from the manufacturer.
- Specifications for each window in a set of drawings should appear in a window schedule.

Internet Resources

Andersen Windows and Doors
Manufacturer of windows and doors

Jeld-Wen Windows and Doors
Manufacturer of windows and doors

Marvin Windows and Doors
Manufacturer of windows and doors

Pella Corporation
Manufacturer of windows and doors

Velux
Manufacturer of skylights, blinds, and home automation products

Review Questions

Answer the following questions using the information in this chapter.

1. List five functions of doors and windows.
2. Name eight types of interior doors.
3. Interior flush doors are usually _____ thick.
4. What are the horizontal cross members in panel doors called? What are the vertical cross members called?
5. What is the main use of bifold doors in residential construction?
6. Explain how pocket doors are different from sliding doors.
7. A door that swings through a 180° arc is called a _____ door.
8. Name two ways in which exterior wood doors are different from interior wood doors.
9. What is the most popular type of garage door?
10. What is the function of a drip cap?
11. Explain the purpose of a door sill.
12. The three parts of a door jamb are the two side jambs and a _____ jamb across the top of the frame.
13. Why is it important to design and place windows properly in a residential structure?
14. The window glass area should be at least _____ percent of the floor area of the room.
15. What is the difference between muntins and mullions?
16. What does the rough opening size of a window represent?
17. Which window is hinged at the side and swings out?
18. Name one type of window that does not provide ventilation.
19. Explain the difference between a bay window and a bow window.
20. What information should a window schedule include?

Suggested Activities

1. Construct a scale model of an exterior or interior door, jambs, and rough framing. Use CADD or manual drafting techniques to make plan, elevation, and section drawings. Present the model and drawings to the class and explain the features.
2. Select a floor plan for a small- to medium-size house. Using CADD, draw the floor plan. Then, plan the windows for the house following the guidelines presented in this chapter for ventilation, light, and view. Insert window symbols into the walls. Design and draw new symbols as needed. Finally, create a window schedule for the house.
3. Visit a local lumber company and examine the cutaway models of the windows available from the company. Measure the various parts of one model and prepare a sketch. Identify the type of window and the manufacturer. Collect specification data about the windows and bring the material to class for reference purposes.
4. Using CADD, draw various window and door symbols as shown in this chapter. Add these to your symbol library.

Problem Solving Case Study

Your client has asked you to design a cottage "getaway" to be built in the Blue Ridge Mountains in Maryland. The cottage only needs a bedroom, one bathroom, and a general living/kitchen area. The client wants to make the most of the mountain views, and because he is an artist, needs plenty of natural light. However, he wants the cottage to be as energy-efficient and sustainable as possible.

Design the cottage to meet the client's specifications and create a floor plan drawing in CADD. Search the Internet to find suitable doors and windows for the cottage and incorporate them into your design. Add a door schedule and a window schedule to your floor plan. Present your final drawings to the class.

ADDA Certification Prep

The following questions are presented in the style used in the American Design Drafting Association (ADDA) Drafter Certification Test. Answer the questions using the information in this chapter.

1. Which of the following statements are true about doors and windows?
   A. A Dutch door is composed of two parts—an upper and lower section.
   B. Picture windows are fixed-glass units and are usually rather small.
   C. An awning window has sashes that are hinged at the top and swing out at an angle.
   D. Muntins are large vertical and horizontal bars that separate the total glass area into smaller units.
   E. The basic unit size represents the overall dimensions of the window unit.
2. Match each type of door with its description.
   Doors: 1. French door, 2. Double-action door, 3. Panel door, 4. Bifold door, 5. Flush door
   A. Smooth on both sides.
   B. Has cross members called stiles and rails.
   C. Made of two parts hinged together.
   D. A panel door in which all of the panels are glass.
   E. A door that can swing through an arc of 180°.
3. Match each type of window with its description.
   Windows: 1. Double-hung, 2. Casement, 3. Hopper, 4. Jalousie, 5. Clerestory
   A. Has sashes hinged at the side that swing outward.
   B. Hinged at the bottom and swings to the inside of the house.
   C. Has narrow, horizontal glass slats held in metal clips.
   D. Placed high on a wall to admit light.
   E. Has two sashes that slide up and down in grooves.

Curricular Connections

1. **Language Arts.** Research the history of the use of glass windows in homes. Compose an essay on how glass changed the building industry and the possible uses for homes and other residential structures.
2. **Social Science.** Research the origins of clerestory windows and how they got their name. Write a summary of your findings.

Review Questions. Questions designed to reinforce the content covered in the chapter.

Curricular Connections. Activities and assignments designed to relate the book's content to other curriculum, such as language arts and social science.

ADDA Certification Prep. Practice questions reinforcing chapter topics, presented in the style of the American Design Drafting Association (ADDA) Drafter Certification Test.

Procedures.
Detailed, step-by-step instructions for completing architectural drawings using manual or CADD methods.

370 Section 3 Plan Development

CADD Drawing Techniques

The procedure for drawing a foundation or basement plan with CADD is basically the same as that used with manual drafting techniques. However, there are a couple of major differences. The biggest difference is that the drawing is created at full scale. Then, an appropriate scale is selected when the drawing is plotted. The following steps outline drawing a foundation or basement plan using CADD.

Procedure
CADD

Drawing a Foundation or Basement Plan

1. Make a copy of the floor plan on a new layer in the foundation plan drawing. As you develop the foundation plan, place items on the appropriate layers using the correct line width and linetype. If you are drawing the foundation plan in the same file as the other drawings in an architectural set of drawings, place the foundation plan on its own set of layers.
2. Draw the outside line of the foundation walls and delete the outside line of the floor plan wall, if they do not coincide. Generally, the outside lines of the foundation walls are identical to the outside lines of the rough stud walls on the floor plan in a frame structure with siding. Brick or other veneer is added to the outside of this point. The foundation wall is wider than a frame wall; therefore, the inside line will fall inside the floor plan. Generally, the foundation wall will be 8″, 10″, or 12″ thick, although there are exceptions. A 12″ thick wall will be used in this example. Some CADD software programs draw all the lines of a footing and stem wall automatically when you change the type of wall. This example assumes that you will draw them individually.
3. Draw all footings. The footings and foundation walls should be drawn on separate layers because the line widths and linetypes are different. Piers and their footings may be added to these layers since they use similar linetypes and are part of the foundation. **Figure 15-14** shows the foundation walls,

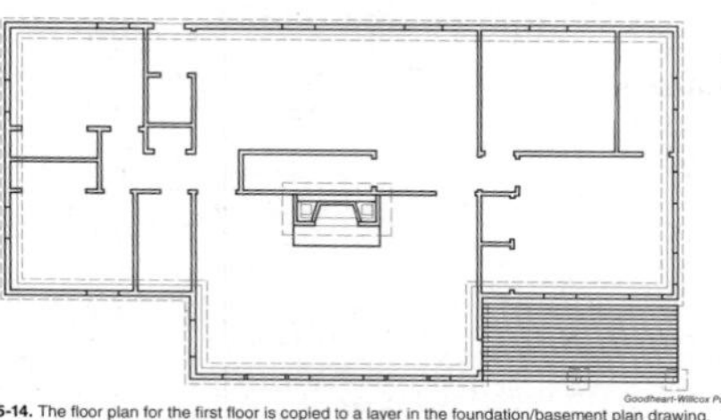

Figure 15-14. The floor plan for the first floor is copied to a layer in the foundation/basement plan drawing. Footings and piers are then added on another layer. The floor plan layer is shown here for reference.

STEM Connections.
Activities and assignments designed to relate the book's content to the science, technology, engineering, and mathematics (STEM) education paths.

Communicating about Architecture.
Group and individual activities designed to facilitate class participation.

544 Section 4 Construction Systems and Supplemental Drawings

STEM Connections

1. **Technology.** Skylights are very useful for increasing the amount of natural light in a room. One of the complaints about skylights in the past has been that there was no way to "shut off" the light or to dim it if a room becomes too bright. Skylight manufacturers today have found ways to prevent the problem. Research skylights and write a report on the ways skylights today can be controlled or shaded.

Communicating about Architecture

1. **Reading.** With a partner, make flash cards of the key terms in this chapter. On the front of the card, write the term. On the back of the card, write the pronunciation and a brief definition. Use this chapter and a dictionary for guidance. Then take turns quizzing one another on the pronunciations and definitions of the key terms.
2. **Speaking.** Using the same flash cards developed in the previous activity, explain to the class what you like about certain types of doors and windows. Describe in detail what is appealing to you and what is not, and identify which types of doors and windows you would want for your home.

350 Section 3 Plan Development

Parametric Modeling | Creating a Floor Plan

Parametric modeling is a special type of 3D modeling introduced in Chapter 12, *Building Information Modeling*. Constructing a 3D parametric model in architectural design often begins with creating the floor plan. The process of creating a floor plan in parametric modeling is similar to that used with a general-purpose CADD system, but there are different steps and workflows because of the nature of 3D modeling and the way in which the drawing is prepared. For example, instead of drawing 2D lines to represent the walls on a 2D floor plan, you place the walls as 3D components on the plan. Walls are still drawn by picking points and they still appear as lines when working in a 2D view, but each wall is made up of a "block" of lines that represents a 2D section of the wall. Changing to a 3D view allows you to view the wall in its full width, height, and depth. Other components of the model are constructed in similar fashion.

The setup steps involved in creating a floor plan in parametric modeling are different from those in other types of CADD work. One of the first steps before modeling starts is to create the levels and views that will be used in the project. ***Levels*** are assigned elevations that define key heights of the building. For example, a level named First Floor can be used to establish the height of the first floor. Additional levels, such as Second Floor and Roof, can be used to establish other key heights. As each level is created, you have the option to create a named plan view that is associated with the corresponding elevation. Typically, one or more default levels are available when you start a project based on a default template. For example, Level 1 is a typical default level defining an elevation of 0′-0″ and Level 2 is a typical default level defining an elevation of 10′-0″. See **Figure 14-29.** A default view is associated with each of these levels.

Levels can be created by switching to an elevation view and using the **LEVEL** command. The levels you use in a project will vary depending on the type of home being drawn and the type of construction. The following are examples of typical levels that could be used in a residential design project:

Levels Above Grade	Levels Below Grade
First Floor	Top of Footing
Second Floor	Basement Floor
Top of Plate	Top of Foundation

The following procedure is based on using the First Floor level to create a floor plan. Once you have established the level of the first floor, open the first floor plan view to begin working. This procedure is designed for a one-story home with wood frame construction and a basement. Elements of the basement and foundation are explained in Chapter 15, *Foundation Plans*. See Chapter 17, *Roof Designs*, for details on roof construction. See Chapter 24, *Stair Details*, for details on stair construction. The following is presented as a typical sequence, but specific steps will vary depending on the program used and the type of construction.

Level 2 10′-0″
Level 1 0′-0″

Figure 14-29. Levels are elevations that identify key heights of a building. Shown are the default levels typically available when starting a project in a parametric modeling program.

Parametric Modeling.
Features addressing tools and processes used in parametric modeling software, including step-by-step instructions for creating a 3D model and related drawing documentation.

Student Resources

Textbook

The **Architecture: Residential Drafting and Design** textbook provides an exciting, full-color, and highly illustrated learning resource. The textbook is available in print or online versions.

Workbook

The student Workbook provides hands-on practice with questions, problems, and activities to reinforce textbook content. Each chapter corresponds to the text and reinforces key concepts and applied knowledge.

Online Learning Suite

Available as a classroom subscription, the Online Learning Suite provides the foundation of instruction and learning for digital and blended classrooms. An easy-to-manage shared classroom subscription makes it a hassle-free solution for both students and instructors. An online student text and workbook, along with rich supplemental content, brings digital learning to the classroom. All instructional materials are found on a convenient online bookshelf and are accessible at home, at school, or on the go.

Online Learning Suite/ Student Textbook Bundle

Looking for a blended solution? Goodheart-Willcox offers the Online Learning Suite bundled with the printed text in one easy-to-access package. Students have the flexibility to use the print version, the Online Learning Suite, or a combination of both components to meet their individual learning style. The convenient packaging makes managing and accessing content easy and efficient.

Instructor Materials

Instructor resources provide information and tools to support teaching, grading, and planning; class presentations; and assessment.

Instructor's Presentations for PowerPoint®

These presentations help visually reinforce key concepts. The presentations are designed to allow for customization to meet daily teaching needs. They include objectives, outlines, and images from the textbook.

ExamView® Assessment Suite

Quickly and easily prepare, print, and administer tests with the ExamView® Assessment Suite. With hundreds of questions in the test bank corresponding to each chapter, you can choose which questions to include in each test, create multiple versions of a single test, and automatically generate answer keys. Existing questions may be modified and new questions may be added. You can prepare pretests, formative assessments, and summative assessments easily with the ExamView® Assessment Suite.

Instructor's Resource CD

One resource provides instructors with time-saving preparation tools such as answer keys; lesson plans; drawing problem files; correlation charts to Precision Exams standards; and other teaching aids.

Online Instructor Resources

Online Instructor Resources provide all the support needed to make preparation and classroom instruction easier than ever. Available in one accessible location, support materials include answer keys, lesson plans, Instructor's Presentations for PowerPoint®, ExamView® Assessment Suite, and more. Online Instructor Resources are available as a subscription and can be accessed at school or at home.

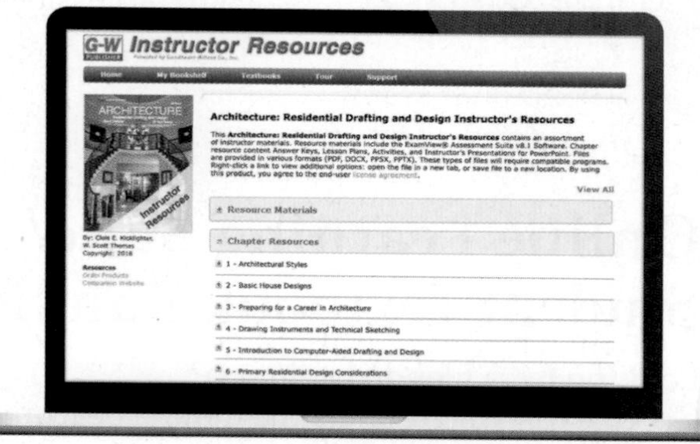

G-W Online

G-W Online enhances your course with course management and assessment tools that accurately monitor and track student learning. The ultimate in convenient and quick grading, G-W Online allows you to spend more time teaching and less on administration.

Brief Contents

Expanded Contents

Section 3
Plan Development

Section 4
Construction Systems and Supplemental Drawings

Section 6

Electrical, Plumbing, and Climate Control

Section 7
Specifications and Estimating Costs

Features

Green Architecture

Employability

Drafting Procedures

Parametric Modeling

Section 1

Architectural Drafting Fundamentals

pics721/Shutterstock.com

Chapter 1

Architectural Styles

Objectives

After completing this chapter, you will be able to:

- Describe traditional architectural styles used in the United States.
- Explain how social and cultural ideas influence architecture.
- Explain the historical design influences on today's residential homes.
- Identify types of multifamily housing.
- Describe current trends in architecture.

Key Terms

adobe
apartment
architectural style
condominium
cooperative
Craftsman period
half-timbering
mail-order house
mansard roof
Modernism
multifamily housing
pattern books
period home
Postmodernism
Romanticism
townhouse
Victorian period

The study of architecture encompasses sensitivity to design, skill in drawing techniques, knowledge of construction, and awareness of technological advancements. It is the combination of these abilities that yields today's outstanding architects, designers, and builders. They design and build the massive high-rise buildings, quaint lakeshore cottages, modern churches, and family homes required to meet the needs of our society.

Throughout civilization, architecture has changed and adapted to people's desires and needs. This chapter explores the architectural styles of the home, how they are influenced by the past, how they are used in the present, and how they will continue to influence our environment in the future. See **Figure 1-1**. An ***architectural style*** is a classification of a structure based on its appearance, the materials used, structural and decorative details, building techniques, and artistic expression.

Traditional Architectural Styles

Over the centuries, numerous architectural styles have been developed for residential construction. Many were developed to suit the climate and needs of families in various parts of the country. Some styles became so popular that they took on names related to their shape, period of time, or the area of the country in which they were designed and constructed.

Most American architectural styles have evolved from the past. The Native Americans,

Arthur Rutenberg Homes, Inc.

Figure 1-1. Styles from the past often influence the design of new homes. This home borrows the tile roof and arches of the Spanish Colonial style.

along with English, Spanish, French, German, Dutch, and other people who settled in North America, contributed to the vast number of architectural styles that are used throughout the country. Traditional architectural styles provide a historical background that still influences the design of today's homes.

Native American Houses

The evolution of the American house started with the dwellings of the Native American inhabitants. The Native Americans developed their building techniques over thousands of years. They used locally obtained natural resources such as rock, clay, wood, bark, plants, and animal hides to construct their shelters.

Wigwam

The wigwam was a small house usually made of wood frames covered with woven mats. See **Figure 1-2**. Many people think of wigwams as round structures with domed roofs, but they could also be cone-shaped or oblong. The typical size of a wigwam was about 10′–16′ in diameter and 8′–10′ high. The grass houses used in the Southern Plains were a variation of the wigwam.

Tipi

In the North American Plains region, many Native American tribes moved often, following bison and other food and clothing resources across the plains. Their shelter had to be lightweight and easy to assemble and break down. Their main form of housing was the tipi, a cone-shaped structure covered with animal (usually bison) hides. The typical size of a tipi is 12′ in diameter and 10′–12′ tall. See **Figure 1-3**.

Longhouse

The longhouses built by the Iroquois and Algonquian tribes in the Northeast were much larger structures than wigwams and tipis, although the construction was similar to that of wigwams. They were usually rectangular and consisted of wood pole frames covered by bark or grass mats. They could be as large as 200′ long,

A

Nancy Catherine Walker/Shutterstock.com

B

Gunter Nezhoda/Shutterstock.com

Figure 1-2. A—The framework for a wigwam was constructed of supple wood from young trees. B—The framework was covered by thick mats woven of grasses and other plant material.

Philip Lange/Shutterstock.com

Figure 1-3. To form a tipi, poles made from saplings or long branches were tied together at the top to support a covering that was typically made of animal hides.

20′ wide, and 20′ tall and were used as permanent shelter to house up to 60 family members. See **Figure 1-4**. Depending on the region, the longhouse evolved into many forms. Some had thatched roofs. Others, such as the chickee used by the Seminoles, had roofs supported by poles, but the sides were left open. In the Northwest coastal region, a heavy, timber-framed structure with a gabled roof covered with flat wood planks was typical.

Adobe

The Pueblo Indians in the Southwest used adobe brick with stone, earth, and timber to build their houses. ***Adobe*** is a natural building material made of water, sand, clay, and straw mixed together, then formed into the desired shape. The Pueblo Indians built flat-roofed dwellings that were multiple stories high. The buildings were joined together in rows much like townhouses to create a shared environment. See **Figure 1-5**. The thick adobe walls supported a roof system consisting of earth and large horizontal timbers that extended beyond the perimeter of the walls. Adobe dwellings later became the inspiration for Spanish Colonial, Spanish Eclectic, southwestern, and eco-friendly houses. The adobe process is still used throughout the world.

Earthen Houses

In the Great Plains and Eastern Woodlands, many dwellings were constructed of earth or sod. See **Figure 1-6**. The hogans built by the Navajo, the earth lodges built by the Sioux, and the pit houses on the West Coast are all examples of earthen houses. The igloo was a variation of an earthen house that was made of snow and ice. Earthen houses were often built partially underground. The timber framework was covered with a layered system of smaller sticks, long grasses, woven mats, and earth. It was common for the earth to be covered in sod. An opening at the top allowed light into the windowless structure while allowing smoke to escape from the fire pit below.

SF photo/Shutterstock.com

Figure 1-4. An example of an Iroquois longhouse.

Gary Yim/Shutterstock.com

Figure 1-5. The adobe homes built by the Native Americans in the Southwest were community structures that shared common walls.

akva/Shutterstock.com

Figure 1-6. Earthen homes were built partly underground to protect the inhabitants from heat in the hot summer months and from cold in the winter months.

American Colonial Houses

The earliest non-native houses were built by European settlers in the early 1600s. The early settlers of Colonial America brought with them the building traditions and styles of their homelands. They adapted their techniques to their new location, incorporating local building techniques and using native building materials to construct their shelters.

Log Homes

One of the earliest Colonial homes was the log cabin, which was introduced in the early 1600s by Swedish and Finnish immigrants. These settlers came from areas with rich resources of timber and brought with them the building techniques of their homeland. The log cabin was originally a simple one-room, gabled-roof house built from large logs with a centrally located door and chimney. See **Figure 1-7**. Over time, one-room cabins were replaced by log houses with multiple rooms.

The walls of a log home consisted of logs stacked one on top of another. The ends of the logs were notched to allow the walls to interlock in the corners, forming a square or rectangular structure that supported the roof. The small narrow cracks or slits between logs were filled and weatherproofed.

Michael Shake/Shutterstock.com

Figure 1-7. The one-room log cabin was an early Colonial design. The style was adapted over time to build larger structures with multiple rooms.

Saltbox

By the early 1700s, demand for more interior space led many settlers in New England to construct an additional "lean-to" structure, one half-room deep, to the rear of the house. The additional space changed the roof line, giving the house a distinctive look. The shape of the house resembled the shape of a box that was commonly used during the Colonial period for keeping salt and other sundries. This style, therefore, became known as the Saltbox. See **Figure 1-8**. The low, slanting roof also helped combat the bitter winds common to New England winters.

Cape Cod

Further advances in building techniques allowed the roof to span more than one room, allowing for a wider ground plan. This change introduced the New England Cape Cod, one of the earliest and best known of the Colonial styles. Built by the English colonists, the Cape Cod was a fairly small house with a gable roof and a massive central chimney located in line with the front door. The roof had very little overhang and the eaves line was always near the top of the symmetrically placed windows that flanked the entrance. See **Figure 1-9**.

The early Cape Cods were built with a small hall and one to three rooms on the first level and one to two additional rooms in the attic. A later addition to the Cape Cod was the *dormer*, a projecting structure on a roof that had walls, a front-facing window, and a roof. It provided daylight, ventilation, and additional usable space. Today, the same features are incorporated in larger houses that accommodate the needs of the modern family.

Tidewater

The Tidewater style was developed in the 1700s along the southeastern coastline to help people live comfortably in the moist heat. This style was noted for its full-width front porches, which provided cool shelter from the hot sun and frequent rainstorms of the region. The porch was built under an uninterrupted roof

Goodheart-Willcox Publisher

Figure 1-8. This modern home is an excellent reproduction of the New England Saltbox style.

Gregory James Van Raalte/Shutterstock.com

Figure 1-9. This is a refined version of the traditional Cape Cod style. Later Cape Cod houses had dormers on the second floor, as shown here.

line and became an extension of the house. See **Figure 1-10**. The wood, log, or masonry structures were usually built on pilings to raise the house above ground. This helped provide some protection against flooding from occasional tidal surges associated with hurricanes and other major storms.

Like the Saltbox, the Tidewater started out as a small one-story, one-room house. Eventually, it grew into a hall and parlor plan containing two rooms separated by a centrally located stairway leading to the attic. Often, a pair of chimneys was placed at the gable ends at opposite ends of the house. Tidewater became the dominant style throughout the rural south and is still influencing architecture to this day.

Spanish Colonial

In 1565, the Spaniards established North America's first colonial settlement in St. Augustine, Florida. Like the English, the Spaniards had a major influence on American domestic architecture. They combined Native American building techniques with their own and used local building materials to create the style of Spanish Colonial.

The Spanish Colonial house was built of thick walls made of adobe brick or rubble stone, with few windows and multiple doors, and a pitched or flat roof. For both protection and decoration, the interior and exterior walls were often covered with mud plaster, lime plaster, whitewash, or cement stucco.

Georgian

The Georgian style originated in England and is named after the English kings George I, II, and III. It was introduced into the American colonies in the early 1700s, mainly through the use of ***pattern books*** (publications of treatises,

Mark Winfrey/Shutterstock.com

Figure 1-10. This modern adaptation of a Tidewater home shows the raised construction and an integrated roof over the deep, full-length front porch. The metal roof helps reflect the sun and heat, keeping the house cooler during the hot summer months.

essays, and books on architectural design and construction). Georgian was the dominant style of the American colonies until the end of the Revolutionary War in 1783. The classical architecture of the Italian Renaissance influenced the Georgian style. An emphasis on symmetry, geometrical proportions, and classic formal lines with ornamental trim are elements of Georgian style, as shown in **Figure 1-11.**

The Georgian house was one or two stories with a gabled roof. It was typically two rooms deep with symmetrically placed windows and a centered entrance located on the front facade. The Georgian house originally consisted of two rooms on each side of a central entry hall. A staircase in the entry hall led to four similar rooms on the second floor.

Federal/Adam

The Federal style, also known as the Adam style, symbolizes the period of American history just after the American Revolution. Similar to the Georgian style, the Federal style was influenced by French Rococo and inspired by the classical architecture of Greece and Rome. The Federal style was more delicate and refined than the Georgian, yet it could be more ornamental.

Like Georgian houses, Federal style houses were symmetrical, multistory dwellings with a low-pitched or flat roof. The entrance was centered on the front facade with windows arranged symmetrically around the structure. It was common for the windows to have a flat stone lintel and sill, often with a keystone and a decorative frieze (horizontal band) placed above.

The front entrance of Federal style houses was the distinguishing feature that set them apart from Georgian houses. Federal style buildings had a semicircular or elliptical fanlight above the front door, whereas the Georgian style did not. Often the door was flanked by sidelights (side windows). See **Figure 1-12**.

PRILL Mediendesign und Fotografie/Shutterstock.com

Figure 1-11. The Longfellow house in Cambridge, Massachusetts is an excellent example of the Georgian style. Note the perfect symmetry and formal lines.

Pattie Steib/Shutterstock.com

Figure 1-12. Notice the semicircular fanlight above the front door of this Federal style home.

Romantic Styles

After the War of 1812, growing bitterness against England pushed America away from England's traditional ways. The new social movement of ***Romanticism*** began to spread throughout Europe and into the United States. Romanticism was a revolt against the Enlightenment movement. Enlightenment, also called the *Age of Reason*, was a social movement that challenged the role of religion and emphasized the ability of humans to reason and change society. In Romanticism, the focus was on nature, antiquity (ancient times), emotion, individuality, democracy, and art. The main Romantic architectural styles in the United States were Greek Revival, Gothic Revival, and Italianate.

Greek Revival

The main feature of the Greek Revival style was a covered entry or porch with classical columns. The columns often dominated the facade of the building, giving it the look of a Greek temple. Another common feature was a wide band of trim separating the roofs from the main body of the house, porches, and entrances. Other features included a low-pitched gabled or hip roof, symmetrical window placement, a front door surrounded by sidelights and a transom, and decorative window crowns and door pediments with Greek designs such as egg-and-dart, Greek key and fret, knotted rope, and honeysuckle leaf. See **Figure 1-13**.

Gothic Revival

The Gothic Revival style first appeared in England in the mid-1700s. Andrew Jackson Davis, an American architect, introduced Gothic Revival to the United States in 1832. Gothic Revival was widely used on public buildings such as churches, universities, and prisons, but houses also adopted some of its elements.

Denton Rumsey/Shutterstock.com

Figure 1-13. The distinctive feature of the Greek Revival style was the use of columns supporting a covered front porch or entryway.

The common feature of a Gothic Revival house was a steeply pitched, cross-gabled roof with decorative gable trim. The Gothic (pointed) arch of windows extending into the gable area was another distinguishing feature. Finials were often applied to the top of the gables to accentuate the roof. Also, a one-story entry or full-width porch with a flattened Gothic arch was common.

Italianate

The Italian villas (country houses) of rural Central and Northern Italy were the inspiration for the Italianate style. Italianate houses were wood-frame or masonry. In its simplest form, an Italianate house was square or rectangular and two or three stories high, with a flat or low-pitched roof. A distinctive feature was wide overhanging eaves supported by decorative brackets. See **Figure 1-14.** The tall, narrow windows were framed with decorative trim and embellished with crowns, often supported with brackets. Windows were double-hung with single-pane or double-pane glazing, often placed in groups of two or three. The entryway had tall arched or curved double doors with a large single pane of glass. The entry often had a small porch with a bracketed roof, supported by square columns with beveled corners. A square cupola or tower was also common.

Victorian Styles

The ***Victorian period*** flourished during the Industrial Revolution from 1860 to 1900. Also known as the *Gilded Age*, it was a time of prosperity, a time when the house represented the wealth of the family. New technology and mass-produced building materials allowed the construction of extremely ornate homes. Therefore, Victorian homes were seldom simply boxes

Gary Yim/Shutterstock.com

Figure 1-14. These apartments in New York were built in the Italianate style. Notice the highly decorative trim on the overhanging eave.

to be lived in. New construction techniques allowed for complex floor plans and exteriors. Several different styles are associated with the Victorian period. It was common to mix different elements from one style to another. In addition, regional variations exist within each style.

Second Empire

The Second Empire style originated in France during the 1850s and became popular in America during the 1860s. Its most distinctive feature was the ***mansard roof***, which was developed by Francois Mansart, a 17th-century French Renaissance architect. It had a double-pitched hip roof that allowed the top level to be used for additional living space. The lower slope of the roof often had patterned shingles and dormer windows. See **Figure 1-15**.

The Second Empire style had the same architectural elements as the Italianate, except the windows were less elaborate. Often, the windows were arched. The new style was more functional than previous styles and was considered modern for its time. The Second Empire lost its desirability after the economic downturn in 1873 and was out of fashion by 1880.

Stick

From 1860–1890, the Stick style emphasized the exterior wall surface as the decorative element, often suggestive of timber framing. Drawing from the medieval past, the main features of the Stick style were exposed horizontal, vertical, and diagonal boards (stickwork). The raised stickwork was not functional; it was just decoration. Other features included steeply pitched roofs, cross gables, exposed roof trusses, overhanging eaves with exposed rafter ends, wood clapboards or shingles (often patterned), and patterned masonry.

Susan Law Cain/Shutterstock.com

Figure 1-15. The Second Empire style allowed people to use the space under the double-pitched mansard roof as living space.

Queen Anne

The Queen Anne style is arguably the most recognized of all Victorian styles. The style was popularized in America by Boston architect Henry Hobson Richardson. It became the dominant style in the 1880s and remained popular until the early 1900s.

Inspired by the English Renaissance and the American Colonial style, the Queen Anne house had asymmetrical forms, steeply pitched roofs, projecting gables, patterned shingles and masonry, massive chimneys, stucco, diamond pane windows, and half timbers. See **Figure 1-16**. A full-length or "wraparound" porch (one that extends around more than one wall) was common on the Queen Anne, as well as an integrated porch. The asymmetrical structure was adorned with patterned shingles, decorative fretwork, spindles, posts, bay windows, finials, towers, and many other decorations.

Period Home Styles

The social and economic problems of the Industrial Revolution pushed people to seek a simpler life. People wanted to leave the excessive Victorian era to return to a "traditional" way of life. A ***period home*** represented the past, when the virtues of tradition were important. It provided the needed balance and stability the people desired.

Colonial Revival

The Colonial Revival movement began near the end of the Queen Anne period and lasted well into the 1950s. Early examples of the Colonial Revival style were loose interpretations of the Colonial past. Typically, they were asymmetrical Queen Anne structures with classical elements of Roman and Greek design. By 1915, however, the popularization of the nostalgic past created a need for more accurate representations. The Colonial Revival style borrowed many features

Lori Martin/Shutterstock.com

Figure 1-16. Queen Anne is a complex style that was made possible by the introduction of mass-produced materials, such as the spindles and decorative fretwork on this house.

from the early Colonial period. The Cape Cod and Saltbox were common forms; however, Georgian and Federal architecture became the major influences for design. The rectangular shape, often with a one-story wing (addition on the side) had rectangular, double-hung windows, often grouped in adjacent pairs. A centrally located door was decorated with a pediment, typically enclosed within a covered porch or portico.

A popular Colonial Revival style was the Garrison, **Figure 1-17**. A distinguishing feature of the Garrison was the overhanging second story, which made it possible to add extra space to the second level at little extra cost.

Spanish Eclectic

The Panama-California Exposition (a celebration of the Panama Canal opening) in 1915 inspired America's interest in Spanish architecture. The Spanish Eclectic style, popular from 1920 to 1940, included elements from the Native American, Colonial American, Arts and Crafts, and Spanish architectural periods. The mixture of decorative elements from multiple eras is what distinguished the style as "eclectic." Although the Spanish Eclectic style was found mainly in the southwestern and southeastern United States, it was also used in the north.

Distinguishing features of Spanish Eclectic included an asymmetrical facade, low-pitched tile roofs, a prominent arch above the main doorway, arched main windows, stucco walls, decorative tile or stucco vents, and chimneys with clay or tile roofs. The houses often had round or square towers, carved stone decoration, and open or roofed balconies with wood or iron railings. See **Figure 1-18**.

Thomas Paradis, Northern Arizona University

Figure 1-17. A traditional Garrison style home. Distinguishing features are an overhanging second story, wood siding, and a steep pitch roof.

Paul Matthew Photography/Shutterstock.com

Figure 1-18. The Spanish Eclectic style takes many different forms. This example has a decorative clay roof over the chimney, as well as the tile roof, arched entry, and square tower that were typical of this style.

Employability

Keeping Up with Architectural Trends

The field of architecture is constantly changing. New materials become available, and new processes are established to increase quality or decrease costs. Employers look for job candidates who know how to keep up with current trends. You can keep your architectural knowledge up-to-date using several different types of sources. Examples include:

- Internet searches
- American Institute of Architects
- Local architects
- Trade journals and magazines such as *Architectural Digest*

When you look for information about current trends, be sure to evaluate the sources you use. How reliable is the source? Is a source reputable? How current is the information it provides? Asking these questions can help you stay current in the field without falling victim to false or misleading information.

Activity

Find out more about architectural trends in your area. Which architectural styles are most popular? Which styles are increasing in popularity? Which are decreasing in popularity? Do most people live in a single family home or in multifamily homes? Write a report on your findings. At the end of your report, list all of the sources you used, and indicate your level of confidence in each source.

Tudor Revival

The Tudor Revival style imitated the English Tudor architecture from the 15th to the 17th centuries. The Tudor Revival house had one-and-one-half or two-and-one-half stories. It had steeply pitched roofs and prominent cross-gables, often overlapping and having various eave heights. The casement or double-hung windows were tall and narrow with small windowpanes. The wood-frame structure was covered with stucco, brick, stone, or wood, often with ***half-timbering*** (exposed, hand-hewn wood framing with masonry-filled spaces). Unlike the half-timbering in English Tudor architecture, however, the half-timbering in the Tudor Revival was false. The boards were used only as decoration to resemble timber framing. See **Figure 1-19**. Other distinguishing features included a massive chimney made of brick or stone, often with a decorative top. Many Tudor Revivals also had towers.

Styles of the 20th Century

As the turn of the 20th century approached, some people were inspired by the past, while others looked toward the future. These differences stirred the Modern movement in America. ***Modernism*** rejected the classical European constraints of the orderly past and the industrialization of the nation. It strove to bring back quality of life through craftsmanship.

Craftsman Period

The ***Craftsman period***, inspired by the English Arts and Crafts movement, lasted from 1860 to 1930. The Arts and Crafts movement was social and cultural backlash against the Industrial Revolution. The movement's purpose was to renew the human spirit by reuniting art, labor, and the artist while promoting hand workmanship.

Most people accredit the original Craftsman style to Charles and Henry Greene in Pasadena, California. By the early 1900s, Craftsman architecture had spread throughout the country by the expansion of magazines, pattern books, and mail-order houses. ***Mail-order houses*** were affordable, mass-produced, unassembled houses in a "do-it-yourself kit" that were available through various catalogs. The popularity of mail-order houses kept Craftsman-style homes in demand until the 1930s. The two basic Craftsman styles were the *foursquare* and the *bungalow*.

Susan Law Cain/Shutterstock.com

Figure 1-19. This Tudor Revival home contains decorative woodwork and other details that mimic the original English Tudor style.

Foursquare

A foursquare house is simply a square house, one- to two-and-one-half stories, divided into four rooms per floor. Foursquare homes mimicked many different styles, but the Craftsman foursquare was one of the most popular. See **Figure 1-20**.

The Craftsman foursquare house was two- to two-and-one-half stories high with a pyramidal, hipped roof. The roof often had wide eaves and exposed gable ends with beams and a large central dormer. The shape was square with a simple, closed floor plan divided into four rooms per floor. The facade was symmetrical with large double-hung windows, a large front porch supported by square columns, and wide stairs. The Craftsman foursquare could be built with wood siding, brick, stone, stucco, or concrete block.

Greg Henry/Shutterstock.com

Figure 1-20. An example of the Craftsman foursquare style.

Bungalow

Gustav Stickley, an Arts and Crafts furniture designer and publisher, was a major influence on the Craftsman movement in America. Stickley promoted the idea that a house has natural character when it is built in its simplest form using local materials. The natural character allows the house to blend with its surrounding landscape.

Stickley promoted the Craftsman bungalow style in his magazine *The Craftsman*. The Craftsman bungalow was a rectangular one- or one-and-one-half-story dwelling, usually with a low-sloping gable roof with a wide overhang, and a full or partial porch. See **Figure 1-21**. On the main floor, all the rooms were placed around a centrally located living room, usually with a fireplace. The adjoining rooms were connected to each other. The dining room, kitchen, bathroom, and often a bedroom were located on the main floor. Additional bedrooms were located on the second floor.

Several mail-order house catalogs offered their versions of the Craftsman bungalow. The demand resulted in the development of several different designs. These included the California bungalow, Chicago bungalow, Milwaukee bungalow, and Michigan bungalow, to name a few.

Prairie

The Prairie style, created by a group of Chicago architects, was a true American style designed to meet the needs of the American people. Architect Louis H. Sullivan started the movement with his ideals on "form follows function," open interior spaces, and merging architecture with nature. The most noted Prairie architect, however, was Frank Lloyd Wright. Sullivan, Wright, and others formed a group now known as the "Prairie School."

Their belief was a house should reflect not the past, but the time in which it was built.

Steve Holderfield/Shutterstock.com

Figure 1-21. The Craftsman bungalow was a one- or one-and-one-half-story building with most of the rooms on the main floor and a wide porch along the front of the house.

Green Architecture
Green Design

As environmental issues become mainstream topics, people are becoming more environmentally conscious. Many architects and designers are incorporating green design and sustainability into their work. In architecture, the goal of *green design* is to create buildings that conserve resources while being "environmentally friendly" (having little impact on the environment). *Sustainability* is the ability to last a long time without having a negative impact on the environment and future generations of people. Regardless of style, any new home can have a green design.

They developed an architectural style designed to blend into the Midwest prairie landscape. The rectangular, one- or two-story house had a flat or low-hipped roof with wide overhanging eaves. Horizontal lines visually lowered the house, making it harmonious with its surroundings. The use of natural building materials such as stone and wood strengthened the union of house and land. See **Figure 1-22**.

Robert Crow/Shutterstock.com

Figure 1-22. Frank Lloyd Wright's Fallingwater is an example of the Prairie style. Notice how well it fits into the natural setting.

Art Deco

The Art Deco style emerged in the 1920s. Art Deco united smooth surfaces, geometric shapes, and projections with strong vertical or horizontal lines to emphasize architectural features. Buildings were often decorated with stylized motifs that included geometric designs, glass block, and bright accent colors that accentuated the architecture, as shown in **Figure 1-23**. The style was mainly used for commercial buildings, but was also used for houses and multifamily dwellings.

Travel Bug/Shutterstock.com

Figure 1-23. The Art Deco style emphasized geometric designs that were often accented with bright colors.

Art Moderne

Art Moderne, which had its roots in the *Bauhaus* movement in Germany, became a dominant architectural style around 1930. Houses built in this style were asymmetrical with smooth surfaces, often with curved corners, and a flat roof. Art Moderne houses shared features such as curved glass-block windows or wall sections and round windows with the Art Deco style. They were usually white, however, and they had few of the decorative features of Art Deco.

International

The Bauhaus movement was also a major influence on the International style, often referred to as the "modern" style. The International style embraced form, function, and new building technology. All decoration from past styles was removed because it was nonfunctional. International style houses were rectangular with asymmetrical facades, sometimes with cylindrical forms, and often emphasizing horizontal planes with rows of windows and cantilevered sections. They incorporated manufactured materials such as glass, steel, and concrete. Buildings in this style have multiple roof lines, flat roofs, smooth surfaces, and plain columns. See **Figure 1-24**.

Ranch

Another architectural style that is still commonly used today is the Ranch. The Ranch style is a long and low, one-story house style that developed from the homes built by ranchers in the southwestern United States. The basic Ranch design is rectangular with a low-pitched, gabled roof and wide overhanging eaves. The wide eaves provide extra protection from the weather. The Ranch house was traditionally built on a concrete slab. However, over the years, the Ranch house has taken on many newer features. Ranch houses now usually have a two-car attached garage and sometimes a basement. See **Figure 1-25**. Many contemporary Ranch houses have an L-shape layout to add interest and break up the straight-line effect. Skylights and cathedral ceilings are other variations found in some modern Ranch houses.

photobank.ch/Shutterstock.com

Figure 1-24. The International style had little or no decoration, resulting in clean lines and smooth surfaces.

Steve Holderfield/Shutterstock.com

Figure 1-25. Most Ranch homes today have a garage, and many borrow elements from other architectural styles, such as the front porch on this home.

Postmodern

Postmodern architecture first appeared in the 1950s, but did not become a recognized movement until the late 1970s. ***Postmodernism*** marked the return of embellishment, and injected wit and character into architecture. It was a direct response to the sterility of the International style. Postmodernism reintroduced decoration. Suggestion and adornment returned to the forefront, replacing the forcefully stark approach of Internationalism. Appearance was no longer clearly defined by realistic requirements.

Postmodern style was generally characterized by the use of sculptural forms, ornaments, and materials to make a "statement" about the owner or architect. Postmodernism was very individualistic—no two homes of this style were ever the same. See **Figure 1-26**.

bbbb/Shutterstock.com

Figure 1-26. In direct opposition to the International style, the Postmodern style introduced humor and fantasy into architecture.

Neomodern

Neomodern architecture embodies the same basic principles associated with the International style. Buildings designed in the neomodern style emphasize form and function and reject the use of decoration and elements borrowed from past architectural styles. Neomodernism emerged in the late 20th century as a response to postmodernism and revitalized the "modern" architectural style.

Residential Architecture Today

Contemporary houses are the result of years of architectural design and evolution. In this context, the terms *contemporary* and *modern* are not associated with any special style of house. They simply refer to a house that is current and is not from the past. However, most contemporary house designs borrow some distinctive features from traditional styles. See **Figure 1-27**.

The needs and finances of a family generally dictate the type and style of today's construction. The rapid development of new building materials and methods of construction and fabrication have made it possible to design homes that require minimal maintenance, which is often a high priority for people with busy lifestyles.

The ability of the architect or building designer to meet the client's needs is equally important. Depending on client interests, an architect has many options, such as making extensive use of glass for appearance and interior light. Alternatively, an architect may choose to place emphasis on exposed structural members to create a distinctive look reminiscent of a specific style, such as Craftsman. In fact, architects take inspiration from many different styles to create functional, yet interesting, designs for their customers. See **Figure 1-28**.

Multifamily Housing

The homes discussed to this point in the chapter are single-family residences. This means that a single family lives in the home. Today, many people choose to live in ***multifamily housing***, buildings that provide homes for more than one family. Examples of multifamily housing include cooperatives, condominiums, townhouses, and apartments.

Alexander Chaikin/Shutterstock.com

Figure 1-27. Today's architects draw from many different ideas and styles to please their clients. The architect of this house used a large amount of glass with Craftsman overtones to create a light, airy feel.

Goodheart-Willcox Publisher

Figure 1-28. Architects today combine styles of the past with new features and designs to meet the needs of their clients.

Cooperative

The term ***cooperative***, or *co-op*, refers to a type of ownership, rather than a type of building. The building is owned and operated by a corporation. Each family's living space is called a *unit*. Each buyer purchases stock in the corporation to become a shareholder. In return, each shareholder receives a lease that grants the shareholder the right to occupy the unit's space. The unit's value determines the purchase price of the stock. See **Figure 1-29**.

Since members own a share of the corporation, they do not pay rent. They do, however, pay a monthly fee that is proportionate to what the corporation pays to manage and operate the building. The corporation uses the money to pay mortgage payments, property taxes, insurance, utilities, management fees, reserved funds, maintenance, and repairs.

The main advantage of co-op ownership is affordability. Co-op ownership requires lower down payments and lower closing costs, and often offers longer mortgage terms. Co-ops combine the advantages of home ownership with the convenience of apartment living. Another advantage of co-op ownership is community control. Each stockholder has a voice in running the co-op. The stockholders have the right to approve decisions that protect the interests of the corporation. A board of directors is formed to represent the majority.

Some disadvantages of a co-op may include excessive record keeping, a longer process for decision making, and conflicts between shareholders. Some co-ops do not allow shareholders to gain equity in their investment, resulting in less incentive to invest additional capital. The success of a co-op depends on participation. All members must abide by the wishes of the majority. However, if the members of the co-op collectively make a bad decision, all of the members are affected.

Condominium

A ***condominium*** is similar to a co-op in that it is a type of ownership. However, unlike the owner of a unit in a cooperative, who buys stock in a corporation, the owner of a condominium buys the unit and a share of the common ground. See **Figure 1-30**. The owner receives a deed to the unit and pays taxes on it. Owners of condominium units have a shared interest in all the common property and facilities. Common

Steve Rosset/Shutterstock.com

Figure 1-29. People who live in cooperatives (co-ops) purchase stock in the corporation that owns the building.

AMA/Shutterstock.com

Figure 1-30. Owning a unit in this condominium includes partial ownership of the facilities, including the pool.

property and facilities may include hallways, laundry areas, parking lots, sidewalks, lawns, tennis courts, and swimming pools. Common property is maintained using association fees paid monthly by the owners of the condominium units.

Any type of dwelling can be a condominium. A condominium complex may consist of a single building or a group of buildings and surrounding property. It may include a mixture of converted apartments, single-family homes, townhouses, duplexes, and high-rise buildings.

The main benefit of a condominium is pride of ownership with the ability to gain equity. Also, condominiums are generally more affordable than single-family houses. Other benefits include amenities such as security, recreation and fitness areas, and the convenience of not having to perform maintenance.

A condominium is not without some potential disadvantages. Privacy can be a major problem in buildings that do not have proper sound insulation. Association fees, as well as maintenance and repair fees, may be costly and are not tax deductible.

Townhouse

A ***townhouse*** is typically a two- to four-story house connected to one or more similar houses by a common wall. Typically, a townhouse occupies less land than a single family house. Townhouses, also sometimes known as rowhouses, are commonly placed next to each other in a row to form a close community. See **Figure 1-31**.

A townhouse has the same benefits and disadvantages as a condominium, with some additional conditions. The buyer purchases not only the unit, but also the land it sits on. A townhouse generally includes a small yard and often a basement. Maintenance can be a disadvantage

Konstantin L./Shutterstock.com

Figure 1-31. Townhouses share a common wall, but they are often detailed differently to help distinguish the units from one another and to add style to the building.

to some because it is the owner's responsibility to maintain the interior and the exterior of the unit, including the yard.

Apartment

Any type of dwelling may be rented, but apartments are the most common rentals. An ***apartment*** is living space that is available for rent. Rent is money paid in exchange for the right to occupy and use the space. The tenant (occupier) pays the owner or landlord a monthly fee that is specified in a lease (contract between tenant and landlord). The lease also defines additional rules and requirements, such as the length of the lease, amount of security deposits, and pet policies. See **Figure 1-32**.

Apartments are available in many types of buildings. An apartment can be in a duplex (a building with two units, both with separate entrances), or in an apartment building containing three or more units. In some cases, several apartment buildings are planned and built at the same time in a group called an apartment complex. This option makes good use of the land; it helps provide greater security and may provide additional amenities, such as recreational areas.

Apartments have definite advantages for large segments of the population. Renting is popular with people who may not have the means to buy property. Apartments offer many choices of style, size, price range, and facilities. Another advantage is that they require little time or effort from the renter for upkeep and maintenance.

Disadvantages of rental apartments relate mostly to loss of control over living space. Renters have little or no voice in how the apartment building is managed and maintained. Also, money spent on rent is not applied toward ownership. However, in spite of these disadvantages, apartments are the best answer to the housing needs of many people.

Trends in Architecture

Today's architectural trends give the architect a tremendous amount of freedom. Architectural styles reflect client requests for comfortable, environmentally conscious living space. Architects

Linda Johnsonbaugh/Shutterstock.com

Figure 1-32. Apartment rentals appeal to many people because repairs and maintenance are the responsibility of the apartment owner, rather than the people who rent the units.

borrow from the more formal styles of the past, but also incorporate unique structural and decorative elements in new homes.

More homes are being developed using environmentally friendly building materials and construction techniques. See **Figure 1-33**. Trends include creating designs for homes that use or re-use:

- existing building materials
- newly developed materials that have a less harmful effect on the environment
- materials and processes that are free of toxic chemicals and other items that can damage the environment or human, plant, or animal life
- materials that are easily recyclable or are reusable indefinitely, or that are biodegradable in common landfill conditions
- "smart" materials that can respond to environmental conditions
- sustainable materials harvested from renewable natural resources

Sustainable Housing

In many areas, home builders now offer sustainable housing. These homes are guaranteed to be built using materials that have been harvested and processed using sustainable processes. For example, sustainable lumber is lumber that was planted, grown, and cut in a way that protects the forest's long-term health. After the lumber was cut, it was processed and transported by companies that use responsible environmental practices.

svic/Shutterstock.com

Figure 1-33. Architects can be environmentally responsible by designing houses to use sustainable materials or newly developed materials that are easily recyclable and free from toxic chemicals. This house is being built entirely of sustainable lumber.

Summary

- Traditional architectural styles were first brought to the American colonies by settlers from Europe and were adapted to use local materials and methods.
- Social and cultural attitudes affect architectural design in many ways, including use of materials and the extent of ornamentation.
- Today's architectural designs draw from traditional styles developed over hundreds of years.
- Cooperatives, condominiums, and rental apartments are common forms of multifamily housing.
- Trends in residential architecture include designing for comfortable living and environmentally friendly housing.

Internet Resources

American Design Drafting Association (ADDA)
Resources for the design drafting profession and drafter certification

American Institute of Architects (AIA)
Educational and industry resources for the architectural profession

Builder Magazine Online
Home building news, sample home plans, and information about building products

Inhabitat Weblog
Forum discussions and news articles related to green architectural technology

Review Questions

Answer the following questions using the information in this chapter.

1. What is an *architectural style?*
2. Name and briefly describe five types of Native American houses.
3. Explain how the environment along the southeastern coast of the United States influenced the architectural features of the Tidewater architectural style.
4. Which of the following Colonial styles was known for a "lean-to" structure at the rear of the house and a low, slanting roof?
   A. Cape Cod
   B. Spanish Colonial
   C. Adam
   D. Saltbox
5. What is the major difference between the Federal and Georgian architectural styles?
6. Briefly explain the influence of Romanticism on the Greek Revival style.
7. What was the most distinctive feature of the Second Empire style, and what advantage did it provide?
8. The _____ _____ was a popular Victorian style home that commonly included a full-length or "wraparound" porch as well as an integrated porch.
9. Which architectural style was available through mail-order catalogs?
10. Which two 20th-century architectural styles in the United States were influenced by the German *Bauhaus* movement?
11. The Ranch home is a long and low, one-story house style with a low-pitched, _____ roof and overhanging eaves.
12. Examples of _____ housing include cooperatives, condominiums, townhouses, and apartments.
13. Briefly explain the differences between a condominium and a cooperative.
14. What factors often dictate the style of today's architecture?
15. Describe some ways in which sustainability can be applied to residential housing design.

Suggested Activities

1. Call on a local architect and ask the following questions. Compose a brief report on the architect's responses.
   A. What style of home is most in demand today in your region?
   B. Describe the educational requirements to obtain a degree in architecture.
   C. Describe the process to become a registered architect with the American Institute of Architects.
   D. Describe the job description of an entry-level design drafter in this company.
2. Using a variety of sources, develop an architectural design folder illustrating as many home styles as you can find. Indicate on each home any design features that have been borrowed from the past or demonstrate a futuristic trend.
3. Visit a local residential construction contractor and inquire about current building materials and new environmentally friendly building materials being used for exterior structural features and sustainability. Ask for an explanation of each product and how each is used in construction. Make a list of these materials and make an oral presentation of your research to the class.
4. Select one of the architectural styles described in this textbook. Cut out and glue together a cardboard model of that design.
5. Find an example of mass media advertising for homes in your area. Obtain a copy of the ad. Attach the copy to the top of a sheet of paper. Then analyze each claim made in the ad. Below the ad, list further questions that you would need to ask before you considered buying a home from this builder or in this community.

Problem Solving Case Study

A new client has come to your architectural office in Denver, Colorado, to discuss ideas for her family's new residence. She is moving to Colorado from a rural area in southern Georgia to take a new job. She has not yet decided whether to build a home or buy an existing one. The client is about 35 years old and has three children, ages 9, 5, and 2.

When you ask about her family's priorities, she tells you that the home must be close to good schools and daycare facilities. Although her new job is downtown, she does not want to live downtown because she thinks that would be too big of a change for her children. She wants a house with at least three bedrooms, with room for expansion. Given this preliminary information, answer the following questions.

1. What type of housing would you recommend for this client?
2. What home style might be most suitable?
3. What further questions would you need to ask the client to help narrow down the choices?

Certification Prep

The following questions are presented in the style used in the American Design Drafting Association (ADDA) Drafter Certification Test. Answer each question using the information in this chapter.

1. Which of the following are traditional architectural styles?
   A. Adam
   B. Contemporary
   C. Spanish Eclectic
   D. Saltbox
   E. Cooperative

2. Which of the following statements are true?
   A. Many of today's homes are built in the modern architectural style.
   B. The Cape Cod is a traditional architectural style that was developed in Colonial times.
   C. When you buy a condominium, you are buying one unit in a building and a share of the common ground.
   D. The most important job for today's architect is to design homes that reflect the traditional architectural styles.
3. Identify the type of housing as single family (S) or multifamily (M).
   A. Ranch
   B. Cooperative
   C. Condominium
   D. Tidewater

Curricular Connections

1. **Social Science.** Historically, culture has played an important part in architectural design. For example, one type of ancient Chinese architecture reflects the cultural belief that people are an integral part of nature. Its distinguishing features include simplicity and honesty in design. Research cultural influences on each of the following styles of architectural design.
   - Ancient Greek architecture
   - Chinese Siheyuan architecture
   - Gothic European architecture
   - Ancient Mayan temple architecture

   Collect illustrations of each, and assemble them into an illustrated multimedia presentation. In your presentation, include a summary section that compares and contrasts these styles with contemporary styles. Show your presentation to the class.
2. **Language Arts.** How much influence does advertising have on the homes people buy? Home builders often use billboards, newspaper ads, television and radio commercials, and even Internet sites to promote their products. It is important to realize that builders design these messages specifically to persuade people to buy their homes. Suppose you see a newspaper ad that contains the following claims for a new housing community:
   - Near parks and recreational facilities
   - Great schools
   - Low utilities
   - Prices starting at $150,000!

   Think critically about these claims. What do these things really tell you? What further questions would you need to ask before deciding to live in the community?

STEM Connections

1. **Engineering.** The original English Tudor home style used half-timbering as a structural element. In the Tudor Revival style, however, the half-timbering was decorative, not structural. Investigate the structural elements of these two styles. What engineering advances allowed the Tudor Revival style to use half-timbering for decoration only? What supported the walls and roofs in Tudor Revival homes?

Communicating about Architecture

1. **Speaking and Listening.** Working in small groups, create a poster that illustrates different architectural styles. Add labels to identify the different features that distinguish each style from the others. Afterward, display your posters in the classroom as a convenient reference aid for discussions and assignments.
2. **Speaking and Listening.** Working in groups, use the same posters you previously created or similar posters, this time without the labels. Use these posters to quiz one another about the architectural styles they represent. As you present each style, use a one-sentence description to summarize the main features of that particular style.

Chapter 2

Basic House Designs

Objectives

After completing this chapter, you will be able to:

- Identify four basic house designs.
- Explain the advantages of each house design.
- Recognize the disadvantages of each house design.
- Explain the variations of split-level designs.

Key Terms

attic
basement
crawl space
daylight basement
dormer
footprint
habitable space
intermediate level
living level
one-and-one-half-story
one-story
shotgun house
slab construction
sleeping level
split-entry
split-level
square foot
two-story
walkout basement

A residential home designer has four basic designs to choose from: one-story, one-and-one-half-story, two-story, and split-level. Each design has specific strengths and weaknesses. The designer considers these, along with factors such as site requirements, climate, environmental impact, surroundings, and the client's personal preferences, budget, and needs when deciding on a design for a particular client.

One-Story Designs

In a ***one-story*** house, all the regular living space is on one level, as shown in **Figure 2-1**. Like all house designs, a one-story house may be built with a full basement or a crawl space, or on a slab. See **Figure 2-2**. With ***slab construction***, the walls rest on a foundation with a concrete floor at ground level. A ***crawl space*** is an area less than full height, located at or below the ground level of the main floor, that is used for maintenance and storage. A ***basement*** is a full-height area located fully or partially below the ground level of the main floor. It is used for utilities, storage, and additional livable space. The additional work of excavating and constructing foundation footings and walls makes the basement the most costly to build, followed by the crawl space. The slab is the least expensive option.

The main advantage of the one-story design is having all the living space on one level. A one-story house without a basement is popular with people who do not want stairs. The elderly, the disabled, and families with small children often avoid stairs for safety and mobility reasons.

Travis Houston/Shutterstock.com

Figure 2-1. In a one-story house, all of the normal living space is on one level.

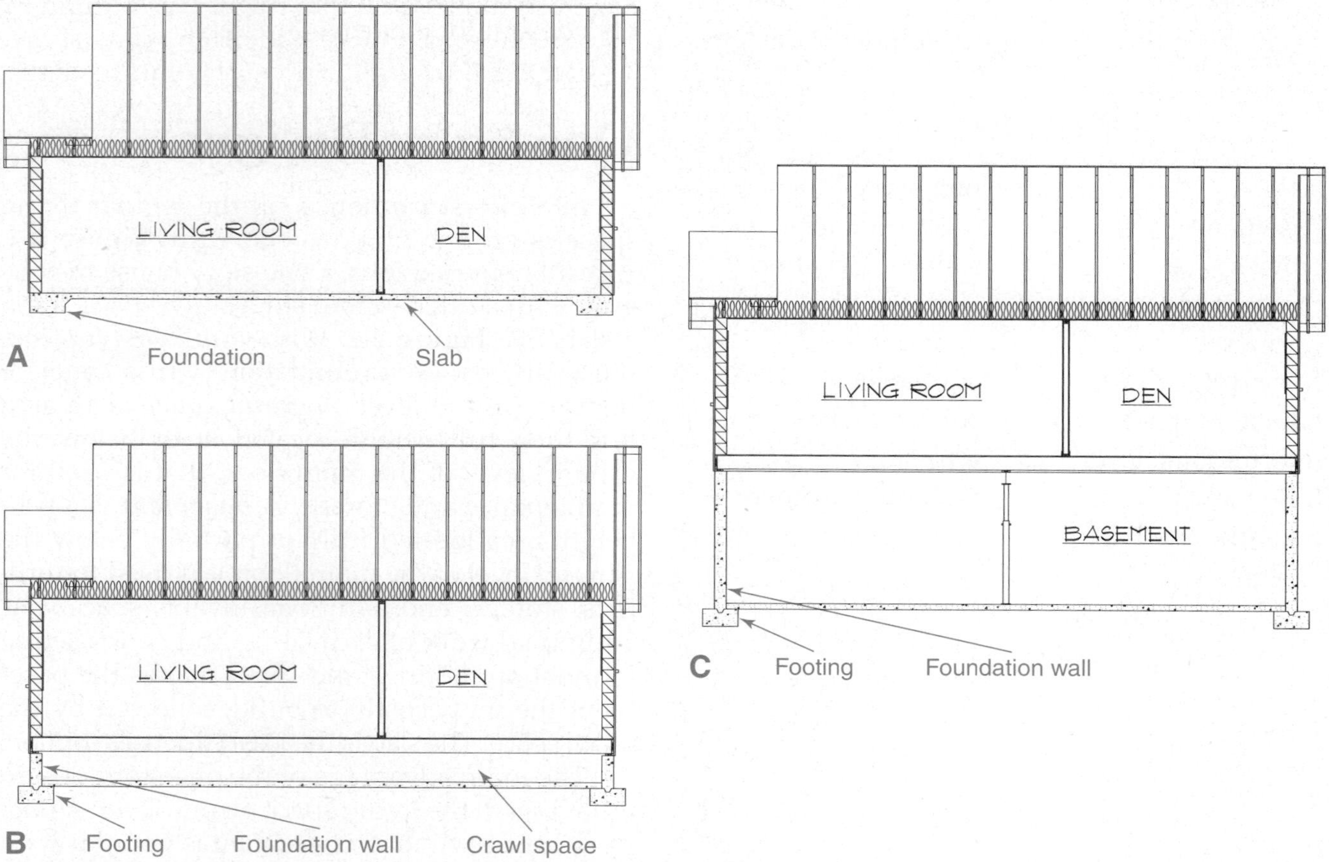

LIVING ROOM
DEN
A Foundation Slab

LIVING ROOM
DEN
B Footing Foundation wall Crawl space

LIVING ROOM
DEN
BASEMENT
C Footing Foundation wall

Goodheart-Willcox Publisher

Figure 2-2. A—A house design with a concrete slab floor reduces cost and simplifies construction. B—A crawl space adds accessibility for service and maintenance. C—A full basement adds valuable living space to a house.

Another advantage of the one-story house is that it offers plenty of opportunities for indoor-outdoor living. Any room that has an exterior wall can have a patio, porch, or terrace. See **Figure 2-3**. Windows along the perimeter walls bring the outdoor surroundings inside and make the interiors appear larger. In addition, a one-story house lends itself to expansion and remodeling. Many variations are possible. See **Figure 2-4**.

Christina Richards/Shutterstock.com

Figure 2-3. The quality of this outdoor space greatly enhances the living area of the home and allows for casual entertaining.

A one-story house also has disadvantages. It usually costs more to build than other designs with the same square footage. The ***square foot*** (ft^2 or sq. ft.) is the US architectural standard of measurement of a $1' \times 1'$ area. A one-story house spreads out, rather than up, and has a larger footprint than other designs. A ***footprint*** is the area of land occupied by a building. A one-story house requires a larger lot, additional roof area, and a longer foundation length. All of these items add to the cost of construction. See **Figure 2-5**. Furthermore, considerable hall space may be required to provide access to all rooms. See **Figure 2-6**.

Heating and cooling can also be challenging. Larger rooms at longer distances from the heating, ventilation, and air conditioning (HVAC) systems may be difficult to heat or cool. Proper space and utility planning can keep the distance that heated or cooled air has to travel to a minimum.

The one-story house has taken many styles throughout the years. The most common is the traditional Ranch house, shown in **Figure 2-1**,

Anne Kitzman/Shutterstock.com

Figure 2-4. One-story homes are adaptable to many styles. In this home, the owner chose to add an octagonal room reminiscent of a tower, as well as a front porch.

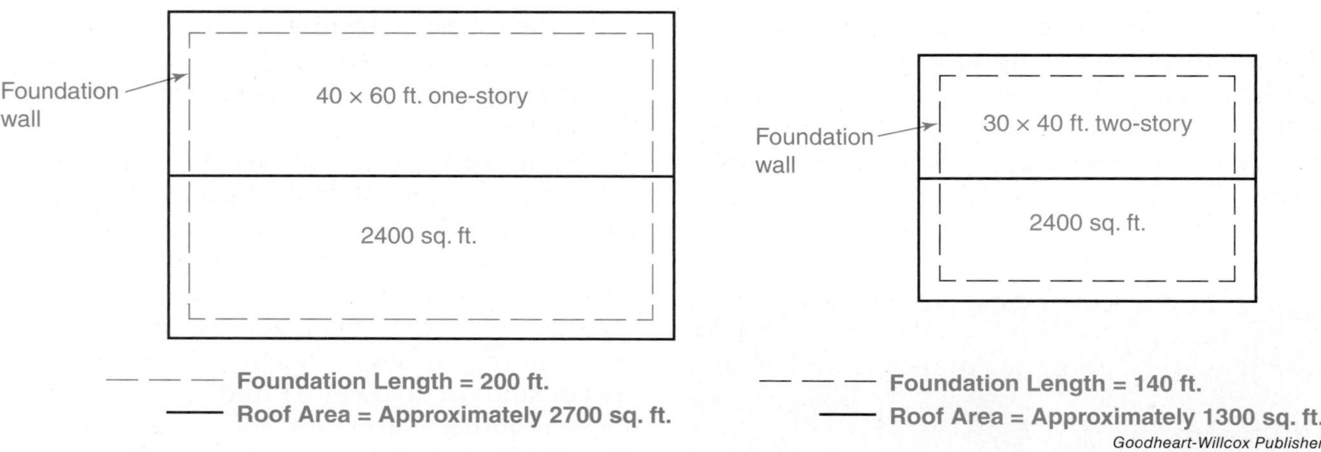

Goodheart-Willcox Publisher

Figure 2-5. A comparison of the foundation length and roof area of a one-story house and a two-story house with a similar amount of living area reveals why a one-story is usually more expensive to build.

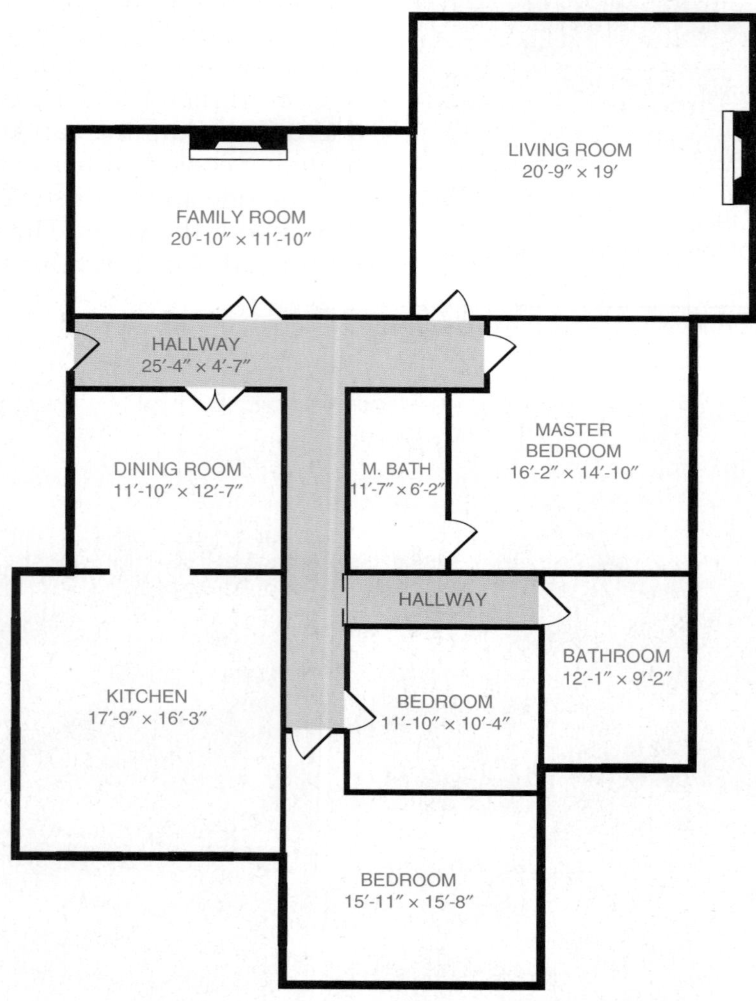

Joingate/Shutterstock.com

Figure 2-6. The hallways needed to access all of the rooms in this one-story house waste a lot of space that could be used for other purposes. Many one-story homes today are arranged in an open pattern that reduces the necessity for hallways.

with its low-pitched roof and wide roof overhangs. Since extra space is not required above the ceiling, a low roofline is used. The eight-foot walls and low-pitched roof simplify construction. The low height makes outside maintenance easy. Cleaning gutters, washing windows, and painting do not require long ladders or other special equipment.

Besides the Ranch house, other variations of the one-story house are popular throughout the country. For example, log homes are often built with only one story. Craftsman bungalows and Prairie style homes are other examples.

Another style, the ***shotgun house***, is a traditional style from the southern states. It is a one-story house that has a long rectangular plan in which all rooms are in line with and directly connected to one another from the front to the back of the house. Its name came from the idea that if you were to fire a gun through the front door, the bullet would travel straight through all the rooms and exit through the back door. See **Figure 2-7**. The shotgun house design influenced replacement housing for the post-Hurricane Katrina disaster area of New Orleans. In these designs, the rooms often connect to a common hallway that runs from the front of the house to the back. The hallway has entrances at the front and rear of the house, in the traditional shotgun style.

One-and-One-Half-Story Designs

The ***one-and-one-half-story*** house is a one-story design with a tall, wide roof that allows for expansion of living space into the attic. The ***attic*** is the space between the ceiling and the roof of a structure. Identifying features of a one-and-one-half-story house are dormers, windows and vents in the gable, and angular ceilings on the second level. See **Figure 2-8**. ***Dormers*** are

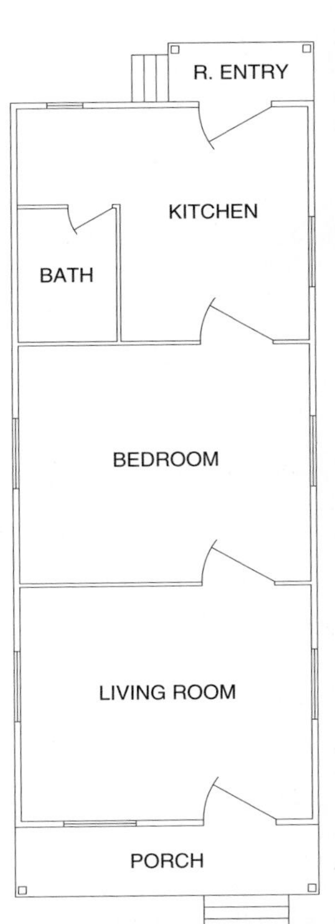

A

B

Goodheart-Willcox Publisher; Josh Gibson

Figure 2-7. A—Floor plan for a traditional shotgun house. B—A Katrina cottage with traditional shotgun influences.

Photo courtesy of James Hardie® Siding Products

Figure 2-8. The identifying features of a one-and-one-half-story house are dormers, angular second-story ceilings, and windows and vents on the gable ends.

projecting structures on a roof that have walls, a front-facing window, and a roof. In addition to enhancing the look of the exterior, they provide light and additional usable space in the attic area.

The amount of habitable space in the attic is determined by the width and height of the house. ***Habitable space*** is the total living area in a building. In most areas of the country, any space with less than five feet of headroom is considered unusable. The pitch of the roof limits the usable area in the attic to about half that of the first level. See **Figure 2-9**. A finished attic generally contains bedrooms and a bathroom. Other common rooms are a home office, an entertainment room, and storage areas. To comply with local building codes, bedrooms on the second level are typically located on the end walls of the structure to provide emergency egress, or exit, out of the structure.

The main advantage of a one-and-one-half-story house is that it occupies less ground than a one-story house that has the same amount of living space. Because some of the living space is upstairs, the footprint is smaller, and less land is required.

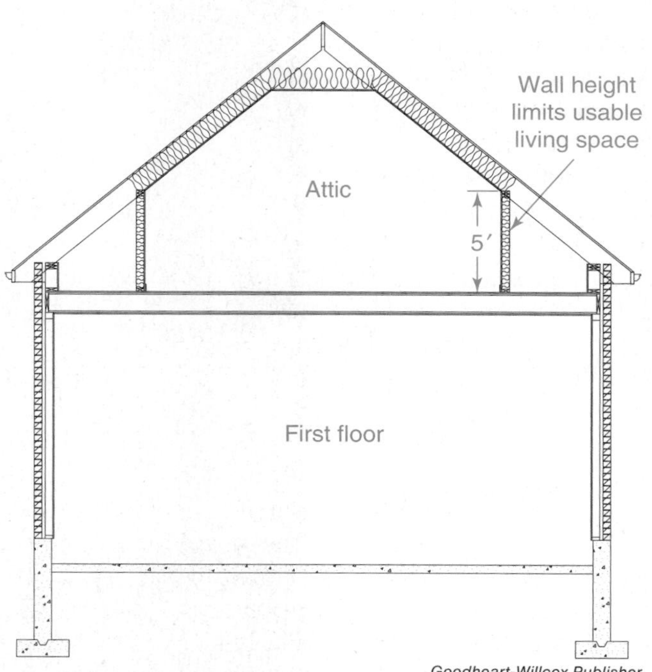

Goodheart-Willcox Publisher

Figure 2-9. The habitable space on the second floor of a one-and-one-half-story house is limited by the slope of the roof.

Green Architecture

Container Housing

One efficient type of green housing is the *container house*, which is made from a shipping container, also known as an *Intermodal Steel Building Unit (ISBU)*. See **Figure A**. ISBU construction is a good option for affordable housing, emergency housing, and storage. The trend started from a "grass roots" movement to re-use salvaged or surplus metal shipping containers from land and sea transportation of goods. There is no longer a surplus, however, and most container housing today uses new material.

The containers are made of non-corrosive *Corten steel*, a durable metal designed to withstand the elements by making its own protective layer of rust. Although each container is structurally independent, the ISBUs fit together to form "building blocks" for house construction. They can be stacked and connected in various geometric shapes and sizes to provide the framework of the house. See **Figure B**. Openings cut into the containers accommodate doors, windows, and walls.

By leaving the metal exposed, the designer can give the house an industrial look. For a more traditional look, the exterior can be covered with siding, masonry, or stucco. The interior can be finished with the same materials used in traditional construction.

A container house qualifies as "green" because it is made of sustainable and reusable materials. Converting a container into a house uses less energy than recycling the steel. A container has a life span of about 100 years. In addition, a container house can be designed and built for energy efficiency.

A

Hansenn/Shutterstock.com

B

Martin Bilek/Shutterstock.com

Figure A—These student apartments were made from recycled steel shipping containers.
Figure B—Windows and doors are cut into the ISBUs, often before they are set in place. In this design, two sides have also been removed to increase the size of the living area to span two or more containers.

The one-and-one-half story house has some additional building costs that are not incurred with a one-story house. Stairs, dormers, and complicated roofs are the principal sources of additional costs. Other disadvantages include less mobility (stairs), low ceilings and limited window space on the second level, and more difficult maintenance due to the added height.

The one-and-one-half-story design is versatile. It can be adapted to various styles such as the Saltbox, Tudor Revival, and Craftsman. The most recognizable is the traditional Cape Cod. See **Figure 2-10**. It can be built as a small two-bedroom, one-bath house with the attic unfinished. The attic can be finished later, deferring the costs of expansion until additional space is needed.

Harris Shiffman/Shutterstock.com

Figure 2-10. This traditional Cape Cod house is one of many variations of the one-and-one-half-story house design.

Two-Story Designs

The ***two-story*** house has two full levels of living space. The wall and ceiling heights are 8′ or more on both levels. See **Figure 2-11**. The main advantage of the two-story house compared to the one-story and one-and-one-half-story designs is that it can have a smaller footprint with the same amount of interior space. This makes the two-story house more economical to build. Privacy is another advantage of the design. Bedrooms are often on the second floor, with the remaining livable space on the first level. **Figure 2-12** shows a section of a typical two-story house with a basement.

Electrical wiring and plumbing in a two-story house are comparatively economical. The common walls between levels allow systems to share components and to be centrally located. This decreases the amount of materials and labor needed for construction.

Heating and cooling are easier on a two-story house because the ceiling is below air space in the attic instead of directly under the roof. Even though the second level is usually far from the furnace, it is easy to heat. Heat from the first level naturally rises to the second level. In addition, routing ductwork through insulated spaces increases efficiency.

The height of a two-story house makes exterior maintenance challenging and costly. See **Figure 2-13**. For some people, the necessity of climbing stairs from level to level is a disadvantage. Many houses, however, can include a stairway lift or elevator to provide greater accessibility.

Two-story houses are adaptable to many of the architectural styles described in Chapter 1,

ARENA Creative/Shutterstock.com

Figure 2-11. A two-story house has the same amount of habitable space on the first floor and the second floor.

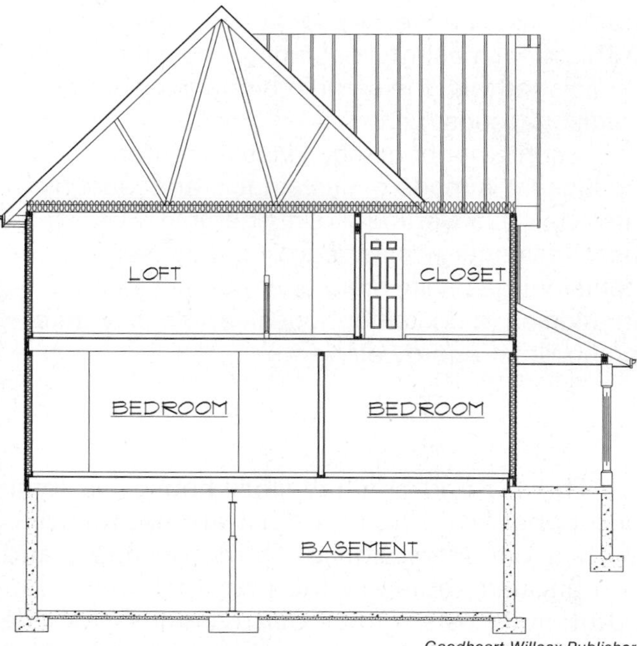

Goodheart-Willcox Publisher

Figure 2-12. A two-story house has a relatively small footprint because half of the square footage is on the second level.

Lawrence Roberg/Shutterstock.com

Figure 2-13. Maintenance on a two-story house can be a challenge. Using low-maintenance materials such as vinyl siding can help reduce the time and money needed to maintain a two-story home.

Architectural Styles. In many cases, two-story houses built in a traditional style look best when placed with similar styles. See **Figure 2-14**.

Split-Level Designs

The ***split-level*** house is a multi-level house that solves the problem of a sloping or hilly lot by shifting floor levels to accommodate the site. See **Figure 2-15**. The design goal of the split-level house is to merge architecture with land to create a visually pleasing and balanced design. Split-level houses have two to four levels, usually separated at half-story heights (4′), with short sets of connecting stairs.

The general arrangement of a split-level house separates sleeping, living, and recreation areas on different levels. See **Figure 2-16**. Little or no hall space is required in a split-level house due to its basic design. Minimal excavation, often with a cost savings, allows the lower level to become a finished room.

Split-level houses do have some challenges. Heating and cooling may be difficult if the HVAC systems are not designed properly. Unlike floor

Lindsay Dean/Shutterstock.com

Figure 2-14. These two-story houses have different styles, yet they complement each other because they have the same basic size and similar design elements.

Karamysh/Shutterstock.com

Figure 2-15. A contemporary, Craftsman style split-level house designed to take advantage of the natural surroundings.

Grafica/Shutterstock.com

Figure 2-16. The interior of a split-level home. Notice how the stairs separate the living area from the bedrooms on the upper level.

plans in other house types, the open floor plan in a split-level house allows free movement of air among all levels. Adequate insulation with a zoned heating and cooling system usually solves any problems. This method uses separate thermostats to control the temperature of various zones (areas) of the house.

Daily activity in a split-level house requires access to all levels. This makes it a poor choice for people who do not want stairs. Providing access is difficult because of space restrictions and costly equipment such as multiple lifts or a double-entry elevator.

Four-Level Split Design

A four-level split design has four levels of usable space consisting of three living areas and a basement level. See **Figure 2-17**. The lowest level, a full-height basement, accommodates the heating and cooling equipment, a storage area,

Kenneth Sponsler/Shutterstock.com

Figure 2-17. In this four-level split design, the garage is located on the basement level.

and perhaps a shop or a bathroom. The basement's footprint is about 40 to 60 percent of the house floor plan. This is usually enough for efficient use without wasted space.

An alternative to a regular basement is a daylight basement or a walkout basement. A ***daylight basement*** is similar to a regular basement except the topography allows the placement of windows on an exterior wall. This allows additional daylight into the recessed area. Daylight basements are often finished to create livable space. A ***walkout basement*** is similar, but also has an entry that provides access to the outdoors. The basement-level garage in **Figure 2-17** is an example of a walkout basement.

The level above the basement is the ***intermediate level***. Depending on the slope of the land, it can be located below or at ground level. Often, it includes the garage and a recreation area. Patios and terraces added to the recreation area further enhance its use. See **Figure 2-18**. The intermediate level can have a large foyer, mudroom, or family room.

The ***living level*** is located above the intermediate level. This level includes the kitchen, dining room, living room, and a full or half bathroom. The sloping grade allows this multifunctional area to be at or slightly above finished grade level.

The highest elevation is the ***sleeping level***. This area contains the bedrooms and one or two bathrooms. The half-level difference between the living and sleeping levels increases privacy and reduces noise.

Three-Level Split Design

A three-level split design is similar to a four-level design, except there is no basement. See **Figure 2-19**. The intermediate level is the lowest in elevation. The area can accommodate a family room or recreation room (rec room), bathroom, laundry room, storage room, or garage. The intermediate level also gives access to the crawl space, which is located underneath the living level. The crawl space provides an area for maintenance, ventilation, and extra storage. Above the crawl space and located at ground level is the living level. The kitchen, dining room, living room, foyer, mudroom, and a bathroom are generally located on the living level. As with the four-level split design, the highest elevation is the sleeping level, containing the bedrooms and additional bathrooms.

Paul Saini/Shutterstock.com

Figure 2-18. A terrace or patio can extend a recreation or entertainment area on the intermediate level into the outdoors.

Publio Furbino/Shutterstock.com

Figure 2-19. An unusual three-level home built into the side of a mountain.

Split-Entry Design

A ***split-entry*** house has two levels separated by the entrance's foyer stairway. The main living area is on the top floor, and a secondary living area or basement is on the lower level. Commonly referred to as a *bi-level* or *raised ranch*, it is essentially a one-story house with a raised basement. Exterior stairs going up to the entrance are a common feature when the foyer is above ground. See **Figure 2-20**.

Split-Level Layouts

The split-level house has three variations: side-by-side, front-to-back, and back-to-front layouts. See **Figure 2-21**. The grade or slope of the lot determines the variation best suited for a given application.

Lots that slope from one side to the other are suited for the side-by-side layout. This layout places the living area opposite the sleeping and intermediate areas.

The front-to-back variation of the split-level house is suited for lots that are high in front and low in the back. This variation looks like a

V.J. Matthew/Shutterstock.com

Figure 2-20. A split-entry house with exterior steps leading to the main living area.

one-story home from the front and a two-story home from the rear. The living area faces the street, and the bedrooms are on the uppermost level to the rear of the structure.

The back-to-front variation of the split-level house is just the opposite. It requires a lot that is low in front and high in back. The intermediate level faces the street at ground level. The bedrooms are above the intermediate level and also face the street. The living level is located at the rear of the house.

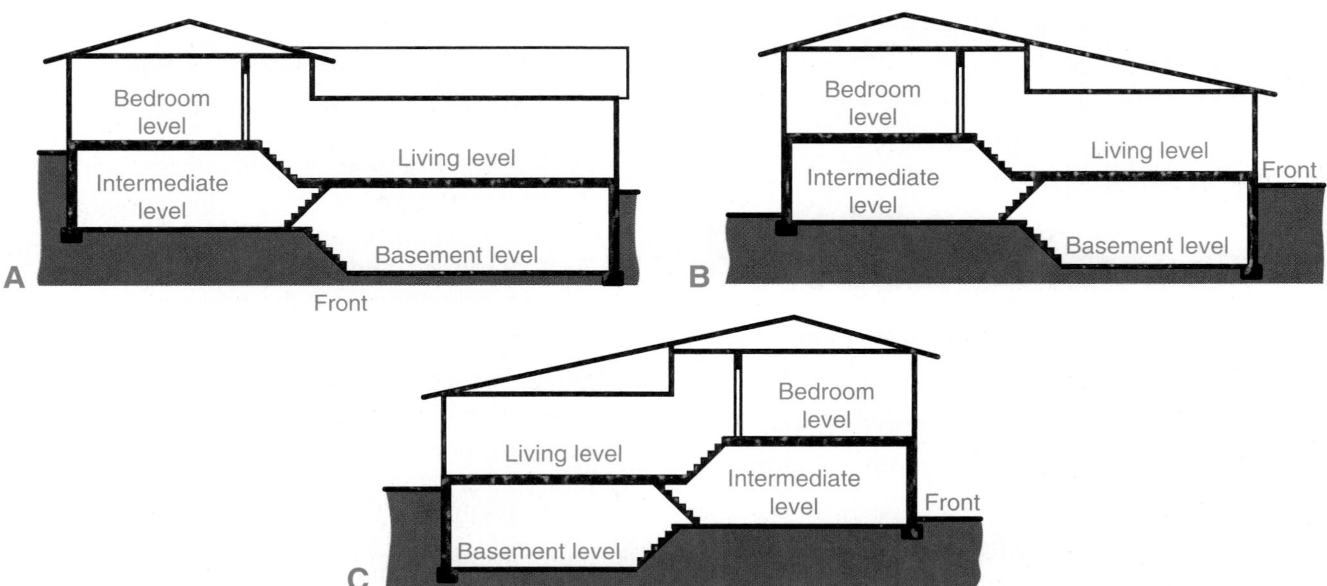

Goodheart-Willcox Publisher

Figure 2-21. Variations of the split-level house design. A—A front view section of a side-by-side split-level house. B—A side view section of a front-to-back split-level house, which adapts to a lot that slopes down to the back. C—A side view section of a back-to-front split-level house, which adapts to a lot that slopes down to the front.

Summary

- The four basic house designs are the one-story, one-and-one-half-story, two-story, and split-level designs.
- In a one-story house, all the regular living space is on one level, with no stairs, so access is easier for people with limited mobility.
- The one-and-one-half-story house is a single-story design with a wide, tall roof that allows for additional habitable space in the attic.
- The two-story house has two full levels of living space.
- The split-level house was developed to solve the problems presented by a sloping or hilly lot by shifting floor levels to accommodate the site.
- Split-level houses may have two, three, or four levels, depending on the site and the customer's preference.
- The three basic variations of the split-level house are the side-by-side, front-to-back, and back-to-front layouts.

Internet Resources

ISBU Association
Resources for container home construction

Jetson Green
Information about green architectural technology

Split-Level Home Design Guide
Information about all types of split-level housing

Review Questions

Answer the following questions using the information in this chapter.

1. List four basic residential home designs.
2. Identify three advantages of the one-story house.
3. What are the identifying features of a one-and-one-half-story house?
4. How much living space is typically available on the second level of a one-and-one-half-story house?
5. What is the main advantage of a one-and-one-half-story house?
6. Which house design is the most economical to build?
7. Describe the advantages and disadvantages of a two-story house.
8. Which house design was developed to take advantage of a sloping or hilly building site?
9. Name the four levels of a four-level split design.
10. Which house design variation looks like a two-story from the front and a one-story from the rear?

Suggested Activities

1. Form a group of four students. Assign each member, including yourself, one of the basic house designs (one-story, one-and-one-half-story, two-story, and split-level). Have each member:
   A. Identify a house in the community that represents the assigned design type.
   B. Photograph or sketch the house from various angles. Try to include all sides of the house.
   C. Write a report describing the design, style, key features, materials, colors, and location.
   D. Explain the design's advantages and disadvantages relating to the occupants and their community.
   E. Coordinate and prepare a group presentation about the findings.
2. Visit a contractor or architectural firm and ask for copies of basic house designs. Bring these to class and lead a class discussion to compare and contrast the designs. Identify the type of family that would be best suited to each design.
3. Invite an architect or building designer to your class to discuss how basic house designs are selected for various areas of your community.

Problem Solving Case Study

One of the first steps in the design process is gathering information. It is important for a designer to learn about a client's lifestyle and understand the client's needs before suggesting a particular design.

Client Profile: Mr. and Mrs. Wilson are not happy with their present house. They want to build a new one that fits their lifestyle. They are asking for your recommendation on a house design.

Invite two people to role-play the clients. Gather information that will allow you to become familiar with their lifestyle. Items to consider include likes and dislikes about their present house, needs and wants, budget, space requirements, location, accessibility, maintenance costs, function (daily activities), and future requirements. Organize the information using a word processor program. Carefully study the information and choose a house design to recommend to the Wilsons.

Prepare a report summarizing your findings and your recommendations. Present it to the "clients" for approval. Ask for their thoughts about your recommendations and incorporate any changes they suggest.

Certification Prep

The following questions are presented in the style used in the American Design Drafting Association (ADDA) Drafter Certification Test. Answer the questions using the information in this chapter.

1. Match the house designs with their descriptions.

   House designs: 1. One-story, 2. One-and-one-half-story, 3. two-story, 4. split-level
   A. Second floor has half as many square feet as the first floor.
   B. The most economical house design.
   C. No stairs are needed unless a basement is present.
   D. Adapted to uneven terrain.

2. Which of the following statements are true?
   A. The attic of a one-story house can be used for additional living space.
   B. One disadvantage of a one-story house is that it frequently costs more to build than other designs of the same square footage.
   C. The one-story house solves the problems presented by a sloping or hilly lot.
   D. A split-entry house has two levels.

3. Match each of the following terms with its definition.

   Terms: 1. Habitable space, 2. Footprint, 3. Crawl space, 4. Basement
   A. A full-height area located fully or partially below the ground level of the main floor.
   B. The area of land occupied by a building.
   C. An area less than full height located below the ground level of the main floor, used for maintenance and storage.
   D. The total living area in a building.

Curricular Connections

1. **Language Arts.** Media presentations take many forms, including print media (magazines and books), e-media (online articles), and visual media (television, movies, and podcasts). All of these media have one thing in common: The presentation influences how the information is perceived by the reader or viewer. Choose a medium and find an article or presentation related to the topic "green design." The topic should be current, and it should relate to architecture. Carefully analyze the content and determine if the writer or presenter achieved his or her purpose. Consider the following questions:
   - What is the writer's message?
   - Did the writer accomplish his or her goal?
   - Were facts or opinions used as information?
   - Is the information biased (one-sided)?
   - Was the information adequate to create a viewpoint?
   - In what other ways did the content influence your viewpoint?

   In your own words, write a brief summary of the content and describe how the writer influenced your opinions. Form a small group with other classmates to discuss your findings.

2. **Social Science.** "People skills" can be an important asset to an architect. Consider this scenario: An enthusiastic client tells you he wants a two-story house design. He explains that he wants plenty of room for indoor-outdoor entertaining, so he thinks a two-story design would be best. He has many ideas to contribute to the design. Having studied architecture, you know that there are at least two other house designs that might work better for his intended use. Consider how best to explain the other options to this client. Which house designs might work best? How can you present the information to help the client choose a better option without hurting his feelings or losing his enthusiasm?

STEM Connections

1. **Math.** A new client is looking to construct a one-and-one-half-story home with a total of 2100 square feet. Assuming that the second floor has half as much square footage as the first floor, how many square feet of living space will be on the first floor? How many square feet will be on the second floor?

Communicating about Architecture

1. **Speaking.** Working in groups of four, assign each member a design style (one-story, one-and-one-half story, two-story, or split-level) of his or her ideal home. Have each member make drawings or create model sets of the home. Each member should describe the ideal home in detail—room by room, feature by feature. At the end of all four presentations, poll the group members to see which house they like best.
2. **Speaking and Listening.** As classmates describe their ideal homes, take notes on their presentations. Write down any questions that occur to you. Then, give your vote to the house you like the best and explain your selection.

Chapter 3

Preparing for a Career in Architecture

Objectives

After completing this chapter, you will be able to:

- Compare the duties and educational requirements of various career options in architecture.
- Explain the advantages and disadvantages of entrepreneurship.
- Describe the skills and traits employers look for when interviewing job applicants.
- List workplace skills that have a positive effect on job performance.
- Describe strategies for increasing your chance for promotion.
- Explain the proper procedure for leaving a job.

Key Terms

active listening
architect
architectural drafter
architectural engineer
architectural illustrator
business etiquette
construction technologist
discrimination
employability skills
entrepreneur
estimator
franchise
harassment
interior designer
job skills
land surveyor
lifelong learning
personal management skills
portfolio
residential building designer
résumé
specifications writer
teamwork
workplace skills

Careers in Architecture

Many different career and job opportunities exist in the architectural field. You may find some of these occupations more interesting and exciting than others. To find the career that is right for you, it is important to look at all of the alternatives. This chapter outlines a number of career opportunities and provides an overall picture of the skills you will need to get and keep a job in the architectural field.

Architect

An ***architect*** designs structures by working closely with the client to make preliminary drawings, sketches, and suggestions for materials to be used. See **Figure 3-1**. When the architect and client agree on a final design for the structure, the architect prepares a set of *working drawings*.

An architect may also help the client select a building contractor and may represent the owner in dealing with the contractor during construction. It is usually the architect's duty to check construction periodically as it proceeds to see that the plan is being followed and the specified materials are being used. See **Figure 3-2**.

To become an architect, you will need a bachelor's or master's degree from an accredited college or university. A bachelor's degree generally involves five years of full-time study. Most states require a degree from a program accredited by the National Architectural Accrediting Board (NAAB) in order to take a licensing examination. In addition, most states require completion of an internship with an architectural firm to gain field experience prior to the licensing examination.

Yuri Arcurs/Shutterstock.com

Figure 3-1. An architect works closely with the client to design a plan that meets the client's preferences, needs, and budget.

Finally, you will take a licensing examination in the state in which you will work. The license indicates that you are a registered architect. It also verifies that you are qualified to design structures that meet the standards for safety, health, and property. Most architects become licensed by taking the Architect Registration Examination (ARE) and are registered with the National Council of Architectural Registration Boards (NCARB). Some states require licensed architects to complete additional education and training each year to learn about building code changes, new construction materials, and new building practices.

Job opportunities for an architect are currently very favorable. Many architects work for large design firms that design commercial buildings. Many others, however, enjoy working for small, residential design firms or even starting their own company.

Architectural Drafter

Architectural drafters generally draw the details of working drawings and make tracings

Monkey Business Images/Shutterstock.com

Figure 3-2. The architect inspects the construction site frequently to make sure the plans are being followed.

Green Architecture

Eco-Entrepreneurship

With the current international emphasis on "going green," starting a business that emphasizes sustainable, environmentally friendly products and services is worth considering. In fact, green entrepreneurship, or *eco-entrepreneurship*, is an excellent alternative for architectural entrepreneurs.

No matter what aspect of architecture interests you, green options are not only available, but can also give your new company a marketing boost. Do you want to be an interior designer? Offer your clients green materials and lighting options. Would you prefer to be an architect or a specifications writer? The opportunities for suggesting and specifying green options are almost endless.

Even if you choose a career that does not involve material or process specifications—such as architectural drafting—you can promote the use of green processes in your office. Computer-aided drafting, which is used in virtually all architectural drafting today, greatly reduces the amount of paper needed in an architectural office. Plans are still printed, but only at certain stages. Errors and change requests can be completed without the use of paper. Storing finished products electronically also saves paper. Choosing environmentally friendly alternatives when furnishing and lighting the office can also help your business project a green image.

Many other green options exist for eco-entrepreneurs. Several websites offer valuable information and tips on how to get started and how to market a green business. Before deciding on the details of a new business, research these options and suggestions.

from original drawings that the architect or designer has prepared, **Figure 3-3**. They often begin as junior drafters and are given more difficult assignments as they gain experience in the architectural firm. Many architectural drafters are satisfied with their position and retain this job as a career. Others may take further coursework and the licensing examination to become architects.

Educational requirements for the architectural drafter usually include graduation from high school with some courses in architectural drawing. Proficiency with a computer-aided drafting (CAD) system is also desirable. Extensive study at a technical institute, vocational school, or community college provides further experience and helps ensure better job placement.

Architectural Illustrator

An ***architectural illustrator*** prepares drawings, sketches, renderings, and other types of illustrations to present ideas to potential clients and create advertisement materials for commercial catalogs and publications. Illustrators typically have a high degree of artistic skill and creativity. See **Figure 3-4**. Today, most of the work is done on computers using illustration software, but some is still done by hand using traditional artistic methods. Chapter 27, *Presentation Drawings*, provides an overview of the various techniques

Inga Ivanova/Shutterstock.com

Figure 3-3. Architectural drafters are responsible for creating the final architectural drawings. Today, almost all working drawings are created using a computer with computer-aided drafting (CAD) software.

A

B

Figure 3-4. Architectural illustrators create drawings for many different purposes. A—Highly realistic drawings show potential clients proposed construction details and give them an idea of how the house will look on their property. B—Conceptual drawings may be used to illustrate broad concepts. This type of illustration may also be used on company brochures to imply that the company is up-to-date and forward-looking.

used by architects and illustrators to prepare presentations and renderings.

As you study architectural drafting and design, you may find you have a flair for preparing illustrations. Many architectural illustrators begin their study in architectural drafting or art and branch off into this specialized field. The educational requirements are similar to those of the architectural drafter or commercial artist. Job opportunities are normally found in larger architectural firms.

Specifications Writer

The job of the ***specifications writer*** is to prepare all the written information needed to describe materials, methods, and fixtures to be used in the structure. See **Figure 3-5**. Chapter 35, *Specifications*, provides a broad overview of the types of information a specifications writer prepares.

Like architects, specifications writers must be knowledgeable in all phases of construction, building materials, hardware, and fixtures. A college degree is normally required, with emphasis on technical drawing, industrial materials, and building construction. In some cases, a specifications writer may advance to this position from experience in the construction industry and related study, but these opportunities are rare.

Estimator

The person who calculates the costs of materials and labor for a building is the ***estimator***. See **Figure 3-6**. An estimator has a large amount of responsibility, because any error in judgment or material estimates could prove very costly to the company. The estimator must prepare all the paperwork necessary to inform the architect or builder of what the total cost of the structure will be. Selling prices and profits are then determined from this information.

A college degree with an emphasis in mathematics is necessary for an architectural estimator, especially one who works for a large company or corporation. Computer experience is normally required, and familiarity with a computer-based estimating package is advisable. A good background in economics and structural materials is also valuable. In smaller companies, an estimator may be promoted from drafting work or the building trades and given additional training to master the necessary job skills.

Surveyor

In architectural work, a ***land surveyor*** is primarily concerned with establishing areas and boundaries of real estate property. A surveying team usually includes a rod worker, chain worker,

Department of Veterans Affairs

DESCRIPTION OF MATERIALS

PRIVACY ACT NOTICE: VA will not disclose information collected on this form to any source other than what has been authorized under the Privacy Act of 1974 or Title 38, CFR 1.576 for routine uses (for example: Authorizing release of information to Congress when requested for statistical purposes) as identified in the VA system of records, 55VA26, Loan Guaranty Home, Condominium and Manufactured Home Loan Applicant Records, Specially Adapted Housing Applicant Records, and Vendee Loan Applicant Records - VA, 17VA26, Loan Guaranty Fee Personnel and Program Participant Records - VA, and published in the Federal Register. Your obligation to respond is required to obtain or retain benefits.

RESPONDENT BURDEN: We need this information to establish the value and or cost of adaptations or new construction before work begins. Title 38, U.S.C. authorizes collections of this information. We estimate that you will need an average of 30 minutes to review the instructions, find the information, and complete this form. VA cannot conduct or sponsor a collection of information unless a valid OMB control number is displayed. You are not required to respond to a collection of information if this number is not displayed. Valid OMB control numbers can be located on the OMB Internet Page at www.reginfo.gov/public/do/PRAMain. If desired, you can call 1-800-827-1000 to get information on where to send comments or suggestions about this form.

☐ PROPOSED CONSTRUCTION ☐ UNDER CONSTRUCTION CASE NO.

PROPERTY ADDRESS (*Include City and State*)

NAME AND ADDRESS OF CONTRACTOR OR BUILDER

NAME AND ADDRESS OF LENDER OR SPONSOR

INSTRUCTIONS

1. For additional information on how this form is to be submitted, number of copies, etc., see the instructions in the VA Lender's Handbook.
2. Describe all materials and equipment to be used, whether or not shown on the drawings, by marking an X in each appropriate check-box and entering the information called for each space. If space is inadequate, enter "See misc." and describe under item 27 or on an attached sheet. **The use of paint containing more than the percentage of lead by weight permitted by law is prohibited.**
3. Work not specifically described or shown will not be considered unless required, then the minimum acceptable will be assumed. Work exceeding minimum requirements cannot be considered unless specifically described.
4. Include no alternates, "or equal" phrases, or contradictory items. (Consideration of a request for acceptance of substitute materials or equipment is not thereby precluded.)
5. Include signatures required at the end of this form.
6. The construction shall be completed in compliance with the related drawings and specifications, as amended during processing. The specifications include this Description of Materials and the applicable Minimum Property Requirements.

1. EXCAVATION

Bearing soil, type

2. FOUNDATIONS

Footings concrete mix ______ strength psi ______ Reinforcing

Foundation wall material ______ Reinforcing

Interior foundation wall material ______ Party foundation wall

Columns material and sizes ______ Piers material and reinforcing

Girders material and sizes ______ Sills material

Basement entrance areaway ______ Window areaways

Waterproofing ______ Footing drains

insulation

vents

Department of Veterans Affairs

Figure 3-5. Specifications writers have a solid knowledge of architectural materials and methods, as well as an understanding of the complex forms needed to describe an architectural job.

instrument worker, and party chief. They are involved with the planning and subdivision of land and the preparation of property descriptions. See **Figure 3-7**. It is also their responsibility to prepare maps and plats that show defined areas and natural or artificially created features above and below the ground level. Surveyors prepare drawings and written specifications to show property lines and features of the land.

Surveyors are skilled in the use of surveying equipment. They collect data accurately and are knowledgeable about mapping. An understanding of the principles of real estate property law is also valuable. Many features of a residential structure depend on the surveyor's skill in measuring grade level and property lines. Many building code requirements are based on these data.

OtnaYdur/Shutterstock.com

Figure 3-6. An estimator prepares the costs of materials and labor for a building.

Dmitry Kalinovsky/Shutterstock.com

Figure 3-7. One of the first steps before construction can begin on a new home is a detailed survey of the property.

Educational requirements for a surveyor include a bachelor's degree in surveying or civil engineering. However, many technical institutes and community colleges offer two-year programs that allow a person with practical experience to become a surveying technician. Education in CAD and surveying software is also desirable.

Teaching Architectural Drafting

A teaching career in architectural drafting is an interesting and rewarding experience for many people. There are considerable opportunities to teach architecture in high schools, trade or vocational schools, community colleges, and universities. See **Figure 3-8**.

The educational requirements for teaching architecture include a bachelor's degree in architecture or industrial technology, but other requirements vary according to the type of school and program. Teaching architectural technology or graduate programs in architectural drafting

Goodluz/Shutterstock.com

Figure 3-8. Introducing students to the world of architecture can be an extremely rewarding career.

normally requires an advanced degree—either a master's or doctorate—as well as practical experience.

Architectural Engineer

If you enjoy looking at the details that make up the "big picture," you may be interested in a career as an architectural engineer. ***Architectural engineers*** work with all of the systems within a building to integrate the design, construction, and operation of the building. See **Figure 3-9**. They concentrate on the stability of the structural components and make sure the architect's design is safe. In the wake of damage from hurricanes, tornadoes, and other natural disasters in recent years, public concern about the structural integrity of buildings has increased. As a result, job opportunities for architectural engineers have also increased.

To become an architectural engineer, you will need at least a bachelor's degree in either architectural engineering or civil engineering. The courses are more technical than those for an architect and include training in thermodynamics and engineering physics. As with all architectural careers, experience in an architectural firm is usually preferred.

Andresr/Shutterstock.com

Figure 3-9. The architectural engineer is responsible for ensuring that the structural design is strong enough to withstand common hazards. Depending on the area of the country, houses are built to resist hurricane-force winds, earthquake damage, or damage from other natural disasters.

Construction Technologist

Construction technologists are qualified for both supervisory and technical roles in the construction industry. In addition to managing construction, the duties of a construction technologist may include purchasing, expediting, specifications writing, estimating and bidding, quality control, and site supervision. See **Figure 3-10**.

A construction technologist typically has a bachelor's degree in construction technology. This major requires a strong background in science and knowledge of construction methodology. Experience in construction, although not essential, is extremely helpful.

Residential Building Designer

Residential building designers are specialists who are familiar with the complex process of planning and designing a residential structure. See **Figure 3-11**. They must know the applicable building codes and ordinances, as well as design options and product choices.

Although the work of a building designer is similar to that of an architect, building designers do not have to register with the state, and in many states, the requirements for becoming a building designer are not regulated. Therefore, for those who have chosen the building design profession, there is no greater evidence of competency than becoming a Certified Professional Building Designer (CPBD). Residential designers may or may not hold a degree in architecture, but they must have at least six years of professional design experience or equivalent higher education training to receive National Council of Building Designer Certification (NCBDC) credentials. The organization that represents this group of professionals is the American Institute of Building Design (AIBD).

Interior Designer

Although their specialty is designing interior spaces, ***interior designers*** are sometimes consulted during the planning stages of new construction. They may review proposed floor plans and offer ideas for architectural highlights in high-end homes. See **Figure 3-12**.

Brocreative/Shutterstock.com

Figure 3-10. An experienced construction technologist may be responsible for site supervision or quality control inspections.

Brandon Bourdages/Shutterstock.com

Figure 3-11. Residential building designers concentrate on the design and construction of single-family homes.

Shawn Zhang/Shutterstock.com

Figure 3-12. The recessed ceiling, decorative columns, and wainscoting in this home theater room show the influence of an interior designer.

Many interior designers work for design or architectural firms; however, about 30% of interior designers are self-employed. To become an interior designer, you will need a bachelor's degree in interior design. Additional training or experience is required for some positions.

Entrepreneurship

Some day you may want to have your own business. A person who starts, manages, and assumes the risks of a business is called an ***entrepreneur***. Every year many new businesses are started, but most fail. The reasons generally cited for failure include lack of adequate financing, poor management, and lack of required knowledge. These issues need not prevent you from starting a business, however. If you understand the possible problems and make a plan to deal with them, you can be a successful business owner.

Owning your own business has both positive and negative aspects. Advantages of owning a business include being your own boss, setting your own hours, the chance to make more money, and the satisfaction of building a successful enterprise. See **Figure 3-13**. Disadvantages include the enormous responsibility of making decisions, long hours required to start and run the business, risk of failure, and—if you hire employees—responsibility for the livelihood of others. However, the rewards of running a successful business generally outweigh the disadvantages. To own a business, you can buy an existing business, buy a franchise, or start your own business "from the ground up."

Buying an Existing Business

The first decision for owning your own business is what type of business you want to own. You

Oliveromg/Shutterstock.com

Figure 3-13. As an entrepreneur, this architectural designer enjoys the freedom to work in his own home. He can dress casually, unless he is meeting clients. With the help of his computer and smartphone, his "office" can be in the kitchen, the living room, or even outside.

Nataliiap/Shutterstock.com

Figure 3-14. Before agreeing to buy an existing business, investigate it thoroughly. Review the company's annual report and other documents to make sure it is in good financial condition.

may have seen many "business opportunities" advertised in the newspaper or online. Most of these are not really opportunities at all. If it seems too good to be true, it probably is. To find out if a business opportunity is legitimate, research the company's background. Find out how well the company is doing. Why does the owner want to sell? See **Figure 3-14**.

If the company appears to be in good shape, you should still ask questions such as:

- What business skills and knowledge do you have that apply to this business?
- What government regulations apply to this business?
- Can you get financing?
- How much overhead, such as utilities, taxes, payroll, and insurance, does the business have?
- Is the location good?
- What about the competition?

Consider all of these things carefully. If you are still interested after answering these questions, this may be the company for you.

Buying a Franchise

A ***franchise*** is a license to sell an established company's products or services. Allstate® Insurance, SportClips®, and Chili's® are examples of franchises. See **Figure 3-15**. The biggest advantage of purchasing a franchise is that the product or service is already well-known. Many franchised businesses also offer training and advice for the franchise owners. The disadvantages include

KzlKurt/Shutterstock.com

Figure 3-15. Restaurants provide a large number of franchising opportunities. Although many people associate restaurant franchises with fast food, several fine dining establishments are also franchised.

having to pay a monthly licensing fee to the owner of the company and having to abide by the company's rules for selling and advertising.

Starting a New Business

Starting your own new business is a little trickier than buying an existing business. Just having a good idea or quality product or service is not enough to have a successful business. Success requires constant attention to detail and solid planning. After you decide on the type of business, many of the questions listed previously for buying an existing business apply. Can you get financing? What government regulations apply? How much will your monthly overhead be? Where should you locate your business? What is the competition?

In addition, several other questions need to be addressed for a new business. Depending on the type of business you choose, these questions may include:

- Do you have the strength and determination to own and manage a business?
- Can you manage a work force? See **Figure 3-16**.
- What type of business organization should you choose?
- How will you hire good employees?
- How will you advertise your product or service?
- What government agencies offer help?
- What are the long-term consequences to you and your family? Are you prepared to risk failure?

Finally, you will need to make decisions regarding the day-to-day details of the business. Consider these questions:

- How will you organize your business to maintain high efficiency and quality?
- Who will purchase your product or service, and what type of advertising is most likely to reach them?
- How much should you charge?
- How will you reward productive workers?
- How will you protect your workers against injury on the job?

Kelly Young/Shutterstock.com

Figure 3-16. All but the smallest businesses need at least a few employees. The owner needs to hire good employees and then manage the team efficiently and fairly.

As you can see, owning a business is not a simple process. It can be very rewarding, however, if you take the time necessary to plan the business before you start. Many resources exist to help you prepare to open a business. Contact organizations such as the Small Business Administration (SBA) for advice and help. The SBA can suggest financing alternatives and help you understand government regulations, among other things. Conducting thorough research and contacting organizations that provide assistance to small businesses can help make your business a success.

RAGMA IMAGES/Shutterstock.com

Figure 3-17. A good résumé provides the information a potential employer wants to know in a neat, concise format.

Employability Skills

Choosing a career is an exciting task, but it is only the first of many steps that must be taken to find employment. After you decide which career path is right for you, the next steps are to prepare yourself for employment and to obtain the job you want.

Employability skills are skills that help you get and keep a job. They do not include ***job skills***, which are the technical skills you need to perform a job correctly, such as creating working drawings. Employability skills are needed in addition to job skills. To learn job skills, you can get a degree in your field or participate in on-the-job training. Some employability skills can be learned, but many are developed through experience.

Job-Seeking Skills

You can find job opportunities in many places: in newspapers, online, or at employment agencies, for example. You may also hear of a job that interests you by word of mouth from friends or relatives. Regardless of how you find the job, the first thing you will need to do is apply for it. Applying for a job involves more than just filling out an application for employment. Prepare yourself so that you can make a good impression on the company.

Create or update your ***résumé*** to summarize your job qualifications, experience, and education. See **Figure 3-17**. This is one of the first steps, because you will need to send your résumé along with your job application. See the Employability feature "Developing a Résumé" for more information about creating your résumé. If the employer is impressed by your résumé, you may then be called in for an interview.

Making a good impression during an interview requires both advance preparation and good communication skills. If the company has a website, browse the site to learn as much as you can about the organization before you apply. Being knowledgeable about the company makes a good first impression. The more you know about the company, the better equipped you will be to explain how you can contribute to the company's success.

Tips for successful interviews include:

- *Dress appropriately.* Wear conservative clothing that is appropriate for the job.
- *Arrive promptly.* Showing up on time demonstrates your punctuality, which is a quality most employers require.
- *Use good posture.* Sit up straight, with your shoulders back and your head up. Good posture helps convey that you have confidence in yourself and your work.
- *Be prepared.* Conduct an online search to find common interview questions and be prepared to answer them. Also, if you have a ***portfolio*** of professional design drafting work, bring it with you and offer to show examples of your work.
- *Do not use slang.* Express yourself clearly and concisely using standard English grammar.

Employability

Developing a Résumé

A good résumé can help convince a prospective employer to hire you. The actual content of a résumé may vary according to the type of job you are applying for. Typical information includes contact information, present job position, work history, educational background, professional and personal accomplishments, and recognitions.

Résumés can be organized into several different formats. The most common are reverse chronological and functional résumés. A *reverse chronological résumé* organizes the content in order of time, starting with your current job and working through past jobs. A *functional résumé* focuses on work skills or job functions, rather than specific jobs. Regardless of its format, your résumé should be concise (to the point), free of errors, and no more than two pages long. Many employers will not read a résumé that is longer than two pages.

Equally important is the computer file format you use. Most employers receive résumés by e-mail. The Microsoft Word document format (.docx or .doc) is often the preferred format. Other popular formats include Adobe PDF, HTML, and plain ASCII text. For best results, check with the potential employer to find out which format the company prefers.

You do not have to create or format your résumé from scratch. Many word processing and desktop publishing programs include résumé templates that can help you get started. There are also many examples of résumés on the Internet.

Activity

Compose a résumé using a template from a software program or an Internet source. Be sure to include action verbs to add energy and interest to your résumé. Examples of action verbs include *achieved*, *delivered*, *established*, and *organized*. When you are satisfied with the content, check your résumé for errors in grammar, and double-check the spelling. Have someone do a final check to find any errors you may have overlooked. When you are finished, save your résumé for future use. It is best to update your résumé on a regular basis so it will be ready when you need it.

- *Demonstrate self-confidence.* Show that you are confident in yourself and your abilities. See **Figure 3-18**.
- *Thank the interviewer.* At the end of the interview, thank the interviewer for granting the interview.

Workplace Skills

After you have received and accepted a job offer, your next task is to keep it. There are many factors that affect your job performance and how your employer views you. These factors can determine how you advance in a job and even whether you remain employed. The employability skills related to keeping a job and advancing in a career are often called ***workplace skills***. Workplace skills include several different sets of skills, including communication, personal management, and teamwork skills.

Communication Skills

Communication skills, both oral and written, are among the most important workplace skills for anyone in the architectural field. The ability to explain new ideas and concepts clearly to potential clients helps draw in new business. See **Figure 3-19**. The ability to translate those ideas into the plans needed for an architectural project is critical to complete the job.

When you think of "communication skills," you may think of speaking and writing skills. It may surprise you to learn that listening is also an important communication skill. Listening is more than just hearing; it includes understanding what is being said. Many companies encourage their employees to use ***active listening***. This technique involves giving your full attention to the speaker. Nod to show understanding, and ask questions to clarify anything that is not clear. Active listening is a good communication tool, whether you are talking to your supervisor, your coworkers, or clients.

AISPIX by Image Source/Shutterstock.com

Figure 3-18. This job applicant is ready to make a good impression during her interview. Her neat appearance and confident smile show enthusiasm, and she has brought her portfolio to show the interviewer that she is competent, well-organized, and efficient.

Alexander Raths/Shutterstock.com

Figure 3-19. Being friendly, knowledgeable, and willing to listen as well as talk can help you communicate ideas to potential clients.

Personal Management Skills

The way you conduct yourself on the job has a direct relationship to how well you perform your job. The skills that allow you to perform your job well are ***personal management skills***. These skills include social skills, productivity, the ability to balance your work and personal life, goal setting, responsibility, and a willingness to accept constructive criticism.

Social skills are the skills that help you get along with others. Examples include being polite, caring about the feelings of the people around you, and working well with people from diverse cultures. See **Figure 3-20**.

Another part of social skills is avoiding discrimination and harassment. ***Discrimination*** is treating someone unfairly, either personally or professionally, based upon the person's age, race, religion, or gender. ***Harassment*** is tormenting, teasing, or intentionally bothering someone, especially if the person has asked you to stop. Sexual harassment is one type of harassment, but other types exist as well. Making fun of someone, for any reason, is a form of harassment. Discrimination is prohibited by federal law, and harassment is also illegal in most states. Be aware of situations that may involve harassment or discrimination, and avoid them.

Productivity in the workplace requires many different personal management skills. These include:

- Punctuality
- Efficiency and organization
- Leadership
- Work ethic
- Safety consciousness
- Positive attitude
- Responsibility and accountability
- Critical thinking and problem-solving skills
- Ability to accept constructive criticism
- Willingness to learn new skills to keep your job skills current (***lifelong learning***)

For more information about these and other employability skills, read the Employability features included in many of the chapters in this textbook.

Teamwork Skills

Employers seek employees who can work well with others. Due to the nature of most work

Yuri Arcurs/Shutterstock.com

Figure 3-20. You will encounter people from many different social, cultural, and ethnic backgrounds on the job. Respecting each person's opinions, even if they are different from yours, will help you get along with others and will improve your efficiency.

today, ***teamwork***, or working closely with others toward a common goal, is absolutely necessary. Teamwork skills include:

- Ability to cooperate with others
- Flexibility
- Willingness to try new ways to get things done
- Honesty and openness
- Willingness to accept the ideas of others

A big advantage of a team is its ability to develop plans and complete work faster than individuals working alone. Therefore, you will be more desirable as an employee if you know how to be a team player. See **Figure 3-21**.

Auremar/Shutterstock.com

Figure 3-21. The members of this team have worked together to develop ideas and a model for a new housing development. Each member shares ideas that contribute to the success of the project.

Strategies for Promotion

The skills and strategies needed to be promoted in your job are not very different from those needed to keep a job. The first step is to do your current job to the best of your ability. Act professionally at all times. If you are not sure how to do something, ask someone who knows. Asking for help is *not* a strike against you. Rather, it shows that you are responsible enough to ask for help when needed to do your job properly.

Keep a positive outlook, even when things go wrong. Avoid complaining, and never blame someone else for a problem. Following this advice will help you gain a reputation for fairness and a good attitude—characteristics that will help at promotion time. See **Figure 3-22**.

In addition to doing your job well and having a good attitude, there are several other things you can do to position yourself for promotion. If you finish your work ahead of schedule, ask for more work. After proving that you are capable of doing your job, ask for more responsibilities. This shows an eagerness to learn and contribute to the success of the company.

Odua Images/Shutterstock.com

Figure 3-22. This woman was promoted partly because of her positive attitude and her "can-do" approach to tough business problems.

Try to gain new knowledge and skills. If your company does not offer training, many outside opportunities are available. For example, the American Design Drafting Association (ADDA) offers professional training and continuing education for architectural drafters. The ADDA also offers a certification program. If you have not already done so, obtain this or another national certification that applies to your current position. Certification adds credibility and improves your chance for promotion.

If you are hoping to be promoted to a specific position, think ahead. What skills are needed for that position? Work to learn those skills so that you will be qualified for the position you seek. While you are doing this, however, be careful to continue to meet your current responsibilities. In addition, continue to be a team player. If you are one of several people being considered for a promotion, do not say anything negative about the other people. Be considerate of your coworkers, and always give credit to people who have good ideas or who contribute to a successful project.

Demonstrate good ***business etiquette***. Having good etiquette means conducting yourself appropriately and courteously at all times. For example, allowing your cell phone to ring during a meeting is considered poor etiquette. Answering the phone is even worse. If your company offers personal or professional etiquette courses, take them. Professional and personal manners go a long way in getting the promotion you seek.

Finally, be patient. Employers may watch employees carefully for months, and in some cases even years, before offering a promotion. They want to be sure that you are a good fit for the new position. They look not only at your technical skills, but also at your personal management and teamwork skills.

Leaving a Job

More money, more responsibility, and better benefits are some of the reasons for leaving a job. There are others, too, but all job departures need to be handled in a way that is considerate of the employer.

When you make the decision to leave your job, submit a letter of resignation at least two weeks before your last day. See **Figure 3-23**. Your letter of resignation should state your reason for leaving and the date you expect to leave. The letter allows the employer to begin looking for your replacement. Perhaps there will be enough time to hire someone who can work with you during your final days.

Many people have found that a past employer became their greatest ally when they needed a good reference for a future position. Therefore, it is to your advantage to maintain your professional attitude and be courteous throughout the job exit process, even if you are angry or upset. Keeping a good business relationship with your employer makes good business sense.

Michael Jung/Shutterstock.com

Figure 3-23. Giving your employer written notice two weeks or more before you leave the company is the courteous thing to do.

Summary

- A variety of career options are available in architecture, ranging from designing structures to preparing the drawings from which the structure will be built and estimating the cost of materials and labor.
- Entrepreneurship has both advantages, such as being your own boss and being able to set your own hours, and disadvantages, such as long hours and many responsibilities.
- The skills employers look for in job applicants include those that make employees productive, including communication skills, personal management skills, and teamwork skills.
- Many different skills have a positive effect on a person's job performance. Examples include punctuality, efficiency, having a positive attitude, and exhibiting critical thinking and problem-solving skills.
- Strategies for promotion include doing your current job well; having a positive attitude; gaining new knowledge, skills, or certifications, especially those needed for the promotion; and using good business etiquette.
- Being courteous and professional and providing sufficient notice to the employer when leaving a job helps an employee maintain a good relationship with the employer.

Internet Resources

American Institute of Architects (AIA)
Educational and industry resources for the architectural profession

American Institute of Building Design (AIBD)
Resources for residential home design and designer certification

Architectural Digest
News articles and resources for the architectural profession

Association of Technology, Management, and Applied Engineering (ATMAE)
Technology and engineering resources for students

Builder Magazine Online
Home building news, sample home plans, and information about building products

Ecopreneurist Weblog
Forum discussions for entrepreneurs interested in sustainable design

Insurance Institute for Business & Home Safety
Resources for designing buildings to withstand fire and weather hazards

National Institute of Building Sciences (NIBS)
Resources and standards for building technology and systems

National Institute of Standards and Technology (NIST)
Reference materials for measurement science

Résumé Templates
Downloadable résumé templates

US Department of Labor
Occupational Outlook Handbook

Review Questions

Answer the following questions using the information in this chapter.

1. What is the difference between an *architectural drafter* and an *architectural illustrator*?
2. Why must an estimator wait until after the specifications writer finishes his or her work to finalize the estimate for a job?
3. In general, what are the job qualifications for an *architectural engineer*?
4. List at least five duties a *construction technologist* might have.
5. What is an *entrepreneur*?
6. What three methods can an entrepreneur use to become a business owner?
7. What is the difference between *employability skills* and *job skills*?
8. List at least five tips for a successful interview.
9. What are social skills?
10. Why are teamwork skills considered an advantage for a potential employee?

Suggested Activities

1. Using library references such as the *Occupational Outlook Handbook*, select a career related to architecture. Write a report covering topics such as job opportunities, educational requirements, job responsibilities, and predicted factors for success.
2. Prepare a presentation in PowerPoint format that depicts the many types of jobs involved in architecture. Make use of electronic pictures, sketches, and clip art to illustrate the ways in which the architect influences the construction of a residential structure.
3. Visit a local architect's office or an architectural firm to ask questions and observe the operation. Prepare a list of the various responsibilities and skills required by those involved with residential architecture and construction. Note the use of any new techniques or equipment in architectural designing.
4. To become better acquainted with educational offerings in architecture, obtain catalogs from community colleges, technical schools, and universities, or use the Internet to review offerings. Write down the names of courses available and prerequisites. Discuss with your class the many directions a person may take in making architecture a career.
5. Invite an entrepreneur to class to discuss the pros and cons of owning your own business.
6. Contact a local architectural firm and inquire about the employability skills required by that firm. Compose a written report to describe your findings.

Problem Solving Case Study

At Georgia's previous job as a junior residential building designer, her supervisor consistently passed off her ideas as his own. The company was impressed by many of these ideas, so the supervisor was well-respected by the owners. One day, the supervisor stopped at Georgia's desk and chuckled. "It doesn't look like you will be promoted any time soon, Georgia," he said softly. "I need those ideas of yours."

After considering the situation, Georgia submitted her written resignation and left the company. Now she is interviewing for a similar job at another company. The interviewer asks, "Why did you leave your previous job?"

Given this scenario, answer the following questions.

1. How should Georgia reply to the interviewer's question?
2. What workplace skills does the supervisor at Georgia's first job lack? What other problems do you see in his behavior?
3. If she had decided not to leave the first company, what other options might Georgia have had?

Certification Prep

The following questions are presented in the style used in the American Design Drafting Association (ADDA) Drafter Certification Test. Answer the questions using the information in this chapter.

1. Identify each of the following as a job skill (J) or an employability skill (E).
   A. Creating working drawings
   B. Accepting constructive criticism
   C. Sketching new design ideas
   D. Working as a team
   E. Thinking critically to solve problems
2. Match each job title with its description.

   Job titles: 1. Residential building designer, 2. Estimator, 3. Interior designer, 4. Architect, 5. Specifications writer, 6. Architectural drafter
   A. Describes all the materials, methods, and fixtures to be used in a structure.
   B. Works with the client to develop suggestions and drawings for a structure.
   C. Calculates the costs of materials and labor to build a structure.
   D. Plans and designs residential structures.
   E. Offers suggestions for interior architectural details of a structure.
   F. Draws details of working drawings from the original drawings and sketches.

3. Which of the following statements are true?
   A. An entrepreneur who purchases a franchise is in complete control of the business.
   B. The Small Business Administration helps entrepreneurs by suggesting financing alternatives.
   C. Before buying an existing business, an entrepreneur should thoroughly examine the financial records of the business.
   D. One of the disadvantages of owning your own business is being able to set your own hours.

Curricular Connections

1. **Language Arts/Communication.** Think about current methods of teaching architecture, including physical classrooms and online courses. How do students and instructors communicate? How is this different from communication in classrooms when your parents or grandparents were in school? Write a paragraph comparing and contrasting communication techniques in the classroom now and then.
2. **Social Science.** The development of computer-aided drafting software and illustration software changed fields of architectural drafting and illustrating dramatically in only a few years. How did this impact the careers of people who worked in these fields before the software was developed? What adjustments have these people had to make?

STEM Connections

1. **Technology.** The process of searching and applying for a job has changed considerably in the last 10 years. Conduct research, if necessary, to find out more about how job searching processes have changed. Then consider today's advancing technology. What further changes might be expected in these processes in the next 10 years?

Communicating about Architecture

1. **Speaking and Listening.** In groups of two or three, role-play a job applicant and an interviewer in a job interview. Have one member of the group simulate the person being interviewed and one or two others pose questions. Research typical job interview questions and proper responses. Try to use as many of the interview tips mentioned in this chapter as possible. Take turns being the interviewer and the job applicant.
2. **Speaking and Writing.** You want to start your own architecture business, but you need money to get your company started. You made an appointment with some potential financiers whom you need to cover your start-up costs. Explain the type of company you would run. Remember, you are trying to convince these people to give you their financial backing, so you need a strong sales pitch. Describe as many details as possible, including the size and location of the company, the service you will provide, the customers you will target, and your vision for your company's success. If necessary, bring visual aids to support your presentation. Have your classmates ask you questions as if they are making the decision of whether to invest in your company.

Chapter 4

Drawing Instruments and Technical Sketching

Objectives

After completing this chapter, you will be able to:

- Describe the drawings and views commonly used in architectural drafting.
- List and explain the use of architectural drafting equipment.
- Apply technical sketching techniques.
- Interpret the standard alphabet of lines.
- Demonstrate an acceptable architectural lettering style.

Key Terms

alphabet of lines
border line
centerline
construction line
cutting-plane line
dimension line
elevation
ellipse
extension line
floor plan
guideline
hidden line
leader
long break line
multiview drawing
object line
orthographic projection
plan view
proportion
section lines
section view
short break line
template
working drawings

A strong understanding of the discipline of architecture is independent of an understanding of the tools used to produce architectural drawings and plans. To be competent in an architectural field, you will certainly need to know how to use the tools of manual or computer-aided drafting. However, there is much more to architecture than the use of tools. You will need a solid knowledge of building materials and general construction techniques. An understanding of residential architectural design principles is critical. You will also need to understand the various systems that make up a house, such as the electrical, plumbing, and climate control systems.

This textbook addresses all of these topics and will help you learn how to apply architectural design principles. First, however, you need to understand how to use the tools and processes for creating drawings. An understanding of basic drafting practices is a necessary introduction to architectural drawing and style. This chapter provides brief descriptions of the types of drawings created by architectural drafters. This chapter also describes manual drafting processes. The next chapter focuses on computer-aided processes.

Multiview Drawings

A ***multiview drawing*** is one that contains enough views of an object or structure to represent its true size and shape from all sides. Multiview drawings are necessary to communicate the information needed to build a structure. All structures can be viewed from six basic sides: above, below, front, back, left side, and right side. Typically, the view from below the structure is not used in architecture. All of the other views are needed, as well as additional views to show the interior of the structure and various construction details.

To show a building (or any other object) at its true size and shape, drafters use a technique called ***orthographic projection***. See **Figure 4-1**. This fundamental drafting technique shows the height, width, and depth of a three-dimensional object on two-dimensional paper from a viewpoint of infinity. The infinite viewpoint allows the projection lines to be parallel to each other. This, in turn, allows drawings to show the true size and shape of the structure.

Plan Views

The top view of a structure is called a ***plan view***. The plan view is used as the basis for most of the other views in a set of working drawings for a building. ***Working drawings*** are a set of drawings that contain all of the information needed to bid on and construct a building. The drawings in a set of working drawings include a roof plan, floor plan, foundation plan, and plans of the various systems that make up the structure, such as electrical plans and plumbing plans. All of these are developed from the basic plan view.

The ***floor plan*** is one of the most important plans in a set of working drawings because it serves as a frame of reference for all the other views. A floor plan is a horizontal ***section view*** that shows the building as if part of it had been removed so that you can see what is inside. The section is cut about 4′ above the floor, and everything above that point is removed. This allows you to see the shape of the floor, the configuration of the walls, and the locations of doors and windows. See **Figure 4-2**.

Elevations

The front, back, and side views in an architectural drawing are called ***elevations***. Architectural drafters ordinarily draw an elevation of all sides of the structure. These elevations are sometimes named according to their directional relationship to the site. For example, if the front

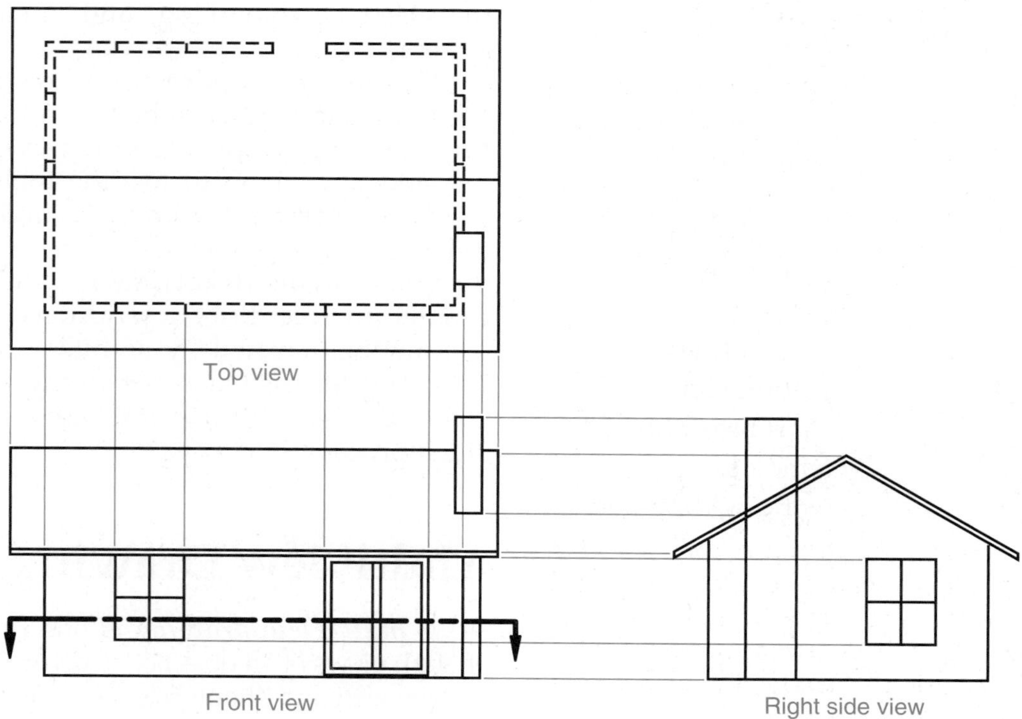

Goodheart-Willcox Publisher

Figure 4-1. This camp cottage shows the normal orthographic projection of views.

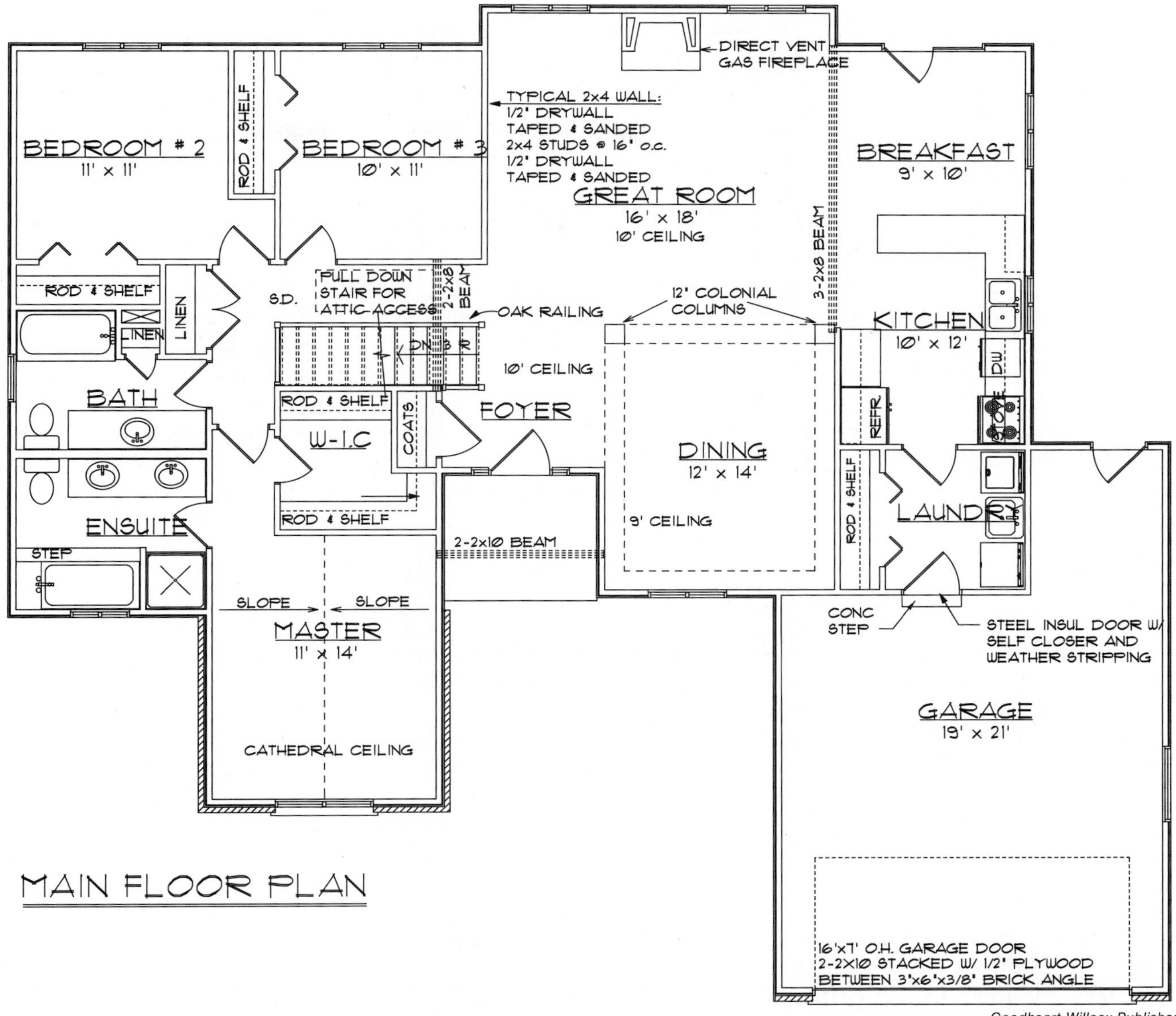

Goodheart-Willcox Publisher

Figure 4-2. A floor plan is a section view taken at about 4′ above the floor surface to show the arrangement of walls, windows, and doors.

of the building faces north, this view would be called the north elevation. If there is no directional information on the plan, then the elevations are called front, rear, left, and right elevations. **Figure 4-3** shows how the floor plan is used to project the elevations. In an actual drawing, the elevations are not presented upside-down and sideways as shown in this illustration. Each elevation is shown upright in its natural position.

Elevations include vertical height dimensions to show information for construction. Typical vertical height dimensions on exterior elevations include the existing grade, finished floor height, and finished ceiling height. The dimensions provided vary depending on dimensioning standards, building code requirements, and office practice.

Some complex structures require more than four elevations to provide a complete description. In certain cases, additional types of elevation views may be used, depending on the shape of the home. An auxiliary elevation may be included when the home has an inclined feature, such as an angled exterior wall. An auxiliary view is an

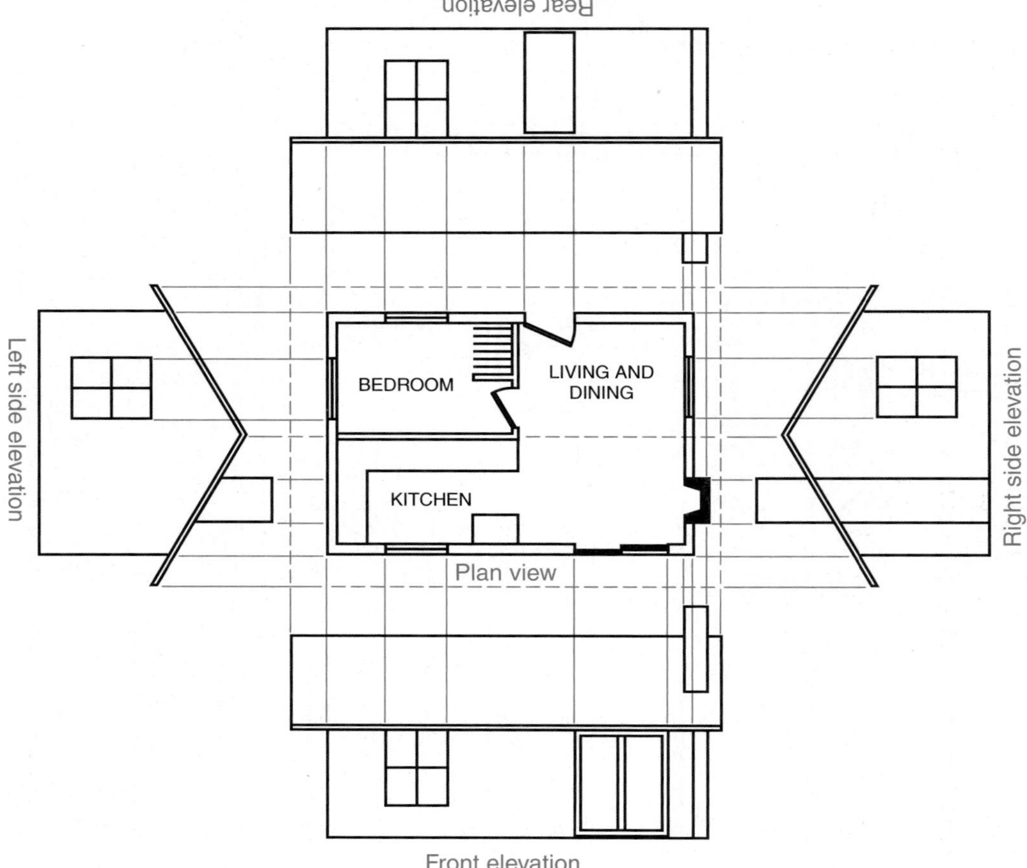

Goodheart-Willcox Publisher

Figure 4-3. The floor plan of the camp cottage from Figure 4-1, showing how the elevations are projected.

additional view used to provide a true size and shape description of an object surface, typically a surface inclined to the principal planes. An auxiliary view is projected from a principal view where the inclined surface appears as an "edge." The plane of projection is parallel to the surface and features are projected perpendicular from the surface to construct the auxiliary view.

The projection techniques used in constructing auxiliary views are applied to determine spatial relationships such as the true length of a line, the point view of a line, the edge view of a plane, and the true size of a plane. Similar projection techniques are used in constructing revolutions and intersections. The use of projection techniques to construct views defining spatial relationships is referred to as *descriptive geometry*. Principles of descriptive geometry are used by drafters and engineers in solving and visualizing design problems.

Sections

As previously discussed, a section view is produced by removing or "cutting" a portion away to show interior detail. Section drawings are used when more information is needed to fully describe how the construction is to be completed. Sections are commonly drawn to show the type of construction used for exterior walls and roofs. Building sections are taken through the interior to show features such as stairs that are not visible from outside the building. See **Figure 4-4**. These views are named by location, direction, or letter designation.

Manual Drafting Equipment

An architectural drafter uses equipment and tools designed specifically for drafting.

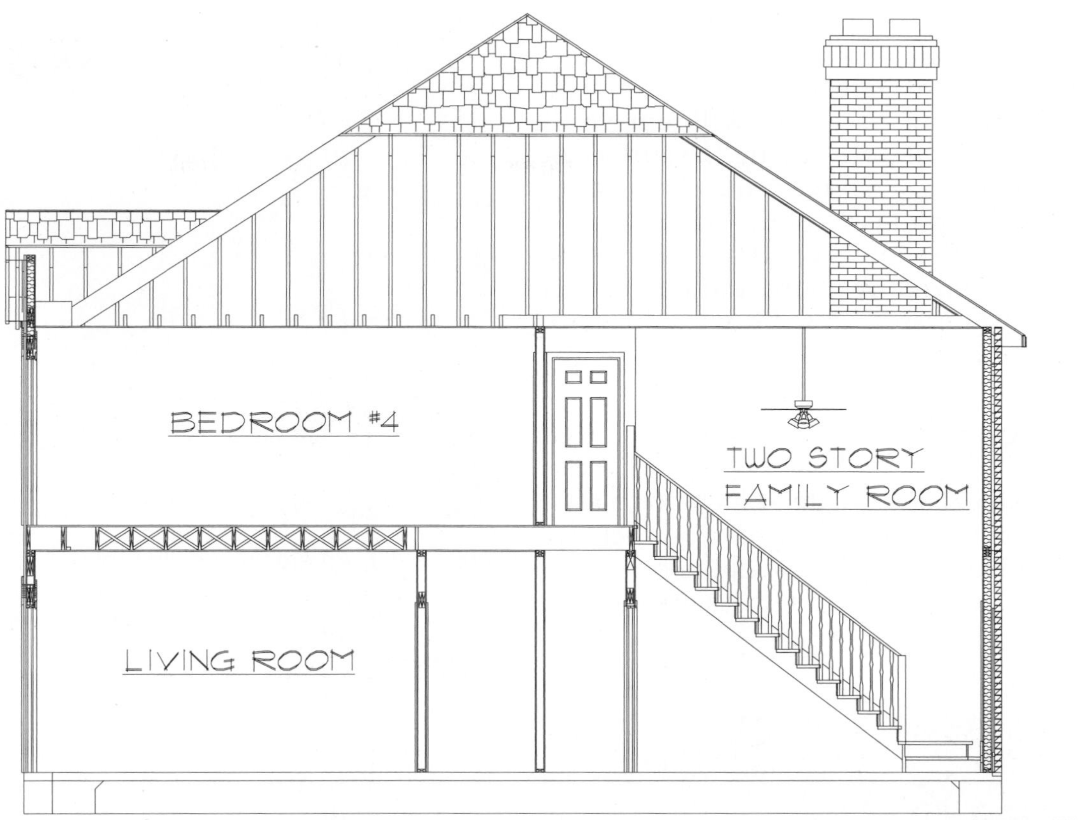

Goodheart-Willcox Publisher

Figure 4-4. Building sections show structures such as staircases that are not visible in other views.

Traditional drafting equipment, such as triangles, scales, and compasses, can be used to produce architectural drawings manually. The following sections describe drafting equipment and tools that are used to produce architectural working drawings manually. See Chapter 5, *Introduction to Computer-Aided Drafting and Design*, for information about computer-aided drafting equipment.

Pencils

Most manual drafters today use mechanical pencils. Lead holders are still used by some drafters, but mechanical pencils offer several advantages. See **Figure 4-5**. The main benefits are that mechanical pencils do not require sharpening and they come in pre-determined thicknesses. Wooden pencils are also used, but generally only for sketching.

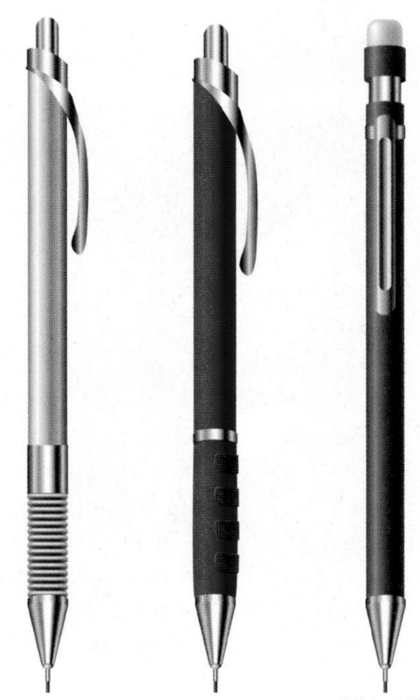

Wildstyle/Shutterstock.com

Figure 4-5. Mechanical drafting pencils come in a variety of styles and are now used for most manual drawings because they save time.

Erasers

Most drafters use erasers that are not attached to a pencil. Select an eraser that will remove all traces of lead without destroying the surface of the paper or leaving colored marks. Some pink erasers leave a pinkish color that mars the appearance of the finished drawing. Plastic erasers are preferred by many drafters for this reason. Electric erasers can be used to erase large areas quickly. See **Figure 4-6**.

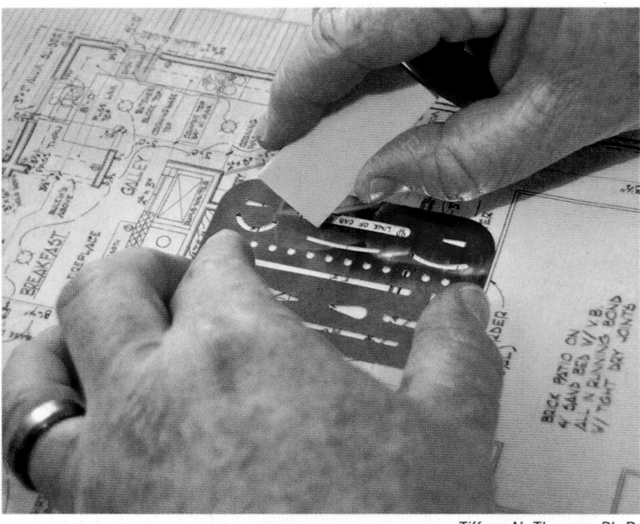

Tiffany N. Thomas, Ph.D.

Figure 4-7. An erasing shield protects the drawing so that you can erase a line of lettering or a feature without smudging the drawing or accidentally erasing nearby lines.

Erasing Shields

Erasing shields are made of metal or plastic and are usually thin to provide for accurate erasing. See **Figure 4-7**. The shield allows lines to be erased without removing surrounding lines. Always use the erasing shield when there is a possibility of touching another line that you wish to save.

Tiffany N. Thomas, Ph.D.

Figure 4-6. An electric eraser reduces the time required to erase large areas.

Paper

Most architectural drawings are finished on some type of tracing paper, vellum, or drafting film. Preliminary drawings are sometimes made on opaque drawing paper and then later traced for reproduction. Drafting paper, vellum, and film can be purchased in standard size sheets or rolls. The sheets are easier to use but are usually more costly. **Figure 4-8** shows two systems of standard drawing sheet sizes and the letter designation for each size.

Presentation plans are often completed on illustration board or some other special medium designed for the particular artistic technique used in the presentation. As a general rule, the type of medium selected depends on the presentation technique used.

Drawing Boards

Traditional drawing boards are made in standard sizes of 12″ × 18″, 18″ × 24″, 24″ × 36″, and 30″ × 42″. Most boards are white pine or

Standard Drawing Sheet Sizes (Inches)		
Multiples of 8-1/2″ × 11″	**Letter Designation**	**Multiples of 9″ × 12″**
8-1/2″ × 11″	A	9″ × 12″
11″ × 17″	B	12″ × 18″
17″ × 22″	C	18″ × 24″
22″ × 34″	D	24″ × 36″
34″ × 44″	E	36″ × 48″

Relative Sheet Sizes (Multiples of 9″ × 12″ Shown)

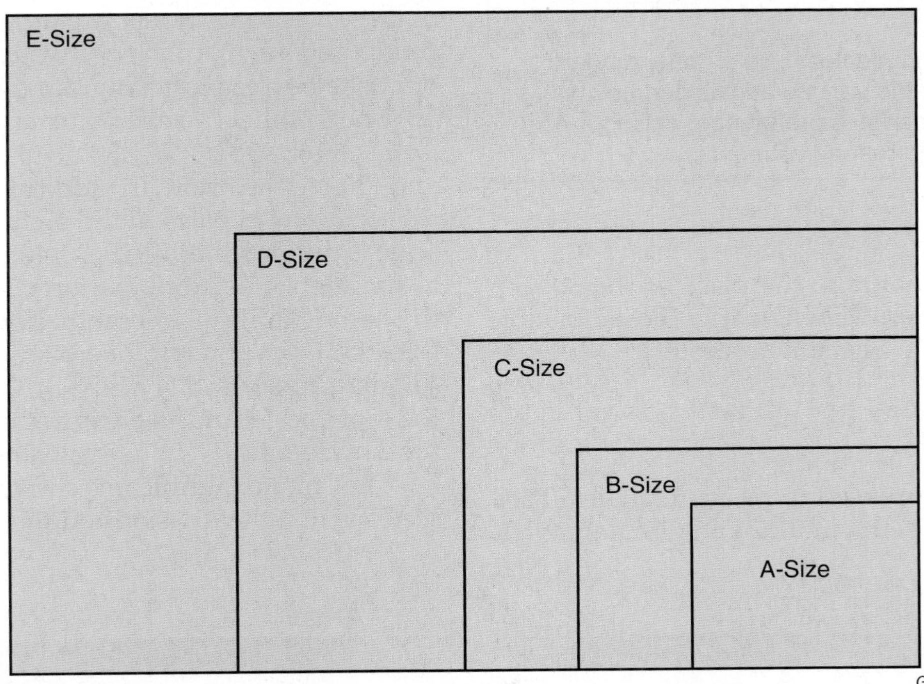

Goodheart-Willcox Publisher

Figure 4-8. Standard drawing sheet sizes for architectural drafting.

basswood, or plywood with a vinyl cover. For those who still draft manually, drafting tables that have drawing board tops are used most often. See **Figure 4-9**.

T-Square

The T-square is a traditional drafting instrument that is manufactured from wood, metal, plastic, or a combination of these materials. The T-square slides along one edge of the drafting board and is used to draw horizontal lines. It also provides an edge against which triangles are placed to draw vertical and inclined lines.

Triangles

Triangles are used in combination with a T-square to draw lines that are not horizontal. The most commonly used triangles for drafting work are 45° and 30°-60° triangles. They are available in metal or plastic, but plastic is preferred by many drafters because of its transparency. See **Figure 4-10**. Adjustable triangles are

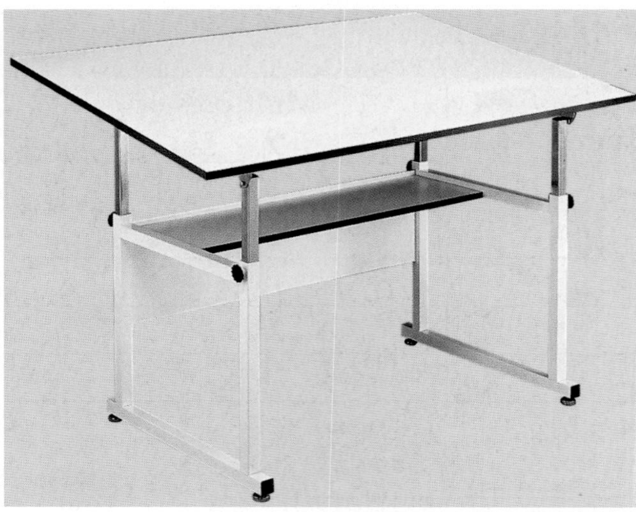

Alvin & Company

Figure 4-9. Drafting tables have a drafting board top that can be set to various angles and heights according to the drafter's preference. This four-post table has front and rear adjustments.

also available that take the place of the 30°-60° and 45° triangles. When using the adjustable type, take care to adjust it accurately.

Protractors

Protractors are used to measure angles. They are available in semicircular and circular styles. See **Figure 4-11**. The semicircular type is extensively used by most architectural drafters. Measurements of less than half a degree are not possible with most common protractors. However, metal protractors with a vernier scale allow measurements that are accurate to one minute.

Scales

The scales used in drafting are primarily the architect's scale, engineer's scale, and combination scale. A typical architect's scale and engineer's scale are shown in **Figure 4-12**. Scales can be made of wood, plastic, metal, or a combination of these materials. Scales are designed in various configurations that include two-bevel, four-bevel, opposite bevel, and triangular shapes.

The architect's scale is usually divided into 3/32″, 3/16″, 1/8″, 1/4″, 1/2″, 3/8″, 3/4″, 1″, 1-1/2″, and 3″ to the foot. In addition, one edge is divided into 16 parts to the inch. The engineer's scale is divided into 10, 20, 30, 40, 50, and 60 parts to the inch. The combination scale is just what the name implies—a combination of scales from the architect's and engineer's scales. It has scales divided into 1/8″, 1/4″, 1/2″, 3/8″, 3/4″, and 1″ to the foot and 50 and 16 parts to the inch. Decimal measurements can be made using the 50 scale.

The most significant difference in these scales is that the divisions on the architect's scale

Tiffany N. Thomas, Ph.D.

Figure 4-10. To draw accurate vertical lines, place the base of the triangle against the T-square, as shown here. For inclined lines, you can use more than one triangle as necessary to achieve the correct angle.

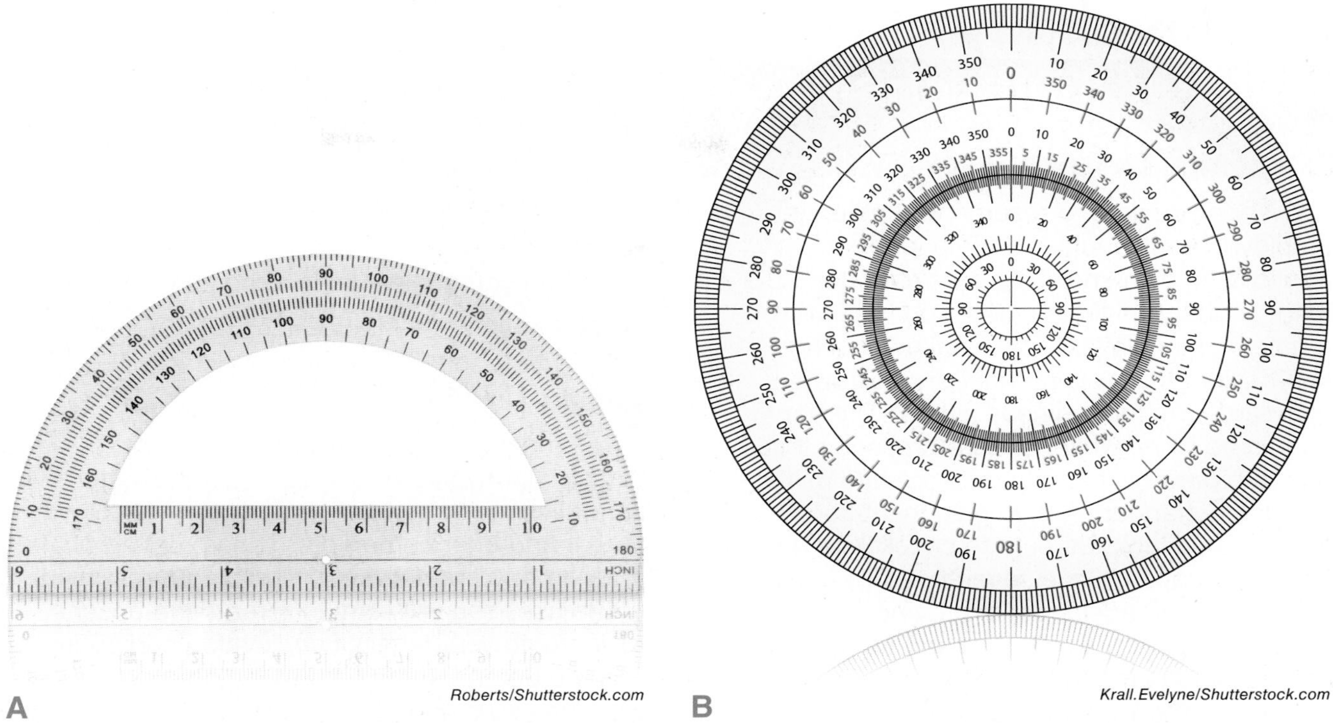

A Roberts/Shutterstock.com
B Krall.Evelyne/Shutterstock.com

Figure 4-11. Protractors allow drafters to mark off lines at any angle. A—The semicircular protractor is placed against a T-square to ensure accuracy. B—The circular protractor allows drafters to mark angles that are greater than 180°.

are based on twelve units to the foot, and the divisions on the engineer's scale are based on ten units to the inch. The combination scale is designed to provide both features. An architectural drafter usually needs both an architect's scale and an engineer's scale because certain drawings, such as topographical drawings and site plans, require measurements in tenths.

Size vs. Scale

The words *size* and *scale* mean different things. In drafting terminology, one may say the drawing is "half size." This means the drawing is one half as large as the real object. If the real object is 10″ long, a half-size drawing of the object would be 5″.

When the notation at the bottom of the drawing states Scale: 1/2″ = 1′-0″, the drawing is half scale, not half size. Half scale (1/2 scale) in architectural drafting means that 1/2″ on the drawing is equal to 1′-0″ on the object or building. If you were to make a *half-size* drawing of a 40′ × 60′ house, you would need a piece of paper a little over 20′ × 30′. By contrast, if you were to make a *half-scale* drawing of the same house,

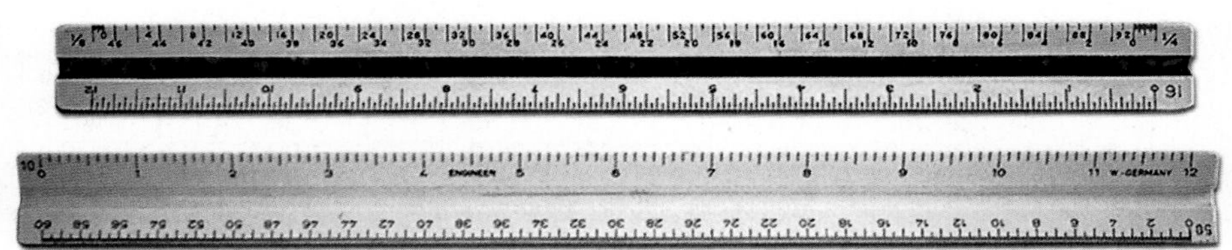

Goodheart-Willcox Publisher

Figure 4-12. An architectural drafter uses both an architect's scale and an engineer's scale.

Employability

Letter of Application for Employment

When you send a résumé to a potential employer, you should include a letter of application, also known as a *cover letter*. This letter is often the first contact you have with a potential employer. It can make a lasting impression. It should be neat and follow a standard form for business letters. The paper should be ivory, white, or a neutral color. Make sure the paper is free of smudges and mistakes.

Use a standard font to give the letter a professional look. Be sure to check your spelling and punctuation. Have several people read the letter and offer advice for improving it.

The letter should be brief and to the point. It should include the following items:

- Title of the job you seek
- Where you heard about the job
- Your strengths, skills, and abilities for the job
- Reasons you should be considered for the job
- When you are available to begin work
- Request for an interview

Activity

Compose a letter of application for employment to accompany your résumé. Check the letter carefully, and ask two or three classmates to read it and offer comments. Then create a final draft on good paper. Keep it with your résumé for future use. You will want to reread and possibly revise both your letter of application and your résumé before you use them, but this exercise will give you a good head start.

you would need a sheet of paper 20″ × 30″. Most residential floor plans are drawn at 1/4 scale, at which 1/4″ on the drawing equals 1′-0″ on the house.

Using a Scale

Study the 1/4 scale shown in **Figure 4-13**. (Be careful not to confuse the 1/4 scale with the 1/8 scale that appears on the same face, but starts from the opposite end.) Notice the last 1/4″ on the right-hand side of the 1/4 scale. It is divided into twelve parts that represent the 12 inches in one foot.

The scale shown in **Figure 4-14** shows the correct way to measure 16′-4″ on the 1/4 scale. Always begin at zero on the scale and lay off the whole number of feet. Then, measure back from zero to the number of inches. Use a sharp pencil and be very careful in pinpointing the exact length. Always draw as accurately as possible.

Dividers

The dividers have many uses in manual drafting. They can be used to divide a line into proportional parts, measure a length that must be used a number of times, and perform other, similar operations. See **Figure 4-15**. Divider points are shaped like needles. They must be kept sharp to be useful.

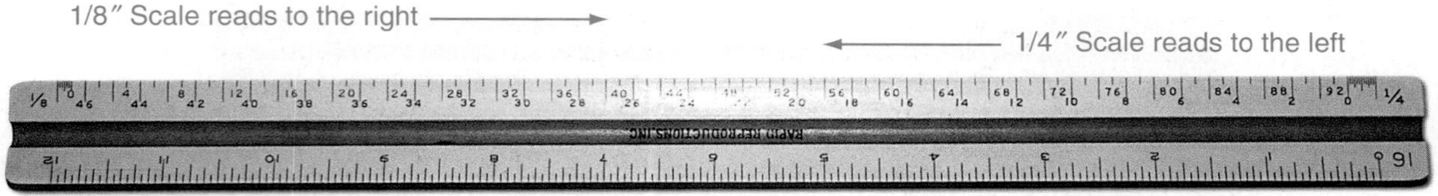

Goodheart-Willcox Publisher

Figure 4-13. The 1/8″ = 1′-0″ and 1/4″ = 1′-0″ scales are printed on the upper edge of this architect's scale. The 1/4″ = 1′-0″ scale is standard in most architectural work.

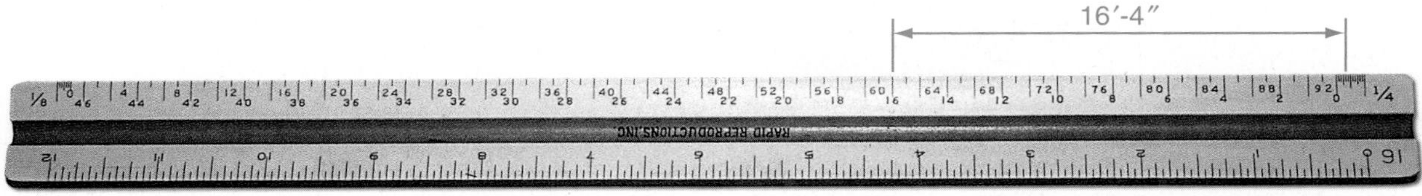

Goodheart-Willcox Publisher

Figure 4-14. The proper method for measuring 16′-4″ using the 1/4″ = 1′-0″ scale.

Architectural drafters use dividers in two sizes: large (about 6″) and small (about 4″). The small dividers usually have an adjustment wheel in the center or on the side to allow fine adjustments. The large dividers sometimes have a friction device.

Compass

The compass is used to draw circles, arcs, or radii. It is available in different styles and sizes to match the dividers. The varieties most commonly used by architectural drafters are the small, medium, and large bow compass (about 6″ in length). **Figure 4-16** shows a center-wheel compass.

Use an F or H hardness lead. Place a fine point on the lead and adjust it to be slightly shorter than the center point. Some practice is required to draw sharp, smooth arcs. Hold the compass between your thumb and forefinger, and rotate the compass clockwise while leaning it slightly forward. See **Figure 4-17**.

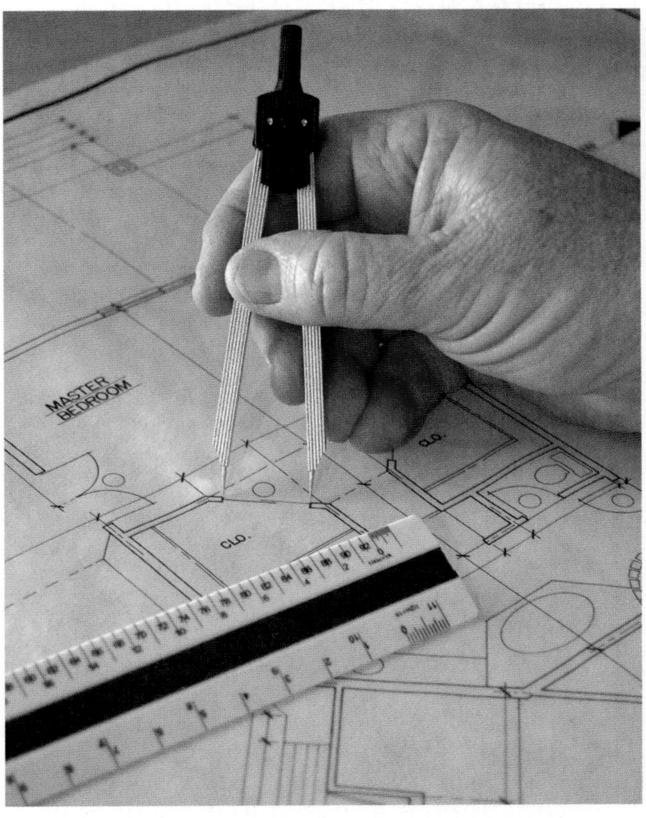

A

B

Tiffany N. Thomas, Ph.D.

Figure 4-15. Dividers can be used for many purposes. In this case, the drafter is checking the exact width of a closet doorway. A—Measuring the opening on the drawing. B—Reading the measurement on the 1/4″ = 1′-0″ scale.

Goodheart-Willcox Publisher

Figure 4-16. A center-wheel compass allows you to make small adjustments to the circle radius by turning the wheel.

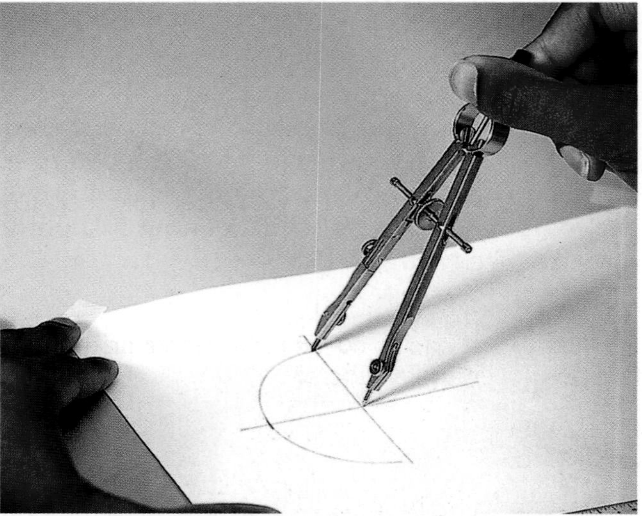

Goodheart-Willcox Publisher

Figure 4-17. Use a sharp lead and hold the compass as shown here to draw a circle.

The center point of a compass is different from points on the dividers. The compass center point may be cup-shaped or have a point with a shoulder. This prevents the point from going too deep into the drawing board or vinyl cover.

Lettering Guides

Guidelines are light lines that are used to help letter a drawing neatly. Lettering guides are used to draw these guidelines. A common lettering guide is the *Ames Lettering Guide*. See **Figure 4-18**. This guide has a rotating disk that allows you to draw evenly spaced lines for letters up to 1-1/2″ high. A lettering guide is used with a T-square to keep the guidelines perfectly horizontal.

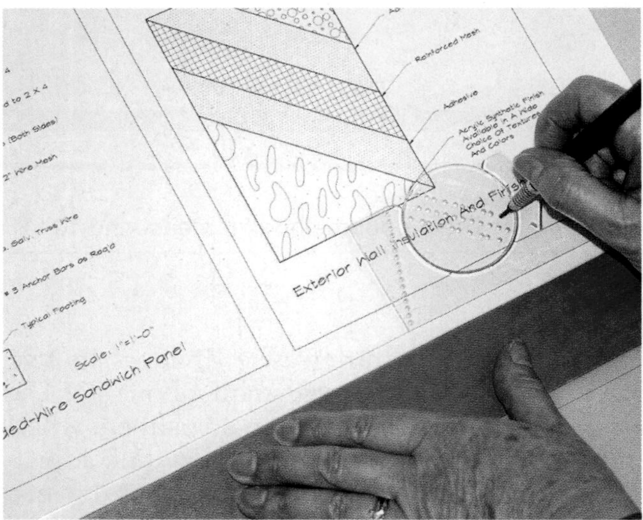

Goodheart-Willcox Publisher

Figure 4-18. An Ames Lettering Guide has a disk that you can rotate to align holes properly for creating guidelines. After aligning the guide, place the pencil in the correct hole and slide the guide along the T-square to draw the guideline.

Irregular and Flexible Curves

Curves that are not circular have a series of different centers and are difficult to construct with a compass. Irregular curves and flexible curves are used instead to produce a smoothly curved line. See **Figure 4-19**. Traditional irregular curves, also called *French curves*, are usually made of metal or clear plastic. They come in several shapes and sizes and consist of curved edges that can be aligned in various positions to achieve the desired curve.

When using an irregular curve, line up at least four points and draw the line through three of them. Continue this process until the curve is completed. This procedure produces a smooth line.

Flexible curves can be reshaped as necessary to provide complex curves without the need for repositioning. They provide additional flexibility, but may be difficult to position or align exactly.

Technical Pens

Technical pens are used to draw lines with ink. Pen points are interchangeable and range in size from very fine to about 1/16″ wide. See **Figure 4-20**. In addition to being used for drafting

A

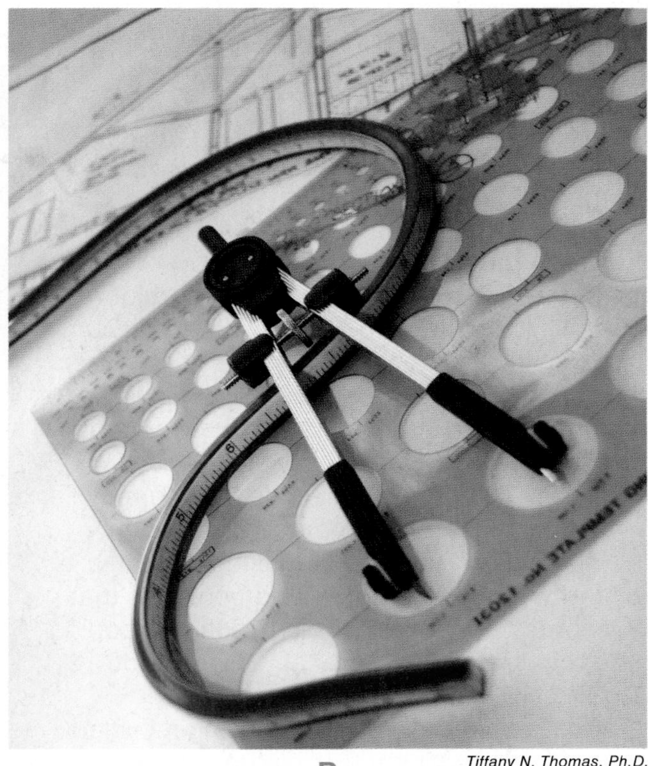
B

Tiffany N. Thomas, Ph.D.

Figure 4-19. A—Place an irregular curve so that it fits the three points you want to connect. B—Unlike an ellipse template or a compass, a flexible curve can be bent to follow complex curves accurately.

work, technical pens are often used by architectural illustrators for design and promotional drawings.

Templates

Templates serve as a guide for drawing special lines or symbols. Most templates are made of flexible plastic. **Figure 4-21** shows a typical plastic template used in architectural drafting. The cutouts represent standard symbols or shapes and can be traced to form the symbol on the

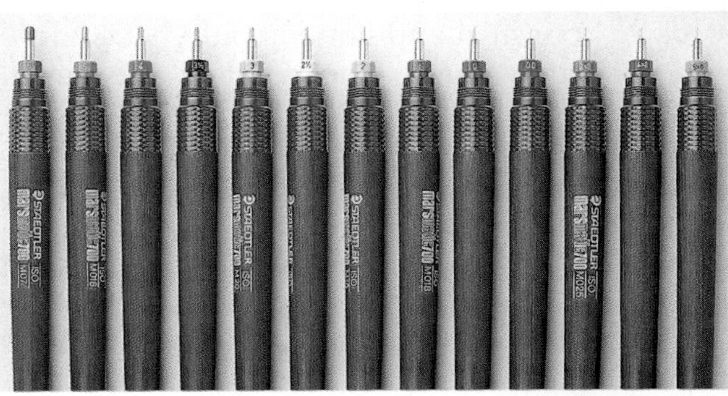

Staedtler Mars GmbH & Co.

Figure 4-20. A typical set of technical pens.

Tiffany N. Thomas, Ph.D.

Figure 4-21. Templates help drafters draw standard symbols and shapes accurately.

Green Architecture
Eco-Friendly Vellum

Is vellum an environmentally friendly choice for architectural drawings that are created manually? The answer is yes...and no. Vellum can be manufactured in different ways.

In the direct method, which is used for most of the vellum sold in the United States, vellum is manufactured from the same cellulose fibers as regular opaque paper, but using a different process. The vellum consists entirely of tightly packed cellulose fibers, without chemical additives. This type of vellum is easy to recycle, so it is considered environmentally friendly.

The indirect method of making vellum is to start with opaque paper and treat it so that it becomes transparent. This is done by adding a petroleum-based chemical, which is not eco-friendly.

Some paper mills are now using recycled paper to make vellum. This method is eco-friendly, but some of the benefit is lost if chemicals are used to treat the paper.

To be sure you are purchasing eco-friendly vellum, read the information on the package. You can also look up the manufacturer's website and read more about the company and its environmental policies.

drawing. Some of the features on the templates are general shapes that can be used to form symbols not represented on the template. A wide variety of templates can be purchased in various scales to suit the requirements of almost any architectural working drawing.

Maintaining and Storing Manual Drafting Equipment

Manual drafting equipment requires periodic inspection and regular maintenance to remain reliable and safe. Drafting equipment such as triangles, T-squares, irregular curves, and protractors should be inspected periodically for warping, chips, or other physical defects. Damaged instruments should be replaced. Also, triangles and straightedges can collect lead dust; they should be kept clean. An inventory of manual drafting equipment and consumables, such as paper, vellum, erasers, and pencils, should be maintained to prevent work stoppage.

All manual drafting equipment must be properly stored. For example, compasses and dividers have sharp points. These instruments must be stored in cases to prevent damage to the points.

Manually prepared drawings must be properly stored. They should be identified by a properly drawn title block. All drawings must be identified by some sort of naming convention, which appears in the title block. Then, the sheets must be stored in a flat file or carefully rolled and stored in a tube.

Technical Sketching

The process of making a drawing without the use of conventional drafting instruments is known as *technical sketching*. Most designers use sketches to visualize an idea before they create a drawing. Sketching is also useful for sharing ideas when an idea is still flowing and developing.

Technical sketching requires only a pencil, preferably with a soft lead, and paper. You can use either plain paper or paper with a grid pattern. It is generally easier in the beginning to sketch on grid paper than on plain paper. Grid paper is available in standard sizes, with 4, 8, 16, or 32 squares per inch. Perspective grid paper is also available for use with design sketches. See **Figure 4-22**.

Sketching Technique

For best results when sketching, hold the pencil with a grip firm enough to control the strokes. Your arm and hand should have a free and easy movement. The point of the pencil should extend approximately 1-1/2″ beyond your fingertips. Use your third and fourth fingers to steady your hand. See **Figure 4-23**.

As you sketch, rotate the pencil slightly between strokes to retain the point longer. Initial lines should be sharp and light, not fuzzy. Use light pressure to avoid making grooves in the paper.

Strive for neatness and good technique when sketching, but do not expect a technical sketch to

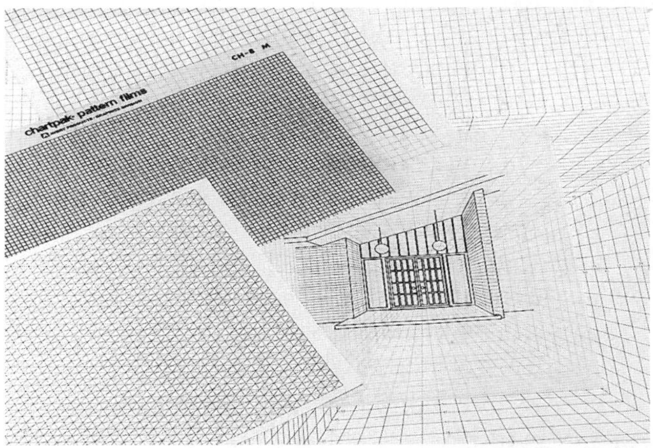

Goodheart-Willcox Publisher

Figure 4-22. A variety of useful grids are available for architectural drafting. Grid paper is available in square, isometric, and perspective patterns.

look like an instrument drawing. Good technical sketches have a character all their own.

Sketching Straight Lines

When you sketch straight lines, your eye should be on the point where the line will end. This will help coordinate your eye and hand movements to help ensure a straight line. Use a series of short strokes to reach that point. When you have sketched all of the lines, go back and darken the lines. When you darken lines, your eye should be on the tip of the lead.

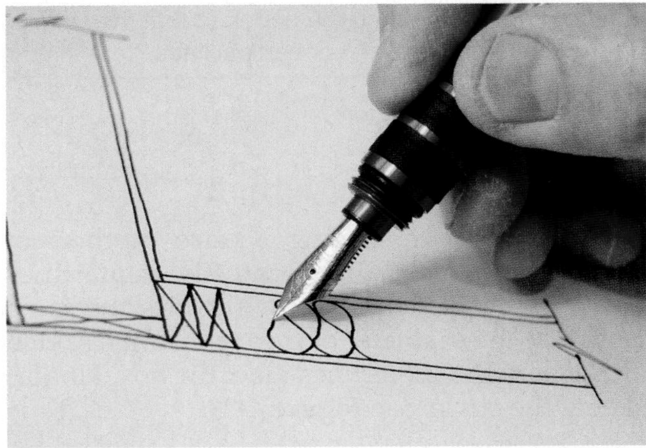

Tiffany N. Thomas, Ph.D.

Figure 4-23. As you become more comfortable sketching, you can use a pen to sketch lines. This drafter is sketching irregular curves to represent batt insulation.

Horizontal Lines

To sketch a horizontal line, first locate both endpoints of the line. Next, position your arm for a trial movement, keeping the forearm approximately perpendicular to the line being sketched. Then, sketch a series of short, light lines to connect the two endpoints. Finally, darken the line in one continuous motion. See **Figure 4-24**.

Vertical Lines

Sketch vertical lines from top to bottom. When making the strokes, position your arm comfortably at about 15° to the vertical line. You may find it easier to sketch vertical or horizontal lines if you place the paper at a slight angle. Using a finger and wrist movement or a pulling arm movement is best for sketching vertical lines.

The procedure for drawing vertical lines is similar to that for drawing horizontal lines. First, locate the endpoints of the line. Next, position your arm for a trial movement. Then, sketch several short, light lines. Finally, darken the line in one continuous motion. See **Figure 4-25**.

Inclined Lines and Angles

Straight lines that are not horizontal or vertical are called *inclined lines*. To sketch inclined lines, sketch between two points or at a designated angle. Use the same strokes and

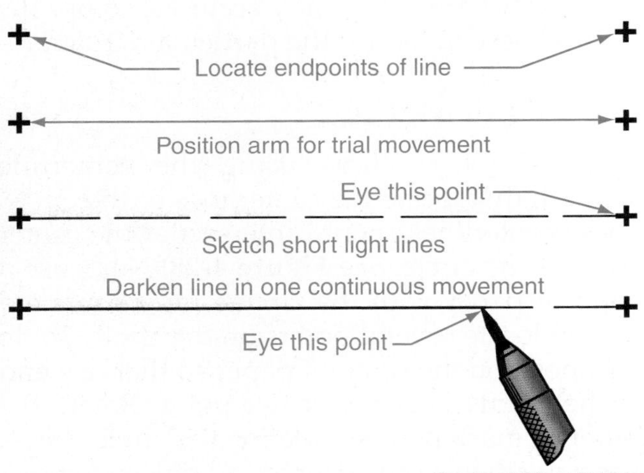

Goodheart-Willcox Publisher

Figure 4-24. The four basic steps to sketching a horizontal line.

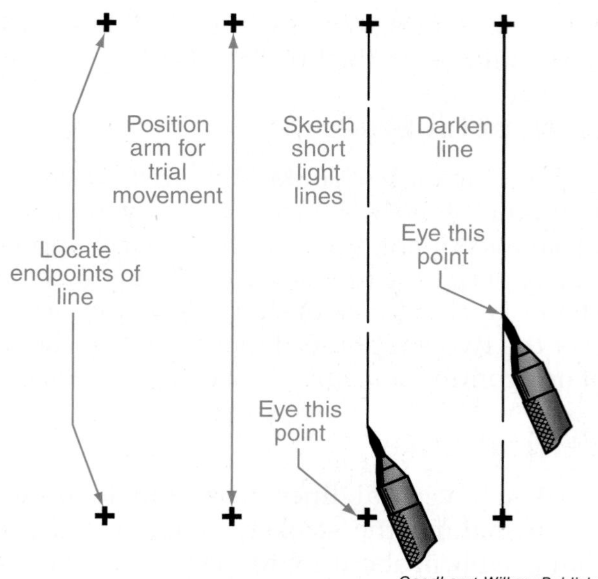

Goodheart-Willcox Publisher

Figure 4-25. The four basic steps to sketching a vertical line.

techniques as for sketching horizontal and vertical lines. See **Figure 4-26**. If you prefer, rotate the paper to sketch these lines as if they were horizontal or vertical lines. To estimate angles accurately, first sketch a right angle (90°). Then subdivide it to get the desired angle. See **Figure 4-27**.

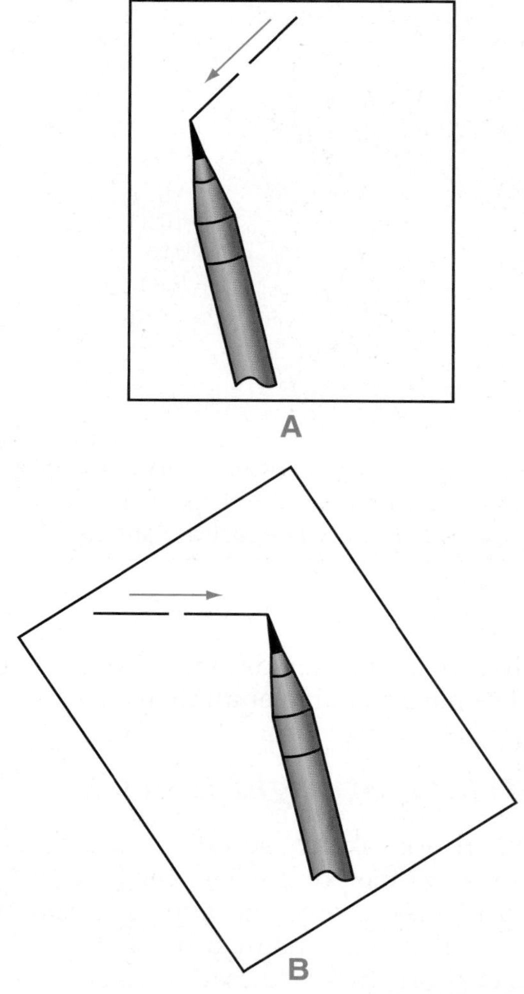

Goodheart-Willcox Publisher

Figure 4-26. Use the same techniques to sketch inclined lines as for horizontal and vertical lines. A—Inclined lines can be sketched with the paper square to the drawing surface. B—Alternatively, they can be drawn by rotating the paper so that they can be sketched as horizontal or vertical lines.

Sketching Circles and Arcs

There are several methods of sketching circles and arcs: the centerline method, enclosing square method, hand-pivot method, and free-circle method. All are sufficiently accurate, so use the method best suited for the particular situation.

Centerline Method

To sketch a circle using the centerline method, first locate the centerlines of the circle. These centerlines should intersect at the center point of the circle. See **Figure 4-28**. Next, use a scrap of paper with the circle's radius marked on it to locate several points on the circle. To do this, position the scrap of paper so that one end of the radius is at the center point. Rotate the paper to mark points to define the circle shape. Then position your arm for a trial movement and sketch the circle in short sweeps. Darken the line to finish the sketched circle.

Enclosing Square Method

To use the enclosing square method of sketching a circle, first locate the centerlines of the circle. Sketch a box with sides the same length as the diameter of the circle. Then sketch arcs where the centerlines meet the box. Finally, sketch the circle. See **Figure 4-29**.

Hand-Pivot Method

The hand-pivot method is a quick and easy technique for sketching circles. First, locate the center of the circle. Next, using your small finger

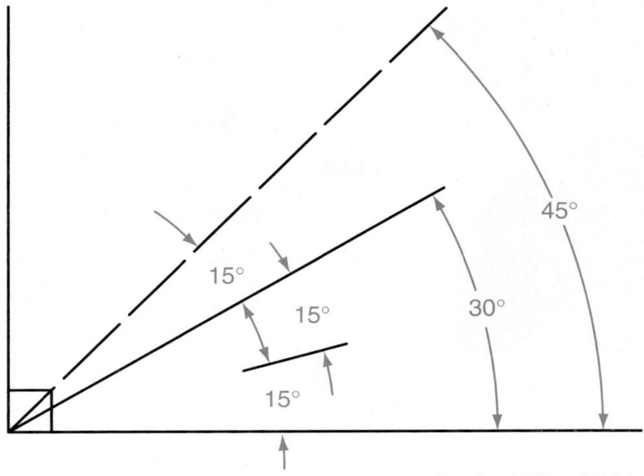

Goodheart-Willcox Publisher

Figure 4-27. Estimating an angle for a technical sketch. First, sketch a 90° angle. Then divide the 90° angle into the appropriate angle using estimation (without instruments).

as a pivot and holding the pencil in the normal manner, rotate the paper 360°. Your small finger should remain stationary on the center of the circle as you rotate the paper. See **Figure 4-30**.

Free-Circle Method

The free-circle method of sketching circles involves more skill, but you can achieve good circles with practice. With this method, you do not use any guides to help you sketch. You sketch the circle using only your hand-eye coordination.

Sketching Ellipses

Occasionally, it is necessary to sketch an ellipse. An ***ellipse*** is a regular oval shape that has a major (longer) diameter and a minor (shorter)

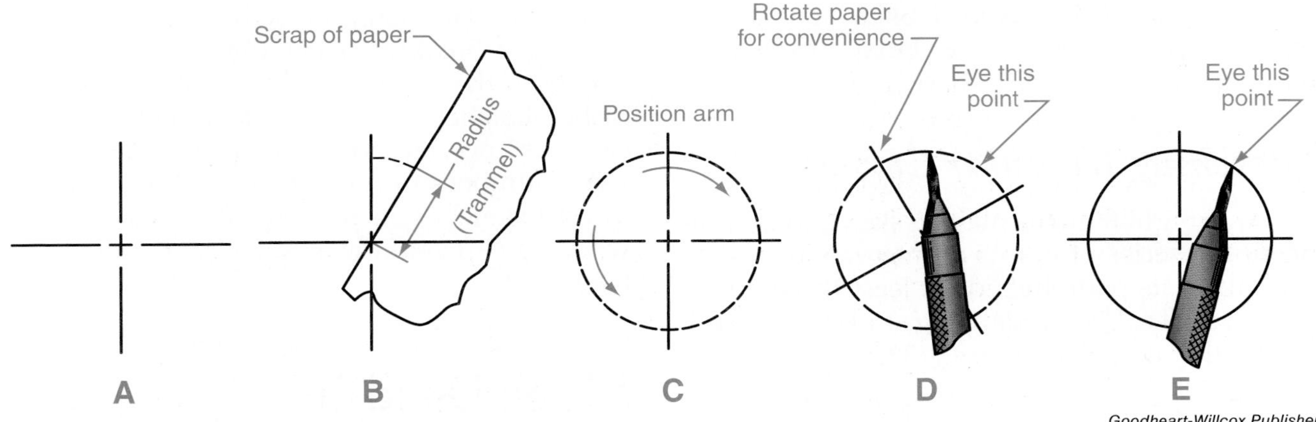

Goodheart-Willcox Publisher

Figure 4-28. The centerline method of sketching a circle.

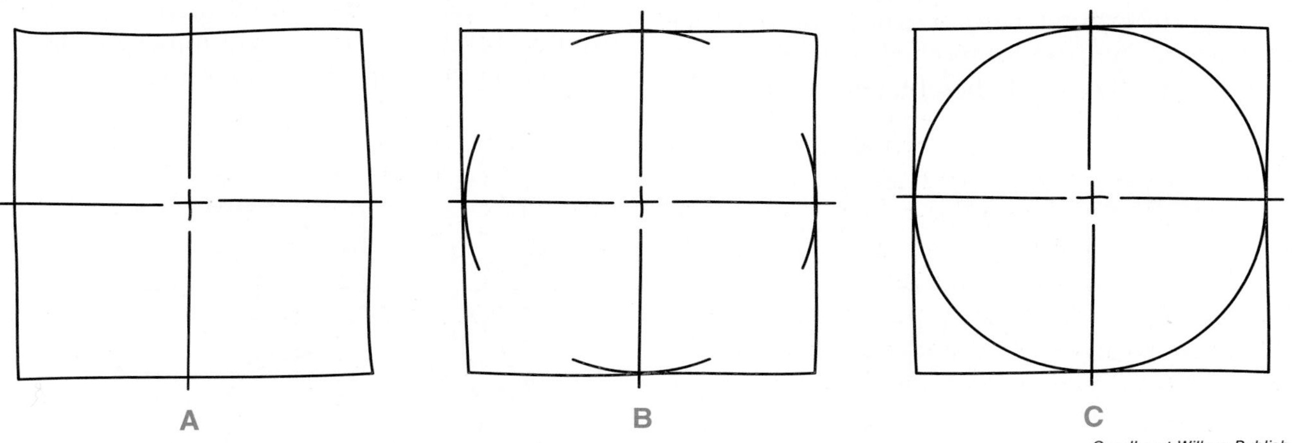

Goodheart-Willcox Publisher

Figure 4-29. The enclosing square method of sketching a circle.

Goodheart-Willcox Publisher

Figure 4-30. The hand-pivot method of sketching a circle.

diameter. The procedure for sketching an ellipse is similar to that for sketching a circle using the enclosing square method. First, locate the centerlines of the ellipse. Then draw a box with side lengths equal to the major and minor diameters of the ellipse. See **Figure 4-31**. Sketch arcs where the centerlines meet the box. Finally, sketch the ellipse.

Sketching Irregular Curves

An irregular curve may be sketched by connecting a series of points at intervals of 1/4″ to 1/2″ along its path. Include at least three points in each stroke. Use overlapping strokes to achieve a smooth curve. See **Figure 4-32**.

Proportion in Sketching

There is more to sketching than making straight or curved lines. Sketches must contain correct proportions. ***Proportion*** is the size relationship of one part to another, or to the whole object. Keep the width, height, and depth of the object in your sketch in proportion to those of the object itself to provide an accurate description of the object.

A useful technique in estimating proportions is the unit method. This method involves establishing a relationship between distances on an object by breaking each distance into units. Compare the width to the height of the object to be sketched, and select a unit that will fit each distance, as shown in **Figure 4-33**. Use the same number of units for the width and height in your sketch. This method is especially useful when you are making a sketch from a picture of the object.

Lines Used in Architectural Drawing

The main purpose of a drawing is to communicate design ideas accurately and clearly. Architectural drafters use a number of different line types to help the reader understand the

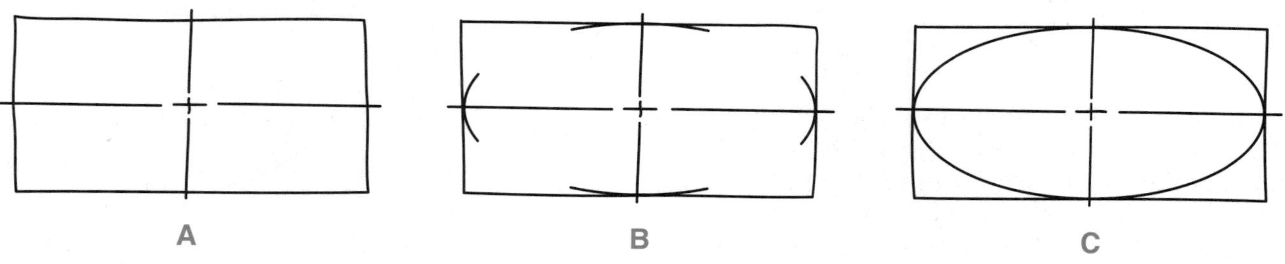

Goodheart-Willcox Publisher

Figure 4-31. Sketching an ellipse is similar to using the enclosing square method of sketching a circle.

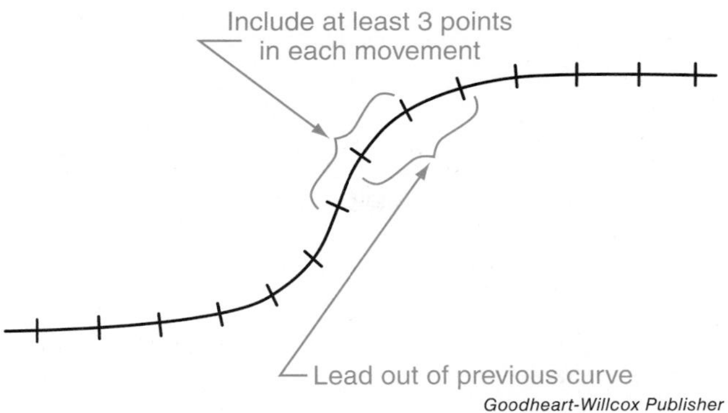

Figure 4-32. When you sketch an irregular curve, include at least three points in each segment you sketch. Also, overlap each section with the previous section to create a smooth curve.

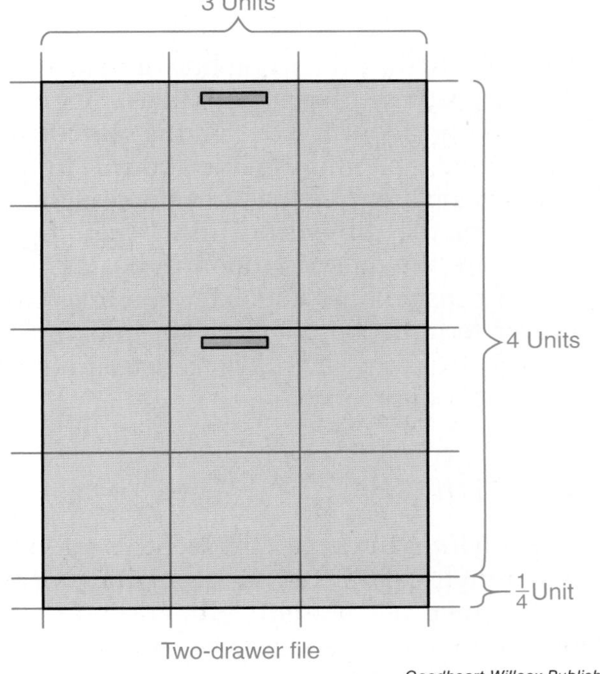

Figure 4-33. To use the unit method of gauging proportions, divide the object into equal-sized squares. The proportion can be changed by increasing or decreasing the size of the units in your sketch.

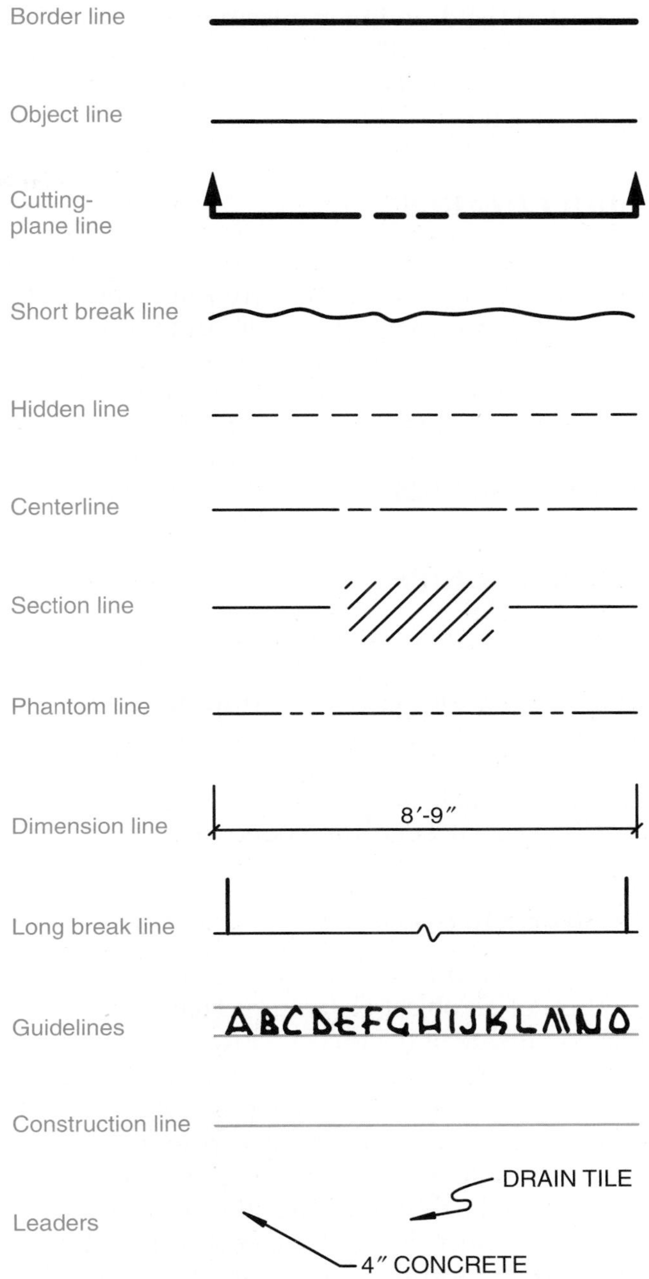

Figure 4-34. The general line types used in architectural drawing. Together, these line types are known as the alphabet of lines.

drawing. Drafters refer to the collection of line types used in drafting as the ***alphabet of lines***. **Figure 4-34** shows the different types of lines included in the alphabet of lines.

Lines are defined by their appearance and line weight, or thickness. For some line types, the line thickness is a matter of office practice or office standards. General guidelines and recommendations are provided here for each line type.

Border Lines

Border lines are very heavy lines used to form a boundary for the drawing. These lines assure the person who reads the drawing that no part of the drawing is missing. The lines also provide a "finished" appearance to the drawing. A line weight of .047″ (1.20 mm) should be used for border lines.

Object Lines

Object lines show the outline of the main features of the object. They are important lines and should be easy to see. On an architectural drawing, features such as interior and exterior walls, steps, driveways, patios, fireplaces, doors, and windows are represented by object lines. In general, object lines are drawn between .024″ (0.60 mm) and .028″ (0.70 mm) wide.

Hidden Lines

Hidden lines represent an edge that is behind a visible surface in a given view. In a floor plan, hidden lines are also used to indicate features above the cutting plane, such as an archway or wall cabinets in a kitchen. Hidden lines are usually not as thick as object lines. A line weight of .020″ (0.50 mm) is recommended for hidden lines.

Dimension Lines

Dimension lines are used to show size and location of an object or feature. They are usually placed outside of the object. However, it is sometimes proper to place them within the object if the area is large and not too cluttered with other lines. All dimension lines include numbers (dimension text) denoting the length of the dimension. The dimension text is usually placed halfway between the ends, either above the dimension line or within a break in the dimension line. Some form of symbol, such as an architectural "tick" mark (slash) or arrowhead, is placed at both ends of the dimension line. **Figure 4-35** shows accepted methods of terminating dimension lines and placing the dimension text. Dimension lines are usually drawn with a line weight of .012″ (0.30 mm), although a line weight of .014″ (0.35 mm) is sometimes used.

Extension Lines

Extension lines show the termination point of a dimension line. They extend from a portion of the object to the dimension lines and to a short distance past the dimension lines. Begin an extension line about 1/16″ from the object being dimensioned, and end the line about 1/16″ past the dimension line. Use the same line weight that you use for the dimension line. "Tick" marks (slashes) are the most common indicators used where dimension lines and extension lines cross. However, termination points can be dots, arrows, or a variety of other symbols as determined by office or school practice.

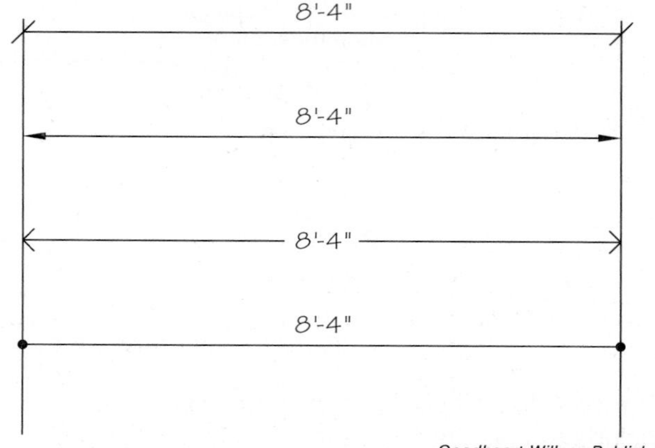

Goodheart-Willcox Publisher

Figure 4-35. Examples of accepted terminators for dimension lines on architectural drawings. Notice that the dimension text can be placed just above the dimension line or in a break in the dimension line.

Centerlines

Centerlines indicate the centers of holes and symmetrical objects, such as windows and doors. Centerlines simplify dimensioning, but they should not be used as extension lines. The line weight of centerlines can be .012″ (0.30 mm) or .014″ (0.35 mm).

Long and Short Break Lines

Break lines are used to show that not all of the part is drawn. For example, a break line might be drawn across a paved driveway indicating that the drive is longer than shown on the plan.

When the break is two or three inches in length, a ***long break line*** is usually used. ***Short break lines*** are used when part of the object is shown broken away or removed to reveal an underlying feature. Long break lines are thin and straight; they are drawn with a line weight of .014″ (0.35 mm) or .012″ (0.30 mm). Short break lines are heavy and are drawn using a .031″ (0.80 mm) line weight.

Cutting-Plane Lines

Cutting-plane lines are heavy lines used to show where an object is to be sectioned. Ordinarily, cutting-plane lines are labeled with a letter at each end or a flag at one end and a direction arrow at the other so that the section detail can be easily identified. A line weight of .031″ (0.80 mm) should be used for these lines.

Section Lines

Section lines, also called *crosshatch lines,* are thin lines used to show that a feature has been sectioned. General section lines are usually drawn at a 45° angle. However, there are specific patterns to represent various types of material. A .012″ (0.30 mm) line weight is generally used for section lines.

Guidelines

Guidelines are used for hand lettering. They are drawn very light and are for the drafter's use. Guidelines help improve the quality of lettering and are therefore well worth the time and effort required to draw them.

Guidelines are drawn in pencil only. Some drafters use a non-photo blue pencil lead for guidelines, especially if the drawing will be reproduced. The blue is not picked up by the camera, so the drawing looks clean and crisp.

Construction Lines

Construction lines are very light lines used in the process of constructing a drawing. They are for the drafter's use only and should not reproduce when a print is made. Draw your construction lines sharp and light.

Leaders

Leaders are thin lines that lead from a note or dimension to a feature on the drawing. Leaders often terminate with an arrowhead, but a dot or other accepted type of terminator may be used. Leader lines may be drawn straight or curved. Often, straight leaders are drawn with an optional shoulder placed on the end of the leader before the note. The angle at which the leader is drawn can be any angle, but it is preferable to use an angle from 15° to 75°.

Line Type Application

Figure 4-36 shows most of the general line types used in a floor plan. Other line types are explained in this textbook in the areas pertaining to their specific use. All lines on a manual drawing are black.

In manual drafting, hard leads are used to draw thin lines. Soft leads are used to draw thick lines. Pencil lead grades range from 9H (very hard) to 9B (very soft). However, the leads from B to 9B are generally considered too soft for use on architectural working drawings.

Architectural Lettering

There is no one correct architectural lettering style. Many acceptable styles present a certain artistic flair. Many architects develop their own unique style. **Figure 4-37** shows three individual styles developed by architecture students. Each of the styles is different, but each is in keeping with the sensitivity of architecture.

In computer-aided drafting, lettering is called *text*. Placing text on CADD drawings is discussed in Chapter 5, *Introduction to Computer-Aided Drafting and Design*. Most CADD programs provide text fonts specifically designed for architectural drafting. See **Figure 4-38**.

Developing a Lettering Style

You may wish to develop your own style of lettering. See **Figure 4-39**. Follow these guidelines to create a style that is acceptable for architectural drawings, but is also uniquely yours:

1. Draw guidelines and use them.
2. Experiment with variations of uppercase (capital) letters to determine the ones you like best. Lowercase letters are not used for architectural lettering.

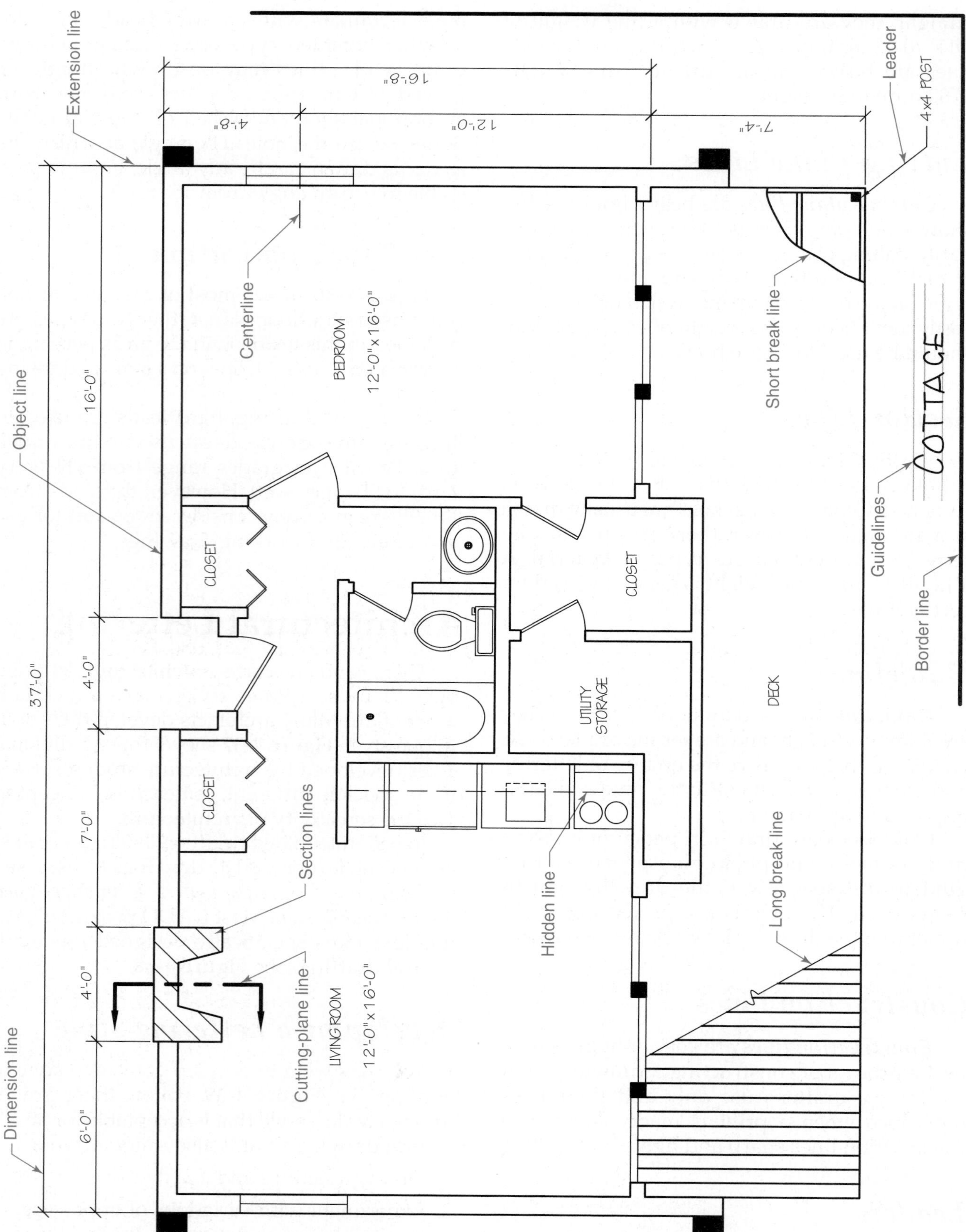

Goodheart-Willcox Publisher

Figure 4-36. This simplified floor plan illustrates most of the line types used by the architectural drafter.

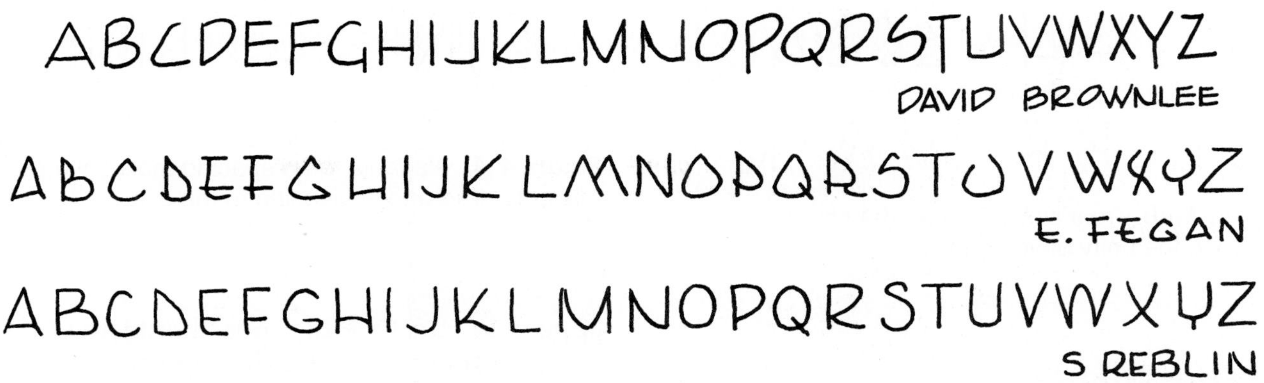

ABCDEFGHIJKLMNOPQRSTUVWXYZ
DAVID BROWNLEE

ABCDEFGHIJKLMNOPQRSTUVWXYZ
E. FEGAN

ABCDEFGHIJKLMNOPQRSTUVWXYZ
S REBLIN

Goodheart-Willcox Publisher

Figure 4-37. Architectural students should develop their own personal lettering style.

FINISHED GRADE — Stylus BT

FINISHED GRADE — CityBlueprint

FINISHED GRADE — CountryBlueprint

FINISHED GRADE — Archstyl

FINISHED GRADE — Arial

Goodheart-Willcox Publisher

Figure 4-38. Examples of common CADD text fonts used on architectural drawings.

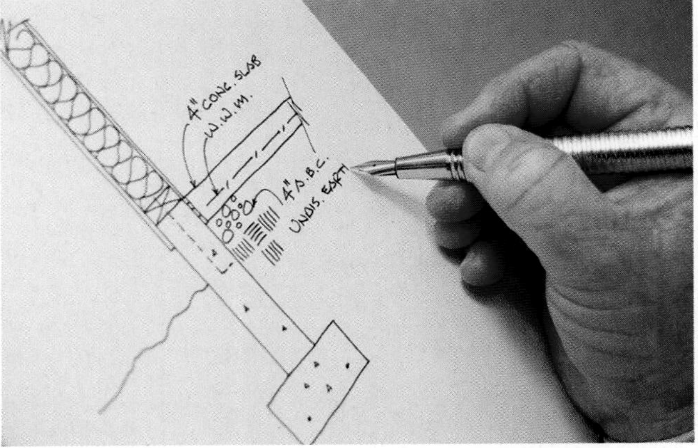

Tiffany N. Thomas, Ph.D.

Figure 4-39. If you frequently letter drawings by hand, develop your own distinctive lettering style. Your style should be clear and easy to read, but uniquely yours.

3. Select letter styles that produce artistic letters that are easily identified.
4. Apply the same style to all similar letters. See **Figure 4-40**.
5. Letter the entire alphabet large enough so that the letters are easy to read.
6. Make a mental picture of each letter so that you can draw it the same each time.
7. Practice your style until it becomes a part of you and flows without difficulty.
8. Use your style at every opportunity. The more you use it, the better it will become.

Architectural lettering is vertical, not slanted (oblique). If you learn to letter vertically, you should never have to worry whether your method will be acceptable. Oblique letters are used only for words that should be in italics.

Goodheart-Willcox Publisher

Figure 4-40. Treat similar letters the same way to increase the unity of your style.

Goodheart-Willcox Publisher

Figure 4-41. Variable letter spacing makes words easier to read and is pleasing to the eye.

Letter Spacing

The space between letters in a word is not constant. **Figure 4-41** shows an example of a word with constant spacing between each letter, and with variable spacing that makes the word easier to read and more pleasing to the eye. Judging the space between letters is a skill that you will perfect only with constant practice.

Word Spacing

Proper spacing between words is as important as the spacing between letters. Words must not appear to run together, nor should they be so far apart that they waste drawing space. A good rule to follow is to allow approximately a letter-height distance between words.

Letter Size

There are no absolute rules concerning lettering size, but most lettering in an architectural drawing should be 1/8″ or 3/32″ high. Remember to use only capital letters. Titles are usually lettered larger—often 1/4″—with bold underlines. Underlining text also helps to call attention to essential information within the drawing.

Summary

- Architectural working drawings consist of multiview drawings, including plan views and elevations, that completely describe the structure to be constructed.
- Traditional drafting equipment is used to construct architectural drawings manually, without the aid of a computer.
- Technical sketching is a method of making a drawing using only a pencil or pen and paper, without drafting instruments.
- Architectural drafters use a number of line types to help the reader clearly understand the drawing.
- Architectural lettering style varies with the individual drafter, but all lettering should be of a consistent height and easy to read.

Internet Resources

Alvin & Company
Drafting products and supplies

American Institute of Architects (AIA)
Educational and industry resources for the architectural profession

American National Standards Institute (ANSI)
Published US and international standards

Drafting Equipment Warehouse
Drafting products and supplies

International Organization for Standardization (ISO)
Published international standards

Review Questions

Answer the following questions using the information in this chapter.

1. For what types of architectural drawings is the plan view of a structure used?
2. What are the dimensions of an architectural C-size drawing sheet?
3. Which manual drafting instrument is used with triangles, lettering guides, and other instruments to ensure that lines are drawn perfectly horizontal, perfectly vertical, or at accurate angles?
4. The most commonly used triangles for drafting work are the _____ and _____ triangles.
5. Which manual drafting instrument is used to draw circles and arcs?
6. A scale that is divided into 10, 20, 30, 40, 50, and 60 parts to the inch is the _____ scale.
7. If a drawing is one half as large as the real object, then the drawing is said to be _____.
8. Technical _____ is the process of making a drawing without the use of conventional drafting instruments.
9. Briefly describe the procedure for sketching a vertical line.
10. When sketching _____ lines, you may want to rotate the paper to sketch the lines as if they were horizontal or vertical lines.
11. Name the four methods that can be used to sketch a circle.
12. Which line type should be used to draw the walls of a structure in a plan view?
13. Lines that are used to represent an edge that is behind a visible surface in a given view are called _____ lines.
14. What is the difference between section lines and cutting-plane lines?
15. Which two line types are for the drafter's use only and should not show up in reproductions or prints of the drawing?
16. About how far apart should words be placed in hand lettering?

Suggested Activities

1. Using an architectural lettering style, letter the alphabet and numbers 0 through 9 on a sheet of grid paper. Make the lettering at least 1/4″ high so the proportions will be distinct.
2. Draw the alphabet of lines using proper line weights. Next to each line, letter the name of the line using an architectural lettering style.

3. Visit a drafting supply store and make a list of the types of time-savers available in stock that can be used in architectural drawing. Include the prices in your list.
4. Obtain a sketch pad with square grid lines. Measure your drafting lab and sketch a plan view showing the walls, doors, and windows. Dimension the plan as illustrated in this chapter. Use proper line symbols and line weights. Make the drawing at a scale of 1/4″ = 1′-0″.
5. Search online for traditional drafting equipment and supplies. Prepare a bulletin board display by printing and mounting illustrations of pieces of equipment used by architectural drafters to create drawings manually.

Problem Solving Case Study

You are designing a small vacation cottage for a client. The client asks you to bring your initial drawings to his home for review before you create the final drawings. You have finished the initial floor plan and have arrived at the client's home to get his opinion. The client is pleased overall, but asks you to move the bedroom window three feet to the left and to add a window over the kitchen sink. He also wants to add a back door to the cottage. You want to make these changes immediately so the client can see the revised plan, but your erasing shield and other instruments are back at your office. How can you make the client's suggested changes without making a mess on the drawing?

Certification Prep

The following questions are presented in the style used in the American Design Drafting Association (ADDA) Drafter Certification Test. Answer the questions using the information in this chapter.

1. Which of the following items are considered manual drafting equipment?
   A. Architect's scale
   B. Engineer's scale
   C. Printer
   D. Adjustable triangle
   E. Erasing shield
   F. Keyboard
2. Which of the following statements are true?
   A. A French curve is used to draw curved lines.
   B. Technical sketching is usually done with drafting instruments.
   C. The space between letters in a word should be consistent.
   D. All of the lines on a manual technical drawing are black.
   E. An ellipse has both a major diameter and a minor diameter.
3. Match each line type with its use.

   Line types: 1. Hidden, 2. Border, 3. Centerline, 4. Cutting-plane line, 5. Object line

   A. Heavy line used to show where an object is to be sectioned.
   B. Dashed line used to show an edge behind a visible surface in a given view.
   C. Heavy line used to form a boundary around a drawing.
   D. Line that shows the outline of an object's features.
   E. Dashed line used to show the center of a symmetrical object or the center point of a circle.

Curricular Connections

1. **Social Science.** Today, most new architectural drawings are created using computer systems. However, manual skills are still needed for some purposes. Conduct research to find out when and where manual drafting methods are used today. Will manual drafting still be needed 10 years from now? 20 years from now? Explain your answer.
2. **Language Arts/Writing.** Conduct research to find out more about proportion and how it is used in creating both technical and nontechnical drawings. Write an essay comparing the use and importance of proportion in the fine arts (for example, painting or sculpture) and in architectural drafting.

STEM Connections

1. **Math.** You are creating a set of working drawings manually for a small vacation cottage. You are using an overall scale of 1/4″ = 1′-0″. The basic dimensions of the cottage are shown in the illustration below. Use this information to answer the following questions.

A. What will be the actual drawn length of dimension line A in the drawing?

B. What will be the actual drawn length of dimension line B in the drawing?

C. What will be the actual drawn length of dimension line C in the drawing?

D. What will be the actual drawn length of dimension line D in the drawing?

E. What will be the actual drawn length of the front wall labeled E in the drawing?

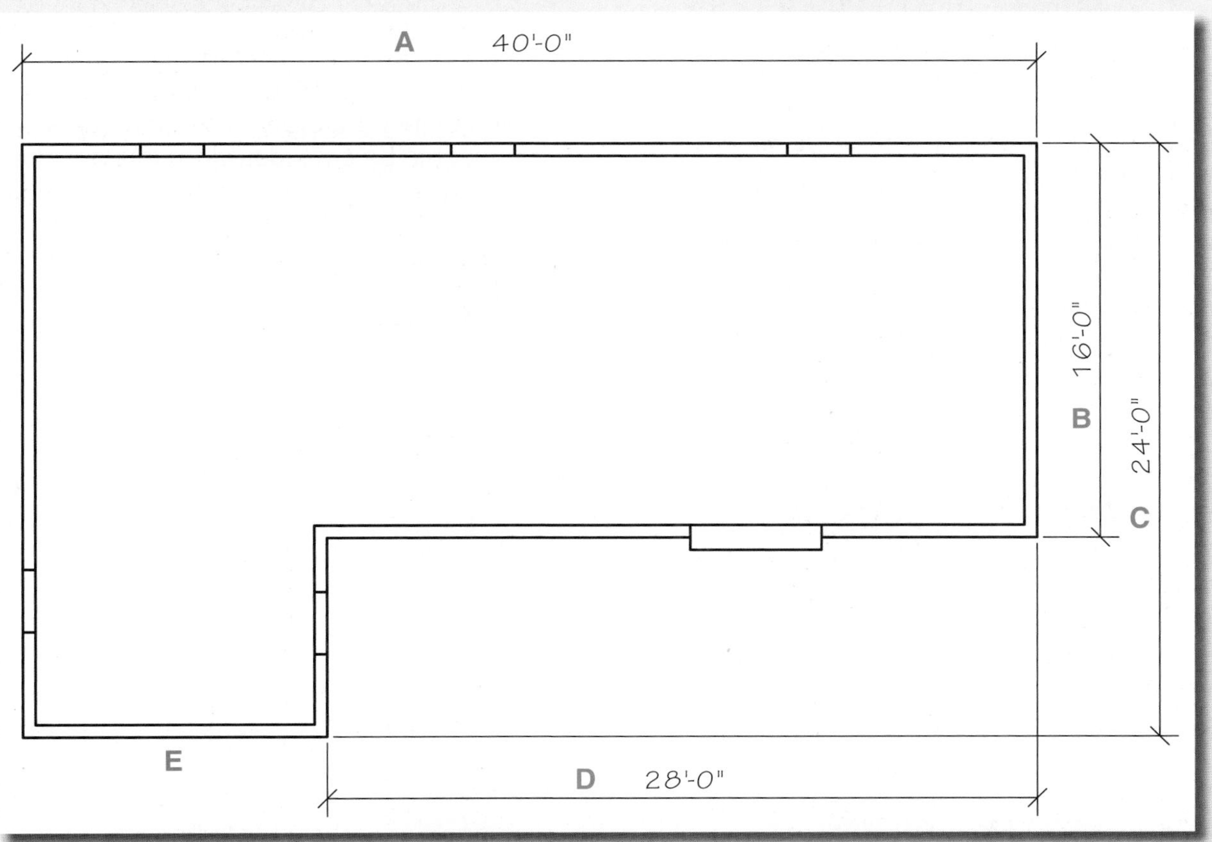

Goodheart-Willcox Publisher

2. **Engineering.** Conduct research to find out more about descriptive geometry and the types of spatial relationships that are found by constructing auxiliary views, revolutions, and intersections. Write an essay that describes applications for descriptive geometry in architectural drafting and other drafting disciplines. For example, auxiliary views are used to show the true size and shape of inclined features, such as an angled exterior wall or a roof section. Intersections are used to show relationships between intersecting features, such as a roof opening for a chimney or transition sections of different shapes used in piping or ductwork. Compare how these types of views are developed in manual drafting and computer-aided drafting (CAD). Explain the tools and methods used to automatically generate auxiliary views and intersections in a CAD system.

Communicating about Architecture

1. **Writing.** Create a cover letter and résumé. Use the information in this chapter to include all necessary information in your cover letter. Also, go online to job search websites (Monster.com or Careerbuilder.com, for example) to see templates of résumés and cover letters. Decide which examples are most effective and then insert your information. Pay attention to spelling, punctuation, and grammar. Share your résumé with your classmates and get their feedback.
2. **Reading and Speaking.** Research job openings at local or national architecture firms. Determine what types of skills the firms are seeking. Identify a specific position you are interested in. How much more experience do you need, if any, before you can apply for this particular position? Determine what additional schooling or experience you would need before you could reasonably expect to be considered for this position. Share your findings with the class. Discuss the wages and benefits being offered. Is the compensation package close to what you were expecting when reading the job description?

Chapter 5

Introduction to Computer-Aided Drafting and Design

Objectives

After completing this chapter, you will be able to:

- Explain how computer-aided drafting and design can simplify architectural drawing tasks.
- List the components of a typical CADD workstation.
- Evaluate features of CADD programs for use in architectural drafting.
- Describe file management, drawing, editing, display, dimensioning, and other commands that are typically included in CADD programs.

Key Terms

absolute coordinates
AEC-specific CADD package
animation
annotative objects
attribute
block
CAD
CADD
Cartesian coordinate system
command
display grid
ergonomics
fillet
grid snap
hatching
laser scanner
layer
mirror line
object
object snap
parametric
point cloud
polar coordinates
primitive
relative coordinates
rendering
round
snap
solid modeling
surface modeling
symbol library
template
tracking
wireframe

What Is CADD?

CAD is an acronym for computer-aided (or computer-assisted) drafting. ***CADD*** (with two Ds) includes both drafting and design. It integrates design, analysis, and often pre-manufacturing, as well as drafting. See **Figure 5-1**. Because this textbook emphasizes both drafting and design, the term CADD is used for all applications of computer-aided drafting, computer-aided design, and computer-aided drafting and design.

Simply put, CADD is a tool that replaces the traditional pencil and paper for the drafter and designer. While CADD makes the process of designing a product or structure much easier, the fundamentals of design have not changed. Knowledge of how to use CADD software cannot replace a solid knowledge of accepted drafting practices, drafting techniques, building materials, and construction details.

Nevertheless, CADD can simplify many drawing tasks. A drafter or designer using a computer system and the appropriate software can:

- draft a part, structure, or other needed product
- modify a design without having to redraw the entire drawing
- call up symbols or base drawings from computer storage
- re-use frequently needed forms and shapes
- produce schedules or analyses
- produce hard copies of complete drawings or drawing elements in a matter of minutes

All types of architectural, engineering, and construction (AEC) drawings can be produced

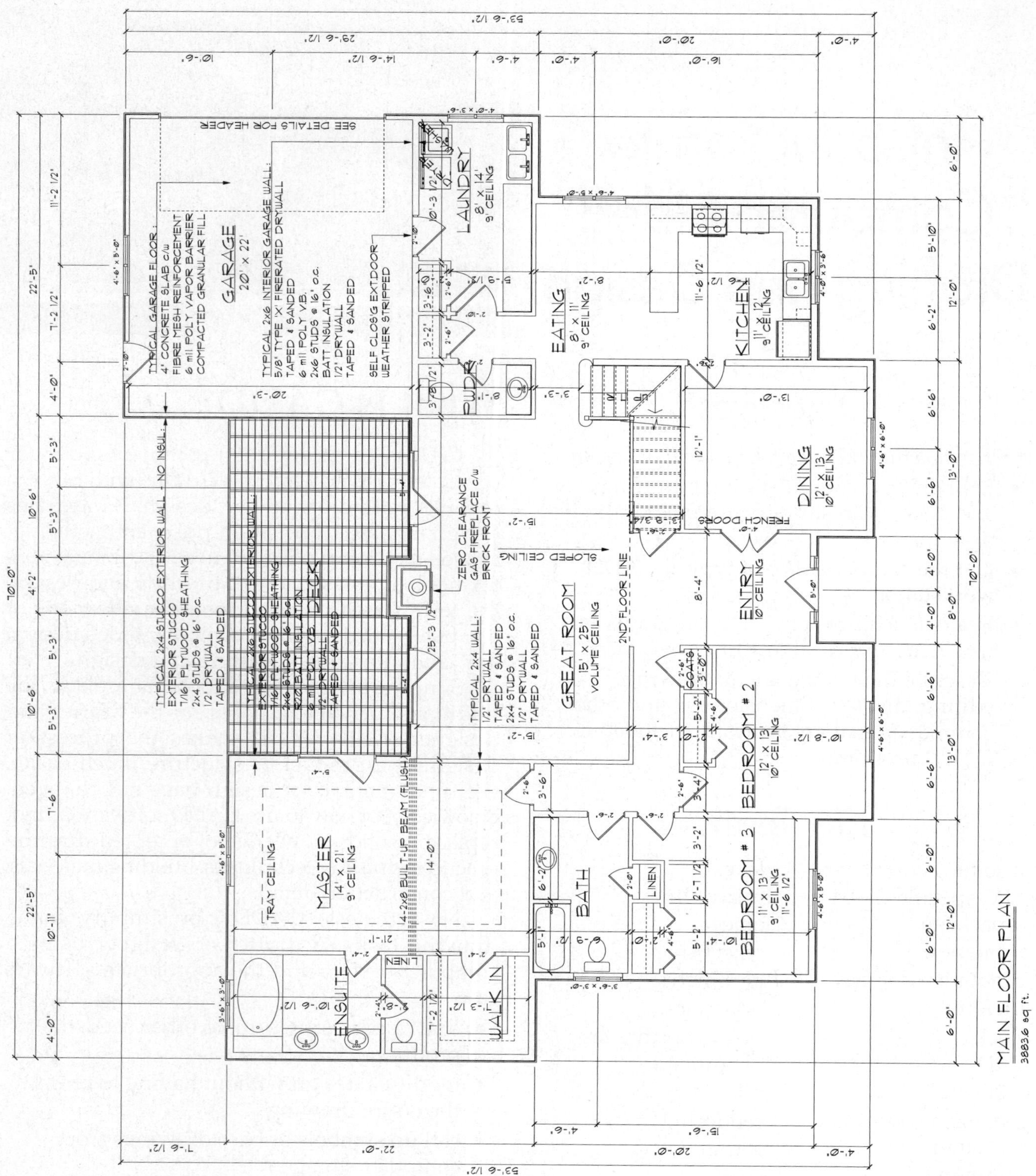

Goodheart-Willcox Publisher

Figure 5-1. CADD has greatly improved the process of designing and creating complex drawings, such as this floor plan.

with CADD software. See **Figure 5-2**. CADD software programs range from very basic programs that can be purchased for under $100 to programs that cost many thousands of dollars.

Why Use CADD?

There are many reasons to use CADD, but the most important is that CADD saves time and money. Once a design has been completed and stored in the computer, it can be called up whenever needed for copies or revisions. Revising CADD drawings is one of the greatest time- and money-saving benefits. Frequently, a revision that requires several hours to complete using traditional (manual) drafting methods can be done in a few minutes on a CADD system. In addition, some CADD packages automatically produce updated schedules after you revise the original plan, thus eliminating the need to update the schedules manually.

Other reasons for using CADD include:

- *Productivity*. CADD programs allow the drafter or designer to quickly develop and communicate ideas in a precise and professional manner.
- *Flexibility*. Once a design is complete, a drawing can be plotted at any scale and on different media, depending on the intended use.
- *Uniformity*. Drawings produced on a CADD system possess a high degree of uniformity regardless of who makes the drawings. See **Figure 5-3**.
- *Quality*. CADD makes it easy to ensure consistency in line thickness and pattern scales, and eliminates both smudged lines and sloppy lettering.

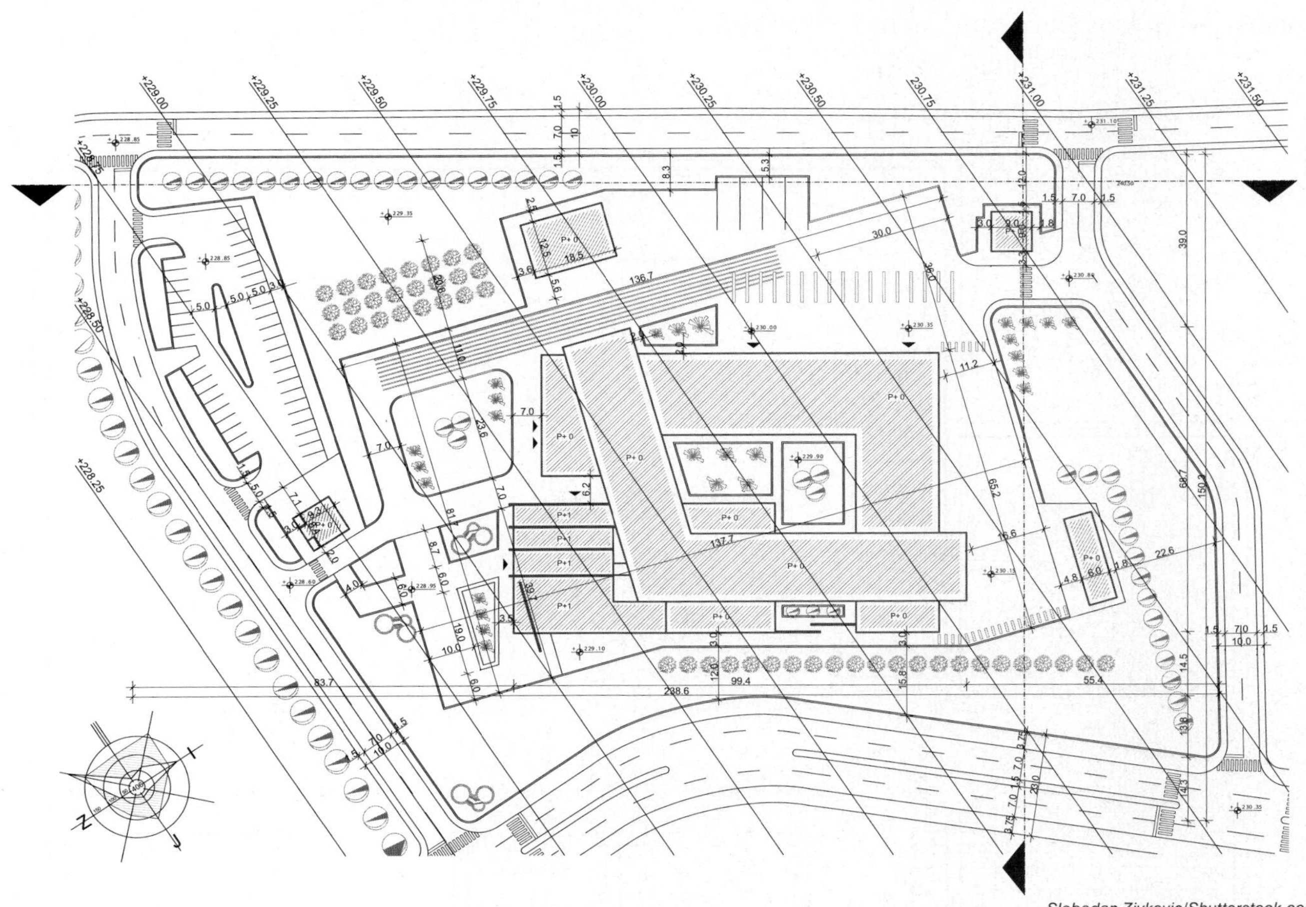

Slobodan Zivkovic/Shutterstock.com

Figure 5-2. This site plan for a new industrial park is an example of the many types of drawings that can be created using CADD software.

- *Scale*. In CADD, objects are always drawn at their true size and are then plotted or printed at the appropriate plot scale for each sheet.

CADD Hardware

Most CADD programs, even high-end software, can be run on home computer systems. These stand-alone systems are inexpensive and powerful and can be purchased at most appliance and electronics stores. See **Figure 5-4**. A computer is made up of a central processing unit (CPU), one or more input devices, one or more output devices, and a storage device. The CPU contains the processor or microprocessor, memory, and input/output interfaces.

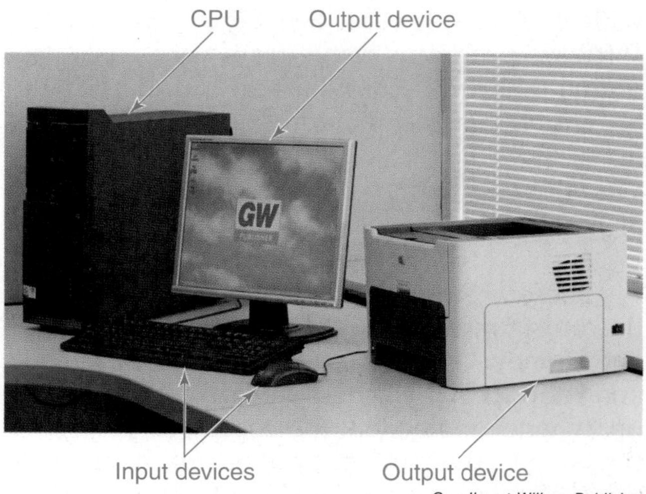

Goodheart-Willcox Publisher

Figure 5-4. A typical CADD workstation.

Input Devices

The input devices for a CADD system usually consist of a keyboard and a mouse or other pointing device. These devices allow you to enter commands and data into the computer system. Although considered older technology, some specialty systems may use a light pen or a digitizer and puck to input information into

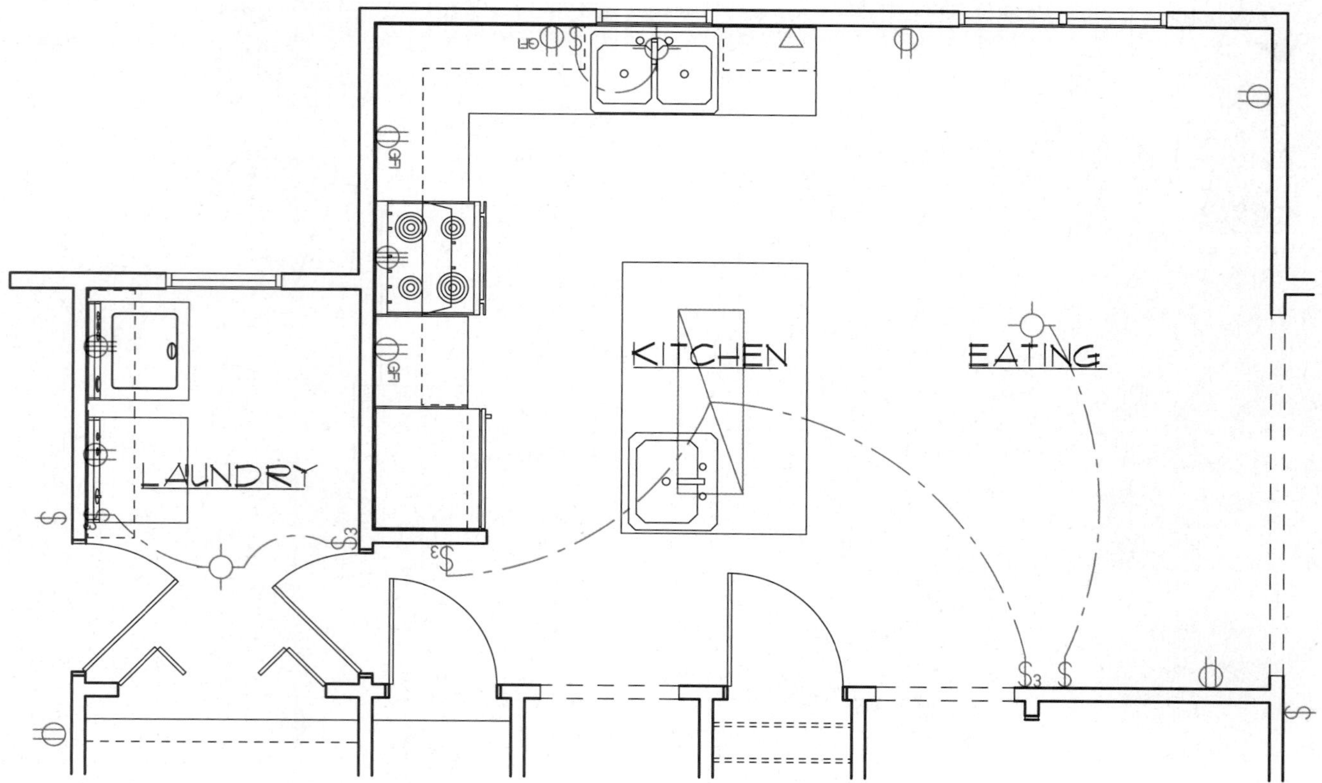

Goodheart-Willcox Publisher

Figure 5-3. All of the electrical symbols in this drawing are uniform. The only variable is the rotation of the symbols.

a CADD system. A puck is similar to a mouse, but can sense its exact position on a calibrated digitizer pad. In the past, digitizers were useful for converting existing paper drawings to electronic CADD drawings. However, they are seldom used today. Most drawings today are created using CADD, so a mouse and keyboard are sufficient for most architects.

Recently, tablet computers have reduced the need for a separate input device. These devices have touch screens that use the human finger as an input device. They are very portable and can be used on the construction site or in the client's living room to make quick changes to a design. See **Figure 5-5**.

Monitors

The monitor is the most common output device. Most monitors are now LCD or LED flat-screen monitors. Monitors are generally described in terms of size and screen properties. The size of a monitor is measured diagonally. Generally, a 17″ monitor is the smallest that can be used effectively with CADD. With small monitors, most of the computer screen may be taken up by toolbars and menus. Many desktop CADD systems have a 21″ or larger monitor. See **Figure 5-6**.

Another important aspect of a CADD system's display device is the video card. The video card is the device that transmits data from the CPU

Vovan/Shutterstock.com

Figure 5-5. Tablet computers allow architects to make quick design changes in the field with just the touch of a finger.

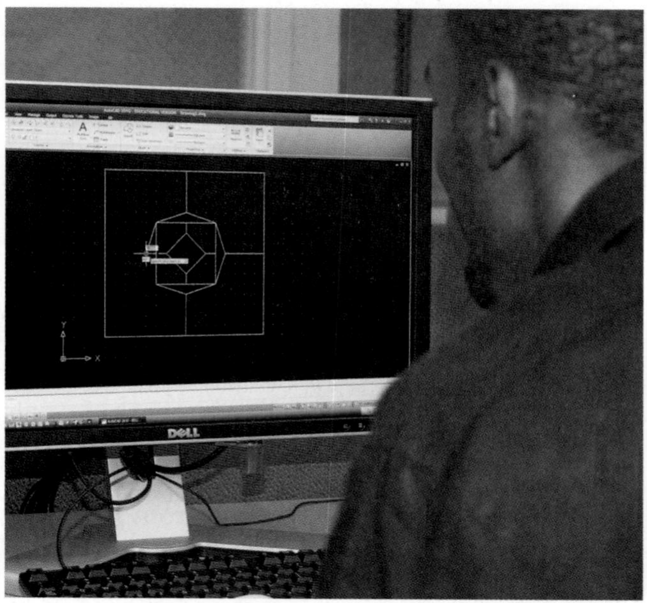

Goodheart-Willcox Publisher

Figure 5-6. Large monitors are considered required equipment by many architectural firms.

to the monitor. Some video cards are specifically designed for CADD and high-end graphics. However, each card has advantages and disadvantages. Before selecting a card, locate a hardware review in a computer or CADD magazine. Use this information to help determine which video card is best suited for your application. Also, be aware that some CADD software programs require an approved or recommended video card to operate at peak performance. Check the software company's website or the user's guide for information about video card requirements.

Printers and Plotters

Printers and plotters are output devices that provide a way to produce hard copies of CADD drawings. For smaller drawings, such as A-size and B-size drawings, most of the printers sold by electronics and computer stores can be used. The most common of these are inkjet and laser printers.

Laser printers are fast and provide crisp, clean images. The biggest disadvantage of laser printers is the lack of color. Color laser printers exist, but they are generally expensive to purchase and operate. They also typically do not produce very good color.

Employability
Conducting a Meeting

One employability skill that often goes overlooked by employees is the ability to conduct a meeting efficiently. Whether the meeting is a small team meeting, a large group meeting, or a department meeting, most employers want their employees to be able to conduct a meeting when called upon.

Meeting protocols vary. For formal meetings, Robert's Rules of Order are generally used. For informal staff or small team meetings, the rules are not so rigid. However, if you are responsible for conducting the meeting, keep the following tips in mind.

- Keep order in the meeting by insisting that only one person speak at a time.
- Make sure everyone has a chance to express his or her thoughts and ideas.
- If the meeting gets sidetracked from its intended subject, keep the meeting on target by guiding members back to the topic being discussed.
- Near the end of the meeting, summarize what was accomplished.
- If the meeting resulted in additional responsibilities for any team members, make sure each team member knows what is expected and when it must be accomplished.
- Thank all of the team members for participating in the meeting.

Activity

You should be familiar with Robert's Rules of Order because they are used in many different clubs and organizations. Research the basic rules of Robert's Rules of Order. With a group of four or five classmates, practice chairing a meeting and following these rules.

Inkjet printers are slower than laser printers, but they are easy to use. An advantage of inkjet technology is that it allows you to produce hard copies of ***renderings*** in full color. When making prints on special "photo paper," it is sometimes hard to tell a good rendering from a photograph. In the architectural field, this can be a great asset.

For larger drawings, plotters are needed. Most plotters today are inkjet plotters. They are similar to the inkjet printers, but can produce up to E-size prints. See **Figure 5-7**.

Another type of printer used in CADD applications, called a 3D printer, is a device used to generate a physical model from CADD data. This is discussed in Chapter 28, *Architectural Models*.

DesignJet Division, Hewlett-Packard

Figure 5-7. Inkjet plotters are well-suited to producing larger CADD drawings, such as this E-size drawing.

Storage Devices

Storage devices save data, such as drawings, for later use. A storage device places the data on digital storage media. A computer's hard drive is a storage device with self-contained media. Other storage devices, such as DVD-RW drives and USB drives, allow data to be stored on a removable device. USB drives are particularly useful for transporting large working drawings and other electronic data for architectural projects. See **Figure 5-8**.

Networks

Often, several stand-alone systems are connected in a network. This allows each computer to share information through the network wiring. A network typically allows devices such as printers and plotters to be shared among the computers. It may also provide a server where entire sets of working drawings and projects can be stored or archived.

Types of CADD Software

A variety of CADD software programs are available. These range from very basic programs that can draw simple two-dimensional (2D) objects to high-end programs that can create three-dimensional (3D) models and renderings and have advanced features such as automated schedules. CADD programs can be classified into two broad groups: general-purpose and AEC-specific.

General-Purpose CADD Packages

General-purpose CADD packages are designed for making typical mechanical drawings and other general drafting applications. Some general-purpose CADD programs are high-end programs that offer many advanced capabilities. Others provide only basic functions and are typically used for CADD education or home use.

Iwona Grodzka/Shutterstock.com

Figure 5-8. CADD systems are compatible with many different types of storage devices. Clockwise from top left: USB ("thumb") drive, DVD discs, internal hard drive, and portable external hard drive.

AEC-Specific CADD Packages

AEC-specific CADD packages are those that are designed for use in the architectural, engineering, and construction (AEC) industries. These packages generally include all of the functionality of general-purpose CADD programs. However, they include tools and features for use in the AEC fields. The extra functions improve the workflow for AEC drafters. Architectural and construction drawings can be created using general-purpose CADD packages. However, an AEC-specific program streamlines common architectural drawing tasks and may therefore be more efficient.

Selecting a CADD Program

In order to get the best CADD system for your needs, you must first decide what you want to accomplish with the software. If all you plan to do is produce 2D drawings, then you do not need all of the "bells and whistles" of a high-end system. If you are going to be producing 3D models and renderings, then you will probably need a high-end system. The answers to these basic questions may help you select the best package for you:

- How well does the package meet your needs? Is it useful to you?
- Is the program easy to learn and use? Does it provide help tools and clear instructions?
- What type of support does the company provide after you purchase the software? Does the company provide updates, either free or for a reasonable cost? Will the company answer your questions over the phone? Is training available at a local college or trade school? Remember, some CADD programs can be quite complex and you may need some help learning to use them.
- What are specific features of the software? Is it 2D or 3D? Is it compatible with other popular packages?
- What are the hardware requirements of the package?
- Does the program require special hardware not common to other packages?
- Check the warranty. What is covered, and for how long?
- How much does it cost? How does the cost compare with similar packages?

You may be able to think of other questions to add to this list. If possible, use the program before you purchase it, or at least talk to someone who has used it.

Common General-Purpose CADD Features

Certain basic features are common to all CADD programs. An overall knowledge of these features can help you select the CADD program that is best for you, because different programs handle the features in different ways. Some CADD programs are more capable than others. The following sections provide an overview of the common features available in popular general-purpose CADD packages. This is not intended to be a comprehensive list or to recommend one software brand over another. You are the best judge of which CADD package best suits your requirements.

Objects

Objects are the elements used to create drawings. They include items such as lines, points, circles, and arcs. More advanced objects, such as polylines, fillets, and chamfers, add function to the program. These may not be available with low-end CADD programs.

Drawing Units

Most CADD programs support different units of measure. Commonly supported unit formats include architectural (fractional), engineering, scientific, and decimal. The decimal unit format is used for both US Customary and metric units.

Angular units of measure can also be available in a variety of formats. Some common angular units of measure include decimal degrees, degrees/minutes/seconds, grads, radians, and surveyor's units. Being able to choose from several formats can be useful if you will be using the CADD program for multiple applications. For example, surveyor's units are commonly used on site (plot) plans, whereas architectural units are used for floor plans.

Coordinate Entry and Command Entry

A basic requirement to make drawings is the ability to tell the software where to place objects. There are generally several ways to do this in any given CADD program. For example, when drawing a line, you can generally type coordinates or pick points with the mouse.

To precisely locate points, most CADD programs use a standard point location system called the ***Cartesian coordinate system***. In 2D drafting applications, this system consists of a horizontal axis called the X axis and a vertical axis called the Y axis. The system is divided into four quadrants and the axes intersect at the 0,0 origin. See **Figure 5-9**. In a 3D modeling environment, a third axis, the Z axis, is added. Points in 2D drafting are located using X and Y coordinate values and are represented as X,Y. Coordinates can be positive or negative depending on their location in relation to the origin. Referring to **Figure 5-9**, a point located in the upper-right quadrant has a positive X coordinate value and a positive Y coordinate value. A point located in the lower-right quadrant has a positive X coordinate value and a negative Y coordinate value. Points located in the two left quadrants have negative X coordinate values and positive or negative Y coordinate values.

Three basic forms of coordinate entry used in 2D drafting are absolute, relative, and polar coordinate entry. See **Figure 5-10**. ***Absolute coordinates*** are exact point locations measured from the origin. For example, the absolute coordinate 2,4 is located two units from the origin in the positive X direction and four units from the origin in the positive Y direction. See **Figure 5-10A**. ***Relative coordinates*** define a location from a previous point. The @ symbol is typically used to specify a relative coordinate entry. For example, suppose you have located the first point of a line at the coordinate 3,3 shown in **Figure 5-10B**. Entering the relative

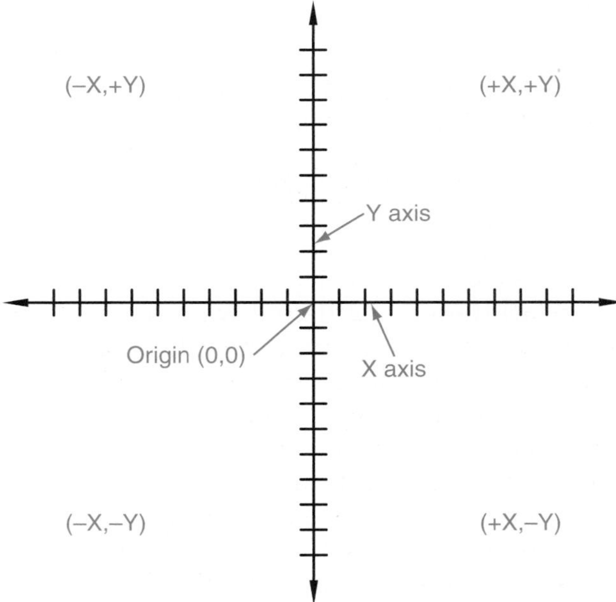

Goodheart-Willcox Publisher

Figure 5-9. The Cartesian coordinate system is a standard point location system used in CADD programs. For 2D drafting applications, the X and Y axes are used and the system is divided into four quadrants. Coordinates have positive or negative values depending on their location in relation to the origin.

Green Architecture

Electronic Waste

Although digital technology is helping reduce the damage from existing threats to the environment, its continuing use and constant growth comes at a price. For example, newer and faster CADD programs often require computer hardware upgrades. When computers and other types of electronics are replaced, the older machines that are thrown out become *e-waste*. E-waste is the fastest growing cause of toxic waste in the United States.

The toxic chemicals found in e-waste can consist of lead and mercury. While these toxins can damage the environment, they are also harmful to your health. Exposure to lead can cause neurological damage and cancer. Mercury poisoning can cause damage to the nervous and endocrine systems. Recent policies regarding the disposal and recycling of e-waste have been adopted in several countries. Several electronics manufacturers have initiated recycling programs for their products. More information is available from Regional Computer Recycling & Recovery (RCR&R).

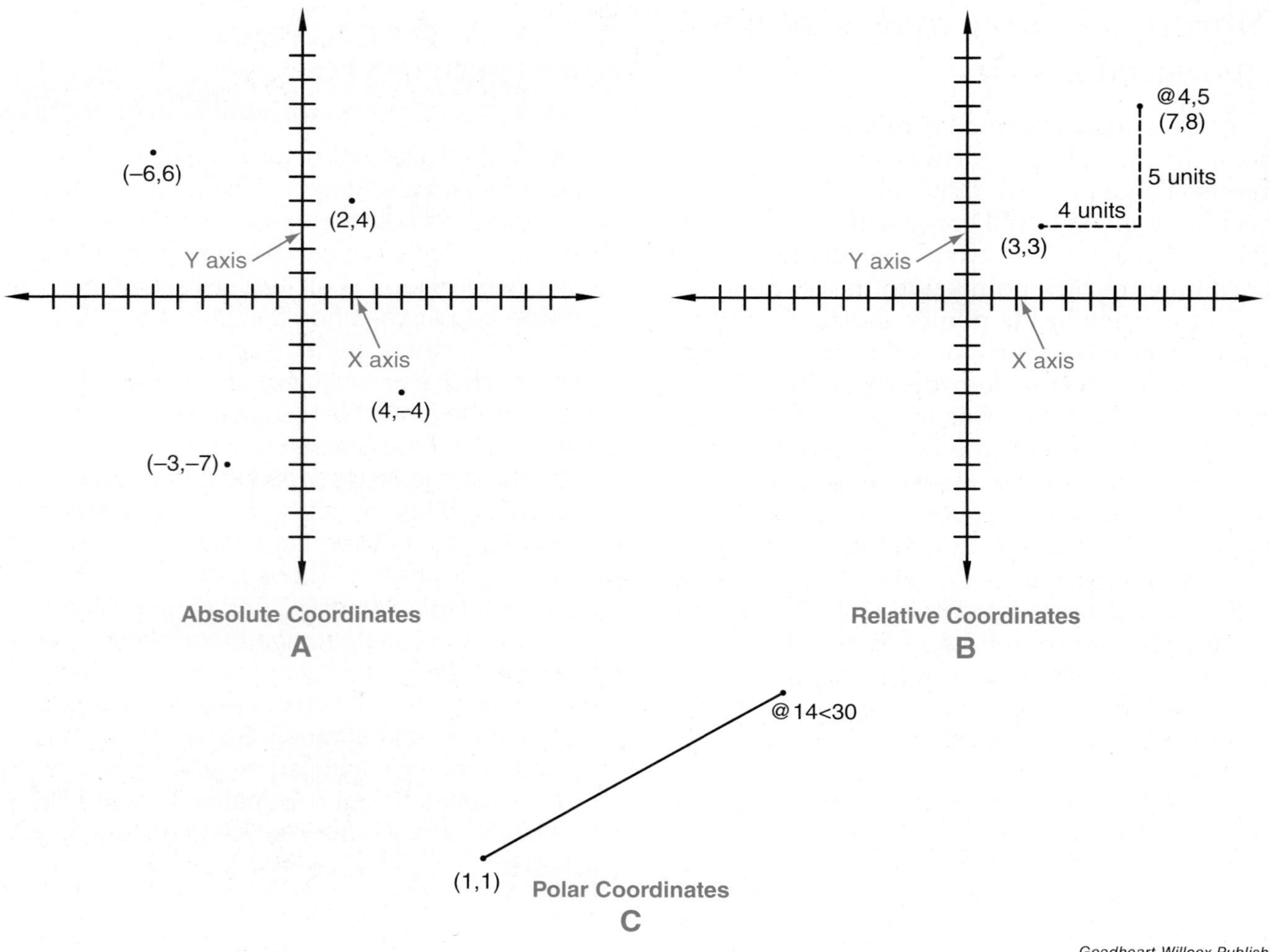

Goodheart-Willcox Publisher

Figure 5-10. Methods of 2D coordinate entry. A—Absolute coordinates are located in relation to the origin. B—Relative coordinates are located in relation to a previous point. C—Polar coordinates are located by specifying a distance and angle relative to a given point.

coordinate @4,5 would place the endpoint of the line four units to the right and five units above the previous point at the coordinate 7,8. ***Polar coordinates*** are relative coordinates that define a location at a given distance and angle from a fixed point (most typically a previous point). The entry format *@distance<angle* is normally used to specify polar coordinates. Typically, angular values are measured counterclockwise from 0° horizontal. For example, in **Figure 5-10C**, after locating the first point of a line at the coordinate 1,1, entering the polar coordinate @14<30 locates the endpoint 14 units away from the first point at an angle of 30° counterclockwise in the XY plane.

Just as there are different ways of providing point locations, there are generally a variety of ways to give instructions to the software. These instructions are called ***commands***. Generally, a command can be entered in several ways. Most commands can be accessed from a palette called the *ribbon* at the top of the display screen. In addition, most commands can be entered by typing the command name on the command line or in an input field on screen. Other methods include accessing commands from pull-down menus or shortcut (right-click) menus. The manner in which a command is entered does not change the function of the command. However, entering a command by different methods may change the steps needed to complete the command.

Dimensions

Properly dimensioning a drawing is one of the fundamentals of drafting. Dimensions are added to a drawing to specify the exact length, width, diameter, location, or other measurement related to the objects in the drawing. When done manually, dimensioning is time-consuming and can be a major source of errors or omissions. Most CADD packages provide the ability to automate the placement of dimensions. For example, when dimensioning a line, instead of drawing each extension line and dimension line separately, you can specify a dimension style, enter the appropriate dimensioning command, and select the endpoints of the dimension. The CADD software does the rest. The software automatically calculates the length of the line and inserts the correct measurement as dimension text.

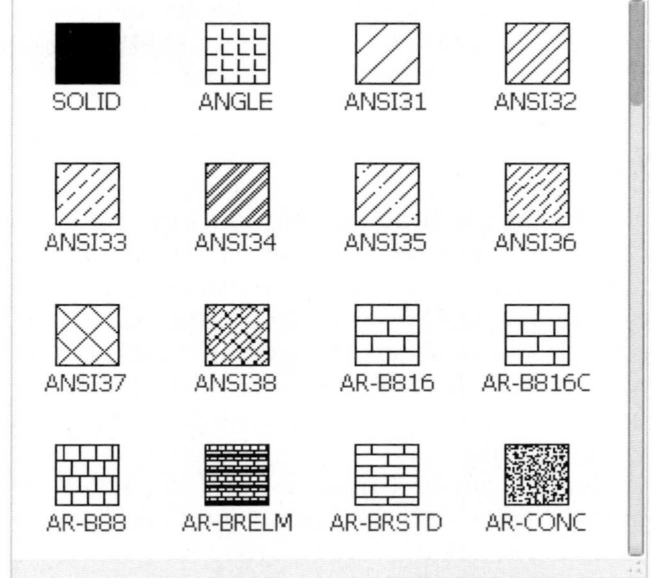

Goodheart-Willcox Publisher

Figure 5-11. General-purpose CADD programs typically provide a variety of hatch patterns to represent building materials and other items.

Hatch Patterns and Materials

Hatching is an important feature for any drawing that requires a section view. Placing hatch patterns on a CADD drawing is equivalent to drawing section lines in manual drafting. In architectural drafting, hatching is also used to represent bricks, shingles, grass, siding, insulation, and many other features. General-purpose CADD packages include several standard hatch patterns. See **Figure 5-11**. Some CADD programs also allow you to design your own patterns.

When you create a hatch in a CADD program, the entire hatch exists as one object. You do not have to draw the individual lines. Like automatic dimensions, this feature saves drafters a great amount of time.

AEC-specific CADD programs offer hatch patterns that are specifically designed for the AEC field. A general-purpose CADD program may not offer the patterns needed in the AEC field, such as shakes or shingles, various brick patterns, earth, sand, concrete, and foliage. These patterns can be difficult to create if they are not included in the program.

If you are going to be modeling in 3D, hatching is not necessarily as important to you. Instead of using hatch patterns, you can define materials and apply them to objects in the drawing. When you render the drawing, the material appears. For example, you could define a wood-grain material pattern and apply it to the cabinets in an elevation section that shows the kitchen. When you render the drawing, the cabinets appear to be made of wood.

Text

The ability to place text on a drawing is very important in most drafting situations. It is therefore important for CADD software to have good text support. You should try to find a program that can use several different text fonts. Most Windows-based CADD software can use any font installed in Windows for text on a drawing.

Lettering style is very important in architectural drafting. Some CADD packages allow the drafter to design and use a custom font. Many architects prefer to use a personalized lettering style. For them, this custom feature is an important part of the CADD package.

Editing Tools

The ability to edit a drawing is one of the most important aspects of CADD. Editing includes operations such as copying, erasing, moving, scaling, rotating, trimming, dividing, mirroring, and stretching. Some of the low-end CADD programs offer limited editing capabilities. Select a CADD program that has several editing tools from which to choose.

Layers

One of the fundamental tools in any good CADD program is the ability to draw on and manage layers. A ***layer*** is a virtual piece of paper on which CADD objects are placed. All objects on all layers, or sheets of paper, are visible on top of each other. If you are familiar with traditional (manual) drafting, you can think of layers as vellum overlays.

Layers can be turned on and off, resulting in the display of only those objects needed. For example, in a floor plan, you may have one layer for walls, one for the electrical plan, and one for the plumbing plan. This allows you to turn off the plumbing plan layer to display only the walls and electrical plan. See **Figure 5-12**.

Most CADD programs allow you to create and manage layers. Generally, you can assign a unique layer name and color to each layer. In addition, some CADD programs allow you advanced control over layers. For example, some CADD programs allow you to prevent certain layers from printing.

Proper layer management is very important to effective CADD drawing. This is especially true when the drawing is jointly worked on by several drafters, designers, or engineers. In an effort to standardize layer use in industry, several organizations have attempted to develop layer naming and usage standards. There is no one universally accepted standard. However, the American Institute of Architects (AIA) has developed the *AIA CAD Layer Guidelines*. These guidelines are part of the US National CAD Standard and are used by many organizations, either directly or as a basis for the organization's own standards.

It is important to follow the standards required by your company, department, or client. While you should always attempt to follow accepted industry standards, such as the AIA guidelines, it is more important that everyone working on a project follow the same convention. For example, instead of following the AIA conventions, your company may adopt a simple naming convention such as *WALLS*, *FOUNDATION*, and *LANDSCAPE*. If this layer naming scheme meets your needs, then adopt it and make sure everyone follows the convention.

Colors

Another important feature in CADD programs is object display color. If all objects in a drawing are displayed in the same color, it can be hard to identify the individual features. On the other hand, if all walls are displayed in red, all doors are displayed in yellow, and all windows are displayed in green, anybody who is familiar with this color scheme can quickly determine what is represented. Notice how color is used in **Figure 5-12** to distinguish the electrical layer and other layers. Just as with layer names, it is important to adopt a color usage convention and make sure everybody sticks to it.

Display colors are often assigned to layers, so that an object's color is determined by the layer on which it is drawn. This is one reason that layer conventions are so important, as described in the previous section.

Linetypes

Managing the types of lines used on a drawing is also important. The alphabet of lines is an important part of drafting, whether the drawing is created by hand or on a CADD system. See Chapter 4, *Drawing Instruments and Technical Sketching*, for more information about the alphabet of lines. In order to follow the alphabet of lines, the CADD system you choose should have the ability to use different linetypes. See **Figure 5-13**. The system should also have the ability to set line thickness or width. Most CADD programs provide a variety of linetypes that conform to the alphabet of lines. Typically, as with display colors, you can assign a specific linetype and line weight to each layer. When layers are set up in this manner, all lines are displayed on screen and printed or plotted according to the assigned settings. This provides a way to establish line conventions for a particular application. It is also possible to set the scale of each line (or all lines) to adjust the length of dashes and spaces so your drawing better conforms to an accepted standard or office practice.

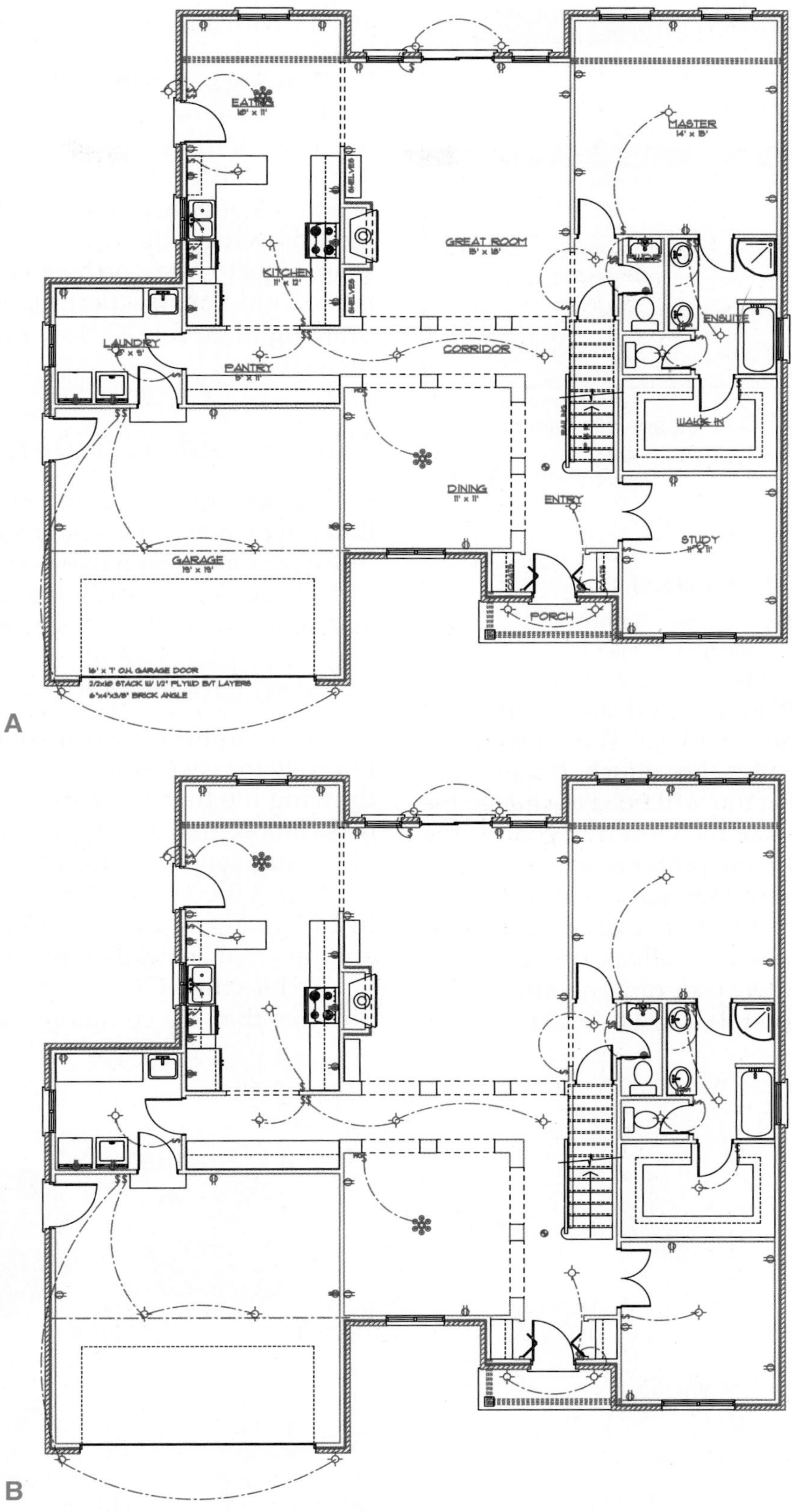

Goodheart-Willcox Publisher

Figure 5-12. Controlling the display of layers to show items on a floor plan. A—The complete drawing with all layers turned on. B—The same drawing with the electrical layer turned on and the text layer turned off so that the electrical fixtures are easier to see.

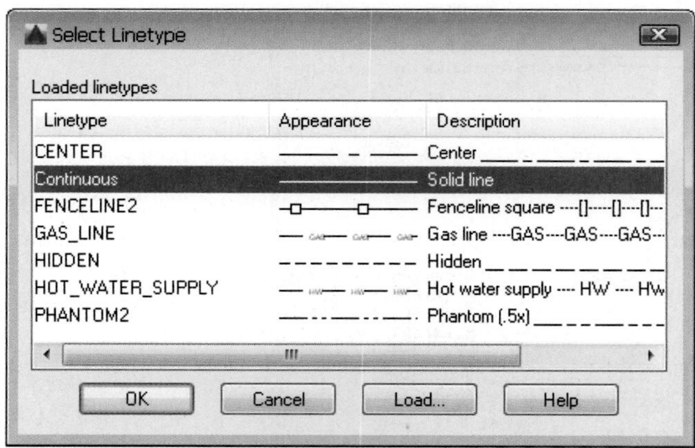

Goodheart-Willcox Publisher

Figure 5-13. Most CADD packages allow you to define or select various types of lines.

Display Controls and Drawing Aids

In CADD, all drawings are created at full scale. If a wall is 40′ long, you draw the line that represents the wall 40′ long. Therefore, most architectural drawings are much larger than the computer screen. You will need to change the magnification factor of the view and change the view itself to see different portions of the drawing. The functions that allow you to do this are called *display controls* and include zooming and panning commands, as well as other related commands. All CADD programs should have a variety of display controls. Most CADD programs also provide a way to save views to be restored later.

Drawing aids help you locate a specific position on the screen or on existing objects. They make the task of drawing easier, faster, and more accurate. All mid-range and high-end CADD programs offer a variety of drawing aids. Common drawing aids include a display grid, grid snap, object snaps, orthogonal mode, isometric mode, and construction planes. Without good drawing aids, CADD drawings can be hard to manage.

Blocks and Attributes

Blocks are special objects that can best be thought of as symbols that can be inserted into a drawing. Once you have spent the time to create a block, you can insert it into the drawing again and again without having to redraw it.

Symbol Libraries

Most drafters save their blocks as symbol libraries for easy access. A ***symbol library*** is a drawing file that contains a collection of blocks or symbols that are typically related, such as plumbing symbols, electrical symbols, or landscaping symbols. See **Figure 5-14**. When stored in this manner, a block can be located quickly and inserted as needed into any drawing.

Architectural CADD packages include symbol libraries that are commonly used in both plan

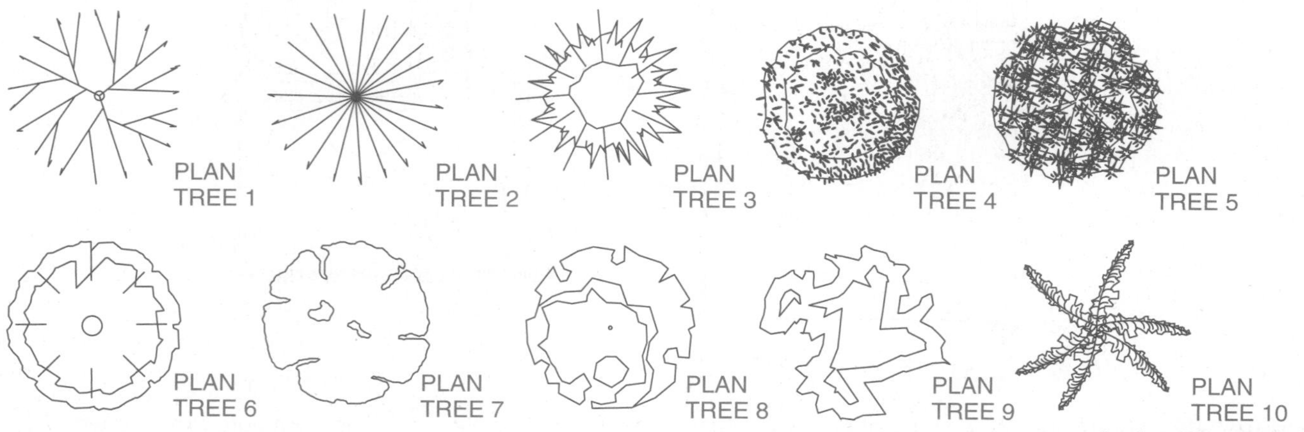

Goodheart-Willcox Publisher

Figure 5-14. These tree symbols are stored in a symbol library. Any of these symbols can be quickly inserted into a CADD drawing, repeatedly if needed.

drawings and elevations. For example, trees, furniture, doors and windows, and common appliances are usually included in architectural drawings. Symbol libraries developed specifically for AEC applications include:

- standard door types
- standard window types
- plumbing symbols
- electrical and lighting symbols
- heating, ventilation, and air conditioning (HVAC) symbols
- furniture symbols
- tree and plant symbols
- appliance symbols
- vehicle symbols
- title symbols
- construction details

Most AEC-specific CADD packages include at least some of these collections. Many CADD programs also allow you to add third-party symbol libraries to the software.

Attributes

Most CADD systems support both blocks and attributes. An ***attribute*** is text information saved with the block when it is inserted into a drawing. For example, you may create a block that consists of all the lines needed to represent a case-molded window. When you create the block, you assign attributes to it describing the window size, style, and manufacturer.

Attributes are often assigned to a block when it is created. However, another feature supported by many CADD programs is to prompt the user for attributes when the block is inserted. This allows a single block, or symbol, to serve for many different sizes, styles, and manufacturers. Using the case-molded window example, you may draw a generic window and prompt the user for a size, style, and manufacturer when the block is inserted.

Annotative Objects

As previously discussed, all objects in CADD are drawn at full scale. For example, a room that measures 12′ × 14′ is created by drawing lines 12′ and 14′ long to represent the walls. When the drawing is printed or plotted, the appropriate plotting scale is selected to fit the drawing on a B-size or C-size sheet. The plotting scale that is selected requires initial planning for items such as dimensions and notes. This is because text for dimensions and notes is typically 1/8″ high on architectural drawings. At a plotting scale of 1/4″ = 1′-0″, text that is drawn 1/8″ high becomes too small to read when the drawing is plotted to scale. To account for this, the drafter can calculate a scale factor and apply it to the text so that it appears at the appropriate size when plotted. However, some CADD programs have special tools to automatically scale text without applying a user-defined scale factor.

Annotative objects are drawing objects that are automatically scaled to the correct size by the software when the drawing is plotted. Automatic scaling of annotative objects is based on the *annotation scale*. The annotation scale is a separate setting from the plotting scale, but the same scale is typically specified for both settings so that annotative objects are scaled correctly. For example, if annotative text is drawn at a height of 1/8″ with an annotation scale of 1/4″ = 1′-0″ and the drawing is then plotted at a scale of 1/4″ = 1′-0″, the plotted (paper) size of the text is 1/8″. By using this method, the correct text height is calculated automatically and a special calculation for the scale factor is not required. Annotative text is created by setting an annotative text style current and then specifying an annotation scale prior to drawing the text. In similar fashion, other types of objects can be created as annotative objects. These include dimensions, blocks, attributes, and hatch patterns. As with text, the objects are automatically sized based on the annotation scale. Using annotative objects saves the drafter time in calculating the drawing scale and helps ensure that objects are plotted at the correct size.

Drawing Setup

When creating a new drawing file, it is common to start with a previously saved file that contains frequently used settings and drawing content. This method is especially useful in architectural projects, where it is common to have multiple drawing files that use the same unit format, layer definitions, and title block format. A ***template*** is a file configured with user-specified settings and drawing content that can be applied to new files. Many of the features previously discussed in this chapter can be incorporated into a template.

Using templates speeds the setup process by eliminating repetitive startup tasks. In addition, templates improve drawing efficiency and accuracy because the same file settings and content can be applied by different drafters in a network environment. It is common to create a number of templates for different applications. For example, different templates can be created for use with different sheet sizes, title block formats, and drafting standards.

Program Customization

Program customization includes displaying and hiding menus or toolbars, modifying menus or toolbars, creating new menus or toolbars, and writing macros, commands, or "programs" to help streamline the drawing process. The degree to which you can customize the software is especially important to an experienced CADD user. By customizing the program to suit specific needs, the drafter can become highly efficient. In addition, program customization can help a CADD manager better standardize a department's drafting procedures.

3D Modeling and Rendering

Three-dimensional modeling capability is an advanced capability of some CADD programs. Much of the drafting done in CADD is in two dimensions, just like a manual drawing on paper. However, 3D modeling programs create a "virtual" object in the computer that has width, length, and depth. The 3D object can be shaded or colored, assigned materials, rotated, and animated.

Surface modeling creates 3D objects by drawing a skin, often over a wireframe. A ***wireframe*** is a group of lines that represent the edges of a 3D model, but does not have a skin or "thickness." Surface modeling is used for rendering and animation. However, it is not often used for engineering applications because a surface model does not have volume or mass properties.

Solid modeling creates 3D objects by generating a volume. If you think of surface modeling as blowing up a balloon to obtain a final shape, solid modeling is obtaining the final shape by filling it with water. A solid model can be analyzed for mass, volume, material properties, and many other data. Many CADD packages that can produce solid models also allow you to create cross sections, which is difficult or impossible to do with a surface model. In addition, a solid model can be rendered and imported into many animation software packages.

An important part of architectural design is preparing the presentation drawings used to show a client the proposals. A 3D CADD drawing that is properly set up can be used to create a computer rendering, or presentation drawing. Just as 2D working drawings are needed to build the project, renderings of 3D models help sell the project to the client. The solid model in **Figure 5-15** has been detailed so carefully that it almost looks like a photograph. However, by changing the materials assigned to the exterior of the house, the architect can show potential clients the effects of various materials and color choices on the exterior. For example, the stone could be changed to brick, or the paint on the second floor could be changed from yellow to brown.

Animations

Related to presentation drawings are animations. ***Animations*** show motion, so they can show features such as windows and doors opening and the changing effect of sunlight on a room. Animations can also be used to present a room or building as a person would see it walking through. With the right CADD software and a skilled drafter, a client or review board can be shown a very accurate representation of what the final construction will look like.

AEC-Specific CADD Features

Most CADD programs designed for use in architecture offer specific time-saving features for architects and building designers. The following sections cover features that are typically offered in AEC-specific CADD programs.

jl661227/Shutterstock.com

Figure 5-15. Because this is a solid model, it can be rotated and viewed from any angle to show a client the sides and back of the house. In addition, the model can be altered to show different materials on the exterior.

Schedule Automation

One of the biggest advantages of using blocks and attributes in an architectural drawing is the ability to generate schedules automatically. A schedule is a list of all items of a specific type that are needed for construction. For example, if you insert all windows as blocks with correctly defined attributes, AEC-specific CADD systems can generate a window schedule that includes every window in the drawing, complete with its size, style, material, manufacturer, and any other attributes that you have defined. See **Figure 5-16**. The window schedule can then be used for design, estimating, and purchasing. Many AEC-specific CADD programs can generate window and door schedules, kitchen cabinet schedules, plumbing fixture schedules, lighting fixture schedules, and other schedules, as well as various reports.

In addition to creating schedules, some AEC-specific CADD programs can automatically update or correct a schedule when an item on the drawing is changed. For example, if your client wants to add a 30×60 double-hung window to the floor plan, the window is automatically included in the schedule when you add it to the drawing. Using CADD, such a change requires only a few seconds to complete.

Wall Generation

Architectural packages generally provide more than one method of generating walls. Features such as intersection cleanup, wall thickness specification, and wall alignment are important time-savers that can be found in most AEC-specific CADD programs.

Stair Generation

Stair design requires a considerable effort, both to calculate and to draw. Some AEC-specific CADD programs include automated stair design features. The drafter enters data from the

PRODUCT CODE	SIZE	COUNT	R.O. SIZE	TYPE	WIDTH	HEIGHT	R.O. WIDTH	R.O. HEIGHT	OPENING ID	JAMB SIZE
30X60 DOUBLE HUNG 1	2'-6" x 5'-0"	1	R.O. 2'-6" x 5'-0"	WINDOW	2'-6"	5'-0"	2'-6"	5'-0"	1	3"
60X60 DOUBLE HUNG 2	5'-0" x 5'-0"	1	R.O. 5'-0" x 5'-0"	WINDOW	5'-0"	5'-0"	5'-0"	5'-0"	2	3"
48X48 DOUBLE HUNG 2	4'-0" x 4'-0"	1	R.O. 4'-0" x 4'-0"	WINDOW	4'-0"	4'-0"	4'-0"	4'-0"	3	3"
24X42 DOUBLE HUNG 1	2'-0" x 3'-6"	1	R.O. 2'-0" x 3'-6"	WINDOW	2'-0"	3'-6"	2'-0"	3'-6"	4	3"
30X60 DOUBLE HUNG 1	2'-6" x 5'-0"	1	R.O. 2'-6" x 5'-0"	WINDOW	2'-6"	5'-0"	2'-6"	5'-0"	5	3"
30X60 DOUBLE HUNG 1	2'-6" x 5'-0"	1	R.O. 2'-6" x 5'-0"	WINDOW	2'-6"	5'-0"	2'-6"	5'-0"	6	3"
30X60 DOUBLE HUNG 1	2'-6" x 5'-0"	1	R.O. 2'-6" x 5'-0"	WINDOW	2'-6"	5'-0"	2'-6"	5'-0"	7	3"
30X60 DOUBLE HUNG 1	2'-6" x 5'-0"	1	R.O. 2'-6" x 5'-0"	WINDOW	2'-6"	5'-0"	2'-6"	5'-0"	8	3"
30X60 DOUBLE HUNG 1	2'-6" x 5'-0"	1	R.O. 2'-6" x 5'-0"	WINDOW	2'-6"	5'-0"	2'-6"	5'-0"	9	3"
30X60 DOUBLE HUNG 1	2'-6" x 5'-0"	1	R.O. 2'-6" x 5'-0"	WINDOW	2'-6"	5'-0"	2'-6"	5'-0"	10	3"
48X48 DOUBLE HUNG 2	4'-0" x 4'-0"	1	R.O. 4'-0" x 4'-0"	WINDOW	4'-0"	4'-0"	4'-0"	4'-0"	11	3"
108X84 CLASSIC NARROW	9'-0"	1	R.O. 9'-3"	GARAGE	9'-0"	7'-0"	9'-3"	7'-1"	A	3"
108X84 CLASSIC NARROW	9'-0"	1	R.O. 9'-3"	GARAGE	9'-0"	7'-0"	9'-3"	7'-1"	B	3"
36X80 COLONIAL A 1	3'-0"	1	R.O. 3'-3"	DOOR	3'-0"	6'-8"	3'-3"	6'-9"	C	3"
30X80 COLONIAL A 1	2'-6"	1	R.O. 2'-8"	DOOR	2'-6"	6'-8"	2'-8"	6'-9"	D	3"
28X80 COLONIAL A 1	2'-4"	1	R.O. 2'-6"	DOOR	2'-4"	6'-8"	2'-6"	6'-9"	E	3"

Goodheart-Willcox Publisher

Figure 5-16. Some CADD programs have the ability to generate window schedules automatically when the drawing is properly set up.

architect's sketches, and the software automatically draws the stairs. See **Figure 5-17**. Data that is typically entered includes the finished-floor-to-finished-floor height, the stair width, and the run of the stairs. Some AEC-specific CADD programs also offer the ability to extract details from the drawn stairs. Generally, options are provided for wood, metal, and concrete/steel stairs. High-end CADD packages also include elevators and escalators.

Point Cloud Support

There are many different design tools and workflows available to the architectural drafter when using an AEC-specific CADD system. As part of the design process, it may be useful to collect dimensional data or site data in electronic form from existing construction and import it into a new design project. This approach can be useful in a building remodeling or renovation project or a historic preservation project. One method for collecting data in building construction is to create a point cloud. A ***point cloud*** is a three-dimensional digital representation of an existing building or construction site consisting of millions of points. A point cloud is similar to a 3D model, but it uses points to represent the object and does not contain any surface geometry or vector data. The data in a point cloud is generated through a process called laser scanning. A ***laser scanner*** is a device that captures point data from a building or site by recording XYZ coordinates of individual points in space. One or more scans may be made from the existing work in order to produce scan files, which are then processed by the scanner or in a separate software program to generate the point cloud file. Once the point cloud file is generated, it is imported into the CADD program and used as a basis for the new design. Typically, 3D modeling software is used to work with the point cloud data. Some AEC-specific CADD programs with 3D modeling capability provide tools for working with point clouds. Common tools include display controls, point cloud object snaps, cross

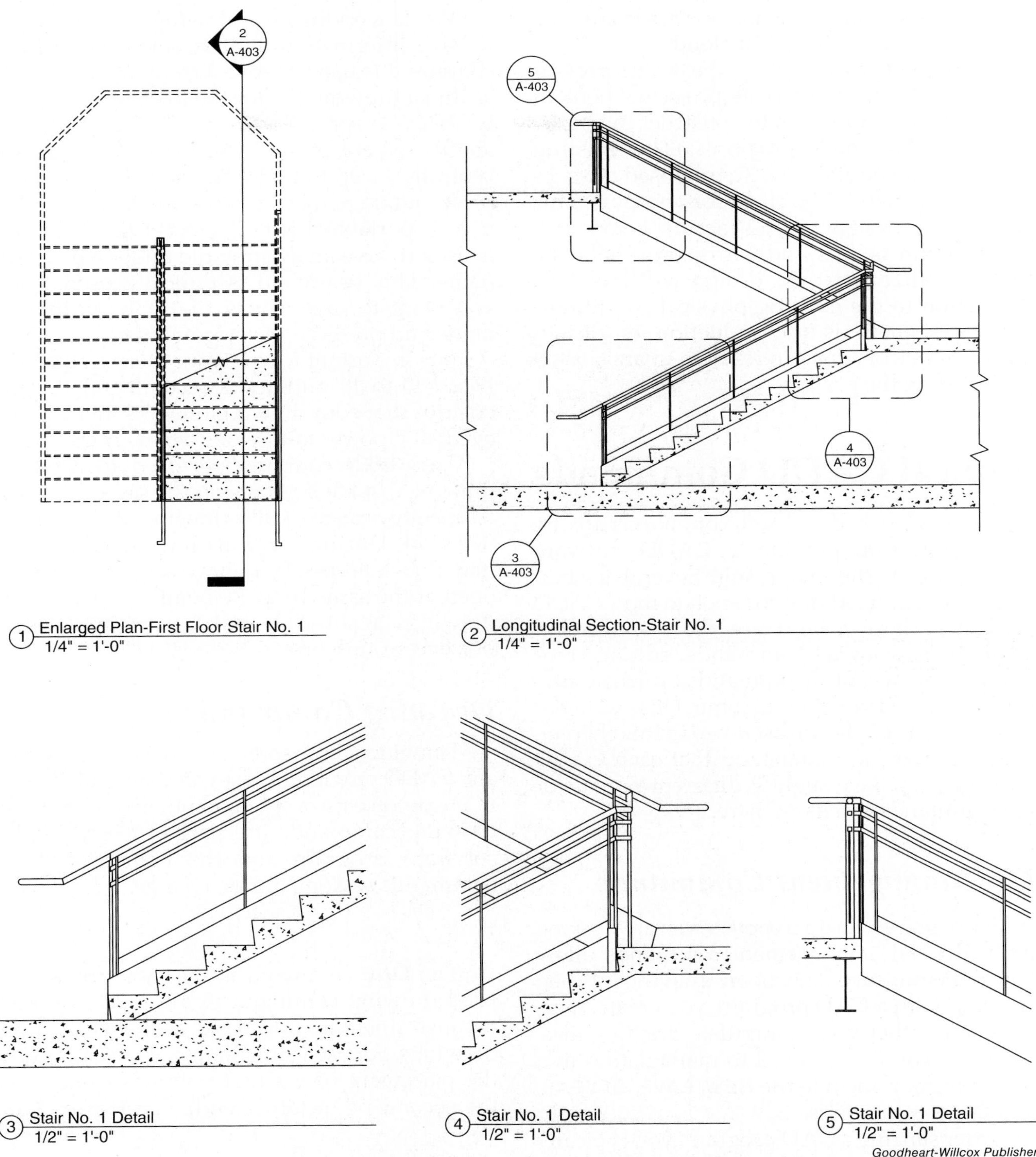

Goodheart-Willcox Publisher

Figure 5-17. These standard stair construction details are generated automatically from data supplied by the drafter.

section tools, and extraction tools for creating 2D geometry from the point cloud.

Using point cloud data in the design process can be useful for large-scale projects where an architectural firm needs to construct "as-built" drawings for study purposes. The existing drawings can be altered with proposed changes and then shown to the client for approval. This part of the design process occurs before any construction begins and can greatly help the firm visualize what the design will look like in relation to the existing physical conditions. Another benefit is the reduction of design changes or errors that can result in unanticipated costs during the project.

Typical CADD Commands

As previously discussed, commands are the instructions you provide to CADD software to accomplish the end result. Several general groups of commands are common to most CADD software. These groups are file management commands, drawing commands, editing commands, display control commands, dimensioning commands, and drawing aid commands. Examples of these commands are discussed in this chapter. It is important to understand that each CADD package may have slightly different names for the commands discussed here.

File Management Commands

Each time you use a computer, you are working with files. File management commands allow you to begin, save, and open drawings. When working with a CAD program, you create, save, open, and otherwise manipulate drawing files. Common commands used to manage files in a CAD program include the **NEW**, **SAVE**, **SAVEAS**, and **OPEN** commands.

After starting a CAD program, you typically have a choice between beginning a new drawing or opening an existing drawing. The **NEW** command is used to start a new drawing file. This command typically gives you the option of starting a new drawing from "scratch" or from a template. As previously discussed, a template is a drawing file with preconfigured settings for a specific application.

While working on a drawing, you will want to save information as it is added. The **SAVE** command is used to save a drawing. If you are saving a drawing file for the first time, you will be asked to specify a file name. You must also specify where to save the file. CAD files are typically saved to folders on a local or network drive, but there may be cases when you want to save to portable media. The **SAVEAS** command is used to save an existing file under a different name. This command is typically used when you want to save a new file with a different name and preserve the original file.

It is important to save your work frequently. Every 10 to 15 minutes is recommended. This ensures that your drawing remains intact in the event of a power failure or system crash.

The **OPEN** command is used to access a drawing that has been previously saved. You will frequently need to recall a drawing file for continued work. During a typical drawing session, you may find it necessary to have several drawings open at the same time. Remember to save your drawings again after making any updates to preserve your work.

Drawing Commands

Drawing commands form the foundation of any CADD program. These commands allow you to create objects on the computer screen. Basic drawing commands are part of every CADD software program and the names of these commands seldom, if ever, change.

Line

The **LINE** command is the most frequently used drawing command in a CADD program because lines are the basic elements of most drawings. For each straight line, you will specify the placement of the first point (one end) and the second point (other end). See **Figure 5-18**.

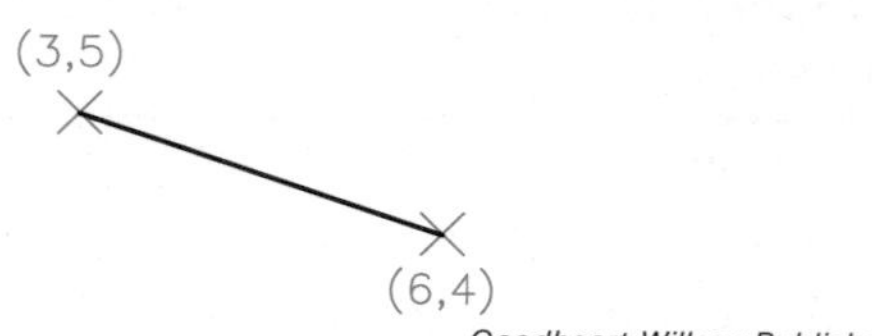

Goodheart-Willcox Publisher

Figure 5-18. The **LINE** command draws a straight line between two endpoints that you specify.

Generally, you can enter specific coordinates for the endpoints or pick the endpoints on screen.

Some CADD packages provide a **DOUBLE LINE** command, although it may not have this name. This command is useful in creating walls on floor plans and similar applications where parallel lines are required. Most CADD programs allow you to set the distance between the double lines. In addition, some programs allow you to control how the corners and intersections are formed. Some AEC-specific CADD packages even allow you to draw all of the lines to create a wall, including the building materials in each wall.

Circle

The **CIRCLE** command automates the creation of a circle object. Most CADD software allows you to select from several common methods of defining a circle. See **Figure 5-19**. These methods include:

- Center and radius
- Center and diameter
- Three points on the circle
- Two points on the circle
- Radius and two lines or two circles to which the circle should be tangent

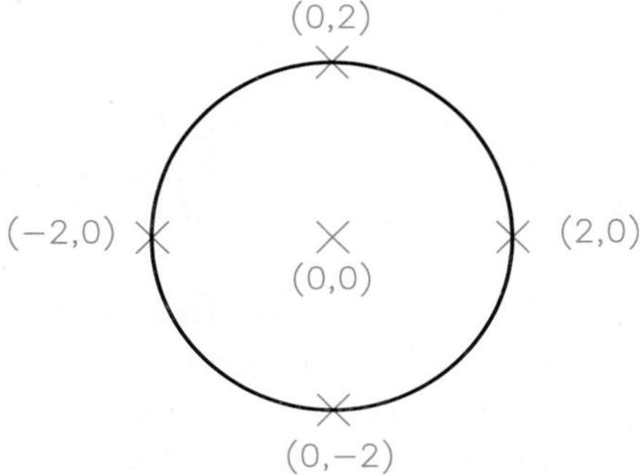

Goodheart-Willcox Publisher

Figure 5-19. There are several ways to define a circle. Using the information shown here, you could use the center/radius, center/diameter, two points, or three points methods.

Arc

An arc is a portion of a circle. Most CADD software allows you to select from several methods of defining an arc. See **Figure 5-20**. Examples include:

- Three points on the arc
- Starting point, center, and endpoint
- Starting point, center, and included angle
- Starting point, center, and length of chord
- Starting point, endpoint, and radius
- Starting point, endpoint, and included angle
- Starting point, endpoint, and a starting direction

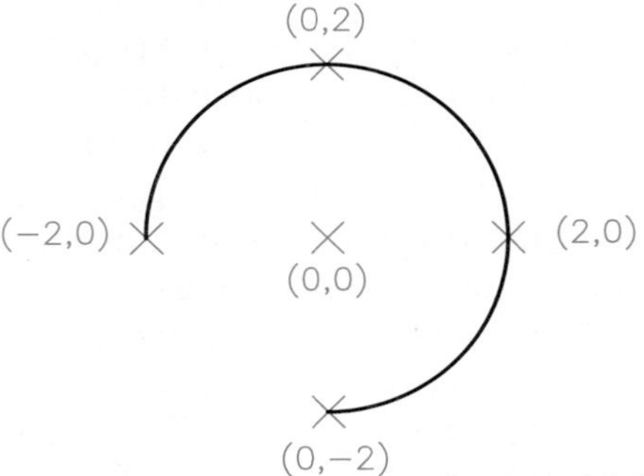

Goodheart-Willcox Publisher

Figure 5-20. An arc can be defined using several methods.

Rectangle

A square or rectangle can be drawn using the **LINE** command. However, the **RECTANGLE** command automates the process of creating a square or rectangle. Most CADD software provides at least two methods for constructing a rectangle. These are specifying the width and height of the rectangle or specifying opposite corners of the rectangle. See **Figure 5-21**.

Polygon

The **POLYGON** command automates the construction of a regular polygon. A regular polygon is an object with sides of equal length and equal included angles. The **POLYGON** command can

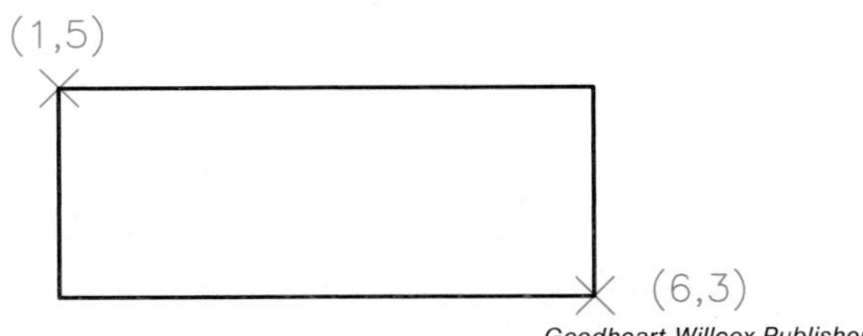

Goodheart-Willcox Publisher

Figure 5-21. You can draw a rectangle by specifying opposite corners.

create an object with three or more sides. A common approach used in many CADD programs is to either inscribe the polygon within a circle or circumscribe it about a circle. See **Figure 5-22**. The information required in these instances is radius of the circle, method desired, and number of sides for the polygon. Another method available in some CADD programs is to define the endpoints of one side of the polygon and the number of sides. The software calculates and generates the remaining sides to create a regular polygon.

Text

You can add text to a drawing using the **TEXT** command. This is important for placing notes, specifications, and other information on a drawing. Most CADD packages provide several standard text fonts to choose from, and some packages offer more than one command for generating text. Some are designed to place a single line of text on a drawing, and others are better for creating complex notes.

Hatch

Hatching is a fundamental part of drafting. In architectural drafting, hatching is used in section views to show cutaway parts and to represent specific materials. It is often used in elevation drawings, such as for siding or bricks. Hatching is also used on site plans to represent ground coverings, masonry features, water, and other features.

The **HATCH** command is used to hatch an area of a drawing. Areas to be hatched are selected with the pointing device and elements within the boundary can be excluded, if desired. See **Figure 5-23**.

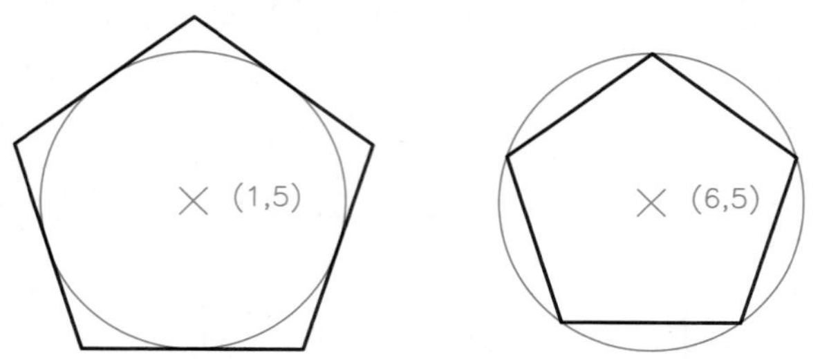

Goodheart-Willcox Publisher

Figure 5-22. A polygon can be circumscribed (left) or inscribed (right).

Editing and Inquiry Commands

Editing commands allow you to modify drawings in several ways. Inquiry commands are used to list the drawing database records for selected objects and to calculate distances, areas, and perimeters. Editing and inquiry commands described in this section include: **ERASE**, **UNDO**, **MOVE**, **COPY**, **MIRROR**, **ROTATE**, **SCALE**, **FILLET**, **CHAMFER**, **EXTEND**, **ARRAY**, **LIST**, **PROPERTIES**, and **MEASURE**. These commands can be found in almost all CADD software programs.

Erase

The **ERASE** command permanently removes selected objects from the drawing. Many CADD programs provide a "select" option in the command that allows you to select the objects to erase. Some CADD software programs have a "block erase" or window feature that will erase items within the block or window that you specify.

Undo

The **UNDO** command reverses the last command. If the last command was **ERASE**, as an example, the objects that were deleted are restored. You can sequentially step back through previous commands, but you cannot "jump" a command in the sequence. Certain limits are usually applied to this command.

Move

The **MOVE** command allows one or more objects to be moved from the present location to a new one without changing their orientation or size. Generally, you must pick a starting point and a destination point. Relative displacement is often used for this operation. With relative displacement, you pick any starting point. Then, you specify a displacement from that point in terms of units, or units and an angle.

Copy

The **COPY** command usually functions in much the same way as the **MOVE** command.

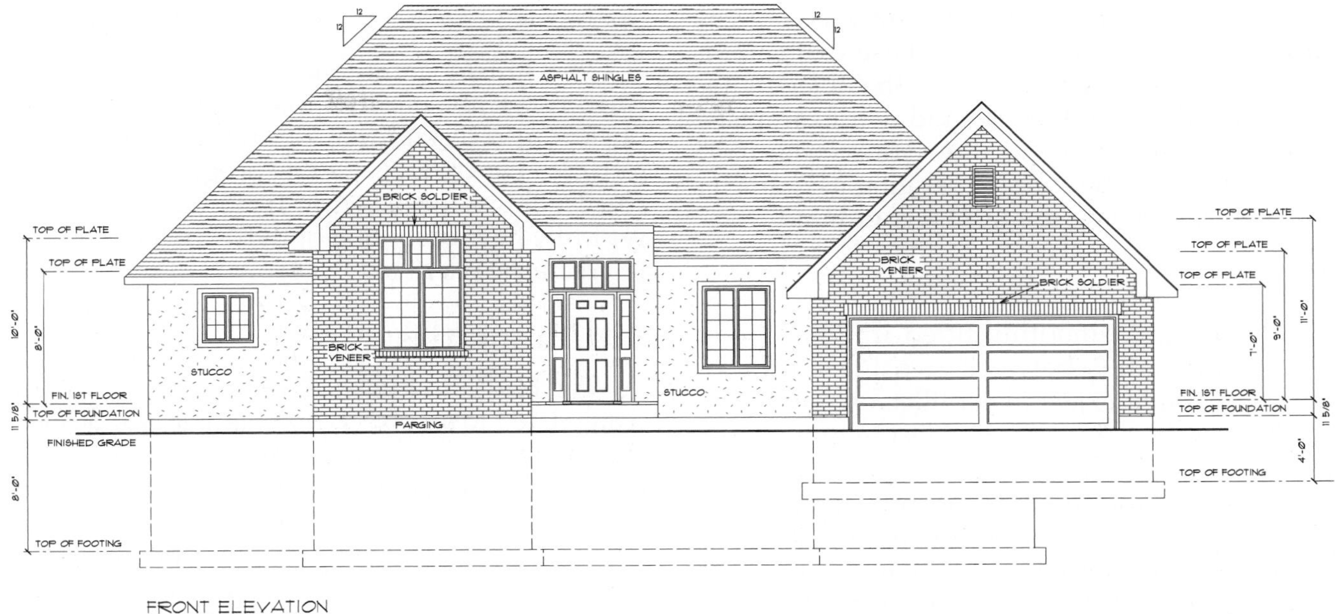

Goodheart-Willcox Publisher

Figure 5-23. Hatch patterns can be used to show materials in an elevation drawing.

However, it is used to place copies of the selected objects at the specified locations without altering the original objects.

Mirror

The **MIRROR** command draws a mirror image of an existing object about a centerline. This command is especially useful when you are creating symmetrical objects. For example, if you draw one side of ornate scrollwork on a door, you can use the **MIRROR** command to reflect the scrollwork to the other side of the door. See **Figure 5-24**. The **MIRROR** command in most CADD programs allows you to either keep or delete the original object during the operation. To mirror an object, you specify a ***mirror line***, which is the centerline about which the mirror operation takes place. The mirror line can generally be specified at any angle.

Rotate

The **ROTATE** command is used to alter the orientation of objects on the drawing. Typically, you must specify a center point for the rotation. The amount of rotation can generally be specified in degrees or selected using the pointing device.

Scale

The size of existing objects can be changed using the **SCALE** command. When using the **SCALE** command, most CADD programs require you to specify a base point for the operation. This point is generally on the object, often a reference corner or the center of the object.

Goodheart-Willcox Publisher

Figure 5-24. The scrollwork on this door was first mirrored vertically. Then the original and the mirrored copy were mirrored horizontally. The mirrored copies and the final scrollwork on the door are shown here in color.

Some CADD programs are ***parametric.*** This means that you can change the base size parameter, or any other parameter, of the object without using the **SCALE** command. For example, a parametric program will allow you to scale a ∅5 circle up by 50% by simply changing its diameter to 7.5 without using the **SCALE** command.

Fillet

A ***fillet*** is a smoothly fitted internal arc of a specified radius between two lines, arcs, or circles. A ***round*** is just like a fillet, except it is an exterior arc. See **Figure 5-25**. Most manufactured parts, including those for architectural applications, have some fillets or rounds. The **FILLET** command is used to place fillets and rounds. After drawing the curve, the command trims the original objects to meet the curve perfectly.

Chamfer

The **CHAMFER** command is very similar to the **FILLET** command. However, instead of a curve, a straight line is placed between the chamfered lines. Just as with the **FILLET** command, the original lines are trimmed to meet the straight line (chamfer). Depending on the CADD program, this command may require that the two objects to be chamfered be lines, not arc segments.

Extend

The **EXTEND** command is used to lengthen an object to end precisely at a boundary edge. The boundary edge is defined by one or more objects in the drawing. Most CADD programs place limitations on which types of objects can be extended. In addition, only certain types of objects can be used as boundary edges.

Array

The **ARRAY** command is essentially a copy function. It makes multiple copies of selected objects in a rectangular or circular (polar) pattern. See **Figure 5-26**. CADD programs that have the capability of drawing in three dimensions typically have an option of the **ARRAY** command to create arrays in 3D.

List/Properties

The **LIST** and **PROPERTIES** commands show data related to an object. For example, the properties for a line may include the coordinates of the endpoints, the length, the angle from the start point, and the change in X and Y coordinates from the start point. The **LIST** and **PROPERTIES** commands can be useful for determining the object type, the layer the object is drawn on, and the object's color and linetype settings.

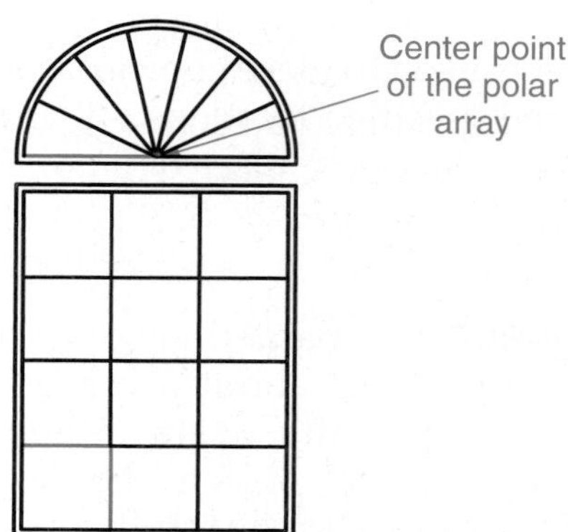

Goodheart-Willcox Publisher

Figure 5-26. The panels of glass in the semicircular fan light were drawn as a polar array. The rectangular panes of glass were drawn as a rectangular array. The original objects are shown in color.

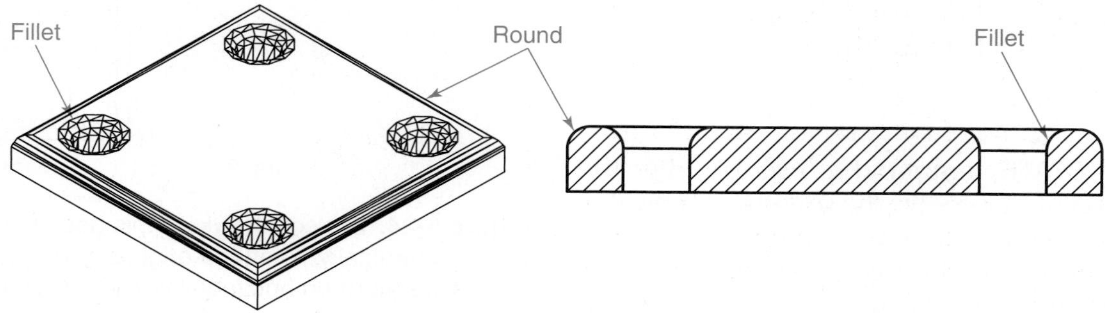

Goodheart-Willcox Publisher

Figure 5-25. Fillets and rounds on a drawing.

Measure

The **MEASURE** command is used to calculate several geometric properties, including distance, radius, angle, area, circumference, and volume of the specified objects. Depending on the program, the **DISTANCE** or **AREA** command may be used to measure geometric properties. Often, you can select a closed object or simply pick points on an imaginary boundary to calculate a measurement. Most CADD programs allow you to remove islands, or internal areas, when calculating area or volume. The **MEASURE** command has many applications in architecture, from calculating the square footage of a house to determining the surface area of a garage floor, which is needed to determine the amount of concrete for the floor.

Display Control Commands

Many CADD programs allow you to control the size of the display using the scroll wheel on a mouse. Scrolling away from you increases the display magnification, and scrolling toward you decreases the magnification. This is by far the simplest way to magnify the objects on the screen or to "zoom out" to see more of the drawing. Display control commands are also available to provide more precise control over how a drawing is displayed on the screen. These commands are used to control the position and magnification of the screen window, save views for later use, and regenerate or "clean up" the screen. Although different CADD packages have different advanced commands for these purposes, almost all contain basic **ZOOM**, **PAN**, **VIEW**, and **REDRAW** or **REGEN** commands.

It should be noted that there is a difference between changing the display size of objects on the screen and changing their physical size. Remember, all objects are drawn at their true size in a CADD program. To change their physical size, you would use editing commands, such as **SCALE** or **EXTEND**. To change the size at which they appear on the screen, without altering their physical size, you use display control commands.

Zoom

The **ZOOM** command increases or decreases the magnification factor, which results in a change in the apparent size of objects on the screen. The actual size of the objects does not change. You can think of this as using the zoom feature on a camera. **ZOOM** may be the most-used display control command. Generally, it has several options that include zooming to the drawing limits or extents, dynamically zooming, and zooming to a specific magnification factor.

Pan

The **PAN** command moves the drawing in the display window from one location to another. It does not change the magnification factor. If you think of the drawing as being on a large sheet of paper behind the screen, panning is moving the sheet so a different part of the drawing can be seen. It is useful when you are using a high magnification factor to work on details. See **Figure 5-27**.

Many CADD programs also allow you to pan without entering a formal command. You can hold down the scroll wheel on the mouse and move the mouse to pan to a different location in the drawing.

View

When constant switching back and forth between views and magnification factors on a large drawing is required, the **VIEW** command can be used to speed the process. This command allows you to save a "snapshot" of the current

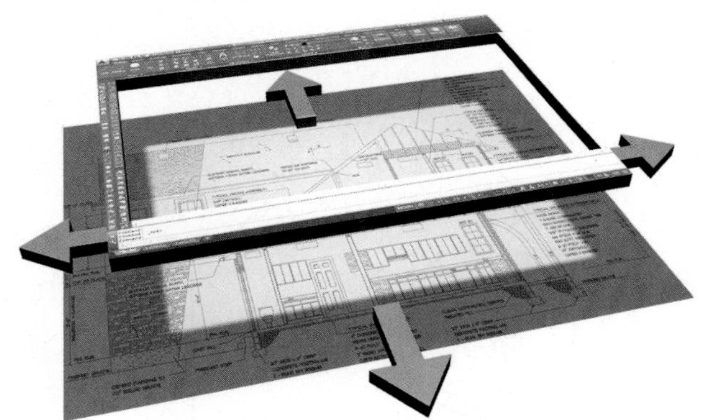

Eric K. Augspurger; print courtesy of SoftPlan Systems, Inc.

Figure 5-27. You can think of panning as moving a drawing sheet around underneath the CADD drawing screen. Only the portion of the drawing directly "below" the drawing area on the screen will be visible.

drawing display, including the view and magnification factor. After saving a view, you can quickly recall it later. This can be much faster than zooming and panning to return to the desired view.

Redraw/Regenerate

The **REDRAW** command "cleans up" the display by removing marker blips. Some commands redraw the screen automatically. For example, a redraw occurs when a grid is removed or visible layers are changed. However, it is sometimes useful to request a redraw when other operations are being performed.

The **REGENERATE** command is similar to **REDRAW**, except that it forces the software to recalculate all of the objects in the entire drawing and redraw the screen. This command is useful when you change the magnification to show small curved objects at a larger size. This sometimes results in the curves looking segmented. Regenerating the screen recalculates the curves so that they appear smooth again.

Dimensioning Commands

One of the advantages of using CADD is automated dimensioning. In almost all drafting applications, the drawing must be dimensioned to show lengths, distances, and angles between object features. The five basic types of dimensioning commands are **LINEAR**, **ANGULAR**, **DIAMETER**, **RADIUS**, and **LEADER**. See **Figure 5-28**.

A linear dimension measures a straight line distance. The distance may be horizontal, vertical, or at an angle. Typically, you have several choices on how the dimension text is placed. The text may be aligned with the dimension lines, always horizontal on the drawing, or placed at a specified angle. In architectural drafting, dimension text for a linear dimension is never perpendicular to the dimension line.

An angular dimension measures the angle between two nonparallel lines. The lines can be actual objects or imaginary lines between an origin and two endpoints. Typically, you have the same text placement options as with linear dimensions. In architectural drafting, dimension text for arcs and angles may be unidirectional (always horizontal).

Diameter and radius dimensions are very similar. A diameter dimension measures the distance across a circle through its center. A radius dimension measures the distance from the center of an arc to a point on that arc. A radius dimension can also be used for a circle, but is not typically used in that manner.

A leader is used to provide a specific or local note. A leader consists of an arrowhead or a different terminating symbol (such as a dot), a leader line, and the note. Often, an optional shoulder is placed on the end of the leader before the note.

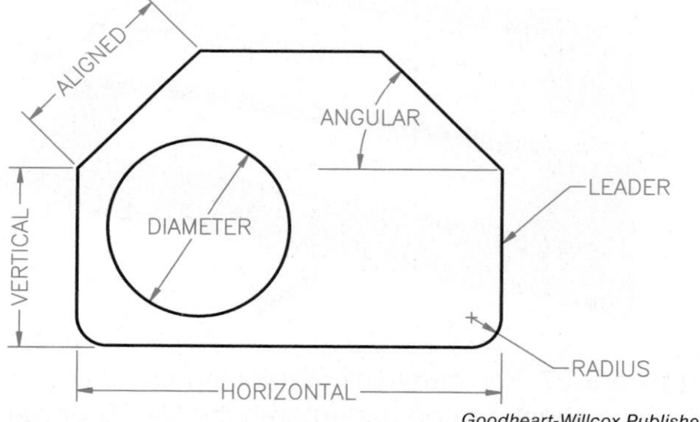

Goodheart-Willcox Publisher

Figure 5-28. Several types of dimensions may appear on a drawing.

Drawing Aids

Drawing aids are designed to speed up the drawing process and, at the same time, maintain accuracy. Most CADD packages provide several different drawing aids. These can range from a display grid or viewport ruler to various forms of snapping and tracking.

Grid

A ***display grid*** is a set of visual guidelines in the drawing area, much like the lines on graph paper. How the grid appears when displayed depends on which CADD program you are using. See **Figure 5-29**. In most CADD programs with a grid function, you can change the density, or spacing, of the grid. The appearance of the grid is controlled with the **GRID** command.

Some CADD programs also have rulers that can be displayed along the horizontal and vertical edge of the drawing screen. The display of these rulers is often controlled by a single command.

However, the display may also be controlled by an **OPTIONS** or **SETTINGS** command, depending on the CADD program.

Snap

Snap is a function that allows the cursor to "grab onto" certain locations on the screen. There are two basic types of snap: grid snap and object snaps. A ***grid snap*** is controlled with the **SNAP** command and uses an invisible grid, much like the visible grid produced by the **GRID** command. When grid snap is turned on, the cursor "jumps" to the closest snap grid point. In most CADD programs, it is impossible to select a location that is not one of the snap grid points when grid snap is on. Just as with a grid, you can typically set the snap grid density or spacing.

An ***object snap*** allows the cursor to "jump" to certain locations on existing objects. Object snaps provide a very quick way of connecting new objects accurately to existing objects. Most CADD programs have several different object snaps. These can include endpoint, center, midpoint, perpendicular, tangent, quadrant, and intersection, as well as many others. See **Figure 5-30**. Depending on the CADD program you are using, there may be additional object snaps available. Generally, you can turn on the object snaps that you want to use while another command is active. For example, suppose you have a line already drawn and you want to draw

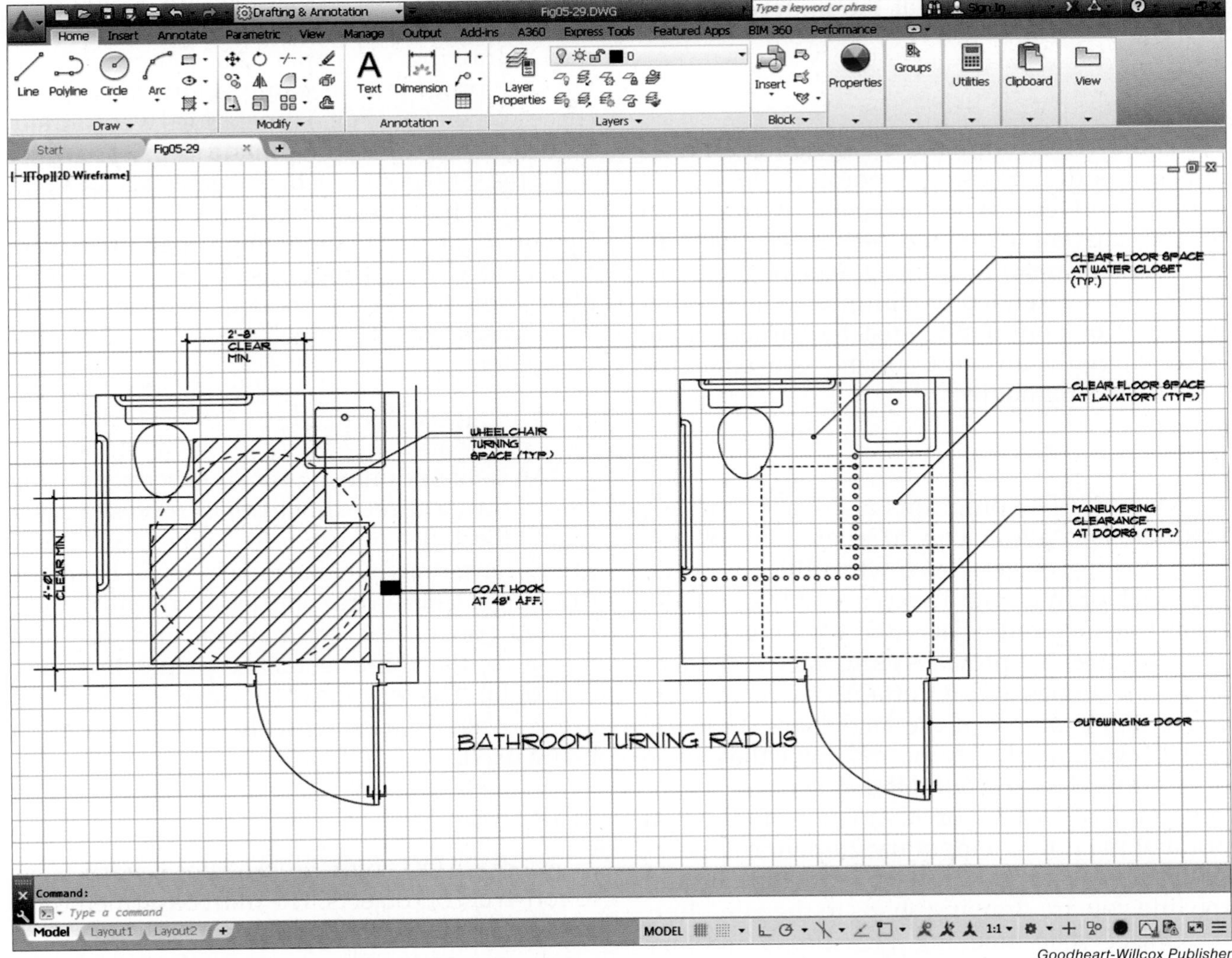

Goodheart-Willcox Publisher

Figure 5-29. The grid is a nonprinting set of guidelines that look like graph paper.

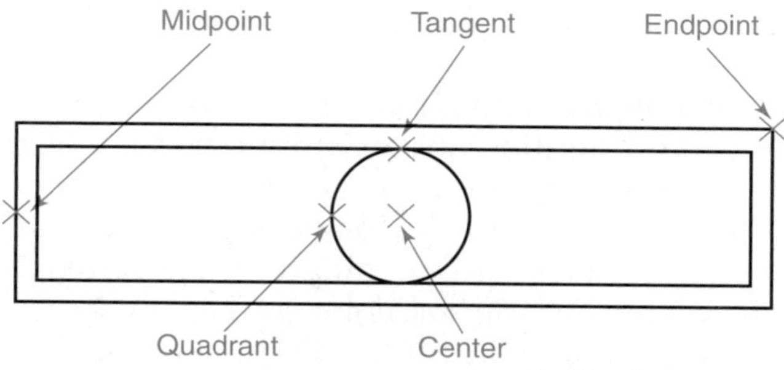

Goodheart-Willcox Publisher

Figure 5-30. This fluorescent light symbol contains several common object snap locations: the midpoint and endpoints of a line, the center and quadrants of a circle, and points of tangency.

another line from its exact midpoint. You can enter the **LINE** command, temporarily set the midpoint object snap, and pick the first endpoint of the second line at the midpoint of the first line.

Ortho

The **ORTHO** command ensures that all lines and traces drawn using a pointing device are orthogonal (vertical or horizontal) with respect to the current drawing plane. The **ORTHO** command is useful in drawing "square" lines that will be later extended or trimmed to meet other objects. The command must be turned off to draw a line at an angle unless you enter the coordinates manually.

Tracking

Many CADD programs also have ***tracking*** features that allow you to align new objects with existing objects, even when the objects do not touch or intersect. Two types of tracking are polar tracking and object snap tracking.

Polar tracking provides temporary guidelines at preset angles when certain commands are active. For example, if the angles are set to 45° and 90°, you can start a line and move the mouse or pointing device around the screen. Whenever you get close to a 45° or 90° angle from the first point of the line, a temporary guideline appears on the screen to show you the exact angle, and the line you are drawing snaps to the guideline.

Object snap tracking provides temporary guidelines from object snap points on existing objects. For example, suppose you want to start a line at the exact midpoint of another line, but about three feet to the right of the existing line. You can move the mouse over the midpoint of the existing line to "acquire" the midpoint object snap, and then move away from the object snap. A temporary tracking line shows you the exact horizontal or vertical path from the midpoint so that you can start the new line exactly aligned with the midpoint of the existing line. Note that the midpoint object snap has to be active for this example to work.

3D Drawing and Viewing Commands

When CADD programs were first developed, they were used to create two-dimensional (2D) drawings. This was the natural progression from traditional (manual) drafting, which produces a 2D drawing on paper. As computers and CADD programs became more advanced, three-dimensional (3D) capabilities were added. At first, these capabilities made it easier to draw 3D representations, such as isometrics and perspectives, but these are really 2D drawings. Eventually, true 3D modeling capabilities were added to CADD programs. These capabilities allow you to design, model, analyze, and in some cases "pre-machine" a part all within the computer.

Isometric Drawing

An isometric drawing is a 2D pictorial drawing that shows a three-dimensional representation of an object. See **Figure 5-31**. Some CADD programs have drawing aids to help make isometric drawings. These drawing aids typically are a rotated grid, orthographic cursor, and snap representing the three isometric planes (top, left, and right). The way in which these drawing aids are activated varies with the CADD program being used.

3D Modeling

Most CADD software provides several ways to construct 3D objects. The most basic method is to use primitives. ***Primitives*** are 3D objects that can be placed together to construct 3D models. Common primitives used in CADD programs

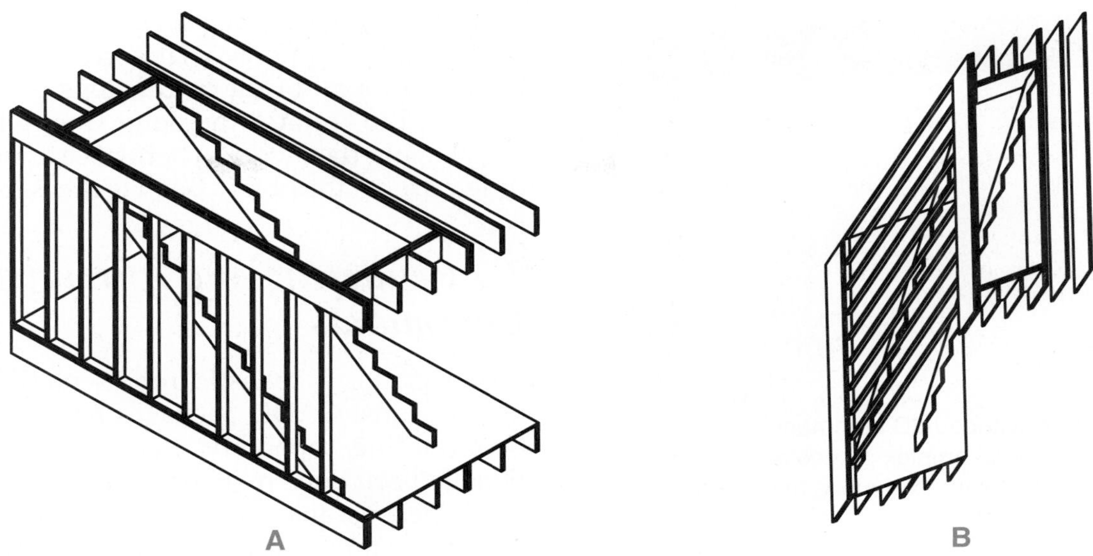

Eric K. Augspurger

Figure 5-31. A—A 2D isometric drawing of roughed-in stair stringers. Although it looks three-dimensional, it was drawn in only two dimensions. B—When the isometric drawing is viewed from a different viewpoint, you can see that it is only two-dimensional.

are boxes, cylinders, cones, and spheres. See **Figure 5-32**. Commands used to create primitives are generally based on the shape. For example, the **BOX** command creates a box-shaped object, and the **SPHERE** command creates a 3D sphere.

More advanced 3D commands allow you to use extrusion, revolution, or lofting operations to construct 3D models. Commands such as **EXTRUDE**, **REVOLVE**, and **LOFT** are typically used to construct complex 3D shapes from 2D or 3D geometry. See **Figure 5-33**.

3D Views

CADD software with 3D modeling capability typically has a **HIDE** command to remove lines that would normally be hidden in the current view. These are the lines that would be drawn

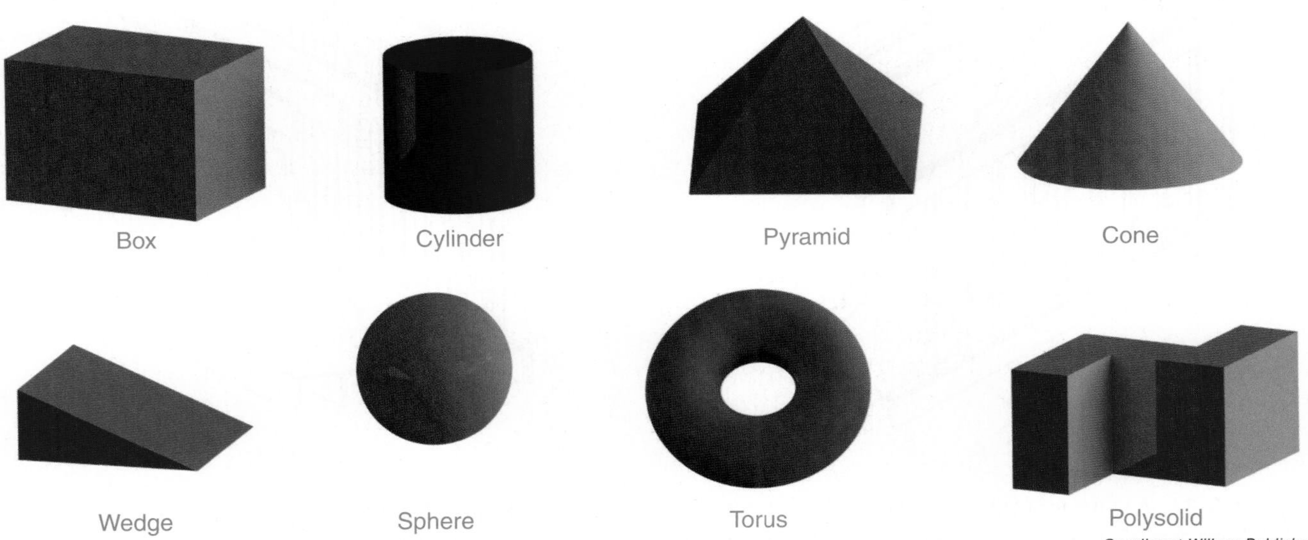

Goodheart-Willcox Publisher

Figure 5-32. Examples of 3D primitives available in CADD programs.

Goodheart-Willcox Publisher

Figure 5-33. Advanced 3D commands allow you to create models with complex curves and features. This table was created from extrusions and loft objects.

as hidden lines in a 2D drawing. Hiding lines can help you visualize the 3D model.

In addition to hiding lines, you also need to be able to see the objects from different angles. It would be nearly impossible to create a 3D model of any complexity only being able to see a top view, for example. Each CADD program has its own unique way of displaying different 3D views. Some CADD programs have preset isometric views. Other programs have an **ORBIT** command that allows you to change the view dynamically. There are also programs that have both of these options and more. However, the basic goal of all of these functions is the same. You need to "rotate" the point from which you are viewing the model to better see another part or feature on the object. See **Figure 5-34**.

3D Rendering and Animation Commands

To create a realistic representation of 3D objects, most CADD packages have some type of rendering capability. Rendering has traditionally been done by hand with paint, charcoal, chalk, pencils, and ink. However, just as the process of creating a drawing has been automated with CADD, so too has the process of rendering the drawing. Generally, a **MATERIAL** command is used to define surface textures and apply them to objects. A **LIGHT** command is used to create lights to simulate various lighting conditions. A **RENDER** command is used to generate the rendering. Many high-end CADD programs can produce very realistic renderings, given enough time to properly set up lights and materials. See **Figure 5-35**.

Some CADD programs have the ability to add movement to 3D objects to create an animation.

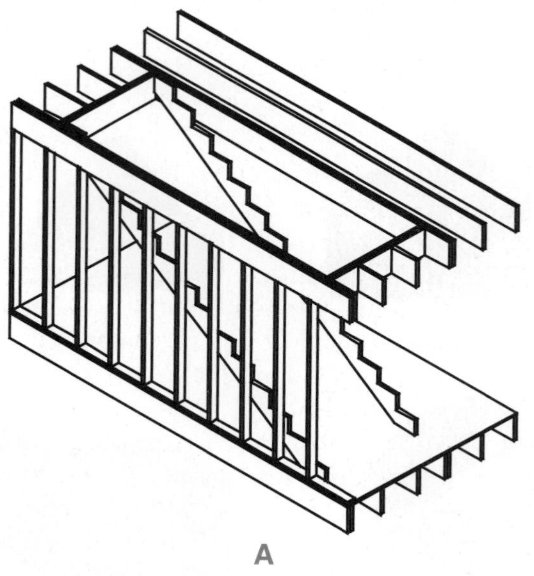

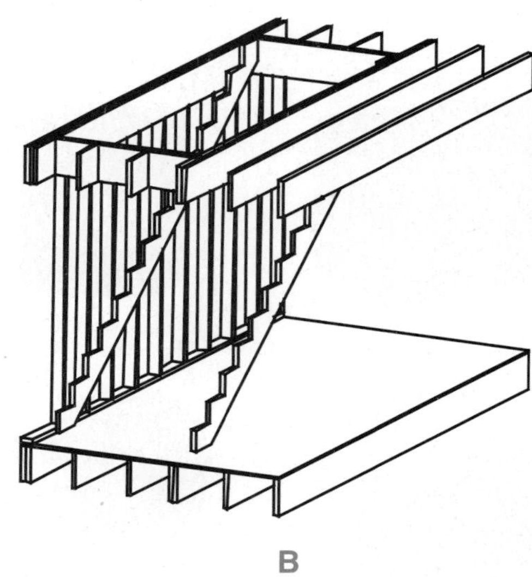

Eric K. Augspurger

Figure 5-34. A—An isometric view of a 3D model. Compare this to Figure 5-31A. The two views are identical. B—When the 3D model is viewed from a different viewpoint, you can see that it is truly three-dimensional. This viewpoint is exactly the same as the viewpoint for the 2D isometric drawing in Figure 5-31B.

Helmuth A. Geiser, Member AIBD

Figure 5-35. This rendering shows a nice setup of lights and materials. Good planning and a lot of time were required to create this model.

An animation is a series of still images played sequentially at a very fast rate, such as 30 frames per second. There are small differences between each frame and, when the frames are viewed quickly in succession, the brain interprets these differences as movement. See **Figure 5-36**. Generally, an **ANIMATE** command is used to add movement to the objects and a **RENDER** command renders the animation.

CADD Equipment Maintenance and Drawing File Storage

Operating a CADD system requires efficient management of resources and proper maintenance of all computer equipment. Regular maintenance is important to keep equipment functioning properly. Plotters, printers, and other electronic equipment should be cleaned and serviced according to the instructions and schedules established by the manufacturers. Equipment should be repaired or replaced as needed. In addition, electronic equipment should be powered through a surge protector.

Printing and plotting supplies should be kept on hand and stored properly. An inventory of replacement toner and ink cartridges, plotter pens, paper, and other consumables should be maintained to prevent work stoppage when these items need to be replaced.

CADD drawing files and all other electronic files associated with projects must be stored properly to ensure that they can be retrieved when needed. Drawing files must be stored using a file naming convention that allows for easy retrieval. For each project, create a system of folders on a network drive so that it is easy to locate files. Use a network drive with automatic file backup capability or establish a backup storage system in a different location. At the end of a project, move files into an archive folder. All drawing files (and all critical electronic data) associated with the project must be archived with some form of backup for safekeeping. As drawings are electronically revised, the backup files must also be replaced.

Material Safety

As a drafter, you may not think about material safety. However, there are many types of materials that you come in contact with, and some may be considered hazardous. The Occupational Safety and Health Administration (OSHA) requires:

- A list be kept of all hazardous materials used on the premises.
- A file be maintained containing material safety data sheets (MSDS) on each hazardous material.
- Employees be trained in the proper use of hazardous materials.

Some materials that you may come in contact with include ammonia, cleaning fluids, inks, and toner. These materials must be properly handled and must be properly disposed of when you are done using them. For example, spent toner cartridges should not be placed in the garbage. They should be returned to a recycling facility for recharging and eventual re-use. When in doubt, check the facility's master list of hazardous materials. If the material is listed as hazardous, check the material's MSDS for hazards. Finally, check with the manufacturer or the Environmental Protection Agency (EPA) for disposal procedures.

Eric K. Augspurger

Figure 5-36. There is not much difference between "neighboring" frames of an animation. However, over the length of the animation, you can see that the window is opening and closing.

The Ergonomic Environment

Like other workers who spend long periods of time doing detailed work with a computer, drafters using computer-aided drafting equipment may be susceptible to eyestrain, back discomfort, and hand and wrist problems. ***Ergonomics*** is the science of adapting the workstation to fit the needs of the drafter. Applying ergonomic principles results in a comfortable and efficient environment. There are many types of ergonomic accessories that may improve a computer workstation, including wrist rests, ergonomically designed chairs, and back supports. In addition, the table in **Figure 5-37** identifies a few things that can be done to create a comfortable environment and help prevent injury or strain to the operator's body.

Cleanliness is another important part of the drafting environment. Keep papers, pens, rules, reference books, storage media, and other materials organized. The work area should not be cluttered with unneeded items.

Ergonomic Guidelines
Eyes
• Position the monitor to minimize glare from overhead lights, windows, and other light sources. Reduce light intensity by turning off some lights or closing blinds and shades. You should be able to see images clearly without glare. • Position the monitor so that it is 18″ to 30″ from your eyes. This is about an arm's length. To help reduce eyestrain, look away from the monitor every 15–20 minutes and focus on an object at least 20″ away for 1–2 minutes.
Wrists and Arms
• Forearms should be parallel to the floor. • Periodically stretch your arms, wrists, and shoulders. • Try using an ergonomic keyboard and mouse. The keyboard keeps the wrists in a normal body position and the mouse will fit your hand more comfortably.
Neck
• Adjust the monitor so that your head is level, not leaning forward or back. The top of the screen should be near your line of sight.
Back
• Use a chair that is comfortable and provides good back support. The chair should be adjustable and provide armrests. • Sit up straight. This maintains good posture and reduces strain. Think about good posture until it becomes common practice. • Try standing up, stretching, and walking every hour. This will also reduce strain.
Legs
• Keep your thighs parallel to the ground. • Rest your feet flat on the floor or use a footrest. • When taking a break, walk around. This will stretch the muscles and promote circulation through your body.

Goodheart-Willcox Publisher

Figure 5-37. Following ergonomic guidelines promotes efficiency, comfort, and safety in the work environment.

Summary

- CAD is an acronym for computer-aided (or computer-assisted) drafting, and CADD includes both computer-aided drafting and computer-aided design.
- CADD is a tool that must be used properly in order to prepare architectural drawings.
- The hardware for a CADD system includes the CPU, one or more input devices, one or more output devices, and a storage device.
- CADD software can be either general-purpose or AEC-specific. AEC-specific CADD packages have features that help architects and architectural drafters work more efficiently.
- Features that are common to most CADD packages include the ability to create objects, use various drawing unit formats, create dimensions automatically, and organize objects on layers.
- Typical CADD commands include file management, drawing, editing, inquiry, display control, and dimensioning commands, as well as drawing aids and 3D drawing and viewing commands.

Internet Resources

American Design Drafting Association (ADDA)
Resources for the design drafting profession and drafter certification

American Institute of Architects (AIA)
Educational and industry resources for the architectural profession

Architectural Record
Continuing Education Center

Autodesk
AutoCAD® and Revit® software publisher

Bentley Systems
MicroStation® software publisher

Chief Architect
Chief Architect® software publisher

Regional Computer Recycling & Recovery (RCR&R)
Electronics recycling services

SoftPlan Systems
SoftPlan® software publisher

US National CAD Standard
US National CAD Standard; AIA CAD Layer Guidelines

Review Questions

Answer the following questions using the information in this chapter.

1. What is the difference between CAD and CADD?
2. Name five reasons for using CADD.
3. List the hardware components of a typical CADD system.
4. What are the two broad types of CADD software most often used for architectural drafting?
5. What is the purpose of dimensions on an architectural drawing?
6. Explain the concept of layers in a CADD program.
7. Explain the term *symbol library.*
8. Explain two reasons why program customization features are important to an experienced CADD user.
9. List three items that can be generated automatically by many AEC-specific CADD programs.
10. List at least five types of commands found in CADD programs.
11. _____ commands allow you to create objects on the computer screen.
12. In general, what do editing commands allow you to do?
13. _____ commands are used to list the drawing database records for selected objects and to calculate distances, areas, and perimeters.

14. What is the difference between a *fillet* and a *round*?
15. List three display control commands.
16. What is the purpose of drawing aids?
17. Define *block* and *attribute*.
18. A _____ is a file configured with user-specified settings and drawing content that can be applied to new files.
19. Briefly describe the purpose of each of the following commands.
    A. **LINE**
    B. **POLYGON**
    C. **UNDO**
    D. **MIRROR**
    E. **CHAMFER**
    F. **ZOOM**
    G. **LEADER**
    H. **ORBIT**
20. _____ modeling creates 3D objects by generating a volume.
21. What are *primitives*?
22. For what is the **HIDE** command available in most CADD systems used?
23. What is *ergonomics*?
24. Name at least two ergonomic accessories that can be used to improve a computer workstation.

Suggested Activities

1. Using the Internet, search for various CADD software programs. Make a list with the software grouped as general-purpose or AEC-specific. Give an oral presentation to your class on your findings.
2. Contact a local AEC firm that uses CADD. Find out which CADD package the firm uses and identify the criteria the firm used to choose it.
3. Some CADD programs, including programs used for architectural drawing, are available for download from the Internet without charge. One example is Trimble SketchUp Make. Download one of these free programs and try to create a few simple drawings. **Important**: Be sure to obtain permission from the owner of the computer before you download software. Write an essay about your experience with the software. How easy was it to learn and use?
4. Obtain electronic examples of AEC renderings or animations. The Internet can be a great source for this, but be sure to download only those files labeled as "freeware" or "freely distribute." All others are copyrighted material.
5. Collect as many different examples of 3D computer-generated illustrations as you can. Search through books, magazines, and online sites. Bring your examples to class to share with others. Classify each one as a wireframe, surface or solid model, or animation.
6. Prepare a list of hazardous materials found in your school's drafting lab or your drafting department. For each material listed, provide a description of disposal procedures. Use guidelines specified by the manufacturer or the Environmental Protection Agency.

Problem Solving Case Study

Your architectural design drafting firm is unhappy with its current general-purpose CADD software and is considering changing to another CADD package. The company has asked you to research the various CADD programs that are available. You are to analyze and compare the available software on the following characteristics: cost, capability, ease of use, and learning curve. Do the required research and create a chart to compare at least four different CADD packages. Based on the results of your research, choose the CADD package that you believe will best fit the needs of the architectural design drafting firm. Write a paragraph explaining why you chose this program over the other three.

ADDA Certification Prep

The following questions are presented in the style used in the American Design Drafting Association (ADDA) Drafter Certification Test. Answer the questions using the information in this chapter.

1. Which of the following are considered to be hardware input devices?
   A. keyboard
   B. monitor
   C. printer
   D. digitizer
   E. mouse
2. Which of the following statements are true?
   A. The monitor is an output device.
   B. The mouse is an output device.
   C. AEC-specific CADD packages have features that make the software more useful to architects than general-purpose CADD packages.
   D. Attributes are text information that can be saved with a block to provide information about the block or the feature it represents.
   E. To change the length of a wall from 40′ to 35′, the best command to use is **ZOOM**.
3. Match each command with its general function.

   Commands: 1. **SCALE**, 2. **PAN**, 3. **ERASE**, 4. **UNDO**, 5. **EXTEND**, 6. **ZOOM**
   A. Moves the drawing window to a different area at the same magnification so that another part of the drawing is visible on the screen.
   B. Lengthens a line or arc to a specified boundary.
   C. Reverses the previous command.
   D. Deletes the specified objects from the drawing.
   E. Increases or decreases the magnification of the drawing on the screen.
   F. Increases or decreases the physical size of objects in the drawing.

Curricular Connections

1. **Social Science.** In the last 30-plus years, CADD software has completely changed the methods used by architectural drafters. For example, knowledge of how to use an erasing shield is much less important now. Knowledge of how to use computer software is much more important. Yet some underlying characteristics remain the same, such as accuracy and attention to detail. Think about the effect these changes have had on older architectural drafters—those who have been working in the field since 1980 or earlier. How have these changes in the architectural drafting field affected their careers? Their personal lives? Also, what other professions have had similar changes? What are some examples of professions in the architectural drafting field that did not exist five years ago? Write an essay describing your thoughts.

STEM Connections

1. **Math.** Newer versions of CADD software are released periodically. The cost of upgrading to the newer versions can be high. Choose two professional CADD packages and find out the initial cost of each. Determine how often, on average, each package is updated and the cost of a typical upgrade. Add the initial cost of each package and the cost of upgrades for a period of 5 years. Which package had the highest initial cost? Which package costs more over a 5-year period? Write a paragraph describing your results. Show your calculations.
2. **Engineering.** Solid modeling has provided scientists and engineers with a completely new method of testing structures: virtual testing. Find out more about the types of structural and materials testing that can now be done virtually. Consider the advantages and disadvantages of performing these tests virtually. Write a report explaining the pros and cons of virtual structural testing.

Communicating about Architecture

1. **Reading and Speaking.** With a partner, make flash cards for each of the CADD commands discussed in this chapter. On the front of each flash card, write the name of the command. On the back, write a description of the command. Take turns quizzing one another on the command names and descriptions.
2. **Speaking and Listening.** Working in small groups, prepare an oral presentation to describe the advantages of using CADD in architectural drafting. Create posters or other visual aids to use in your presentation. Include illustrations of architectural drawings and computer renderings.

Section 2

Architectural Planning

pics721/Shutterstock.com

Chapter 6

Primary Residential Design Considerations

Objectives

After completing this chapter, you will be able to:

- Explain key site planning considerations.
- Evaluate the costs and requirements for building a residential home.
- Describe the working drawings used to build a structure.

Key Terms

building code
building section
construction details
deed
electrical plan
elevation
equity
floor framing plan
floor plan
foundation plan
gross annual income
heating, ventilation, and air conditioning (HVAC) plan
landscaping plan
model building code
pictorial presentation
plumbing plan
roof framing plan
roof plan
site
site plan
specifications
title
title search
topography
working drawings
zoning

Most people have a "dream home" that they hope to build some day. However, few people consider beyond the house itself. They seldom take into consideration the location and characteristics of the site, local building codes, community attributes, and their family lifestyle and quality of living. These considerations, in many cases, are just as important as the size and room arrangement of the house.

Site Considerations

The ***site*** is more than just a piece of property—it is part of a larger community. See **Figure 6-1**. It is located in a certain school district and is a certain distance from shopping areas. An airport or major freeway may be nearby. The local community may be a growing metro area or a rural, less populated area. Next to the house itself, the site is probably the most expensive item in a residential housing project. It should be evaluated carefully to realize its potential as a vital part of the home.

Topography

The physical characteristics of the land on a site are known as its ***topography***. The topography may be rolling or flat, it may contain steep slopes and cliffs, or it may have a lake or pond. It may be located in a warm or cold climate. See **Figure 6-2**.

Study the topographical drawings of the site to determine its slope, contour, size, shape, and

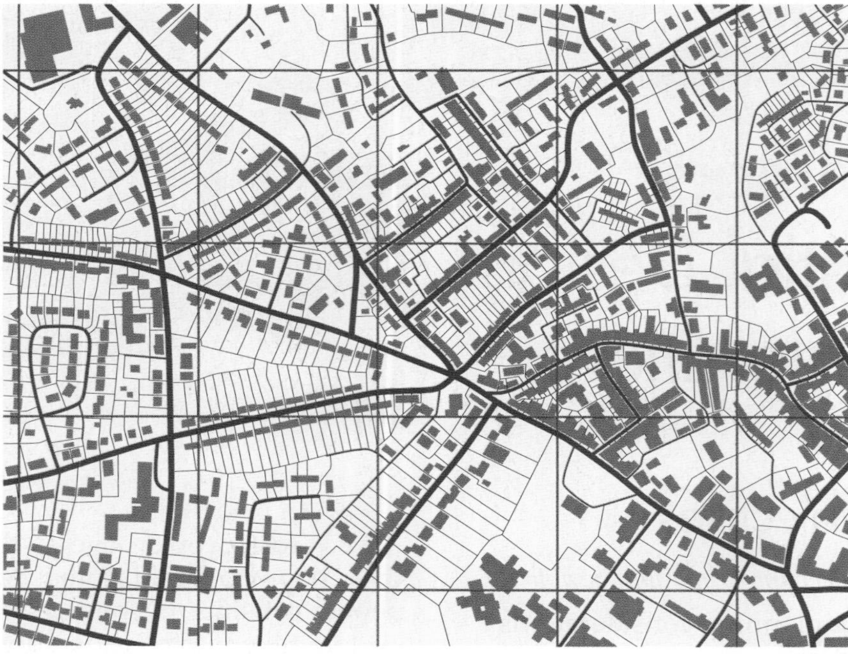

Robert Adrian Hillman/Shutterstock.com

Figure 6-1. A home site is always a part of a larger community, with shopping centers, schools, and other community structures.

EugeneF/Shutterstock.com

Figure 6-2. A well-planned community neighborhood takes advantage of the natural site characteristics.

elevation. Trees, rocks, and soil conditions may also be indicated on the drawings. These factors may limit or suggest the type of structure that may be built on the site. For example, a flat site lends itself to a ranch or two-story house. A hilly or sloping site is ideal for a split-level home. A site that has many trees may be ideal for a house with large windows and liberal use of natural materials. When planning a home, every effort should be made to take full advantage of site characteristics. The structure should appear to be part of the site. It should blend in with the surroundings rather than stand apart from them.

If the site is in a rural area, you may have to provide water and septic systems. In these cases, extra care must be taken to select a proper site. Hard water, iron water, and the lack of availability of drinkable water are problems that must be considered before the house is built. Some soil types can prevent or hinder the installation of a water or septic system. In such instances, equipment used for installation is expensive and the work is labor-intensive. Also, after the home is built, a septic system requires regular maintenance.

The shape of the site is another important factor. A long and narrow site, or one that is oddly shaped, may limit construction possibilities. See **Figure 6-3**. The site measurements and property lines should be checked by a surveyor before construction begins. Having correct site information at the beginning of the design stage is essential to avoid later problems. Having this information can also assist in determining the final design.

Costs and Restrictions

The price of the site or lot should be examined carefully. Take into consideration any needed improvements, such as grading, fill, tree removal, and drainage. These will add to the final cost of the lot. Also take into account the amount of road frontage the lot has and whether it is a corner lot. Any future assessments for road, sewer, or other improvements are usually proportional to the length of frontage. Corner lots generally have higher assessments because roads run along two sides of the property.

Ownership of the property is transferred through a legal document called a ***deed***. See **Figure 6-4**. A ***title*** provides evidence of ownership and is where any liens, easements, or restrictions on the property are listed. A ***title search*** is required by law in many areas before a deed can be transferred to a new owner to determine if there are any legal claims against the property. Even if not required by law, a title search should be conducted for your own protection. After the title search, the title company may offer title insurance that protects the homeowner if any

Brykaylo Yuriy/Shutterstock.com

Figure 6-3. This narrow hillside lot is beautiful, but perhaps impractical. Building a home in this rural area would require a septic system, as well as special site preparation to accommodate the steep hillside.

Green Architecture

Working with Nature

Many people who want a "green home" concentrate on the features of the home itself. But what about the site on which the home is built? What effect will building a home on the site have on the environment?

One interesting way to work with nature and the environment when you build a new home is to choose your landscaping carefully. Use plants that are native to the area, rather than bringing in "exotic" species from other areas of the country. Plants that are native to the area do a better job of supporting the local wildlife. They are also better suited to the local environment. This has many benefits for the homeowner. For example, native plants usually do not need to be watered often, if at all. Because the plants are suited to the local soil, the soil does not have to be "improved" to ensure that they will flourish.

Another idea is to avoid large expanses of concrete or paved areas on the property. Keep as much of the property as possible covered with greenery and growing plants, such as the native plants previously described. In addition to adding beauty to the property, green plants and trees absorb carbon dioxide and produce oxygen. They provide a natural air filter to help keep the air cleaner and healthier.

WARRANTY DEED

The Above Space for Recorder's Use Only

THE GRANTOR(S), Kenneth R. Warner, as Successor Trustee of the Joan P. Warner Trust dated August 7, 2006, of the City of Chicago, County of Cook, State of Illinois, for and in consideration of TEN ($10.00) DOLLARS, and other good and valuable consideration in hand paid, CONVEY(S) and Warrant(s) to Benjamin Mays, 10329 S. Hoyne, Chicago, IL 60643, of the County of Cook, all interest in the following described real estate, being situated in the County of Cook, in the State of Illinois, to-wit:

LOT FIVE (5) IN BLOCK FOUR (4) IN AUGUST JERNBERG'S SUBDIVISION IN THE SOUTH WEST QUARTER OF THE NORTH WEST QUARTER OF SECTION EIGHTEEN (18), TOWNSHIP THIRTY SEVEN (37) NORTH, RANGE FOURTEEN (14), EAST OF THE THIRD PRINCIPAL MERIDIAN, IN COOK COUNTY, ILLINOIS.

SUBJECT TO: covenants, conditions and restrictions of record, private, public and utility easements and roads and highways, party wall rights and agreements, general taxes for the year 2015 and subsequent years including taxes which may accrue by reason of new or additional improvements during the year(s) 2015

Permanent Index Number: 25-18-122-014-0000
Common Address: 10620 S. Claremont, Chicago, IL 60643

Hereby releasing and waiving all rights under and by virtue of the Homestead Exemption laws of the State of Illinois.

DATED this 14 day of Sept., 2015

Kenneth R. Warner

Kenneth R. Warner, as Successor Trustee of
the Joan P. Warner Trust dated August 7, 2006

State of Illinois)
) ss:
County of)

I, the undersigned, a Notary Public in and for said County and State aforesaid, Do Hereby Certify that Kenneth R. Warner, as Successor Trustee of the Joan P. Warner Trust dated August 7, 2006, is/are the person(s) whose name(s) are subscribed to the foregoing instrument, appeared before me this day in person, and acknowledged that they signed, sealed and delivered the said instrument as their free and voluntary act, for the uses and purposes therein set forth, including the release and waiver of the right of homestead.

Given under my hand and official seal, this 14 day of Sept, 2015.

Commission Expires 4/23/2016

Karen Carlyle
Notary Public

This instrument prepared by:

Karen Carlyle
8128 Ripple Ridge
Tinley Park, IL 60477

"OFFICIAL SEAL"
Karen Carlyle
Notary Public, State of Illinois
My Commission Expires 4/23/2016

Send Subsequent Tax Bills to and return to:

Benjamin Mays
10620 S. Claremont
Chicago, IL 60643

Goodheart-Willcox Publisher

Figure 6-4. A typical property deed containing a legal description of the site.

unexpected liens are discovered after the property has been purchased. The deed, title, and title insurance are very important documents and should be examined carefully by a competent attorney before the property is purchased.

Restrictions on the property may specify the style of house that may be built, the size of the house, the type of landscaping, or even the types of vehicles that can be parked on the property. Easements may allow utilities to cross the property or may prevent the filling of a low area that must remain for drainage purposes. Be sure you understand and agree with the restrictions before closing the sale.

Zoning and Building Codes

Zoning is a planning tool used by communities to restrict the kinds of structures built in various areas. Zoning is usually based on local building codes according to the type of business or residence, such as commercial, single-family, or multifamily use. See **Figure 6-5**. Investigate the zoning laws in the area where the site is located. If it is zoned for commercial use or for multifamily dwellings, you cannot build a single-family home on the property. Even if the selected site is zoned for single-family structures, you might find that the large open area nearby that plays a large part in your site decision is zoned for light industry. Check the zoning!

Another area that many prospective buyers fail to explore is local building codes. Codes are different from zoning. ***Building codes*** specify requirements for construction methods and materials for plumbing, electrical, and general building construction. For example, the building code in a particular area may require all electrical wiring to be in grounded conduit. It is important to understand building codes because they may be so restrictive that the type of house planned for the site cannot be built. Building codes also affect construction costs. Very strict codes may raise the cost of construction significantly. On the other hand, codes may be so lax that the quality of homes in the area is poor.

Model building codes are rules developed by independent agencies that can be adopted or incorporated into law by state and local governments. Two widely adopted model building codes in the United States are the International Residential Code and the International Building Code, both published by the International Code Council (ICC). The International Residential Code sets design and construction regulations

Gary Blakeley/Shutterstock.com

Figure 6-5. In many towns, zoning is arranged to place schools and businesses close to the homes they serve. In this community, the high school and a grocery store are within easy walking distance of several neighborhoods.

for residential structures, with an emphasis on one- and two-family dwellings and townhouses. The International Building Code sets design and construction regulations for building systems. The International Building Code is typically used by communities to set guidelines for commercial and multifamily structures, but it is applicable to all building types, including one-family residences. In order to comply with local building requirements, it is important to know which building codes apply in a given community. International Residential Code requirements are referenced throughout this textbook.

It is common for states and municipalities to adopt model codes and establish additional requirements based on local needs and safety provisions. For example, California has seismic design requirements for construction of earthquake-resistant structures. Florida has design requirements addressing construction to withstand high wind loads.

Generally, all construction and remodeling requires a building permit from the county, town, city, or village. If you live in a town or city, you may need to comply with both county and city building codes. Talk with a local building inspector to determine the cost of permits, required inspections, and other building regulations. **Figure 6-6** shows a typical building permit form.

The Community

Before selecting a building site, evaluate the surrounding community and neighborhood. Consider the following questions:

- Is the neighborhood a well-planned community? Or has the neighborhood developed naturally, with no central theme or forethought? Which do you prefer?
- Are the existing homes in the community in the price range of the house you are considering buying or building?
- Is the community alive and growing, or is it rundown and dying?

Employability
Completing a Job Application

A prospective employer may ask you to complete a job application form before having an interview. The job application form highlights the information the employer needs to know about you, your education, and your prior work experience. Employers often use these forms to screen applicants for the skills needed on the job. You might complete a form in a personnel or employment office. Sometimes, you may get the form by mail.

The appearance of the application form can give an employer the first opinion about you. Fill out the form accurately, completely, and neatly. How well you accomplish this task can determine whether you get the job. When asked about salary, write *open* or *negotiable*. This means you are willing to consider offers. Be sure to send or give the form to the correct person, whose name often appears on the form. In larger companies, job applications are usually handled by the human resources department.

Many employers now request electronic applications, either through the employer's website or an independent job-search website. When filling out an online application, it is extremely important to include key terms for which the employer may search. This will help you stand out from the many other applicants the employer will consider.

When preparing your application, be sure to save it in the appropriate file format. If a preferred format is not given, it is best to save the application in Microsoft Word .docx or .doc file format, or save it as a PDF file. This will enable the employer to find specific search terms in your document. Be sure to complete all the fields of the application. Many job-search sites have sample forms on which you can practice before attempting to complete a real application.

Activity

Search online to find a sample job application that you can download free, or one with which you can practice online. Fill out the application as if you were applying for a job as an architectural drafter.

VIGO COUNTY
BUILDING PERMIT APPLICATION
VIGO COUNTY BUILDING INSPECTION DEPARTMENT
201 CHERRY STREET, TERRE HAUTE, INDIANA 47807

Applicant to complete numbered spaces only. This form must be signed by owner and/or contractor.

1	JOB ADDRESS			
	LOT NO.	BLK	TRACT	
2	OWNER	MAIL ADDRESS	ZIP	PHONE
3	CONTRACTOR	MAIL ADDRESS	PHONE	
4	ARCHITECT OR DESIGNER	MAIL ADDRESS	PHONE	
5	ENGINEER	MAIL ADDRESS	PHONE	
6	LENDER	MAIL ADDRESS		BRANCH
7	USE OF BUILDING	PRESENT	PROPOSED	

8 Class of work: NEW ADDITION REMODEL REPAIR MOVE REMOVE (WRECKING)

9 Describe work:

10 Valuation of work: $

PLEASE DO NOT WRITE IN SHADED AREAS

SPECIAL CONDITIONS:	Required	Received
RE-ZONING		
BOARD OF ZONING APPEALS		
HEALTH DEPT.		
FIRE DEPT.		

APPLICATION ACCEPTED BY	PLANS CHECKED BY	APPROVED FOR ISSUANCE BY

PLUMBING
NEW OR ALTERED SEWER LINES NECESSARY YES ☐ NO ☐
PLUMBING NECESSARY: ☐ YES ☐ NO | PLUMBING PERMIT FEE:
Number of fixtures to be installed
Sewers must be approved by Board of Health.

ELECTRICAL
NEW SERVICE: Required ☐ YES ☐ NO
Number of circuits to be installed
NEW SERVICE: Amperage
Electrical Permit Fee: $

NOTICE
THIS PERMIT BECOMES NULL AND VOID IF WORK OR CONSTRUC-TION AUTHORIZED IS NOT COMMENCED WITHIN 120 DAYS, OR IF CONSTRUCTION OR WORK IS SUSPENDED OR ABANDONED FOR A PERIOD OF 120 DAYS AT ANY TIME AFTER WORK IS COMMENCED.

I HEREBY CERTIFY THAT I HAVE READ AND EXAMINED THIS APPLICATION AND KNOW THE SAME TO BE TRUE AND CORRECT. ALL PROVISIONS OF LAWS AND ORDINANCES GOVERNING THIS TYPE OF WORK WILL BE COM-PLIED WITH WHETHER SPECIFIED HEREIN OR NOT. THE GRANTING OF A PERMIT DOES NOT PRESUME TO GIVE AUTHORITY TO VIOLATE OR CANCEL THE PROVISIONS OF ANY OTHER STATE OR LOCAL LAW REGULATING CON-STRUCTION OR THE PERFORMANCE OF CONSTRUCTION.

11 SIGNATURE OF CONTRACTOR OR AUTHORIZED AGENT (DATE)

12 SIGNATURE OF OWNER (IF OWNER BUILDER) (DATE)

ENGINEERS DEPT.

DRAINAGE			
SET BACK LINES			
ENTRANCE & EXITS			
PARKING SURFACE			
OFF STREET PARKING	SPACES AVAIL.	SPACES NEEDED	

AREA PLANNING
ZONED
OTHER:

Goodheart-Willcox Publisher

Figure 6-6. A building permit must be obtained before construction can begin.

- Does the community have room for growth, or is it restricted?
- Are the residents of the community people who take pride in their homes and keep them well maintained, or are many homes in disrepair? See **Figure 6-7**.
- Does the community have good schools and convenient shopping areas?
- Are services such as fire protection, water service, sewer service, natural gas service, and garbage collection available in this community? What is the average monthly cost for utilities?
- Is the site near your place of employment?
- Is public transportation available and close by?

Housing Considerations

After you decide on a site, the next consideration is the house you will build on it. You will need to consider your family's needs and how much you can afford to spend for housing.

Lisajsh/Shutterstock.com

Figure 6-7. Check the other houses in the neighborhood. Well-maintained houses indicate pride of ownership and help keep housing prices stable.

Family Needs

A functional house represents the lifestyle of those who occupy it. Rather than try to change your lifestyle to fit the house, build the structure to meet the needs and lifestyle of the people who will use it.

Family size is a major consideration in a house design. Do not forget to consider future family growth as well. Plan for ample space for all members of the family to perform their chosen activities. See **Figure 6-8**. Consider providing space for:

- Accommodating guests
- Bathing
- Dressing
- Dining
- Entertaining
- Family recreation
- Hobbies
- Housekeeping
- Laundering
- Preparing food
- Relaxing
- Sleeping
- Storage
- Studying
- Working/home office

These activities should not necessarily be thought of in relation to specific rooms. Some activities are performed throughout the house, while others are restricted to certain areas. The important point is to provide enough space for the activities in which the family will be engaged. Let the structure take the shape and arrangement that best serves these needs.

Yeko Photo Studio/Shutterstock.com

Figure 6-8. Be sure to consider present and future needs of the family, including children and pets.

Budgeting for Housing

A home is the most expensive item an individual or family will buy. When choosing a house to build or buy, you need to consider several factors—income, other expenses and obligations, housing needs, and expected future income.

Since housing is generally a monthly expense, you might begin by calculating how much you can afford to spend on housing over a long period of time. Most financial advisors recommend that monthly housing cost no more than one-third of your monthly take-home pay. Take-home pay is your earnings after taxes and other deductions have been subtracted. In other words, it is the amount of your paycheck or direct deposit.

A homeowner's housing cost is not limited to the monthly mortgage payment. It also includes utility costs, property taxes, and homeowner's insurance. If the site you select is in a flood zone, you should also consider the cost of flood insurance.

To arrive at a rough estimate of the amount you can afford for housing, add all of your monthly nonhousing expenses. See **Figure 6-9**. These include food, clothing, transportation, recreation, and payments on outstanding loans. Be sure to also include scheduled savings and retirement planning expenses. Next, find the amount you have available to spend each month. Be sure to include all of your income and earnings. Finally, subtract the monthly nonhousing expenses from the total monthly income. This is the *maximum* amount you can afford to spend for housing each month. You will probably want to keep your housing costs under the maximum that you can afford. Allow yourself some free income each month for unexpected expenses. For example, if your car breaks down or your refrigerator stops working, you will need to pay for repairs.

JohnKwan/Shutterstock.com

Figure 6-9. A good way to determine your monthly expenses is to track them for a period of several months. This will help you know how much you spend, on average, for utilities, clothing, food, and other expenses.

A rule of thumb for determining how much you can spend on a home is a price that is no more than 2-1/2 times your gross annual income. ***Gross annual income*** is the amount of money you earn before taxes and other deductions. For example, if your gross annual income is $42,000, you should be able to afford a $105,000 home.

Mortgage lenders may have more specific rules. In general, most lenders will not provide a mortgage that requires payments of more than 28% of your gross monthly income. The actual amount of the mortgage payment is determined by the sale price of the house, the amount of money paid as a down payment, and the current interest rate. Most mortgage lenders require between 3% and 5% of the sale price as a down payment. In addition, until the owner has 20% equity in the home, most mortgage lenders require private mortgage insurance (PMI). ***Equity*** is the amount the house is worth minus the amount owed. The remainder is the amount of money a homeowner would get from the sale of the house. PMI is insurance against the owner defaulting on the mortgage; in other words, PMI protects the lender from losing money if the owner defaults on the loan.

Working Drawings

A set of plans or ***working drawings*** is all of the drawings and related specifications needed to construct a house. All sets of plans include certain types of drawings. Other drawings are needed for individual projects, depending on the job requirements.

Primary Plans

Most sets of plans for residential construction include the following items:

- Site plan
- Foundation plan
- Floor plan
- Elevations
- Electrical plan
- Construction details
- Building sections
- Specifications

The ***site plan*** shows the location of the house on the site, as shown in **Figure 6-10**. It shows utilities, topographical features, site dimensions, existing trees or vegetation, and any other buildings on the property.

The ***foundation plan*** specifies the foundation size and materials used. See **Figure 6-11**. It provides information about excavation, waterproofing, and supporting structures. It may also include the basement plan if the house has a basement.

The ***floor plan*** shows all exterior and interior walls, doors, windows, patios, walks, decks, fireplaces, mechanical equipment, built-in cabinets, appliances, and bathroom fixtures. See **Figure 6-12**. If the house has more than one story, a separate plan is drawn for each floor of the house.

Elevations are drawn for each side of the house. See **Figure 6-13**. These drawings are orthographic projections showing the exterior features of the building. They show the placement of windows and doors, the type of exterior building materials used, exterior steps, the chimney, rooflines, overhang dimensions, and other exterior details.

The ***electrical plan*** is drawn from the floor plan. See **Figure 6-14**. It locates switches, electrical outlets, ceiling fixtures, television and cable jacks, LAN connections, the service entrance location, and the panel box. The electrical plan also provides general information concerning circuits and special installations. A legend or key is typically included on the electrical plan to explain the meaning of the electrical symbols used on the plan.

Construction details are drawn when more information is needed to fully describe how the foundation, wall, or roof construction is to be completed. Typical drawings include details of kitchens, stairs, chimneys, fireplaces, windows and doors, and foundations.

Building sections are vertical "cuts" or "slices" through the structure that illustrate the type of foundation, wall, and roof construction to be used. See **Figure 6-15**. Building sections typically illustrate unique or different construction techniques. Another purpose of building section drawings is to clarify the change in floor levels throughout a structure.

Specifications describe the materials and quality of work. They provide additional information that is not noted or shown on the drawings. The drawings and the specifications, or *specs*, form the basis of a legal contract between the owner and the builder. If there is a conflict between the specification sheets and the actual working drawings, the specifications take legal precedence and are considered the final answer to any question related to the construction or materials used on the project.

Other Plans

Several other types of drawings may be incorporated into a set of residential working drawings. These often include a roof plan, roof framing plan, floor framing plan, heating and cooling plan, and plumbing plan. All of these are based on the floor plan. Additional plans may include a landscaping plan, which is often based on the site plan, and pictorial presentations.

A ***roof plan*** should be included if the roof is intricate and not clearly shown by the standard drawings. The roof plan may be incorporated into the site plan. A ***roof framing plan*** may be drawn to clarify construction aspects associated with the roof. This plan should be included when the roof is complex and requires special construction techniques. The roof framing plan shows the rafters, ceiling joists, fascia boards, and supporting members such as headers and beams.

A ***floor framing plan*** shows the direction of floor joists and major supporting members. It

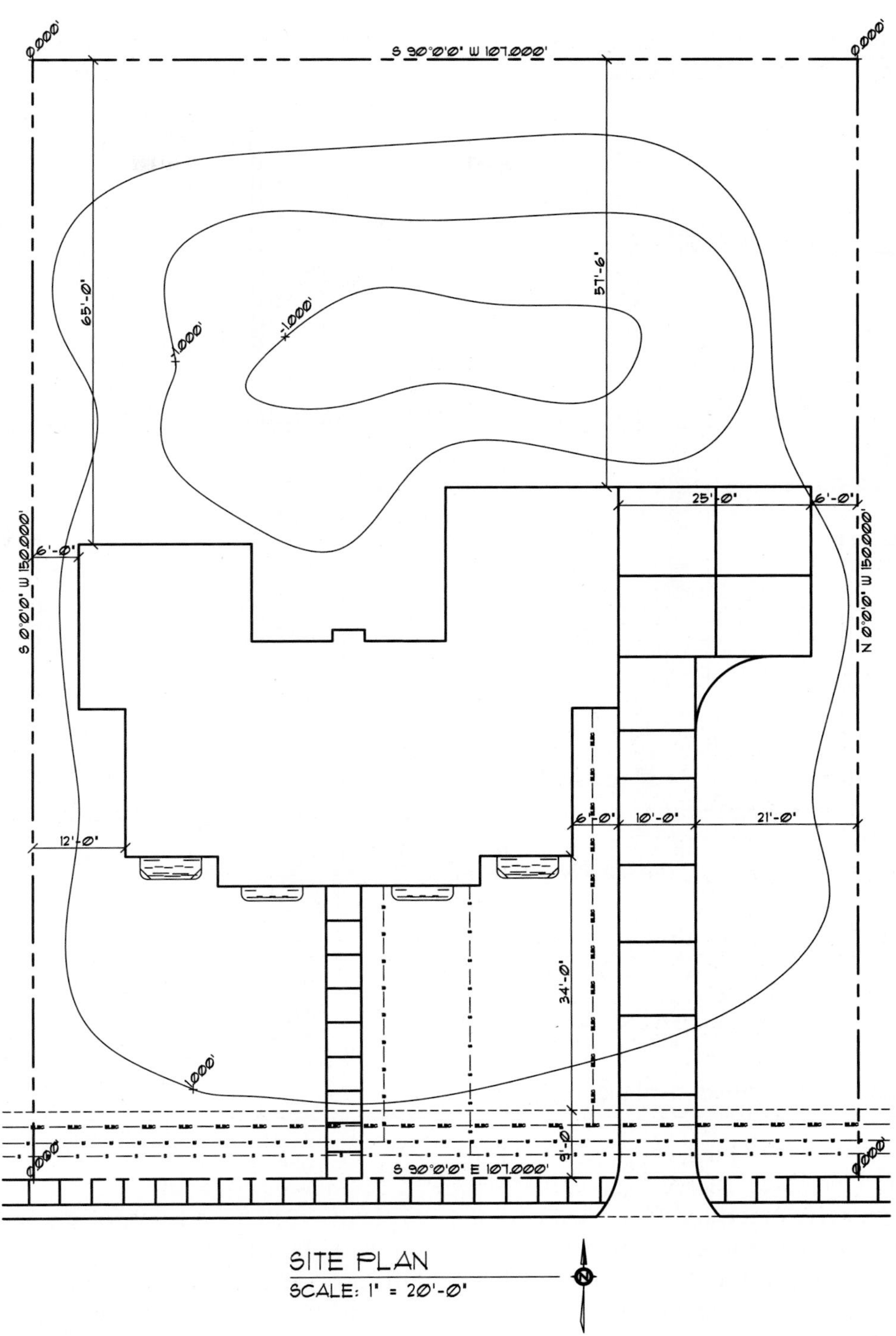

Goodheart-Willcox Publisher

Figure 6-10. A residential site plan.

does not show the layout of rooms and locations of walls. The floor plan shows those items.

The ***heating, ventilation, and air conditioning (HVAC) plan*** shows components of the climate control system of the house. These components include the furnace, air conditioner, heating and cooling ducts, and hot water pipes used for heating purposes. Typically, each system is designed by the contractor who installs the system.

A ***plumbing plan*** shows the location of pipes and plumbing fixtures. These features include the hot and cold water pipes, waste lines, vents,

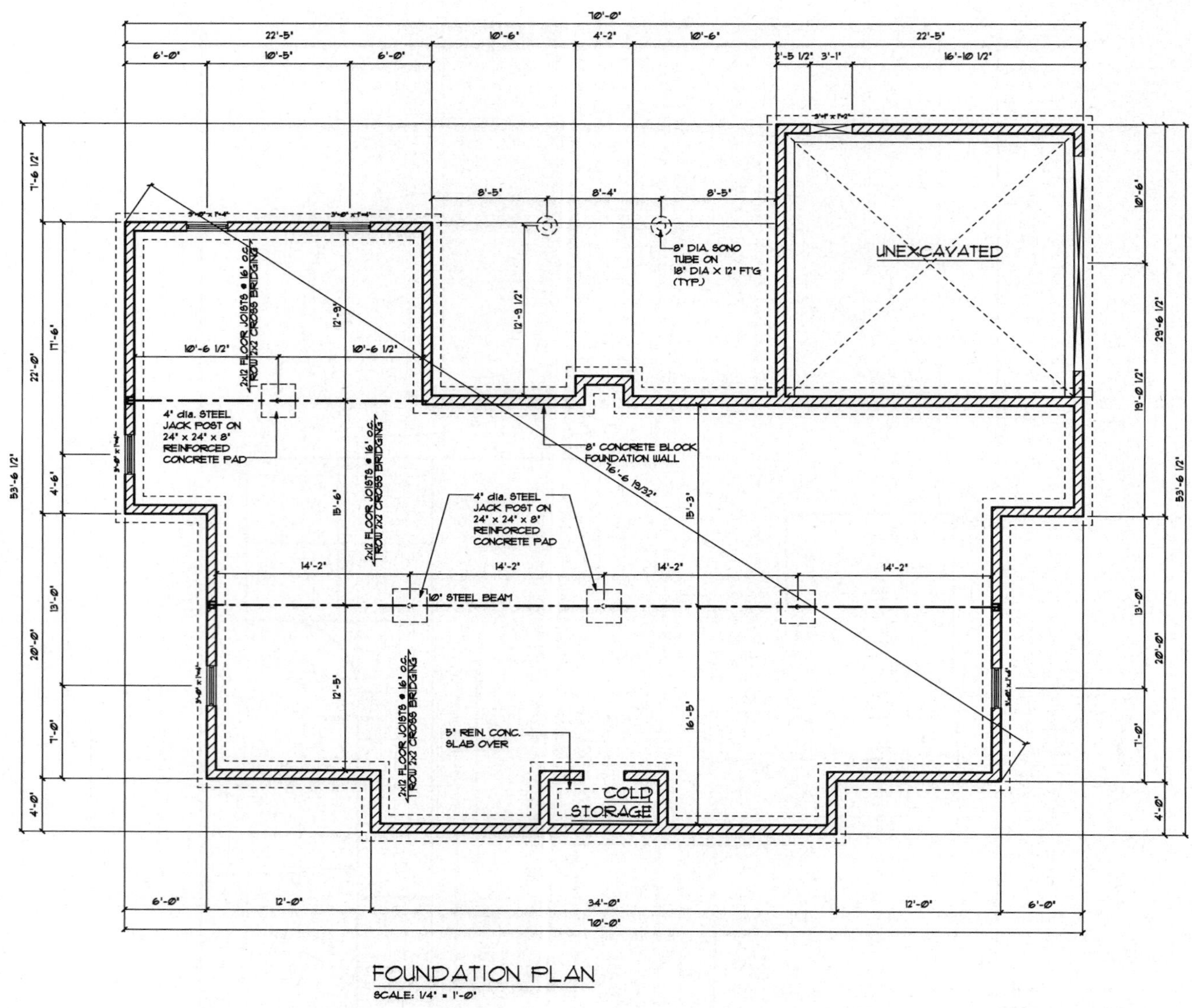

Goodheart-Willcox Publisher

Figure 6-11. A foundation plan for a residence.

and a storage tank when needed. The locations of plumbing fixtures and cleanouts are also included.

The ***landscaping plan*** locates and identifies plants and other elements included in landscaping the site. A plant legend is often included on the landscaping plan to show what plants are being planted and the quantity needed of each type of plant. This plan is often combined with the site plan.

A ***pictorial presentation*** or rendering is often included to show how the structure will appear when finished. See **Figure 6-16**. The pictorial method used in manual drafting typically utilizes a two-point perspective with a picture plane line, true height line, station point, left and right vanishing points, ground line or ground point, and horizon line. See Chapter 26, *Perspective Drawings*, and Chapter 27, *Presentation Drawings*, for a description of these terms and how to construct a pictorial presentation. When using a CADD program, computer-generated pictorials, including perspective views, can be created from a 3D model after the model is constructed. In some cases, a physical model is used instead of, or in addition to, a pictorial drawing to depict the total structure in greater detail.

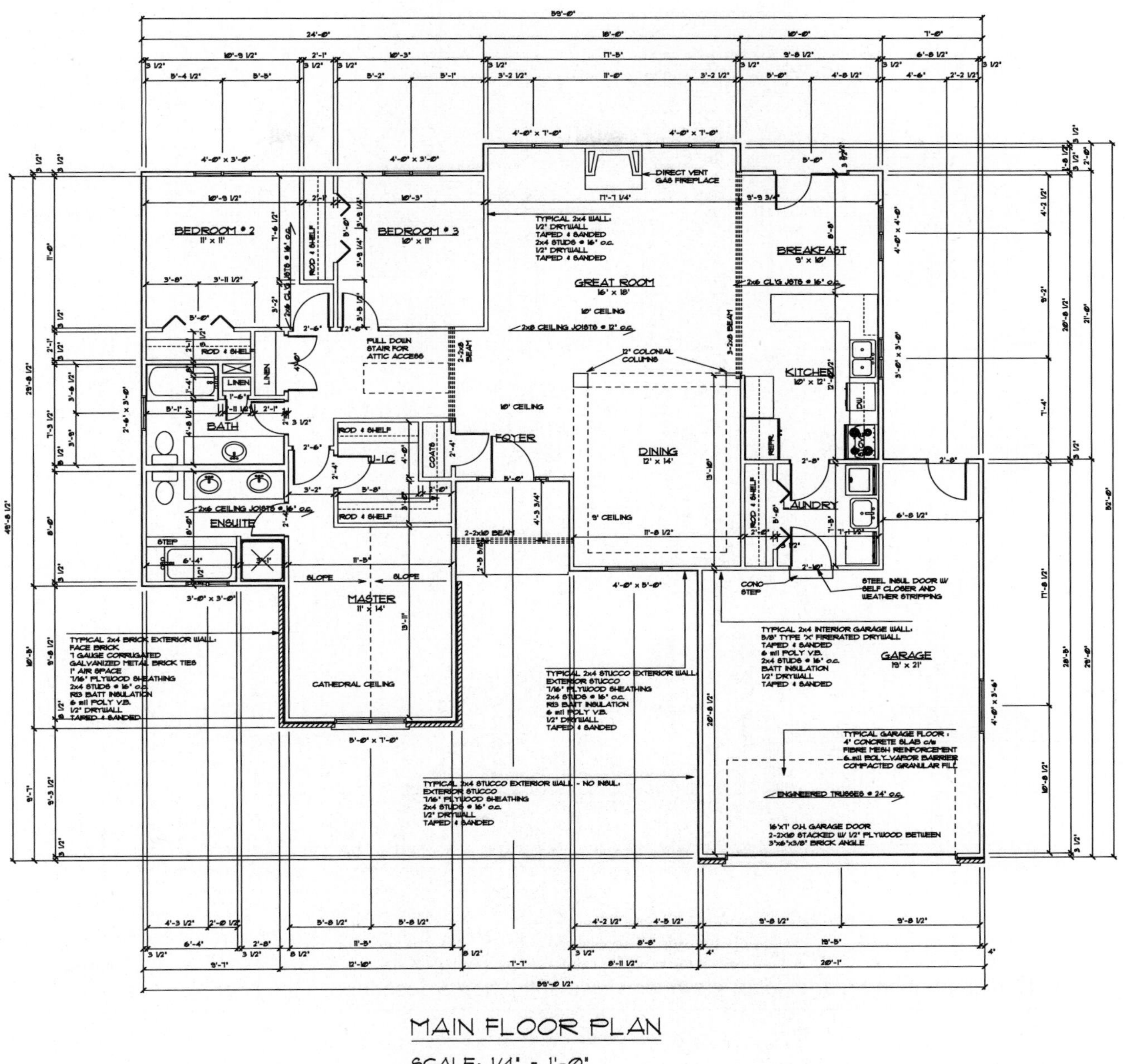

Goodheart-Willcox Publisher

Figure 6-12. The floor plan is the basis for many other plans in a set of working drawings.

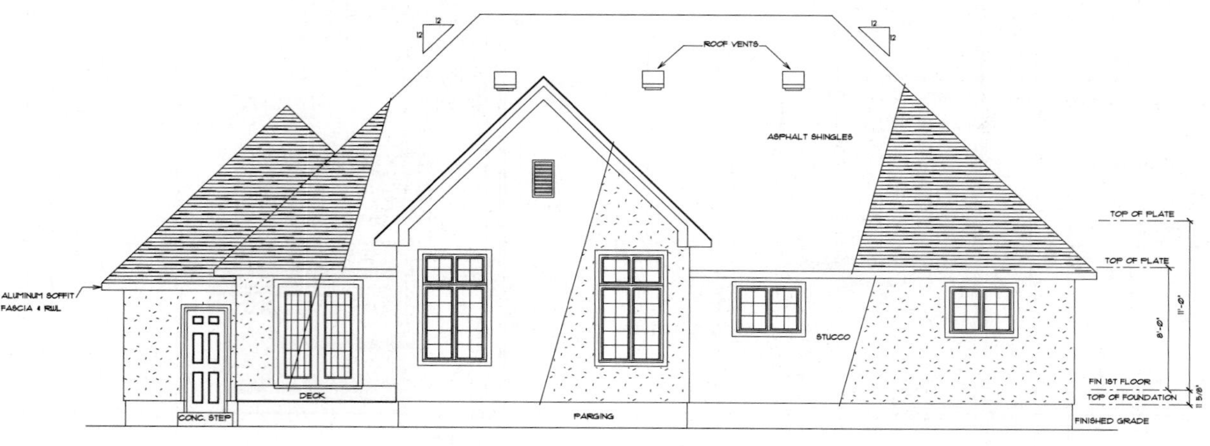

Goodheart-Willcox Publisher

Figure 6-13. The front and rear exterior elevation views of the home described in the floor plan in Figure 6-12.

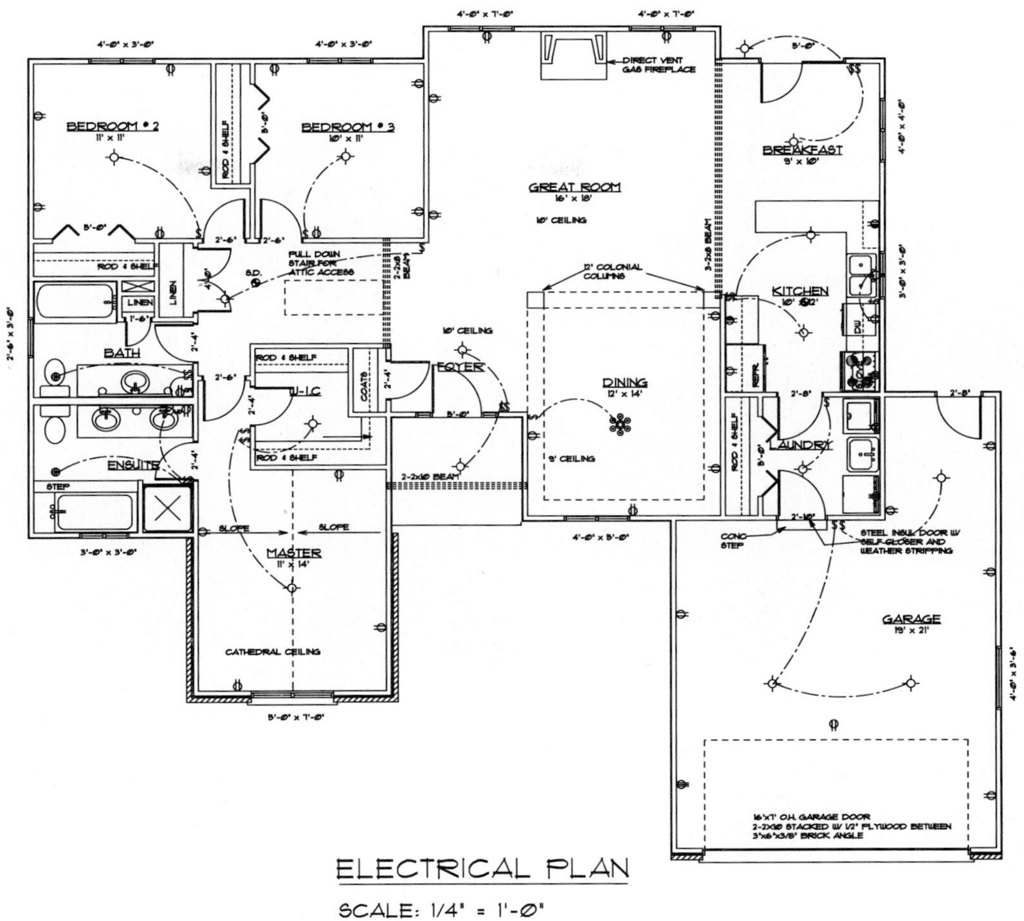

Goodheart-Willcox Publisher

Figure 6-14. The electrical plan is drawn from the floor plan and, in many cases, is actually the same CADD drawing with electrical layers displayed.

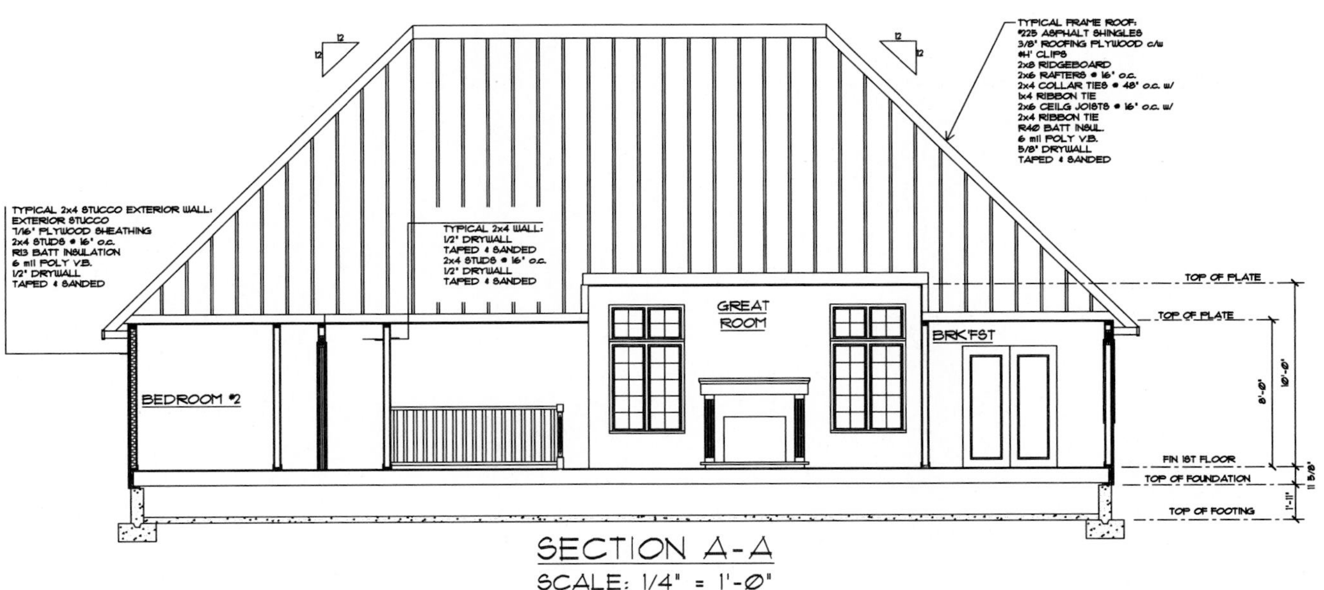

Goodheart-Willcox Publisher

Figure 6-15. Building sections are vertical cuts through the structure to illustrate construction methods and changes in floor heights.

jl661227/Shutterstock.com

Figure 6-16. This expertly rendered perspective shows the finished structure realistically and serves as an important communication device.

Summary

- The characteristics of a site frequently affect the type of house that can be built on the site.
- Site considerations include the topography of the site, costs and restrictions, zoning, building codes, and the community in which the site is located.
- When considering the requirements for a new home, consider future family growth and allow ample space for all members of the family to perform their chosen activities.
- To find the maximum amount you can afford to spend on housing each month, subtract all of your nonhousing expenses from your total monthly take-home pay.
- The primary plans included in a set of working drawings are the site plan, foundation plan, floor plan, elevations, electrical plan, construction details, building sections, and specifications.
- Other plans that may be included in a set of working drawings are a roof plan, roof framing plan, floor framing plan, HVAC plan, plumbing plan, landscaping plan, and a pictorial presentation of the finished home.

Internet Resources

B4UBUILD
Residential building codes, construction standards, building permit information, and links

International Code Council (ICC)
Published building codes and standards

US Environmental Protection Agency (EPA)
Resources for green building design

Review Questions

Answer the following questions using the information in this chapter.

1. How does the topography of a site affect the home that can be built on it?
2. In addition to the actual price of a building site, what other factors contribute to its cost?
3. What is the difference between *zoning* and *building codes*?
4. When planning for a new house, what two housing considerations should you address?
5. In addition to the monthly mortgage or rent payment, what other monthly costs are considered housing costs?
6. Describe a method of estimating the maximum monthly amount that you can spend on housing.
7. In general, what is the highest percentage of monthly gross income a mortgage lender will approve for payments on a home loan?
8. What are *working drawings*?
9. List at least five primary plans that are included in a set of working drawings.
10. What is the purpose of specifications in a set of working drawings?

Suggested Activities

1. Visit your local city or county building inspector and ask to be shown copies of the codes that are used in your community. Inquire how the cost of permits is calculated and what is required by the building department when applying for a permit.
2. Make a list of the activity areas (spaces) that you would provide if you were planning a new home for your family's needs. Be sure to include all the needs of each member of your family and special group activity areas.
3. Look around your neighborhood for a vacant lot or piece of property. Make a list of considerations that should be addressed if a house were to be constructed on this property.
4. Prepare an oral presentation to describe the advantages of proper site consideration when planning a house. Create posters or other graphics to use in your presentation.
5. Contact a local civil engineer and ask what type of site preparation must be done before a residential structure is built in your area. Write an informative report on your findings.

Problem Solving Case Study

Harold Jordan has always dreamed of owning his own split-level home nestled in the mountains. He has saved $50,000 to purchase the building site and is excited to begin looking for an appropriate site. His initial search turned up three properties he thinks would work:

A. A 5-acre lot halfway up a mountain in a very rural area with an asking price of $35,000.

B. A 3-acre lot on flat land in a small town with a great view of the mountains in the distance, with an asking price of $45,000.

C. A 5-acre lot in gently rolling foothills, in a highly developed area, with an asking price of $40,000.

Given this information, answer the following questions.

1. What other factors should Mr. Jordan consider before he makes his final choice?
2. If you were Mr. Jordan, which lot would you choose, and why?

ADDA Certification Prep

The following questions are presented in the style used in the American Design Drafting Association (ADDA) Drafter Certification Test. Answer the questions using the information in this chapter.

1. Which of the following statements are true?
   A. A site is more than just a piece of property—it is part of a larger community.
   B. Flat topography lends itself to a ranch or two-story house.
   C. The site measurements and property lines should be verified by a surveyor before construction begins.
   D. Building sections are orthographic projections that show the exterior features of each side of a house.
2. Which of the following statements is true?
   A. The foundation plan shows all exterior and interior walls, doors, windows, patios, walks, decks, fireplaces, mechanical equipment, built-in cabinets, appliances, and bathroom fixtures.
   B. The electrical plan is drawn from the exterior elevations.
   C. Construction details are usually drawn when more information is needed to fully describe how the foundation, wall, or roof construction is to be completed.
3. Which of the following items in a set of working drawings are based on or developed from the floor plan?
   A. Roof plan
   B. Foundation plan
   C. Landscaping plan
   D. Electrical plan

STEM Connections

1. **Math.** Imagine that you are a loan officer working for a local bank. Three families have come to you for a home loan. Assuming that the bank will approve a loan for no more than 2-1/2 times each family's income, determine the maximum loan the bank will approve for each family.
   A. Family #1: Annual income of $250,000.
   B. Family #2: Annual income of $75,000.
   C. Family #3: Annual income of $125,000.
2. **Math.** Consuelo recently graduated from an architectural program and is now working at a small architectural firm. Her starting salary is $27,900, and her take-home pay is $23,715 per year. She is thinking about building a home, so she has been tracking her expenses for the last several months. In an average month, she spends $95 for electricity, $46 for natural gas, $84 for telephone service, $68 for cable TV, $250 for groceries, $50 for clothing, and $50 for transportation expenses. She also has a car payment of $230 per month and credit card payments of $325. What is the *maximum* monthly amount Consuelo can afford to spend on housing?

3. **Science.** It has been known for some time that large cities create "hot spots." In other words, the temperature in the city is often several degrees higher than in surrounding rural areas. Investigate to find out possible reasons for this fact. What can people who live in cities do to help reduce the temperature to match the temperature in the surrounding rural areas?

Communicating about Architecture

1. **Reading.** With a partner, make flash cards of the different types of plan drawings (site plan, foundation plan, etc.) used in residential construction. On the front of the card, write the description of what is found in that particular plan. On the back, write the name of the plan. Take turns reading the descriptions and quizzing each other.
2. **Speaking.** Select 10 of the key terms in this chapter and imagine them being used by architects in a real-life context. With a partner, role-play a situation in which an architectural firm is designing a new split-level home for a client.

bikeriderlondon/Shutterstock.com

This luxurious living room is spacious and provides access to a large backyard patio.

Chapter 7

Planning the Living Area

Objectives

After completing this chapter, you will be able to:

- Identify the three main areas in a typical residence.
- Explain why designers take special needs into account when designing a new home.
- Describe the rooms and areas that comprise the living area.
- Apply design principles to planning a living room.
- Analyze a dining room using good design principles.
- Design a functional entry and foyer.
- Communicate the primary design considerations for a family room.
- Integrate designs for outdoor living areas into the total floor plan of a dwelling.

Key Terms

accessibility
aging-in-place
balcony
closed plan
courtyard
deck
foyer
gazebo
great room
living area
main entry
open plan
patio
porch
service area
service entry
sleeping area
special-purpose entry
special-purpose room
traffic circulation
universal design
verandah

Areas of a Residence

A residential structure can be divided into three basic areas: the sleeping area, living area, and service area. See **Figure 7-1**. The focus of this chapter is the ***living area***, where the family relaxes, entertains guests, dines, and meets together. The living area may include a living room, dining room, entry and foyer, family room, special-purpose rooms, and porches or patios. The ***sleeping area*** is where the family sleeps, rests, and bathes. This area is discussed in Chapter 8, *Planning the Sleeping Area*. The ***service area*** is the part of the house where food is prepared, clothes are laundered, goods are stored, cars are parked, and equipment for upkeep of the house is stored. The service area is discussed in Chapter 9, *Planning the Service Area*. To develop a functional home, the designer must understand the purpose of each area and the rooms it contains.

Designing for Accessibility

In addition to the purpose of the room, the designer should know how the room will be used and by whom. According to the *Americans with Disabilities: 2010* report issued by the US Census Bureau, 56.7 million people in the United States have some level of disability. Of those, 3.6 million use wheelchairs, and another 11.6 million use canes, walkers, or crutches. More than half of those people who use wheelchairs and more than half of those who use canes, walkers, or crutches are over the age of 65. As the "baby boomers" (the large number of people born between 1946 and 1964) become elderly, those numbers are expected to increase dramatically.

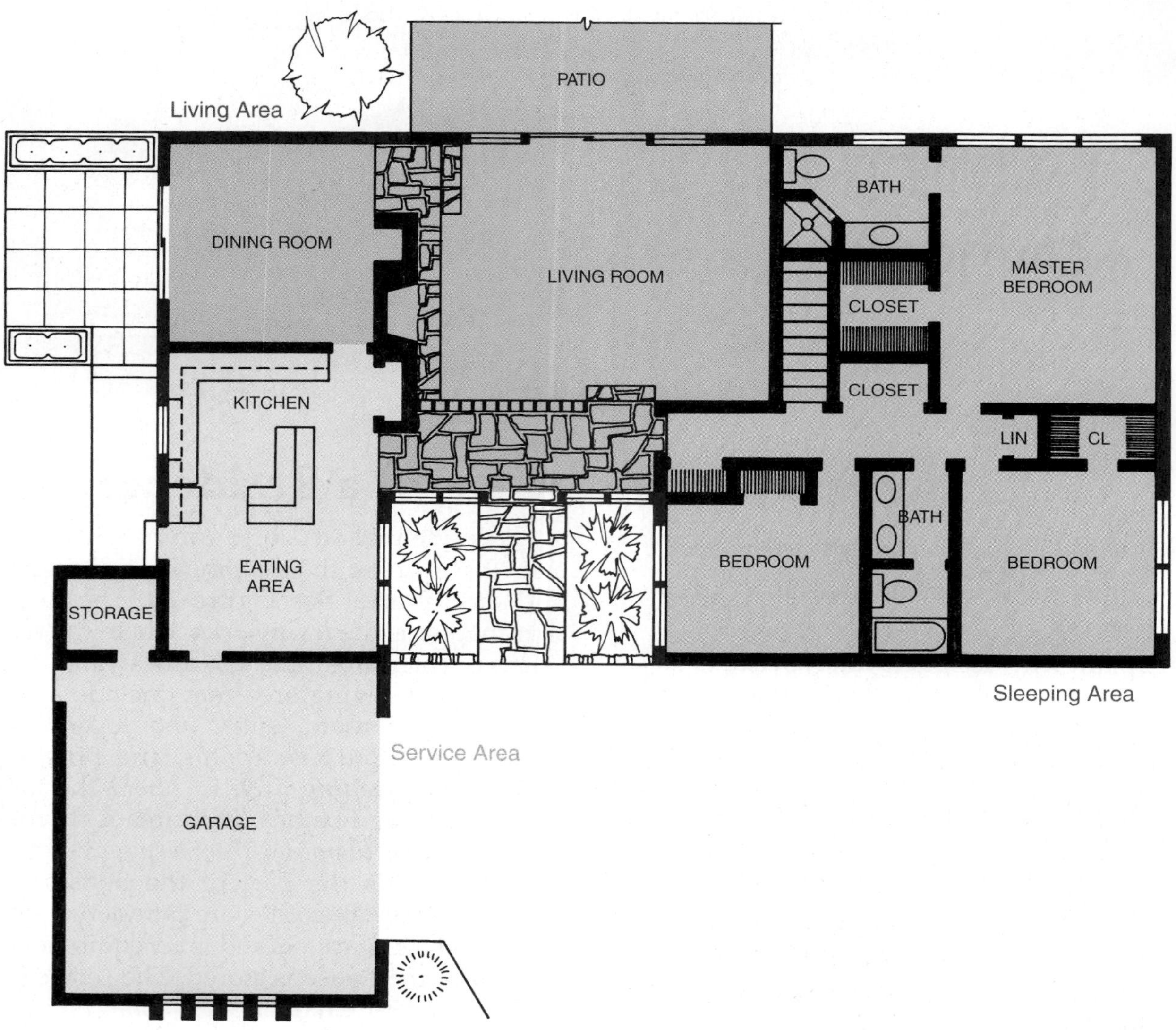

Goodheart-Willcox Publisher

Figure 7-1. A residence can be divided into three basic areas: the living area, sleeping area, and service area.

Accessibility is a measure of how easily all people, including those who are physically handicapped or have limited mobility, can access or use something. It is important to consider how all areas of a home can be made accessible to people with special needs, including the disabled and the elderly.

The International Residential Code (IRC) establishes regulations for residential design and construction, such as the minimum amount of space in various rooms and areas of a home. The IRC, published by the International Code Council (ICC), is a model building code widely used by communities to set building guidelines. The IRC was developed to specifically address building guidelines for residential structures, with an emphasis on one- and two-family dwellings and townhouses.

Guidelines for designing structures to meet accessibility standards are provided in the ICC A117.1 *Accessible and Usable Buildings and Facilities* standard. This standard sets accessibility guidelines for commercial and residential structures and is approved by the American National Standards Institute (ANSI). As you read this chapter and the rest of the textbook, you will notice many references to the International Residential Code and the *Accessible and Usable Buildings and Facilities* standard.

Accessibility design guidelines applying to the Americans with Disabilities Act (ADA) are addressed in the *ADA Standards for Accessible*

Design. The *ADA Standards for Accessible Design* are geared toward commercial, public, and government buildings, but they also apply to multifamily housing and even single-family housing in certain circumstances.

Designing for Aging-in-Place

Designing a functional home requires an understanding of the day-to-day needs of a family. However, it is also important to consider future needs. The areas and working features of a home should be planned so that the occupants can live comfortably in their surroundings and remain comfortable as they age. Designing for *aging-in-place* helps address this concern. ***Aging-in-place*** is the ability of people to live comfortably and remain in their home as they become older. Planning for aging-in-place takes into account design factors such as accessibility, safety, and convenience. For example, a kitchen can be designed with easier access to cabinets by using roll-out shelves or racks. Another option is to include one or more lazy Susans. A home can also have safety features such as non-slip flooring and stairway lighting. Provisions for future safety features, such as grab bars in bathrooms, can be made by designing the appropriate framing in bathroom walls. Additional design features for aging-in-place include the following:

- At least one no-step entrance to provide easier access into the home.
- Wide doorways (36″ wide) and hallways (42″ wide) to accommodate wheelchair users.
- A single-story floor plan with no stairs and all rooms on the same level.
- Lever-type door handles and water faucets for easier operation.

Employability

Preparing for a Job Interview

A job interview gives you the opportunity to learn more about a company and to convince the employer that you are the best person for the position. The employer wants to know if you have the skills needed for the job. Adequate preparation is essential for making a lasting, positive impression. Here are some ways to prepare for the interview:

- *Research the employer and the job*. Know the mission of the employer and specifics about the job. Also, try to learn what the company looks for when hiring new employees.
- *Be prepared to answer questions*. Go online to find questions frequently asked by employers in job interviews and prepare answers for each.
- *List the questions you want answered*. For example, do you want to know if the company offers on-the-job training? Opportunities for advancement?
- *List the materials you plan to take to the interview*. This seems simple enough. However, if you wait to grab items at the last minute, you may forget something important.
- *Decide what to wear*. Dress appropriately, usually one step above what is worn by your future coworkers. For instance, casual clothing is acceptable for individuals who will do manual labor or wear a company uniform. If the job involves greeting the public in an office environment, a suit is more appropriate. Always appear neat and clean.
- *Practice the interview*. Have a friend or family member interview you in front of a mirror until you are happy with your responses.
- *Know where to go for the interview*. Verify the address of the interview location by checking the site beforehand, if possible. Plan to arrive ready for the interview at least 10 minutes early.

Activity

With a classmate, gather a list of questions that are frequently asked by employers in job interviews. Take turns being the employer and applicant. Identify the questions that make you most uncomfortable and concentrate on them. Practice answering the questions until both of you are comfortable.

Designing for aging-in-place is expected to become more widespread in future years to meet the needs of the large "baby boomer" generation. Many residential design projects that address aging-in-place will consist of home remodeling projects because of the desire of older homeowners to stay in their existing home.

Universal Design

Universal design is a design approach concerned with meeting the needs of all people regardless of age, health, or ability. Universal design is similar to designing for accessibility and aging-in-place, but it takes additional factors and functions into consideration. For example, wall-mounted grab bars in a shower improve accessibility for an elderly person with limited mobility. However, the same design feature may be useful for a young adult recovering from knee surgery or a broken foot. Another example is a one-story floor plan, which allows easier access to different rooms for wheelchair users as well as young children.

As people become more inclined to stay in their homes as they age, homes constructed with universal design features take on greater significance. Also, home designs that can be universally used by the young or elderly are much more appealing to certain buyers—such as a multigenerational family or someone who intends to live in a home for many years.

Designing with CADD

Today's CADD packages include tools to make the design of all the areas of a residence easier. With a CADD system, time required to develop a suitable design is greatly reduced through the use and re-use of symbols to produce a variety of designs. In addition, proposed designs can be rendered and shown to clients. **Figure 7-2** shows the realism that can be presented with today's high-end CADD software.

Mayer George Vladimirovich/Shutterstock.com

Figure 7-2. This 3D CADD rendering of a dining room is difficult to distinguish from a photograph.

Traffic Circulation

A primary consideration in designing a functional house plan is traffic circulation. ***Traffic circulation*** is the movement of people from one area or room to another. Circulation must be planned for maximum efficiency of movement. Travel distances should be short and, if possible, not pass through private areas such as bedrooms. See **Figure 7-3**. An analysis should be made of traffic circulation to determine if the plan is as functional as it should be. Frequently, a slight change in the floor plan can smooth the flow of traffic to the desired locations.

Living Room

For many families, the living room is the center of activity. Depending on the specific occasion, it may be a playroom for the children, a TV room, or a conversation place. Its size and arrangement depend on the lifestyle of the members of the family who will ultimately use it.

The living room, like all other rooms in the house, should be used; it should not be planned just as a showplace. A properly designed living room can be a functional part of the house and, at the same time, a beautiful and usable area. See **Figure 7-4**.

Size

Living rooms are of all sizes and shapes. A small living room may be as small as 150 square feet. An average-size living room may be around 250 square feet. A large living room may be around 400 square feet (or larger). See **Figure 7-5**.

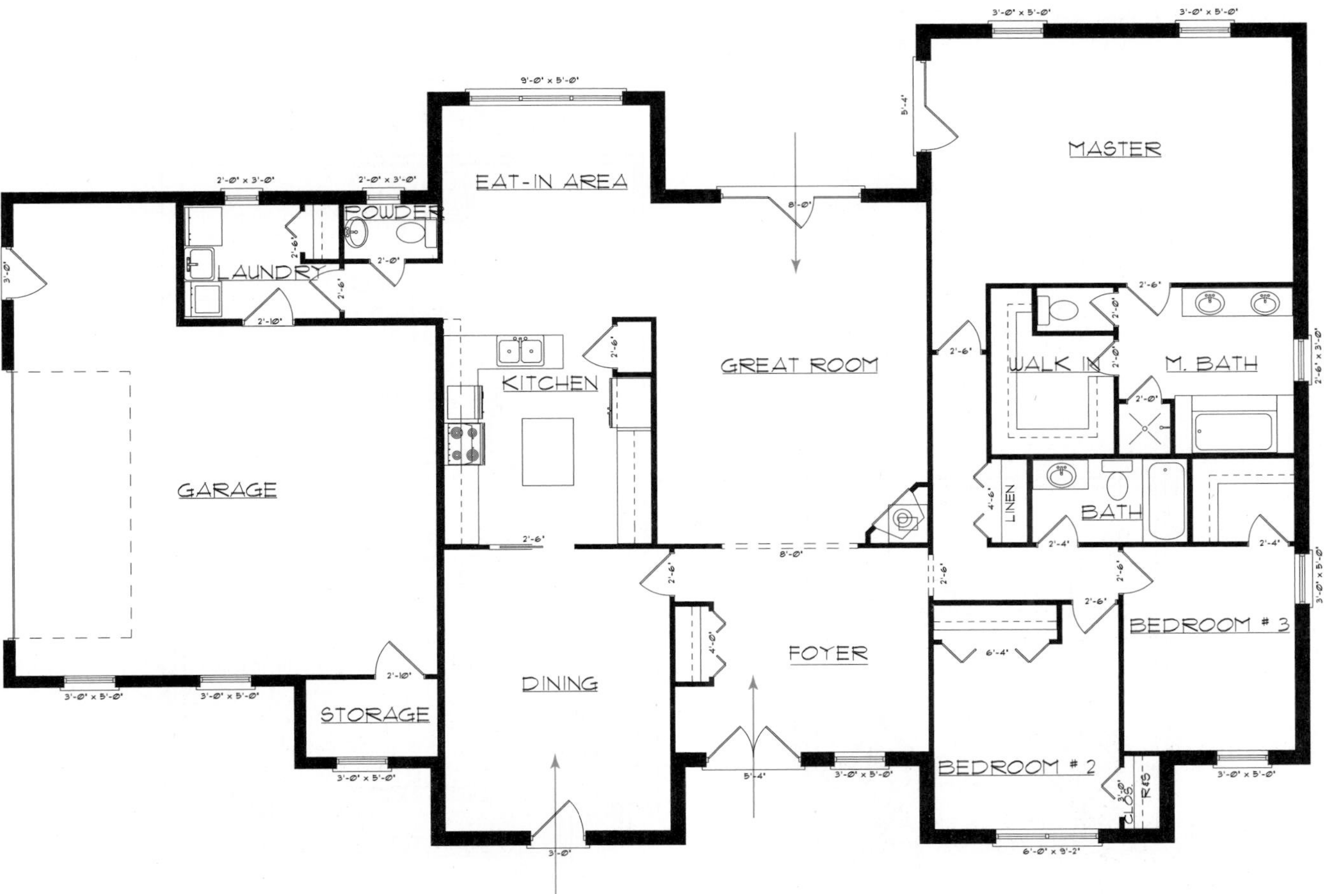

Goodheart-Willcox Publisher

Figure 7-3. Analyze the traffic patterns in this home. Notice that the bedrooms are separated from the main living areas but are easily accessible from the foyer. The dining, kitchen, and eat-in areas are also grouped for easy access, and all areas can be reached quickly from the main living areas.

Breadmaker/Shutterstock.com

Figure 7-4. This attractive living room is designed for both entertaining and relaxing.

The most important questions to ask regarding size and design of a living room are:

- What furniture is planned for this room? **Figure 7-6** shows common furniture sizes.
- How often will the room be used?
- How many people are expected to use the room at any one time?
- Is this a multipurpose room? If so, how many functions are combined in this room?

The answers to these questions should help establish the broad specifications for the room, including its size.

Specific furniture should reflect the use to which the room will be subjected. For instance, if the room is to be used primarily for viewing television, the arrangement should indicate that use. Conversely, if a separate room is provided for TV, then this activity will probably not be a consideration. It is important to analyze the functions to be performed and provide space for them.

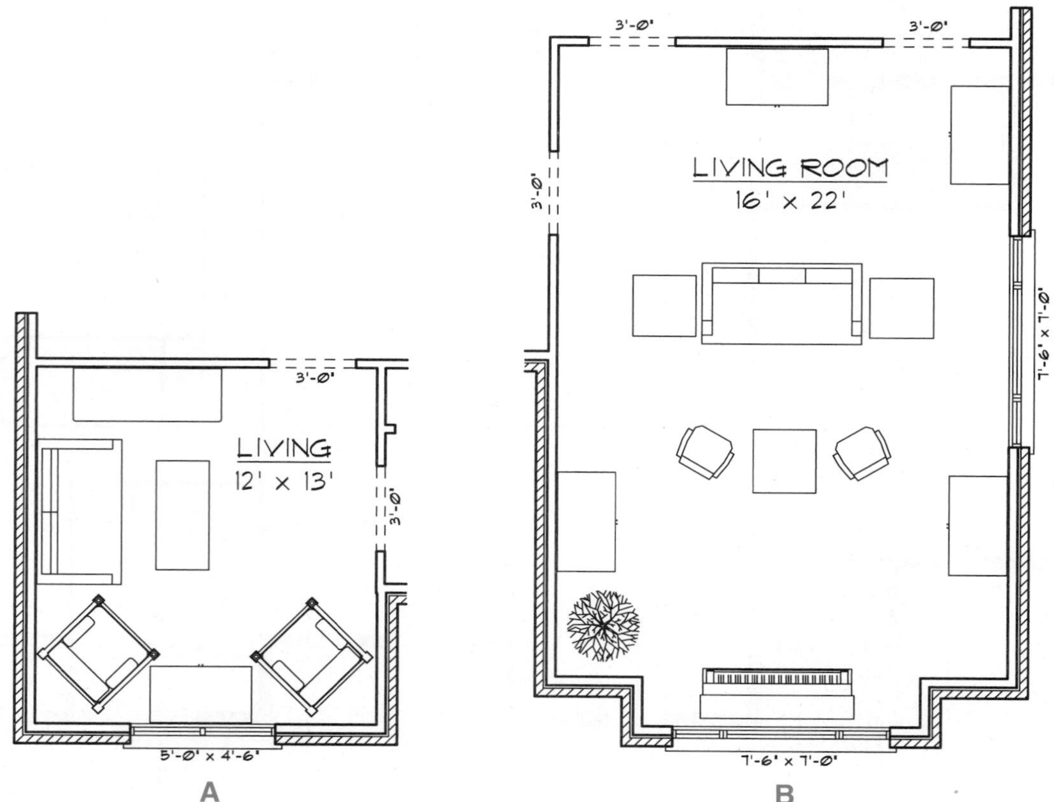

Goodheart-Willcox Publisher

Figure 7-5. A—This small living room has only about 150 square feet. B—A larger living room with about 350 square feet.

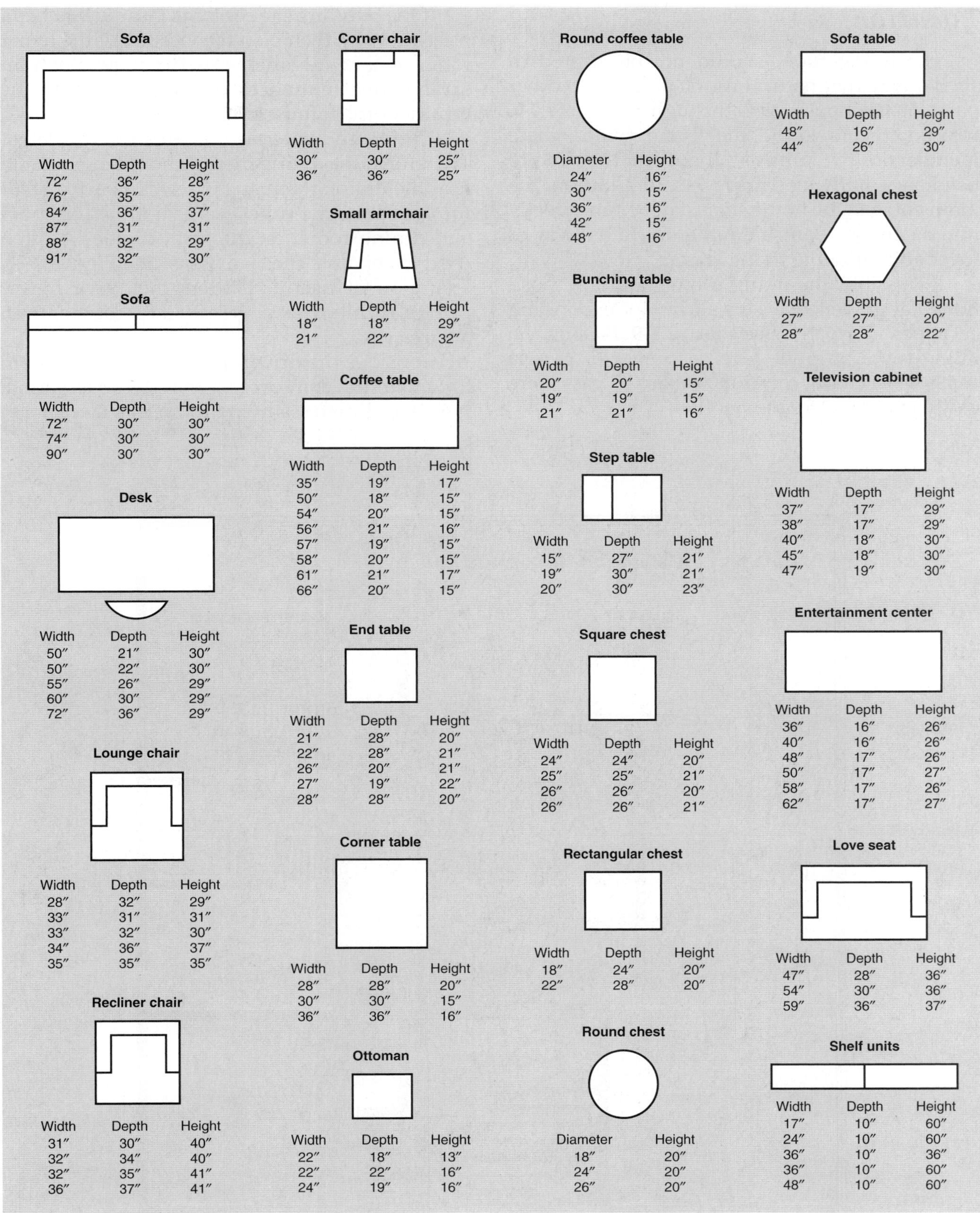

Goodheart-Willcox Publisher

Figure 7-6. Standard sizes of typical living room furniture.

Location

The living room should not be located in such a way that natural traffic patterns to other parts of the house pass through it, **Figure 7-7**. Instead, try to locate the living room where members of the family will not feel the need to use it as a hall. See **Figure 7-8**. In addition, the main entry to the home should not open directly into the living room, but rather into a hallway or foyer adjoining the living room.

If possible, the living room should be positioned at grade level. This allows for expanding activities to a patio. See **Figure 7-9**. Placing the living room at grade level also enables people using wheelchairs, canes, or walkers to pass more easily from one area to another.

If the building site contains an area that has a pleasing view, then plan the location of the living room to take advantage of the view. Such an arrangement enhances the use and often the beauty of the living room.

Dining and entertaining are closely related. Therefore, the living room should be located near the dining room. In homes that have a ***great room*** or area that functions as both living room and dining room, an informal divider is often used to separate the two areas. See **Figure 7-10**. Examples of useful dividers include a flower planter, furniture arrangement, or screen, or even an area rug.

Consider the orientation of the living room for maximum comfort and energy conservation. In warm climates, a living room that faces north

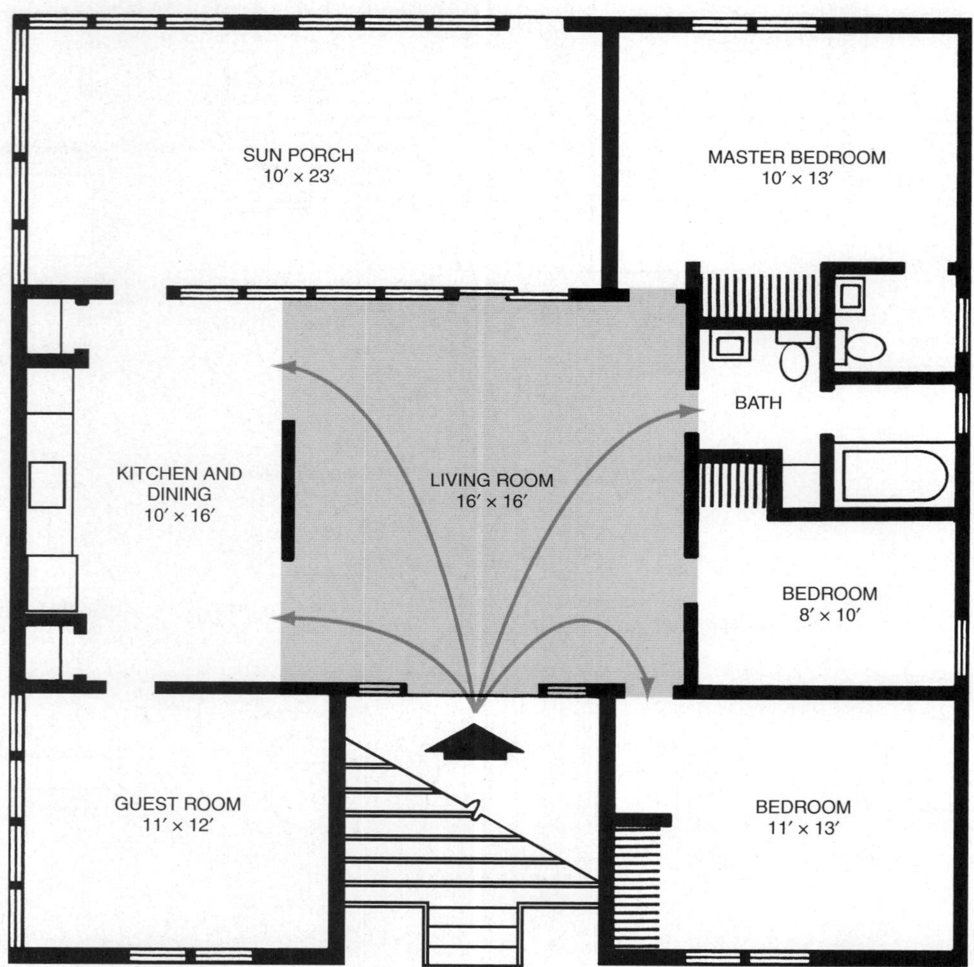

Goodheart-Willcox Publisher

Figure 7-7. Notice how the traffic patterns from all of the surrounding rooms pass through this poorly located living room.

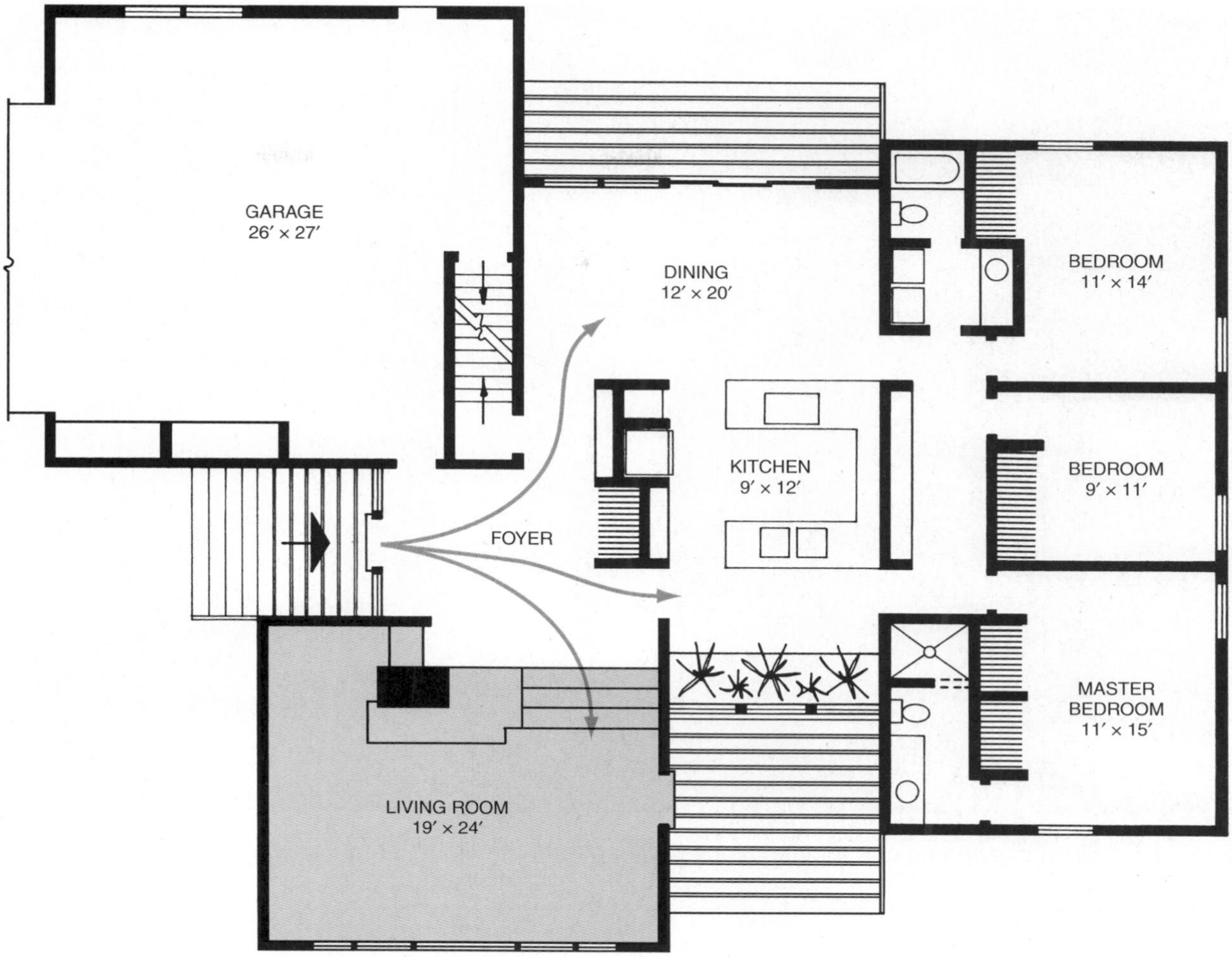

GARAGE
26′ × 27′

DINING
12′ × 20′

BEDROOM
11′ × 14′

KITCHEN
9′ × 12′

BEDROOM
9′ × 11′

FOYER

MASTER
BEDROOM
11′ × 15′

LIVING ROOM
19′ × 24′

Goodheart-Willcox Publisher

Figure 7-8. This living room is located near the kitchen and dining areas, yet no traffic patterns pass through it.

pics721/Shutterstock.com

Figure 7-9. A small living room at ground level with excellent access to the patio beyond.

Sklep Spozywczy/Shutterstock.com

Figure 7-10. Ceiling treatments and a glass block wall separate the dining area from the living area and kitchen in this great room.

will help keep the living areas cool. The north side is usually shaded, while the south side receives sun almost constantly. In cool climates, place the living room on the south side of the house to take advantage of winter sun.

The use of large windows or sliding doors further encourages the feeling of spaciousness and increases the enjoyment of the living room. See **Figure 7-11**. Avoid breaking up exterior wall areas with too many small windows. Also, plan for adequate wall space for all of the required furniture.

Décor

The décor of the living room can vary widely. The styles should be selected by or for the homeowner to reflect his or her personal preferences. Keep in mind that color, texture, and design can be used to emphasize a room's good points and minimize any weak aspects.

If the exterior of the home follows a specific style, such as Georgian or Victorian, it is a good idea to design the interior rooms, including the living room, to reflect the exterior design. For example, a home with a Queen Anne Victorian exterior should have furnishings, wall and floor coverings, and window treatments that enhance the Victorian flavor of the house. See **Figure 7-12**. Contemporary furniture and décor are appropriate for a modern or postmodern house.

Dining Room

Around the beginning of the 1900s, most new homes had a dining room. For economic reasons, shortly after World War II, fewer houses were built with dining rooms. Currently, the trend has changed again and separate dining rooms are popular. However, for each home, the determining factor of whether to include a

Breadmaker/Shutterstock.com

Figure 7-11. The picture window in this living room brightens the room and showcases the beautiful lake view.

Baloncici/Shutterstock.com

Figure 7-12. This room, which opens to the patio of a Victorian-styled home, contains furnishings that blend well with the external appearance of the home.

separate dining room should be the lifestyle of those who will live in the house, rather than fad or fancy.

The main function of a dining room is to provide a special, dedicated place for family dining. See **Figure 7-13**. However, informal meals are often taken in the kitchen rather than in a separate room or area. Many modern homes provide eating facilities in the kitchen for informal meals and a separate dining room for more formal gatherings.

Plan

When planning the dining room, a decision should be made early as to whether an open or closed plan is more desirable. **Figure 7-10** shows an example of a dining room in an ***open plan***. In a ***closed plan***, the dining room is a separate room, as shown in **Figure 7-13**. From a maintenance and cleanup standpoint, a separate dining room is typically out of view from the rest of the living area of the house. If the dining room is used only rarely, the upkeep is relatively easy.

Size

In most cases, the dining room size depends on the number of people who will use the room at a given time, the furniture to be included in the room, and clearance allowed for traffic through the room. A small room, capable of seating four to six people around a table and providing space for a buffet, requires an area of about 120 square feet. A medium-size room, about 12′ × 15′, provides space for six to eight people with a buffet and china closet. Large dining rooms are 14′ × 18′ or larger. See **Figure 7-14**.

Typical dining room furniture includes the table, chairs, buffet, china closet, and sometimes a server or cart. See **Figure 7-15**. Arrangement and spacing may depend on the layout of the room, a pleasant outdoor vantage point, or orientation to other rooms. At least 2′-3″ should be allowed from center-to-center of chairs around the table. Be certain to provide ample space for serving. Usually, 2′-0″ is sufficient space between the back of the chairs and the wall.

Chris Rodenberg Photography/Shutterstock.com

Figure 7-13. In this home, which was designed for year-round entertaining, the formal dining room opens up to the patio and garden areas.

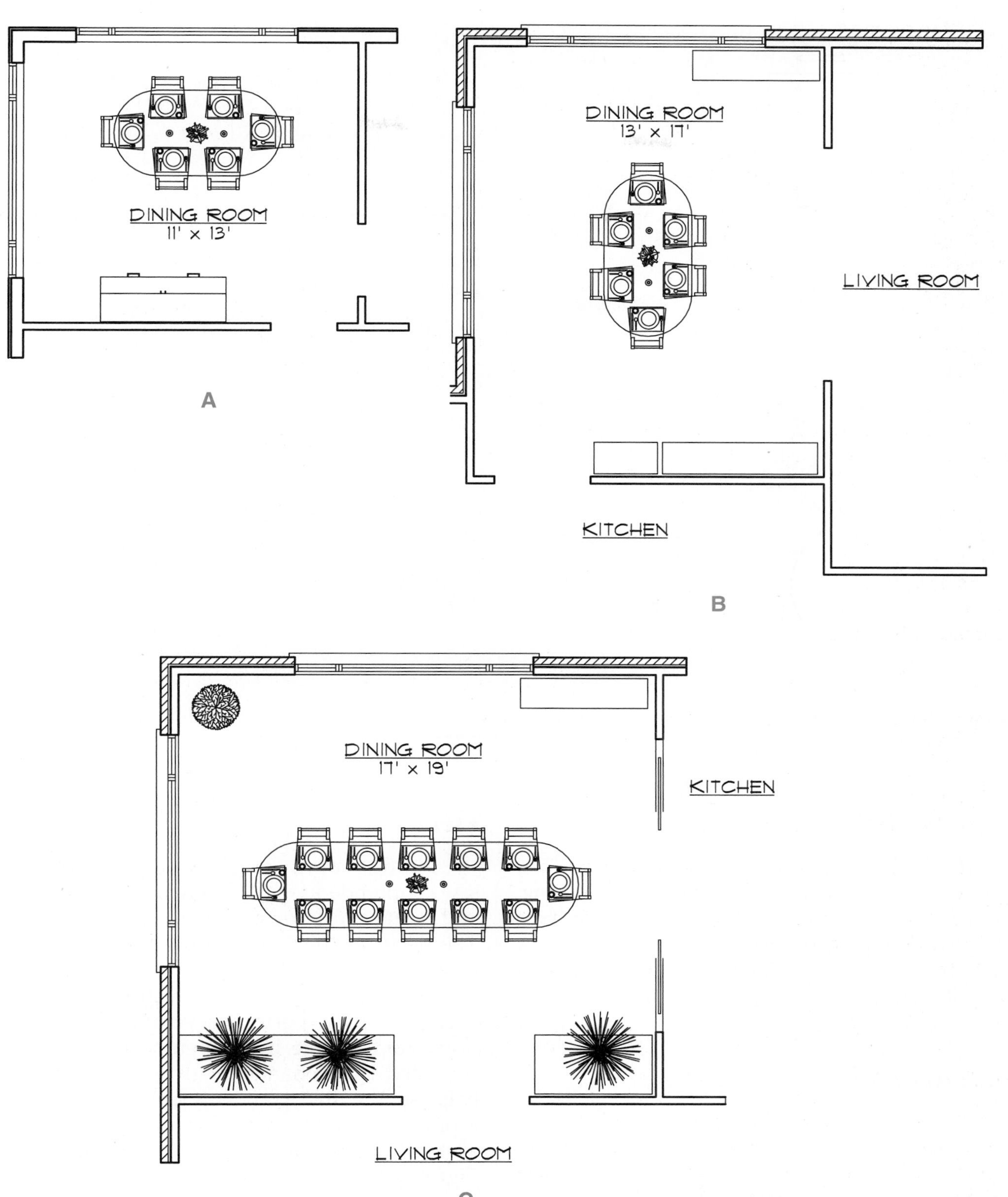

Goodheart-Willcox Publisher

Figure 7-14. A—A floor plan for a small dining room that seats four to six people. B—A medium-size dining room arranged in respect to the other living areas. C—A large dining room seats eight or more people and is best suited for a large family or one that entertains frequently.

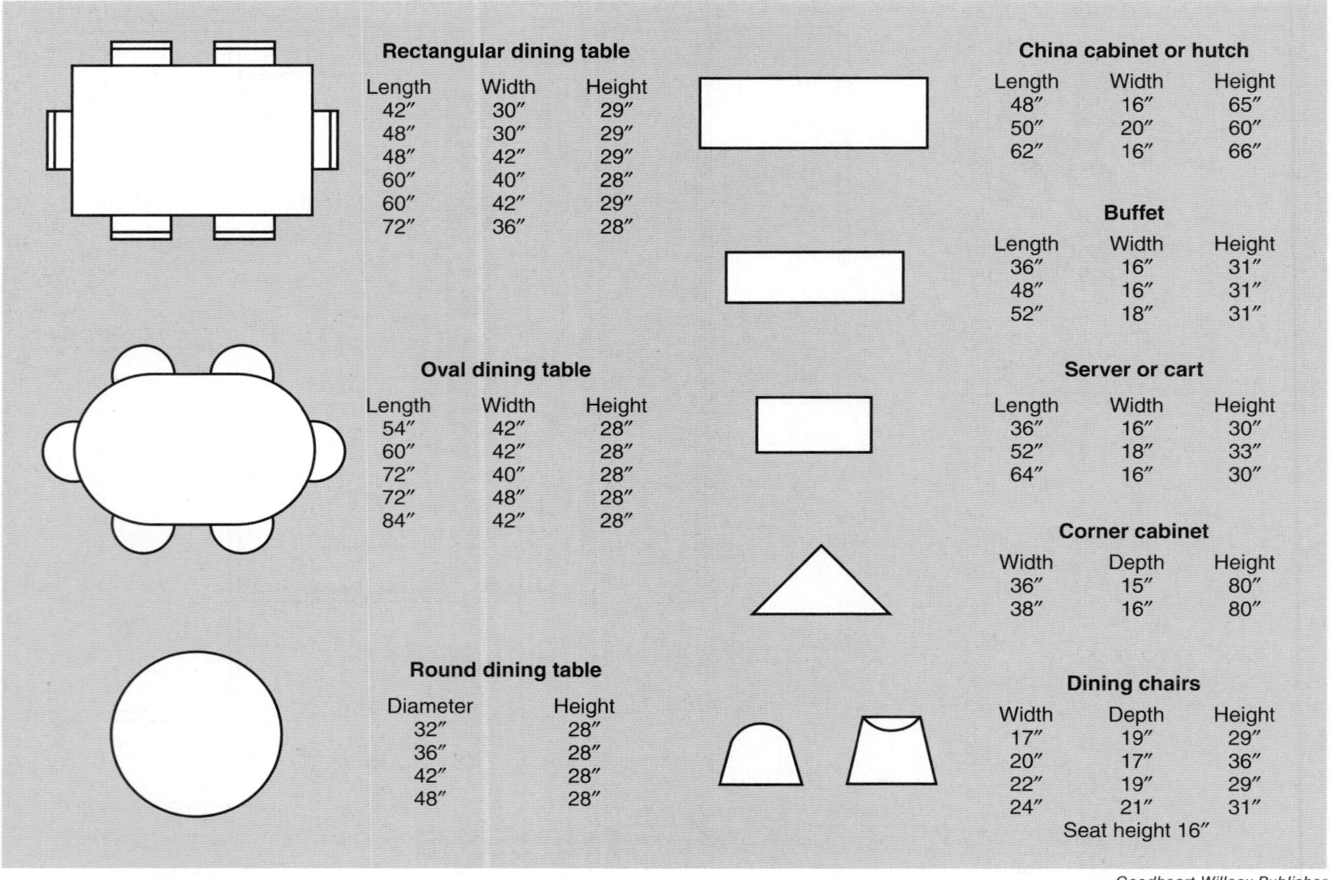

Figure 7-15. Typical dining room furniture and dimensions.

Accessibility

To enable people in wheelchairs to use the dining room, open leg space is needed for dining. Tables with legs that are far apart or that have pedestal legs provide space for wheelchair use. A minimum of 32″ is needed for passing between furniture pieces or walls. See **Figure 7-16**.

Location

For efficient use, the dining room should be adjacent to the kitchen and living room. An arrangement in which the dining room is between the living room and kitchen provides for natural movement of guests from living room to dining with minimum confusion. Furthermore, added space is available in the living room if needed. This is especially true in an open plan.

Décor

Dining rooms are relatively small, intimate spaces intended for the enjoyment of gathering and eating a relaxing meal with family or friends. The décor of the room should be inviting and comfortable.

Lighting is an important feature in a dining room, and it can perform several different functions. For example, in an open plan, the lighting provided by a chandelier over a dining table helps set the dining area off from the rest of the room. If the light is on a dimmer switch, it can also help set a variety of different moods. See **Figure 7-17**.

Entry and Foyer

The living areas of a house include the entry and foyer. Every house has at least one main

Ambient Ideas/Shutterstock.com

Figure 7-16. This large dining room has ample space for the china cabinet, buffet, table, and eight chairs, with plenty of room for a wheelchair to maneuver easily.

ep_stock/Shutterstock.com

Figure 7-17. The chandelier in this dining area performs several functions. It provides plenty of light, identifies this area as the dining area, and also makes an interesting design statement.

entry, and most houses have two or three. Many, but not all, houses also have a foyer, an area just inside the entrance.

Entry

The three basic types of entries are the main entry, the service entry, and the special-purpose entry. Refer again to **Figure 7-3**. What types of entries are included in this floor plan?

Main Entry

The ***main entry*** should be designed to be impressive because it is the first part of the house that guests see when they arrive. An entry need not be large to be attractive. Creative use of materials and a functional arrangement can enhance beauty and design. See **Figure 7-18**.

The main entry should be centrally located to provide easy access to various parts of the house. A main entry opening into a foyer is usually preferable to an entry leading directly into the living room. The entry should be designed in such a way that callers may be viewed without opening the door. Glass side panels provide visibility, add natural light, and contribute to the design. In addition, protection from the weather is a major consideration in the design of an entry. Either an overhang may be provided or the entry may be recessed.

The main entry should be not only functional, but also visually interesting. A recessed entry is impressive and helps to break up a long, plain front that might otherwise be dull. An extended overhang may also add design and interest to a plain roof. An extra-tall door and ornate wood-work can add visual interest to the entry. See **Figure 7-19**. Well-styled doors are a key element in any entry. Doors should be carefully selected to conform to the overall design of the house and add a special touch of creative design. Added emphasis may be obtained by using two doors instead of one. This technique places more

Karamysh/Shutterstock.com

Figure 7-18. The size of this entry suits the overall size of the house. The designer relied on a complementary color and arches to make the entry attractive. Notice the overhang that protects visitors from the weather.

pics721/Shutterstock.com

Figure 7-19. The woodwork detailing and repetitive angles in this covered entry add style and a touch of elegance.

emphasis on the entry and also increases its function. Regardless of the technique used, the style of the entry should be compatible with the remainder of the house. See **Figure 7-20**. The use of totally different materials or a drastic change in proportion usually does not produce desirable results.

Bobkeenan Photography/Shutterstock.com

Figure 7-20. Notice how the arched doors in this entry carry through the same theme of styling as the rest of the house.

The size of the entry depends somewhat on the size and design of the house. However, sufficient space should be provided to accommodate several people at any given time.

Service Entry

The ***service entry*** is usually connected to the kitchen. The overall design may be improved by placing a mudroom or utility room between the kitchen and service entry. ***Special-purpose entries*** are those providing access to patios, decks, and courts. Sliding doors are often used for this type of entry. Service and special-purpose entries are not intended to be as striking as the main entry. See **Figure 7-21**.

Accessibility

The typical size for an entry door is 3′-0″ wide, 6′-8″ high, and 1-3/4″ thick. To be handicapped accessible, the entry should be large

Iriana Shiyan/Shutterstock.com

Figure 7-21. This service door to the rear of the house is designed to match the house style. However, convenience, rather than beauty, is the main purpose of this entry.

enough to permit the door to open a full 90°. The International Residential Code specifies a minimum clear width of 32″ and a minimum clear height of 78″ for the door opening. To allow for proper positioning of a wheelchair, there should be 12″ to 18″ of space on the doorknob side of the entry and the foyer.

Foyer

The ***foyer*** is a place to greet guests and, in colder climates, remove overcoats and boots. Consequently, the flooring material must be unaffected by water or dirt. It should also be easy to clean. See **Figure 7-22**. Materials such as slate, terrazzo, ceramic or asphalt tile, linoleum, or urethane-finished hardwood are often used for foyer floors.

In cold climates, the foyer should have a coat closet. The typical minimum inside dimensions are 2′ × 3′. A more desirable size would be 2′-6″ deep by 4′-0″ wide. The floor covering in the closet should also withstand mud and water.

Frequently, the foyer provides access to other rooms of the house through halls. The International Residential Code recommends a minimum hall width of 3′-0″. A width of 3′-6″ or 4′-0″ is more desirable.

Size

The size of the foyer depends on several factors:

- Size of the house
- Location
- Personal preference

The minimum size for a foyer is about 6′ × 7′. A typical small foyer is shown in **Figure 7-23**. An average size is 8′ × 10′. Anything larger than 8′ × 10′ is considered a large foyer.

Décor

Décor of the foyer generally reflects or coordinates with the color schemes and materials used in the living room and other adjacent rooms. Yet, because the foyer is often an extension of the entry, it should capitalize on the design aspects of the entry when possible. See **Figure 7-24**. For

Joy Brown/Shutterstock.com

Figure 7-22. The tile in this foyer serves two purposes. It is waterproof and easy to clean, and it serves as a visual divider between the foyer and the hardwood in the living room.

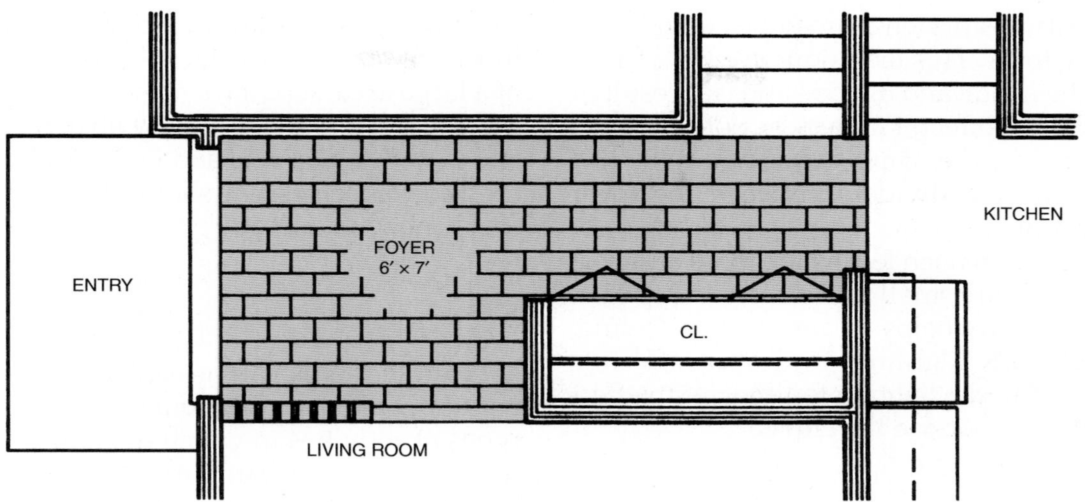

Goodheart-Willcox Publisher

Figure 7-23. This small foyer has a coat closet and serves as an access to the living room, stairs, and kitchen.

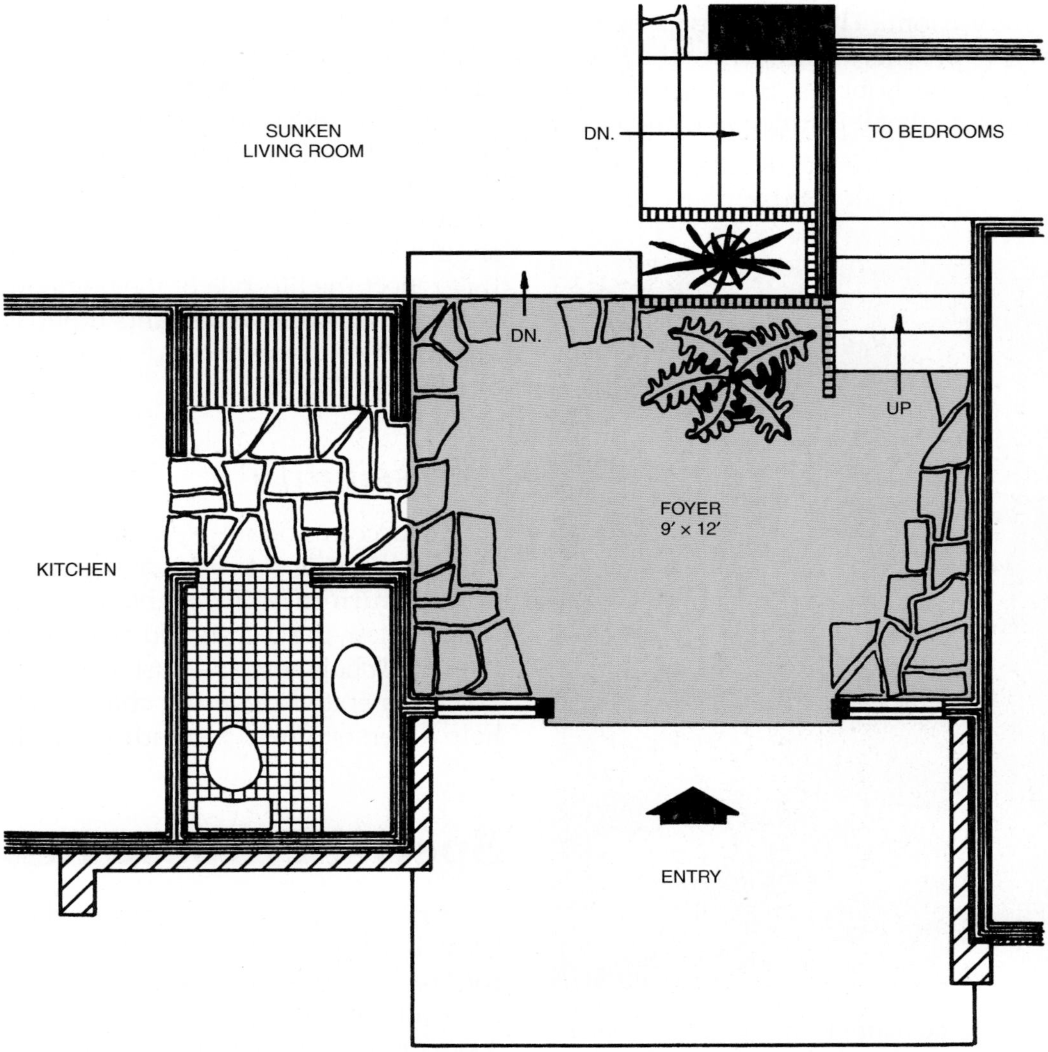

SUNKEN LIVING ROOM
DN.
TO BEDROOMS
DN.
UP
FOYER
9′ × 12′
KITCHEN
ENTRY

Goodheart-Willcox Publisher

Figure 7-24. Notice that this large foyer is the same width as the entry, making it a visual extension of the entry.

example, a two-story entry may be extended to include the foyer. This technique creates a unity between the inside and outside and can result in a very pleasing effect. Planters or potted plants may be used in the same way. They may also serve as informal dividers between the foyer and other rooms.

Foyers with an open feeling are more desirable than those that are small and closed. Using mirrors and windows helps create an open feeling. See **Figure 7-25**. Lighting is also an effective design tool. Plan the lighting for maximum effect both inside and outside the entry.

Family Room

Many homes have a room for family enjoyment. It may be called a family room, recreation room, or hobby room. The basic purpose of a family room is to provide a place where the family can play or pursue hobbies. See **Figure 7-26**. Design the room so that it is functional and easily maintained.

Tomasz Markowski/Shutterstock.com

Figure 7-25. The large mirror in this tiled foyer makes the room appear to be much larger than it is. Notice the lighting that showcases the mirror.

Some designers favor placing the family room in the basement. This location takes advantage of a large area, separates noise from other living areas, contains the necessary structural details, and is easy to decorate and keep clean. Wherever the room is located, it should be convenient to everyone who uses it.

Size

Family rooms vary greatly in size. The number of people planning to use the room and the types of activities in which the family members will be engaged are important considerations in determining the size. A common size is 12′ × 20′.

Décor

Furniture selection for the room is very important and depends on the anticipated activities. The family room typically receives a great deal of use. Therefore, choose furniture that is serviceable and resistant to wear.

Family rooms are planned for the enjoyment of family and friends. The décor of the room should be welcoming with furniture and colors that reflect the lifestyle of the homeowner. Large-screen TVs, pool tables, and other game tables are common items placed in the family room. See **Figure 7-27**.

Accessibility

To accommodate a person using a wheelchair, a space of 4′ to 5′ wide should be provided around furniture. To enable easy transfer to a sofa or chair, the seat should be the same height as the wheelchair seat and cushions should be firm. Power-operated elevating chairs are available to help a person get to a standing position.

Special-Purpose Rooms

After the primary rooms of the living area have been planned, consider special-purpose rooms. ***Special-purpose rooms*** may include a dedicated home office, library, music room, sunroom or atrium, greenhouse, or even a ham radio room. See **Figure 7-28**.

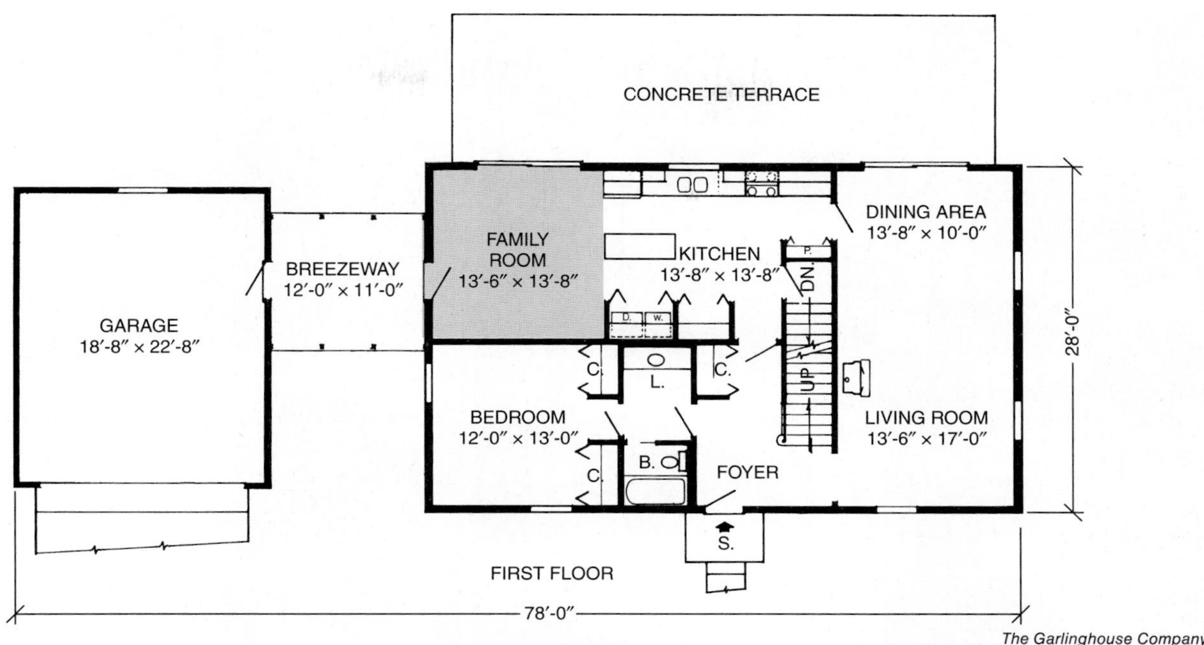

The Garlinghouse Company

Figure 7-26. The location of this family room is ideal for games, family hobbies, and indoor-outdoor activities.

Christopher Edwin Nuzzaco/Shutterstock.com

Figure 7-27. This basement family room provides plenty of space for playing games, sharing casual meals with family and friends, and watching the large-screen TV. Notice the easy-to-clean flooring and décor.

pics721/Shutterstock.com

Figure 7-28. Although many people use a corner of another room as a home office, having a dedicated room is preferable, especially if one or more members of the family will spend a great deal of time working at home.

Some special-purpose areas may be placed in the corner of another room. When more space is needed, a dedicated room can be designed and placed in an appropriate location. Some special-purpose rooms, such as a music room or sunroom, may be located to the side or rear of the house. See **Figure 7-29**. Rooms that require a great deal of privacy, such as a darkroom, should be placed in a remote area of the home.

In addition to location, many special-purpose rooms have other specific requirements that should be addressed in the design process. These requirements may include storage, lighting, ventilation, plumbing, and electrical use. For example, an art room may need a certain quality and quantity of light.

pics721/Shutterstock.com

Figure 7-29. This sunroom provides a pleasant spot for sipping tea on a chilly morning. The sun and natural surroundings make up most of the "décor" in this room.

Outdoor Living Areas

The living facilities in a well-designed house extend beyond its walls, as shown in **Figure 7-30**. Patios, porches, decks, courtyards, and gazebos can effectively enlarge the area and function of a house.

Diane Uhley/Shutterstock.com

Figure 7-30. This screened porch provides a smooth transition from indoors to outdoors. It allows people to relax in a comfortable outdoor area.

Lighting is an important feature of any outdoor living space. Without proper lighting, use after dark may be limited. Lighting should be used as a design tool to assist in accomplishing an atmosphere and extend the usefulness of the structure. Lighting also adds safety and security.

Patios

Patios are usually near the house but not structurally connected to it. Patios are located at ground level and are constructed for durability. Concrete, brick, stone, tile, redwood, pressure-treated wood, and synthetic decking are commonly used construction materials. The patio shown in **Figure 7-31** is an example of how a well-designed patio can add to the overall function of a house.

Patios are used for relaxing, playing, entertaining, and living. Each function requires consideration as to location, size, and design. Try

Phase4Photography/Shutterstock.com

Figure 7-31. The owners of this house have furnished the patio to make a pleasant outdoor living area.

to locate patios designed for relaxing on a quiet side of the house near the bedrooms where there is privacy. Privacy may be achieved through the use of screens, walls, or plants. A patio designed for entertaining and playing will most likely be large and located off of the living room, dining room, or family room. Play patios are usually less encumbered with furniture, planters, and screens. The play patio is usually designed for use by children and adults for physical activities that require open space. See **Figure 7-32**. The entry on a play patio sometimes doubles as a service entry.

Consider the orientation of the patio in relation to sunlight, wind, and the view. In warm climates, providing shade may be a major factor. In colder regions, ensuring ample sun may be a prime objective. If the surrounding area lacks natural beauty, more emphasis should be placed on design and styling. The use of flowers, pools, and screens helps to create a beautiful setting for dining, relaxing, or entertaining.

If the house has a swimming pool, the area around the pool can be designed as a patio. **Figure 7-33** shows an example of a patio with a swimming pool as the main feature. This type of patio may be used as a living, entertaining, or play patio, or merely as a place to relax.

Porches

Porches and decks differ from patios in several ways. They are generally structurally connected to the house. See **Figure 7-34**. Porches that are not under a roof are called ***decks***. Decks differ from patios in that they are typically above grade. The deck in **Figure 7-35** provides

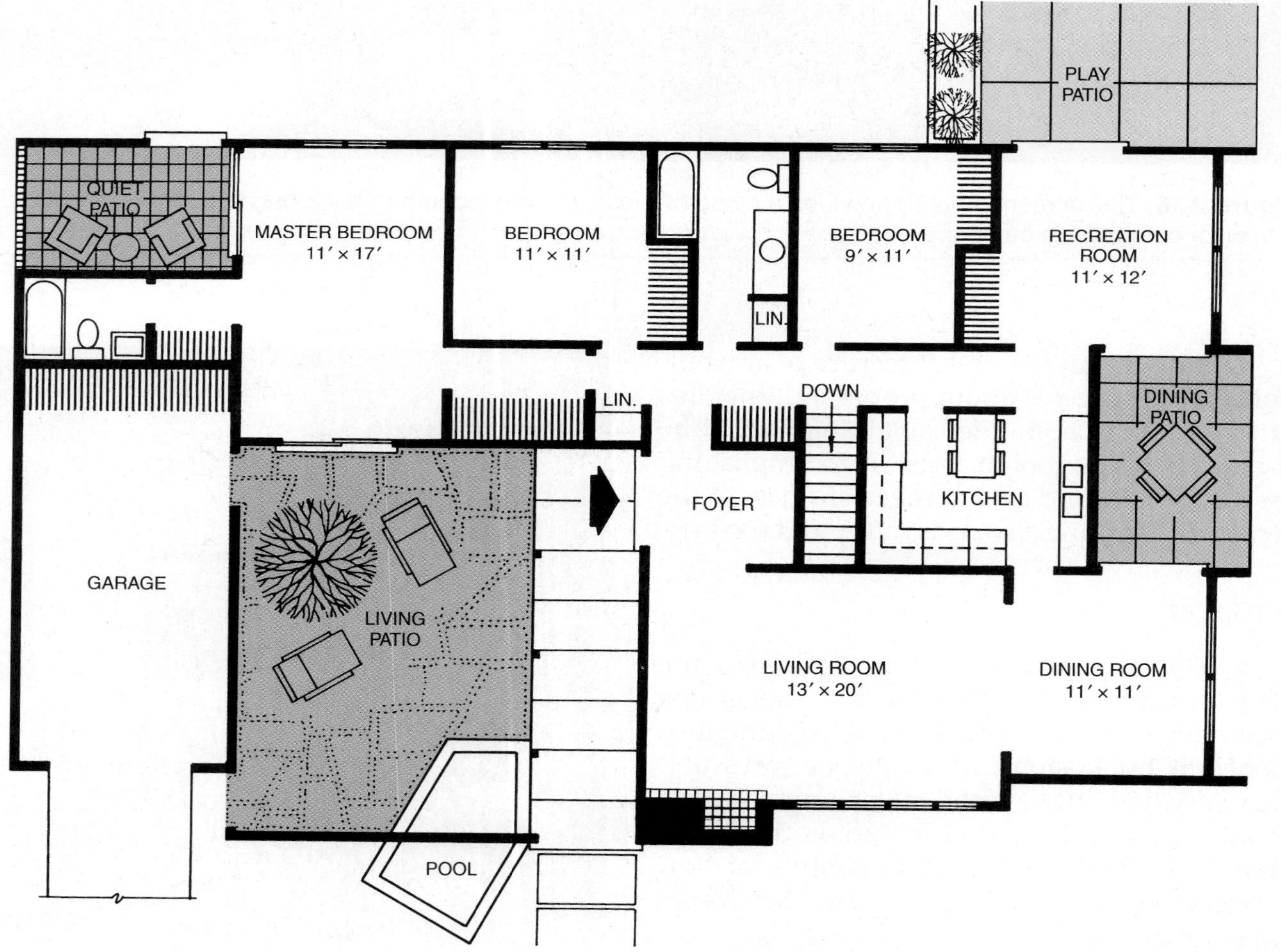

Figure 7-32. This floor plan has four patios designed for different types of activities. Notice their locations in relation to the rest of the house.

Elena Elisseeva/Shutterstock.com

Figure 7-33. This pool patio was designed to blend in with its surroundings. Notice the fence and shrubbery that provide privacy for the homeowner.

Christopher Edwin Nuzzaco/Shutterstock.com

Figure 7-34. Unlike patios, porches are part of the structural design of the home.

Green Architecture

Porches and Green Design

Have you ever noticed that many older houses have deep porches on one or more sides of the house? Have you ever wondered why?

Porches were a "green" design feature long before people started thinking about environmentally friendly home designs. In the days before air conditioning, porches were used to help keep a home cooler by preventing the sun from entering the home directly. See **Figure A**. Because they are structurally attached to the house and generally under the roof line, they may also help protect the exterior walls of the house from direct exposure to rain and snow.

After air conditioning became widespread in residential homes, many designers stopped including large porches. In fact, porches were considered to be an excess, unnecessary expense. Now, however, some designers are realizing the potential of porches to reduce electricity use while moderating the temperature of the home. When you design a home, consider adding porches as an environmentally friendly feature.

Ekaterina Kamenetsky/Shutterstock.com

Figure A. Porches can be incorporated into any housing style. Notice how the porches in this home keep the direct sun from reaching the exterior walls. This allows many more windows to be used, brightening the interior while moderating the outside temperature.

Iriana Shiyan/Shutterstock.com

Figure 7-35. A large deck like this one provides outdoor dining space, as well as plenty of room for other outdoor activities.

a large entertaining space overlooking a lake view. Balconies and verandahs are other types of porches. ***Balconies*** are narrow porches generally located on the upper floor of a home. A ***verandah*** is a large porch that typically extends along an entire wall of the house.

Porches may function as outdoor dining areas and entry extensions. The usefulness of the porch may be increased by the addition of screens or glass. Screens help keep flying insects out of the dining area, and glass allows the porch to be used during the winter months in northern climates.

Since porches and decks are above grade, a ramp is required for access by the disabled. Plan for a ramp with a slope between 1:12 and 1:20. A steeper slope is hard to navigate with a wheelchair or walker.

Courtyards

Courtyards are outdoor spaces that are at least partially enclosed by walls or a roof. They are similar to porches and patios and may have characteristics of both. See **Figure 7-36**. Courtyards may be used for dining, relaxing, talking, or entertaining. They may also serve as gardens to add a touch of spring throughout the year. Courtyards are sometimes used to break up floor plans, add interest, or provide natural light to an interior part of the house that has no exterior wall.

Darryl Brooks/Shutterstock.com

Figure 7-36. A courtyard is similar to a porch or patio, but is enclosed by walls on at least two or three sides.

Gazebos

A beautiful gazebo or garden structure can provide an architectural focal point. See **Figure 7-37**. A ***gazebo*** is a roofed structure that is similar to a porch, but is detached from the house. It typically has open sides. A gazebo can be a place from which to view the surrounding beauty of the lawn and gardens. Gazebos are often screened, and some are even enclosed with glass in colder climates to make them more comfortable and usable on cold days.

Darryl Brooks/Shutterstock.com

Figure 7-37. A gazebo can be the focal point of a garden or provide a quiet place to read or to rest after a long walk.

Summary

- The three major areas of a house are the living area, the sleeping area, and the service area.
- More than 15 million people in the United States use a wheelchair, walker, cane, or crutches. A good home design takes the special needs of these people into account.
- Movement of people throughout the house should be considered to allow traffic to flow smoothly from one room to another.
- A properly designed living room is both attractive and useful for a family's daily activities.
- Before planning the dining room, the designer must decide whether the house should have an open plan or a closed plan.
- There are three basic types of entries—main entry, service entry, and special-purpose entry.
- The foyer is a place to greet guests and, in colder climates, remove overcoats and boots.
- The family room is a relaxed space where a family can play games, watch television, and conduct other activities.
- Special-purpose rooms may include a dedicated home office, sunroom or atrium, greenhouse, music room, or any other type of room that fits the family's lifestyle and needs.
- Outdoor living areas such as patios and porches increase the living area of the house.

Internet Resources

Architectural Digest
News articles and resources for the architectural profession

Armstrong World Industries
Supplier of flooring and ceiling products

Better Homes and Gardens
News articles and resources for home improvement projects

Congoleum Corporation
Supplier of flooring products

International Code Council (ICC)
Published building codes and standards

Marvin Windows and Doors
Supplier of windows and doors

Schulte Corporation
Manufacturer of storage solutions

Sweets Network
Sweets™ Product Catalogs

Review Questions

Answer the following questions using the information in this chapter.

1. What rooms are typically included in the living area of a home?
2. What set of standards address accessibility design guidelines applying to the Americans with Disabilities Act (ADA)?
3. List two characteristics of good traffic circulation in a home.
4. About how many square feet are in an average-size living room?
5. What is a *great room*, and what rooms might it replace in a house with an open plan?
6. What are the advantages of having a closed plan with a separate dining room?
7. List the three basic types of entries.
8. What is the purpose of the *foyer*?
9. Identify three special-purpose rooms that may be included in the living area of a home.
10. How does a *porch* differ from a *patio*?

Suggested Activities

1. Design a medium-size living room with furniture. Present your plan in color for a bulletin board display. Prepare a short description of the intended use for the room.
2. Design plans for a dining room that is designed to accommodate six people. Include furniture that is appropriate for a modern or postmodern home and show the furniture on the plans. Use manual or CADD drafting.

3. Prepare a bulletin board display of different entries. Use color illustrations from magazines or color prints from the Internet. Try to represent a broad range of designs.
4. Find a plan for a house that has no patio. Using CADD, design a porch or patio for the house. Print the patio on vellum or film. Present the patio design as an overlay on the house plan.
5. Using CADD, design a special-purpose room. Specify the equipment and furniture required. Explain the special requirements that must be met in the room.
6. Using CADD, design symbols for furniture and other items that may be found in the living area of a home. Add these symbols to your symbol library for future use.

Problem Solving Case Study

You are working with Mr. and Mrs. Delgado in the design of their new custom home. They have a building site in the Adirondack Mountains in New York. They want a comfortable home that can easily accommodate their extended family and friends, because they frequently entertain. Mr. Delgado does not think a foyer is necessary, but Mrs. Delgado disagrees. She would like your opinion as to the placement of the foyer and the main entry and the size of these proposed areas. They would like to discuss this with you at the next meeting. What will you tell Mr. and Mrs. Delgado?

ADDA Certification Prep

The following questions are presented in the style used in the American Design Drafting Association (ADDA) Drafter Certification Test. Answer the questions using the information in this chapter.

1. Which of the following rooms are considered part of the living area of a home?
   A. Master bathroom
   B. Kitchen
   C. Dining room
   D. Laundry room
   E. Library
   F. Patio
   G. Foyer
2. Which of the following statements are true?
   A. The foyer is a type of closet.
   B. The main entry should be placed in a convenient location.
   C. Courtyards are similar to porches and patios but are at least partially enclosed by walls or a roof.
   D. Family rooms take the place of dining rooms and living rooms in an open plan.
   E. According to the *Americans with Disabilities: 2010* report, 3.6 million Americans use wheelchairs.
3. Match each type of outdoor living area with its description.

   Outdoor living areas: 1. Balcony, 2. Verandah, 3. Patio, 4. Courtyard, 5. Deck
   A. Similar to a patio but typically above grade.
   B. A narrow porch extending from the upper floor of a residence.
   C. A large porch that extends across an entire side of the house.
   D. A feature near the residence, but not attached to it; usually at ground level.
   E. An outdoor space that is partially or fully enclosed by walls or a roof.

Curricular Connections

1. **Social Science.** Compare the entertainment possibilities in a house with an open plan and one with a closed plan. For a family that entertains frequently, which plan might be better? Why?
2. **Language Arts.** World War II had a dramatic impact on architectural design. Conduct research to find out more about the trend away from having separate dining rooms that occurred after World War II and write an essay explaining why this trend may have occurred.

STEM Connections

1. **Math.** A client has requested that the family room in his new house have 400 square feet. When you ask what he plans to use the room for, he explains that he wants an area big enough to accommodate a Ping-Pong table, as well as a comfortable seating arrangement for at least eight people. Design a room that has exactly 400 square feet and will provide enough space for the client's intended use. (You may need to research the size of a Ping-Pong table before designing the room.) Show the dimensions of the room on your drawing.

Communicating about Architecture

1. **Reading.** Working in groups of three, create flash cards for the key terms in this chapter. Have each student select several terms and make flash cards for the terms. On the front of the card, write the term. On the back of the card, write the pronunciation and a brief definition. Use this chapter and a dictionary for guidance. Then take turns quizzing one another on the pronunciations and definitions of the key terms.
2. **Speaking.** Working in a group, brainstorm ideas for creating classroom tools (posters, flash cards, and/or games, for example) that will help your classmates learn and remember the different rooms in the living area of a house. Choose the best idea(s), then delegate responsibilities to group members for constructing the tools and presenting them to the class.

Chapter 8

Planning the Sleeping Area

Objectives

After completing this chapter, you will be able to:

- Discuss factors that are important in the design of bedrooms.
- Plan a furniture arrangement for a bedroom.
- Implement important design considerations for a bathroom.
- Plan a bathroom for accessibility by people who are disabled or have limited mobility.

Key Terms

1/2 bath
3/4 bath
bidet
comfort-height toilet
full bath
ground fault circuit interrupter (GFCI)
lavatory
sleeping area
split bedroom plan
vanity
water closet

Typically, about one-third of the house is dedicated to the ***sleeping area***. This area includes bedrooms, bathrooms, and accessory rooms such as dressing rooms or saunas. Normally, the sleeping area is in a quiet part of the house away from vehicular traffic and other noise.

The design of bedroom and bathroom spaces may be developed easily and rapidly using a CADD system. Many of the elements used in the design of these rooms are commonly available as symbols. Often, manufacturers provide CADD symbols of their furniture, cabinets, and other items that can be used in designing a home. You can also develop custom symbols as needed. In addition, CADD systems allow you to render proposed designs and show them to clients for approval. **Figure 8-1** shows a CADD-generated rendering of a bathroom design.

Bedrooms

Bedrooms are so important that houses are frequently categorized by the number they contain, such as "two-bedroom," "three-bedroom," or "four-bedroom." The size of the family usually determines the number of bedrooms needed. Ideally, a home has enough bedrooms that each family member can have one. In the case of a couple with no children living at home, at least two bedrooms are desirable. The second bedroom could be used as a guest room and for other activities when there are no guests. See **Figure 8-2**. A home with only one bedroom may be difficult to sell. Three-bedroom homes usually have the greatest sales potential. A three-bedroom

Alexey Kashin/Shutterstock.com

Figure 8-1. This CADD-generated presentation drawing demonstrates the usefulness of computer-generated images to describe a design idea.

pics721/Shutterstock.com

Figure 8-2. An extra bedroom can be used for other purposes, such as a home office or a hobby room.

home can provide enough space for a family of four. It may be wise to include an extra bedroom in the plan that can be used for other purposes until needed. It is usually more economical to add an extra room at the outset rather than expand later.

There are several options for placing bedrooms in a home. Grouping the bedrooms together in a separate wing or level of the house, as shown in **Figure 8-3**, affords seclusion and privacy. In a ***split bedroom plan,*** the master bedroom is separated from the remaining bedrooms to provide even greater privacy. See **Figure 8-4**. Another option is to include a bedroom in another area of the home for an employee, live-in relative, or overnight guests. Each bedroom should have its own access to the hall. An attempt should be made to place each bedroom close to a bathroom. Some bedrooms may have their own private baths.

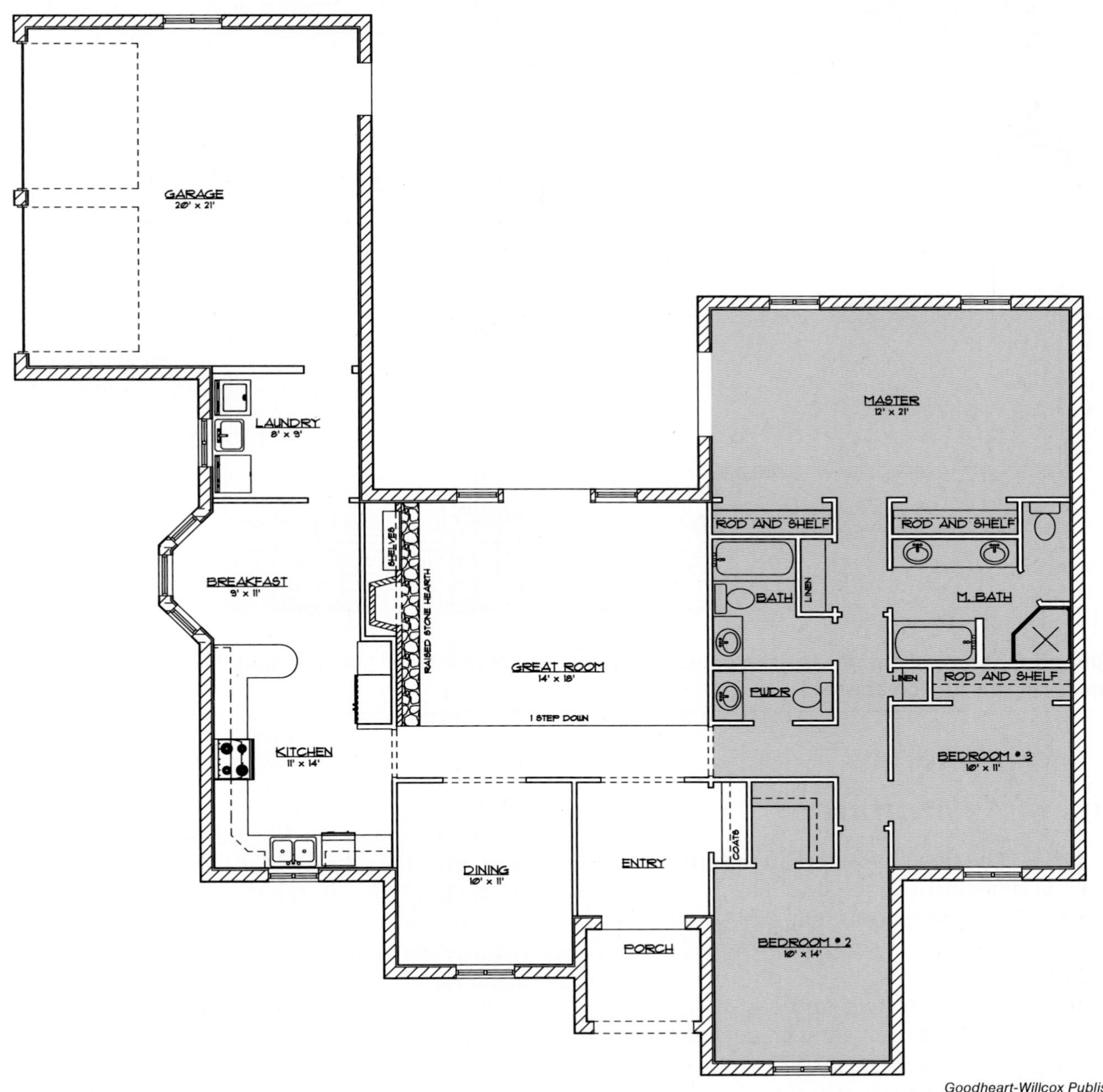

Goodheart-Willcox Publisher

Figure 8-3. Bedrooms that are grouped together in a wing or level of the house away from other activities help reduce noise in the sleeping area.

Goodheart-Willcox Publisher

Figure 8-4. A split bedroom plan separates the master bedroom from all the other bedrooms to provide even greater privacy for homeowners.

Size and Furniture

One of the first challenges in designing a bedroom is determining its size. The International Residential Code recommends 70 square feet as the minimum size. A small bedroom is shown in **Figure 8-5**.

It has 99 square feet and can hold the bare essentials in furniture. An average-size bedroom contains between 125 and 175 square feet. See **Figure 8-6**. Such a room provides ample space for a twin or double bed, chest of drawers, dresser, and other small pieces of furniture. A large bedroom has more than 175 square feet of floor space, as shown in **Figure 8-7**. A room of this size provides space for additional furniture. A desk, chair, or television may be included as bedroom furniture. The largest bedroom is usually considered to be the master bedroom. It often has its own private bath.

Bedroom design is directly related to the amount and size of the furniture to be used. Common furniture sizes are shown in **Figure 8-8**. It is not necessary to design the bedroom with a specific arrangement in mind.

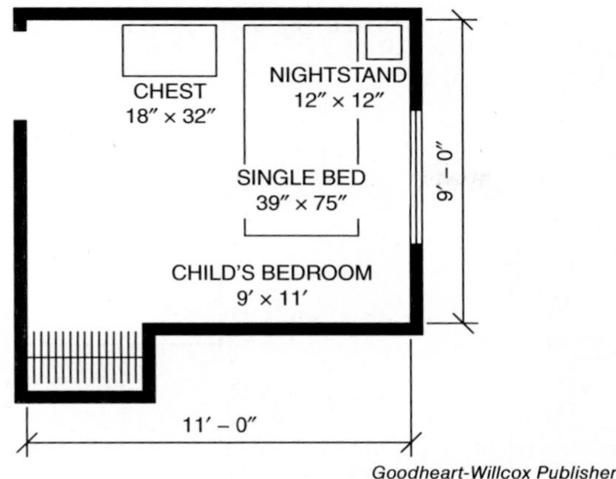

Figure 8-5. A small bedroom with the minimum furniture: a single bed, nightstand, and chest of drawers.

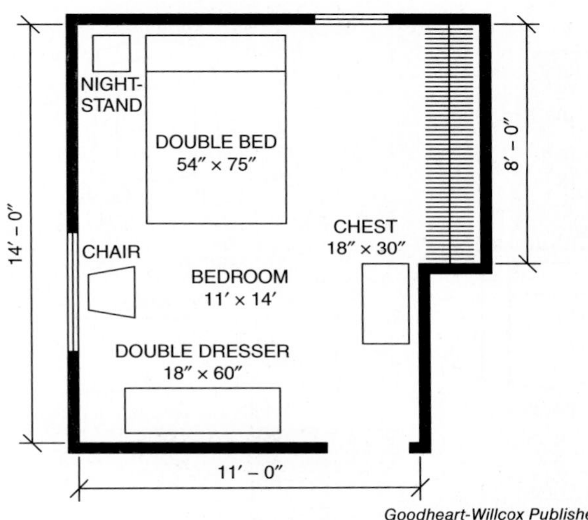

Figure 8-6. An average-size bedroom has room for a double bed, chest, chair, double dresser, and nightstand.

In fact, it is best to allow for several different arrangements so the homeowner can change the furniture around or purchase different pieces. Just make sure that all of the items the homeowner wants to place in the bedroom will fit in the room you design.

Closets

Each bedroom typically includes a closet. The minimum width of a closet is usually 6′-0″. The minimum depth of a closet is 24″. When possible, closets should be located along interior walls. This provides noise insulation between rooms and does not reduce exterior wall space. A bedroom normally has no more than two exterior walls. The use of one of these for closets reduces the possibility of cross ventilation through windows.

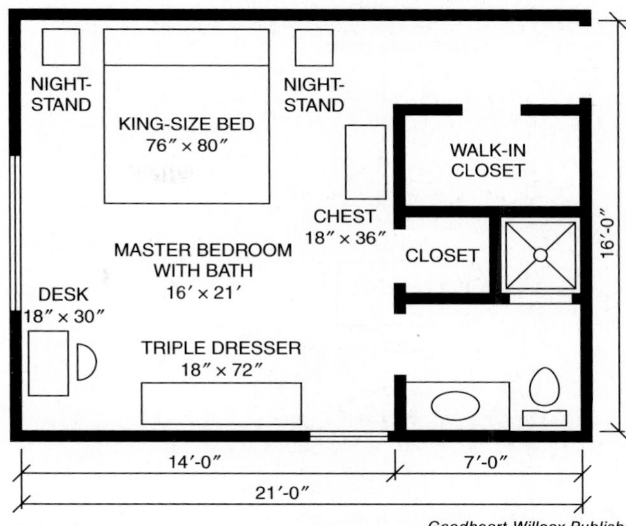

Figure 8-7. An arrangement for a large master bedroom with a private bath.

A variety of closet doors can be used to provide access to the closet: sliding, bi-fold, accordion, or flush. The usual height of a door is 6′-8″, but most doors are also available in 8′-0″ heights. In general, plan to use doors that provide easy accessibility yet require little space. See **Figure 8-9**. Good lighting is also a necessity. For all except the smallest closets, plan to include a light fixture inside the closet.

Doors and Windows

Windows and doors are important bedroom features. An ideal bedroom has windows on two walls to allow cross ventilation. Each bedroom has at least one entry door. The door should swing into the bedroom. Allow space along the wall for the door when it is open. Locating a door near a corner of the room usually results in less wasted space. To further conserve space, pocket or sliding doors may be used.

Interior doors are usually 1-3/8″ thick and 6′-8″ high. Standard widths range from 2′-0″ to 3′-0″ in increments of 2″. The minimum recommended bedroom door width is 2′-6″. A wider

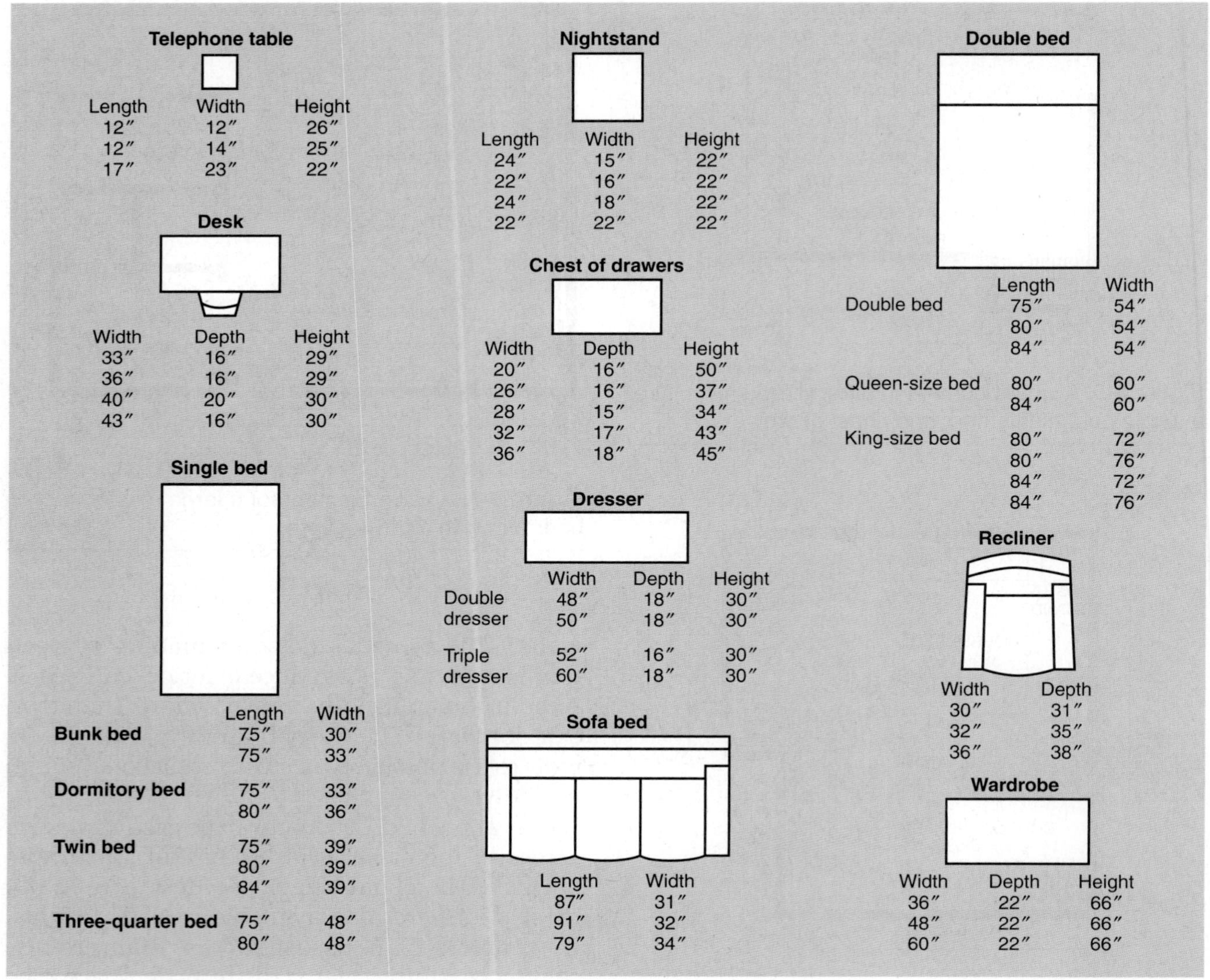

Figure 8-8. Common sizes of standard bedroom furniture.

door, 2′-8″ or 2′-10″, provides for easier movement of furniture, especially adjacent to a hall. To accommodate a wheelchair, doorways should be at least 2′-8″ wide.

Décor

A well-planned bedroom is a cheerful, but restful, place. Carefully select colors that help to create a quiet and peaceful atmosphere. **Figure 8-10** shows an example of a well-designed, tastefully furnished bedroom. Notice the two small windows on the back wall and the window on the right. Their placement ensures adequate ventilation in the room.

Accessible Bedrooms

When designing a bedroom for the disabled, allow ample space for maneuvering a wheelchair around furniture without obstructions. In addition, space must be allowed for easy transfer into and out of bed. See **Figure 8-11**. A space of 3′ should be provided on at least one side of the bed for transfer. Four or more feet should be allowed between stationary objects. A clear space of 5′ square usually is required for turning a wheelchair in front of a closet.

Beds intended to be accessible to a disabled person must be the same height as the seat of a wheelchair. That is, the mattress should be

Iriana Shiyan/Shutterstock.com

Figure 8-9. The sliding doors on this closet allow easy access without taking up space in the room when they are open.

Stephen Coburn/Shutterstock.com

Figure 8-10. The décor in a bedroom should be tranquil and peaceful, yet cheerful and inviting.

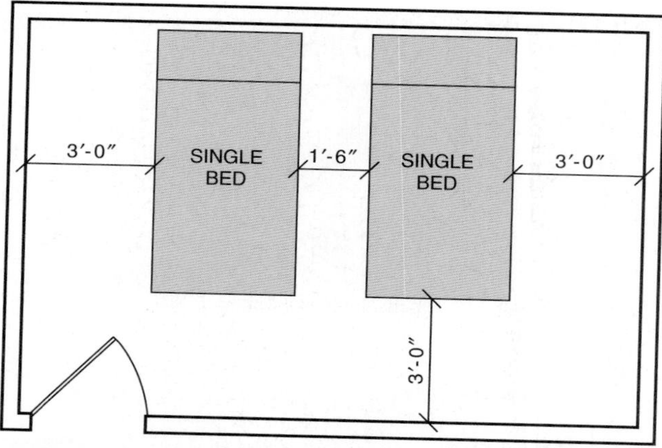

Goodheart-Willcox Publisher

Figure 8-11. An example of minimum space clearances for bedroom furniture in a bedroom designed for a person in a wheelchair.

the same height as the wheelchair seat and firm enough for easy transfer. An adjustable bed can also be used. A clearance space of 10″ is required under the bed for the footrests of the wheelchair.

Bi-fold, accordion, or sliding doors generally allow for partial closet entry by wheelchair users. To be accessible to the disabled, clothing rods should be located 40″ to 48″ from the floor. Adjustable shelves provide greater accessibility and may be placed at various heights from 40″ to 48″ above the floor. Clothes hooks should not be more than 40″ from the floor.

Bathrooms

The small, drab bathroom of the late 1900s is almost a thing of the past. Homes today have larger, more pleasant baths. Today's homes also have more bathrooms than were used in the past. All homes require at least one bathroom, and most modern homes have two or more. Ideally, every bedroom should have its own bath, although this is often impractical due to the added expense of plumbing walls that contain water supply lines, waste lines, and vent pipes.

Bathrooms may be simple, with only the necessary fixtures, or elaborate in design and function. See **Figure 8-12**. A dressing or exercise area may be incorporated into the bath. These activities require more space and added facilities. Plan the bath around the functions to be provided.

Number, Location, and Size

Often, the design of the house indicates the minimum number of baths needed. If the house is very small, one bath may be sufficient. In this case, locate the bathroom where it is most convenient. See **Figure 8-13**. Locate the door in a hall common to all the bedrooms. A person should not be required to go through another room, such as a bedroom, to reach the bath. In some

A Iriana Shiyan/Shutterstock.com

B pics721/Shutterstock.com

Figure 8-12. A—Small bathrooms do not have to be dull or plain. The colors and interesting floor tile add interest to this small bath. B—A large, luxury bathroom may contain a whirlpool tub with a separate shower, dual sinks, and other attractive features.

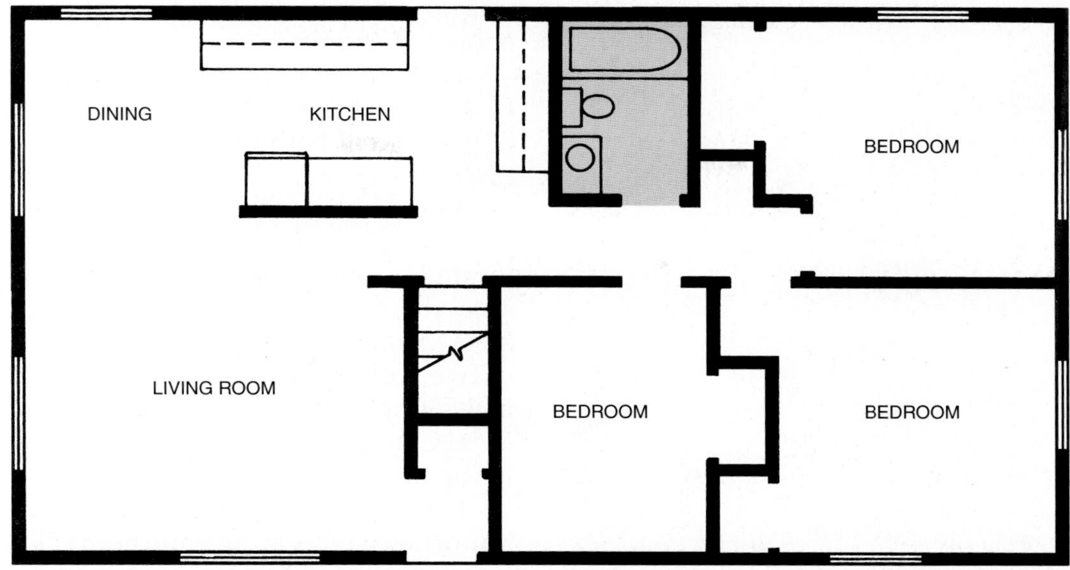

Goodheart-Willcox Publisher

Figure 8-13. A well-planned, centrally located bathroom in a small house.

designs, it is convenient to have two bedrooms sharing the same bathroom. A double-entry bath, as shown in **Figure 8-14**, illustrates one design solution.

A ***full bath*** contains a sink, toilet, and tub or tub/shower combination. A ***1/2 bath*** is one that typically has only a sink and toilet. See **Figure 8-15**. A ***3/4 bath*** is functional for basement or attic conversions. It contains a sink, toilet, and shower,

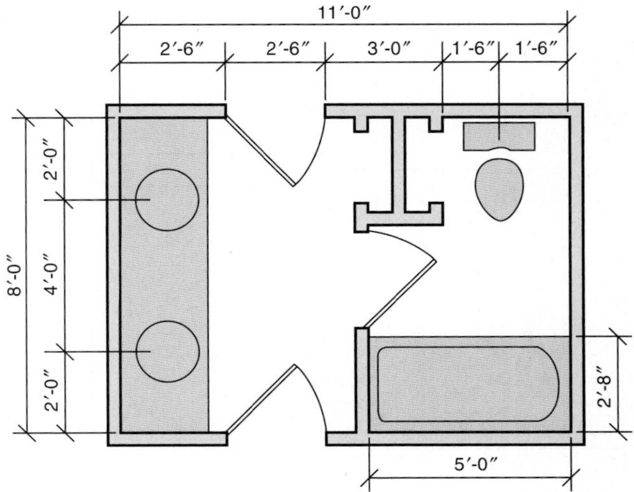

Goodheart-Willcox Publisher

Figure 8-14. A double-entry bath allows two bedrooms to share a bath directly. Notice the additional privacy door that separates the sinks from the tub and toilet.

Green Architecture

Volatile Organic Compounds (VOCs)

Volatile organic compounds (VOCs) are toxic substances that evaporate into the atmosphere. The evaporation of VOCs contributes to the development of environmental hazards such as smog, but VOCs can also reduce the quality of air indoors. Not only are VOCs harmful to the environment, but they can also be harmful to your health. Continued exposure to these toxins can produce symptoms such as headaches and nausea, or more severe damage such as organ damage and cancer. Products that contain VOCs include substances such as paint and cleaning supplies, but VOCs are also found in fabrics or carpets.

As you plan a home design, you can reduce the homeowner's exposure to VOCs being released into the home. Many VOC-containing products are offered in more organic alternatives. These products use plant-based materials rather than chemicals such as benzene. Plan to use zero-VOC paints, and choose carpets and other flooring materials carefully. Take the time to research the materials. In general, choose materials with natural finishes or fabric that is made from organic cotton.

Iriana Shiyan/Shutterstock.com

Figure 8-15. A half bath is often sufficient for the lower floor of a two-story house if all of the bedrooms are upstairs.

but no bathtub. A 3/4 bath and a full bath are shown in **Figure 8-16**.

A two-story house in which all of the bedrooms are upstairs requires at least 1-1/2 baths—a full bath on the second level near the bedrooms and a 1/2 bath on the first floor near the living area. A split-level house also requires at least 1-1/2 baths. Since the bedrooms are located on the upper level away from the living area, there is a need for another bath on a lower level. A large ranch house requires a minimum of two baths. The bedrooms are usually located in a wing of the house away from the living area. Convenience dictates a second bath in the living area.

For years, designers have emphasized the importance of locating bathrooms close together and near the kitchen to reduce cost. Granted, the cost will be less if bathrooms share a common plumbing wall. However, this is a minor consideration compared to convenience and function. It is desirable to design functional baths and place them in the most convenient locations.

A small-size bath is 5′ × 8′. A large bath may be 10′ × 10′, 10′ × 12′, or larger. A family bathroom requires more countertop and storage space than a guest bath. Most people prefer ample space

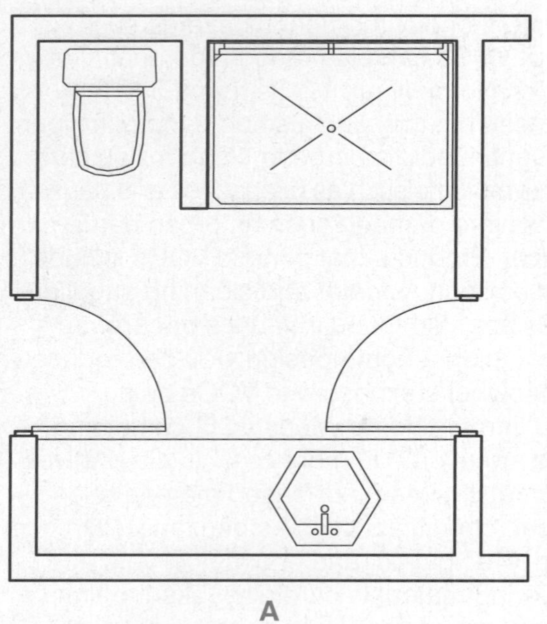

A

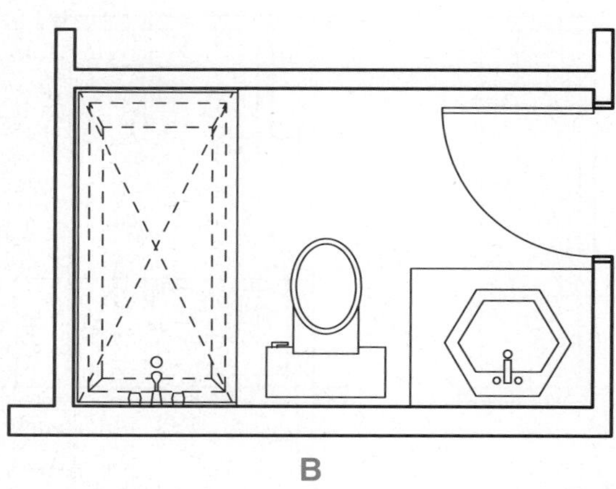

B

Goodheart-Willcox Publisher

Figure 8-16. A—A 3/4 bath includes a shower but no bathtub. B—A full bath has a bathtub or a bathtub/shower combination.

Employability

Evaluating Job Offers

When considering a job offer or comparing two or more positions, you should explore the following work factors:

- *Physical surroundings*. Where is your workspace located? Is the atmosphere conducive to your style of working? Is parking provided? Is public transportation close by?
- *Work schedule*. Will the workdays and work hours mesh with your lifestyle? Is occasional overtime work required?
- *Income and benefits*. Is the proposed salary fair? Will you receive benefits that are just as valuable as extra income? How much sick leave is granted during the year? Is personal or emergency leave available? What is the vacation leave policy? Are there medical and life insurance benefits? Is there a credit union? Will the company pay tuition for college courses or special programs related to your job? Is a cafeteria on the premises? Does it offer food to employees at reduced cost?
- *Job obligations*. Will you be expected to join a union or other professional organization? If so, what are the costs? Will you be expected to attend meetings after work?
- *Advancement potential*. Is there opportunity for advancement? After demonstrating good performance, how soon can you seek a position with more responsibilities? Before you can advance, are there special expectations, such as a higher degree? Are training programs provided?

Talking about advancement requires considerable diplomacy. After all, you should not appear too eager to leave the job for which you are interviewing. Many employers expect a new employee to remain at least one year at that job. If you place undue emphasis on advancement, you will appear uninterested in the current opening.

Activity

Contact two companies in your area and ask for a list of benefits they offer their employees. Alternatively, visit the websites of two companies that post job and benefits information online. Compare the benefits offered by the two companies. On the basis of benefits alone, which company would you choose to work for? Why?

for dressing, linen storage, and personal items. Larger bathrooms also allow for luxury or oversize tubs. See **Figure 8-17**. A large bathroom is most convenient for a wheelchair user. To be handicapped accessible, the bathroom must have a minimum of 5′ × 5′ clear space to allow turning of the wheelchair.

Doors

Bathroom doors are ordinarily not as wide as bedroom doors. A door width of 2′-6″ or even 2′-4″ is usually sufficient. If provisions are being made for wheelchair use, then the door should be a minimum of 2′-8″ wide. Doors should swing into the bathroom and not interfere with any fixtures. In some instances, a pocket door is used to subdivide the bath into two or more areas.

Ventilation and Electricity

A bathroom *must* have ventilation. This may be provided by windows or an exhaust fan. If windows are used, care must be taken to locate them properly. Windows should be placed such that a draft is not produced over the tub and maximum privacy is secured. The exception might be in a luxury bathroom, in which the homeowner might want a picture window over the tub with a view of a secluded area.

If an exhaust fan is used, it should be located near the tub and toilet area. *Electrical switches should be placed so that they cannot be reached from the tub.* In addition, ***ground fault circuit interrupter (GFCI)*** receptacles should be used in the bathroom. These are fast-acting devices that detect short circuits and immediately shut off power to the receptacle.

pics721/Shutterstock.com

Figure 8-17. This bathroom, with a retro art deco style, has plenty of space for a whirlpool tub and a separate shower.

Primary Fixtures

The three primary fixtures found in most bathrooms are the sink, toilet, and tub or shower. The sink is often called a ***lavatory***, and the toilet is often called a ***water closet*** (abbreviated WC on floor plans). Provide ample space for each fixture in the room. For toilets and sinks, the International Residential Code recommends a clearance space of 30″ center-to-center between fixtures and a clearance space of 15″ from the center of a fixture to a side wall. Typical fixture sizes are shown in **Figure 8-18**.

Sinks

A sink cabinet, or ***vanity***, can provide much-needed countertop and storage space, especially in a family bathroom. Sinks are usually circular, oval, or rectangular, but other shapes are used as well. Twin sinks are desirable when more than one person must share the bathroom. Another trend is the use of vanities built to look like furniture. **Figure 8-19** shows common sizes of bathroom vanities. Wall-mounted and pedestal sinks may be used to enhance the look of a small bathroom or to provide sufficient knee space for wheelchair users. A mirror or a mirrored medicine cabinet should be placed above the sink. Arrange the mirror so it is well lighted and away from the tub to prevent fogging.

Toilets

Toilets are produced in a number of styles. Most toilets require a space at least 30″ wide for installation. Allow 36″ for a handicapped person. Toilets should be placed so that they are not visible from another room when the bathroom door is open.

Bathtubs and Showers

Regular bathtubs range in size from 54″ to 72″ long and 28″ to 32″ wide. The most common size is 30″ × 60″. Often, a shower is installed above the tub. This provides the convenience of both and does not require two separate facilities. See **Figure 8-20**.

Many homes have a tub and separate shower stall. Prefabricated showers are available in metal, fiberglass, and plastic. Hand-held shower heads may be more convenient and shower controls should be within reach of the user. Tub and shower floors should be flat and slip resistant. Common shower sizes range from 30″ × 30″ to 36″ × 48″.

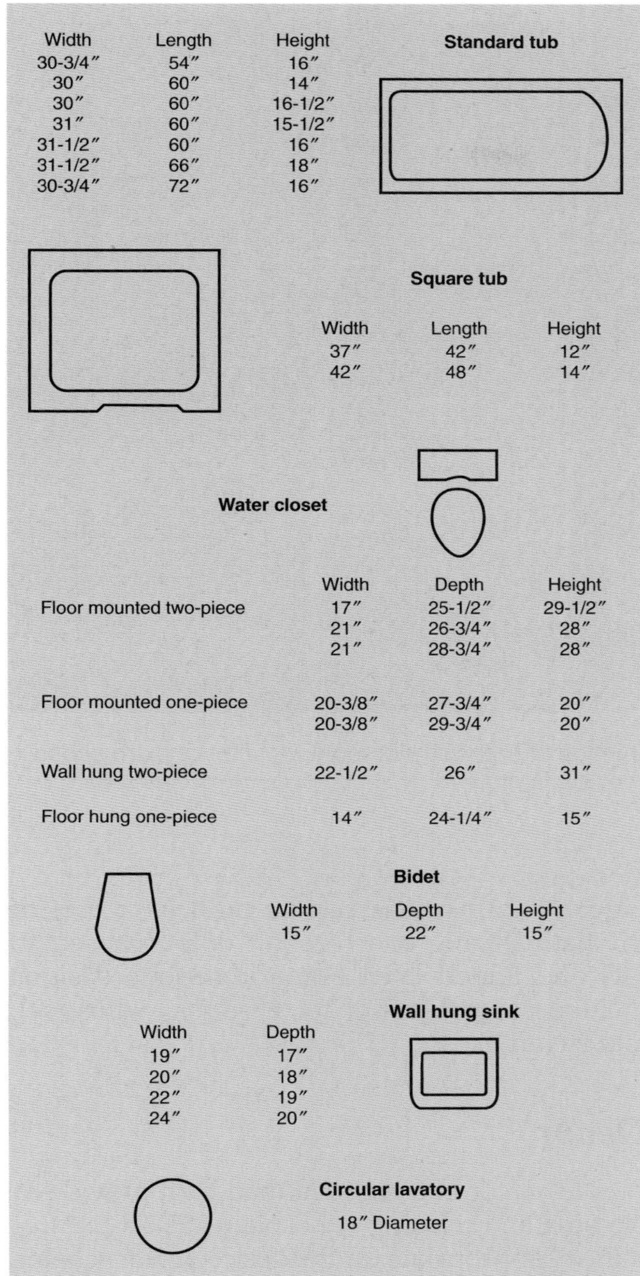

Goodheart-Willcox Publisher

Figure 8-18. Common sizes of bathroom fixtures.

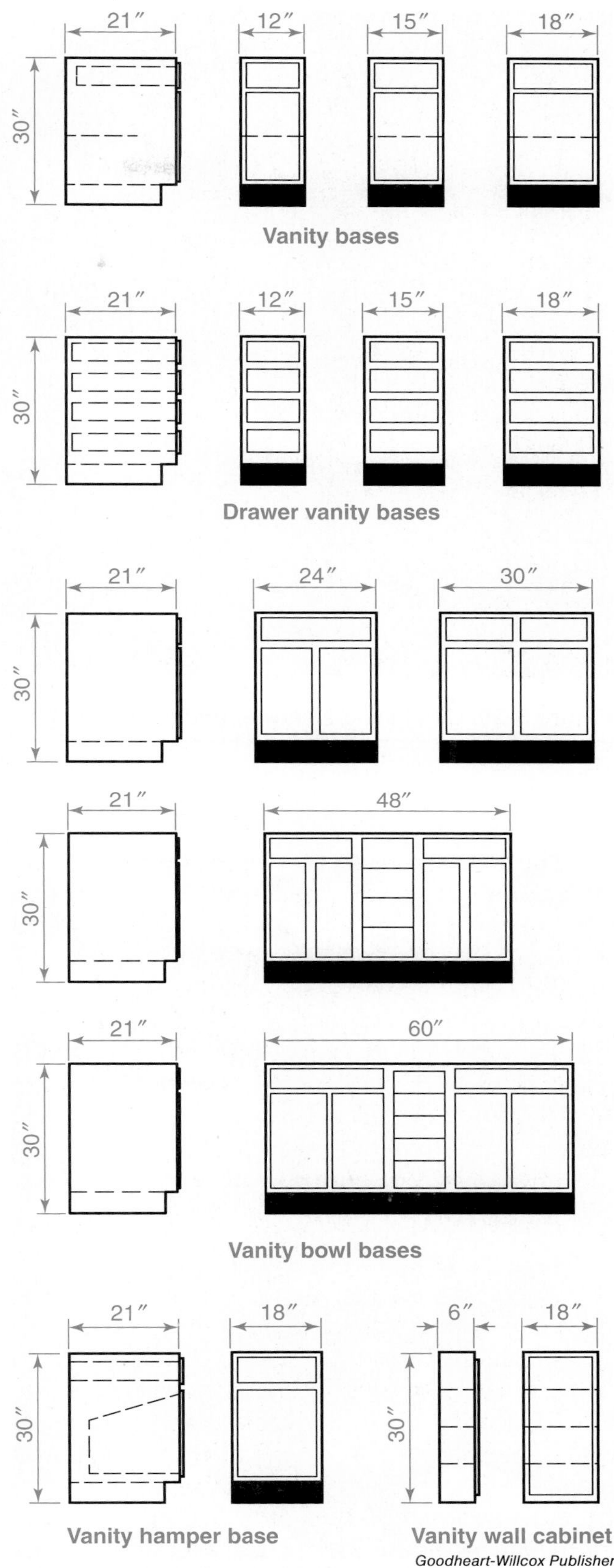

Goodheart-Willcox Publisher

Figure 8-19. Common sizes for bathroom vanities.

Additional Fixtures

Some luxury homes include a ***bidet*** in the bathrooms. See **Figure 8-21**. Usually, a bidet is installed only in the master bath. However, some home designs include a bidet in the main bath as well.

Whirlpools, hot tubs, and saunas can be installed in or near the bathroom. See

haveseen/Shutterstock.com

Figure 8-20. Combining a shower and tub offers the convenience of both without requiring a lot of extra space.

Mayer George Vladimirovich/Shutterstock.com

Figure 8-21. A luxurious master bathroom with a bidet next to the toilet.

Figure 8-22. Saunas can be built as a part of the bath during construction or purchased in kits and added later. Some luxurious designs include a combination of a sauna, whirlpool, and steam bath.

Décor

The décor of a well-planned bath provides a pleasing and relaxing atmosphere. Select fixtures that are appropriate for the desired color scheme or style of the room. Plants and art pieces may be added to enhance the beauty of the room.

Figure 8-23 shows a small bath that provides maximum convenience and practicality at a nominal cost. Economy is partially obtained by the supply and drains being placed on a single wall. Also, there is no wasted space in this functional bath. Open-shelf cabinetry helps add the illusion of space to the room. Also notice the bath seat that blends with the tub. This seat provides access for elderly people and people with limited mobility, without requiring a large amount of space.

photosphobos/Shutterstock.com

Figure 8-22. This high-end design includes an enlarged bath area with a full sauna. A sauna of this size must usually be designed into the house, rather than added later.

Safety

Safety should be a prime consideration when planning the bath. A well-planned bath is constructed from materials that are easy to clean and resistant to moisture, mildew, and mold. Flooring materials that become slick when wet should not be used. Devices should be installed in tub and shower faucets to control water temperature to eliminate scalding from hot water. Also, devices can be installed to control the water pressure so that when the cold water pressure is reduced, the hot water flow is automatically reduced. Non-shatter or safety glass should be used in shower and tub enclosures.

Accessibility

Wall-mounted toilets are more accessible for people in wheelchairs. A toilet seat that is 17″ to 19″ high is about the same height as most wheelchair seats and will provide for easy transfer. See **Figure 8-24**. Elevated toilet seats are also available to provide access. Many people are now installing ***comfort-height toilets*** in their

Photo courtesy of Kohler Co.

Figure 8-23. An example of a shower/tub combination that is accessible to people with limited mobility. Notice the four grab bars and the sliding bath seat.

Kevin Penhallow/Shutterstock.com

Figure 8-24. Notice the height of this toilet, which is fully equipped for use by people with various disabilities. The grab bar on the left swings up out of the way when not in use, but can be lowered to provide support when needed.

homes, even if the house is not being equipped for disabled access. The seats on these toilets range from 17″ to 19″ high. They make access easier not only for people in wheelchairs, but also for elderly people and people who have joint problems or other physical conditions.

Allow at least 27″ from the underside of the bathroom sink to the floor for wheelchair armrests. The top of the sink should be at a maximum height of 34″. If countertop sinks are used, insulate any exposed pipes to prevent burns. For easy reach, faucet handles should be a maximum of 20″ from the front of the sink. Lever-type handles provide greater usability.

If the home is being designed for a person in a wheelchair, the mirror should be tilted slightly downward or mounted low enough for a wheelchair user to see. Another option is to install a full-length mirror on a bathroom wall or door. A medicine cabinet should be mounted so that the top shelf is not more than 48″ from the floor. The cabinet should be lower if mounted over a counter or sink.

Bathtub rims should not be lower than 18″ from the floor to provide access from a wheelchair to the tub. Tubs may also have safety features such as nonskid bottoms and grab rails. In addition, various types of seats, stools, transfer seats, or lifts for use in bathtubs or showers are available. See **Figure 8-25**. Bathtubs are available with a built-in bath seat or platform on the opposite end of the tub from the drain. Walk-in bathtubs with built-in seats can make it easier for people with limited mobility to bathe.

Walk-in or "roll-in" shower stalls are also available for wheelchair users. In addition, special

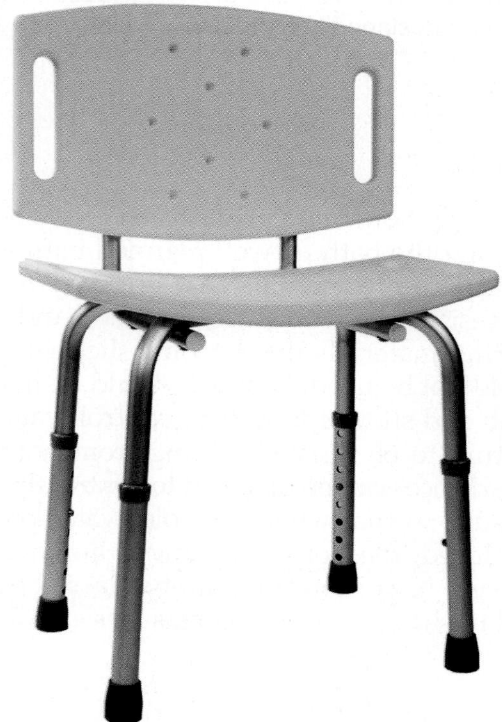

B. Speckart/Shutterstock.com

Figure 8-25. Adjustable bath chairs like this one allow people with limited mobility to use a bathtub without worrying about how to get in and out of the tub. The chair is placed in the tub, and the person slides from a wheelchair or the side of the tub onto the bath chair. The nonskid tips on the chair legs prevent the chair from slipping.

bathing wheelchairs that can be wheeled right into the shower area are available. See **Figure 8-26**. Some shower designs include a wall-mounted seat that allows people to transfer from a wheelchair to the seat. The seat folds against the wall when not in use. Placing a shower head over the center of the shower makes it more accessible for wheelchair users.

Special safety provisions should be made for anyone of limited mobility who might use the bathroom. This may include a specially designed shower or tub, as described earlier. In addition, grab bars should be provided, especially in the areas where the toilet, tub, and shower are located. Horizontal bars are designed for pushing up, while vertical bars are designed for pulling up. Grab bars must be well anchored. They should be 1-1/4″ to 2″ in diameter with a profile that is easy to grasp and contains no sharp edges. Grab bars should be no further than 1-1/2″ away from the wall. Refer again to **Figure 8-24**.

A B Brown/Shutterstock.com

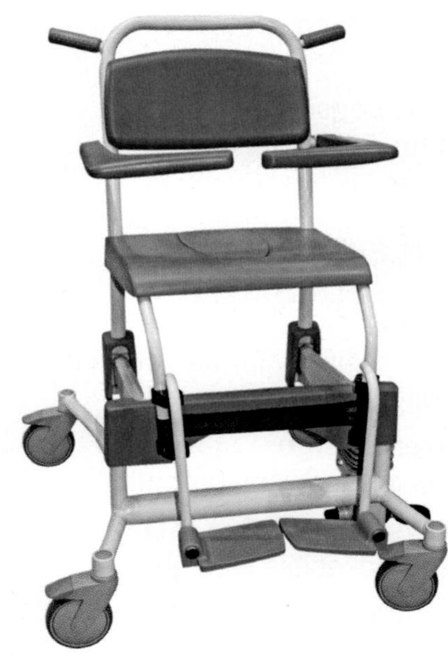

B daseaford/Shutterstock.com

Figure 8-26. A—This shower stall was designed for a wheelchair to be rolled in. The bench swings up out of the way if the person is in a shower wheelchair. Otherwise, the person transfers to the bench and the wheelchair is removed. B—A shower wheelchair that can remain in the shower while the water is running.

Summary

- The sleeping area includes bedrooms, bathrooms, and accessory rooms such as dressing rooms or saunas.
- The size of the family that will live in the house usually determines the number of bedrooms needed.
- When possible, closets should be located along interior walls.
- Ideally, bedrooms should have windows on two walls for cross ventilation.
- All homes require at least one bathroom, but most homes have two or more.
- All bathrooms must be ventilated by either a window or an exhaust fan.
- The primary bathroom fixtures are the sink (lavatory), toilet (water closet), and bathtub or shower.
- Safety is a prime consideration when planning a bathroom.

Internet Resources

Accessibility Design
Design ideas for accessibility for seniors and people with disabilities

Accessible Shower Design
Accessible designs for showers, bathtubs

Americans with Disabilities Act (ADA)
ADA Standards for Accessible Design

Home & Garden Television (HGTV)
Home design ideas

International Code Council (ICC)
Published building codes and standards

Jacuzzi
Bath fixtures

Kohler Company
Plumbing fixtures

Moen
Plumbing fixtures

Pfister
Plumbing fixtures

Sterling Plumbing
Plumbing fixtures

Review Questions

Answer the following questions using the information in this chapter.

1. Explain why it is better to design and build a house that has at least two bedrooms, even if only one of the bedrooms is currently needed.
2. Describe the characteristics of a split bedroom plan.
3. What is the minimum acceptable size for a bedroom according to the International Residential Code?
4. List four common types of doors generally used for closets.
5. Explain the difference between a 3/4 bath and a full bath.
6. What is the minimum number of bathrooms needed for a two-story house if all of the bedrooms are upstairs? How many bathrooms are needed for a large ranch house?
7. Describe the ventilation required for a bathroom.
8. List two electrical safety concerns that must always be addressed in a bathroom.
9. What is a comfort-height toilet, and when should you consider specifying one?
10. How much space should be allowed from the underside of the bathroom sink to the floor for wheelchair armrests?
11. List at least three safety features that should be included in a bathroom.
12. What are the specifications for a grab bar?

Suggested Activities

1. Design a small bathroom (5′ × 10′). Show the location and size of each fixture in a plan view.
2. Design and draft a plan view for a clothes closet that is 3′ deep and 8′ in length. Show the maximum door access, clothes rod, and shelf storage area. Refer to the illustrations in this chapter for examples.

3. Design and draft an average-size bedroom. Make a plan view drawing of the room. Include the bed, a dresser, a chest of drawers, and other furniture to meet the needs of your own activities. You may want to include a study or reading area.
4. Look through a number of home design and planning magazines for closet arrangements. Prepare a display of clippings that illustrates maximum use of closet space for clothes, shoes, and other apparel.
5. Locate agencies and organizations that specify requirements for bath facilities to be handicapped accessible. Enlist the help of your local librarian or use the Internet to find at least two different sources. Then, obtain a list of these requirements from each source. Finally, design and draft a bathroom for a disabled person that meets all of the requirements.
6. Using CADD, design and draft bedroom and bathroom symbols and add them to your symbol library for future use.
7. Select a floor plan of a house from a newspaper, magazine, or other literature. Using CADD, recreate the basic floor plan. Use the symbols in your symbol library to furnish the bedrooms. If you want to include something that is not in your symbol library, create a new symbol and add it to your symbol library.

Problem Solving Case Study

Mrs. Wilson has asked you to prepare a simple sketch of a proposed bathroom remodel. Her parents are moving in with her. Her mother is confined to a wheelchair, and her father walks with a cane. Mrs. Wilson has a room available with a private bath, shown in **Figure A**, but the bath needs to be remodeled to make it accessible for her parents. Consider the following questions:

1. Is this bathroom large enough to accommodate the necessary changes for wheelchair use?
2. Specifically, what changes would need to be made?

Make a sketch or a CADD drawing to show the changes you would make.

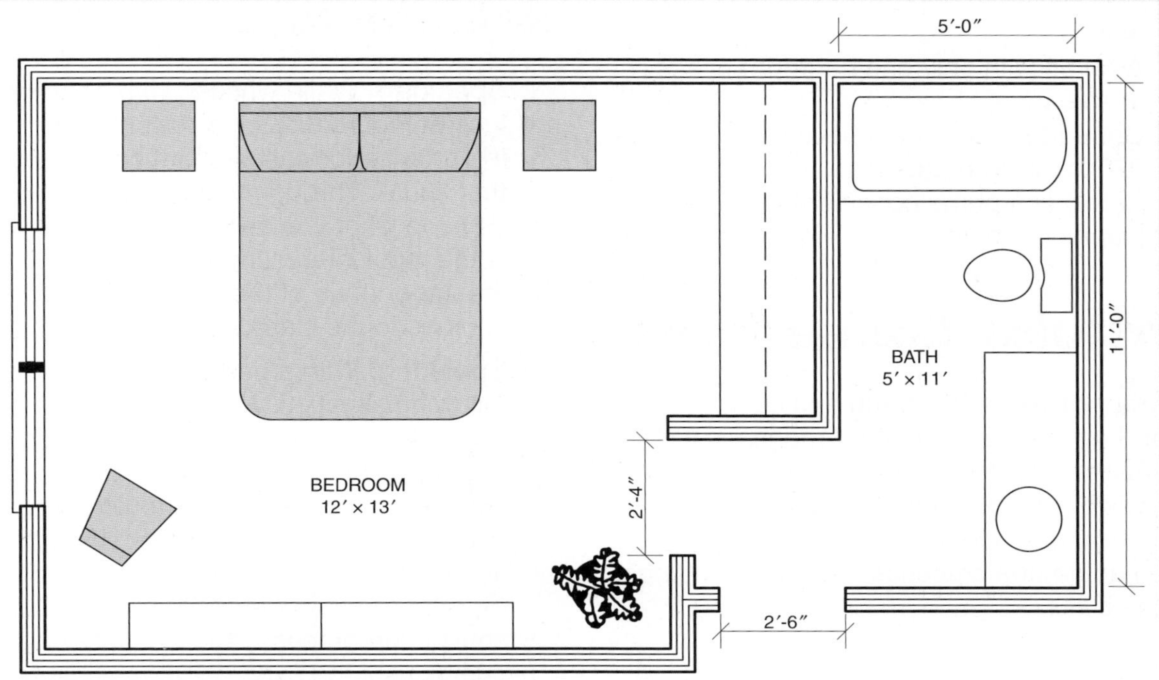

Goodheart-Willcox Publisher

Figure A. Use this plan to complete the Problem Solving Case Study.

ADDA Certification Prep

The following questions are presented in the style used in the American Design Drafting Association (ADDA) Drafter Certification Test. Answer the questions using the information in this chapter.

1. Which of the following rooms are considered part of the sleeping area of a home?
   A. Master bedroom
   B. Family room
   C. Bathroom
   D. Guest bedroom
   E. Sauna
   F. Dressing room
2. Which of the following statements are true?
   A. The largest bedroom is generally considered to be the master bedroom.
   B. All homes require at least one bathroom.
   C. The International Residential Code recommends 90 square feet as the minimum size of a bedroom.
   D. A minimum size bathroom is 10′ × 10′.
   E. All bathrooms are required to have ventilation.
3. Which of the following statements are *false*?
   A. The minimum depth of a clothes closet is 24″.
   B. A home with only one bedroom is easy to sell.
   C. Comfort-height toilets have seats that are 22″ to 24″ from the floor.
   D. Safety is a prime consideration when planning a bath.

Curricular Connections

1. **Language Arts.** Research and compose a report on the history of the Americans with Disabilities Act (ADA) and give examples of accessibility requirements provided in the ADA Standards for Accessible Design. Give a five-minute oral presentation of your findings to the class.

STEM Connections

1. **Math.** In recent years, major improvements have been made in the design of the flush toilet. High-efficiency toilets use only 1.28 gallons of water per flush. Older toilets used approximately 3.5 gallons per flush. A typical family of four flushes the toilet an average of 20 times per day. If a family of four replaced all of its toilets with high-efficiency toilets, how much water would the family save in one year?
2. **Technology.** In recent years, several new types of bathtubs and showers have been developed, including roll-in showers and walk-in bathtubs. Conduct research to find various bathtubs and showers designed specifically for people with physical challenges or limited mobility. Choose one that interests you and find out how it works and what requirements it has for space and installation. Write a report describing the specific model you investigated. Explain the advantages and disadvantages of using this fixture in a residence.

Communicating about Architecture

1. **Speaking.** While working with a partner, look at Figure 8-22 and describe the important information being conveyed by that figure. Through your collaboration, develop what you and your partner believe is the most interesting verbal description of the importance of the figure. Present your findings to the class.
2. **Speaking.** With a partner, role-play the following situation. An architect must explain to a client what it will take to convert a regular bathroom to one that is handicapped accessible. One student should play the role of the architect; the other should act as the client. Use the figures in this chapter for reference. As the architect explains the conversion process, the client should ask questions if the explanation is unclear. Switch roles and repeat the activity.

Chapter 9

Planning the Service Area

Objectives

After completing this chapter, you will be able to:

- Plan the service area of a home by applying good design principles.
- Design a functional kitchen to meet a family's needs.
- Plan an efficient laundry room.
- Describe appropriate dimensions for garage or carport space.

Key Terms

corridor kitchen
island kitchen
L-shaped kitchen
mudroom
overhead doors
peninsula kitchen
service area
straight-line kitchen
U-shaped kitchen
work centers
work triangle

The ***service area*** supplements the living and sleeping areas of the house. It supplies equipment and space for maintenance, storage, and service. The service area includes the kitchen, laundry room, mudroom, garage or carport, and utility or storage space. See **Figure 9-1**. Due to its varied functions, the service area requires careful thought and planning on the part of the designer and the client.

CADD systems can speed up the design of a home's service area. Specialized software and CADD add-ons are available for designing kitchens and creating pictorial representations of them. **Figure 9-2** shows two very different types of CADD drawings.

Kitchen

Food preparation is the intended purpose for a kitchen. Its use may, however, be extended to include informal dining and entertaining. The table and chairs in **Figure 9-2B** provide the perfect spot for a casual meal.

Kitchen design can present unique challenges. Inefficiency and added cost will result if the challenges are not solved. From the standpoint of cost, the kitchen is usually the most expensive room in the house per square foot. It also receives the most use of any room.

Kitchen Planning

Proper location of the kitchen is important. It is the prime element of the service area and its

Goodheart-Willcox Publisher

Figure 9-1. The service area of this house includes the garage, kitchen, laundry, and mudroom, a bathroom, and some storage.

A 3d Pictures/Shutterstock.com

B tangyan/Shutterstock.com

Figure 9-2. A—Many kitchen design packages allow you to create pictorial line drawings similar to this one. B—A rendering of a proposed kitchen design.

relation to other areas of the house requires careful evaluation. The kitchen should be located near the service entrance to the garage, because this is where groceries are brought into the house. Also, outside trash containers are usually located close to the service entrance. The kitchen should also be located near the dining room.

Planning an efficient kitchen involves the proper placement of appliances, adequate storage cabinets, and food preparation facilities. This placement creates the ***work centers***—the food preparation center, cleanup center, and cooking center. In designing kitchens, give considerable thought to the general location of each of the kitchen work centers. The arrangement should be logical and should minimize the amount of movement necessary to prepare a meal.

The ***work triangle*** is one measure of kitchen efficiency. It is determined by drawing a line from the front-center of the range to the refrigerator, from the refrigerator to the sink, and then from the sink back to the range. The lengths of these three lines are added together to produce the length of the work triangle, as shown in **Figure 9-3**. For an efficient kitchen, this distance should not exceed 21′.

Accessibility

Almost any kitchen can easily be adapted for a handicapped person. A kitchen that is handicapped accessible may follow the same layout as any other plan. However, the work surfaces should be lower, sinks should have clearance underneath, and cooking units should be accessible. See **Figure 9-4**.

Ample space must be provided for wheelchairs. Toe space of 6″ deep and 9″ high is needed under the cabinets for wheelchair footrests. Knee space of 30″ wide, 27″ high, and 25″ deep can be provided by an overhang or extended kitchen counter space.

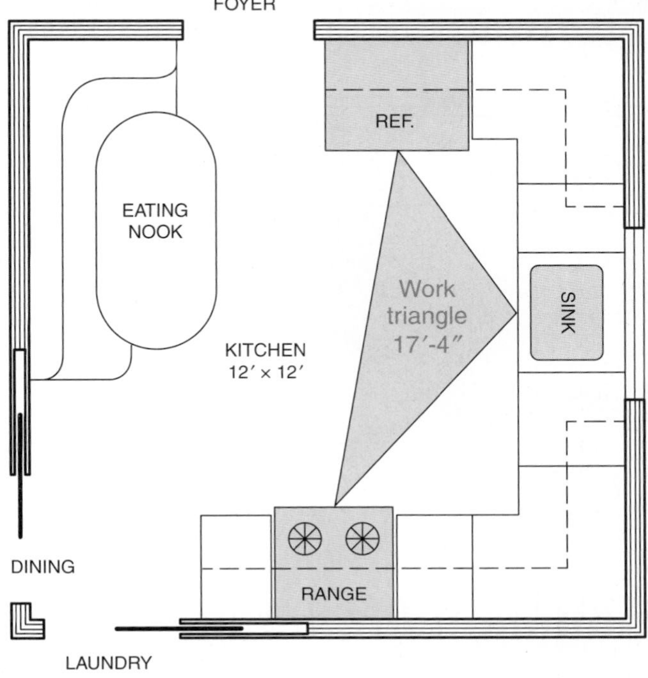

Goodheart-Willcox Publisher

Figure 9-3. The work triangle is a good measure of kitchen efficiency. The combined length of the three sides should not exceed 21 linear feet.

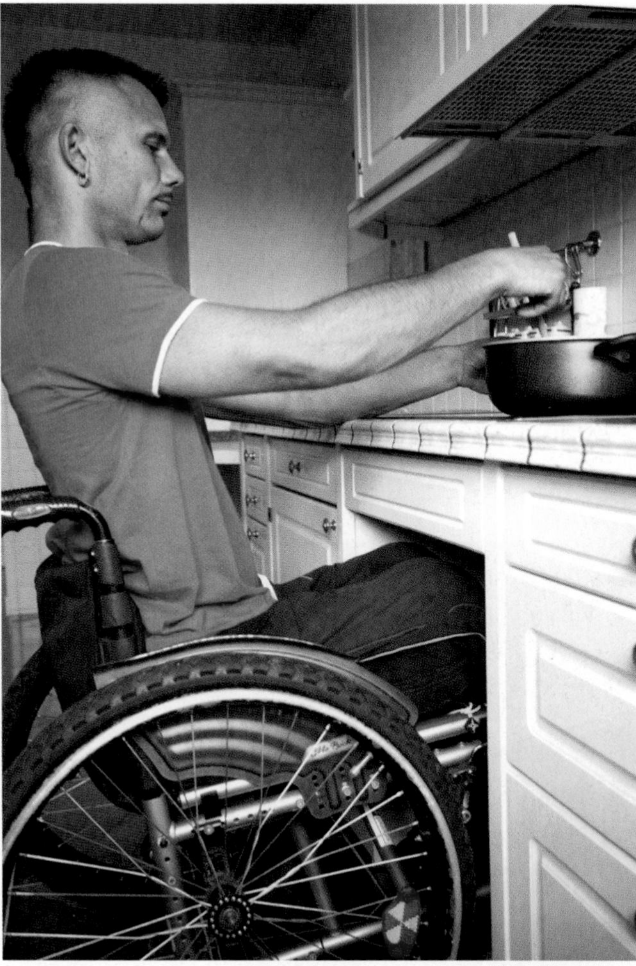

peppi18/Shutterstock.com

Figure 9-4. The knee space beneath this stove is one example of a design modification that can help make a kitchen accessible.

Kitchen Styles

There are six basic kitchen styles:

- Straight-line
- L-shaped
- Corridor
- U-shaped
- Peninsula
- Island

Each style has advantages and disadvantages. The style selected for a particular home may depend on the preferences of the person who will be spending the most time working in the kitchen.

Straight-Line Kitchen

The ***straight-line kitchen*** style is frequently used in small houses, cottages, and apartments. See **Figure 9-5**. Little space is required for this style and it usually provides for an efficient arrangement of kitchen facilities. Two disadvantages of the style are that it provides a limited amount of cabinet space and the result is usually not visually pleasing. The straight-line kitchen is seldom used unless space is very limited.

L-Shaped Kitchen

The ***L-shaped kitchen*** is located along two adjacent walls, as shown in **Figure 9-6**. This style results in an efficient workspace. Two work centers are generally located along one wall and the third on the adjoining wall. This style is not intended for large kitchens because the efficiency of the plan is lost if the walls are too long.

Corridor Kitchen

The ***corridor kitchen,*** also called a *galley kitchen,* is located on two walls opposite each

A

Rade Kovac/Shutterstock.com

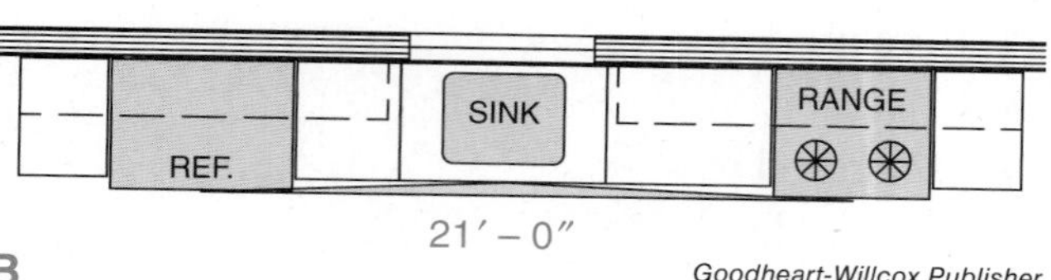

B

Goodheart-Willcox Publisher

Figure 9-5. A—An example of a straight-line kitchen. B—The work triangle in a straight-line kitchen.

A

mirounga/Shutterstock.com

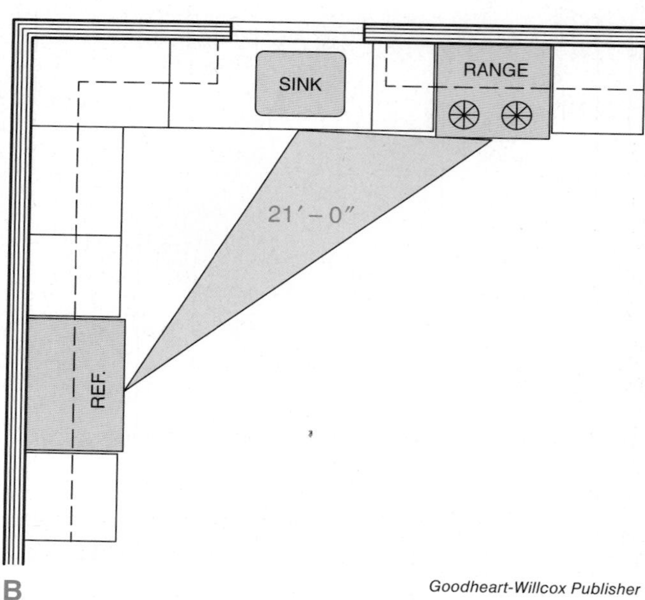

B

Goodheart-Willcox Publisher

Figure 9-6. A—An L-shaped kitchen is located on two adjoining walls. B—Notice the efficient, traffic-free work triangle.

other. Corridor kitchens are usually small to medium in size and are ideal for long, narrow rooms. See **Figure 9-7**. The open space between opposing cabinets should be at least four feet. A corridor kitchen tends to be an efficient workspace. However, the style is not recommended if traffic will be heavy through the kitchen.

U-Shaped Kitchen

The work triangle in a ***U-shaped kitchen*** is compact and functional. See **Figure 9-8**. Most U-shaped kitchens are medium in size with the open space between the legs of the U being about 5′ or 6′. If the kitchen is much larger than this, it becomes less efficient as the work triangle becomes larger. Two potential disadvantages of this type of kitchen design are that the resulting corner space may be difficult to access and more expensive corner cabinets may be required.

Peninsula Kitchen

The ***peninsula kitchen*** is a popular style because it provides plenty of workspace. See **Figure 9-9**. The peninsula is often used to join the dining area with the kitchen, using the peninsula as a divider. It may be used as the cooking center, food preparation center, or eating area. As in a U-shaped kitchen, the work triangle is small.

A Iriana Shiyan/Shutterstock.com

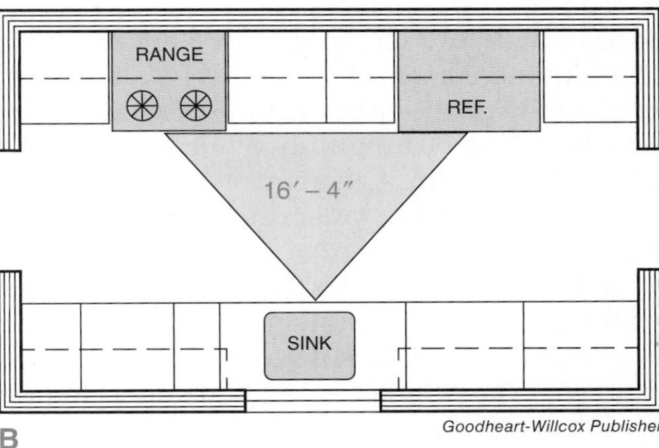

B Goodheart-Willcox Publisher

Figure 9-7. A—This typical corridor kitchen has plenty of cabinet space. B—The work triangle in a corridor kitchen is very efficient, unless many people will be traveling through it during meal preparation.

A eurobanks/Shutterstock.com

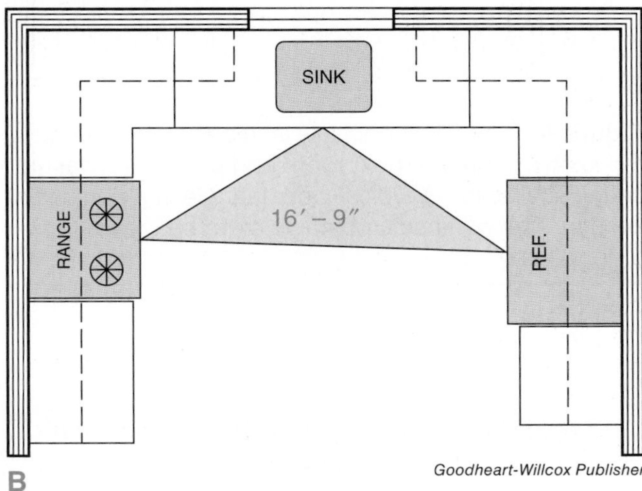

B Goodheart-Willcox Publisher

Figure 9-8. A—An example of a U-shaped kitchen. B—In a U-shaped kitchen, each of the three items in the work triangle may be on a different wall. Although this may lengthen the work triangle, it also allows ample counter space for food preparation.

A pics721/Shutterstock.com

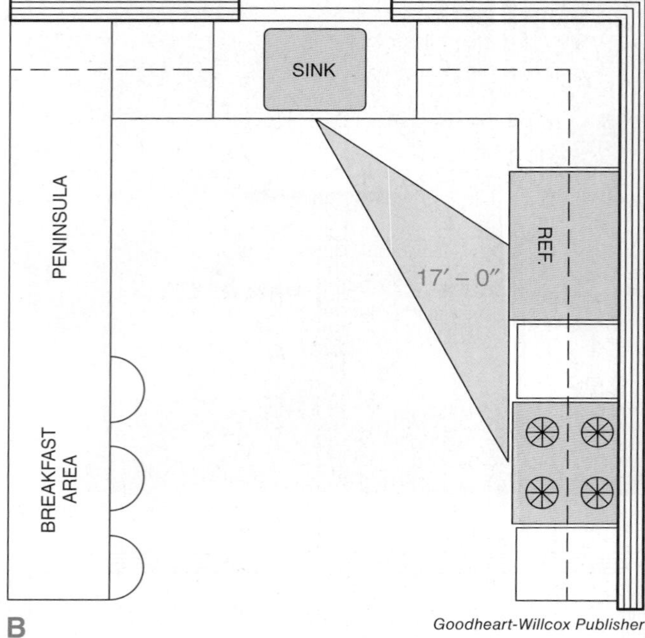

B Goodheart-Willcox Publisher

Figure 9-9. A—The peninsula in this kitchen separates the kitchen from the next room and provides a casual eating space. B—A typical work triangle in a peninsula kitchen. The peninsula contains extra space for food preparation.

Island Kitchen

The ***island kitchen*** may be a modification of the straight-line, L-shaped, or U-shaped kitchen style. See **Figure 9-10**. The island may house the sink, cooking center, or food preparation area. In some cases, it may also serve as a countertop or snack bar. At least 4′ of clearance should be allowed on all sides of the island for easy access.

Green Architecture

The Green Kitchen

The kitchen is one of the most active areas in the home for recycling. Most food packaging today can be recycled. Some communities allow you to mix all of your recyclables together, and others require that they be separated according to type.

To serve your architectural clients well, become familiar with the recycling rules in the communities for which you are designing homes. Then think about how you can design the kitchen to make recycling easier. For example, some cabinet manufacturers have base cabinets that hold two or three waste bins. Including one of these cabinets in a kitchen would make it easier for the homeowner to separate recyclable items.

Composters are another green design idea for the kitchen. Several companies now make small composters that can be used on a countertop or hidden in a base cabinet. Discuss these ideas with your clients at the design stage to determine which ones work best for them. Designing a kitchen to be green is much easier than trying to retrofit an existing kitchen.

Cabinets

Kitchen cabinets provide the majority of storage space in most kitchens. They are produced in standard sizes, but may be made to custom sizes if required. Most standard base cabinets are 34-1/2″ high and 24″ deep. They are available in width increments of 3″, such as 15″, 18″, or 21″. Wall cabinets are either 12″ or 13″ deep. They may be 12″ to 30″ high (in 3″ increments) and 12″ to 36″ wide (in 3″ increments). Wall cabinets are also produced in taller dimensions, some as tall as 45″.

Figure 9-11 illustrates the standard base and wall cabinets that most manufacturers produce as standard units. Be sure to check the specifications of the cabinets selected before drawing the kitchen plan.

Options for Accessibility

In base cabinets, compartmentalized drawers instead of shelves can bring the full depth of the

A

Chris Rodenberg Photography/Shutterstock.com

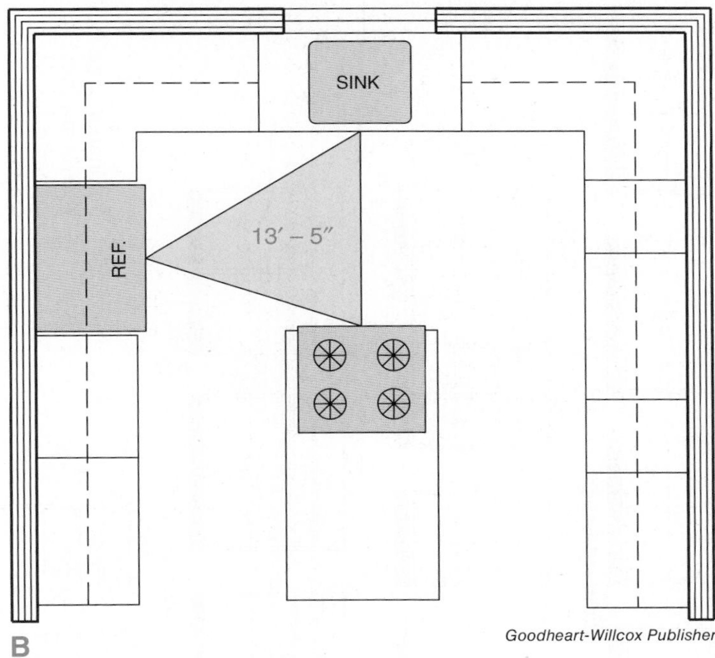

B

Goodheart-Willcox Publisher

Figure 9-10. A—The island in this kitchen holds the sink and doubles as an elegant eating area. B—Take care when designing an island kitchen to avoid interrupting the work triangle. This kitchen would be much less efficient if the stove was located on the left wall.

base cabinets within reach of a handicapped user. Roll-out shelves, racks, and baskets can be used to make base cabinets usable. See **Figure 9-12**. A lazy Susan is convenient for wall or base cabinets in corners.

It is difficult for people in wheelchairs to reach shelves higher than 48″. The bottom of wall cabinets should be situated so the first shelf can be reached from a seated position, usually not more than 17″ above the counter. Cabinets over stoves and refrigerators are exceptions. Mechanical assistance must be provided for these cabinets to be used by people in wheelchairs. Shelves in wall cabinets should be adjustable.

Kitchen Drawings

A typical section through the base and wall cabinets is shown in **Figure 9-13**. **Figure 9-14** shows the plan view and elevations of a kitchen. Notice how the wall and base cabinets are identified in the plan view. The numbers shown

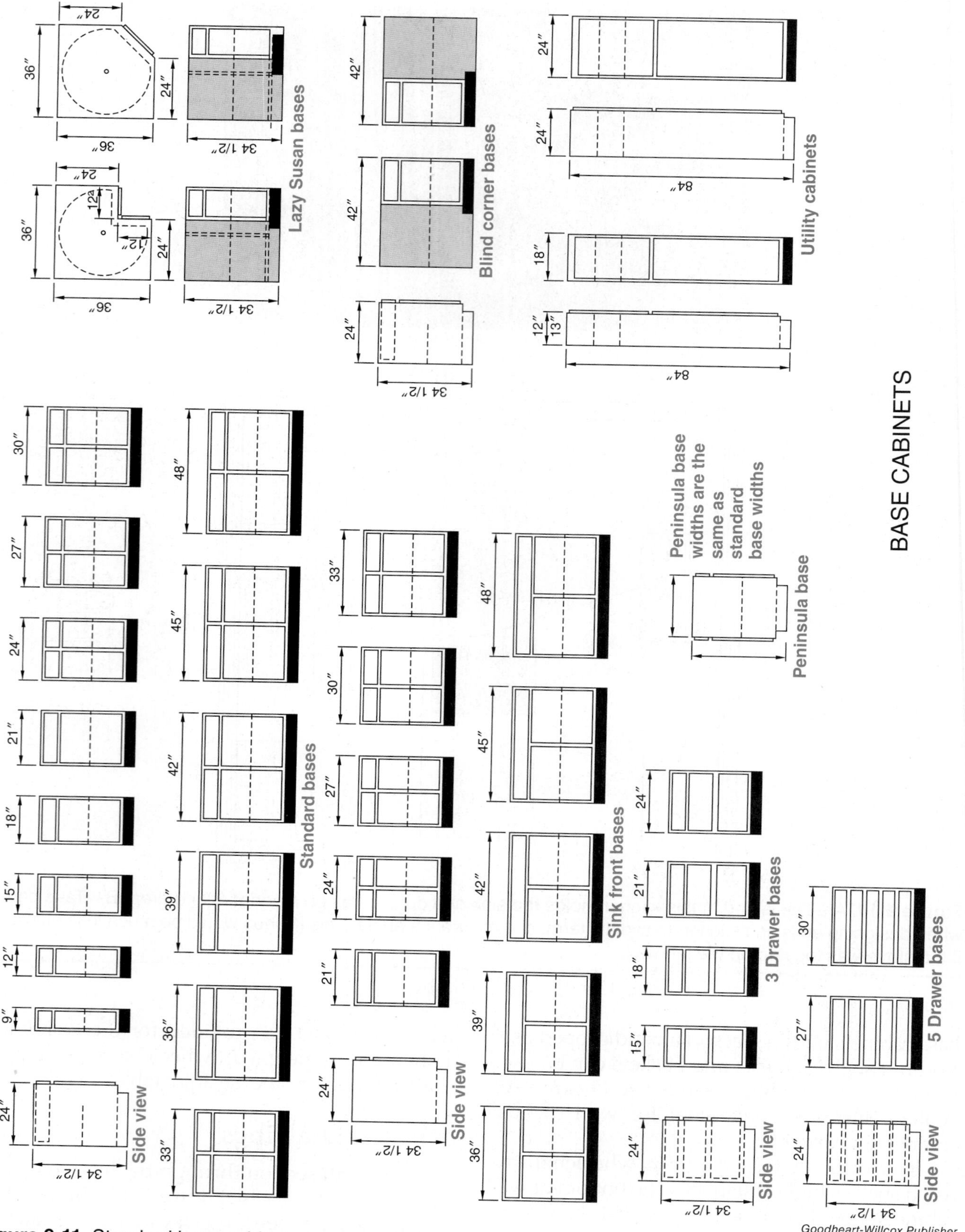

Figure 9-11. Standard base cabinet sizes and designs.

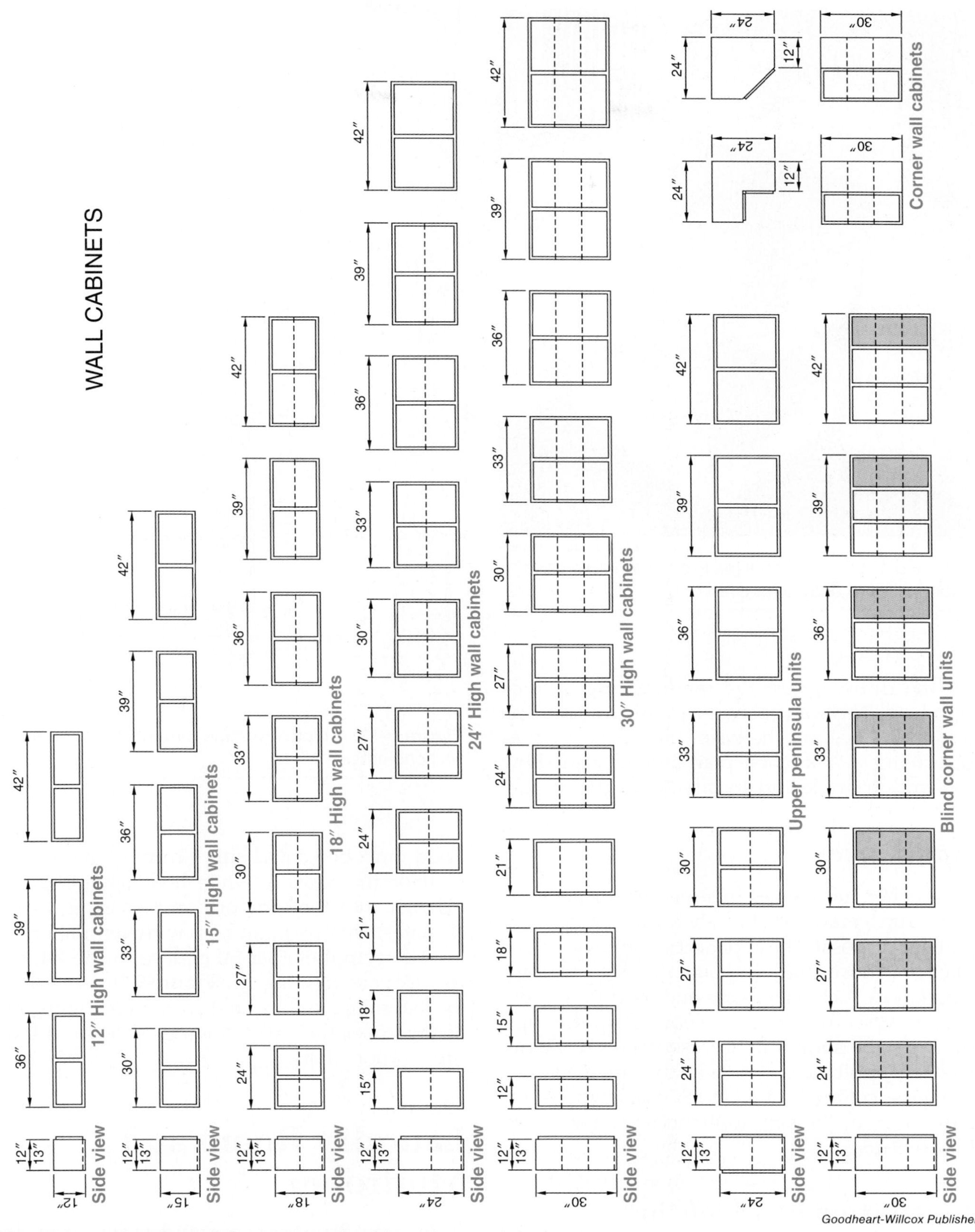

Figure 9-11. (Continued) Standard wall cabinet sizes and designs.

Olivier Le Queinec/Shutterstock.com

Figure 9-12. Roll-out shelves like these make base cabinets more usable for everyone.

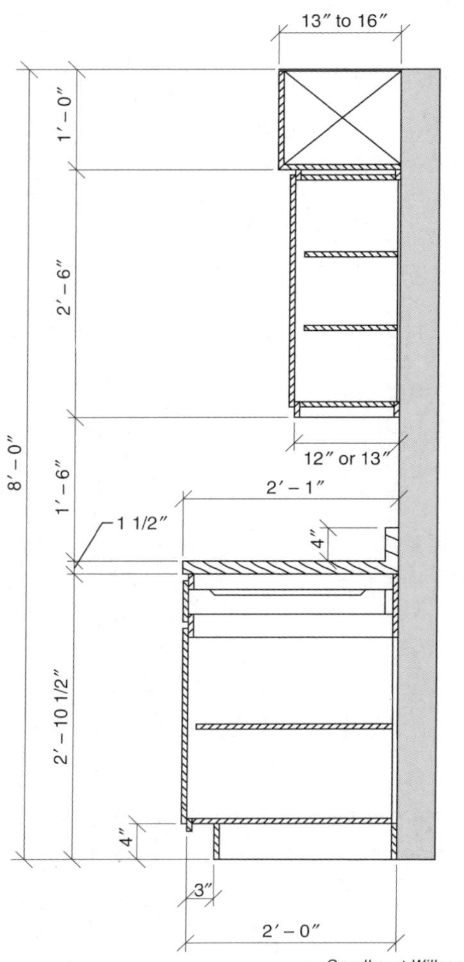

Goodheart-Willcox Publisher

Figure 9-13. A typical section through the base and wall cabinets.

on the drawing are the manufacturer's stock numbers. The wall cabinets are illustrated with a hidden line, and the base units are shown as object lines. A kitchen plan should also show the work triangle and specify its length.

Appliances

Kitchen appliances include the stove/range, oven, refrigerator, dishwasher, microwave, and garbage disposal. The appliances shown on a floor plan are those that are generally not movable. Appliances such as toasters and food processors are not typically shown on a floor plan, although they may be shown in a presentation drawing. Kitchen appliances are available in a variety of styles, colors, and sizes. Symbols and standard sizes of kitchen appliances are shown in **Figure 9-15**.

Ventilation and Lighting

Good ventilation is a must in the kitchen. When using a range hood with a fan, the range hood must be vented either through an outside wall or the roof. A range hood should never exhaust into the attic or crawl space. In some climates, windows can help with ventilation.

The activities that take place in the kitchen require good lighting. See **Figure 9-16**. In addition to the main ceiling fixtures, task lights are needed over the sink, cooking center, and food preparation areas.

Laundry Room and Mudroom

A laundry room provides an area for washing, drying, pressing, and folding clothes. See **Figure 9-17**. A spacious laundry room with

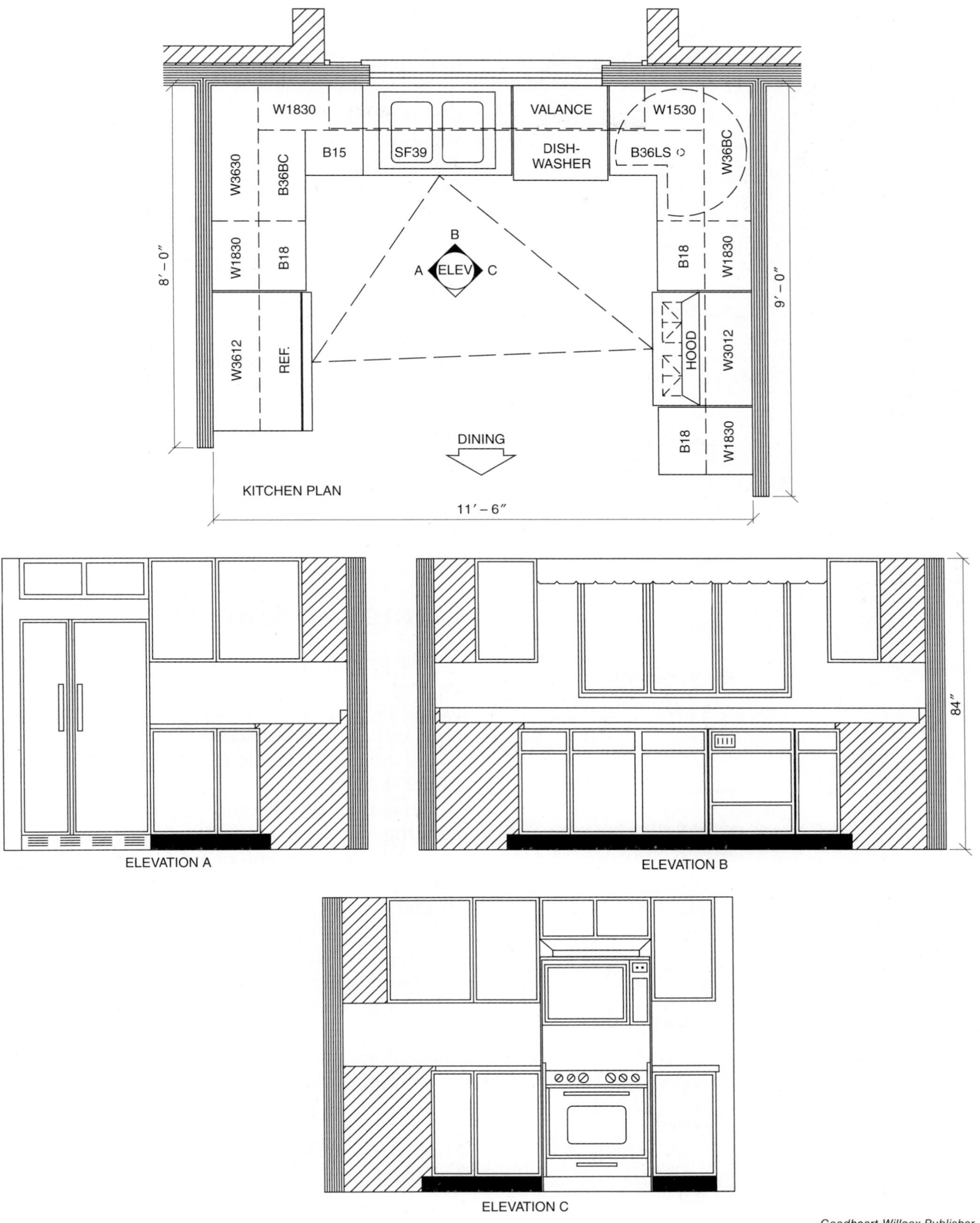

Goodheart-Willcox Publisher

Figure 9-14. Construction drawings for a kitchen.

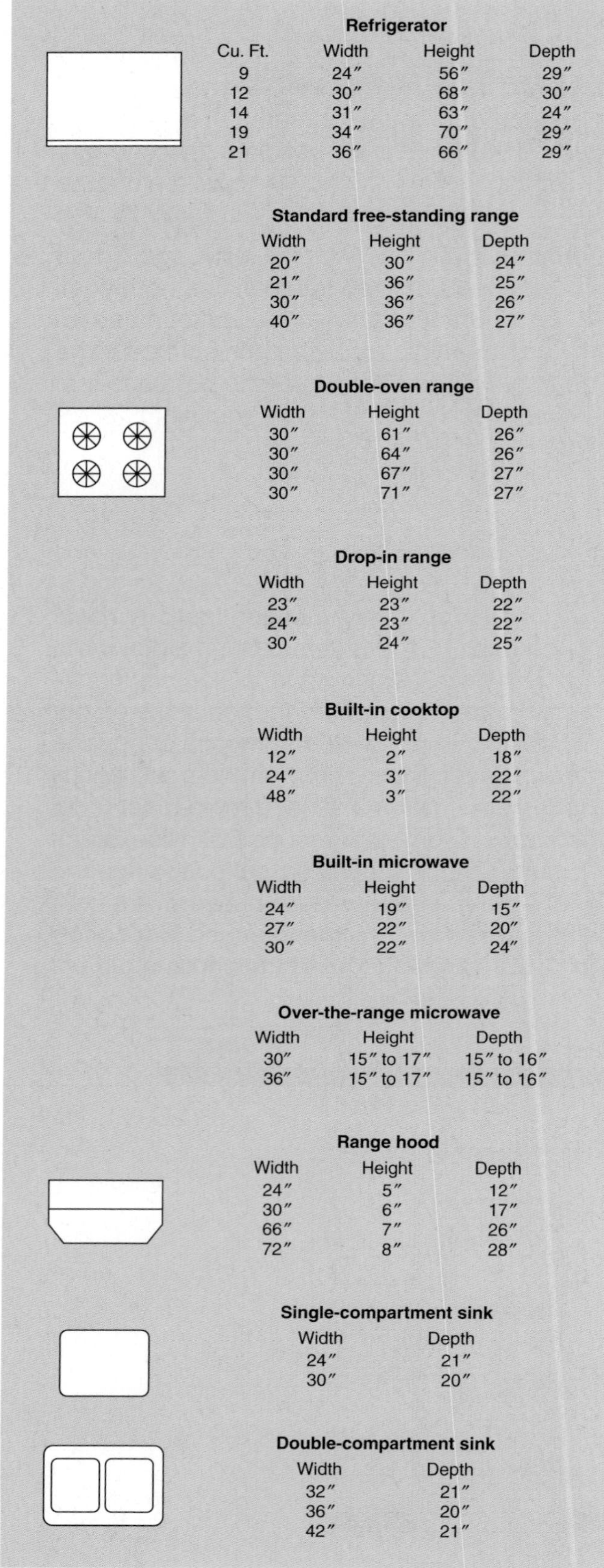

Refrigerator

Cu. Ft.	Width	Height	Depth
9	24″	56″	29″
12	30″	68″	30″
14	31″	63″	24″
19	34″	70″	29″
21	36″	66″	29″

Standard free-standing range

Width	Height	Depth
20″	30″	24″
21″	36″	25″
30″	36″	26″
40″	36″	27″

Double-oven range

Width	Height	Depth
30″	61″	26″
30″	64″	26″
30″	67″	27″
30″	71″	27″

Drop-in range

Width	Height	Depth
23″	23″	22″
24″	23″	22″
30″	24″	25″

Built-in cooktop

Width	Height	Depth
12″	2″	18″
24″	3″	22″
48″	3″	22″

Built-in microwave

Width	Height	Depth
24″	19″	15″
27″	22″	20″
30″	22″	24″

Over-the-range microwave

Width	Height	Depth
30″	15″ to 17″	15″ to 16″
36″	15″ to 17″	15″ to 16″

Range hood

Width	Height	Depth
24″	5″	12″
30″	6″	17″
66″	7″	26″
72″	8″	28″

Single-compartment sink

Width	Depth
24″	21″
30″	20″

Double-compartment sink

Width	Depth
32″	21″
36″	20″
42″	21″

Goodheart-Willcox Publisher

Figure 9-15. Appliance symbols and sizes.

base cabinets and wall cabinets can also serve as a storage area for extra sheets, towels, and other miscellaneous items, as shown in **Figure 9-18**.

If you are designing the home for someone who is physically challenged, be certain to plan for accessibility for the use of the washer and dryer and utilization of the base and wall cabinets. Doors leading into and out of the laundry room will also need to be a minimum of 2′-8″ wide. Sizes and shapes of common appliances and furnishings used in a laundry room are shown in **Figure 9-19**.

A ***mudroom*** is a room connected directly to a service entrance. Its purpose is to provide a place to remove and store overcoats, muddy boots, and other outdoor gear. Mudrooms are particularly useful in cold climates. Not only do they keep snowy gear out of the main part of the house, but they also provide a windbreak between the outside entry and the interior of the home. In some homes, the mudroom and laundry room may be combined.

Garage or Carport

The primary purpose of a garage or carport is to provide shelter for the homeowner's cars. The garage or carport may be small and simple or large and complex. In addition, it can be attached to the house or detached (freestanding). See **Figure 9-20**.

Several factors should be considered when deciding between a garage and a carport. A carport is open on one or more sides. As such, it provides less protection and security for the car than a garage. However, certain house styles look better with a carport, while other styles look better with a garage. In very cold or very hot climates, a garage may be more desirable in order to protect the cars against extreme temperatures. Carports are less expensive to build than garages and are often an excellent choice for temperate climates.

Size and Location

The size and location of the garage or carport will depend on the number of cars to be housed, the size and layout of the house, and the space available. A single-car facility may

Breadmaker/Shutterstock.com

Figure 9-16. The natural, ceiling, and task lighting in this kitchen provides enough light for food preparation at any time of day or night.

pics721/Shutterstock.com

Figure 9-17. Design the laundry room with plenty of space for ironing or folding clothes.

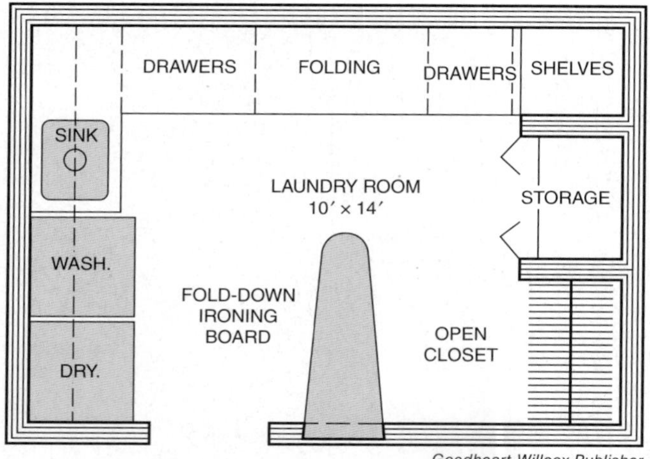

Goodheart-Willcox Publisher

Figure 9-18. A laundry room that provides space for washing, drying, ironing, folding, and storage.

Ironing board

Width	Length	Height
15″	54″	23″ – 37″

Laundry tub

Width	Depth	Height
24″	20″	34″
24″	23″	34″
28″	26″	34″

Dryer

Width	Depth	Height
29″	26″	43 1/2″

Washer

Width	Depth	Height
29″	26″	43 1/2″

Goodheart-Willcox Publisher

Figure 9-19. Symbols and sizes for common items used in a laundry room.

Employability

Honesty and Ethics in the Workplace

When you accept a job, your employer counts on you to be honest and act with integrity. Unfortunately, some people abuse this trust. For example, they may arrive at work a few minutes late every morning or leave a few minutes early in the afternoon. This may not sound like much, but someone who consistently arrives 5 minutes late and leaves 5 minutes early is cheating the employer out of 50 minutes of work time every week. Over the course of a year, this adds up to more than 40 hours—a full week! This is one form of dishonesty in the workplace.

Theft is another common form of dishonesty in the workplace. In many cases, it may be something small, such as a pen or a pad of sticky notes. Even though the item may not be worth much, theft is theft, and it costs employers millions of dollars each year.

A good employee is aware of these issues and takes care to avoid dishonesty in any form. But what if you notice someone else being dishonest? Do you report the individual to your supervisor? If you do choose to report it, will this jeopardize your working relationship with the accused employee? Will you feel guilty for reporting the issue? Will you question your decision to act in a responsible way? You should think about these issues so that you can act appropriately when such situations occur.

Activity

You have just started to work for an architectural design firm. The supervisor has assigned you to train with another employee who has two years of work experience with this firm. Your trainer is in charge of ordering and stocking the numerous office supplies that are in use at the firm. When the office supply company delivers a rather large order, you see your trainer loading three boxes of ink cartridges into her car. Should you confront the person with your knowledge of this alleged theft? Should you report this matter to the supervisor? Do you think this is a test on the trainer's part to see if you will say anything about this alleged theft? Answer these questions and share your opinions with the class.

Jessie Eldora Robertson/Shutterstock.com

A

Linda Johnsonbaugh/Shutterstock.com

B

Figure 9-20. A—This home includes a two-story carport. B—The garage in this house is designed to fit well with the style of the rest of the house.

range in size from 11′ × 19′ to 16′ × 25′. A space designed for two cars may be as small as 20′ × 20′ or as large as 25′ × 25′.

To be handicapped accessible, a garage or carport should be a minimum of 24′ long. This will provide space for a wheelchair to pass in front or in back of the car. A minimum of 5′ should be planned on the side of the car for a door to be fully opened and a wheelchair placed next to the car. A width of 12′ to 14-1/2′ is recommended for one car and a wheelchair. See **Figure 9-21**.

Goodheart-Willcox Publisher

Figure 9-21. The size of the garage or carport depends on its intended use. A—The single-car carport on the left is small with no storage facilities. The single-car carport on the right has ample storage and provides enough space for wheelchair access. B—The two-car garage on the left has adequate storage. The two-car garage on the right is much larger and can provide both storage and wheelchair access.

Design

A garage or carport should be designed as an integral part of the style of the total structure. This does not mean that the facility must be attached. However, if care is not taken, an attached or detached garage or carport can detract from the appearance of the house.

If the garage is detached, a walkway should be provided to the house. The walkway should lead to the service entrance and provide easy access to the kitchen. In some climates, a covered walkway may be desirable. See **Figure 9-22**.

Plan the garage or carport with storage in mind. Provide space for outdoor recreation equipment and gardening tools, if no other specific facility is provided for that purpose. Many homes have a garage that is full of tools and other equipment and the cars cannot be parked inside. This is often a result of poor planning.

As you design the garage or carport for a home, keep the following ideas in mind:

- The floor of the garage or carport should be concrete at least 4″ thick and reinforced with steel or wire mesh.

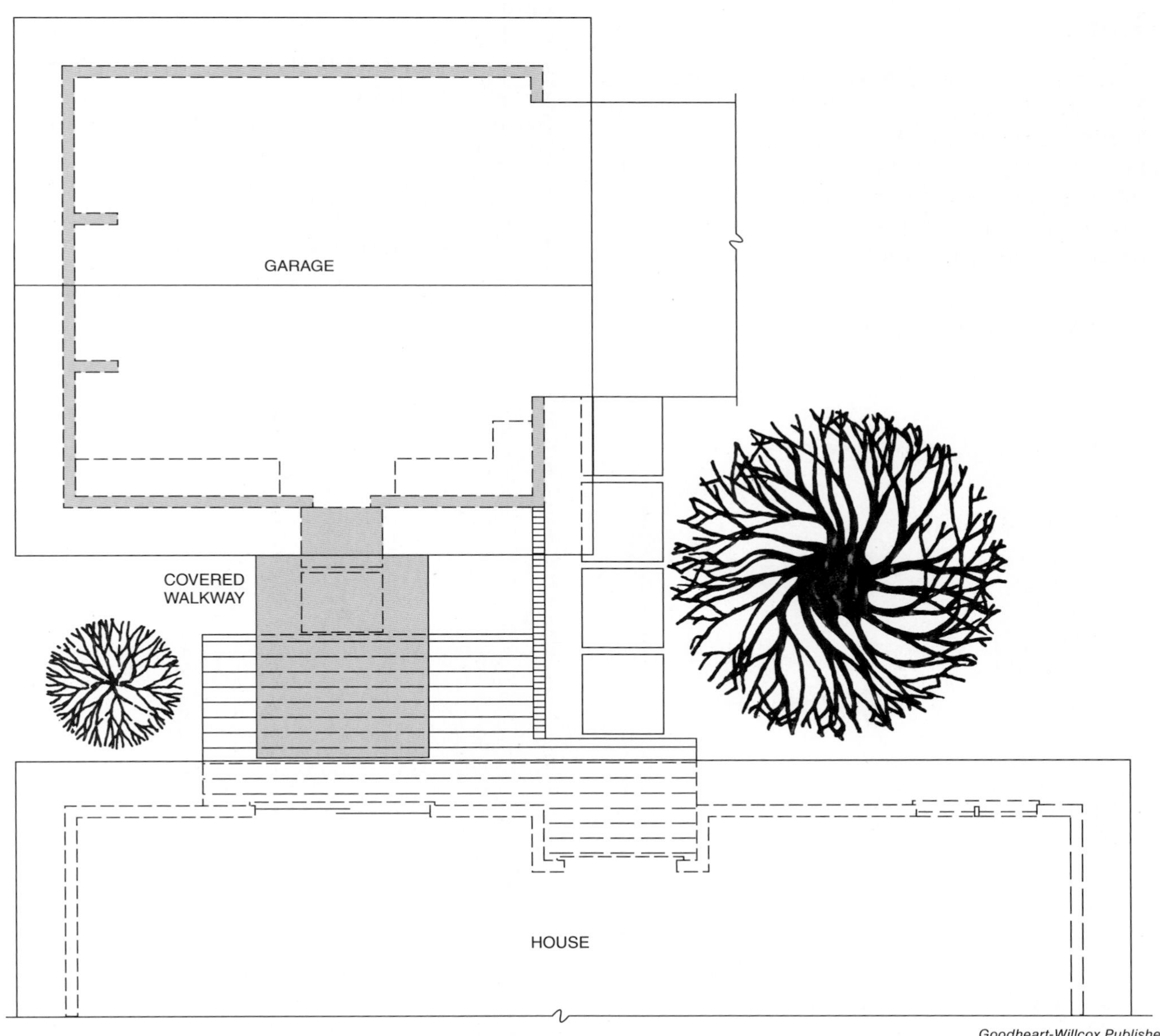

Goodheart-Willcox Publisher

Figure 9-22. This plan shows a detached garage with a covered walkway to the house.

- Good floor drainage is important. However, many cities prohibit a floor drain in the garage.
- Include an ample number of windows for ventilation and natural lighting in a garage.
- Supplement natural lighting with artificial lighting.
- If the garage is attached to the house, be sure to check the local building codes for special requirements regarding fire protection.
- Be sure to plan the garage or carport for a standard-size car, even though the prospective owner may have a compact car. If necessary, adjust the design for larger vehicles.

Doors

Garage doors are often called ***overhead doors***. They are available in standard sizes and come in wood, fiberglass, plastic or vinyl, aluminum, and steel. Wood has been a traditional choice and is still preferred by many, but it requires frequent painting and is expensive. Metal doors are inexpensive and require little maintenance. Fiberglass is very durable and may allow some natural light to come through even when the door is closed.

A single-car garage door is usually 8′ or 9′ wide and 7′ or 8′ high. A two-car garage door is usually 16′ wide and 7′ or 8′ high. Recreational vehicles may require a higher garage door. Garage doors are also produced in widths of 18′.

Driveway

The driveway should be planned along with the garage. The minimum driveway width is 10′ for a single-car garage. A two-car garage requires a wider driveway, at least at the entrance to the garage.

If space is available, a turnaround is often recommended. This allows the driver to turn the vehicle around when exiting the driveway and drive forward onto the street. Backing the vehicle directly onto the street should be avoided when possible, but is not always achievable due to the constraints of a subdivision. **Figure 9-23** shows two turnarounds with dimensions.

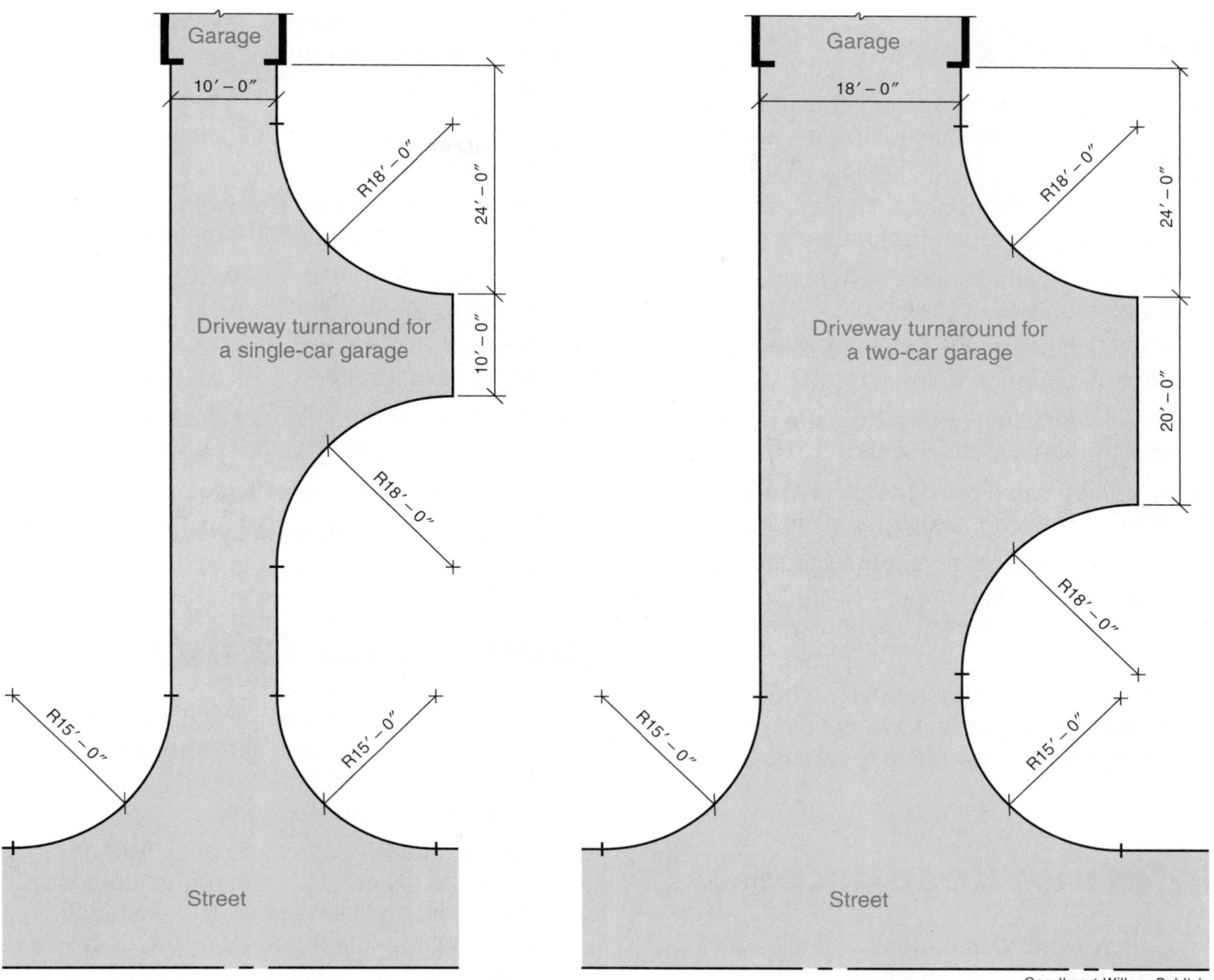

Goodheart-Willcox Publisher

Figure 9-23. Standard dimensions of turnarounds for single- and two-car garages.

Summary

- The service area supplies equipment and space for maintenance, storage, and service.
- Planning an efficient kitchen involves the proper placement of appliances, storage cabinets, and food preparation facilities.
- For an efficient kitchen work space, the work triangle should not exceed 21′.
- The kitchen should be located near the service entrance to the garage.
- Good ventilation and lighting are important requirements in the kitchen.
- A laundry room provides an area for washing, drying, pressing, folding, and storing clothes.
- The size and location of the garage or carport depends on the number of cars to be housed, the size and layout of the house, and the space available.
- If the garage is attached to the house, be sure to check the local building codes for special requirements regarding fire protection.

Internet Resources

Americans with Disabilities Act (ADA)
ADA Standards for Accessible Design

Kraftmaid
Source for kitchen cabinets and ideas

Merillat
Source for kitchen cabinets and ideas

Overhead Door
Residential and commercial garage doors

Raynor
Residential and commercial garage doors

Whirlpool
Appliances and kitchen collections

Review Questions

Answer the following questions using the information in this chapter.

1. Which rooms or areas in a house are included in the service area?
2. What is a *work triangle*, and how does it affect kitchen design?
3. Identify the six basic kitchen styles.
4. How is a straight-line kitchen different from a corridor kitchen?
5. What is the difference between an L-shaped kitchen and a U-shaped kitchen?
6. How high and deep are most standard base cabinets for kitchens?
7. Name three options to make a kitchen more accessible for a person in a wheelchair.
8. Which kitchen appliances are routinely shown on the floor plan for a kitchen?
9. What is the purpose of a *mudroom*?
10. What is the difference between a garage and a carport?

Suggested Activities

1. Visit an appliance store and obtain literature on the newest kitchen appliance designs. Prepare a bulletin board display using pictures from the literature.
2. Secure specifications and price lists of kitchen cabinets from a manufacturer. Using CADD, plan a kitchen using the cabinets from that manufacturer. Draw the plan view and elevations. Identify the cabinets using the manufacturer's numbers and dimension the drawings. Calculate the total cost of the cabinets you specified.
3. Obtain three floor plans from magazines or other sources. Analyze the provisions for laundering clothes in each plan. Explain the strengths and weaknesses of each. Propose improvements where needed.
4. Measure the length and width of a standard-size car. Using CADD, design a full-size plan (top) view symbol for a car.
5. Using CADD, design a single-car garage that provides adequate space for the car you drew in the previous activity, plus space for extra storage. Use the car symbol to help plan the garage.
6. Using CADD, draw kitchen symbols from this chapter. Add these to your symbol library for future use.

Problem Solving Case Study

A longtime client has come to your architectural office to discuss ideas for an addition to his home. His home is at the edge of a large wooded park that has many trails and provides much entertainment for his family. However, his entire family is tired of having to clean up the debris that they constantly track in from the surrounding woods. Also, the washer and dryer are currently in the garage, which makes laundry a hot chore in the summer and a cold one in the winter. He wants to add a combination mudroom and laundry room, but he wants to keep the laundry area separate from the dirtier mudroom area.

Given this basic preliminary information, answer the following questions.

1. What type of additional service area square footage would you recommend for this client?
2. What cabinets and appliances will be needed?
3. How could you keep the laundry area separate from the mudroom area?

Certification Prep

The following questions are presented in the style used in the American Design Drafting Association (ADDA) Drafter Certification Test. Answer the questions using the information in this chapter.

1. Which of the following are considered to be kitchen styles?
   A. Corridor
   B. U-shaped
   C. Split-level
   D. Contemporary
   E. Island
2. Which of the following statements are true?
   A. The minimum driveway width is 12′ for a single-car garage.
   B. The straight-line kitchen style is frequently used in small houses, cottages, and apartments.
   C. The peninsula kitchen is a popular style because it provides plenty of workspace.
   D. *Mudroom* is another term for a laundry room.
3. Which of the following statements are *false*?
   A. The kitchen should be located near the service entrance to the garage.
   B. Most U-shaped kitchens are large, with the open space between the legs of the U being about 9′ or 10′.
   C. Careful consideration of all specifications and design requirements is an essential part of developing the kitchen plan.
   D. To be handicapped accessible, a garage should be a minimum of 20′ long.

Curricular Connections

1. **Social Science.** Culture has played an important part in the development of service areas in residential architectural design. Research cultural influences on the inclusion of kitchens, pantries, and laundry rooms from the earliest home designs to the most modern. Collect illustrations of each, and assemble them into an illustrated presentation for PowerPoint. In your presentation, include a summary section that compares and contrasts these styles.
2. **Language Arts.** If you were going to design a home for yourself, which of the six basic kitchen styles would you use? Why? Would you make any changes to the basic style? Prepare a three-minute speech and present it to the class. Use visual aids to illustrate your points.

STEM Connections

1. **Technology.** Think about the technology that is used every day in the kitchen. For example, people cook with stovetops, ovens, or ranges, keep food chilled or frozen in a refrigerator, wash dishes in a dishwasher, and grind up wastes in a food disposer. You may take these items for granted, but the first practical dishwasher for residential use was not introduced until the 1920s. Dishwashers did not become standard kitchen appliances until as late as the 1970s.

   Today, technology is advancing at a rapid rate. How will technology affect the appliances we use in the kitchen? Conduct research to find out what ideas inventors are developing for kitchen appliances. Then write an essay describing what you think the kitchen of the future will be like.

Communicating about Architecture

1. **Reading.** With a partner, make flash cards for the different types of kitchens discussed in this chapter. Place an illustration of the kitchen style on the front of the card. On the back of the card, write the kitchen name and description. Take turns quizzing one another on the kitchen types.
2. **Reading and Speaking.** Interview an architect. Ask the architect to describe a typical day at work. Here are some questions you might ask:
   - What is the work environment like?
   - What are the job duties?
   - What kinds of challenges does the architect have to deal with?
   - What other types of professionals does the architect work with?

   Report your findings to the class, giving reasons why you would or would not want to pursue a career similar to that of the person you interviewed.

Chapter 10

Designing for Health and Safety

Objectives

After completing this chapter, you will be able to:

- Identify fire hazards around the home and explain preventive measures.
- Explain the hazards associated with carbon monoxide and discuss preventive measures.
- Explain the hazards associated with radon in residential housing and describe preventive measures.
- Discuss problems in residential structures associated with excess moisture.
- Compare building techniques used in different areas of the United States to minimize damage from natural and weather-related disasters.
- Identify safety tips to increase general home safety.

Key Terms

carbon monoxide (CO)
condensation
earthquake zone
flash flood
floodplain
hurricane code
hurricane tie
Indoor Radon Abatement Act
mold
radon
radon mitigation
safe room
seismic area
smoke detector
storm surge
ventilation
water vapor

Contrary to what you may think, the home is generally not a safe place. Experts say that more injuries occur in the home than anywhere else. Therefore, an intensive effort should be made to design structures that are safe for the occupants. Building codes help ensure the structural strength and safety of a home. This chapter focuses on certain additional areas, beyond structural integrity, that deserve special consideration.

Smoke and Fire Detection

Structural fires are a significant danger to every home. See **Figure 10-1**. According to the "Home Structure Fires" report released in 2013 by the National Fire Protection Association (NFPA), an average of 366,600 residential fires occurred each year from 2007 to 2011. Residential fires resulted in an average of 2570 deaths per year during this time. The leading cause of residential fires is cooking equipment, followed closely by people falling asleep while smoking. Other common causes include:

- Using flammable materials improperly to start a fire.
- Operating unsafe electrical or heating equipment.
- Placing flammable materials too close to a potential source of ignition.

linerpics/Shutterstock.com

Figure 10-1. No residential home is immune to the danger of fire, no matter how well the homeowners maintain it.

Fire Prevention

Some common sense rules can help prevent a fire in your home. Here are a few of the most obvious ones.

- Keep a fire extinguisher in an obvious location and check it periodically to be sure it works. This will not prevent a fire, but it may allow you to extinguish a small fire before it gets out of control.
- Do not overload electrical circuits. Overloaded circuits generate excess heat that may ignite nearby materials. See **Figure 10-2**.
- Have your heating system inspected yearly. A dirty or improperly operating heating system can ignite a fire.
- Keep matches and lighters out of the hands of children.
- Store flammable liquids in approved containers.
- Dispose of trash on a regular schedule. An accumulation of trash can be fuel for a fire.
- Select upholstered furniture that is fire-resistant.
- Use seasoned wood in wood-burning stoves and fireplaces. Green wood creates creosote buildup, which can lead to a chimney fire.
- Have fireplaces and wood-burning stoves cleaned on a regular basis.

Smoke Detectors

A ***smoke detector*** is a small appliance that gives a loud warning signal when it detects smoke in the house. Detectors for the hearing impaired

Barnaby Chambers/Shutterstock.com

Figure 10-2. In today's world of computers, smartphones, portable media players, and other electronic gadgets, people tend to use power strips like these to charge their electronics. Use power strips with great caution to avoid overloading the circuit. Never plug one power strip into another one, as shown here.

set off an ultra-bright strobe light. There are two basic types of smoke detectors—*ionization* and *photoelectric*. The ionization type responds more rapidly to fires in which flames are visible, but the photoelectric detector is faster in detecting a smoldering or slow-burning fire. Both types provide early warning of a fire.

Make sure your home has an adequate number of detection devices to provide real protection. Fewer than one-third of all homes have sufficient smoke alarms. According to the US Consumer Product Safety Commission, you need at least one smoke detector on each floor of the house, including the basement and finished attic, and detectors should be installed in each bedroom and outside sleeping areas. The International Residential Code specifies that smoke detectors be located in each bedroom, in the immediate area outside the bedrooms, and on each additional level, including basements and habitable attics.

On the first floor, the living room or family room is often a good central location for a smoke detector. Another central spot is the top of the stairwell between the first and second floors. In this location, a detector will "sniff out" the first signs of a fire on either floor and sound an early warning. For detailed instructions on where to install detectors, be sure to refer to the specific smoke detector model's user guide.

Some smoke alarms are powered by batteries or by household current with a battery backup. See **Figure 10-3**. If a battery runs down, a chirping detector alerts you to replace the battery. New lithium batteries last about 10 years, but you must still check each device at least once a year to see that it is working properly. Your life may depend on it.

Serenethos/Shutterstock.com

Figure 10-3. Replace 9-volt batteries in smoke detectors once a year, even if they are only a backup system in case of power failure.

Fire Safety Code Requirements

Model building codes specify minimum requirements for fire safety. Requirements commonly cited by building codes for fire safety include the following:

- Every occupied room in a residence must have at least two exits. One of these exits must be a doorway. Also, bedrooms located in basements must be directly accessible to the outside.
- Folding stairs, a ladder, or a trapdoor cannot be the only access to an occupied room.
- Every bedroom must have a window that can be easily opened by hand from the inside, unless the room has two interior exits or a direct exterior door. The window must have a clear opening of at least five square feet, no less than 20″ in width and 24″ in height, and must be no more than 44″ from the floor to the bottom of the window.
- Exit paths from bedrooms to exits must be at least 3′ wide.
- Exit paths from any room must not pass through a space that is subject to locking or a room controlled by another family.
- All exit doors must be at least 24″ wide.
- All stairs must be at least 36″ wide with treads at least 10″ wide and risers not more than 7-3/4″ high.
- Quick-opening devices must be used on all storm windows, screens, and burglar guards.
- Inside quick-release catches must be used as door-locking devices for easy exit.

- Bathroom door locks must provide for opening from the outside without a special key. See **Figure 10-4**.
- Children must be able to easily open closet doors from the inside.
- Smoke detectors should be installed in bedrooms, outside each sleeping area, and on every level of the house used for occupancy.
- Escape must not be blocked in the event of a malfunction of a combustion heater or stove.

More information is available from the NFPA. Also, check your local building code for additional requirements. Many areas, such as large metropolitan areas, may have codes that exceed these requirements.

Fire Extinguishers

Every residence should have at least one functioning fire extinguisher. Place the fire extinguisher where it can be found easily when needed. Fire extinguishers are classified according to the type of fire on which they are to be used. The Class A extinguisher should be used for fires involving paper, wood, fabric, and other ordinary combustible materials. Class B extinguishers are to be used for burning liquids, such as a grease fire. Class C extinguishers are for use on electrical fires. Many fire extinguishers are labeled ABC and can be used on all of these types of fires. **Figure 10-5** provides more detail about the different types of fire extinguishers.

Goodheart-Willcox Publisher

Figure 10-4. This bathroom door lock set can be opened from the outside with any slender probe or "key."

Carbon Monoxide (CO) Detection

Carbon monoxide (CO) is an odorless, tasteless, invisible gas that is potentially deadly. Carbon monoxide consists of one atom each of carbon (C) and oxygen (O). Dangerous CO concentrations may be produced by improperly vented wood stoves, gas or oil furnaces, fireplaces, gas ranges, clothes dryers, water heaters, space heaters, charcoal grills, or even cars in an attached garage.

The risk posed by properly installed and functioning appliances is minimal. However, sloppy installation, damaged equipment, or improper construction practices can allow CO to enter the living space in harmful concentrations. Today's more energy-efficient, airtight home designs can compound the problem by trapping CO-polluted air in the home.

Carbon Monoxide Poisoning

Carbon monoxide is absorbed into the body through the lungs and binds to the hemoglobin in red blood cells. This reduces the blood's ability to transport oxygen. Eventually, CO displaces enough oxygen to result in suffocation, brain damage, or death. One-third of all survivors of CO poisoning have lasting memory disorders or personality changes. In addition, heart attacks have been associated with high CO levels.

CO concentrations are measured in parts per million (ppm). A CO concentration of 15,000 ppm can kill you in minutes, and longer exposures to small concentrations are also dangerous. The longer exposure allows the CO to build up to lethal concentrations in the blood.

Symptoms of CO poisoning include headaches, drowsiness, fatigue, nausea, and vomiting. Since these symptoms can be mistaken easily for flu, some health experts believe that CO poisoning has been underreported. Medical experts estimate that one-third of all cases of CO poisoning go undetected. According to the Centers for Disease Control and Prevention, accidental exposure to CO in the home contributes to more than 400 deaths annually. In addition, more than 20,000 persons in the United States seek medical attention because of CO inhalation.

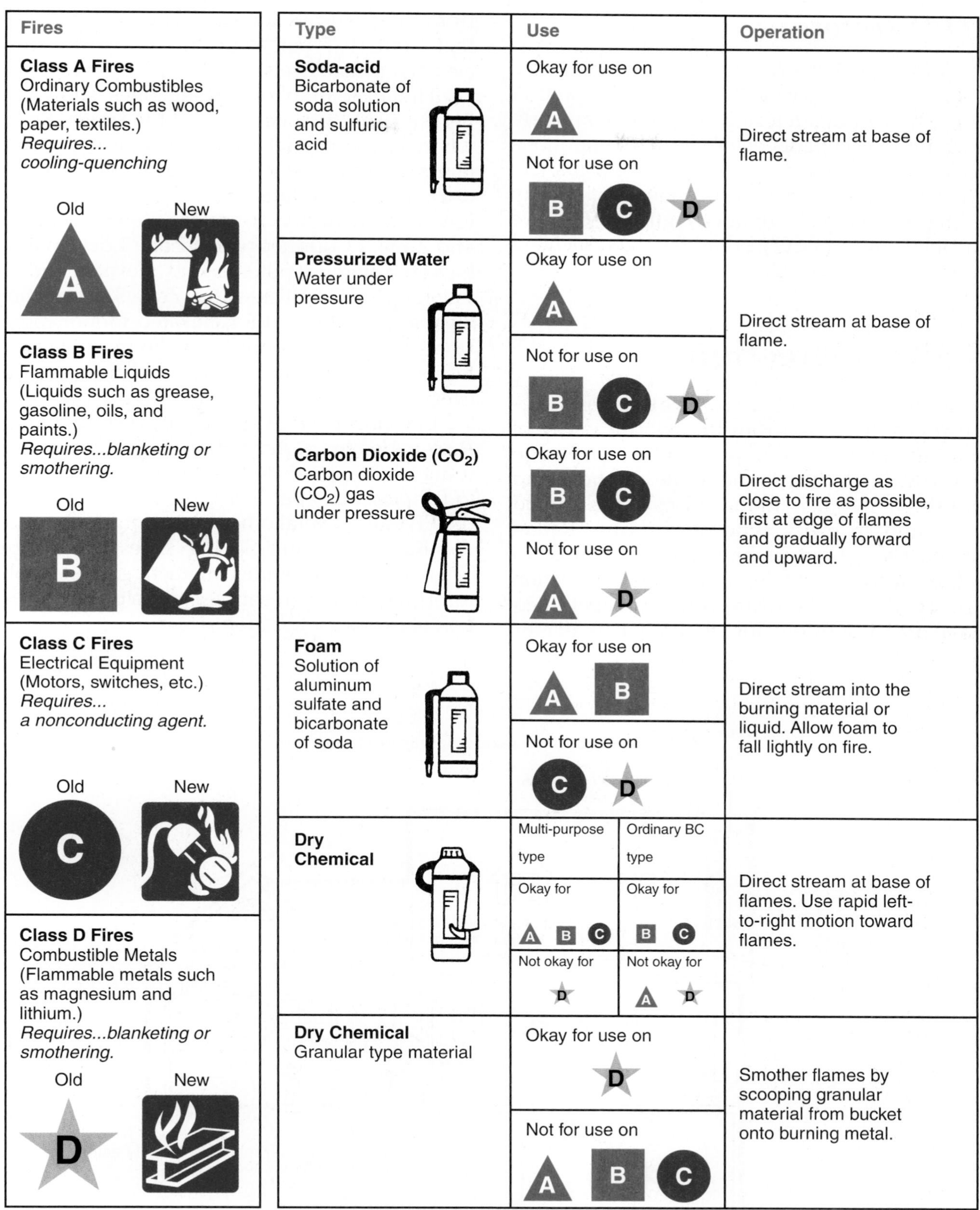

Fires
Class A Fires Ordinary Combustibles (Materials such as wood, paper, textiles.) *Requires... cooling-quenching* Old: A   New
Class B Fires Flammable Liquids (Liquids such as grease, gasoline, oils, and paints.) *Requires...blanketing or smothering.* Old: B   New
Class C Fires Electrical Equipment (Motors, switches, etc.) *Requires... a nonconducting agent.* Old: C   New
Class D Fires Combustible Metals (Flammable metals such as magnesium and lithium.) *Requires...blanketing or smothering.* Old: D   New

Type	Use	Operation
Soda-acid Bicarbonate of soda solution and sulfuric acid	Okay for use on A Not for use on B C D	Direct stream at base of flame.
Pressurized Water Water under pressure	Okay for use on A Not for use on B C D	Direct stream at base of flame.
Carbon Dioxide (CO_2) Carbon dioxide (CO_2) gas under pressure	Okay for use on B C Not for use on A D	Direct discharge as close to fire as possible, first at edge of flames and gradually forward and upward.
Foam Solution of aluminum sulfate and bicarbonate of soda	Okay for use on A B Not for use on C D	Direct stream into the burning material or liquid. Allow foam to fall lightly on fire.
Dry Chemical	Multi-purpose type Okay for A B C Not okay for D Ordinary BC type Okay for B C Not okay for A D	Direct stream at base of flames. Use rapid left-to-right motion toward flames.
Dry Chemical Granular type material	Okay for use on D Not for use on A B C	Smother flames by scooping granular material from bucket onto burning metal.

Goodheart-Willcox Publisher

Figure 10-5. The different classes of fires and the types of fire extinguishers that can be used on each.

CO Detectors

A CO detector is reasonably priced insurance against unnecessary health risks in the home. A properly working detector can provide an early warning to occupants before gas concentrations reach a dangerous level. Like smoke alarms, CO detectors should be mounted on the hallway ceiling outside the bedrooms. **Figure 10-6** shows possible sources of CO gas and the recommended locations of CO detectors.

Radon Detection

Radon is an invisible, odorless, tasteless, radioactive gas. It comes from the natural decay of uranium found in soil, rock, and water. Radon moves through the ground to the air above and into the home. It is found all over the United States and in every type of building. Radon can be dangerous in high concentrations. In fact, according to the Environmental Protection Agency (EPA) and the Surgeon General's Office, radon is responsible for about 21,000 deaths from lung cancer each year. The EPA estimates that 1 out of 15 homes in the United States has elevated radon levels.

The EPA map of radon zones shown in **Figure 10-7** illustrates areas of the United States where the potential exists for elevated radon levels. The map assigns zone designations to the counties in each state. There are three zone designations identified by color—Zone 1, Zone 2, and Zone 3. Counties with a Zone 1 designation have the highest potential for elevated indoor radon levels. Counties with a Zone 3 designation have a low potential for elevated indoor radon levels. However, as noted on the map, elevated levels of radon have been found in homes in every state.

In October 1988, Congress passed the ***Indoor Radon Abatement Act***, setting the goal of reducing indoor radon levels to those of outdoor air—0.2 to 0.5 picocuries per liter (pCi/L) of air. In 2008, the EPA and several other organizations founded the Radon Leaders Saving Lives Campaign. This campaign provides interactive online tools, information, and resources to help reduce the risk of exposure to radon.

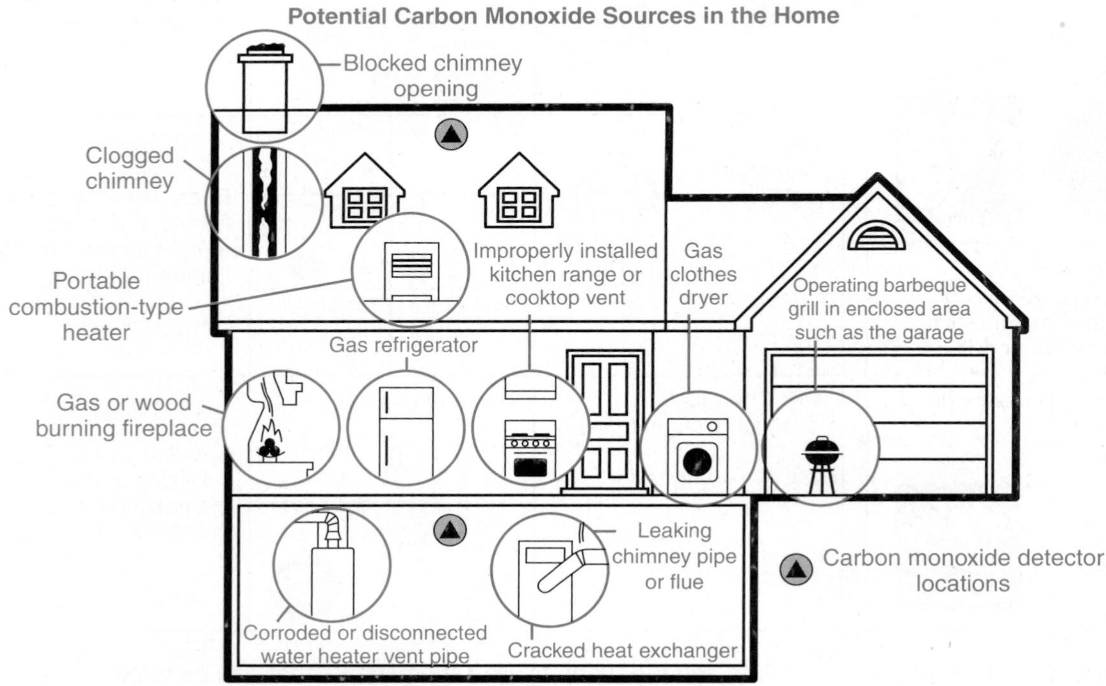

Provided by First Alert®

Figure 10-6. This drawing identifies potential carbon monoxide sources in the home and where carbon monoxide detectors should be located.

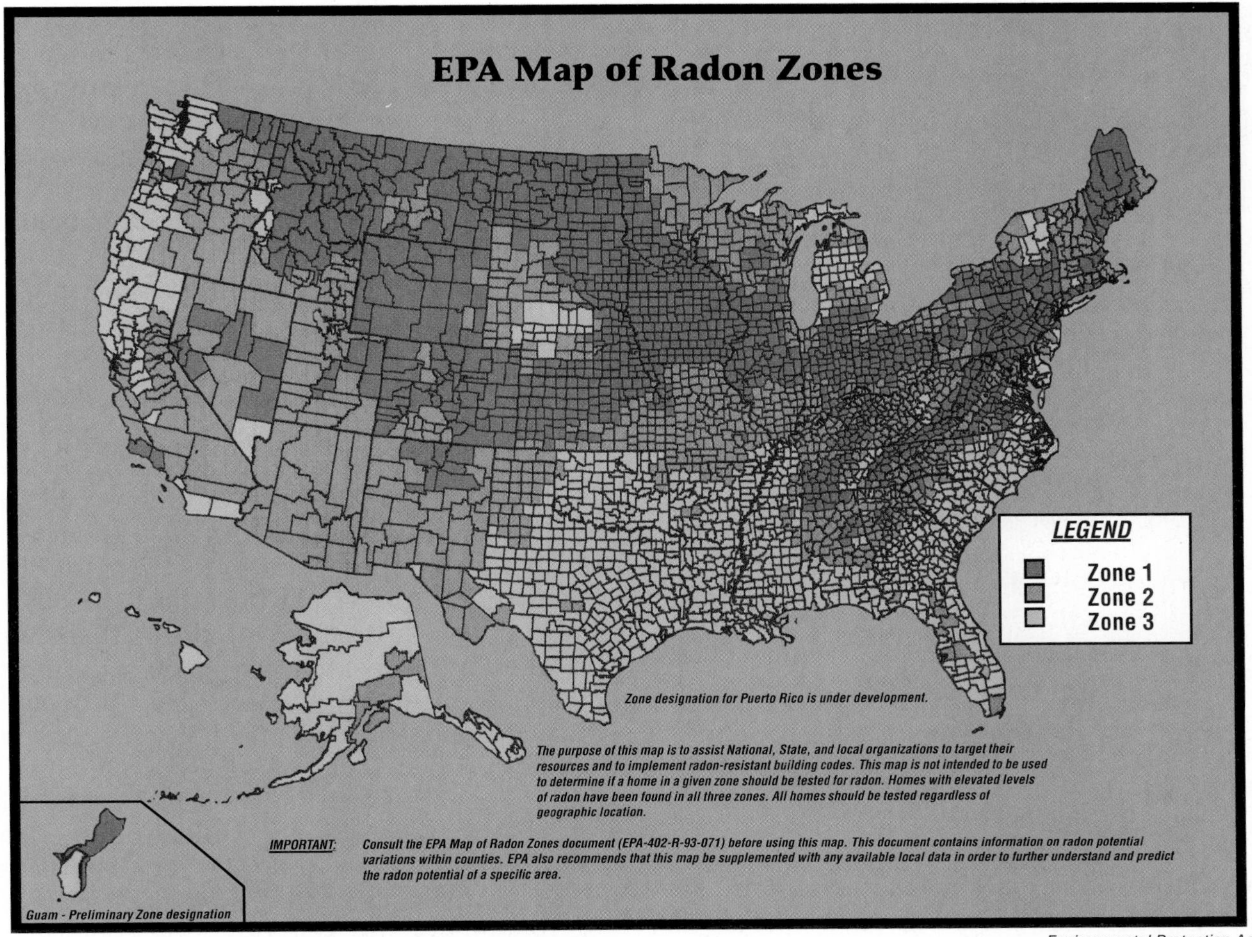

Environmental Protection Agency

Figure 10-7. This map from the Environmental Protection Agency shows radon level designation zones for counties in the United States.

Radon in the Home

Any home, whether old or new, can be subject to high levels of radon. Radon enters the home through cracks in solid floors and walls, construction joints, gaps in suspended floors, gaps around service pipes, cavities inside walls, and the water supply. Typically, radon levels from water are not as great as those from soil. The rate at which radon enters a home depends on the amount of radon in the soil, the number of cracks and openings between the home and the soil, and ventilation in the home.

Fresh air dilutes radon. When homes are closed up for winter heating or summer air conditioning, the radon levels start to build. Unoccupied homes trap and build up higher levels than homes that are occupied.

Radon Testing

The EPA recommends that radon levels be checked in all homes. The test is very simple and requires only a few minutes to administer. Several kinds of testing devices are available. See **Figure 10-8**. The two general types of testing devices are short-term and long-term. When selecting a test kit, look for the statement "Meets EPA Requirements" on the package.

Short-term testing requires 2 to 90 days, depending on the device. An advantage of using a short-term device is that the results of the test are available within a short period of time. A disadvantage of this type of testing device is that it does not provide year-round average radon levels. Radon levels vary from day to day and from season to season.

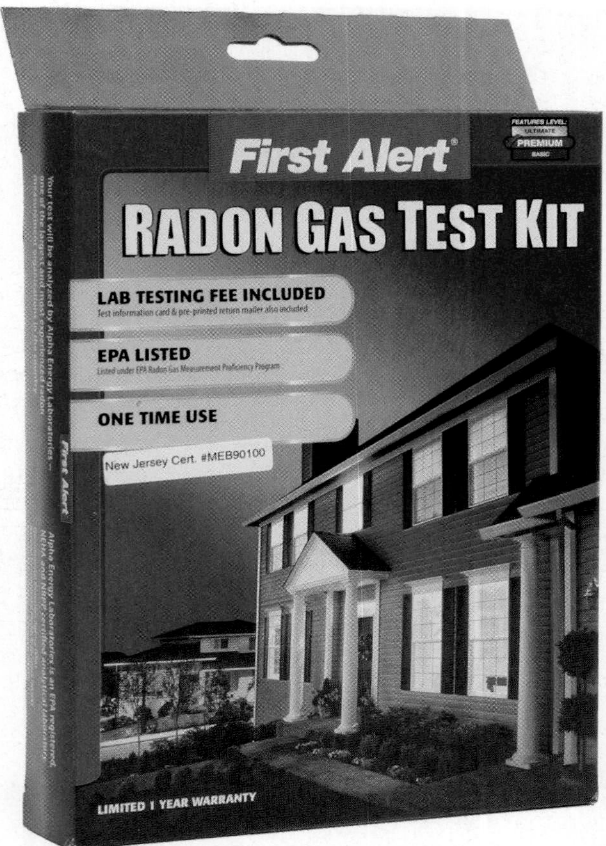

Goodheart-Willcox Publisher

Figure 10-8. This inexpensive radon gas test kit allows homeowners to collect appropriate samples and send them to an EPA-listed lab for analysis. The cost of the kit includes the lab testing fee.

Long-term testing devices take more than 90 days. The advantage of using a long-term device is that it provides a year-round average of radon levels. A disadvantage is that it requires a longer period of time to obtain the test results.

Radon testing should be carried out when the house is occupied. Doors and windows should be kept closed as much as possible. The detector should be placed in the lowest level, such as the basement or first floor. Place the detector 20″ above the floor and away from drafts, high heat, high humidity, and exterior walls.

At the completion of the test, the testing device is sent to a laboratory for analysis. If the reading on a short-term test is 4 pCi/L or higher, a second test is recommended. If the results on a long-term or second short-term test are 4 pCi/L or higher, take steps to remove the radon from the house. For readings between 4 and 20 pCi/L, take action within a few years. If the readings are above 20 pCi/L, take action within a few months. Readings below 4 pCi/L may provide some risk, and future testing is suggested. The EPA recommends testing for radon every few years to determine if larger amounts of radon are seeping into the house.

Radon Mitigation

The term *mitigation* means to reduce the effects of something. The process of reducing radon levels in a building is called ***radon mitigation***. There are several methods of radon mitigation for homes and several factors to consider when selecting a method. The radon level, costs of installation and system operation, house size, and foundation type are all factors that should be taken into consideration when selecting the method to use. When selecting a contractor to mitigate the radon from your house, use one who is state-certified or one who has been certified by the National Environmental Health Association (NEHA) or the National Radon Safety Board (NRSB). If you plan to do the repairs yourself, help is available from your state or the EPA.

Basements and slab-on-grade construction require the following three-step process:

1. Minimize soil-gas entry by sealing joints, cracks, and other openings in slabs, below-grade walls, and floors, including openings for the sump pump. In addition, gas-retarding barriers—polyethylene membranes under floors and parging (a thin coat of mortar) on outside walls—should be installed.
2. Install an active, fan-driven radon-removal vent-pipe system as shown in **Figure 10-9**. A passive system may also be installed that can be activated later by adding a fan, usually in the attic.
3. Reduce the "stack" or "chimney" effect in basements, which can draw soil gas into the home. This can be done by closing air passages between floors and providing air from outside for combustion devices and exhaust fans.

In crawl spaces, radon must be diverted before it reaches the living space. The crawl space should be adequately vented to outside air. To

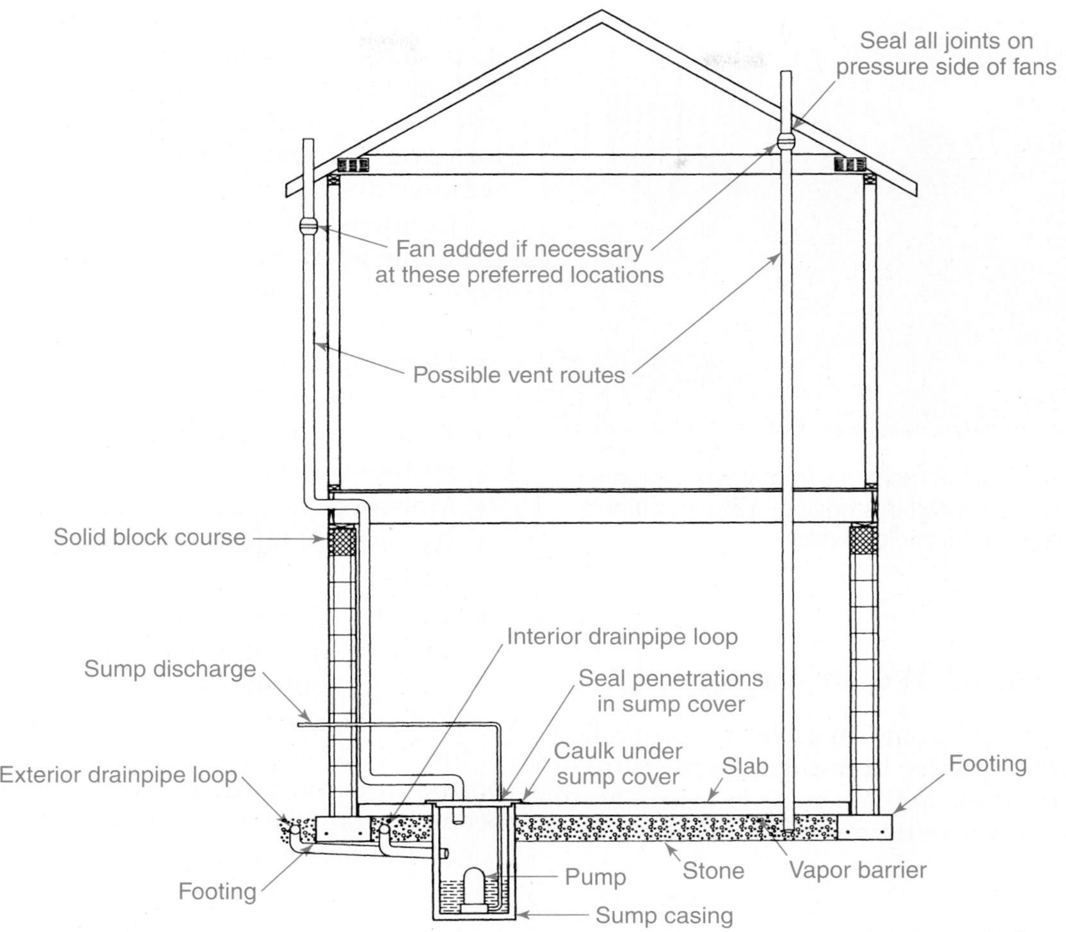

Goodheart-Willcox Publisher

Figure 10-9. This diagram shows an active, fan-driven radon-removal vent-pipe system.

prevent radon gas from seeping into the structure, the soil should be covered with a polyethylene membrane or concrete, and the tops of block foundation walls should be sealed. Seal openings in floors and ductwork with caulks, foams, and tapes. More information on radon mitigation is available from the EPA, the NRSB, the National Safety Council (NSC), and the International Residential Code, which specifies construction methods for passive radon systems used in different foundation designs.

Moisture and Mold Problems

The incidence of moisture and mold problems in residential structures has increased appreciably in recent years. One of the reasons for this is that new buildings are constructed to have less air infiltration and heat loss/gain. In fact, some studies by the EPA have shown that many new homes have poorer air quality inside the home than outside the home. This condition has resulted in the term "sick house syndrome."

In many cases, the root of the problem is excessive moisture within the structure. This is due to unwanted moisture entering the building from a variety of locations. When moisture remains over time, the growth of unhealthy mold sets in, as shown in **Figure 10-10**. Gradual deterioration of the building materials accompanies mold growth. Once this cycle begins, the space inside the dwelling may rapidly reach a point where it is not healthy for occupants. Several health hazards are associated with excessive mold.

Cynthia Farmer/Shutterstock.com

Figure 10-10. Excess moisture from a small plumbing leak not only discolored this ceiling, it also provided an excellent place for mold to grow.

Migration of Water Vapor

All air contains some invisible moisture called ***water vapor***. Relative humidity is a measure of water vapor in the air. When air is warm, it can hold more moisture than when it is cold. When water vapor comes into contact with a cold surface, it condenses to form water or, if the surface is 32°F or lower, frost. The most common visual example of ***condensation*** in the home is the formation of water or frost on the glass in a window during cold weather.

Condensation becomes a serious problem in the home when it occurs on or within the walls, floors, and ceilings. Evidence of condensation may be seen as:

- Damp spots on ceilings and the room side of exterior walls.
- Water and frost on inside surfaces of windows. See **Figure 10-11**.
- Moisture on basement walls and floors.
- Water-filled blisters on outside paint surfaces.
- Marbles of ice on attic floors resulting from condensation of water on points of nails through roof sheathing.

Excessive moisture in a warm house is forced to the outside in cold weather and condensation on the inner surfaces or within the walls may occur. By controlling the amount of water vapor, condensation can be prevented.

Employability

Being an Efficient Employee

No matter what your job is or how long you have had it, you can always improve your efficiency. Efficiency is a measure of how much you can do—and how well you can do it—with the resources you have. Like the world in general, the workplace is constantly changing. Look critically at the work you do, whether it is schoolwork or work at a part-time or full-time job. Examine the methods you use to get your work done. Methods that have been useful in the past can sometimes be replaced with newer, more efficient methods made possible by new technology.

General tips that may help you improve your efficiency include:

- At the beginning of each day, think about what you need to accomplish that day and set your priorities accordingly.
- Consider your energy levels during the day and match your energy level to your tasks. For example, if you think better in the morning, do tasks that require the most thought or brainpower in the morning.
- Organize your work environment. Identify items you need on a daily basis and keep them within easy reach. Not having to spend time searching for these items not only saves time, but also helps you retain your focus on the task at hand.

Activity

Perform a self-analysis using the tips provided here. How well are you doing? In what ways can you improve your efficiency? Set yourself three written goals that you believe will increase your efficiency within the next month. At the end of the month, review your list. Did you achieve your goals?

Joe Belanger/Shutterstock.com

Figure 10-11. When warm, moisture-filled air comes into contact with colder air, it loses some of its moisture-carrying capacity. As a result, water vapor condenses to liquid water or frost.

Since water vapor is not visible or easily detected until it condenses, occupants are generally not aware of a problem. As a result, little thought is generally given to control of water vapor until condensation problems arise.

Sources of Water Vapor

Everyday household activities produce considerable moisture inside the home. Some of the most obvious sources include people, bathing facilities, cooking processes, laundry, and open gas flames. Sources of water vapor in the structure itself may include wet plaster, seepage in basements, unexcavated basements, and foundation leaks. Water vapor will always be present inside the home from routine activities, but with proper ventilation, the moisture is not excessive or harmful. See **Figure 10-12**. However, moisture from leaks, wet basements, and other sources should be prevented.

Water condensation is not only a cold-weather problem, but a summertime problem as well. For example, what happens if warm, moist air from the outside on muggy days enters the cool basement air? Condensation occurs when the warm air comes into contact with cool basement walls, floors, and cold-water pipes. This is just like the condensation on a cold glass of ice water. Also, houses built on a concrete slab may have condensation problems in the summertime.

Preventive Measures

The methods used to control moisture vapor or humidity and condensation vary with the type of structure and the parts of a house. There are three principal cures that may reduce condensation problems. These can be used individually or in combination.

- Reduce interior humidity by controlling water vapor at the source and ventilating.
- Use vapor barriers to prevent the flow of moisture through building materials.
- Raise inner surface temperatures by insulating.

To avoid condensation in a house built over a crawl space, the crawl space must be kept dry. The following points should be considered.

- Grade the lot appropriately for good drainage.
- Use gutters and downspouts or wide overhangs to eliminate rain seepage.

Broan-NuTone, A Nortek Company

Figure 10-12. A typical bathroom ventilation fan removes water vapor from inside the house, thus reducing the chance of mold growing.

- Lay a moisture-proof cover on the ground of the crawl space to prevent the rise of moisture. Generally, a 4-mil or 6-mil polyethylene film will serve this function.
- Provide foundation vents to allow moisture to escape from the crawl space.
- Where floor insulation is used, establish a vapor barrier either directly above it or between the subfloor and the finish flooring.

To avoid condensation in slab floor construction, follow these recommendations.

- Insulate by using gravel, cinders, crushed rock, or other insulating material beneath the floor.
- Provide good drainage.
- Install insulation at the edges of the slab and install a vapor barrier under the slab to prevent ground moisture from entering the building. See **Figure 10-13**.

Ventilation

Ventilation in the home can be used to reduce excessive humidity that cannot be controlled at its source. Model building codes generally specify the number and size of vents to use in a given structure. There are so many variables, however, that the minimum proposal may not be sufficient in every case. It is more satisfactory to provide controlled (powered) ventilation than to depend on uncontrolled vents and cracks around windows and doors. See **Figure 10-14**. If a home is heated by a combustion-type furnace, an outside air intake can be added to the system. The same is true for a combustion-type water heater and fireplace. Proper ventilation may be the solution to most moisture vapor problems in the home.

Broan-NuTone, A Nortek Company

Figure 10-14. This fan-powered roof vent is capable of cooling an attic of up to 1800 square feet.

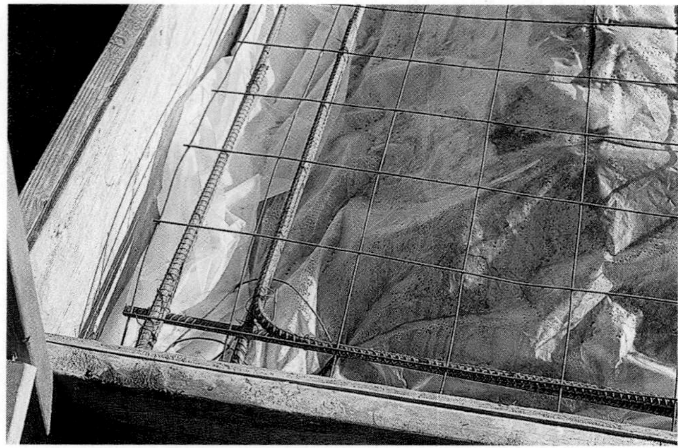

Goodheart-Willcox Publisher

Figure 10-13. A polyethylene film placed under a concrete slab reduces moisture penetration through the slab.

Health Hazards Associated with Mold

Mold is the common term for several types of fungus that reproduce through spores. These spores are always present in the air inside and outside our homes. There are molds that can grow on wood, paper, carpet, and foods. In fact, molds can be found almost anywhere moisture is present. Therefore, the best way to reduce mold growth in the home is to control moisture.

According to the EPA, all molds can be health hazards. Exposure to mold has been identified as a potential cause of many health problems, including asthma, sinusitis, nosebleeds, chest congestion, and upper respiratory infections. Infectious diseases caused by molds include athlete's foot and yeast infections. Allergic responses to mold are also common. Symptoms of allergies to mold include:

- Breathing difficulties
- Coughing
- Sore throat

Green Architecture

Eco-Friendly Mold Removal

Traditional mold removal products rely on harsh chemicals—mainly chlorine bleach—to remove mold from inside the home. These chemicals are effective, but dangerous to breathe and harmful to the environment.

Fortunately, there are several environmentally friendly ways to remove mold, and most of these methods are safer for humans, also. The product you choose may depend on the size of the mold problem. For routine bathroom cleaning, vinegar or ammonia can help remove mold and keep it from coming back. Hydrogen peroxide can also be used, although it must be used exactly according to directions to be effective. Many commercial eco-friendly mold removal products are also available. Read the packaging carefully to be sure the product is not only eco-friendly but also safe for humans and pets.

For large areas, or for repeated use, an ozone generator is a good choice. Although it is an expensive option, ozone has about 3000 times more disinfecting power than chlorine. While the generator is running, the area is not safe for humans or pets. However, after the cycle has finished, the ozone breaks down into ordinary oxygen, leaving no harsh chemicals, and the area is completely safe.

- Nasal and sinus congestion
- Skin and eye irritation

Mold Prevention and Removal

It is always better to prevent mold from growing when possible, so that you do not have to worry about removing the mold later. Tips to help prevent mold from forming in a home include:

- Clean and dry drip pans in your appliances on a regular basis.
- Vent clothes dryers to the outside.
- When bathing, cooking, or using the washing machine, use an exhaust fan or open a window.
- Take steps to reduce indoor humidity to between 30% and 50% relative humidity.

If you discover a mold problem in your home, you should take steps to have the mold removed as soon as possible. In many cases, you can remove the mold yourself. However, it is very important to follow EPA or other accepted mold removal guidelines. In general:

- Wear protective clothing, including an N-95 respirator, long rubber gloves, and goggles.
- For hard surfaces, use a sponge to apply a mixture of household bleach and water. Allow the mixture to work for 15 minutes, then dry.
- Soft materials that contain mold (such as carpet and ceiling tiles) generally cannot be cleaned adequately and should be replaced.
- Remove the *cause* of the mold, such as a leaky faucet, to prevent the mold from recurring.
- When in doubt, consult a professional.

In some cases, it is better not to try to remove the mold by yourself. If a large area is affected; if the heating, ventilation, and air conditioning (HVAC) system is contaminated with mold; or if the mold damage was caused by sewage or other contaminated water, leave cleanup to the professionals. See **Figure 10-15**. Mitigation (removal) of mold growth can be very costly in states with higher temperatures and humidity levels such as Mississippi and Florida. Be sure the company you choose is experienced in mold removal.

Weather- and Nature-Related Safety

Every area of the United States is faced with one or more destructive forces of nature, such as flooding, hurricanes, tornadoes, and earthquakes. Every residential structure should be designed and built to reasonably resist the destructive forces of nature. However, some areas are more prone to certain types of natural destructive forces. Therefore, building codes vary somewhat in their requirements to help prepare homes to withstand the natural disasters that are most common in a given area. Be sure to

RioPatuca/Shutterstock.com

Figure 10-15. If a large area of mold is present, leave the cleaning to the professionals. They use special techniques to remove the mold and make a home safe for habitation.

check the building codes in the area for which you will be designing homes.

Earthquakes

An ***earthquake zone***, also known as a ***seismic area***, is an area that is prone to earthquakes. Most people think of California when earthquakes are mentioned. The fact is, earthquakes can and do happen all over the United States. The most severe earthquake on record in the United States was along the New Madrid fault, which runs through northern Arkansas, southern Missouri, and western Tennessee. Other active earthquake zones include the southern Appalachians, New England, and Alaska.

As indicated on the seismic zone map in **Figure 10-16**, there is some chance of earthquake damage in all regions of the country. Areas that have a very low chance of damage include much of Florida and Texas, as well as parts of many states in the north central United States.

Reducing Earthquake Damage to Homes

Five basic areas need to be addressed to reduce the hazards of earthquakes—site considerations, soil and foundation types, building shapes and mass, structural details, and drainage. A thorough analysis of any existing or proposed structure should take all of these factors into account.

The notion that a structure can be "earthquake-proof" is misleading. However, the need to reduce the risk of serious structural failure is valid. Four kinds of structural elements need careful consideration to determine what kinds of strengthening strategies are practical. They include:

- The foundation that supports the building
- The horizontal members, such as floors
- The columns, posts, and other vertical members that transfer the weight of the structure to the foundation
- All points of connection

House Structure

Examples of the destructive forces of earthquakes on residential structures are shown in **Figure 10-17**. The following summary describes structural design specifications that can be made to reduce structural damage from an earthquake.

- Attach the sill plate to the foundation with anchor bolts spaced in accordance with local building code requirements. See **Figure 10-18**.
- Reinforce cripple walls (short walls) with a plywood shear wall that connects the sill plate, cripple studs, and wall plates. Generally, 1/2″ CDX plywood is used for one-story homes, 5/8″ plywood for two-story houses, and 3/4″ plywood for three-story structures.
- Install blocking at the midspan and ends of floor joists. Long spans may require additional blocking. Use angle steel or metal angle clips to attach the joist ends to the rim joists and between the rim joist and sill plate.

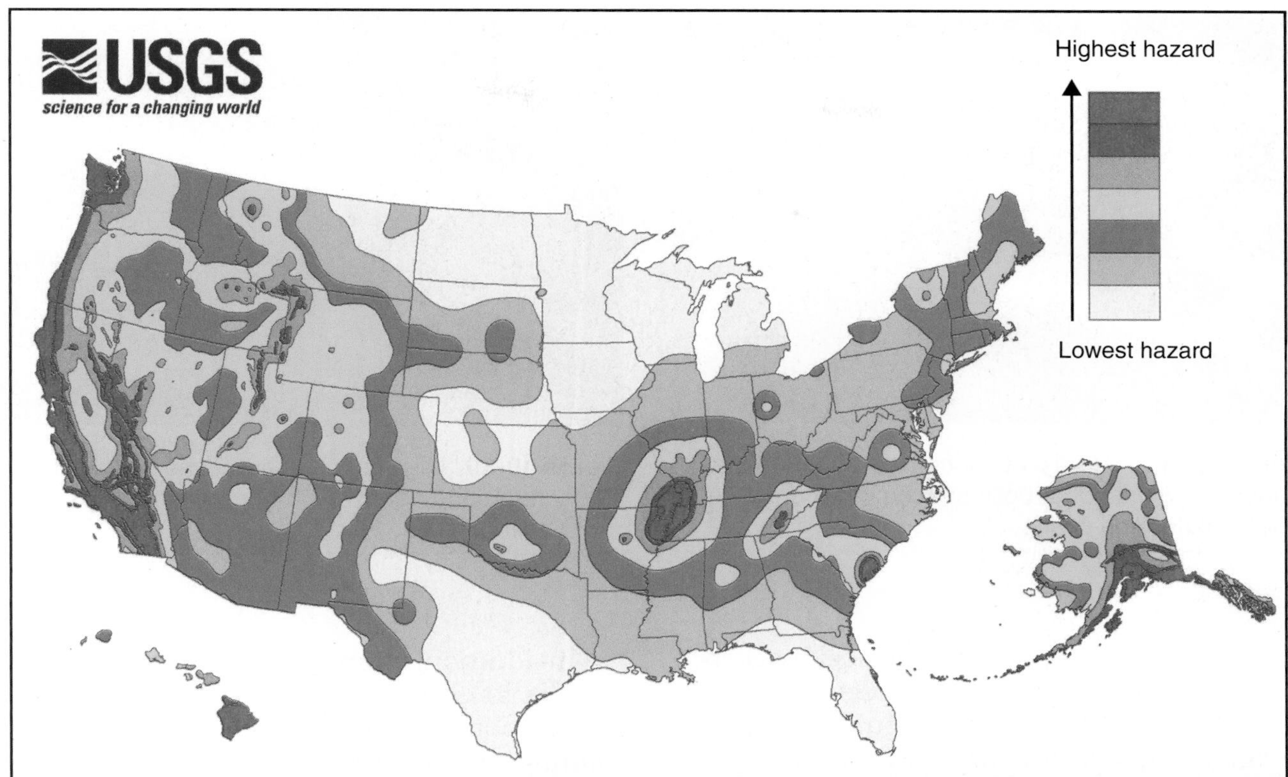

United States Geological Survey

Figure 10-16. This seismic map from the US Geological Survey shows areas of the United States that are most likely to experience earthquakes.

A

B

FEMA/Eilis Maynard

Figure 10-17. These homes were damaged by the August 2014 Napa earthquake in California. This was a 6.0 magnitude earthquake.

Goodheart-Willcox Publisher

Figure 10-18. The sill plate should be bolted to the foundation with anchor bolts spaced in accordance with local building codes.

Goodheart-Willcox Publisher

Figure 10-20. This roof uses hurricane ties set into a concrete bond beam to anchor each roof truss to resist uplift forces.

- Add metal clips, T-straps, or steel brackets at all connections between posts and beams. See **Figure 10-19**. Beams should be securely attached to piers with heavy metal straps and anchor bolts.
- Install hurricane ties between the top plates or bond beams and the rafters and ceiling joists, as shown in **Figure 10-20**. ***Hurricane ties*** are straps or clips that anchor the roof components to the house. Although they were developed for hurricane protection, they also help strengthen homes in earthquake-prone areas.

Goodheart-Willcox Publisher

Figure 10-19. Thick metal straps have been added to the connections between the posts and beams in this structure to resist lateral forces.

In addition, chimneys are particularly vulnerable to earthquake damage. A large, reinforced footing, structural steel bracing, ties to framing, and reduced weight above the roof line can reduce the potential for damage.

Floods

Each year, flooding is responsible for more property damage and deaths than hurricanes, tornadoes, and earthquakes combined. Every state in the United States experiences flooding at some point. Communities located in low-lying areas, near a body of water, or downstream from a dam have the highest risk. See **Figure 10-21**. ***Flash floods*** are especially dangerous because they represent a high volume of fast-moving water that can appear suddenly. Consider these facts:

- The force of 6″ of swiftly moving water can cause you to lose your footing.
- Flash flood waters move at very fast speeds and can move boulders, uproot trees, demolish buildings, and wash out bridges.
- It takes only 2′ of moving water to sweep away an automobile.

Floodplain Risk

Historically, people have built their homes next to bodies of water—rivers, lakes, the ocean—for many reasons. Water is needed for drinking and for irrigating crops. In many places, it has also been the main route of transportation. Building

Tony Campbell/Shutterstock.com

Figure 10-21. This home in Indiana was built in a low-lying area and was flooded when a nearby river overran its banks.

planet5D LLC/Shutterstock.com

Figure 10-22. This home was built on the west coast of Florida in an area that is known to flood when a hurricane approaches. All of the living spaces in the home are raised 14′ above ground level. Some people enclose the ground level and use it as garage or storage space, but building codes forbid having living space at the ground level.

next to a body of water has benefits, but there are drawbacks as well.

Natural ***floodplains*** have been identified throughout the United States according to the average number of years between flooding, such as a 100-year floodplain or a 500-year floodplain. These areas are referred to by local building departments when issuing building permits. Generally, new buildings are prohibited in floodplains that flood frequently. In some places, buildings are permitted only if the elevation of the structure is located significantly above the floodplain. See **Figure 10-22**.

Flood Mitigation

Examples of flood mitigation include relocating homes out of the floodplain, elevating homes above the base floodplain (usually the 100-year floodplain), and minimizing the vulnerability to flood damage through both structural and nonstructural means. See **Figure 10-23**. Check your local building code for information regarding building in flood-prone areas before selecting a site for a new home or purchasing an existing home.

Tornadoes

"Tornado Alley" covers the part of the United States that runs north from Texas, through eastern Nebraska, and northeast to Indiana. It is known for the number and severity of tornadoes that occur there. However, even though Texas, Oklahoma, and Kansas may have more tornadoes

FEMA News Photo

Figure 10-23. When a structure is elevated to mitigate flood damage, all exterior appliances, including the air conditioning unit, must be elevated as well.

than other states, the rest of the country also has tornadoes on a regular basis. See **Figure 10-24**.

Homes that are built strictly to current model building codes for high-wind regions have a much better chance of surviving tornadoes and other violent windstorms than homes that do not meet these requirements. In spite of what you might think, wind speeds in most tornadoes are at or below the design speeds specified in most typical building codes. Records show that about 85% of all reported tornadoes have wind speeds of 112 mph or less. In other words, a house built to code will resist the majority of tornadoes.

Building to Resist Tornadoes

No above-ground structure is completely tornado-proof. However, there are steps that can be taken to give a house a better chance of surviving a tornado. The following recommendations are intended to aid the design and building processes.

Windows. Install impact-resistant windows. These windows are specially designed to resist high winds and are commonly available in tornado- and hurricane-prone areas.

Entry doors. Exterior doors should have at least three hinges and a 1″-long dead bolt security lock. Anchoring the door frames securely to the wall framing is very important.

Sliding glass doors. These doors are more vulnerable to wind damage than most other doors because of their large exposure. Install impact-resistant door systems made of laminated glass, plastic glazing, or a combination, or substitute French doors with small panes of glass.

Garage doors. Garage doors are highly susceptible to wind damage because of their size and construction. Have a qualified inspector determine if both the door and frame will resist high winds. If purchasing a new door, check the wind rating and select a door that will withstand at least 110-mph winds.

Ernest R. Prim/Shutterstock.com

Figure 10-24. Tornadoes can occur in any state, and no structure is completely tornado-proof.

Roofs. Be sure the roof covering and sheathing will resist high winds. Not all roofing materials are equal in this respect. If you are replacing an existing roof, a qualified roofing contractor can take the following steps to increase the stability of the roof.

1. Remove the existing roofing materials down to the sheathing.
2. Inspect the rafters or trusses to be sure they are securely connected to the walls.
3. Cut out and replace any damaged sheathing. Be sure it is nailed according to the schedule required by the local building code.
4. Install a roof covering that is designed for high-wind areas. Attachment must follow the manufacturer's specifications.

Gables. Gable end walls must be braced properly to resist high winds. Check the current building code for "high-wind regions" for guidance or consult your local building department.

Connections. Connections between the foundation and walls, floor and walls, and roof structure and walls are critical points. See **Figure 10-25**. Appropriate connectors must be used and attached properly.

Anchors. The exterior walls must be properly anchored to the foundation. Approved anchor bolts or straps and fasteners can be used for this purpose.

Upper stories. If the house has more than one story, be sure the wall framing of the upper stories is properly connected to the lower wall framing. Use approved straps and fasteners.

Goodheart-Willcox Publisher

Figure 10-25. Joist hangers were used in this structure to increase the strength of the structure and resist damaging winds.

Roof framing. Anchor the roof framing to the exterior walls with approved straps, clips, and fasteners. Consult the local building code for specifications or get help from your local building department.

Tornado Preparedness

No home is completely tornado-proof, so you should take steps to protect yourself and your family when a tornado threatens. A tornado watch is issued when conditions are favorable for tornado formation. A tornado warning is issued when a tornado has been sighted or detected on radar.

Most communities have a severe weather warning system. Be familiar with it. Make sure every member of your family knows what to do when a watch is issued or a warning is sounded. During the watch phase of the storm, remove anything in your yard that can become flying debris before the storm strikes. Do *not* attempt this after a warning is sounded.

When a tornado warning is sounded, seek shelter immediately. Decide ahead of time where you will go. It could be a local community shelter or your own underground storm cellar. See **Figure 10-26**. Some newer homes have a ***safe room*** within the house that has been constructed to withstand tornado-force winds. Stay away from windows and preferably position yourself under something sturdy, such as a workbench or staircase. Seek the center and lowest section of the building.

Develop a family plan for protection, escape, and a meeting place to reunite if members become separated. Assemble an emergency kit that includes:

- Three-day supply of drinking water and food
- First aid supplies
- Portable NOAA weather radio
- Basic tools
- Flashlight
- Work gloves
- Emergency cooking equipment
- Portable lantern
- Fresh batteries
- Clothing
- Blankets

Cheryl A. Meyer/Shutterstock.com

Figure 10-26. Know where the nearest tornado or emergency shelter is in your community and make plans to meet there when a tornado warning is issued.

- Prescription medications
- Extra keys
- Eyeglasses
- Credit cards and cash
- Important documents, including insurance policies

Contrary to what you may have heard, do not open your windows. This only increases water and wind damage to the inside of the house. Do not stay in a trailer, mobile home, or manufactured home during a tornado. These units are too light to resist tornadoes even if they have tie-downs. Do not attempt to ride out the storm in an automobile. A strong tornado can pick up a vehicle and destroy it.

Hurricanes

A hurricane is a tropical cyclone with winds that have reached a constant speed of 74 miles per hour (64 knots) or more. Hurricane winds blow in a large spiral around a relatively calm center called the *eye*. The eye is usually 20 to 30 miles across, but the storm may extend out 400 miles or more. See **Figure 10-27**.

Storm systems similar to hurricanes are called by different names in different parts of the world. For example, in the western North Pacific and Philippines, these systems are referred to as *typhoons*. In the Indian Ocean and South Pacific Ocean, they are called *tropical cyclones*.

US Hurricanes

Areas in the United States that are the most vulnerable to hurricanes include the Atlantic and Gulf coasts from Texas to Maine; the Caribbean

Vladislav Gurfinkel/Shutterstock.com

Figure 10-27. Hurricanes are so large that they can be seen clearly in satellite images. The eye of this hurricane is east of Florida, but the storm is so large it covers almost the entire state.

territories; and tropical areas of the western Pacific that include Hawaii, Guam, American Samoa, and the Northern Mariana Islands. August and September are the peak months of the hurricane season, but the season lasts from June 1 through November 30.

When a hurricane approaches land, it usually brings torrential rains, high winds, and storm surges. Of these three events, the storm surge is generally the most dangerous. A ***storm surge*** is a dome of ocean water fueled by the hurricane that can be 20′ at its highest point and up to 100 miles wide. The power of the surge can demolish communities along the coast as it sweeps ashore. The greatest property damage from hurricanes occurs as they make landfall. Damage is caused by strong winds, storm surge, flooding, tornadoes, and riptides. Together, these forces can demolish most any structure in their path.

On average, 10 tropical storms develop each year in the North Atlantic. Of these, six usually reach hurricane strength and two may strike the coast of the United States. The most deaths in US history caused by a single hurricane resulted from the Galveston, Texas hurricane in 1900. This hurricane took 6000 lives.

There are only two major hurricanes in a typical year. On average, there are 10 named storms each year, six of which become hurricanes. In 2005, the worst hurricane season in decades, there were 27 named tropical storms, 13 of which became hurricanes. Seven of the hurricanes were considered major and three were category five (the strongest). Hurricane Katrina hit the Gulf Coast in 2005 and became the second deadliest hurricane in US history. See **Figure 10-28**. Nearly 1300 people lost their lives. In addition, reconstruction costs were estimated at more than $200 billion. Another major storm, Hurricane Sandy, hit the United States in 2012, causing billions of dollars in damage.

Robert A. Mansker/Shutterstock.com

Figure 10-28. Hurricane Katrina devastated the Gulf Coast. After the storm surge and floodwater receded, some homes were repairable. However, many homes, like this one, were completely destroyed.

Hurricane Mitigation through Codes

Many states and local governments in coastal areas of the United States have enacted ***hurricane codes***. These codes are designed to reduce damage to property during a hurricane. For example, Florida has instituted the Coastal Construction Control Line (CCCL) program. This defines the extent of a zone from the coastline inland that is subject to flooding, erosion, and other impacts during a 100-year storm. Properties located between the ocean and the CCCL are subject to state-enforced elevation and construction requirements. The CCCL foundation and elevation requirements in this area are even more stringent than National Flood Insurance Program (NFIP) coastal (V-Zone) requirements. Likewise, the CCCL wind load requirements for properties between the ocean and the CCCL are more stringent than the wind load requirements of the model building codes.

There is emerging proof that more stringent codes and enforcement work in limiting property damage. The beach home shown in **Figure 10-29** is located seaward of the CCCL and was built to the strict building code required for housing in the CCCL zone. In 2005, Hurricane Wilma destroyed homes in this area that were not built to these standards. Most of the damage was caused by coastal flooding that included storm surge, wind-generated waves, and flood-induced erosion. Although the home shown in **Figure 10-29** was also damaged, the structure remains intact.

Colman Lerner Gerardo/Shutterstock.com

Figure 10-29. This home survived Hurricane Wilma in 2005 with little major structural damage because it was built to meet the CCCL code requirements.

It is very clear that increased structural requirements and stricter enforcement are worth the efforts.

Building to Resist Hurricanes

The following recommendations are intended to provide broad guidance in the design and building of a dwelling that will more likely resist the forces of a hurricane. However, local and state codes should always be consulted.

Landscaping. Use shredded bark as a landscaping material instead of gravel or rock. Remove weak branches and trees that could fall on the house during a storm.

Windows. Install impact-resistant window systems or hurricane shutters or panels that cover window openings to prevent glass from being broken by flying debris. See **Figure 10-30**.

Entry doors. Install at least three hinges on exterior doors that are 6′–8″ high. Four hinges should be installed on exterior doors that are 8′–0″ high. Install a dead bolt security lock with a bolt at least 1″ long. Be sure door frames and hinges are securely anchored to the wall framing. Doors should be solid-core or steel doors, or they should be rated to resist hurricane-force winds.

Sliding glass doors. Reduce the vulnerability of sliding glass doors to wind damage by installing an impact-resistant door system or hurricane panels that completely cover the entire opening.

Garage doors. Garage doors are highly susceptible to wind damage because of their large area. Purchase a door that is certified to withstand at least 110-mph winds. Be sure the track system has the same rating and is solidly anchored to the wall with bolts or screws. Doors wider than 8′ must have metal stiffeners to resist hurricane-level winds, as shown in **Figure 10-31**.

Roofs. The roof structure and covering are areas of significant concern during very high winds. Select a roofing material that is designed to resist high winds. See **Figure 10-32**. Be sure to follow recommended installation procedures. Roof sheathing should be fastened as prescribed by the building code in your area. This may include the use of construction adhesive as well as nails. Every truss or rafter must be secured to the exterior wall with hurricane ties. Proper nailing is very important to the quality of the installation. In addition, the roof structure must

A

B

Goodheart-Willcox Publisher

Figure 10-30. A—These accordion-style hurricane shutters protect two sets of glass doors in this home when a hurricane approaches. Notice that all furniture has been removed to prevent any of the objects from becoming an airborne "missile" in hurricane winds. B—When not in use, the hurricane shutters fold back to the sides of the door or window. Since they match the trim on the house, they are unobtrusive, yet easy to close when a hurricane threatens.

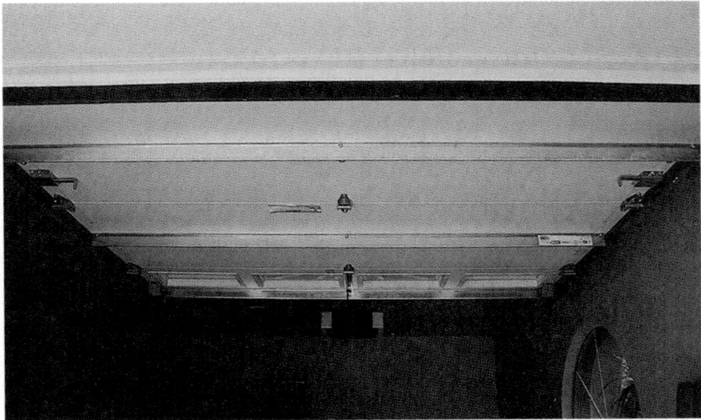
Goodheart-Willcox Publisher

Figure 10-31. The strength of garage doors can be increased greatly by adding metal stiffeners to each panel of the door. This door will resist 120-mph winds.

Goodheart-Willcox Publisher

Figure 10-32. The roofing material being applied to this home is colored concrete tile. When attached properly, it will resist typical hurricane-strength winds.

be braced inside to produce a rigid structure able to resist hurricane winds.

Gables. The end walls of a gable roof are particularly vulnerable to high-wind damage. Make certain they are braced properly. Check with your local building department or truss manufacturer.

Connections. Reinforce the points where the roof and the foundation meet the exterior walls of the structure. This is generally accomplished through the use of anchors, straps, or clips. Walls are usually anchored to the foundation using anchor bolts or straps placed at intervals specified by the local building code. See **Figure 10-33**. Second-story framing must be securely fastened to the lower level through the use of straps that bridge the floor joist area.

Hurricane Preparedness

Prepare an escape plan for when a hurricane threatens. Most communities have a disaster

Goodheart-Willcox Publisher

Figure 10-33. Anchor bolts are used in this slab-type foundation to connect the exterior walls to the foundation.

preparedness plan and you should be familiar with it. Create a family plan as well. Identify escape routes and select an emergency meeting place for your family to gather if you become separated. Contact relatives and loved ones to relieve their concern.

Also, prepare your home for the storm before it arrives. Hurricanes usually take several days to develop, and that provides time to get ready. Develop an emergency kit that includes:

- Three-day supply of drinking water and food that does not require refrigeration or cooking
- First aid supplies
- Portable NOAA weather radio
- Toolbox with basic tools
- Flashlight and extra batteries
- Work gloves
- Personal hygiene items
- Emergency cooking equipment
- Portable lanterns
- Clothing and blankets
- Prescription drugs
- Extra house and car keys
- Eyeglasses
- Credit cards and cash
- Important documents, including insurance policies
- Food and other necessities for pets

Prepare a complete description of your personal belongings. Recording a video of every room in your home and its contents or at least photographing every room is a good idea. Store recordings or photographs in a safe place.

Remove items from outside the home that might be blown about during the storm. Follow news reports about the weather so you know what to expect. Shut off the water and gas supply. Disconnect all electrical appliances except food storage. Wrap outside electric motors with plastic to prevent water damage. Be sure to fill the fuel tanks in your vehicles because fuel may not be available for evacuation or for several days following the storm. Finally, always obey evacuation orders from local authorities.

General Home Safety

The majority of us believe that our homes are safe. Survey evidence shows, however, that most are not. So, what can be done to improve the safety of a home? First, take a look at some of the statistics related to home safety.

- According to the National Safety Council, about one-third of the accidental deaths that occur in homes each year in the United States are from falls.
- Each year, about 250,000 people older than 65 end up in the hospital after suffering a broken hip in a fall. Many of these falls happen in the home.
- Three of every five fire-related deaths in the United States occur in residences without smoke detectors.
- Most electrical shocks in the home result from the misuse of household appliances.
- The major causes of accidents in the home are falls, burns, electrical shock, and poisonings.

The first step in preventing accidents and injuries in the home is to be sure that your home meets the building code in your area. The major purpose of the code is to improve safety. Newly constructed homes are inspected and must pass inspection in order to receive an occupancy permit. However, older homes or homes that are not well maintained may not pass such an inspection.

Secondly, many common sense actions that relate to everyday living can improve home safety. For example:

- Keep stairs free of toys and other items.
- Remove trip hazards from traffic circulation patterns.
- Keep the area around a fireplace or heater free of combustible materials.
- Secure flammable and toxic liquids. Properly handle and dispose of environmentally hazardous materials.
- Limit the use of extension cords.
- Keep electrical and mechanical appliances and devices in good repair.
- Choose rugs with nonskid backing. See **Figure 10-34**.
- Provide adequate lighting in hazard-prone areas.
- Childproof your home if you have young children.
- Follow good housekeeping practices.

Loskutnikov/Shutterstock.com

Figure 10-34. Slick stair surfaces are a fall hazard. Cover them, when possible, with nonskid rugs or rugs that are held in place mechanically. The rug in this home is held in place by stair rods that reduce the fall hazard while adding a touch of elegance.

Summary

- Structural fires are a significant danger to every home, but a combination of fire safety code requirements and common sense precautions can reduce the risk of fire in a home.
- Carbon monoxide (CO) is an odorless, tasteless, invisible gas that is potentially deadly.
- Radon is an invisible, odorless, tasteless, radioactive gas that moves up through the ground to homes and other structures.
- If not controlled, condensation of water vapor can cause structural damage and increase mold growth in a residence.
- Building codes across the United States address common weather- and nature-related destructive forces.
- Complying with building codes and taking common sense precautions can improve general safety in the home.

Internet Resources

Centers for Disease Control and Prevention
Resources promoting public health and safety

Federal Emergency Management Agency (FEMA)
Reference materials for disaster mitigation and preparedness

International Code Council (ICC)
Published building codes and standards

National Radon Safety Board (NRSB)
Radon testing information and technician certification programs

National Safety Council (NSC)
Safety training courses and certification programs

Radon Leaders Saving Lives
Radon testing information and service providers

US Environmental Protection Agency (EPA)
Resources for green building design

Review Questions

Answer the following questions using the information in this chapter.

1. What are the two leading causes of residential fires, according to the National Fire Protection Association?
2. Identify three locations in the home where a smoke detector should be installed.
3. Why are today's homes more likely to have dangerous levels of carbon monoxide than older homes?
4. What is the primary health concern associated with radon?
5. List four signs that condensation may be a serious problem in a home.
6. What health problems have been associated with exposure to mold?
7. List three examples of flood mitigation.
8. What should you do when a tornado warning is issued?
9. What is a *hurricane code*?
10. List at least three ways you can reduce the chance of people tripping or falling in your home.

Suggested Activities

1. Examine your home and prepare a list of fire hazards. Then, prepare a plan to eliminate the hazards.
2. Go to your local home building center or hardware store. Examine the carbon monoxide detectors that are available. Make a list of the features of the products, prices, and general information given on the packaging. Prepare a written report describing your findings.
3. Research the topic of radon gas. Determine those sections of the country where the radon hazard is most prevalent. Identify common methods of radon mitigation in those areas. Prepare a report on your findings.

4. Prepare a report on one of the major weather- or nature-related hazards. This may be on earthquakes, floods, tornadoes, or hurricanes, but select a hazard common to your area. Be sure to include topics such as areas of the country that are most vulnerable, frequency, cost in lives and dollars, and preventive measures. Record your sources.

Problem Solving Case Study

A client has come to you for design services for a new custom home to be built in Iowa City, Iowa. You are aware that according to the EPA, the entire state of Iowa has a probability of high indoor concentrations of radon. Conduct research to find the answers to the following questions for your client.

1. What building codes have been adopted that affect the construction of new homes in this location?
2. What provisions are made for radon protection in the construction of new homes?
3. How will this affect your client's new home structurally and financially?

ADDA Certification Prep

The following questions are presented in the style used in the American Design Drafting Association (ADDA) Drafter Certification Test. Answer the questions using the information in this chapter.

1. Which of the following statements about radon are correct?
   A. Radon smells like rotten eggs.
   B. Radon is found only in remote areas of the United States.
   C. Radon is not dangerous.
   D. Radon comes from the natural decay of uranium.
   E. Unoccupied homes build up higher radon levels than occupied homes.
2. Which of the following statements are true?
   A. The home is generally not considered a safe place.
   B. Structural fires are a significant danger to every home.
   C. A smoke detector is a small appliance that gives out a loud warning signal when it detects radon in the home.
   D. Every occupied room in a home must have two exits.
3. Which of the following supplies should be included in a hurricane preparedness kit?
   A. Toolbox with basic tools
   B. Small refrigerator with chilled foods
   C. Portable NOAA weather radio
   D. Three-day supply of drinking water
   E. Electric fans
   F. Credit cards

Curricular Connections

1. **Language Arts.** Conduct research to find out more about carbon monoxide and radon. Compose a five-page report comparing and contrasting carbon monoxide poisoning and radon gas poisoning. Be sure to list the sources you used to create the report. Present your findings to the class.

STEM Connections

1. **Science.** Conduct research to find out more about radon gas. What are its chemical properties? What radioactive particle does it emit? From a structural viewpoint, why is it more likely than many other gases to penetrate building materials such as concrete block, mortar, and insulation?
2. **Engineering.** In order to develop requirements for hurricane codes, engineers must design building products and methods and then test them under hurricane conditions. Find out more about how engineers test building products and methods. Prepare a report explaining your findings.

Communicating about Architecture

1. **Listening and Speaking.** Listen closely as your classmates present their findings on carbon monoxide poisoning and radon poisoning. Take notes on anything you find particularly interesting, or write down any questions you think of during the presentations. Once your classmates are finished presenting, share with the class one thought or question you had regarding their research.
2. **Listening and Speaking.** On paper, create a table with two columns. Label one column Carbon Monoxide and label the other Radon. In each column, write down symptoms and illnesses that can be caused by excessive exposure. Working in a small group, describe each condition and see if the group members can identify if the condition is from carbon monoxide exposure, radon exposure, or both.

Chapter 11

Designing for Sustainability

Objectives

After completing this chapter, you will be able to:

- Explain the difference between sustainability and green building.
- List seven major sustainable design concepts and explain how they apply to residential design.
- Explain the concept of building information modeling.
- Identify national certification programs for green building.

Key Terms

building information modeling (BIM)
daylighting
dioxins
ecosystem
fly ash
geothermal energy
gray water
green building
greenwashing
net zero energy building
nonrenewable energy source
persistent bioaccumulative toxicants (PBTs)
reclaiming
recycling
renewable energy source
semi-volatile organic compounds (SVOCs)
solar energy
solar harvesting
sustainability
sustainable building
volatile organic compounds (VOCs)
weatherization
xeriscaping

"Sustainability," "green building," "going green"—you have almost certainly heard these terms. Surprisingly, many people do not have a clear understanding of their meanings. Most of us are aware that our current lifestyles have had unintended negative consequences on the environment. We are beginning to realize that practices that harm the environment, along with the depletion of natural resources, will have a long-term effect on our ability to survive on this planet. Sustainability is a positive response to this problem. It involves people who are looking for ways to reduce our "footprint," or impact on the environment, and help preserve the Earth and its resources for future generations. See **Figure 11-1**. This chapter explains the concepts of sustainability and green building as they apply to residential architecture and construction.

Sustainability vs. Green Building

Many people use the terms *sustainability* and *green building* to mean exactly the same thing. In fact, they are different. Strictly speaking, the concept of ***sustainability*** includes meeting the needs of humans for food, housing, and other needs and wants, without using up resources that cannot be replaced, and without affecting the environment negatively. By extension, a ***sustainable building*** is one that can be built, used for a long time, and then reused or recycled, all without using up resources and impacting the environment negatively. Achieving true

stefanolunardi/Shutterstock.com

Figure 11-1. This botanist is recording data about the poplar trees in this tree farm. Tree farming is one way people have begun to help the environment while providing wood and wood products for buildings and other purposes.

sustainability will involve many complex changes in how people think about resource use. Although people around the world are working on it, we are still a long way from accomplishing sustainability.

Green building is not as ambitious as sustainability. While recognizing that sustainability is the "gold standard," ***green building*** strives to use materials and processes more efficiently, reduce pollution, and cause as little damage to the environment as possible. Green building is, in other words, the ongoing process of trying to become sustainable. As an example of the difference between green building and sustainability, a home that uses a solar space heating system for heat in the winter is considered "green." However, if the same home occupies 5000 square feet and requires a high output of energy from an air-conditioning system in the summer, it is not considered "sustainable." As discussed later in this chapter, from the standpoint of energy efficiency, a home must be a "net zero energy" home to be considered truly sustainable. This chapter uses the term *sustainability* to identify the general concepts relating to green building technology and sustainable design. Keep in mind, however, that these concepts are evolving and that many buildings being constructed using environmentally friendly practices are still in the "green building" phase.

Sustainable Design Concepts

To create a home that is truly sustainable, designers and architects need to consider the entire life cycle of the home. This includes the design and construction stage, the occupancy or use stage, and the end-of-life stage. See **Figure 11-2**. Throughout their life cycle, traditional home designs typically use many nonrenewable resources, use resources inefficiently, and release potentially harmful substances into the environment.

More specifically, the goals of sustainable design are to:

- Avoid depleting (using up) natural resources
- Prevent damage to the environment throughout the building's life cycle

There are many ways to accomplish these goals. Unfortunately, an effort to achieve one goal often causes a negative impact in other ways. The use of recycled steel for structural members is one example. The concept of recycling materials is good, but the energy resources required to recycle the steel, and the pollution created in this process, make some people wonder if recycling steel is really a sustainable practice. As you can see, there is still much disagreement on exactly *how* to make buildings sustainable. Most people agree, however, that sustainable building design requires the following elements:

- Proper site selection
- Efficient placement of the house on the site

Alexey Fateev/Shutterstock.com

Figure 11-2. Part of designing sustainably is planning what will happen to the home at the end of its life. After reading this chapter, look again at this photo. What parts of this house might have been reclaimed?

- Use of sustainable materials and processes
- Improved energy choices and use
- Water conservation and protection
- Low-impact or no-impact operation and maintenance
- Adaptability to meet multiple purposes

Site Selection

One important, but often overlooked, aspect of sustainable residential building design is the selection of a suitable site. Site selection should occur well before the home itself is designed. Traditional site selection considerations are described in Chapter 6, *Primary Residential Design Considerations*. In sustainable design, other factors should also be taken into consideration.

First, consider the impact of developing the site on the area's ecosystem. An ***ecosystem*** is the interaction of plants and animals with each other and the environment. See **Figure 11-3**. It goes without saying that you should not develop environmentally sensitive lands; development on many of those areas is prohibited by law. However, constructing a building has multiple effects on the ecosystem no matter where it is built. So, you should ask yourself how much the site will need to be modified prior to building the home. For example, will the modifications change the contour of the land? Examples of changing the contour include adding fill dirt to low-lying areas or digging into or removing high areas. Changing the contour affects patterns of water runoff not only for the building site, but also for all the land surrounding it. See **Figure 11-4**. To be sustainable, a building must be built on a site in such a way that harmful storm-water runoff is reduced or at least controlled.

Another common modification is the removal of trees that provide habitat for wildlife and the right amount of shade for other plants in the ecosystem. Many builders are conscientious in replacing the removed trees with new ones after construction. In fact, some building codes require this. However, the new trees are rarely

Goodheart-Willcox Publisher

Figure 11-3. An ecosystem includes not just the trees and ground cover, but also the many animal species that depend on them for food and shelter.

as large as those removed, so the impact of their removal on the local ecosystem should be considered.

Next, consider how much energy will be required not only to build a home in this location, but also to live in the home after it has been built. Energy use is discussed later in this chapter, but during the site selection phase, try to imagine the energy that will be needed to travel back and forth for work, school, shopping, and entertainment. What transportation options are available at this site? Is the site within walking or bicycling distance of stores and schools? See **Figure 11-5**.

Although motorized transportation is becoming more energy-efficient, the majority of the motorized vehicles on the road today use nonrenewable energy sources, contribute to pollution, or both. A *truly* sustainable home would minimize or eliminate the need for these types of vehicles. Of course, this is an area where we

George Burba/Shutterstock.com

Figure 11-4. The construction of this house changed the water runoff pattern for the entire hillside. Water is deflected around the house, which causes new flow patterns that affect everything downhill from the house.

Nick_Nick/Shutterstock.com

Figure 11-5. Selecting a building site that is within bicycling distance of stores and schools helps make a home more sustainable.

are currently at the "green building" phase. Rather than insist on true sustainability, we try to minimize the negative impacts. This is a large enough goal for the present, while we work on technologies and methods that may, in the future, enable complete sustainability.

Locating the House

The next step after selecting a site is to determine where on the site the house will be located and how it will be oriented. This step is sometimes combined with site selection because the two are closely related. Try to place the house in a location that requires removal of the smallest number of trees. Use the existing trees to your advantage. For example, mature deciduous trees (those that lose and regrow their leaves on a seasonal basis) can provide shade. This helps reduce the amount of energy needed to cool a house in the summer months. In the fall, the trees lose their leaves, which allows the sun to warm the house during the winter months. See **Figure 11-6**.

Before designing the house, spend some time at the building site. Notice the shade patterns at various times of day, and whether there is a prevailing wind (wind that blows in the same direction most of the time). Take these items into consideration so that you can place windows and doors to maximize the use of natural breezes to cool the house.

Plan to pave as little of the site as possible. If you choose a concrete driveway, place the house to minimize the length of the driveway. Concrete holds heat and reduces the natural filtering processes of the land. It also contributes to runoff in heavy rains.

Nejron Photo/Shutterstock.com

Figure 11-6. The large tree on the right side of this home helps protect it from the heat of the summer sun.

Designing a Sustainable Home

The design stage of building a home is critical to its long-term sustainability. At this stage, you can plan not only materials, but also building processes that minimize impact on the environment. Consider ways to incorporate recycled or recyclable components and to reduce or eliminate the use of toxic substances.

Reclaimed and Recycled Building Materials

According to the Environmental Protection Agency (EPA), building construction accounts for 60% of the raw materials used in the United States for purposes other than food and fuel. Salvaging, or ***reclaiming***, materials from buildings that are being torn down, as well as from other sources, is a good way to boost sustainability. Reclaiming materials reduces the need for waste disposal and can even add character to a home. See **Figure 11-7**. Lumber, bricks, doors, windows, fixtures, and cabinets are examples of items that can be reclaimed. For more ideas about designing with reclaimed materials, consult recognized organizations such as PlanetReuse, Habitat for Humanity, and the Building Materials Reuse Association (BMRA). Habitat for Humanity also operates stores that sell reclaimed building materials.

You are probably familiar with many different ***recycling*** programs. They are available for everything from plastics to electronic components. For recycling to work, however, people need to buy products made of recycled materials. Building a home offers many opportunities for incorporating recycled materials. For example, recycled paper can be used to make drywall. Concrete can be made with a high percentage of ***fly ash***, which is ash recovered as a byproduct of coal-burning energy plants. Insulation can be made of a mixture of organic and recyclable materials such as cellulose, cotton, and fiberglass. Metal roofing and siding products, glass tiles, and even kitchen countertops can also be made from recycled materials.

Daniel Goodchild/Shutterstock.com

Figure 11-7. Examples of reclaimed marble in a salvage yard. These marble slabs can be reused to make countertops, mantels, and other items for a new home.

Another consideration is whether the building materials can be recycled at the end of the home's useful life. Many of the recycled materials that go into a home can be recycled again later. This concept of using materials again and again is central to sustainability.

Toxic Substances to Avoid

Many traditional building components contain toxic chemicals. Some of them, such as polyvinyl chloride (PVC) and other chlorinated plastics, are relatively safe for use, but are toxic during their production and again when they are disposed of. Their production and incineration produces ***dioxins***, which are some of the most carcinogenic (cancer-causing) agents known.

Dioxins and heavy metals are known as ***persistent bioaccumulative toxicants (PBTs)***. These items do not break down quickly. They can last for many years or even decades. *Bioaccumulative* means that they build up, or accumulate, in living organisms. They can enter your body through the air you breathe, the food you eat, or even the soil you touch. Not only are PBTs toxic, but many of them have been known to cause mutations and reproductive disorders.

Relatively green alternatives to PVC include polypropylene, polyethylene, and some thermoplastics. See **Figure 11-8**. In the future, possibly the best choice will be to use a sustainably grown bioplastic, which not only removes the toxicity, but also helps reduce our dependence on the

Green Architecture

Aluminum: A Sustainable Material

Recycling aluminum cans is nothing new. People have been doing it for many years. What you may not know is that aluminum recycling is a perfect example of sustainable manufacturing. Aluminum is 100% recyclable, and it can be recycled again and again.

The aluminum recycling process is not complex. It consists of removing contaminants, such as paint, and then melting the aluminum. It can then be molded into storage shapes such as ingots (bars) or rolls. These products are supplied to the manufacturers for use in new products.

Recycling aluminum also saves energy. The recycling process requires only 5% of the energy needed to mine aluminum from bauxite ore. In addition to helping the environment, this lowers the cost of producing aluminum products.

Many communities also accept other types of aluminum products for recycling besides aluminum cans. Accepted items may range from aluminum foil to used lawn furniture. This is important because although aluminum is easily recycled, it decomposes very slowly. If it ends up in a landfill, it may take 400 years or more to break down.

Aluminum can be incorporated into a home design in several ways. Aluminum chips or "flakes" can be incorporated into roofing material to reduce heat absorption, which in turn lowers the cost of cooling the home. Aluminum can also be used with other metals to create alloys that are lightweight, resistant to corrosion, and structurally stable. Because it is sustainable, aluminum is being used more and more in green building designs.

Maryunin Yury Vasilevich/Shutterstock.com

Figure 11-8. Polypropylene is one alternative to PVC for plumbing applications.

Viridian Reclaimed Wood

Figure 11-9. This reclaimed Douglas fir flooring was treated with a low-VOC finish at the factory. It is considered a sustainable product because it is both reclaimed and free of harmful levels of volatile organic compounds.

petroleum that is used in traditional plastics. Sustainably grown bioplastics are not widely available yet; they are still in the research stage.

Other toxins that are commonly found in building materials include ***volatile organic compounds (VOCs)***. These chemicals contain carbon compounds that vaporize at room temperature. We then breathe in the vapor, which often contains known carcinogens such as formaldehyde, toluene, xylene, and benzene. VOCs also contribute to smog and other environmental hazards.

VOCs are commonly present in composite woods, insulation, flooring, paints, and adhesives, among other sources. Read the label carefully when choosing these products. Try to choose low- or no-VOC products as much as possible. See **Figure 11-9**.

Semi-volatile organic compounds (SVOCs) are similar to VOCs, but they release vapor much more slowly. Whereas VOCs are most hazardous during installation and shortly after, SVOCs are released from building materials for much longer periods. SVOCs are commonly added to building materials to increase water resistance or as flame retardants.

Pressure-treated lumber is chemically treated to protect it against decay due to moisture or bugs. Traditionally, pressure-treated lumber contained chemicals, including a type of arsenic, considered both carcinogenic in humans and harmful to the environment. However, this chemical was phased out in 2004 for residential use. It is still a good idea to find out what chemicals were used to treat the wood before using it.

Greenwashing

Many companies are finding that "being green" is an excellent sales tool because green building is currently in fashion. People want to be able to say they have "gone green." Unfortunately, this has led to many false claims that advertise a product as green or environmentally friendly when in fact, it is not. In some cases, the product may even be environmentally harmful.

This practice is known as ***greenwashing***. When looking for green alternatives, both for building materials and for household products, be sure to read the label carefully. Look at the contents or ingredients. If you have any doubt, research the product or its ingredients before purchasing it.

Energy Choices

From an energy perspective, a home is sustainable if it uses net zero energy. A ***net zero energy building*** is one that produces as much energy per year as it consumes, or one for which the net energy cost for a year is $0. Although it was once considered improbable, a few net zero buildings exist now, and both government and private builders are planning to increase that number significantly within the next few decades.

One of the basic principles of designing a net zero building is relying completely on renewable energy sources. A ***renewable energy source*** is one that can supply electricity or other forms of energy from continually replenished sources. Today, many alternatives exist for reducing our dependence on ***nonrenewable energy sources***, such as petroleum. Some of them are still in their infancy. Others, although well established, are not quite as efficient as we would like them to be. Here again, we can plan to be "green" as we work toward sustainability. Renewable energy sources include solar, geothermal, wind, hydropower, and some forms of biomass energy. Of these, both solar and geothermal energy are suitable for direct use in carefully designed residential homes.

Solar Energy

Solar energy, or energy harvested from the sun, can be a completely renewable source of energy. Even when nonrenewable materials are used to create the photovoltaic cells (cells that convert sunlight into electrical energy), solar energy can be a green alternative to petroleum-based energy sources. See **Figure 11-10**.

There are many ways to incorporate solar energy into the design of a home. Probably the best-known example is a solar water heater. Solar energy can be used in many other ways, however, using both active and passive techniques. With careful design, a solar water heater can also power radiant floor heating. Because heat rises, this is an efficient use of a renewable energy source.

An example of a completely renewable solar energy system is a passive solar heating and cooling system. This type of system should be planned for early during the design of the home. This enables the materials for the roof, walls, flooring, and windows to be selected specifically to work with the passive system. The only requirements are a south-facing exposure, the proper materials to allow the sun to enter (glass

Federico Rostagno/Shutterstock.com

Figure 11-10. This home is powered by solar energy. The solar panels and other solar features, such as large expanses of glass on the southern face of the house, were included in the original design of the home.

or plastic), and the proper materials to absorb and store the heat or cold for future use. The materials used in passive solar heating and cooling systems vary according to the temperatures in the region in which the house is built.

Passive solar systems may or may not meet a home's total energy needs. Most homes that incorporate passive systems also have a traditional system as a backup. However, combining a passive solar system with other energy-saving techniques (such as placing windows to catch breezes) can greatly decrease the home's need for nonrenewable energy.

Geothermal Energy

Energy from heat within the Earth is known as ***geothermal energy.*** With the use of a geothermal heat pump, a home can be designed to use the Earth's heat for both heating and cooling. See **Figure 11-11**. Some systems also supply the house with hot water, eliminating the need for a separate water heater.

Unlike passive solar systems, which cost almost nothing as long as they are designed into the house, geothermal heat pumps are expensive. They are very reliable, however, and in most cases, they pay for themselves within 5 to 10 years.

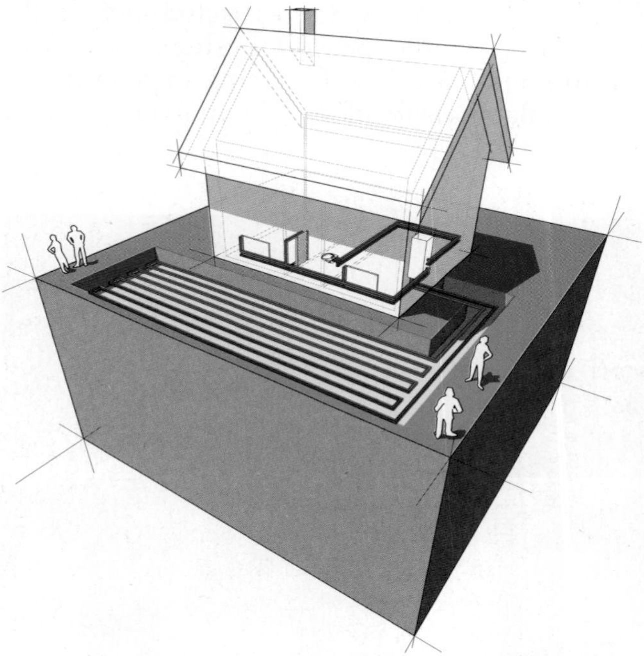

Energy-Efficient Design

Another principle used in designing a net zero building is to reduce the energy requirements of the home. Passive solar heating and cooling help accomplish this, but other tools are used as well. For example, sophisticated air barriers and "super insulating" insulation keep conditioned air from leaking to the outside, and prevent bacteria, toxins, and other unwanted matter from entering the home.

A related method is ***weatherization,*** which helps prevent air from leaking around windows and doors. Weatherization techniques include low-cost processes such as caulking around windows and installing weatherstripping around doors. See **Figure 11-12**. Storm doors and storm windows are also considered forms of weatherization.

Another design technique that can lower energy costs is daylighting. ***Daylighting*** means using windows and skylights to provide natural sunlight for the home. Light from the sun is free and reduces the need to run electric lights. When you design the house and its rooms, place windows and skylights to bring natural light into the home.

Slavo Valigursky/Shutterstock.com

Figure 11-11. A horizontal closed-loop geothermal system like this one is a good choice for a new home. The trenches for the system need to be only four or five feet deep, which helps keep costs down.

LesPalenik/Shutterstock.com

Figure 11-12. Caulking around windows and doors greatly reduces air leaks into and out of the home.

Some designers are now using a technique called ***solar harvesting***. In one form of solar harvesting, interior electric lights are fitted with light and motion sensors. When no one is in the room, or when the natural daylight is sufficient, the sensors turn off the lights automatically. Used with daylighting, this can be an excellent way to reduce the amount of energy consumed in a home.

Water Conservation and Protection

Water is a somewhat renewable resource in the sense that it constantly recycles itself by evaporating from the Earth and then falling again as rain. However, Earth has only a fixed amount of water. As the human population increases, and fresh water supplies become more in demand, conserving and protecting fresh water supplies becomes a priority.

There are many ways to design water conservation into a home. For example, plan to use only water-efficient plumbing fixtures such as high-efficiency toilets and low-flow showerheads.

If the home will have an outdoor irrigation system, plan for one that can use gray water. ***Gray water*** is water that has been used in baths, showers, clothes washers, and bathroom sinks. It does not include wastewater from toilets or from kitchen sinks or dishwashers—that water is called *black water* and must be treated at a sewage facility before reuse. Gray water has been used successfully in many areas for irrigation purposes, greatly reducing the amount of water used by a household. See **Figure 11-13**. The reuse of gray water requires the separation of gray water from black water, so this system is best included as part of the overall, original home design.

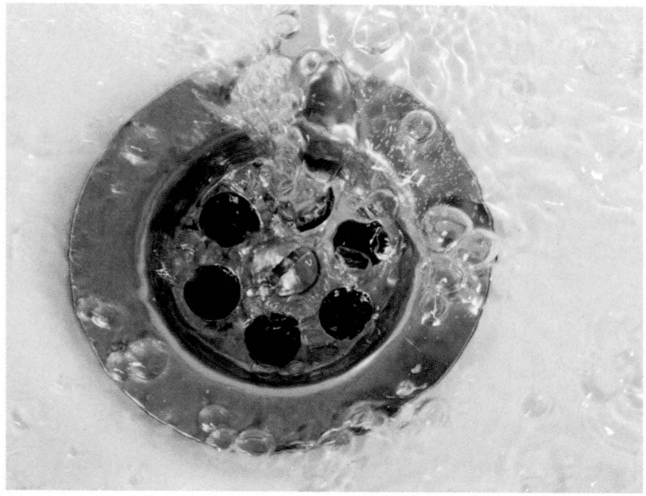

Tiplyashin Anatoly/Shutterstock.com

Figure 11-13. In a traditional home, water used in the shower or bath flows down the drain and into the wastewater or sewage system. Gray water irrigation systems reuse this water to irrigate the landscaping around the home.

Operation and Maintenance

By incorporating a few additional low-cost design ideas, you can help the homeowner live more sustainably over the lifetime of the home. For example, plan for ceiling fans in all of the living spaces, such as the bedrooms, family room, and living room. Running a ceiling fan costs a fraction of what it costs to run a typical air conditioner. Although ceiling fans do not cool the air, they stir a breeze and greatly reduce the need for air conditioning, which reduces energy consumption.

For all electrical appliances, including a traditional air conditioner, be sure the product has earned the ENERGY STAR. See **Figure 11-14**. The ENERGY STAR program was developed jointly by the EPA and the US Department of Energy as a measure to help protect the environment. To earn the ENERGY STAR, a product must meet strict guidelines for energy efficiency.

If you are designing the landscaping as well as the home, incorporate water-efficient landscaping methods to help the homeowner conserve water on an ongoing basis. ***Xeriscaping*** is landscaping using only native plants or plants that are appropriate for the local climate and ecosystem. These plants require less water than "exotic" plants that are better suited for another area of the country (or world). See **Figure 11-15**. Native plants have the additional bonus of being more pest-resistant than exotics, which results in less need for pesticides and other groundwater contaminants.

Irrigation systems—even gray-water systems—can be used efficiently or inefficiently. Encourage the homeowner to practice water conservation by using a few basic techniques:

- Use a controller to turn the irrigation system on and off automatically.

U.S. Environmental Protection Agency, ENERGY STAR program

Figure 11-14. To earn the ENERGY STAR, an appliance or home must meet the energy efficiency guidelines provided by the EPA and the US Department of Energy.

Juha Sompinmäki/Shutterstock.com

Figure 11-15. Using native plants helps reduce the need for irrigation. Notice also the gravel used between stepping stones in this path. Unlike solid concrete surfaces, the gravel allows water to flow naturally into the ground.

- Limit the amount of time the system runs to the minimum needed.
- Irrigate at night to minimize water loss from evaporation.
- Set the controller to water for a shorter amount of time to avoid runoff.

Many people over-water their lawns without realizing it by using a controller to set a certain number of hours per week throughout the year. In reality, plants and grasses require a different amount of water at different times of the year. The amount of irrigation needed also depends on the amount of rainfall the area receives. Some states, such as California, have online calculators that can help people determine exactly how much water their landscaping needs at specific times of the year. If you are responsible for landscaping the site, educate the homeowner about how much water is needed for irrigation and provide tips for conserving water.

Adaptability

Finally, consider what will happen to the home when it is no longer needed or wanted. This may happen when people begin a family, or when their children grow up and move away. Sometimes a homeowner has to move to take a job in another location. The usual result is that the home is sold to another homeowner. Sometimes, however, the needs of the entire community change. The land on which the home was built may be rezoned for a different type of use. Will the home be torn down, or can it be repurposed? As a designer of sustainable housing, you should consider both of these possibilities.

In general, the more flexible a structure is, the better its chances of being repurposed. See **Figure 11-16**. Although it is difficult to look ahead and know what purposes a home may serve many years from now, there are certain

BELL Architects headquarters in Washington, DC; photo by Anice Hoachlander

Figure 11-16. This historic building, a former row house constructed in the late 1800s, was converted to office space by an architectural firm. The style of the original home was retained, both inside and out. The interior space features a restored staircase, exposed ceiling beams, and refinished pine floors.

things a designer can do to make the building more flexible. For example, by designing the home to meet Americans with Disabilities Act (ADA) standards, you can make it easier to convert the home for commercial purposes later. See Chapters 7, 8, and 9 for more information about ADA guidelines and other accessibility guidelines.

Another idea that can make a home more flexible is movable walls. Several manufacturers now offer wall systems that can be installed, moved, or uninstalled in just a couple of hours by homeowners without a knowledge of construction. Being able to move walls allows a homeowner to carve a new bedroom out of excess space, or to join a living room and dining room to make a great room. This flexibility may allow the homeowner to keep the house even when his or her needs change. If the property has been rezoned, movable walls allow the home to be repurposed more easily into commercial or industrial space.

In some cases, no matter how flexible the building design, a home must be torn down. This raises other sustainability issues that should be addressed during the original design stage. From the roof to the foundation, what will happen to the materials from the home? In a sustainable design, every material in the home can be either reused or recycled, without generating waste.

We are not yet capable of zero waste, but we can design homes using materials and processes that significantly reduce waste, use renewable resources, and increase efficiency. The ideas presented in this chapter are merely a starting point. New and better processes, techniques, and materials are being developed every day. As a potential home designer of tomorrow, you can make a big difference by keeping up with new ideas for sustainability and incorporating them into your designs.

Building Information Modeling (BIM)

Many tools are available to help architects and building designers meet the challenges of sustainable design. One such tool is ***building information modeling (BIM)***. BIM is actually a process that utilizes software tools to streamline building design, analysis, and management. BIM provides a way of looking at a building project that includes not only design and construction, but also managing the building throughout its life cycle. It is generally used to meet functional and physical design requirements while minimizing impacts on the environment. BIM is considered a very efficient approach to building design because the architect, engineers, client, and various contractors are all included in decision making from the beginning of the project. The information each of these individuals contributes helps keep the project on track and minimizes delays.

Although BIM is sometimes used in the design of individual homes, it is more commonly used in commercial building projects. BIM is covered in more detail in Chapter 12, *Building Information Modeling.*

Green Certifications

Several national organizations and associations offer certification that a home meets specific "green" standards. Probably the best known is the Leadership in Energy and Environmental Design (LEED) for Homes certification. Another widely recognized certification is the National Green Building Standard certification. ENERGY STAR also certifies new homes, but that certification is based entirely on energy efficiency. Both LEED and the National Green Building Standard certification use a more comprehensive approach.

Another certification used in construction is the Green Globes certification. The Green Globes certification rating systems are primarily for commercial construction, but they can also be used for multifamily buildings. In the United States, Green Globes certification is administered by the Green Building Initiative.

Certification programs are also available at the state level. State certification guidelines can help you tailor your sustainability efforts to suit the environment and ecosystems found in your state. To find programs available in your state, you can search online for "green building certification programs."

LEED for Homes Program

In 2000, the US Green Building Council (USGBC) developed a green building certification program called the LEED Green Building Rating System. Within this program, there are several systems of ratings suited specifically for different applications, such as new and existing residential, commercial, hospital, and school structures. LEED for Homes is the rating system that applies to residential homes. LEED certification verifies that the home has been designed and constructed according to the organization's specific guidelines. See **Figure 11-17**.

LEED for Homes rates buildings on several different factors to achieve a "whole-building approach" to sustainability. The categories addressed for LEED certification include:

- Location and transportation
- Sustainable sites
- Water efficiency
- Energy and atmosphere
- Materials and resources

Employability
Dress Codes

As an employee, you are a representative of your company. Therefore, your employer expects you to be neat and clean on the job. Taking care of yourself gives the impression that you want people to view you as a professional.

Your daily grooming habits should consist of bathing or showering, using an antiperspirant, and putting on clean clothes. Regularly brushing your teeth and using mouthwash will promote healthy teeth and fresh breath. Keep your hair clean and styled in a way that will not be distracting.

Employers also expect their employees to dress appropriately. Many companies have a dress code. If your workplace does not, use common sense and avoid extremes. Refrain from wearing garments that are revealing or have inappropriate pictures or sayings. Some employers have rules requiring that tattoos or piercings other than pierced ears remain covered. Good appearance is especially important for employees who have frequent face-to-face contact with customers.

Activity

Contact an architectural firm in your area and ask about the dress code used in the office. Does the dress code change if an architect needs to visit a client or a construction site? Use the information you learn to propose a general dress code for an architect in the office and in the field.

- Indoor environmental quality
- Innovation
- Regional priority

LEED also offers several levels of professional credentials to architects and building designers who are interested in sustainable design. Applicants must pass an exam administered by the Green Building Certification Institute in order to become certified. The USGBC offers handbooks for each level of credential to help people prepare to take the exam.

National Green Building Standard Certification

The ICC 700 National Green Building Standard was developed by the National Association of Homebuilders (NAHB) and the International Code Council (ICC). This standard, which was approved by the American National Standards Institute (ANSI), addresses design and construction practices for residential buildings. Certification based on practices specified in this standard is administered by Home Innovation Research Labs. Like LEED certification, the National Green Building Standard certification is based on several different categories:

- Site design
- Resource efficiency
- Water efficiency
- Energy efficiency
- Indoor environmental quality
- Building operation and maintenance

Professional certification is available for individuals who are interested in becoming accredited for verifying National Green Building Standard projects.

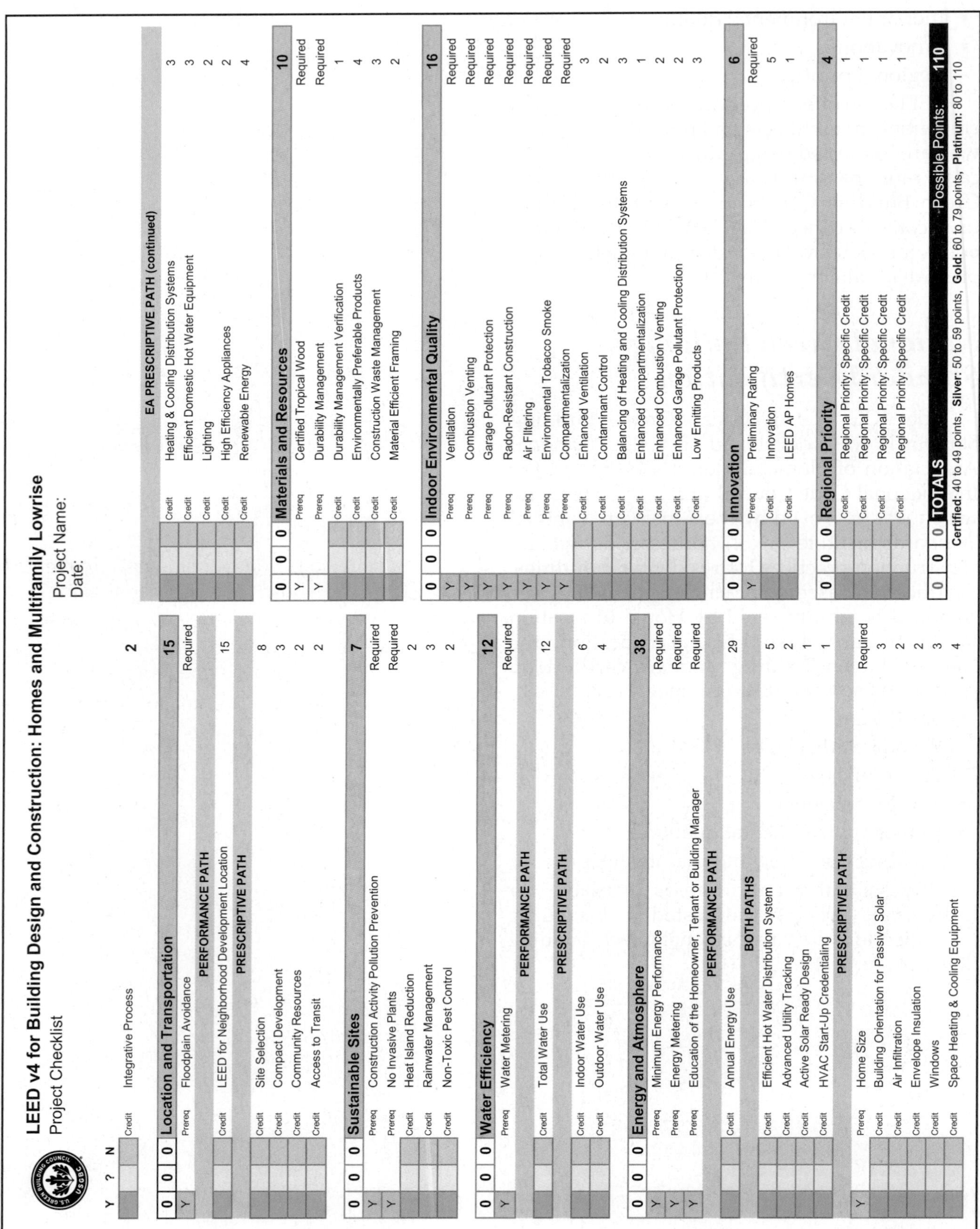

LEED v4 for Building Design and Construction: Homes and Multifamily Lowrise

Project Checklist

Project Name:
Date:

Y	?	N			
			Credit	Integrative Process	2
0	0	0		**Location and Transportation**	**15**
Y			Prereq	Floodplain Avoidance	Required
				PERFORMANCE PATH	
			Credit	LEED for Neighborhood Development Location	15
				PRESCRIPTIVE PATH	
			Credit	Site Selection	8
			Credit	Compact Development	3
			Credit	Community Resources	2
			Credit	Access to Transit	2
0	0	0		**Sustainable Sites**	**7**
Y			Prereq	Construction Activity Pollution Prevention	Required
Y			Prereq	No Invasive Plants	Required
			Credit	Heat Island Reduction	2
			Credit	Rainwater Management	3
			Credit	Non-Toxic Pest Control	2
0	0	0		**Water Efficiency**	**12**
Y			Prereq	Water Metering	Required
				PERFORMANCE PATH	
			Credit	Total Water Use	12
				PRESCRIPTIVE PATH	
			Credit	Indoor Water Use	6
			Credit	Outdoor Water Use	4
0	0	0		**Energy and Atmosphere**	**38**
Y			Prereq	Minimum Energy Performance	Required
Y			Prereq	Energy Metering	Required
Y			Prereq	Education of the Homeowner, Tenant or Building Manager	Required
				PERFORMANCE PATH	
			Credit	Annual Energy Use	29
				BOTH PATHS	
			Credit	Efficient Hot Water Distribution System	5
			Credit	Advanced Utility Tracking	2
			Credit	Active Solar Ready Design	1
			Credit	HVAC Start-Up Credentialing	1
				PRESCRIPTIVE PATH	
Y			Prereq	Home Size	Required
			Credit	Building Orientation for Passive Solar	3
			Credit	Air Infiltration	2
			Credit	Envelope Insulation	2
			Credit	Windows	3
			Credit	Space Heating & Cooling Equipment	4
				EA PRESCRIPTIVE PATH (continued)	
			Credit	Heating & Cooling Distribution Systems	3
			Credit	Efficient Domestic Hot Water Equipment	3
			Credit	Lighting	2
			Credit	High Efficiency Appliances	2
			Credit	Renewable Energy	4
0	0	0		**Materials and Resources**	**10**
Y			Prereq	Certified Tropical Wood	Required
Y			Prereq	Durability Management	Required
			Credit	Durability Management Verification	1
			Credit	Environmentally Preferable Products	4
			Credit	Construction Waste Management	3
			Credit	Material Efficient Framing	2
0	0	0		**Indoor Environmental Quality**	**16**
Y			Prereq	Ventilation	Required
Y			Prereq	Combustion Venting	Required
Y			Prereq	Garage Pollutant Protection	Required
Y			Prereq	Radon-Resistant Construction	Required
Y			Prereq	Air Filtering	Required
Y			Prereq	Environmental Tobacco Smoke	Required
Y			Prereq	Compartmentalization	Required
			Credit	Enhanced Ventilation	3
			Credit	Contaminant Control	2
			Credit	Balancing of Heating and Cooling Distribution Systems	3
			Credit	Enhanced Compartmentalization	1
			Credit	Enhanced Combustion Venting	2
			Credit	Enhanced Garage Pollutant Protection	2
			Credit	Low Emitting Products	3
0	0	0		**Innovation**	**6**
Y			Prereq	Preliminary Rating	Required
			Credit	Innovation	5
			Credit	LEED AP Homes	1
0	0	0		**Regional Priority**	**4**
			Credit	Regional Priority: Specific Credit	1
			Credit	Regional Priority: Specific Credit	1
			Credit	Regional Priority: Specific Credit	1
			Credit	Regional Priority: Specific Credit	1
0	0	0		**TOTALS** Possible Points:	**110**

Certified: 40 to 49 points, **Silver:** 50 to 59 points, **Gold:** 60 to 79 points, **Platinum:** 80 to 110

US Green Building Council

Figure 11-17. The LEED for Homes Design and Construction Checklist.

Summary

- *Sustainability* and *green building* are related terms, but they mean different things; we use green building techniques in our efforts to make homes sustainable.
- Sustainability is a complex concept, and there is much debate about exactly how to achieve it.
- Common sustainable home design programs take into consideration the site on which the home will be built, the materials and processes used in the home, and what will happen to the home at the end of its useful life.
- Building information modeling (BIM) is a method of designing that includes not only the physical design, but also the functional design and management throughout the building's life cycle.
- Certifications are available on the national and state levels to verify that a home meets minimum standards for a "green home."

Internet Resources

Autodesk
BIM software

Building Materials Reuse Association (BMRA)
Design ideas and resources for reclaimed materials

Eco-Structure
News about sustainable building projects and developing technology

Green Home Building
Examples of natural and sustainable building

Home Innovation Research Labs
National Green Building Standard certification

US Green Building Council (USGBC)
LEED certification resources

PlanetReuse
Online resource that matches reclaimed materials with designers, builders, and homeowners

US Department of Energy (DOE)
Information about geothermal heat pumps

US Environmental Protection Agency (EPA)
Resources for sustainable design

Review Questions

Answer the following questions using the information in this chapter.

1. What is the difference between *sustainability* and *green building*?
2. What stages are included in the life cycle of a typical home?
3. Name two goals of sustainable design.
4. Describe two possible impacts on an ecosystem as a result of developing a site and building a home on it.
5. Explain how to position a house on a site to take advantage of existing trees.
6. Name three types of building materials that can be reclaimed and used in new building construction.
7. List at least three relatively green alternatives to using PVC in building construction.
8. What conditions does a home have to meet to be considered a net zero energy home?
9. Explain how daylighting and solar harvesting techniques can be used together to lower the amount of energy consumed in a home.
10. Name two national certifications that are available for sustainable homes and the organizations that offer them.

Suggested Activities

1. Contact your local government or chamber of commerce to find out if your community has any green initiatives or programs. Write a report describing any programs that exist.
2. Contact building supply companies in your area and research the available "green" or sustainable building materials they offer. Prepare a multimedia presentation of your findings.
3. Conduct research to find out more about recycling programs in your area. What items can be recycled? What items *cannot* be recycled? What can people do with items that cannot be recycled in your area but may be recyclable somewhere else? Write a report describing your findings.

4. Find a product at a local grocery or hardware store that is labeled as a "green" product. Read the label carefully and conduct research if necessary to learn more about the product. Is the product really green, or is this an example of greenwashing? Write a report explaining whether you consider the product to be green and why.
5. Conduct an interview with a LEED-certified professional in your area. Ask the professional to explain how he or she became certified and to describe any challenges he or she faced. Prepare a brief oral presentation and present your findings to the class.
6. Like LEED certification, the National Green Building Standard certification is available to professionals as well as buildings. Find out more about the levels of certification for professionals and what certification at each level means. Write a report explaining your findings.
7. Clean, pure drinking water is not available to many people in various parts of the world. Identify key areas where this is a problem. What are some cost effective ways to provide clean, pure drinking water? What are the social and economic impacts of countries failing to provide basic water purification for its citizens? Participate in a group discussion about how citizens can address these concerns.

Problem Solving Case Study

A client has contacted your architectural office in Seattle, Washington, to discuss ideas for her family's new residence. The client wants to incorporate green building concepts and make the home as sustainable as possible. She wants a house with at least three bedrooms, with room for expansion. Given this basic preliminary information, answer the following questions.

1. What type of building materials would you recommend for this client?
2. What further questions would you need to ask the client before you begin the design process?

Certification Prep

The following questions are presented in the style used in the American Design Drafting Association (ADDA) Drafter Certification Test. Answer the questions using the information in this chapter.

1. Match each term with its description.

   Terms: 1. Gray water, 2. Daylighting, 3. Greenwashing, 4. Weatherization, 5. Xeriscaping

   A. Falsely advertising a product as green.
   B. Landscaping using only native plants or plants appropriate for the ecosystem.
   C. Preventing air from leaking around a building's windows and doors.
   D. Using windows and skylights to provide natural sunlight for a home.
   E. Water that has been used in baths, showers, clothes washers, and bathroom sinks.
2. Which of the following statements are true?
   A. An ecosystem is the interaction of plants and animals with each other and the environment.
   B. When selecting a site for a new home, you should consider energy needs for transportation to and from the finished home.
   C. Most lumber naturally contains a high level of dioxins.
   D. At this time, there is no such thing as a net zero energy home.
   E. Passive solar systems increase the cost of a house very little if they are included in the original house design.
3. Which of the following are considered ways to conserve water?
   A. Using high-efficiency toilets throughout the home.
   B. Using gray water for irrigation.
   C. Running dishwashers once a week, whether or not they are full.
   D. Xeriscaping to reduce the amount of water needed by landscaping plants.
   E. Irrigating during daylight hours.

Curricular Connections

1. **Social Science.** The EPA sponsors an Environmentally Preferable Purchasing (EPP) program to help people locate products that are recycled or otherwise considered green. Conduct research to find out more about this program. What effect do you think such a program will have on building supply companies that make an effort to offer green or sustainable products? What effect will it have on companies that offer only traditional products?
2. **Language Arts.** An important skill when you are reading articles about green building (or any other topic) is to be able to distinguish truth from "hype." Find an article in a magazine or on the Internet that discusses any aspect of green building technology. Read the article carefully. Note any statements that seem untrue or make a claim that seems extreme. Conduct further research if necessary to find out whether the claims are true. Then, write a summary paragraph stating whether you think the article is a reliable source of information, and why.

STEM Connections

1. **Technology.** Conduct research to find a new and innovative building material or process that is considered green or sustainable. Write a report describing the new or existing technology used to make the material or process green.

Communicating about Architecture

1. **Speaking.** Conduct a debate on the topic of green building. Divide into two groups. Each group should gather information on a specific country moving toward green building, with one group supporting the movement and the other opposing it. Use definitions and descriptions from this chapter to support your side of the debate and to clarify meanings as necessary. You may need to perform further research to find costs associated with green building, expert opinions, arguments against green building, and other relevant information.
2. **Listening.** As your classmates deliver their presentations on green building, listen carefully to their arguments. Take notes on important points and write down any questions you have. After the presentations, ask questions to obtain additional information or clarification from your classmates as necessary.

Image courtesy of Autodesk

Building information modeling (BIM) has a variety of applications in sustainable design. Shown is a rendered BIM model of a modern office design. In this building, more than 80% of the materials used in the interior spaces are recyclable.

Chapter 12

Building Information Modeling

Objectives

After completing this chapter, you will be able to:

- Explain the principles of building information modeling (BIM).
- Describe the characteristics of a BIM model.
- Explain applications for BIM in commercial and residential architecture.
- List and describe major BIM processes used in a building project.
- Explain the common tools and processes used in parametric modeling.
- Describe common processes used to coordinate models between different engineering disciplines.
- Explain applications for a BIM model in facility management.

Key Terms

BIM model
building information modeling (BIM)
clash detection
construction simulation
detail components
detailing
detail lines
family
file interoperability
front-loading
levels
material takeoff
parametric model
project
project template
schedule
sheet
view range
view template

Building information modeling (BIM) is a design, coordination, construction, and building management process in which a virtual building model physically and functionally replicates the actual building. BIM provides a complete management system for building projects from design through construction and operation.

BIM involves a different approach to design and construction in comparison to traditional practices. Constructing a building as a 3D model allows designers to visualize the building and analyze its performance before construction begins. When used properly and accurately, the tools of a BIM system can produce increased efficiencies throughout design and construction.

While BIM has been used more extensively in commercial construction, the benefits of BIM apply to both commercial and residential architecture. This chapter focuses on the technological aspects of BIM and the ways in which it is impacting the world of architectural design.

Introduction to BIM

Architectural design professionals work in a highly competitive, rapidly evolving industry. The challenges faced by an architectural firm are similar to those in other businesses. In order to succeed, a firm must be able to earn jobs and produce work that meets expectations. The firm must be able to complete design projects on schedule and coordinate work with engineers and contractors. In addition, the firm must be able to stay current with changes in the field and adapt to the use of new technologies and construction processes. Because the construction industry is so competitive, firms are always looking for ways to become more efficient and effective. The ability to manage projects to completion in the most efficient manner possible is critical to a firm's success.

BIM is an approach to building design that allows for management of all aspects of a building project. While BIM is often associated with the use of 3D modeling software, the term *BIM* does not just refer to the use of 3D software to create a virtual building model. BIM encompasses a number of processes that take place throughout a design project and the lifetime of the building. Some of these processes are:

- Conceptual design
- Building analysis
- Model construction and documentation
- Design collaboration
- Cost estimating
- Construction management
- Data management
- Facility management

BIM provides a mechanism for coordinating all of these processes, managing related data, and making the data available to all stakeholders in the project—from designers and engineers to consultants, contractors, building owners, and facility managers.

The virtual building model in a BIM project, called a ***BIM model***, serves as the foundation of the project. See **Figure 12-1**. A BIM model is a 3D solid model that represents the complete building. It contains all required design data for construction. The objects in a BIM model include components such as walls, floors, and stairs. A BIM model is referred to as a ***parametric model*** because each object has editable properties. In this type of model, objects have "smart" relationships with one another. When a change is made to an object, the complete model updates to reflect the change. In addition, each object contains material properties and parameters that identify product data. For example, a wall has thickness and height properties, material properties, and parameters such as fire rating and cost. The wall consists of a system of framing

Model courtesy of Autodesk

Figure 12-1. A BIM model is a virtual representation of a building. This is a custom home developed as a BIM model. The home has photovoltaic panels and wind turbines to provide sources of energy and includes wide expanses of glass to admit natural light.

members and elements that make up the wall assembly. For example, a typical interior wall consists of a 3-1/2″ stud frame with 1/2″ gypsum board on both sides. Each object in the model is an asset that can be used for scheduling, cost estimating, and monitoring in construction and management of the building.

BIM software programs provide predefined objects that can be used "out of the box," as well as tools for creating custom objects to meet specific requirements. This allows the designer to create an accurate model representing the actual items used in construction. However, a BIM model can be used by anyone involved in the project, not just the designer. It provides a live record of the building that can be used for both construction and building management. There are a number of BIM software programs used in building design. Some of the most common are Autodesk® Revit, Graphisoft® ArchiCAD, Bentley® AECOsim Building Designer, and Nemetschek Vectorworks®.

Because a BIM model is a complete representation of a building, the elements making up different building systems can be viewed to verify the validity of the design. For example, the electrical and plumbing systems can be examined to determine if there is interference between electrical conduit and mechanical ductwork. This helps identify design flaws before construction begins. The ability to study a 3D model of the building before it is constructed is one of the key advantages of BIM over traditional design methods.

In a typical CADD workflow, 2D drawings are created to represent the building. The drawings are assembled into a set of documents used in construction. Many architectural firms continue to use this approach because it is efficient and reliable. However, while this method is more efficient than creating drawings manually, the actual process is 2D-based. It is not much different from manual drafting in that 2D lines are used to represent building objects. BIM offers a fundamentally different approach to building design and drawing documentation. A 3D model is created to represent the work and 2D drawing views are generated from the 3D model. All views are stored in a central file, eliminating the need to create and manage separate 2D drawing files. This increases design efficiency and eliminates traditional change management of 2D drawings. In some cases, 2D drawings are not even used in the field. Information for construction can be accessed on site by workers using electronic tablets or other viewing devices.

The use of parametric modeling software instead of a 2D-based CADD system is the most fundamental difference between BIM and traditional design processes. However, there are a number of other differences. BIM provides opportunities to adopt processes that are tailored specifically for 3D modeling, such as computer-generated model simulations, construction simulations, and model collaboration. The 3D modeling process facilitates coordination of work between different engineering disciplines. It allows designers to link models and monitor modeling status in another file, as discussed later in this chapter.

When a firm decides to transition to a BIM system from traditional design processes, there is more involved than just switching to 3D modeling software. Firms face many challenges in making this transition. The extent to which a firm utilizes BIM and coordinates work with other companies are two of the most important issues to consider. Standards have been developed to help address these issues.

The National BIM Standard-United States (NBIMS-US), developed by the BuildingSMART Alliance, specifies information exchange standards for BIM projects. Some countries in Europe have adopted comprehensive BIM standards. In the United Kingdom, the AEC (UK) BIM Technology Protocol specifies software-based practices to meet an acceptable "level" of BIM in construction projects. This standard specifies software-based practices for achieving Level 2 BIM, which refers to 3D modeling collaboration between different engineering disciplines. Level 2 BIM builds on Level 1 BIM, which refers to single-discipline 3D model development without multidisciplinary model sharing. In 2016, the United Kingdom made Level 2 BIM required practice for public works projects. This mandate is part of an initiative to cut construction costs and reduce impact on the environment. In the future, standards development will likely continue as firms explore uses for BIM and seek ways to implement it in projects.

Implementing BIM

Companies that adopt BIM do so with the intent to achieve greater efficiencies in building projects. However, this decision requires careful planning and strategy. Usually, implementation occurs gradually in phases, rather than overnight. One common approach is to implement BIM over a series of projects. For example, a firm may decide to use BIM in a pilot project by creating a 3D model and using it to produce the drawing documentation. After the initial project, the firm may decide to share models and coordinate work with other disciplines. As this process becomes more familiar, subsequent projects may involve greater use of coordination and data exchange. This transition continues to evolve as the firm employs greater use of BIM, and additional parties, including the building owner, become more involved in the process.

Because implementing BIM requires a major shift in how a company operates, proper planning is essential. One of the first steps in implementing BIM is to appoint a BIM manager. This should be someone who can guide the company in its transition and provide the necessary leadership. The BIM manager is usually the person who is most knowledgeable about a certain type of BIM software, but this individual must have a combination of knowledge and management skills. The BIM manager's responsibilities may include the following:

- Software training
- IT management
- Identifying projects that are suitable for BIM
- Assigning roles to team members
- Coordinating work with other disciplines
- Standards development

Firms frequently find it necessary to employ an outside consultant to help with the transition. The consultant can help with training and project coordination. The consultant can also help identify standard practices to implement and mistakes to avoid. In working through this process, the firm must be able to establish a strategy for using BIM to effectively reduce costs. BIM provides very powerful tools, but specific applications and uses must be understood by the firm before it makes BIM part of its business model.

Applications for BIM in Residential and Commercial Architecture

The majority of companies using BIM in architectural design are in commercial construction. See **Figure 12-2**. BIM is also used in residential building projects, but to a lesser extent. There are several reasons for this. Most commercial construction projects are more complex in scope than residential projects. Large commercial projects usually have much longer time frames and sequences that require greater monitoring. Typically, large commercial projects have a larger economy of scale and tend to have higher profit margins than residential projects. Projects in the commercial sector stand to benefit more from BIM because the improvements in efficiency produce greater savings and have more impact.

Botswana Innovation Hub - SHoP Architects

Figure 12-2. BIM is commonly used in commercial building projects. This is a BIM model of a science and technology center. The wing shown is the central building, which serves as a collaboration area for the building tenants.

By comparison, since many residential projects are less complex and have tighter profit margins, there is the belief that BIM offers only marginal benefit in residential architecture.

For some residential firms, the startup costs involved in implementing BIM can present a significant challenge. Commercial firms typically have larger staffs and more resources to work with than residential firms, so they are usually better equipped to invest in the necessary training and development. Many commercial firms view BIM as an opportunity to save on costs and generate new business in a growing area of the industry.

One of the biggest reasons that BIM has had more growth in the commercial sector is competition. Not only are some governments mandating use of BIM in certain projects, there is growing demand from private clients who want BIM to be part of the contracted work. Many owners are interested in acquiring a BIM model of the building once construction is completed. A BIM model has valuable applications for owners. It can be used to track building operation costs and schedule equipment maintenance. Because commercial building owners have become more interested in BIM, commercial firms that do not adopt BIM risk falling behind and losing business to other firms. For the most part, these issues have not been as important in residential construction because there has been less demand from home buyers.

One area in which BIM has measurable benefits to residential designers is custom home design. See **Figure 12-3**. A BIM model can be analyzed in the early design stages to determine whether it meets the criteria in a green building standard, such as the Leadership in Energy and Environmental Design (LEED) certification. The LEED for Homes certification is popular with home buyers who are interested in sustainability issues, such as renewable energy and water conservation.

GRAPHISOFT
The Eco-house 3.0|NOEM - noem.com|photo © Meritxell Arjalaguer

Figure 12-3. This custom home is a prefabricated design constructed from locally sourced wood. The home was designed using BIM software. Design and construction of the home was completed in 10 weeks.

Regardless of whether a firm is involved in commercial or residential architecture, BIM offers a number of advantages to consider. Some of the primary advantages are described below.

- **Productivity.** After implementation has been accomplished, a firm has the potential to produce work that is more accurate and easier to manage. All of the drawing documentation associated with a BIM model is stored in a single file. Editing a BIM model updates all associated geometry and views simultaneously. This is much more efficient than editing multiple drawing files and updating printed drawings individually.
- **Visualization.** The ability to view a structure in three dimensions offers a powerful design tool. Displaying plan views and 3D views on screen helps in visualizing the design and verifying that it is accurate. In addition, renderings and animations of 3D models are usually much easier for clients to visualize than 2D drawings. See **Figure 12-4**. Model renderings, as well as the model itself, can be shared with clients early in the design process to obtain feedback.
- **Collaboration.** BIM helps streamline coordination with different disciplines involved in the design process. By referring to a 3D model prepared by an architect, for example, a structural engineer can model the necessary structural elements. The same process can be used by mechanical, electrical, and plumbing engineers, as discussed later in this chapter. This process helps foster communication and cooperation between different engineers. It also helps reduce design errors and rework.
- **Marketing.** A firm using BIM can promote itself as a provider of BIM services. See **Figure 12-5**. The firm can leverage BIM to attract new business by educating clients on the benefits of BIM processes. Additionally, BIM can be used to earn repeat business from clients who "buy in" and decide to use it for future projects.

The decision to adopt BIM also involves challenges and risks. It is very likely that a firm will experience growing pains during implementation. Adopting BIM requires re-thinking of traditional office practices and can require significant effort to learn new skills and delivery

Image courtesy of Archaus Architects Limited

Figure 12-4. Renderings of BIM models are effective tools in communicating the design to clients. The interior of this apartment features a gas fireplace and a spectacular bayside view.

Image courtesy of Autodesk

Figure 12-5. Model renderings are commonly prepared for marketing purposes. This medical building was designed in BIM software and rendered in presentation software.

methods. Disadvantages associated with implementation of BIM are described below.

- **Initial investment.** There are a number of costs to consider in implementing a BIM system. Among the most significant are investment in new software and hardware, software training, investment in infrastructure to support large file storage and exchange, and IT management. Software training is one of the most difficult costs to project. In some cases, training can require a significant amount of time. Other startup costs are related to new technical processes that emerge as a result of switching to 3D modeling software. During the transition, company drafting standards must be revised and an accepted modeling standard must be developed. Company drafting standards are typically used to cover dimensioning and detailing practices, while a modeling standard is used to cover processes such as 3D modeling practices, content library development, and template development.
- **Level of implementation.** The extent to which BIM is used in actual practice and the manner in which information is organized and shared present major questions for many firms. There are many different aspects to BIM and successful implementation depends on many factors. In order to support model coordination, for example, one key factor is the ability to exchange data between different software programs. This is called ***file interoperability***. The software used by a firm must be able to produce files that can be opened by others involved in design, construction, and building management. File exchange standards have been established to address this issue. The Industry Foundation Classes (IFC) file format is a standard exchange format used for BIM software programs. However, file exchange is just one aspect of BIM management. There are other aspects that require definition of standard practices. In the future, standards may address issues such as level of BIM compliance, ownership of model data, and data management protocols.

Ultimately, architectural firms must weigh the benefits and risks and decide whether BIM can produce greater profitability. For residential firms, this decision will likely be guided by customer demand, growth and acceptance in industry, and development of industry standards.

BIM Processes

One of the key objectives in using BIM is to streamline coordination with the different contributors in a building design project. The design, scheduling, construction, and data management tools of a BIM system are used to help achieve this objective.

Major BIM processes that take place over the course of a building design project include model design, model construction, model collaboration, data management, and facility management. Each process is coordinated so that all stakeholders have the opportunity to provide input. The following sections discuss these processes and related tools.

Model Design

A building design project typically begins with design studies. The design studies are intended to serve as a comprehensive analysis of the design. For example, a building site is initially studied to evaluate existing conditions and environmental impacts of the proposed structure. Factors such as solar orientation, wind patterns, and building code requirements are studied. This phase of design is commonly referred to as schematic design. It is during this phase that conceptual designs and models are prepared and evaluated. In a BIM project, these may consist of hand sketches, computer-generated renderings, or a combination of the two. See **Figure 12-6**. Once the initial design concept is approved, the project moves from schematic design into the design development phase, where more detailed development occurs.

To gain the most benefit from BIM, it is customary to involve as many stakeholders as possible in the early design stages. This allows information to be collected from engineers,

Employability

Community Service

Most people in the United States act as responsible and contributing citizens. As communities look for ways to improve housing for citizens and protect the environment, opportunities exist for people and their employers to take action. Some companies encourage their employees to become involved in community service. There are a number of organizations that provide opportunities for volunteering in community service projects. For example, Rebuilding Together is an organization that makes free repairs to homes owned by people with limited income. Rebuilding Together's volunteer programs are designed to improve homes owned by people such as older adults, people with disabilities, and veterans.

Activity

Your employer asks you to organize and lead a team of employees to help improve living conditions for citizens in your community. To start the community service project, your employer agrees to give participating employees one workday to initiate a project. You and several team members decide to attend a city council meeting to identify housing and environment issues in your community that negatively impact citizens. The workday following the council meeting, plan to take the following steps.

- Identify the community concerns. Brainstorm ways to address one or more of the problems. Evaluate the list and narrow it down to one project on which the team members agree.
- Have the team set a goal. Determine what resources your team needs to meet the goal.
- Create a plan for achieving the goal. How can individual team members continue to help meet the team goal after the initial action?
- Carry out the team plan and evaluate the results. How was your team able to meet its goal and your employer's goal of getting involved in the community? In what ways have team members carried on with the project to meet the needs of other citizens in the community?

A

B

C

Dennis Dixon
BluPrint Design + Build

Figure 12-6. Conceptual sketches and models are commonly used in the early design stages to communicate design ideas. A—A hand-drawn sketch used to develop an initial design concept for a custom home. B—An exterior rendering created from a BIM model of the home. Presentation software was used to render the model in a "sketched" style. C—An interior rendering of the home.

contractors, consultants, material suppliers, and the building engineers who will ultimately be responsible for maintaining the building. This is called ***front-loading*** the project. This approach is intended to minimize design errors and reduce the need for changes during construction. For example, input from the contractors helps establish how the building will be constructed, which helps minimize change orders and construction waste. This input also helps ensure that the appropriate building materials will be used in the design and that accurate quantities of materials can be ordered.

Front-loading is an efficient approach because all stakeholders are included in decision making from the beginning of the project and there is a greater chance that the appropriate design decisions are made. This improved efficiency allows more time to focus on design, which helps drive innovation.

One of the most important factors considered during the early stages of design is sustainability. The design is studied to identify opportunities for using sustainable materials and improving the energy efficiency of the building. This is typically achieved through model analysis and design simulations.

Model Analysis

Sustainability is an important objective in architectural design. Issues such as energy consumption, water use, and efficient use of resources are key factors to consider in building projects. These issues have become more important to building owners because of rising energy costs and the desire to protect the environment. In response to these issues, green building efforts have become common. Many buildings are designed to meet requirements in green building certifications and standards such as LEED, ENERGY STAR, and the International Green Construction Code. Sustainable design is introduced in Chapter 11, *Designing for Sustainability*.

BIM processes help designers integrate sustainable design principles. As part of the design process, a 3D model can be analyzed using design simulations. Design simulations are software-based tools used to simulate conditions and analyze building performance. By analyzing models in this manner, designers can study alternative scenarios and enhance performance factors such as energy efficiency. Model analysis occurs during the early stages of design so that input from different sources is considered. This is a powerful tool for reducing energy costs.

Design simulations can be used to evaluate aspects such as site conditions, carbon emissions, water management, wind patterns, ventilation, thermal performance, daylighting and lighting loads, shadows and reflections, and energy use. See **Figure 12-7**. The results of a simulation can be compared with established LEED or ENERGY STAR standards to determine whether the design is in compliance.

Some software programs that are primarily used for modeling work provide analytic tools for performing simulations. However, this varies.

Green Architecture

Carbon Footprint

A carbon footprint is a measurement of how much the everyday behaviors of an individual, company, or nation can impact the environment. It includes the average amount of carbon dioxide put into the air by energy and gas used at home and in travel, as well as other more detailed aspects. The construction industry as a whole has a large carbon footprint. The processes used in transporting building materials and operating construction equipment greatly impact the environment. The electricity that goes into producing certain building products, such as brick, causes the emission of great quantities of carbon dioxide.

Design simulations can be used to evaluate the carbon performance of a building. Usually, a whole-building energy analysis can be used to generate a carbon emissions report. The report indicates the annual carbon output based on the geographic location and other factors, such as the heating and cooling systems used by the building. Also included in the report are the annual usage and cost of electricity for the building.

Based on the simulation results, adjustments can be made to improve the building's carbon output and thermal performance. For example, the designer can change the site orientation, select different exterior window glazing, or adjust the window-to-wall percentage.

London Blackfriars station, courtesy of Network Rail and Jacobs®

Figure 12-7. Design simulations can be used to simulate construction conditions for visualization purposes. This simulation is being used to isolate the structural and mechanical building systems in an integrated model to coordinate multidisciplinary work.

In some cases, software add-ons or separate programs are used for more comprehensive analysis.

To perform a simulation, the designer configures the model for a specific type of study. The software calculates the results based on criteria such as the geographic location, local climate patterns, time and date, size of the building envelope, and thermal zones of the building. The analysis results are displayed in a visual format to assist the designer in interpreting information. Still or animated simulations are usually performed, depending on the type of analysis. An energy analysis can be animated, for example, to show the effects of natural light and shadows in an indoor space. Still simulations typically use a surface-mapped display to illustrate the results. See **Figure 12-8**. This example shows an energy analysis simulation to determine the effects of adding window shades to the building. Notice the color variations between the still images.

A solar study can be used to determine the effects of sunlight and the location of the sun at different times of day relative to the site. See **Figure 12-9**. The solar study in this example displays the path of the sun from sunrise to sunset and the total sun area over the period of a year. The position of the sun is based on the current time of day. Additional tools can be used to analyze other factors. For example, an animation can be created from the solar study to show shadow casting at different times of day for a given geographic location.

A structural analysis can be used to analyze loads. This type of analysis is common in commercial construction. For example, a structural design can be analyzed to check strength data for beam and column connections and verify that sizes of structural components are correct. See **Figure 12-10**.

The results of a design simulation can be used to optimize the model by making the appropriate design changes. For example, based on the results of a heating and cooling study, the designer can select different exterior window glazing to improve thermal performance. The ability to optimize energy efficiency early in the design process provides a powerful tool to reduce building costs and pass along the savings to the owner.

A

B

Images courtesy of ARBA Studios

Figure 12-8. These are still images generated from an energy analysis simulation. The simulation is used to study how artificial lighting can be minimized in the indoor space and determine the effects of adding window shades to reduce glare. A summary of values in lighting units is included. A—The indoor space without shading devices. B—The space after adding the proposed shading devices.

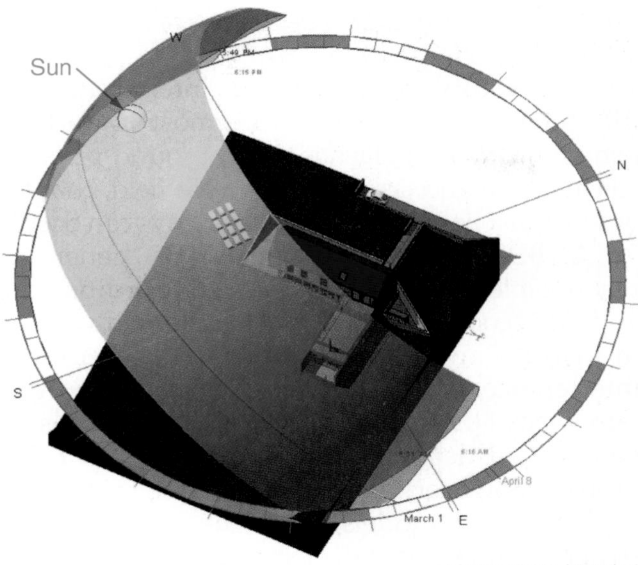

Model courtesy of Autodesk

Figure 12-9. A solar study can be used to simulate the location and path of the sun in relation to the home. Shown are the afternoon location of the sun and the total sun area over a period of a year.

Cost Estimating

One of the first steps in a design project is to prepare a preliminary estimate of material and labor costs to construct the building. The preliminary estimate is used to obtain approval from the client and helps in making design decisions. Generally, the preliminary estimate is a rough estimate of costs. Once the design has been approved, a more accurate estimate, called a detailed estimate, is prepared. The tools of a BIM system help streamline this process.

A BIM model supplies all of the building data used in cost estimating. Each object in a BIM model has properties that identify information such as material, type, manufacturer, part number, and size. This information can be used to create a material takeoff. A ***material takeoff*** is a list of quantities of materials used in constructing a building. A material takeoff accounts for all building materials used in construction. For example, each material in a 2 × 6 exterior wall with brick veneer, including the brick, plywood

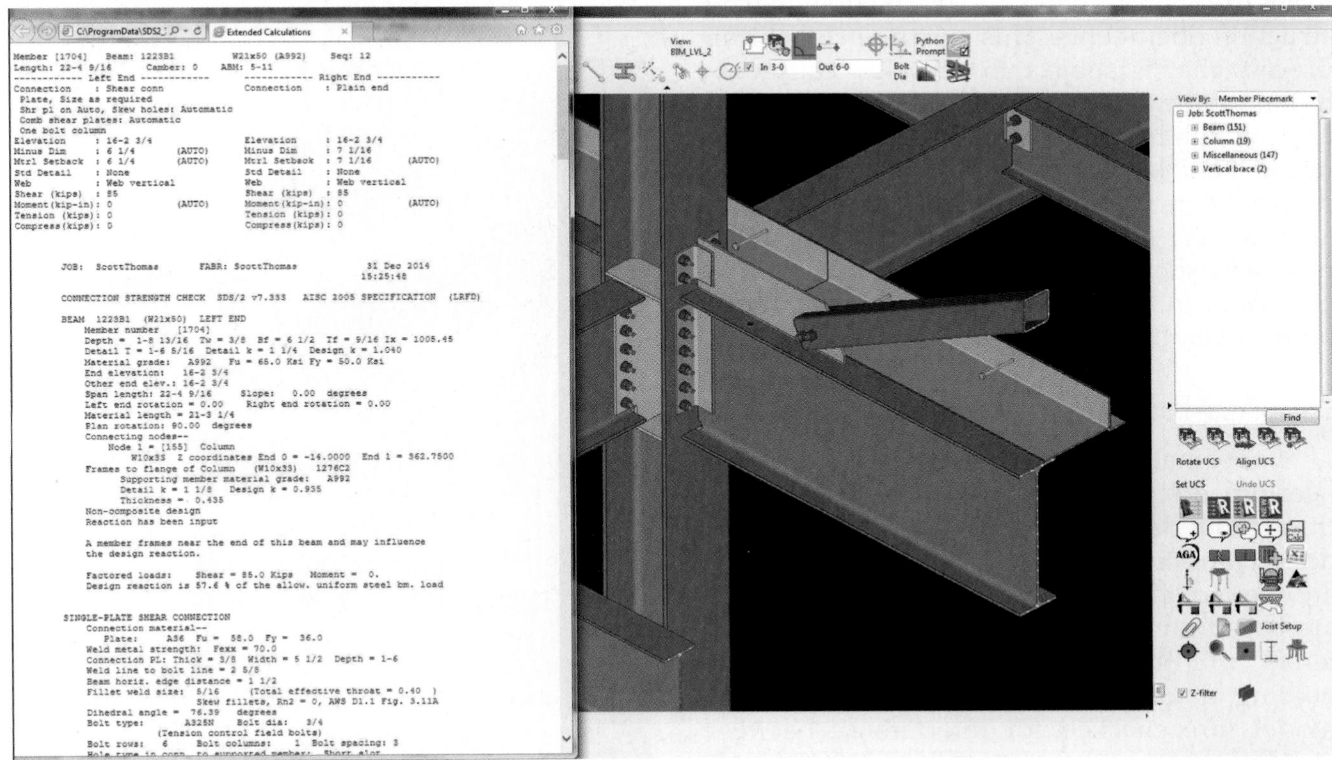

Goodheart-Willcox Publisher

Figure 12-10. This structural analysis shows load and strength calculations for a beam and column assembly.

sheathing, stud, insulation, vapor barrier, and gypsum board, is considered and listed individually. This provides accurate quantities for estimating costs and ordering materials.

Some modeling software programs provide tools for creating a material takeoff automatically. The material takeoff appears similar to a spreadsheet and can be formatted to include material counts and quantities in units such as linear feet, square feet, and cubic feet. However, a more common method to create a material takeoff is to import the design model into an estimating software program. The software is then used by an estimator to prepare the estimate. The estimator creates a material takeoff from the model and adds material prices and labor costs to calculate the estimate. The imported model file is linked so that if changes are made to the design model, information in the material takeoff updates automatically and changes are reflected in the estimate. This allows estimates to be precisely calculated. Estimating is discussed in more depth in Chapter 36, *Estimating Building Costs*.

Traditionally, estimators prepared cost estimates manually by hand by working from the construction documents. This is a time-consuming process that is subject to mistakes caused by human error. Preparing estimates directly from information in a BIM model is much more accurate and efficient. It also provides flexibility to the design team in managing costs and exploring alternatives. For example, different brands of products, such as windows or cabinets, can be compared in the model to determine the impact on the overall cost.

Clash Detection

Coordination of work with different engineering disciplines plays an essential role throughout design and construction. In a typical design project involving BIM, a number of models are created in different disciplines. The models are based on the same design, but contain different building systems related to each engineering discipline. Prior to construction, the models are checked for interference between building components. Interference checking in BIM software is commonly referred to as ***clash detection***. This process takes place before construction begins. It helps ensure that conflicts are found and design revisions are in place to correct the errors.

The ability to check for interference in different models is one of the most important benefits of BIM. If clashes are not found prior to construction and errors occur in the field, change orders must be issued and costly delays can occur.

A BIM project coordinator is generally responsible for managing model coordination. Typically, coordination meetings are held weekly to identify and resolve conflicts. To check for interference, the different models are imported into special software. The number of models to be checked depends on the complexity of the project. However, in a typical project, there may be individual models from the architectural, structural, mechanical, electrical, and plumbing trades.

In a clash detection study, the software evaluates model geometry and highlights areas in the building where interference exists. This process identifies clashes between elements such as structural members, mechanical ductwork, plumbing lines, and electrical conduit. See **Figure 12-11**. Preventing these types of clashes from happening

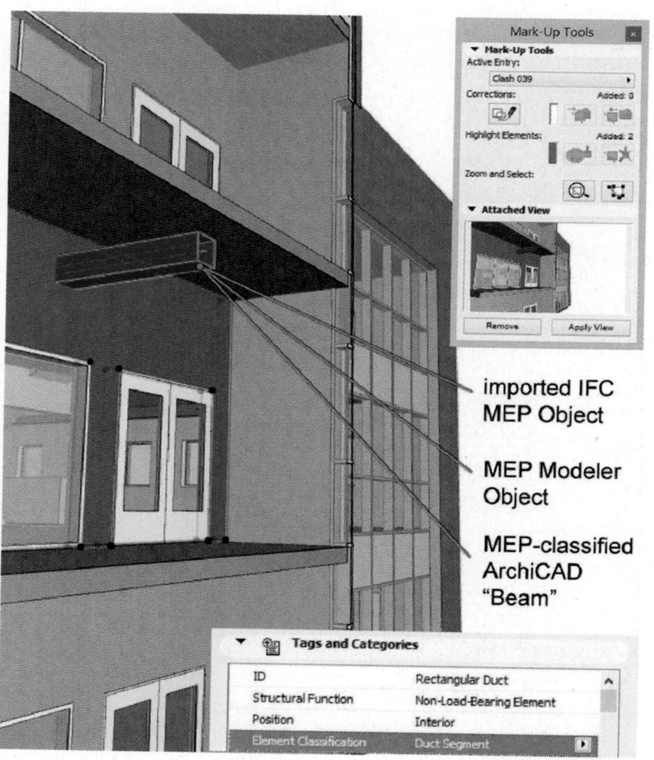

GRAPHISOFT

Figure 12-11. A clash detection study. This study indicates that the rectangular duct requires redesign.

in the field is critical for construction efficiency and helps reduce material waste.

Simulating Construction

Designing and constructing a building model in 3D modeling software is much like constructing the actual building. Creating a building model requires knowledge of building materials, building systems, and construction processes. See **Figure 12-12**. In order to create an accurate model, the designer must know how these processes work so that the building reflects sound building practices.

Before construction takes place in a BIM project, it is possible to create a construction simulation to verify constructability of the building. A ***construction simulation*** is an animation that illustrates construction processes in sequential order. The animation is created in special software and is based on an installation schedule. The installation schedule specifies construction tasks and related information, such as start and end dates. To create the animation, components in the building are grouped into selection sets and associated to tasks in the installation schedule. During playback of the animation, components move into place according to the scheduled tasks. This is a powerful tool for visualizing when specific construction activities occur and checking the status of the project at a certain date.

Construction simulations are particularly important to contractors, who can determine which methods to use for specific processes ahead of construction. These types of simulations can also help contractors predict potential conflicts in construction and manage scheduling so the project is built on time. A construction simulation can also be shared with building owners, who can view the expected sequence of activities before crews break ground.

Model Construction

BIM model construction is based on a parametric modeling workflow. In this type of

Model courtesy of DesignGroup and the National Audubon Society

Figure 12-12. In order to construct a BIM model accurately, the designer must be familiar with building materials, building systems, and construction processes. Notice the exposed ductwork, steel joists, and steel beams in this model.

modeling, elements such as walls, floors, doors, and windows are created as 3D objects. Objects can be edited parametrically and have "smart" relationships with one another. All model edits have a downstream effect so that any geometry associated with an edit is automatically updated.

As previously discussed, creating a BIM model is similar to constructing the actual building. The designer must have an understanding of construction principles to construct the model accurately. For example, it is important to have an understanding of common framing methods used to construct walls, floors, ceilings, and roofs. The designer must also have an understanding of structural construction and the typical materials and fasteners used. Construction systems used in residential construction are covered in later chapters of this text.

A BIM model serves a number of purposes. On one hand, the model can be studied to analyze building performance and conflicts in construction, as previously discussed. In addition, a BIM model can be used to create the construction drawings used in the building project. One of the major advantages in creating a BIM model for this purpose is that work takes place in a 3D environment, allowing the model to be viewed in its physical form from different viewpoints. The display can be quickly switched between plan, section, elevation, and 3D views to make it easier to visualize features during modeling work. The following sections discuss the typical processes involved in creating a BIM model.

Model Setup

The first step in constructing a BIM model is to create a new project. A ***project*** is a file that stores all of the model geometry and views associated with the model. A project template provides a starting point for creating a new project. A ***project template*** is a file configured with predefined settings, model content, and views that can be applied to a new project. Usually, a project template is set up for a specific discipline, such as architectural, structural, or mechanical design. As the designer becomes more familiar with the modeling process, template development becomes more important. For example, project templates are typically created to incorporate office drafting standards and discipline-specific content. Project templates are powerful standardization tools that can save considerable setup time.

Modeling software used in BIM provides a 3D design environment for creating a building model and preparing the drawing documentation. The model is constructed by working in different views. Each view provides a working space in which to construct model geometry. For example, walls can be created by working in a plan view, such as a floor plan view. Objects that are created are visible in other views. In addition, changes made in a given view are reflected in other views.

The views in the model file are usually set up to coordinate with the major types of views and working drawings used in architectural drafting. Typical types of views include plan views, sections, elevations, and discipline-specific views, such as mechanical, electrical, and plumbing plan views. The views are named to identify the content and relationship to the building. For example, a view named First Floor Plan is used to represent the first floor plan view of the model. Each view can be prepared for drawing documentation purposes. Then, views are inserted onto sheets. A ***sheet*** is different from a view. A sheet is a layout that contains a title block and a view for printing.

Views in the model file are organized in a logical order by the software. In the modeling interface, views are listed in a window similar in appearance to a file explorer window. See **Figure 12-13**. Views are organized under named categories such as Floor Plans, Ceiling Plans, Sections, and Elevations. This helps keep track of all the views in a model. A similar organization is used for sheets, as shown in **Figure 12-13**.

The method in which views and sheets are organized in the model file differentiates BIM from traditional CADD processes. For example, in CADD work, the different drawings created in a project may be organized by using different layers, different drawing files, or a combination of the two. In this approach, it is common to have multiple drawing files that host other drawings. This requires an additional level of project management. In a BIM model, all of the model views and drawing documentation are stored in a single file. This greatly simplifies file storage and makes it much easier to locate drawing views, provided that the views are properly named and organized.

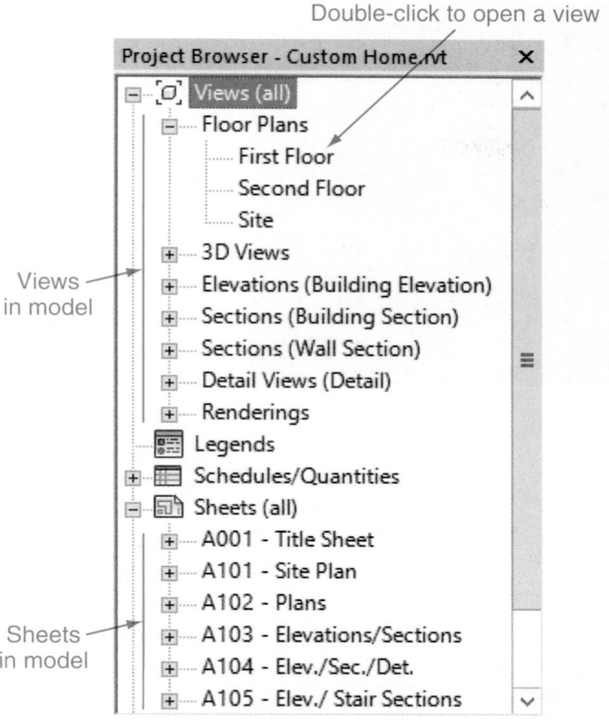

Model courtesy of Autodesk

Figure 12-13. The views in a parametric model file are logically organized and grouped under named categories. Sheets are organized in the same manner.

The organization of views in a BIM model helps the designer manage content in other ways. For example, object visibility can be controlled within each view by adjusting the view's visibility settings. In a floor plan view, objects that are normally set to display include walls, floors, casework, doors, and windows. Objects that are turned off include topographic components used in site plan development. The visibility settings for a view can be saved to a ***view template***. View templates are typically built into a project template. In addition to visibility settings, a view template can include settings such as the view scale, graphic display style, and view range. The ***view range*** defines the range of visibility for objects in a plan view.

The most common views that are used in new projects are usually saved in a project template. Any additional views that are needed can be created after starting a new project or during the modeling process.

Another common step during model setup is to create the levels that will be used in the project. ***Levels*** are assigned elevations that define key heights of the building. Each level is assigned a name and an elevation height. For example, a level named First Floor can be used to establish the elevation of the first floor. Levels are assigned to plan views and are usually created in an elevation view, as discussed later in this chapter.

Once the model file is set up with the appropriate views and levels, modeling can begin. Creating views is discussed in the following sections.

Creating Plan Views

In a residential design project, model construction typically starts with creating the floor plan view. See **Figure 12-14**. Often, the floor plan view serves as a basis for other views. This section introduces basic processes for creating a floor plan and other typical plan views for a residential home. Procedures with specific steps for creating plan views, section views, and elevations in parametric modeling are presented in later chapters. These procedures address modeling processes in greater depth. For example, creating a floor plan is covered in Chapter 14, *Floor Plans*.

Normally, the first step in creating the floor plan is to create the exterior and interior walls. Walls are created using the **WALL** command. After accessing the command, a wall type representing the materials used in construction is selected and the wall is drawn by picking start and end points. If one of the default wall types in the program does not include the necessary materials, a new wall type can be created. This is usually done by duplicating a default wall type and editing it to define the required materials. This is a common process that can be used with other object types when a default object does not meet the design requirements.

After the exterior and interior walls are created, additional features used on the floor plan are modeled. Doors and windows are added by selecting the appropriate components and inserting them in the exterior walls. It may be necessary to load a family containing the required door or window types if they are not available in the model. A ***family*** is a collection of components that represent variations of the same item in different sizes and orientations. Families containing items such as doors, windows,

A

B

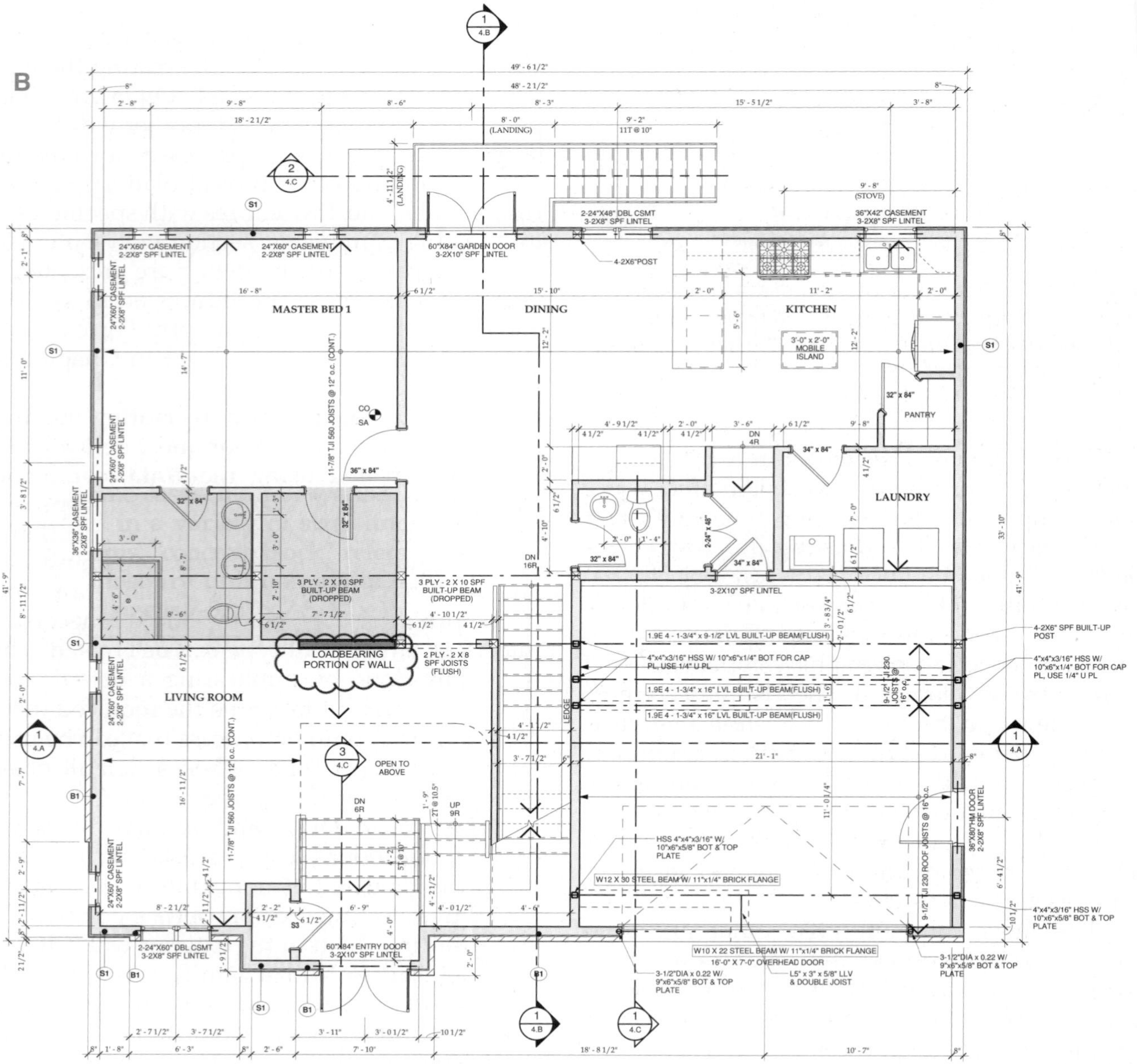

MASTER BED 1

DINING

KITCHEN

LAUNDRY

PANTRY

LIVING ROOM

LOADBEARING PORTION OF WALL

OPEN TO ABOVE

3'-0" x 2'-0" MOBILE ISLAND

60"X84" GARDEN DOOR 3-2X10" SPF LINTEL

60"X84" ENTRY DOOR 3-2X10" SPF LINTEL

16'-0" X 7'-0" OVERHEAD DOOR

W10 X 22 STEEL BEAM W/ 11"x1/4" BRICK FLANGE

W12 X 30 STEEL BEAM W/ 11"x1/4" BRICK FLANGE

3 PLY - 2 X 10 SPF BUILT-UP BEAM (DROPPED)

2 PLY - 2 X 8 SPF JOISTS (FLUSH)

11-7/8" TJI 560 JOISTS @ 12" o.c. (CONT.)

9-1/2" TJI 230 ROOF JOISTS @ 16" o.c.

1.9E 4 - 1-3/4" x 16" LVL BUILT-UP BEAM(FLUSH)

1.9E 4 - 1-3/4" x 9-1/2" LVL BUILT-UP BEAM(FLUSH)

49' - 6 1/2"

48' - 2 1/2"

41' - 9"

Dennis Dixon
BluPrint Design + Build

Figure 12-14. A—This custom home design was developed using BIM software. B—The first floor plan for the home.

and furniture are usually included with the software and can be loaded into a project as needed. Some product manufacturers supply files on their websites for the same purpose.

The floor of the building is commonly modeled when creating the floor plan. A floor is created using the **FLOOR** command. The appropriate floor type is selected and a sketch is made to define the area of the floor. The floor represents the type of floor framing used and is made up of the structural materials used in construction, such as wood joists or a concrete slab.

To complete the floor plan, additional components, such as casework, appliances, fixtures, and stairs, are added. As components are placed, editing tools can be used to help in the process. Editing tools are used for moving or rotating components, making copies of existing components, creating mirror copies, creating arrays, and trimming and extending geometry. These tools are similar to standard editing commands used in 2D CADD software.

The floor plan can be duplicated if a similar type of plan is needed in the construction documents. For example, to create a furniture plan, a duplicate of the floor plan can be made and used to add the furniture. The visibility settings in the floor plan are then adjusted to turn off the display of furniture.

If the building has a second floor, another floor plan view can be created by creating a level named Second Floor and assigning it to a view named Second Floor Plan. Then, objects are added to the second floor of the model. If there are objects from the first floor that are in the same locations on the second floor, such as interior walls, they can be copied using a copy-and-paste operation.

Other views are used in similar fashion to construct additional building systems in the model. For example, to create the building foundation, a view named Foundation Plan can be used. The view is set to the appropriate level for creating the foundation walls. Once the walls are created, structural components such as footings, columns, and beams are added. A foundation with a basement also includes a structural floor, interior walls, and any additional components located in the basement. See **Figure 12-15**.

The roof of the structure is added by creating a roof system that uses the materials in construction. A roof is created using the **ROOF** command. The roof can be modeled in a view that corresponds to a level at the top of the exterior walls, such as the Top of Plate level. The roof is modeled based on the specific style of roof used for the building. For example, the roof can be modeled as a gable, hip, or flat roof. The exterior walls of the structure are used as a location reference and a sketch is made to define the area of the roof. For gable and hip roofs, the roof slope and slope direction are specified. Additional features, such as fascia boards, soffits, and gutters, are added to complete the roof.

The same basic modeling process is used for the other building systems used in the structure. For example, additional views can be used to model the mechanical, electrical, and plumbing systems. The components of each system are modeled in the appropriate view and each view is named to identify the content.

Section views and elevation views can be prepared in similar fashion for the construction drawings. However, these views are also useful for design and visualization purposes. These views are discussed in the following sections.

Section Views

A section view shows a portion of a building as if it has been "cut." In parametric modeling, a section view is created by drawing a cutting-plane line to represent where the section is to be "cut." This process requires picking two points to locate the cutting-plane line. Then, the section view is automatically generated by the program.

The **SECTION** command is used to create a section view. Section views can be created as building sections, wall sections, and detail sections. Building sections and wall sections are normally used in the drawing documentation to clarify construction requirements. See **Figure 12-16**.

Creating section views plays an important role during the modeling process. Often, creating a section helps the designer verify feature locations or visualize features to be modeled. A common process is to create a section view in order to edit the profile of a feature, such as a wall. After creating the section view, the view is displayed and the wall is edited by editing the sketch of the wall. This technique can be used to create a "cutout" in a wall or an architectural feature, such as a radial curve at the top.

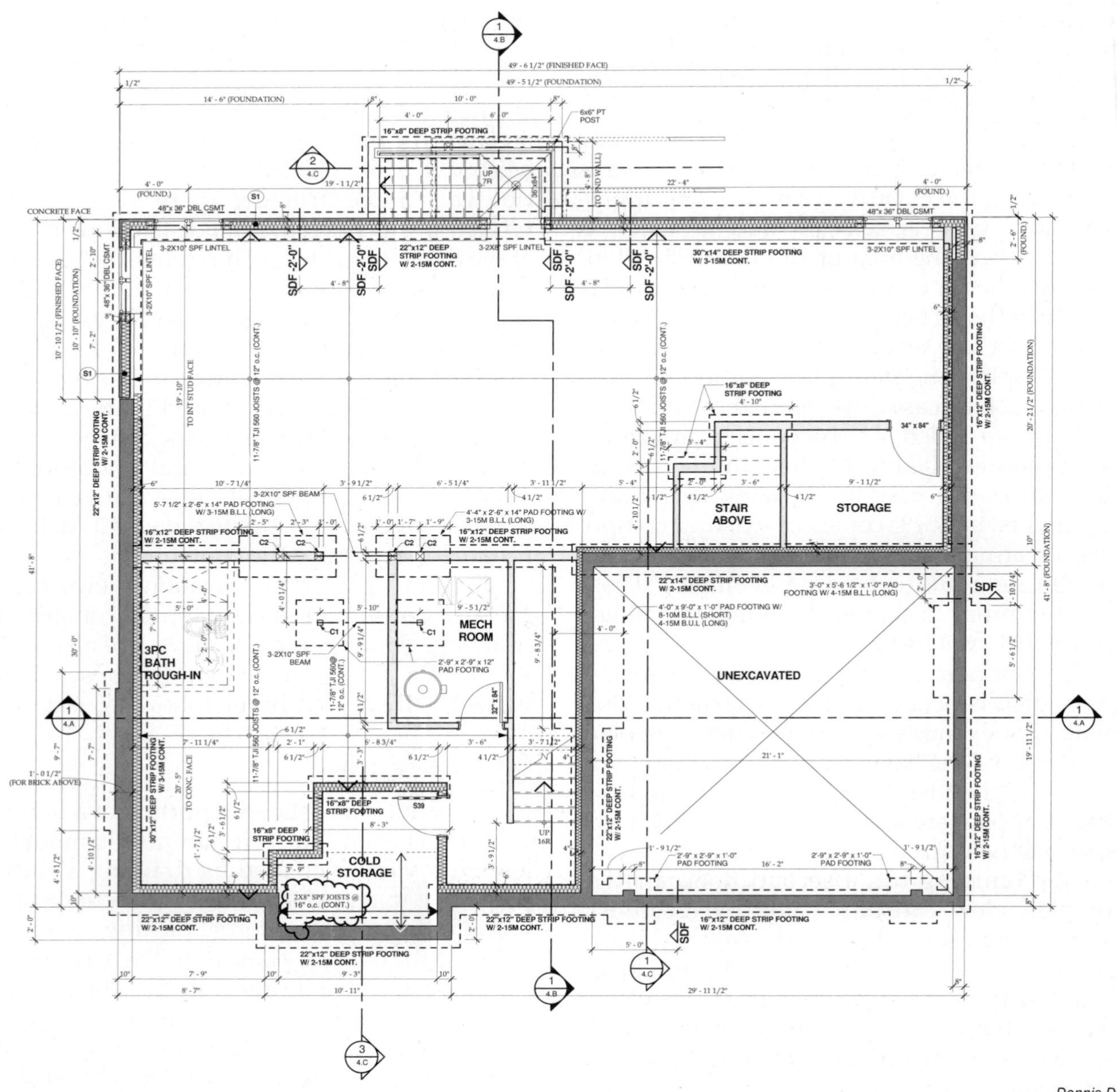

Dennis Dixon
BluPrint Design + Build

Figure 12-15. A basement plan shows the foundation construction and the layout of the basement. This basement plan is for the home shown in Figure 12-14.

Elevations

Elevations are views that illustrate the exterior features of each side of a building. Usually, there are four default elevations in a model file showing the north, south, east, and west views of the building. Elevations are commonly included in the drawing documentation to show the finished appearance of the building. See **Figure 12-17**.

The **ELEVATION** command is used to create an elevation view. The view can be an exterior or interior elevation. An elevation is created by aligning an elevation symbol with a feature in the model, such as an exterior wall. The placement of the symbol orients the viewing direction. Then, the elevation is automatically generated by the program.

Elevations are used to create the levels used in the model. The **LEVEL** command is used to

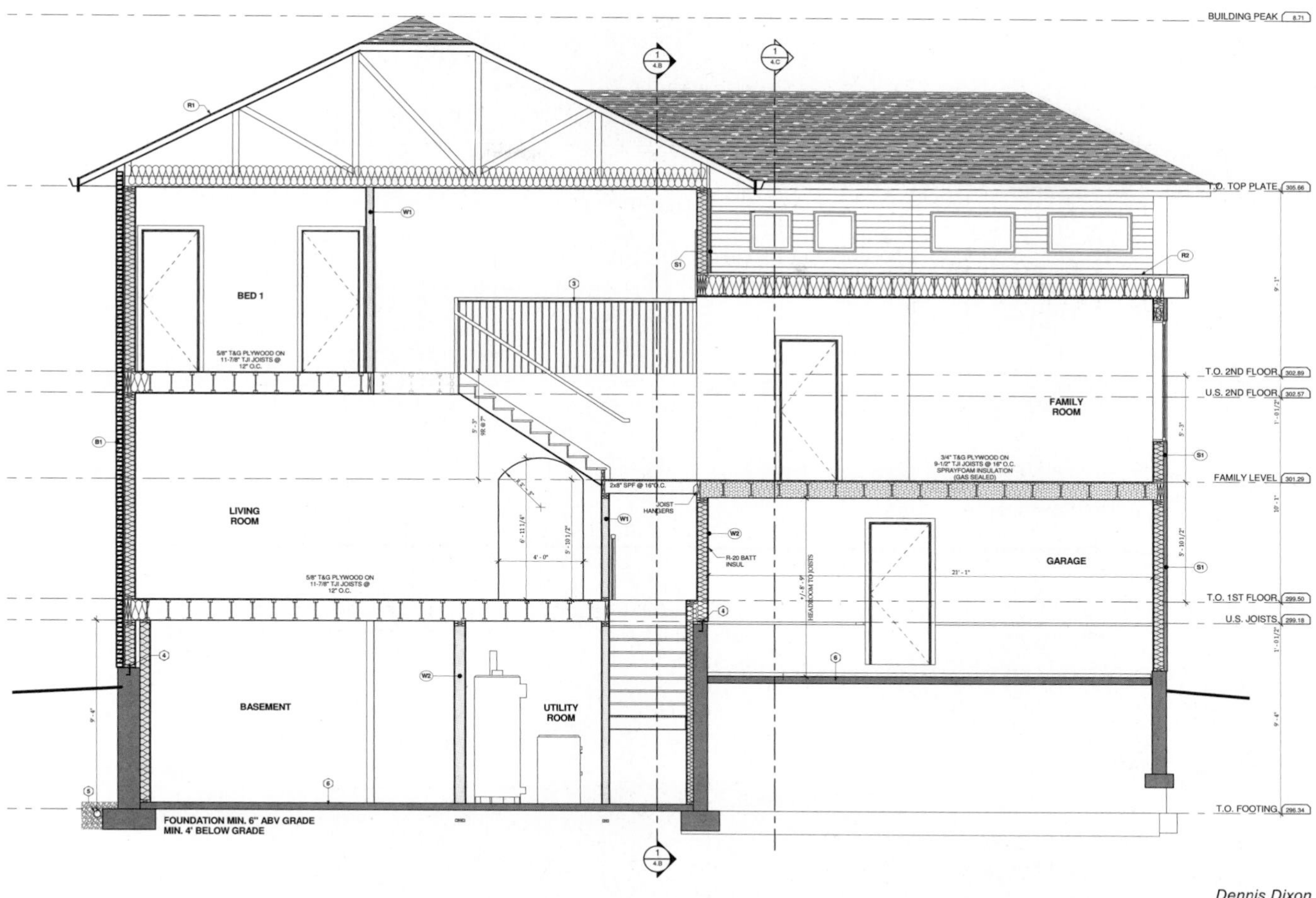

Dennis Dixon
BluPrint Design + Build

Figure 12-16. A building section cuts through the entire structure. This building section is for the home shown in Figure 12-14 and shows the layout of rooms, height information, and construction details.

create levels. As each level is created, the program asks the user whether to create a named plan view associated with the corresponding elevation. This provides a way to create levels and views in the same sequence. Levels are usually included on elevations in the construction drawings to identify important heights of the building.

Schedules

A ***schedule*** is a list of all items of a specific type that are needed for construction. Schedules are used to organize information for items such as rooms, doors, windows, cabinets, lighting fixtures, and plumbing fixtures. Information in a schedule is linked to the model and updates automatically when items are added or existing data changes. This provides a powerful tool for verifying quantities and keeping information up to date.

A schedule is created by specifying the type of item to be listed. The schedule can then be formatted to list properties such as part number, type, size, cost, material, and finish. Once this information is specified, the schedule is automatically generated by the program. Schedules usually accompany views in the drawing documentation and can be inserted onto sheets in the same way as views.

Schedules can be used for processes such as estimating, ordering, and installation. A schedule can typically be exported to a spreadsheet software program or an external database. This helps coordinate construction data with other stakeholders in the project who do not have access to the modeling software.

Dennis Dixon
BluPrint Design + Build

Figure 12-17. Elevations show the exterior features of a building. These elevations are for the front and rear sides of the home shown in Figure 12-14. Note the levels used to identify important heights. A—Front elevation. B—Rear elevation.

Detailing

The tools of a parametric modeling program make it possible to model with great accuracy and precision. However, it is not necessary to model every item for construction purposes or to complete the drawing documentation. Depending on the level of detail required, it is common to create some features on detail drawings by drawing 2D geometry, rather than modeling in 3D. Often, the designer must consider the time involved and decide which process is most efficient.

Detailing is the process of using 2D geometry to represent non-modeled features in views. Detailing is accomplished using detail lines and detail components. ***Detail lines*** are view-specific lines that appear only in the view in which they are created. ***Detail components*** are view-specific symbols that appear only in the view in which they are created. Using detail lines and detail components in a view is commonly referred to as drawing "on top of" the model geometry in a view. Detail lines and detail components are used when additional detail is needed to clarify the construction requirements.

Detailing is commonly used when preparing drawings such as wall sections, which include detailed features such as brickwork, wood framing members, and fasteners. These features can be created as detail components instead of modeling them. Modeling programs typically provide a library of predefined detail components for this purpose. See **Figure 12-18**.

Detailing plays a key role in the modeling process because it provides flexibility to the designer. It also provides a way to meet accepted drafting standards when preparing the detail drawings.

Sheet Preparation

Each view created in the model can be completed by adding dimensions, annotations, and any other information needed for construction. Then, each view is inserted onto a sheet for printing or plotting. The sheet contains a title block and is named to identify the content. A sheet naming convention that follows accepted school or office practice should be followed. Sheets with inserted views can be included in a project template to save layout time.

Sheets have the same relationship to the model as views. If a view has been inserted onto a sheet and changes are made to the model, the view updates on the corresponding sheet.

Sheets are commonly plotted to an electronic file format, such as portable document format (PDF). Each sheet can be saved as a separate PDF file when it is plotted. However, depending

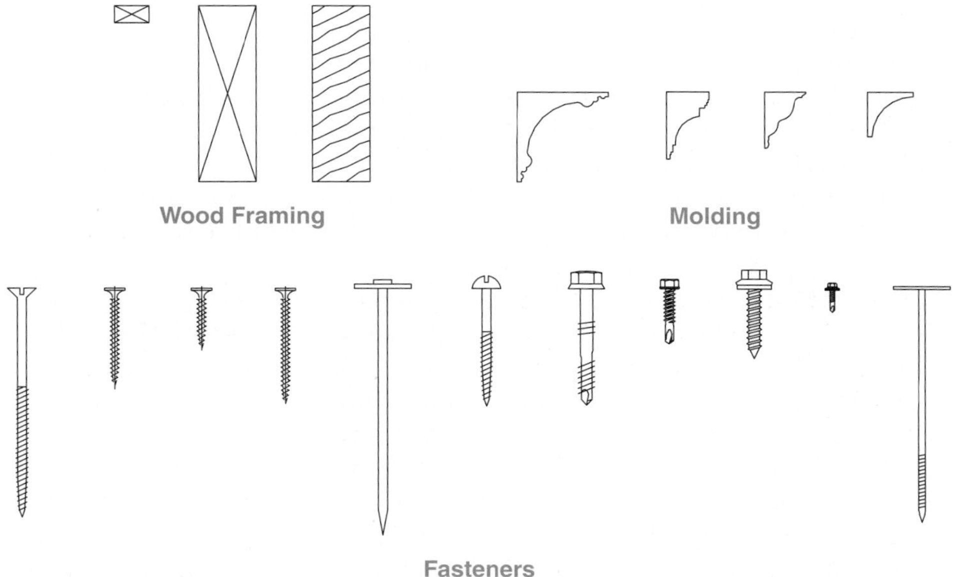

Images courtesy of Autodesk

Figure 12-18. Detail components are view-specific 2D symbols used for detailing. A library of predefined components is typically supplied with parametric modeling software.

on the size of the project, it is common to plot multiple sheets to a single PDF file that contains all of the sheets in the model. Plotting files in this manner may require a batch printing utility or an additional printer driver. Once the PDF file is created, it can then be plotted to hard copy or viewed electronically using the appropriate software. This provides the flexibility to work from printed drawings, a tablet, or a mobile viewing device during construction.

Model Collaboration

BIM facilitates a collaborative design process. Modeling work in different engineering disciplines can be closely managed and coordinated using special tools in the software. These tools allow designers to share models and track the work of others as the building design is developed.

During design development, it is common for the architect and the engineers in other disciplines to exchange models in order to coordinate work. This approach requires a definition of responsibilities and expectations to be met by the different designers. In a typical commercial design project, for example, the architect is normally responsible for developing an architectural design model. The structural engineer uses the architectural design model as a basis to create a structural model and add components such as columns and beams. This work must be coordinated so that when revisions are made in either model, components are prevented from clashing and design intent is maintained.

It is also possible for different disciplines to coordinate a project by working on a single model file. In this case, edits are made in locally copied files that are linked to a central file. However, this type of collaboration is not widely used when multiple disciplines are involved. It is more commonly used by a design team within a specific discipline, such as a group of designers in an architectural office. This approach requires a highly coordinated process and a precise definition of responsibilities for each modeler.

Coordination of work in different disciplines is achieved by linking models and monitoring changes as they occur. Typically, this process works by inserting a model from another engineering discipline into a host file. This establishes a link to the other model. Then, elements from the linked model can be copied into the host file using a special copying function. The copied elements have a link to the external model, enabling changes to be monitored and reported. For example, if the structural columns in a linked structural model are copied by the architect and one of the columns is moved by the structural engineer in the structural model, an alert is issued in the architect's host file. The architect can then review the change and decide what action to take. The architect can accept the change, reject the change, or leave the status unresolved without taking immediate action. The architect can also issue a comment to address the change and generate a coordination report.

In order for model collaboration to be effective, regular communication should take place between the different engineers and offices. See **Figure 12-19**. This helps resolve design conflicts and ensures that everyone is on the same page. Usually, changes in design that occur can be resolved through meetings or e-mail correspondence.

Data Management

The amount of data generated during a building project and the need to share it among different stakeholders are major considerations for companies using BIM. Data must be organized and stored in such a way that it is readily available to the different contributors in the project. Usually, this requires a database system for managing all of the different types of data collected.

Enterprise software designed for project information management is commonly used for this purpose. This type of software is used for organizing and storing project data such as e-mail correspondence, construction schedules, contract documents, notes and photographs from construction, and building operation and maintenance information. This data is stored in a centralized location along with the models and drawing documentation developed during the project.

Regardless of the type of data management system used, the system must have safeguards for file security and backup. In addition, files should be organized to permit easy retrieval of content. This can be achieved by using file naming standards and a system with a function to search for key terms across multiple file formats.

Monkey Business Images/Shutterstock.com

Figure 12-19. Regular communication between design teams is necessary to coordinate work in different offices.

Facility Management

From the building owner's perspective, BIM offers many tangible benefits. The involvement of designers, engineers, contractors, consultants, and the owner throughout the building process helps in achieving the best design outcome for the owner. Incorporating input from the different stakeholders helps improve the performance of the building, which in turn enhances the value to the owner. See **Figure 12-20**.

One of the primary goals of BIM is to construct buildings that perform more efficiently. This directly benefits owners. However, there are other benefits that extend beyond energy efficiency. A BIM system has important applications in facility management and operations. Throughout the life of the building, the tools of a BIM system can be used by the owner to track and control operations.

After construction is completed, an as-built model can be prepared by the contractor and given to the owner. In some commercial projects, this is a required provision. An as-built model reflects changes from the original design that have occurred during construction. It serves as an up-to-date record of the building and provides valuable information, such as the building measurements, the existing layout of equipment, and the age and condition of the equipment. This information can be used for a number of purposes. For example, the owner can use the BIM model to project annual energy costs, estimate landscaping costs, schedule preventive maintenance, and plan for when equipment must be repaired or replaced. The as-built model can also be used for space planning and to help determine needs for renovation projects. Because the building systems are represented in digital form, the desired information can usually be retrieved quickly. This is more efficient than the traditional method of working from plan drawings.

Implementing BIM in facility management involves some of the same types of technological challenges faced by design firms. For example, making the transition from traditional facility management processes to a BIM-based system requires software training for building engineers and maintenance managers. More than likely, these needs will continue to evolve in the future as building owners gain more familiarity with the technology.

Image courtesy of Autodesk

Figure 12-20. This building model is designed with solar panels to provide a renewable energy source, helping to save on energy costs.

Summary

- BIM is an approach to building design that allows for management of all aspects of a building project.
- A BIM model is a 3D solid model that provides a complete representation of a building.
- Custom home design is an area in which BIM has measurable benefits to residential design firms.
- Front-loading allows information to be collected from as many stakeholders as possible in the early design stages of a building project.
- Design simulations can be used to analyze building performance and help reduce energy costs.
- Clash detection helps ensure that conflicts are found prior to construction.
- A project template contains predefined settings, model content, and views and provides a starting point for creating a new project.
- Detail lines and detail components are view-specific objects used to represent non-modeled features.
- An as-built model can be used by building owners to project annual energy costs, estimate landscaping costs, schedule preventive maintenance, and plan for when equipment must be repaired or replaced.

Internet Resources

American Institute of Architects (AIA)
Educational and industry resources for the architectural profession

Architectural Record
Continuing Education Center

Autodesk
Revit software publisher

Bentley
AECOsim Building Designer software publisher

Graphisoft
ArchiCAD software publisher

National Institute of Building Sciences (NIBS)
BuildingSMART Alliance National BIM Standard-United States

Nemetschek
Vectorworks software publisher

Review Questions

Answer the following questions using the information in this chapter.

1. How does BIM differ from traditional practices used in design and construction?
2. List five BIM processes that take place during a design project and throughout the lifetime of a building.
3. Why is a BIM model referred to as a parametric model?
4. Why has BIM been more widely used in commercial design than residential design?
5. Explain why BIM has benefits in custom home design.
6. Name three advantages of BIM that apply regardless of whether a firm is involved in commercial or residential architecture.
7. Explain the term *front-loading*.
8. List at least four aspects of a 3D model design that can be evaluated using design simulations.
9. What is the purpose of clash detection?
10. What is a *construction simulation*?
11. What is the purpose of a project template?
12. What is the difference between a *view* and a *sheet*?
13. What is the purpose of a view template?
14. In which type of view are levels usually created?
15. What is a *family*?
16. How is a section view created in a parametric model?
17. How is a schedule created in a parametric model?
18. View-specific lines that appear only in the view in which they are created are called _____ lines.

19. Briefly describe the process used to link a model from a different discipline in order to coordinate work.
20. What is the purpose of an as-built model in facility management?

Suggested Activities

1. Write a short essay that explains the reasons why BIM has been more widely adopted by commercial firms than residential firms. Contact a local residential architectural firm to ask about the type of design and documentation process the firm uses and the reasons why the firm uses it.
2. Conduct research to find out more about BIM standards such as the National BIM Standard-United States (NBIMS-US) and the AEC (UK) BIM Technology Protocol. Write a report on your findings.
3. Search online to find a residential design firm that is using BIM for custom home projects. Determine whether the firm uses BIM for all projects. Write a report on your findings.

Problem Solving Case Study

You have a design drafting firm in Bakersfield, California, that specializes in home remodeling projects. Mr. and Mrs. Anderson have contacted you regarding the remodeling of their 50-year-old residence. They want to increase the energy efficiency of the home. To achieve this, they also want to use new sustainable building materials and construction methods.

Given this preliminary information, perform any necessary research and answer the following questions.

1. How would BIM assist you in the design and construction of this project?
2. If your firm does not utilize BIM, what additional costs would be incurred on your part to acquire BIM software and the computer hardware needed to run BIM software?

Certification Prep

The following questions are presented in the style used in the American Design Drafting Association (ADDA) Drafter Certification Test. Answer the questions using the information in this chapter.

1. Which of the following statements about BIM is true?
   A. BIM assists in visualizing a building design.
   B. A BIM model is a 3D surface model that represents the complete building.
   C. The virtual building model in a BIM project is called a BIM model.
   D. BIM model construction is based on a parametric modeling workflow.
   E. A view template is used to start a new project.
2. Match each term with its description.

   Terms: 1. Schedule, 2. Family, 3. Detail components, 4. Material takeoff
   A. A collection of components that represent variations of the same item in different sizes and orientations.
   B. View-specific symbols that appear only in the view in which they are created.
   C. A list of quantities of materials used in constructing a building.
   D. A list of all items of a specific type that are needed for construction.
3. Which of the following statements are *false*?
   A. Interference checking is commonly referred to as clash detection.
   B. Front-loading is the process of using 2D geometry to represent non-modeled features in views.
   C. Levels are commonly created in plan views.
   D. A construction simulation is an animation that illustrates construction processes in sequential order.

Curricular Connections

1. **Social Science.** One of the primary advantages of BIM is that it facilitates collaboration and data exchange between companies involved in the construction process. Research two local architectural firms that have used BIM to share and coordinate models. Interview architects from both firms to learn about how much success they have had with this process. Write a short report on your findings.

STEM Connections

1. **Engineering.** BIM is commonly used in commercial building projects, but there are certain types of commercial buildings for which BIM is especially suited. This is usually because of the complexity involved in construction and the efficiencies gained in facility management. In some facilities, space planning and equipment management are particularly important to the operation. Conduct research to find out more information about facility management in BIM and buildings in which space management is a key concern. Write a report on your findings.
2. **Math.** BIM can involve expensive startup costs for a design drafting firm. Conduct research on five different BIM software programs. Examine the cost of the software, as well as the cost of upgrading computer hardware in order to operate the software. Calculate the potential savings on projects and the time it will take to recoup the cost of installing BIM software for each of the five programs. Write a short report on your findings and present your report to the class.

Communicating about Architecture

1. **Reading.** With a partner, make flash cards of the key terms in this chapter. On the front of the card, write the term. On the back of the card, write the pronunciation and a brief definition. Use this chapter and a dictionary for guidance. Then take turns quizzing one another on the pronunciations and definitions of the key terms.
2. **Speaking and Listening.** Assemble a collection of illustrations that show custom homes designed in BIM. Include the different types of views discussed in this chapter. Present the illustrations to the class.

David Wright House, LLC

This home, a residence in Arizona designed by Frank Lloyd Wright, is a candidate for historical preservation. The building has a unique spiral design and is constructed of concrete block. Built in the mid-20th century, the building was one of Wright's last designs.

Chapter 13

Planning for Remodeling and Renovation

Objectives

After completing this chapter, you will be able to:

- List the reasons that people remodel and the factors they should consider before beginning a remodeling project.
- Compare the four main types of remodeling according to cost, complexity, and time required.
- Describe the different types and purposes of renovation.
- Understand the role of the family, architect, interior designer, and contractor in a remodeling or renovation project.

Key Terms

adaptive reuse
addition
attic
dehumidifying system
dormer
moisture barrier
preservation
remodeling
renovation
restoration
R-value
sump pump

Not all architectural design involves new construction. The needs of homeowners are not static—they change over time. For example, a young couple may start a family, or someone who has been laid off from a job may decide to start a business at home. Sometimes, the best answer to changing needs is to buy or build a new home. In many cases, however, an existing home can be changed to meet the new needs. See **Figure 13-1**.

Changes to an existing home generally fall into one of two categories: remodeling or renovation. This chapter describes the processes involved in remodeling and renovation, including the architectural planning needed for each.

Remodeling

Remodeling is changing an existing space into a new form. It can be a wise investment that will increase the value of a home. It may also be a way to change part or all of a home's appearance. The least complex type of remodeling involves making changes to a room that is already used or changing an unused space so it can be used as a living area. Adding on to a home generally requires more complex changes.

A family may decide to remodel for several reasons:

- As a family grows, its living patterns and needs may change.
- Older homes may need newer equipment or better insulation to keep up with higher energy costs. See **Figure 13-2**.

Photoroller/Shutterstock.com

Figure 13-1. As families grow and change, their housing needs change. This outdoor kitchen addition is modern and efficient and expands the functional space of the home.

- As the work schedules of family members become busier, a more efficient home may be needed.
- Increases in income may result in more disposable income and spur the desire for updated styles and appliances.
- Entertaining may become more common, requiring more adequate kitchen and living spaces.
- New family members may need their own bedrooms.

Remodeling an existing home has many advantages. It is usually much less expensive than purchasing a new home. It also avoids the hassles and additional expenses involved with moving. Families may have close ties with neighbors, schools, and community organizations. The home may also hold sentimental

Goodheart-Willcox Publisher

Figure 13-2. This well-maintained older house is a prime candidate for remodeling to improve the heating and air-conditioning, plumbing, and electrical systems.

value. These factors and the high cost of building or buying a new home may make remodeling a more practical alternative.

Local building ordinances and property taxes are also considerations when making remodeling choices. Remodeling may require several building permits, and all changes must comply with local codes. See **Figure 13-3**. If remodeling increases the value of a home, it may also increase the property taxes on the home. Usually, adding on to the structure and exterior remodeling are more likely to require building permits and increase taxes. Remodeling of unused spaces within the home may be a better choice if building ordinances and higher taxes are concerns.

The cost, time, and effort required to remodel must also be considered before starting a project. All three factors are affected by the size and complexity of the remodeling project. An accurate estimate of all costs of remodeling, including all building materials, utility additions, and labor, should be obtained before starting any project. Larger projects can be very expensive and may require financing. However, the costs can be spread out over months or even years by remodeling in stages. The disadvantage of this approach is the prolonged inconvenience of having a remodeling project extend over a long period.

A remodeling project can vary in cost depending on the amount of time and effort spent by family members. If all work is contracted to professionals, the job will be finished quickly with little effort from family members. However, contracted work is usually expensive. In addition, good communication and supervision by a family member is critical to ensure that work is done as desired.

At the other extreme, all work may be done by family members. This method can save a great deal of money in labor costs. The finished work may also be more personalized than would have been possible with contractors. However, the project will probably require much more time and considerable skill. Unless the homeowner is very familiar with the type of work involved, serious errors in remodeling may occur or building codes may not be followed correctly.

Many families choose to do some remodeling on their own and contract professionals for the most difficult jobs. For instance, paneling and painting may be done by family members, but complex wiring changes should be handled by an electrician. This method allows good results at a lower cost. It also ensures safe construction and eliminates frustration with jobs that are too difficult for an amateur. See **Figure 13-4**.

Remodeling is not just an option used by homeowners who do not want to move. It also offers choices to home buyers who cannot afford custom-built housing. Many people buy less expensive housing and remodel to meet their own needs.

Jim Parkin/Shutterstock.com

Figure 13-3. After the city or county issues a building permit, it sends inspectors to approve the work at various stages of construction. Work that does not meet local ordinances must be redone.

Goodheart-Willcox Publisher

Figure 13-4. Professional subcontractors may be hired to do complex jobs such as building walls or a roof structure safely and according to local building codes.

Types of Remodeling

Remodeling may be divided into four main types: changing lived-in areas, making unused space livable, adding on, and buying to remodel. Each category varies in the level of change, complexity, cost, and time required for remodeling. Many remodeling projects may include more than one type of remodeling.

Changing Lived-In Areas

Used or "lived-in" rooms are generally remodeled to update equipment, improve traffic patterns, or give a room a new appearance. Kitchens are most commonly changed and, generally, the most expensive room to remodel. Bathrooms, bedrooms, and other rooms may be changed as well.

Remodeling a lived-in room usually does not require major changes, such as tearing down a wall or rewiring. Occasionally, a window or door may be enlarged or moved. Kitchen or bathroom remodeling may require relocation of some plumbing and wiring receptacles. However, changes are usually less complex than the changes required in other types of remodeling.

Kitchens

Kitchens are usually remodeled when the homeowner wants to update or add appliances. See **Figure 13-5**. While updating appliances, the homeowner may also want to improve the use of space, traffic patterns, availability of storage, and the efficiency of the work triangle. Information on kitchen planning in Chapter 9, *Planning the Service Area*, can help you evaluate a client's present kitchen and plan a new one.

Iriana Shiyan/Shutterstock.com

Figure 13-5. The owner of this older kitchen updated it by refinishing the cabinets, installing new appliances, adding recessed light fixtures, and installing floor tile in an interesting pattern.

Many changes can be made to increase the efficiency of a kitchen. The traffic circulation path can be improved by moving doors so that traffic patterns do not interfere with the work triangle. An appliance may be moved to make a more efficient work triangle. General and local lighting may be enhanced.

Counter space may be added to make room for food preparation or to allow space for countertop appliances. Storage space may be added, or present storage space may be improved for more efficient use of space. For instance, a corner cabinet with space that is difficult to reach may be replaced with a lazy Susan. Pull-out storage may also be used to improve access to items in cabinets.

If several new appliances are added or major appliances are moved, rewiring will be necessary. Additional circuits may also be needed. Changes in plumbing lines will be needed if the sink is moved, if a refrigerator with an automatic ice maker is added, or if a built-in dishwasher is moved or added. New ventilation must be installed when the range is moved.

pryzmat/Shutterstock.com

Figure 13-6. Moving a sink involves changes in plumbing lines. A professional plumber is usually required to make sure the lines are installed correctly.

Bathrooms

Like kitchens, bathrooms are often remodeled to make updates, such as replacing old fixtures. Bathrooms can be costly to remodel if changes in plumbing lines are needed. Water supply and waste lines must be checked to make sure that they are the correct size for new plumbing installations. See **Figure 13-6**. Locating new fixtures in the same positions as old ones can reduce remodeling costs.

Other improvements may be made in bathrooms as well. Bathrooms may be enlarged by moving a wall. They may be improved by adding storage space. Skylights may be added for natural lighting and ventilation. New floor and wall treatments, such as ceramic tile, may be installed for easier maintenance.

Other Rooms

The appearances of bedrooms, living rooms, dining rooms, and other rooms that do not house major appliances can be changed dramatically with relatively minor remodeling projects. Most often, floor, wall, and ceiling treatments are updated. See **Figure 13-7**. New lighting fixtures may also be added. Partial walls or built-in storage may be added to a room. Many times, these projects are simple enough for family members to do on their own.

More complicated changes may include moving or widening a doorway to improve traffic circulation. Windows may also be added or enlarged to improve the view and increase ventilation. A wall may be removed so that two rooms are made into one. These changes are more complicated and should be done by someone with experience. The changes may affect the structural support of the house. In addition, wiring and insulation may have to be altered.

Making Unused Space Livable

Many homes have areas that are not used as living space. These areas include garages, porches, unfinished basements, and attics. Although these areas need changes to make them suitable for living, they already have sound roofs, walls, and floors. It may be less expensive to remodel these areas than to add on to a home. Also, remodeling unused space is often quicker and more convenient than adding on space.

Domenic Gareri/Shutterstock.com

Figure 13-7. The character of this dining area is defined entirely by the wall treatment and furnishings. Imagine the same dining area with a completely different look. How would you achieve it?

Garages and Porches

Garages and porches are often converted into bedrooms, baths, dining rooms, family rooms, sunrooms, or studies. See **Figure 13-8**. These areas are often chosen for remodeling because they are conveniently located in relation to other rooms in the house. For instance, a porch adjoining a kitchen would make a convenient breakfast room.

The foundations under these areas should be checked to see if they are deep enough to comply with local building codes. Foundation requirements for garages and porches may be different than for living areas. A ***moisture barrier*** should be placed between the foundation and flooring materials. This is a membrane that retards the flow of moisture vapor and reduces condensation. Insulation should be added to meet the ***R-value*** recommended for living spaces. Additional wiring may be needed for lighting and outlets.

Windows and doors are often changed or added when remodeling garages and porches. Insulated glass windows or storm windows may replace the original windows. The garage door may be replaced with a sliding glass door or with a window. Doors from a garage or porch to the house may be relocated for more logical access. Sliding glass doors, panel doors, or open doorways may be used to connect the remodeled area to the home.

Some type of heating and cooling system is needed in remodeled porches and garages. To ensure proper heating and cooling of the remodeled area, it may be wise to consult an HVAC professional for this aspect of the project. If the

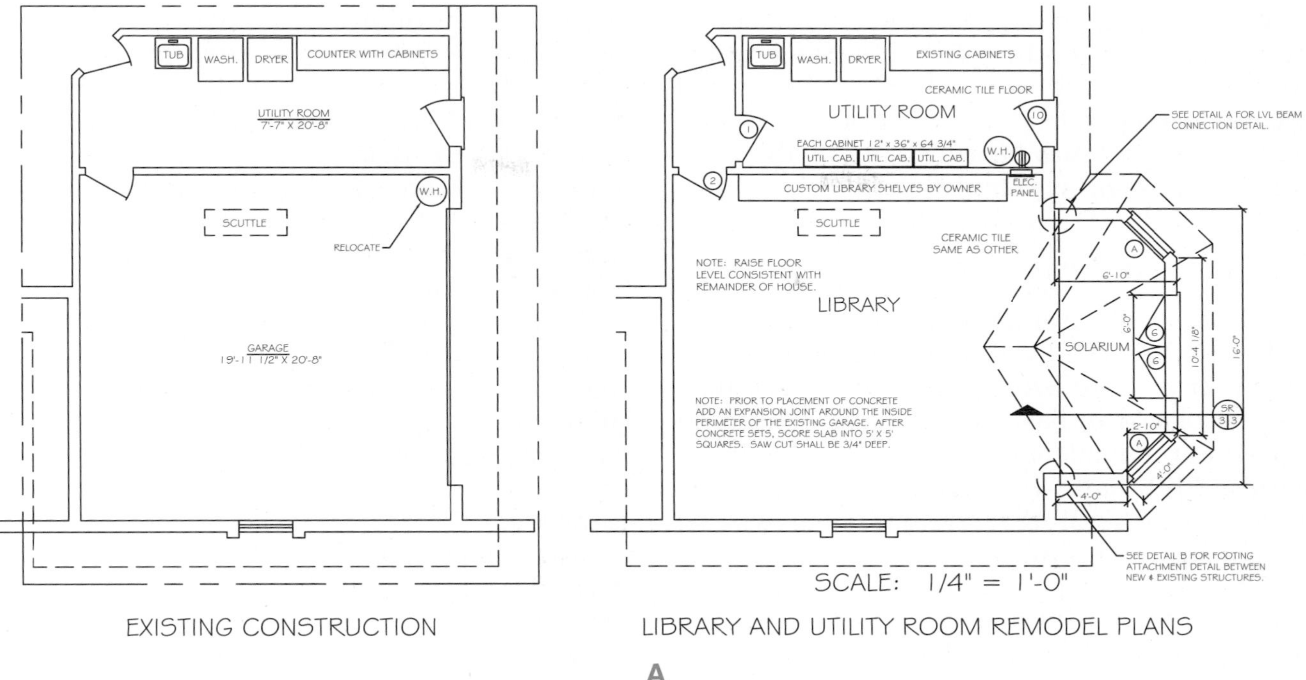

A

B

C

D

Goodheart-Willcox Publisher

Figure 13-8. The conversion of a two-car garage into a library/solarium. A—The working drawings. B—The garage before remodeling. C—Remodeling in progress. D—The completed project.

room is open to an original room in the house, heating and air conditioning from the original room may be enough for both areas. However, if the room is separate, it will need its own supply. Ducts and vents may be extended into the room from the existing system.

Unfinished Basements

Unfinished basements are often remodeled to be used as family rooms, recreation areas, hobby areas, and workshops. Bedrooms may also be placed in basements if sufficient lighting and an outside entrance are provided. See **Figure 13-9**. Bathrooms and a small kitchen area may be desired if the basement will be used for entertaining.

Basement areas are often damp, so vapor barriers and a dehumidifying system should be added for comfort. A ***dehumidifying system*** removes moisture vapor from the air to reduce the relative humidity in the space. If flooding or seepage is common, a ***sump pump*** should be added. Also, any leaks in the walls or floors should be properly repaired before installing wall and floor materials. If the foundation is sound, flooring materials can be applied directly to the surface. Paneling and drywall should be applied to furring strips to allow space for wiring and insulation.

Basements can be gloomy if sufficient light is not provided. Window wells and windows may be enlarged to increase natural light. Illuminated ceilings and recessed lighting provide excellent artificial lighting for basements. Additional wiring for light fixtures and outlets will be needed.

Additional plumbing lines will also be needed if a bath or kitchen area is added to the basement. New fixtures should be placed as close as possible to existing plumbing lines to reduce cost.

Kelly MacDonald/Shutterstock.com

Figure 13-9. This unfinished basement is being remodeled to provide an additional bedroom as well as a storage closet under the stairs.

Finally, if a basement is converted into a living area, a direct exit to the outdoors may be required. Check local fire protection codes and laws to be sure the remodeling project meets regulations.

Attics

An ***attic*** is the space between the ceiling and roof of a structure. In some house styles, such as a Cape Cod, the attic is frequently converted to a bedroom, hobby room, or conversation area. See **Figure 13-10**. If a bedroom is placed in this area, a bathroom should also be added.

Before converting an attic, ceiling joists, which will now become floor joists, should be checked to determine if they are strong enough to support the appropriate live load. Adequate headroom and usable floor space should also be available. At least 7′ of height should be allowed between the floor and the finished ceiling. The ceiling may slope from 7′ to 5′ high, but the areas that have a low ceiling will be limited in use.

Windows and skylights can be added to an attic for natural lighting. ***Dormers*** allow in natural light and increase the amount of usable space in an attic by adding headroom. However, they are more costly to add than skylights and regular windows because they require modifications in the roof structure.

Adequate insulation for a living area should be placed in the attic ceiling and walls. Proper ventilation is especially important because warm air tends to get trapped in attics. Ceiling fans and vents may be helpful. Additional wiring may also be required. If a bathroom is added, plumbing lines will be needed.

Adding On

Converting existing unused spaces may not be possible or practical. In these situations, the family may choose to build additional space onto a home. This new space is called an

Veremeenko Irina/Shutterstock.com

Figure 13-10. A growing family found space in this attic for an imaginative child's bedroom. The nautical theme fits well with the roof lines.

addition. Any type of space, such as a bedroom, bathroom, den, or garage, may be added to a home. Additions may also be used to enlarge an existing room, such as a living room or kitchen. In any case, the new addition should harmonize with other rooms in the house, both on the inside and on the outside.

Building permits and inspections are almost always necessary with additions. Also, local zoning laws may restrict the types of additions allowed on a home. Usually, the exterior walls of a home must be kept a minimum distance from lot lines. Timing is important because weather conditions can hamper much of the work involved in building an addition.

Ground-Level Additions

Adding on is more complex than changing areas within the original structure. A new area is created from the foundation to the roof, which alters the exterior appearance of the home. A ground-level addition may have a crawl space or basement below and a second floor and/or attic space above.

Adding on to a home often involves the removal of part or all of an existing exterior wall. See **Figure 13-11**. Most exterior walls are bearing walls, except for end walls of a one-story house with a gable roof. Temporary supports must be used when such a wall is removed, and some type of permanent load-bearing support must be in place before the remodeling is finished.

Walls that are to be removed usually contain wiring and plumbing. Rerouting of these lines may be necessary. Also, you must check for underground plumbing mains and cables before digging for an addition's foundation. In most states, this is required by law.

Any planned addition should blend well with the architectural style of the existing home. The size, shape, and placement of the addition should not be obtrusive or overpowering. The exterior design should be in the same style as the original house. See **Figure 13-12**. The placement, size, and style of windows and doors in the addition should blend with the original structure. Landscaping elements can be used to blend the new addition into the original house.

Employability
Continuing Education

The field of architecture has changed dramatically in the last few decades, and even today, it continues to change rapidly. Companies look for employees who are willing to adapt to change and to continue their education throughout their career.

Many opportunities are available for continuing education in the architectural field. Here are some examples:

- The American Design Drafting Association/American Digital Design Association (ADDA) provides annual conferences, as well as training opportunities in specific drafting applications.
- The American Institute of Architects (AIA) offers virtual conventions and workshops and has an entire continuing education system based on learning units.
- The *Architectural Record* has a Continuing Education Center website where architects and engineers can earn AIA Continuing Education learning units in the latest architectural trends and customs.

These and other opportunities are easy to access online. Some organizations require membership. Some, such as the ADDA, even have student divisions. Even though you are just now learning about architecture, joining one or more of these associations shows potential employers that you are serious about working in the field. After you become a licensed architect, continuing education may become one of your top priorities to remain a productive employee in this fast-changing field.

Sue Smith/Shutterstock.com

Figure 13-11. The kitchen in this home is being expanded to provide an informal breakfast and sitting area. Much of the original bearing wall will be retained, but the windows will be removed to create a pass-through for food and other items.

A

B

C

Goodheart-Willcox Publisher

Figure 13-12. The raised entry element added to the existing entry blends seamlessly with the existing structure. A—Entry before remodeling. B—Remodeling in progress. C—The completed project.

The type of space to be added, location of rooms in the original home, and availability of space should be considered when deciding where to place the addition. For instance, a game room or party room should not be located adjacent to the sleeping area. However, this would be a good location for another bedroom. Also, lot boundaries may eliminate some areas of the home as a location for the addition.

Second-Story Additions

Some homes may not have enough yard space for a ground-level addition. Often, these homes are already at the permitted boundary limit. In addition, many areas have "green space" requirements that dictate a certain ratio of yard area to house area. For these homes, the addition of a second story may be considered. These additions are usually much more expensive and complex than ground-level additions. The roof must be removed and replaced to make room for the second story. In addition, the foundation and first floor walls must be strong enough to support the weight of a second story. Stairways connecting the first and second floors must also be built.

Basement Additions

In addition to "green space" requirements, some areas also have height restrictions. In these cases, if the house does not have a basement, one can be added. Adding a basement is very expensive and requires professional planning and construction. Generally, adding a basement should only be considered when all other options have been eliminated.

Buying to Remodel

Many home buyers would like a custom-built home, but cannot afford one. Often, these people buy less-expensive housing and remodel to meet their own needs and tastes. For example, most subdivisions contain a limited number of house styles. Yet, with additions, exterior changes, and interior changes, these houses can be remodeled to fit the lifestyle of individual families.

Another recent trend is "flipping" houses. This is a process in which a building contractor or private individual purchases a house that is currently in poor condition. The person remodels the house or restores it to a livable condition, often putting in much of the labor personally. See **Figure 13-13**. Then the person sells the home at a profit. Some people flip houses for fun; for others, it is a business. Care must be taken, however. The purchase price of the house, plus the cost of materials and any paid labor used to remodel it, must be low enough that the house can be resold at a profit.

Ernest R. Prim/Shutterstock.com

Figure 13-13. This man is installing a glue base for new flooring in the house he is flipping. He will make this and other improvements to the home, then put the home back on the market to make a profit.

Renovation

Many older houses have suffered from neglect for various reasons. For example, a house that has been rental property may be slightly damaged by each tenant over a number of years. Instead of making proper repairs, the landlord performs only the bare minimum of repairs. Over the span of several years, the value of this house drops as it becomes less desirable to live in. ***Renovation*** is the process of returning a home to a desirable condition. See **Figure 13-14**. Current styles, new materials, and state-of-the-art appliances are often used in the renovation. Often, renovation is called "rehab," short for *rehabilitation*. Many metropolitan areas have several building rehab programs to encourage renovation of deteriorating homes in declining areas.

Renovation is a major process that requires much time, money, and careful planning. Preliminary planning is especially important. Building codes must be strictly followed. Several lengthy and expensive projects may be needed to reach the "finished" home. Many of these projects will require contracted work.

Some home buyers include the cost of renovation in the amount of their house mortgage. Others obtain a mortgage for the cost of the house only and pay for the renovation without financing. Another option is to refinance the house after all work is completed and use the equity from the increase in value to pay off the renovation expenses.

Before buying a home to renovate, inspect it carefully. Consider the types of changes that will be required and their estimated costs. Some homes may be very inexpensive, but renovating them would cost more than building a new home. A sound foundation and floor substructure are essential. All wood should be checked for insects and dry rot. If support beams are unsound, renovation will probably be too expensive to be worthwhile. Other areas to check are wiring, heating, roofing, walls, and insulation. Renovation can be expensive if major changes in these areas are needed.

A

B

Norandex/Reynolds Building Products

Figure 13-14. A—This old home is in very poor condition. B—Renovation has made the home a nice place to live.

Restoration

Restoration is a type of renovation that involves returning a home to the "look and feel" of its original state. Great care is taken to show the character of the home, including its form and features, as they were initially meant to be. Many historic homes of an earlier period are painstakingly restored in every detail. See **Figure 13-15**. Authentic materials, designs, and colors are researched to ensure accuracy. Later additions to the home are torn down, and any part of the original structure that is missing is rebuilt. Furnishings of the period are collected for use in the home. In short, an intense effort is exerted to restore its original appearance.

Some changes to the original systems are made in restoration. For example, electrical and plumbing systems can and should be updated to meet the current building code. This work should be done very carefully to maintain their original character. For example, wall sconces

A

B

Norandex/Reynolds Building Products

Figure 13-15. Restoring a home is a process that remains true to the original character of the house. Much work has been done to this house, but notice that all of the structural details remain exactly the same as the originals. A—Before. B—After.

that were originally gaslights can be converted to use electricity, or they can be replaced with new fixtures that have a similar appearance.

Preservation

Like restoration, ***preservation*** is a type of renovation that helps return a home to its original state. Unlike restoration, preservation concentrates on saving and maintaining the original structure and materials.

To illustrate the difference between restoration and preservation, consider the tin wall panel from a historic home in Louisiana shown in **Figure 13-16**. A restorer would analyze the properties of the panel, perhaps make a plaster cast of it, and have new panels made as necessary to restore the look of the wall. The new panels would look exactly like the old one, but they would be new, and possibly made with different materials. A preservationist, on the other hand, would attempt to do whatever is necessary to return the existing panel to its original state. The emphasis in preservation is on stabilizing and protecting the existing structures and materials.

As with restoration, certain changes are allowed in preservation, on a limited basis. If the home was originally wired for electricity, the wiring can be updated and brought up to code. However, electricity would not usually be installed in a home that originally did not have electricity. See **Figure 13-17**.

K. Chelette/Shutterstock.com

Figure 13-16. A tin wall panel from a historic home in Louisiana.

Adaptive Reuse

True preservation is not always practical or even possible. To save homes and other buildings that have historic significance or are beautiful examples of architecture, compromises are sometimes required. It is often possible to maintain the original, restored exterior appearance while remodeling the interior to meet new needs. Without interior remodeling, the building would be unable to meet the needs and may be demolished.

Adaptive reuse is the process of changing the purpose of a building. One of the most common ways to repurpose a historic home is to restore it to its original appearance and use it as a historical museum. Examples include the Hope mansion, built by North Carolina Governor David Stone in 1803, and Rancho Los Cerritos in California, built in 1844. Old railroad depots, hotels, and even stagecoach stops have also been repurposed as museums.

Not all old buildings are repurposed as museums. In many cases, private homes become shops or businesses, such as offices for attorneys, accountants, architects, and other professionals. Sometimes larger buildings, such as old factory buildings and warehouses, may sit idle because they need extensive repairs or are no longer needed for their original function. They become eyesores and locations for crime and mischief. As a result, there is significant pressure from community groups and individuals to regain these buildings as functional structures. Through adaptive reuse, they can once again be functional resources to the community, as shown in **Figure 13-18**.

Planning for Remodeling or Renovation

A good remodeling or renovation job is carefully planned before any work begins. Planning involves appraising the original

Mark Winfrey/Shutterstock.com

Figure 13-17. The John Oliver cabin in the Smoky Mountains is an example of a home that has been preserved, rather than restored. It was carefully stabilized using methods that would have been used when it was originally built.

Photo courtesy of James Hardie® Siding Products

Figure 13-18. These old warehouses have been converted into restaurants, shops, and condominiums. This is an example of adaptive reuse.

house, determining the changes needed, and drawing plans.

Analyzing and Organizing the Project

The first step of planning involves determining the weak and strong points of the present home. Limited space and storage, inefficient appliances, and poor natural lighting are examples of items that may need changing. However, walls, molding, and flooring materials may be worth saving.

For both remodeling and many types of renovation, the existing plumbing, heating and cooling, wiring, and insulation should be evaluated. If updating or repairs will be needed within a few years, it may be less expensive and more convenient to make changes during the current project. Replacing windows and doors to increase a home's energy efficiency may also be considered. In renovations and some restoration projects, original windows are sometimes replaced with insulated or even hurricane-resistant glass. See **Figure 13-19**.

After the area to be worked on has been evaluated, the next step in the project is to create a rough sketch of the original space. The sketch should include any architectural details such as windows, doors, steps, and fireplaces. Desired changes can be drawn, evaluated, and altered in order to complete a final plan. The final plan should be used when consulting contractors, ordering materials, and applying for building permits.

Hiring Professionals

For larger projects, or when the homeowner has no experience with remodeling or renovation, it is often a good idea to hire professional help. Depending on the project, architects, interior designers, and contractors may be consulted.

Architect

An architect can help analyze the current structure and can make suggestions to improve a remodeling or renovation plan. The architect can make sure that the overall style of the home's exterior will remain well designed. An architect can also help determine whether remodeling or renovation plans comply with building, plumbing, and electrical codes. The architect will make final drawings of the proposed plan and write specifications for materials. See **Figure 13-20**. The family may consult an architect only to evaluate and draw plans, or the family may use the architect to contact a contractor and supervise the work to completion.

A

B

Norandex/Reynolds Building Products

Figure 13-19. The original windows in this renovated home have been replaced with insulated glass. A—Before. B—After. Although the new owner chose to remove the porch railing and attic windows and add shutters to the remaining windows, the basic character of the home remains intact.

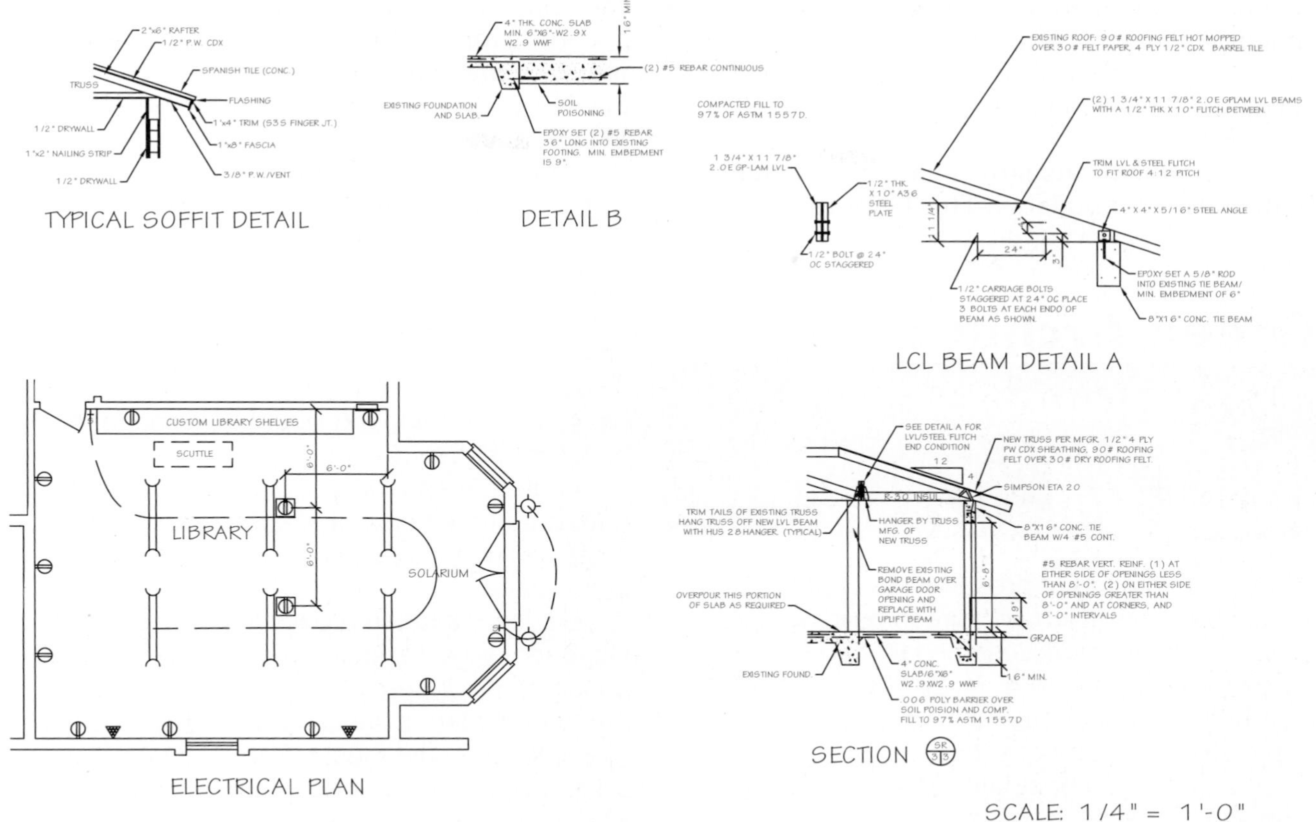

Goodheart-Willcox Publisher

Figure 13-20. The architect can provide the drawings needed to accomplish a remodeling project. These are detail drawings for the garage conversion shown in Figure 13-8.

For restoration and preservation projects, an architect is almost always essential. Architects have the resources to research the history of a home and are knowledgeable about materials and processes. Some architects specialize in restoration or preservation projects.

Interior Designer

An interior designer may be consulted in the planning stages of remodeling or renovation. Some decorating, department, and home improvement stores offer the free services of a decorator if products are purchased from their store. A freelance designer or a design firm may also be consulted.

Designers can also help to put the needs and desires of a family into concrete plans. They can make suggestions to improve the design or the function of any material within a room. They can also help select materials that will be both functional and tasteful. Fabric samples, paint chips, and samples of other materials to be used in a room can be coordinated by the designer. The designer can also help the family choose materials that fit within a budget.

Interior designers can also help in evaluating the overall floor plan of a room. They can make suggestions for improving the efficiency of circulation and the overall use of space. The interior designer can be consulted separately or with an architect.

Interior designers may also be needed for restoration projects. They can help research the original period furnishings and suggest ways to imitate and incorporate them, even if the building will be adaptively reused.

Contractor

After planning is finished, a contractor may be hired to do the actual work. Many contractors specialize in remodeling, and some specialize in renovation or preservation. The contractor will obtain any necessary building permits and schedule the work of any subcontractors needed for the project. Subcontractors may include carpenters, plumbers, electricians, masons, and painters.

A contractor usually charges one fee for both materials and labor. This helps to eliminate the chance of unexpected expenses. However, a contractor is not always needed. A family member may choose to serve as the contractor and hire any specific subcontractors needed. When a contractor is not used, an interior designer or architect can help to estimate costs, or the family can make their own estimates.

Green Architecture

Restoration vs. Preservation: Which Is Better?

Any restoration or preservation project should be undertaken with green building and sustainability in mind. Just the fact that the building will be reused is, in itself, a "green" idea. Beyond that, though, the concept of restoration or preservation can get sticky.

Imagine that a beautiful old home in your area, built in 1903, is being considered for restoration or preservation. The frame structure seems to be intact, but the foundation needs some work. The ancient paint is peeling badly both inside and outside the home. The windows fit badly because the foundation has shifted slightly, so the entire building is drafty. The object of the renovation is to make the building usable as a historical museum. Which process should be used: restoration or preservation?

Restoration would allow windows to be replaced with newer, energy-efficient replicas. Low- or no-VOC paints could be used. Preservation, on the other hand, would probably be less expensive, and would be fitting for a historical museum.

From a "green" perspective, restoration makes more sense in this case. The original paint most likely contained lead, which cannot be used in any case.

But is restoration always the best answer? No. Each project should be planned individually based on the types of repairs needed and the "green" alternatives that are available. For example, even the most efficient air-conditioning system would not be better than a home that was originally designed more than 100 years ago to take advantage of natural breezes—and many homes were designed with this in mind. Preservation may be a better idea for these homes. Also take into consideration what would happen to the original materials if they are replaced by new materials. Can the original materials be used in some other way?

The question is complex, and you will find that many people consistently advocate either restoration or preservation. The important point is to analyze the project carefully and determine the best route to restore or preserve each individual property.

Summary

- People remodel their homes for many reasons, including updating appliances, making the home more energy-efficient, and meeting changing needs for space.
- A remodeling project can vary in cost depending on the scale of the project and the amount of time and effort spent by family members.
- Remodeling can be divided into four main types: changing lived-in areas, making unused space livable, adding on, and buying to remodel.
- Renovation is the process of returning a home to a desirable condition.
- Two special types of renovation are restoration and preservation.
- Professionals such as architects, interior designers, and contractors may be helpful for any remodeling or renovation project.

Internet Resources

Advisory Council on Historic Preservation
Training courses for federal historic preservation compliance

Better Homes and Gardens
Ideas for renovating interiors and exteriors of older homes

National Trust for Historic Preservation
News about historic preservation projects and historic property listings

Restoration Hardware
Reproductions of period furniture and antique hardware

This Old House
Expert advice on repairing, remodeling, and renovating older homes

US Environmental Protection Agency (EPA)
Rules and regulations for handling lead in renovation jobs

Review Questions

Answer the following questions using the information in this chapter.

1. List five reasons a family may choose to remodel a home.
2. Why might a family choose remodeling over buying a new house?
3. List the four main types of remodeling.
4. What special considerations or equipment are necessary when converting an unfinished basement into living space?
5. Explain the factors that must be considered when changing an unfinished attic into a livable room.
6. What precautions should you take when you are adding onto a home and removing an existing exterior wall?
7. What is the main difference between remodeling and basic renovation?
8. Compare the purpose of restoration with the purpose of preservation.
9. Explain the concept of adaptive reuse.
10. Name three types of professionals that may be helpful in a remodeling or restoration project.

Suggested Activities

1. Write a short essay discussing the planning that would be needed to remodel an attic into a studio workplace.
2. Write a report that justifies the use of reclaimed building materials for the renovation of a client's home. Address pricing differences and sustainability impact by using recycled or reclaimed building materials.
3. Find a residence in your community that is a candidate for historical preservation. Take a series of photographs of the building. Research the history of the building and the area in which it resides. Determine if restoration, preservation, or adaptive reuse is suitable for this building. Present your analysis to the class.

4. Use traditional drafting or CAD software to draw the existing layout of your kitchen. Then, draw a remodeled layout for your kitchen. Present your designs to the class in an oral presentation. Explain why you believe the remodeled layout would improve the existing kitchen.

Problem Solving Case Study

You have a design drafting firm in Atlanta, Georgia, that specializes in home remodeling projects. Mr. and Mrs. Cooper have contacted you regarding the remodeling of their home. The home is 30 years old and is difficult to heat and cool. They want to increase the energy efficiency of the home as well as increase their comfort during the hot, humid Atlanta summers.

Given this preliminary information, perform any necessary research and answer the following questions.

1. What ideas should you present to the Coopers to help increase energy efficiency in their home?
2. What suggestions can you make that will increase their comfort during the summer months?

ADDA Certification Prep

The following questions are presented in the style used in the American Design Drafting Association (ADDA) Drafter Certification Test. Answer the questions using the information in this chapter.

1. Which of the following statements are true about remodeling?
   A. Remodeling can change an existing space into a new form.
   B. Adding on to homes generally requires more complex changes than altering lived-in spaces.
   C. Local building ordinances do not need to be considered when you are remodeling an interior space.
   D. The cost, time, and effort required to remodel should be considered before starting a project.
   E. The most commonly remodeled rooms in a typical home are the kitchen and bathrooms.
2. Match each term with its description.
   Terms: 1. Restoration, 2. Renovation, 3. Remodeling, 4. Preservation
   A. Concentrates on stabilizing and preserving the original materials and structures of a building.
   B. Changes an existing space into a new form.
   C. Returns a building to its original "look and feel."
   D. Returns a run-down building to a desirable condition.
3. Which of the following statements are *false*?
   A. The basic purpose of renovation is to make a house desirable.
   B. When restoring a historic home, it is considered wrong to update the plumbing.
   C. New materials are often used to replace the original materials when a house is undergoing preservation.

Curricular Connections

1. **Social Science.** One of the largest considerations in the restoration of a home is the original appearance of the home. This often requires historical research. Choose a historic home in your area—preferably one that has not yet been restored. Conduct research to find out as much as possible about when the home was built, its appearance when it was first built, whether any additions have been made, and the styles of furnishings that were popular when the house was new. Write a report on your findings. Be sure to list your sources.
2. **Language Arts.** Conduct research to find an old, historic building that is currently in danger of being demolished. Many such places exist in the downtown areas of major cities. Find one that interests you and conduct research to learn more about it. Why might it be demolished? How could it be adaptively

reused instead? Prepare and deliver a persuasive speech to your class to convince them that the building should be reused instead of demolished.

STEM Connections

1. **Math.** Retrofitting an existing home to add or update an air-conditioning system can be both difficult and expensive. Many new technologies are available on the market today that allow you to incorporate "green" air-conditioning systems into older homes. Research and compose a report comparing and contrasting older, newer, and "green" heating and air-conditioning systems. Research initial start-up costs and yearly energy costs for one specific older model, one new model, and one "green" model. Calculate potential savings and the time it will take to recoup the cost of installing the new unit and the "green" unit.

Communicating about Architecture

1. **Reading.** With a partner, make flash cards of the key terms in this chapter. On the front of the card, write the term. On the back of the card, write the pronunciation and a brief definition. Use this chapter and a dictionary for guidance. Then take turns quizzing one another on the pronunciations and definitions of the key terms.
2. **Speaking.** Select five of the key terms in this chapter and imagine them being used by architects in a real-life context. With a partner, role-play a situation in which an architectural firm is asked to remodel a 30-year-old home for a client.

Section 3

Plan Development

pics721/Shutterstock.com

Chapter 14

Floor Plans

Objectives

After completing this chapter, you will be able to:

- List the information required on a typical floor plan.
- Represent typical materials using standard architectural hatch patterns (symbols).
- Design and draw a residential floor plan using accepted manual drafting techniques.
- Create a floor plan using accepted CADD techniques.
- Dimension a floor plan in a clear and precise manner.

Key Terms

expansion floor plan
family
floor plan
hatch pattern
levels
material symbol
overall dimension
parametric modeling
space diagram

The ***floor plan*** is the heart of a set of construction drawings. It identifies the location and dimensions of exterior and interior walls, windows, doors, major appliances, cabinets, fireplaces, stairs, and other fixed features of the house. The floor plan is the one plan to which all trade workers refer. For a residence, the floor plan is usually the first drawing created. It is the basis for many other plans. Because modifications are frequently required as other plans are developed, however, the floor plan may not be finished until near the end of the design process.

The floor plan is not a typical top view; it is actually a section drawing. An imaginary cutting plane passes through the structure about 4′ above, and parallel to, the floor. The cutting plane may be higher or lower as necessary to cut through the required details. In some instances, an offset plane is required to change levels, as in the case of a split-level or multi-level house.

Figure 14-1 shows a floor plan of a single-story, three-bedroom house. Many features commonly found on a floor plan are shown in the figure. Sometimes when the structure is not complex, the floor plan may include information that would ordinarily be found on other drawings. For example, the electrical plan, heating and cooling plan, or plumbing plan might be combined with the floor plan. If you are using traditional drafting methods, be careful not to include too much information on a single drawing or the drawing will become cluttered and confusing. If you are using CADD, you can put all of the information for the additional plans on separate layers and hide the layers when they are not needed.

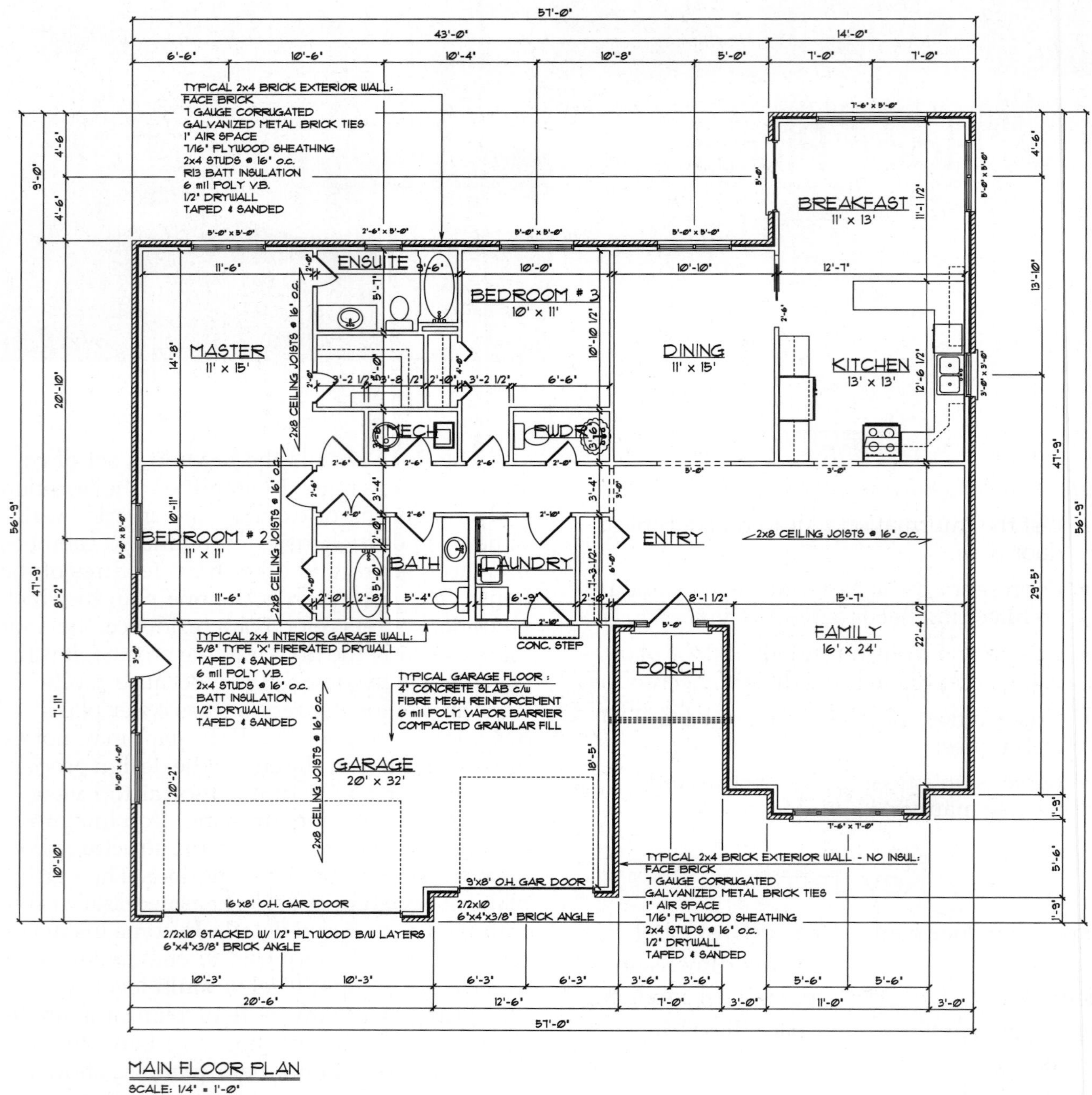

Goodheart-Willcox Publisher

Figure 14-1. A—A floor plan of a three-bedroom house showing the locations of walls, windows, doors, appliances, and fixtures.

Required Information

At a minimum, a floor plan includes the following information. See **Figure 14-2**.

- Location and orientation of exterior and interior walls
- Size and location of windows and doors
- Placement of built-in cabinets and appliances
- Location of permanent fixtures
- Location of stairs
- Location of fireplaces
- Size and location of walks, patios, and decks
- Room names
- Materials used (material symbols)

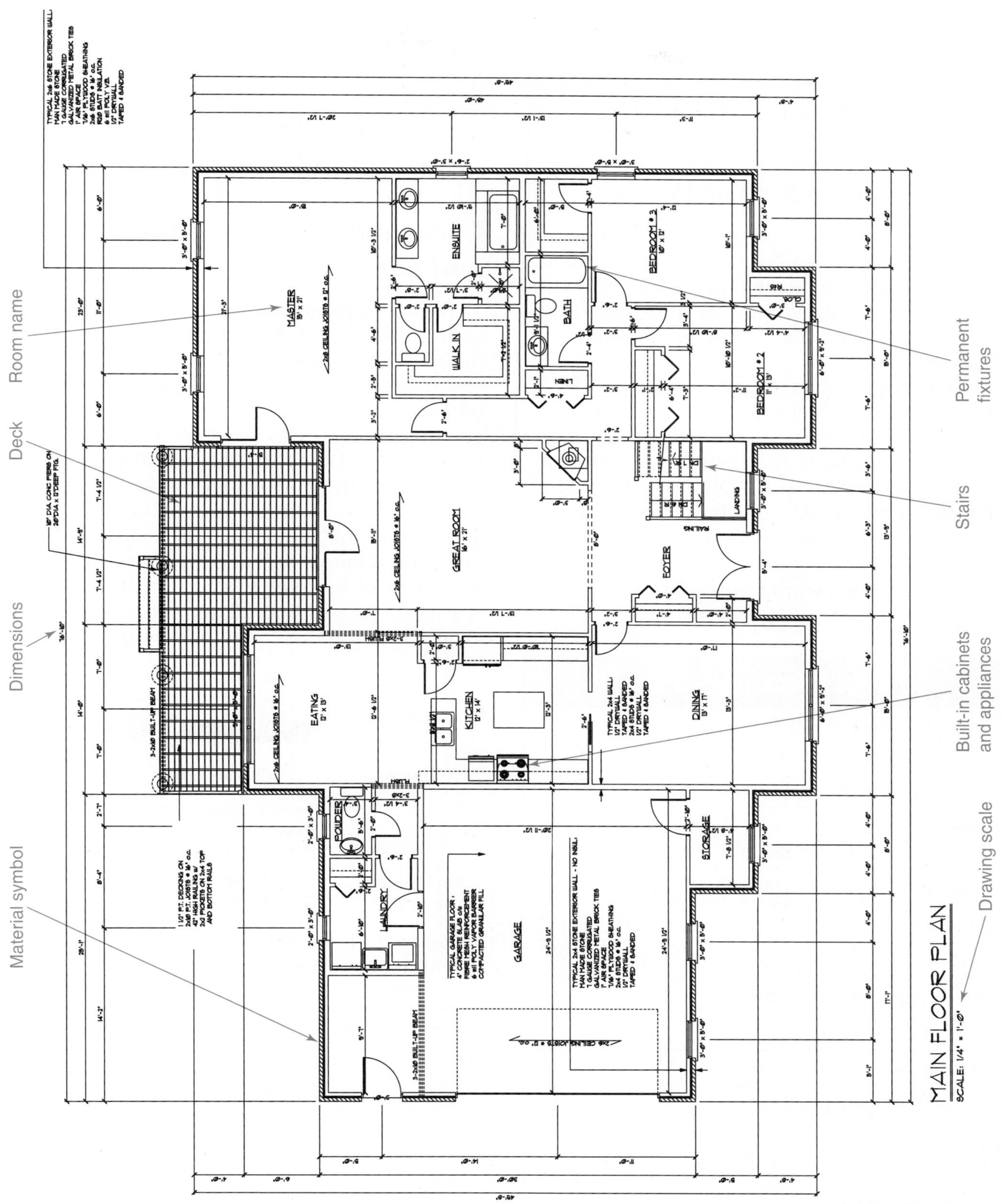

Goodheart-Willcox Publisher

Figure 14-2. The required elements of a floor plan.

- Location and size dimensions
- Drawing scale

Frequently, related structures such as a detached garage or swimming pool are also shown on the floor plan.

Location and Size of Walls

Be careful to draw all of the walls accurately. Any variations in wall thicknesses on a drawing will be readily evident and detract from the neatness of the drawing. Use the chart shown in **Figure 14-3** as a guide to nominal wall thicknesses.

When drawing manually, set your dividers to the proper wall thickness dimension. Then use the dividers to measure wall thickness rather than try to measure each time with your scale. When drawing using CADD, use the **OFFSET**, **DOUBLE LINE**, **WALL**, or similar command to draw the wall at the proper thickness.

Since the floor plan is a section drawing, hatch patterns (symbols) should be used to indicate materials. See **Figure 14-4** for examples of hatch patterns that are commonly used for walls. Notice that three different patterns are shown for frame walls. Although the meaning of most symbols is standardized, there is some variation. Be sure to follow the practices of your school or office when selecting hatch patterns.

Location and Size of Windows and Doors

When locating windows and doors on frame walls, place a centerline through the middle of the opening, as shown in **Figure 14-5**. In masonry construction, the centerline is not needed because dimensions are to the opening. The opening shown in the wall for windows is the sash width. For doors, the actual door width is shown as the opening in the wall. The door swing must be indicated on the floor plan. Sills are drawn for windows and exterior doors. Common window and door symbols are shown in **Figure 14-6**. Refer to Chapter 21, *Doors and Windows*, for additional symbols and more detailed information on windows and doors.

Wall Thickness Chart	
Wood Frame Walls	
Exterior walls (with sheathing and siding)	6″
Interior walls (with drywall both sides)	5″
Concrete Block Walls	
Exterior walls	8″, 10″, or 12″
Interior walls	4″ or 8″
Brick Veneer Exterior	
Veneer on frame	10″
Veneer on concrete block	12″
Brick Exterior Walls	
Two courses of brick	8″
Two courses with 2″ air space	10″
Three courses of brick	12″

Goodheart-Willcox Publisher

Figure 14-3. This chart shows nominal thicknesses for several common wall types.

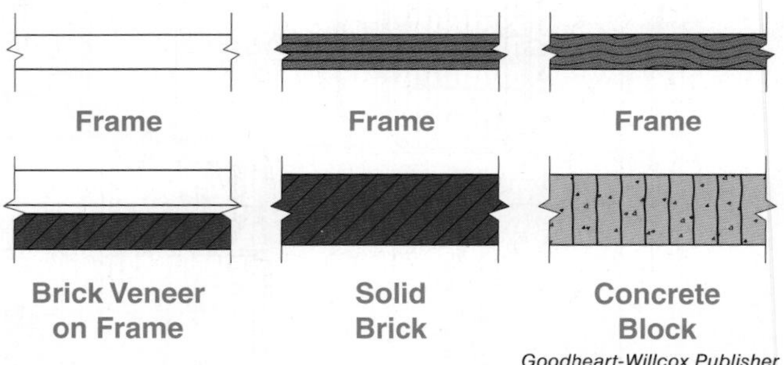

Goodheart-Willcox Publisher

Figure 14-4. These are several common hatch patterns (symbols) used to indicate wall materials on the floor plan.

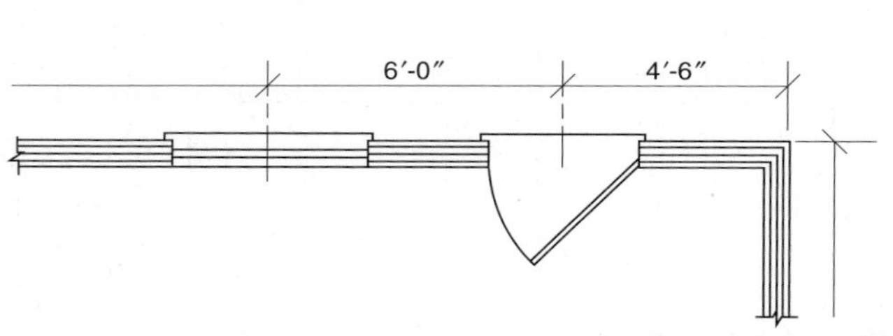

Goodheart-Willcox Publisher

Figure 14-5. Windows and doors are located using a centerline in frame construction. The type of window and the door swing direction should be shown.

Occasionally, a plain opening or archway may be desired rather than a door. In this case, hidden (dashed) lines are used to show that the opening does not extend to the ceiling. See **Figure 14-7**. Hidden lines are used on the floor plan to indicate that a feature is above the cutting plane or hidden by some other detail.

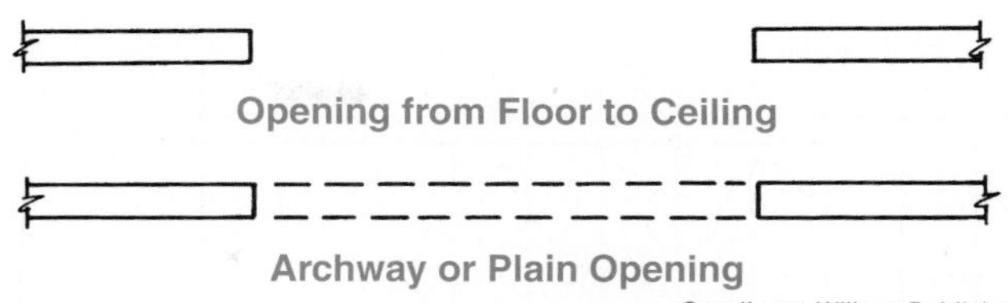

Figure 14-7. Two methods of representing interior wall openings other than windows and doors.

Cabinets, Appliances, and Permanent Fixtures

The location and size of kitchen cabinets, bathroom vanities, fixtures, and appliances must be indicated on the floor plan. These features are drawn using standard symbols that represent specific sizes. Never guess at the size of an appliance or fixture. Obtain information related to each item, record the necessary dimensions and specifications, and include that information in the plans.

Refer to symbols and location procedures covered in Chapter 8, *Planning the Sleeping Area,* and Chapter 9, *Planning the Service Area.* Also, examine local codes related to clearances and installation procedures acceptable in your area.

Stairs and Fireplaces

If a stairway or fireplace is to be included, only information about the basic size and location needs to be recorded on the floor plan. Detail drawings will be included in the set of drawings for these two features.

For stairs, the direction of flight, number of risers, and width of the stairs are given on the floor plan. The minimum clear width for stairs required by the International Residential Code is 3′-0″ in the space above the handrail and below the minimum headroom. See **Figure 14-8**. The riser height and tread width for stairs may be specified on the floor plan or on a stair detail drawing. Additional information on stair design is provided in Chapter 24, *Stair Details.*

For a fireplace, the basic width, length, location, and shape of the opening are shown on the floor plan. Either a simplified or detailed symbol may be used to identify the fireplace, as shown in **Figure 14-9**. The detailed symbol is usually preferred. Additional flues that may be housed in the chimney are frequently included on the floor plan.

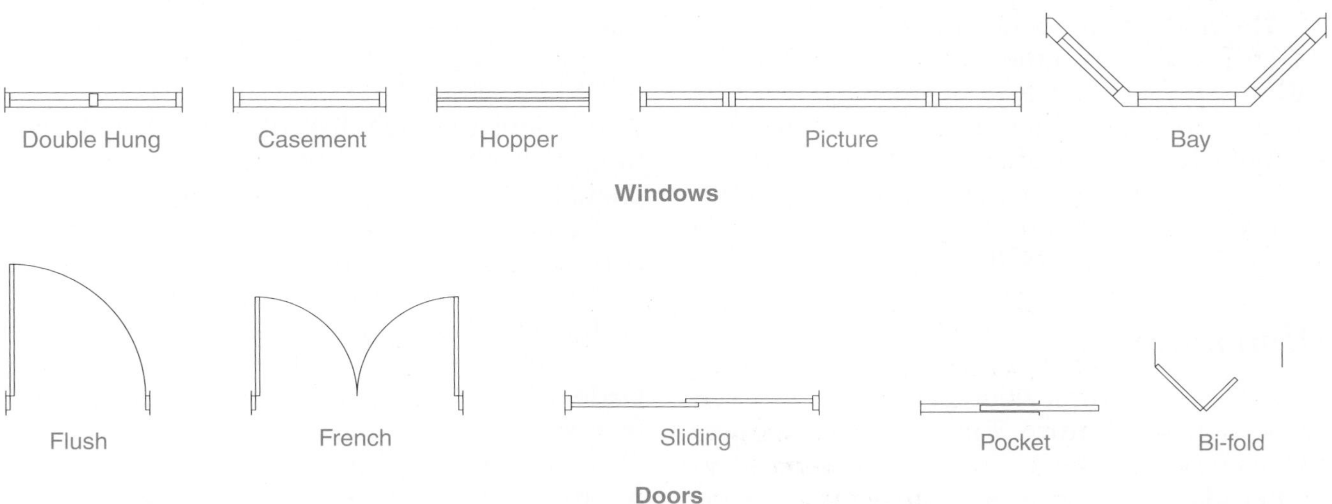

Figure 14-6. Common window and door symbols used on residential floor plans.

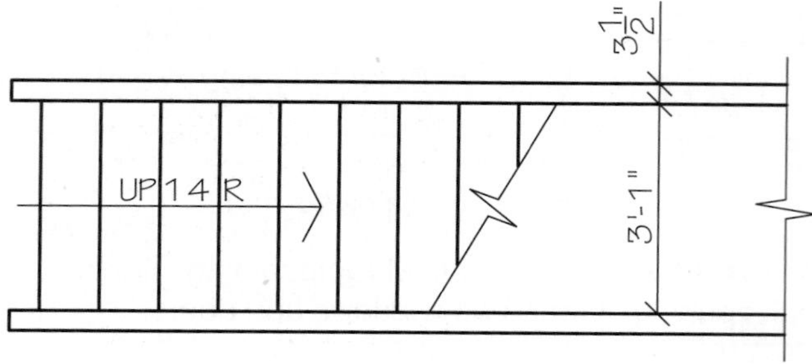

Goodheart-Willcox Publisher

Figure 14-8. The direction of flight, number of risers, and width of stairs are shown on the floor plan.

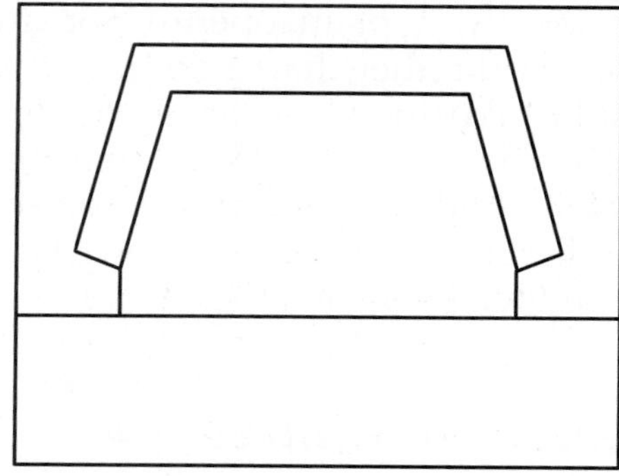

Simplified Fireplace Symbol

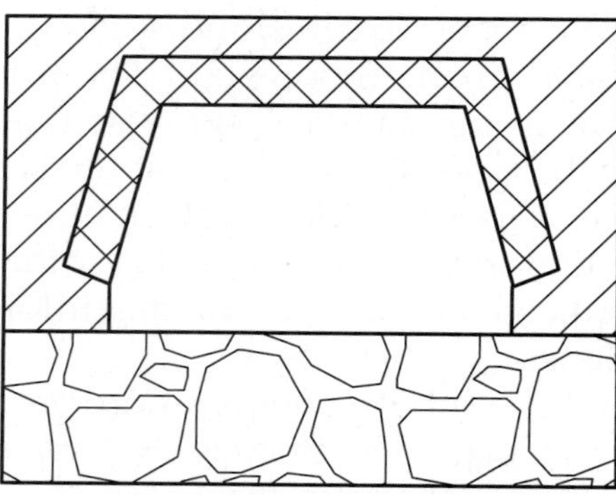

Detailed Fireplace Symbol

Goodheart-Willcox Publisher

Figure 14-9. A fireplace can be represented on a floor plan using a simplified or detailed symbol.

Walks, Patios, and Decks

Several outside features of the house are commonly included on the floor plan. Walks, patios, decks, and swimming pools are examples. Sizes and materials should be indicated on the plan, as well as locations.

Room Names and Material Symbols

Room names add information that is important in communicating the plan to others. The room name should be lettered slightly larger (3/16″) than the surrounding lettering. Ideally, the room name should be in the center of the room, but it may be shifted to one side or lowered if needed. The approximate size of the room may be added immediately below the name. This can be helpful for viewers who are not familiar with construction drawings.

Material symbols or ***hatch patterns*** are a type of shorthand for the drafter. Symbols (hatch patterns) are used instead of words to describe the materials being specified. Use a material symbol whenever the material should be identified. If the symbol is not a standard one, identify it. Several common building material symbols are shown in **Figure 14-10**.

Dimensioning

Dimensions on a floor plan show the size or location of a feature. *The importance of proper and careful dimensioning cannot be overemphasized.* Proper placement of dimensions requires good judgment. Locate dimensions where viewers will logically look for them.

Dimension lines in architectural drafting are generally continuous lines with the dimension figure placed above the line. Dimension figures are always parallel (never perpendicular) to the dimension line. Any accepted termination symbol may be used as long as you are consistent throughout the set of drawings.

When drawings are so crowded with dimensions that it is difficult to see the objects, move dimension lines out from the drawing far enough (at least 3/4″) so the dimension, as well as the object lines, can be clearly seen. Spacing between the dimension lines may be 1/4″ or 3/8″ as desired. Dimension lines may be located within the house area if that seems to be the logical place for them. Refrain from using long leaders. The maximum length of a leader should be two inches.

Dimensions in architectural drawing are recorded in feet and inches. Depending on school or office practice, foot and inch marks may be omitted on plan drawings and other architectural

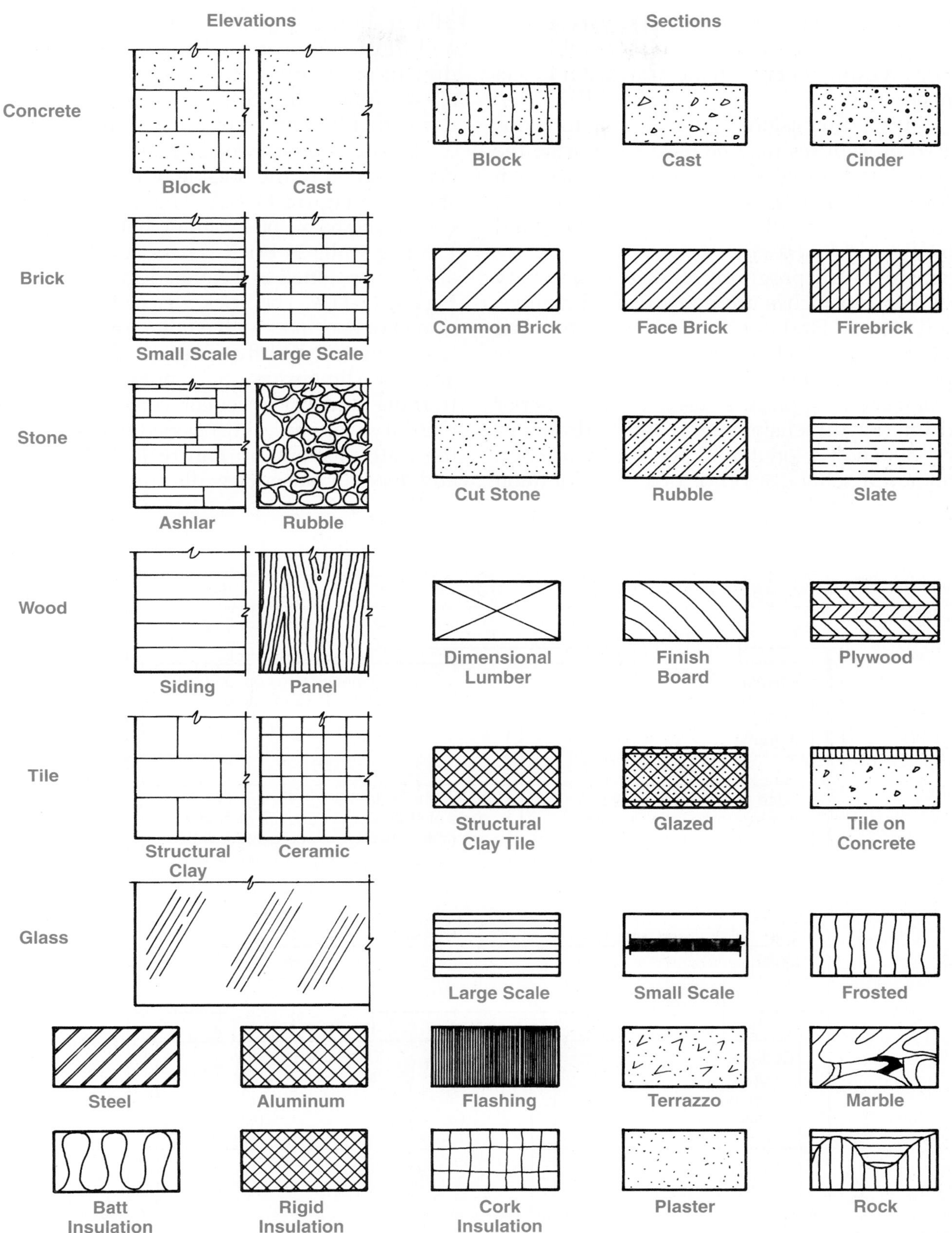

Goodheart-Willcox Publisher

Figure 14-10. Building material symbols commonly used on residential floor plans.

working drawings. In such cases, it is understood that a dimension such as 12-6 could not mean anything other than the dimension 12 feet 6 inches.

When a dimension is less than one foot, one of two procedures may be used to indicate the length. Either place a zero in the foot location followed by the number of inches (0′-6″ or 0-6) or record the length as so many inches and show the inch mark (6″).

Some CADD programs allow you to specify how feet and inches are marked on drawings; others do not. Find out the CADD settings that are used in your school or office and follow the appropriate practice.

Dimensioning practices used to locate exterior and interior dimensions on working drawings vary depending on the type of construction shown and school or office practice. Common dimensioning practices are discussed here and illustrated in this chapter. While different dimensioning practices exist, it is important to always follow the accepted conventions or standards required by your school or office.

Exterior walls in wood frame construction are dimensioned to the outside of the stud wall, as shown in **Figure 14-11A**. This usually includes the weatherboard or sheathing but not the siding. Exterior walls in brick veneer construction are also dimensioned to the outside of the stud wall, **Figure 14-11A**. The brick veneer is also dimensioned or specified with a note. Another practice is to dimension to the exterior of the structure and use dimensions or a note to specify the framing and brick veneer construction. Solid masonry walls are dimensioned to the outside of the wall, as shown in **Figure 14-11B**. Windows and doors in masonry walls are dimensioned to

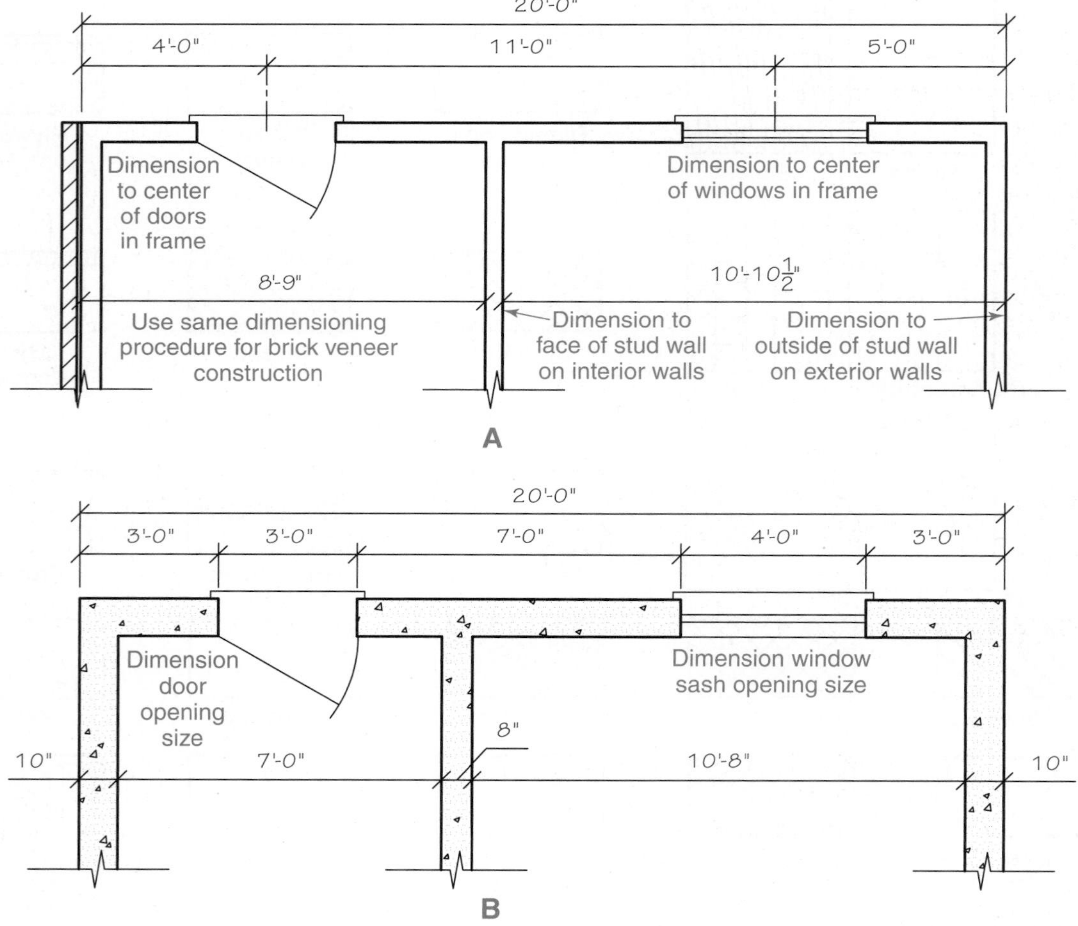

Figure 14-11. A—Recommended method of dimensioning frame wall and brick veneer construction. B—Solid masonry walls (cast concrete, block, brick, or stone) are usually dimensioned as shown.

the opening, rather than a centerline. In concrete masonry unit construction, some drafters prefer to dimension the window and door openings to their centers rather than to the rough openings.

Interior walls are commonly dimensioned to the faces of stud walls. Refer to **Figure 14-11A**. One method is to give the dimensions to the same side of the walls throughout the drawing. Depending on school or office practice, dimensions may also be given to both sides of interior walls. Another practice is to dimension interior walls to their centers. In this case, a short line is drawn down the middle of the wall at the termination point of the dimension to show that the center is indicated.

Overall dimensions are necessary to provide the total length and width of the structure. Always verify the dimensions by adding all the partial dimensions together. Their sum should equal the overall dimension. For example, in **Figure 14-11A**, 4′ + 11′ + 5′ equals 20′, which matches the overall 20′ dimension. One of the most frequent errors in dimensioning is that partial dimensions do not add up to equal the total distance.

The overall length and width of major wall segments should be lengths that are multiples of 4′. Building material sizes are keyed to this dimension and much unnecessary waste will result if this rule is not applied.

Frequently, notes are required to present information that cannot be represented by a conventional dimension or symbol. These notes

Employability

Creating a Portfolio

When you interview for an architectural job, your interviewer will expect you to present samples of your work to showcase your qualifications. A *portfolio* is a selection of work that you collect and organize to show your qualifications, skills, and talents.

Some people prefer a print portfolio that contains actual drawings and other items they have created. Others choose to create an e-portfolio, or digital portfolio. Both types have advantages and disadvantages. For example, an e-portfolio is much easier to transport than a print portfolio—all you need is a USB drive. However, a print portfolio may have more impact because it is easier for the interviewer to see the quality of the actual drawings you have made by hand (in manual drafting) or the neatness and appropriateness of the prints you have made (in CADD).

Now is a good time to think about which type of portfolio you want to create and to actually start it. You do not need a lot of finished drawings to begin your portfolio. In fact, a portfolio is a "living" tool. In other words, you will constantly add to it, and occasionally remove items from it.

What should you include in your portfolio? In general, you should include items that show your technical skills and level of accomplishment. For example, for an architectural job, you would almost certainly include examples of architectural working drawings, including at least one floor plan.

Activity

After completing this chapter, use the Internet to search for *print portfolio* and *e-portfolio*. Read articles about each type of portfolio and locate examples of portfolio work created by others. Determine which type of portfolio you will create and review the floor plans you have created. Choose one that you consider to be your best work so far and place it in your portfolio. If you are building a print portfolio, print the drawing on good-quality paper or vellum and place it in a folder or envelope that is large enough to hold the drawing without folding it. Some companies make professional portfolio cases; you may want to consider one of these at some point. For now, a large envelope may meet your needs just as well.

If you are building an e-portfolio, obtain a USB drive that you can dedicate entirely to your portfolio. Do not use the drive for anything else. Label it carefully so that you do not accidentally overwrite or delete the contents. If you created your floor plan drawing using CADD, copy the drawing to the USB drive. If you created the drawing using manual techniques, you can scan the drawing using a scanner and save the resulting file on your USB drive. In most cases, however, CADD drawings work better with e-portfolios.

should be brief and located where they are easy to see. Include only required information. Notes may be lettered 1/8″ high or slightly smaller. They should be read from the bottom of the sheet, not from the edge.

Scale and Sheet Identification

Residential floor plans are usually drawn to a scale of 1/4″ = 1′-0″. A detail may be drawn at a larger scale and the site plan at a smaller scale, but the other drawings in a set of architectural drawings should be 1/4″ = 1′-0″. The size of paper selected for the plans is determined by the size of the structure. A sheet of 18″ × 24″ paper is large enough for most plans. The scale must appear at the bottom of each drawing, except on the pictorial representation of the total house.

Number the sheets in a set of construction drawings so the reader may determine if the set is complete. This is important. One method that works well is to number each sheet as Sheet 1 of 6, Sheet 2 of 6, and so on. The sheet number should appear in the lower right-hand corner of each sheet.

Metric System of Dimensioning

The metric system of measurement is standard in most countries outside the United States. Many US companies, especially those having international business, use the metric system or dual dimensioning, which shows both metric and inch dimensions. However, in the US residential construction industry, the US Customary (inch) system is standard. Before the metric system can be accepted by the US building industry, new lumber sizes and standards must be decided on and accepted.

Even though the metric system is not standard in the United States, a simple floor plan is shown in **Figure 14-12** to illustrate metric

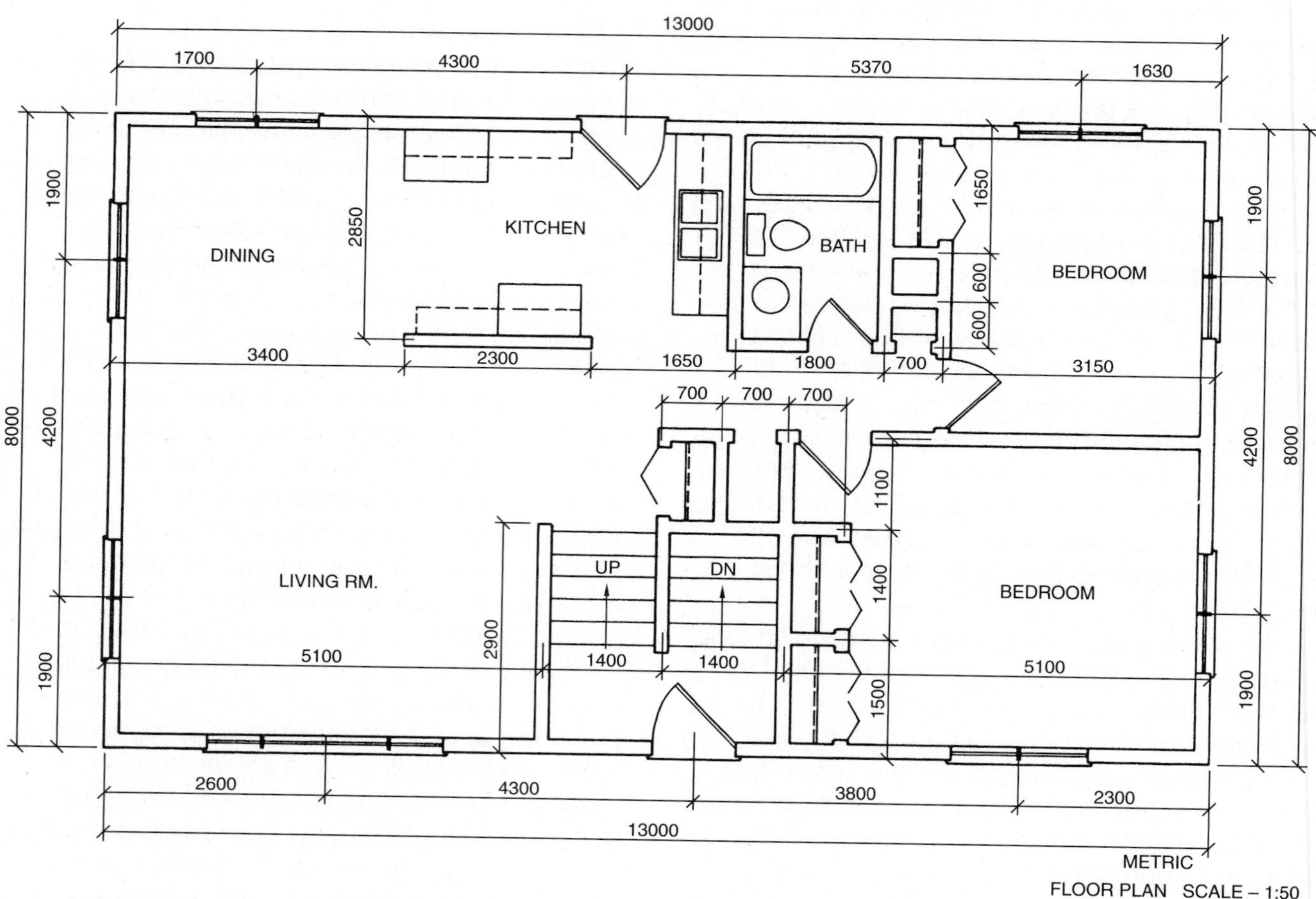

Figure 14-12. This floor plan is dimensioned in metric units.

dimensioning. The basic units for linear measurement in the construction industry should be restricted to the meter (m) and the millimeter (mm). Thus, on drawings, whole number dimensions always indicate millimeters, and decimal numbers (to three decimal places) always indicate meters.

Drawing a Floor Plan

The first step in designing a house is to determine the requirements of the structure and record them as preliminary sketches. These rough sketches will provide direction for drawing the plan to scale. The steps in the following sections should aid you in drawing a floor plan once the basic requirements are determined and some preliminary sketches are developed.

Some drafters prepare a *bubble diagram* from preliminary design sketches. This is a freehand sketch or computer-generated drawing that uses "bubble" shapes to represent rooms and spaces in the home. The bubble diagram serves as a basis for the design and provides a way to evaluate spatial relationships before making a scaled drawing. A series of sketches are typically made during this phase to plan room locations and spaces based on a site analysis. The site analysis accounts for factors such as the natural site contour, building code restrictions, style of home to be built, and solar orientation. Additional considerations for locating a structure on the site and guidelines for drawing site plans are discussed in Chapter 16, *Site Plans*.

Figure 14-13 shows a floor plan for a single-story house. First- and second-level floor plans for a two-story house are shown in **Figure 14-14**.

Some floor plans take future expansion into account during the initial design stage. These ***expansion floor plans*** have much to offer. If additions are planned when the house is originally designed, the expanded house does not later appear as being "added on to." Also, fewer basic changes are required when additions are ultimately made. The plan shown in **Figure 14-15** is designed for expansion. The basic house, 28′ × 52′, contains the necessary space for a small family. As the family grows, the house can be enlarged to meet the family's needs. A bedroom and bath could be added first and the breezeway, bath, and mudroom added later. Finally, the garage, storage, and porch may be built to complete the expanded plan, which measures approximately 34′ × 74′.

Procedure
Manual Drafting

Drawing a Floor Plan

It is important to always follow the practices of your school or company when you create any kind of architectural plan. Certain general steps apply to most drawing tasks, however. Follow these basic steps to create a floor plan for a home with frame wall construction using manual drafting techniques.

1. Lay out the exterior walls. Draw the walls as light construction lines. Be sure that the overall length and width of the house are measured to the proper place on the walls and that walls are the correct thickness. Steps 1 and 2 are shown in **Figure 14-16**.
2. Locate the interior walls. Use light construction lines. Set your dividers to the desired wall thickness and use them to transfer the dimension. The manner in which interior walls are dimensioned is determined by school or office practice. In this example, interior walls are dimensioned to their centers, so the centers of the walls are used to locate their position.
3. Determine the location of the windows and doors. Both of these features will be dimensioned to the centerline of the opening in frame wall construction, so locate the centerline first. Indicate the swing of doors and type of window. Darken lines used for windows and doors. Include sills if appropriate. Steps 3, 4, and 5 are shown in **Figure 14-17**.
4. Draw the stairs. (If the house has no stairs, go to the next step.) Measure the width of the stairs and lay out the treads. Draw equally spaced lines to represent the stair treads. Show the direction of travel and the number of risers. Note that the height between finished floors must be determined and the tread depth and riser height calculated before this step can be completed accurately. See Chapter 24, *Stair Details*, for instructions on performing these calculations.

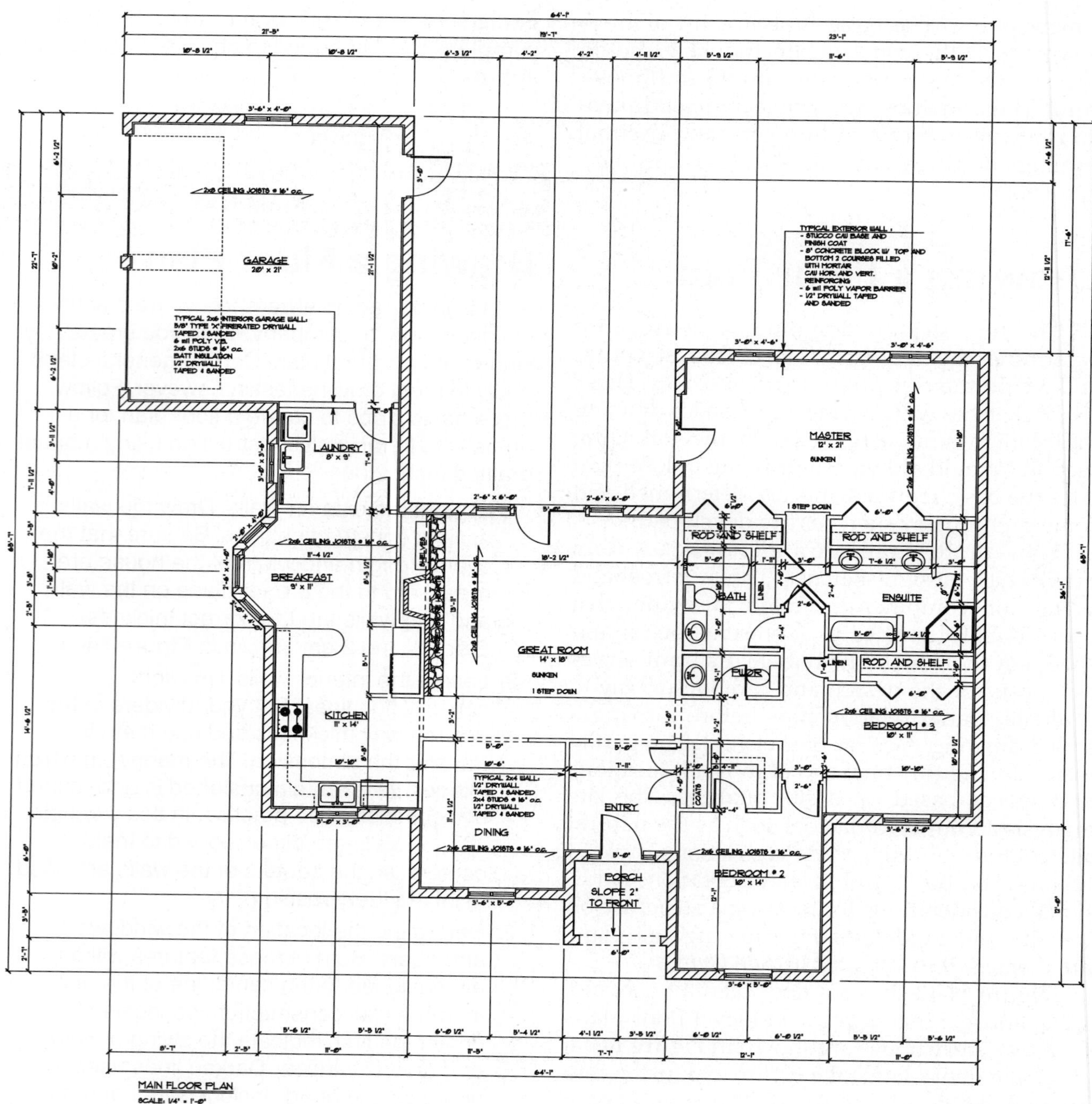

Goodheart-Willcox Publisher

Figure 14-13. A floor plan for a single-story house with concrete block construction for exterior walls.

5. Draw the fireplace(s). (If the house does not have a fireplace, go to the next step.) Since the dimensions of a fireplace must be exact to ensure proper operation, some preliminary work must be done before the fireplace can be drawn on the floor plan. Identify the type and size of fireplace to be used and record these dimensions for further use. Darken the fireplace outline and fire chamber size. See Chapter 25, *Fireplace, Chimney, and Stove Details*, for more information. You may now darken all exterior and interior walls.
6. Draw walks, patios, and decks. Select materials and designs that will complement

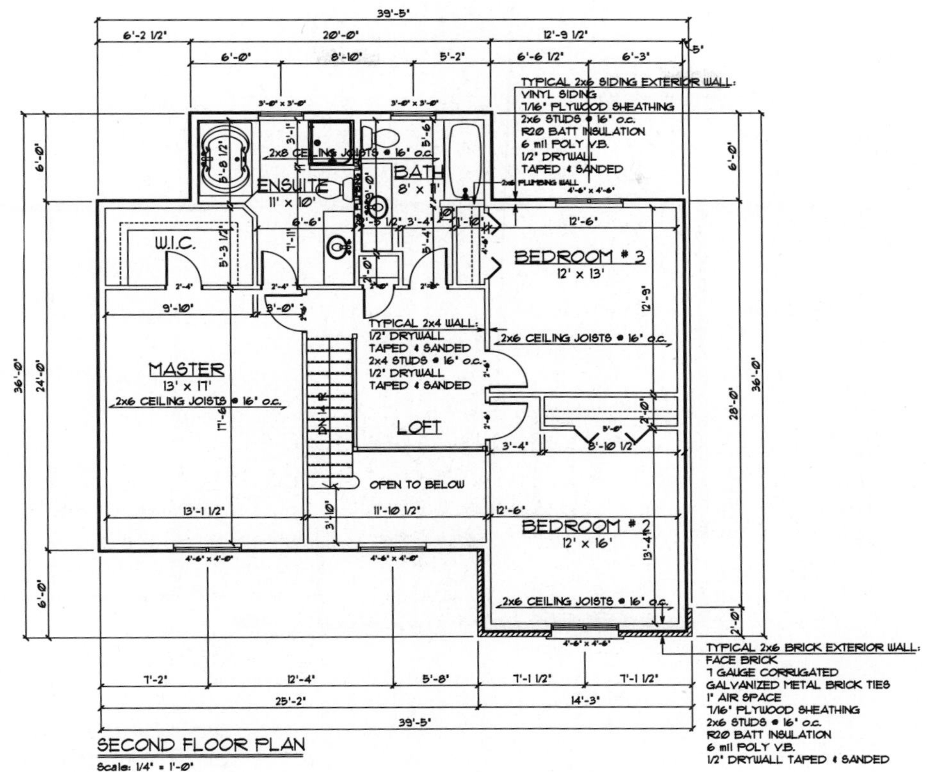

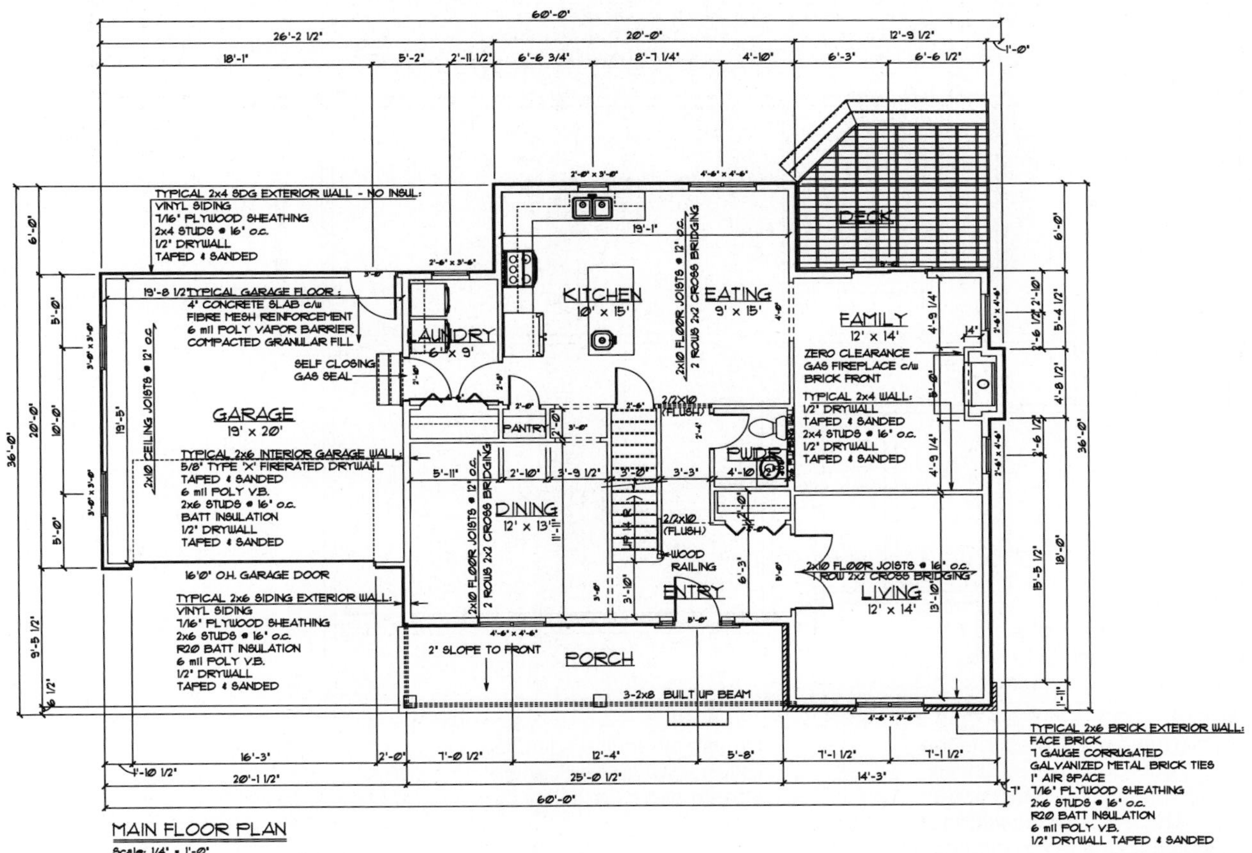

Goodheart-Willcox Publisher

Figure 14-14. The first floor and second floor plans for a two-story house with frame construction.

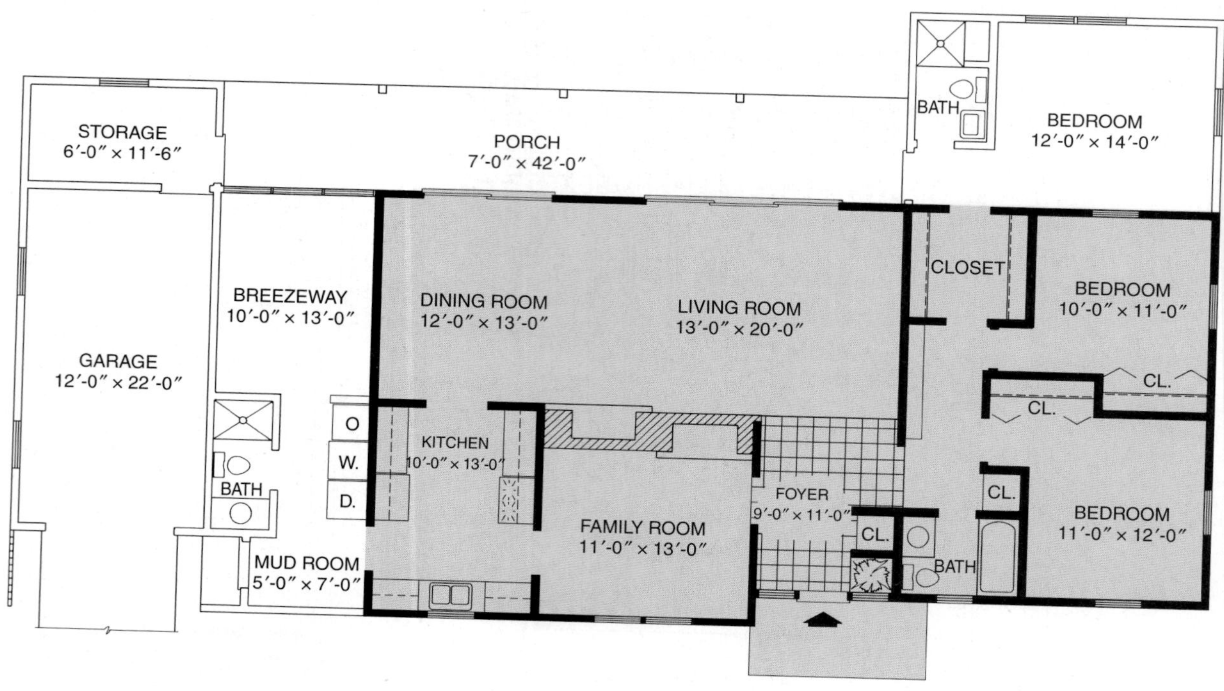

Goodheart-Willcox Publisher

Figure 14-15. An expansion floor plan for a house that can be expanded from 1456 to 2516 square feet.

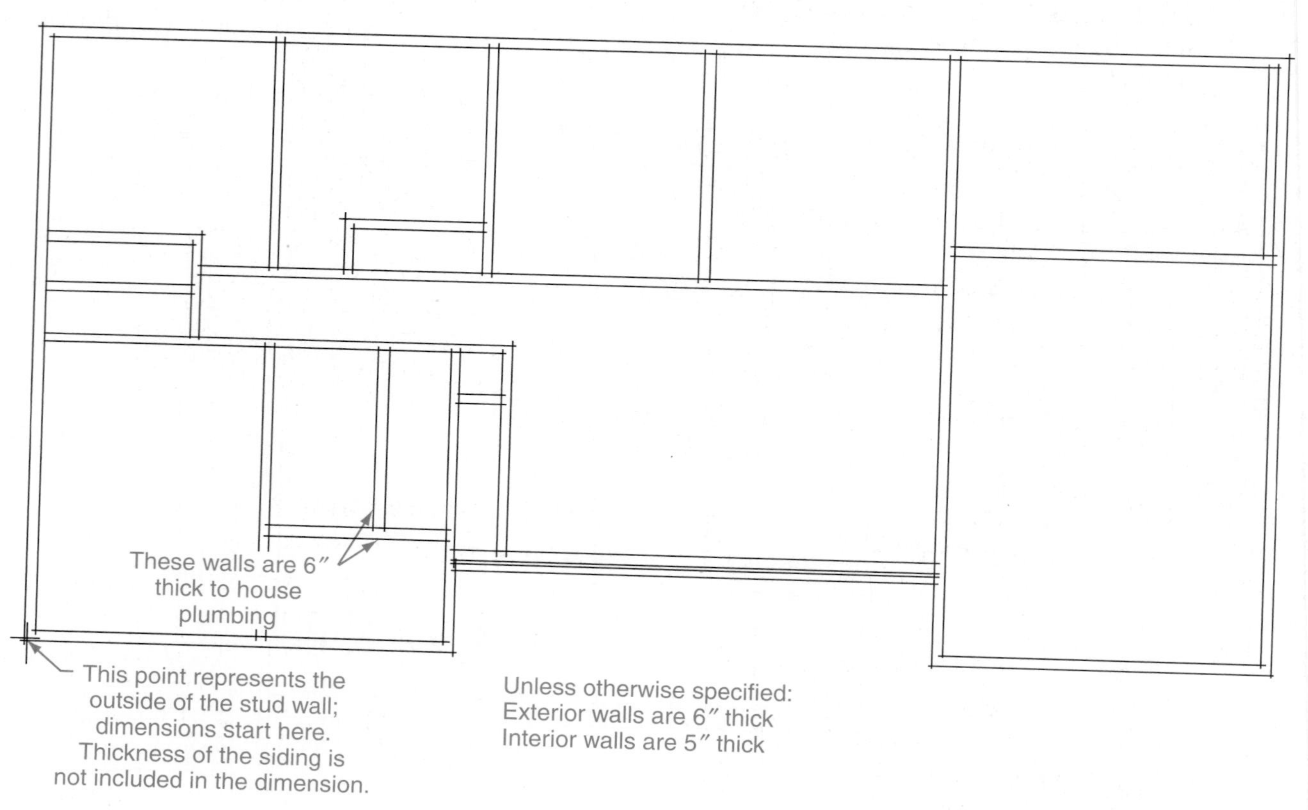

Goodheart-Willcox Publisher

Figure 14-16. Lay out the interior and exterior wall locations as light construction lines.

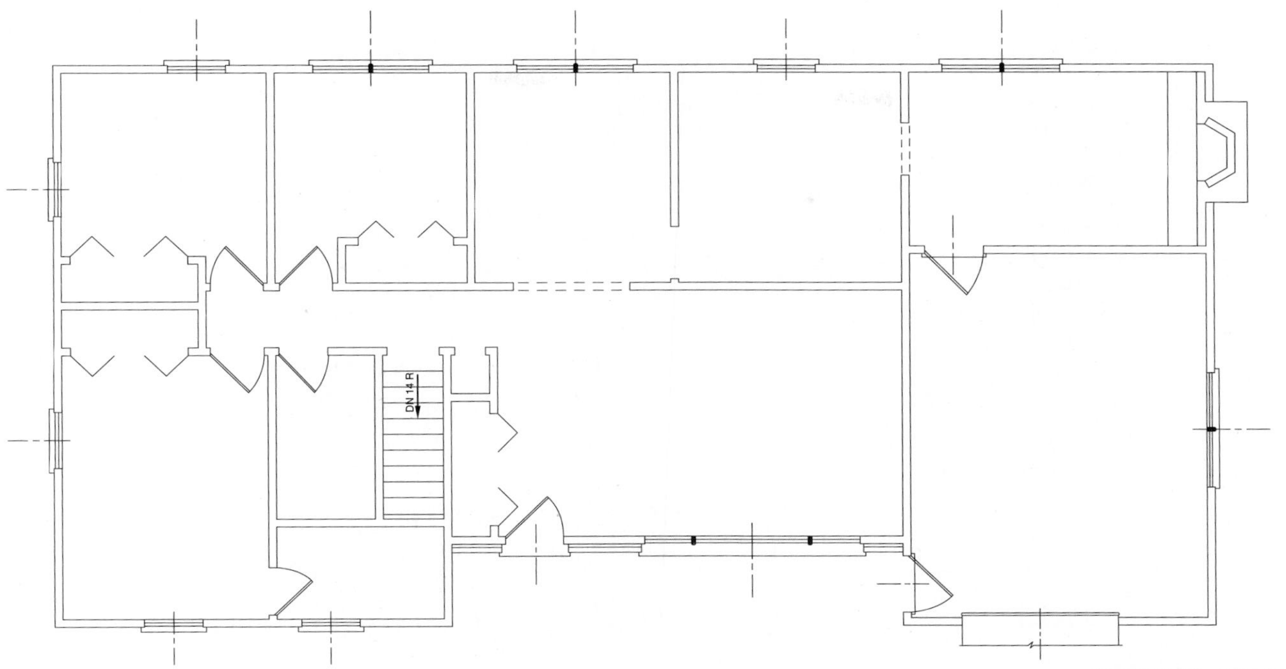

Goodheart-Willcox Publisher

Figure 14-17. Windows, doors, a fireplace, and stairs have been added to the layout. Lines showing walls and symbols have been darkened.

the total structure. Lay out and draw these elements. Steps 6, 7, and 8 are shown in **Figure 14-18**.

7. Draw the kitchen cabinets, appliances, and bathroom fixtures. Kitchen base cabinets are usually 24″ deep; wall cabinets are 12″ deep. The base units are shown as solid lines, and the wall cabinets are indicated using a hidden linetype. The refrigerator and range are usually deeper than 24″ and should be represented as such. Bathroom vanities and fixtures should be located and drawn in the same way as kitchen cabinets and appliances. Be sure to check local codes for required fixture clearances. Refer to Chapter 8, *Planning the Sleeping Area*, and Chapter 9, *Planning the Service Area,* for information on bathrooms and kitchens, respectively.
8. Add dimensions, notes, and room names. Keep in mind the dimensioning guidelines presented earlier in this chapter. Make sure the dimensions are accurate and complete. Letter the room name in the center of each room and show the approximate room size below the name if desired. Look over the drawing and add any general or specific notes that seem warranted. *Note:* It is important to show dimensions for all exterior wall features on the wall where they are located.
9. Add material and identification symbols. It is better to wait until the drawing is nearly finished to add material symbols so they do not interfere with dimensions or notes. Add the necessary symbols and darken remaining light lines. *All object lines, hidden lines, centerlines, etc., on a drawing should be black and only vary in width.* Exceptions are guidelines and construction lines. You may wish to remove the construction lines, but do not remove the guidelines. Steps 9 and 10 are shown in **Figure 14-19**.
10. Draw the title block and add the scale. The scale is important and should be placed in a prominent location near the bottom of the drawing. It may be located in the title block if all drawings on the sheet are the same scale. The title block should include the sheet number, name of the drawing, scale, date, name of the client, name of the drafter, and any other necessary information. The title

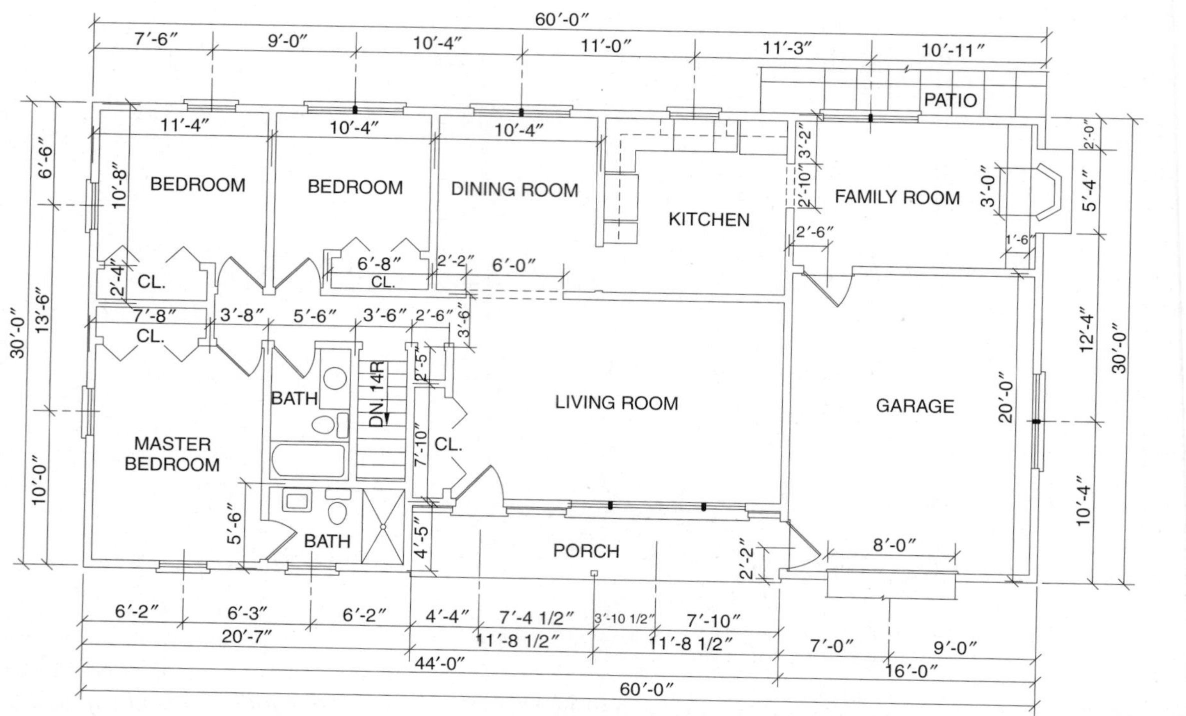

Goodheart-Willcox Publisher

Figure 14-18. A patio and porch, kitchen cabinets, bathroom fixtures, room names, and dimensions have been added to the plan.

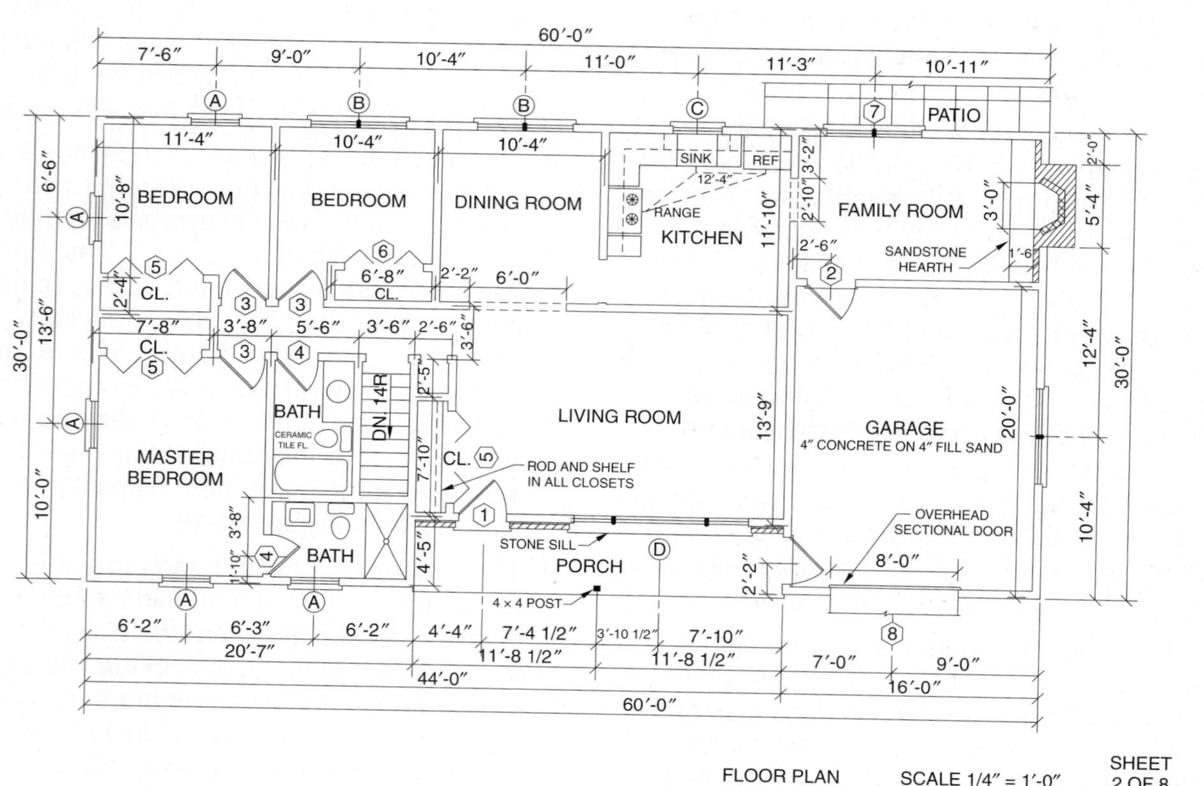

Goodheart-Willcox Publisher

Figure 14-19. The floor plan is completed by adding material and identification symbols, notes, the drawing scale, and the name of the drawing.

block typically appears along the bottom or right edge of the drawing sheet. A typical title block used in architectural drafting is shown in **Figure 14-20**.

11. Check the entire drawing. Examine all aspects of the drawing for accuracy and completeness.

Procedure CADD

Drawing a Floor Plan

A CADD system greatly speeds the process of drawing and designing a floor plan. Automatic wall generation, repetitive use of symbols, dimensioning features, and elimination of hand lettering cut the design and drafting time to a fraction of that required by a traditional (manual) drafter. You must still know the basics of design, but the actual representation of your design is fast and accurate. See **Figure 14-21**.

Most generic CADD packages can be used to draw floor plans, but a package designed especially for architectural work is much preferred. Most have an extensive symbol library and dimension styles that are generally used by architects. Some software also includes an architectural font for lettering that can give the drawing a hand-drawn appearance.

The following steps can be used with most CADD systems. The specific commands will vary from one software program to another, but the basic procedure should still apply.

1. Prepare a space diagram. A ***space diagram*** is an effective tool for determining how the various rooms and areas fit together. The diagram should be drawn at full size, with each room or area identified and the number of square feet noted for each. A space diagram should be placed on its own layer. **Figure 14-22** shows a completed space diagram. The total area of the floor plan is 1778.91 square feet.
2. Draw the exterior and interior walls. Use a layer dedicated to the floor plan. The **DOUBLE LINE**, **OFFSET**, **DRAW WALL**, or similar command can be used to draw the walls, as shown in **Figure 14-23A**. Clean up the wall intersections as required. **Figure 14-23B** shows wall areas that usually require cleanup.

   Two important things to remember when locating and drawing exterior and interior walls on a floor plan are their proper thickness and measurement location. The thickness of all walls should be drawn as accurately as possible. When using a CADD system, walls can be drawn to the exact dimensions instead of to a nominal thickness. This is determined by school or office practice. For example, interior walls are generally 4-1/2″ thick, which allows for drywall on both sides of a 3-1/2″ (actual size) stud. Exterior walls vary considerably depending on type and construction technique. A typical exterior frame wall might be 5-3/32″ in actual thickness. This thickness is the result of 1/2″ drywall, 3-1/2″ stud, 3/4″ rigid foam insulation, and 11/32″ siding. In CADD, it is just as easy to draw a wall 5-3/32″ thick as it is one 6″ thick. Draw the wall to the exact dimension if this is the required school or office practice.

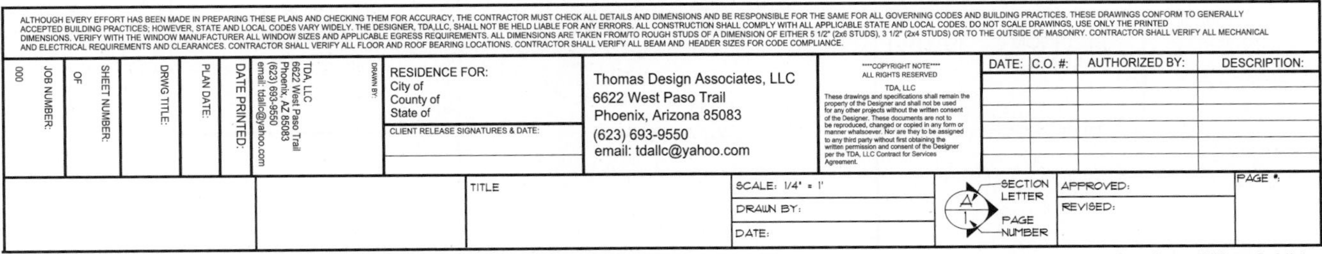
ALTHOUGH EVERY EFFORT HAS BEEN MADE IN PREPARING THESE PLANS AND CHECKING THEM FOR ACCURACY, THE CONTRACTOR MUST CHECK ALL DETAILS AND DIMENSIONS AND BE RESPONSIBLE FOR THE SAME FOR ALL GOVERNING CODES AND BUILDING PRACTICES. THESE DRAWINGS CONFORM TO GENERALLY ACCEPTED BUILDING PRACTICES; HOWEVER, STATE AND LOCAL CODES VARY WIDELY. THE DESIGNER, TDA,LLC, SHALL NOT BE HELD LIABLE FOR ANY ERRORS. ALL CONSTRUCTION SHALL COMPLY WITH ALL APPLICABLE STATE AND LOCAL CODES. DO NOT SCALE DRAWINGS, USE ONLY THE PRINTED DIMENSIONS. VERIFY WITH THE WINDOW MANUFACTURER ALL WINDOW SIZES AND APPLICABLE EGRESS REQUIREMENTS. ALL DIMENSIONS ARE TAKEN FROM/TO ROUGH STUDS OF A DIMENSION OF EITHER 5 1/2" (2x6 STUDS), 3 1/2" (2x4 STUDS) OR TO THE OUTSIDE OF MASONRY. CONTRACTOR SHALL VERIFY ALL MECHANICAL AND ELECTRICAL REQUIREMENTS AND CLEARANCES. CONTRACTOR SHALL VERIFY ALL FLOOR AND ROOF BEARING LOCATIONS. CONTRACTOR SHALL VERIFY ALL BEAM AND HEADER SIZES FOR CODE COMPLIANCE.

000 JOB NUMBER:
OF SHEET NUMBER:
DRWG TITLE:
PLAN DATE:
DATE PRINTED:
TDA, LLC
6622 West Paso Trail
Phoenix, AZ 85083
(623) 693-9550
email: tdallc@yahoo.com
DRAWN BY:

RESIDENCE FOR:
City of
County of
State of
CLIENT RELEASE SIGNATURES & DATE:

Thomas Design Associates, LLC
6622 West Paso Trail
Phoenix, Arizona 85083
(623) 693-9550
email: tdallc@yahoo.com

****COPYRIGHT NOTE****
ALL RIGHTS RESERVED
TDA, LLC
These drawings and specifications shall remain the property of the Designer and shall not be used for any other projects without the written consent of the Designer. These documents are not to be reproduced, changed or copied in any form or manner whatsoever. Nor are they to be assigned to any third party without first obtaining the written permission and consent of the Designer per the TDA, LLC Contract for Services Agreement.

DATE:	C.O. #:	AUTHORIZED BY:	DESCRIPTION:

TITLE
SCALE: 1/4" = 1'
DRAWN BY:
DATE:
SECTION LETTER
PAGE NUMBER
APPROVED:
REVISED:
PAGE #:

Goodheart-Willcox Publisher

Figure 14-20. The title block includes information such as the drawing scale, the name of the drawing, the sheet number, the name of the drafter, and the name of the client the drawing has been prepared for.

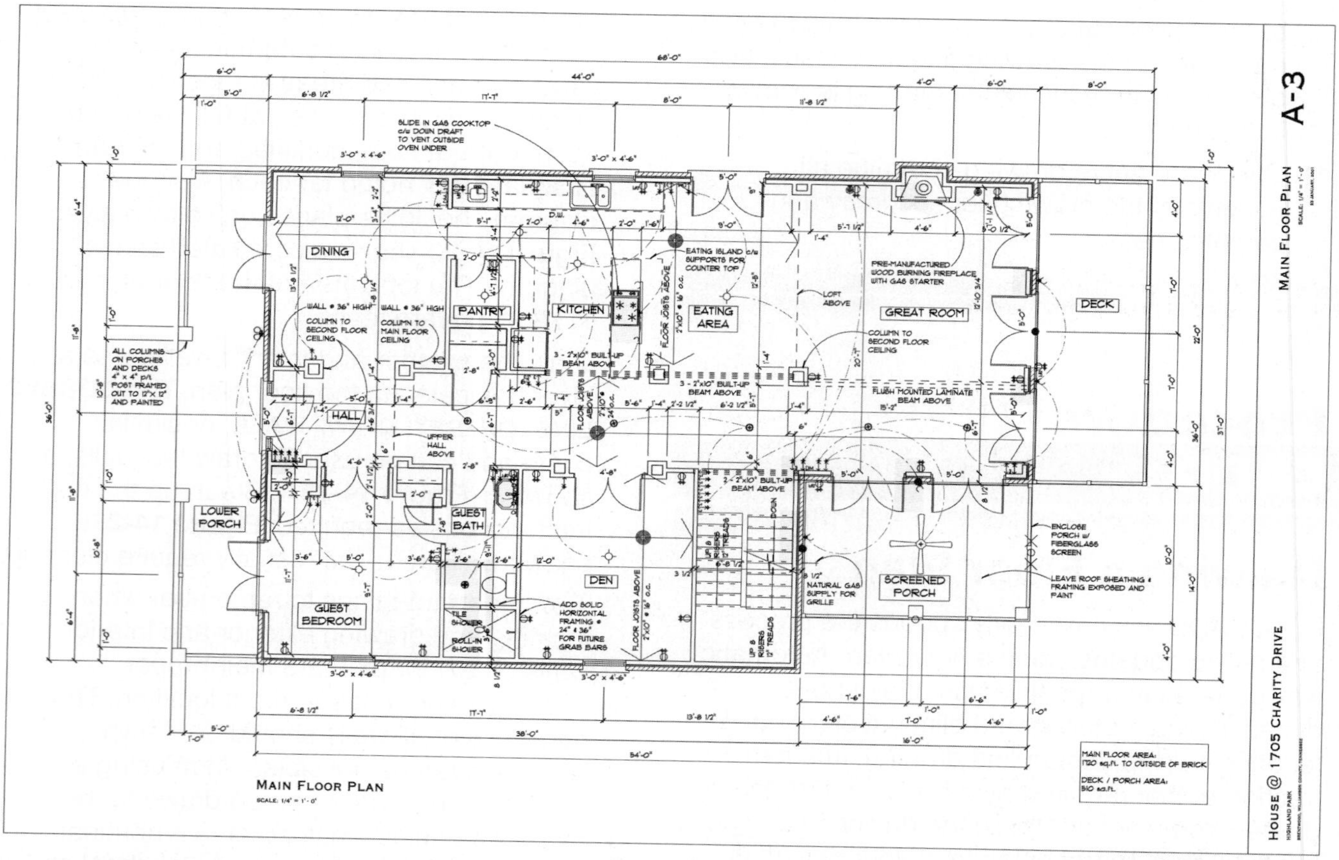

SoftPlan Systems, Inc.

Figure 14-21. The use of standard symbols from a symbol library greatly reduced the time required to draw this combination floor and electrical plan in CADD.

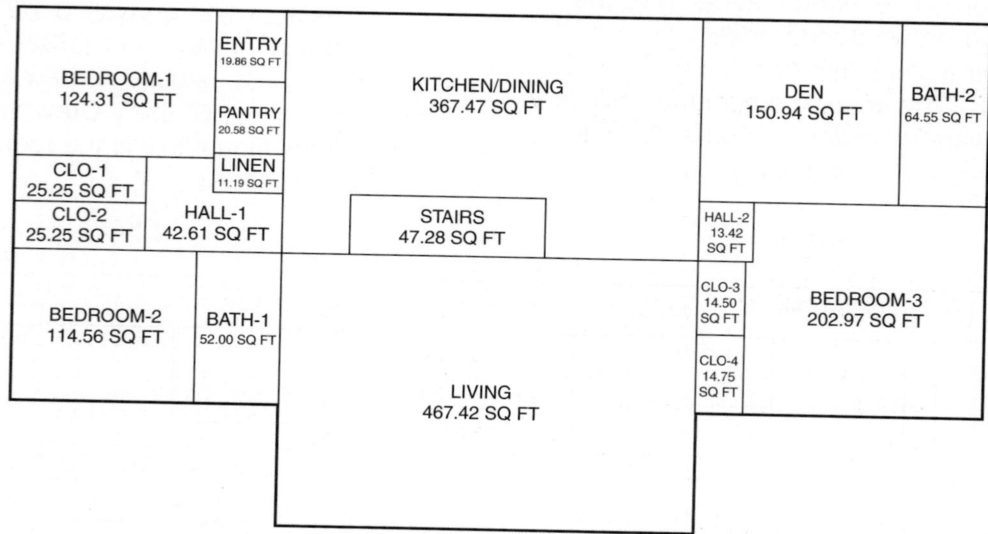

Goodheart-Willcox Publisher

Figure 14-22. This computer-generated space diagram shows the designated room name and area. Many CADD programs can calculate the square footage for you.

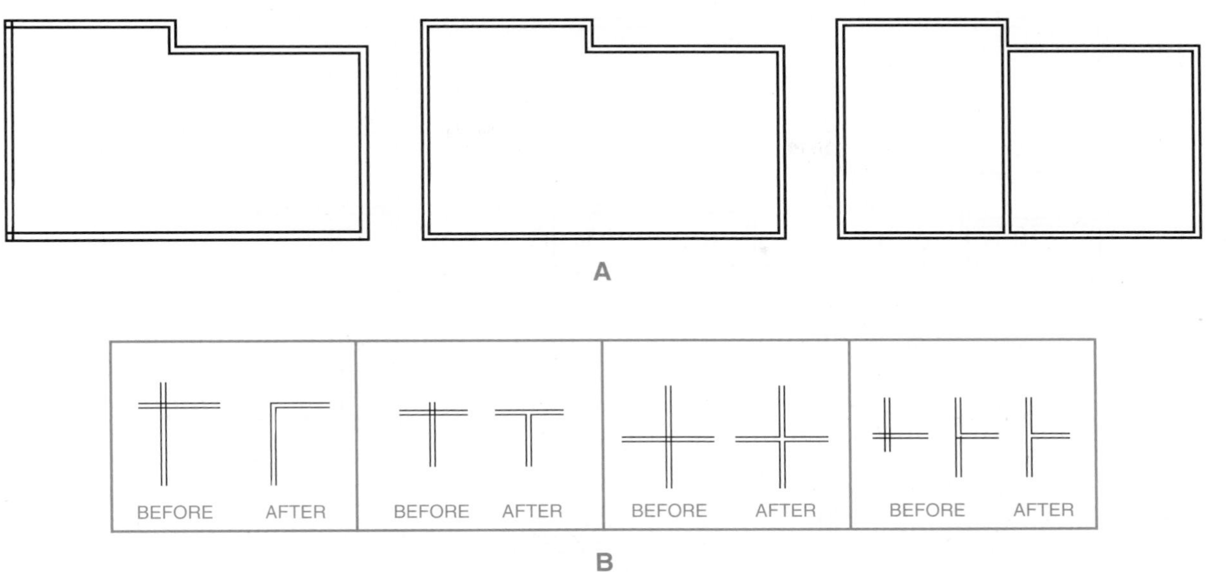

Goodheart-Willcox Publisher

Figure 14-23. A—Developing a floor plan using the **DOUBLE LINE** command. B—Four kinds of wall intersections that typically require cleanup.

The measurement location is to where the wall is dimensioned. The manner in which interior walls are dimensioned is determined by school or office practice. In this example, interior walls are dimensioned to the stud faces. Therefore, an automatic dimension to the stud face of an interior wall should produce a reasonable figure such as 6′-2″ or 12′-3″, but not 10′-1-7/16″. Exterior frame walls are usually dimensioned to the outside of the rough frame wall, which includes the weatherboard or rigid foam insulation on the outside of the studs, but not the siding or veneer. These lengths should also be reasonable. Try to plan a structure so that the overall length and width are multiples of 2′ or 4′, if possible.

Figure 14-24 shows the floor plan for the space diagram in **Figure 14-22** after this step is completed. Note the difference in thickness of the exterior and interior walls. Also note how the intersections are handled where an interior wall becomes an exterior wall in the large center area.

3. Add the window and door symbols. When windows and doors are located in a frame wall structure, they are dimensioned to the center of the unit. This is true even if the unit has more than one door or window. Plan

Green Architecture

Designing a Green Floor Plan

You can incorporate many green ideas into the actual footprint of a home by making eco-friendly design decisions while you are developing the floor plan. For example, air moves more freely through the rooms in an open floor plan, so incorporating an open floor plan can help lower energy bills in the finished home.

Another, related idea is to design rooms for multiple purposes. For example, when one room can function as both a bedroom and an office or sitting room, less floor space is needed. You can save hundreds of square feet by designing rooms to meet more than one need. This is a green idea because a home with a smaller footprint consumes fewer materials and uses less energy than a larger home.

Yet another idea that is often overlooked is to design a location for the furnace in the middle of the house. Heat naturally radiates outward in all directions. If you place the furnace in an unheated space, such as a garage, or against an outside wall, some of the heat produced will be wasted.

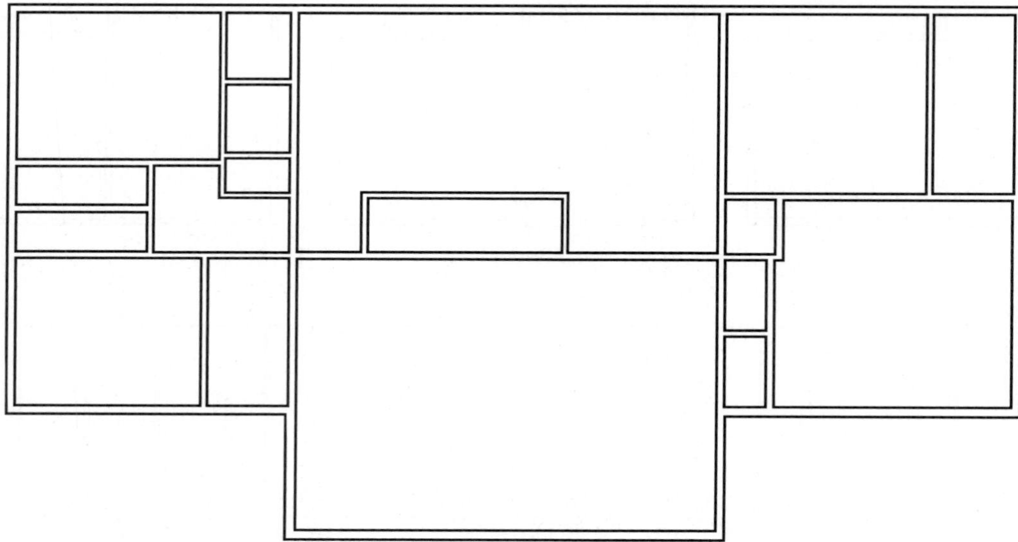

Goodheart-Willcox Publisher

Figure 14-24. The floor plan developed from the space diagram in Figure 14-22. All wall intersections have been cleaned up.

the location of these elements so that they complement the overall design, but also use location dimensions that are at least multiples of 1″. Window sills may or may not be included, depending on the designer's preferences. **Figure 14-25** shows the plan with windows and doors added. These elements should be plotted with thinner lines than the walls. Therefore, place them on a separate layer or assign a different object color. In CADD drawings, color is often used on-screen to identify objects on different layers.

4. Draw the stairs. Put the stairs on a separate layer for easy modification of the floor plan. Also, consider the final plotted line thickness and adjust the layer settings as appropriate.

   The one-story house in this example has a basement. The total distance from the finished basement floor to the finished first floor must be determined before the stairs can be designed. The total distance for this house is 10′-2″. This is greater than usual because rather large wood floor trusses will be used.

   Some CADD programs can calculate the tread width and riser height for each step and automatically draw the stairs. Whether or not you have this option, the stairs should conform to good design principles. The stair treads, handrails, and direction of travel should be shown on the floor plan. See Chapter 24, *Stair Details*, for complete details on stair design and calculations. **Figure 14-26** shows steps 4 through 7.

5. Draw or insert the fireplace. If your plan has a fireplace, locate and draw the fireplace in its proper location using appropriate hatch patterns. Place the fireplace on its own layer. Also, consider the final plotted line thickness and adjust the layer settings as appropriate.

   Proper design is essential to satisfactory operation. Identify the type and size of fireplace.

6. Locate and draw walks, patios, and porches. These elements should be considered extensions of the floor plan. You may want to use a separate layer for these elements. Consider the final plotted line thickness when selecting a layer and object color.

7. Draw the kitchen cabinets, appliances, and bathroom fixtures. Review Chapter 8, *Planning the Sleeping Area*, and Chapter 9, *Planning the Service Area,* before adding these elements. Good planning in these areas is essential. Add the kitchen cabinets, appliances, and bathroom fixtures using standard symbols from the symbol library. Add these elements using the appropriate layers and linetypes.

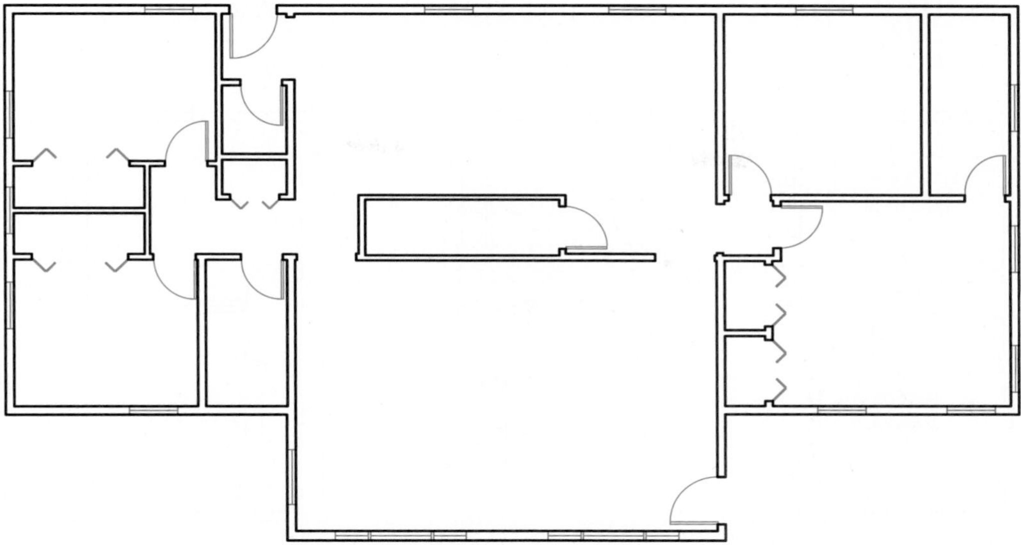

Goodheart-Willcox Publisher

Figure 14-25. Windows and doors have been added by inserting symbols from the symbol library.

8. Add dimensions. Place the dimensions on a separate layer. All construction features on the floor plan should be dimensioned unless the location or size is very obvious. For example, a door placed at a standard 4″ offset or a set of bi-fold doors that fills the space in front of a closet need not be dimensioned. However, if there is any doubt, dimension the feature. Remember, the extension lines begin at the outside of the rough stud wall and do not include the thickness of the siding or veneer.

   Every window, door, intersecting wall, or offset in the exterior wall must be dimensioned. Each exterior segment should have partial dimensions, as well as an overall length dimension. Study the arrangement of dimensions in **Figure 14-27** to see how dimensions should be arranged on a drawing. Be sure your dimensions are accurate and

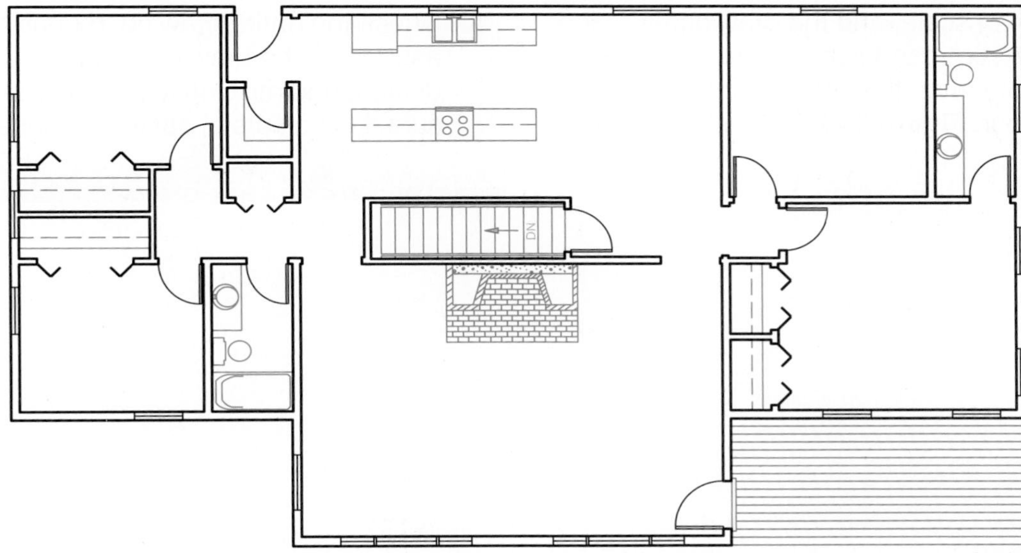

Goodheart-Willcox Publisher

Figure 14-26. Stairs, the fireplace, a porch, cabinets, fixtures, and appliances have been added to the floor plan.

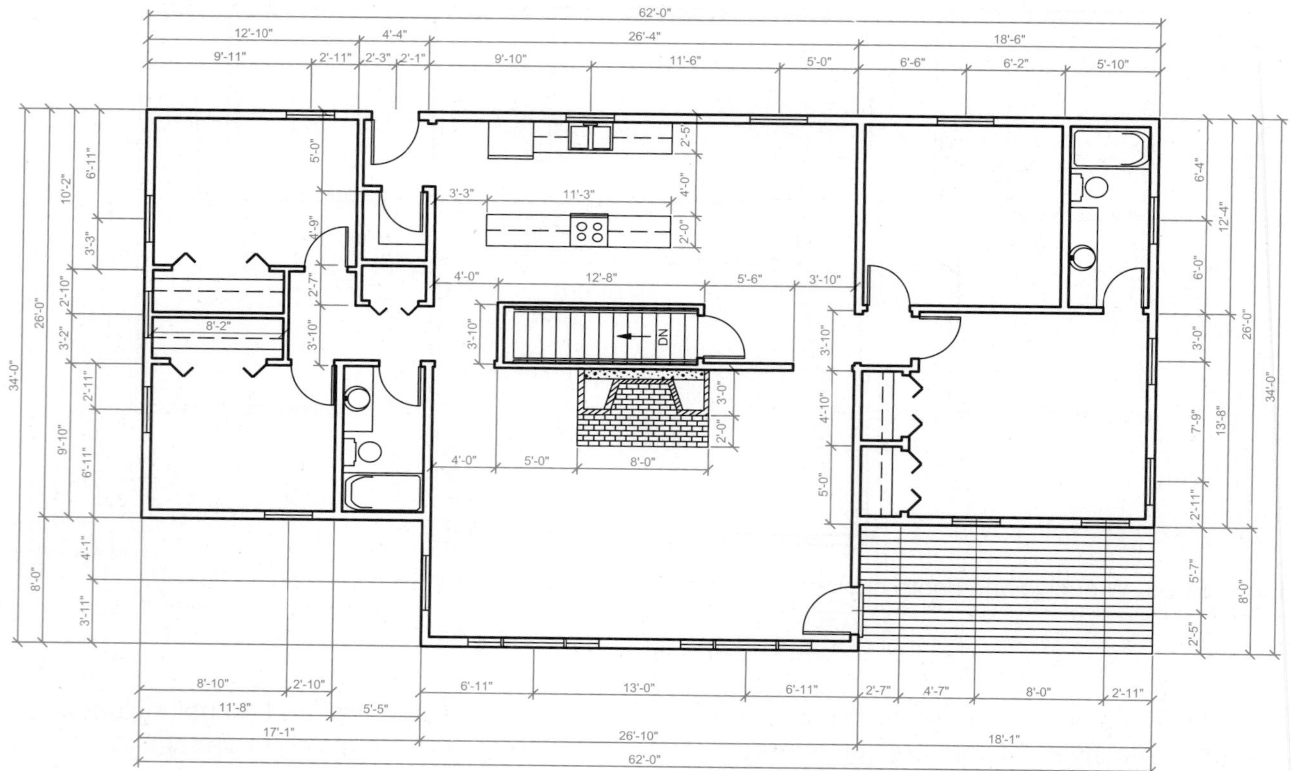

Goodheart-Willcox Publisher

Figure 14-27. The dimensions have been added to the floor plan following proper guidelines.

add up properly. Use the dimensioning capabilities of your CADD program to accomplish this task. Be sure to set up the dimensioning layer with the correct linetype and thickness.

9. Add room names, notes, material symbols, the drawing scale, and the drawing title. Use the **TEXT** command to enter room names and sizes, notes, the scale, and the title, as shown in **Figure 14-28**. Construct a title block, if required by your school or company. Place these items on one or more dedicated layers with the correct linetype and thickness. Add any necessary material symbols that were not already inserted as part of a symbol, but do not overdo it.
10. Check the entire drawing. Examine all aspects of the drawing for accuracy, good design, and missing items. When you are sure it is complete, save and plot the drawing.

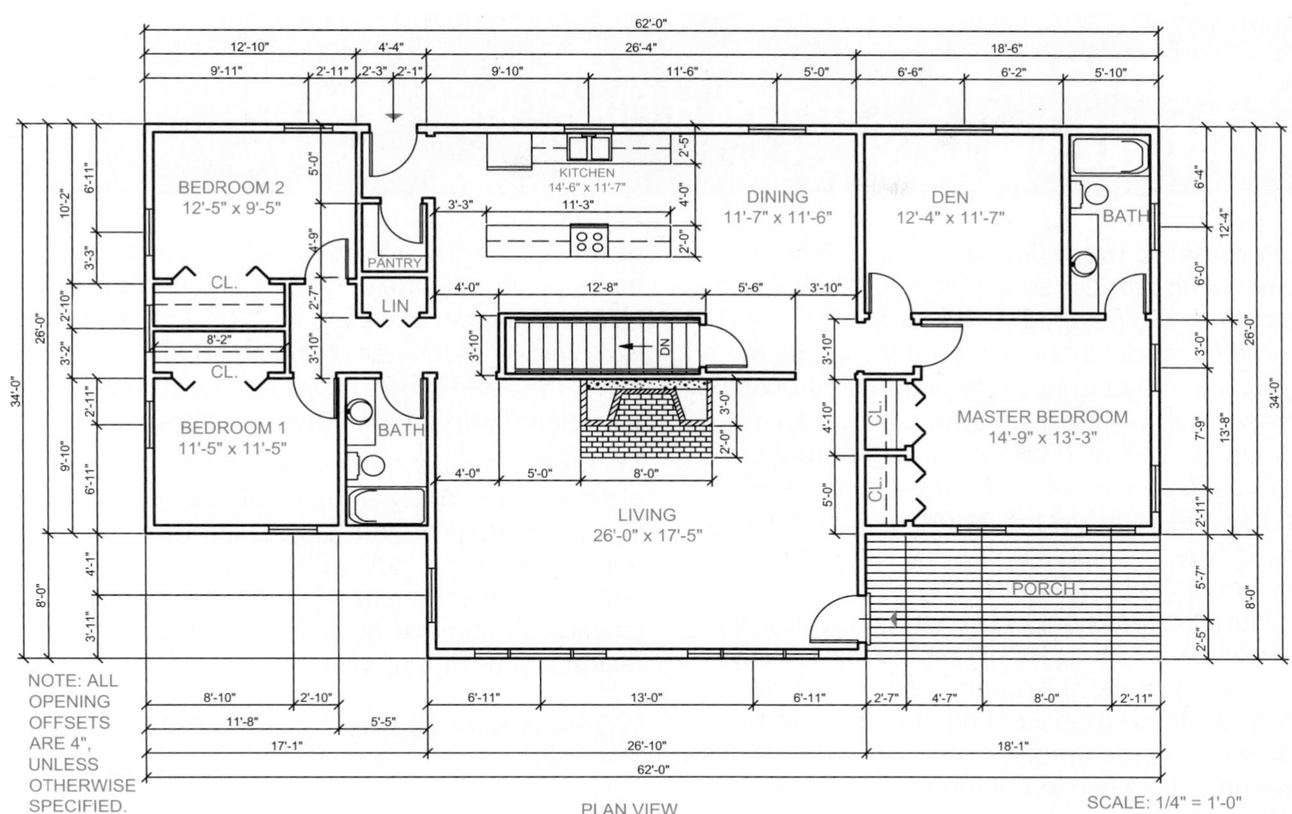

Goodheart-Willcox Publisher

Figure 14-28. Labels and room sizes have been added to the floor plan.

Parametric Modeling

Creating a Floor Plan

Parametric modeling is a special type of 3D modeling introduced in Chapter 12, *Building Information Modeling*. Constructing a 3D parametric model in architectural design often begins with creating the floor plan. The process of creating a floor plan in parametric modeling is similar to that used with a general-purpose CADD system, but there are different steps and workflows because of the nature of 3D modeling and the way in which the drawing is prepared. For example, instead of drawing 2D lines to represent the walls on a 2D floor plan, you place the walls as 3D components on the plan. Walls are still drawn by picking points and they still appear as lines when working in a 2D view, but each wall is made up of a "block" of lines that represents a 2D section of the wall. Changing to a 3D view allows you to view the wall in its full width, height, and depth. Other components of the model are constructed in similar fashion.

The setup steps involved in creating a floor plan in parametric modeling are different from those in other types of CADD work. One of the first steps before modeling starts is to create the levels and views that will be used in the project. ***Levels*** are assigned elevations that define key heights of the building. For example, a level named First Floor can be used to establish the height of the first floor. Additional levels, such as Second Floor and Roof, can be used to establish other key heights. As each level is created, you have the option to create a named plan view that is associated with the corresponding elevation. Typically, one or more default levels are available when you start a project based on a default template. For example, Level 1 is a typical default level defining an elevation of 0′-0″ and Level 2 is a typical default level defining an elevation of 10′-0″. See **Figure 14-29**. A default view is associated with each of these levels.

Levels can be created by switching to an elevation view and using the **LEVEL** command. The levels you use in a project will vary depending on the type of home being drawn and the type of construction. The following are examples of typical levels that could be used in a residential design project:

Levels Above Grade	Levels Below Grade
First Floor	Top of Footing
Second Floor	Basement Floor
Top of Plate	Top of Foundation

The following procedure is based on using the First Floor level to create a floor plan. Once you have established the level of the first floor, open the first floor plan view to begin working. This procedure is designed for a one-story home with wood frame construction and a basement. Elements of the basement and foundation are explained in Chapter 15, *Foundation Plans*. See Chapter 17, *Roof Designs*, for details on roof construction. See Chapter 24, *Stair Details*, for details on stair construction. The following is presented as a typical sequence, but specific steps will vary depending on the program used and the type of construction.

Goodheart-Willcox Publisher

Figure 14-29. Levels are elevations that identify key heights of a building. Shown are the default levels typically available when starting a project in a parametric modeling program.

1. Draw the exterior walls. Access the **WALL** command and specify the appropriate wall type. Select a wall type that represents the materials used in construction. In some programs, many of the default wall types may be designed for heavy commercial construction. This often requires duplicating a default wall type, such as a generic wall, and editing it to create a wall with the necessary materials. For example, to create a 2 × 4 frame wall with vinyl siding, define materials to create a wall consisting of 1/2″ siding, 3/4″ rigid foam insulation, 7/16″ plywood sheathing, 3-1/2″ stud, and 1/2″ gypsum board. This produces a wall measuring 5-11/16″ thick. Once the wall type is created, make sure it is selected and set the base constraint to the First Floor level. Set the top constraint to the Top of Plate level. The base and top offsets should be 0′-0″. Set the appropriate justification and draw the exterior walls in a clockwise direction. Normally, the justification for exterior walls is set to core face exterior. This aligns the cursor to the outside structural face (the outside stud face of the wall). Draw the walls to the exact dimensions.
2. Draw the interior walls. Access the **WALL** command and specify the appropriate wall type. Use a default wall type or make a duplicate and edit it to create a wall with the necessary materials. For example, a typical 4-1/2″ interior frame wall consists of a 3-1/2″ stud with 1/2″ gypsum board on both sides. Once the desired wall type is selected, set the base constraint to the First Floor level and the top constraint to the Top of Plate level. The base and top offsets should be 0′-0″. Set the appropriate justification, such as exterior finish. Draw the walls to the exact dimensions. To help locate walls accurately, use the offset function with an appropriate offset distance and pick on existing wall lines, or use construction aids such as reference planes. Remove construction geometry when it is no longer needed.
3. Add doors and windows. For each door and window, insert the appropriate component. If a certain component you are looking for is not available within the project file, load a family containing the component into the project. A ***family*** is a collection of components similar to a symbol library containing blocks. A family is a separate file from the project file and is typically made up of variations of the same item in different sizes and orientations. For example, a door family may consist of a flush design available in different widths and heights. Doors and windows are referred to as *hosted items* and require a wall for placement. Place doors at the appropriate wall locations, paying attention to the correct swing orientation. Place windows in similar fashion. Specify the appropriate sill height and place the window in the correct orientation within the wall. Switch between the plan view and a 3D view to help verify that you are placing items correctly.

   If the structure has a large expanse of glass, an alternative to placing a window is to create a curtain wall. A curtain wall is a special type of wall made of glass. A curtain wall is typically constructed by drawing the wall within an existing wall and "cutting" the host wall in order to embed the curtain wall. Once the curtain wall is placed, a grid is created to divide the wall into panels. The panels can then be edited. Panels can be changed to materials other than glass, such as stone, and even different building components, such as doors or different wall types. Horizontal and vertical aluminum members called mullions are typically inserted between panels to establish a framework. Curtain walls are very common in commercial buildings, but they can also be used in residential construction and have a variety of design applications.
4. Create a floor system. Access the **FLOOR** command and specify the appropriate floor

Parametric Modeling | Creating a Floor Plan *(Continued)*

type. Use a default floor type or make a duplicate and edit it to create a floor structure with the necessary material. A typical floor system consists of two separate floors—a structural floor and a finish floor. The structural floor is supported by the foundation and the finish floor rests on top of the structural floor. It is important to note in this type of modeling that unlike walls, which are extruded upward in a positive Z direction from the host level, floors are extruded downward in a negative Z direction from the host level. In other words, the top of the floor is level with the host level. To create a floor system, create the structural floor first. Use an appropriate material, such as wood joists, and assign the appropriate thickness. The thickness of the structural floor should extend to the foundation wall below. To place the floor, pick the appropriate wall lines on the plan to form a sketch defining the perimeter. If necessary, draw lines manually and use editing tools to complete the sketch. The sketch should be made so that the perimeter of the structural floor extends into the exterior walls. Also, ensure that the sketch forms a closed boundary before completing the command. The finish floor is created in a similar manner. Use an appropriate material, such as wood flooring, tile, or carpet. Assign the thickness of the finish material. When placing the floor, use the thickness measurement to specify an offset height above the structural floor elevation. Pick the inside wall lines on the plan or draw lines manually to form a sketch defining the perimeter. The perimeter of the finish floor should *not* extend into the exterior walls. An alternative to modeling a finish floor as a separate unit from the structural floor is to note all finish floor materials on the detail drawings.

5. Locate and draw patios and porches. For slab construction, use the **FLOOR** command. Create a structural floor system with the desired thickness and assign concrete as the floor material. Create a sketch for the slab that is oriented at the appropriate level. For example, a patio that meets an exterior wall can be constructed so that it is offset just below the first floor level and extends to grade.
6. Insert kitchen cabinets, appliances, and fixtures. Load families containing the desired components into the project. If your software does not provide a certain item, conduct a search online. Some manufacturer websites and "freeware" websites provide predefined components for use in parametric models. Once the appropriate families are loaded into the project, insert each component on the plan. To change the orientation of a component, press the space bar while the component is selected. Make sure that you place items at the correct elevation in relation to the floor. For example, if the model has a finish floor offset above the first floor level, adjust the component to the correct elevation. Switch between the plan view and an elevation or 3D view to help verify that you are placing items correctly. When placing kitchen cabinets, insert both base and wall cabinets. After placing base cabinets, add countertops over the cabinets. Grips can typically be used to resize the countertops to align with the cabinet edges. If you need to create a more complex countertop, an alternative is to create a floor with the appropriate thickness and finish material.
7. Add dimensions. All construction features should be dimensioned using appropriate practices. Use the specific tools of your program to accomplish this task. In cases where you need to change the default property of a dimension, such as the precision, but you want to maintain the default precision for most dimensions, create a new dimension style. Edit the unit format of the new style and apply the style to dimensions that require the different precision format.

Dimensions added to a parametric model have parametric properties. Making a change to a dimension updates the associated geometry and affects the entire model. For example, if you dimension the distance between two walls, you can quickly adjust the distance by simply changing the dimension. This is a powerful design tool that allows you to quickly make changes and evaluate the effects on the model.

8. Create rooms to define all of the rooms on the plan. If needed, create separator lines to establish boundaries where there are open areas. Room tags are normally inserted automatically when creating rooms. Typically, the default room tag contains a room name and number. To create a room tag that does not use a number, duplicate the default room tag and edit it to remove the room number. After creating each room, edit the room tag text to display the correct room name.
9. If it is necessary to create additional floor plans, such as a floor plan for a second floor, components can typically be copied from one level to additional levels by using a "copy and paste" operation. This technique is useful for copying items such as interior walls, doors, and windows when the same items are used at similar locations on multiple floors.
10. Create a new sheet that will be used for the first floor plan view. Use an appropriate sheet size and title block. If necessary, load a sheet format used by your school or office into the project. Change the default name and number of the sheet to reflect an accepted naming convention. Next, insert the floor plan view onto the sheet. Typically, this can be done using a drag-and-drop operation. Text for the view title and scale normally appears below the view when inserting the view. Position the text appropriately. The scale identifies the annotation scale used for dimensions and other annotations when plotting. This should typically be 1/4″ = 1′-0″ for the floor plan.
11. Check the entire floor plan. You may need to adjust dimensions or other items so that the entire view fits on the sheet. If needed, return to the floor plan view to make changes. When you are sure the plan is complete, print or plot the sheet.

Summary

- The floor plan is not a typical top view; it is actually a section drawing.
- Material symbols or hatch patterns are a type of shorthand used by the drafter to represent construction materials.
- Dimensions in architectural drawing are recorded in feet and inches.
- Dimensioning practices used to locate exterior and interior dimensions vary depending on the construction technique and school or office practice.
- Overall dimensions are necessary even though all of the partial dimensions add up to the same number.
- Specific CADD commands vary from one software program to another, but the basic drawing procedure for floor plans is similar in all of them.

Internet Resources

Autodesk
AutoCAD® and Revit® software publisher

Chief Architect
Chief Architect® software publisher

Donald A. Gardner Architects
Examples of floor plans

SoftPlan Systems
SoftPlan® software publisher

The Sater Design Collection
Examples of floor plans

Review Questions

Answer the following questions using the information in this chapter.

1. What is the purpose of a floor plan?
2. At what height above the floor is the section shown in a floor plan taken?
3. Identify the material indicated by the following material symbols in a section view.

   A.

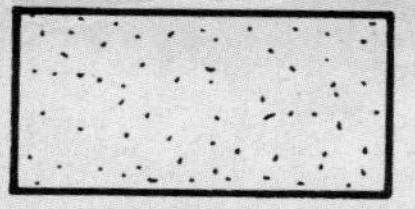

   B.

   C.

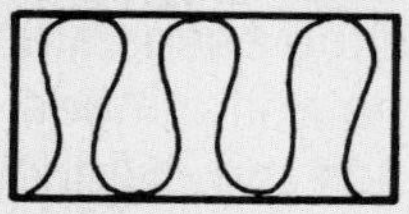

   D.

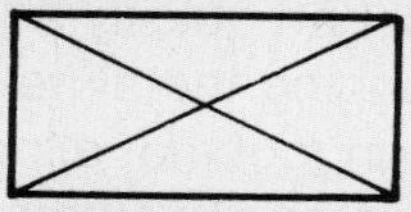

   E.

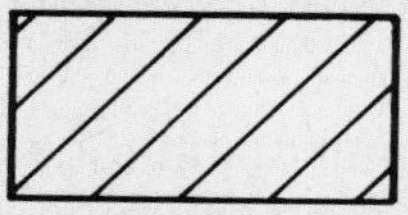

   F.

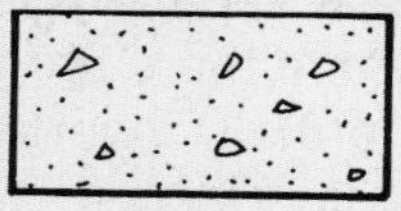

4. Explain the difference in dimensioning windows and doors in frame construction and in masonry construction.
5. The actual thickness of an exterior frame wall with 1/2″ insulation board, 1/2″ drywall, and 5/8″ siding on a 1-1/2″ × 3-1/2″ framing member (stud) is 5-1/8″. However, an exterior frame wall may be represented as a nominal thickness of _____ on the floor plan.
6. How is an archway commonly indicated on a floor plan?
7. What information about stairs is included on a floor plan?
8. At what size should the room names be lettered on a floor plan?
9. Describe two methods of showing a dimension that is less than one foot.
10. Explain the difference in dimensioning exterior frame walls and solid masonry walls.
11. Explain how you can double-check your accuracy on the partial dimensions on a drawing.
12. What is a *bubble diagram*?

13. A(n) ______ is an effective tool for determining how the various rooms and areas fit together.
14. In CADD, kitchen cabinets, appliances, and bathroom fixtures can be inserted from a ______.
15. What is the scale of most residential floor plans?

Suggested Activities

1. Find a floor plan for a small house or cottage from a magazine, newspaper, or other source. Draw it to 1/4″ = 1′-0″ scale. Show all necessary dimensions, notes, and symbols. Present your drawing along with a copy of the original. Use traditional (manual) drafting or CADD.
2. Draw a floor plan for a one-bedroom apartment with a living room, combined kitchen and dining area, bath, and a small storage area. Interior walls are frame and exterior walls are brick veneer on 8″ concrete block. Show the calculated living space on the floor plan.
3. Design a ranch-style house that:
   - Is on a flat lot.
   - Has three bedrooms.
   - Has two bathrooms.
   - Includes a living room, kitchen, and dining room.
   - Has a patio and a fireplace.
   - Has a two-car attached garage.
   - Is frame construction.

   Draw and dimension a floor plan for the house.
4. Find a floor plan for a house or apartment that you feel has a poor arrangement and use of space. Redesign this plan using CADD to achieve proper use of space and room arrangement. Present both for comparison.
5. Make a preliminary design sketch of a floor plan for a new home and use it to prepare a bubble diagram. Use circles or squares for the bubble shapes and make the sketch using correct proportions. Label the rooms and spaces and indicate the approximate dimensions of each room. If necessary, make additional sketches and modify the bubble diagram to refine the design. Then, use the bubble diagram to draw and dimension a floor plan using manual drafting or CADD.

Problem Solving Case Study

Mr. and Mrs. Livingston have their hearts set on the home shown in **Figure A**, shown on the next page, which was designed for them several years ago by an architect in a different city. The dimensioned version of this floor plan is shown in Figure 14-13 in this chapter. The Livingstons were waiting until retirement to build the home. Now they have retired and are moving to your area. They have also found and purchased the "perfect" lot on which to build the house. Unfortunately, the lot is long and narrow, measuring 200′ × 80′, and the property setbacks are 10′ across the front and back of the property. They have asked you to revise the floor plan to fit on the lot they have chosen.

Determine the best way to modify the house to fit on the lot without sacrificing the character or key elements of the floor plan. Sketch the rough shape of the lot, or draw it on a separate layer in a CADD drawing, and draw the revised floor plan. Make a list of the changes you are making so you can explain them when you show the Livingstons the revised plan.

ADDA Certification Prep

The following questions are presented in the style used in the American Design Drafting Association (ADDA) Drafter Certification Test. Answer the questions using the information in this chapter.

1. Which of the following statements are true about floor plans?
   A. The floor plan is actually a horizontal section "cut" through the floor plan at a height of about 4′.
   B. A residential floor plan is typically drawn to a scale of 1/8″ = 1′-0″.
   C. Add all the partial dimensions that together equal the overall dimension to verify proper dimensions.
   D. Windows in masonry walls are located by dimensioning to the center of the window.
   E. Floor plans drawn in most countries outside the United States use the metric system of measurement.

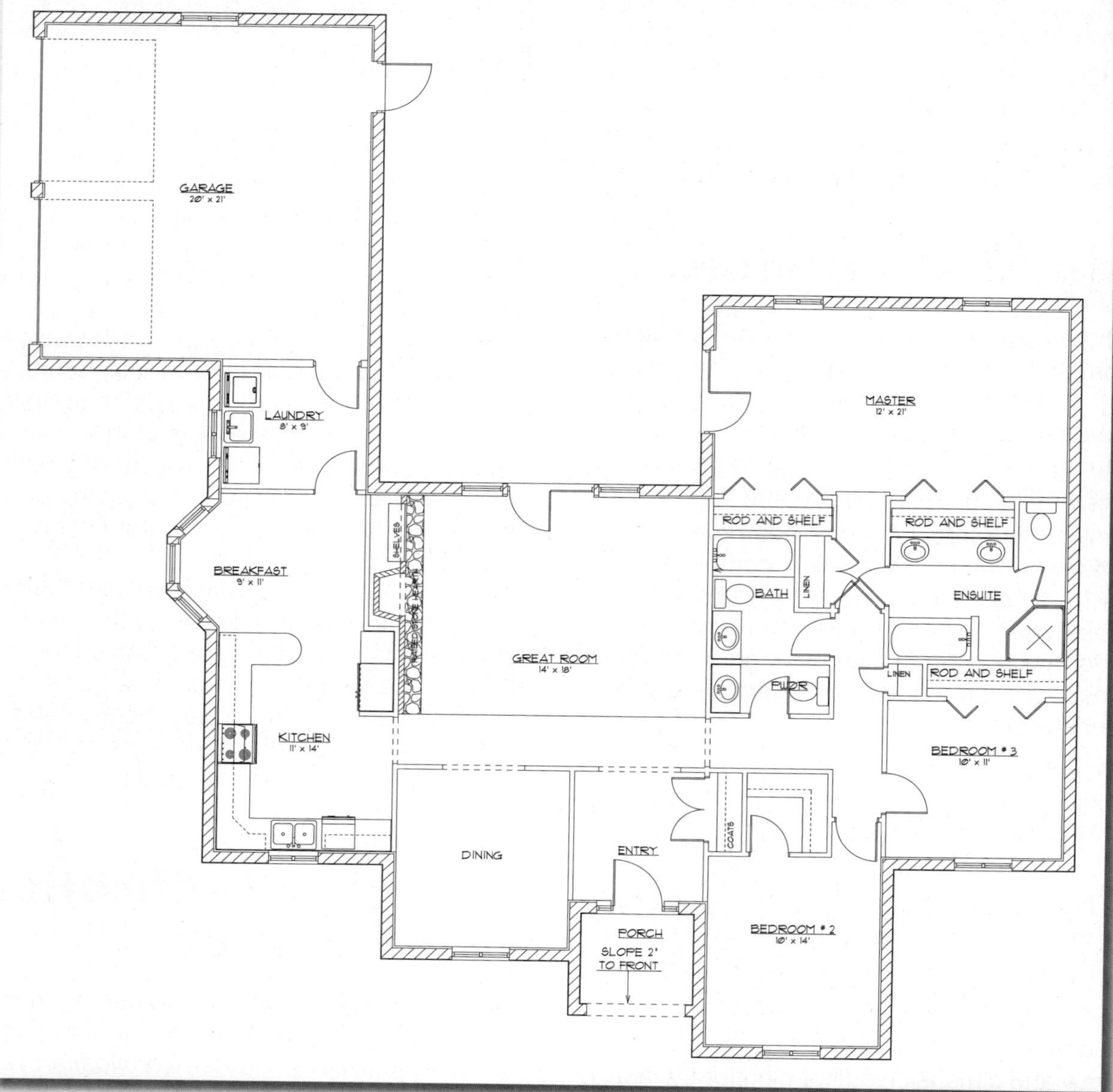

Figure A

Goodheart-Willcox Publisher

2. Which of the following statements are true about drawing a floor plan using manual drafting techniques?
   A. The first step is to draw the exterior walls using dark lines of the correct lineweight.
   B. Dividers should be used to locate interior wall lines to represent the correct wall thickness.
   C. Draw the stairs using an estimate of the number of steps and their width.
   D. Wall cabinets in the kitchen should be drawn 24″ deep using hidden lines.
   E. All lines should be black; only the thickness and types of lines should vary.

3. Which of the following statements about floor plans created using CADD are *false*?
   A. Space diagrams are not useful when you create a floor plan drawing using CADD.
   B. Using symbols from a symbol library generally increases the amount of time needed to create a floor plan.
   C. One way to create wall lines of the correct thickness in a CADD program is to use the **OFFSET** command or a similar command.
   D. The final plotted thickness should be considered when assigning a layer to dimensions.

Curricular Connections

1. **Social Science.** Go to a local building supply store or search on the Internet to find and record common sizes of structural building materials such as plywood, concrete block, and dimensional lumber. List your results or make a table to display them neatly. Examine the sizes closely. Then write an analytic report explaining how standard sizes help reduce the cost of building and also reduce the amount of waste generated in the construction of new homes.
2. **Language Arts.** Write a creative, fictional short story about what might happen if an architect failed to dimension a floor plan accurately. Your story can be funny or serious, but be sure to develop the plot carefully so that someone who does not know much about architectural drawing can enjoy the story. Use correct grammar and good paragraph development. Be sure to check your spelling.

STEM Connections

1. **Math.** You are preparing to create a detail drawing of a staircase. In the floor plan, which is drawn to the typical 1/4″ = 1′-0″ scale, the lines that represent the stair treads in the staircase are 3/4″ long. Your stair detail will be drawn to a scale of 1/2″ = 1′-0″. How long will you draw the lines that represent the stair treads?

Communicating about Architecture

1. **Listening.** In small groups, discuss with your classmates—in basic, everyday language—your knowledge of floor plans and what should be included in them. Conduct this discussion as though you had never read this chapter. Take notes on the observations expressed. Then review the points discussed, factoring in your new knowledge of floor plans. Develop a summary of what you have learned about floor plans and present it to the class, using the terms that you have learned in this chapter.
2. **Speaking and Listening.** Working in small groups, create a portfolio that illustrates architectural designs that you admire. Search online for examples of printed or digital portfolio work. Gather and organize material for your portfolio as if it were your own and present it to the class. Point out features that you admire and explain how these works stand out from others.

Dorn1530/Shutterstock.com

An accurate foundation plan is important to ensure that the house is properly constructed.

Chapter 15

Foundation Plans

Objectives

After completing this chapter, you will be able to:

- Identify the primary features included in a foundation plan.
- Discuss the differences between a foundation plan and a basement plan.
- Design and draw a foundation plan for a typical residential structure using traditional or CADD methods.
- Design and draw a basement plan for a typical residential structure using traditional or CADD methods.

Key Terms

basement plan	foundation plan
brick ledge	pier
footing	pilaster

The foundation plan is one of the most critical plans in a set of architectural working drawings. If the foundation plan is flawed, the foundation may not be strong enough to support the house. If the foundation fails, major damage to the house can result. Therefore, it is important to understand all of the factors that must be considered before the foundation plan can be drawn.

Foundation and Basement Plans

The ***foundation plan*** is a section view that provides all of the information needed by the excavators, masons, carpenters, cement workers, and others who build the foundation. A typical foundation plan is shown in **Figure 15-1**. A foundation plan ordinarily includes:

- Footings for foundation walls, piers, and columns
- Foundation walls
- Piers and columns (posts)
- Dwarf walls (low walls built to retain an excavation or embankment)
- Openings in the foundation wall, such as for windows, doors, and vents
- Beams and pilasters
- Direction, size, and spacing of floor joists or trusses
- Drains and sump (if required)
- Details of foundation and footing construction

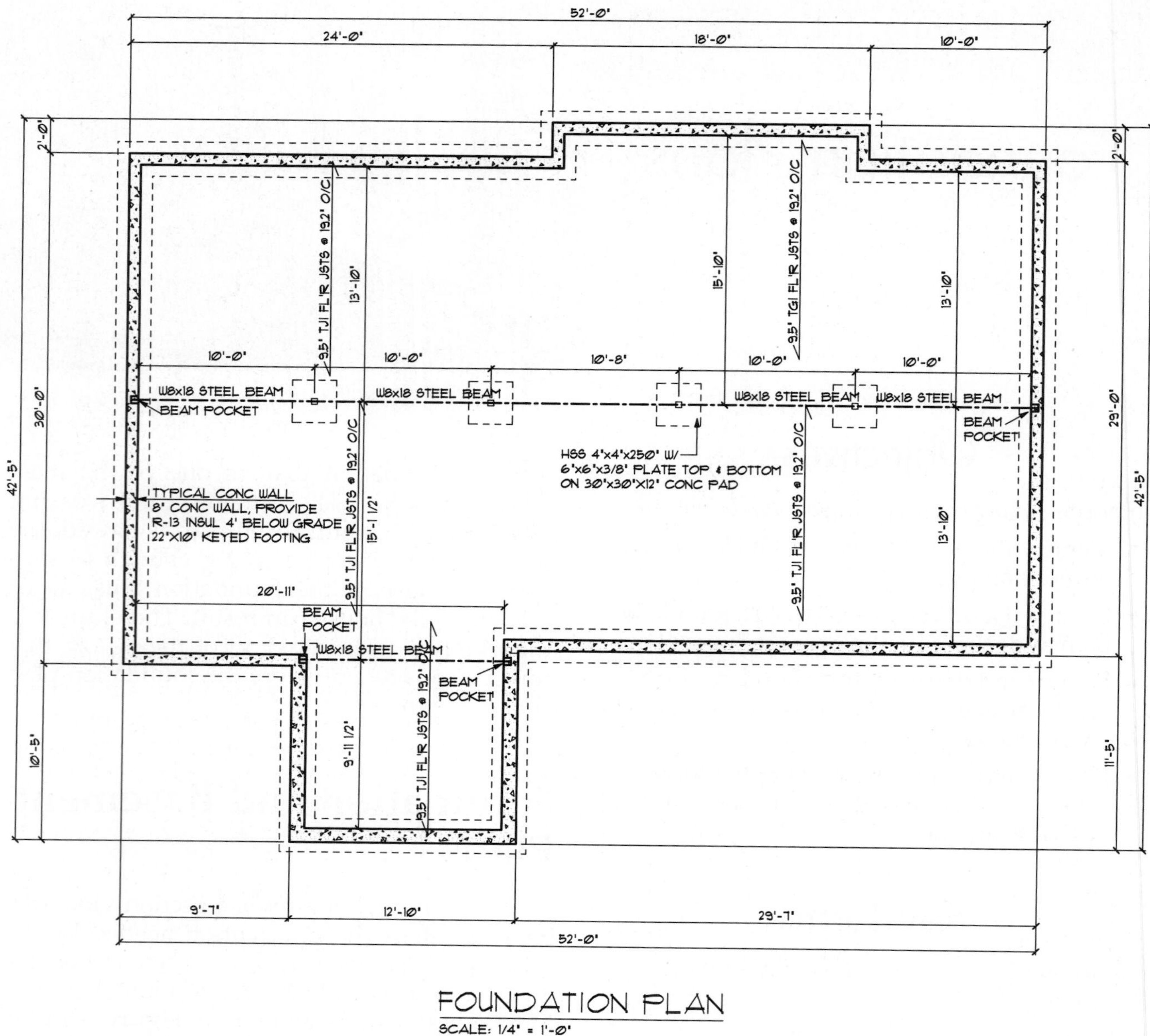

Goodheart-Willcox Publisher

Figure 15-1. A typical foundation plan for a residence.

- Complete dimensions and notes
- Scale of the drawing

The foundation plan is usually drawn after the floor plan and elevations have been roughed out. As on a floor plan, symbols or hatch patterns are typically used on a foundation plan to show various materials. Common hatch patterns are shown in **Figure 15-2**. Notice that many of these symbols are the same as those used on the floor plan.

In climates where the frost penetration depth is several feet, basements are usually included in home designs. Since the footings must be below the frost depth, it is comparatively inexpensive to excavate the soil under the house and extend the foundation down a few more feet to create a basement. This additional excavation provides usable space at much less cost per square foot than the first floor level. Basements are also popular in crowded areas where building sites are small.

A ***basement plan*** is a combination foundation and floor plan. See **Figure 15-3**. It includes the information commonly shown on the foundation

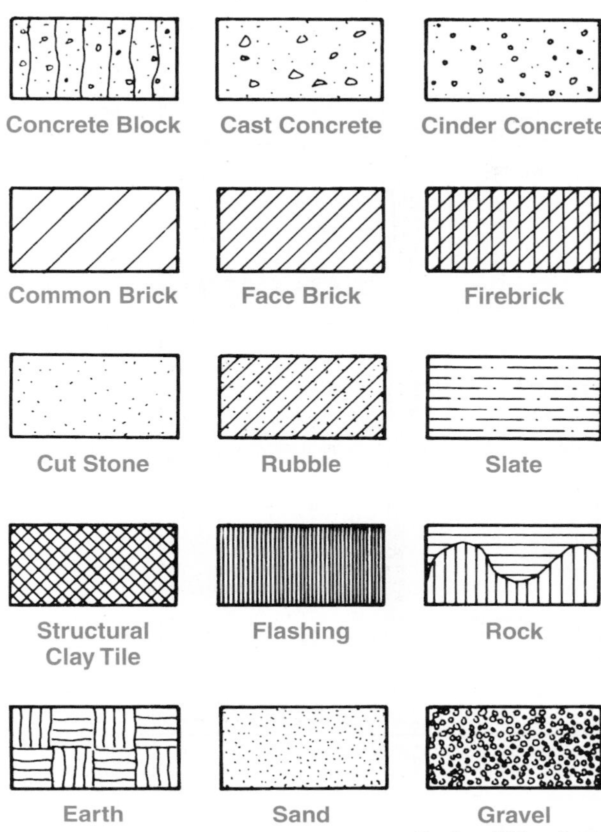

Figure 15-2. Symbols or hatch patterns that are commonly used to represent materials on foundation plans.

plan, but also shows interior walls, stairs, windows, doors, and any built-in appliances or fixtures in the basement. In some structures, such as a split-level house, a foundation plan is required for one section of the house and a basement plan is needed for the other.

Preparing to Draw a Foundation or Basement Plan

The foundation or basement plan is drawn from information presented on the floor plan, site plan, and elevations. The dimensions on the foundation plan and floor plan must be accurate and consistent. The preliminary floor plan may be used as an underlay for drawing the foundation plan. These procedures reduce the time required to make the drawing and help keep errors to a minimum.

Before drawing the foundation plan, determine the type of exterior walls specified on the floor plan. This step is important because the dimensions of the foundation will differ for different types of exterior walls. For example, the foundation size will be larger for a brick veneer house than for a house with a stud wall frame. The reason for the difference is that the basic house size is measured to the outside of the stud wall for both types of construction. However, a 4″ ***brick ledge*** to support the brick is required for the brick veneer house. This adds 8″ to the total length and width of the foundation needed for a frame structure with a masonry veneer. See **Figure 15-4**. The site plan and elevations should also be examined to determine whether

Employability

Time Management

Employers use time management techniques to develop and maintain work schedules and meet deadlines. As an employee, you can increase your value to your employer by understanding time management and meeting, or beating, any deadlines you are given. Do not make the mistake of thinking that meeting a deadline is the most important task, however. Meeting a deadline is never an excuse for sloppy work. Your work must be done accurately and precisely, as well as within the assigned deadline. You can accomplish this by using time management techniques similar to those used by your employer.

Activity

Many resources are available to help you hone your time management skills. Conduct research to find time management techniques that you can incorporate into your school or office setting. Make a list of those you think will work best for you. Then, one at a time, try incorporating them into your daily schedule. Observe the results.

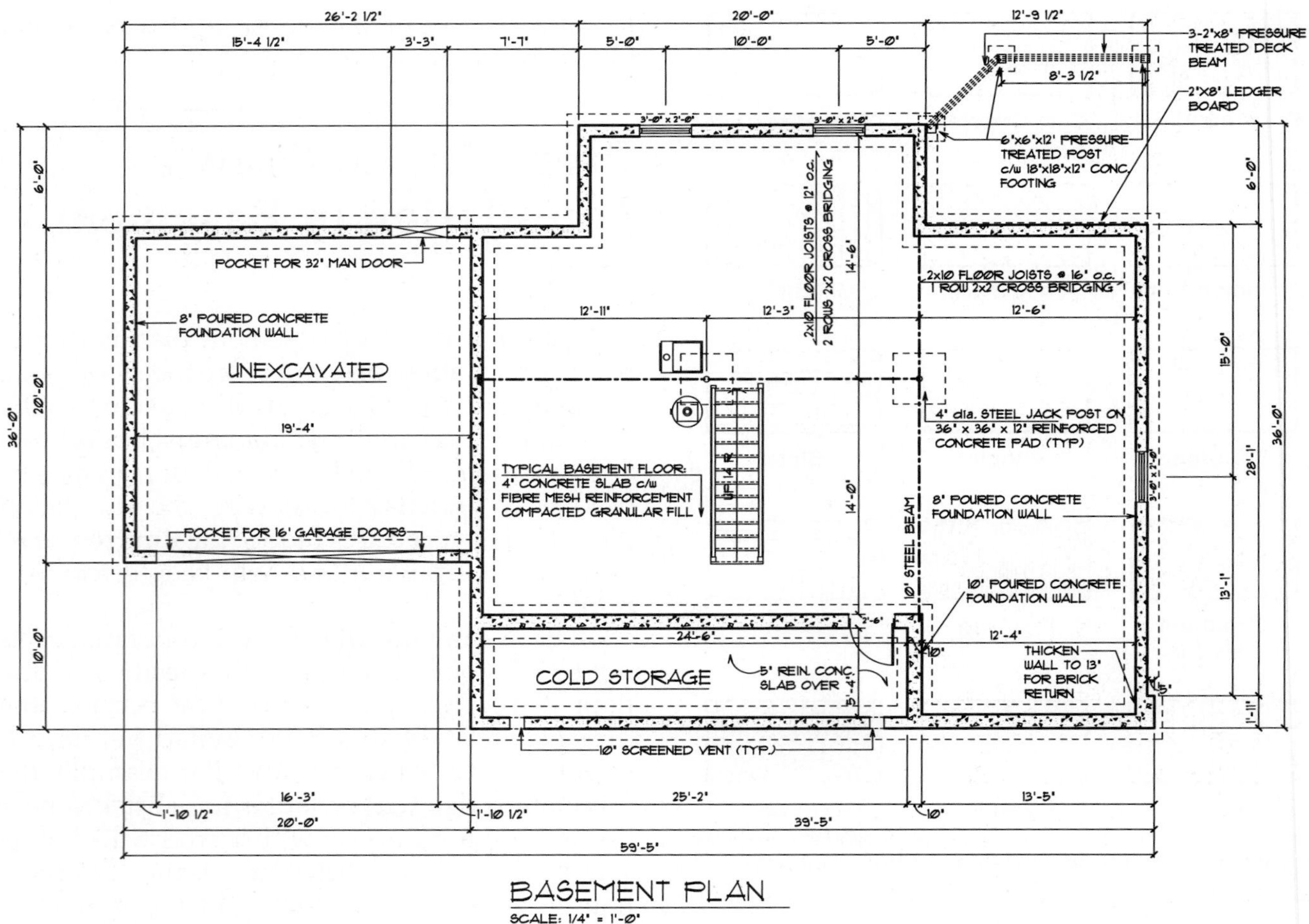

Goodheart-Willcox Publisher

Figure 15-3. A typical basement plan for a residence.

stepped footings or retaining walls are needed. See **Figure 15-5**.

Determine the required size of footings and foundation walls from the available information. Also check the maximum frost penetration depth for the area. If the soil bearing capacity is questionable, conduct a soil bearing test. See **Figure 15-6**. Refer to the local building code to be sure that all requirements are met before proceeding.

Traditional Drawing Techniques

The steps for drawing a foundation plan and a basement plan are similar. However, extra steps are needed to create the basement plan. The steps for both procedures are listed in the following sections.

Procedure Manual Drafting

Drawing a Foundation Plan

The following steps describe the general procedure for drawing a foundation plan using manual drafting techniques. Not every item will apply to every situation.

1. Select the scale. As you may recall, residential structures are usually drawn to 1/4″ = 1′-0″ scale. Be sure to use the same size tracing sheets for all drawings in the set. Steps 1 through 4 are shown in **Figure 15-7**.
2. Locate the outline of the foundation walls on the paper. Allow ample space for dimensions, notes, and a title block. Use the floor plan as

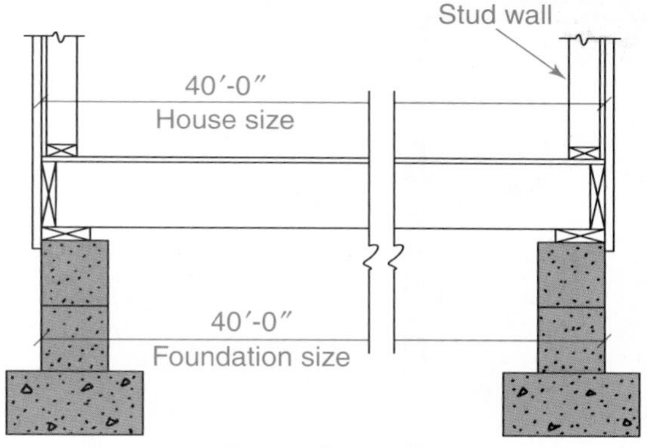

Stud wall
40′-0″
House size
40′-8″
Foundation size
Brick Veneer Structure

Goodheart-Willcox Publisher

Figure 15-4. A brick veneer house requires a foundation wall that is 8″ longer and wider than the foundation wall for a frame structure.

K & S Testing and Engineering, Inc.

Figure 15-6. A soil bearing test is being made to determine the load-bearing capacity of the soil.

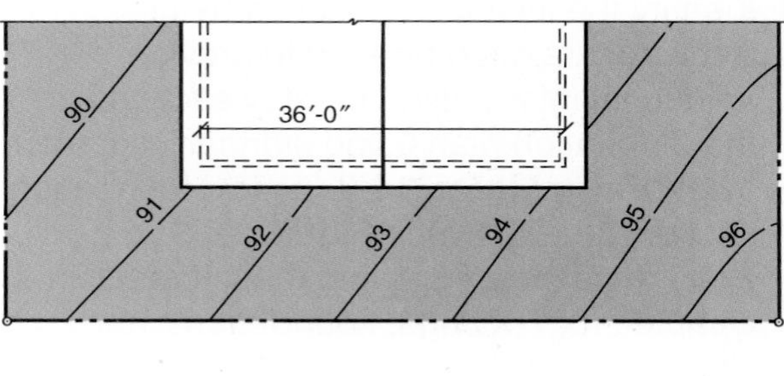

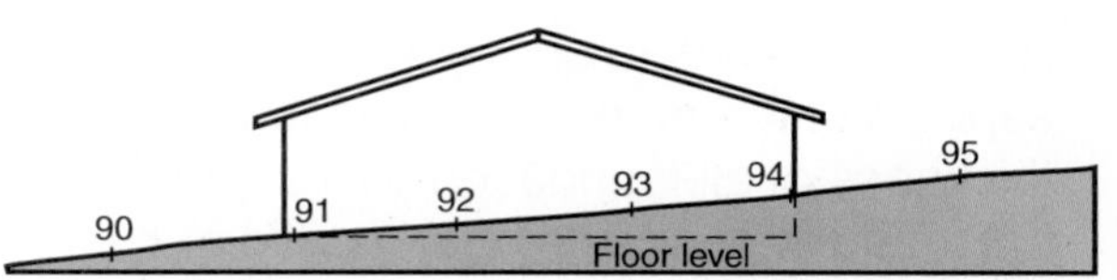

Goodheart-Willcox Publisher

Figure 15-5. In this example, no consideration was given to the existing grade as shown by the contour lines on the site plan. As a result, the finished floor level is below grade, which most likely violates the building code.

an underlay or draw the foundation plan from dimensions obtained from the floor plan.

3. Draw the foundation walls, piers, and pilasters. A ***pier*** is a masonry pillar that supports the floor framing. A ***pilaster*** is a rectangular column that projects from a wall. It can be used for additional girder or beam support. Also draw the foundation for a fireplace and chimney, if the home will have a fireplace.
4. Indicate breaks in the foundation wall. Examples include breaks needed for windows, doors, access holes, and vents.
5. Lay out and draw the footings for the foundation walls. A ***footing*** is a masonry section usually constructed of reinforced concrete. The footings support the foundation wall and structure by spreading the weight over a larger area. Use a hidden line for the footings. Steps 5 through 10 are shown in **Figure 15-8**.
6. Draw the footings for the piers and columns (posts).

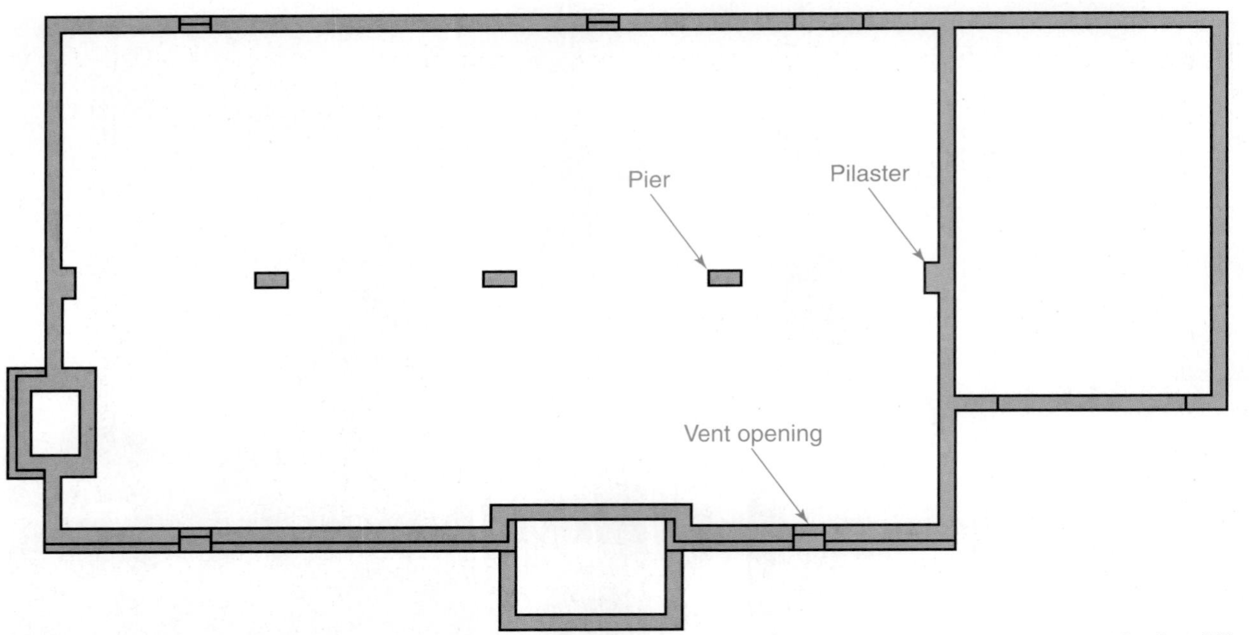

Goodheart-Willcox Publisher

Figure 15-7. A partially completed foundation plan that shows the foundation walls, piers, pilasters, and vent openings.

Green Architecture

Green Foundations

Many builders automatically choose to build a solid foundation using poured concrete or concrete masonry unit (CMU) construction. However, greener options exist. For example, as described in Chapter 11, *Designing for Sustainability*, you can choose concrete with a high percentage of fly ash (the reclaimed ash from coal combustion).

Another option is to use pressure-treated lumber for the footing and stem walls of a house. A foundation made from pressure-treated lumber is as sturdy and structurally sound as concrete. Before using pressure-treated lumber, make sure that the local building code allows the use of pressure-treated lumber for foundations, because building codes may be very strict in dictating the use of specified building materials for foundations. Also, make sure the lumber was pressure-treated within the last few years. Older pressure treatments contained arsenic, which is a harmful carcinogen. The newer pressure-treated lumber does not contain arsenic or other harmful compounds.

7. Draw the footings for the fireplace and chimney.
8. Locate the supporting beam if one is required. Draw the beam using a single, thick centerline.
9. Show the size, spacing, and direction of floor joists or trusses. Use the standard notation, as shown in **Figure 15-8**.
10. Identify the location of section details. Sections are often needed to provide additional information. Identify sections on the foundation plan using standard notation, as shown in **Figure 15-8**. Typical foundation sections are shown in **Figure 15-9**. You will learn more about drawing these details in Chapter 18, *Footings, Foundations, and Concrete*.
11. Add dimensions to show the size of all aspects of the foundation. The length and thickness of all foundation wall segments must be dimensioned. Pier locations are dimensioned to the center rather than to the edge. Steps 11 through 15 are shown in **Figure 15-10**.
12. Letter any necessary notes.
13. Add the proper material symbols.

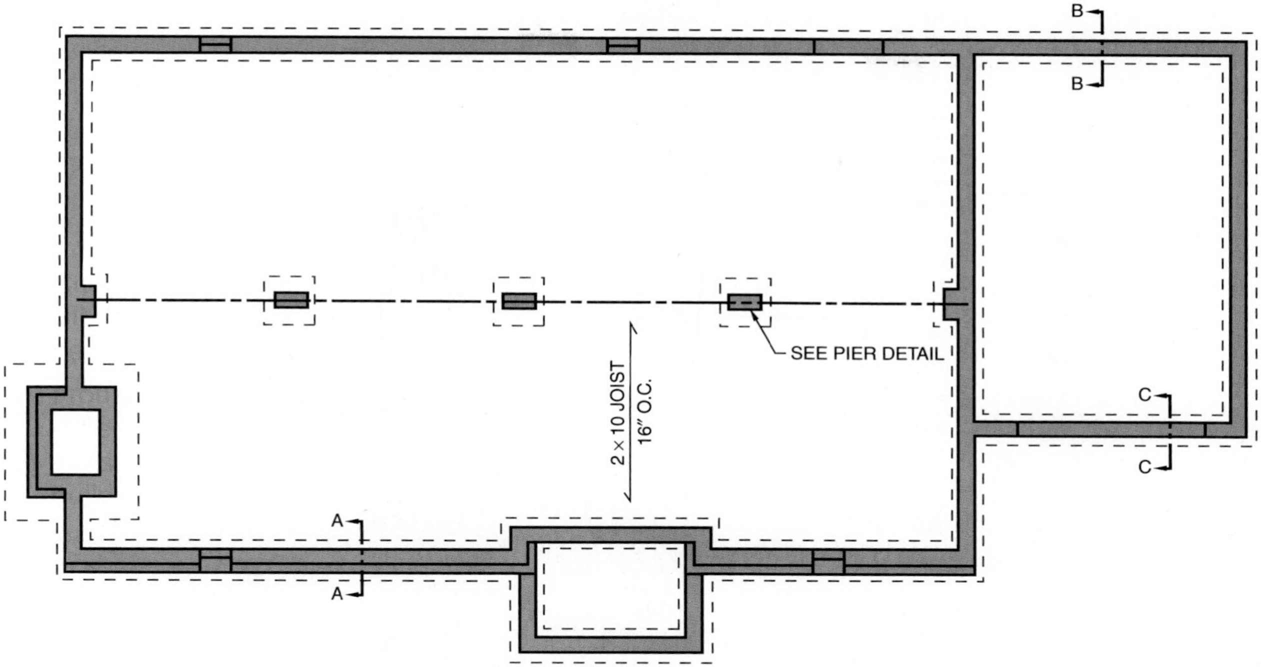

Goodheart-Willcox Publisher

Figure 15-8. Footings for the foundation walls and the piers, the supporting beam, all section symbols, and the floor joist data have been added to the foundation plan.

14. Add the title block, scale, and name of the drawing.
15. Check the drawing. Be sure you have included all of the information necessary to construct the foundation.

Procedure
Manual Drafting

Drawing a Basement Plan

As noted earlier, a basement plan is similar to a foundation plan, but there are several additional features on a basement plan. Use the following steps to draw a basement plan using manual drafting techniques.

1. Select the scale. Like foundation plans, most residential basement plans are drawn at 1/4″ = 1′-0″ scale. Steps 1 through 4 are shown in **Figure 15-11**.
2. Draw the exterior foundation walls. Use the floor plan as an underlay or use information taken from the floor plan. Be sure the foundation walls are correctly positioned with respect to the first floor walls.
3. Draw the footings for the foundation walls, chimney, and fireplace. Also draw the piers and columns (posts).
4. Locate and draw the beam and supports or bearing wall partition(s).
5. Design the room layout in the basement area. Darken the lines. Steps 5 through 9 are shown in **Figure 15-12**.
6. Indicate breaks in the basement walls for windows or doors.
7. Locate and draw the stairs leading to the basement.
8. Show the size, spacing, and direction of floor joists or trusses. Use the standard notation.
9. Identify the location of sections required to provide additional information about the basement construction. Indicate the sections on the basement plan using standard notation.

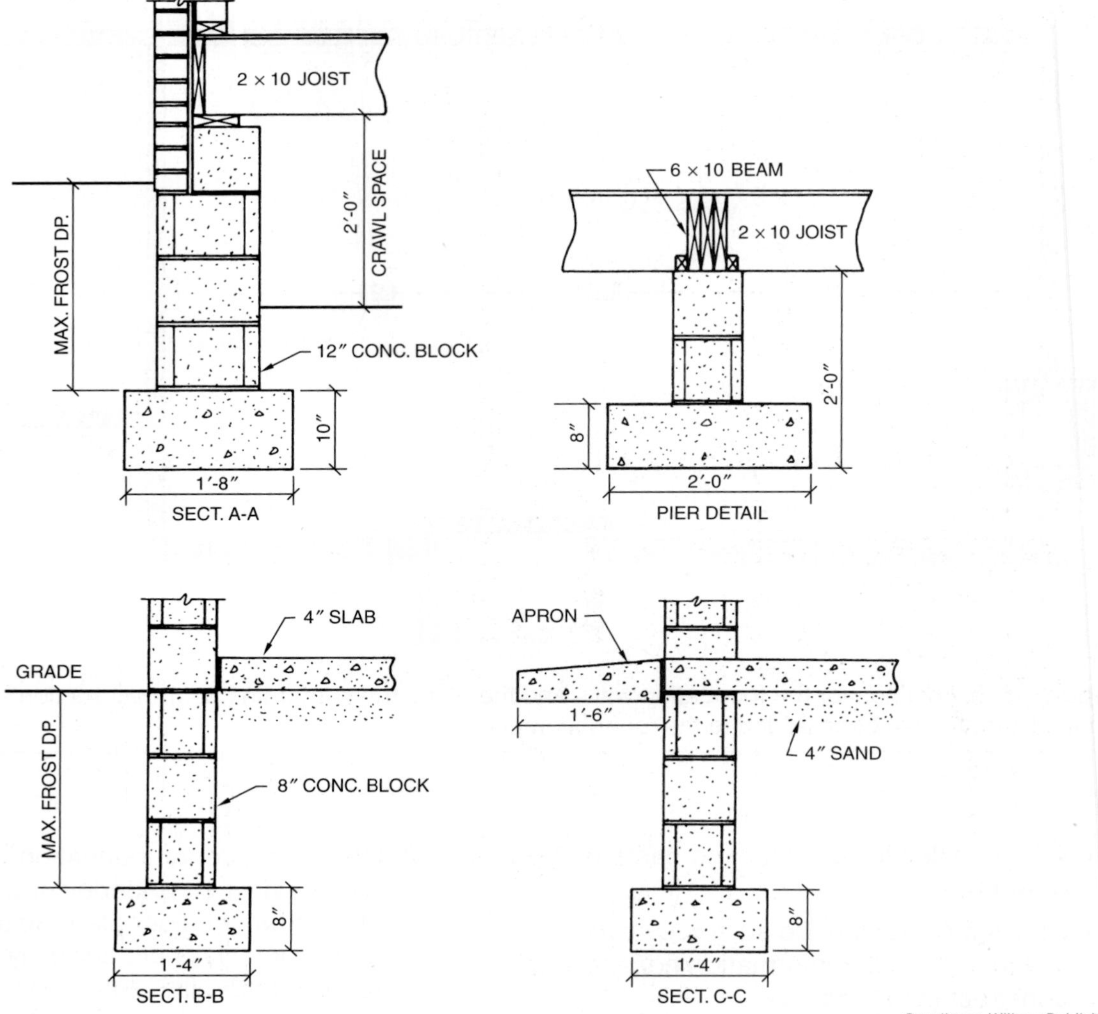

Goodheart-Willcox Publisher

Figure 15-9. These foundation details are required to further describe the foundation construction.

10. Locate and draw permanent bath fixtures such as a toilet, tub, and sink. Also, locate the furnace, hot water heater, water storage tank, water softener, sump, and floor drains. Not all of these items are necessary on every plan. Steps 10 through 16 are shown in **Figure 15-13**.
11. Add dimensions to show all features. Dimension interior frame walls using the practices of your school or office. In **Figure 15-13**, interior frame walls are dimensioned to the center of the walls. If using this practice, do not dimension to the center of foundation walls.
12. Letter any necessary notes.
13. Show electrical switches, outlets, and fixtures. This step is required if a separate basement electrical plan is not going to be included in the set of drawings.
14. Add the proper material symbols.
15. Add the title block, scale, and name of the drawing.
16. Check the drawing. Be sure you have included all of the information necessary to construct the foundation and basement.

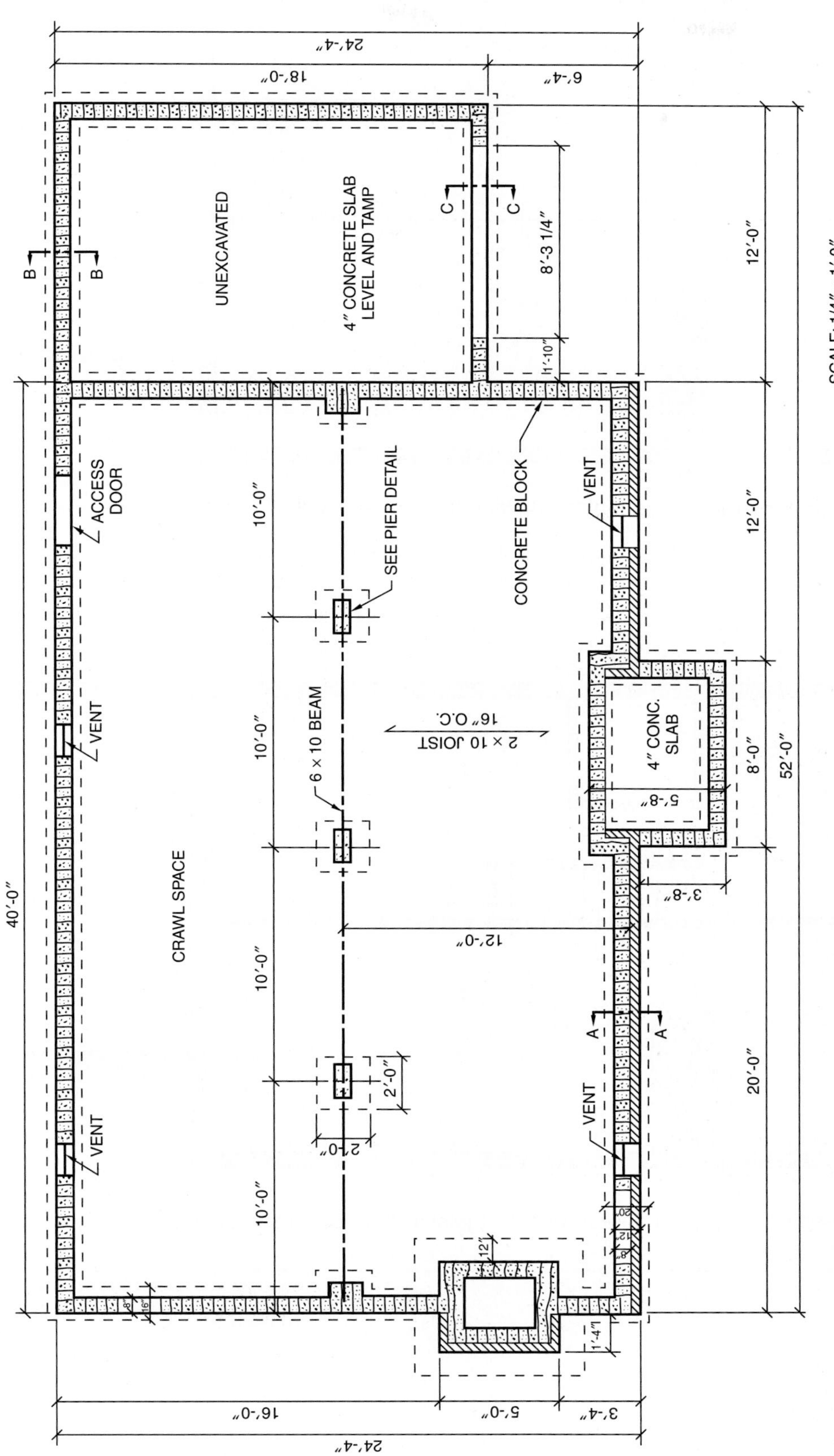

Goodheart-Willcox Publisher

Figure 15-10. The completed foundation plan showing dimensions, notes, foundation material hatch patterns, and the drawing scale. This house has a stud wall frame with a brick veneer along the front.

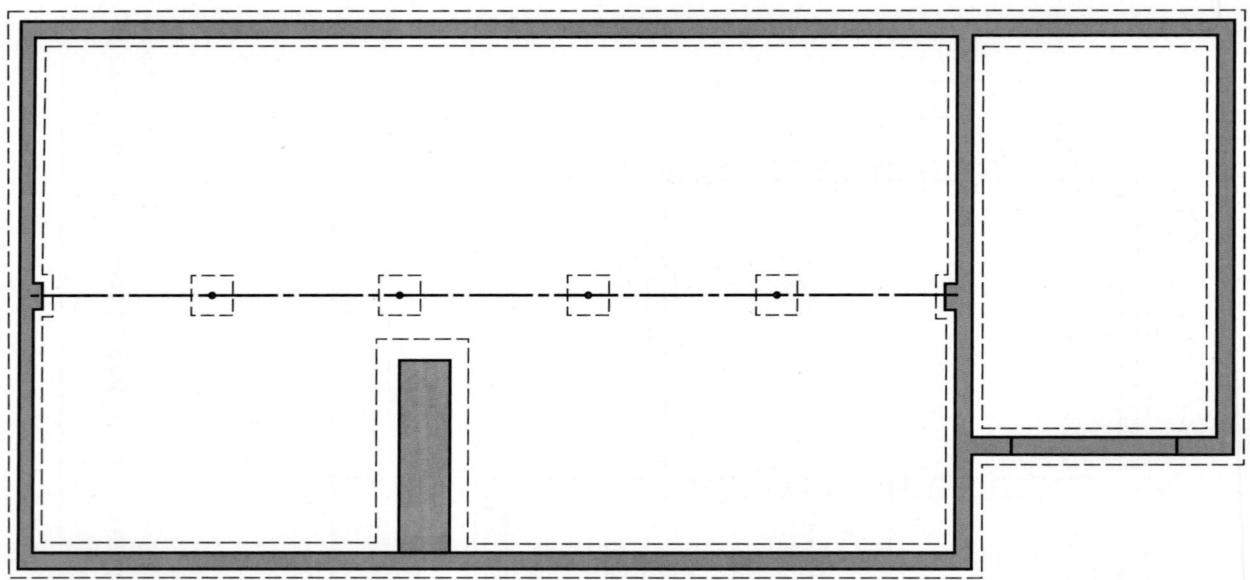

Goodheart-Willcox Publisher

Figure 15-11. A partially completed basement plan showing the foundation walls, footings, supporting beam, and posts/columns.

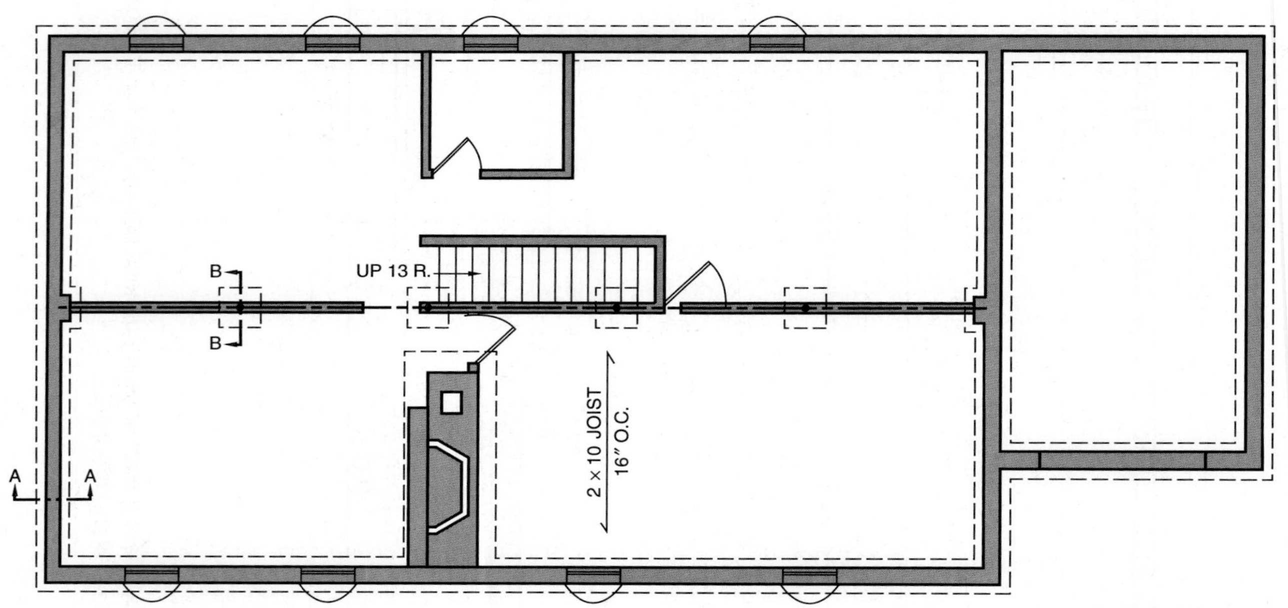

Goodheart-Willcox Publisher

Figure 15-12. Interior basement walls and doors, windows, joist information, stairs, and section symbols have been added to the partially completed plan.

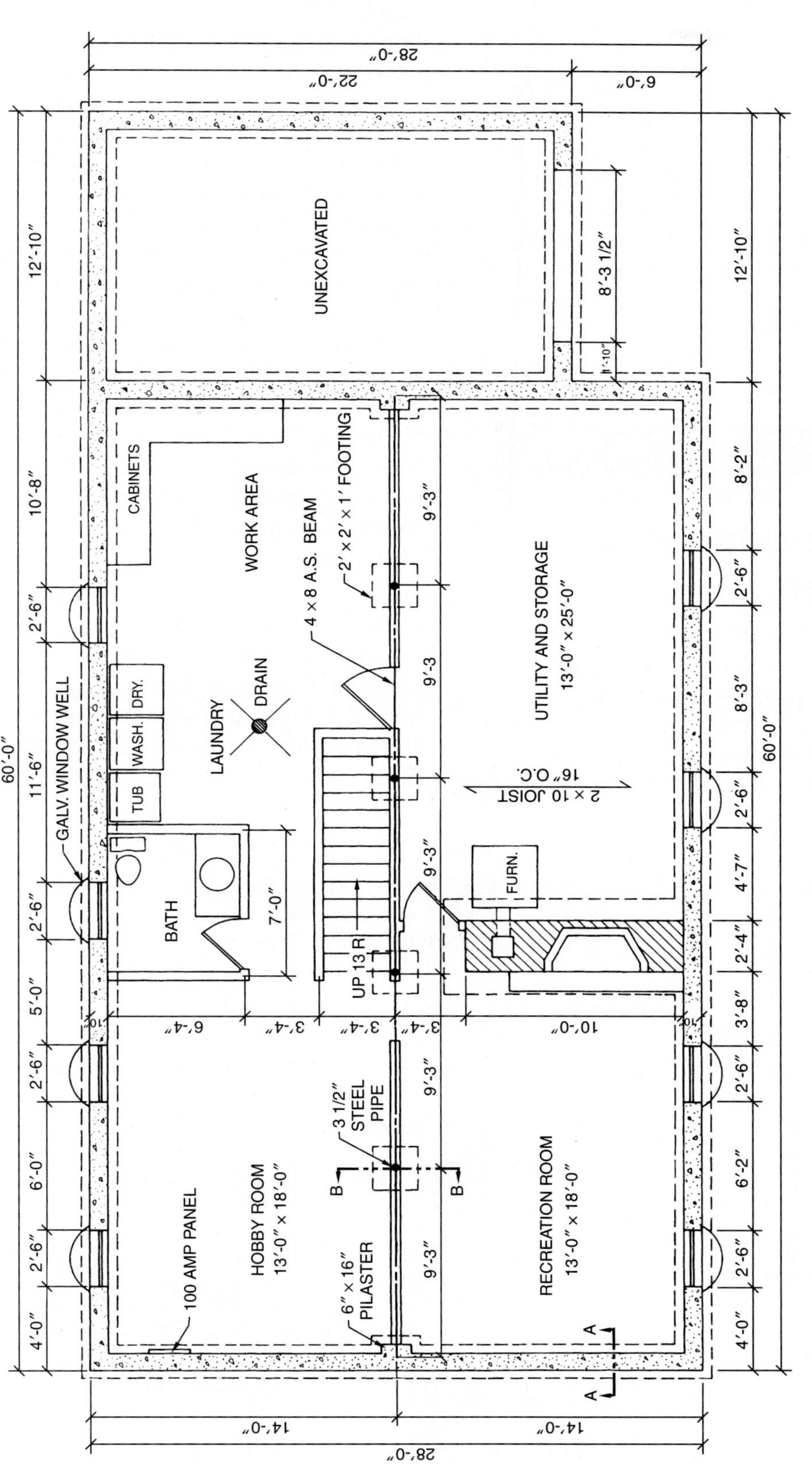

Figure 15-13. A completed basement plan. The foundation walls are cast concrete and the structure has a stud wall frame.

CADD Drawing Techniques

The procedure for drawing a foundation or basement plan with CADD is basically the same as that used with manual drafting techniques. However, there are a couple of major differences. The biggest difference is that the drawing is created at full scale. Then, an appropriate scale is selected when the drawing is plotted. The following steps outline drawing a foundation or basement plan using CADD.

Procedure CADD

Drawing a Foundation or Basement Plan

1. Make a copy of the floor plan on a new layer in the foundation plan drawing. As you develop the foundation plan, place items on the appropriate layers using the correct line width and linetype. If you are drawing the foundation plan in the same file as the other drawings in an architectural set of drawings, place the foundation plan on its own set of layers.
2. Draw the outside line of the foundation walls and delete the outside line of the floor plan wall, if they do not coincide. Generally, the outside lines of the foundation walls are identical to the outside lines of the rough stud walls on the floor plan in a frame structure with siding. Brick or other veneer is added to the outside of this point. The foundation wall is wider than a frame wall; therefore, the inside line will fall inside the floor plan. Generally, the foundation wall will be 8″, 10″, or 12″ thick, although there are exceptions. A 12″ thick wall will be used in this example. Some CADD software programs draw all the lines of a footing and stem wall automatically when you change the type of wall. This example assumes that you will draw them individually.
3. Draw all footings. The footings and foundation walls should be drawn on separate layers because the line widths and linetypes are different. Piers and their footings may be added to these layers since they use similar linetypes and are part of the foundation. **Figure 15-14** shows the foundation walls,

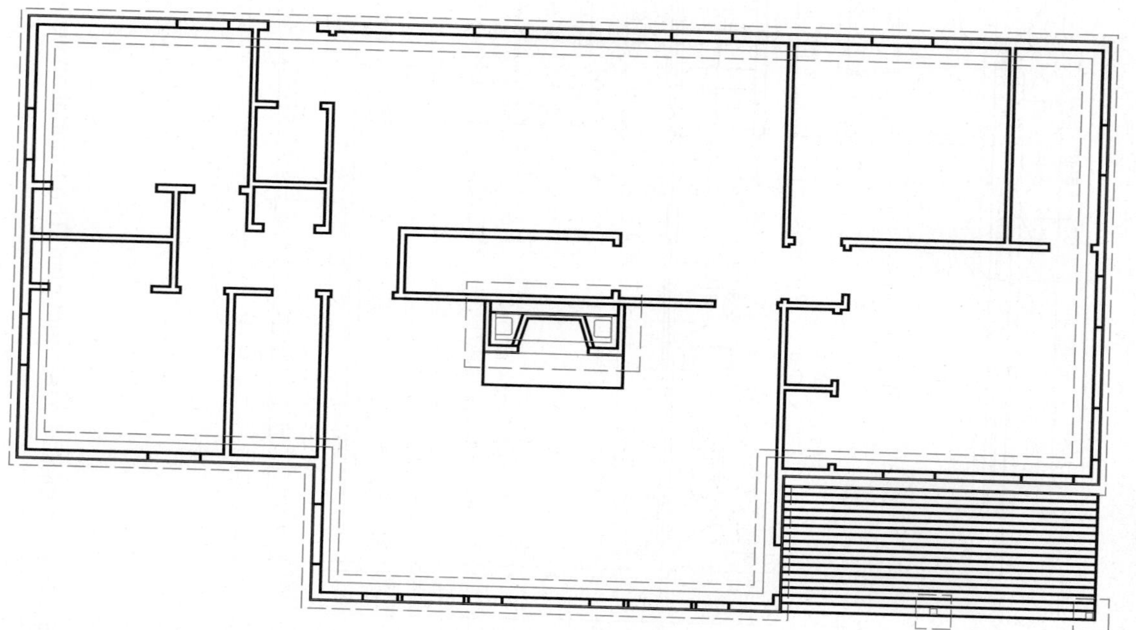

Goodheart-Willcox Publisher

Figure 15-14. The floor plan for the first floor is copied to a layer in the foundation/basement plan drawing. Footings and piers are then added on another layer. The floor plan layer is shown here for reference.

footings, and chimney located and drawn.

4. For a basement plan, draw the stairs, interior walls, windows, and doors. Place the stairs on their own layer for easy use with other layers/plans. This is an appropriate time to turn off the floor plan layer since it is no longer needed for the foundation/basement plan. Again, you may not have to do this step if your CADD program works differently.
5. Draw all interior walls and insert door and window symbols into the plan. Place walls on their own basement floor plan layer. In similar fashion, use a separate basement floor plan layer for symbols. When inserting symbols, take advantage of an existing symbol library or begin one of your own. Also at this point, add other features such as the joist direction arrow and window wells. See **Figure 15-15**.
6. Dimension the plan. Use the dimensioning capabilities of your CADD program to accomplish this task. If you use automatic dimensioning functions, check the dimensions carefully to be sure they are appropriate.
7. Insert symbols for appliances, fixtures, and the furnace, if any. These should be placed on a symbols layer.
8. Add cutting-plane symbols where required.
9. Label room names and sizes.
10. Add the scale and title to the foundation plan layer.
11. Look over the plan to be sure it is complete. **Figure 15-16** shows the completed foundation/basement plan.

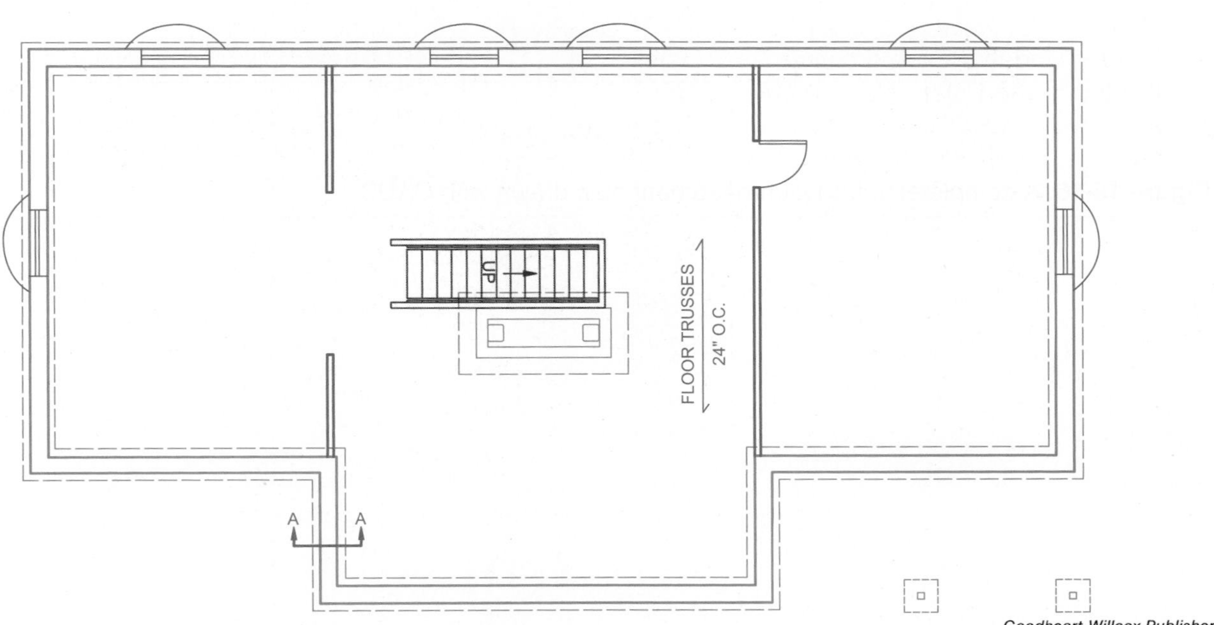

Figure 15-15. The interior walls, stairs, windows, and doors in the basement are added.

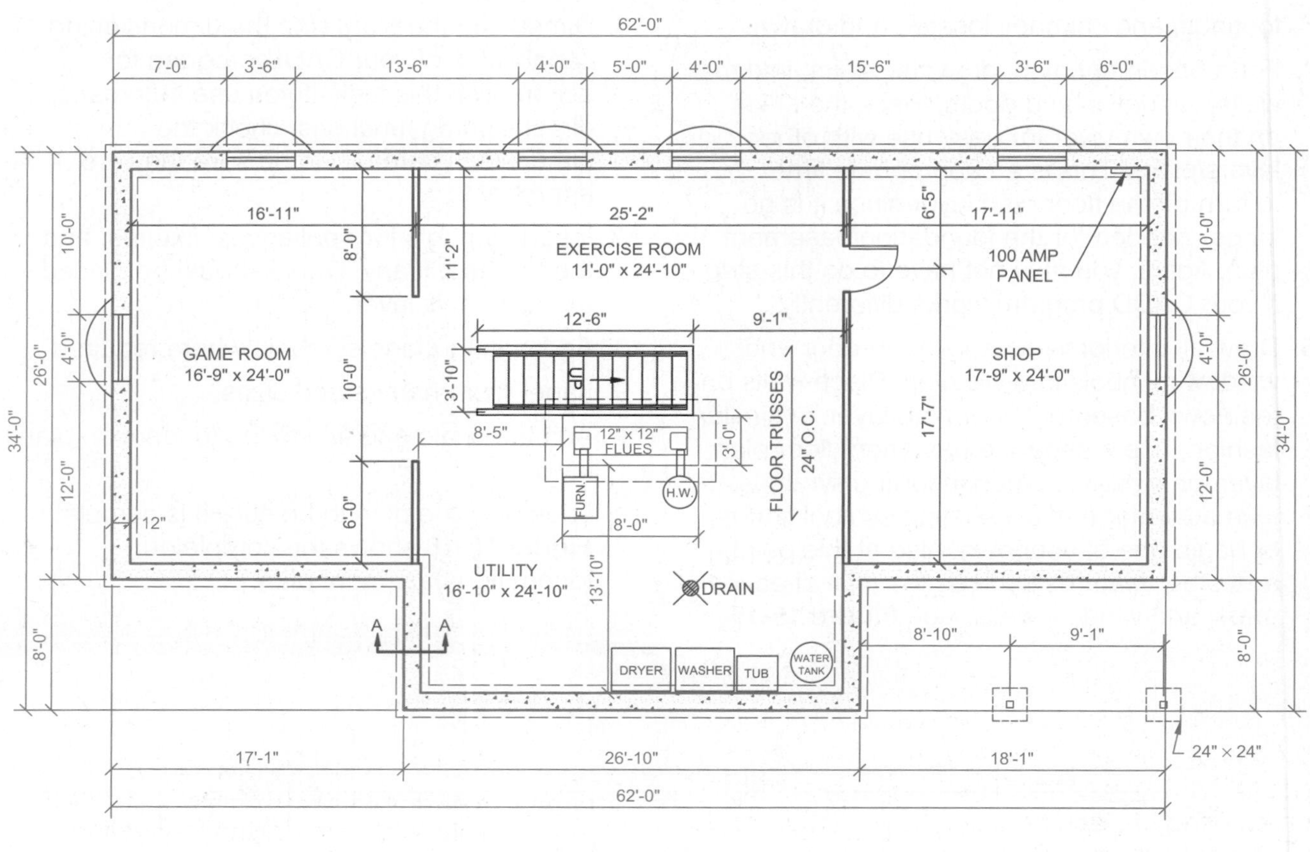

Goodheart-Willcox Publisher

Figure 15-16. A completed foundation/basement plan drawn with CADD.

Parametric Modeling | Creating a Foundation or Basement Plan

Creating a foundation plan in parametric modeling involves some of the same steps used with a general-purpose CADD system. However, instead of creating 2D line work, you construct the plan by placing 3D components into the model. This procedure builds on the parametric modeling procedure presented in Chapter 14, *Floor Plans*. Refer to that procedure if needed. If you have not added levels and views appropriate for the foundation plan, do so now. Typical levels used for a foundation plan include Top of Footing, Basement Floor, and Top of Foundation. Establish each level at the appropriate elevation. In certain cases, you will find it helpful to create grids for the placement of structural columns. This can be done at the very beginning of the project or prior to placing columns. The **GRID** command can be used to place horizontal and vertical grids locating the column centerlines.

The following procedure is designed for a one-story home with wood frame construction and a basement. This procedure is presented as a typical sequence, but specific steps will vary depending on the program used and the type of construction.

1. Draw the foundation walls. Draw the walls in the first floor plan view. This will enable you to use the first floor walls as a location reference. In order to see the foundation walls form as they are created, adjust the view range to an appropriate level below the First Floor level. Access the **WALL** command and select a foundation wall type. The foundation wall will generally be 8″, 10″, or 12″ thick, depending on the type of construction used for the first floor walls. Use a default wall type or make a duplicate and edit it to create a wall with the necessary material, such as cast-in-place concrete. Once the desired wall type is selected, set the base constraint to the Top of Footing level and the top constraint to the Top of Foundation level. The base and top offsets should be 0′-0″. Set the appropriate justification, such as core exterior, and draw the walls using the first floor walls as a reference. Pick points that align with the stud wall face along the first floor walls so that the foundation walls are correctly positioned.
2. Create the foundation wall footings. Create these footings in the Top of Footing plan view. Adjust the view range to an appropriate level below the Top of Footing level to see the footings as they are created. The **WALL** command can be used to select and place a structural footing. Select a default type or make a duplicate and edit it to create a concrete footing with the required dimensions. Note that footings are typically extruded downward in a negative Z direction from the host level. In other words, the top of the footing is level with the host level. To create each footing, pick each of the foundation walls. This centers each footing under the corresponding foundation wall as it is created.
3. Draw the structural slab representing the basement floor. Switch to the Basement Floor plan view. Access the **FLOOR** command and select a concrete floor type. Generally, the basement floor will be 4″ thick. To create the floor, pick the inside wall foundation lines on the plan or draw lines manually to form a sketch defining the perimeter. The perimeter of the basement floor should *not* extend into the exterior walls. Ensure that the sketch forms a closed boundary before completing the command.
4. Create the columns and the footings supporting the columns. Create these components in the Basement Floor plan view. Access the **COLUMN** command to select and place a column. Select a default type or make a duplicate and edit it to create a column with the required dimensions. Set the base constraint to the Basement Floor level. Specify a negative base offset of –4″ so that the base of the column is beneath the slab floor. Specify an appropriate top constraint. This can typically be done by setting the top

Parametric Modeling | Creating a Foundation or Basement Plan *(Continued)*

constraint to a specific level and entering an offset value. The column should extend to the proper elevation located under the supporting beam above. To create the footing supporting the column, use the **WALL** command. If necessary, adjust the view range in the plan view. Select a default footing type or make a duplicate and edit it to create a footing with the required dimensions. Pick the center of the column to place the footing. After the footing is created, confirm that the top surface of the footing is aligned with the bottom of the column. Use the **COPY** command to place the additional columns and footings.

5. Create the supporting beam above the columns. Switch to a plan view that corresponds to the base elevation of the beam. If needed, adjust the view range so that the columns are visible. The beam should be centered on the columns and should meet the bottom surface of the structural floor above. To make it easier to center the beam over the columns, create a reference plane that locates the beam centerline. Access the **BEAM** command and select a steel beam type that meets the structural requirements, such as a wide flange beam. To place the beam, pick two points along the reference plane that locate the endpoints. Switch to a 3D view to verify the beam is correctly positioned.

   If the design includes pilasters or beam pockets to support the ends of the beam, these features can be added to the model. However, it may be more efficient to note or draw these features on detail drawings. In parametric modeling, there are often cases where not all building features are modeled in 3D in order to represent them on 2D drawings. As an alternative, 2D lines called *detail lines* can be added to a view in order to represent non-modeled features. Detail lines are view-specific and do not appear in other views in the model. Some modeling programs provide a library of predefined 2D detail symbols called *detail components* intended for drawing features in 2D. Using detail geometry is common on views such as wall sections, where there may be many detailed features that require extra drafting work. This technique is often used in conjunction with 3D modeling and provides flexibility in conveying detailed information about the design.

6. Draw the interior walls of the basement. Locate doors and windows on the plan. For each item, insert the appropriate component. Insert components for appliances, fixtures, and the furnace.
7. Dimension the plan. Use the dimensioning capabilities of your program to accomplish this task. Check the dimensions carefully to be sure they are appropriate.
8. Add cutting-plane symbols where required to indicate sections. Working with sections in a parametric model is discussed in Chapter 22, *Building Sections*.
9. Create rooms to define the rooms on the plan. Adjust the placement of text for room names and tags so that the text does not obstruct dimension text.
10. Create a new sheet for the foundation plan view. Insert the foundation plan view onto the sheet. If needed, adjust the placement of text for the view title and scale. The scale for the foundation plan should be 1/4″ = 1′-0″.
11. Check the entire foundation plan. When you are sure the plan is complete, print or plot the sheet.

Summary

- A foundation plan is a plan view section drawing that provides all of the information necessary to construct the foundation.
- A basement plan is a combination foundation and floor plan.
- The foundation plan is drawn from information presented on the floor plan, site plan, and elevations.
- Before drawing a foundation plan, it is necessary to determine the type of exterior walls specified on the floor plan.

Internet Resources

Georgia-Pacific LLC
Supplier of building products

Louisiana-Pacific (LP) Corporation
Manufacturer of building materials

Portland Cement Association
Information about cement and concrete and their uses in residential construction

Anchor Wall Systems
Retaining wall systems and design tips

Review Questions

Answer the following questions using the information in this chapter.

1. Explain the purpose of a foundation plan.
2. List eight features that are usually shown on a foundation plan.
3. Hatch patterns are used on the foundation plan to show various _____.
4. What is the difference between a *foundation plan* and a *basement plan*?
5. What is the purpose of a brick ledge?
6. Why is a basement a logical and economical choice for cold climates?
7. List three things you should check before drawing a foundation or basement plan.
8. At what scale is a foundation plan drawn when using traditional drafting methods?
9. What is the purpose of a footing?
10. What kind of line is used to indicate the supporting beam?
11. When drawing a foundation plan in CADD, how is the floor plan initially used?
12. When a foundation plan is drawn in CADD, at what scale is the plan drawn?

Suggested Activities

1. Select a floor plan for a garage or storage shed. Develop a foundation plan for the structure with a slab foundation. Add necessary dimensions, symbols, and notes. Provide sufficient information so that the foundation can be constructed from your drawings without additional resources.
2. Locate a floor plan for a cottage or vacation home. Then, design and draw the foundation for this house using CADD. Completely dimension the drawing and indicate details needed to explain the construction.
3. Using CADD, draw the foundation plan for a two-car garage that has a slab foundation. Assume the garage is stud wall construction and is 24′-0″ × 24′-0″. Check the required footing depth for your area and make the design meet the requirement.
4. Select a house floor plan from a magazine or other source. Draw a foundation plan for the house.

Problem Solving Case Study

You are creating a home design and set of architectural plans for the Bellinghams. The foundation plan for their new home is shown in Figure 15-10 in this chapter. The Bellinghams are delighted with the floor plan for their new home, but they have decided they want a basement, instead of just a crawl space, under the first floor. They want to include a recreation room, one bedroom, and a bathroom in the basement. What adaptations must you make? Create a new basement plan that shows the new features. Add fixtures and dimensions as needed.

ADDA Certification Prep

The following questions are presented in the style used in the American Design Drafting Association (ADDA) Drafter Certification Test. Answer the questions using the information in this chapter.

1. Which of the following statements are true about foundation plans?
   A. The foundation plan is drawn from information presented on the floor plan, site plan, and elevations.
   B. The foundation plan is a section drawing.
   C. The foundation plan is prepared primarily for the excavators, masons, carpenters, and cement workers who build the foundation.
   D. The type of exterior walls specified on the floor plan make little difference in the specifications for the foundation walls.
   E. The site plan and elevations should be examined to determine the need for stepped footings and retaining walls.
2. Which of the following statements are true?
   A. The foundation plan is a combination basement and floor plan.
   B. The procedure for drawing a foundation or basement plan with CADD is basically the same as when using manual drafting techniques.
   C. The outside lines of the foundation walls are usually identical to the outside lines of the rough stud walls on the floor plan of a frame structure with siding.
   D. Material symbols are not needed on foundation drawings.
3. Which of the following statements is *false*?
   A. The split-level house may need a foundation plan for one section of the house and a basement plan for another.
   B. The preliminary floor plan is often used as an underlay for drawing the foundation plan.
   C. Soil bearing tests should be performed after the foundation has been built.

Curricular Connections

1. **Social Science.** The earliest form of concrete was first invented by the Romans many thousands of years ago. Numerous Roman architectural works were constructed using this newly developed building material. Research early Roman architecture and compose a report describing at least three of these Roman structures. Compare and contrast each building or structure's use of concrete, the design of the structures, and the purpose for which each structure was intended.
2. **Language Arts.** Consider the advantages and disadvantages of including a basement in the plans for a new home. Decide which option you would choose if you could build a "dream" home for yourself anywhere in the world. Write an essay explaining where you would build your house and why you would or would not include a basement in the plans. Give at least three reasons for your decision.

STEM Connections

1. **Science.** Investigate the scientific principle behind using a footing to spread the weight of a foundation wall and structure over a larger area. Why must the footing extend below the frost line? In your own words, explain this concept to a classmate.

Communicating about Architecture

1. **Reading.** With a partner, make flash cards of the key terms in this chapter. On the front of the card, write the term. On the back of the card, write the pronunciation and a brief definition. Use this chapter and a dictionary for guidance. Then take turns quizzing one another on the pronunciations and definitions of the key terms.
2. **Speaking.** Select five of the key terms in this chapter and imagine them being used by architects in a real-life context. With a partner, role-play a situation in which an architectural firm is asked to design the foundation for a new home for a client.

Chapter 16

Site Plans

Objectives

After completing this chapter, you will be able to:

- Identify and describe the features shown on a typical site plan.
- Visualize land elevations from contour lines.
- Properly locate a building on a site.
- Explain the purpose of a landscaping plan.
- Draw a site plan or landscaping plan using correct symbols and conventions.

Key Terms

bearing	plot plan
benchmark	property lines
contour interval	setbacks
contour line	site plan
interpolation	topographical features
landscaping plan	topographical surface
mean sea level	
north arrow	

Plans that show the land or site on which a house will be built are just as important as the foundation and floor plans. In fact, the foundation plan depends partly on the original or modified contours of the land.

A ***site plan*** is a plan (top) view drawing that shows the contours of the building site and the location and orientation of proposed new construction on the property. This drawing is used to show the land and how the house will be situated on it. A site plan plays an important role in the construction of a new home. The site plan is sometimes called a ***plot plan***. In some architectural or civil drafting firms, these terms are interchangeable. A *plot* can be described as an empty piece of land.

A ***landscaping plan*** is sometimes included as well. The landscaping plan is similar to a site plan, but it shows how the building site will be landscaped, if landscaping is included in the overall architectural plans. It shows the type and placement of trees, shrubs, flowers, gardens, and pools on the site.

The Site Plan

The purpose of a site plan is to show the property lines and the existing topography of the site. See **Figure 16-1**. *Topography* refers to the physical characteristics of the land. If modifications need to be made to the topography, the site plan also shows planned changes or improvements. For example, a low spot may be filled in, or a hill may be partially leveled. See **Figure 16-2**.

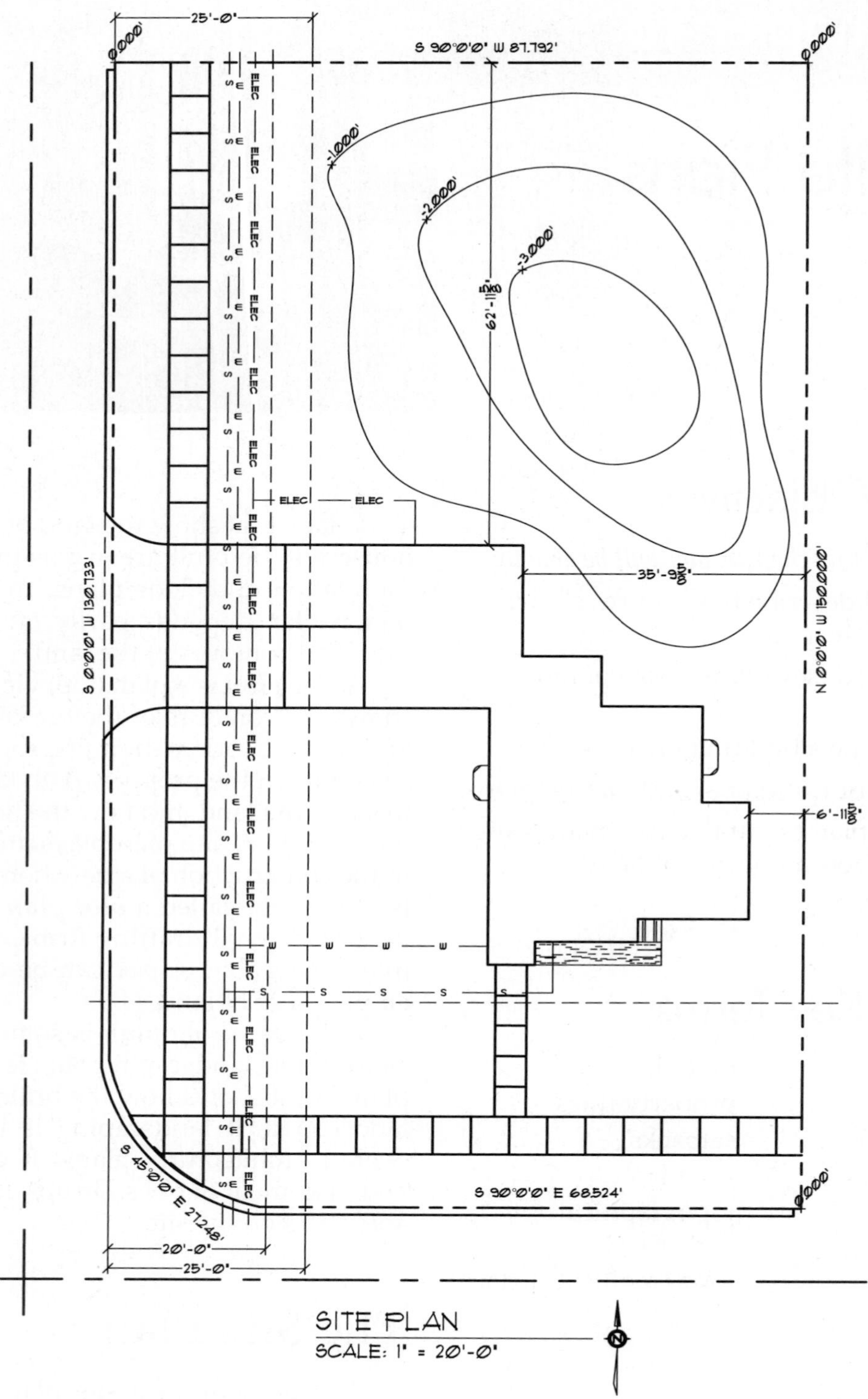

Goodheart-Willcox Publisher

Figure 16-1. A site plan is prepared from information provided by a surveyor.

The site plan shows several specific features, including:

- Length and bearing (direction) of each property line
- Contour of the land
- Elevation of property corners and contour lines
- ***North arrow*** (a symbol that shows the direction of north; also called a *meridian arrow*)

Racheal Grazias/Shutterstock.com

Figure 16-2. Residential property is often graded before the home is built. The grading changes the contours of the land. The original and proposed contours can be shown on a site plan.

- Trees, shrubs, streams, and gardens
- Location, outline, and size of existing buildings
- Existing streets, driveways, sidewalks, and patios
- Location of existing utilities
- Easements for utilities and drainage (if any)
- Existing well, septic tank, and leach field
- Existing fences and retaining walls
- Lot number or address of the site
- Scale of the drawing

Property Lines

Property lines define the site boundaries. The length and ***bearing*** (direction) of each line must be identified on the site plan. Property line lengths are measured with an engineer's scale to the nearest 1/100 foot. **Figure 16-3** shows a property line that is 175.25′ long and has a bearing of N 89° E (north eighty-nine degrees east).

Bearing angles are recorded in degrees from north or south and, if required, minutes and seconds are included. There are 360 degrees in a circle, 60 minutes in a degree, and 60 seconds in a minute. An example of a typical bearing might be S 63° W, while a more precise bearing would read S 63° 13′ 05″ W. **Figure 16-4** shows a number of lines with bearings identified.

A ***benchmark*** is a permanent object used by surveyors to establish points of reference. If the property corner begins or ends on a benchmark, it is identified on the drawing with a benchmark symbol. All other corners are represented by drawing a small circle centered on the exact property corner. See **Figure 16-5**. A point of beginning is shown if a benchmark is not readily available.

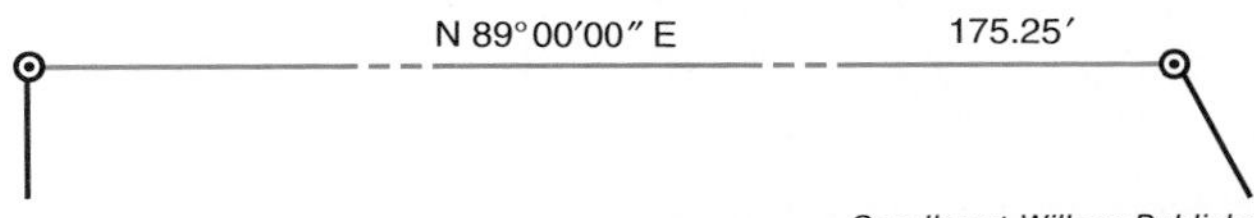

Goodheart-Willcox Publisher

Figure 16-3. This property line is 175.25′ long and has a bearing of N 89° E.

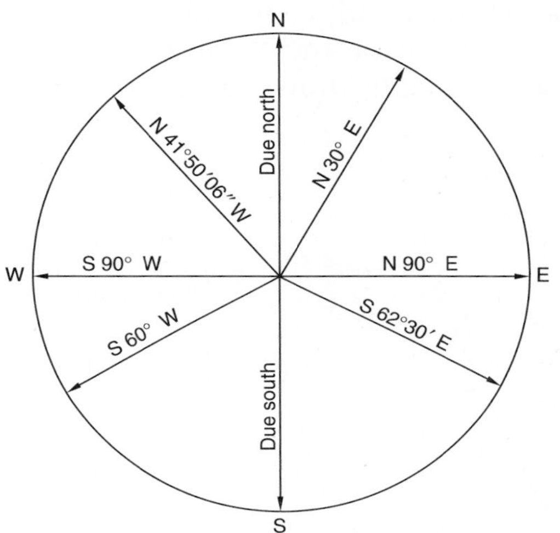

Goodheart-Willcox Publisher

Figure 16-4. Bearings are measured from north or south and may include degrees, minutes, and seconds.

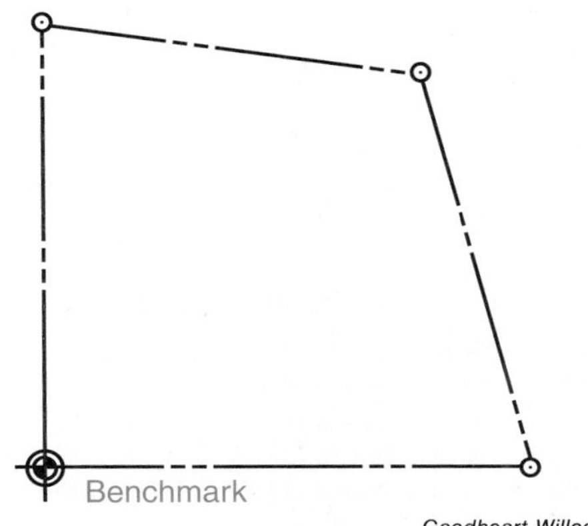

Goodheart-Willcox Publisher

Figure 16-5. Identification of property corners. The lower left corner of the property is on a benchmark, so it is identified with a benchmark symbol.

It is customary when drawing the property lines of a site to begin at one corner and proceed in a clockwise manner. **Figure 16-6** shows the procedure for drawing the property lines of a site.

Contour Lines

Contour lines help describe the topography of a site by depicting shape and elevation of the land. A contour line connects points that have the same elevation. The shoreline of a lake is a good example of a contour line. All points where the water meets the shore have the same elevation. Looking at several characteristics of contour should help to clarify the use of contour lines:

- The ***contour interval*** is the vertical distance between two adjacent contour lines. This interval may be any distance that is relevant for the specific drawing. **Figure 16-7** illustrates a contour interval of five feet. Be sure to identify the elevation of each contour line.
- Closely spaced contour lines on a site plan indicate a steep slope, as shown in **Figure 16-8**. Widely spaced contour lines indicate relatively level ground.
- When contours are smooth and parallel, the ground surface is even. When contours are irregular, the ground surface is rough and uneven. See **Figure 16-9**.

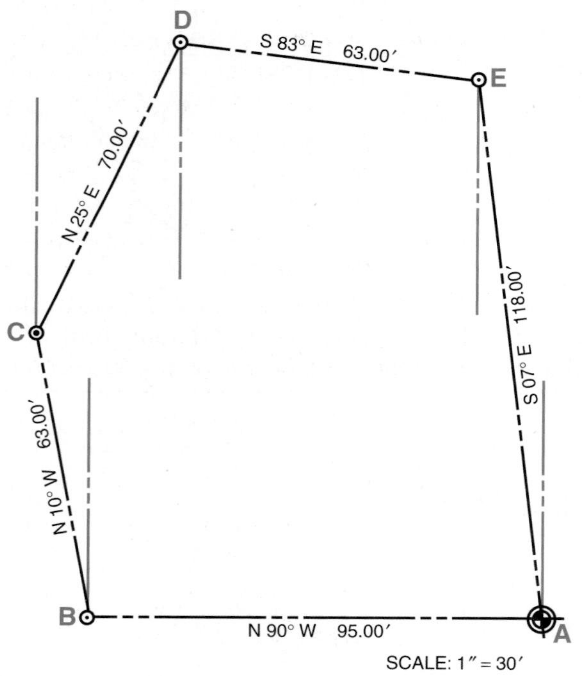

Goodheart-Willcox Publisher

Figure 16-6. These property lines are drawn to scale based on the property line descriptions provided. Begin drawing at the benchmark, if one is provided.

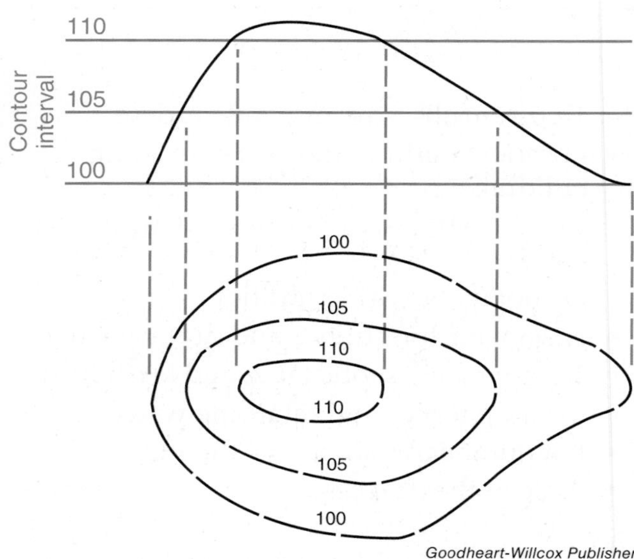

Goodheart-Willcox Publisher

Figure 16-7. The contour lines shown on the bottom describe the contour shown in the elevation view based on a contour interval of 5 feet.

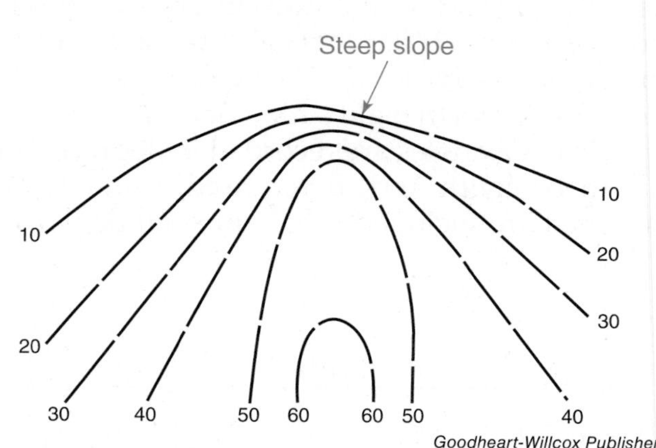

Goodheart-Willcox Publisher

Figure 16-8. The relative spacing of contour lines represents the slope of the land. Contour lines that are close together indicate a steep slope.

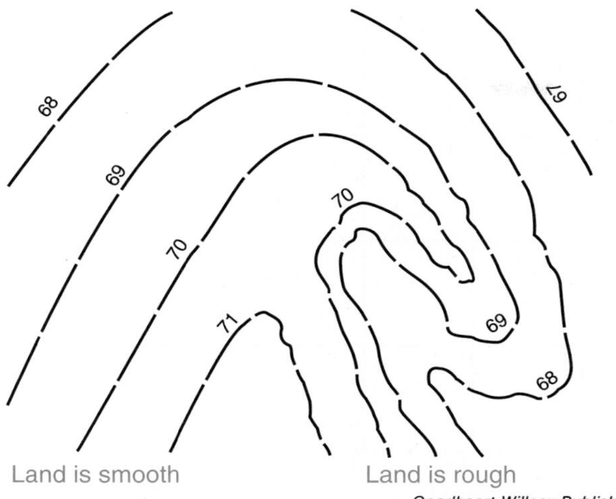

Goodheart-Willcox Publisher

Figure 16-9. The smoothness of contour lines indicates the relative roughness of the land.

- Summits and depressions are represented by closed contour lines, as shown in **Figure 16-10**. The elevation in relation to the adjacent contour line indicates whether the feature is a summit or depression.
- Contour lines of different elevations do not cross. In a steep vertical slope, however, they may be so close that they appear to touch.
- Contour lines cross watersheds and ridge lines at right angles. At ridges, the concave side of the curve faces the higher elevation. At valleys, the convex side of the curve faces the higher elevation.
- Proper symbols should be used to identify valleys and ridges, as shown in **Figure 16-11**.

The accepted reference elevation point for topographical surveys is ***mean sea level***. This is a standardized elevation. Many times, however, it is not important to know how far a point is from sea level, but what the relative difference is between two or more points. In residential home construction, relative elevations are usually sufficient.

Contour lines that are the result of a survey are usually represented by a series of thin freehand lines about 1″ to 2″ in length. Estimated contours are represented by a line of short dashes similar to a hidden line. See **Figure 16-12**.

Figure 16-13 shows contour lines plotted from a grid of elevations developed using survey data. The more survey measurements taken for a given area, the more accurately the contour lines represent the topography. When insufficient data is given, the resulting contour may be only moderately accurate or not accurate at all. In the example shown in **Figure 16-13**, ***interpolation*** is used to locate elevation points for plotting the contour lines. First, elevation measurements from survey data are recorded at each grid intersection. In the given example, elevations are measured in feet. The contour lines are plotted by estimating point locations in reference to the elevation measurements. Notice that grid intersections representing elevations in whole feet establish exact points for plotting the contour

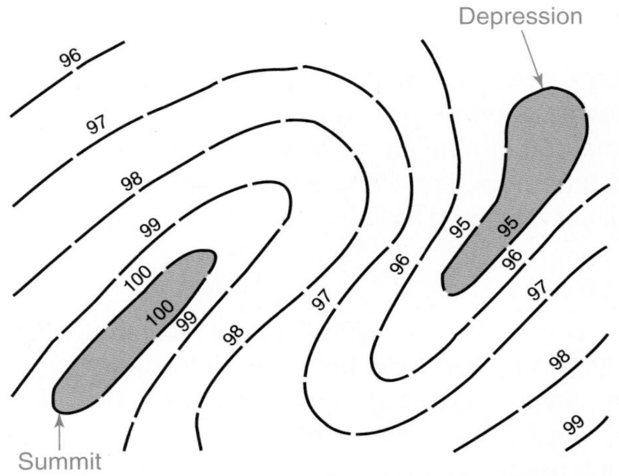

Goodheart-Willcox Publisher

Figure 16-10. Summits (left) and depressions (right) are represented by closed contour lines.

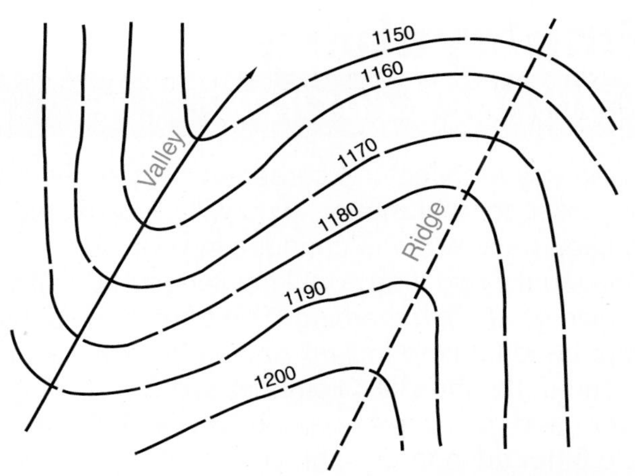

Goodheart-Willcox Publisher

Figure 16-11. The proper symbols for showing ridges and valleys on a site plan. Notice that the contour lines meet the ridge and valley lines at a 90° angle.

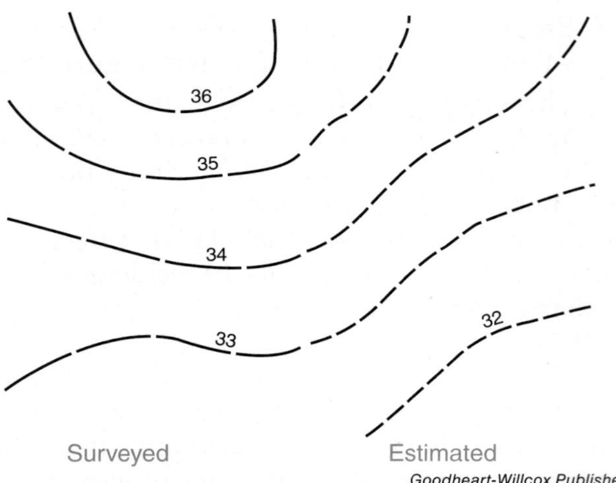

Goodheart-Willcox Publisher

Figure 16-12. Surveyed contours are represented by thin lines about 1″ or 2″ long. Estimated contours are shown with a dashed line.

	A	B	C	D	E	F
1	15.5	14.8	14.0	13.4	13.2	12.7
2	15.0	14.0	13.4	13.0	12.5	12.0
3	14.6	13.7	14.7	12.0	11.7	11.0
4	14.3	13.6	12.5	11.5	10.8	10.3
5	14.2	13.5	12.2	11.0	10.0	10.5

Goodheart-Willcox Publisher

Figure 16-13. The contour lines, shown in color, were plotted from an elevation grid using data supplied by a surveyor.

lines. For example, the grid intersections at points B-2 and C-1 represent the elevation 14.0′. Additional points are obtained by analyzing differences in elevation and locating approximate points at proportional distances between adjacent grid elevations.

Topographical Features

Topographical features include trees, shrubs, streams, roads, utilities, fences, and similar features. These features are represented on a site plan by symbols. When possible, use standard symbols that are easily recognizable. If you must use a nonstandard symbol, identify it in a legend on the drawing.

Figure 16-14 shows some of the more common topographical symbols. In some topographical drawings, color plays an important role. See **Figure 16-15**. When color is used, follow these guidelines:

- Black is used for lettering and human-built works, such as roads, houses, utilities, and other structures.

Employability

Lifelong Learning

In any architectural career—or any other type of career, for that matter—you will be expected to keep pace with the changes in your field. Continually updating your knowledge and skills is known as *lifelong learning*. The term implies that your need for learning will never end. You cannot assume that the skills you have will be all you ever need during your career. New technology and other advances mean you must continue to learn to keep up with changes in the field.

Employers usually provide some training or incentives to pursue training. In fact, some companies offer tuition reimbursement plans. However, employees are often expected to use time outside the job to stay up-to-date in their field of expertise. People who enjoy their work will view lifelong learning as an exciting challenge.

Activity

Conduct research to find out about lifelong learning opportunities offered by three major employers in your area. Also research the learning opportunities provided by organizations such as the American Institute of Architects. Prepare a table to compare the opportunities from all of these sources.

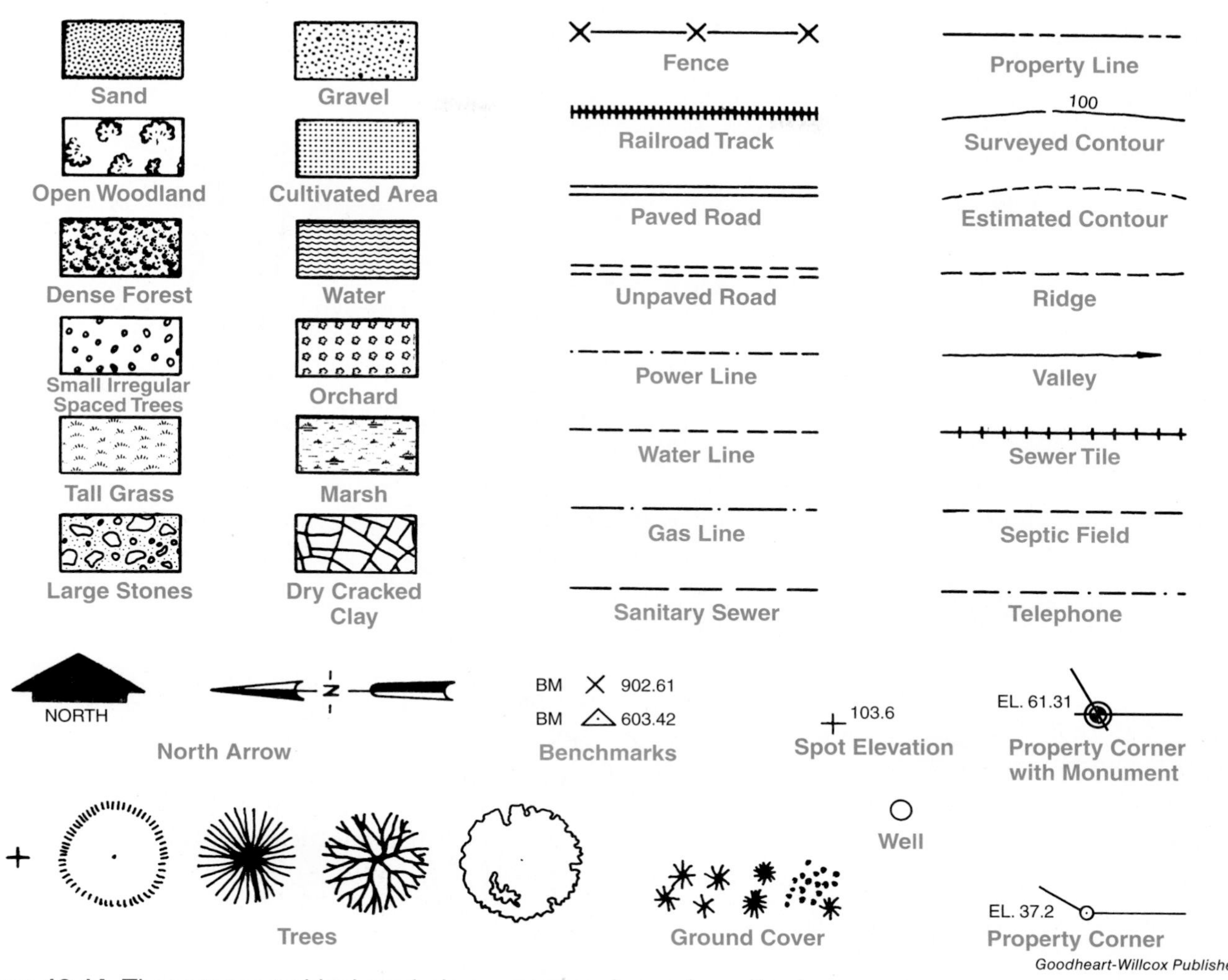

Figure 16-14. These topographical symbols are commonly used on site plans.

- Brown represents all land forms, such as contour lines.
- Blue is used for water features, such as streams, lakes, marshes, and ponds.
- Green is used for vegetation.

Location of the Structure on the Site

A complete analysis should be made of the site to determine the ideal location for the home. The analysis should include factors such as natural contour, trees, view, surrounding houses, code restrictions, style of house to be built, solar orientation, winds, placement of well and septic system, and size and shape of the site. Not all of these factors will apply in every situation, but they should be examined to determine their importance.

Once a specific location is decided on, the structure is drawn on the site plan. There are three commonly accepted methods of representing the house on the site plan. The first method is to lay out the outside of the exterior walls, omitting all interior walls and roof. Shade or crosshatch the area covered by the house, as shown in **Figure 16-16A**. The second method is to draw the exterior walls as hidden lines and show the roof using solid lines, as you would on a typical roof plan. See **Figure 16-16B**. The third method shows exterior walls thickened, as shown in **Figure 16-16C**. Again, all interior walls, windows, and doors are omitted.

The location of the house on the site must be dimensioned. The standard procedure is to

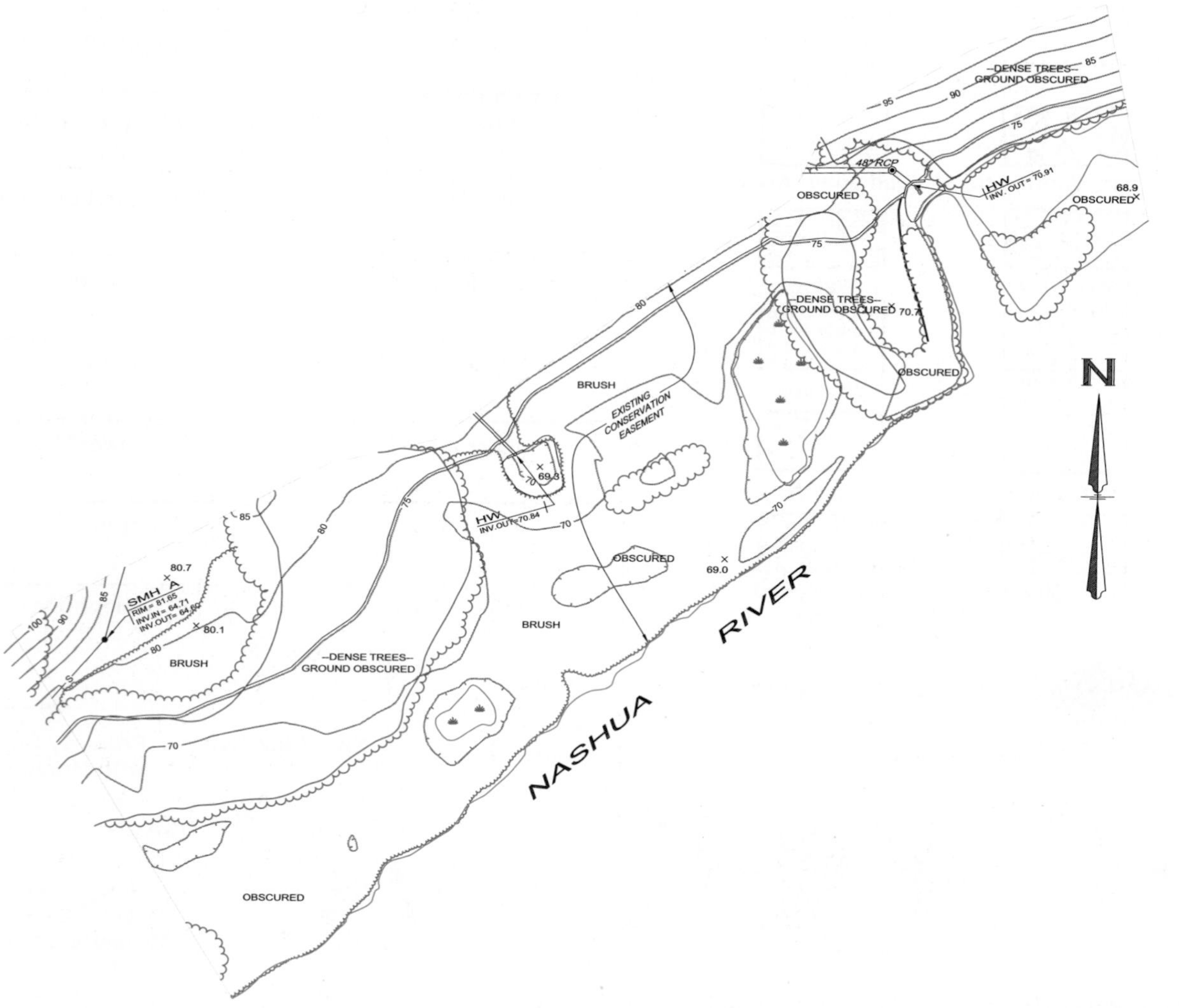

Goodheart-Willcox Publisher

Figure 16-15. Maps and some other types of topographical drawings use colors in specific ways to make the drawing more easily readable.

Green Architecture

Re-Using Existing Vegetation

As you plan where on a piece of property to place a house, be sure to consider the existing vegetation. This includes trees, bushes, and other growing things on the property. Building around existing trees is a good way to make a site more sustainable. At the same time, you can save the client money that might otherwise be needed to purchase new trees and shrubs. Also, keeping mature trees in their original location and designing the home around them can have a pleasing aesthetic value because the structure will be designed to work with the natural surroundings.

If it is not possible to work around one or more trees, consider relocating them to another place on the property. Even mature trees can be moved successfully. Always work with a reliable landscaping or tree service. These professionals know what precautions are needed to prevent damage to the trees or the surrounding structures and nearby equipment, such as electrical or telephone wires.

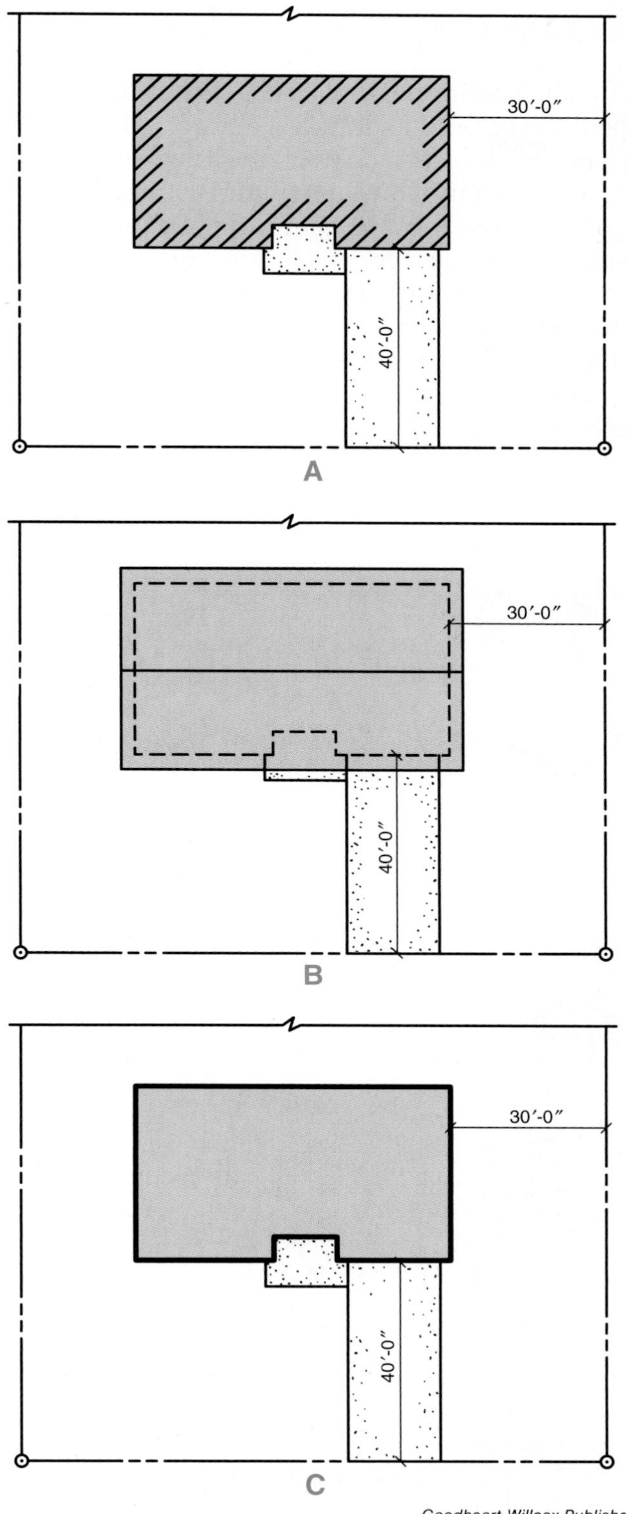

Goodheart-Willcox Publisher

Figure 16-16. The size and location of a house are represented on a site plan in one of three ways. A—Shading or crosshatching the area covered by the house. The roof is not included. B—Using a roof plan. Exterior walls are represented as hidden lines. C—Using thickened exterior walls.

dimension the distance of one corner of the house from adjacent lot lines, as shown in **Figure 16-16**. In some instances, this is not sufficient to clearly locate the structure. **Figure 16-17** shows how to dimension the placement of a home that is not parallel to the property lines. In each instance, dimension the distance from the outside of the exterior wall, or from the roof if this location is critical, to the property line. If required, show the roof overhang distance, too.

The Landscaping Plan

The purpose of the landscaping plan is to show the type and placement of trees, shrubs, flowers, gardens, and pools to be added on the site. It provides an excellent way to plan the total setting for the home. A landscaping plan is not always required, but may be completed even when it is not required.

Much of the information presented on the site plan is also shown on the landscaping plan. The boundary lines, north arrow, outline of the house, driveway, walks, patios, and contour lines are needed to place the landscape elements into their proper perspective. Symbols are used to represent various types of plants. However,

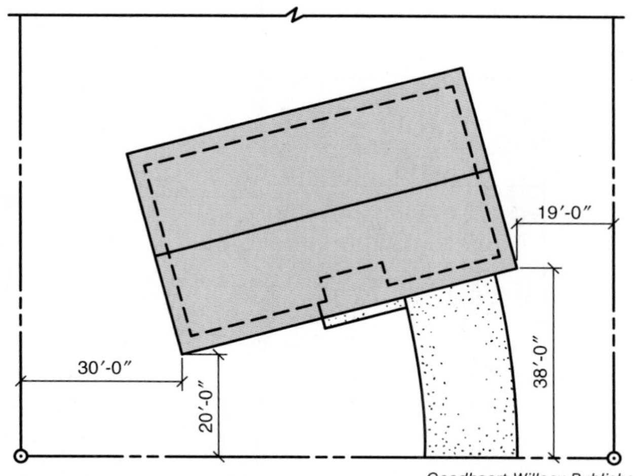

Goodheart-Willcox Publisher

Figure 16-17. A house that is not positioned parallel to the property lines may require more than two dimensions to locate it properly on the site. A bearing line could also be used to show the position of the house.

there are more types of ornamental plants in the world than you can practically have symbols to use. Therefore, the same symbol is often used for different types of plants. These symbols are then keyed to a chart or schedule to avoid confusion.

Figure 16-18 shows a typical landscaping plan. Notice that the drafter has used letters keyed to a landscaping schedule to identify the individual plants. When practical, the plant symbols should be drawn to proper scale. This produces a realistic idea of the components on the plan.

Drawing a Site Plan

The traditional and CADD procedures given here can be used to draw a site plan or landscaping plan. However, drawing a site plan is more complex than drawing a landscaping plan. If you are drawing a landscaping plan, ignore any steps not needed for the landscaping plan.

To draw a site plan accurately, you may first need to conduct research to find any survey data that has been collected for the area. This can greatly simplify the process of drawing accurate contour lines and locating any topographical

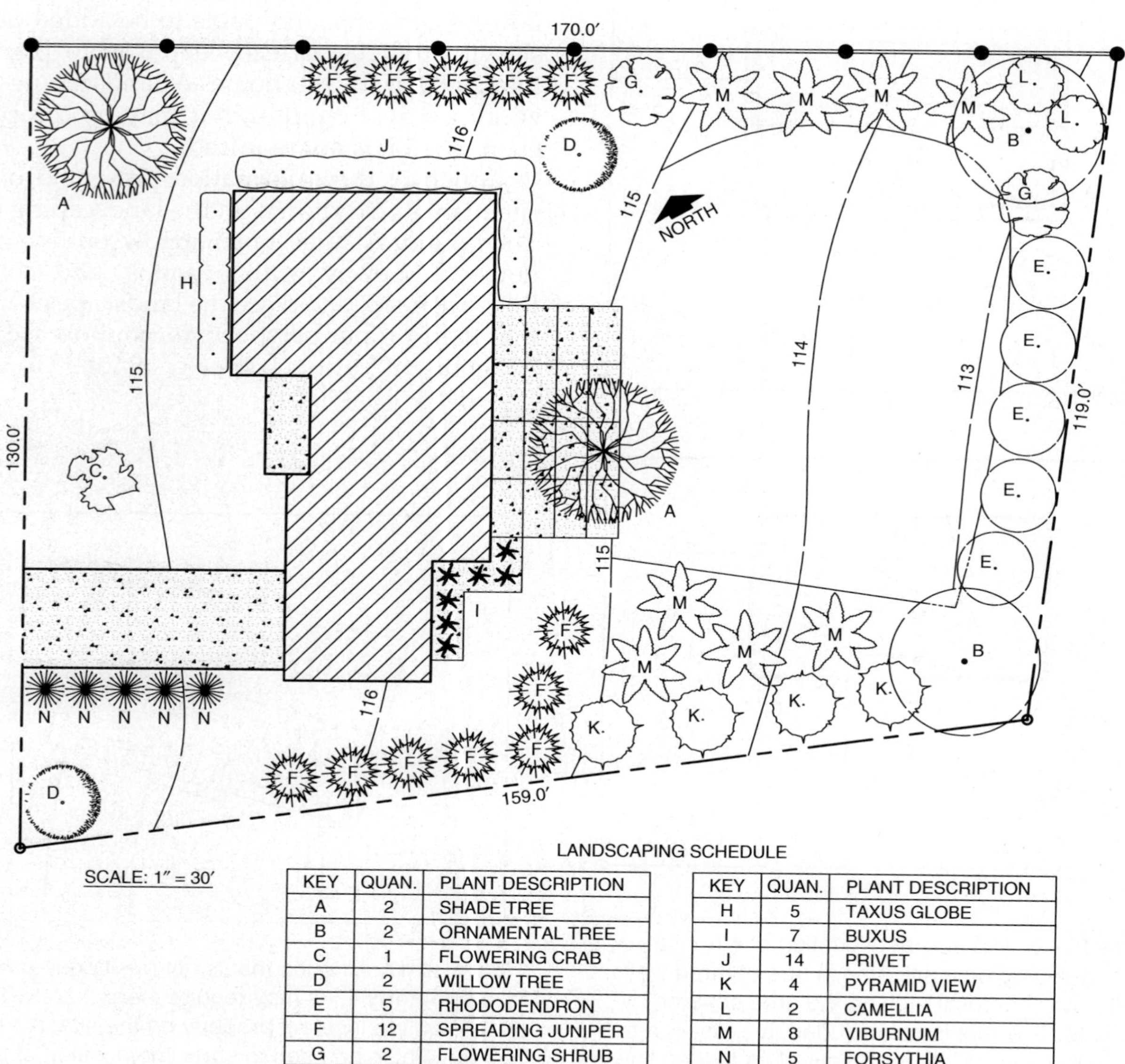

LANDSCAPING SCHEDULE

KEY	QUAN.	PLANT DESCRIPTION
A	2	SHADE TREE
B	2	ORNAMENTAL TREE
C	1	FLOWERING CRAB
D	2	WILLOW TREE
E	5	RHODODENDRON
F	12	SPREADING JUNIPER
G	2	FLOWERING SHRUB

KEY	QUAN.	PLANT DESCRIPTION
H	5	TAXUS GLOBE
I	7	BUXUS
J	14	PRIVET
K	4	PYRAMID VIEW
L	2	CAMELLIA
M	8	VIBURNUM
N	5	FORSYTHIA

Goodheart-Willcox Publisher

Figure 16-18. This is a typical landscaping plan that shows the type and location of trees and shrubs on the property.

features. If no survey data is available, in some cases it is acceptable to estimate these items. Be aware, however, that the accuracy of the site plan can affect the entire building project. If the contour of the site is to be changed, accuracy is critical.

Procedure Manual Drafting

Drawing a Site Plan

The following steps are recommended for drawing a site plan using traditional or manual drafting techniques. Omit any steps or items that do not apply to your situation.

1. Select a scale that provides the largest drawing on the paper size that you have chosen. All of the sheets in a set of drawings should be the same size for ease of handling. The property lines should be placed sufficiently inside the border to provide room for adding dimensions, notes, and a title block. Scales commonly used for site plans range from 1/8″ = 1′-0″ to 1″ = 30′-0″ and smaller.
2. Lay out the property lines using data supplied by the surveyor or other source. Be extremely careful in this step to ensure an accurate drawing. Steps 2 through 7 are illustrated in **Figure 16-19**.
3. Letter the bearing and length of each property line. Letter the scale near the bottom of the drawing.
4. Some communities require setbacks from the property lines. ***Setbacks*** are boundaries that establish minimum distances from the property lines where structures cannot be located. Setbacks are designated to prevent a building from being constructed too close to a property line. On

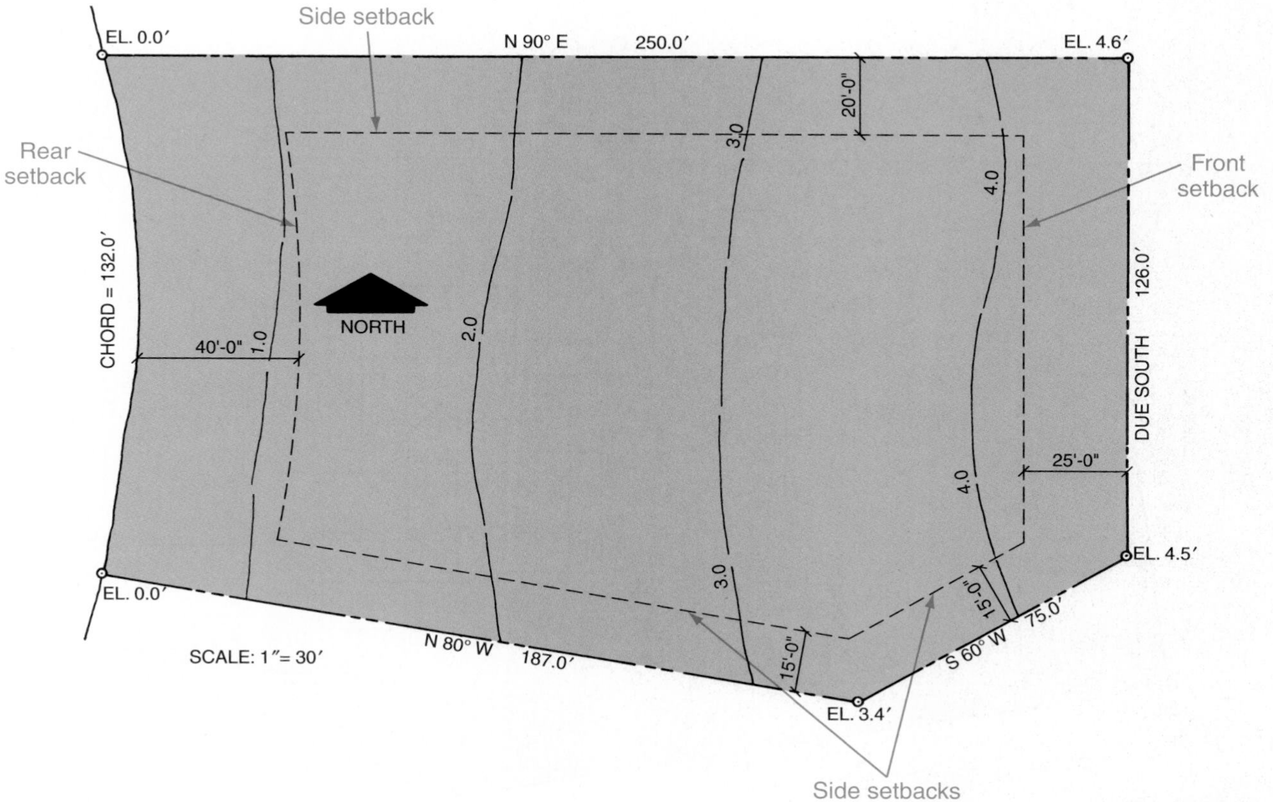

Goodheart-Willcox Publisher

Figure 16-19. This is a partially complete site plan. The property lines and setbacks have been located. The north arrow, drawing scale, contour lines, and corner elevations have also been added.

the site plan, setbacks are drawn parallel to the property lines using hidden lines. If setbacks are required by the local building code, make sure the proposed structure does not fall within the setback area. In **Figure 16-19**, there are 25′ and 40′ setbacks for the east and west ends of the property and 20′ and 15′ setbacks for the north and south.

5. Locate the north arrow in a place on the drawing where it will be easy to see, yet not interfere with the drawing.
6. Select a contour interval that is appropriate for this plan and plot the contour lines. Draw the lines lightly at this point.
7. Letter the elevation of each contour line and property corner.
8. Locate the house on the site. Steps 8 through 10 are shown in **Figure 16-20**.
9. Dimension the distance from the house to two adjacent property lines. The elevation of a reference corner of the house is sometimes given.
10. Draw surrounding features such as the driveway, sidewalks, and patios. The size and elevation may be given for each if required.
11. Determine the centerline of the street and location of utilities. Draw these features using the correct linetypes, and dimension their location. If a well and septic system are required, draw them at this point. Steps 11 through 14 are illustrated in **Figure 16-21**.
12. Draw other topographical features, such as trees and shrubs. Darken in all light contour lines at this point.
13. If you are drawing a landscaping plan, place the plants, garden areas, and other site improvements at this time.
14. Check your drawing to be sure you have included all necessary elements.

Figure 16-22 shows a typical site plan for a larger home site. The house has its own septic system and well. Notice the symbols and methods used to indicate these features.

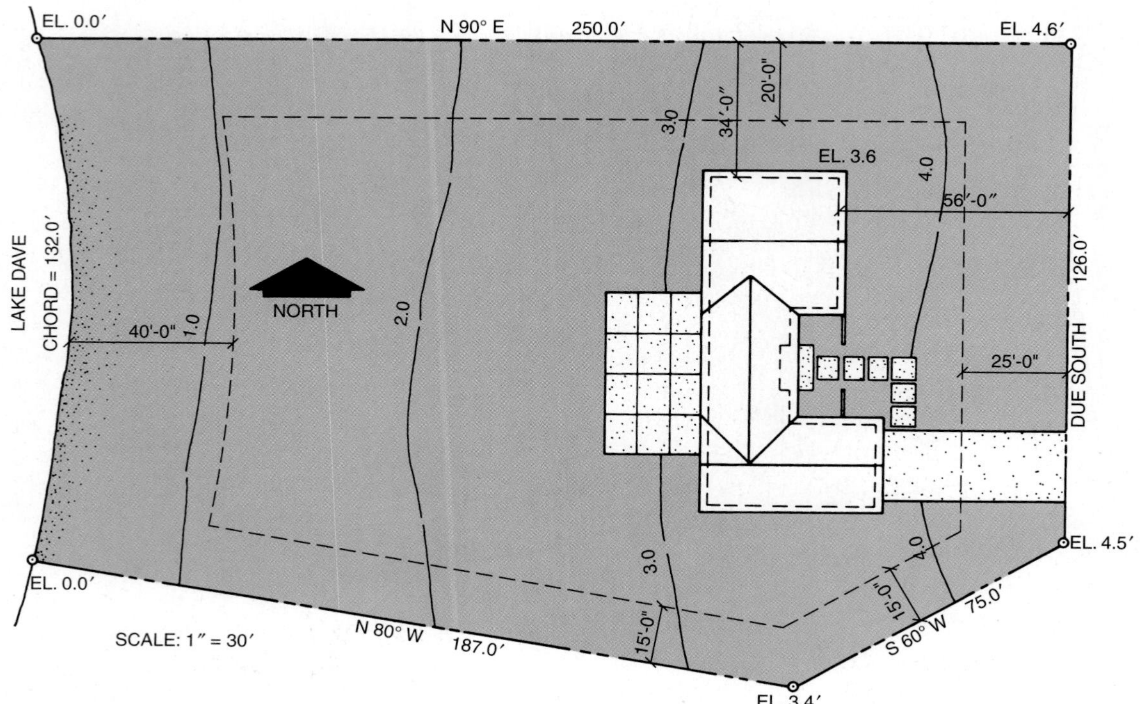

Figure 16-20. The house, drive, and patio are drawn on the plan and dimensions are added.

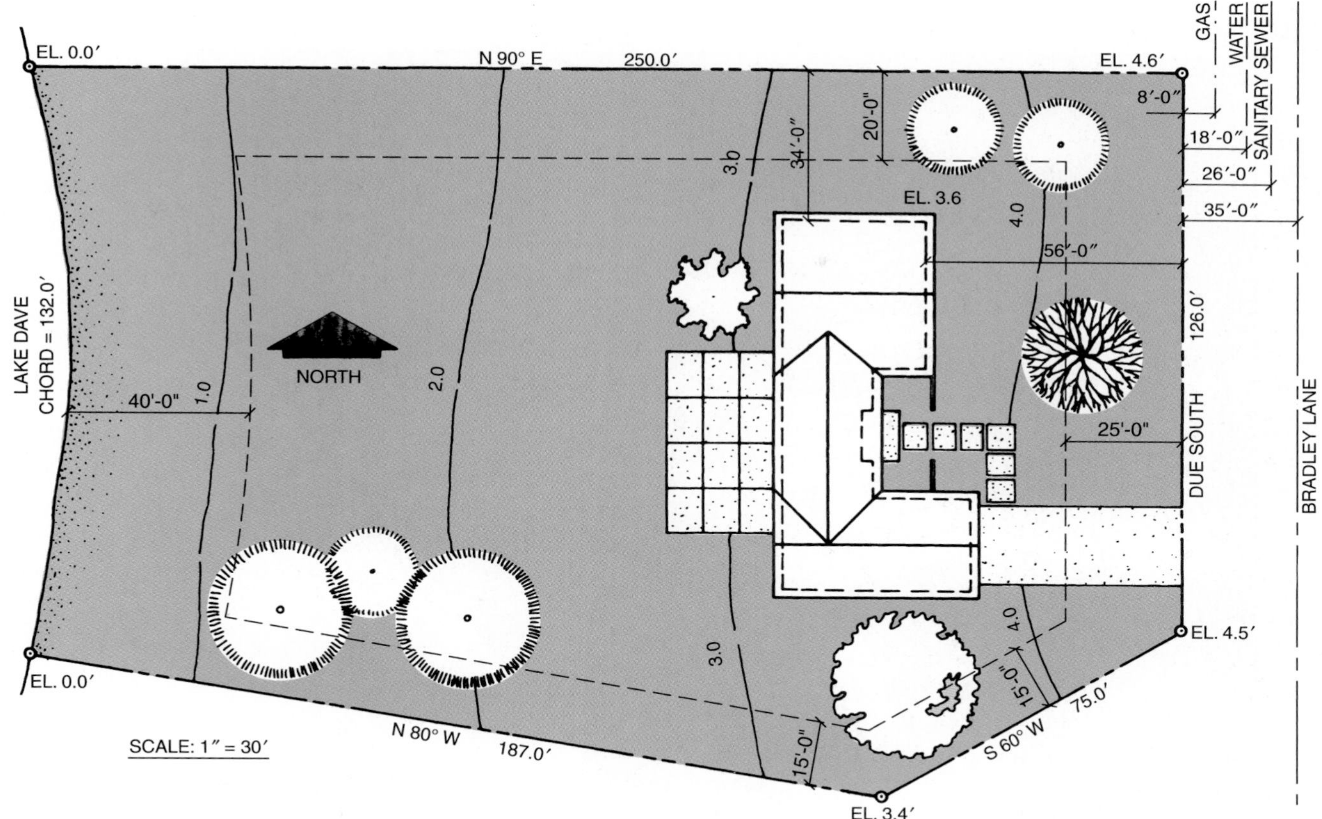

Goodheart-Willcox Publisher

Figure 16-21. This is a completed site plan showing the property lines, setbacks, house location, north arrow, topographical features, centerline of the street, and utilities.

Procedure
CADD

Drawing a Site Plan

A site plan can be drawn with almost any CADD package. However, software programs designed specifically for this purpose are available. These packages greatly facilitate drawing property lines and contour lines using standard data provided by surveyors. Compatibility is always a concern when two or more packages are to be used together. Be sure that your basic CADD package supports any specific-use software that you purchase.

This procedure assumes that you are using a basic CADD package, rather than special-purpose software, to develop the plan. Use the following steps to draw a site plan or landscaping plan using CADD. Draw all objects at their full size. If you are drawing the plan in the same file as the other drawings in an architectural set of drawings, place the plan on its own set of layers.

1. Determine the final plot (print) scale before you begin. When setting up the drawing to plot, select a plot scale that will provide the largest drawing on the size of paper that you have chosen for the set of drawings. Scales commonly used in drawing site plans range from 1/8″ = 1′-0″ to 1″ = 30′-0″ and smaller. The scale should be noted on the plan and used to determine the proper lettering height for notes and dimensions.
2. Lay out the property lines using proper linetypes and symbols. Draw the property lines on their own layer because the linetype is unique. Start at the reference corner, if there is one, and lay out each line in a clockwise manner until you reach the starting point.

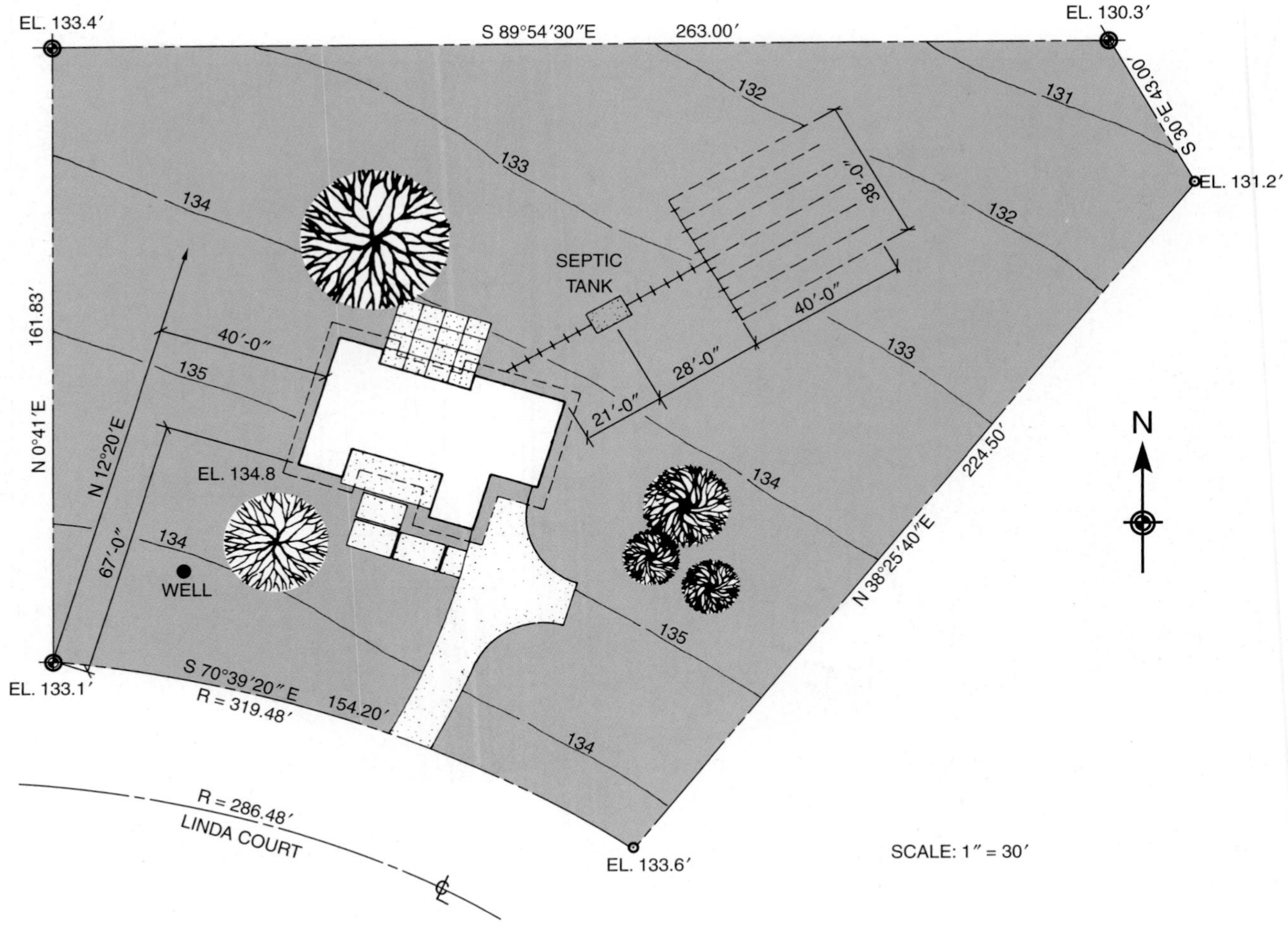

Figure 16-22. A site plan for a house that has a septic system and well.

3. Locate the building(s) on the site. Be careful to position the buildings according to code. Locate setbacks from the property lines if required. The driveway, patios, walks, and other flatwork may also be located at this time. Add property corner elevations. Place the building perimeter, drive, and walks on a single layer of their own. See **Figure 16-23**.
4. Choose an appropriate contour interval for the site. Draw the contour lines on their own layer. If you have survey data, plot the points on your drawing and connect them using the CADD software's spline command. Alternatively, if your CADD software has a "freehand" function, use it to draw the contour lines. Label the elevation of each contour line. Steps 4 through 6 are shown in **Figure 16-24**.
5. Select a reference corner for the house to locate the house properly on the site with respect to the grade. Locate the corner relative to a property corner or two property lines that form a right angle. Label the reference corner and provide its elevation. Add the dimensions on their own layer.
6. Draw additional features of the house, such as roof lines. Long dashed lines are appropriate for the roof line. Place the roof line on a separate layer.
7. Add other topographical features, such as trees, streams, and right-of-ways. Choose appropriate layers for these features. Use symbols from the symbol library or design your own symbols. If you design your

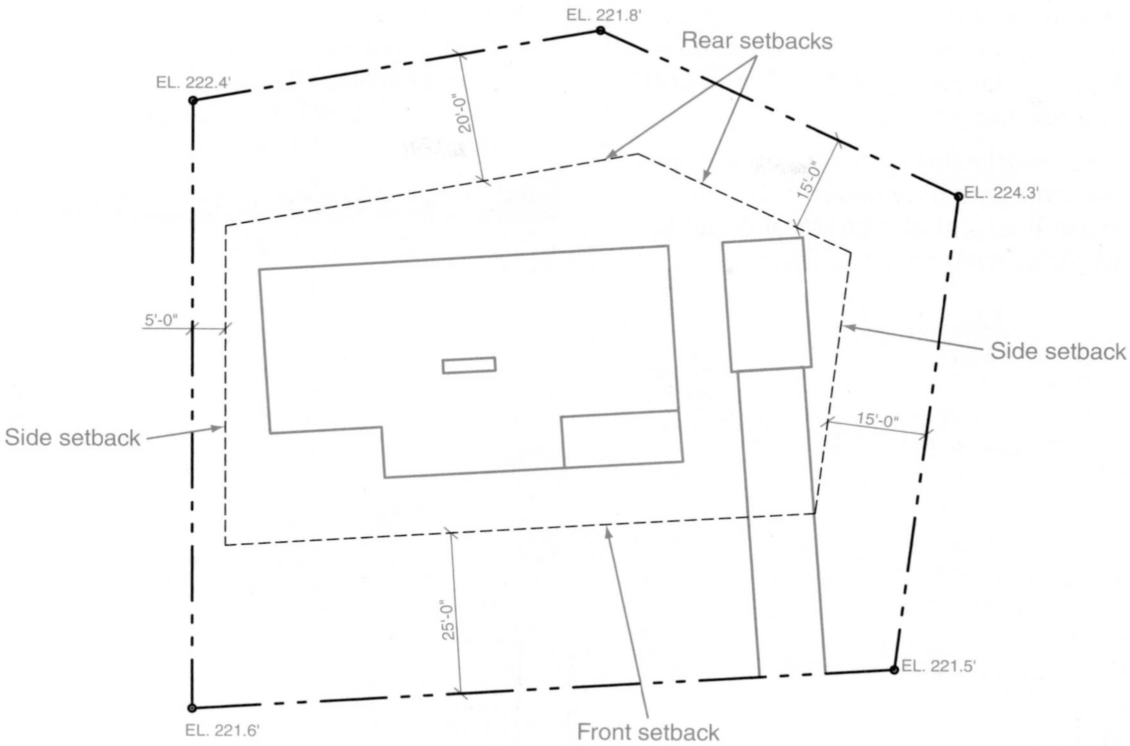

EL. 221.8'
Rear setbacks
EL. 222.4'
20'-0"
15'-0"
EL. 224.3'
5'-0"
Side setback
Side setback
15'-0"
25'-0"
EL. 221.5'
EL. 221.6'
Front setback

Goodheart-Willcox Publisher

Figure 16-23. Begin the site plan by drawing the property lines, setbacks, and structures.

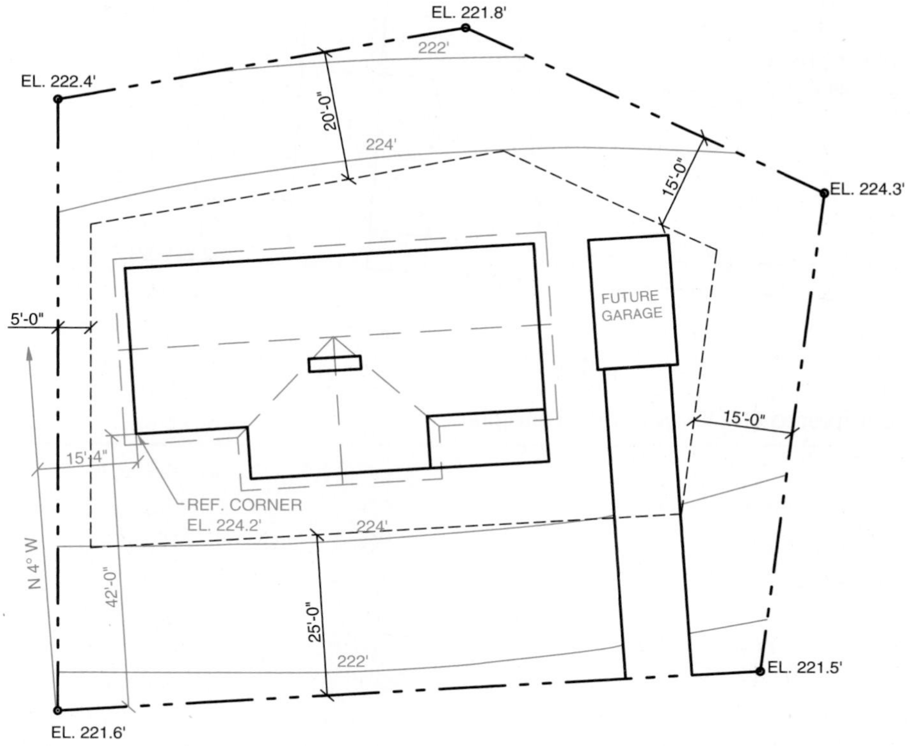

EL. 221.8'
222'
EL. 222.4'
20'-0"
224'
15'-0"
EL. 224.3'
FUTURE
GARAGE
5'-0"
15'-0"
15'-4"
REF. CORNER
EL. 224.2'
224'
N 4° W
42'-0"
25'-0"
222'
EL. 221.5'
EL. 221.6'

Goodheart-Willcox Publisher

Figure 16-24. The contour lines, roof line, and reference corner location dimensions have been added to the site plan.

own, you may want to update your symbol library for future use. If you are creating a landscaping plan, add the new plants and other landscaping features.

8. Include property line data and a north arrow. Property line data may be added to the drawing in the form of a chart, or it can be placed along each property line.
9. Add the scale, title, utilities, septic tank and field, lot number, and well. All site plans should include the scale and title. Add the other items as needed. **Figure 16-25** shows the completed site plan.

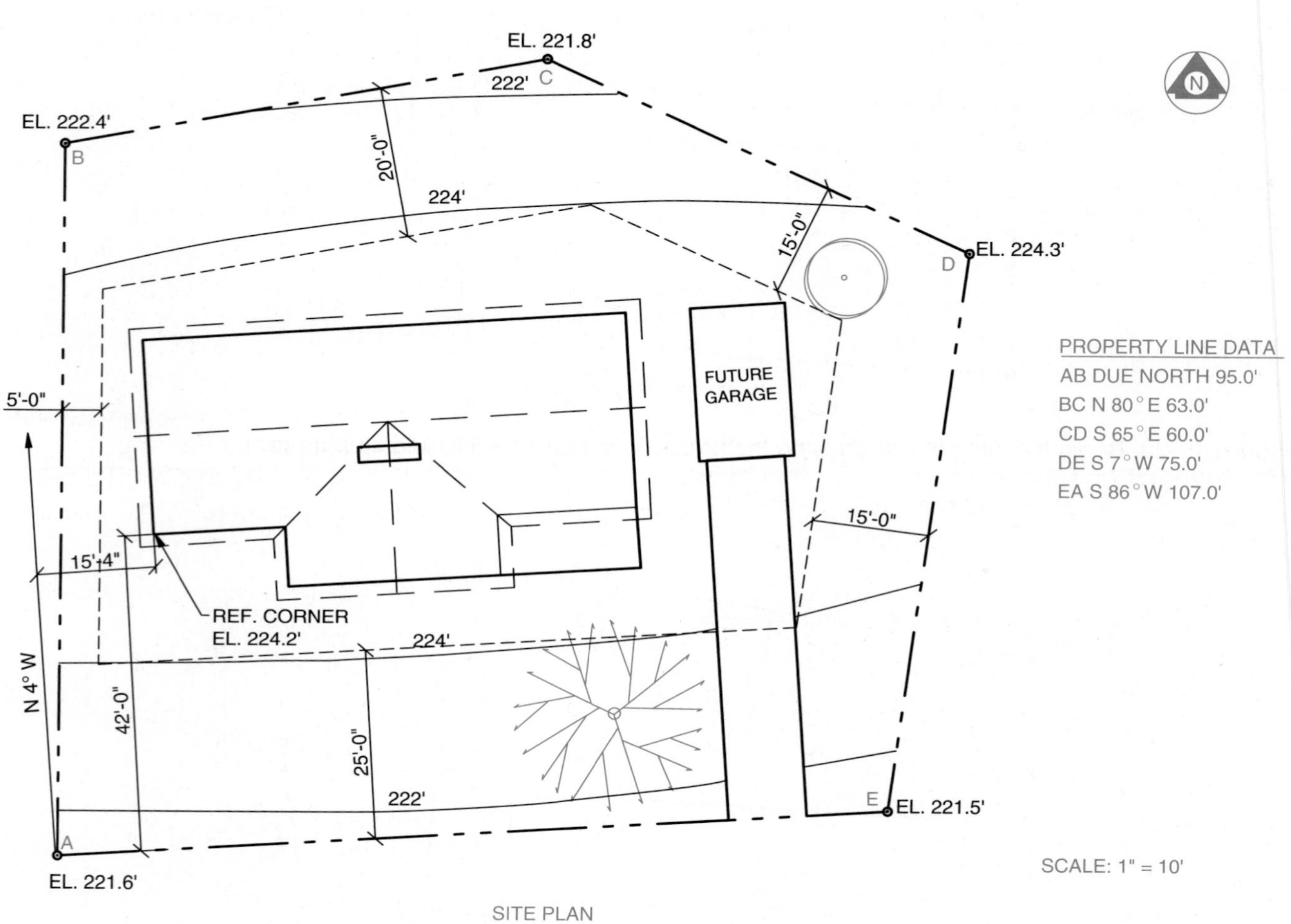

Goodheart-Willcox Publisher

Figure 16-25. The completed CADD-generated site plan.

Parametric Modeling | Creating a Site Plan

Parametric modeling programs used in architectural design provide specific tools for creating a site plan. These tools make it possible to work from survey data and create a site plan that shows contour lines, property lines, and topographical features. However, creating a site plan in a parametric modeling program involves different processes in comparison to those used in a basic CADD system. The main difference is that the actual site is modeled in 3D and represents the physical characteristics and contours of the land. The site component in a parametric model is called a ***topographical surface***. After adding a topographical surface to the model, the building and the surrounding land can be displayed in a 3D view to evaluate the entire design. Often, this type of view is rendered for presentation purposes. See **Figure 16-26**. As with other views in the model, a 2D view of the site plan can be prepared for the construction drawings.

Depending on the program used, a default site plan view is typically available for modeling the site when the project is created from a default template. The following procedure describes the steps for creating a site plan and is designed for a one-story home with a basement. This is a typical sequence, but specific steps will vary depending on the program used.

1. Open the site plan view and create the topographical surface for the model. Access the **TOPOSURFACE** command to create a topographical surface. The default command option is used to pick points defining elevations along the surface. Use survey measurements to establish each point location. The points picked are used by the program to triangulate faces defining the topographical surface. After completing the command, the resulting object has contour

Anthony J. Panozzo

Figure 16-26. This site plan shows the surrounding topography of a proposed home design and was rendered for presentation purposes.

Parametric Modeling Creating a Site Plan *(Continued)*

lines connecting points with the same elevation. If needed, edit the topographical surface by adding points or adjusting the elevations of existing points. The more points used, the more accurate the results. If needed, adjust the contour interval of the topographical surface to change the spacing between contour lines.

Another way to create a topographical surface is to import a site plan drawing or model from another CADD program. Some architectural drafters prefer to import a drawing or model prepared by a civil engineer because it represents accurate design data. When importing a site plan drawing file from another CADD program, the drawing should be prepared for this specific purpose. For best results, each contour line in the drawing is assigned an elevation value defining a Z axis height. In addition, a base point is recorded in the drawing to serve as a location reference. The XYZ coordinates of the base point are used to establish a survey point in the parametric model. Additional setup steps in the parametric model file may be necessary, such as orienting the north direction of the site. Once the model has been configured appropriately, import the drawing and use the **TOPOSURFACE** command to create the topographical surface. Access the appropriate command option and select the imported file. The topographical surface is generated by the program from the contour lines in the imported drawing.

2. Adjust the topographical surface if part of it passes into the structure and needs to be removed. This can typically be accomplished by creating a building pad. A building pad establishes a footprint that determines where material is "cut" out of the model. Typically, a building pad is created by sketching a boundary around the building perimeter. Make the sketch in the appropriate plan view, such as the Basement Floor plan view, so that the top of the building pad is located at the appropriate elevation. Access the appropriate command and sketch a boundary by picking the foundation wall lines. Ensure that the sketch forms a closed boundary before completing the command. Switch to a 3D view or a section view to verify that the topographical surface passes around the exterior walls and below the building.
3. Modify the material properties of the topographical surface to create the appropriate appearance. For example, change the surface material to an appropriate material, such as grass. Set the hatch pattern used to represent the material in a section view to an earth pattern.
4. Place additional elements to define the features of the site plan. Add property lines using the appropriate command. There are typically two ways to create property lines. One method is to specify the length and bearing of each line in a table. Another method is to sketch the lines. This method can be used to trace over property lines in an imported survey drawing. Setbacks can be created in similar fashion. For example, create the setback lines by drawing property lines and editing the lines to use a hidden linetype.
5. Add features such as the driveway, sidewalks, and other flatwork. This can typically be accomplished by defining areas on the topographical surface that use a different material from the site's surface material. These areas, called subregions, are used to "subdivide" the topographical surface. To create a subregion, access the appropriate command and make a sketch using standard sketch tools. Then, change the material property of the subregion to the appropriate material. For example, assign a concrete or asphalt material to a subregion used to represent a driveway.

6. Add topographical features by inserting the appropriate components. Add features such as trees, bushes, and plants. Typically, a library of items is available in the program to create these features. Place components by picking points on the topographical surface. The components are oriented based on the contour of the land.
7. Determine if it is necessary to add more features to show certain details. Some elements of the site plan can be added using view-specific 2D detail lines or detail components. These elements do not appear in other views in the model. Items such as utility lines and curbs can be added in this manner.
8. Add dimensions and other text as needed to complete the site plan. Label contour lines to identify elevations and tag property lines to show bearings and distances. Set the view scale of the site plan to the appropriate scale for plotting annotations.
9. Create a new sheet for the site plan. Insert the site plan view onto the sheet. If needed, adjust the placement of text for the view title and scale.
10. Look over your work to be sure that you are finished. When you are sure the plan is complete, print or plot the sheet.

Summary

- A site plan shows the contours of the building site and the location and orientation of proposed new construction on the property.
- Property lines define the site boundaries.
- A benchmark is a permanent object used by surveyors to establish points of reference.
- Contour lines help describe the topography of a site by depicting shape and elevation of the land.
- Some sets of architectural plans have landscaping plans to show the placement of new trees, shrubs, flowers, gardens, and pools.

Internet Resources

Autodesk
Publisher of AutoCAD® and Revit® software

Bobcat
Supplier of construction equipment

CAD Depot
Landscaping symbols and other CADD information

Caterpillar
Supplier of heavy equipment for construction

US Environmental Protection Agency (EPA)
Information about environmental effects of modifying land contours

Review Questions

Answer the following questions using the information in this chapter.

1. What is a *site plan*?
2. Explain the purpose of the north arrow.
3. What information is included with the property lines on a site plan?
4. Briefly describe the process of drawing property lines for a site.
5. What type of line on a site plan connects points of the same elevation?
6. How are estimated contours represented on a site plan?
7. What four colors are commonly used on topographical drawings, and for what is each color used?
8. List at least five factors that should be analyzed to help determine the ideal location for a house on a site.
9. Describe the standard procedure for dimensioning the location of the house on the site.
10. What type of plan shows the type and placement of trees, shrubs, flowers, gardens, and pools to be added to a building site?
11. How are various types of plants distinguished on a landscaping plan?
12. If you are using a single CADD drawing for all of the plans in a set of working drawings, how should you organize the items to be included on the site plan?

Suggested Activities

1. Select a vacant site in your community that is suitable for a home. Measure the site, determine north with a compass, and draw a site plan of the property using CADD. Show any trees or other features that may be on the site and indicate approximate contour lines.
2. Select a floor plan of a house from a newspaper, magazine, or other source that is appropriate for the site you drew in Activity 1. Locate the house on the site. Add the appropriate dimensions.
3. Compile a list of 15 ornamental trees and shrubs that grow in your area. Describe the mature size and characteristics of each. Develop a plan view symbol for each one and add the symbols to your symbol library for future use.
4. Using the site plan you developed in Activity 2 and the symbols you created in Activity 3, draw a landscaping plan for the property.

Problem Solving Case Study

You have been asked to create a landscaping plan for the home shown in **Figure A**. The basic footprint of the house is 40′ wide by 20′ deep, and it sits parallel with the edges of the rectangular 96′ by 64′ building lot. The front right corner of the house is 28′ from the right property line and 23′ from the front property line. The land slopes evenly from back to front across the width of the property. The elevation at the back property line is 146′, and the elevation at the front property line is 132′. A 12′-wide driveway will run from the front of the property to the right side of the house. The house is located on the outskirts of Muncie, Indiana.

Given this information, create a landscaping plan for the house. Be sure to specify plants that are native to the area. Keep the contour of the site in mind and develop a plan that will reduce water runoff.

ADDA Certification Prep

The following questions are presented in the style used in the American Design Drafting Association (ADDA) Drafter Certification Test. Answer the questions using the information in this chapter.

1. Which of the following statements are true about site plans?
   A. Site plans are also known as elevation drawings.
   B. Site plans contain contour lines.
   C. Site plans are section drawings.
   D. Site plans show proposed new construction on the property.
2. Which of the following items in a set of architectural working drawings are developed from the site plan?
   A. Plumbing plan
   B. Electrical plan
   C. Landscaping plan
   D. Roof plan

Figure A *whitehoune/Shutterstock.com*

3. Match each feature with the plan that contains it. *Note:* Some items may be contained on more than one plan.

   Plans: 1. Site plan, 2. Landscaping plan

   A. Contour lines
   B. New septic system
   C. Existing septic system
   D. New plantings
   E. Topographical features such as a stream or pond

STEM Connections

1. **Engineering.** The United States contains numerous soil types. Research at least five different soil types that occur in your area. Find out their chemical makeup and their ability to support structures such as houses. Compose a report explaining how these soil types affect the building code requirements in your area. Explain what, if anything, would need to be done to the soil before building a home on it.
2. **Technology.** Several computer programs now exist for modeling water runoff given a specific soil type, slope, and type and amount of vegetation on a site. Conduct research to find out more about these programs. Then prepare a multimedia report on how technology can help architects and landscape designers improve a building site. Also describe the potential effects of these efforts on sustainability.
3. **Science.** Conduct research to find out the methods surveyors use to determine the exact elevation of a specific point on a piece of property. In general, surveyors base their elevations on mean sea level. How do they know how far above sea level a piece of property is located if the property is nowhere near any coastline? Prepare a 3-minute oral presentation of your findings.

Communicating about Architecture

1. **Reading.** With a partner, make flash cards of the chapter terms. On the front of the card, write the term. On the back, write the phonetic spelling. (You may also choose to use a dictionary.) Practice reading aloud the terms, clarifying pronunciations where needed.
2. **Speaking.** Select five of the key terms in this chapter and imagine them being used by architects in a real-life context. With a partner, role-play a situation in which an architectural firm is asked to draw a site plan for a new home.

Chapter 17

Roof Designs

Objectives

After completing this chapter, you will be able to:

- Identify and sketch 12 different types of basic roof designs.
- Draw a roof that has a typical roof slope.
- Describe the construction of a typical frame roof.
- Explain the importance of proper attic ventilation and roof flashing.
- Compare the advantages and disadvantages of different roofing materials.
- Explain the purpose of a roof plan.

Key Terms

box cornice	plumb cut
clear span	rafter
close cornice	rake
cornice	rise
downspout	roof framing plan
flashing	roof pitch
free-form roof	roof plan
gable end	roof sheathing
gusset	roof slope
gutter	roof truss
lookout	run
open cornice	warped roof

Types of Roofs

The overall appearance of a home is greatly affected by the roof lines and materials used for roof construction. See **Figure 17-1**. The designer has many standard styles from which to choose. The chosen style should complement the basic design of the home being constructed. **Figure 17-2** shows several roof types used in residential construction. These types are discussed in the following sections.

Gable Roof

The gable roof is a triangular roof with a gable at each end. This type of roof is easy to build, sheds water well, provides for ventilation, and can be applied to a variety of house shapes and designs.

Winged Gable Roof

The winged gable roof is essentially a gable roof extended at the peak. Lookout rafters are necessary to provide support for the increased overhang. This style of roof provides an attractive design feature on the roof.

Hip Roof

A hip roof is similar to a gable roof, but the hip roof has a sloped roof section, or hip, at the ends instead of gables. It is slightly more difficult to build than a gable roof, but it is still a popular choice. It does not provide for ventilation as well as some other roof designs.

Photo Courtesy of James Hardie® Siding Products

Figure 17-1. The architect's complex roof design and choice of roofing materials had a significant impact on the finished appearance of this residence. Notice that although the roof line is complex and two different roofing materials are used, the overall design fits the style of the house.

Dutch Hip Roof

The Dutch hip roof is basically a hip roof with a small gable at each end. The gable typically extends up at a steeper angle than the hips. These gables can provide ventilation if vents are installed. However, the vents also increase the chance of leakage.

Flat Roof

A flat roof is the most economical roof to construct, but it does not add much to the design of most houses. It requires a "built-up" or membrane roof covering rather than conventional shingles. A built-up roof consists of layers of roofing felt and tar or some other material, such as rubber topped with gravel. Actually, most so-called flat roofs are pitched at about 1/8″ to 1/2″ per foot to aid in drainage. The flat roof is popular in warmer areas of the country where wide overhangs are desirable for shade and where little or no snow falls.

Shed Roof

A shed roof is similar to a flat roof, but has more pitch. It is frequently used for additions to existing structures or in combination with other roof styles. A built-up roof is generally required unless the roof has a pitch of more than 3:12, or three feet of rise for each 12 feet of run.

Gambrel Roof

The gambrel roof is sometimes called a barn roof because it has been used extensively on barns. The roof has two different slopes. The steeper side slopes provide additional headroom in the attic or second story of a building. In residential housing, a gambrel roof is often used to make the attic usable for additional living space.

Mansard Roof

The mansard roof is a French design named after the French architect Francois Mansart. It is similar to the gambrel roof, but the space under the roof is almost always used as living space. Like the gambrel, it is more difficult to construct than the hip or gable roof.

A-Frame Roof

The A-frame roof provides not only a roof, but also the walls of the structure. Originally, it was used for cottages. However, it has also been applied to homes, churches, and other structures. The pitch of the roof generally allows for two floors, but the second floor is much smaller than the first floor and is often used as a loft.

Butterfly Roof

The butterfly roof is not widely used. From the 1950s through the early 1970s, some contemporary homes were built with a butterfly roof. However, this type of roof is now rare in new construction. A butterfly roof has the advantage of providing plenty of light and ventilation. However, drainage is a problem. Flashing should

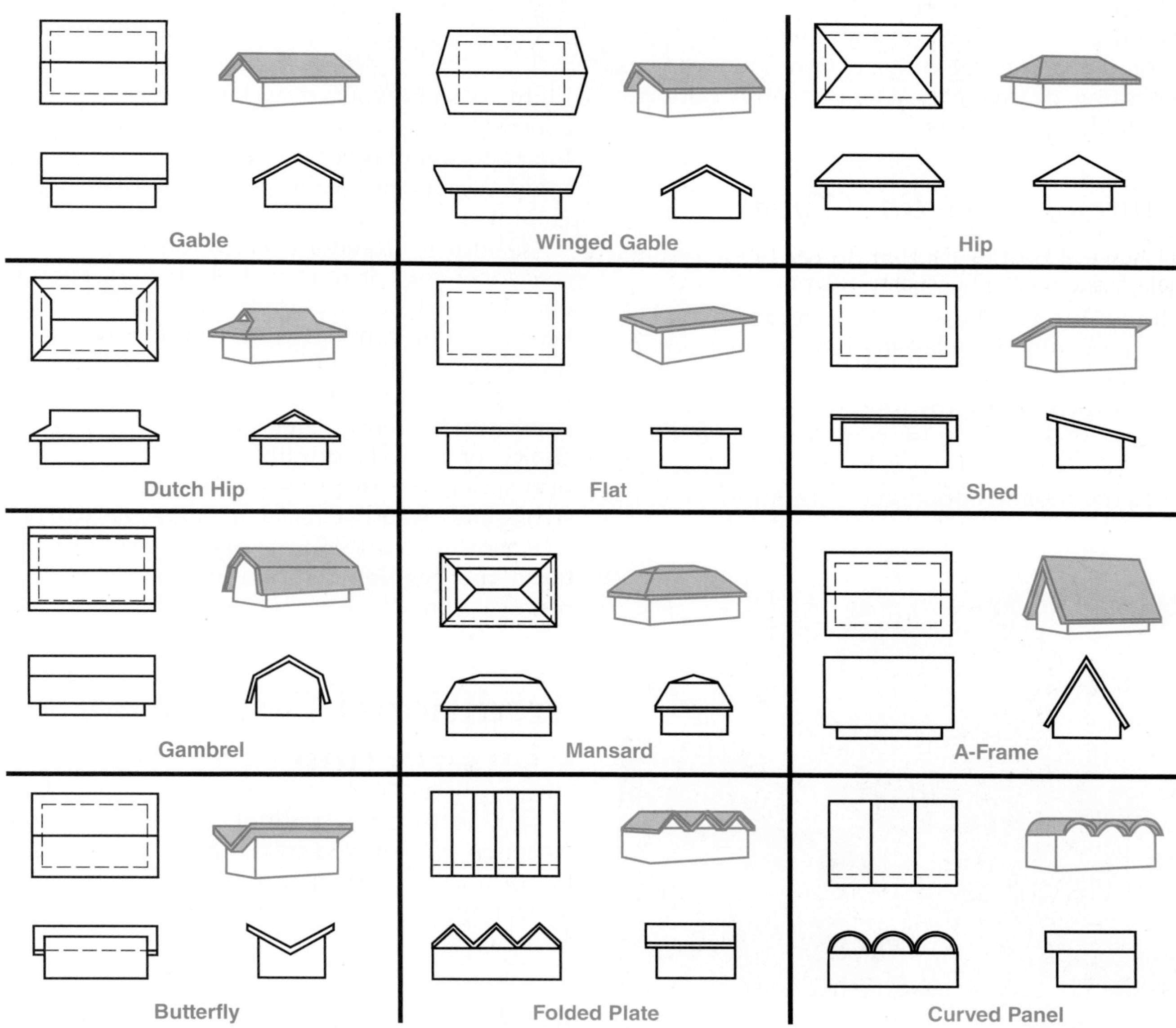

Figure 17-2. Any of these roof designs may be used in residential construction. Some designs are more popular than others.

extend far up each slope along the valley to prevent leaking.

Folded Plate Roof

The folded plate roof has limited use in single-family houses. However, it is sometimes used in small condominiums, motels, and small commercial buildings. Modular, prefabricated roof units are available. However, this roof has the same drainage problems as the butterfly roof.

Curved Panel Roof

The curved panel roof is similar to the folded plate roof in style and application. It has limited use in home construction. This roof has the same drainage problems as the butterfly and folded plate roofs.

Contemporary Roof Types

Several roof types that do not belong to the other categories have been used in recent years. Although the details of these roofs vary, they can generally be classified as contemporary styles.

Warped roofs are limitless in design. See **Figure 17-3**. The most common shape for a warped roof is a hyperbolic paraboloid, which gives the roof an appearance similar to a kite in flight. Warped roofs may be constructed from concrete, molded plywood, or plastics. Because this type of roof is very complex and expensive to build, its application for residential construction is limited.

Jorge Salcedo/Shutterstock.com

Figure 17-3. The roof of the Kresge Auditorium at MIT is an example of a warped roof. The curvature of the roof is controlled by complex mathematical formulas.

Green Architecture

Living Roofs

In many cities across the United States, "living roofs" are becoming a popular alternative to traditional roofs. A living roof is one that has been covered with soil and is capable of growing live plants. Living roofs provide many benefits. They can be used to grow food, for example. They also provide excellent insulation for the building, which can reduce heating and cooling costs. In addition, they help reduce storm water runoff, create habitat for wildlife, and may even help lower air temperatures in large cities.

Complete freedom is possible with the ***free-form roof***. It may include planar, curved, and warped surfaces. See **Figure 17-4**. This type of roof can be produced in any shape that can be achieved by stretching fabric over a support frame. The final roofing material is applied to the fabric. Urethane foam is a popular choice of material for this roof. It is sprayed over a network of pipes and net material. It is strong and weather resistant. Like the warped roof, however, a free-form roof is expensive to build and has limited application in residential construction.

Traditional Frame Roof Construction

The features of traditional frame roof construction are covered in the next sections. It is important to understand these features and their impact on the roof before designing a frame roof.

Rafters

The roof framing is designed to support the roof covering materials. The framing must be

Ambient Ideas/Shutterstock.com

Figure 17-4. This detail photo of the roof of Denver International Airport shows the complex shapes that can be accomplished in a free-form roof.

strong and rigid. Roof framing consists of several distinct structural elements. The first and most basic of these elements is the ***rafter***. Common rafters are perpendicular to the top wall plate. They extend from the ridge of the roof to the plate or beyond. **Figure 17-5** shows a plan view of the roof framing for a combination hip and gable roof. Note that several types of rafters other than common rafters are identified.

Rafters are cut to the proper dimensions by locating the ridge cut, seat cut, plumb cut, and tail cut, as shown in **Figure 17-6**. Note that a ***plumb cut*** is any cut that is vertical or perpendicular to the ground. Technically, both the tail cut and the ridge cut are also plumb cuts.

The precise layout of these cuts is determined by the slope of the roof and the clear span of the building. Terms that must be understood before calculating rafter dimensions and roof pitch are *clear span*, *rise*, and *run*. The ***clear span*** is the horizontal distance from the inside of one exterior stud wall to the inside of the opposite exterior stud wall. The ***rise*** of a roof is the vertical distance measured from the top of the wall

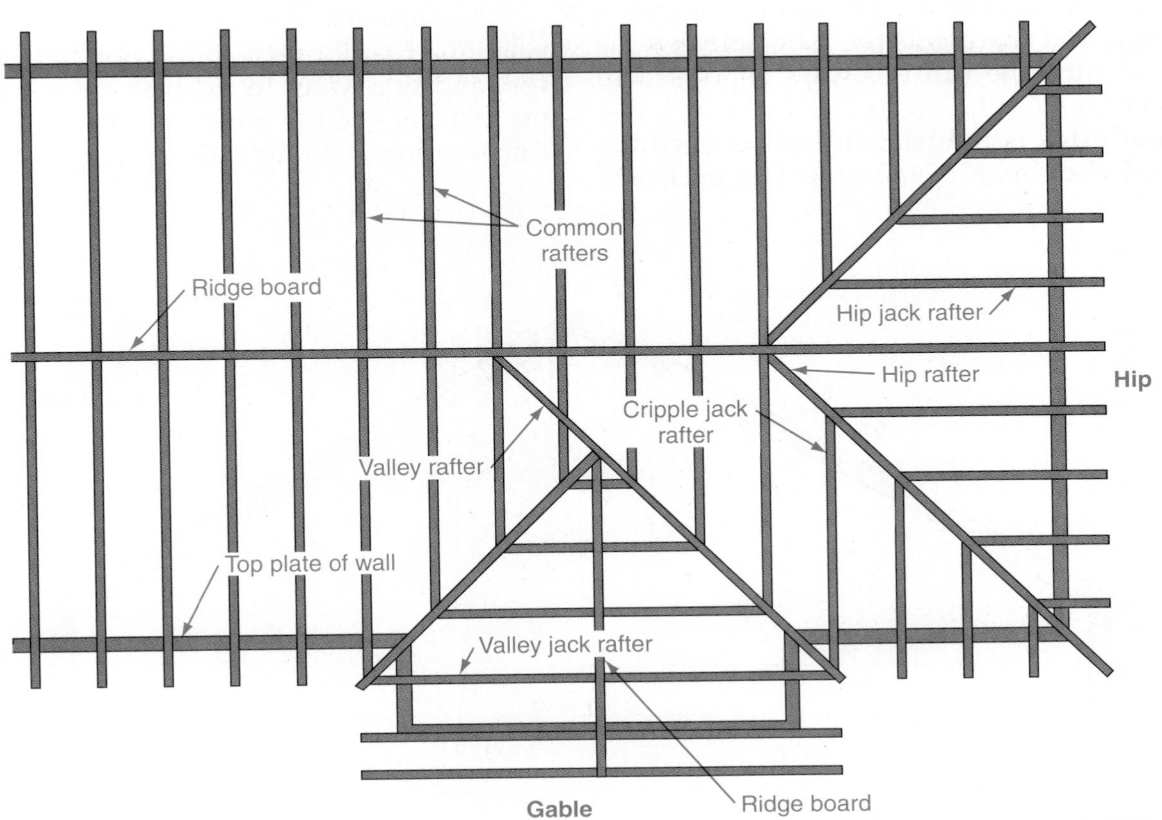

Goodheart-Willcox Publisher

Figure 17-5. The structural members of typical roof framing are identified here.

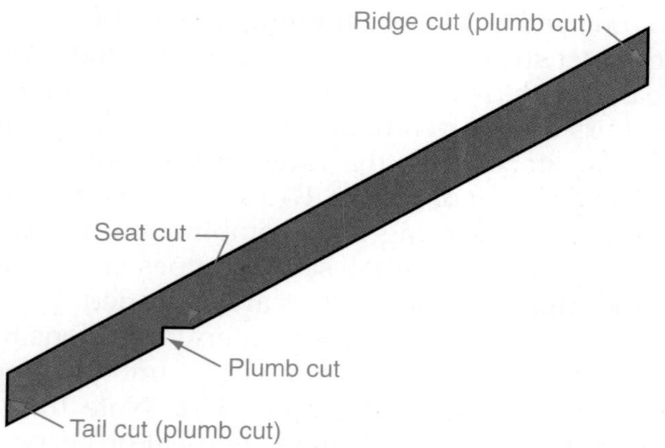

Figure 17-6. A common rafter with the various cuts labeled.

plate to the underside of the rafters. The ***run*** of a roof is one-half the distance of the clear span. See **Figure 17-7**.

The terms *roof slope* and *roof pitch* refer to the slant of the roof. ***Roof slope*** is the relationship between the rise and run of the roof. The slope may be given on a drawing with a slope diagram, as shown in **Figure 17-7**. The slope diagram is a triangle that represents the ratio between the rise and run. The run is always expressed in this ratio as 12 units.

Roof pitch is the relationship between the rise and clear span of the roof. The pitch is a fractional expression calculated using this formula:

Pitch = Rise / Clear Span

Figure 17-8 shows several roof pitches that are commonly used in residential construction. When designing a roof, you can help keep costs down by using one of these standard roof pitches.

The slope of a roof may also be indicated using an angular dimension. For example, a roof with a 45° slope has a 12:12 slope or 1/2 pitch. However, this method is seldom used because it is difficult to measure as accurately as the other methods.

Rafter sizes depend on the distance to be spanned, spacing of the rafters, and weight to be supported. Rafter span data for common species of wood is given in **Figure 17-9**. Rafters for roofs with low slopes may also serve as a base for the finished ceiling. In this instance, they are acting as both rafters and ceiling joists. See **Figure 17-10**.

Cornice

The ***cornice*** is the overhang of the roof at the eave line that forms a connection between the roof and side walls. In a gable roof, it is formed on two sides of the building. The cornice continues around all four sides on a hip or flat roof.

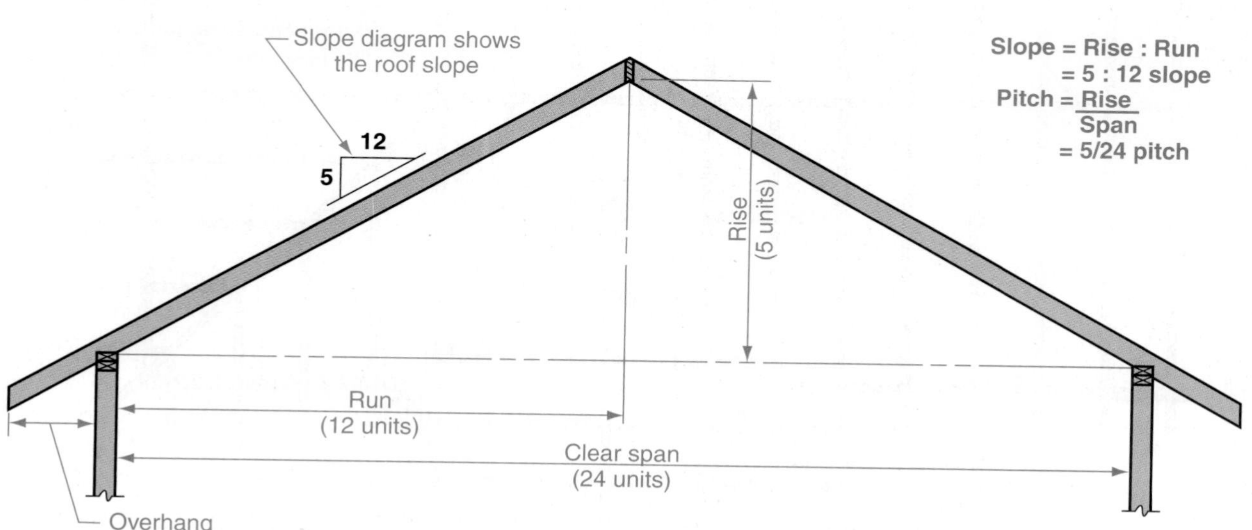

Figure 17-7. This illustration shows the roof rise, run, and clear span, and methods of calculating the slope and pitch of the roof.

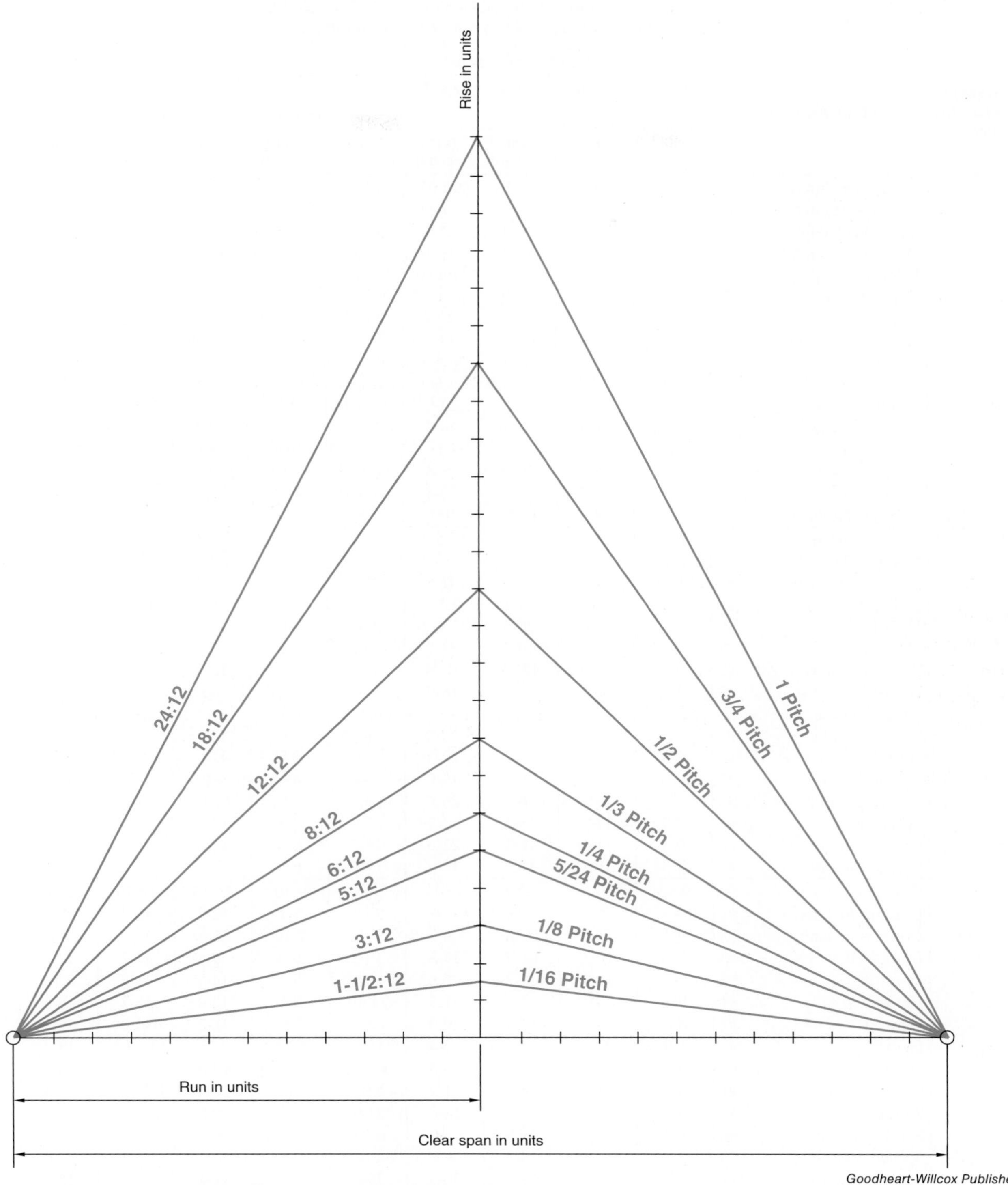

Goodheart-Willcox Publisher

Figure 17-8. Several roof pitches used in residential construction.

The three types of cornices frequently used in residential buildings are the open cornice, box cornice, and close cornice. The ***open cornice*** may be used with exposed-beam construction, contemporary, or rustic designs. See **Figure 17-11**. Rafter ends are exposed and are usually tapered or curved to prevent a bulky appearance.

In a ***box cornice***, the space between the end of a projecting rafter and the wall is enclosed with a soffit board. There are three basic types

RAFTER SPANS FOR COMMON LUMBER SPECIES
(Roof live load = 20 psf, ceiling not attached to rafters, L/Δ = 180)

RAFTER SPACING (inches)	SPECIES AND GRADE		DEAD LOAD = 10 psf					DEAD LOAD = 20 psf				
			2 x 4	2 x 6	2 x 8	2 x 10	2 x 12	2 x 4	2 x 6	2 x 8	2 x 10	2 x 12
			Maximum rafter spans[a]									
			(feet - inches)	(feet - inches)	(feet - inches)	(feet - inches)	(feet - inches)	(feet - inches)	(feet - inches)	(feet - inches)	(feet - inches)	(feet - inches)
12	Douglas fir-larch	SS	11-6	18-0	23-9	Note b	Note b	11-6	18-0	23-9	Note b	Note b
	Douglas fir-larch	#1	11-1	17-4	22-5	Note b	Note b	10-6	15-4	19-5	23-9	Note b
	Douglas fir-larch	#2	10-10	16-10	21-4	26-0	Note b	10-0	14-7	18-5	22-6	26-0
	Douglas fir-larch	#3	8-9	12-10	16-3	19-10	23-0	7-7	11-1	14-1	17-2	19-11
	Hem-fir	SS	10-10	17-0	22-5	Note b	Note b	10-10	17-0	22-5	Note b	Note b
	Hem-fir	#1	10-7	16-8	22-0	Note b	Note b	10-4	15-2	19-2	23-5	Note b
	Hem-fir	#2	10-1	15-11	20-8	25-3	Note b	9-8	14-2	17-11	21-11	25-5
	Hem-fir	#3	8-7	12-6	15-10	19-5	22-6	7-5	10-10	13-9	16-9	19-6
	Southern pine	SS	11-3	17-8	23-4	Note b	Note b	11-3	17-8	23-4	Note b	Note b
	Southern pine	#1	10-10	17-0	22-5	Note b	Note b	10-6	15-8	19-10	23-2	Note b
	Southern pine	#2	10-4	15-7	19-8	23-5	Note b	9-0	13-6	17-1	20-3	23-10
	Southern pine	#3	8-0	11-9	14-10	18-0	21-4	6-11	10-2	12-10	15-7	18-6
	Spruce-pine-fir	SS	10-7	16-8	21-11	Note b	Note b	10-7	16-8	21-9	Note b	Note b
	Spruce-pine-fir	#1	10-4	16-3	21-0	25-8	Note b	9-10	14-4	18-2	22-3	25-9
	Spruce-pine-fir	#2	10-4	16-3	21-0	25-8	Note b	9-10	14-4	18-2	22-3	25-9
	Spruce-pine-fir	#3	8-7	12-6	15-10	19-5	22-6	7-5	10-10	13-9	16-9	19-6
16	Douglas fir-larch	SS	10-5	16-4	21-7	Note b	Note b	10-5	16-3	20-7	25-2	Note b
	Douglas fir-larch	#1	10-0	15-4	19-5	23-9	Note b	9-1	13-3	16-10	20-7	23-10
	Douglas fir-larch	#2	9-10	14-7	18-5	22-6	26-0	8-7	12-7	16-0	19-6	22-7
	Douglas fir-larch	#3	7-7	11-1	14-1	17-2	19-11	6-7	9-8	12-12	14-11	17-3
	Hem-fir	SS	9-10	15-6	20-5	Note b	Note b	9-10	15-6	19-11	24-4	Note b
	Hem-fir	#1	9-8	15-2	19-2	23-5	Note b	9-0	13-1	16-7	20-4	23-7
	Hem-fir	#2	9-2	14-2	17-11	21-11	25-5	8-5	12-3	15-6	18-11	22-0
	Hem-fir	#3	7-5	10-10	13-9	16-9	19-6	6-5	9-5	11-11	14-6	16-10
	Southern pine	SS	10-3	16-1	21-2	Note b	Note b	10-3	16-1	21-2	25-7	Note b
	Southern pine	#1	9-10	15-6	19-10	23-2	Note b	9-1	13-7	17-2	20-1	23-10
	Southern pine	#2	9-0	13-6	17-1	20-3	23-10	7-9	11-8	14-9	17-6	20-8
	Southern pine	#3	6-11	10-2	12-10	15-7	18-6	6-0	8-10	11-2	13-6	16-0
	Spruce-pine-fir	SS	9-8	15-2	19-11	25-5	Note b	9-8	14-10	18-10	23-0	Note b
	Spruce-pine-fir	#1	9-5	14-4	18-2	22-3	25-9	8-6	12-5	15-9	19-3	22-4
	Spruce-pine-fir	#2	9-5	14-4	18-2	22-3	25-9	8-6	12-5	15-9	19-3	22-4
	Spruce-pine-fir	#3	7-5	10-10	13-9	16-9	19-6	6-5	9-5	11-11	14-6	16-10
19.2	Douglas fir-larch	SS	9-10	15-5	20-4	25-11	Note b	9-10	14-10	18-10	23-0	Note b
	Douglas fir-larch	#1	9-5	14-0	17-9	21-8	25-2	8-4	12-2	15-4	18-9	21-9
	Douglas fir-larch	#2	9-1	13-3	16-10	20-7	23-10	7-10	11-6	14-7	17-10	20-8
	Douglas fir-larch	#3	6-11	10-2	12-10	15-8	18-3	6-0	8-9	11-2	12-7	15-9
	Hem-fir	SS	9-3	14-7	19-2	24-6	Note b	9-3	14-4	18-2	22-3	25-9
	Hem-fir	#1	9-1	13-10	17-6	21-5	24-10	8-2	12-0	15-2	18-6	21-6
	Hem-fir	#2	8-8	12-11	16-4	20-0	23-2	7-8	11-2	14-2	17-4	20-1
	Hem-fir	#3	6-9	9-11	12-7	15-4	17-9	5-10	8-7	10-10	13-3	15-5
	Southern pine	SS	9-8	15-2	19-11	25-5	Note b	9-8	15-2	19-7	23-4	Note b
	Southern pine	#1	9-3	14-3	18-1	21-2	25-2	8-4	12-4	15-8	18-4	21-9
	Southern pine	#2	8-2	12-3	15-7	18-6	21-9	7-1	10-8	13-6	16-0	18-10
	Southern pine	#3	6-4	9-4	11-9	14-3	16-10	5-6	8-1	10-2	12-4	14-7
	Spruce-pine-fir	SS	9-1	14-3	18-9	23-11	Note b	9-1	13-7	17-2	21-0	24-4
	Spruce-pine-fir	#1	8-10	13-1	16-7	20-3	23-6	7-9	11-4	14-4	17-7	20-4
	Spruce-pine-fir	#2	8-10	13-1	16-7	20-3	23-6	7-9	11-4	14-4	17-7	20-4
	Spruce-pine-fir	#3	6-9	9-11	12-7	15-4	17-9	5-10	8-7	10-10	13-3	15-5

(continued)

RAFTER SPANS FOR COMMON LUMBER SPECIES *(continued)*
(Roof live load = 20 psf, ceiling not attached to rafters, L/Δ = 180)

RAFTER SPACING (inches)	SPECIES AND GRADE		DEAD LOAD = 10 psf					DEAD LOAD = 20 psf				
			2 x 4	2 x 6	2 x 8	2 x 10	2 x 12	2 x 4	2 x 6	2 x 8	2 x 10	2 x 12
			Maximum rafter spans[a]									
			(feet - inches)	(feet - inches)	(feet - inches)	(feet - inches)	(feet - inches)	(feet - inches)	(feet - inches)	(feet - inches)	(feet - inches)	(feet - inches)
24	Douglas fir-larch	SS	9-1	14-4	18-10	23-9	Note b	9-1	13-3	16-10	20-7	23-10
	Douglas fir-larch	#1	8-7	12-6	15-10	19-5	22-6	7-5	10-10	13-9	16-9	19-6
	Douglas fir-larch	#2	8-2	11-11	15-1	18-5	21-4	7-0	10-4	13-0	15-11	18-6
	Douglas fir-larch	#3	6-2	9-1	11-6	14-1	16-3	5-4	7-10	10-0	12-2	14-1
	Hem-fir	SS	8-7	13-6	17-10	22-9	Note b	8-7	12-10	16-3	19-10	23-0
	Hem-fir	#1	8-5	12-4	15-8	19-2	22-2	7-4	10-9	13-7	16-7	19-3
	Hem-fir	#2	7-11	11-7	14-8	17-10	20-9	6-10	10-0	12-8	15-6	17-11
	Hem-fir	#3	6-1	8-10	11-3	13-8	15-11	5-3	7-8	9-9	11-10	13-9
	Southern pine	SS	8-11	14-1	18-6	23-8	Note b	8-11	13-10	17-6	20-10	24-8
	Southern pine	#1	8-7	12-9	16-2	18-11	22-6	7-5	11-1	14-0	16-5	19-6
	Southern pine	#2	7-4	11-0	10-11	16-6	19-6	6-4	9-6	12-1	14-4	16-10
	Southern pine	#3	5-8	8-4	10-6	12-9	15-1	4-11	7-3	9-1	11-0	13-1
	Spruce-pine-fir	SS	8-5	13-3	17-5	21-8	25-2	8-4	12-2	15-4	18-9	21-9
	Spruce-pine-fir	#1	8-0	11-9	14-10	18-2	21-0	6-11	10-2	12-10	15-8	18-3
	Spruce-pine-fir	#2	8-0	11-9	14-10	18-2	21-0	6-11	10-2	12-10	15-8	18-3
	Spruce-pine-fir	#3	6-1	8-10	11-3	13-8	15-11	5-3	7-8	9-9	11-10	13-9

Check sources for availability of lumber in lengths greater than 20 feet.

For SI: 1 inch = 25.4 mm, 1 foot = 304.8 mm, 1 pound per square foot = 0.0479 kPa.

a. The tabulated rafter spans assume that ceiling joists are located at the bottom of the attic space or that some other method of resisting the outward push of the rafters on the bearing walls, such as rafter ties, is provided at that location. Where ceiling joists or rafter ties are located higher in the attic space, the rafter spans shall be multiplied by the following factors:

H_C/H_R	Rafter Span Adjustment Factor
1/3	0.67
1/4	0.76
1/5	0.83
1/6	0.90
1/7.5 or less	1.00

where:

H_C = Height of ceiling joists or rafter ties measured vertically above the top of the rafter support walls.

H_R = Height of roof ridge measured vertically above the top of the rafter support walls.

b. Span exceeds 26 feet in length.

Figure 17-9. Determine the maximum allowable rafter span by referring to this table. The rafter span is the horizontal distance between supports. This is not to be confused with rafter length, which must be calculated using the rise and run of the roof. The table assumes a maximum deflection of 1/180th of the span with a normal live load.

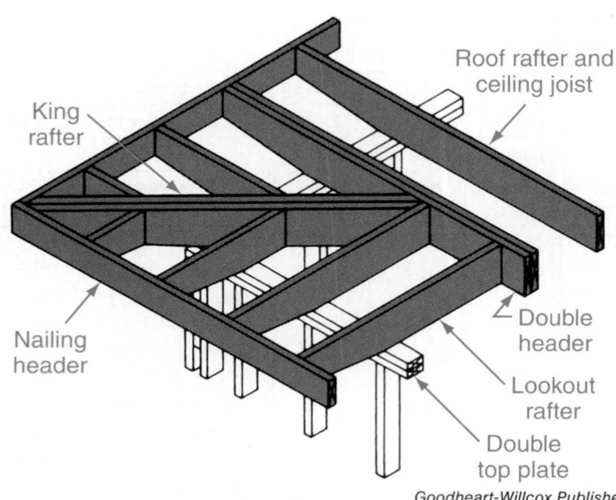

Figure 17-10. The rafters in this low-pitched roof also serve as ceiling joists.

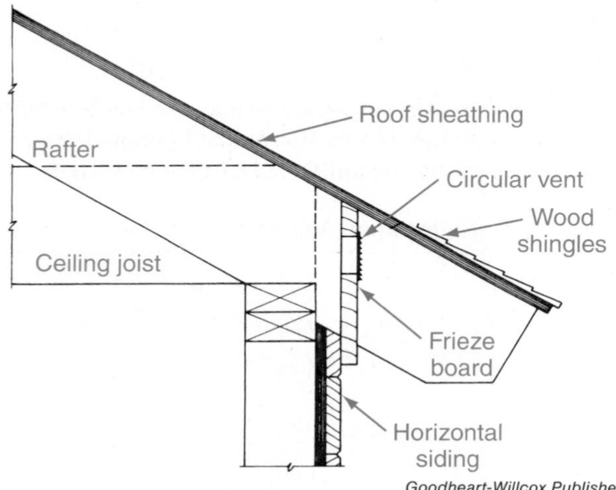

Figure 17-11. This section view shows an open cornice.

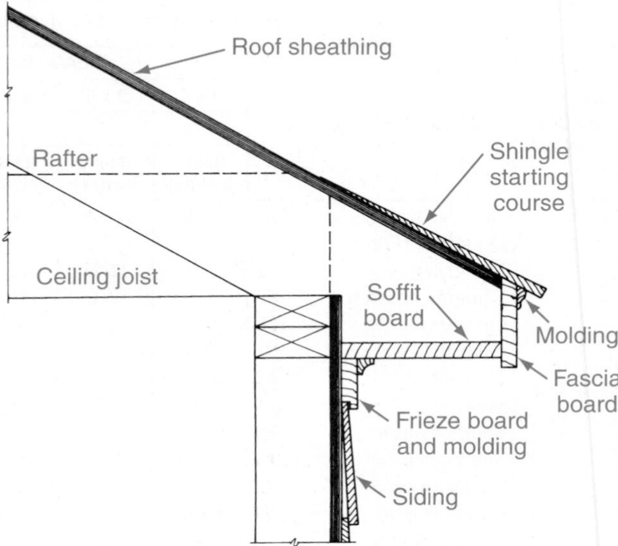

Figure 17-12. This section view shows a narrow box cornice.

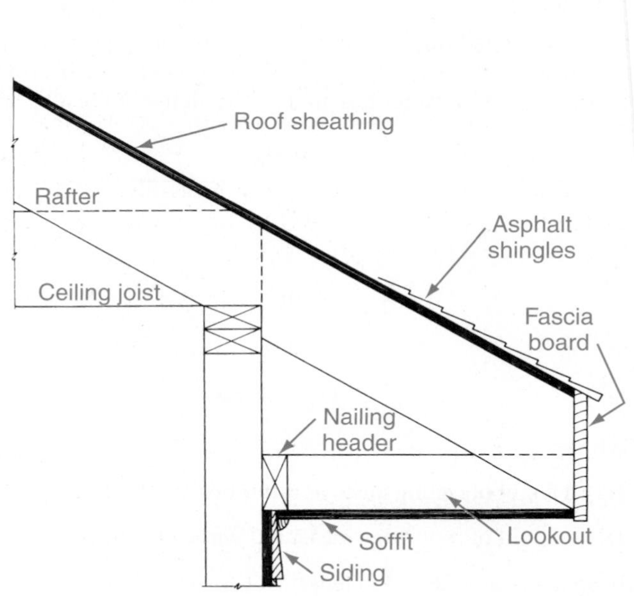

Figure 17-13. This section view shows a wide box cornice with lookouts.

of box cornices: the narrow box, wide box with lookouts, and wide box without lookouts. A narrow box cornice is usually between 6″ and 12″ wide. The soffit board is nailed directly to the bottom side of the rafters, as shown in **Figure 17-12**. A wide box cornice with lookouts normally requires additional support members, called ***lookouts***, for fastening the soffit. **Figure 17-13** shows a wide box cornice with lookouts. A wide box cornice without lookouts has a sloped soffit. The soffit material is nailed to the underside of the rafters. This type of cornice is frequently used when the overhangs are very wide. See **Figure 17-14**.

A ***close cornice*** is one in which the rafter does not project beyond the wall. The roof is terminated by a frieze board and molding. See **Figure 17-15**.

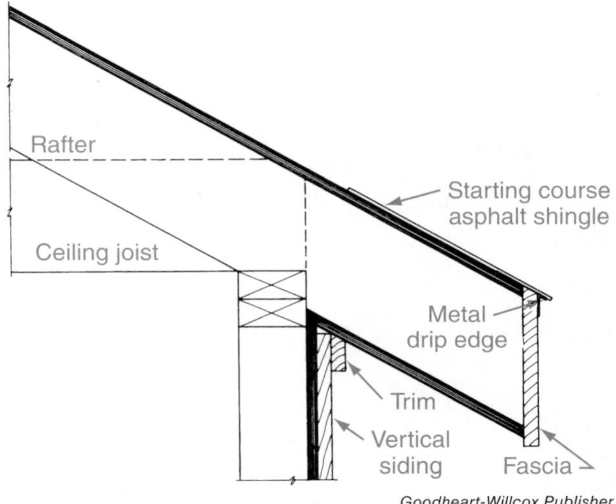

Figure 17-14. This section view shows a wide box cornice without lookouts.

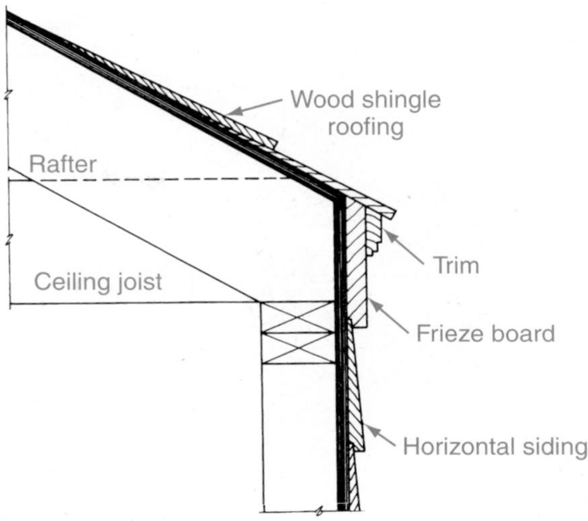

Figure 17-15. This section view shows a typical close cornice.

Rake or Gable End

The ***rake*** or ***gable end*** is the extension of a gable roof beyond the end wall of the house. The amount of overhang and treatment at the gable should be about the same as the cornice. The style of house must be considered when designing the gable end. A narrow box cornice is normally used for Cape Cod or colonial homes. The same proportions should be extended to the gable end. For example, if a close cornice is used, then a close rake should also be used. **Figure 17-16** shows the framing for a gable end with a wide overhang. A close rake is less expensive to build, but wide overhangs provide for side wall protection and less frequent painting.

Roof Trusses

The ***roof truss*** is an assembly of members that form a rigid framework of triangular shapes.

Employability
Computer Ethics

In most jobs today, the computer is an essential tool. The employer provides a computer for your use as a tool for research or to accomplish tasks, such as drawing a set of architectural plans. It is unethical to use the computer, without permission, for personal activities such as playing games, shopping, or other activities that are outside of your assignments.

It is also unethical to access confidential information, download copyrighted material, or harass others while using company- or school-owned equipment. Unapproved use of computers may open up the computer network for viruses and other issues that may jeopardize the integrity of the network.

Many organizations monitor computer users to make certain that the computer activity is ethical and legal. Users may also be required to sign an agreement that the computer will only be used for specific purposes.

Activity

To learn more about ethical use of company or school equipment, talk to a network administrator at a local business. Ask what his or her experiences have been with the unethical use of equipment. Also talk with an administrator at your school. What rules have been put in place for computer use in the classrooms and labs?

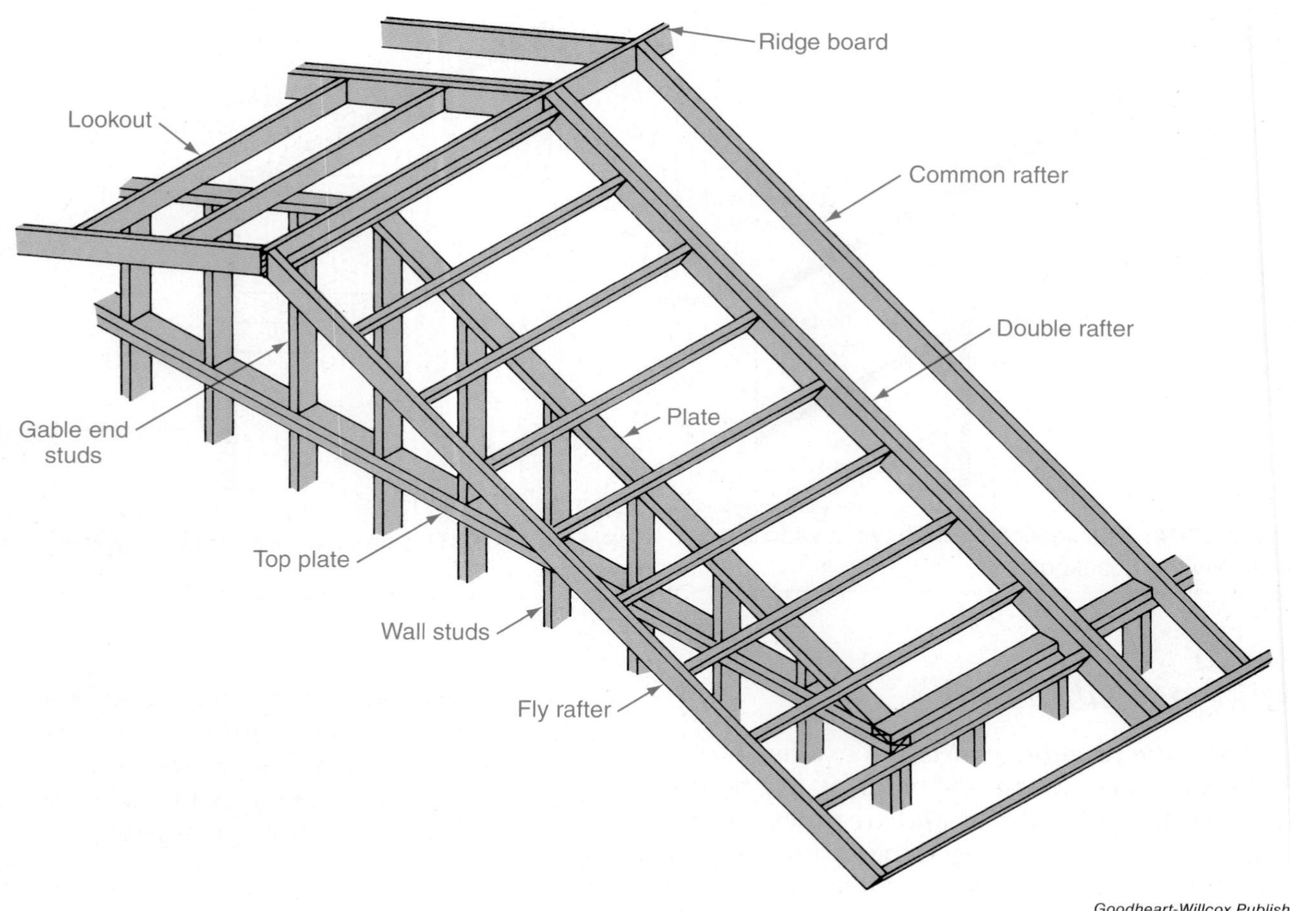

Figure 17-16. This framing is for a gable end with a wide overhang.

This arrangement permits wide, unsupported spans with a minimum amount of material. **Figure 17-17** shows several roof truss designs.

The information needed to purchase the proper truss for a house includes the span, roof pitch, spacing of the trusses, and anticipated roof load. A roof that can support a load of 40 pounds per square foot is adequate for most applications.

Most roof truss manufacturers provide design services. Some manufacturers also use CADD software that produces a truss design that will support the required load for the specified span. Similar software is available to individuals.

Lightweight wood roof trusses are designed to span distances of 20′ to 32′, and in some instances even more. Most lightweight trusses are made from 2 × 4 lumber; however, 2 × 6 lumber may be used for wider spans and heavier loads. Prefabricated trusses are readily available for standard widths and pitches. In many cases, they are less expensive than conventional framing. Trusses for nonstandard dimensions may be built on the site or factory-produced.

Wood trusses that are commonly used in residential construction are the Fink (W) truss, king-post (K-post) truss, and scissors truss. Details of these truss designs are shown in **Figure 17-18**. Most trusses are designed to be placed 24″OC. Ceiling materials are nailed to the bottom of the trusses. ***Gussets*** made from metal or 3/8″ or 1/2″ plywood are frequently used to fasten the members of a wood truss together, as shown in **Figure 17-19**. The gussets add strength to the truss assembly.

Roof trusses that extend the top chord vertically using a "raised heel" design provide additional space for ceiling insulation, as shown in **Figure 17-20**. This construction allows the ceiling insulation to be extended to the outside of the exterior wall without interfering with attic ventilation. This amount of insulation is generally not possible with traditional roof framing methods.

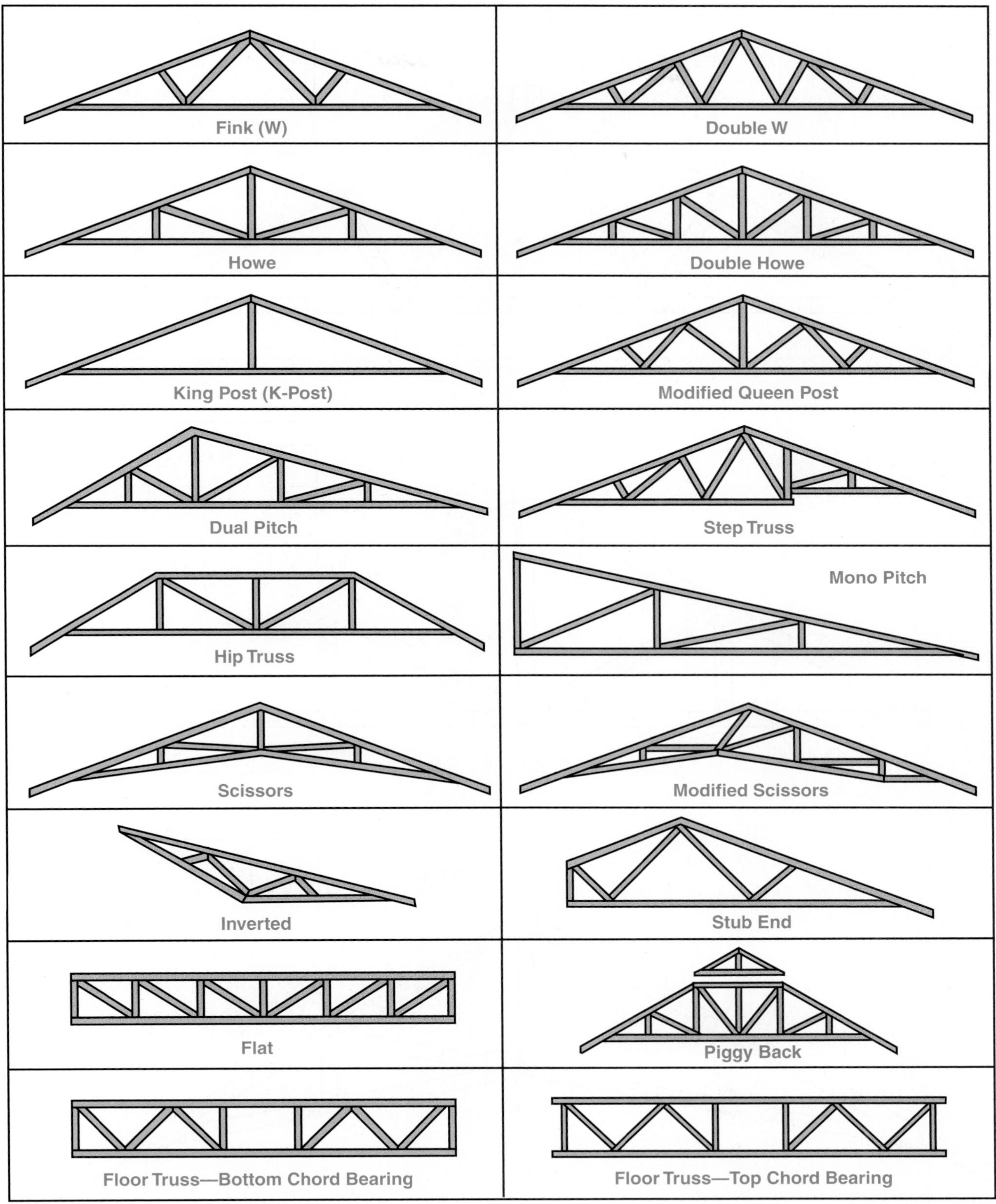

Goodheart-Willcox Publisher

Figure 17-17. Examples of roof truss designs. Note that the number of webs and web configurations may vary from those shown here.

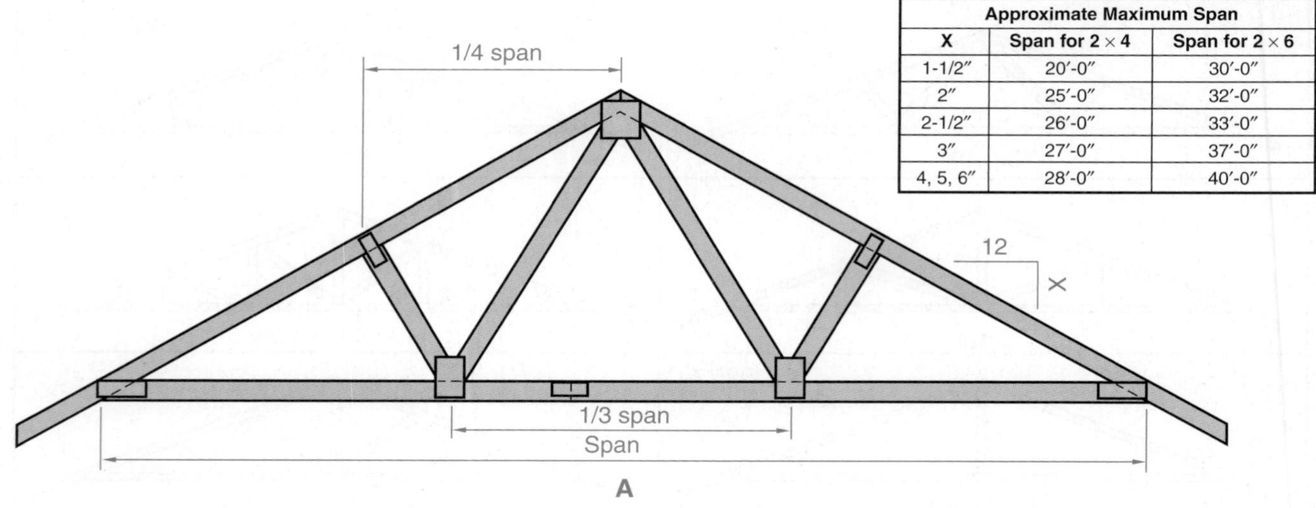

Approximate Maximum Span		
X	Span for 2 × 4	Span for 2 × 6
1-1/2″	20′-0″	30′-0″
2″	25′-0″	32′-0″
2-1/2″	26′-0″	33′-0″
3″	27′-0″	37′-0″
4, 5, 6″	28′-0″	40′-0″

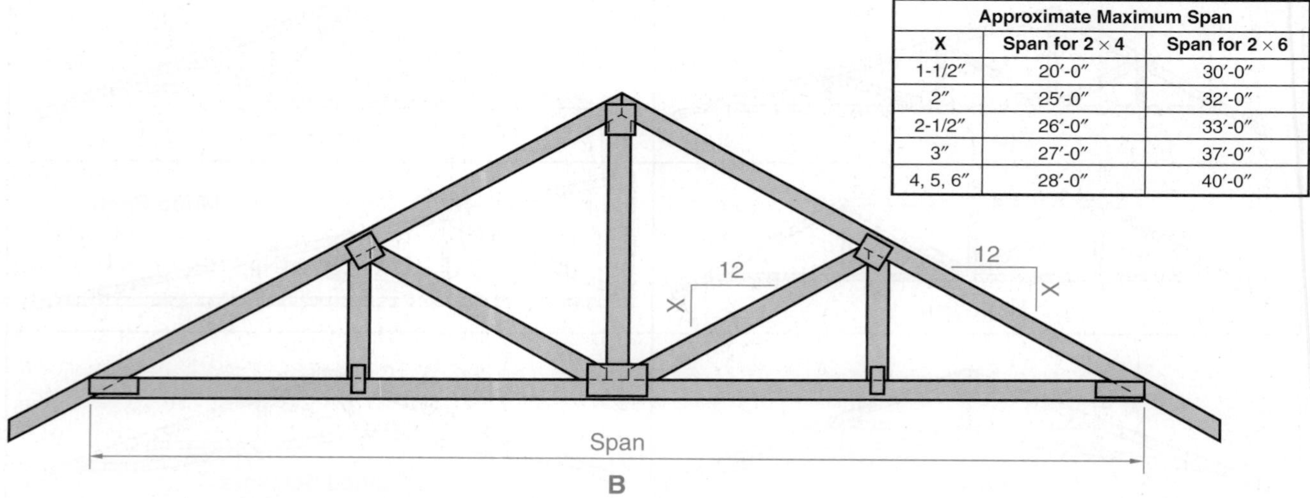

Approximate Maximum Span		
X	Span for 2 × 4	Span for 2 × 6
1-1/2″	20′-0″	30′-0″
2″	25′-0″	32′-0″
2-1/2″	26′-0″	33′-0″
3″	27′-0″	37′-0″
4, 5, 6″	28′-0″	40′-0″

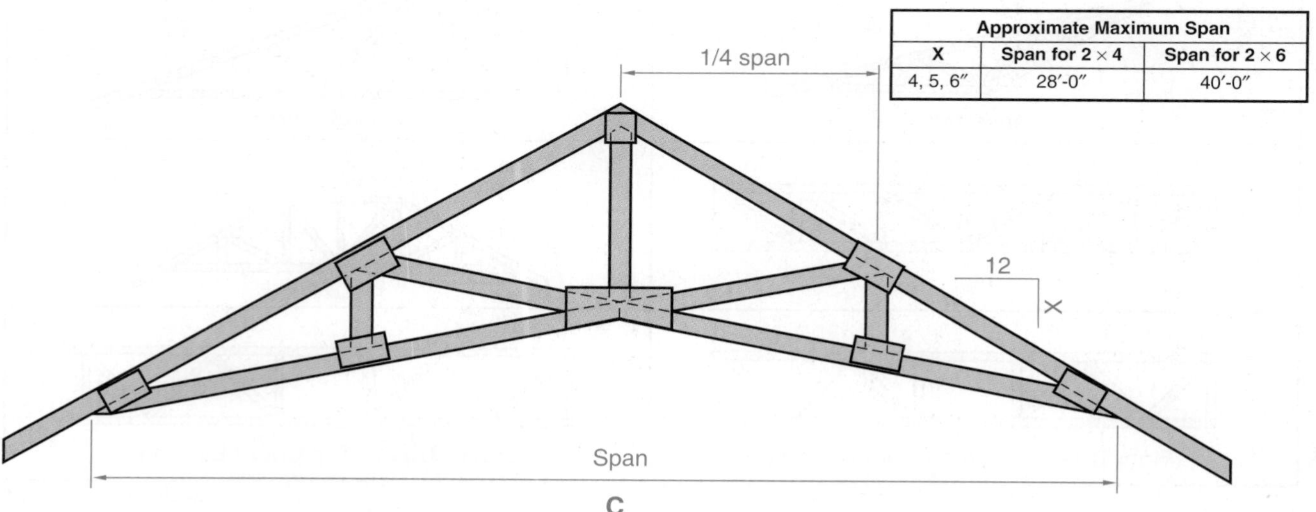

Approximate Maximum Span		
X	Span for 2 × 4	Span for 2 × 6
4, 5, 6″	28′-0″	40′-0″

Goodheart-Willcox Publisher

Figure 17-18. There are three common types of trusses. A—The Fink or W truss. B—The king-post or K-post truss. C—The scissors truss.

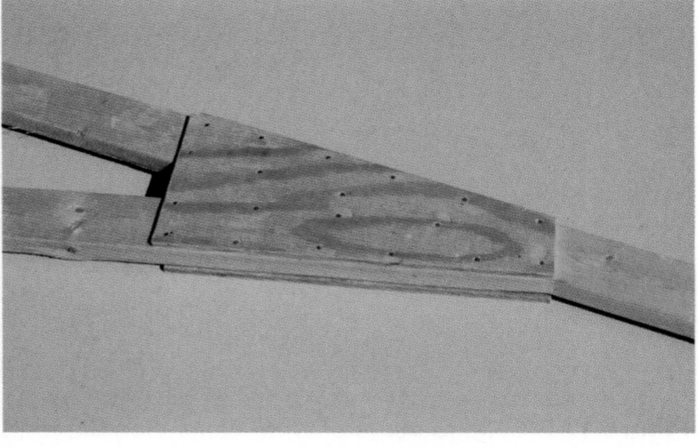

Goodheart-Willcox Publisher

Figure 17-19. Trusses are often assembled with gussets. A—Metal gussets. B— Plywood gussets.

The increased airflow reduces moisture condensation on the underside of the roof sheathing and prevents damage to the structure.

Ventilation

Providing for adequate ventilation in the attic space is a necessity. If sufficient ventilation is not provided, moisture will form on the underside of the roof sheathing and, in time, damage will result. Also, a well-ventilated attic will help to cool the interior of the house during the summer by allowing heat to escape.

Ventilation in the attic space is usually accomplished through the use of louvered openings in the gable ends and along the underside of the overhang. Ridge ventilators also provide an efficient means of expelling hot air when coupled with soffit openings. See **Figure 17-21**. The difference between the temperature of air in the attic and the outside causes air movement and thus reduces the temperature inside.

The total area of ventilator openings should be at least 1/300th of the ceiling area. For example, if the ceiling area is 1200 square feet, then the ventilator area should be a minimum of four square feet. **Figure 17-22A** shows several louvered gable-type ventilator openings. **Figure 17-22B** shows a number of other types of ventilators that can be added to the roof to improve airflow.

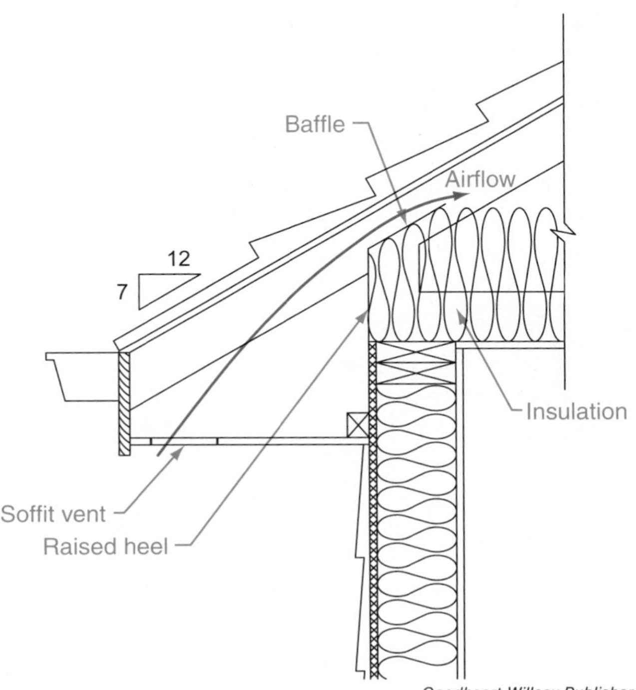

Goodheart-Willcox Publisher

Figure 17-20. Raised heel trusses provide space for extra insulation without interfering with ventilation.

Flashing

Flashing is used to shed water away from areas of potential leakage. Flashing should be used where the roof comes into contact with a wood or masonry wall, chimney, or roof valley—any element that penetrates the roof. Wide strips of weather-resistant metal, such as aluminum, copper, and galvanized sheet steel, are commonly used as flashing. Flashing is placed beneath the surface material at a distance sufficient to

Cor-A-Vent, Inc.

Figure 17-21. Ridge vents provide ventilation along the ridge of the roof.

prevent the penetration of water. **Figure 17-23** shows flashing around a chimney.

Roof valleys may be flashed with metal or two thicknesses of 90# roll-type roofing. The width of valley flashing should be no less than specified in the table in **Figure 17-24**.

Figure 17-25 shows valley flashing under an asphalt shingle roof. Often, a ribbon of asphalt-roofing mastic is used under the shingles adjacent to the valley flashing to aid in waterproofing the roof.

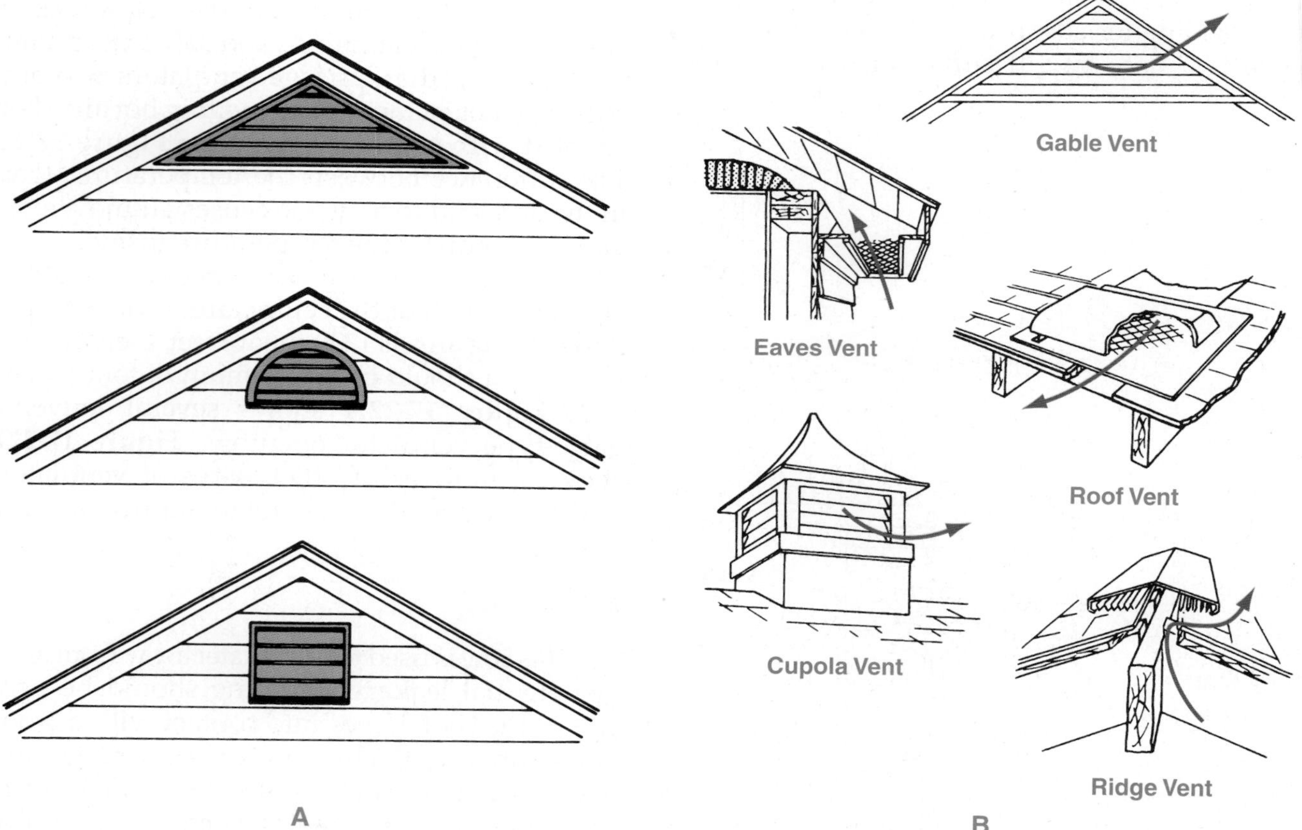

Goodheart-Willcox Publisher

Figure 17-22. A—Typical louvered gable-type ventilators. B—Several different methods of roof ventilation are possible.

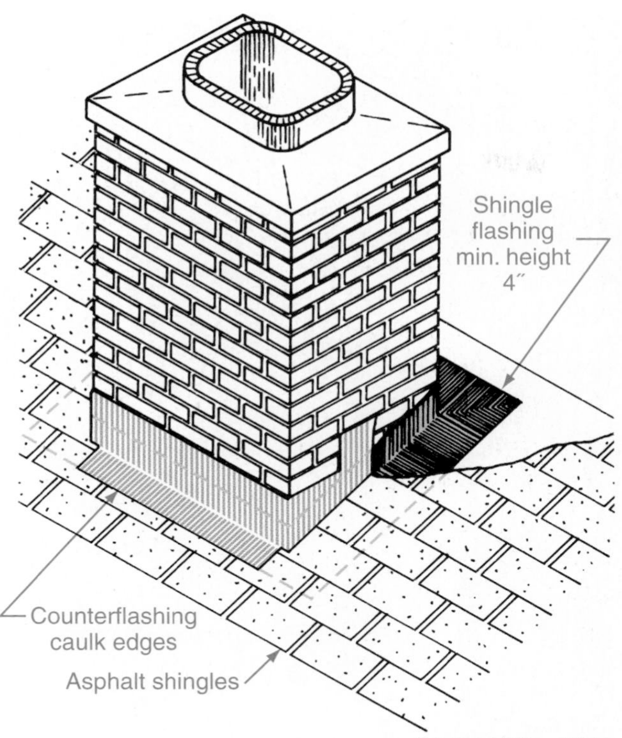

Goodheart-Willcox Publisher

Figure 17-23. Flashing around a chimney is composed of shingle flashing and counterflashing.

Roof Slope	Flashing Width
Less than 4:12	24″
4:12 to 7:12	18″
Over 7:12	12″

Goodheart-Willcox Publisher

Figure 17-24. Minimum flashing widths for various roof slopes.

A small metal edging is normally used at the gable and eaves line to act as a drip edge. This flashing prevents water from entering behind the shingles and protects the fascia and rake boards. See **Figure 17-26**.

Gutters and Downspouts

Gutters collect water from the roof and direct it to an outlet. A ***downspout*** is a vertical pipe that receives the water from the gutter outlet. An extension at the bottom of the downspout directs water away from the house. This prevents water from running directly off the eaves and splattering the house and running down the foundation wall. Gutters are usually pitched 1″ to 1-1/2″ per 2′. This slope permits even flow and prevents water from standing in the gutter.

Several styles of gutters and downspouts are available in copper, vinyl, aluminum, and galvanized sheet metal. Several common shapes and sizes of gutters are shown in **Figure 17-27**. Gutters can be painted or finished to match the trim on a house, or they can be painted a contrasting color to add a design element.

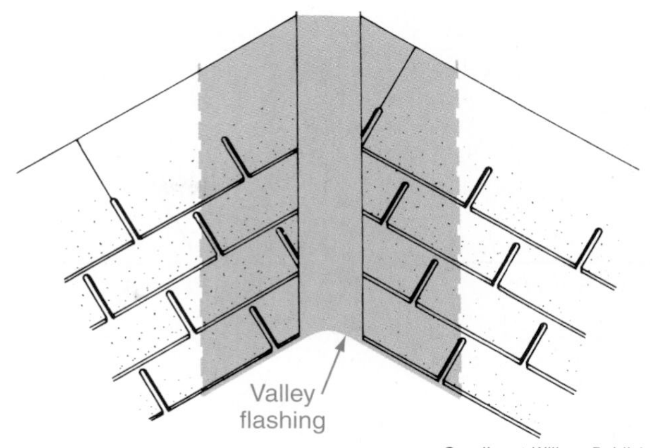

Goodheart-Willcox Publisher

Figure 17-25. The width of valley flashing is dependent on the roof slope, but should be a minimum of 12″.

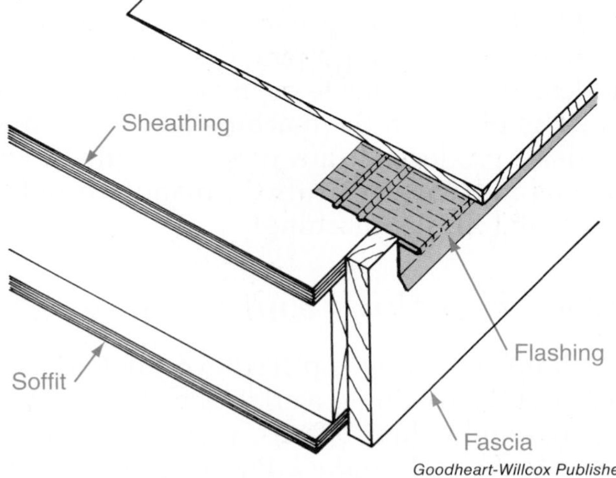

Goodheart-Willcox Publisher

Figure 17-26. Drip edge flashing set above the sheathing and down the side of the fascia board prevents water from entering behind the shingles and protects the fascia.

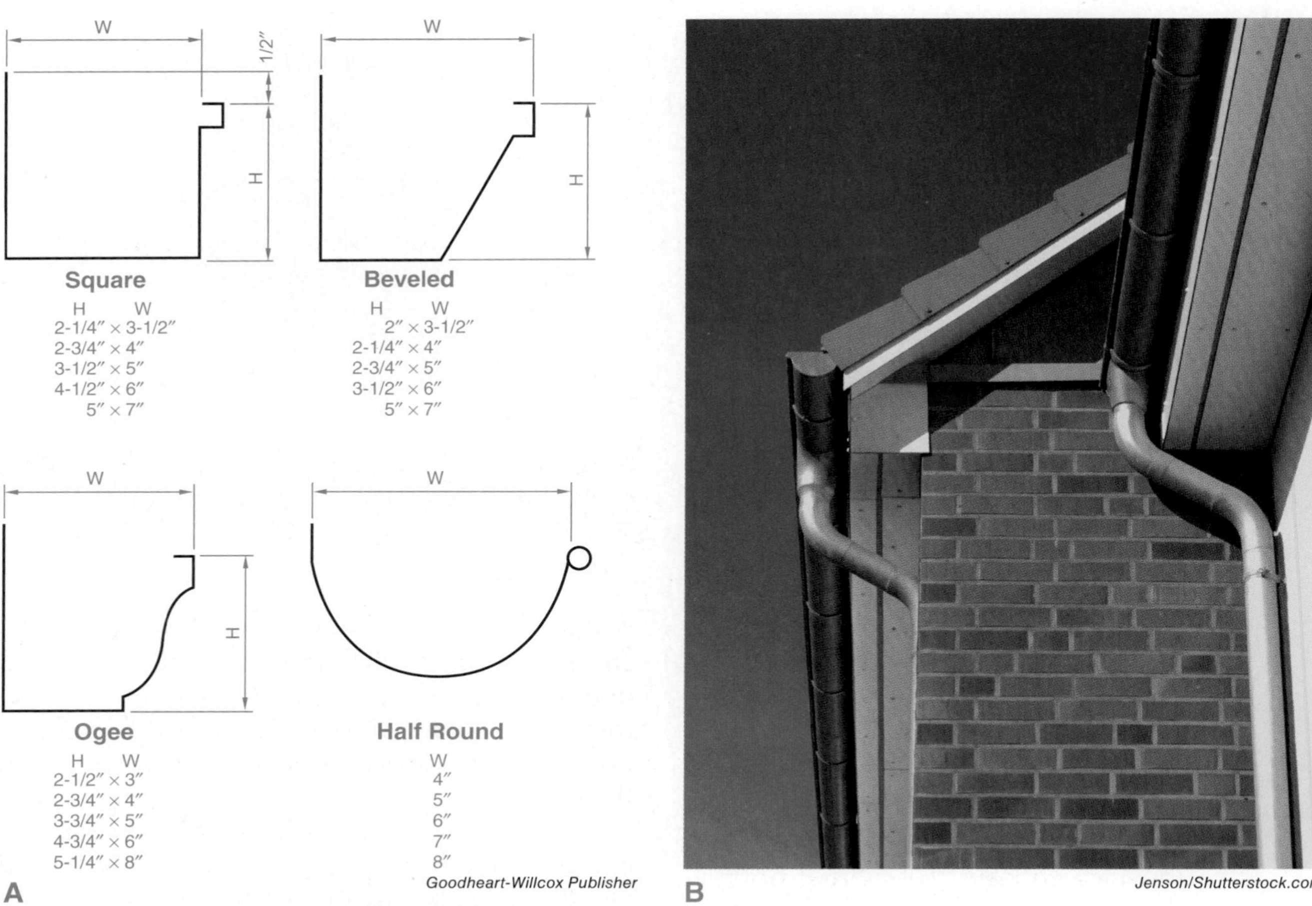

Figure 17-27. A—Typical gutter designs and sizes. B—Half-round style gutter made from aluminum, with downspouts.

The standard length for a gutter segment is 10′. However, many installers offer seamless gutters. Seamless gutters are manufactured to length either on site or in the shop. Flat roll stock is placed in the machine and the formed gutter is produced to any needed length. Downspouts and elbows can also be manufactured on site using similar machines.

Roof Sheathing and Roofing

Roof sheathing is placed over the rafters to support the roofing material. Sheathing may be planks, individual boards, plywood, or other approved panel product. Plywood is a popular choice, except when wood shingles are used as the roofing material. Usually, 1 × 3, 1 × 4, or 1 × 6 boards are used for wood shingle roofs. See **Figure 17-28**.

The thickness of sheathing varies with the spacing of the rafters or supporting beams. For rafters spaced 16″OC or 24″OC, 1/2″ standard sheathing-grade plywood is used. The plywood must be laid with the face grain perpendicular to the rafters, as in floor sheathing. The sheets should be staggered so that two sheets side-by-side do not end on the same rafter.

When individual boards are used as sheathing, they are usually no wider than 6″ or 8″. For rafters 16″OC or 24″OC, the minimum board thickness is 3/4″. Each board should be long enough to span a minimum of two rafters. Longer boards are preferred for gable ends.

The roofing material used on a house should have a long life and provide a waterproof surface. Typical materials include asphalt shingles, wood shingles, tile, slate, roll roofing, copper, aluminum, galvanized steel, layers of felt and

Goodheart-Willcox Publisher

Figure 17-28. This roof has wood shingles. You can see the wood boards used to support the shingles.

tar, and rubber membrane roofing. Factors that influence the selection of the roofing material are cost, local codes, roof pitch, design, and individual preference.

More homes have asphalt shingle roofs than any other type of roofing material. The usual recommended minimum weight of asphalt shingles is 235 pounds per square for square-butt strip shingles. A "square" of shingles will cover 100 square feet. Therefore, if the roof area is 200 square feet, two squares of shingles are needed for the roof. The square-butt strip shingle is 12″ × 36″ and is laid on 5″ intervals. See **Figure 17-29**. A layer of 15-pound, saturated-felt building paper is ordinarily placed on the sheathing before laying the shingles. This acts as a moisture barrier.

Roofing Materials

New roofing materials are always being designed. These materials are stronger to reduce damage from severe storms. Also, an effort is being made to make them attractive and, in some cases, simulate the look of traditional roofing materials. Three options for roofing materials are asphalt laminate shingles, metal roofing, and clay tile.

Asphalt Laminate Shingles

Traditional asphalt shingles are slowly being replaced by asphalt laminate shingles, **Figure 17-30**. Laminates are thicker and heavier than traditional asphalt shingles. This makes them more wind resistant and, therefore, less likely to be blown off the roof during high winds.

Laminate shingles have other advantages in addition to wind resistance. They can add a raised, three-dimensional appearance to the roof. They can also provide the appearance of greater depth to lower-pitched roofs.

However, laminate shingles are more expensive than traditional asphalt shingles. Their increased thickness makes installation more difficult. They are heavier to handle and harder to cut.

Christina Richards/Shutterstock.com

Figure 17-29. Asphalt shingles are designed to be laid at 5″ intervals.

Photo Courtesy of James Hardie® Siding Products

Figure 17-30. The laminate shingles on this roof add considerable depth and eye appeal to this structure. Notice how they simulate the appearance of traditional wood shingles.

Metal Roofing

Metal roofing is gaining wider acceptance for residential construction across all regions of the United States. It is compatible with most roof designs because of the wide range of styles available.

One of the big advantages of metal roofing is its ability to resist high winds. Some products claim a wind resistance of up to 230 miles per hour. Some metal roofing styles simulate the appearance of clay tile, cedar shingles, or slate. Others are designed to look like metal and are incorporated into the overall home design. In fact, the metal roof is a key characteristic of some house styles. See **Figure 17-31**.

Chuck Wagner/Shutterstock.com

Figure 17-31. The aluminum roof on this Key West home is resistant to high wind, as well as visually pleasing.

Metal roofing has many advantages. It has a long life and requires little maintenance. It can be used with most roof assemblies and looks good with many different home styles. It can even simulate the appearance of other roofing materials, while providing a very high wind resistance not possible with other roofing materials.

Metal roofing has disadvantages, too. It typically costs more than a comparable asphalt shingle roof. The installation must be more precise as compared to installation for other types of roofing. Some metal finishes also fade over time.

Clay Tile

A clay tile roof is a decorative, prominent feature that enhances the appeal of the entire structure. See **Figure 17-32**. Clay tile is available in many colors, styles, and shapes and can be designed for compatibility with any architectural style. Roof tile is available in other materials besides clay, including concrete, metal, and synthetic resin.

The primary advantages of clay tile are appearance and durability. It is energy efficient, fireproof, and resistant to wind and rot. Clay tile is strong and designed to last for many years. If installed and maintained properly, a clay tile roof can last for several decades or longer.

However, clay tile is significantly more expensive than other roofing materials. In addition, larger framing is required to support clay tile because of its weight. Clay tile also requires careful installation to prevent cracking or breakage.

Boral Roofing

Figure 17-32. The colored clay tile roof on this home stands out visually and adds appeal to the overall design.

Roof Plans

Roof plans are used to show the shape of the roof and information such as roof pitch and the size and location of framing members used to construct the roof. There are two types of roof plans that may be prepared for a set of architectural working drawings: a roof plan and a roof framing plan.

A ***roof plan*** is a plan (top) view that shows the shape of the roof. It shows the perimeter of the roof and the ridge lines to indicate the direction of the slopes. The roof plan may also show the size and location of roof vents. See **Figure 17-33**.

A ***roof framing plan*** shows the exterior roof lines, the size and location of all roof framing members, and any additional information required for constructing the roof. See **Figure 17-34**. The roof framing plan often shows the exterior house walls for reference. The exterior roof lines and roof framing members are drawn using solid lines, and the exterior house walls, which are hidden by the roof, are drawn using hidden (dashed) lines. Depending on office practice, the

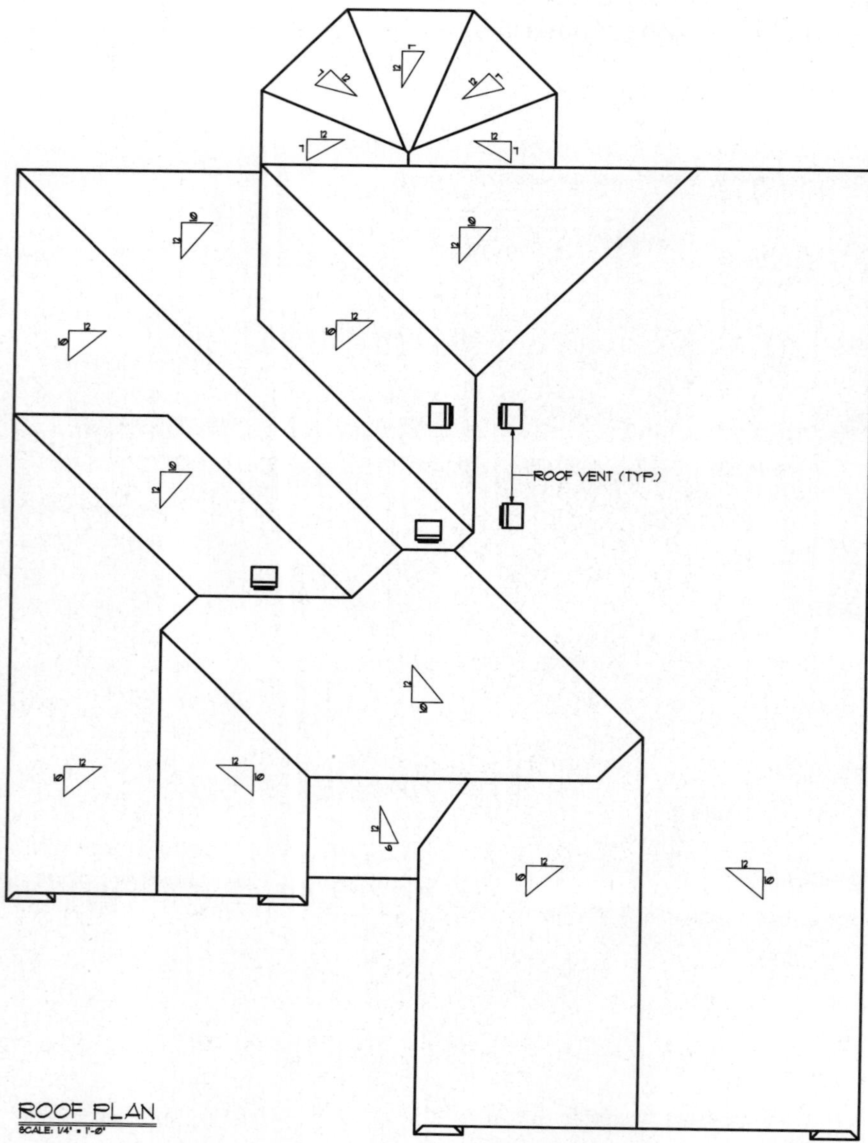

Goodheart-Willcox Publisher

Figure 17-33. A roof plan shows all exterior roof lines to describe the shape of the roof. This roof plan includes the locations of roof vents.

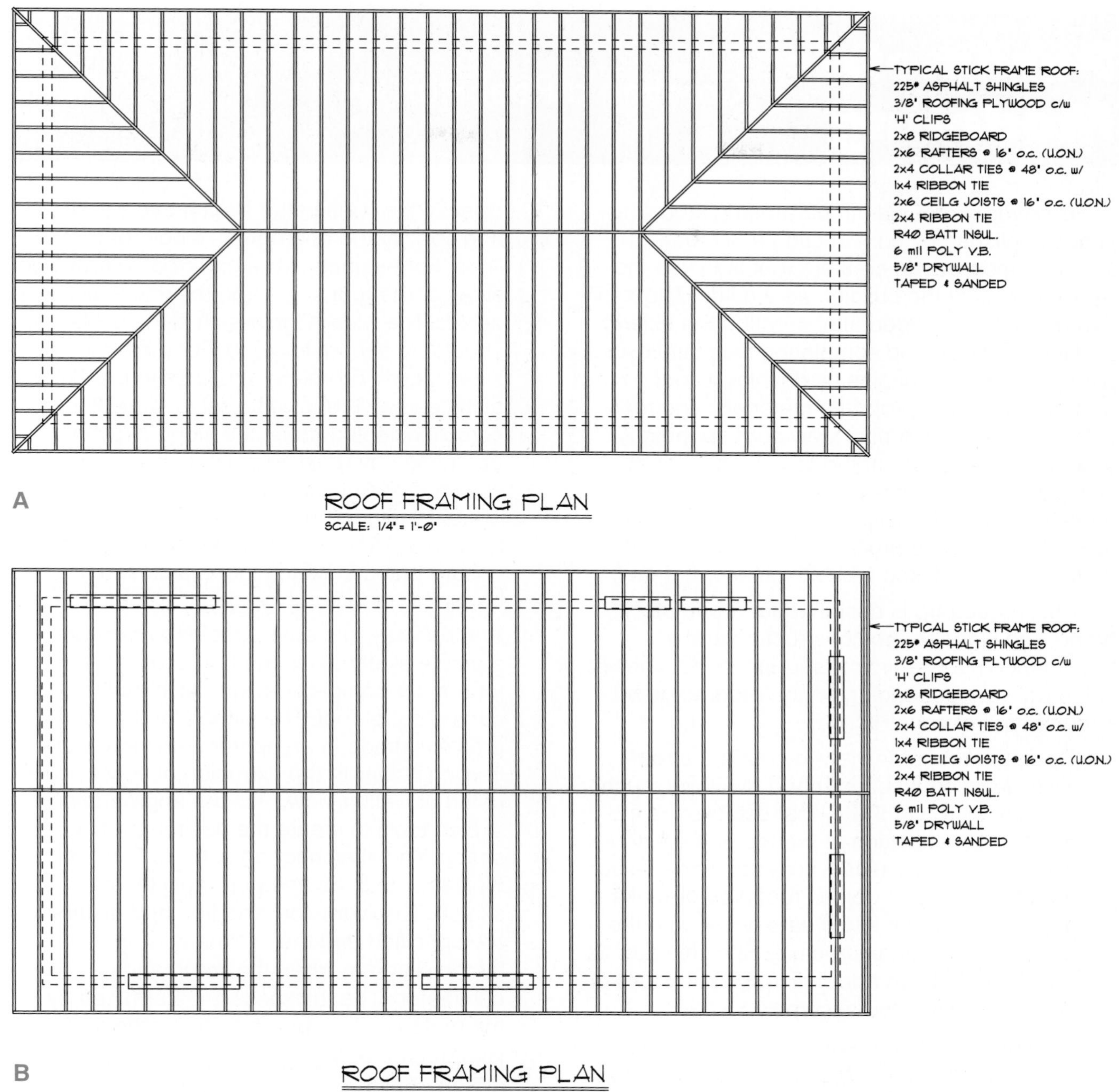

Ryan Verpooten

Figure 17-34. A roof framing plan shows the exterior roof lines and all of the roof framing members to clarify roof construction requirements. A—A roof framing plan for a hip roof with the exterior house walls shown. B—This roof framing plan for a gable roof shows the exterior house walls and header locations for reference.

locations of headers on bearing walls may also be shown for reference.

A separate roof plan or roof framing plan is not always included in a set of architectural drawings. A roof plan is required only if the roof design is complicated and is not shown clearly by other plans. In some cases, the roof plan is shown on the elevation drawings or on a sheet including framing details, such as truss details. The roof plan may also be combined with another drawing in a set of plans, such as the site plan.

Parametric Modeling

Creating a Roof Plan

Creating a roof plan in parametric modeling is accomplished by constructing a 3D roof. One common way to create a roof is to use the exterior walls of the building as a guide. The roof can normally be added after creating the exterior and interior walls and completing the initial floor plan. The process begins by defining a roof system with the appropriate materials. The roof is then modeled in a plan view corresponding to a level established at the top of the exterior walls. A variety of tools are usually available for modeling flat, gable, hip, and many other types of roofs. The following procedure describes typical methods for modeling a basic gable or hip roof.

This procedure is designed for a one-story home with wood frame construction and a basement. This is a typical sequence, but specific steps will vary depending on the program used and the type of construction.

1. Open the roof plan view to create the roof. This view should correspond to a level, such as Roof or Top of Plate, that establishes the appropriate elevation at the top of the exterior walls. Access the **ROOF** command and select a roof type. Use a default roof type or make a duplicate and edit it to create a roof with the necessary material structure. Specify rafter or truss construction and define the thickness of each material in the assembly.
2. A common way to create a roof is to make a sketch based on the footprint of the building. Select each of the exterior walls to create the sketch. You can also draw lines and other objects defining the roof perimeter by using the appropriate sketch tools. If required, set an offset distance defining the roof overhang extending past the walls. The sketch reflects the offset value.
3. Specify the lines in the sketch that will slope and specify the appropriate slope for those lines. For example, for a basic gable roof, two sides of the roof slope and the end walls have gables. The lines in the sketch at the gable ends should be set not to slope. For a hip roof, all sides slope. Therefore, the lines in the sketch at the end walls should be set to slope. For more complex sloping roofs, the slope direction can be defined by drawing a slope arrow on the sketch in the upward direction of the slope. Then, the appropriate slope for the roof is specified. After the slope has been defined, ensure that the sketch forms a closed boundary before completing the command.
4. Another way to create a roof is to extrude a profile sketch. This method can be used for a more complex design, such as a curved panel roof. The sketch for the roof profile is made in an appropriate view that is perpendicular to the extrusion direction, such as an elevation view. Use the appropriate sketch tools to create the desired profile shape. The sketch for an extruded roof is typically made as an open (not closed) sketch. The extrusion direction and distance are specified and the thickness is applied by the program when the command is completed. The thickness is determined by the material structure defined for the roof.
5. Depending on the type of roof created and the heights of exterior walls, it may be necessary to attach the exterior walls to the roof. This adjusts the walls to meet the roof and typically alters the wall profile to align with the roof profile. Access the appropriate command and attach the top of the walls to the roof if the walls are below the roof. Attach the base of the walls to the roof if the walls are above the roof. In some cases, you may need to edit a wall profile in order to properly join the wall to the roof. This type of edit is usually completed in a section view. Using section views in parametric modeling is discussed in Chapter 22, *Building Sections*.

6. Create the additional components that are part of the roof. Typically, commands are available to create components such as fascia boards, soffits, and gutters. Create these components in the appropriate view. Fascia boards and gutters can sometimes be quickly created in a 3D view by picking edges of the model.
7. Complete the roof plan by adding the appropriate annotations. To display the exterior walls and framing below the roof, it may be necessary to adjust the view range. Change the display of the exterior walls to use a hidden linetype. Add notes and roof slope symbols as needed to show information about the roof construction.
8. Create a new sheet for the roof plan view. Insert the roof plan view onto the sheet. If needed, adjust the placement of text for the view title and scale. The scale for the roof plan should be 1/4″ = 1′-0″.
9. Check the entire roof plan. When you are sure the plan is complete, print or plot the sheet.

Summary

- Common roof designs include gable, hip, mansard, and gambrel roofs, but several other roof designs also exist.
- A roof is supported by rafters or roof trusses.
- Adequate ventilation in the attic space is necessary to avoid the formation of moisture underneath the roof sheathing.
- Flashing is used to shed water away from areas of potential leakage.
- The roofing material used on a house should have a long life and provide a waterproof surface.
- A roof plan or a roof framing plan is included in a set of architectural working drawings when it is necessary to clarify construction requirements for the roof.

Internet Resources

ATAS International
Manufacturer of metal roofs, walls, and accessories

CertainTeed
Manufacturer of sustainable building products

Cor-A-Vent
Manufacturer of roof vents

GAF Building Materials
Manufacturer of residential and commercial roofing materials

McElroy Metal
Manufacturer of Met-Tile (metal roofing that simulates tile)

Review Questions

Answer the following questions using the information in this chapter.

1. Give the names of at least 10 distinct roof types.
2. The roof framing member that extends from the ridge to the top plate or beyond is called a(n) _____.
3. What formula is used to calculate the fractional pitch of a roof?
4. The _____ of a roof is one-half the span.
5. The pitch of a roof that has a slope of 45° is _____.
6. List three things that determine rafter size.
7. The _____ is the overhang of the roof at the eave line that forms a connection between the roof and side walls.
8. What is the difference between an *open cornice* and a *box cornice*?
9. Name three types of roof trusses that are commonly used in residential construction.
10. List information required to purchase roof trusses for a home.
11. What is a *gusset*?
12. Explain what can happen if sufficient ventilation is not provided in an attic space.
13. The total area of ventilator openings should be a minimum of _____ of the ceiling area.
14. What is the purpose of roof flashing?
15. Name two materials commonly used for roof flashing.
16. How wide should the flashing be if the roof slope is 5:12?
17. Identify five roofing materials that are used on residential structures.
18. When is a roof plan required in a set of architectural working drawings?

Suggested Activities

1. Contact several manufacturers of roof covering materials and ask for specifications and descriptive literature about their products. Display the literature and then add it to the classroom collection.
2. Build a scale model of an open cornice, a box cornice, or close cornice. Use a scale of 1″ = 1′-0″ and label the various parts. Display your model.
3. Using CADD, design a roof for a 24′ × 36′ cottage or a small house of your choice. Draw a roof plan and a roof framing plan. Dimension the drawings and describe the materials used.

4. Build scale models of three different types of trusses. Compare their strength by applying weight to each model until it breaks. Write a description of your testing procedure and record your results. Present your data to the class.

Problem Solving Case Study

A new client has come to your architectural office in Idaho Falls, Idaho, to discuss ideas for her family's new residence. She is moving to Idaho from a metropolitan area in New York state in order to take a new position with a law firm. She has requested a Southwest-style flat roof for her new house.

Given this preliminary information regarding the requested roof design, answer the following questions.

1. Why might a flat roof be a poor choice in Idaho Falls?
2. What type of roof design would you recommend for this client?

ADDA Certification Prep

The following questions are presented in the style used in the American Design Drafting Association (ADDA) Drafter Certification Test. Answer the questions using the information in this chapter.

1. Which of the following statements are true about roof design and construction?
   A. A roof truss is an assembly of members that form a rigid framework of triangular shapes.
   B. Roof framing is designed to support the roof covering materials.
   C. Most flat roofs are pitched at about 1/8″ to 1/2″ per foot to aid in drainage.
   D. Cornices are cut to the proper dimensions by locating the ridge cut, seat cut, plumb cut, and tail cut.
2. Which of the following statements are *false*?
   A. The thickness of sheathing is the same regardless of the spacing of the rafters.
   B. In a box cornice, a soffit board encloses the space between the end of a projecting rafter and the wall.
   C. The curved panel roof is similar to the gable roof in style and application.
   D. The clear span is the horizontal distance from the inside of one exterior stud wall to the inside of the opposite exterior stud wall.
3. Match each type of roof with its description.
   Roof types: 1. Gambrel, 2. Butterfly, 3. Warped, 4. Mansard, 5. Shed
   A. Similar to a flat roof, but has more pitch.
   B. Has a valley in the middle instead of a ridge.
   C. Named for a French architect.
   D. Often used on barns to provide more vertical space.
   E. Has complex curvature; the most common shape is a hyperbolic paraboloid.

Curricular Connections

1. **Social Science.** To a certain extent, the style and pitch of a roof reflect the area of the country in which you live. Research three regions in the United States with different climates, including the region in which you live. For each region, list the most common roof styles and their roof pitches. Compare and contrast these roof styles and pitches in a written report.

STEM Connections

1. **Math.** A client has requested a design for a flat-roof cottage in south Texas. The cottage will be 32′ square. You have designed the roof to have a pitch of 1/8″ per foot, sloping from the front to the back of the house, to aid in drainage. What is the difference between the roof height at the front of the house and the back of the house?

2. **Engineering.** Roof trusses allow larger areas to be spanned with a minimum amount of material. Conduct research to determine why roof trusses are stronger than simple beams or joists of the same length. Prepare a multimedia presentation to show examples of why this is true.

Communicating about Architecture

1. **Writing and Speaking.** Create an informational pamphlet on roof designs in the United States. Include the different types of roofs, their designs, and the regions in the country where they can be found. Include illustrations in your pamphlet. Present your pamphlet to the class.
2. **Speaking.** Interview a roofer who works in residential construction. Ask the person to describe a typical day at work. Here are some questions you might ask:
   - What is the work environment like?
   - What are the job duties?
   - What are some of the hazards that exist on the job site?
   - What other types of professionals does he or she work with?

   Report your findings to the class, giving reasons why you would or would not want to pursue a career similar to that of the person you interviewed.

Photo Courtesy of James Hardie® Siding Products

Roof style and the selection of roofing materials are important elements in the overall design of the structure. The raised seam metal roof on this home is attractive and provides resistance to high winds.

Section 4

Construction Systems and Supplemental Drawings

Karamysh/Shutterstock.com

Chapter 18

Footings, Foundations, and Concrete

Objectives

After completing this chapter, you will be able to:

- Describe the procedure for staking out a house location.
- List the major considerations when designing a footing for a residential foundation.
- Analyze a residential building project to determine the appropriate type of foundation wall.
- Discuss the design considerations for wood, concrete, and masonry foundation walls.
- Calculate the load to be supported by a beam.
- Describe the characteristics of concrete, concrete blocks, masonry, and pavers used in residential construction.

Key Terms

9-12-15 unit method
batter boards
bearing wall
cement
concrete
contraction joints
creep
dead load
excavate
flexible paving system
float
footing
foundation walls
kip
lintel
live load
monolithic slab foundation
parge coat
pier foundation
pilaster
post (column) foundation
reinforcement bars (rebar)
rigid paving system
screed
screed board
slab foundation
stem wall
stepped footing
T-foundation
trowel
wood foundation

A good house foundation that will support the structure adequately requires careful planning and design. The architect or building designer can select from masonry, all-weather wood, or slab styles of foundation for the structure. See **Figure 18-1**. Each type of foundation requires careful measuring and calculations.

Specialty CADD software packages are available to calculate permissible spans for various materials, generate details, and draw foundation plans. Many architects and building designers take advantage of these CADD packages.

Staking Out the House Location

"Staking out" the house is the process of placing stakes in the ground at the corners of the building. This is done to provide reference points while the foundation is built. The site plan provides the necessary dimensions for staking out the location of the house on the lot. A measuring tape and contractor's level are used to stake out the building accurately. When angles other than 90° must be measured, a surveyor's transit is also required.

The first step in staking out the house is to locate each corner by laying off the distances indicated on the site plan. A stake is driven into the ground at the location of each corner to identify its position. Square corners can be laid out using the ***9-12-15 unit method*** shown in **Figure 18-2**. These proportions define a right triangle and establish a 90° angle corner. To use this method, measure 9 units along one leg of

A Goodheart-Willcox Publisher

B The Engineered Wood Association

C Goodheart-Willcox Publisher

Figure 18-1. Three different types of residential foundations. A—Typical masonry foundation. B—All-weather wood foundation. C—Slab foundation.

the corner and 12 units along the other leg. The distance between these two endpoints should be 15 units. Adjust the angle between the legs until the distance is exactly 15 units. The position of all corners should then be checked for accuracy by diagonal measurement, as shown in **Figure 18-3**. Both diagonal measurements should be equal in a rectangle with perfect 90° corners.

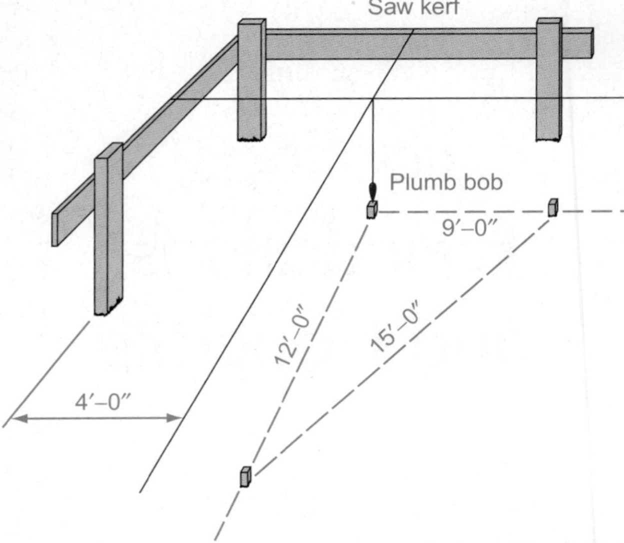

Goodheart-Willcox Publisher

Figure 18-2. Squaring a corner using the 9-12-15 unit method.

Batter boards are used to retain the location of the foundation during excavation and construction. These are constructed of 2 × 4 stakes and a pair of 1 × 6 boards. The stakes are sharpened on one end and driven into the ground about 4′ outside of where the footing will be. A 1 × 6 board is nailed horizontally to the stakes so it is level. Each corner of the house will have two batter boards. All horizontal batter boards should be

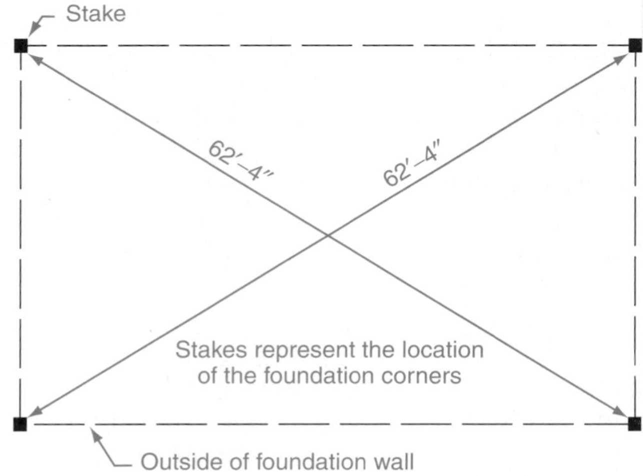

Goodheart-Willcox Publisher

Figure 18-3. The accuracy of the layout may be checked by comparing diagonal measurements. Both measurements must be equal if all corners are 90°.

in the same horizontal plane and have the same elevation. A strong cord or string is stretched across the boards at opposite ends of the building and located directly above the corner stakes. A plumb bob is used for accurate placement of each stake. Refer again to **Figure 18-2**. This is done for each side of the building. A saw kerf is usually made at the exact point on the horizontal batter board where the string is located. This prevents the string from moving along the board. After cuts are made in all batter boards and the strings are run, the strings locate the lines of the house. See **Figure 18-4**.

A control point is needed to determine the depth of excavation and foundation wall height. The corner with the highest elevation is usually selected for the control point. All depth or height measurements are made from this point. The finished floor should be at least 8″ above the finished grade.

Excavation

The equipment used to ***excavate***, or remove the top soil, depends on the size of the excavation and type of soil. A bulldozer or a tractor with a blade is usually used for footings and foundation walls. A trencher or backhoe may be used to excavate for foundations when either slab construction or a crawl space is planned. If the excavation needs to be deeper, such as when the home will have a basement, excavation is generally done using a backhoe or power shovel. The removed soil is saved for final grading.

Excavation for footings should be at least 6″ below the average maximum frost penetration depth. See **Figure 18-5** for the approximate frost depth in your area. In areas with a shallow frost depth, the footings should extend a minimum of 6″ into undisturbed earth. Local building codes usually specify the minimum footing depth for a given area.

Do not backfill under the proposed footings because uneven settling of the house may occur. In instances where part of the footings sit on rock, about 6″ of the rock should be removed under the proposed footing and replaced with compacted sand to equalize settling.

On sites that have recently been filled and regraded, the footings should extend down to the original undisturbed earth. The exception is when soil tests prove that the earth is sufficiently compacted to properly support the structure.

Excavation must be large enough to allow space to work when constructing the foundation wall and installing drain tile. A back slope is an outward taper of the excavation wall. The gradient of the back slope depends on the type of soil. Sandy soil is likely to cave in and therefore requires a gentle back slope. On the other hand, an excavated wall in clay may be nearly vertical.

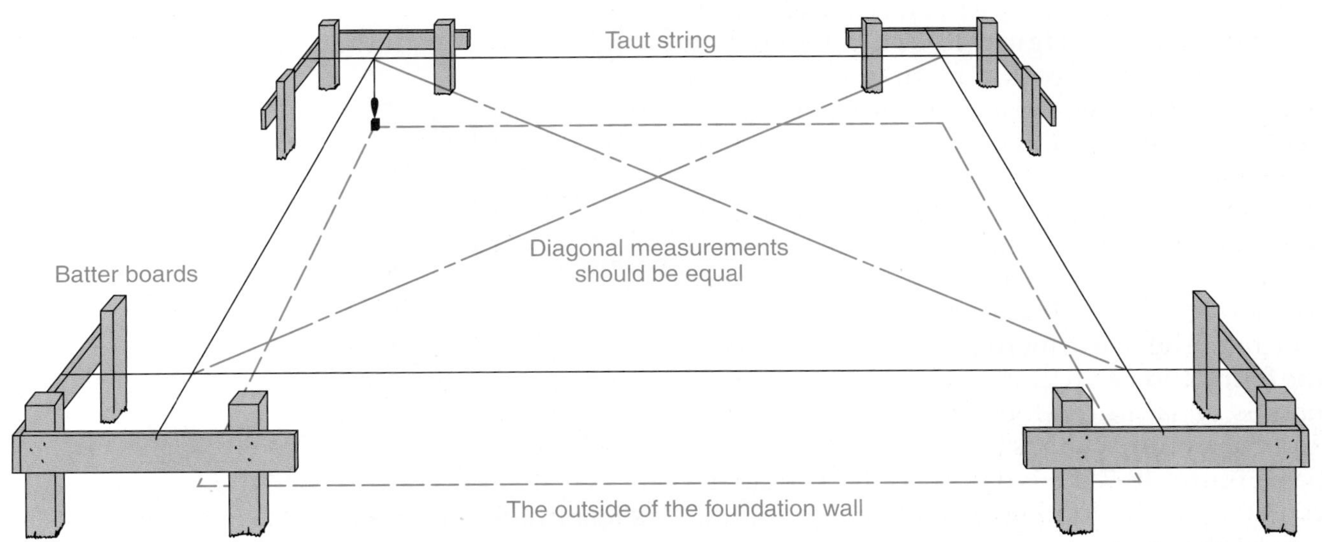

Figure 18-4. Batter boards are placed at each corner around the proposed foundation.

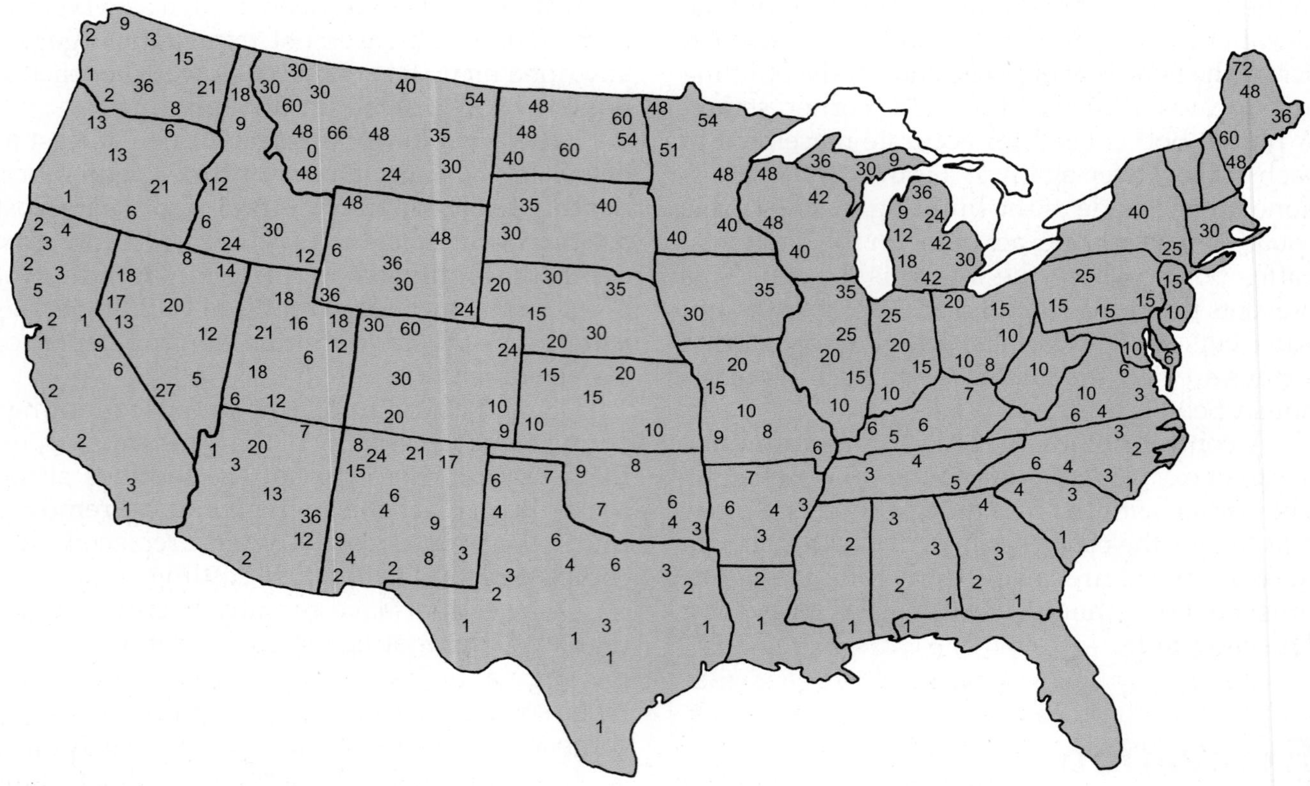

US Department of Commerce Weather Bureau

Figure 18-5. The average depth of frost penetration in inches for locations throughout the United States.

Footing Shapes and Specifications

Footings increase the supporting capacity of the foundation wall by dispersing the load over a larger area. See **Figure 18-6**. If a foundation were to be built on rock, a footing would not be essential. However, most houses are not built on such solid material and need footings to support the heavy loads.

The size and type of footing should be appropriate for the weight of the building and the load-bearing capacity of the soil. Footings for most residential structures are made of poured concrete. The size of footing is normally based on the foundation wall thickness. The footing thickness is equal to the foundation wall thickness and the footing width is twice the wall thickness. See **Figure 18-7**. Foundation walls should be centered on the footing. Therefore, the footing projects beyond each side of the foundation wall a distance equal to one-half the thickness of the foundation wall. This footing size is designed for most normal soil conditions ranging from sand to clay. If the soil load-bearing capacity is very poor, the size of footings should be increased and the footings should be reinforced with steel.

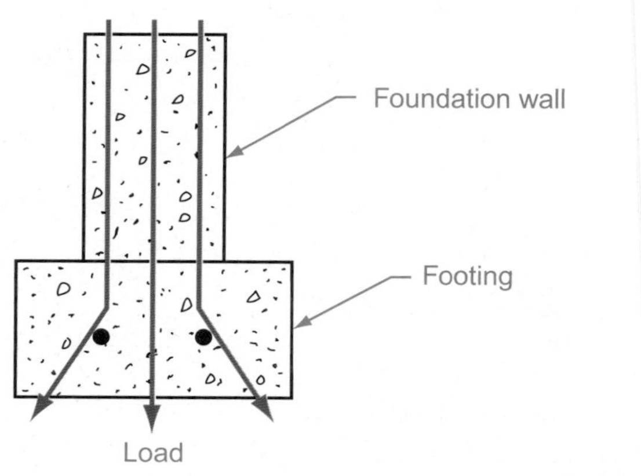

Goodheart-Willcox Publisher

Figure 18-6. The footing distributes the weight of the building, which is transmitted through the foundation wall, over a broad area.

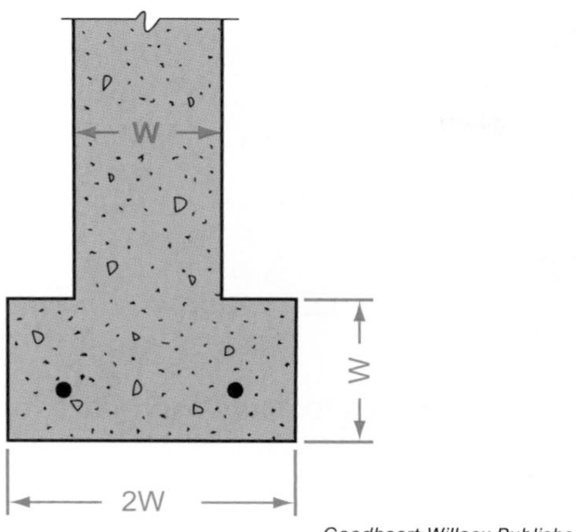

Goodheart-Willcox Publisher

Figure 18-7. The proportions of the footing are typically based on the foundation wall thickness.

During construction, the load increases on the footing and compresses the average subgrade soil. This compression causes a slight settlement of the structure. Whenever there are two or more different subsoils under various parts of the house, a deviation in settlement may occur due to the unequal compressibility of the soil. Also, the weight of most homes is greater on two of the four walls, which causes unequal loading. It is recommended that footings be large enough to minimize any of these differences in settlement to reduce cracking. Check your local building code for recommended minimum footing size.

When footings must be located over soft or poorly drained soils, soils that are not uniform, or backfilled utility trenches, two #6 (3/4″) steel ***reinforcement bars (rebar)*** should be placed as reinforcement along the length of the footing 2″ from the bottom. Adding rebar to any footing will provide further stability to the structure. Again, check local building codes for the required size of steel reinforcement on concrete footings and foundation walls.

Footings for fireplaces and chimneys are more massive than regular house footings because they must support greater weight. A solid footing reinforced with steel is usually required. The footing should be 12″ thick and extend 6″ beyond the perimeter of the chimney on all sides. The chimney footing should be cast integrally with the foundation wall footing if the chimney is located on an outside wall.

Stepped footings are frequently necessary when building on hilly terrain. See **Figure 18-8**. If stepped footings are required, the steps should be placed horizontally and the height of the vertical step should not be more than three-fourths of the distance between the steps. Step height and length should be multiples of 8″ if the foundation is made of concrete block. Good building practice requires two #4 (1/2″) steel reinforcement bars in the horizontal and vertical footing where steps are located. If steel bars are not used, the footing will probably crack at these points.

Foundation Walls

The ***foundation walls*** are the part of the house that extends down from the first floor to the footing. A foundation wall may also be a basement wall. Materials used to build foundation walls include cast (poured) concrete, concrete block, pressure-treated wood, and stone or brick. Cast concrete and concrete block are widely used in residential structures. Pressure-treated wood foundations are gaining acceptance for residential structures. Brick is much more expensive than cast concrete, block, or wood, and is seldom used. Stone was once used extensively, but is now rarely used as a foundation material. **Figure 18-9** illustrates these common foundation materials in section.

There are four basic types of foundations: foundation wall and footing, slab foundation, pier or post foundation, and wood foundation. See

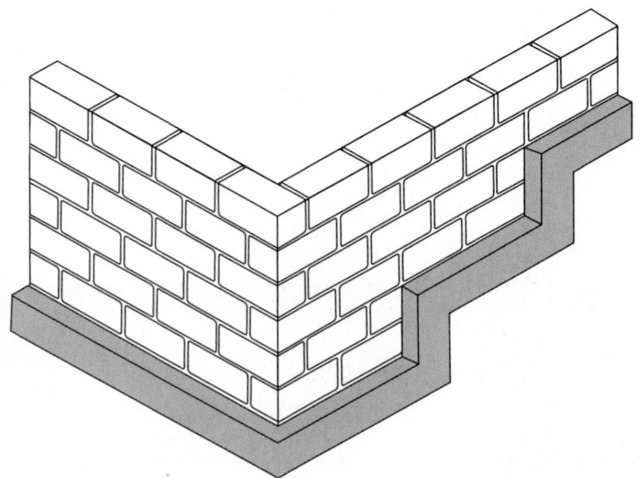

Goodheart-Willcox Publisher

Figure 18-8. A stepped footing and foundation wall are required for a sloping or hilly site.

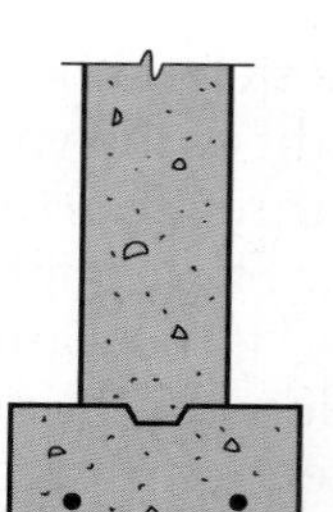

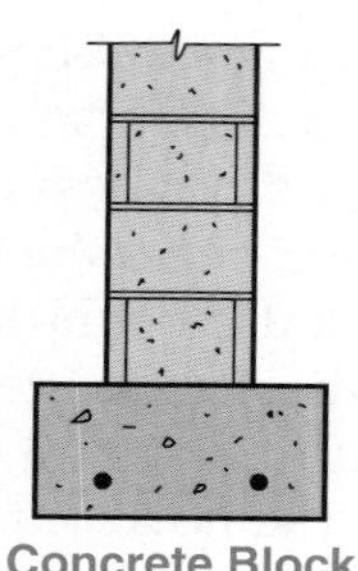

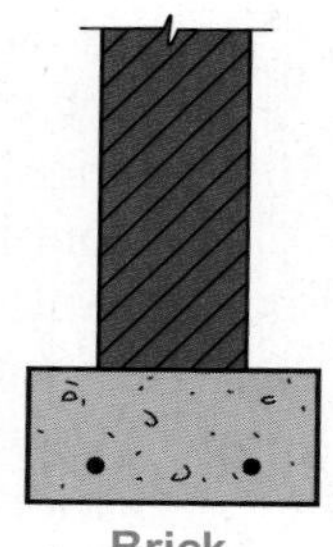

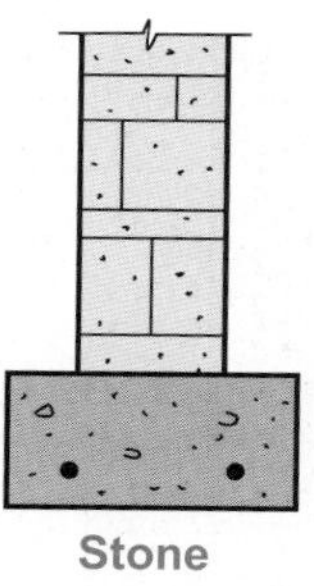

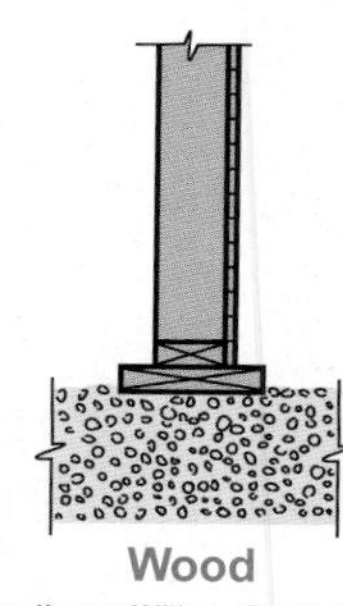

Goodheart-Willcox Publisher

Figure 18-9. Cast concrete, concrete block, and wood are commonly used for foundation walls. Brick and stone were once popular but are now rare in new construction.

Figure 18-10. The type chosen for a particular situation will depend upon the weight to be supported, load-bearing capacity of the soil, location of the foundation in the building, climate, local building codes, and preferred building practice. All of these factors should be considered when designing a foundation.

Foundation Wall and Footing

The most common type of foundation is the foundation wall and footing. This combination is commonly known as a ***T-foundation***. The foundation and footing are usually two separate parts, but may be cast as a single unit. **Figure 18-11** shows several applications of the T-foundation that are commonly found in residential construction.

The concrete for the footings of a T-foundation is usually placed in forms made from 2″ thick construction lumber, as shown in **Figure 18-12A**. The level form boards are nailed to stakes to prevent movement while the concrete is being cast. After the concrete is set, the forms are removed. A product that combines the form and drain tile is also available, as shown in **Figure 18-12B**. This form remains as part of the structure to provide drainage around the foundation.

Slab Foundations

A ***slab foundation*** is a floor and foundation system constructed with a concrete slab floor. There are different types of slab foundations in residential construction. The foundation may be placed at the same time the floor is cast, or the foundation may be a separate unit from the slab floor. Examples and dimensions of typical slab foundations are illustrated in **Figure 18-13**.

A ***monolithic slab foundation*** is an extension of a slab floor. It is placed at the same time as the floor is cast and is not a separate unit. It is sometimes called a *thickened-edge slab*. The foundation wall should extend down below the frost line, as in the case of the foundation wall and footing. The addition of steel rebar or mesh is

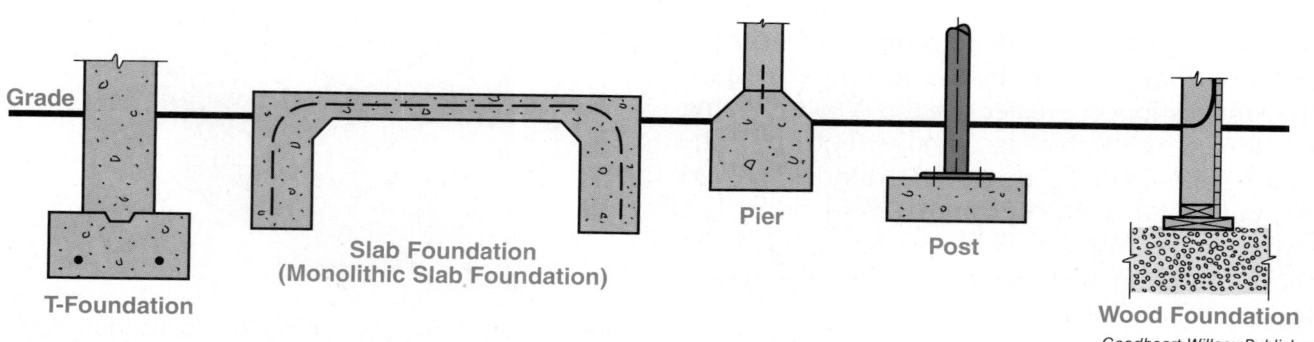

Goodheart-Willcox Publisher

Figure 18-10. Common types of foundations used in residential construction.

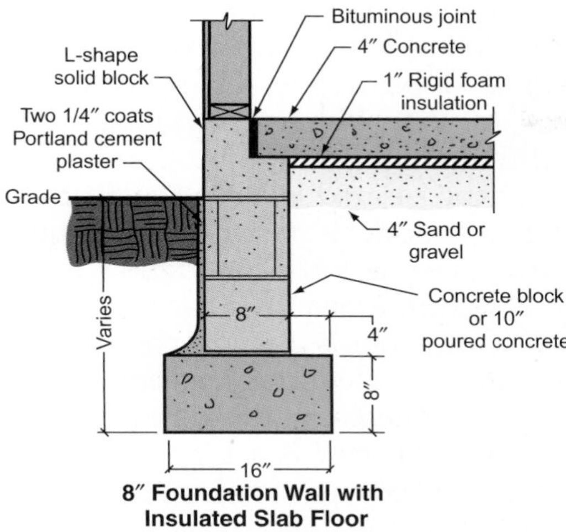

8″ Foundation Wall with Insulated Slab Floor

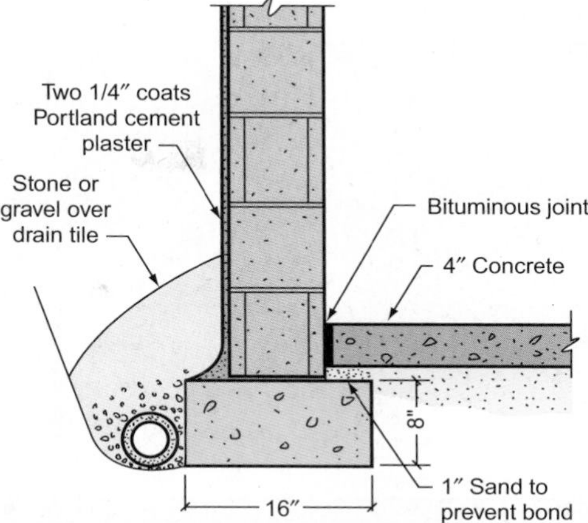

8″ Basement Wall and Footing

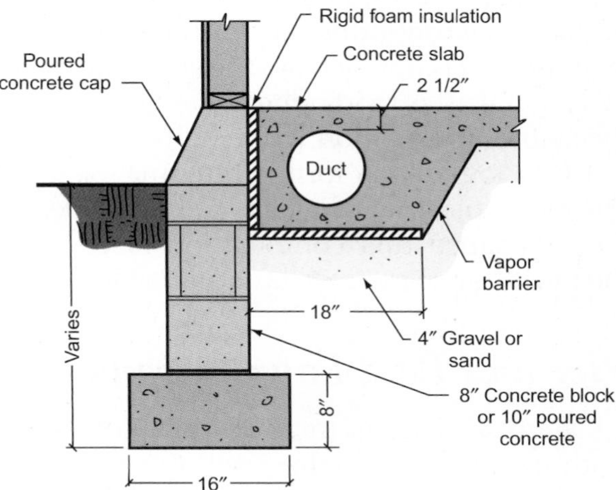

Insulated Slab for Perimeter Heat with Concrete Block Foundation

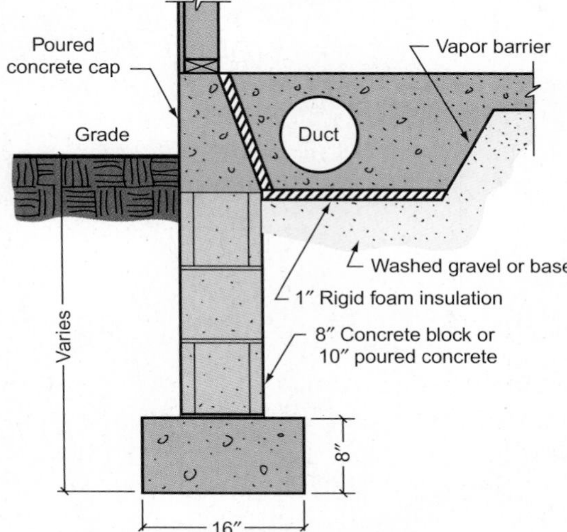

Insulated Slab for Perimeter Heat with Concrete Block Foundation

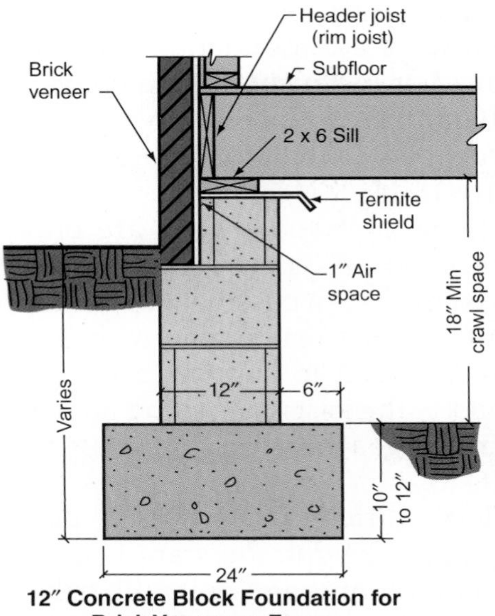

12″ Concrete Block Foundation for Brick Veneer on Frame

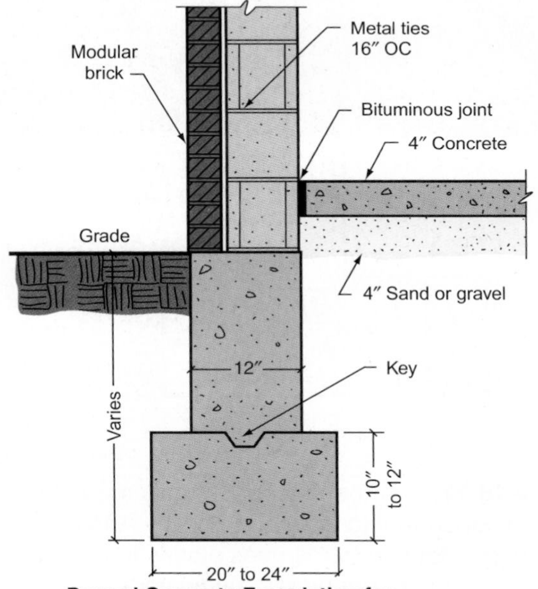

Poured Concrete Foundation for Composite Brick and Block Wall

Goodheart-Willcox Publisher

Figure 18-11. Typical T-foundation details.

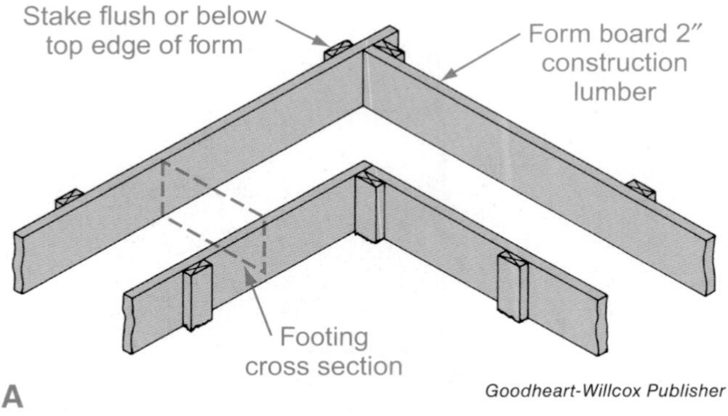

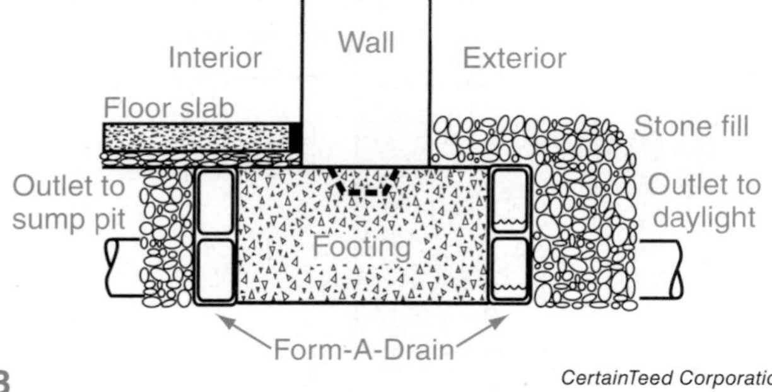

Figure 18-12. A—Footings are usually made by pouring concrete into form boards. B—Another approach to footing forms uses plastic forms that remain in place to remove groundwater.

recommended to prevent the foundation from cracking due to settling. This type of foundation is also used for bearing wall partitions.

Some of the primary advantages of the monolithic slab foundation are that it requires less time, expense, and labor to construct. Since no separate footing is required, excavation is not as extensive as for a foundation wall and footing. Less time is required because the entire foundation and floor is placed in one operation.

You may hear the terms *foundation wall* and *stem wall* used interchangeably, but the two are different. A ***stem wall*** is a type of foundation wall typically used in a crawl space foundation or slab foundation to support the above-grade walls. In a slab foundation, the stem wall may be part of a monolithic slab foundation, or it may be poured separately from the slab. The purpose of a stem wall is to join the above-grade walls to the slab or foundation while helping to provide a sturdy foundation for the building. Stem walls are often used with slabs in hurricane-prone areas because this combination is considered the most hurricane-resistant type of foundation.

Pier and Post Foundations

Many situations in residential construction lend themselves to the use of either a ***pier foundation*** or a ***post (column) foundation***. The basic components of these foundation types include a footing and a pier or post. Frequently, it is cheaper and just as satisfactory to use piers instead of a T-foundation under parts of a building. For instance, when a crawl space is planned and the distance is too great for a single span, a pier foundation is a logical choice. See **Figure 18-14**.

The terms *post* and *column* are often used interchangeably. A common application that involves columns is a basement or garage where the distance is too great to span with floor joists. Columns are used to support a beam that in turn supports the joists, providing an alternative to constructing a bearing wall partition. See **Figure 18-15**.

The basic difference between a pier and a column is their height. Piers are usually much shorter than columns and are ordinarily located under, not within, the house. **Figure 18-16** illustrates a few of the common styles of piers used in residential construction. **Figure 18-17** shows

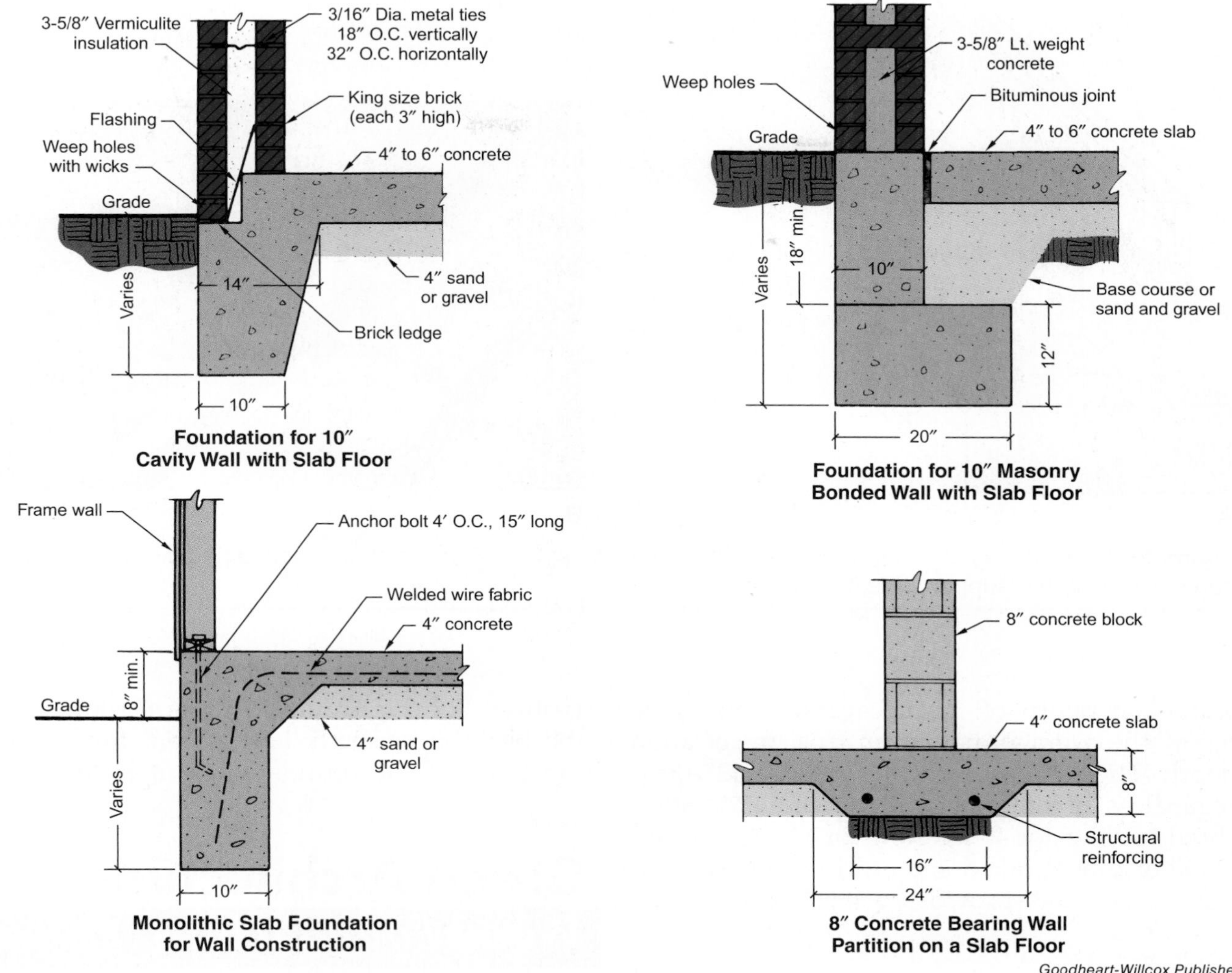

Figure 18-13. Typical slab foundation details.

a column (jack post) application in a basement.

The footing for a post foundation is usually square or rectangular. The minimum thickness for one-story construction is 8″ with a minimum projection of 5″ beyond the face of the column or post. Two-story homes require a minimum thickness of 12″ and a minimum projection of 7″ beyond the face of the column or post. The column or post may be masonry, steel, or wood. If wood is used, it should be pressure-treated to resist decay.

Wood Foundations

Wood foundations are known by several names: *permanent wood foundation (PWF)*, *all-weather wood foundation (AWWF)*, and *treated wood foundation*. Basically, a wood foundation is a below-grade, plywood-sheathed, pressure-treated stud wall. See **Figure 18-18**. The wood foundation is generally used in warmer climates where freezing of the ground is infrequent.

All wood used in the foundation is pressure-treated with chemical solutions that make the wood fibers useless as food for insects or fungus. The system is accepted by major model building codes, including the International Residential Code (IRC). A wood foundation may be used in full basement or crawl space construction and is adaptable to almost any site and light-frame building design.

For a structure with a crawl space, a trench is excavated to receive the footing and foundation

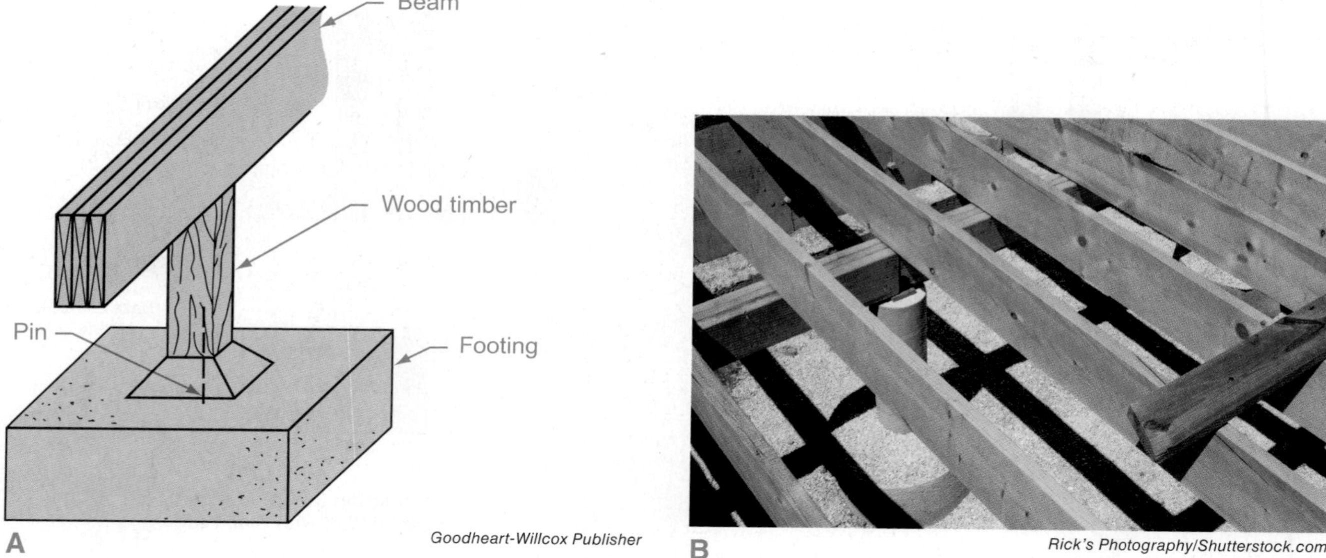

Figure 18-14. A—Parts of a pier foundation. B—A typical application in which the footing and pier support a beam, which in turn supports the floor joists.

wall. The depth of the excavation should be below the average maximum frost penetration depth. The trench should be at least 12″ deep regardless of the frost depth. The excavation should allow for 2″ of sand or 6″ of crushed stone or gravel raked smooth in the bottom of the trench. This provides a level base for the footing. See **Figure 18-19**. It is essential that the base be perfectly level to ensure that the top plate of the foundation unit is level and

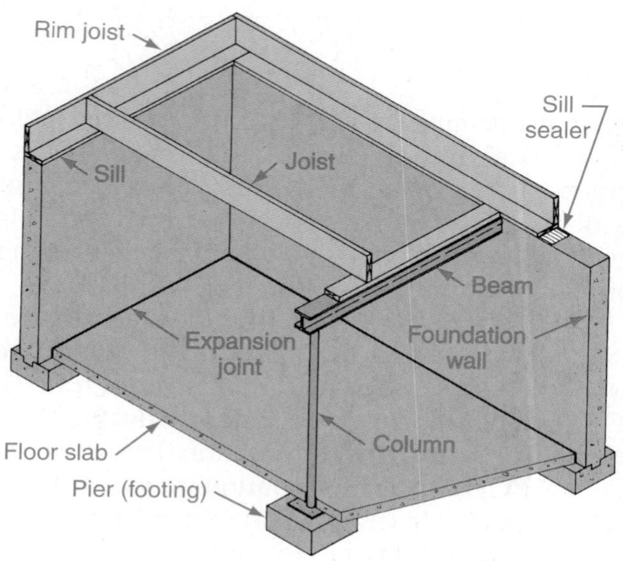

Figure 18-15. This column is supported by a footing and supports a beam.

Green Architecture

Wood Foundations

The use of wood for footings, foundation walls, and stem walls is considered by many people to be a sustainable alternative to traditional concrete materials. Wood can be grown sustainably and is ultimately recyclable if the time comes to demolish the structure.

When planning for a wood foundation, however, you must consider several important points. For example, you should determine the feasibility of using wood as opposed to traditional concrete construction in areas that have high water tables and/or a high level of annual rainfall. Check the local building codes for regulations regarding use of wood materials for a foundation. Finally, carefully check the chemicals that are used to preserve the wood. Most pressure-treated wood today is safe, but you should make very sure before you use it in the foundation of a house. Also check to be sure the chemicals used do not make the wood unrecyclable.

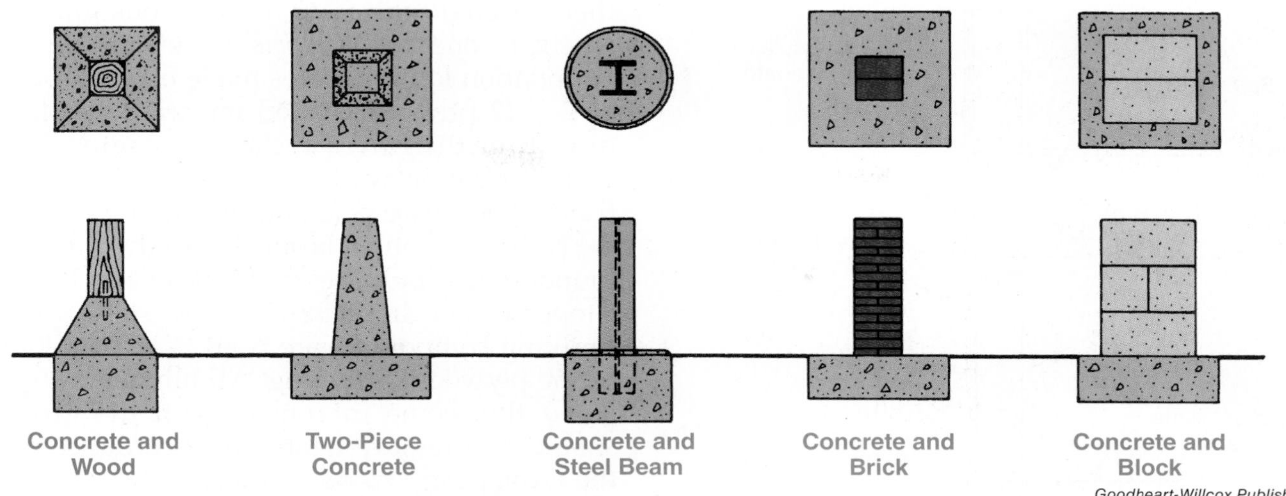

Figure 18-16. Piers are constructed in a variety of styles.

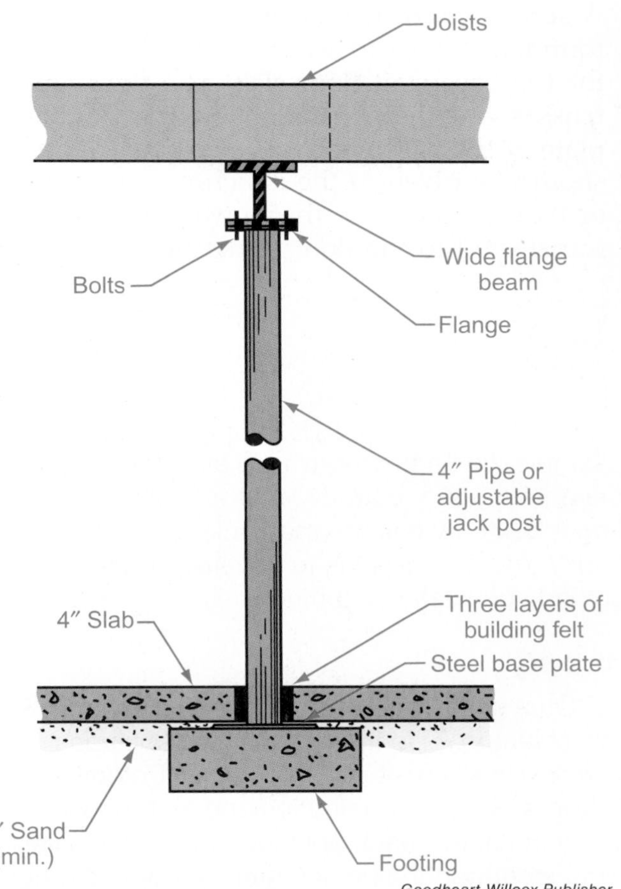

Figure 18-17. A pipe or adjustable jack post is frequently installed in a basement and used to support a steel beam on which floor joists rest.

Figure 18-18. This home is being built with an all-weather wood foundation.

accurately located. The actual footing, generally 10″ or 12″ wide, that bears (rests) on the ground must conform to the local building code.

When a wood foundation is used for a house with a basement, the site is excavated to the same depth as for other foundations. Plumbing lines are installed and provisions are made for foundation drainage according to local requirements. A basement sump should be installed in poorly drained soils or where groundwater is a problem. The bottom of the excavation is

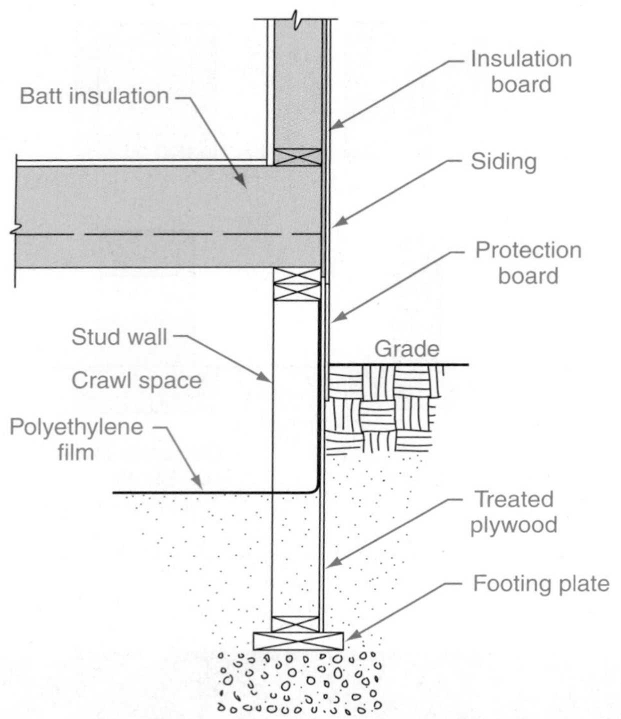

Figure 18-19. This is a section of a typical wood foundation for a crawl space.

then covered with 6″ to 8″ of porous gravel or crushed stone. This material is carefully leveled. Foundation footing plates made of 2 × 8, 2 × 10, or 2 × 12 pressure-treated material are placed directly on the gravel, as shown in **Figure 18-20**. The foundation walls are 2 × 4 or 2 × 6 stud frame. They are erected on the footing plates.

Nails and other fasteners used in a wood foundation should be made of silicon bronze, copper, or hot-dipped zinc-coated steel. Special caulking compounds are used to seal all joints in the plywood sheathing. All lumber and plywood that come in contact with the ground should be pressure-treated in accordance with the American Wood Protection Association (AWPA) U1 standard.

After the basement wall is in place, the porous gravel or crushed stone base is covered with a polyethylene film 6 mil (.006 inch) thick. A ***screed board*** is attached to the inside of the foundation wall to serve as an elevation guide for the basement floor slab. The floor joists or trusses are then installed on the double top plate of the basement wall. Particular attention should be given to the attachment of the joists or trusses to ensure that inward forces will be transferred to the floor structure. On the sides

Employability

Aptitudes and Abilities

Spending a lifetime—or even a few years—in a career for which you are not suited can be frustrating, to say the least. As you are considering your future career, take into account your aptitudes and abilities.

An *aptitude*, or natural talent, is an ability to learn something quickly and easily. Are some of your subjects in school much easier than others? Knowing this can help determine some of your talents. You may not be aware of all of your aptitudes if you have never been challenged to use them. A school counselor can give you an aptitude test to help reveal your strengths.

Abilities are skills you develop with practice. As you prepare to handle a new responsibility, you will learn that it requires certain skills. Can you develop those skills with practice? For example, can a person who is afraid of heights become a good roofer? Can someone lacking finger dexterity learn to manipulate precision tools? You may be able to develop different skills, so find out what you can do well.

Activity

On a sheet of paper, make a table with two columns. Title the left column "Aptitudes and Abilities" and the right column "Potential Careers." List your aptitudes and abilities in the left column. For each aptitude or ability you list, write a corresponding potential career in the right column. You may list the same career more than once. In fact, if you find that one potential career shows up more than once in the right column, you may want to investigate it further. It may be a career at which you can excel.

Osmose Wood Products

Figure 18-20. The footing plate for a wood foundation basement wall bears directly on the stone.

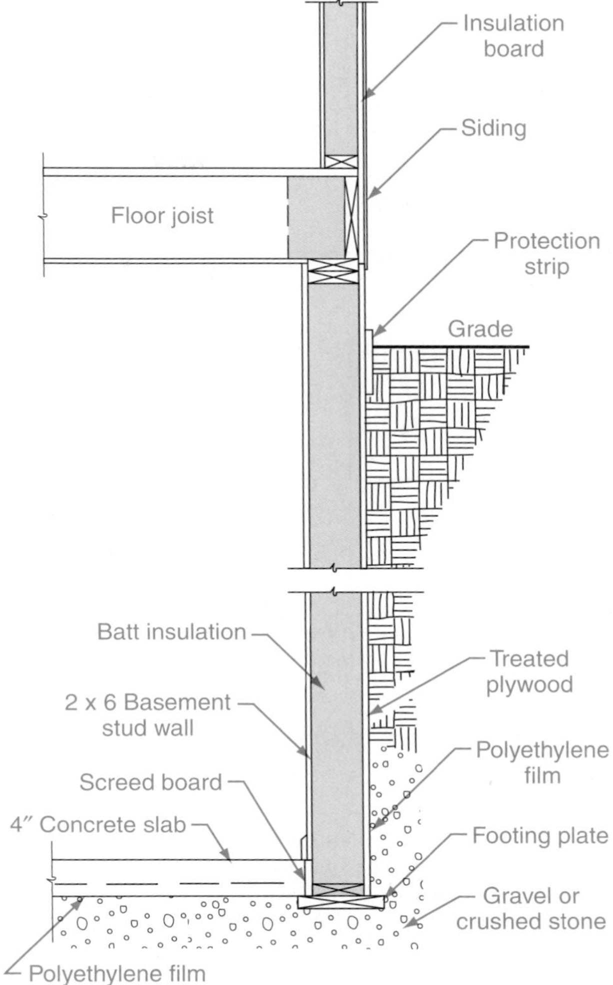

Goodheart-Willcox Publisher

Figure 18-21. A typical wood foundation for a basement.

of the structure where joists run parallel to the wall, blocking should be installed between the outside joists and first interior joists to resist lateral forces.

Before backfilling, a 6 mil polyethylene film should be applied to sections of the wall below grade to serve as a moisture barrier, as shown in **Figure 18-21**. All joints should be lapped at least 6″ and sealed with adhesive. The top edge of the film should be bonded to the wall at grade level with adhesive. A treated wood strip is attached along this edge and caulked. This strip will later serve as a guide for backfilling. *Caution:* Backfilling should not begin until the basement floor has cured and the first floor is installed.

As with any foundation system, satisfactory performance requires full compliance with recommended standards covering design, fabrication, and installation. Standards for wood foundations are available from the American Wood Council (AWC) and the American Forest and Paper Association (AF&PA).

Concrete and Masonry Basement Walls

The thickness of concrete and masonry (block) basement walls depends on both the lateral earth pressure and the vertical load to be supported. Basement walls should be at least as thick as the walls supported. An 8″ masonry foundation wall is permitted if it supports brick veneer on wood frame construction or a 10″ cavity wall where the total height of the wall supported, including the gable, does not exceed 20′. Recommended minimum wall thicknesses at various depths below grade are shown in **Figure 18-22**. These dimensions are based on conventional residential construction and typical soils. The height of the unbalanced fill is measured from the finished grade (exterior) to the basement floor.

Several factors influence the ability of a concrete or masonry basement wall to resist earth pressure. They include the height and thickness of the wall, bond of the mortar, vertical loading, support from crosswalls, pilasters or wall stiffeners, and support provided by the first floor framing. Lateral earth pressure may vary from

PLAIN MASONRY FOUNDATION WALLS

MAXIMUM WALL HEIGHT (feet)	MAXIMUM UNBALANCED BACKFILL HEIGHT[c] (feet)	PLAIN MASONRY[a] MINIMUM NOMINAL WALL THICKNESS (inches)		
		Soil classes[b]		
		GW, GP, SW and SP	GM, GC, SM, SM-SC and ML	SC, MH, ML-CL and inorganic CL
5	4	6 solid[d] or 8	6 solid[d] or 8	6 solid[d] or 8
	5	6 solid[d] or 8	8	10
6	4	6 solid[d] or 8	6 solid[d] or 8	6 solid[d] or 8
	5	6 solid[d] or 8	8	10
	6	8	10	12
7	4	6 solid[d] or 8	8	8
	5	6 solid[d] or 8	10	10
	6	10	12	10 solid[d]
	7	12	10 solid[d]	12 solid[d]
8	4	6 solid[d] or 8	6 solid[d] or 8	8
	5	6 solid[d] or 8	10	12
	6	10	12	12 solid[d]
	7	12	12 solid[d]	Footnote e
	8	10 grout[d]	12 grout[d]	Footnote e
9	4	6 grout[d] or 8 solid[d] or 12	6 grout[d] or 8 solid[d]	8 grout[d] or 10 solid[d]
	5	6 grout[d] or 10 solid[d]	8 grout[d] or 12 solid[d]	8 grout[d]
	6	8 grout[d] or 12 solid[d]	10 grout[d]	10 grout[d]
	7	10 grout[d]	10 grout[d]	12 grout
	8	10 grout[d]	12 grout	Footnote e
	9	12 grout	Footnote e	Footnote e

For SI: 1 inch = 25.4 mm, 1 foot = 304.8 mm, 1 pound per square inch = 6.895 Pa.

a. Mortar shall be Type M or S and masonry shall be laid in running bond. Ungrouted hollow masonry units are permitted except where otherwise indicated.

b. Soil classes are in accordance with the Unified Soil Classification System. Refer to Table R405.1.

c. Unbalanced backfill height is the difference in height between the exterior finish ground level and the lower of the top of the concrete footing that supports the foundation wall or the interior finish ground level. Where an interior concrete slab-on-grade is provided and is in contact with the interior surface of the foundation wall, measurement of the unbalanced backfill height from the exterior finish ground level to the top of the interior concrete slab is permitted.

d. Solid indicates solid masonry unit; grout indicates grouted hollow units.

e. Wall construction shall be in accordance with either Table R404.1.1(2), Table R404.1.1(3), Table R404.1.1(4), or a design shall be provided.

f. The use of this table shall be prohibited for soil classifications not shown.

Figure 18-22. This table shows recommended minimum thicknesses for masonry foundation walls.

almost zero to as great as the hydrostatic pressure (pressure due to gravity) of a liquid with the density of mud.

When local conditions indicate strong earth pressures (lateral force), pilasters can be used to strengthen the basement wall, as shown in **Figure 18-23**. A ***pilaster*** is a rectangular column that projects from a wall. Pilasters are also used for additional girder or beam support. Pilasters must be built at the same time that the basement wall is laid.

Blocks are frequently used to make pilasters. Pilaster blocks should have a minimum width of 16″ and project 4″ inside an 8″ thick basement wall, or 6″ inside a 10″ thick wall. With 12″ masonry walls, pilasters are not usually required. In 8″ thick walls over 30′ long, the distance between pilasters should not be greater than 15′. In 10″ thick walls over 36′ long, this distance should not be greater than 18′. Pilasters may also be required to stiffen concrete foundation walls. Since concrete walls are generally 10″ thick, cast-in-place pilasters are spaced every 18′ along the perimeter of the wall.

Wall stiffeners provide another method of strengthening the walls. This is accomplished

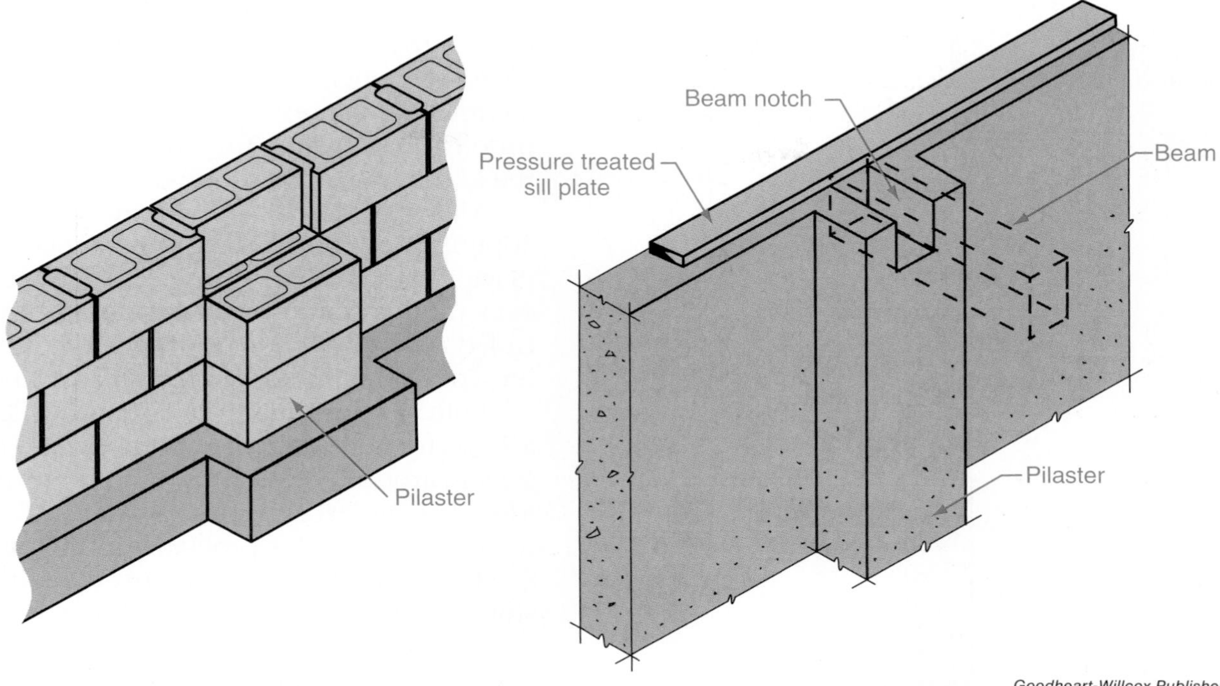

Goodheart-Willcox Publisher

Figure 18-23. Pilasters add strength to a basement wall and may be used to support a beam.

by placing a #4 bar in one core of the block from the top of the wall to the footing. The core of the block is then filled with concrete.

A third procedure is to use continuous horizontal steel joint reinforcement at 16″ intervals vertically. This method provides additional lateral support to the basement wall and helps prevent cracking.

Basement walls should extend at least 8″ above the finished grade in wood frame construction. Wood sills should be anchored to the basement walls with 1/2″ bolts 15″ long and spaced according to local building codes. Anchor clips can also be used to attach the sill, as shown in **Figure 18-24**. Each sill piece should have at least two bolts. Anchor bolts are placed in the cores of the top two courses of masonry, which are then filled with mortar or concrete. Core filling may be supported by a piece of metal lath or similar material.

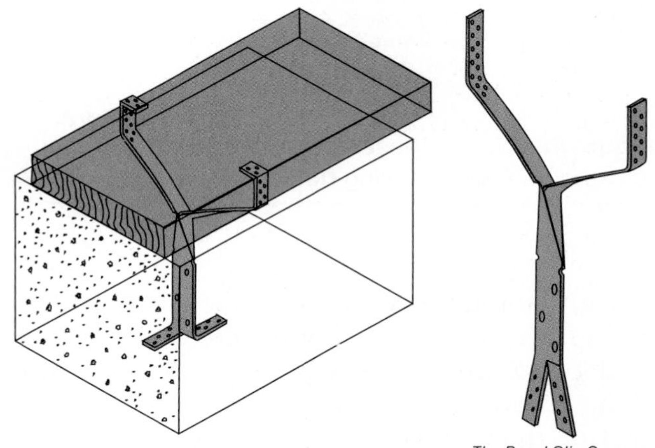

The Panel Clip Company

Figure 18-24. Anchor clips can be used to secure the sill plate to the foundation.

Basement walls may be slightly shorter than first and second floor walls. However, the distance from the top of the basement floor to the bottom of the floor joists above should be no less than 7′. A masonry basement wall that is 11 courses (rows) above the footing with a 4″ solid cap provides a clear height of 7′-5″ from the finished floor to the bottom of the floor joists. See **Figure 18-25**. Some space is generally required for heating ducts, pipes, and beams.

Load-bearing crosswalls in the basement should not be tied to the exterior walls in a masonry bond. Instead, they should be anchored with metal tie bars. The tie bars are usually 1/4″ thick, 1-1/4″ wide, and 28″ long. Each end has a

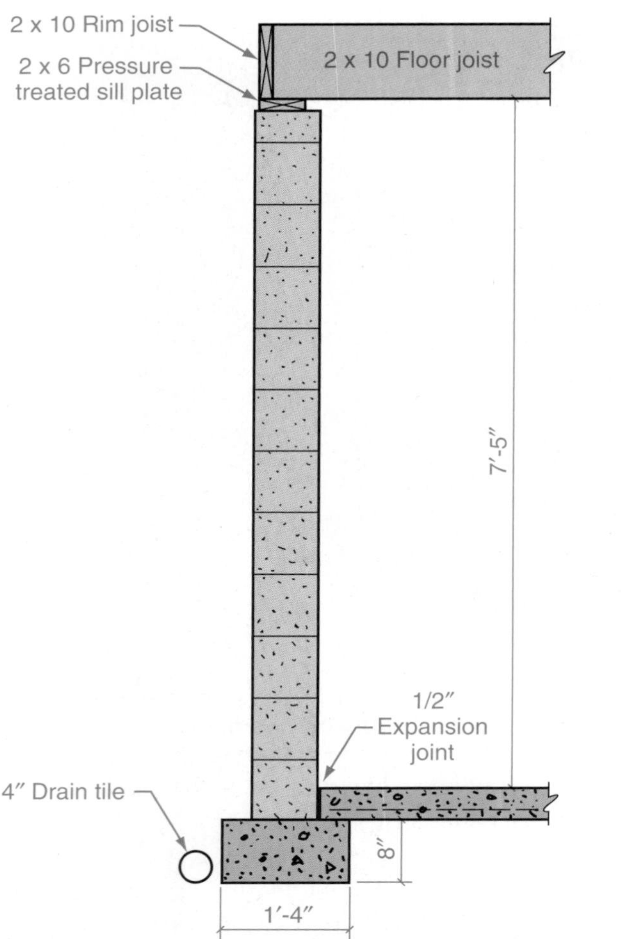

Figure 18-25. This basement wall provides an acceptable floor-to-ceiling height of 7′-5″.

2″ right-angle bend that is embedded in block cores filled with mortar or concrete.

Floor loads are distributed more uniformly along the wall if the top course of block supporting the first floor is capped using one of the following:

- Solid block.
- Solid top block in which the hollow cores do not extend up into the top 4″ of the block.
- Reinforced concrete masonry bond beam.
- Cores in the top course filled with concrete or mortar.

When the wood sill of the first floor bears on both the inner and outer face shells of the block, capping may be omitted.

Basement walls require damp-proofing on the outside to prevent groundwater from seeping through the wall. Cast concrete walls may be damp-proofed with a heavy coat of hot tar or two coats of cement-base paint. These paints are commercially prepared specifically for damp-proofing basements. Tar or paint is applied from the grade line to the footing.

Masonry (block) walls are damp-proofed by applying two 1/4″ thick coats of cement-mortar or plaster to the wall. A thin coat of plaster applied over the foundation wall for damp-proofing is called a ***parge coat***. When the parge coat is dry, it is covered with hot tar or a similar material.

Both cast concrete and masonry walls require a 4″ perforated drain tile or other water removal system around the perimeter of the footing. This tile removes excess groundwater and reduces the chance of water problems in the basement. See **Figure 18-26**. The tile is covered with coarse stone or gravel to a depth of about 18″ to allow water to seep into the tile.

In poorly drained and wet soils, added precautions may be advisable to ensure against water damage. A sump pump may be installed in the basement to remove any water that seeps in. The floor slab may be reinforced to resist uplift by groundwater pressure. A check valve in the floor drain will prevent water from flowing in through the drain from the storm sewer.

Beams and Girders

Most houses have a span that is too great to have unsupported floor joists. Therefore, a beam or girder is required to support the joists and prevent excessive sagging. The beam is usually placed an equal distance from each outside wall or under a bearing wall. A ***bearing wall*** is designed to support part of the load of the structure. The beam runs perpendicular to the direction of the floor joists.

Beams may be either wood or metal. There are two types of traditional wood beams: built-up and solid. Built-up beams are used more frequently than solid ones because they are easier to handle, more readily available, and they do not check (crack) to the extent of solid beams. However, solid beams are generally stronger and more fire-resistant.

Two types of steel beams are commonly used. These are S-beams and wide flange beams (W-beams). See **Figure 18-27**. The S-beam was

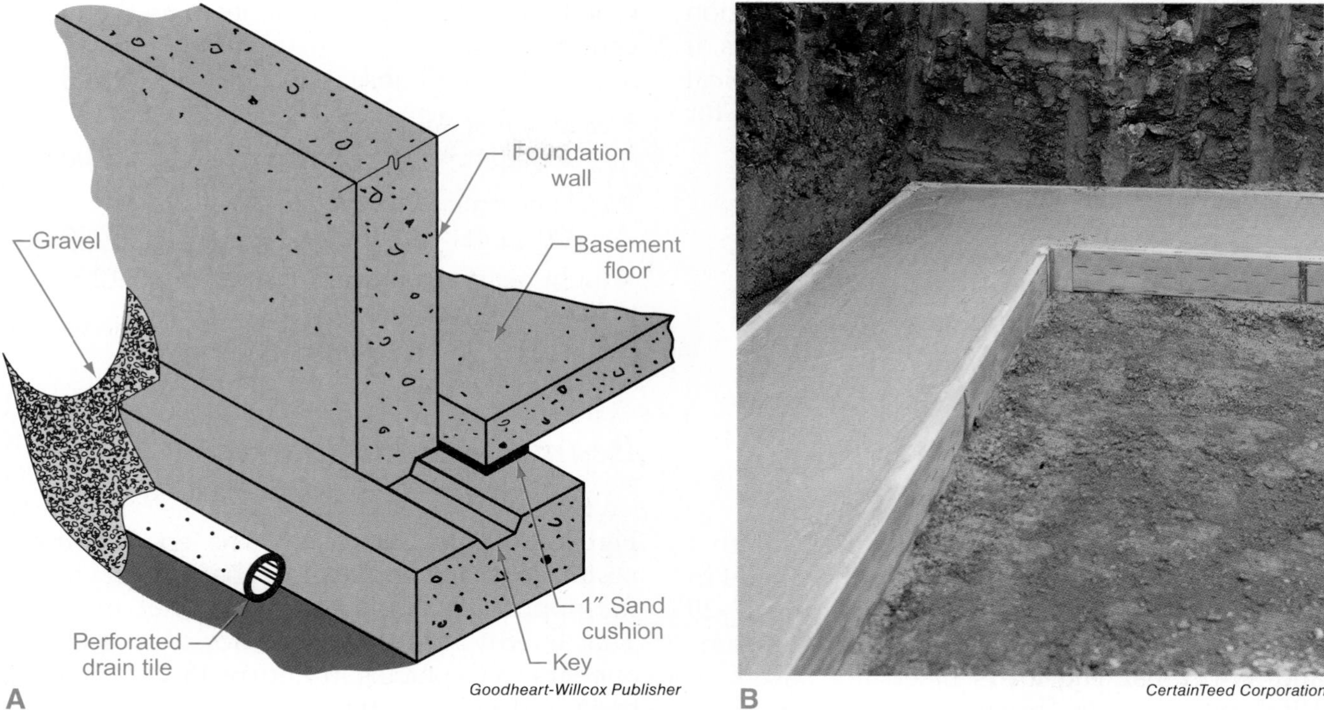

Figure 18-26. A—Drain tile placed along the footing helps prevent water problems in the basement. B—The product shown here is used as forms for the footings and then stays in place to serve as the drain tile.

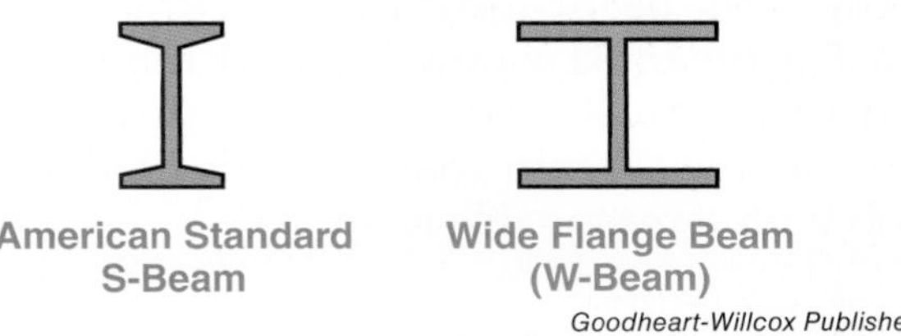

Figure 18-27. These are cross sections of two typical steel beams used in residential construction.

formerly called an I-beam. The W-beam supports greater weight and is more stable than the S-beam. For these reasons, the W-beam is more popular for residential construction.

The size of the beam needed is based on the weight of the structure. **Figure 18-28** shows the approximate area supported by a beam in a two-story home. The weight of this area must be known when calculating the beam size. Weights are designated either as live loads or dead loads. ***Live loads*** are those fixed or moving weights that are not a structural part of the house. Examples include furniture, occupants, snow on the roof, and wind. ***Dead loads*** are the static or fixed weights of the structure itself. Examples of dead

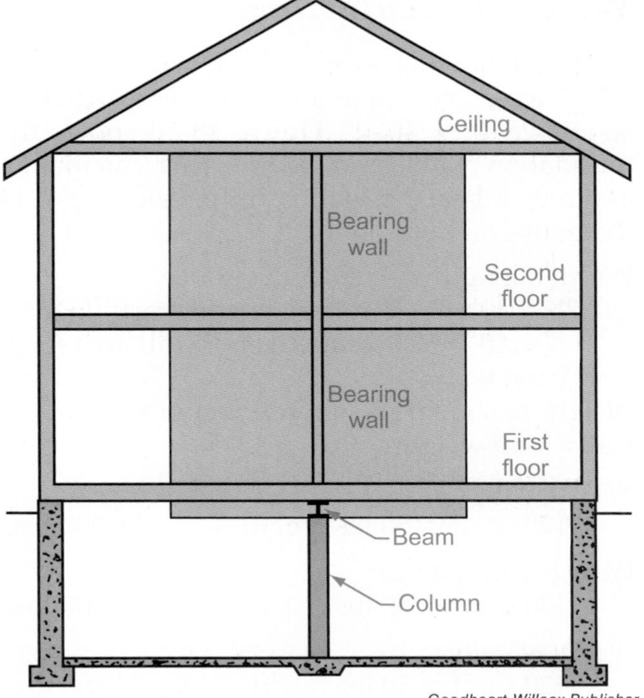

Figure 18-28. The shaded area represents the weight supported by the W-beam.

loads are the weights of roofing, foundation walls, siding, and joists. To simplify matters, it will be assumed that loads found in a typical residence are as follows. Use these figures for load calculations in this text.

- **First Floor.** Live load plus dead load = 50 pounds per square foot.
- **Second Floor.** Live load plus dead load = 50 pounds per square foot.
- **Ceiling.** Live load plus dead load = 30 pounds per square foot.
- **Walls.** Dead load = 10 pounds per square foot.
- **Roof.** No load on the beam. Exterior walls generally support the roof.

Tables that give the greatest safe loads that beams will support usually record the weight in kips. One *kip* equals 1000 pounds. **Figure 18-29** shows span data for American Standard S-beams and W-beams. The loads listed are based on allowable strength design (ASD) calculations. Check local building codes for specific requirements related to load specifications for structural framing and design.

Weight Calculations

The following example calculates the load for a two-story frame structure. The structure size is 28′-0″ × 40′-0″. **Figure 18-30** shows the foundation walls and beam. This calculation assumes a bearing wall running the length of the house on both floors.

Width × length = Area of the house
28′ × 40′ = 1120 square feet for each floor
8′ × 40′ = 320 square feet of wall area for each wall

Weight per square foot × number of square feet = total weight

Weight of first floor
1120 sq. ft. × 50 lbs./sq. ft. = 56,000 lbs.

Weight of second floor
1120 sq. ft. × 50 lbs./sq. ft. = 56,000 lbs.

Weight of ceiling
1120 sq. ft. × 30 lbs./sq. ft. = 33,600 lbs.

Weight of roof on beam
(none in this example) = 0 lbs.

Total = 145,600 lbs.

One-half of the total weight bears on the center beam.
1/2 × 145,600 lbs. = 72,800 lbs.

Weight of first floor wall
320 sq. ft. × 10 lbs./sq. ft. = 3200 lbs.

Weight of second floor wall
320 sq. ft. × 10 lbs./sq. ft. = 3200 lbs.

Weight bearing on beam = 79,200 lbs.

Convert to kips by dividing by 1000. The weight in kips is 79.2 kips.

Beam Calculations

Since no posts are used, as shown in **Figure 18-30**, the span is 40′. The length of beam needed in this example is 40′. A beam large enough to support 79.2 kips over 40′ is not practical. That is why no information for this condition appears in the tables in **Figure 18-29**. The span must be decreased by the addition of one or more support posts. Study the table in **Figure 18-31** and the illustrations in **Figure 18-32**. Notice how the beam size and the weight on the beam decrease with the addition of support posts. Any of the beam and post configurations shown in **Figure 18-31** would support the load of the structure. Steel is sold by the pound, so choose the smallest beam that will adequately do the job with a reasonable span.

Post Calculations

Once the size of beam and number of post supports have been determined, the size of each post must be calculated. This process is not as complex as the procedure for calculating beam sizes. If three posts are used for this example, each beam segment or 10′-0″ span must sustain 19.8 kips (79.2 kips divided by four 10′-0″ spans = 19.8 kips). Each post must also support this weight because it must bear the weight on either side halfway to the next post. See **Figure 18-33**. Steel post design information is given in **Figure 18-34**. Find the required post diameter by finding the weight to be supported and the length of the post in the table.

The unbraced length in this example is 8′ and the weight that must be supported by each post is 19.8 kips. The smallest column shown in the table in **Figure 18-34** is a nominal size of 3″.

Maximum Allowable Uniform Loads for American Standard S-Beams with Lateral Support — Span in Feet																				
Size of Beam	Weight of Beam Per Foot	4	6	8	10	12	14	16	18	20	22	24	26	28	30	32	34	36	38	40
4 x 2-5/8	7.7	12.6	8.4	6.3	5.0															
4 x 2-3/4	9.5	14.5	9.7	7.3	5.8															
5 x 3	10.0	20.3	13.6	10.2	8.1	6.8														
6 x 3-3/8	12.5	30.4	20.2	15.2	12.1	10.1	8.7													
6 x 3-5/8	17.2	37.7	25.1	18.9	15.1	12.6	10.8													
8 x 4	18.4	59.3	39.5	29.6	23.7	19.8	16.9	14.8	13.2	11.9										
8 x 4-1/8	23.0	69.0	46.0	34.5	27.6	23.0	19.7	17.2	15.3	13.8										
10 x 4-5/8	25.4	89.6	67.8	50.8	40.7	33.9	29.1	25.4	22.6	20.3	18.5	16.9								
10 x 5	35.0	127	84.8	63.6	50.9	42.4	36.3	31.8	28.3	25.4	23.1	21.2								
12 x 5	31.8	121	100	75.1	60.1	50.1	42.9	37.5	33.4	30.0	27.3	25.0	23.1	21.5	20.0					
12 x 5-1/8	35.0	148	107	80.1	64.1	53.4	45.8	40.1	35.6	32.0	29.1	26.7	24.7	22.9	21.4					
12 x 5-1/4	40.8	160	126	94.7	75.7	63.1	54.1	47.3	42.1	37.9	34.4	31.6	29.1	27.0	25.2					
12 x 5-1/2	50.0	219	146	109	87.5	72.9	62.5	54.7	48.6	43.8	39.8	36.5	33.7	31.3	29.2					
15 x 5-1/2	42.9		166	124	99.4	82.9	71.0	62.2	55.2	49.7	45.2	41.4	38.2	35.5	33.1	31.1	29.2	27.6		
15 x 5-5/8	50.0	238	184	138	111	92.2	79.0	69.2	61.5	55.3	50.3	46.1	42.6	39.5	36.9	34.6	32.5	30.7		
18 x 6	54.7		239	187	149	125	107	93.4	83.0	74.7	67.9	62.3	57.5	53.4	49.8	46.7	44.0	41.5	39.3	37.4
18 x 6-1/4	70.0	369	297	223	178	149	127	111	99.0	89.1	81.0	74.3	68.5	63.6	59.4	55.7	52.4	49.5	46.9	44.6
20 x 6-1/4	66		291	250	200	166	143	125	111	99.9	90.8	83.2	76.8	71.3	66.6	62.4	58.8	55.5	52.6	49.9
20 x 6-3/8	75.0		364	273	218	182	156	137	121	109	99.3	91.0	84.0	78.0	72.8	68.3	64.2	60.7	57.5	54.6

Loads are in kips. 1 kip = 1000 pounds

Maximum Allowable Uniform Loads for Wide Flange W-Beams with Lateral Support — Span in Feet																				
Size of Beam	Weight of Beam Per Foot	4	6	8	10	12	14	16	18	20	22	24	26	28	30	32	34	36	38	40
8 x 4	13	56.9	37.9	28.4	22.8	19.0	16.3	14.2	12.6											
8 x 5-1/4	18	74.9	56.6	42.4	33.9	28.3	24.2	21.2	18.9	17.0										
8 x 5-1/4	21	82.8	67.9	50.9	40.7	33.9	29.1	25.4	22.6	20.4										
8 x 6-1/2	24		76.8	57.6	46.1	38.4	32.9	28.8	25.6											
8 x 8	31		91.2	75.8	60.6	50.5	43.3	37.9	33.7	30.3										
10 x 5-3/4	22		86.5	64.9	51.9	43.2	37.1	32.4	28.8	25.9	23.6	21.6								
10 x 8	33		113	96.8	77.4	64.5	55.3	48.4	43.0	38.7	35.2	32.3								
10 x 10	49			136	121	100	86.1	75.3	67.0	60.3	54.8	50.2								
12 x 6-1/2	26		112	92.8	74.3	61.9	53.0	46.4	41.3	37.1	33.8	30.9	28.6	26.5	24.8					
12 x 8	40			141	114	94.8	81.3	71.1	63.2	56.9	51.7	47.4	43.8	40.6						
12 x 10	53				155	130	111	97.2	86.4	77.7	70.7	64.8	59.8	55.5	51.8					
12 x 12	65				189	158	135	119	105	94.8	86.2	79.0	72.9	67.7	63.2					
14 x 6-3/4	30		149	118	94.4	78.7	67.4	59.0	52.5	47.2	42.9	39.3	36.3	33.7	31.5	29.5	27.8			
14 x 8	43			167	139	116	99.2	86.8	77.2	69.5	63.1	57.9	53.4	49.6	46.3	43.4	40.9			
14 x 10	61				204	170	145	127	113	102	92.5	84.8	78.3	72.7	67.9	63.6	59.9			
14 x 10-1/8	74				251	210	180	157	140	126	114	105	96.7	89.8	83.8	78.6	74.0			
14 x 14-1/2	90					247	218	191	170	153	139	127	117	109	102	95.4	89.8			
16 x 7	36		187	160	128	106	91.2	79.8	71.0	63.9	58.1	53.2	49.1	45.6	42.6	39.9	37.6	35.5	33.6	
16 x 7-1/8	57			262	210	175	150	131	116	105	95.3	87.3	80.6	74.9	69.9	65.5	61.6	58.2	55.2	52.4
16 x 10-1/4	77				299	250	214	187	166	150	136	125	115	107	99.8	93.6	88.1	83.2	78.8	74.9
18 x 7-1/2	50			252	202	168	144	126	112	101	91.6	84.0	77.5	72.0	67.2	63.0	59.3	56.0	53.1	50.4
18 x 7-5/8	65			330	265	221	190	166	147	133	121	111	102	94.8	88.5	83.0	78.1	73.7	69.9	66.4
18 x 7-5/8	71			364	291	243	208	182	162	146	132	121	112	104	97.1	91.1	85.7	80.9	76.7	72.9
21 x 8-1/4	62			336	287	240	205	180	160	144	131	120	111	103	95.8	89.8	84.5	79.8	75.6	71.9

Loads are in kips. 1 kip = 1000 pounds

American Institute of Steel Construction

Figure 18-29. Span and load tables for American Standard S-beams and W-beams.

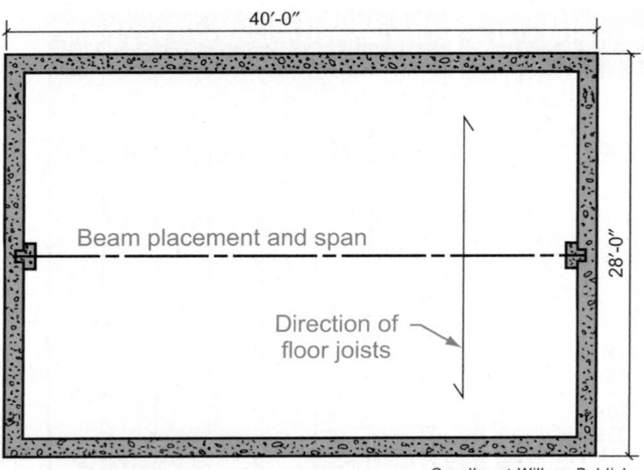

Figure 18-30. This is the foundation wall for the calculations in the text. Notice the direction of the joists and placement of the supporting beam.

This size is more than adequate since it will support 34 kips at a length of 8′. Therefore, the support posts should be 3″ in diameter; each weighs 7.58 pounds per foot or 60.64 pounds total.

Steel posts must have a fillet welded on both ends and provision for attachment to the beam. The post may be bolted or attached with clips. The size of the top flange is determined by the width of the beam to be supported. The bottom flange (often 8″ × 8″) should be larger than the top flange to provide a larger bearing surface on the footing.

Lintels

A ***lintel*** is a horizontal structural member that supports the load over an opening such as a door or window. Lintels may be constructed of precast concrete, cast-in-place concrete, lintel blocks, or steel angles. See **Figure 18-35**.

Openings in cast concrete walls do not require lintels. When lintels are used in a masonry wall, the ends must extend at least 4″ into the wall on either side of the opening. **Figure 18-36** shows a precast lintel over a door in a concrete block wall. Common precast lintel sizes for residential construction are 4″ × 8″, 4″ × 6″, and 8″ × 8″ in a variety of lengths.

Lintels are also made of steel angles. They are available as equal angles (both legs the same size) or as unequal angles. The table in **Figure 18-37** identifies the size of steel angles required to support a 4″ masonry wall above an opening. **Figure 18-38** shows a steel angle lintel supporting the load over a window opening in a brick wall.

Concrete and Masonry Characteristics

Concrete is the result of combining cement, sand, aggregate (usually stone or gravel), and water. ***Cement*** is composed of a mixture of lime, silica, alumina, iron components, and gypsum. The proportions of the ingredients vary with the

Effect of Adding Support Posts

	Span	Weight on Beam	Size of Beam and Weight	Kips Beam Will Support
One post S-beam W-beam	 20′-0″ 20′-0″	 39.6 kips 39.6 kips	 12″ x 5-1/2″ x 50.0 lbs./ft 14″ x 6-3/4″ x 30.0 lbs./ft	 43.8 kips 47.2 kips
Two posts S-beam W-beam	 13′-4″ 13′-4″	 26.4 kips 26.4 kips	 10″ x 4-5/8″ x 25.4 lbs./ft 8″ x 6-1/2″ x 24.0 lbs./ft	 29.1 kips 32.9 kips
Three posts S-beam W-beam	 10′-0″ 10′-0″	 19.8 kips 19.8 kips	 8″ x 4″ x 18.4 lbs./ft 8″ x 4″ x 13.0 lbs./ft	 23.7 kips 22.8 kips

Goodheart-Willcox Publisher

Figure 18-31. This table shows the effect of adding support posts on the load capacity of the beam.

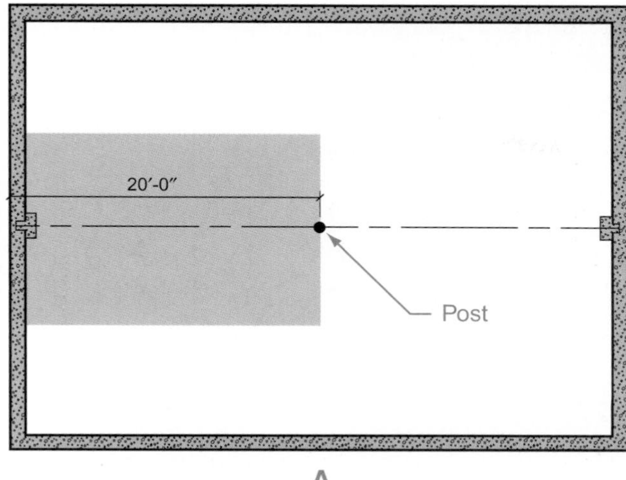

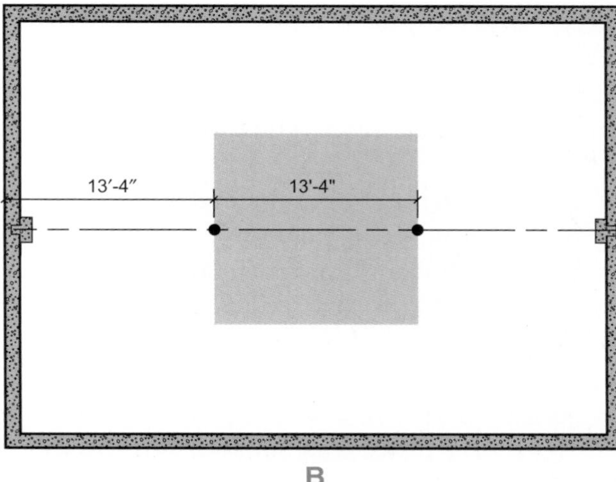

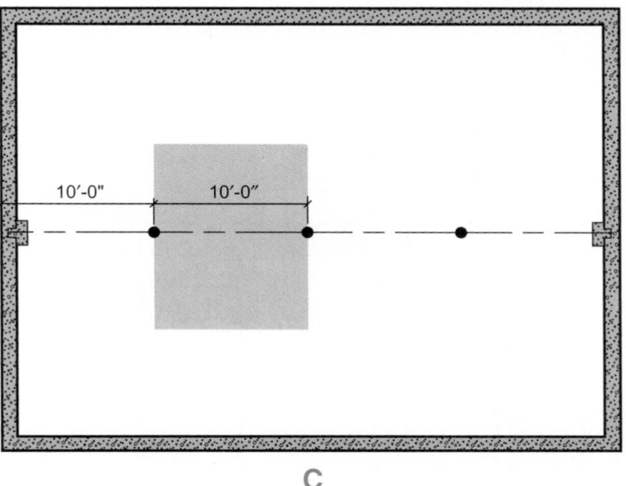

Goodheart-Willcox Publisher

Figure 18-32. The shaded area represents the weight supported by the beam span. A—Effective beam span with one post. B—Effective beam span with two posts. C— Effective beam span with three posts.

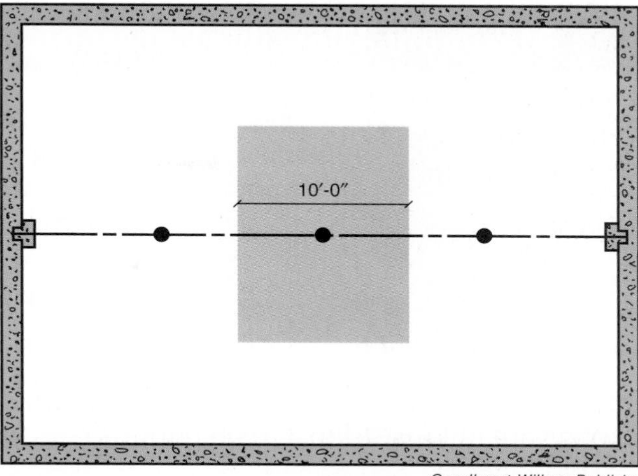

Goodheart-Willcox Publisher

Figure 18-33. Each post must support the weight of the shaded area.

requirements. Concrete sidewalks, driveways, footings, and basement floors usually contain one part cement, three parts sand, and five parts aggregate.

The consistency of concrete is generally specified by how many bags of cement are contained in each yard of mix. A bag of cement is normally 94 pounds. A five-bag mix is considered the minimum for most jobs. A six-bag mix produces a stronger product and should be used when high strength or reinforcing is required.

In general, footings and concrete floors must have both a minimum compressive strength of 3000 psi and minimum cement content of 5 bags (470 lbs.) per cubic yard. The amount of water used will most likely be 6 or 7 gallons for each bag of cement. Check your local building codes for specific requirements.

Concrete is ordered by the cubic yard. The average home requires many cubic yards of concrete. A cubic yard is 27 cubic feet. However, when ordering concrete, figure that only 25 cubic feet of every yard will be useable. Some of the material will remain in the mixer, some will be spilled, and forms may sag. It is better to have a little more concrete than you need than to have too little.

When concrete is placed (poured), air pockets are commonly trapped within the mixture. It is necessary to work these air pockets out by vibrating or tamping. This action helps to form a more dense material and removes weak spots due to air pockets.

Maximum Allowable Concentric Loads for Standard Steel Pipe Columns											
Nominal Size in Inches	Weight per Foot in Pounds	Unbraced Length in Feet									
		6	7	8	9	10	11	12	14	16	18
3	7.58	38	36	34	31	28	25	22	16	12	10
3-1/2	9.12	48	46	44	41	38	35	32	25	19	15
4	10.8	59	57	54	52	49	46	43	36	29	23
5	14.6	83	81	78	76	73	71	68	61	55	47
6	19.0	110	108	106	103	101	98	95	89	82	75

Loads are in kips. 1 kip = 1000 pounds

American Institute of Steel Construction

Figure 18-34. Load table for standard steel pipe columns.

After the concrete has been placed, a screed is used to smooth the surface. The ***screed*** is a long straightedge, usually a board, that is worked back and forth across the surface. This action brings excess water to the surface and settles the aggregate. Power screeds are also available for large jobs.

When screeding is finished, the surface is then worked over with a float. A ***float*** is a short board, about a foot long, with a handle attached to one of the wide sides. The purpose of floating is to:

- Embed the large aggregate just beneath the surface.
- Remove any slight imperfections, lumps, and voids to produce a flat surface.
- Consolidate mortar at the surface in preparation for final steel-troweling.

As the mixture reaches the proper consistency, the troweling process is started. The ***trowel*** is rectangular and is used in a circular motion. See **Figure 18-39**. This troweling action further hardens the surface and develops a very smooth finish. If a slightly rough surface is desired, it

Precast Lintel

Poured Concrete Lintel

Lintel Blocks

Steel Angle Lintel

Goodheart-Willcox Publisher

Figure 18-35. Four types of lintels frequently used in residential building construction.

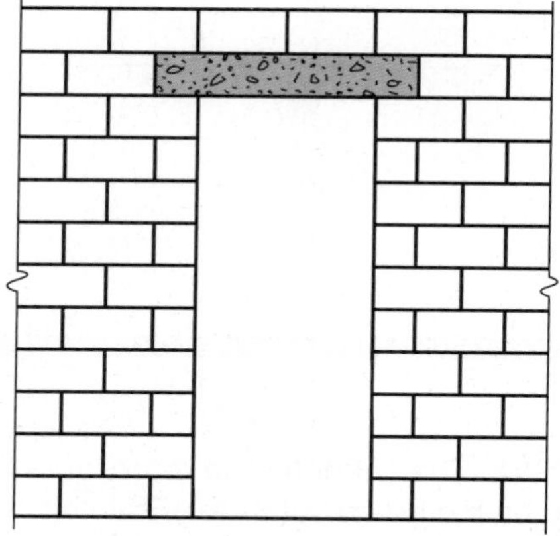

Goodheart-Willcox Publisher

Figure 18-36. This masonry wall doorway has a precast lintel supporting the weight above the opening.

Steel Angles to Support 4″ Masonry Walls	
Span	**Size of Angle**
0′ – 5′	3″ × 3″ × 1/4″
5′ – 9′	3-1/2″ × 3-1/2″ × 5/16″
9′ – 10′	4″ × 4″ × 5/16″
10′ – 11′	4″ × 4″ × 3/8″
11′ – 15′	6″ × 4″ × 3/8″
15′ – 16′	6″ × 4″ × 1/2″

Goodheart-Willcox Publisher

Figure 18-37. This table gives the size of steel angles for lintels.

Goodheart-Willcox Publisher

Figure 18-38. This steel angle lintel supports the load over the window opening in the brick wall.

Orange Line Media/Shutterstock.com

Figure 18-39. This worker is using a trowel to finish the concrete slab for a new residence.

may be swept with a broom after the surface is troweled.

Concrete cures over a long period of time and should be kept moist for several days after it is placed. Failure to do this reduces its strength and may harm the exposed surface. Temperature also affects the setting time of concrete. Cold weather slows down the curing process. Concrete should not be allowed to freeze before it has set. On the other hand, it should not get too hot as it cures because it will form cracks.

Large areas of concrete are likely to crack from expansion and contraction due to changes in temperature and moisture content. This cracking can be minimized or controlled by introducing ***contraction joints.*** These joints are formed by cutting grooves in the freshly placed concrete with a jointing tool. They may also be cut into the slab with a power saw after the concrete has hardened. The depth of joints or grooves should be one-fourth of the thickness of the slab. Contraction joints should be placed in line with interior columns, at changes in the width of the slab, or at a maximum spacing of about 20′.

A concrete slab is usually placed directly on an aggregate base course or firmly compacted sand 4″ to 6″ thick. The slab base should be thoroughly compacted to prevent settlement of the slab. Dry sand should be dampened to prevent absorption of too much mixing water from the fresh concrete. The slab base should also be sloped toward floor drains to ensure a uniform slab thickness. Floor slabs usually have a minimum thickness of 4″.

Floor slabs should not be bonded to footings or interior columns. A sand cushion 1″ thick can be used to separate the slab from the footing. See **Figure 18-40**. A sleeve of three thicknesses of building felt can be wrapped around columns to break the bond. Many different methods and

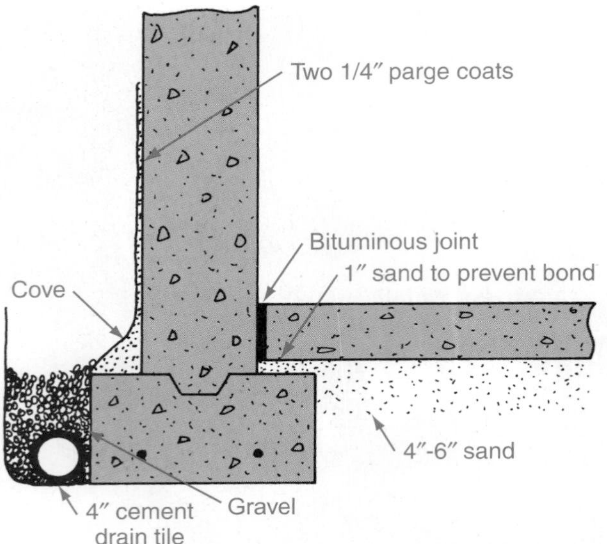

Goodheart-Willcox Publisher

Figure 18-40. Floor slabs should not be bonded to the footing or foundation wall.

techniques are used in this process. This textbook illustrates only a few of them.

Concrete Blocks

Concrete blocks are used extensively in residential buildings. They are used to form exterior and, in some cases, interior walls. They may be purchased in a variety of sizes and shapes. In general terms, "concrete block" refers to a hollow concrete masonry unit nominally 8″ × 8″ × 16″. The actual size is 7-5/8″ × 7-5/8″ × 15-5/8″. These dimensions allow for a 3/8″ mortar joint. The distance from the centerline of one mortar joint to the centerline of the next will be 8″ or 16″. **Figure 18-41** shows a variety of concrete blocks that are frequently used in residential structures.

A wide variety of decorative concrete block is available. Decorative concrete block may be used to form a screen, fence, or wall, as shown in **Figure 18-42**. Use of decorative blocks should not be overlooked when searching for different materials. The applications for concrete blocks are limited only by a designer's imagination.

Paving

Brick or concrete pavers can be installed either as a rigid or flexible system. A rigid paving

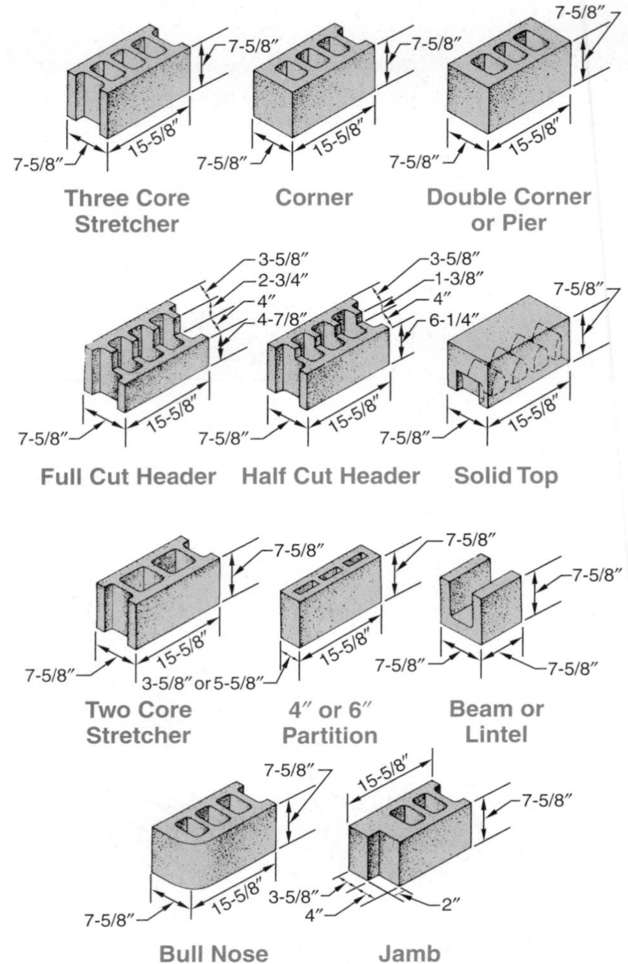

Goodheart-Willcox Publisher

Figure 18-41. These are commonly used concrete blocks. The dimensions are the actual sizes of the blocks.

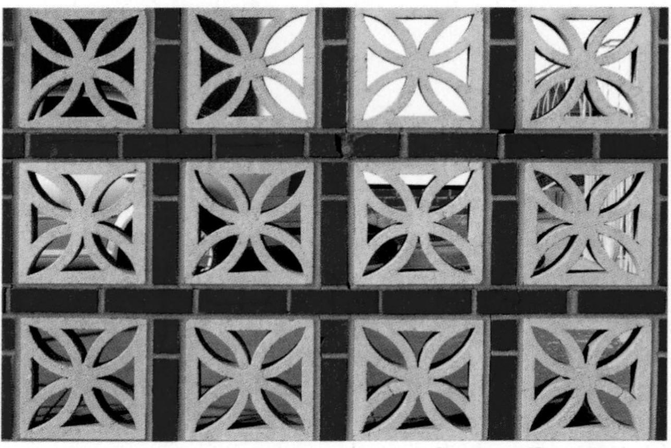

Sam Aronov/Shutterstock.com

Figure 18-42. The designer of this fence combined brick with decorative concrete block to achieve an interesting look.

system is easily recognized by its mortar joints. See **Figure 18-43**. A properly designed ***rigid paving system*** consists of a well-compacted subgrade, a properly prepared base, a reinforced concrete slab, a mortar setting bed, and pavers with mortar joints between them.

Flexible paving has a greater variety of design options than rigid paving. A ***flexible paving system*** consists of a well-compacted subgrade beneath a layer of crushed stone, a sand setting bed, and fine sand between the pavers. A rigid edge restraint must be used to prevent horizontal movement called ***creep***. See **Figure 18-44**.

All brick paving units should conform to ASTM C902, *Standard Specification for Pedestrian and Light Traffic Paving Brick*. For most exterior applications, a brick unit meeting or exceeding the requirements of Class SX should be used. If you use mortar, it should be Type M, conforming to ASTM C270, *Standard Specification for Mortar for Unit Masonry*. Portland cement-lime mortars provide greater durability than other cement types.

Heavy traffic areas, such as driveways, should be constructed of pavers that are at least 2-1/4″ thick, as shown in **Figure 18-45**. Patios and sidewalks may be constructed of 1-1/2″ pavers on a flexible base. Paving should be sloped at least 1/8″ to 1/4″ per foot to provide proper drainage. An expansion joint should be provided every 20′ for rigid paving and every 30′ for flexible paving. Solid curbs that prevent drainage should have weep holes every 16″ along the length.

Rufous/Shutterstock.com

Figure 18-43. This is a rigid paving system; it rests on a mortar setting bed. The thick mortar joints in this example are part of the design of the patio.

Lindsay Douglas/Shutterstock.com

Figure 18-44. This walkway was constructed using a flexible paving system. Notice the edging stones that prevent creep.

AigarsR/Shutterstock.com

Figure 18-45. These pavers are thick enough to withstand the heavy traffic load on the driveway being constructed.

Summary

- "Staking out" a house is the process of placing stakes in the ground at the corners of the building.
- Excavation for footings should be at least 6″ below the average maximum frost penetration depth.
- Footings increase the supporting capacity of the foundation wall by dispersing the load over a larger area.
- Foundation walls are the part of the house that extends from the first floor to the footing.
- The four basic types of foundations include foundation wall and footing, slab foundation, pier or post foundation, and wood foundation.
- The thickness of concrete and masonry (block) basement walls depends on both the lateral earth pressure and the vertical load to be supported.
- Both live loads and dead loads must be considered when determining the size of beams needed in residential construction.
- Concrete cures slowly, over a long period of time, and should be kept moist for several days after it is placed.
- The two basic types of paving systems are rigid and flexible systems.

Internet Resources

American Forest and Paper Association (AF&PA)
National trade association of the forest products industry

ASTM International
Source for standards and engineering publications

Anchor Wall Systems
Manufacturer of retaining wall systems

APA—The Engineered Wood Association
Information about engineered wood products

Boise Cascade
Manufacturer of engineered wood products

Builder Online
Online magazine for builders and designers

Portland Cement Association
Information about concrete homes

Steelworks (American Iron and Steel Institute)
Online resource for the steel industry

Review Questions

Answer the following questions using the information in this chapter.

1. The dimensions necessary for staking out the house are found on the _____ plan.
2. Describe a method of laying out square corners when staking out a house location.
3. What is the purpose of batter boards?
4. What type of equipment is generally used to excavate for a new home if the home will have a basement?
5. What is the purpose of a footing?
6. The excavation for footings must extend at least _____ below the average maximum frost depth.
7. The size and type of footing should be suitable for the building _____ and soil bearing capacity.
8. The thickness of the footing is usually the same thickness as the foundation _____.
9. When are stepped footings required?
10. What is a T-foundation?
11. List two advantages of a monolithic slab foundation.
12. How is a pier foundation different from a post or column foundation?
13. To which type of foundation do the terms AWWF and PWF refer?
14. What prevents the wood in a wood foundation from rotting?
15. Why does the sand or gravel under the footing for a wood foundation need to be perfectly level?
16. Which three materials are used for nails and fasteners in a wood foundation?
17. What is a *pilaster*?
18. What two materials are commonly used to damp-proof cast concrete walls?

19. Which two types of steel beams are commonly used in residential construction?
20. Weights are designated as live loads and dead loads. Snow on a roof is an example of a _____ load.
21. The load that a steel beam will safely support is usually given in _____.
22. A horizontal structural member that supports the load over an opening such as a door or window is known as a _____.
23. List the four ingredients in concrete.
24. In general, what is the minimum compressive strength for concrete used in footings and concrete floors?
25. The nominal size of a concrete block is 8″ × 8″ × 16″. The actual size of this block is _____.
26. What is the minimum thickness of pavers used in heavy traffic areas, such as a driveway?

Suggested Activities

1. Using CADD, draw a plan view of a 12′ × 20′ one-car garage. In a team of at least three students, stake out the garage using string, stakes, and a 50′ measuring tape. Use the 9-12-15 unit method of laying out 90° corners. Check the accuracy by measuring the diagonals. Record the diagonal measurements.
2. Using a carpenter's level on a stool or other fixed surface, determine the difference in elevation at the four corners of the garage you staked out in Activity 1. Have one member of the team hold a pole or strip of wood vertically, with the bottom end resting on the ground over one of the corner stakes. Sight down the level and have your partner make a mark on the pole even with your line of sight. Be sure the level is not tilted. Duplicate this procedure for each corner. Measure the difference between the marks on the rod. These distances represent the variation in elevation. The same procedure can be done much more accurately with a contractor's level. Record your results.
3. Visit an excavation site for a residence in your community. Secure permission from the builder before entering the site. Measure the depth and size of excavation. Determine the size of footings and thickness of foundation walls. Prepare a sketch of the foundation layout with dimensions. Note the type of soil supporting the footings.
4. Select a foundation plan of a small structure with a slab floor, such as a garage or storage building. Calculate the amount of concrete required for the footings, foundation wall, and floor. Show your calculation and draw the foundation plan.
5. Calculate the size of a steel beam and columns required to support a frame house with foundation dimensions of 34′-0″ × 48′-0″. The spacing of your columns should not exceed 12′-0″ for this activity.

Problem Solving Case Study

Mr. Mendel is requesting your assistance. He undertook a "DIY" (do-it-yourself) project to make a paved walkway from the back door of his house. The brick walkway extends about 15′ from the house and then forms a loop through the flower garden. He used a flexible paving system and poured concrete edgings on both sides to avoid creep. He was very careful when preparing the subgrade to keep everything exactly level, and he was extremely proud of the resulting walkway—until the first time it rained. Now he wants your help to "fix" the walkway.

Given this basic information, answer the following questions.

1. What is wrong with Mr. Mendel's walkway?
2. How should the walkway have been constructed?
3. What can you suggest to relieve the problem, now that the walkway has already been built?

ADDA Certification Prep

The following questions are presented in the style used in the American Design Drafting Association (ADDA) Drafter Certification Test. Answer the questions using the information in this chapter.

1. Which of the following statements about foundations are true?
   A. The most common type of foundation is the T-foundation.
   B. Some CADD software programs can calculate the spans permissible for various materials, generate details, and draw foundation plans.
   C. "Staking out" a house means excavating for the foundation walls and footing.
   D. Stem walls are the part of the house that extend from the second floor to the footing.
2. Which of the following statements are *false* regarding wood foundations?
   A. When a wood foundation is used for a house with a basement, the site is excavated to a different depth than for other foundations.
   B. Wood foundations can be used for both full basement and crawl space construction.
   C. The bottom of the excavation for a wood foundation is covered with a coarse wood mulch to aid in drainage.
   D. The foundation walls are 2 × 4 or 2 × 6 stud frame.
3. Match each type of foundation with its description.

   Foundations: 1. Monolithic, 2. Foundation wall and footing, 3. Post, 4. Wood
   A. Also known as a T-foundation.
   B. Consists of a footing and columns.
   C. Chemically treated to prevent decay.
   D. Also known as a thickened-edge slab.

STEM Connections

1. **Math.** A design for a new one-story home has a footprint of 32′ × 54′. It has a bearing wall running the length of the house. Answer the following questions:
   A. What is the total area of the house?
   B. What is the total weight of the house?
   C. How much weight bears on the center beam, in kips?
2. **Science.** Find out more about the chemicals that are used to prevent wood foundations from decaying. What chemicals are used? Do they have any potentially harmful effects if the chemicals leach into the surrounding groundwater? Write an informative report of your findings.
3. **Engineering.** People who live in states that have high water tables generally do not have basements, because the groundwater is so high that water seepage into the basement is a real concern. Conduct research to find accepted methods for constructing a basement in an area that has a high water table. Prepare an informative report of your findings.

Communicating about Architecture

1. **Reading.** With a partner, make flash cards of the chapter terms. On the front of the card, write the term. On the back of the card, write the pronunciation and a brief definition. Use this chapter and a dictionary for guidance. Then take turns quizzing one another on the pronunciations and definitions of the key terms.
2. **Speaking.** Select five of the key terms in this chapter and imagine them being used by architects in a real-life context. With a partner, role-play a situation in which an architectural firm is asked to design a slab foundation for a new home.

Chapter 19

Sill and Floor Construction

Objectives

After completing this chapter, you will be able to:

- Describe the components of a floor system.
- Explain the difference between platform and balloon framing.
- Determine proper joist sizes using a typical span data chart.
- Plan the appropriate floor support using joists or trusses for a structure.
- Select the appropriate engineered wood products for specific applications in residential construction.
- Explain the principles of post and beam construction.

Key Terms

balloon framing
band joist
beam
box sill
cantilevered joist
cement mortar mix
chords
cross bridging
curtain wall
engineered wood products (EWPs)
floor trusses
glue-laminated members
joists
laminated veneer lumber (LVL)
longitudinal method
mudsill
oriented strand board (OSB)
parallel strand lumber (PSL)
platform framing
post and beam construction
ribbon
rim joist
sill
subfloor
transverse method
web
wood I-joist

The commonly used method of floor framing varies from one section of the country to another. Even within a given area, builders may use different methods based on personal preference and experience. Nevertheless, there are two fundamental types of floor framing: the platform method and the balloon framing method. Both types of framing have structural components called *plates, joists,* and *studs.* Another type of construction is the post and beam method. This construction can be used for framing walls and floors.

Platform Framing

In ***platform framing,*** the floor joists form a platform on which the walls rest. Another platform, which is formed by either the ceiling joists or the floor joists of the upper floor, rests on the walls. Platform framing is used more extensively than balloon framing for several reasons. It is satisfactory for both one- and two-story structures, and it is easy and fast to construct. Shrinkage is uniform throughout the structure. Also, the platform automatically provides a firestop between floors. Construction is safe because the work is performed on solid surfaces.

In platform framing, the sill is the starting point in constructing a floor. A ***sill,*** also called a *sill plate,* is the lowest member of the frame of a structure. The sill rests on the foundation and supports the floor joists or the uprights (studs) of the wall. The sill in most residential construction is 2 × 6 dimensional lumber (actual dimensions are 1-1/2″ × 5-1/2″). Platform framing uses a method of sill construction known as ***box sill*** construction. The box sill consists of a 2 × 6 plate called a sill or ***mudsill*** and a header joist, typically called a ***band joist*** or ***rim joist***, that is the same size as the floor joists. See **Figure 19-1**. **Figure 19-2** shows a section of the first and second floor of a structure constructed with platform framing and box sill construction.

In general, a seal is required between the foundation and sill plate. This seal prevents outside air from entering the house. **Figure 19-3** shows one method of sealing the space between the foundation and sill plate.

In areas where termites are a problem, termite shields may also be required by local codes. A termite shield generally consists of a metal strip that runs between a masonry foundation and the wood sill plate. Refer again to **Figure 19-2**.

Balloon Framing

Balloon framing was once used extensively, but has diminished in importance. The distinguishing features of ***balloon framing*** are that the wall studs rest directly on the sill plate and each floor "hangs" from the studs.

Two advantages of balloon framing are small potential shrinkage and good vertical stability.

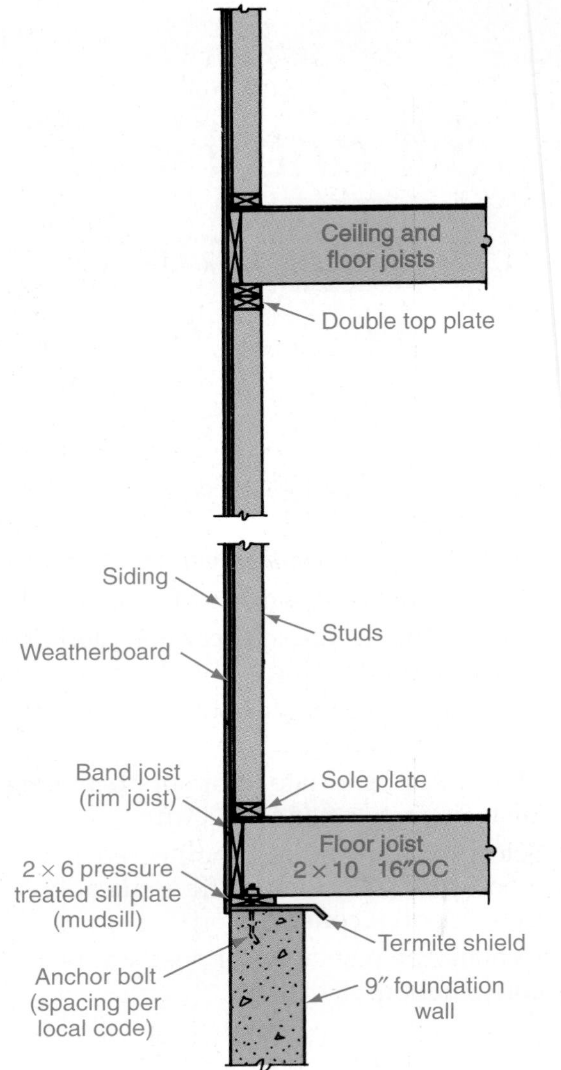

Goodheart-Willcox Publisher

Figure 19-2. This section shows the details of a first and second floor constructed using platform framing and box sill construction.

The vertical shrinkage in a two-story house built with platform framing is sometimes great enough to cause cracking. This is usually not the case with balloon framing. The disadvantages of balloon framing include a less safe surface on which to work during construction and the need to add firestops.

In balloon framing, one of two types of sill construction is used: solid (standard) sill or T-sill. See **Figure 19-4**. In solid sill construction, the studs are nailed directly to the sill and joists. No header is used. Joists are supported by a

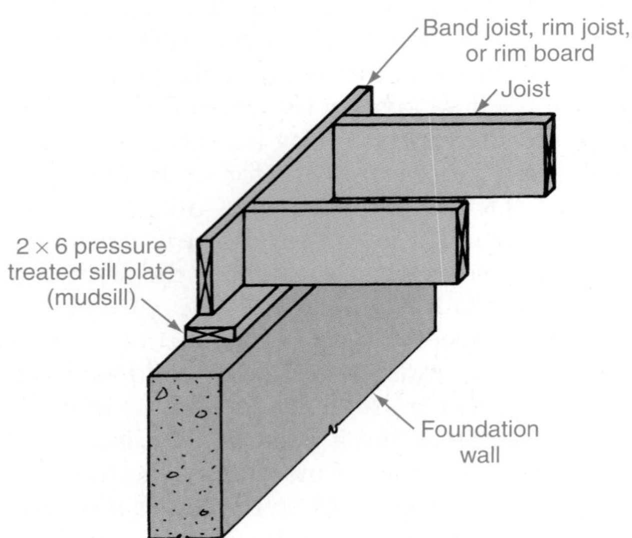

Goodheart-Willcox Publisher

Figure 19-1. Box sill construction consists of a sill on which a header and joists rest.

Goodheart-Willcox Publisher

Figure 19-3. One-inch thick fiberglass insulation is frequently used as a sill sealer.

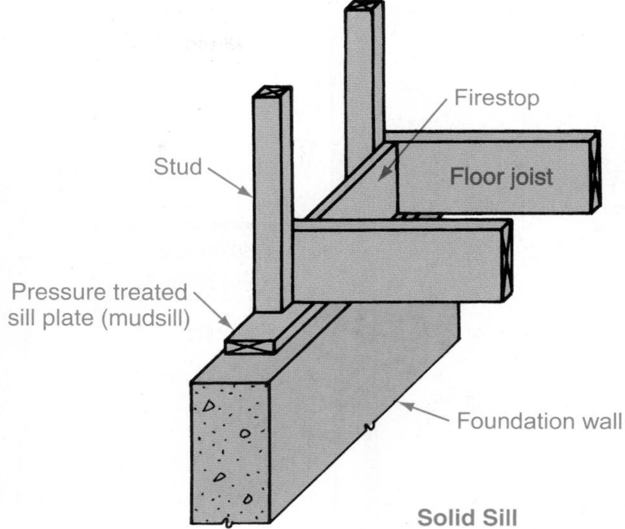

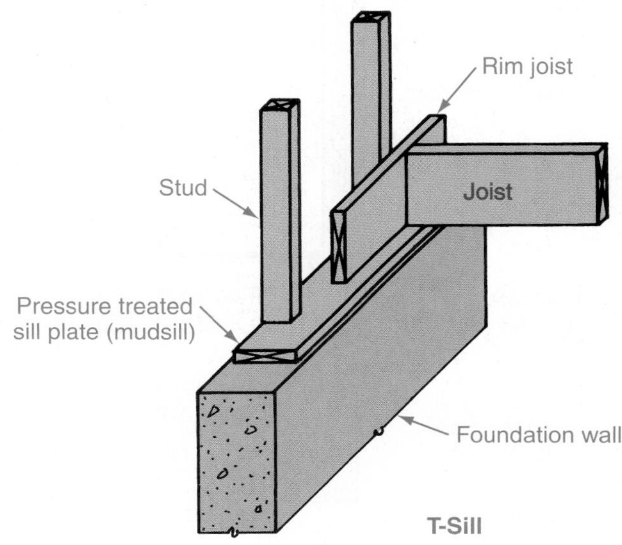

Goodheart-Willcox Publisher

Figure 19-4. In balloon framing, either solid sill or T-sill construction is used.

ribbon (a horizontal member notched into the studs) and nailed to the studs on the second floor level. See **Figure 19-5**. A firestop must be provided between the studs using pieces cut to the proper length. Solid sill construction is used more extensively than T-sill construction in two-story homes.

In T-sill construction, a header rests on the sill and serves as a firestop. The studs rest on the sill and are nailed to the header as well as the sill plate. The sill in T-sill construction may be 8″ or 10″ wide to provide a broader supporting base on which the joists rest.

Joists and Beams

Joists provide support for the floor. They are usually made from common softwood, such as southern yellow pine, fir, larch, hemlock, or spruce. However, engineered wood joists and metal joists are also available.

The size of floor joists ranges from a nominal size of 2 × 6 to 2 × 12. **Figure 19-6** provides the actual dimensions of dimensional construction lumber. The joist size required for a given situation depends on the length of the span, load to be supported, species and grade of wood, and distance the joists are spaced apart. In the case of metal joists, the gage of metal should be considered instead of the species and grade of lumber.

Floor joists may be spaced 12″, 16″, or 24″ on center (OC). A spacing of 16″OC is most common. Floor joist span data for the four most common species of wood joists is given in **Figure 19-7**. The table assumes a maximum deflection of 1/360th of the span with a normal live load, which is the amount that most codes require. The normal live load is 30 or 40 pounds per square foot. The span data in **Figure 19-7** is based on a live load of 30 pounds per square foot and a dead load

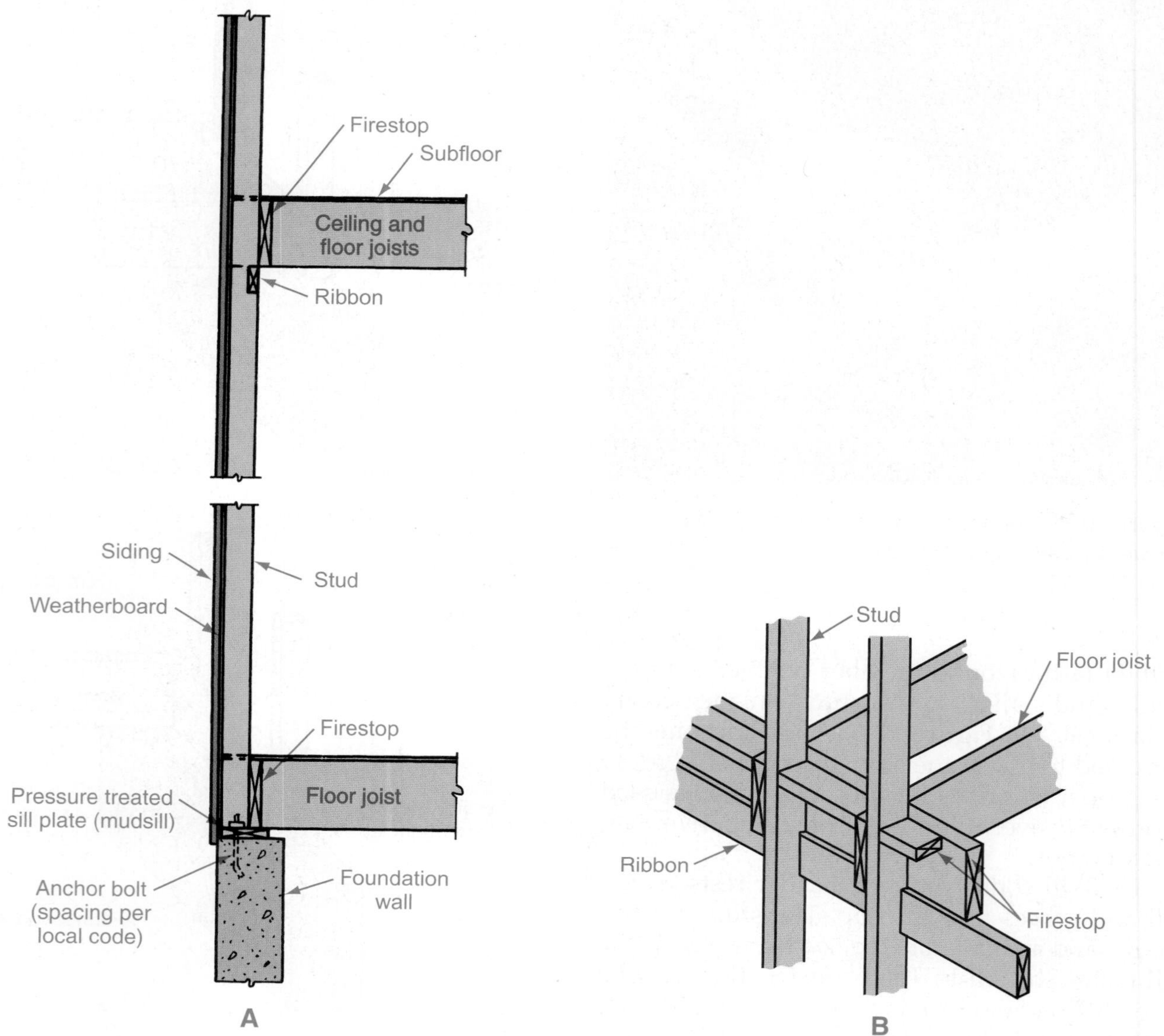

Goodheart-Willcox Publisher

Figure 19-5. A—This section shows the details of a first and second floor constructed using balloon framing and solid sill construction. B—Construction detail showing the location of the ribbon used to support the second floor joists.

of 10 pounds per square foot or 20 pounds per square foot. The Reference Section of this textbook provides additional span data tables. The procedure for using a span data table is:

1. Determine the species of wood to be used.
2. Select the appropriate live load and dead load capacity required for the structure.
3. Determine the lumber grade to be used. Number 2 dense is the usual choice for fir, larch, and southern yellow pine.
4. Scan the lumber grade row and note the maximum spans.
5. Select the joist size and spacing that will adequately support the desired live load and dead load.

Example: The span is 14′-0″ and Number 1 dense southern pine is to be used for the joists. The live load is 30 pounds per square foot and the dead load is 10 pounds per square foot. The table in **Figure 19-7** shows that the following choices would meet these conditions: 2 × 8 joists

Standard Lumber Sizes		
Dimension Lumber		
Product Classification (Nominal Size)	**Actual Sizes**	
	Unseasoned*	**Dry***
2 × 2	1-9/16″ × 1-9/16″	1-1/2″ × 1-1/2″
2 × 3	1-9/16″ × 2-9/16″	1-1/2″ × 2-1/2″
2 × 4	1-9/16″ × 3-9/16″	1-1/2″ × 3-1/2″
2 × 6	1-9/16″ × 5-5/8″	1-1/2″ × 5-1/2″
2 × 8	1-9/16″ × 7-1/2″	1-1/2″ × 7-1/4″
2 × 10	1-9/16″ × 9-1/2″	1-1/2″ × 9-1/4″
2 × 12	1-9/16″ × 11-1/2″	1-1/2″ × 11-1/4″
Board Lumber		
Product Classification (Nominal Size)	**Actual Sizes**	
	Unseasoned*	**Dry***
1 × 2	25/32″ × 1-9/16″	3/4″ × 1-1/2″
1 × 3	25/32″ × 2-9/16″	3/4″ × 2-1/2″
1 × 4	25/32″ × 3-9/16″	3/4″ × 3-1/2″
1 × 6	25/32″ × 5-5/8″	3/4″ × 5-1/2″
1 × 8	25/32″ × 7-1/2″	3/4″ × 7-1/4″
1 × 10	25/32″ × 9-1/2″	3/4″ × 9-1/4″
1 × 12	25/32″ × 11-1/2″	3/4″ × 11-1/4″

* Dry lumber is defined as being 19% or less in moisture content. Unseasoned lumber is over 19% moisture content. The size of lumber changes approximately 1% for each 4% change in moisture content. Lumber stabilizes at approximately 15% moisture content under normal use conditions.

American Forest & Paper Association

Figure 19-6. The actual size of common dimensional and board lumber is smaller than the nominal size.

12″OC or 16″OC; 2 × 10 joists 12″OC, 16″OC, 19.2″OC, or 24″OC; and 2 × 12 joists 12″OC, 16″OC, 19.2″OC, or 24″OC. The most reasonable selection would be 2 × 8 joists placed 16″OC. This will span a maximum of 14′-5″, is the smallest dimensional lumber, and allows the greatest spacing at that size.

Steel floor joists are accepted for residential construction. Builders generally select joist depths ranging from 6″ to 12″ with steel thicknesses from 0.033″ to 0.097″. Continuous span joists are preferred over lapped joists on multiple span conditions. Steel joists are usually spaced 24″OC, but spacing of 12″OC or 16″OC is also used. See **Figure 19-8**.

A floor system may also be constructed using girders or trusses in the place of floor joists, as

Green Architecture

Engineered Floor Joists

One concept of sustainability is the use of fewer materials to achieve the same result. From this point of view, engineered floor joists are a sustainable alternative to solid wood joists. Engineered wood joists can be made from wood chips and other wood products that were formerly considered waste. They are also stronger and can also span longer distances than solid wood joists. This means that fewer joists may be needed to meet building code requirements. These characteristics make engineered floor joists an excellent green alternative.

FLOOR JOIST SPANS FOR COMMON LUMBER SPECIES
(Residential sleeping areas, live load = 30 psf, L/Δ = 360)[a]

JOIST SPACING (inches)	SPECIES AND GRADE		DEAD LOAD = 10 psf				DEAD LOAD = 20 psf			
			2 x 6	2 x 8	2 x 10	2 x 12	2 x 6	2 x 8	2 x 10	2 x 12
			Maximum floor joist spans							
			(ft - in.)	(ft - in.)	(ft - in.)	(ft - in.)	(ft - in.)	(ft - in.)	(ft - in.)	(ft - in.)
12	Douglas fir-larch	SS	12-6	16-6	21-0	25-7	12-6	16-6	21-0	25-7
	Douglas fir-larch	#1	12-0	15-10	20-3	24-8	12-0	15-7	19-0	22-0
	Douglas fir-larch	#2	11-10	15-7	19-10	23-4	11-8	14-9	18-0	20-11
	Douglas fir-larch	#3	9-11	12-7	15-5	17-10	8-11	11-3	13-9	16-0
	Hem-fir	SS	11-10	15-7	19-10	24-2	11-10	15-7	19-10	24-2
	Hem-fir	#1	11-7	15-3	19-5	23-7	11-7	15-3	18-9	21-9
	Hem-fir	#2	11-0	14-6	18-6	22-6	11-0	14-4	17-6	20-4
	Hem-fir	#3	9-8	12-4	15-0	17-5	8-8	11-0	13-5	15-7
	Southern pine	SS	12-3	16-2	20-8	25-1	12-3	16-2	20-8	25-1
	Southern pine	#1	11-10	15-7	19-10	24-2	11-10	15-7	18-7	22-0
	Southern pine	#2	11-3	14-11	18-1	21-4	10-9	13-8	16-2	19-1
	Southern pine	#3	9-2	11-6	14-0	16-6	8-2	10-3	12-6	14-9
	Spruce-pine-fir	SS	11-7	15-3	19-5	23-7	11-7	15-3	19-5	23-7
	Spruce-pine-fir	#1	11-3	14-11	19-0	23-0	11-3	14-7	17-9	20-7
	Spruce-pine-fir	#2	11-3	14-11	19-0	23-0	11-3	14-7	17-9	20-7
	Spruce-pine-fir	#3	9-8	12-4	15-0	17-5	8-8	11-0	13-5	15-7
16	Douglas fir-larch	SS	11-4	15-0	19-1	23-3	11-4	15-0	19-1	23-3
	Douglas fir-larch	#1	10-11	14-5	18-5	21-4	10-8	13-6	16-5	19-1
	Douglas fir-larch	#2	10-9	14-2	17-5	20-3	10-1	12-9	15-7	18-1
	Douglas fir-larch	#3	8-7	10-11	13-4	15-5	7-8	9-9	11-11	13-10
	Hem-fir	SS	10-9	14-2	18-0	21-11	10-9	14-2	18-0	21-11
	Hem-fir	#1	10-6	13-10	17-8	21-1	10-6	13-4	16-3	18-10
	Hem-fir	#2	10-0	13-2	16-10	19-8	9-10	12-5	15-2	17-7
	Hem-fir	#3	8-5	10-8	13-0	15-1	7-6	9-6	11-8	13-6
	Southern pine	SS	11-2	14-8	18-9	22-10	11-2	14-8	18-9	22-10
	Southern pine	#1	10-9	14-2	18-0	21-4	10-9	13-9	16-1	19-1
	Southern pine	#2	10-3	13-3	15-8	18-6	9-4	11-10	14-0	16-6
	Southern pine	#3	7-11	10-0	11-1	14-4	7-1	8-11	10-10	12-10
	Spruce-pine-fir	SS	10-6	13-10	17-8	21-6	10-6	13-10	17-8	21-4
	Spruce-pine-fir	#1	10-3	13-6	17-2	19-11	9-11	12-7	15-5	17-10
	Spruce-pine-fir	#2	10-3	13-6	17-2	19-11	9-11	12-7	15-5	17-10
	Spruce-pine-fir	#3	8-5	10-8	13-0	15-1	7-6	9-6	11-8	13-6

(continued)

Figure 19-7. Floor joist spans for common species of wood. The table assumes a maximum deflection of 1/360th of the span with a normal live load.

FLOOR JOIST SPANS FOR COMMON LUMBER SPECIES *(continued)*
(Residential sleeping areas, live load = 30 psf, L/Δ = 360)[a]

JOIST SPACING (inches)	SPECIES AND GRADE		DEAD LOAD = 10 psf				DEAD LOAD = 20 psf			
			2 x 6	2 x 8	2 x 10	2 x 12	2 x 6	2 x 8	2 x 10	2 x 12
			Maximum floor joist spans							
			(ft - in.)	(ft - in.)	(ft - in.)	(ft - in.)	(ft - in.)	(ft - in.)	(ft - in.)	(ft - in.)
19.2	Douglas fir-larch	SS	10-8	14-1	18-0	21-10	10-8	14-1	18-0	21-4
	Douglas fir-larch	#1	10-4	13-7	16-9	19-6	9-8	12-4	15-0	17-5
	Douglas fir-larch	#2	10-1	13-0	15-11	18-6	9-3	11-8	14-3	16-6
	Douglas fir-larch	#3	7-10	10-0	12-2	14-1	7-0	8-11	10-11	12-7
	Hem-fir	SS	10-1	13-4	17-0	20-8	10-1	13-4	17-0	20-7
	Hem-fir	#1	9-10	13-0	16-7	19-3	9-7	12-2	14-10	17-2
	Hem-fir	#2	9-5	12-5	15-6	17-1	8-11	11-4	13-10	16-1
	Hem-fir	#3	7-8	9-9	11-10	13-9	6-10	8-8	10-7	12-4
	Southern pine	SS	10-6	13-10	17-8	21-6	10-6	13-10	17-8	21-6
	Southern pine	#1	10-1	13-4	16-5	19-6	9-11	12-7	14-8	17-5
	Southern pine	#2	9-6	12-1	14-4	16-10	8-6	10-10	12-10	15-1
	Southern pine	#3	7-3	9-1	11-0	13-1	6-5	8-2	9-10	11-8
	Spruce-pine-fir	SS	9-10	13-0	16-7	20-2	9-10	13-0	16-7	19-6
	Spruce-pine-fir	#1	9-8	12-9	15-8	18-3	9-1	11-6	14-1	16-3
	Spruce-pine-fir	#2	9-8	12-9	15-8	18-3	9-1	11-6	14-1	16-3
	Spruce-pine-fir	#3	7-8	9-9	11-10	13-9	6-10	8-8	10-7	12-4
24	Douglas fir-larch	SS	9-11	13-1	16-8	20-3	9-11	13-1	16-5	19-1
	Douglas fir-larch	#1	9-7	12-4	15-0	17-5	8-8	11-0	13-5	15-7
	Douglas fir-larch	#2	9-3	11-8	14-3	16-6	8-3	10-5	12-9	14-9
	Douglas fir-larch	#3	7-0	8-11	10-11	12-7	6-3	8-0	9-9	11-3
	Hem-fir	SS	9-4	12-4	15-9	19-2	9-4	12-4	15-9	18-5
	Hem-fir	#1	9-2	12-1	14-10	17-2	8-7	10-10	13-3	15-5
	Hem-fir	#2	8-9	11-4	13-10	16-1	8-0	10-2	12-5	14-4
	Hem-fir	#3	6-10	8-8	10-7	12-4	6-2	7-9	9-6	11-0
	Southern pine	SS	9-9	12-10	16-5	19-11	9-9	12-10	16-5	19-8
	Southern pine	#1	9-4	12-4	14-8	17-5	8-10	11-3	13-1	15-7
	Southern pine	#2	8-6	10-10	12-10	15-1	7-7	9-8	11-5	13-6
	Southern pine	#3	6-5	8-2	9-10	11-8	5-9	7-3	8-10	10-5
	Spruce-pine-fir	SS	9-2	12-1	15-5	18-9	9-2	12-1	15-0	17-5
	Spruce-pine-fir	#1	8-11	11-6	14-1	16-3	8-1	10-3	12-7	14-7
	Spruce-pine-fir	#2	8-11	11-6	14-1	16-3	8-1	10-3	12-7	14-7
	Spruce-pine-fir	#3	6-10	8-8	10-7	12-4	6-2	7-9	9-6	11-0

For SI: 1 inch = 25.4 mm, 1 foot = 304.8 mm, 1 pound per square foot = 0.0479 kPa.

Note: Check sources for availability of lumber in lengths greater than 20 feet.

a. Dead load limits for townhouses in Seismic Design Category C and all structures in Seismic Design Categories D_0, D_1 and D_2 shall be determined in accordance with Section R301.2.2.2.1.

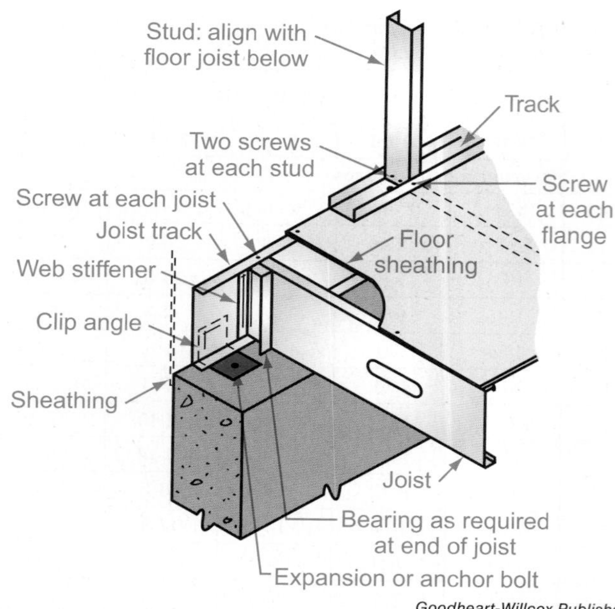

Goodheart-Willcox Publisher

Figure 19-8. This is typical steel framing; the floor joists rest directly on the foundation.

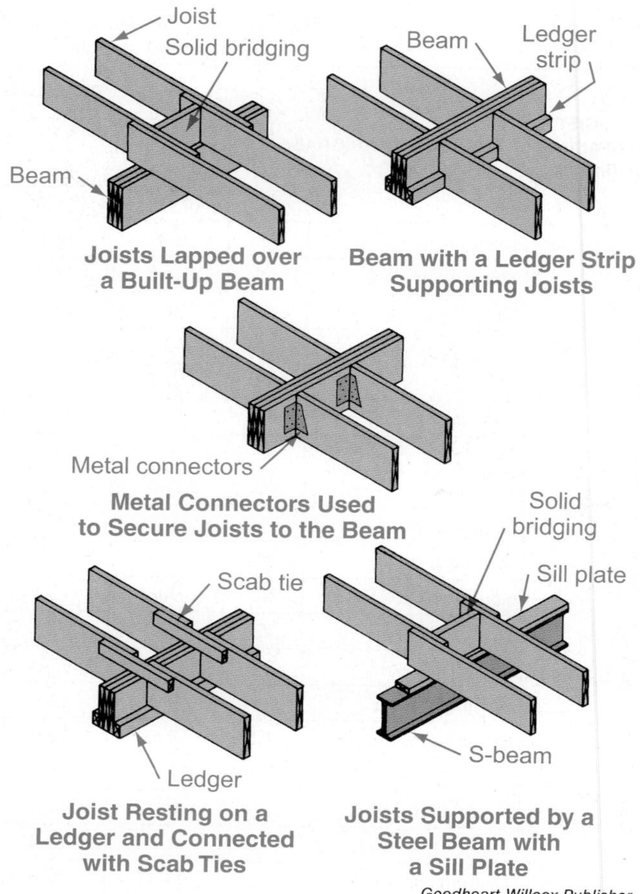

Goodheart-Willcox Publisher

Figure 19-9. These are common methods of supporting floor joists with beams.

discussed in the next section. These are usually 4 × 6, 4 × 8, or 4 × 10 depending on the span. The purpose of this approach is to use fewer support members (joists). The typical spacing of girders or trusses in this system is 48″OC with 1-1/8″ thick tongue-and-groove plywood as the floor decking.

In most house designs, the total distance that joists must span is too great for unsupported joists. A ***beam*** or load-bearing wall is needed to support the joists and effectively reduce the span. The beam may be a solid timber, a built-up beam from dimensional lumber, or a metal S- or W-beam. Load-bearing walls may be concrete block, cast concrete, or frame construction. Several methods of supporting floor joists with a beam are commonly used. **Figure 19-9** shows some of these methods.

Partition walls that run parallel to the floor joists require added support. It is good practice to double the joists under these partition walls, as shown in **Figure 19-10**. If the space between the joists is used as a cold air return duct, solid blocking is used between the joists. Openings in the floor for stairs and chimneys also require double joist framing. **Figure 19-11** shows how such an opening is framed and identifies the various parts.

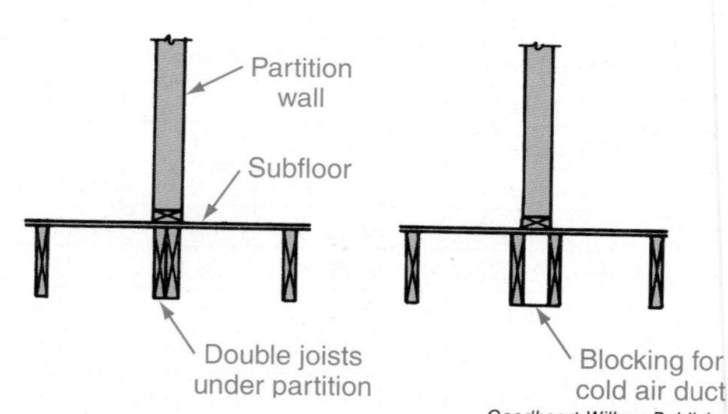

Goodheart-Willcox Publisher

Figure 19-10. Joists should be doubled under partition walls that run parallel to the joists.

Cross bridging is used to stiffen the floor and spread the load over a broader area. See **Figure 19-12**. Bridging boards are ordinarily 1 × 3 with the ends cut at an angle so they fit snugly against the joist. They are nailed securely in

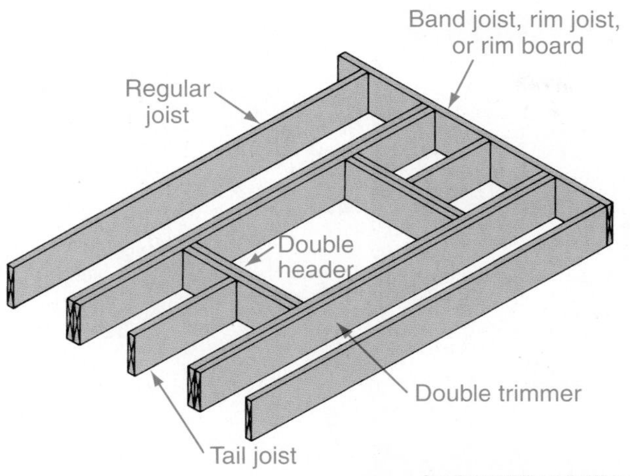

Figure 19-11. Double joists are required for framing around openings for fireplaces and stairs.

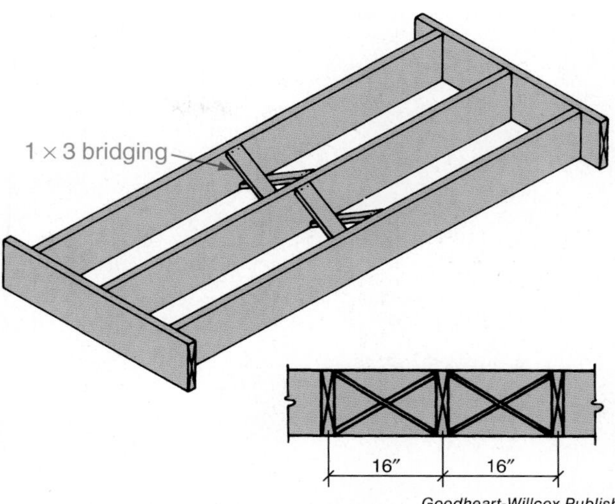

Figure 19-12. Bridging is used to stiffen the floor and is required by many building codes.

place midway between the beam and wall. Metal bridging is also available, as shown in **Figure 19-13**.

Floor Trusses

A truss is a rigid framework designed to support a load over a span. Engineered wood *floor trusses,* designed for light frame construction, are often used in place of floor joists in residential structures. These trusses consist of a top chord, bottom chord, and web. The top and bottom ***chords*** are the horizontal flanges at the top and bottom of the truss. The ***web*** is the framework between the chords. See **Figure 19-14**.

Employability

Respecting Diversity

No matter where you work or attend school, you have probably noticed that your coworkers or classmates come from a variety of different backgrounds and cultures. Gender, race, nationality, social class, and spiritual practice are examples of characteristics that may differ from person to person. These differences between people are called *diversity*. Being able to accept and work with people whose characteristics and beliefs are different from yours is an important skill in today's workplace.

One way to increase your ability to work with people from diverse backgrounds is to get to know them. Find out what they believe, what their attitudes are about various issues, and what they like or dislike. You do not have to agree with everything they say; in fact, you probably will not agree with some ideas. However, by getting to know the individuals, you are less likely to subject them to generalizations and any preconceived biases you may have. You may also make new friends in the process.

Activity

Consider your current attitude about people from various backgrounds. Do you sometimes look at someone from a certain country and automatically think to yourself "that person must be smart," or "what is *she* doing here?" Make a list of generalizations or assumptions you commonly make based on a person's gender, race, nationality, social class, or spiritual practice. For each item on your list, write a specific suggestion for overcoming the generalization or assumption. Then try your suggestions on the people with whom you work or go to school.

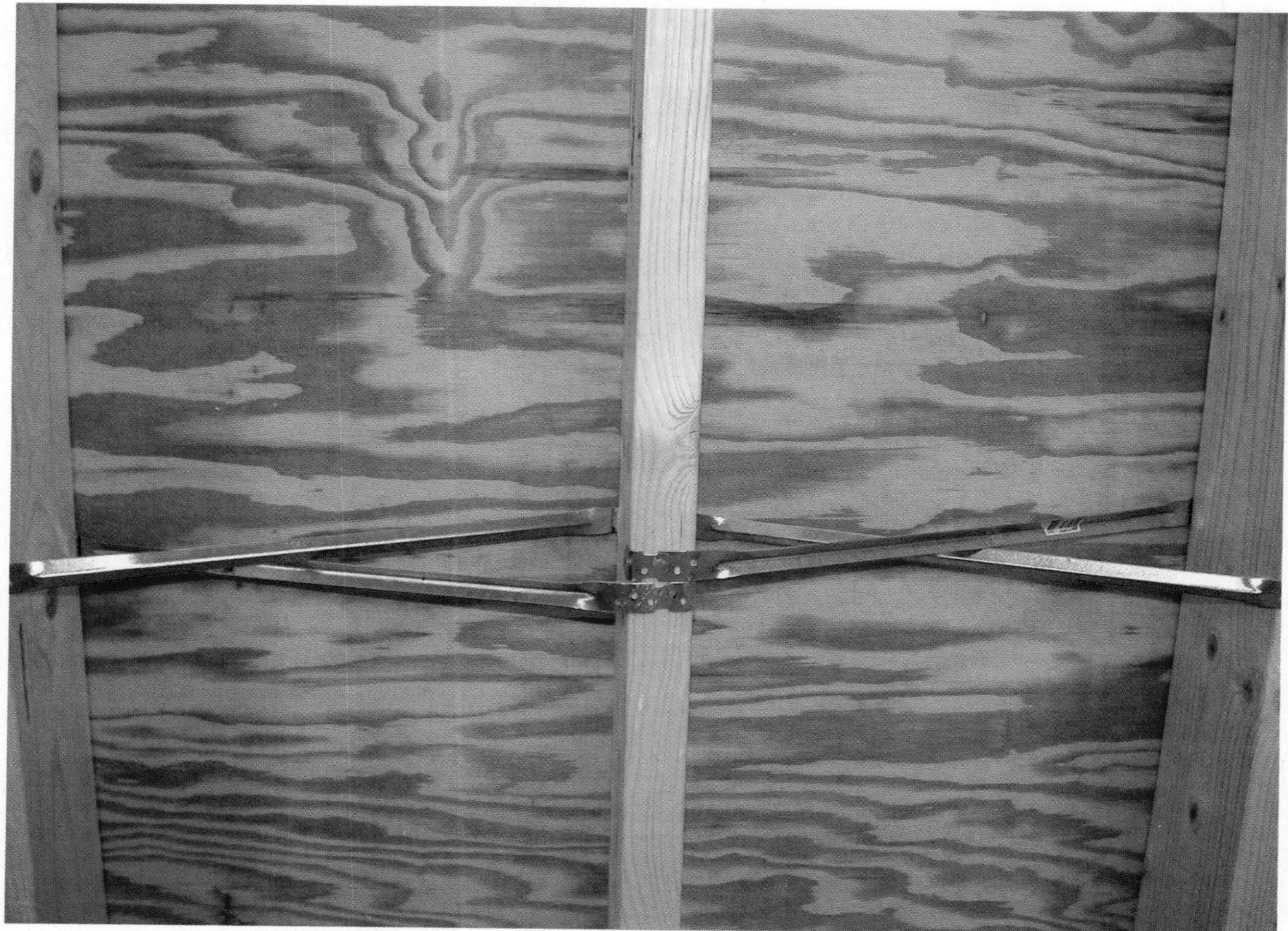

Goodheart-Willcox Publisher

Figure 19-13. Metal bridging can be installed quickly.

Trusses provide clear spans with a minimum of depth in a lightweight assembly that is easy to handle. In addition, the open web construction reduces sound transmission through the floor/ceiling assemblies and makes the installation of plumbing, heating, and electrical systems easier.

Engineered floor trusses are designed with the aid of computer software to ensure accurate load capacities. They are usually fabricated from 2 × 4 or 2 × 6 lumber and are generally spaced 24″OC. **Figure 19-15** shows typical specifications for engineered wood floor trusses. Each truss has a built-in camber (upward curve) so that the floor/ceiling will be level once the load of the house is applied. Stress-graded lumber is used so that a minimum amount of material is required. Some trusses have wood webs. Other trusses are fabricated with wood chords and galvanized steel webs. **Figure 19-16** shows several variations on truss design. The metal webs have teeth that are pressed into the sides of the chords. A reinforcing rib in the metal web withstands both tension and compression forces.

Subfloor

The ***subfloor*** is affixed to the floor joists and provides the surface on which the underlayment for the final finished floor will rest. Plywood, tongue-and-groove boards, common boards, and other panel products are used for subfloors. The large size (4′ × 8′) of plywood and other panel sheets and the comparatively short time required to nail the sheets in place

SpaceJoist/Alpine

Figure 19-14. Engineered wood floor trusses are lightweight, easy to handle, and easy to install.

make these products very popular as subfloors. One-half inch thick plywood, composite board, waferboard, oriented strand board, or structural particleboard may be used when joists are spaced 16″OC. See **Figure 19-17**. However, some builders prefer 5/8″ stock over 1/2″ stock. When these products are used, it is important that the joist spacing is very accurate. All edges of the panels must be supported, as shown in **Figure 19-18**.

In some areas, there is a trend to combine the subfloor and underlayment (usually 5/8″ particleboard) into a single thickness that is generally 1-1/8″ thick. These sheets have tongue-and-groove edges and require no blocking between the joists. A single thickness sheet of 3/4″ tongue-and-groove plywood may also be used for some applications.

Plywood should be installed so that the grain direction of the outer plies is at right angles to the joists. The floor will be stronger when the plywood is positioned in this manner. Panel products should also be staggered so that end joints in adjacent panels are on different joists. A slight space must be allowed between sheets for expansion.

Subfloor panels may also be glued, as well as nailed, to the joists. Structural tests have shown that gluing increases stiffness by 25% with 2 × 8 joists and 5/8″ plywood. Other advantages of gluing are that the system produces a squeak-free structure, eliminates nail-popping, and reduces labor costs.

Span Data for Manufactured Wood Floor Trusses

Maximum Spans: 40-10-5 320 Series

Depth	Deflection	24″ O.C.	19.2″ O.C.	16″ O.C.	12″ O.C.
9-1/4″	L/480	**12′9″**	**13′10″**	**14′8″**	**16′1″**
	L/360	**14′1″**	**15′3″**	**16′1″**	**17′11″**
11-1/4″	L/480	**15′3″**	**16′7″**	**17′8″**	**19′6″**
	L/360	**16′0″**	**18′4″**	**19′7″**	**21′6″**
11-7/8″	L/480	**16′0″**	**17′4″**	**18′6″**	**20′4″**
	L/360	**16′0″**	**19′2″**	**20′5″**	**22′6″**
14″	L/480	**18′3″**	**19′9″**	**20′11″**	**23′3″**
	L/360	**18′6″**	**20′8″**	**23′3″**	**25′7″**
16″	L/480	**18′6″**	**22′2″**	**23′8″**	**26′2″**
	L/360	**18′6″**	**22′11″**	**26′2″**	**28′9″**

Maximum Spans: 40-10-5 420 Series

Depth	Deflection	24″ O.C.	19.2″ O.C.	16″ O.C.	12″ O.C.
9-1/4″	L/480	**14′4″**	**15′6″**	**16′6″**	**18′2″**
	L/360	**15′10″**	**17′1″**	**18′2″**	**19′11″**
11-1/4″	L/480	**16′0″**	**18′8″**	**19′10″**	**21′10″**
	L/360	**16′0″**	**20′0″**	**21′10″**	**24′1″**
11-7/8″	L/480	**16′0″**	**19′6″**	**20′8″**	**22′10″**
	L/360	**16′0″**	**20′0″**	**22′10″**	**25′3″**
14″	L/480	**20′3″**	**22′1″**	**23′8″**	**26′0″**
	L/360	**20′3″**	**24′0″**	**26′0″**	**28′0″**
16″	L/480	**22′0″**	**24′11″**	**26′7″**	**29′3″**
	L/360	**22′0″**	**26′0″**	**29′3″**	**32′0″**

- Up to 12" may be field-trimmed from each end of the SpaceJoist TE truss. Contact your SpaceJoist representative or Engineering Department prior to any additional trimming.
- Span charts reflect the benefit of composite action afforded by a glued-nailed or glued-screwed connection of the sheathing to the top chord of the truss. Consult SpaceJoist for appropriate spans if a nailed-only or screwed-only connection is to be utilized.
- Span dimensions are out-to-out at bearing supports.
  Minimum required bearing length is 1-3/4".
- Span charts are for the uniformly loaded conditions specified in the heading of each chart.
- For SpaceJoist trusses supporting concentrated (point) loads, cantilevered end conditions, or other special loading conditions, contact your SpaceJoist representative.
- Some spans may require top chord supports and/or web stiffeners. Contact SpaceJoist engineering for required reinforcements.

*** Span Charts for additional loadings are available from your SpaceJoist representative.**

SpaceJoist/Alpine

Figure 19-15. Typical design specifications for engineered wood floor trusses. The specified loads refer to a top chord live load of 40 pounds per square foot, top chord dead load of 10 pounds per square foot, and bottom chord dead load of 5 pounds per square foot.

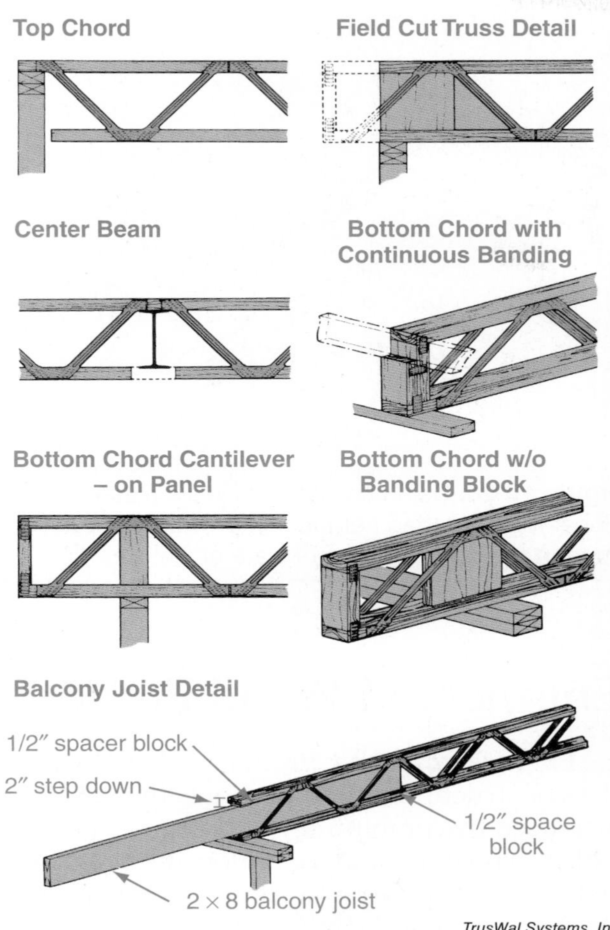

TrusWal Systems, Inc.

Figure 19-16. Examples of trusses with galvanized steel webs.

Georgia-Pacific Corporation

Figure 19-17. Many structural wood panels are manufactured for construction uses. The products shown here are (from top to bottom): waferboard, structural particleboard, composite plywood, oriented strand board, and plywood.

Cantilevered (Overhanging) Joists

Some home designs include a section of the floor that projects beyond a lower level. This design element is called a *cantilever* or overhang. When the floor joists run perpendicular to the cantilevered section, joists with extra length form the cantilever. However, when the joists are parallel to the overhanging area, ***cantilevered joists*** are required. **Figure 19-19** illustrates a typical framing technique for a cantilevered floor section.

A rule of thumb to follow in determining the necessary length of the cantilevered joists is to extend the joists inside the structure a distance at least two to three times the distance that they overhang outside the structure. If the inside

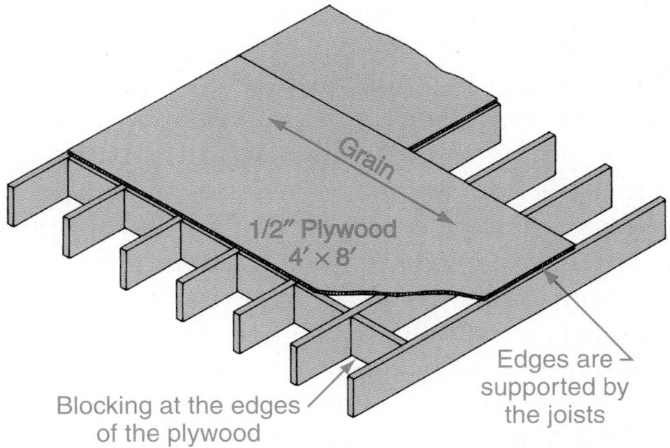

Goodheart-Willcox Publisher

Figure 19-18. Blocking supports the edges of the 1/2″ plywood used for the subfloor. All edges of the panel must be supported. Notice that the outer grain of the plywood is perpendicular to the joists.

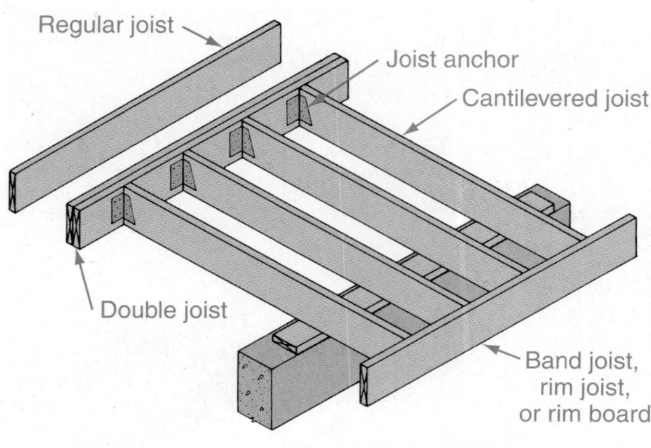

Goodheart-Willcox Publisher

Figure 19-19. Cantilevered joists should extend at least two to three times as far inside the house as they extend outside of it.

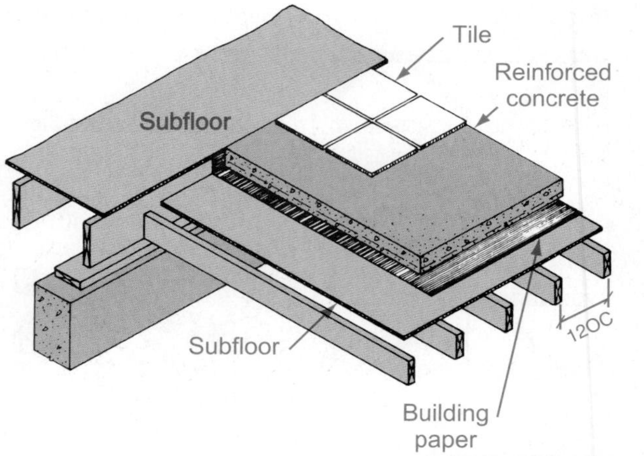

Goodheart-Willcox Publisher

Figure 19-20. Using smaller size joists placed closer together than normal can provide the additional support needed for areas of slate or tile.

distance is too short, the floor along the outside wall may sag over time. If a ledger strip is used to reinforce the joists, it should be located along the top of the inside double header joist. This is because the force will be up rather than down as in a normal situation.

Framing Under Slate or Tile

Certain areas of the home frequently have tile, slate, or stone floors. These materials require a substantial base. If a concrete base is provided, the floor framing must be lowered to provide for the concrete. The dead weight may be as much as 50 pounds per square foot in a bathroom with a tile floor and heavy fixtures. Several techniques are used to provide the needed support. A smaller size joist may be used and the space between joists reduced to provide adequate support, as shown in **Figure 19-20**. Another technique is to use one or more beams under the section to support the added weight.

The concrete base for the tile or stone should be reinforced with wire mesh and cast on a plywood subfloor covered with building paper. A special type of concrete, known as a ***cement mortar mix***, is generally used. It is a mixture of one part Portland cement and six parts sand.

Engineered Wood Products

Engineered wood products (EWPs) are a class of structural wood products that are manufactured by combining wood veneers or fibers with adhesives to produce uniformly high quality and strength. These products are designed to have more strength and consistency than traditional sawn lumber and are being used more and more in new construction. EWPs are used for framing members and components such as beams, headers, joists, and panels. See **Figure 19-21**. EWPs address the lumber industry's most pressing problem—supply—by making more efficient use of material that was previously thought to be unusable. For example, engineered wood products make it possible to use wood from smaller trees and inferior species to manufacture high-quality products.

Engineered wood products have both advantages and disadvantages. These products have better quality and consistency than solid lumber because weaknesses, such as knots, are not found in EWPs. In addition, the uniform drying of EWP components to 8% to 12% moisture content before they are compressed into the final stage produces a more predictable, consistent product from piece to piece. Traditional kiln-dried lumber is usually dried to a 15% to 19% moisture content that is more prone to shrinking and warping. EWPs provide superior design flexibility through greater widths, depths, and beam lengths that are

A

B

Alpine Structures

Figure 19-21. A—Engineered band boards are available in 9-1/4″, 11-1/4″, 12″, 14″, and 16″ depths. They eliminate the need for ripped plywood bands and provide solid backing for deck and siding attachments. B—Engineered headers are available in 1-1/4″ depth and 3-1/2″ width, which matches other framing members for one-piece installation.

not possible with solid lumber. See **Figure 19-22**. Appearance is also a consideration in some applications. Certain EWPs have a distinctive grain-like pattern that can be left exposed for painting or staining.

The greatest disadvantage for EWPs is the lack of industry standards. Products within the same general category can vary greatly because of different proprietary production methods. Each product has its own characteristics, making it difficult to make comparisons.

Goodheart-Willcox Publisher

Figure 19-22. This roof system has long spans that would require support if built with traditional dimensional lumber. However, these parallel strand beams can span the distance with no inner, or intermediate, support.

Oriented Strand Board (OSB)

Oriented strand board (OSB) is a product in which long strands of wood are mixed with resin, placed in layers, and pressed and cured. See **Figure 19-23**. It has been commercially available for many years, first appearing on the

The Engineered Wood Association

Figure 19-23. Oriented strand board is a high-quality, engineered wood panel product that has numerous applications in residential construction.

market in 1978. However, OSB was not readily accepted at the time due to the poor reputation of earlier, low-quality particleboard panels. OSB has since established itself as a quality product and is widely used for roof and wall sheathing, subflooring, siding, and webs for wood I-joists.

Aspen is the preferred wood for making OSB. It is a low-density wood that is easily cut into long strands parallel to the grain. Longer strands produce stronger boards. The strands are mixed with a resin and then mechanically oriented in layers. The outer layers are oriented parallel to the long dimension while the inner layers (core) are parallel to the short dimension. Once the strands are laid, the panel is compressed to its final thickness and the resin is allowed to cure.

Advantages and Disadvantages of OSB

OSB is less expensive to manufacture than plywood because it is made from abundant, fast-growing trees. It also has a unique appearance that is appealing as a design element for certain applications.

However, OSB is subject to swelling because it is manufactured to 2% to 5% moisture content. Plywood is generally about 6%. In addition, OSB is not designed for applications subject to permanent exposure to the elements. Therefore, it is not an acceptable replacement for exterior grade plywood.

Installation of OSB

Oriented strand board is made in panel sizes similar to plywood, typically 4′ × 8′, but it is generally available in sizes up to 8′ × 24′. Manufacturers recommend leaving a space of 1/8″ along all edges to prevent buckling problems when used in roof and wall applications. Installation of OSB near plumbing is not recommended because of potential water drips or leaks. The same nailing schedules that apply to plywood apply to OSB, but it can be nailed to within 1/4″ from the edge of the panel without breaking out.

Parallel Strand Lumber (PSL)

Parallel strand lumber (PSL) is a product in which thin strands of wood are glued together under pressure. See **Figure 19-24**. PSL products have been commercially available in the United States since about 1990. PSL was developed in 1969, but endured 19 years of research and development before being commercialized in Canada in 1988.

PSL is used for beams, columns, and headers. The products provide high strength and span capacity. Low moisture content virtually eliminates shrinking and checking. Pressure-treated PSL is also available for exterior applications. Use of PSL products has increased dramatically in the past few years.

The manufacturing process for PSL begins with debarking logs and peeling them into thin veneers. The veneers are then clipped into 1/2″ wide strands, which are then combined with adhesives and cured under pressure using microwave-generated heat. Large billets 11″ wide by 17″ deep are formed and then sawed to specified sizes.

Alpine Structures

Figure 19-24. Both posts and beams are available as parallel strand lumber.

Advantages and Disadvantages of PSL

PSL has several advantages over conventional lumber. It is very strong and can support heavier loads than solid beams. It also allows long spans, which provides more design flexibility. Because they are available in large widths and lengths, PSL beams eliminate the need for on-site construction of built-up beams.

PSL also has some disadvantages, however. Engineered connections are required for side-loading (hanging joists on only one side of) a multiple-ply PSL beam. Also, PSL should not be drilled or notched. It must be stored on site according to manufacturer's recommendations to avoid swelling.

Installation of PSL

Parallel strand lumber is available in widths ranging from 1-3/4″ to 7″. Two plies of the 2-11/16″ thick members will match a typical 5-1/2″ thick wall. Lengths up to 66′ are available.

A greater bearing area may be required if the PSL beams will be supporting higher loads than solid beams. Contact the manufacturer for tables outlining the required bearing lengths. The proper connectors must always be used. See **Figure 19-25**.

Laminated Veneer Lumber (LVL)

Laminated veneer lumber (LVL) is a product in which veneers of wood are stacked in parallel and glued under pressure. LVL was first used for high-strength aircraft parts in the 1940s. However, commercial production of LVL for high-grade structural members did not begin until 1971. LVL products are now widely used in the construction industry. LVL is used for headers, beams, columns, and joists, and as flanges for wood I-joists. See **Figure 19-26**.

The manufacturing process for LVL is similar to the process used to make plywood. The primary difference between plywood and LVL is that the plies are parallel in LVL, rather than perpendicular, to maximize strength. Southern yellow pine and Douglas fir are generally the woods of choice. Veneer panels are peeled on a veneer lathe in thicknesses of 1/10″ or 1/8″ thick. A waterproof adhesive is applied to the plies before bonding with heat and pressure. The end joints are staggered, which results in a continuous billet of lumber up to 1-3/4″ thick and 4′ wide. Two or more billets can be glued together to form thicker members. The billet is then cut to the desired widths.

Alpine Structures

Figure 19-25. Large parallel strand beams should be connected using structural steel beam connectors.

Trus Joist

Figure 19-26. Laminated veneer lumber has excellent strength and span capacity. It is used as a header in this example.

Advantages and Disadvantages of LVL

The high strength of LVL allows long spans, thereby increasing design flexibility. LVL can also be built up on site to form larger members. However, it is more expensive than solid lumber. Also, LVL is manufactured to a lower moisture content than solid lumber, so it reaches equilibrium on the job site at a different rate than solid lumber. Finally, LVL cannot be used as a standard material. It must be sized for specific load conditions.

Installation of LVL

The 1-3/4″ thick billet is the most common LVL material. It can be used individually for joists or combined with other billets to form headers or beams. It is available in depths from 5-1/2″ to 18″ and in lengths up to 66′.

LVL generally should not be mixed with solid lumber in the same floor assembly due to different moisture content of the products. Like any other girder, header, or beam, LVL beams should not be drilled or notched for electrical or plumbing pass-through.

Glue-Laminated Lumber

Glue-laminated beams, columns, and arches were the first engineered wood products. They were first produced in the 1950s. ***Glue-laminated members***, also called *glulam beams*, consist of 1× or 2× lumber that is glued in stacks to the desired shape and size. See **Figure 19-27**. The individual laminations may be end-joined with adhesives to provide continuous lengths. Therefore, virtually any length and depth can be produced.

Glue-laminated beams are manufactured to a national standard (ANSI/AITC A190.1-2012) that has been accepted by the International Residential Code. Four appearance grades are available: framing, industrial, architectural, and premium. The framing grade, intended to be used in concealed locations, is the least attractive with surface irregularities and visible glue stains. The industrial grade is similar to the framing grade, with visible glue stains, press marks, and knotholes. The architectural grade is sanded on four sides with large knotholes filled with putty. The premium grade beam has all checks and holes filled.

Advantages and Disadvantages of Glue-Laminated Lumber

The high strength of glue-laminated lumber is probably its greatest advantage. Glue-laminated beams are available either straight or with a camber to offset dead-load deflection. The beams are dimensionally stable and can be very attractive. However, the cost of glue-laminated lumber is high. It also requires special handling and storage to prevent damage. The large beams are very heavy and require special equipment to handle them. This product relies on solid sawed lumber produced with traditional milling techniques, which recovers only about 50% of the log. It is therefore a less efficient use of the wood than other engineered wood products.

The Engineered Wood Association

Figure 19-27. A—Glue-laminated lumber is produced in a variety of sizes. B—This home makes extensive use of glue-laminated members.

Installation of Glue-Laminated Lumber

Technical support from the manufacturer is required for most glue-laminated lumber products. Manufacturers provide span charts, installation details, and technical assistance. Special connectors are needed for these large members and heavy loads. Generally, for beams that remain exposed, the connection can be custom made. Manufacturers offer these suggestions to reduce checking and preserve the finished surface.

- Keep the beams covered, but allow the wood to breathe.
- Keep the beams off the ground, even if the wrapper is still on.
- Keep the beams out of the direct sunlight to prevent tanning.
- Keep the beams from rapid or extreme drying.
- Keep the beams from enduring sudden humidity changes.
- Seal the beams as soon as possible after unwrapping.
- Seal any new cuts immediately.
- If possible, condition the beams by allowing them to acclimate slowly to the interior of the building.

Boise Cascade Corporation

Figure 19-28. Wood I-joists are used primarily for long span applications in floor and roof systems.

Wood I-Joists

Wood I-joists or beams are typically made from 2 × 4 machine-stressed lumber or LVL flanges grooved to receive a 3/8″ OSB or plywood web that is glued in place. See **Figure 19-28**. They are high-strength, low-weight, and produced by a variety of manufacturers. Wood I-joists are available in flange widths ranging from 1-1/2″ to 3-1/2″ and depths from 9-1/2″ to 20″. Lengths up to 66′ are produced.

Advantages and Disadvantages of Wood I-Joists

The chief advantage of wood I-joists is probably speed of construction. Members are light for their length and may span the entire width of a house, thereby reducing by half the number of joists that need to be handled. Some wood I-joists have knockout holes to speed the installation of plumbing and electrical cable. Wood I-joists are dimensionally stable and also very straight.

One of the disadvantages of wood I-joists is that they require more effort to cut than solid lumber because of the uneven surface. Some building departments may not allow the use of wood I-joists, so check local codes before specifying them.

Installation of Wood I-Joists

Wood I-joists are used in a manner similar to traditional floor joists or rafters. See **Figure 19-29**. They can be installed using conventional nails and tools and readily available metal connectors. Wood I-joists, like other engineered wood products, are manufactured to a lower moisture content than solid lumber, so wood I-joists and solid lumber should not be used together in the same floor or roof assembly.

Web stiffeners or blocks are normally used at bearing points to help reduce the load on the

Boise Cascade Corporation

Figure 19-29. The floor joists in this home are wood I-joists.

flange-web connection. This is very important in the case of deeper joists. Manufacturers also have recommendations for nail size and the size and location of holes through the web. The flange material should not be cut.

Post and Beam Construction

Post and beam construction uses posts, beams, and planks as framing members that are larger and spaced farther apart than conventional framing members. See **Figure 19-30**. Post and beam construction provides a greater freedom of design than conventional framing techniques.

Most of the weight of a post and beam building is carried by the posts. The walls do not support much weight and are called ***curtain walls***. Curtain walls provide for wide expanses of glass without the need for headers, as shown in **Figure 19-31**. Wide overhangs are also possible by extending the large beams to the desired length. Spacing of the posts is determined by the design of the building and the load to be supported.

The foundation for a post and beam structure may be a continuous wall or a series of piers on which each post is located. The size of the foundation wall or piers is determined by the weight to be supported, soil bearing capacity, and local building codes.

The posts should be at least 4 × 4, or at least 6 × 6 if they are supporting the floor. The vertical height of the posts is also a factor in determining the post size. Check local codes for requirements.

Beams may be solid, laminated, reinforced with steel, or plywood box beams. **Figure 19-32** shows a variety of beam types. The spacing and span of the beams will be determined by the size and kind of materials and load to be supported. In most cases, a span of 7′-0″ may be used when 2″ thick tongue-and-groove subfloor or roof decking is applied to the beams. Thicker beams must be used if a span greater than 7′-0″ is required. See the span tables shown in **Figure 19-33**.

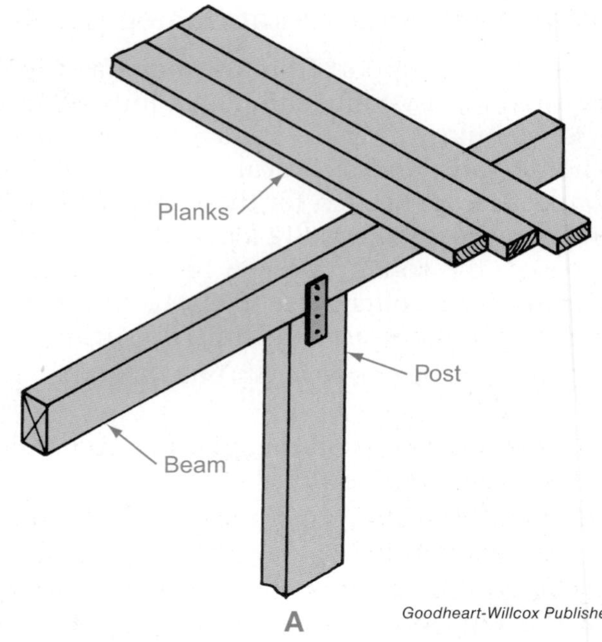

Goodheart-Willcox Publisher

Christian Delbert/Shutterstock.com

Figure 19-30. A—The three components of post and beam construction. B—An example of post and beam construction.

Pozzi Wood Windows

Figure 19-31. Post and beam construction permits broad expanses of glass and provides the warm glow of natural wood finishes.

Two systems of roof beam placement are possible with post and beam construction. See **Figure 19-34**. The first system is the ***longitudinal method,*** in which the beams are placed at right angles to the roof slope. Roof decking is laid from the ridge pole to the eaves line. The second system is called the ***transverse method***. The beams follow the roof slope and decking runs parallel to the roof ridge.

The conventional method of fastening small members by nailing does not provide a satisfactory connection in post and beam construction. Therefore, metal plates or connectors are used. These are fastened to the post and beam with lag screws or bolts. **Figure 19-35** shows a number of metal fasteners used to connect various beam segments.

Decking planks for the roof and floor range in thickness from 2″ to 4″. The planks are usually tongue-and-grooved along the long edges, and they may be tongue-and-grooved on the ends as well. **Figure 19-36** illustrates several plank designs. Roof decking span information is given in **Figure 19-37**. The underside of the planked roof is usually left exposed. If insulation is required, it may be placed above the decking and under the roofing material. Rigid type insulation should be used.

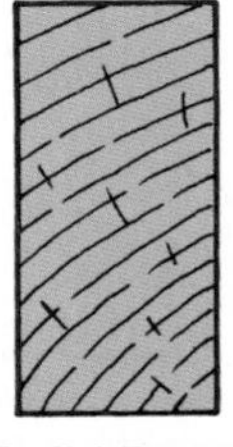

Solid Beam

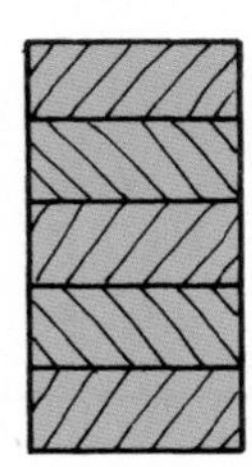

Horizontal-Laminated Beam

Vertical-Laminated Beam

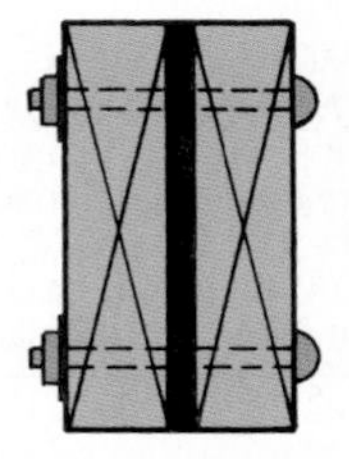

Steel-Reinforced Beam

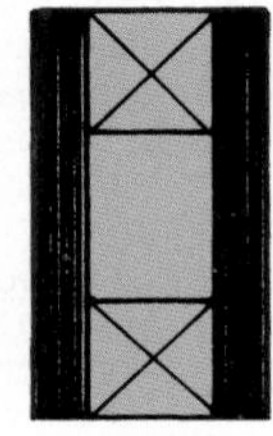

Box Beam

Goodheart-Willcox Publisher

Figure 19-32. A variety of beams can be used in post and beam construction.

Span Data for Glued Laminated Roof Beams*
Maximum Deflection 1/240th of the Span

Beam Size (Actual)	Wgt. of Beam Per Lin. Ft. in Pounds	Span in Feet											
		10	12	14	16	18	20	22	24	26	28	30	32
		Pounds Per Lin. Ft. Load Bearing Capacity											
3″ × 5-1/4″	3.7	151	85										
3″ × 7-1/4″	4.9	362	206	128	84								
3″ × 9-1/4″	6.7	566	448	300	199	137	99						
3″ × 11-1/4″	8.0	680	566	483	363	252	182	135	102				
4-1/2″ × 9-1/4″	9.8	850	673	451	299	207	148	109					
4-1/2″ × 11-1/4″	12.0	1,036	860	731	544	378	273	202	153				
3-1/4″ × 13-1/2″	10.4	1,100	916	784	685	479	347	258	197	152	120		
3-1/4″ × 15″	11.5	1,145	1,015	870	759	650	473	352	267	206	163	128	104
5-1/4″ × 13-1/2″	16.7	1,778	1,478	1,266	1,105	773	559	415	316	245	193	154	124
5-1/4″ × 15″	18.6	1,976	1,647	1,406	1,229	1,064	771	574	438	342	269	215	174
5-1/4″ × 16-1/2″	20.5	2,180	1,810	1,550	1,352	1,155	933	768	586	457	362	290	236
5-1/4″ × 18″	22.3	2,378	1,978	1,688	1,478	1,308	1,113	918	766	598	478	382	311

Example: Clear span = 20′-0″
Beam spacing = 10′-0″
Dead load = 8 lbs./sq. ft. (roofing and decking)
Live load = 20 lbs./sq. ft. (snow)
Total load = Live load + dead load × beam spacing
= (20 + 8) × 10 = 280 lbs./lin. ft.

The beam size required is 3-1/4″ × 13-1/2″, which supports 347 lbs./lin. ft. over a span of 20′-0″.

*Beams may be Douglas fir, larch or southern yellow pine.

Span Data for Glued Laminated Floor Beams*
Maximum Deflection 1/360th of the Span

Beam Size (Actual)	Wgt. of Beam Per Lin. Ft. in Pounds	Span in Feet											
		10	12	14	16	18	20	22	24	26	28	30	32
		Pounds Per Lin. Ft. Load Bearing Capacity											
3″ × 5-1/4″	3.7	114	64										
3″ × 7-1/4″	4.9	275	156	84	55								
3″ × 9-1/4″	6.7	492	319	198	130	89							
3″ × 11-1/4″	8.0	590	491	361	239	165	119						
4-1/2″ × 9-1/4″	9.8	738	479	298	196	134	96						
4-1/2″ × 11-1/4″	12.0	900	748	541	359	248	178	131	92				
3-1/4″ × 13-1/2″	10.4	956	795	683	454	316	228	169	128	98			
3-1/4″ × 15″	11.5	997	884	756	626	436	315	234	178	137	108		
5-1/4″ × 13-1/2″	16.7	1,541	1,283	1,095	732	509	367	271	205	158	123	96	
5-1/4″ × 15″	18.6	1,713	1,423	1,219	1,009	703	508	376	286	221	173	137	109
5-1/4″ × 16-1/2″	20.5	1,885	1,568	1,340	1,170	939	678	505	384	298	235	187	151
5-1/4″ × 18″	22.3	2,058	1,710	1,464	1,278	1,133	886	660	503	391	309	247	200

Example: Clear span = 20′-0″
Beam spacing = 10′-0″
Dead load = 7 lbs./sq. ft. (decking and carpet)
Live load = 40 lbs./sq. ft. (furniture and occupants)
Total load = Live load + dead load × beam spacing
= (40 + 7) × 10 = 470 lbs./lin. ft.

The beam size required is 5-1/4″ × 15″, which supports 508 lbs./lin. ft. over a span of 20′-0″.

*Beams may be Douglas fir, larch or southern yellow pine.

Potlatch Forests, Inc.

Figure 19-33. Span data for glue-laminated floor and roof beams. Local building codes should be checked for specific requirements.

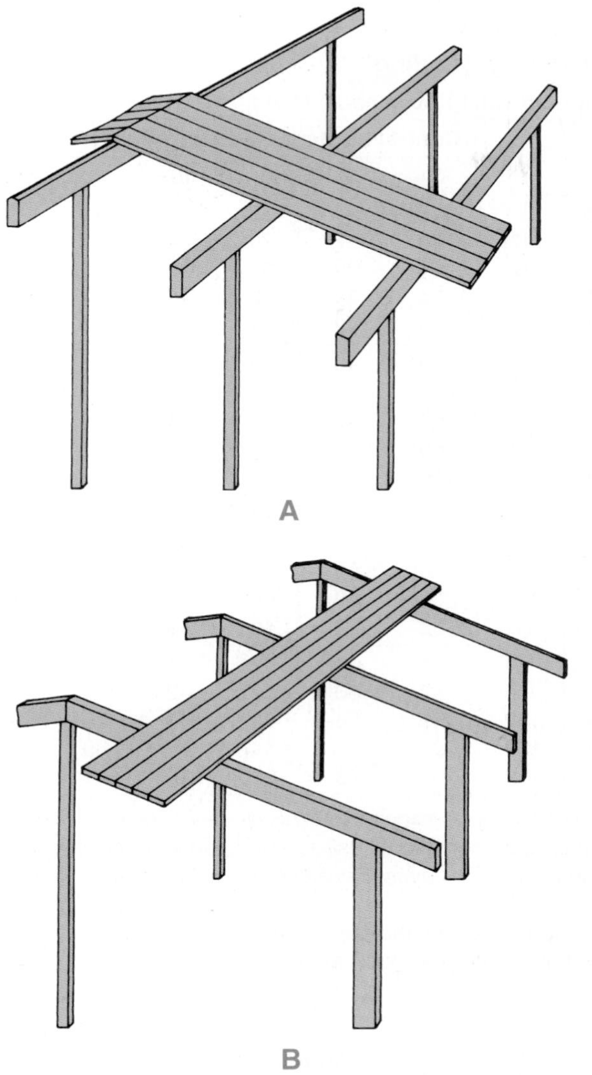

Goodheart-Willcox Publisher

Figure 19-34. A—The longitudinal method of placing roof beams. B—The transverse method of placing roof beams.

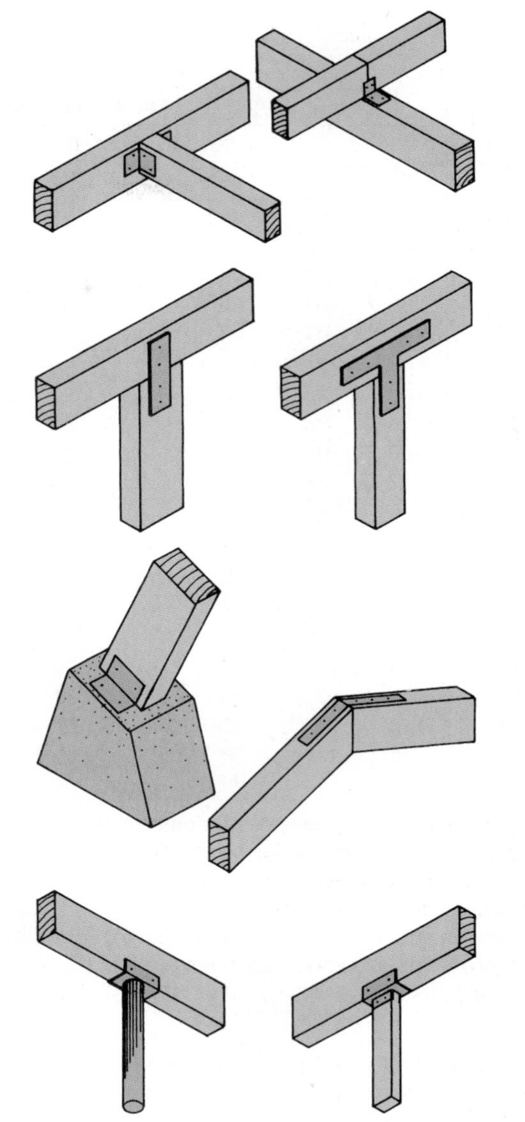

Goodheart-Willcox Publisher

Figure 19-35. Typical metal fasteners used to connect large beam segments.

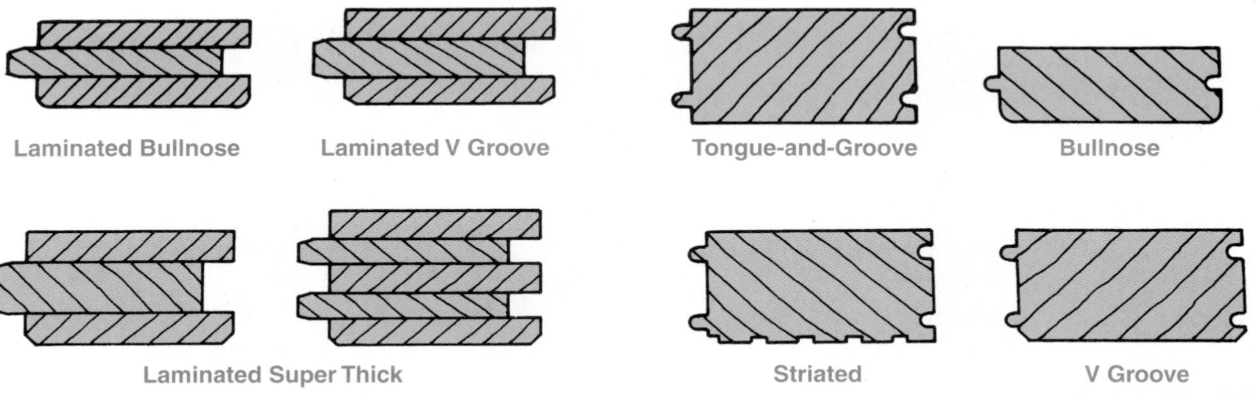

Goodheart-Willcox Publisher

Figure 19-36. Planks are available in several designs for use in post and beam construction.

Two Inch Nominal Thickness[a] Allowable Roof Load Limited By Bending														
Bending Stress, psi	**Allowable Uniformly Distributed Total Roof Load[b,c,d,e], psf**													
	Simple Span, ft							**Controlled Random Layup Span, ft**						
	6	**7**	**8**	**9**	**10**	**11**	**12**	**6**	**7**	**8**	**9**	**10**	**11**	**12**
875	73	54	41	32	26	22	18	61	45	34	27	22	18	15
950	79	58	44	35	28	24	20	66	48	37	29	24	20	16
1000	83	61	47	37	30	25	21	69	51	39	31	25	21	17
1050	88	64	49	39	32	26	22	73	54	41	32	26	22	18
1100	92	67	52	41	33	27	23	76	56	43	34	28	23	19
1150	96	70	54	42	34	28	24	80	59	45	35	29	24	20
1200	100	73	56	44	36	30	25	83	61	47	37	30	25	21
1250	104	76	58	46	38	31	26	87	64	49	39	31	26	22
1300	108	80	61	48	39	32	27	90	66	51	40	32	27	22
1350	112	83	63	50	40	33	28	94	69	53	42	34	28	23
1400	117	86	66	52	42	35	29	97	71	55	43	35	29	24
1450	121	89	68	54	44	36	30	101	74	57	45	36	30	25
1500	125	92	70	56	45	37	31	104	76	58	46	38	31	26
1550	129	95	73	57	46	38	32	108	79	60	48	39	32	27
1600	133	98	75	59	48	40	33	111	82	62	49	40	33	28
1650	138	101	77	61	50	41	34	114	84	64	51	41	34	29
1700	142	104	80	63	51	42	35	118	87	66	52	42	35	30
1750	146	107	82	65	52	43	36	122	89	68	54	44	36	30
1900	158	116	89	70	57	47	40	132	97	74	59	48	39	33
2000	167	122	94	74	60	50	42	139	102	78	62	50	41	35

[a] Based on 1-1/2 in. net thickness. To determine allowable loads for 1-7/16 in. net thickness, multiply tabulated values by 0.918.
[b] To determine allowable uniformly distributed total roof loads for other span conditions, use simple span load values for combination simple span and two-span continuous, and two-span continuous layups; and use controlled random layup road values for cantilevered pieces intermixed layup.
[c] Duration of load, $C_D = 1.0$ used in this table. For other durations of load, adjust by the appropriate factor.
[d] No increase for size effect has been applied ($C_F = 1.00$). F_b values have been previously adjusted.
[e] Dry conditions of use.

American Institute of Timber Construction

Figure 19-37. Span data for tongue-and-groove heavy timber roof decking. *(Continued)*

Three and Four Inch Nominal Thickness Allowable Roof Load Limited by Bending Simple Span And Controlled Random Layups (3 or more spans)																										
Bending Stress, psi	Allowable Uniformly Distributed Total Roof Load[a,c,e,f,g], psf																									
	3 Inch Nominal Thickness[b] Span, ft													4 Inch Nominal Thickness[d] Span, ft												
	8	9	10	11	12	13	14	15	16	17	18	19	20	8	9	10	11	12	13	14	15	16	17	18	19	20
875	114	90	73	60	51	43	37	32	28	25	22	20	18	223	176	143	118	99	84	73	64	56	49	44	40	36
950	124	98	79	65	55	47	40	35	31	27	24	22	20	242	192	155	128	108	92	79	69	61	54	48	43	39
1000	130	103	83	69	58	49	42	37	32	29	26	23	21	255	202	163	135	113	97	83	72	64	56	50	45	41
1050	137	108	88	72	61	52	45	39	34	30	27	24	22	268	212	172	142	119	101	88	76	67	59	53	48	43
1100	143	113	92	76	64	54	47	41	36	32	28	25	23	281	222	180	148	125	106	92	80	70	62	55	50	45
1150	150	118	96	79	66	57	49	42	37	33	30	26	24	293	232	188	155	130	111	96	83	73	65	58	52	47
1200	156	123	100	83	69	59	51	44	39	35	31	28	25	306	242	196	162	136	116	100	87	76	68	60	54	49
1250	163	129	104	86	72	62	53	46	41	36	32	29	26	319	252	204	169	142	121	104	91	80	71	63	56	51
1300	169	134	108	90	75	64	55	48	42	37	33	30	27	332	262	212	175	147	126	108	94	83	73	66	59	53
1350	176	139	112	93	78	66	57	50	44	39	35	31	28	344	272	220	182	153	130	112	98	86	76	68	61	55
1400	182	144	117	96	81	69	60	52	46	40	36	32	29	357	282	229	189	159	135	117	102	89	79	70	63	57
1450	189	149	121	100	84	71	62	64	47	42	37	33	30	370	292	237	196	164	140	121	105	92	82	73	66	59
1500	195	164	125	103	87	74	64	56	49	43	38	35	31	383	302	245	202	170	145	125	109	96	85	76	68	61
1550	202	159	129	107	90	76	66	57	50	45	40	36	32	396	312	253	209	176	150	129	112	99	88	78	70	63
1600	208	165	133	110	92	79	68	59	52	46	41	37	33	408	323	261	216	181	155	133	115	102	90	81	72	65
1650	215	170	138	114	95	81	70	61	54	48	42	38	34	421	333	270	223	187	159	138	120	105	93	83	75	67
1700	221	175	142	117	98	84	72	63	55	49	44	39	35	434	343	278	229	193	164	142	123	108	96	86	77	69
1750	228	180	146	120	101	86	74	65	57	50	45	40	36	447	353	286	236	198	169	146	127	112	99	88	79	71
1900	247	195	158	131	110	94	81	70	62	55	49	44	40	485	383	310	256	216	184	158	138	121	107	96	86	78
2000	260	206	167	138	116	99	85	74	65	58	51	46	42	510	403	327	270	227	193	167	145	128	113	101	90	82

[a] These load values may also be used for cantilevered pieces intermixed, combination simple span and two-span continuous, and two-span continuous layups.

[b] 2-1/2 in. net thickness. To determine allowable loads for 2-5/8 in. net thickness, multiply tabulated loads by 1.10.

[c] All spans to the right of the double line require special ordering of additional long lengths to assure that at least 20% of the decking is equal to the span length or longer.

[d] 3-1/2 in. net thickness.

[e] Duration of load, C_D = 1.0 used in this table. For other durations of load, adjust by the appropriate factor.

[f] No increase for size effect has been applied (C_F = 1.00). F_b values have been previously adjusted.

[g] Dry conditions of use.

American Institute of Timber Construction

Figure 19-37. *(Continued)*

Summary

- The structural components of floor framing include plates, joists, and studs.
- In platform framing, the floor joists form a platform on which the walls rest.
- In balloon framing, the wall studs rest directly on the sill plate and each floor "hangs" from the studs.
- Joists, which provide support for the floor, range from a nominal size of 2 × 6 to 2 × 12.
- Beams support joists when a span is too great for unsupported joists.
- Floor trusses are a lightweight alternative to floor joists in residential structures and consist of a top chord, bottom chord, and web.
- Engineered wood products (EWPs) are manufactured to have uniformly high quality and strength and are used for structural products such as beams, headers, joists, and panels.
- In post and beam construction, posts, beams, and planks are used as framing members and are spaced farther apart than conventional framing members.

Internet Resources

APA—The Engineered Wood Association
Information and research about engineered wood products

Boise Cascade
Manufacturer of engineered wood products

Lumber Specialties
Manufacturer of floor trusses

Southern Forest Products Association
Programs and services associated with southern pine building materials

Western Wood Products Association
Programs and services associated with softwood lumber manufacturers in the western United States and Alaska

Review Questions

Answer the following questions using the information in this chapter.

1. Why is platform framing used more extensively than balloon framing?
2. The lowest member of the frame of a structure, which rests on the foundation and supports the floor joists and wall studs, is the _____.
3. What method of sill construction is used in platform framing?
4. The actual dimensions of a 2 × 6 framing member are _____.
5. Describe the advantages and disadvantages of balloon framing.
6. What are two types of sill construction used with balloon framing?
7. Name three softwoods that are commonly used for joists.
8. What determines the size of joists used in residential construction?
9. The most common spacing for floor joists is _____ OC.
10. What size floor joist should be used if the span is 14′-0″, Number 1 southern pine is to be used, the live load is 30 pounds per square foot, the dead load is 10 pounds per square foot, and the joist spacing is 16″OC? Use the span data chart given in this chapter.
11. What is the purpose of cross bridging?
12. Explain the advantages of using engineered wood floor trusses in residential construction.
13. Why do floor trusses have a built-in camber?
14. Identify four types of structural wood panel products that are used for subflooring.
15. Under what circumstances are cantilevered joists required in residential construction?
16. What type of concrete is used as a base for a slate or tile floor, and what are its components?
17. What is the greatest single disadvantage of EWPs as a group?

18. One of the disadvantages of oriented strand board (OSB) is that it is subject to _____ because it is manufactured to 2% to 5% moisture content.
19. What is the main difference between plywood and laminated veneer lumber (LVL)?
20. What are the three common uses for parallel strand lumber (PSL)?
21. PSL is available in lengths up to _____ feet.
22. What are the three types of framing members used in post and beam construction?
23. What element carries most of the weight of the structure when post and beam construction is used?
24. Identify three types of beams used in post and beam construction.
25. Explain the difference between the longitudinal and transverse methods of roof beam placement in post and beam construction.
26. What type of insulation is used with a planked roof?

Suggested Activities

1. Obtain a set of house plans and identify:
   A. Size of floor joists or trusses required
   B. Spacing of floor joists or trusses
   C. Type of sill construction specified
   D. Thickness and type of subfloor material to be used
   E. Size of sill plate
   F. Type and size of bridging
   G. Type and grade of lumber specified for floor joists or trusses
   H. Method of framing used (such as balloon or platform)
2. Select a floor plan of a house and prepare a list of materials for the first floor, such as the sill, header, floor joist, and subfloor materials.
3. Conduct research to find out more about engineered wood products. Create a table that lists the composition, advantages, and disadvantages of each type of product. Include at least two products that are not described in this chapter.
4. Using CADD, design and draw the floor framing for a house of your own design. Show the spacing, size, type, and grade of floor joists used.

Problem Solving Case Study

Jim and Sandy Morris are a young couple who are very interested in the environment and the concept of sustainability. They looked for a suitable existing home to purchase, but finally decided that it would cost too much to retrofit any of the existing homes on the market to be earth-friendly. They want to build a two-story home with as many sustainable features as possible.

Jim knows that residential construction can be balloon framing, platform framing, or post and beam construction. He wants to know which of these methods, if any, is more sustainable than the others. What will you tell Jim? Conduct research if necessary.

ADDA Certification Prep

The following questions are presented in the style used in the American Design Drafting Association (ADDA) Drafter Certification Test. Answer the questions using the information in this chapter.

1. Which of the following statements are true?
   A. OSB is not subject to swelling because it is manufactured to a 2% to 5% moisture content.
   B. The floor truss is a rigid framework that consists of two webs with a framework of chords between the webs.
   C. Plywood should be installed so that the grain direction of the outer plies is at right angles to the joists.
   D. Platform framing is used more extensively than balloon framing.

2. Which of the following statements are *false*?
   A. In platform framing, the sill plate is the starting point in constructing a floor.
   B. Bridging boards are ordinarily 4 × 8 in size with the ends cut at an angle so they fit snugly against the joist.
   C. The manufacturing process for LVL is completely different from the process used to make plywood.
   D. The conventional method of fastening small members by nailing does not provide a satisfactory connection in post and beam construction.
3. Match each type of engineered wood product with its description.

   Products: 1. Oriented strand board, 2. Parallel strand lumber, 3. Laminated veneer lumber, 4. Glue-laminated lumber
   A. Widely used for roof and wall sheathing, subflooring, siding, and webs for wood I-joists.
   B. The first engineered wood products, made of 1× or 2× lumber glued in stacks to the desired shape and size.
   C. Created by clipping veneers into 1/2″ wide strands, combining them with adhesives, and curing under pressure using microwave-generated heat.
   D. Veneers of wood are stacked so the plies are parallel and are glued under pressure; first used for aircraft parts in the 1940s.

Curricular Connections

1. **Social Sciences.** Conduct research to find building styles that include cantilevered upper floors. Do not restrict your research to the United States. Create a table listing the country or area in which these styles are used and their advantages for the societies in which they are used. Does the physical geography of the region play a part? Write a summary of your findings.
2. **Language Arts.** Write a report comparing and contrasting the various types of natural and engineered structural members used in floor framing. Include the advantages and disadvantages of each.

STEM Connections

1. **Science.** Engineered wood products have become more and more a part of residential construction. Research the glues and adhesives that are used in the manufacture of these products. Are there any indications that these materials may decompose, give off harmful gases, or otherwise pose a threat to people who live in the homes for a number of years? Write a report of your findings.

Communicating about Architecture

1. **Reading.** With a partner, make flash cards of the key terms in this chapter. On the front of the card, write the term. On the back of the card, write the pronunciation and a brief definition. Use this chapter and a dictionary for guidance. Then take turns quizzing one another on the pronunciations and definitions of the key terms.

2 **Speaking.** Select five of the key terms in this chapter and imagine them being used by architects in a real-life context. With a partner, role-play a situation in which an architectural firm is asked to design the floor framing for a new two-story home.

Chapter 20

Wall and Ceiling Construction

Objectives

After completing this chapter, you will be able to:

- List the members of a typical frame wall.
- Explain methods of frame wall construction.
- Describe the applications, advantages, and disadvantages of steel framing in residential construction.
- Explain information shown on a ceiling joist span data chart.
- Describe types of masonry wall construction.
- Identify the basic processes used to produce a quality, three-coat stucco finish.
- Describe the proper application of exterior insulation finish systems.
- Identify the uses of structural insulated panels in residential construction.
- Describe the types of insulated concrete forms used in concrete wall construction.

Key Terms

access hole
ashlar stonework
brick
brown coat
cavity wall
common brick
coursed rubble
cripple stud
exterior insulation finish system (EIFS)
face brick
finish coat
firecut
furring strips
header
header-and-stud framing
insulated concrete forms (ICFs)
jack stud
king stud
lath
lintel
masonry wall
moisture barrier
polygonal rubble
rubble stonework
scratch coat
sole plate
solid blocking
structural C
structural insulated panels
stucco
three-coat stucco system
trimmer
uncoursed cobweb

Residential wall construction is typically one of three types: frame, masonry, or a combination of frame and masonry. The wall panels may be constructed at the building site or prefabricated at a different location and transported to the site for final construction. The trend today is toward more prefabrication and less on-site construction.

CADD software is available to aid in the design of frame walls. Automatic framing plans and material lists are features associated with some of the more sophisticated software packages.

However, a thorough understanding of frame wall construction is required, whether you are using traditional manual drafting methods or a CADD system.

Frame Wall Construction

Frame wall construction involves the proper arrangement of the wall framing members, which are typically construction lumber. The framing members used in conventional wood construction include sole plates, top plates, studs, headers, and bracing. See **Figure 20-1**. Plates and studs are usually nominal 2 × 4 lumber. Headers are typically constructed from larger stock. Bracing may be 1 × 4 stock, metal strap, or plywood sheathing.

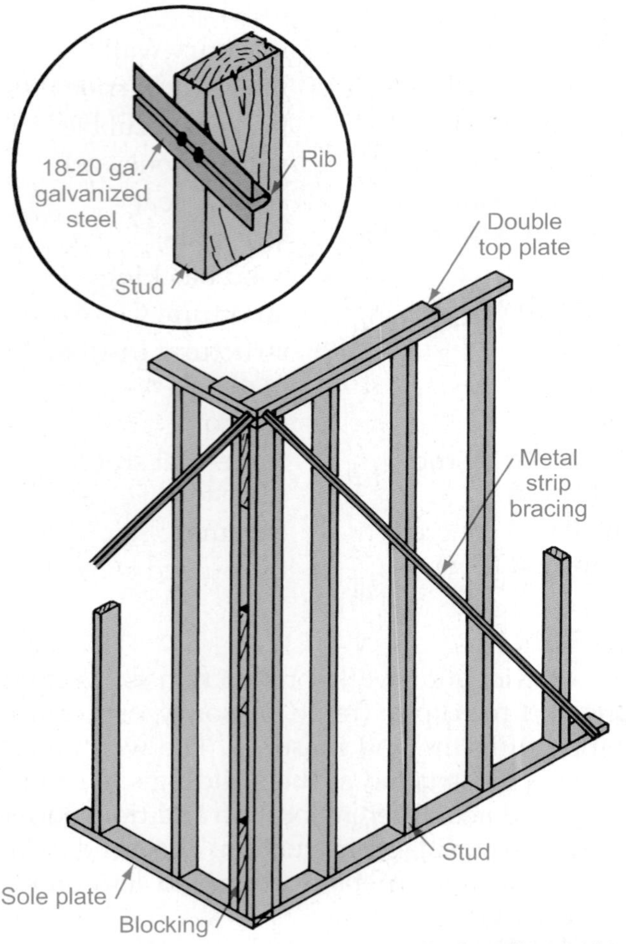

Figure 20-1. This frame wall corner shows many of the typical framing members and their relationship to each other.

Wall framing lumber must have good rigidity and nail-holding properties, be free from warp, and be easy to work. Species that meet these criteria include Douglas fir, southern yellow pine, hemlock, spruce, and larch. The most common lumber grade used is Number 2 or its equivalent. The moisture content of the lumber should be between 15% and 19%.

The wall is usually constructed flat on the subfloor because the subfloor provides a large, flat work surface. The frame is then lifted into its proper vertical position. A wall panel may extend along an entire side of the building if sufficient help is available to raise the wall. Otherwise, the wall may be built in smaller sections. Exterior frame walls may be placed flush with the outside of the foundation wall or moved 1/2″ to 3/4″ to the inside to allow for the thickness of sheathing, weatherboard, or rigid foam insulation. See **Figure 20-2**.

Plates

Frame wall construction usually begins with the ***sole plate***, which is the bottom horizontal member of the wall on which the studs rest. First, the stud spacing is marked off on the sole plate, as shown in **Figure 20-3**. The sole plate acts as an anchor for the wall panels and a nailer for interior and exterior wall sheathing. The sole plates used around the exterior of the house typically are pressure-treated lumber.

Wall studs are cut to length (usually 7′-9″ when 1-1/2″ material is used) and nailed to the sole plate. A top plate is then placed on and nailed to the top of the studs. A second top plate is added after the wall is in place. The ceiling joists rest on this second plate. The distance from the top of the subfloor to the bottom of the ceiling joists is usually 8′-1 1/2″. This distance provides a finished wall height of 8′-0″, which is typical.

Headers

Openings for doors and windows are framed before the wall is moved to the vertical position. Each wall opening requires a ***header*** or ***lintel*** to sustain the weight above the opening. Two basic approaches used in constructing headers are solid blocking and header-and-stud framing.

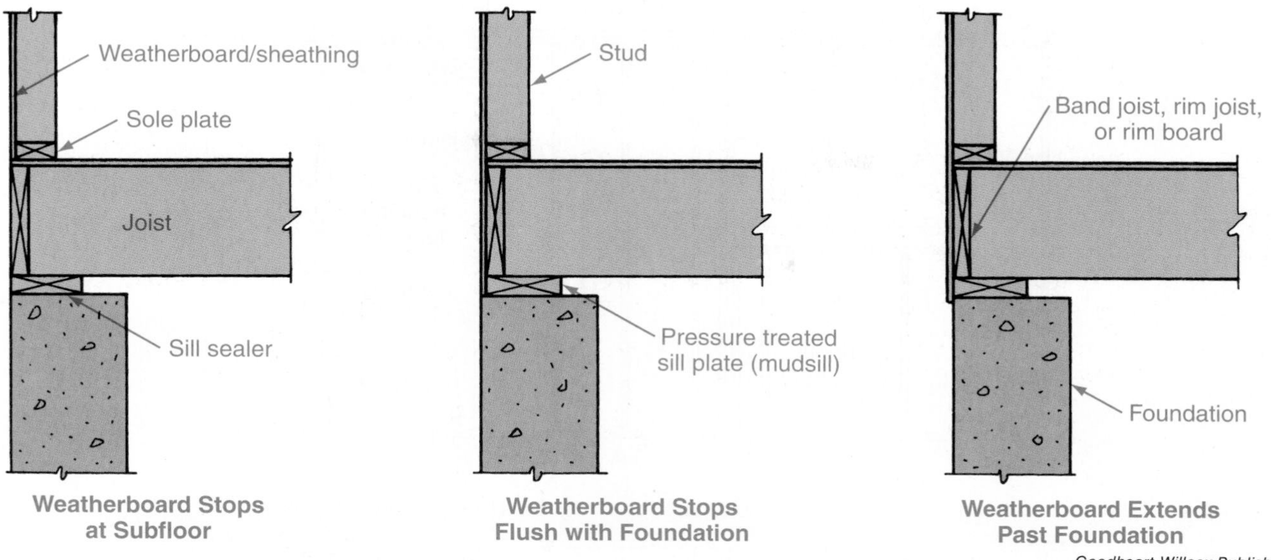

Figure 20-2. The sheathing, weatherboard, or rigid insulation may end at the subfloor or the top of the foundation, or it may extend below the top of the foundation.

In ***solid blocking,*** the header size is increased to completely fill the space from the top of the rough opening to the top plate. See **Figure 20-4.** Two 2 × 12 pieces of dimension lumber are nailed together with a piece of 1/2″ plywood between them to form a 3-1/2″ thick header. ***Trimmers,*** also called ***jack studs,*** are positioned inside the opening to help support the header over an opening in the wall. The trimmers are nailed to full-height ***king studs*** on either side of the opening for additional support. This method reduces construction time, but increases shrinkage.

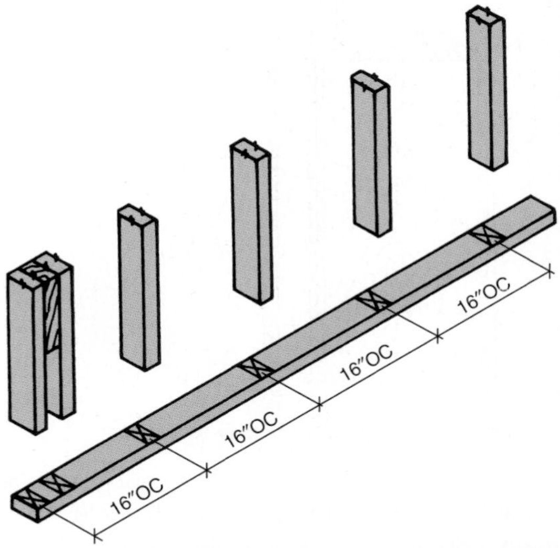

In ***header-and-stud framing, cripple studs*** (also called jack studs) and trimmers are firmly nailed to the sole and top plates. Refer to **Figure 20-4**. Remember, terminology for framing members and construction varies across the country. You should become familiar with the framing terms used in local building codes.

The length of the header is equal to the width of the rough opening plus the thickness of two trimmers (jack studs), as shown in **Figure 20-5**. Header sizes vary with the span and load requirements. The table shown in **Figure 20-6** provides sizes for various spans. *Check the local building code to be sure these specifications are permitted in your area.* Trussed headers are required for openings wider than 8′-0″ or in situations involving extremely heavy loads. **Figure 20-7** illustrates two types of trussed headers.

Rough openings for windows and doors are dimensioned on the floor plan to the center of the opening when located in a frame wall. Specific dimensions are usually provided by the window and door schedule. The width is listed first and the height second. The rough opening height of most doors is 6′-10″. The top of all windows is usually the same distance above the floor.

Goodheart-Willcox Publisher

Figure 20-3. The location of studs is laid out on the sole plate.

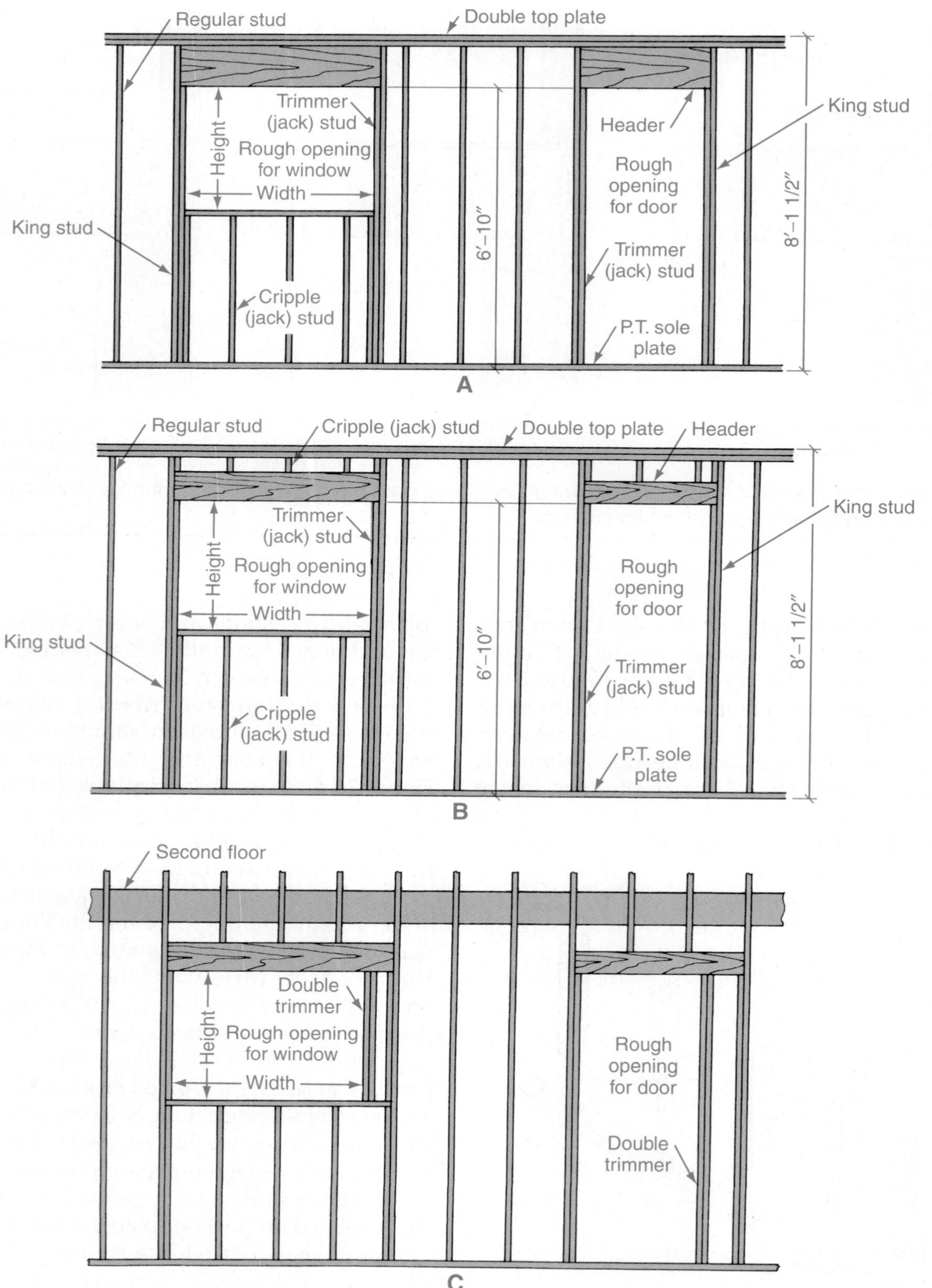

Goodheart-Willcox Publisher

Figure 20-4. A—Solid blocking is used to form the header over a window and door opening in this platform framing example. Studs are 16″OC. B—In header-and-stud framing, cripple studs (also called jack studs) are used above and below the header. Studs are 16″OC in this platform framing example. C—Header-and-stud framing used in balloon framing with 16″OC studs.

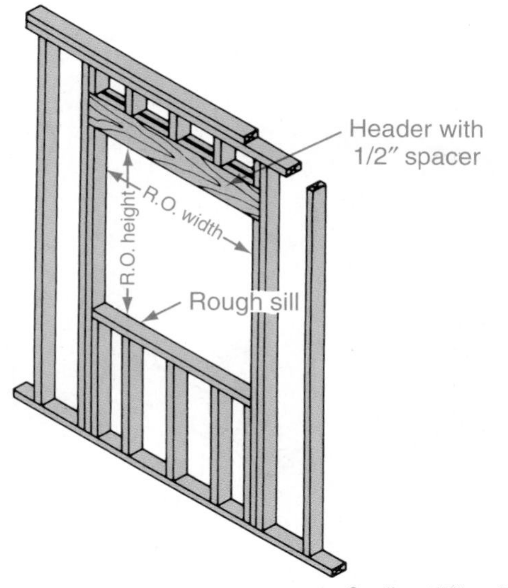

Goodheart-Willcox Publisher

Figure 20-5. The rough opening (R.O.) for a window is the area between the trimmers and the rough sill and header. The header length is the rough opening width plus two trimmer widths.

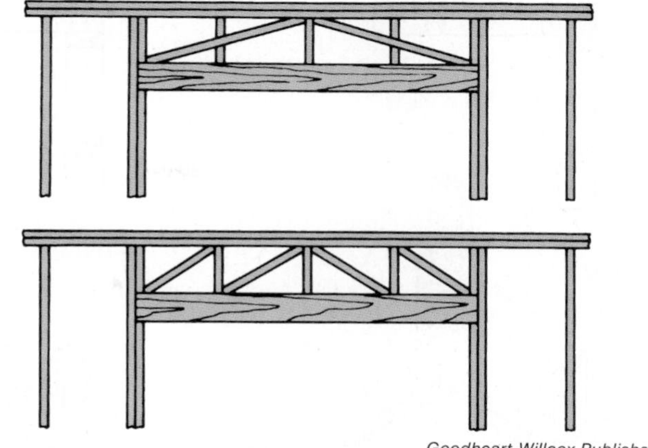

Goodheart-Willcox Publisher

Figure 20-7. Trussed headers increase the supporting strength and possible span.

Exterior Corners and Bracing

Typical methods of framing used to form exterior wall corners are shown in **Figure 20-8**. The corner must provide a nailing edge for the interior wall material and adequate support for the structure.

Corner bracing is required by most codes. Two methods of bracing are commonly used to provide added support. In one method, diagonal corner braces of 1 × 4 lumber or metal straps are used from the top corner of the wall down to the sole plate. This method is shown in **Figure 20-1**. The second method makes use of a sheet of 1/2″ plywood or similar panel nailed to the studs at each corner, as shown in **Figure 20-9**.

Header Size	Maximum Span
2 × 6	3′-6″
2 × 8	5′-0″
2 × 10	6′-6″
2 × 12	8′-0″
Note: Header size refers to size of material used and not the overall size of the header. Each header is constructed of two pieces, on edge, with plywood spacer between.	

Goodheart-Willcox Publisher

Figure 20-6. Typical header sizes for given spans.

Interior Walls

Interior frame walls are constructed in the same way as exterior walls. They have sole plates, studs, and double top plates. Interior walls must be securely fastened to the exterior walls that they intersect. A nailing edge must be provided for the plaster base, drywall, or paneling. This may be accomplished by doubling the exterior wall studs at the intersection of the partition or by using a 2 × 6 nailer secured to cross blocking. **Figure 20-10** illustrates both methods. The same arrangement is used at the intersection of all interior walls.

Steel Framing

Steel as a residential building material was explored shortly after World War II. However, those early steel houses experienced problems and were generally not accepted by the public. Also, once the surplus war steel ran out, steel homes were more expensive than wood homes. Then, in the early 1970s, companies such as US Steel again began to market steel-framed houses due to technological advances in production and materials. However, the public was still not ready to accept the all-steel house.

Today, many things have changed. Wood is becoming scarce and more expensive. The quality

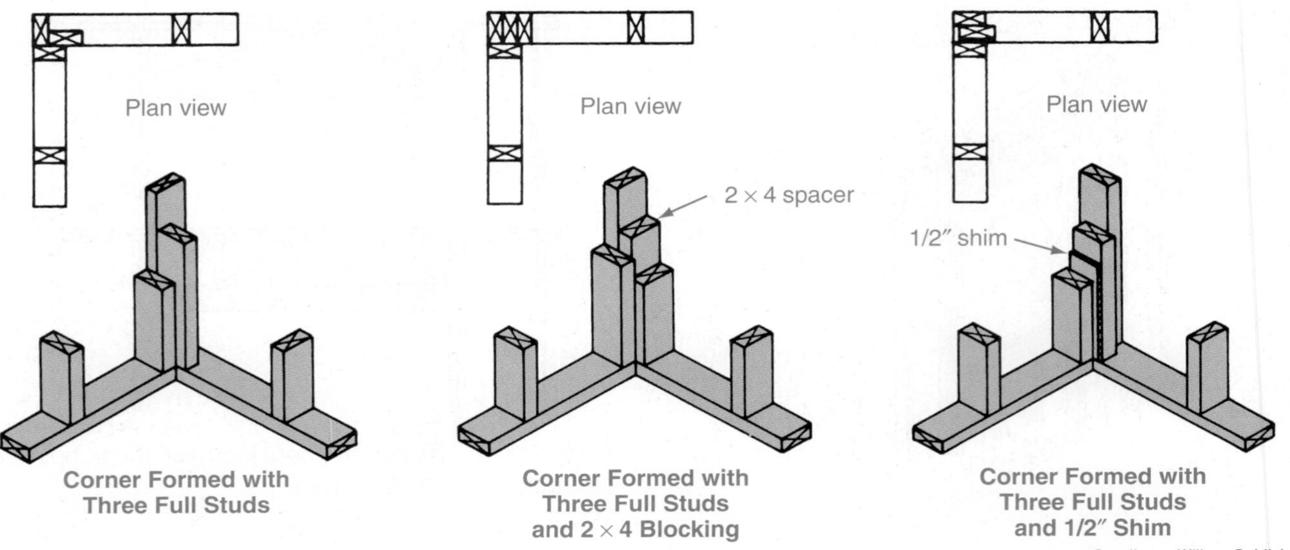

Goodheart-Willcox Publisher

Figure 20-8. Exterior corner posts are framed in a variety of ways. Three accepted methods are shown here.

of new growth lumber is not as good as when timber was cut from older, larger, and stronger trees. Designers and builders are looking for alternatives to wood to improve quality and reduce cost. Vast destruction from hurricanes, fire, earthquakes, and floods has focused new evaluation on building materials, codes, construction methods, and quality of work. Steel framing has performed well and has captured the interest of insurance companies, builders, and prospective home buyers.

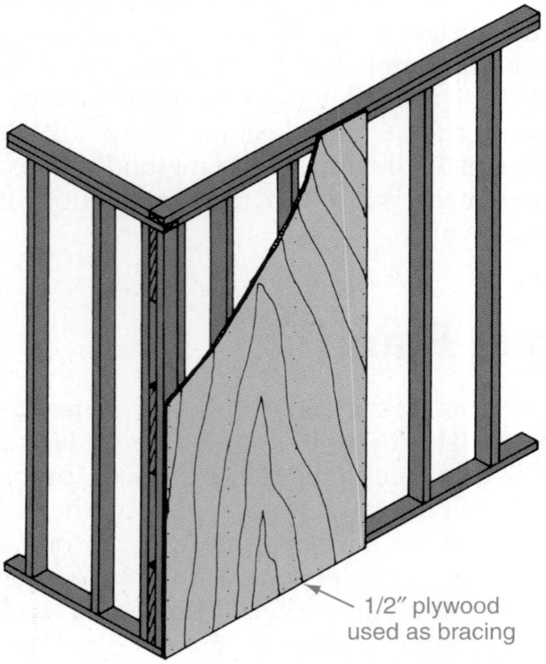

1/2″ plywood used as bracing

Goodheart-Willcox Publisher

Figure 20-9. One-half inch plywood sheathing may be used as bracing for the exterior wall corners, depending on the local building code. Oriented strand board (OSB) is commonly used as well.

Environmental and economic concerns have also forced the building industry to pursue alternative materials and methods. Steel framing is made from a recyclable material and has a proven record in commercial construction. In addition, steel's cost and supply stability make it a viable option for residential framing. Although the initial cost of construction can be higher for steel framing, the long-term durability and sustainable qualities of steel make it competitive with wood.

Advantages of Steel Framing

Several advantages of steel framing are evident for builders, homeowners, and the environment. The benefits to builders include:

- Steel framing can be used with all common types of finishing materials.
- Fewer members are generally required due to the inherent strength of steel.
- Steel will not rot, shrink, swell, split, or warp and is noncombustible.

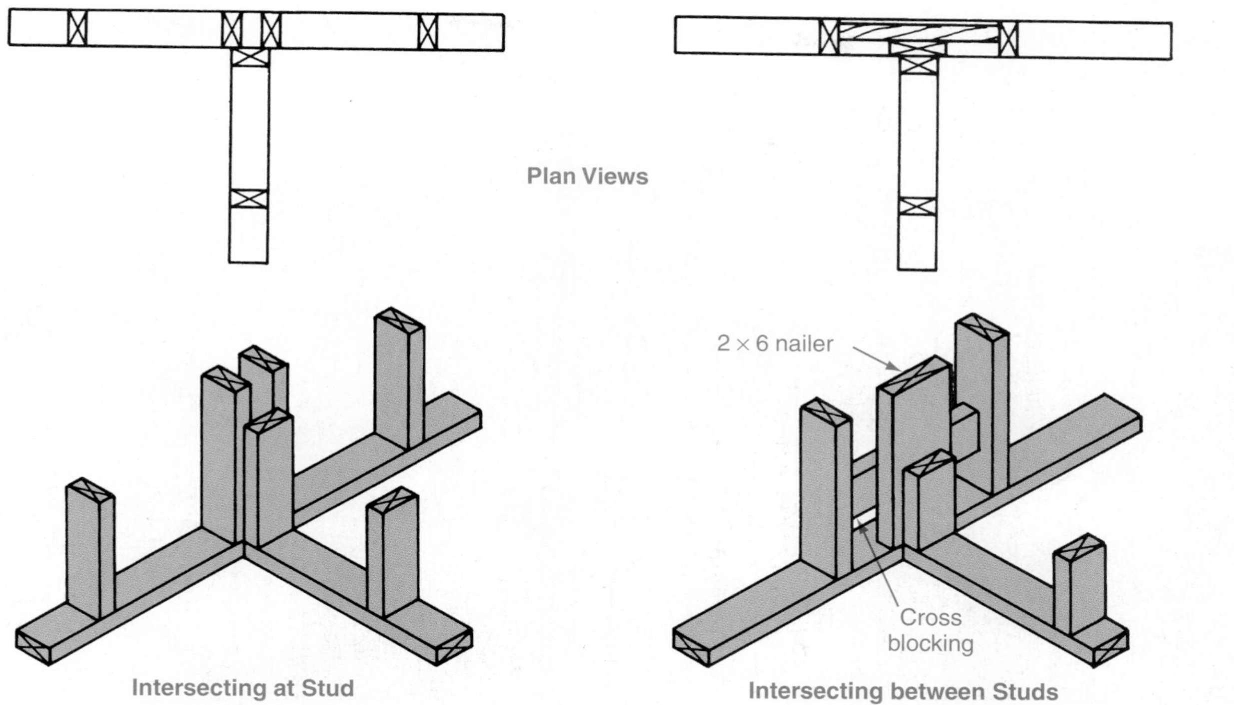

Figure 20-10. The framing for the intersection of partitions and exterior walls is accomplished by using extra studs or blocking and a nailer.

- Steel is consistent in quality and competitively priced.
- Steel members are available in a variety of precut, standard shapes and sizes, as well as custom shapes and sizes. This minimizes construction waste. Lengths up to 40′ are possible. See **Figure 20-11**.
- Steel members are lighter than wood members. Therefore, foundation and seismic loads can be reduced.
- Framing members are manufactured with prepunched holes for pipes and electrical wiring.

Benefits to homeowners include:

- Steel framing does not require treatment for termites. It is free of resin adhesives and other chemicals needed to treat wood framing products.
- Because of its strength, steel can span greater distances, providing larger open spaces and increased design flexibility.
- Steel-framed structures resist fires, earthquakes, and hurricanes because of steel's inherent strength and noncombustible qualities.
- Insurance premiums can be lower for a steel-framed house.
- Remodeling can be easily accomplished because nonbearing walls can be easily removed, altered, and relocated.

In addition to benefits for builders and homeowners, steel framing has significant environmental benefits. These include:

- All steel products are recyclable. In recent years, the recycling rate of steel products in the United States has been above 80%—the highest rate of any material. Millions of tons of steel scrap are recycled every year, reducing waste going to landfills.
- Steel products can be recycled repeatedly without degradation or loss of properties.
- The steel industry is the single largest recycler in North America because recycled steel is an integral ingredient in steel production.
- Magnetic separation makes steel the easiest and most economical material to remove from the solid waste stream.
- The amount of energy required to produce a ton of steel has been reduced by 27% since 1990. (*Source:* American Iron and Steel Institute)

Lev Kropotov/Shutterstock.com

Figure 20-11. Steel framing is available in custom shapes and sizes.

Disadvantages of Steel Framing

Steel framing does have some disadvantages that hinder its acceptance. For example, structures using steel framing require engineering analysis. Even though manufacturers of steel framing systems provide engineering analysis as part of the package, designers and builders need to develop greater familiarity with the capabilities of these systems.

The workability of steel is also a disadvantage. The standard 25-gage nonbearing studs are flimsy and hard to work with. Steel framing components can have sharp edges that will slice the skin if not handled properly. "Hemmed" track is safer than "unhemmed." Steel is hard to cut, and most of a carpenter's tools will not work on steel.

Finally, steel framing is not used in many cases simply because many building officials, designers, and tradespeople are not familiar with it. These people need to be educated about the methods and capabilities of steel framing systems relative to residential construction.

Steel Framing Components

The steel component known as the ***structural C*** or C-section is the predominant shape used for floor joists, wall studs, roof rafters, and ceiling joists. Common sizes of steel framing members are shown in **Figure 20-12**. Standard dimensions are nearly identical to those of dimensional lumber. Flange widths are generally 1-1/2″ and web depths range from 2″ to 12″. Steel thicknesses from 12 to 25 gage are available. Studs used in typical load-bearing applications are 16 to 20 gage. The C-section is available unpunched or prepunched in lengths from 8′ to 16′. Prepunched studs have holes that allow wiring and plumbing to be routed through the stud. A grommet must be placed in every hole through which wires pass to prevent cutting of the wire insulation, unless conduit is used.

A track or channel member is used for rim joists, top and bottom plates, and blocking. It is generally the same gage as the framing material. The track is also available unpunched or prepunched in lengths up to 10′ with flange lengths of 1″ or 1-1/4″.

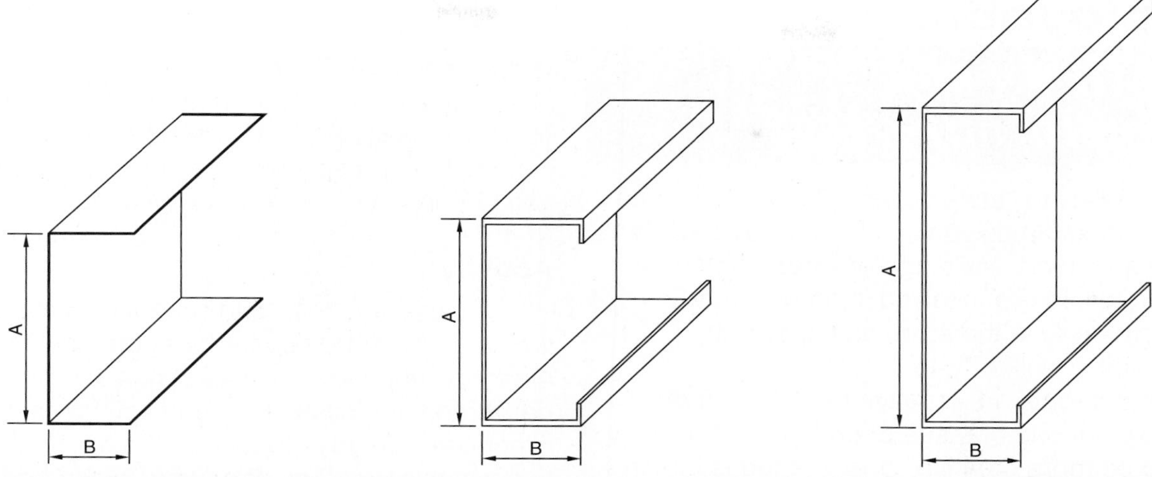

Channel Tracks		C Studs		C Joists	
A	**B**	**A**	**B**	**A**	**B**
2-1/2″	1″	2-1/2″	1-1/4″	5-1/2″	1-7/8″
3-1/4″	1-3/8″	3″	1-3/8″	6″	1-5/8″
3-5/8″		3-5/8″	1-1/2″	7-1/4″	1-3/4″
4″		3-1/4″	1-5/8″	8″	2″
6″		4″		9-1/4″	2-1/2″
		5-1/2″		10″	
		6″		12″	
		7-1/2″			
		8″			

Goodheart-Willcox Publisher

Figure 20-12. Common sizes of the three commonly used steel framing members.

Angle steel can be used as a ledger or a connection bracket. It can also be used for stiffening, bracing, or blocking.

Cold- and hot-rolled channel are similar in shape and gage to the track member. Smaller-size channel is used for stiffening, bracing, and blocking. Hot-rolled channel is used for furring. Cold-rolled Z members may be used in structural applications. These applications include roof purlins and (in lighter gages) furring.

All steel members are fastened with screws. See **Figure 20-13**. These are typically 1/2″ long, low-profile, zinc-coated pan head screws. Steel framing is zinc-galvanized to protect it from corrosion and rust.

Wall and Roof Systems

The construction elements of a framed house include three main assemblies: floors, walls, and roofs. Steel framing is often consistent with wood frame construction, but there are some differences.

Walls

Two types of steel studs are used for walls. Structural C studs are used for interior and exterior load-bearing walls. Drywall studs are used for nonbearing interior partitions. The structural C studs used in wall construction range in size from 2-1/2″ to 8″ and in thickness

Employability

Creativity and Brainstorming

The ability to "think outside the box" to come up with workable design solutions is an important skill for architects, building designers, and most other professionals involved in architectural work. Creativity is therefore an important employability skill.

Some people are creative by nature. Even if you are not one of these people, you can learn to be more creative. One method is to use *brainstorming*. Choose an issue that interests you—architectural or not—and write down as many solutions as you can think of. Do not worry at first about whether your solutions are probable or even possible. There are no right or wrong answers. Just list everything that comes into your head. Give yourself about 10 or 15 minutes to create the list. Then go back over your list and evaluate all of your ideas. The old saying "practice makes perfect" is not quite true; "perfect" is a myth. However, practice can definitely help you become a more creative thinker.

Activity

Consider the following scenario: A client wants a new 1500 square foot home built of solid masonry, but masonry is expensive. When you delivered your initial plans and estimates, the client was very disappointed. The easiest way to solve this problem, of course, would be to use masonry veneer instead. However, the client would really prefer to use solid masonry. Conduct a brainstorming session to determine and list other alternatives that might meet the client's wishes. Set a timer for 10 minutes. At the end of 10 minutes, stop and review your list. How many of your ideas are suitable to present to a "real" client?

from .034″ to .071″. The drywall metal studs are available in sizes from 1-5/8″ to 6″ with thicknesses from .018″ to .034″. Spacing is usually 24″ on center (OC).

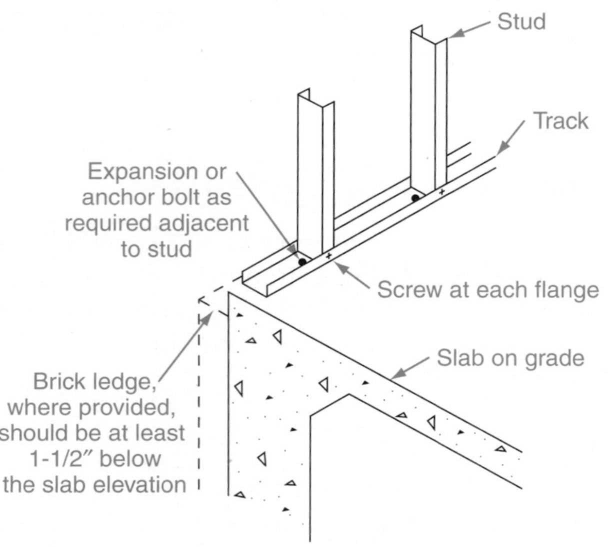

Figure 20-13. This is a typical attachment of a steel-framed wall on slab construction. All steel framing members are screwed together.

Roofs

The broad ranges of available sizes and thicknesses of steel framing members allow steel to be used in virtually any roof system. See **Figure 20-14**. The rafter and ceiling joist systems

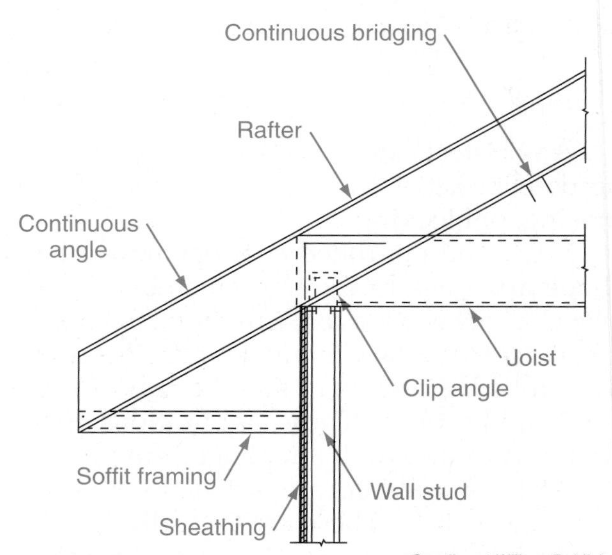

Figure 20-14. Steel framing can be applied to roof construction.

used for traditional lumber-built houses are possible, as well as on-site and off-site trusses. Spacing is usually 24″OC.

Ceiling Construction

After the exterior and interior walls are erected, plumbed, and braced, and the second top plates added, ceiling joists are put in place. These are usually positioned across the width of the house and in the same direction as the rafters. The required size of ceiling joists will depend on the load to be supported, span, wood species, spacing of joists, and grade of lumber used. Span data for ceiling joists in four common species of wood is given in **Figure 20-15**. The span data is based on a live load of 10 pounds per square foot and a dead load of 5 pounds per square foot. The Reference Section of this textbook provides additional span data tables.

Construction of the ceiling is similar to floor construction. The main differences are that a header is not required around the perimeter and a smaller size of lumber is used. Long spans may require support from a bearing wall partition or beam. If a beam is used, it may be located below the joists or placed flush with them using ledger strips. Both methods are illustrated in **Figure 20-16**.

The upper corner of the ceiling joists often interferes with the roof slope. To prevent this interference, the corner is usually cut to match the slope, as shown in **Figure 20-17**.

Roof trusses are now being used in residential construction to a much greater extent than before. This approach eliminates the traditional ceiling joist and rafter. See Chapter 17 for design and construction procedures for roof trusses.

General Framing Considerations

An *access hole* must be provided in the ceiling to allow entry into the attic. This opening is usually in a closet or hallway. The International Residential Code specifies a minimum size of 22″ × 30″ for the opening. Framing around the opening is the same as for openings in the floor. Double headers are used for large holes, such as for a disappearing stairway. However, double headers are not usually required for small openings.

A number of areas in the house require special framing. Openings for heating ducts, wall backing for various fixtures, and extra support for the bathtub are examples of areas that require

Green Architecture
Sustainable Masonry

Masonry is one of the more sustainable building materials. With proper preparation and building techniques, it can be extremely energy-efficient. The life cycle of most types of masonry is long, especially when the home is maintained properly. Most masonry is also recyclable. In addition, some masonry products are designed to be more suitable for the environment than traditional masonry products. For example, traditional clay brick is fired at extremely high temperatures and consumes large amounts of energy when it is manufactured. Newer types of brick are available that are made from fly ash or recycled materials, such as glass or cellulose, instead of clay. These products make use of recycling and do not use firing processes when they are manufactured.

Although masonry products have high strength and durability, just using masonry for exterior walls does not automatically guarantee sustainability. Poor workmanship and inferior materials can reduce the sustainability of masonry considerably. Sustainable building practices and good quality materials must be used. The International Masonry Institute provides educational resources for architects and contractors to help ensure that masonry projects remain “green.” This organization also offers a sustainable masonry certification program to help architects and contractors who want to participate in LEED and other green building programs.

attention. **Figure 20-18** illustrates some of these special framing details.

Framing for a bay window presents special problems. **Figure 20-19** shows one accepted method for framing a bay window. Note that the floor joists extend beyond the wall to provide support for the unit. If the unit is at right angles to the floor joists, then cantilevered joists should be used to support the unit.

Masonry Wall Construction

A ***masonry wall*** is constructed entirely of brick, concrete block, stone, clay tile, terra cotta, or a combination of these materials. Solid masonry walls for residential construction are usually 8" thick. Concrete block walls are popular in many areas of the country. These walls are also called ***cavity walls***. Block walls are relatively inexpensive to construct, and a variety of textures and

CEILING JOIST SPANS FOR COMMON LUMBER SPECIES
(Uninhabitable attics without storage, live load = 10 psf, L/Δ = 240)

CEILING JOIST SPACING (inches)	SPECIES AND GRADE		DEAD LOAD = 5 psf			
			2 × 4	2 × 6	2 × 8	2 × 10
			Maximum ceiling joist spans			
			(feet - inches)	(feet - inches)	(feet - inches)	(feet - inches)
12	Douglas fir-larch	SS	13-2	20-8	Note a	Note a
	Douglas fir-larch	#1	12-8	19-11	Note a	Note a
	Douglas fir-larch	#2	12-5	19-6	25-8	Note a
	Douglas fir-larch	#3	11-1	16-3	20-7	25-2
	Hem-fir	SS	12-5	19-6	25-8	Note a
	Hem-fir	#1	12-2	19-1	25-2	Note a
	Hem-fir	#2	11-7	18-2	24-0	Note a
	Hem-fir	#3	10-10	15-10	20-1	24-6
	Southern pine	SS	12-11	20-3	Note a	Note a
	Southern pine	#1	12-5	19-6	25-8	Note a
	Southern pine	#2	11-10	18-8	24-7	Note a
	Southern pine	#3	10-1	14-11	18-9	22-9
	Spruce-pine-fir	SS	12-2	19-1	25-2	Note a
	Spruce-pine-fir	#1	11-10	18-8	24-7	Note a
	Spruce-pine-fir	#2	11-10	18-8	24-7	Note a
	Spruce-pine-fir	#3	10-10	15-10	20-1	24-6
16	Douglas fir-larch	SS	11-11	18-9	24-8	Note a
	Douglas fir-larch	#1	11-6	18-1	23-10	Note a
	Douglas fir-larch	#2	11-3	17-8	23-4	Note a
	Douglas fir-larch	#3	9-7	14-1	17-10	21-9
	Hem-fir	SS	11-3	17-8	23-4	Note a
	Hem-fir	#1	11-0	17-4	22-10	Note a
	Hem-fir	#2	10-6	16-6	21-9	Note a
	Hem-fir	#3	9-5	13-9	17-5	21-3
	Southern pine	SS	11-9	18-5	24-3	Note a
	Southern pine	#1	11-3	17-8	23-10	Note a
	Southern pine	#2	10-9	16-11	21-7	25-7
	Southern pine	#3	8-9	12-11	16-3	19-9
	Spruce-pine-fir	SS	11-0	17-4	22-10	Note a
	Spruce-pine-fir	#1	10-9	16-11	22-4	Note a
	Spruce-pine-fir	#2	10-9	16-11	22-4	Note a
	Spruce-pine-fir	#3	9-5	13-9	17-5	21-3

(continued)

Figure 20-15. Ceiling joist span data for common species of wood. The maximum deflection assumed is 1/240th of the span with a normal live load.

CEILING JOIST SPANS FOR COMMON LUMBER SPECIES *(continued)*
(Uninhabitable attics without storage, live load = 10 psf, L/Δ = 240)

CEILING JOIST SPACING (inches)	SPECIES AND GRADE		DEAD LOAD = 5 psf			
			2 × 4	2 × 6	2 × 8	2 × 10
			Maximum ceiling joist spans			
			(feet - inches)	(feet - inches)	(feet - inches)	(feet - inches)
19.2	Douglas fir-larch	SS	11-3	17-8	23-3	Note a
	Douglas fir-larch	#1	10-10	17-0	22-5	Note a
	Douglas fir-larch	#2	10-7	16-8	21-4	26-0
	Douglas fir-larch	#3	8-9	12-10	16-3	19-10
	Hem-fir	SS	10-7	16-8	21-11	Note a
	Hem-fir	#1	10-4	16-4	21-6	Note a
	Hem-fir	#2	9-11	15-7	20-6	25-3
	Hem-fir	#3	8-7	12-6	15-10	19-5
	Southern pine	SS	11-0	17-4	22-10	Note a
	Southern pine	#1	10-7	16-8	22-0	Note a
	Southern pine	#2	10-2	15-7	19-8	23-5
	Southern pine	#3	8-0	11-9	14-10	18-0
	Spruce-pine-fir	SS	10-4	16-4	21-6	Note a
	Spruce-pine-fir	#1	10-2	15-11	21-0	25-8
	Spruce-pine-fir	#2	10-2	15-11	21-0	25-8
	Spruce-pine-fir	#3	8-7	12-6	15-10	19-5
24	Douglas fir-larch	SS	10-5	16-4	21-7	Note a
	Douglas fir-larch	#1	10-0	15-9	20-1	24-6
	Douglas fir-larch	#2	9-10	15-0	19-1	23-3
	Douglas fir-larch	#3	7-10	11-6	14-7	17-9
	Hem-fir	SS	9-10	15-6	20-5	Note a
	Hem-fir	#1	9-8	15-2	19-10	24-3
	Hem-fir	#2	9-2	14-5	18-6	22-7
	Hem-fir	#3	7-8	11-2	14-2	17-4
	Southern pine	SS	10-3	16-1	21-2	Note a
	Southern pine	#1	9-10	15-6	20-5	24-0
	Southern pine	#2	9-3	13-11	17-7	20-11
	Southern pine	#3	7-2	10-6	13-3	16-1
	Spruce-pine-fir	SS	9-8	15-2	19-11	25-5
	Spruce-pine-fir	#1	9-5	14-9	18-9	22-11
	Spruce-pine-fir	#2	9-5	14-9	18-9	22-11
	Spruce-pine-fir	#3	7-8	11-2	14-2	17-4

Check sources for availability of lumber in lengths greater than 20 feet.

For SI: 1 inch = 25.4 mm, 1 foot = 304.8 mm, 1 pound per square foot = 0.0479 kPa.

a. Span exceeds 26 feet in length.

designs are possible. Walls that require more than one thickness of masonry must have all thicknesses bonded together. They may be bonded by using a header course every 16″ vertically, or corrugated metal wall ties may be placed in the mortar joints. See **Figure 20-20**. Metal wall ties should be placed no farther apart than 16″ vertically and 32″ horizontally.

One disadvantage of a solid masonry wall is that furring strips are required on the inside of the wall if drywall or paneling is used. ***Furring strips*** are usually 2 × 2 or 1 × 3 lumber affixed to the wall to provide a nailing surface. Insulation can be added on the inside of a solid masonry wall as shown in **Figure 20-21**.

Floor joists are placed directly into openings in solid brick and stone walls. Each joist end is cut at an angle to prevent toppling the wall if the house should catch fire. This cut is known as a ***firecut***. See **Figure 20-22**.

Flashing and termite shields should be used at the base of solid masonry or brick veneer walls,

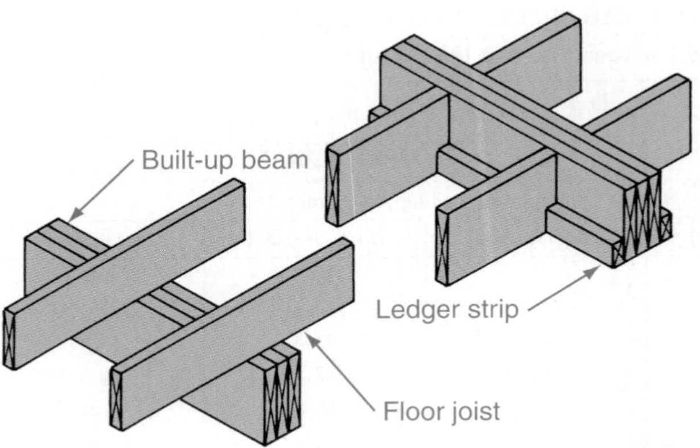

Goodheart-Willcox Publisher

Figure 20-16. Two methods of supporting ceiling joists with a built-up beam.

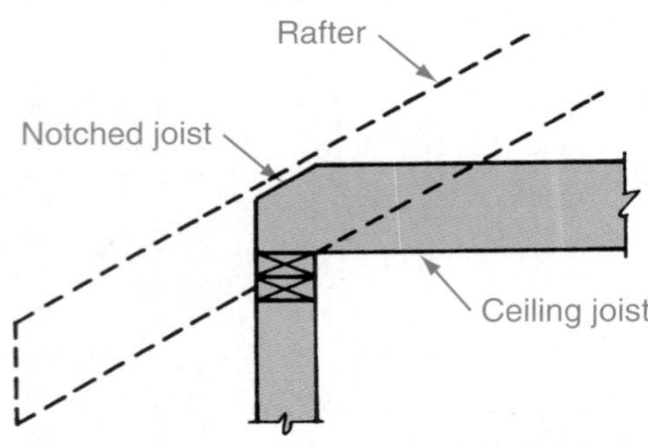

Goodheart-Willcox Publisher

Figure 20-17. Ceiling joists are usually notched to match the roof slope to prevent interference with the roof sheathing.

as shown in **Figure 20-23**. Flashing prevents moisture from entering the structure. Termites are a threat in a large part of the country and cause millions of dollars in damage each year. Termite shields help prevent infestation.

The top plate for the roof must be anchored securely to the solid masonry wall. See **Figure 20-24**. The usual procedure in a brick wall is to place anchor bolts between the bricks. Nuts are threaded onto the bolts to hold the plate in place. A lintel block is used in concrete block construction and anchor bolts are cast in place. The plate is then secured by nuts threaded onto the bolts.

Stonework

Often, stonework is used with a masonry wall to provide a decorative look. The stonework

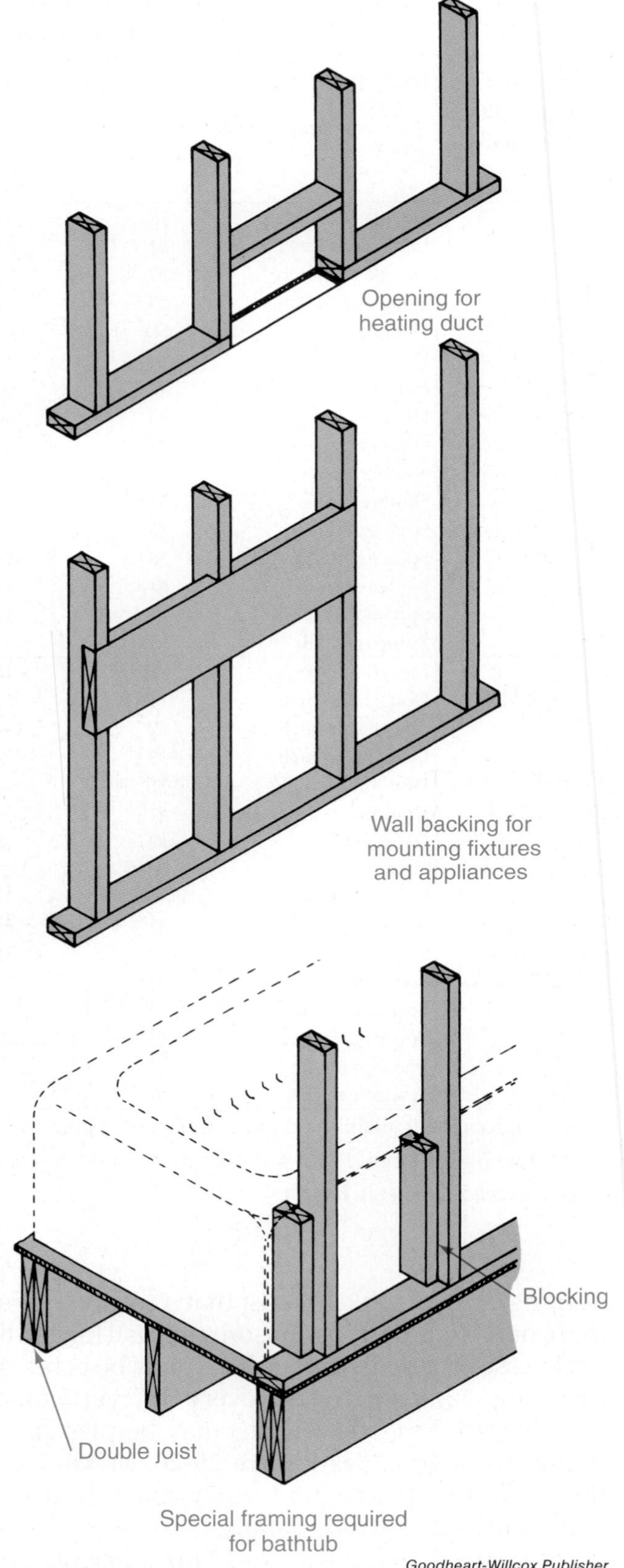

Goodheart-Willcox Publisher

Figure 20-18. These are examples of areas that usually require special framing.

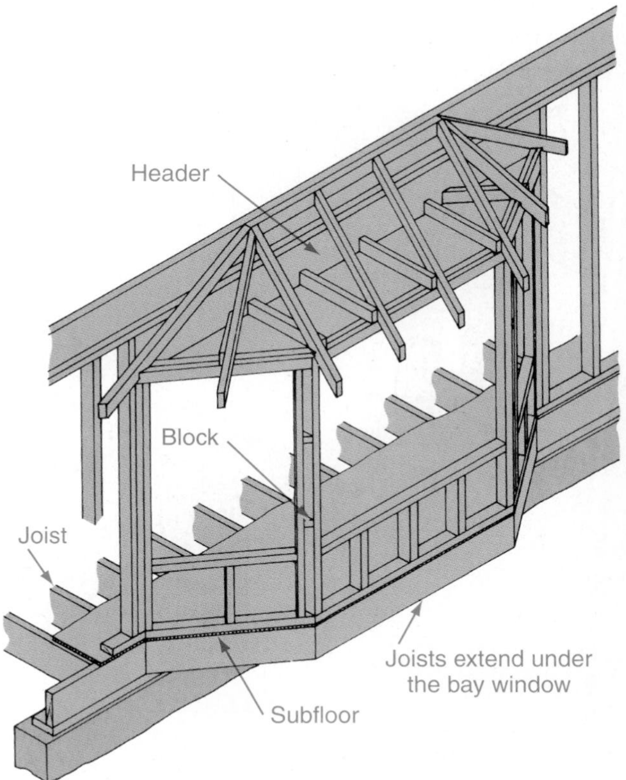

Goodheart-Willcox Publisher

Figure 20-19. This is one accepted method for framing a bay window.

CertainTeed Corporation

Figure 20-21. Insulation can be applied between furring strips on the inside of a solid masonry wall to reduce heat loss.

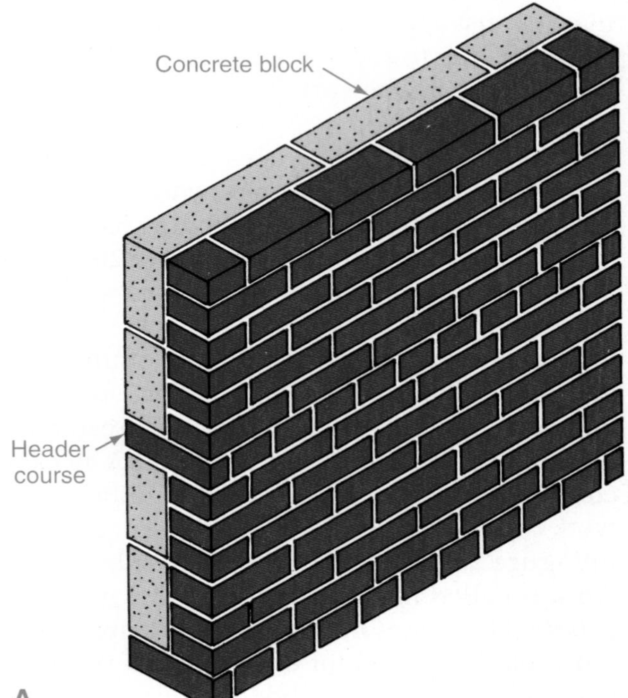

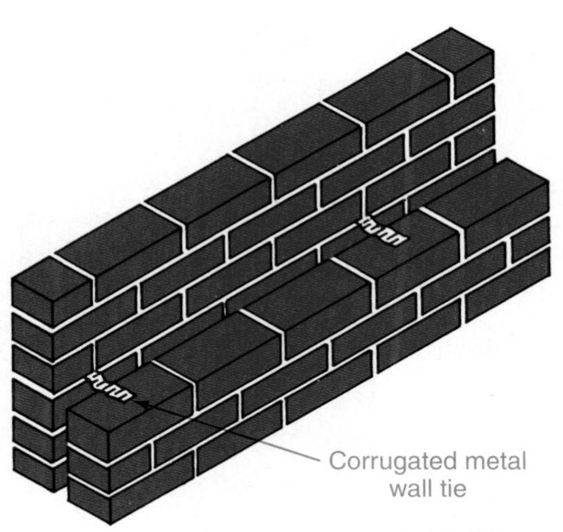

Goodheart-Willcox Publisher

Figure 20-20. A solid masonry wall that has a thickness of more than one piece (brick, block, stone, or tile) must be bonded. A—Using a header course. B—Using corrugated metal wall ties.

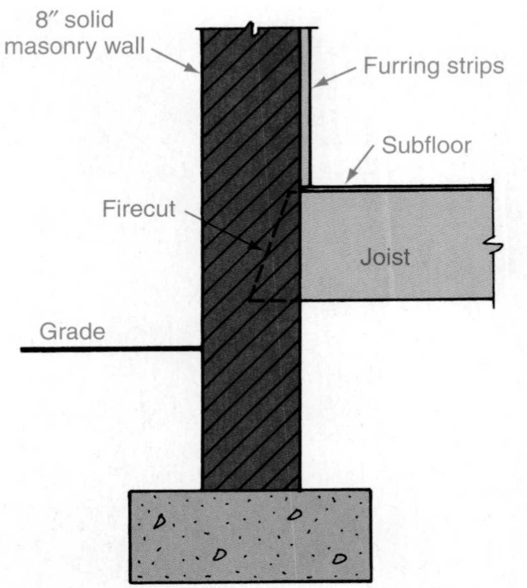

Goodheart-Willcox Publisher

Figure 20-22. Floor joists in a solid masonry wall require a firecut to prevent excessive wall damage in the event of a fire.

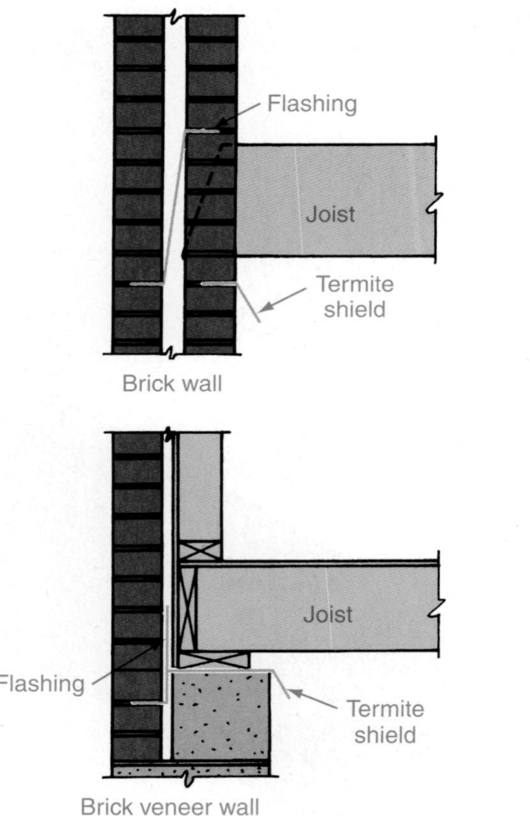

Goodheart-Willcox Publisher

Figure 20-23. Flashing is used to control moisture. Termite shields are required where termites are a threat.

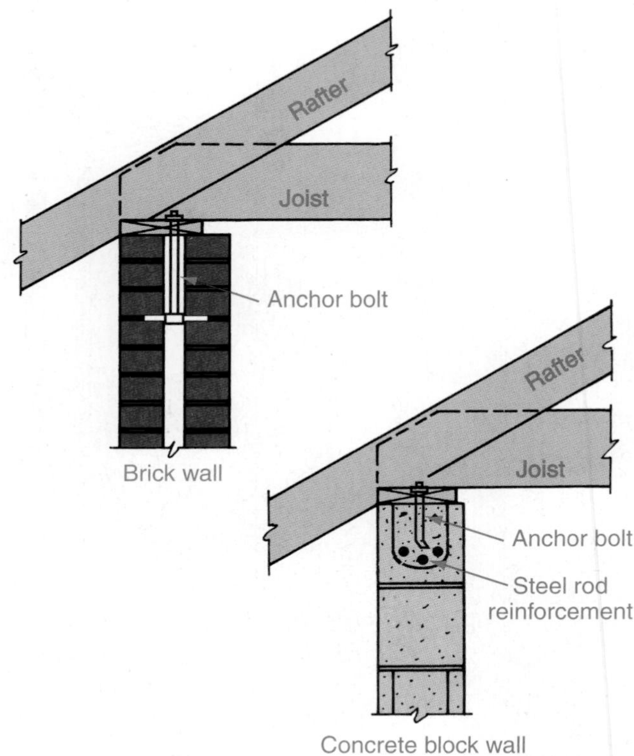

Goodheart-Willcox Publisher

Figure 20-24. The top plate is securely attached to masonry walls with anchor bolts embedded in the wall.

mason must apply a certain amount of artistry to the work due to the varying size and texture of the material. Stonework is commonly classified as ashlar or rubble.

Ashlar stonework uses dressed, cut, or squared stones. Each stone is generally rectangular in shape and a specific size, allowing it to fit in an exact place in the pattern. See **Figure 20-25**. This type of stonework has a more regular pattern or finished appearance.

Rubble stonework is made up of undressed stones of irregular shapes. If the stones are generally flat and rectangular, the result may look like courses (rows) of stone. This is called ***coursed rubble***. See **Figure 20-26A**. Rubble stonework can also have a random pattern, as shown in **Figure 20-26B**. Another type of rubble stonework is called ***uncoursed cobweb*** or ***polygonal rubble***. The stones in this stonework are dressed with relatively straight edges to fit a particular place in the pattern, as shown in **Figure 20-26C**. However, the finished stonework has a rubble, not ashlar, appearance.

Rumo/Shutterstock.com

Figure 20-25. Ashlar stonework has more or less rectangular stones in a fairly regular pattern.

A

Eky Studio/Shutterstock.com

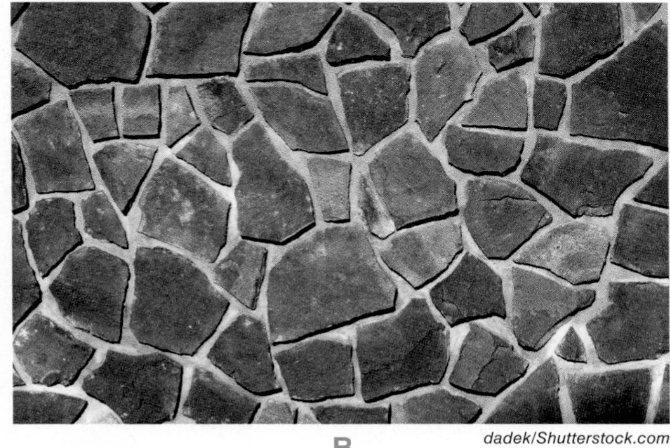

B

dadek/Shutterstock.com

C

holbox/Shutterstock.com

Figure 20-26. A—Coursed rubble stonework. B—Random rubble stonework. C—Uncoursed cobweb or polygonal rubble stonework.

Masonry Veneer

Solid brick and stone walls have been used extensively in years past. However, because of their construction cost, their use is diminishing for residential purposes. The same exterior effect may be obtained with a brick or stone veneer on frame construction. The term *veneer* is commonly used to indicate that a less expensive or desirable material has been covered up with some type of facing material. The veneer does not help support the weight of the building. This type of wall is better insulated, is less expensive to construct, and presents fewer construction problems than a solid wall. **Figure 20-27** shows how a masonry veneer wall is typically insulated on the frame wall side.

Masonry veneer is usually placed 1″ away from the frame wall to provide a dead air space for insulation and a means of escape for moisture that condenses on the inside of the masonry. The veneer is usually 4″ thick, but may range from approximately 1″ to 6″. **Figure 20-28** shows a construction detail of brick veneer over frame construction.

Brick Names and Sizes

Brick is a fired clay product. The final color is ordinarily determined by the natural color of the clay, which is the primary ingredient. However, earth colors are sometimes added to produce a wider variety of colors. Brick may be purchased in single colors or in a mixture to produce a blend.

There are two types of brick used for wall construction—face brick and common brick. ***Face brick*** is usually uniform in size and has sharp corners and lines. ***Common brick*** is not

CertainTeed Corporation

Figure 20-27. Insulation is applied between wall studs on the frame side of a structure with masonry veneer on frame construction. Kraft-faced batt insulation has been installed in the exterior and interior walls of this home.

as uniform in size and color and may have a lip on one or more edges. In recent years, common brick has been used more widely as a facing material and has a character that is quite different from face brick. It produces a rustic appearance and the texture is much more distinct. It looks especially good with a deep rake joint to accent the individual character of each brick.

The names of brick shapes are well established. However, brick sizes are not standardized. The names and sizes of brick frequently used in residential construction are shown in the table in **Figure 20-29**.

Specific terms apply to the position or way in which the brick is laid. **Figure 20-30** illustrates accepted terminology. Note that these terms apply to the position of the brick in the wall, not the type or size of the brick.

Numerous types of mortar joints are used in brickwork. **Figure 20-31** shows some joints used in residential construction. Masons have tools designed specifically for making these joints.

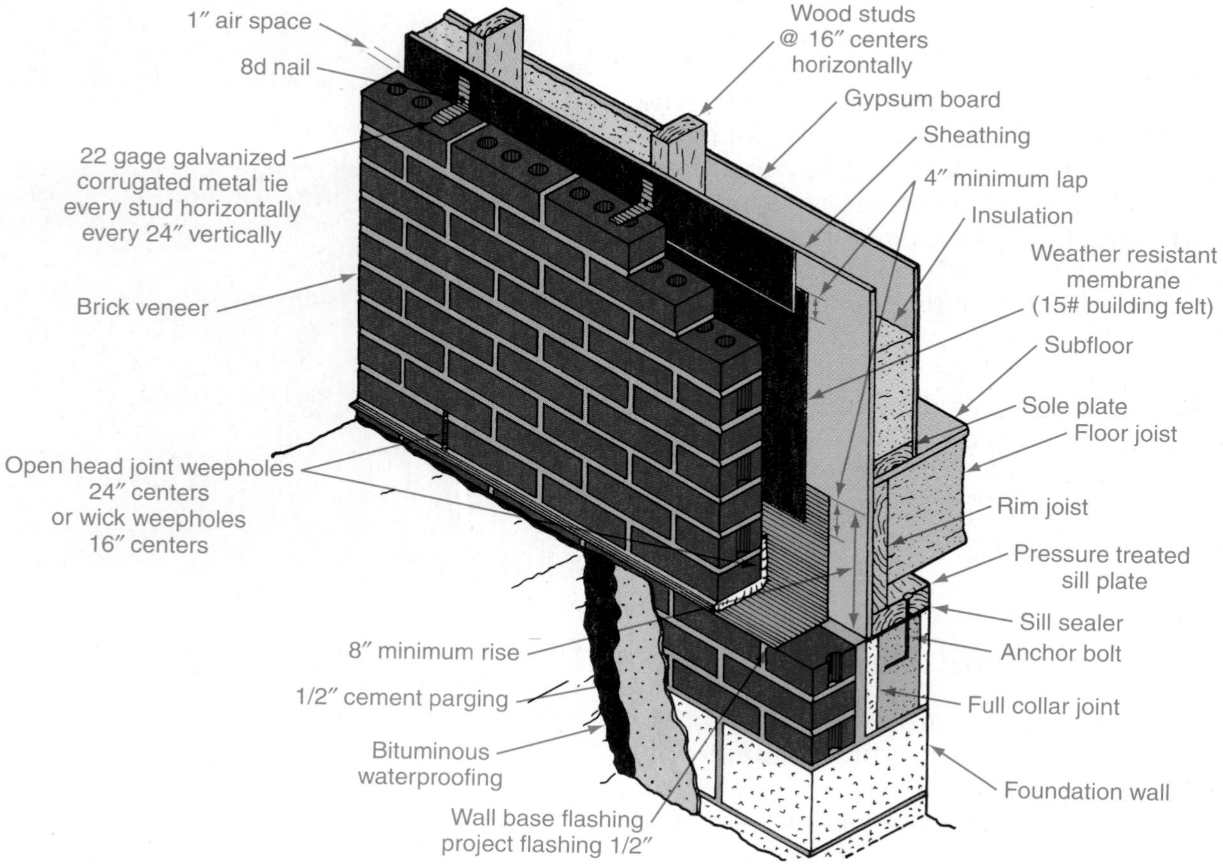

1″ air space
8d nail
22 gage galvanized corrugated metal tie every stud horizontally every 24″ vertically
Brick veneer
Open head joint weepholes 24″ centers or wick weepholes 16″ centers
8″ minimum rise
1/2″ cement parging
Bituminous waterproofing
Wall base flashing project flashing 1/2″
Wood studs @ 16″ centers horizontally
Gypsum board
Sheathing
4″ minimum lap
Insulation
Weather resistant membrane (15# building felt)
Subfloor
Sole plate
Floor joist
Rim joist
Pressure treated sill plate
Sill sealer
Anchor bolt
Full collar joint
Foundation wall

Goodheart-Willcox Publisher

Figure 20-28. This construction detail shows a brick veneer over a frame wall section.

Brick Names and Sizes		
Name	**Nominal Size**	**Actual Size**
Roman	2 × 4 × 12	1-5/8 × 3-5/8 × 11-5/8″
Modular	2-2/3 × 4 × 8	2-1/4 × 3-5/8 × 7-5/8″
SCR Brick	2-2/3 × 6 × 12	2-1/8 × 5-1/2 × 11-1/2″
Standard	Nonmodular	2-1/4 × 3-5/8 × 8″
Norman	2-2/3 × 4 × 12	2-1/4 × 3-5/8 × 11-5/8″
Firebrick*	2-2/3 × 4 × 9	2-1/2 × 3-5/8 × 9″
*Firebrick is not used for exterior wall construction, but is included because it is used in fireplaces.		

Goodheart-Willcox Publisher

Figure 20-29. This table shows the dimensions of common types of bricks.

Goodheart-Willcox Publisher

Figure 20-30. Bricks are laid in basic positions. Each position has a specific name.

A discussion of brickwork would not be complete without mentioning some of the bonds, or bricklaying patterns, that are recognized standards. **Figure 20-32** illustrates a few of the many bonds. The running bond is used extensively in brick veneer construction. The common bond is the most popular for solid masonry walls.

Traditional Three-Coat Stucco

Stucco is a coating applied to the outside of a structure. Generally, the term *stucco* refers to exterior applications, while *plaster* refers to interior spaces. There are three stucco systems in general use today: traditional three-coat stucco, one-coat stucco, and the exterior insulation finish system (EIFS). Each system produces acceptable results when application procedures are followed carefully.

The traditional ***three-coat stucco system*** has been in use for many years and has performed well over time. Successful applications are possible in all areas of the United States. See **Figure 20-33**. The stucco material consists of Portland cement, lime, sand, and water.

Traditional three-coat stucco produces a protective shell around the structure that requires little maintenance. It can be repaired if necessary, however. Since Portland cement stucco resists insects, weather, and rotting, it can have an effective life span of 100 years or more if the underlying structure remains sound.

Problems with stucco applications are generally the result of poor workmanship or improper installation, rather than with the material itself. This is true of any of the three systems. Many builders prefer traditional stucco and continue to use it either in addition to or instead of the newer alternatives.

Preparing for Stucco

The proper preparation for stucco cannot be over-emphasized. Most significantly, a rigid structure is crucial. Three-coat stucco can be applied to most any type of wall system—concrete blocks, poured concrete, brick, metal, or wood frame. See **Figure 20-34**.

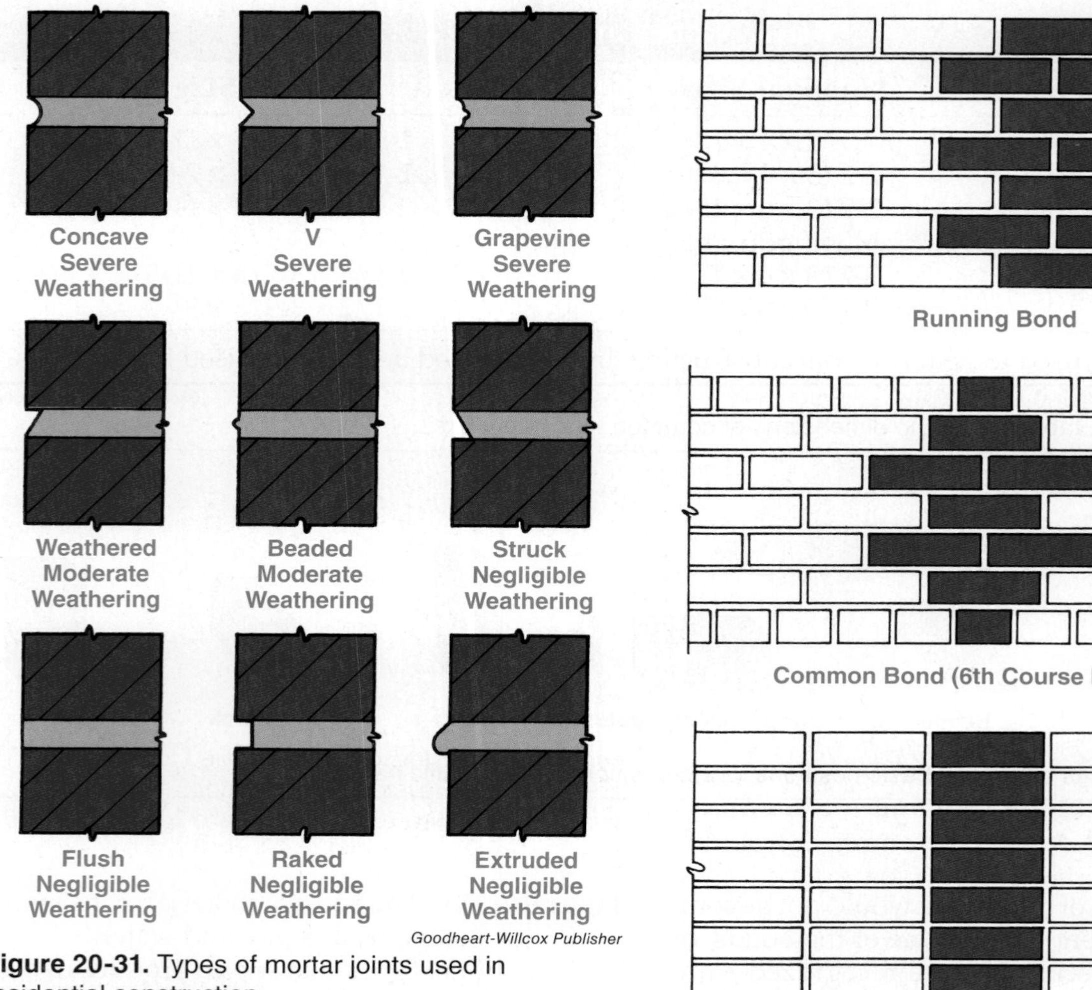

Goodheart-Willcox Publisher

Figure 20-31. Types of mortar joints used in residential construction.

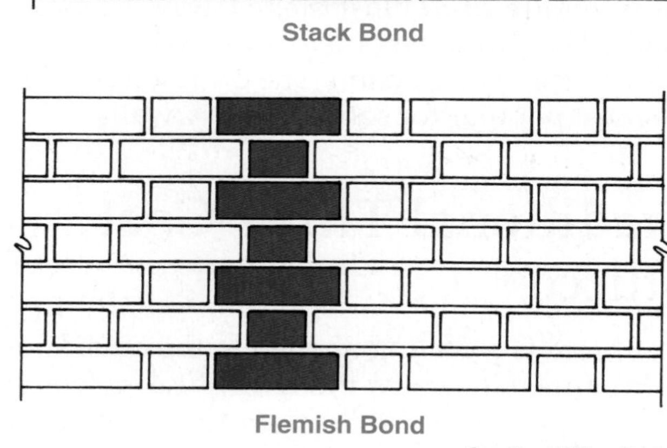

Goodheart-Willcox Publisher

Figure 20-32. Four of the most frequently used brick bonds are shown here.

Stucco is not structural and adds no strength to the building structure. It is a protective shell around the structure. It can resist normal expansion and contraction due to the changes in temperature and moisture, but it cannot resist severe stresses caused by irregular settling or movement in the structure itself.

Cracks in masonry walls will "telescope" through the stucco. Bowed studs can cause thin spots of less than 7/8″ thickness in the stucco that will result in cracking. Movement in plywood that is not properly spaced and nailed will also cause stucco to crack. Integration of engineered lumber and standard lumber framing materials can create uneven expansion and contraction that may result in cracking the stucco shell. It is therefore important to construct the underlying wall with great care to prepare for a long-lasting stucco finish.

Moisture Barrier and Flashing

In order for a stucco application to be successful, moisture must be prevented from entering behind the stucco shell. Even though stucco

Goodheart-Willcox Publisher

Figure 20-33. Many people associate stucco with Spanish-style homes, but stucco can be used with all building styles and in all areas of the country. It will protect the exterior of this home for many years.

allows moisture vapor to pass through readily and is relatively unaffected by moisture, high concentrations will have a devastating effect on the framing members and sheathing that support the stucco in a wood frame structure. Wood frame structures are naturally more susceptible to moisture damage than masonry or concrete buildings.

Moisture barriers and flashing are used to prevent moisture from entering the space behind the stucco. These elements should be viewed as an integral part of the total wall system, with special attention given to joints, openings, and penetrations in the wall.

Moisture barriers are membranes that protect most of the wall area. Kraft paper is used as flashing around wall openings and other areas of wall penetration. The type of Kraft paper used has a layer of asphalt between two sheets of traditional Kraft paper. This paper tears easily, does not resist punctures, and will wrinkle, making it difficult to keep the paper flat. Even though this is the industry standard, it leaves much to be desired as a flashing material. Doubling the thickness increases protection, but is still not completely satisfactory. Another product that may be a better choice is a 20-mil rubberized asphalt membrane sandwiched between a face of 4-mil polyethylene sheet and a back of polyester. This product is extremely water resistant, will enlarge, and resists tearing.

A

B

Goodheart-Willcox Publisher

Figure 20-34. Stucco can be applied to just about any type of wall system. A—Wood frame ready to receive a moisture-resistant barrier prior to stucco. B—Stucco applied directly to concrete block walls.

When a hole or tear does occur in the flashing paper, caulk may be used to repair the spot. Care should be taken to reduce damage and, therefore, the number of repairs. Caulk is also used to seal the flashing at wall openings and penetrations. It is important to select a caulk that adheres to the construction materials under the conditions of use.

Lath (Reinforcement)

The function of ***lath*** is to provide support and attachment for the layers of stucco and to connect the stucco to the structure. See **Figure 20-35**. It is available as self-furring wire lath or rib lath. A moisture-proof membrane is generally attached to the lath at the factory for faster installation. Lath is attached to the sheathing with furring nails or staples that resist corrosion from contact with the mortar. Lath should be installed in the appropriate orientation to enhance adherence of the mortar for the duration of the application.

Goodheart-Willcox Publisher

Figure 20-35. Metal lath and PVC corner bead have been attached with rust-proof fasteners. The weather-resistant barrier can also be seen under the lath.

Scratch or Foundation Coat

The ***scratch coat***, also called the *foundation coat*, is the first stucco layer in the three-coat process. The purpose of the scratch coat is to embed the reinforcement in stucco and provide support for the next coat. See **Figure 20-36**. The scratch coat is a rich mixture of about one part cement to two to four parts sand. It can be applied by hand with a trowel or pumped. Hand-troweled surfaces are understood to be more dense and harder than pumped surfaces, but there are advocates of both methods. The scratch coat is generally 3/8″ thick.

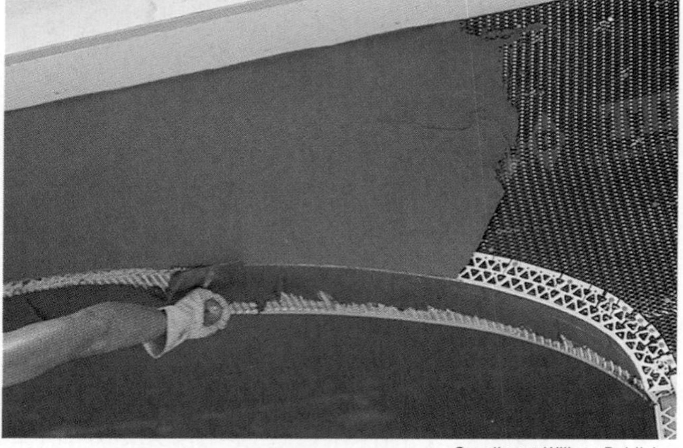

Goodheart-Willcox Publisher

Figure 20-36. The scratch coat of stucco is being applied over the lath by hand, using a trowel.

When the scratch coat has begun to set, the surface should be roughened with a scarifier rake or scratching trowel to secure a better bond for the next coat. Since the scratch coat is relatively thin, it will dry rapidly and should be misted lightly with water to ensure proper curing. Misting is particularly important if the weather is hot and dry.

The scratch coat is ready for the next coat (brown coat) when the surface is hard enough to resist scoring from a nail dragged across the surface. Be sure that at least 95% of the lath is embedded by the scratch coat before proceeding to the next coat.

Brown Coat

The second stucco layer in the three-coat process is called the ***brown coat***. The function of the brown coat is to cover any visible lath, add strength to the shell, true up the surface, and provide an appropriate surface for the final decorative finish coat. The brown coat is applied with a trowel and leveled with a straightedge to a thickness of about 3/8″. Together, the scratch and brown coats should be at least 7/8″ thick. This layer should be flush with the corner bead and ready to receive the final finish coat. Misting may be required if the coat dries too quickly and surface cracks begin to appear.

Finish Coat

The third stucco layer in the three-coat process is called the ***finish coat***. See **Figure 20-37**. This is the decorative layer and is where a detailed texture or design pattern is applied to the surface. Only about 1/8″ of thickness is added by the finish coat. The finish coat may be applied by machine or hand, depending on the desired texture or personal preference. Color may be applied as part of the mortar finish, or the surface may be painted later.

The finish coat should be maintained at the proper temperature for at least 48 hours following application. Stucco should cure for 28 days before painting. Spraying regularly with water, unless prohibited by coloring agents, will aid in curing and removing scum from the textured surface. **Figure 20-38** shows a painted stucco surface.

Bertrand Benoit/Shutterstock.com

Figure 20-37. The finish coat is often given a decorative, textured appearance. A feeling of depth is created by the texture applied to the walls of this modern home.

A

B

Goodheart-Willcox Publisher

Figure 20-38. A—This stucco surface has received a primer and finish coat of paint. B—This close-up view shows the detailed texture that can be achieved with a stucco surface.

Exterior Insulation Finish Systems (EIFS)

An ***exterior insulation finish system (EIFS)*** is a wall covering system that provides thermal insulation and a durable external finish resembling stucco or stone. This system is sometimes called "synthetic stucco." EIFS installations are common in residential construction and provide lots of flexibility with colors and architectural detail, as well as good insulation without thermal gaps. The finished result of a quality installation is very attractive. See **Figure 20-39**.

The exterior coating applied in EIFS construction is a polymer-based material. In a typical EIFS installation, an insulation board is attached to the wall sheathing, a base coat is applied to the insulation board and reinforced with mesh, and a finish coat is applied to the cured base coat. In this system, a moisture barrier must be attached to the wall sheathing to comply with building codes. Water-managed EIFS installations incorporate a drainage track and additional components to divert moisture away from the structure. Refer to the applicable building codes in your area and manufacturer details for additional information. Requirements for EIFS construction are specified in the International Residential Code.

There are advantages and disadvantages to EIFS. Advantages include the reduction in construction time compared to traditional stucco and improved thermal performance of the wall. The disadvantages of EIFS are related to the quality of the work. Problems such as cracking, sealant failure, and water damage can occur when installation is not performed correctly. Installation instructions and details from the manufacturer must be carefully followed to ensure proper performance of the system.

Photo compliments of Dryvit Systems, Inc.

Figure 20-39. The exterior insulation finish system (EIFS) is common in residential construction. A variety of colors and textures are available.

Structural Insulated Panels

Structural insulated panels are structural members that combine two outer "skins" and an insulating foam core into a single unit for framing applications. Structural insulated panels replace three stages in standard construction: framing, sheathing, and insulation. See **Figure 20-40**. The panel structure is strong, rigid, and resistant to twisting, warping, and cracking. The outer skins are typically 7/16″ oriented strand board (OSB) or plywood. The foam core is a lightweight, but relatively thick, low-density expanded polystyrene, extruded polystyrene, or rigid polyurethane. The thick rigid foam core produces a high R-value. Sometimes the inside is faced with wallboard, either above or over the OSB.

Typical wall panels are 3-1/2″, 5-1/2″, or 7-1/4″ thick, while roof panels are either 9-1/4″ or 11-1/4″ thick. These dimensions are similar to traditional construction, but not all panel systems are manufactured or installed in the same way.

AFM Corporation

Figure 20-40. Structural insulated panels are used for framing walls, roofs, and floors in residential construction.

Erecting structural insulated panels requires some special tools. Large roof and wall panels require a small crane to lift the panels in place. Special cutting tools may be needed to cut openings in the panels. Extra-large circular saws are needed to cut through panels at roof ridges and eaves. The foam must be removed to a depth of 1-1/2″ around door and window openings, which is best done using a hot wire tool. Chases for electrical wiring and plumbing present special problems if not planned for early in the design process.

Concrete Wall Systems

The use of concrete in above-grade applications in residential construction has been mainly in moderate climates because of concrete's low-insulative properties. However, the availability of insulated systems has presented alternatives to traditional masonry and concrete wall construction. ***Insulated concrete forms (ICFs)*** can be used to form the foundation and exterior walls for a residence. In this type of construction, forms made of foam insulation remain in place after the concrete is placed and become part of the wall. Wall systems constructed from ICFs improve the thermal performance of concrete and result in a durable structure.

Different ICF systems are available and are classified by the basic shapes of the forms and concrete walls. The most common types of forms are planks, blocks, and panels. Plank forms and block forms are discussed in this chapter.

Plank Forms

Plank forms in ICF construction consist of 2″ × 8″ sections of rigid polystyrene foam insulation. The planks are 4′ or 8′ long and separated with plastic ties so that the space between the panels can be filled with concrete. See **Figure 20-41**. Special form ties and corner ties are required. The wall form is built course by course until the desired height is reached. A typical footing is generally used. The completed form is braced and reinforced before filling with concrete. Typically, a pump truck with a hydraulic boom is used to place the concrete. The resulting concrete wall is insulated on both sides.

Exterior siding or interior paneling can be screwed into the plastic ties. Any polystyrene that is above grade and exposed should be covered with a trowel-applied protective coating. Electrical and plumbing lines can be installed in the 2″ thick insulation. Conduit may be required by some building codes.

Block Forms

Block forms in ICF construction are interlocking blocks of plastic foam insulation that are stackable. See **Figure 20-42**. The block forms have hollow cores that are filled with concrete. Blocks range in size, but are typically 12″ or 16″ high and 40″ or 48″ long.

ICF blocks are stacked course by course and joined with an interlocking tongue and groove. The blocks can be stacked so that the hollow cores are over vertical reinforcing rods placed according to local code requirements. See **Figure 20-43**. Bracing is required as specified by the manufacturer. As with plank forms, a pump truck with a hydraulic boom is necessary to place the concrete properly.

ICF block construction can be finished with most external building finishes. Electrical and plumbing lines can be installed within the thickness of the block shell.

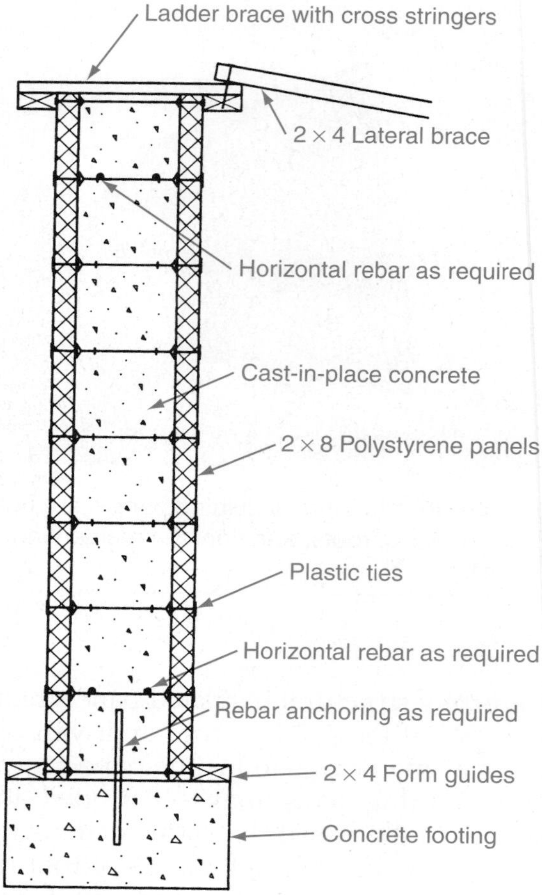

Ladder brace with cross stringers
2 × 4 Lateral brace
Horizontal rebar as required
Cast-in-place concrete
2 × 8 Polystyrene panels
Plastic ties
Horizontal rebar as required
Rebar anchoring as required
2 × 4 Form guides
Concrete footing

Lite-Form™ Wall Section

Lite-Form, Inc.

Figure 20-41. Plank forms in ICF construction are built in courses with plastic ties installed. The forms remain in place and become part of the wall, which results in an insulated concrete wall.

ConForm Global

Figure 20-42. ICF blocks have interlocking ends and hollow cores that are filled with concrete.

Reward Wall Systems, Inc.

Figure 20-43. Concrete is placed with a pump truck in ICF block construction. Reinforcing bars are spaced according to local code requirements.

Summary

- Residential wall construction is typically one of three types: frame, masonry, or a combination of frame and masonry.
- Wall framing lumber must have good rigidity and nail-holding properties, be free from warp, and be simple to work.
- Frame wall construction consists of sole plates, top plates, studs, headers, and bracing.
- Interior frame walls are constructed in the same way as exterior walls and are securely fastened to the exterior walls where they intersect.
- Steel framing has become more popular due to environmental and economic concerns that have forced the building industry to pursue alternative materials and methods.
- The construction elements of a framed house include three main assemblies: floors, walls, and roofs.
- Masonry walls are constructed entirely of brick, concrete block, stone, clay tile, terra cotta, or a combination of these materials.
- The traditional three-coat stucco system has been in use for many years, has performed well over time, and is popular throughout the United States.
- Structural insulated panels are used in framing walls, roofs, and floors.
- Insulated concrete forms (ICFs) can be used to form the foundation and exterior walls for a residence, presenting alternatives to traditional masonry and concrete wall construction.

Internet Resources

APA—The Engineered Wood Association
Information and research about engineered wood products

Georgia-Pacific Corporation
Supplier of building products

International Masonry Institute
Information about sustainable masonry

Portland Cement Association
Information about concrete homes

Steelworks (American Iron and Steel Institute)
Online resource for the steel industry

Review Questions

Answer the following questions using the information in this chapter.

1. Name the five standard framing members used in conventional wood wall construction.
2. Which properties must lumber used for wood framing have, and which species meet these criteria?
3. What is the acceptable range of moisture content for framing lumber?
4. The finished wall height in most residential structures is _____.
5. The framing member used to sustain the weight above an opening in a wall, such as a door or window, is called a _____ or _____.
6. What is the purpose of the trimmers (jack studs) and king studs used at window and door openings?
7. The rough opening height of most doors is _____.
8. What steel component is most often used for floor joists, wall studs, roof rafters, and ceiling joists in residential steel framing?
9. For what purpose are drywall studs used in steel frame structures?
10. List five factors that affect the size of ceiling joists.
11. Name two differences between ceiling construction and floor construction.
12. Name three areas of a house that require special framing consideration.
13. Solid masonry walls for residential construction are usually _____ thick.
14. What is the purpose of a furring strip in masonry wall construction?
15. The angle cut on the end of floor joists to be used with a solid masonry wall is called a(n) _____.
16. In a masonry veneer wall, the air space between the veneer and frame wall is usually about _____ wide.
17. What is the primary ingredient of brick?

18. Describe the differences between face brick and common brick.
19. The most popular brick bond for solid masonry walls is the _____ bond.
20. What is *stucco*?
21. Explain the advantages of applying a three-coat stucco finish to a home.
22. Care must be taken to prevent _____ from entering the space behind stucco.
23. What is another name for exterior insulation finish systems (EIFS)?
24. Name two advantages of an exterior insulation finish system over traditional stucco.
25. Describe the construction of a structural insulated panel.
26. In a wall system that uses insulated concrete forms, what is typically used to place the concrete?

Suggested Activities

1. Construct an accurate scale model at 1″ = 1′-0″ of a wood-framed wall section that has at least one door, one window, and an intersecting partition. Identify the parts.
2. Select a simple floor plan for a frame house. Lay out the wall framing. Indicate headers, trimmers (jack studs), king studs, spacing blocks, and other framing members required.
3. Visit a building site where a house is being constructed using conventional methods. Obtain permission before entering the site. Find out the species and grade of the framing lumber being used. Determine whether solid blocking or header-and-stud framing is used to construct headers in wall openings.
4. Build scale models at 1/4 size of framing for corners, wall intersections, and openings for doors and windows. Prepare plan view drawings for display with the models.
5. Photograph as many different brick bonds as you can find in the area near your home. Prepare a display that identifies each bond.
6. Using CADD, draw the framing illustrations shown in Figure 20-4.

Problem Solving Case Study

Jean and Tom Hendry have come to your architectural office in Mossyrock, Washington to discuss ideas for a new sustainable home. You explain that there are many approaches to making a house environmentally friendly. When you inquire about their priorities, they inform you that they do not want to use traditional building materials for the exterior walls. The exterior must be made of nontraditional building materials that can stand up to large amounts of annual rainfall and snow. The Hendrys have asked you to compile ideas and meet with them again in two weeks.

Conduct research to find out more about nontraditional, sustainable, exterior building materials. Compile a table of these materials with columns for advantages, disadvantages, and suitable climates. Use the table to determine at least two alternatives that might interest the Hendrys. Write a summary of your suggestions to present to the Hendrys.

ADDA Certification Prep

The following questions are presented in the style used in the American Design Drafting Association (ADDA) Drafter Certification Test. Answer the questions using the information in this chapter.

1. Match each type of stonework with its description.

   Stonework: 1. Ashlar, 2. Coursed rubble, 3. Random rubble, 4. Uncoursed cobweb

   A. Undressed stones of irregular shapes that are generally flat and rectangular.
   B. Irregular stonework dressed with relatively straight edges to fit a particular piece in a pattern, with a rubble appearance.
   C. Dressed, cut, or squared stones that fit an exact place in a pattern.
   D. Rubble stonework that has a random pattern.

2. Which of the following statements are *false*?
   A. Frame wall construction usually begins with the top plate, which is the horizontal member of the wall on which studs rest.
   B. Wall studs are cut to length (usually 7′-9″ when 1-1/2″ material is used) and nailed to the sole plate.
   C. Moisture barriers are membranes that protect wood framing from moisture that may seep under a stucco finish.
   D. Rough openings for windows and doors are dimensioned on the floor plan to the edges of the opening when located in a frame wall.
3. Which of the following statements are true?
   A. The distance from the top of the subfloor to the bottom of the ceiling joists is usually 9′-1 1/2″.
   B. The term "veneer" is commonly used to indicate that a less expensive or desirable material has been covered up with some type of facing material.
   C. The two types of brick used for wall construction are face brick and common brick.
   D. Steel framing is becoming more popular as a result of environmental and economic concerns that have forced the building industry to pursue alternative materials and methods.

Curricular Connections

1. **Social Sciences.** Although stucco is an excellent protective coating for homes in almost any environment, public opinion is sharply divided. Some people believe a decorative stucco finish adds value and interest to their home. Other people refuse to have it on their homes. Investigate the reasons people give for or against using stucco on their homes. What economic factors are involved? How do social perceptions differ? Write a summary of your findings.

STEM Connections

1. **Science.** Requirements for wall insulation vary throughout the country. The effectiveness of insulation is given in R-values. Higher R-values indicate better insulating properties. Find out more about the five types of wall insulation used in homes today. Compare their R-values and other characteristics. Determine which type or types might be most effective in your area.
2. **Technology.** The process of recycling steel is fairly straightforward and inexpensive. This is one reason why steel recycling has been so successful. Find out more about the process by which steel is recycled. Write an illustrated report of your findings.

Communicating about Architecture

1. **Speaking.** Pick a figure in this chapter, such as Figure 20-43. Working with a partner, describe and then redescribe the important information being conveyed by that figure. Through your collaboration, develop what you and your partner believe is the most interesting verbal description. Present your narration to the class.
2. **Speaking.** With a partner, explain to the class the differences between ceiling construction and floor construction. Use pictures, poster boards, or any other visual props to help with your presentation.

Chapter 21

Doors and Windows

Objectives

After completing this chapter, you will be able to:

- Compare the types of doors used in a residential dwelling.
- Describe the various types of windows used in residential construction.
- Draw proper door and window symbols on a typical floor plan.
- Prepare door and window schedules.

Key Terms

accordion door
awning window
bay window
bifold door
bow window
brick mold
casement window
casing
clerestory window
door jamb
door schedule
double-action door
double-hung window
drip cap
Dutch door
flush door
French doors
hopper window
jalousie window
mullions
muntins
panel door
pocket door
rails
sash
sill
skylight
sliding doors
stiles
window schedule

Doors and windows perform several functions in a residential structure. They shield an opening from the elements, add decoration, emphasize the overall design, provide light and ventilation, and expand visibility. Windows and doors are necessary features of all residential structures and should be planned carefully to ensure maximum contribution to the overall design and function of the structure.

Many window manufacturers—Andersen, Weather Shield, Pella, and Marvin, to name a few—provide CADD packages that facilitate specifying and drawing their windows and doors. See **Figure 21-1**. Be sure the package is compatible with your CADD software before deciding to use it.

Most manufacturers also provide 2D and 3D window and door symbols for standard CADD packages. These symbols can be manipulated during the design process and then used to create a schedule of the windows and doors. Most CADD software packages also include numerous door and window symbol libraries in their software.

Interior and Exterior Doors

A number of classification systems may be used to identify the various styles and types of doors in residential construction. Two broad classes are interior and exterior doors. Doors may further be grouped according to the method of construction, uses, function, or location.

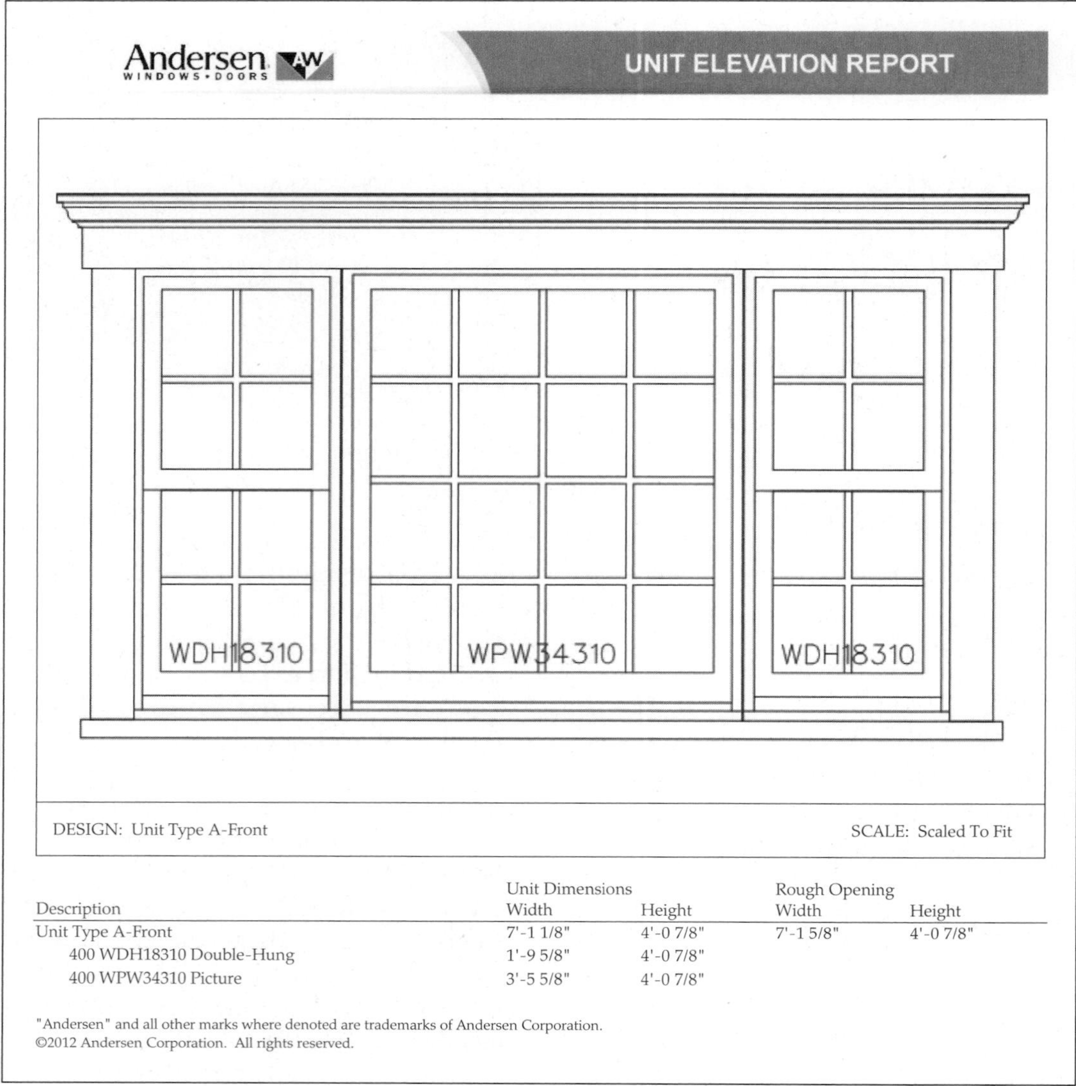

Description	Unit Dimensions Width	Height	Rough Opening Width	Height
Unit Type A-Front	7'-1 1/8"	4'-0 7/8"	7'-1 5/8"	4'-0 7/8"
400 WDH18310 Double-Hung	1'-9 5/8"	4'-0 7/8"		
400 WPW34310 Picture	3'-5 5/8"	4'-0 7/8"		

Andersen Corporation

Figure 21-1. A unit elevation report generated from Andersen Corporation's Window Studio® software. The software provides tools for creating window designs and printing out schedules and product reports.

Interior Doors

Types of interior doors include flush, panel, bifold, sliding, pocket, double-action, accordion, Dutch, and French. Interior doors should be a minimum of 32″ wide to permit comfortable passage of a wheelchair. Lever-type or vertical pull-handles may be easier for a handicapped person to operate. Automatic door openers may be required in some cases.

Flush Doors

Flush doors are smooth on both sides and are usually made of wood. See **Figure 21-2.** Standard interior wood flush doors are 1-3/8″ thick. They are hollow-core doors that have a wood frame around the perimeter. Interior flush doors are produced in a wide range of widths, from 2′-0″ to 3′-0″. The standard width increment is 2″.

Panel Doors

A ***panel door*** has a heavy frame around the outside and generally at least one cross member. The frame and cross members form small panels, **Figure 21-3A**. The vertical members are called ***stiles*** and the horizontal members are ***rails.*** Panels that are thinner than the frame are placed in grooves on the inside edges of the stiles

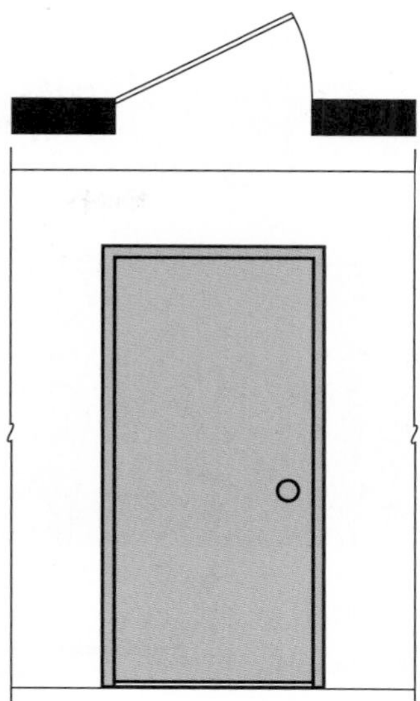

Goodheart-Willcox Publisher

Figure 21-2. A flush door shown with its plan view symbol.

and rails to enclose the space. The panels may be wood, glass, metal, or other material. Panel doors are usually produced in white pine, but may be constructed of other woods or plastic. **Figure 21-3B** shows the plan view symbol and elevation view of a panel door.

Bifold Doors

A ***bifold door*** is made of two parts that together form the door. They may be attached to the side jambs with conventional hinges or secured to the head jamb and floor using a pivot hinge. Bifold doors may be flush, paneled, or louvered. See **Figure 21-4**. They are popular as closet doors, but are seldom used for other applications.

Sliding Doors

Sliding doors, or bypass doors, are popular where there are large openings. See **Figure 21-5**. Any number of doors may be used for a given opening. The width is not critical because the doors are hung from a track mounted on the head jamb. Door pulls are recessed to allow the doors to pass without interference. Glides are installed on the floor to prevent the bottoms from swinging in or out.

Sliding doors may be flush, paneled, or louvered. They are usually constructed from wood, but other materials may be used. The major problem with wood sliding doors is warping, because they are not restrained by hinges.

A

Morgan Products, Ltd.

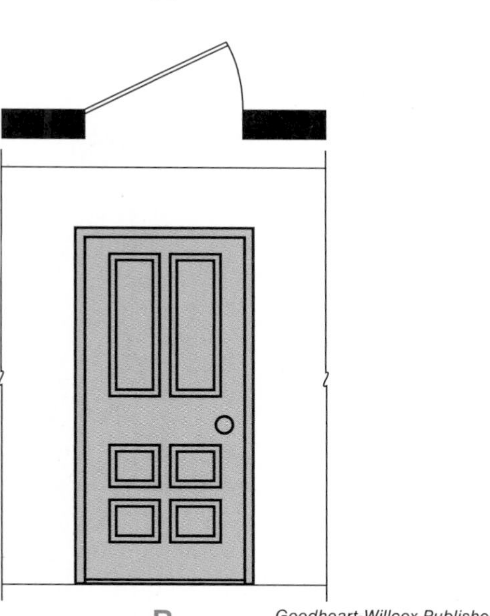

B

Goodheart-Willcox Publisher

Figure 21-3. A—This is a typical panel door used in residential construction. B—A panel door shown with its plan view symbol.

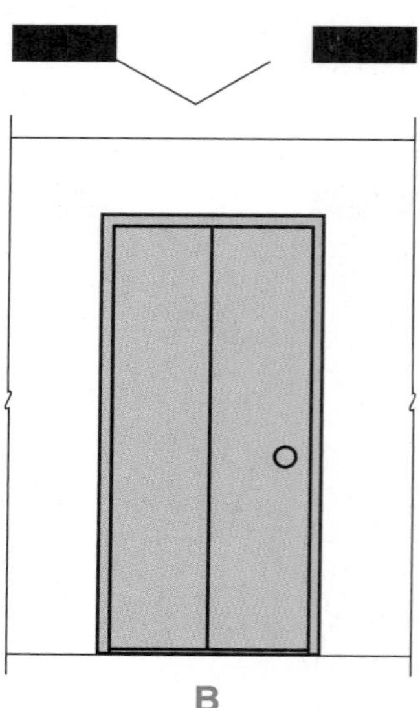

A

B

Goodheart-Willcox Publisher

Figure 21-4. Bifold doors come in many styles. A—These closet doors are louvered to allow air to circulate in the closet. B—Elevation and plan views of a bifold door.

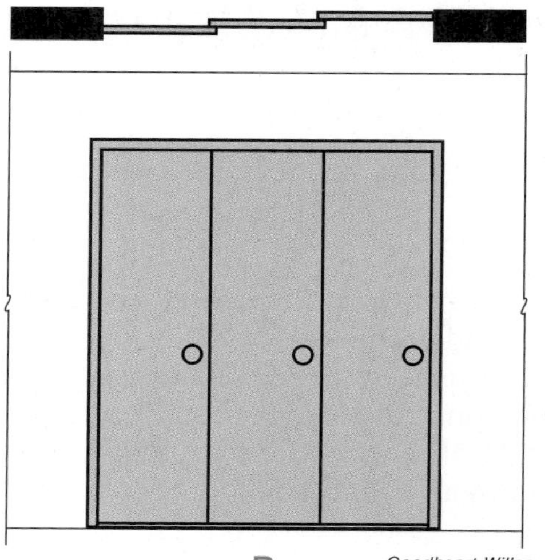

A photobank.ch/Shutterstock.com

B Goodheart-Willcox Publisher

Figure 21-5. A—These sliding doors are designed to close off the dining area when it is not in use. B—Three sliding doors shown with their plan view symbols.

Pocket Doors

Pocket doors are a variation of the sliding door and can be flush or panel doors. A pocket door is hung from a track mounted on the head jamb. Ordinarily, only one door is used to close an opening. The door rests in a wall pocket when open, as shown in **Figure 21-6**.

Pocket doors are frequently used between rooms such as the kitchen and dining room. The chief advantage is that they require no space along the wall when open. However, they cannot be easily installed if outlets or cabinets are to be located on the wall outside of the pocket cavity. Pocket door frames of metal and wood are usually purchased already assembled.

Double-Action Doors

Double-action doors are hinged in such a way that they can swing through an arc of 180°. See **Figure 21-7**. A double-action, spring-loaded hinge is mounted in the center of the side jamb.

This door is generally used between rooms that experience a great deal of traffic, yet require the door to be closed most of the time. Double-action doors may be single or double doors. A flush, panel, or louvered style can be used.

Accordion Doors

Accordion doors are frequently used to close large openings as an alternative to bifold or sliding doors. See **Figure 21-8**. They require little space and are produced in a large variety of materials and designs. They may be constructed from wood, plastic, or fabric. Individual hinged panels are sometimes used, as well as a large folded piece of fabric or other material. The door is supported on a track mounted on the head jamb.

A John Wollwerth/Shutterstock.com

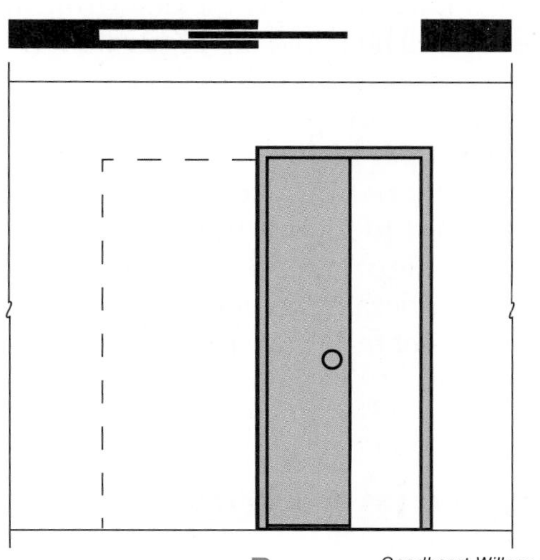

B Goodheart-Willcox Publisher

Figure 21-6. A—This pocket door separates the bedroom from a walk-in closet. B—Elevation and plan views of a pocket door.

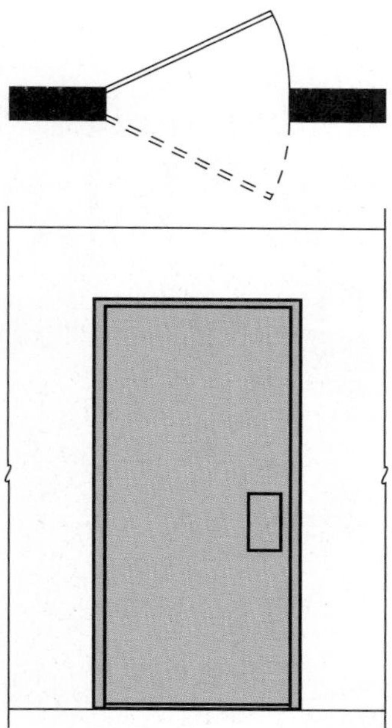

Goodheart-Willcox Publisher

Figure 21-7. A double-action door shown with its plan view symbol.

Exterior Doors

Residential exterior doors are similar to some of the interior types, but also have some differences. Exterior wood doors are usually not hollow core. They are also thicker than interior doors.

Common exterior door styles include flush, panel, and swinging or sliding glass. Dutch doors and French doors can be used as interior doors, but are most commonly used as exterior doors. Garage doors are also exterior doors.

Figure 21-9 shows plan view symbols for various types of exterior doors. Compare these symbols to the interior door symbols shown earlier in this chapter.

Flush Doors

Standard exterior flush wood doors are usually 1-3/4″ thick. These doors are produced from birch, mahogany, oak, and several other woods, as well as metal or reinforced fiberglass. Glass, moldings, or other decorative millwork may be added to the flush door to enhance its appearance. See **Figure 21-10**.

Panel Doors

Exterior panel doors are available in a great variety of styles. They are constructed from

A

Woodfold Manufacturing

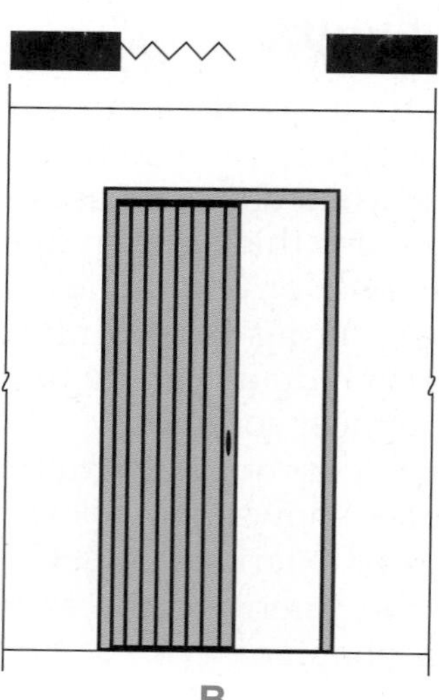

B

Goodheart-Willcox Publisher

Figure 21-8. A—These paneled accordion doors are an effective way to close off the kitchen storage and food preparation space from the dining area. B—An accordion door shown with its plan view symbol.

white pine, oak, fir, and various other woods, as well as metal and reinforced fiberglass. These doors are produced in the same sizes as flush doors. See **Figure 21-11**.

Sliding and Swinging Glass Doors

In recent years, sliding and swinging glass doors have gained popularity, **Figure 21-12**. Sliding doors are usually made of wood and follow typical sliding glass door sizes. Metal units are also available. **Figure 21-13** shows some of the standard sizes of exterior sliding glass doors that are available.

Dutch Doors

A ***Dutch door*** is composed of two parts: an upper section and a lower section. The upper section may be opened independently of the lower section. This allows for light and ventilation. See **Figure 21-14**. A Dutch door is generally used as an exterior door, although it may also be placed between a kitchen and dining room.

French Doors

French doors are panel doors in which all of the panels are glass. See **Figure 21-15**. They are popular for doors that lead to a patio or terrace. They may also be used between rooms to close off a room, such as a dining room, that is used less often than other rooms.

Garage Doors

The most popular type of garage door is the overhead sectional door, shown in **Figure 21-16**. Garage doors are available in wood, metal, and plastics. Each material has its advantages and personal choice is usually the determining factor in selection. The table in **Figure 21-17** shows standard garage door sizes.

If an automatic garage door opener is to be installed, proper space and wiring must be provided. Additional headroom is required above the open door to mount the motor drive on the ceiling. See **Figure 21-18**. An electrical outlet is required to operate the opener. Check the manufacturer's installation requirements for the specific door.

Specifying Doors

Each door identified on the foundation/basement plan and floor plan should appear in a ***door schedule*** with its specifications. Information included on the door schedule should be obtained

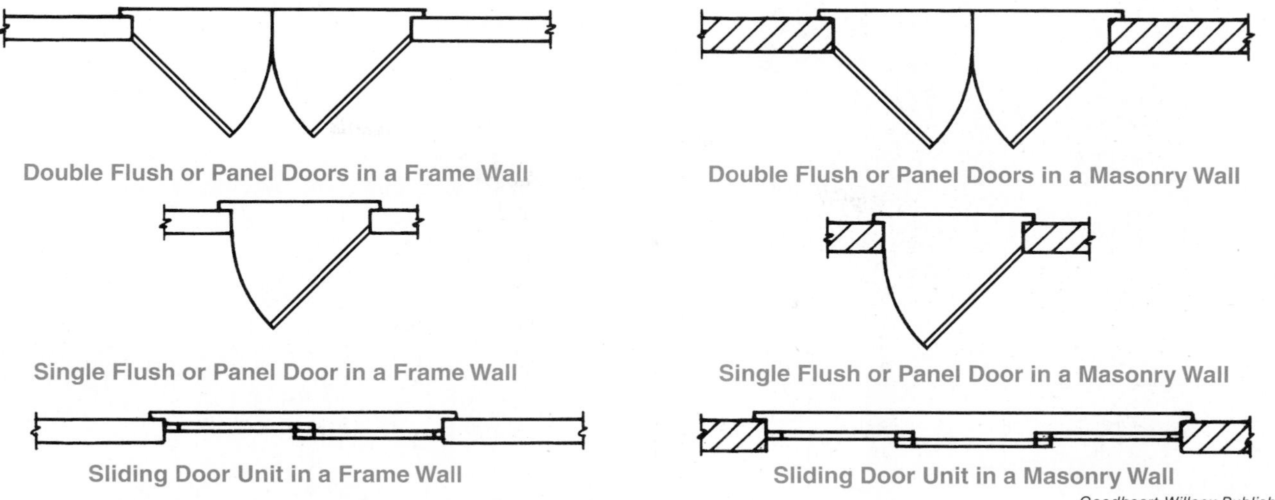

Goodheart-Willcox Publisher

Figure 21-9. These are standard plan view symbols of common exterior doors.

Karen Roach/Shutterstock.com

Figure 21-10. This flush exterior door has an attractive leaded glass inset with matching side and top panels.

Goodheart-Willcox Publisher

Figure 21-11. This traditional panel door is made of metal. This style of door is also available in wood.

A Pella/Rolscreen Company

B The Atrium Door and Window Corporation

Figure 21-12. A—This sliding glass door provides a panoramic view and easy access to the deck. B—This swinging glass door provides access to the deck and allows natural light into the dining room.

Employability
Team Protocol

Residential home design is generally not a one-person task. An entire team may be required to design the home, check the plans for structural integrity, ensure compliance with local building codes, and prepare the final working drawings. In teams, there is a protocol, or set of unspoken rules, that dictates behavior.

Team protocol suggests that a team:

- States a clear unity of purpose
- Has a clear set of performance goals
- Creates an atmosphere that is informal, comfortable, and relaxed
- Encourages everyone to participate and be free to express ideas and feelings
- Leads members to a general consensus through discussion

To be an effective team member, team protocol suggests that you:

- Communicate freely with other team members
- Avoid blaming others
- Support the ideas of other group members; consider all ideas without immediate dismissal
- Do not brag or try to be the "superstar," but more a team player
- Listen actively
- Get involved

Activity

Consider the types of tasks involved in designing a home, from the initial ideas to the final preparation of working drawings. Create a list of the people who might be on the design team. For each person on the list, identify ways that person can contribute to the final goal. Discuss your ideas with other class members.

from manufacturer's literature. Specifications vary and it is important to have exact information for the schedule. A typical door schedule is shown in **Figure 21-19**. The door schedule should be placed on the sheet with the floor plan or elevations, if space permits. Otherwise, it should be located in the details section of the set of drawings.

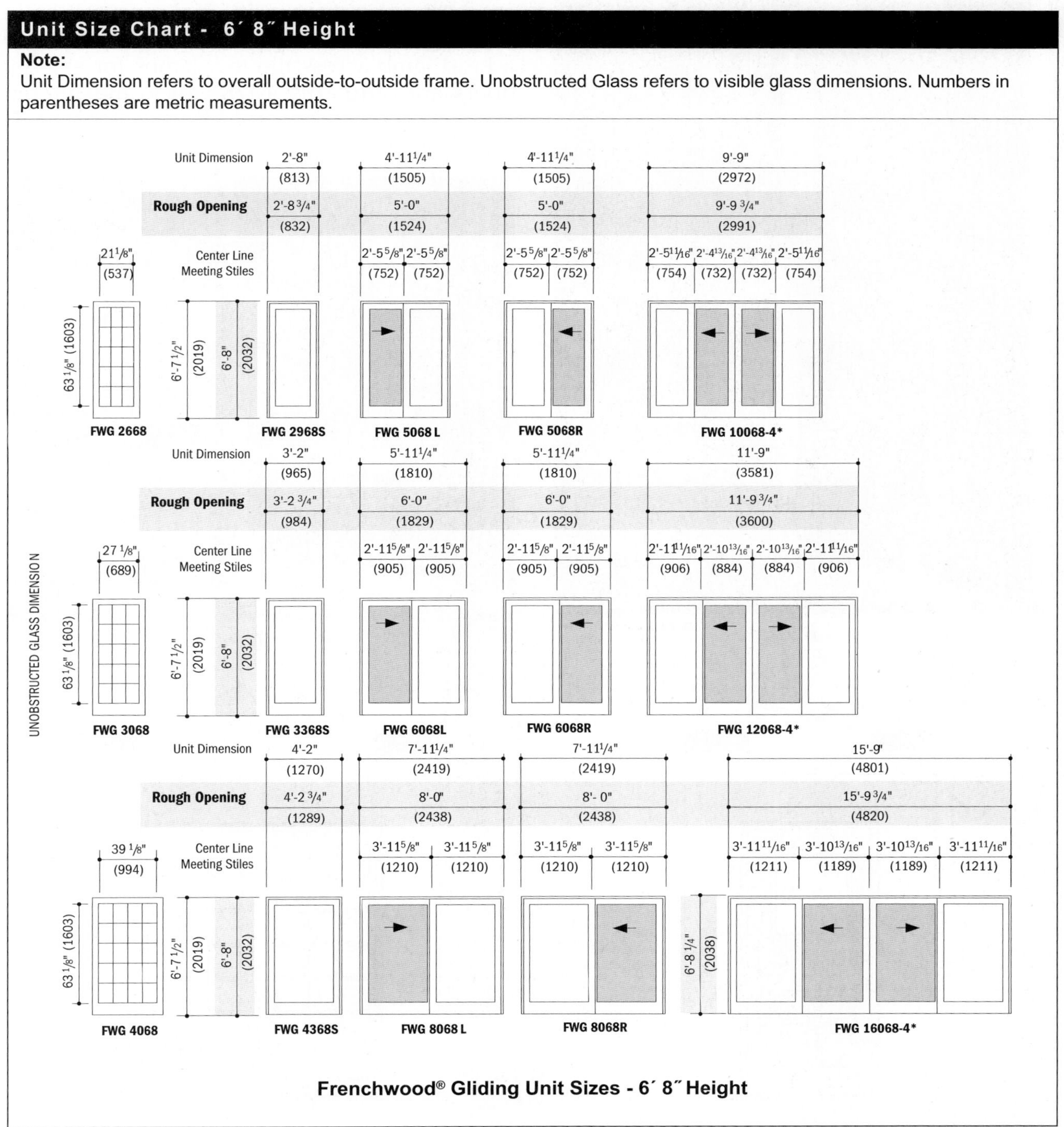

Courtesy Andersen Windows Inc.

Figure 21-13. Standard sizes of glass sliding doors.

Door Details

An interior or exterior door is placed inside a ***door jamb,*** which is the frame that fits inside the rough opening. See **Figure 21-20**. Jambs may be constructed from wood or metal. Wood jambs are more common in residential construction. A jamb consists of three parts—two side jambs and a head jamb across the top. Jambs for exterior doors are ordinarily 1-1/8″ thick and interior

A Ken Schulze/Shutterstock.com

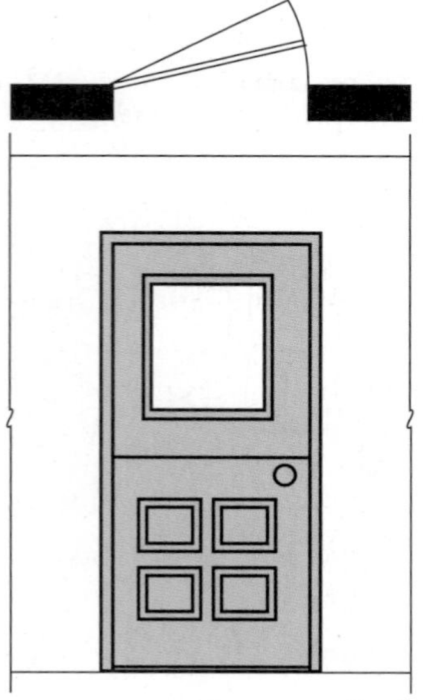

B Goodheart-Willcox Publisher

Figure 21-14. A—The top half of a Dutch door can be opened to allow light and air into a room. B—A Dutch door shown with its plan view symbol.

A Marvin Windows and Doors

B Goodheart-Willcox Publisher

Figure 21-15. A—French doors provide light and a view of the outdoors. B—French doors shown with their plan view symbol.

Goodheart-Willcox Publisher

Figure 21-16. Overhead sectional doors are divided into horizontal sections that travel along rails or tracks on each side of the door. This overhead sectional door is made of steel.

Konstantin L/Shutterstock.com

Figure 21-18. Extra space is required above a garage door to mount a garage door opener.

jambs are 3/4″. The door stop is a rabbet joint in the thicker exterior jambs, but is applied to the face of interior jambs. See **Figure 21-21**.

Jambs are available already assembled with the door hung and ready for installation. These are called *prehung units*. Prehung units are adjustable for slight variations in wall thickness. Consult the manufacturer's literature to determine the preferred rough opening size.

Garage Door Sizes		
Height	Single Door Width	Double Door Width
6′-6″	8′-0″	15′-0″
6′-6″	9′-0″	16′-0″
6′-6″	10′-0″	18′-0″
7′-0″	8′-0″*	15′-0″
7′-0″	9′-0″	16′-0″*
7′-0″	10′-0″	18′-0″
8′-0″	8′-0″	—
*These sizes are the most frequently used.		

Goodheart-Willcox Publisher

Figure 21-17. This table shows common garage door sizes.

Rough openings for interior doors are usually framed 3″ more than the door height and 2-1/2″ more than the door width. This provides ample space for the jambs and the necessary leveling and squaring. The space between the jamb and rough framing is covered with trim called ***casing***. Exterior casing is usually thicker than interior casing. When installed in a masonry wall, casing is called ***brick mold***. In frame construction, a ***drip cap*** is used over the top piece of trim to shed water. A drip cap is not necessary in masonry construction.

Exterior doors require a sill at the bottom of the door opening between the two side jambs. A ***sill*** is designed to drain water away from the door and provide support for the side jambs. Sills are constructed from wood, metal, concrete, or stone. **Figure 21-22** shows a typical exterior flush door detail in frame and brick veneer construction. Door and window construction details are usually drawn in section through the head jamb, the side jamb, and the sill. The head jamb is the jamb across the top of the opening.

Construction details for exterior sliding door units are slightly more complicated than other door construction details. Exterior sliding door jambs vary from one manufacturer to another. The number of door units may also affect the size and shape of the jambs. When specifying exterior sliding doors, it is advisable to secure specifications from the manufacturers to ensure accuracy.

Door Schedule						
Sym.	Quan.	Type	Rough Opening	Door Size	Manufacturer's Number	Remarks
A	2	Flush	3'-2-1/2" x 6'-9-1/4"	3'-Ø" x 6'-8"	EF 36 B	1-3/4" Solid core, birch
B	6	Flush	2'-1Ø-1/2" x 6'-9-1/4"	2'-8" x 6'-8"	IF 32 M	1-3/8" Hollow core, mahogany
C	2	Flush	2'-8-1/2" x 6'-9-1/4"	2'-6" x 6'-8"	IF 3Ø M	1-3/8" Hollow core, mahogany
D	8	Bi-Fold	See manufacturer's specs.	6'-Ø" x 6'-8"	BF 36 AL	Two units each 36" wide, aluminum
E	2	Sliding	4'-2-1/2" x 6'-9-1/4"	4'-Ø" x 6'-8"	IF 24 M	1-1/8" Hollow core, mahogany
F	1	Garage	See manufacturer's specs.	16'-Ø" x 7'-Ø"	G 16 S	Two light overhead sectional, alum.

Goodheart-Willcox Publisher

Figure 21-19. A typical door schedule for a set of residential house plans.

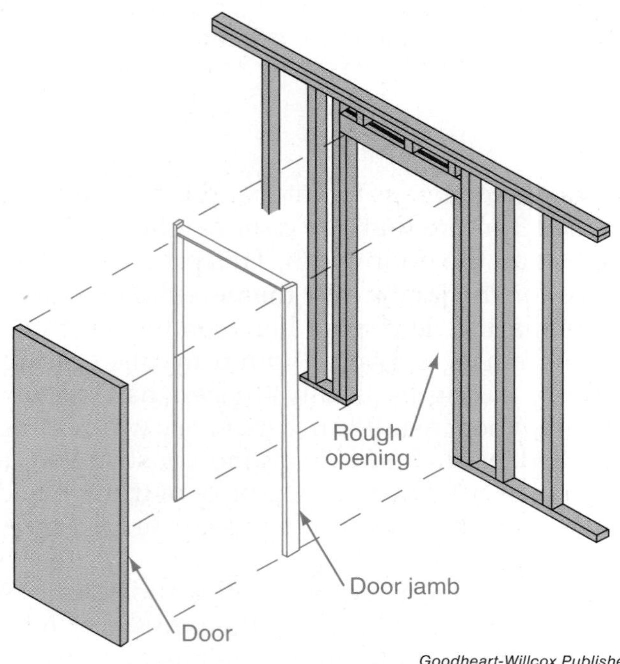

Goodheart-Willcox Publisher

Figure 20-20. The door jamb fits inside the rough opening and supports the door.

Side jamb
Close
Door 1-3/4″ thick
Exterior Door Jamb

Side jamb
Close
Door stop
Door 1-3/8″ thick
Interior Door Jamb

Goodheart-Willcox Publisher

Figure 21-21. Details of interior and exterior wood door jambs.

Ordinarily, it is not necessary to draw detailed window and door section drawings in conventional construction. However, if special framing or uncommon construction is involved, then these drawings are a necessary part of a set of construction drawings.

Windows

When selecting windows for a dwelling, it is important to remember the functions that windows perform. They admit light from the outside; provide fresh air and ventilation to the various rooms; help to create an atmosphere inside by framing an exterior view; and add detail, balance, and design to the exterior of the house.

Proper design and placement of windows will help to eliminate dark corners and provide a uniform amount of light across a room. The following guidelines will help achieve a more evenly lighted room.

- Glass area should be at least 20% of the floor area of the room. This amount of glass will provide suitable natural light even on cloudy days. When the light outside is very bright, the intensity may be controlled with shades or draperies.
- For increased light, the principal windows should face toward the south.
- One large window opening will produce less contrast in brightness than several smaller openings.
- Better distribution of light will be accomplished if windows are placed on more than one wall. See **Figure 21-23**.

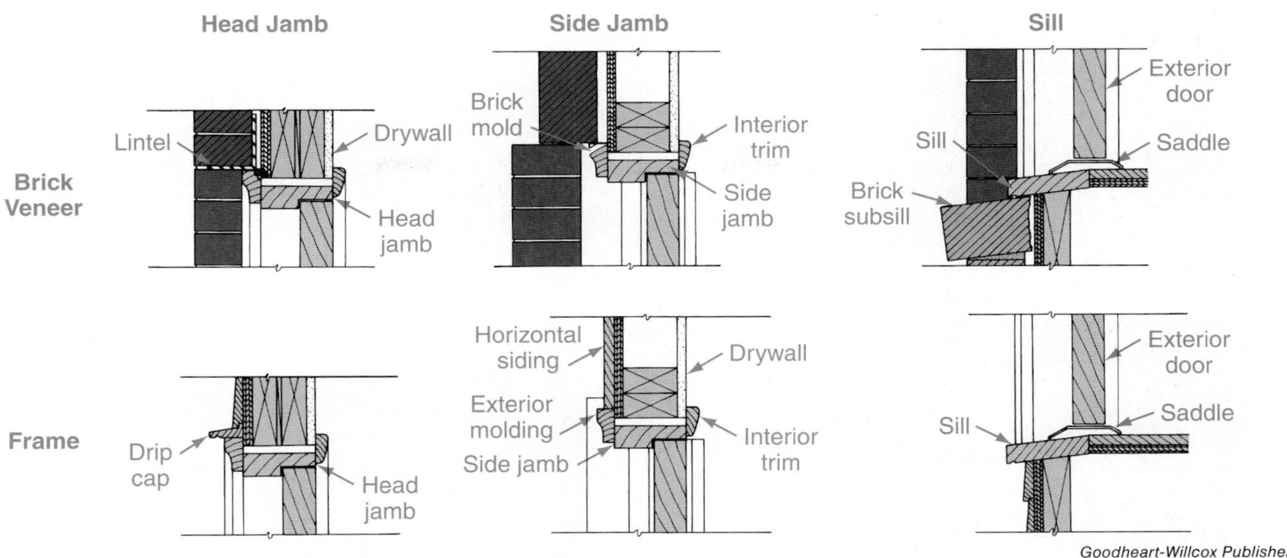

Goodheart-Willcox Publisher

Figure 21-22. Exterior door details for frame and brick veneer construction.

- Windows placed high on a wall provide a greater degree of light penetration into the room than windows placed low.
- Select the window shape that gives the type of light distribution desired in the room. Tall, narrow windows tend to give a thin and deep penetration. Short, wide windows produce a shallow penetration over a broad area.

Natural ventilation in a home is necessary all year long, but is especially important during the summer months. If windows are located with adequate ventilation in mind, comfort will be increased considerably. Apply these guidelines for efficient ventilation.

pics721/Shutterstock.com

Figure 21-23. The even light in this living room comes from multiple south- and west-facing windows.

- Openings for ventilation should be at least 10% of the floor area.
- Placement of openings for ventilation should take advantage of prevailing breezes.
- Locate windows to achieve the best movement of air across the room. Furniture should be placed so it will not interfere with the flow of air through the room.

Windows are often used to enhance an existing view or provide a selective one. Large areas of glass tend to make a room look larger. See **Figure 21-24**. The size and shape of the windows will frame the view, so it is important to select a window of the proper proportions...one that does not have obstructions to the view. Keep the following points in mind when specifying the proper window for a particular view.

- A large area of fixed glass provides clear viewing without obstructions.
- Horizontal and vertical divisions in the window or between windows should be thin to minimize obstruction.
- The sill height of windows should be determined on the basis of furniture, room arrangement, and view.

Designing a home to be functional, efficient, and pleasing to the eye on the exterior is no small task. The placement and number of windows

Iriana Shiyan/Shutterstock.com

Figure 21-24. The window in this kitchen not only provides plenty of natural light, but also makes the room seem larger.

affect the overall design appearance of the home, both inside and outside. They can add to the continuity of the design. Even though windows should be selected to fulfill interior needs, the size, placement, and type may be varied slightly to improve the outside appearance of the home.

The sizing illustrations in this chapter show sizes commonly used throughout the United States. You should be aware, however, that different window specification systems exist. For example, some window manufacturers in the southeast United States use *commodity sizes* to specify product sizes. The products are sized using a numbering system based on nominal width multiples of 18″ and nominal height multiples of 12″. For example, a 23SH window is a single-hung (SH) unit, nominally 36″ wide and 36″ tall.

Window Types

Many types of windows are available for residential construction. See **Figure 21-25.** Windows are constructed differently, depending on whether they are made of wood, metal, or vinyl. In addition, windows of the same general

Green Architecture

Energy-Efficient Windows

When you think of windows, you probably think of glass in a frame. Today, however, some windows are not made of glass at all. For example, acrylic is used in some windows. Although acrylic is as clear as glass, some types of acrylic produced today are 20% more energy-efficient than glass. Acrylic is also more flexible than glass, so it is more difficult to break. Unfortunately, acrylic is made using petroleum products, so although it is energy-efficient, it is not really sustainable. It is much more difficult to recycle than glass.

Glass remains the material of choice for most windows. It can be made more energy-efficient through various coatings. The seal between the glass and frame is also an important factor. Glass can also be laminated to make it wind-resistant. In fact, several window manufacturers offer hurricane-resistant windows that contain laminated glass.

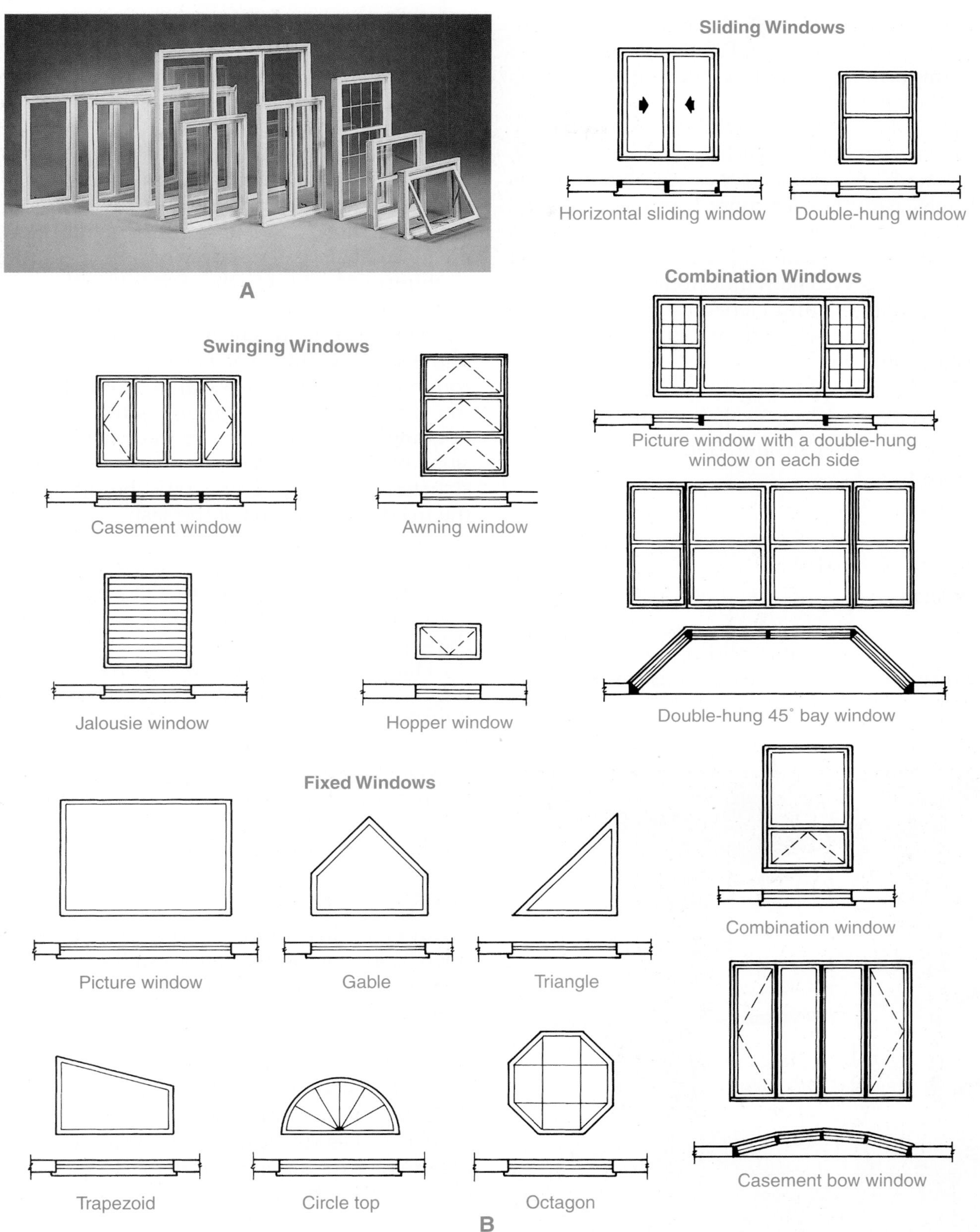

Goodheart-Willcox Publisher

Figure 21-25. A—Typical windows used in residential construction. B—Elevation and plan views of residential windows.

type purchased from different manufacturers are seldom exactly the same. For these reasons, it is very important to obtain window specifications from the manufacturer.

Three basic types of windows are typically used in residential construction: sliding, swinging, and fixed. A fourth type—combination—is possible using two or more types of windows to form a unit. Windows placed in a location other than a typical wall account for a fifth type or category. The windows in this category include skylights and clerestory windows. The specific window selected for a given application depends on:

- The function(s) to be performed
- Architectural style of the structure
- Construction considerations
- Building codes
- Personal taste

Sliding Windows

The two types of sliding windows most commonly used in residential construction are double-hung and horizontal sliding. ***Double-hung windows*** have two sashes. See **Figure 21-26**. The ***sashes*** slide up and down in grooves formed in the window frames. The weight of each sash is usually counterbalanced, or friction devices can be used to hold the sashes in the desired positions.

Marvin Windows and Doors

Figure 21-26. These double-hung windows can be raised to provide a pleasant cross-breeze for the occupants.

Muntins are small vertical and horizontal bars that separate the total glass area into smaller units. ***Mullions***, not to be confused with muntins, are larger horizontal or vertical members that are placed between window units.

Figure 21-27 gives the sizes of double-hung windows produced by one manufacturer. The basic unit size represents the overall dimensions of the window unit. The *rough opening size* is the rough framed space in a wall required to install the window. The *sash opening* is the size of the opening inside the frame or the outside dimensions of the sash. *Glass size* refers to the unobstructed glass size. This would be the same as the inside dimensions of the sash.

Sections are traditionally drawn at the head jamb, side jamb, and sill. See **Figure 21-28**. When a number of windows are placed together to form a unit, it is often necessary to draw a section of the support mullion also.

Horizontal sliding windows ordinarily have two sashes. In some models both sashes are movable; in others, one sash is fixed. A track attached to the head jamb and sill provides for movement. See **Figure 21-29**. Rollers are usually not required for windows unless they are quite large. **Figure 21-30** gives the standard sizes of one brand of horizontal sliding windows.

Swinging Windows

In swinging windows, one or more sashes open by swinging in or out from the frame. The four types of swinging windows most commonly used in residential construction are casement, awning, hopper, and jalousie windows.

A ***casement window*** has sashes hinged at the side that swing outward. See **Figure 21-31**. A single window unit may have a single sash or several sashes separated by vertical mullions. A casement window is opened or closed using a crank, a push-bar on the frame, or a handle on the sash.

Casement windows are produced in a wide variety of sizes. See **Figure 21-32**. Single units may be placed together to form a larger section. The hinge position on a hinged window may be shown in the exterior elevation view by using a

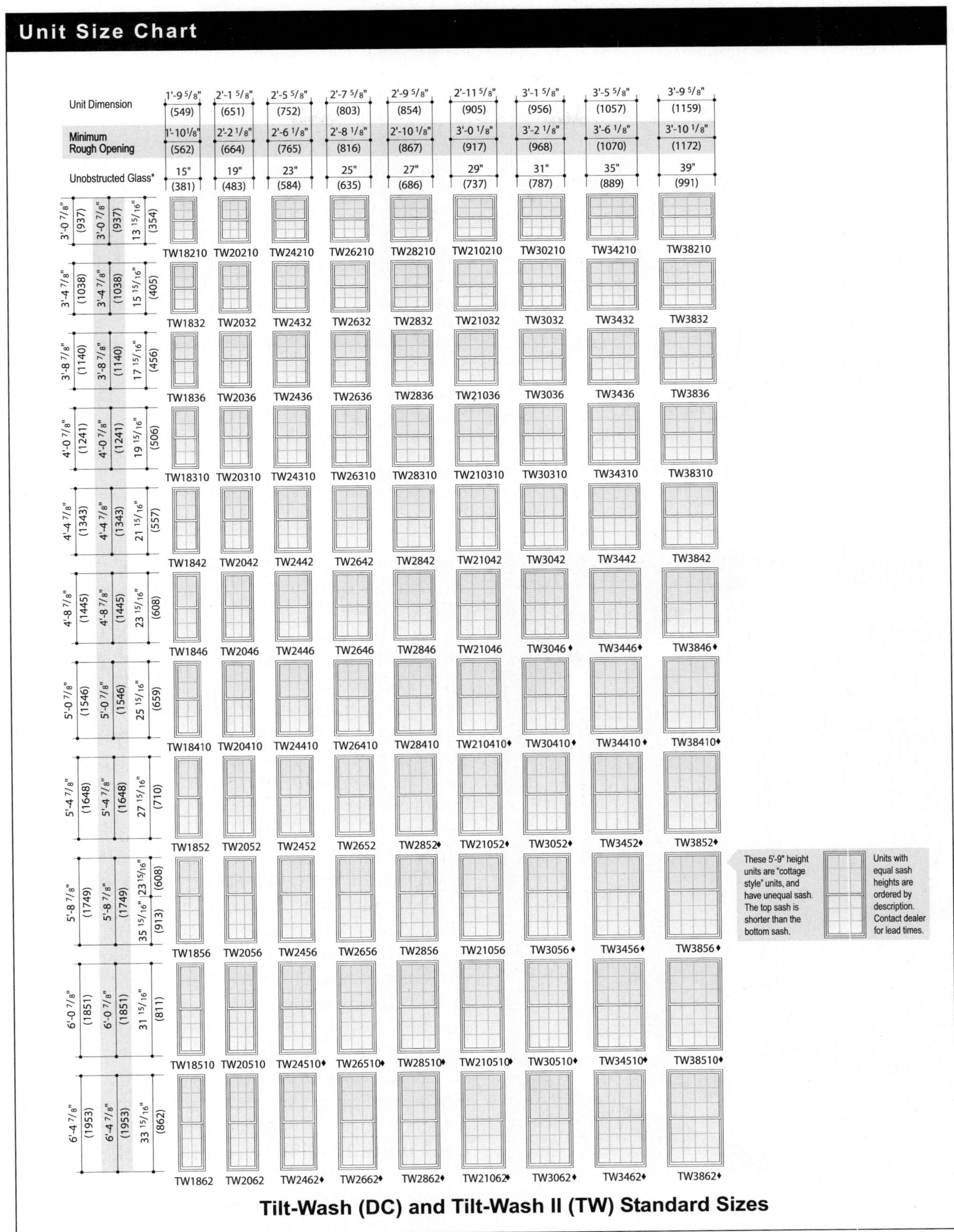

Courtesy Andersen Windows Inc.

Figure 21-27. Standard sizes of double-hung windows.

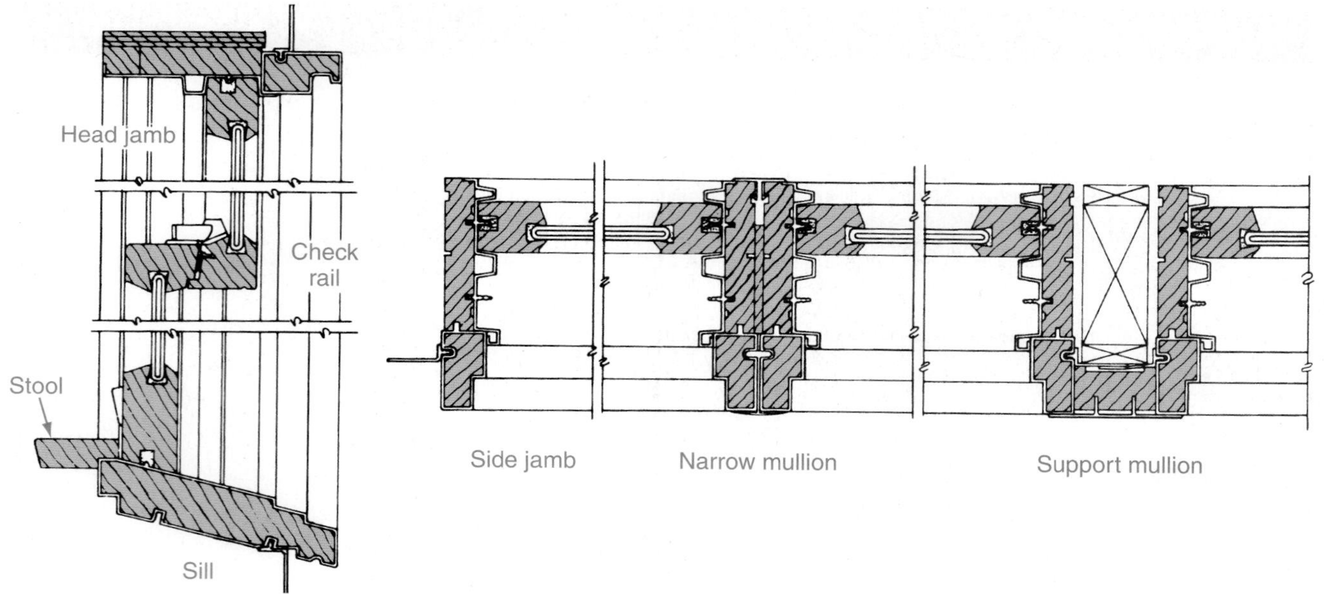

Goodheart-Willcox Publisher

Figure 21-28. Double-hung window details for a vinyl-clad wood window.

Caradco

Figure 21-29. This cutaway of a vinyl-clad sliding window with insulated glass shows the details of its construction.

dashed line, as shown in **Figure 21-33**. It is usually advisable to indicate the direction of swing in this manner.

An ***awning window*** has sashes that are hinged at the top and swing out at an angle. See **Figure 21-34**. An awning window may have several sashes or only a single sash. Crank-operated awning windows are manufactured in a variety of sizes, as shown in **Figure 21-35**.

The ***hopper window*** is hinged at the bottom and swings to the inside of the house. It is opened by a lock-handle at the top of the sash. Hopper windows are usually manufactured as a single unit only. See **Figure 21-36**.

Hopper windows direct air upward and should be placed low on the wall, when not used in a basement, for best ventilation. They are easy to open and wash from the inside. The major disadvantage of a hopper window is the inward swing. This interferes with the use of space in front of the window.

A ***jalousie window*** has a series of narrow, horizontal glass slats that are held in metal clips, which in turn are fastened to an aluminum frame. See **Figure 21-37**. In residential applications, the slats are usually 3″ wide. The slats operate in unison, similar to Venetian blinds or miniblinds.

Jalousie windows are produced in a variety of sizes. Widths range from 18″ to 48″ in increments of 2″. Lengths are available from 17″ to

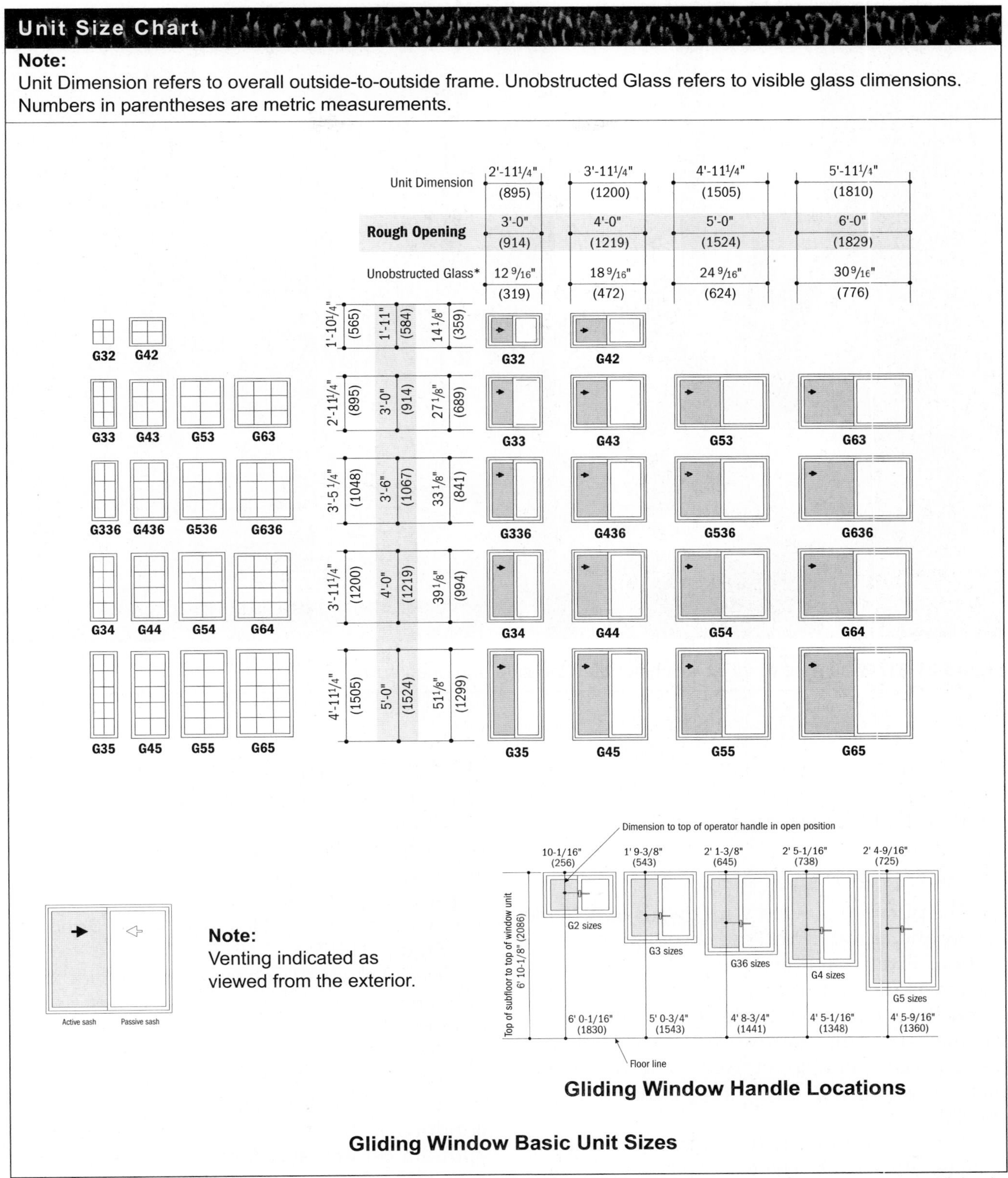

Courtesy Andersen Windows Inc.

Figure 21-30. Sizes of horizontal sliding windows.

CTatiana/Shutterstock.com
Figure 21-31. Casement windows are hinged on the side and open outward.

99-1/2″ in increments of 2-1/2″. Louver (slat) lengths are usually 2″ shorter than the window width (called the *buck size*).

Fixed Windows

The purpose of fixed windows is to provide a view and admit light. They do not permit ventilation. Fixed windows are more likely to be custom made and, therefore, may be sized for a specific application. Since they do not open, weather stripping, hardware, and screens are not required. Examples of fixed windows include picture windows, circle top windows, and special shapes.

Picture windows are fixed-glass units and are usually rather large. The term "picture window" is used because the view is framed, like a picture. These windows are often the center unit of a group of regular windows. See **Figure 21-38**. Picture windows may be purchased in standard sizes or custom-made on the job. **Figure 21-39** gives the standard sizes of picture window units produced by one manufacturer.

Circle top windows are circular windows typically installed above another window. They are available in quarter circles, half circles, ellipses, or full circles. Circle tops can be installed as single units or joined to other types of windows. See **Figure 21-40**.

Special-shape windows provide a wide range of interesting design options that can be used to individualize residential structures. These units are fixed windows in made-to-order shapes and sizes. See **Figure 21-41**. If produced by the same manufacturer as the one used to supply other windows in the house, they may be combined with almost any standard window to create a dramatic effect.

Combination Windows

Combination windows are a mixture of two or more types of windows. The three most

Unit Sizes - Standard Windows

Note:
Handing is viewed from exterior. Unit Dimension refers to overall outside-to-outside frame. Unobstructed Glass refers to visible glass dimensions. Numbers in parentheses are metric measurements.

Unit Dimension	Minimum Rough Opening	Unobstructed Glass							
Unit Dimension			1'-7 1/4" (489)	1'-11 1/4" (591)	2'-3 1/4" (692)	2'-5 1/4" (743)	2'-7 1/4" (794)	2'-9 1/4" (845)	2'-11 1/4" (895)
Minimum Rough Opening			1'-8" (508)	2'-0" (610)	2'-4" (711)	2'-6" (762)	2'-8" (813)	2'-10" (864)	3'-0" (914)
Unobstructed Glass			12 5/8" (321)	16 5/8" (422)	20 5/8" (524)	22 5/8" (575)	24 5/8" (625)	26 5/8" (676)	28 5/8" (727)
1'-11 1/4" (591)	2'-0" (610)	16 3/4" (425)	ACW1820	ACW2020	ACW2420				
2'-3 1/4" (692)	2'-4" (711)	20 3/4" (527)	ACW1824	ACW2024	ACW2424	ACW2624	ACW2824		
2'-7 1/4" (794)	2'-8" (813)	24 3/4" (629)	ACW1828	ACW2028	ACW2428	ACW2628	ACW2828	ACW21028	ACW3028
2'-11 1/4" (895)	3'-0" (914)	28 3/4" (770)	ACW1830	ACW2030	ACW2430	ACW2630	ACW2830	ACW21030	ACW3030
3'-3 1/4" (997)	3'-4" (1016)	32 3/4" (832)	ACW1834	ACW2034	ACW2434	ACW2634	ACW2834	ACW21034	ACW3034
3'-7 1/4" (1099)	3'-8" (1118)	36 3/4" (933)	ACW1838	ACW2038	ACW2438	ACW2638*◆	ACW2838*◆	ACW21038◆	ACW3038◆
3'-11 1/4" (1200)	4'-0" (1219)	40 3/4" (1035)	ACW1840	ACW2040	ACW2440*◆	ACW2640*◆	ACW2840◆	ACW21040◆	ACW3040◆
4'-3 1/4" (1302)	4'-4" (1321)	44 3/4" (1137)	ACW1844	ACW2044	ACW2444*◆	ACW2644*◆	ACW2844◆	ACW21044◆	ACW3044◆
4'-7 1/4" (1403)	4'-8" (1422)	48 3/4" (1238)	ACW1848	ACW2048	ACW2448*◆	ACW2648*◆	ACW2848◆	ACW21048◆	ACW3048◆
4'-11 1/4" (1505)	5'-0" (1524)	52 3/4" (1340)	ACW1850	ACW2050	ACW2450*◆	ACW2650*◆	ACW2850◆	ACW21050◆	ACW3050◆
5'-3 1/4" (1607)	5'-4" (1626)	56 3/4" (1441)	ACW1854	ACW2054	ACW2454*◆	ACW2654*◆	ACW2854◆	ACW21054◆	ACW3054◆
5'-7 1/4" (1708)	5'-8" (1727)	60 3/4" (1543)	ACW1858	ACW2058	ACW2458*◆	ACW2658*◆	ACW2858◆	ACW21058◆	ACW3058◆
5'-11 1/4" (1810)	6'-0" (1829)	64 3/4" (1645)	ACW1860	ACW2060	ACW2460*◆	ACW2660*◆	ACW2860◆	ACW21060◆	ACW3060◆

Venting Configuration

Left Right Stationary

All sizes available left, right and stationary unless noted.

A-Series Casement Standard Window Unit Sizes

Courtesy Andersen Windows Inc.

Figure 21-32. Standard casement window sizes.

Goodheart-Willcox Publisher

Figure 21-33. A dashed line shows the hinged side of casement windows in an elevation view.

Caradco

Figure 21-34. An awning window swings out and resembles an awning when open.

Awning - Single

Unit Dimension	Rough Opening	Unobstructed Glass*	1'-5 1/2" (445) / 1'-6" (457) / 11 1/4" (286)	1'-11 1/2" (597) / 2'-0" (610) / 1'-5 1/4" (438)	2'-5 1/2" (749) / 2'-6" (762) / 1'-11 1/4" (591)	2'-11 1/2" (902) / 3'-0" (914) / 2'-5 1/4" (743)	3'-5 1/2" (1054) / 3'-6" (1067) / 2'-11 1/4" (895)	3'-11 1/2" (1207) / 4'-0" (1219) / 3'-5 1/4" (1048)
1'-5 1/2" (445)	1'-6" (457)	11 1/4" (286)	1616	2016	2616	3016	3616	4016
1'-11 1/2" (597)	2'-0" (610)	1'-5 1/4" (438)	1620	2020	2620	3020	3620	4020
2'-5 1/2" (749)	2'-6" (762)	1'-11 1/4" (591)	1626	2026	2626	3026	3626	4026
2'-11 1/2" (902)	3'-0" (914)	2'-5 1/4" (743)	1630	2030	2630	3030	3630	4030

Awning - Below Picture

Unit Dimension	Rough Opening					
3'-11 1/2" (1207)	4'-0" (1219)	2020 / 2020	2620 / 2620	3020 / 3020	3620 / 3620	4020 / 4020
4'-11 1/2" (1511)	5'-0" (1524)	2026 / 2026	2626 / 2626	3026 / 3026	3626 / 3626	4026 / 4026
5'-11 1/2" (1816)	6'-0" (1829)	2030 / 2030	2630 / 2630	3030 / 3030	3630 / 3630	4030 / 4030
6'-11 1/2" (2121)	7'-0" (2134)	2040 / 2030	2640 / 2630	3040 / 3030	3640 / 3630	4040 / 4030
7'-11 1/2" (2426)	8'-0" (2438)	2050 / 2030	2650 / 2630	3050 / 3030	3650 / 3630	4050 / 4030

Note:
Unit Dimension refers to overall outside-to-outside frame.
Unobstructed Glass refers to visible glass dimensions.

Courtesy Andersen Windows Inc.

Figure 21-35. Standard awning window sizes.

popular types include bay windows, bow windows, and picture windows combined with swinging or sliding windows.

Bay and bow windows are combination windows that project out from the structure. See **Figure 21-42**. They may be constructed using most any kind of windows, including double-hung, casement, and fixed panels.

Bay windows generally have a double-hung window on either side of a fixed center window. The side windows are normally placed at 45° to the exterior wall. A variation on the bay window design is called the *box bay window*. It combines a picture window parallel to the wall with two casement windows placed at 90° to the wall. See **Figure 21-43**. Box bay windows are also called *garden windows*.

Bow windows are a set of windows that form an arc extending out from the wall of the

Courtesy Andersen Windows Inc.

Figure 21-36. Hopper windows are popular for basement applications.

Santiago Cornejo/Shutterstock.com

Figure 21-38. Picture windows are usually meant to frame a specific view. The lack of dividers provides a clear view of the scenery outside.

Dontree/Shutterstock.com

Figure 21-37. Jalousie windows are rarely used, especially in northern climates, because they are not very energy-efficient. However, they can provide interest and a cool breeze when energy efficiency is not a concern, such as in a beach house in the Caribbean.

house. Combinations of four to seven units are common. See **Figure 21-44**.

Skylights and Clerestory Windows

Skylights and clerestory windows are generally used to admit light into areas of the structure that receive little or no natural light. ***Skylights*** are windows that are located on the roof. ***Clerestory windows*** are placed high on a wall. See **Figure 21-45**. These windows not only supply natural light, but also can produce pleasing architectural effects. Some skylights and clerestory windows can be opened for ventilation.

Skylights are available in several basic sizes and shapes. The most common shape is rectangular and designed to fit between the roof trusses. Custom-made skylights are possible to meet most any design situation. Clerestory windows may be custom-made fixed windows or a series of standard windows.

Window Schedules

A ***window schedule*** provides information about all windows in a structure such as type of window, size, identifying symbol, manufacturer's number, and installation. See **Figure 21-46**. The window schedule may be placed on the same sheet as the floor plan or elevation, if space permits. Otherwise, it may be located on one of the other drawings. Care must be taken to ensure that all windows are listed on the schedule and are properly identified.

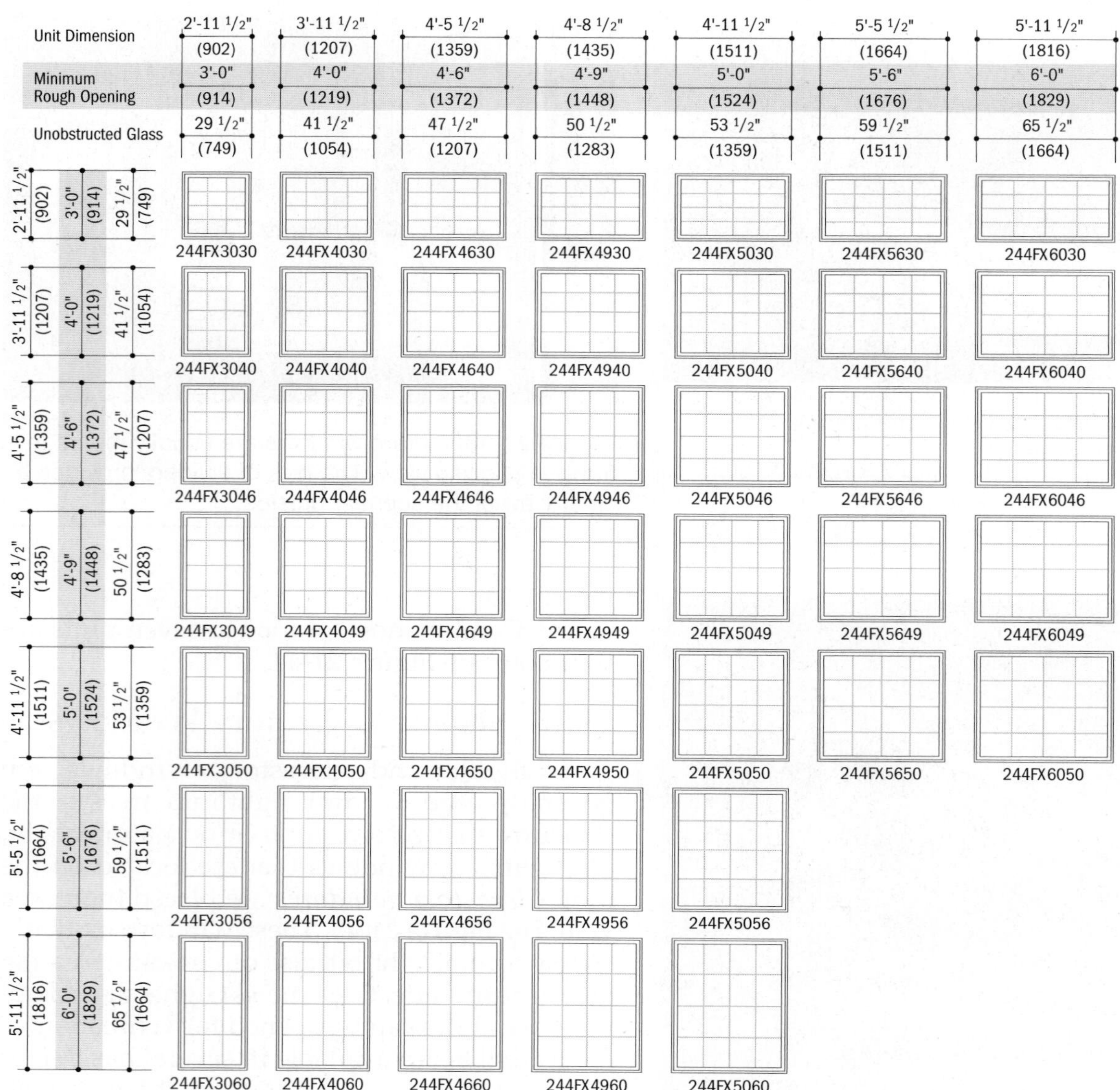

Note:
Unit Dimension refers to overall outside-to-outside frame. Unobstructed Glass refers to visible glass dimensions.

Courtesy Andersen Windows Inc.

Figure 21-39. Standard picture window sizes.

Peachtree Doors, Inc.

A

Unit Dimension	1'-7 1/2" (495)	1'-11 1/2" (597)	2'-3 1/2" (699)	2'-7 1/2" (800)	2'-11 1/2" (902)	3'-3 1/2" (1003)
Minimum Rough Opening	1'-8" (508)	2'-0" (610)	2'-4" (711)	2'-8" (813)	3'-0" (914)	3'-4" (1016)
Unobstructed Glass	13 1/2" (343)	17 1/2" (445)	21 1/2" (546)	25 1/2" (648)	29 1/2" (749)	33 1/2" (851)
Circle Tops (See chart for CT heights)	244CT18	244CT20	244CT24	244CT28	244CT30	244CT34

Finelight ™ Grille Patterns: Sunburst, Renaissance*	Circle Top	
	Unit Dim. Height	Rough Opg. Height
244CT18*	1'-0 5/8" (321)	1'-1 1/8" (333)
244CT20*	1'-2 5/8" (371)	1'-3 1/8" (384)
244CT24	1'-4 5/8" (422)	1'-5 1/8" (435)
244CT28	1'-6 5/8" (473)	1'-7 1/8" (486)
244CT30	1'-8 5/8" (524)	1'-9 1/8" (537)
244CT34	1'-10 5/8" (575)	1'-11 1/8" (587)

*Renaissance pattern not available for 18 or 20 sizes.

Courtesy Andersen Windows Inc.

B

Figure 21-40. A—Circle top windows can be combined with other windows or doors. B—Typical sizes of circle top windows.

A
Weather Shield Mfg., Inc.

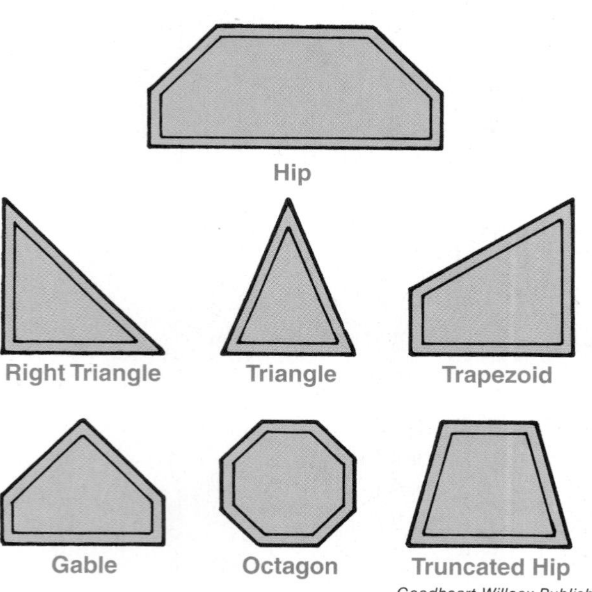

B
Goodheart-Willcox Publisher

Figure 21-41. A—This unique custom window adds an individual touch to a private residence. B—Popular shapes for special-shape windows.

Marvin Windows and Doors

Figure 21-42. A unique bay window especially suited for this location.

karamysh/Shutterstock.com

Figure 21-43. This two-story home has a large box bay window next to the front entrance.

Pozzi Wood Windows

Figure 21-44. This large bow window provides a panoramic view.

Iriana Shiyan/Shutterstock.com

Figure 21-45. This open floor plan has a clerestory window over the sliding doors and several skylights to add natural light to the home.

Window Schedule						
Sym.	Quan.	Type	Rough Opening	Sash Size	Manufacturer's Number	Remarks
A	6	Casement	3'-6-1/8" x 5'-1"	3'-2-1/4" x 4'-9-1/4"	3N3	Primed, screens, insulating glass
B	1	Casement	3'-6-1/8" x 3'-3-1/4"	3'-2-1/4" x 3'-1-1/2"	2N3	Primed, screens, insulating glass
C	1	Casement	5'-6-1/2" x 8'-4-1/2"	5'-2-5/8" x 8'-1"	5N5	Primed, screens, insulating glass
D	1	Casement	2'-5-7/8" x 3'-5-1/4"	2'-2" x 3'-1-3/4"	2N2	Primed, screens, insulating glass
E	5	Hopper	1'-8" x 5'-5"	1'-4" x 5'-2"	314	Exterior casing or subsill not included
F	2	Fixed	2'-4" x 6'-9-1/4"	See remarks	Custom	Glass size-2'-0" x 6'-8" insul.

Goodheart-Willcox Publisher

Figure 21-46. This typical window schedule layout includes all of the necessary information.

Summary

- Windows and doors should be planned carefully to ensure maximum contribution to the overall design and function of the structure.
- Doors are classified as either interior or exterior doors and can be further grouped according to their construction, uses, function, or location.
- Each door identified in a set of drawings should appear in a door schedule with its specifications.
- Windows of the same general type may vary from manufacturer to manufacturer, so it is very important to obtain window specifications from the manufacturer.
- Specifications for each window in a set of drawings should appear in a window schedule.

Internet Resources

Andersen Windows and Doors
Manufacturer of windows and doors

Jeld-Wen Windows and Doors
Manufacturer of windows and doors

Marvin Windows and Doors
Manufacturer of windows and doors

Pella Corporation
Manufacturer of windows and doors

Velux
Manufacturer of skylights, blinds, and home automation products

Review Questions

Answer the following questions using the information in this chapter.

1. List five functions of doors and windows.
2. Name eight types of interior doors.
3. Interior flush doors are usually _____ thick.
4. What are the horizontal cross members in panel doors called? What are the vertical cross members called?
5. What is the main use of bifold doors in residential construction?
6. Explain how pocket doors are different from sliding doors.
7. A door that swings through a 180° arc is called a _____ door.
8. Name two ways in which exterior wood doors are different from interior doors.
9. What is the most popular type of garage door?
10. What is the function of a drip cap?
11. Explain the purpose of a door sill.
12. The three parts of a door jamb are the two side jambs and a _____ jamb across the top of the frame.
13. Why is it important to design and place windows properly in a residential structure?
14. The window glass area should be at least _____ percent of the floor area of the room.
15. What is the difference between muntins and mullions?
16. What does the rough opening size of a window represent?
17. Which window is hinged at the side and swings out?
18. Name one type of window that does not provide ventilation.
19. Explain the difference between a bay window and a bow window.
20. What information should a window schedule include?

Suggested Activities

1. Construct a scale model of an exterior or interior door, jambs, and rough framing. Use CADD or manual drafting techniques to make plan, elevation, and section drawings. Present the model and drawings to the class and explain the features.
2. Select a floor plan for a small- to medium-size house. Using CADD, draw the floor plan. Then, plan the windows for the house following the guidelines presented in this chapter for ventilation, light, and view. Insert window symbols into the walls. Design and draw new symbols as needed. Finally, create a window schedule for the house.

3. Visit a local lumber company and examine the cutaway models of the windows available from the company. Measure the various parts of one model and prepare a sketch. Identify the type of window and the manufacturer. Collect specification data about the windows and bring the material to class for reference purposes.
4. Using CADD, draw various window and door symbols as shown in this chapter. Add these to your symbol library.

Problem Solving Case Study

Your client has asked you to design a cottage "getaway" to be built in the Blue Ridge Mountains in Maryland. The cottage only needs a bedroom, one bathroom, and a general living/kitchen area. The client wants to make the most of the mountain views, and because he is an artist, needs plenty of natural light. However, he wants the cottage to be as energy-efficient and sustainable as possible.

Design the cottage to meet the client's specifications and create a floor plan drawing in CADD. Search the Internet to find suitable doors and windows for the cottage and incorporate them into your design. Add a door schedule and a window schedule to your floor plan. Present your final drawings to the class.

ADDA Certification Prep

The following questions are presented in the style used in the American Design Drafting Association (ADDA) Drafter Certification Test. Answer the questions using the information in this chapter.

1. Which of the following statements are true about doors and windows?
   A. A Dutch door is composed of two parts—an upper and lower section.
   B. Picture windows are fixed-glass units and are usually rather small.
   C. An awning window has sashes that are hinged at the top and swing out at an angle.
   D. Muntins are large vertical and horizontal bars that separate the total glass area into smaller units.
   E. The basic unit size represents the overall dimensions of the window unit.
2. Match each type of door with its description.

   Doors: 1. French door, 2. Double-action door, 3. Panel door, 4. Bifold door, 5. Flush door
   A. Smooth on both sides.
   B. Has cross members called stiles and rails.
   C. Made of two parts hinged together.
   D. A panel door in which all of the panels are glass.
   E. A door that can swing through an arc of 180°.
3. Match each type of window with its description.

   Windows: 1. Double-hung, 2. Casement, 3. Hopper, 4. Jalousie, 5. Clerestory
   A. Has sashes hinged at the side that swing outward.
   B. Hinged at the bottom and swings to the inside of the house.
   C. Has narrow, horizontal glass slats held in metal clips.
   D. Placed high on a wall to admit light.
   E. Has two sashes that slide up and down in grooves.

Curricular Connections

1. **Language Arts.** Research the history of the use of glass windows in homes. Compose an essay on how glass changed the building industry and the possible uses for homes and other residential structures.
2. **Social Science.** Research the origins of clerestory windows and how they got their name. Write a summary of your findings.

STEM Connections

1. **Technology.** Skylights are very useful for increasing the amount of natural light in a room. One of the complaints about skylights in the past has been that there was no way to "shut off" the light or to dim it if a room becomes too bright. Skylight manufacturers today have found ways to prevent the problem. Research skylights and write a report on the ways skylights today can be controlled or shaded.

Communicating about Architecture

1. **Reading.** With a partner, make flash cards of the key terms in this chapter. On the front of the card, write the term. On the back of the card, write the pronunciation and a brief definition. Use this chapter and a dictionary for guidance. Then take turns quizzing one another on the pronunciations and definitions of the key terms.
2. **Speaking.** Using the same flash cards developed in the previous activity, explain to the class what you like about certain types of doors and windows. Describe in detail what is appealing to you and what is not, and identify which types of doors and windows you would want for your home.

Chapter 22

Building Sections

Objectives

After completing this chapter, you will be able to:

- Explain the purposes of building sections.
- Describe the three main types of building sections.
- Explain how to identify the location of a building section.
- List information that must be obtained before a building section can be drawn.
- Draft a full section using either manual or CADD techniques.

Key Terms

building section
cross section
cutting-plane line
full building section
longitudinal building section
partial building section
specific section
transverse building section
typical section
wall section

A set of working drawings must provide all of the information needed to build a structure. The floor and foundation plans provide a wealth of information, but they do not provide all of the details needed to construct a residence. Some features are hidden in these views. In addition, these plans do not show important information about fasteners, methods, and materials. To provide this information, one or more building sections are included in a set of working drawings. ***Building sections*** are vertical "cuts" or "slices" through a structure that illustrate the type of foundation, wall, and roof construction to be used. See **Figure 22-1**. Knowing when and how to include building sections in a set of architectural working drawings is an important skill in the architectural field. It requires an understanding of building materials, their uses in the structure, and what type of building section view is needed.

Purpose of Building Sections

The main purpose of a building section is to inform the contractor or builder of special or unconventional construction methods or techniques to be used in a structure. These may include sunken or raised floor levels, unusual foundations, unique wall or roof construction, and details for split-level or multi-level structures. Building sections also provide important information about size. They show the height of each floor of a building, as well as the heights of windows and other features. Finally, they show the specific materials and fasteners to be used.

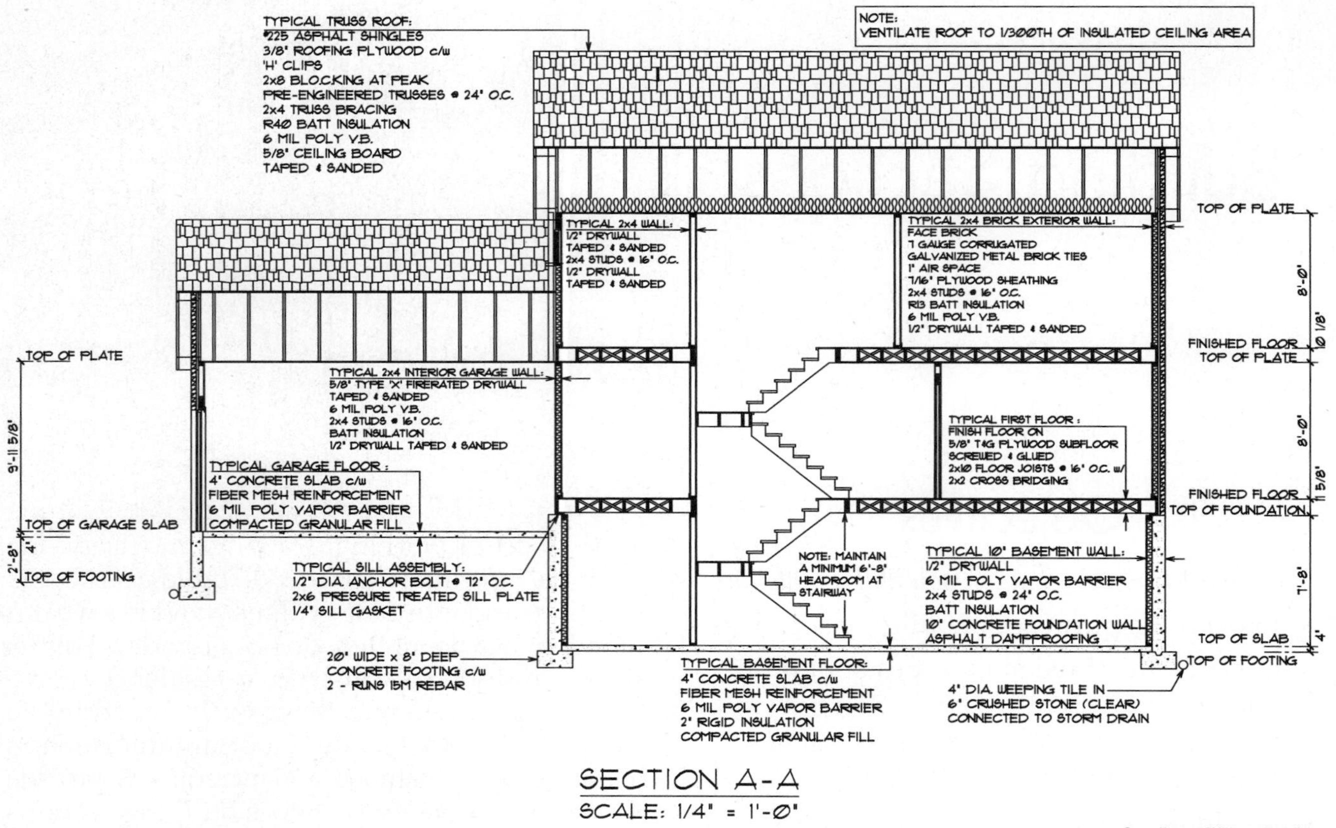

Goodheart-Willcox Publisher

Figure 22-1. A building section cuts vertically through a structure to show foundation, wall, and roof construction, as well as materials and the general relationship of spaces or rooms within the home.

Section views that are created specifically to show one feature, such as stairs, a fireplace, or a deck, are generally called *detail drawings* or construction details. Detail drawings for a deck are shown in **Figure 22-2**. See Chapter 24, *Stair Details*, for information about drawings for stairs. See Chapter 25, *Fireplace, Chimney, and Stove Details*, for information about drawings for fireplaces, chimneys, and stoves.

Types of Building Sections

Different types of building sections are prepared for different purposes. There are three basic types of building sections:

- Full building section
- Partial building section
- Wall section

Each type is described more fully in the following sections.

Full Building Section

A ***full building section***, also called a ***cross section***, cuts vertically through the entire structure. A full building section has three main purposes. First, it shows the relationships among the various interior spaces. The building section shown in **Figure 22-1** is a full building section of a two-story house with a basement. Notice how clearly the layout of the rooms appears in this section. The second purpose is to specify overall height relationships. Notice in **Figure 22-1** that height dimensions are specified for floor slabs, finished floors, and top plates. In addition, a full section provides information about general materials to be used. Materials are often detailed in notes, as shown in the figure. Full building sections are drawn at the same scale as the floor plan, usually 1/4″ = 1′-0″.

Full sections are often required to show foundation information. This is particularly true for pier foundations and post foundations. See

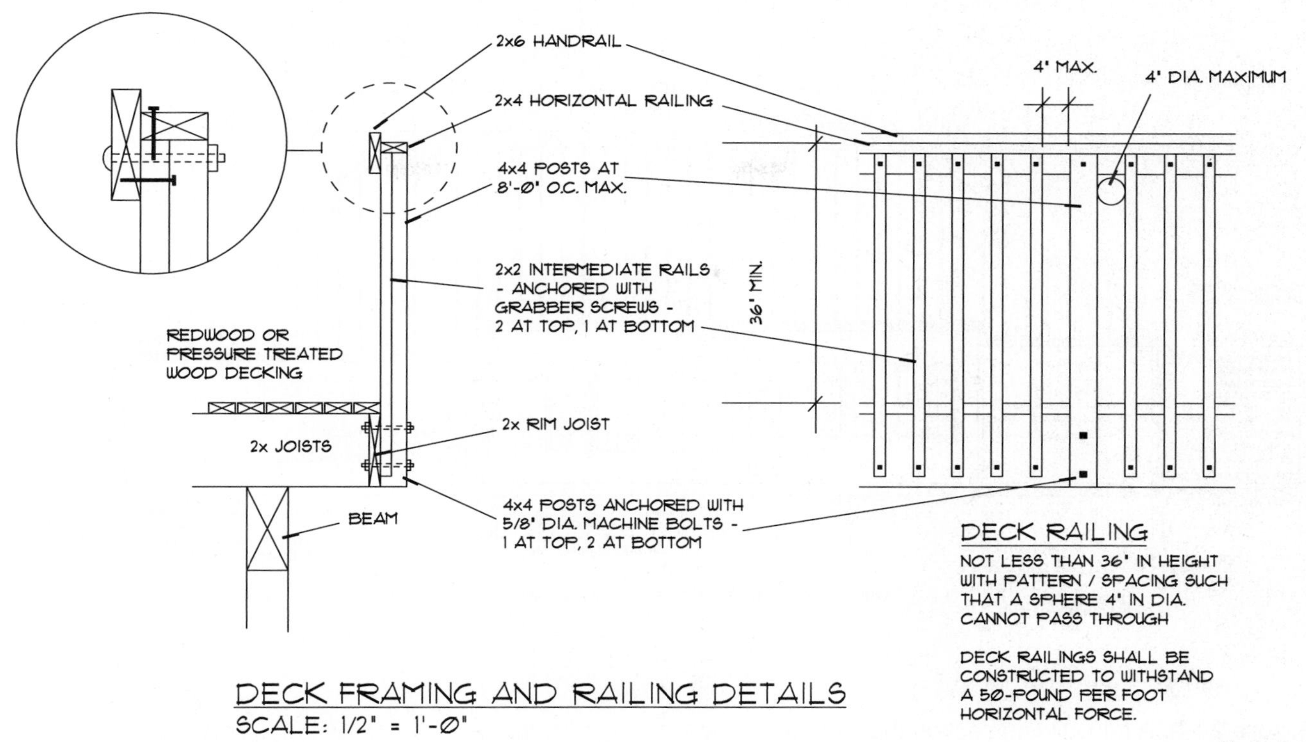

Figure 22-2. Framing and railing details for a deck.

Figure 22-3. The materials to be used for the piers or posts and footings, as well as their spacing, can be shown in a full section.

Partial Building Section

When part of a structure needs to be shown in more detail, an enlarged view is used. A ***partial building section*** cuts through half or more of the structure, but not its entire length. It is drawn at a larger scale—usually 3/8″ = 1′-0″ or larger—to show detailed information about a specific part of the structure. **Figure 22-4** shows a partial building section that details the construction of a master bathroom.

Wall Section

A ***wall section*** cuts through only one wall, typically an exterior wall. See **Figure 22-5**. It shows the foundation system, wall system, and roof system at one location in the structure. Like partial building sections, wall sections are shown at an enlarged scale to show greater detail. They are typically drawn at a scale of 3/4″ = 1′-0″ or larger. Wall sections typically show more specific details in comparison to other types of building sections. Wall sections are also important in constructing accurate elevation drawings. Elevation drawings are discussed in Chapter 23, *Elevations*.

Typical and Specific Sections

Each type of section can be further classified as either a typical section or a specific section. A ***typical section*** is one that represents features or sizes that are used in many different places in the structure. **Figure 22-1** is an example of a typical building section. Notice that the word TYPICAL is included in many of the notes on the drawing. Typical wall sections are included in most sets of construction drawings. See **Figure 22-6**.

A ***specific section***, on the other hand, shows a feature, method, or technique that is used only once, particularly if the information is not clear in the floor plan. **Figure 22-7** shows a specific wall section for a box window over the sink in a kitchen.

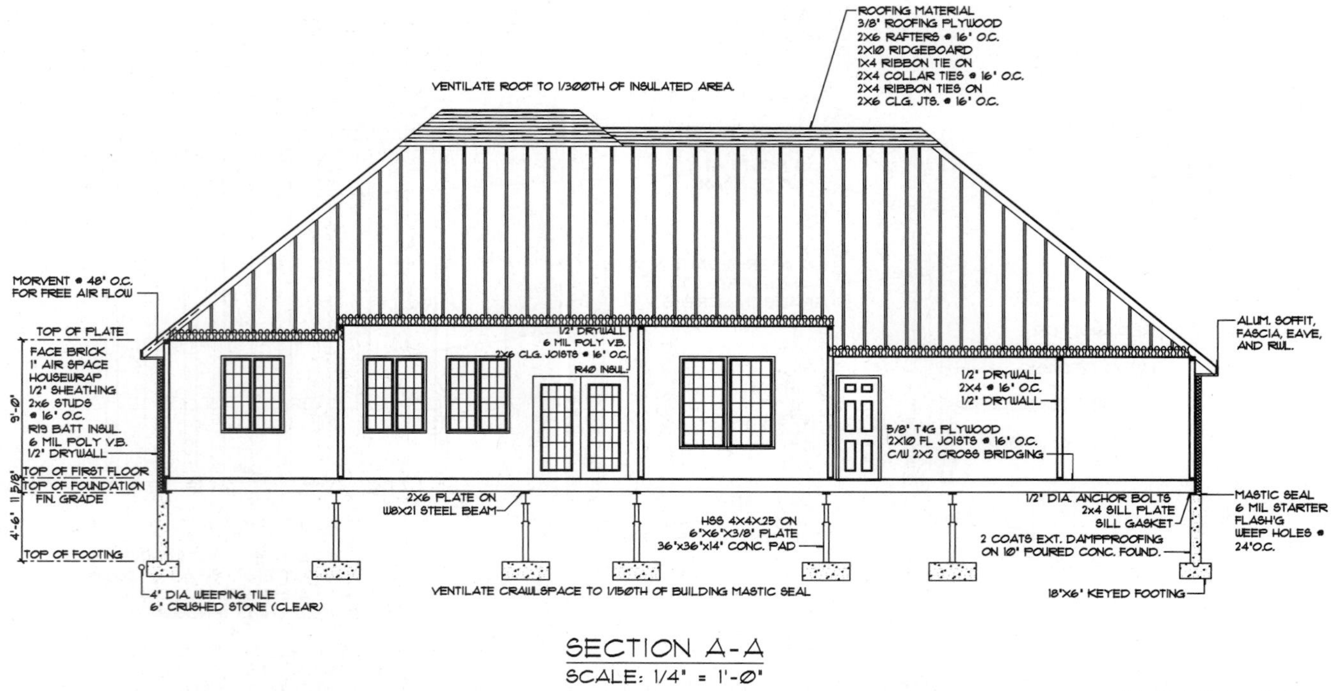

Goodheart-Willcox Publisher

Figure 22-3. A full building section that shows the locations and materials for the piers and footings in a foundation.

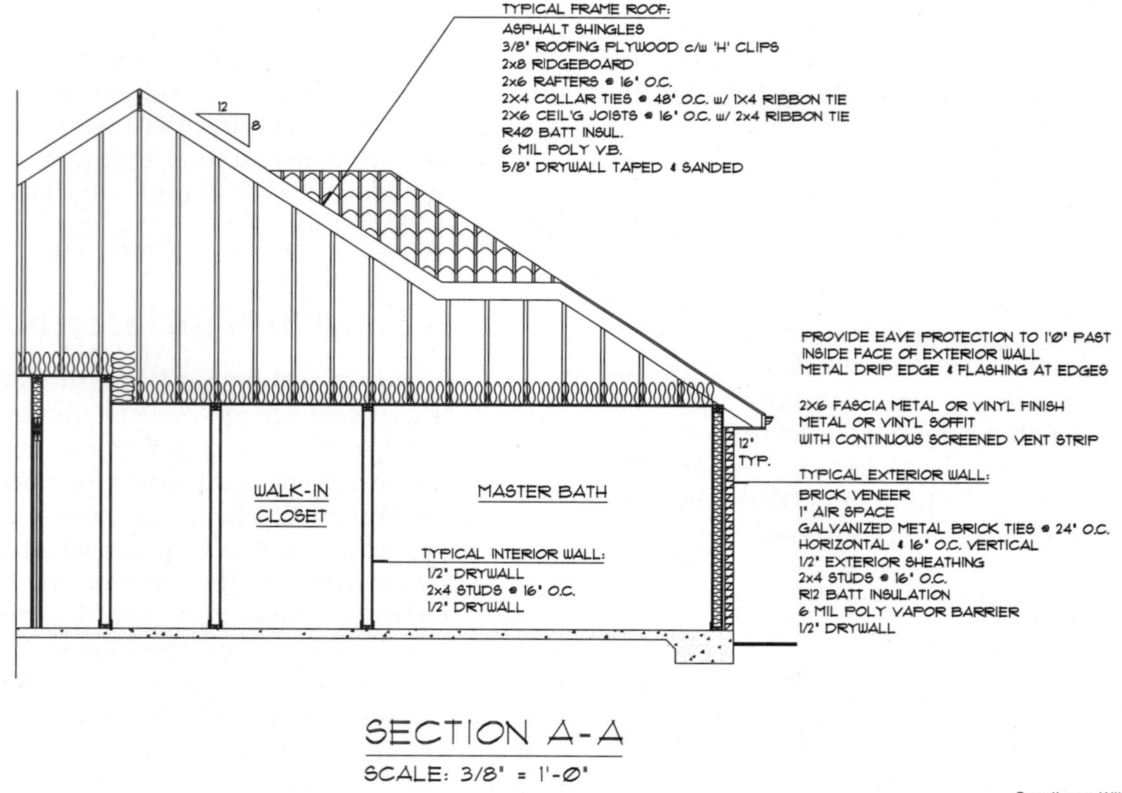

Goodheart-Willcox Publisher

Figure 22-4. An example of a partial building section.

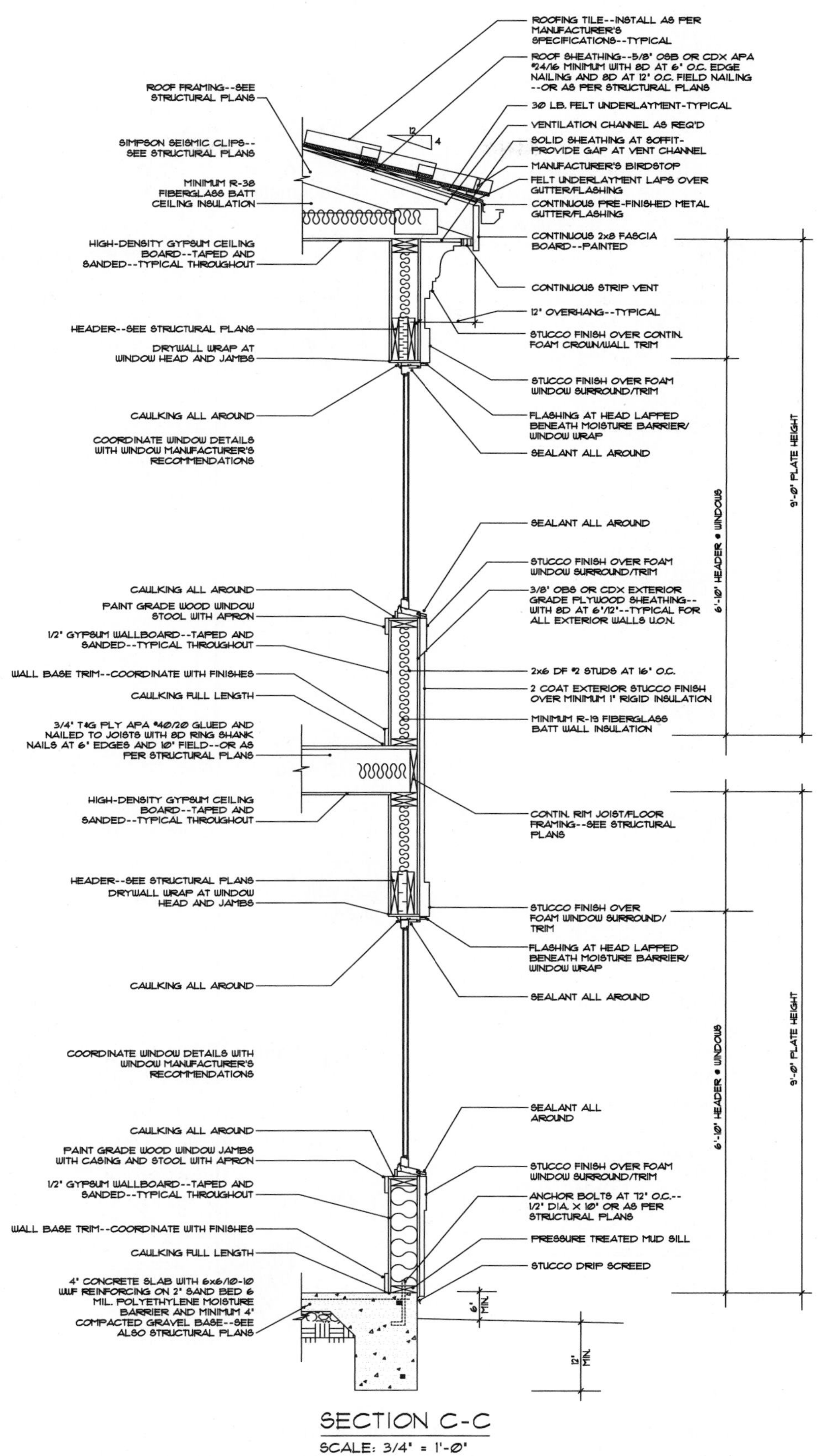

Goodheart-Willcox Publisher

Figure 22-5. A complete wall section for a two-story house.

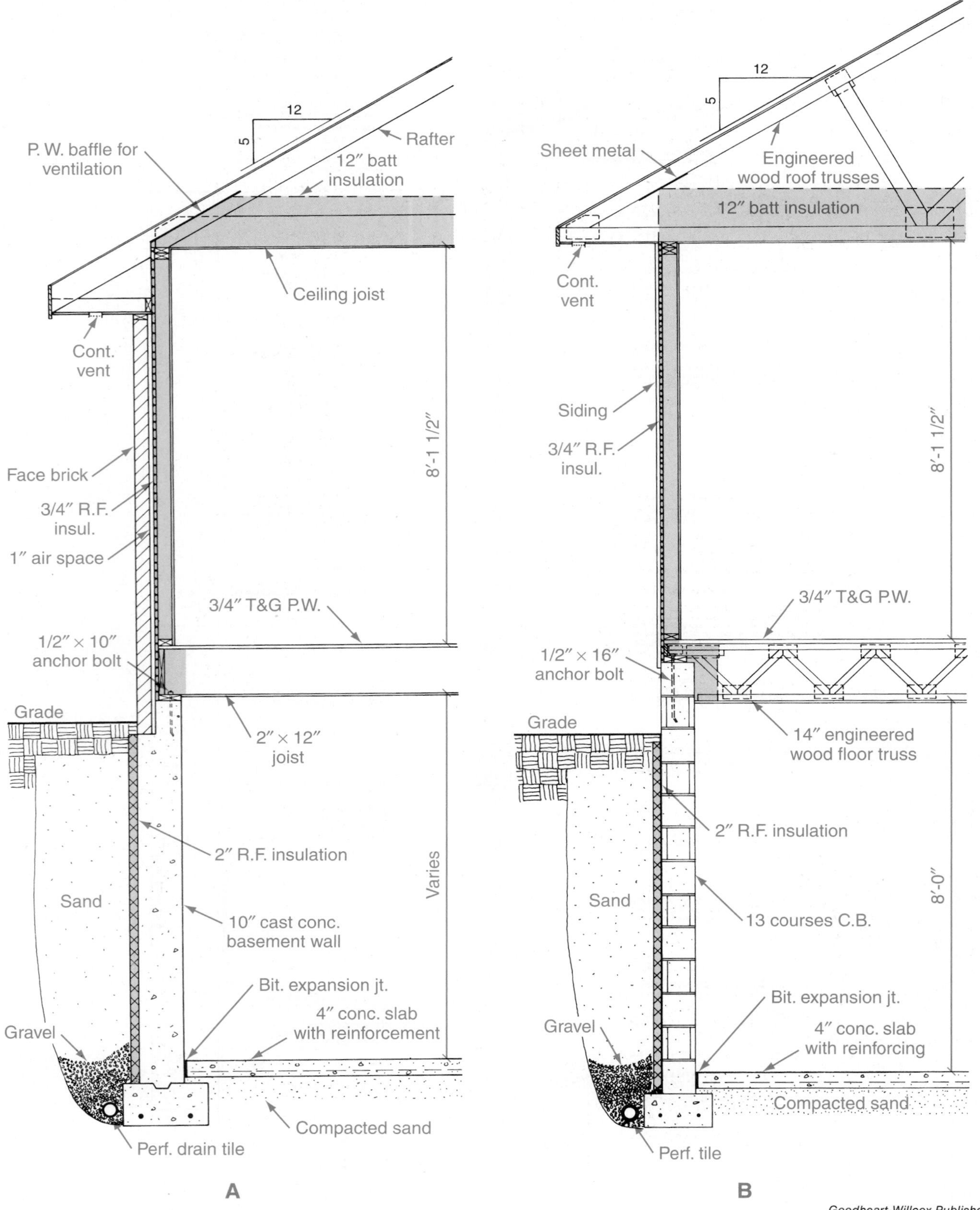

Figure 22-6. A typical wall section shows the construction of the majority of the walls in a structure. A—Typical wall section for a brick veneer structure with a basement. B—Typical wall section for a frame structure with a basement.

Specifying Building Section Location

To read a building section correctly, you need to know where on the building the section was "taken"—where the section cuts through the house. The location of each section in a set of working drawings is typically shown on the floor plan. Depending on the information to be shown, some sections are identified on the foundation plan. A ***cutting-plane line*** is drawn across the plan drawing to identify the location and extent of the section. See **Figure 22-8**.

Identifying Sections

Most sets of plans contain more than one building section. To identify the sections, the first section is labeled A-A, the second is labeled B-B, and so on. The floor plan in **Figure 22-8** has four sections: A-A through D-D. In this case, sections

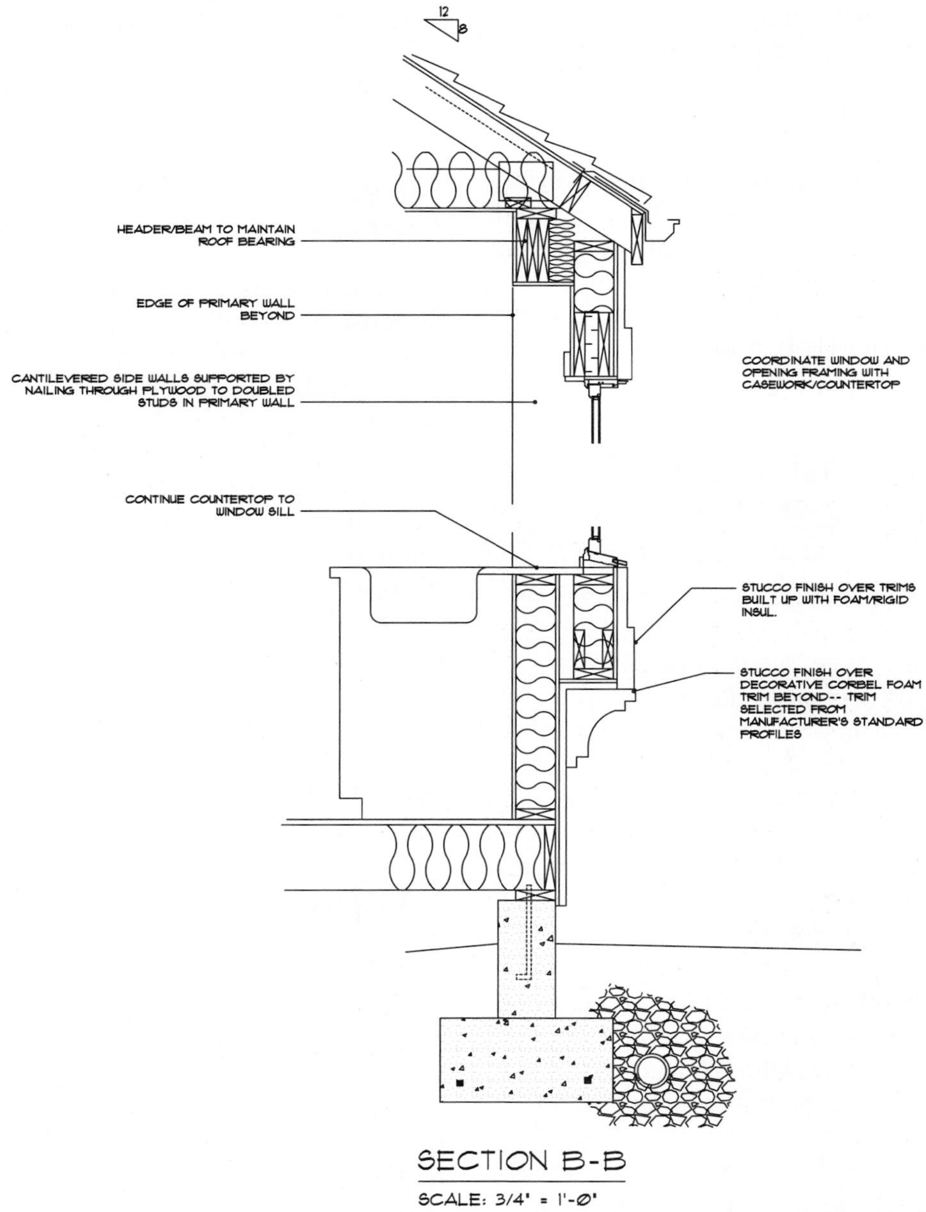

Goodheart-Willcox Publisher

Figure 22-7. A specific wall section was needed for the box window to be built over the sink in this kitchen. This is the only place in the house where a box window will be installed.

Employability
Using Social Media

Social media is used by some architectural firms to reach current customers and find new ones. Because social media is so readily available and easy to use, those who are writing communications for the organization must be prudent when using sites such as Facebook or Twitter for business purposes. Remember that it is unethical to "spam" customers who have not requested to be on an organization's mailing list. Keep your messages honest and return messages from those who have taken time to respond to your communication. Use good judgment and represent the organization in a professional manner.

Activity

Contact several architectural firms in your area and ask how they use social media for marketing and advertising purposes. Find out what guidelines employees are given for using social media for company business. Do any of the firms have rules about using social media for personal business? Write a summary of your findings.

A-A and B-B are full building sections, section C-C is a wall section, and section D-D is a partial building section. Notice that an identifying letter is included at each end of the cutting-plane line. The actual section drawings are labeled SECTION A-A, SECTION B-B, and so on.

Green Architecture
Sustainability Plan

Many companies in the architectural field now include a sustainability plan in their formal company business plans. A *sustainability plan* contains guidelines and procedures to help an organization use and manage resources in a way that meets needs without harming the environment. As the demands on our natural resources increase, companies must implement sustainable practices to safeguard environmental health, economic growth, and quality of life. The creation of a sustainability plan may rely on individual employee input, but the goals are simple. The sustainable practices a company implements must focus on reducing the use of materials, energy, and water; reducing the pollution put out by the company; reducing the amount of waste produced by the company; and using more non-toxic, recycled, and remanufactured materials. Communication and education within the company are necessary to meet these goals.

Longitudinal and Transverse Sections

A full section that runs across the longest dimension of a building is known as a ***longitudinal building section***. Section B-B in **Figure 22-8** is a longitudinal section. A ***transverse building section*** is perpendicular (90°) to the longitudinal building section. It cuts across the width of the building. Longitudinal and transverse sections show different information; therefore, both are often needed in a set of plans. Section A-A in **Figure 22-8** is a transverse section.

If full sections are shown on both the floor plan and the foundation plan, both longitudinal and transverse building sections should be placed in the same location on both plans for consistency. The same is true for partial building sections and wall sections.

Preparing to Draw Building Sections

Many questions will need to be answered before you can draw accurate building sections. Some questions will depend on the individual project. For example, suppose a home is to be built in an area that has a "rainy season." You may need to ask how the foundation and walls should be constructed to best prevent water damage to the home and its foundation in case of high water or flood.

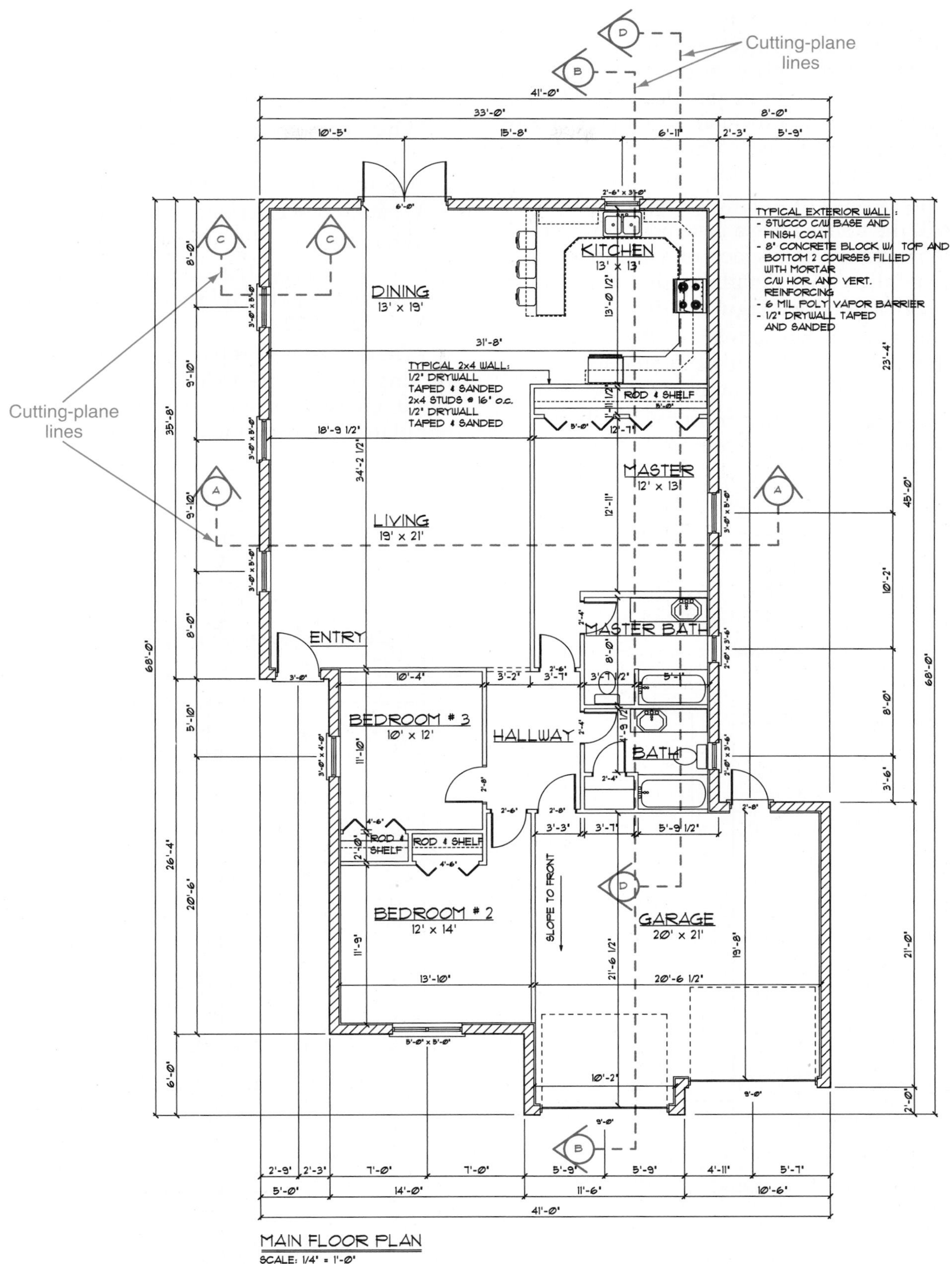

Goodheart-Willcox Publisher

Figure 22-8. The locations of building sections are shown on the floor plan and sometimes on the foundation plan. This floor plan shows the locations of four different building sections.

Other questions, like those that follow, should be asked for every project. These questions are only a few of the most critical questions you should ask before beginning to draw the sections. They certainly do not include all of the questions you may need to answer. Consider each design or building project individually.

- What type of foundation will be used? Will the house have a basement, a raised floor with a crawl space, or a slab-on-grade foundation? Are details needed to clarify its construction? See **Figure 22-9**.
- How will the house relate to the existing grade? Must the grade be altered to accommodate the structure?
- What are the heights from the finished floors to the finished ceilings? Consider the basement and each floor of the house separately.
- Will standard rough opening heights be used for windows and doors? See **Figure 22-10**.
- What type of roof construction is planned? Are details needed to clarify construction requirements? See **Figure 22-11**.
- What kind of exterior materials will be used?
- What type of soffit, if any, will be used?
- Are special construction methods and/or fasteners required for structural connections? See **Figure 22-12**.

When you are preparing to draw building sections, be very careful to ensure that all of your height measurements are precise. Remember that plan view drawings do not include height

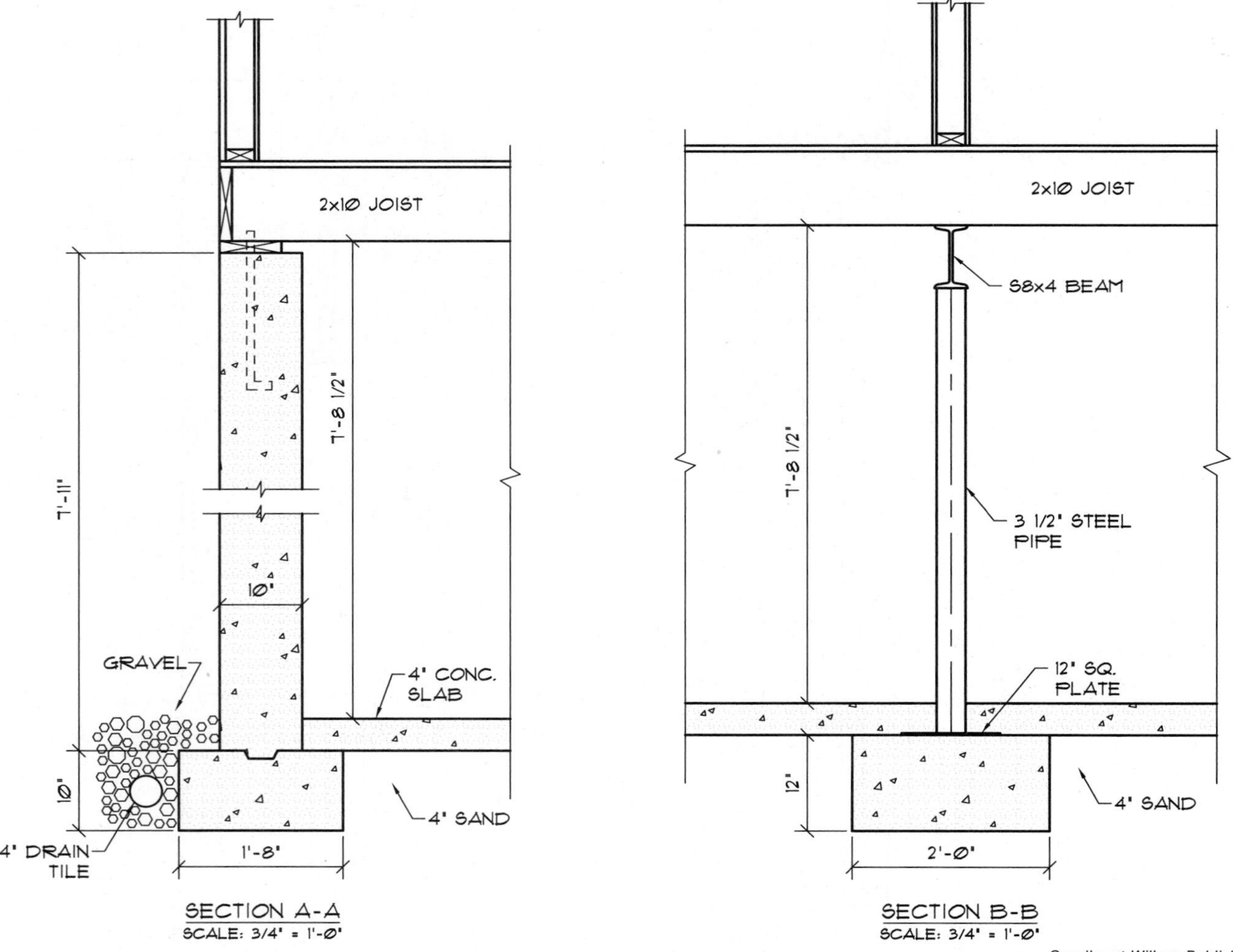

Figure 22-9. Foundation detail sections like these may be needed, depending on the type of foundation to be used and any special circumstances in the design project.

pics721/Shutterstock.com

Figure 22-10. Standard framing would not work for the front entrance to this home. What kind of building section(s) might be required?

information. The contractor will depend on the building sections to make certain the building is constructed correctly.

Drawing Building Sections

After you have gathered all of the necessary information, you can begin drawing the building sections for a project. Procedures are given in this chapter for using both manual and CADD techniques.

Procedure Manual Drafting

Drawing a Full Building Section

The steps that follow describe the procedure for using manual drafting to draw a full building section. The steps can be adapted as necessary to create partial sections and wall sections. Although many of these steps may be automated in your CADD software, understanding the basic steps will give you the foundation you need to use the CADD software wisely.

1. Collect the essential size information as described in the previous section. *A guess is not good enough*. You must know the specific dimensions and construction procedures to be used before you can draw a building section.
2. Choose a scale. Plan to use a scale that will adequately show the elements of the section.

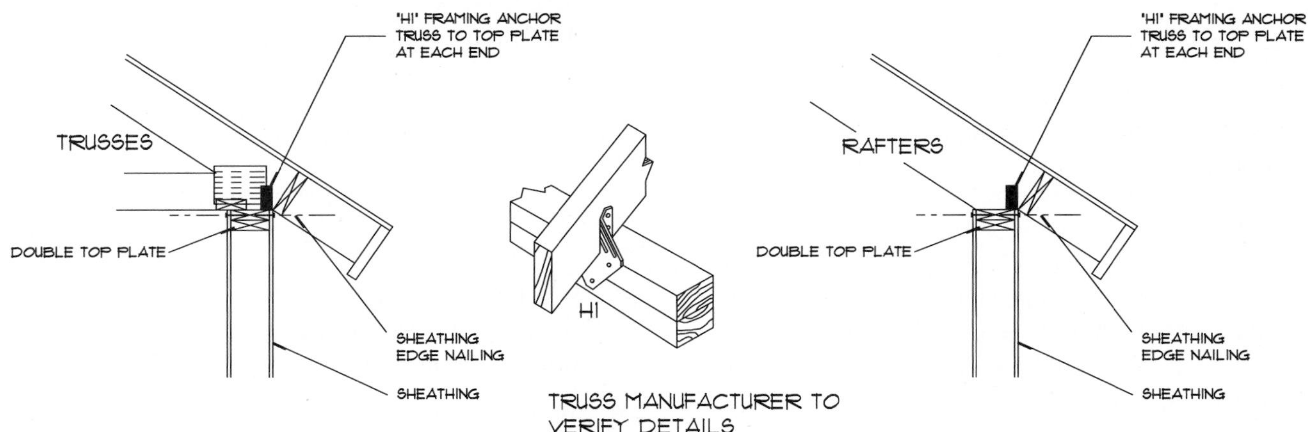

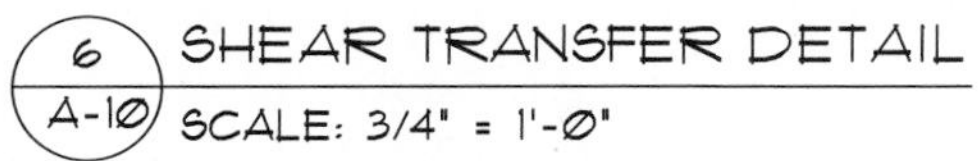

Lizz Layman

Figure 22-11. These sections were drawn to show framing details and structural connections for a roof with trusses or rafters.

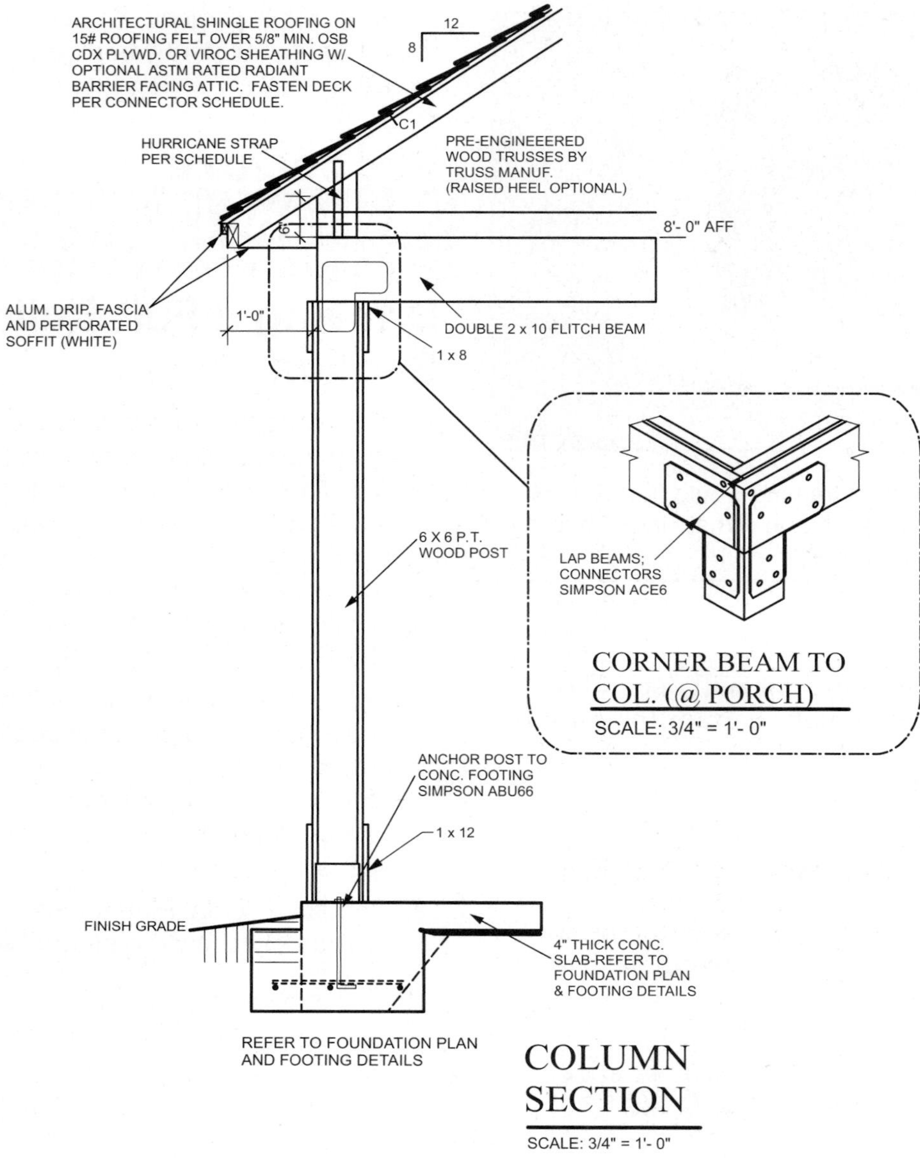

Andrew Ray

Figure 22-12. This column section includes a detail drawing to clarify structural connections between beams and columns.

Common scales used include: 1/2″ = 1′-0″, 3/4″ = 1′-0″, and 1″ = 1′-0″ for wall sections, 1/2″ = 1′-0″ to 3/4″ = 1′-0″ for partial building sections, and 1/4″ = 1′-0″ for full building sections. Remember, these are typical suggested scales for use on the sections. Office or school practices will determine the actual scales you use.

3. Lay out and draw the footing, foundation wall, and floor slab. If the house has a basement, locate the basement slab and show a portion of it. Position and draw the grade line. For this drawing, the house will have a simple monolithic slab foundation. See **Figure 22-13**.
4. After you have properly constructed the foundation, locate and draw the floor joists or trusses and the wall and roof structures. In **Figure 22-14**, the walls and roof have been added. After the walls are completely roughed in, it is wise to sit back and look at the structure carefully to be sure it represents good building practice.

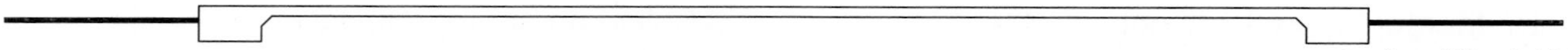

Goodheart-Willcox Publisher

Figure 22-13. Draw the monolithic slab first. Locate and draw the grade line.

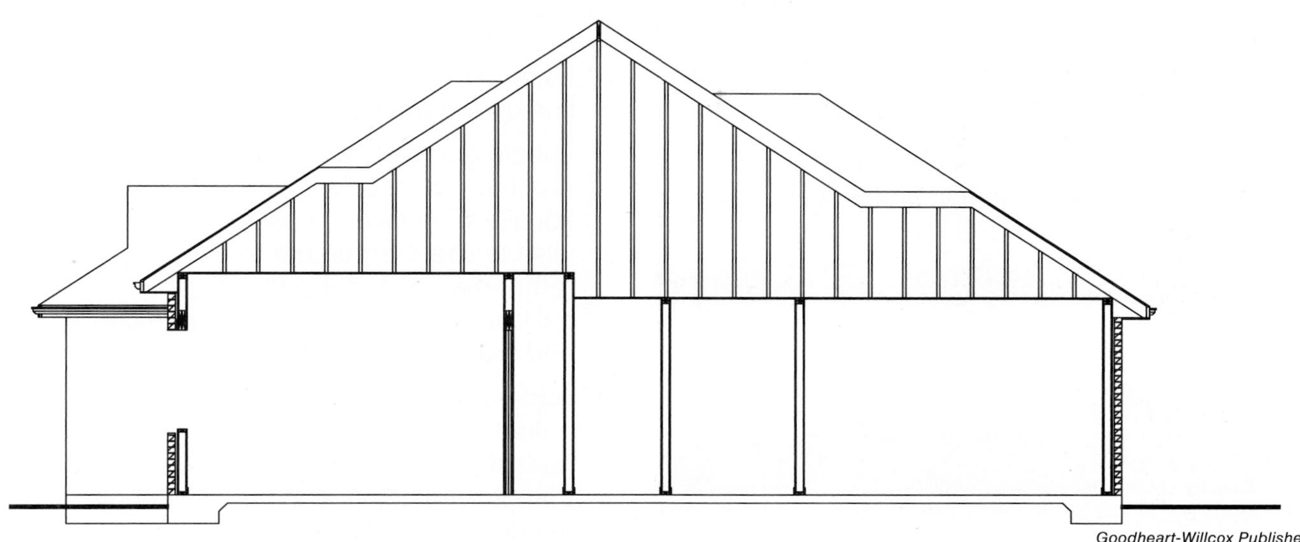

Goodheart-Willcox Publisher

Figure 22-14. Add the walls and roof structures.

5. Add details and material symbols (hatch patterns). Add details such as windows, gusset plates, drain tile, and a roof slope triangle. Include any material symbols needed for insulation, concrete, sand, gravel, or earth. See **Figure 22-15**.
6. Add dimensions and notes. Building sections should include all of the required dimensions—height from the finished floor to the ceiling, thickness of the floor system, footing thickness and width, foundation wall height, overhang length, and so on.

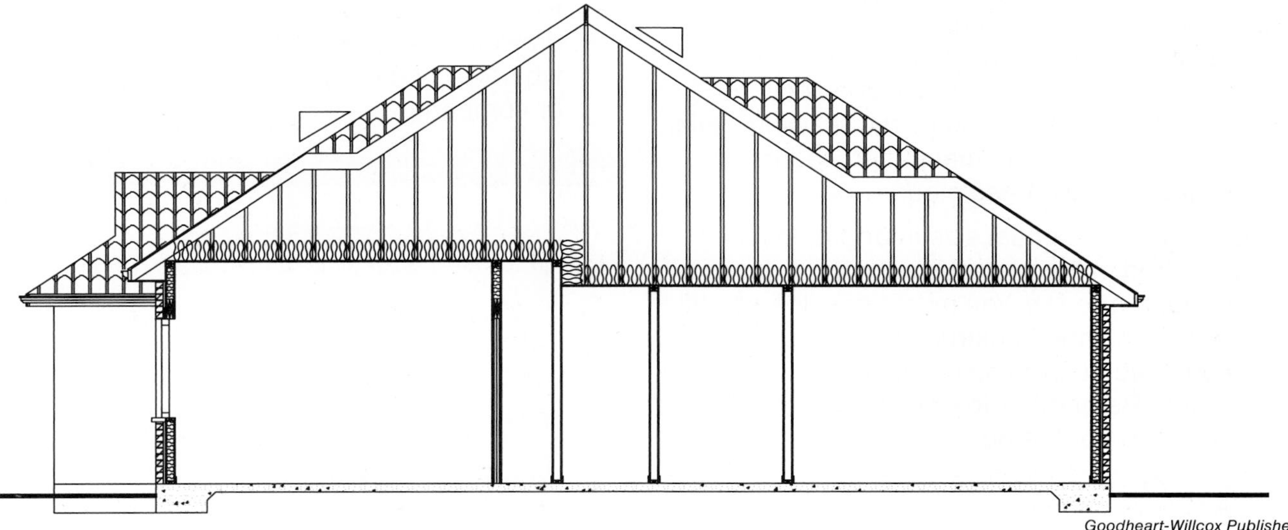

Goodheart-Willcox Publisher

Figure 22-15. Add details and material symbols.

Be thorough. Use local notes to identify materials. Identify the grade elevation. Add any other information that is pertinent for your drawing.

7. Add the title and scale.
8. Look over your work to be sure that you are finished. **Figure 22-16** shows the completed full building section. Remember, a building section—or any other drawing—is not finished until it complies with whatever practices are in force in your school or company.

Procedure

CADD

Drawing a Full Building Section

High-end architectural CADD programs can automate many of the drafting tasks used to create wall, partial, or full sections. You only need to indicate the cutting-plane lines on the floor plan where you want the building sections to be taken. The software automatically creates a completed wall, partial, or full building section drawing.

The following procedure assumes that your software does not generate building sections automatically. The procedure is similar to the manual procedure, although there are some differences. Remember to draw all objects at their actual size—do not scale the drawing. Refer to the illustrations in the manual procedure as necessary to follow these steps.

1. Collect the essential size information as described in the previous section. *A guess is not good enough*. You must know the specific dimensions and construction procedures to be used before you can draw a building section. Remember to draw all objects at their actual size for the building section.
2. Select an appropriate layer for the elements of the foundation or, depending on the CADD software you are using, copy the floor plan and foundation plan into a new drawing. Lay out and draw the footing, foundation wall, and floor slab. If the house has a basement, locate and draw the basement slab. Position and draw the grade line on the appropriate layer.
3. Locate and draw the floor joists or trusses and the wall and roof structures. Be sure to consider the layers, linetypes, and colors you wish to use. Remember to use actual sizes rather than nominal sizes. Zoom in on small parts so that they may be more easily seen and manipulated.
4. Add details and material symbols (hatch patterns). Add details such as windows, gusset plates, drain tile, and a roof slope triangle. Include any material symbols needed for insulation, concrete, sand, gravel, or earth. Some CADD programs will place the hatch patterns automatically for you.
5. Add dimensions and notes. Use local notes to identify materials. Identify the grade elevation. Add any other information that is pertinent for your drawing.
6. Add the scale and title on the appropriate layers.
7. Look over your work to be sure that you are finished. **Figure 22-17** shows the completed full building section drawn in CADD. Remember, a building section—or any other drawing—is not finished until it complies with whatever practices are in force in your school or company.

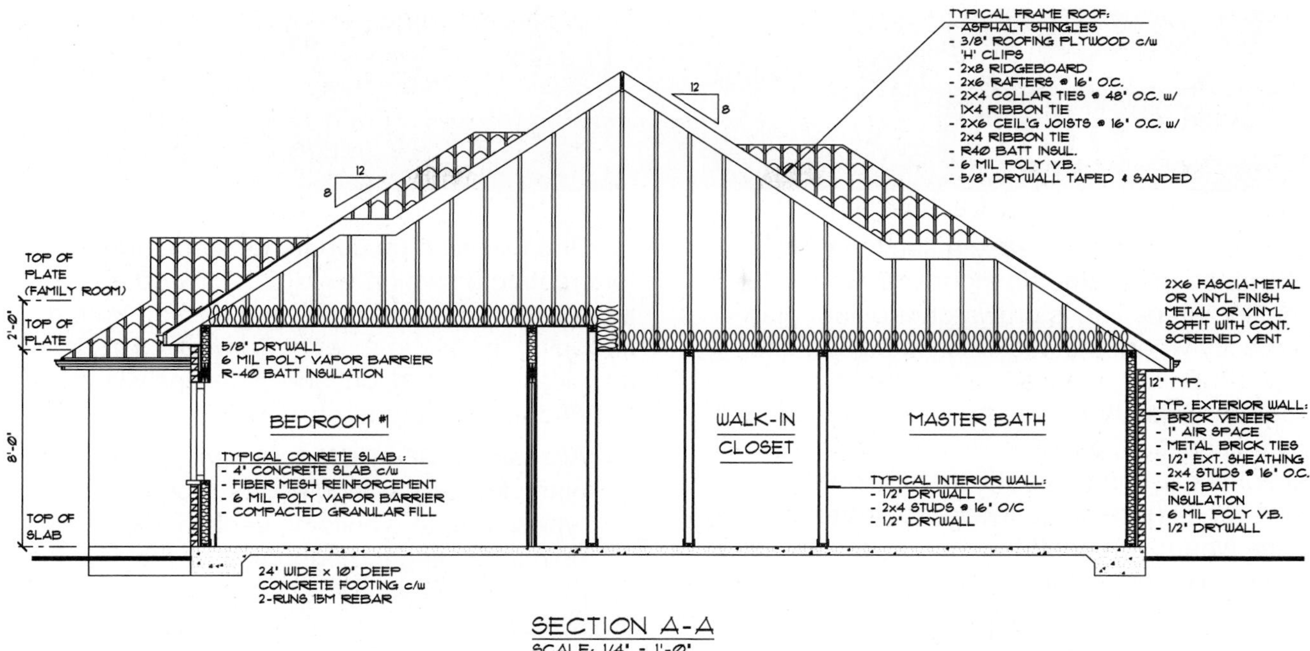

Goodheart-Willcox Publisher

Figure 22-16. The finished building section.

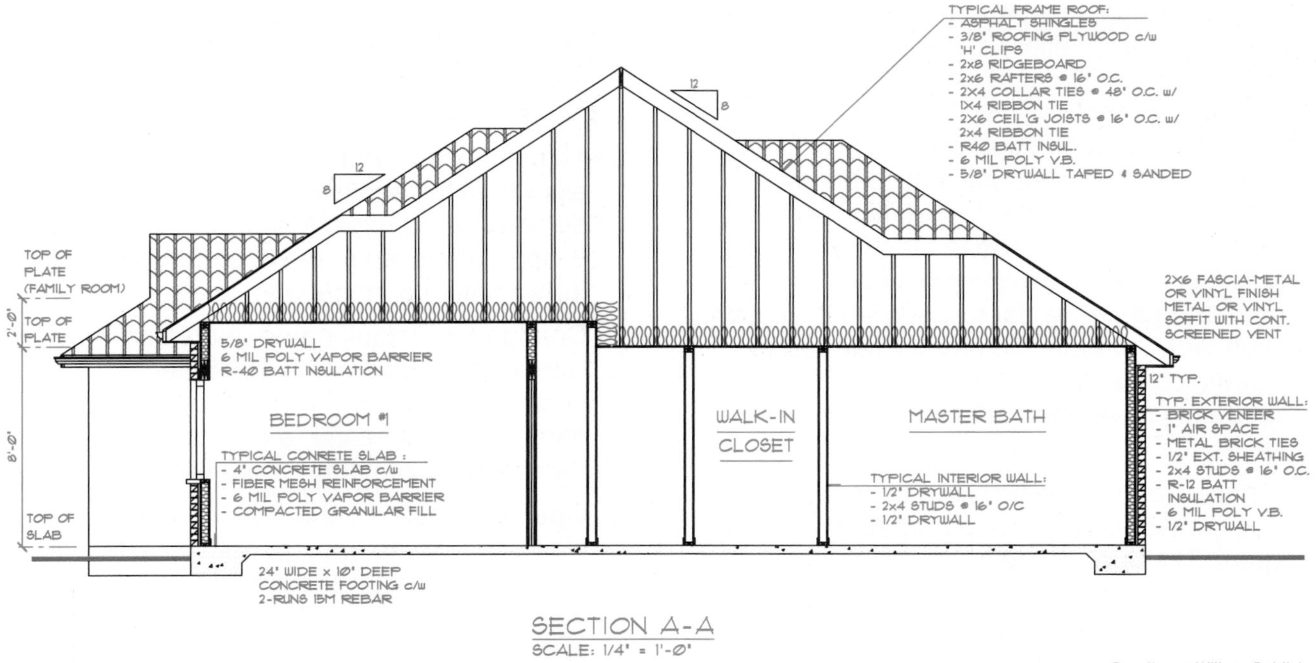

Goodheart-Willcox Publisher

Figure 22-17. The CADD version of the finished building section looks very similar to the manually drawn version, except for the use of color to distinguish various items.

Parametric Modeling

Creating a Section View

The process of creating a section view is automated in parametric modeling. Generally, a cutting-plane line is drawn on the floor plan to specify where the section is to be cut. The view is then automatically generated by the program. This allows you to quickly create a full building section, partial building section, or wall section for use in a set of construction drawings. However, in parametric modeling, there are often cases where you need to create a section view for modeling or visualization purposes, not just for the drawing documentation.

A common example is creating a section view in order to edit a wall profile. After drawing the cutting-plane line in the appropriate view, you can switch to the section view to display a vertical representation of the wall. Using the appropriate editing command, you can then select the wall and edit the wall profile. This activates sketch mode, where you can use sketching tools to adjust the shape of the wall. This is one way to create a wall opening. After you exit the editing command, the model updates accordingly. In parametric modeling, it is important to remember that changes can be made to the model in any view. Section views are commonly used in cases where features are easier to visualize in section. Section views are also commonly referred to in order to check dimensions or to see that components have been added to the model correctly.

There are three basic types of sections that can be created in a typical parametric modeling program. These are building sections, wall sections, and detail sections. A building section is used when it is necessary to show a section of the entire building. A wall section is used to create a section of a single wall. A detail section is used to show an enlarged view of a feature. Each type of section is created in similar fashion.

The following procedure describes the steps for creating a section view. This procedure is intended for creating a building section from a floor plan for use in a set of drawings. This is a typical sequence, but specific steps will vary depending on the program used.

1. Access the **SECTION** command in the floor plan view and select the appropriate view type to create a building section. Pick two points defining the endpoints of the cutting-plane line. Typically, a default section callout symbol appears, but it can usually be changed to a different symbol. The direction of the symbol indicates the viewing direction. If needed, pick the appropriate directional control to change the viewing direction. The section callout symbol is linked to the section view. When the section view is placed on a sheet, the section callout symbol on the floor plan updates to display the sheet and view number.
2. Adjust the section boundary establishing the extents of the section view. Typically, this can be done using grips. Adjusting the boundary is appropriate when the boundary extends further into the model than needed.
3. Change the default name of the section view. Use a descriptive name that reflects the contents of the view. Changing the default name makes it easier to organize different views and locate them when needed.
4. Open the section view and change the view scale to the appropriate scale. Make any adjustments needed to display the appropriate features. It may be necessary to change the appearance of a hatch pattern used for a specific component. For example, you may want to turn the visibility of the pattern on or off. This can be done by adjusting the visibility settings of the view.

5. If necessary, adjust the display of features below grade. Adjust the visibility and thickness of the grade line if needed. If the site plan has been created in the project, the grade line is generated from the topographical surface. To create the proper display of underground material, it may be necessary to access the visibility settings of the hatch pattern applied to the topographical surface.
6. In certain section views, you may want to add features where it is necessary to show more detail. For example, in an exterior wall section, it may be necessary to show where a certain type of brickwork is required. Instead of modeling additional features in 3D, you can add detail lines or detail components to the view. This technique is used when additional detail is needed and it is more efficient to draw the features using 2D lines. Detail lines and detail components are view-specific and do not appear in other views in the model. Some programs provide a library of detail components that can be used to represent common items such as structural blocking and lintels. Showing non-modeled features with detail lines or detail components is often an efficient way to complete sections and detail drawings in parametric modeling.
7. Add dimensions and notes. Use material tags or local notes to identify materials. Add any other information that is pertinent for your drawing.
8. Create a new sheet for the section view. Insert the section view onto the sheet. If needed, adjust the placement of text for the view title and scale.
9. Look over your work to be sure that you are finished. When you are sure the plan is complete, print or plot the sheet.

Summary

- Building sections inform the contractor or builder of any special or unconventional construction techniques to be used in a particular building project.
- The three basic types of building sections are full, partial, and wall sections.
- Full sections are generally drawn at the same scale as the floor plan, but partial sections and wall sections are drawn at a larger scale to show more detail.
- Cutting-plane lines on the floor plan or foundation plan identify the location of building sections.
- The procedures used to create building sections are similar whether using manual techniques or CADD techniques, unless the CADD software has a feature that creates sections automatically.

Internet Resources

Autodesk, Inc.
General and architectural CADD software

CAD Forum
Architectural CADD symbols and blocks

Chief Architect
Architectural CADD software

SoftPlan Systems
Architectural CADD software

Review Questions

Answer the following questions using the information in this chapter.

1. List three purposes for building sections.
2. What is another name for a full building section?
3. How is a wall section different from a partial building section?
4. At what scale is a full building section usually drawn?
5. At what scales are wall sections typically drawn?
6. What is the difference between a typical section and a specific section?
7. Describe how the drafter indicates where on a structure a building section has been taken.
8. List three questions you should ask before beginning to draw the building sections for a project.
9. What three items are the first items to be drawn on a building section, regardless of whether you are using manual or CADD techniques?
10. In what way can high-end CADD software change the procedure for drawing building sections?

Suggested Activities

1. Visit the websites of several window manufacturers to find a "special" window that interests you. Draft a wall section to show how you would incorporate that window into the wall of a home. The exterior construction of the home is up to you. Plot or print the drawing and make a presentation board of your section. Use the board as a visual aid for an oral presentation to the class describing the procedures you used to draft or generate this drawing.
2. Search online to find a floor plan for a home that interests you. Make sure the home has a garage. Recreate the floor plan using manual or CADD techniques. Draft a partial building section for this home to show the foundation and roof details for the garage. Remember to add a cutting-plane line to the floor plan to show the location of the section. Display the floor plan and your building section.
3. Search online to find a ranch-style floor plan that interests you. Recreate the floor plan using manual or CADD techniques. Draft a longitudinal building section and a transverse building section for the floor plan. Be sure to identify both sections on the floor plan.

Problem Solving Case Study

Your client wants to build a custom home in Glendale, Arizona. Like most other cities, Glendale reviews the architectural working drawings for a project before issuing a building permit. Find out more about the requirements for getting a building permit in Glendale. What building sections do you need to include to show sufficient detail to get the building permit for your client?

ADDA Certification Prep

The following questions are presented in the style used in the American Design Drafting Association (ADDA) Drafter Certification Test. Answer the questions using the information in this chapter.

1. Which of the following statements are true about building sections?
   A. A knowledge of construction methods is not necessary for drawing partial building sections.
   B. Building sections inform the contractor or builder of any special or unconventional construction, such as sunken or raised rooms, unusual foundations, or unique wall construction.
   C. A wall section shows more specific detail than a partial or full section.
   D. Dimension lines are used to show where on a building a building section is taken.
2. Which of the following statements are *false*?
   A. A partial building section indicates the least amount of construction detail and information.
   B. Objects in a full building section drawn using CADD are typically drawn at a scale of 1/4″ = 1′-0″.
   C. The only thing you need to know before you begin drawing a building section is where on the building the section will be located.
   D. The first building section to be specified for a building project is typically labeled SECTION A-A.
3. Match each type of building section with its description.

   Building sections: 1. Partial section, 2. Full section, 3. Specific section, 4. Wall section
   A. Runs across the full length or width of a building.
   B. Runs at least halfway across a building.
   C. Contains more detail than other types of sections.
   D. Conveys information about one specific part or feature of the structure.

Curricular Connections

1. **Language Arts.** The notes on a building section are a critical part of the drawing. They must be clear and easy to understand, yet concise enough to fit in a small area. Conduct research to find terminology and abbreviations often used on building sections that are not used in everyday English. For example, the abbreviation OC, o.c., or O.C. is often used to mean "on center." Make a table to show the terms you find, what each term means, and an example of how each can be used on a building section.

STEM Connections

1. **Math.** You are planning to create a wall section using manual drafting techniques and are considering the drawing scale to be used. The vertical dimension of the window to be shown in the wall section is 36″. How long would the lines representing the window be at each of the following scales?
   A. 3/4″ = 1′-0″
   B. 1″ = 1′-0″
   C. 1-1/2″ = 1′-0″
2. **Technology.** Many of the major window manufacturers include illustrations on their websites that show their windows in section. Find such an illustration and read about the window it describes. What special characteristics or features does the window have that are shown in the section drawing? Write a short report explaining why a section drawing might be needed for a wall that contains this window. Be sure to identify the manufacturer and part or model number of the window in your report.

Communicating about Architecture

1. **Reading.** With a partner, make flash cards of the key terms in this chapter. On the front of the card, write the term. On the back of the card, write the pronunciation and a brief definition. Use this chapter and a dictionary for guidance. Then take turns quizzing one another on the pronunciations and definitions of the key terms.
2. **Speaking and Listening.** Put together a collection of illustrations that show the different types of building sections discussed in this chapter. Explain to your classmates the different types of sections and the features they are used to show.

Chapter 23

Elevations

Objectives

After completing this chapter, you will be able to:

- List features that should be included on an exterior elevation.
- Describe the placement of walls, windows, and doors on an elevation.
- Explain how to show roof features on an elevation.
- Identify the dimensions commonly shown on elevations.
- Draw an exterior elevation that demonstrates proper techniques.

Key Terms

elevation
grade line
levels

An ***elevation*** is an orthographic projection drawing that shows one side of the building. The purpose of an elevation is to show the finished appearance of a given side of the building. When the term *elevation* is used in connection with a set of construction drawings, it typically refers to an exterior elevation. A variety of interior elevations may be drawn, but they are usually considered to be details.

Elevations supply height information about basic features of the house that cannot be shown clearly on other drawings. They also indicate the exterior materials, such as siding and roof covering. **Figure 23-1** shows a rendering of a residence and its main floor plan. **Figure 23-2** shows the front elevation of the house. Compare the features shown on the floor plan and elevation.

Required Information

Several features should be included on elevations. These include an identification of the specific side of the house that the elevation represents; grade lines; finished floor and ceiling levels; location of exterior wall corners; windows and doors; roof features; vertical dimensions of important features; porches, decks and patios; and material symbols.

Elevation Identification

Four elevations are customarily drawn—one for each side of the house. See **Figure 23-3**. In some instances, more than four elevations may be

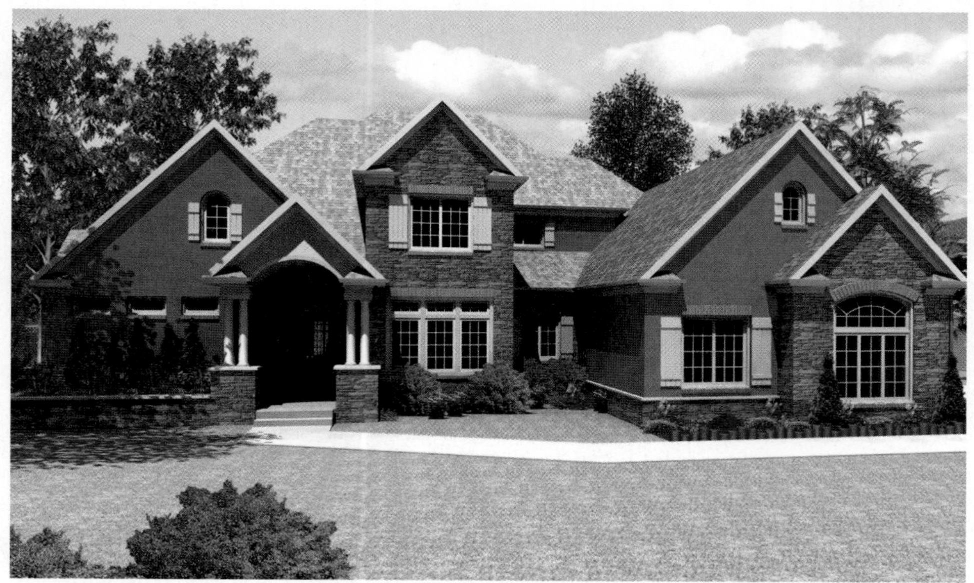

A

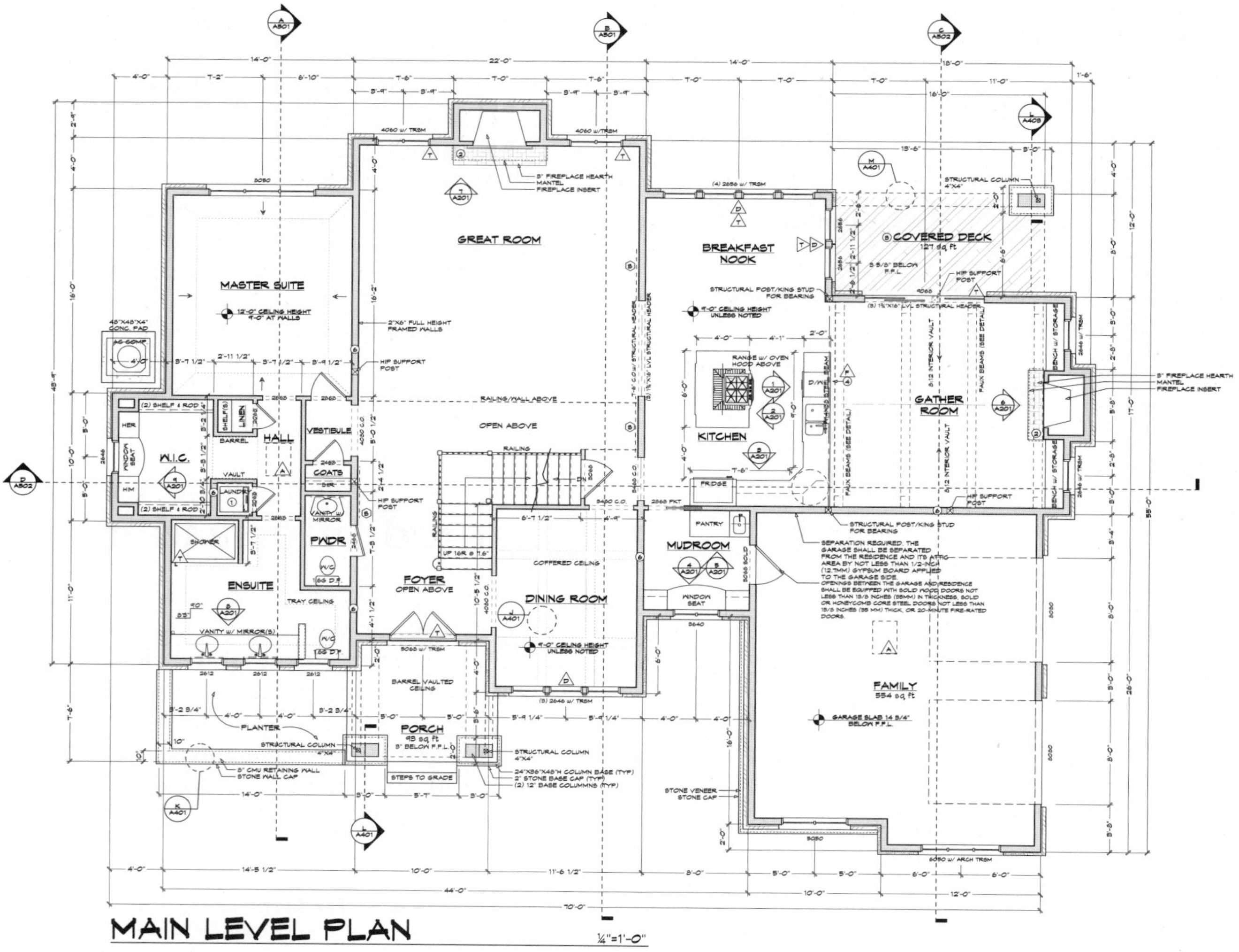
GREAT ROOM
MASTER SUITE
BREAKFAST NOOK
COVERED DECK
KITCHEN
GATHER ROOM
W.I.C.
HALL
VESTIBULE
COATS
PWDR
ENSUITE
FOYER
OPEN ABOVE
DINING ROOM
MUDROOM
PANTRY
FAMILY
PORCH
MAIN LEVEL PLAN
¼"=1'-0"

B

Martin Drafting and Design, Inc.

Figure 23-1. A—This rendering shows a typical residence. B—The main floor plan for the same house. The front elevation for the house is shown in Figure 23-2.

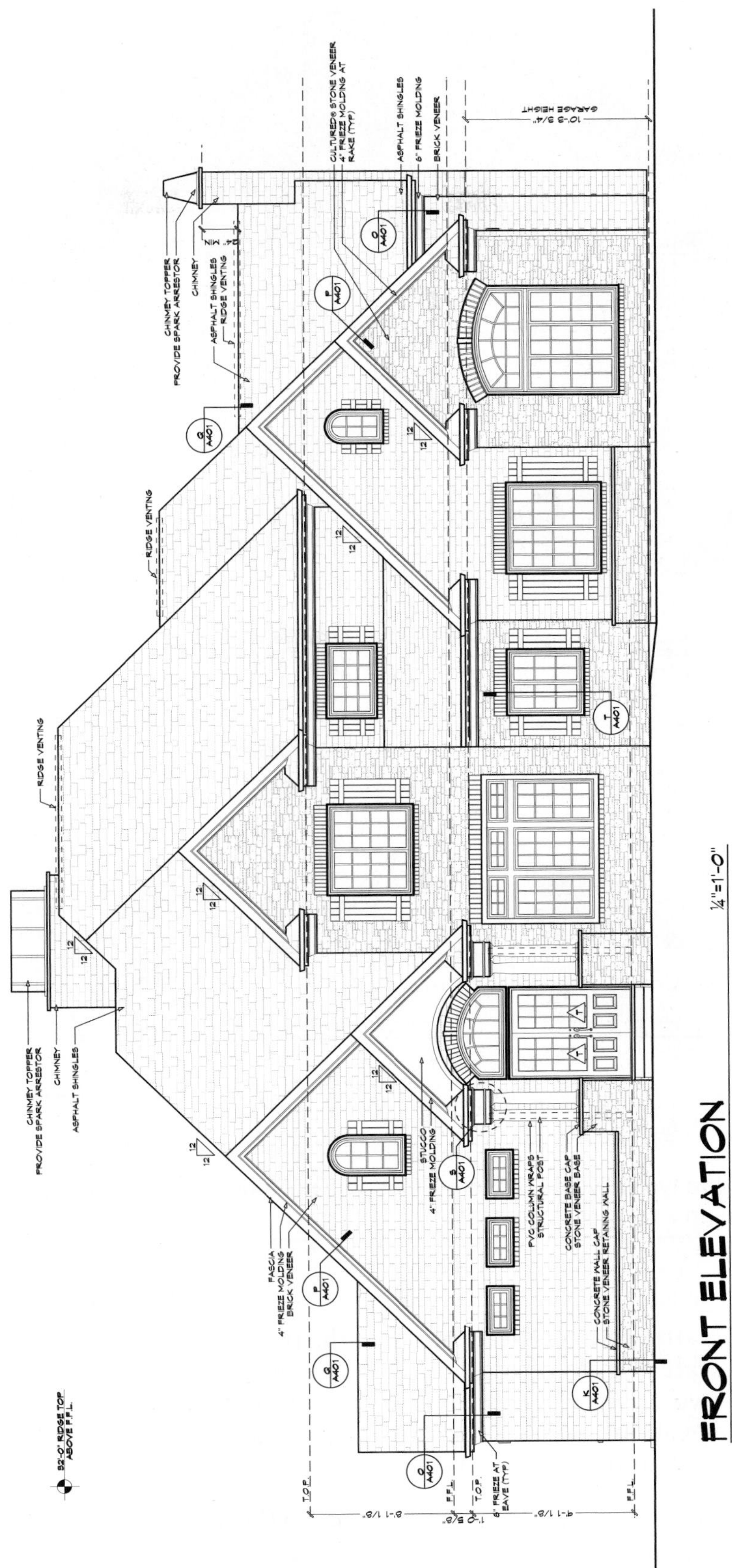

Martin Drafting and Design, Inc.

Figure 23-2. This front elevation is for the house shown in Figure 23-1.

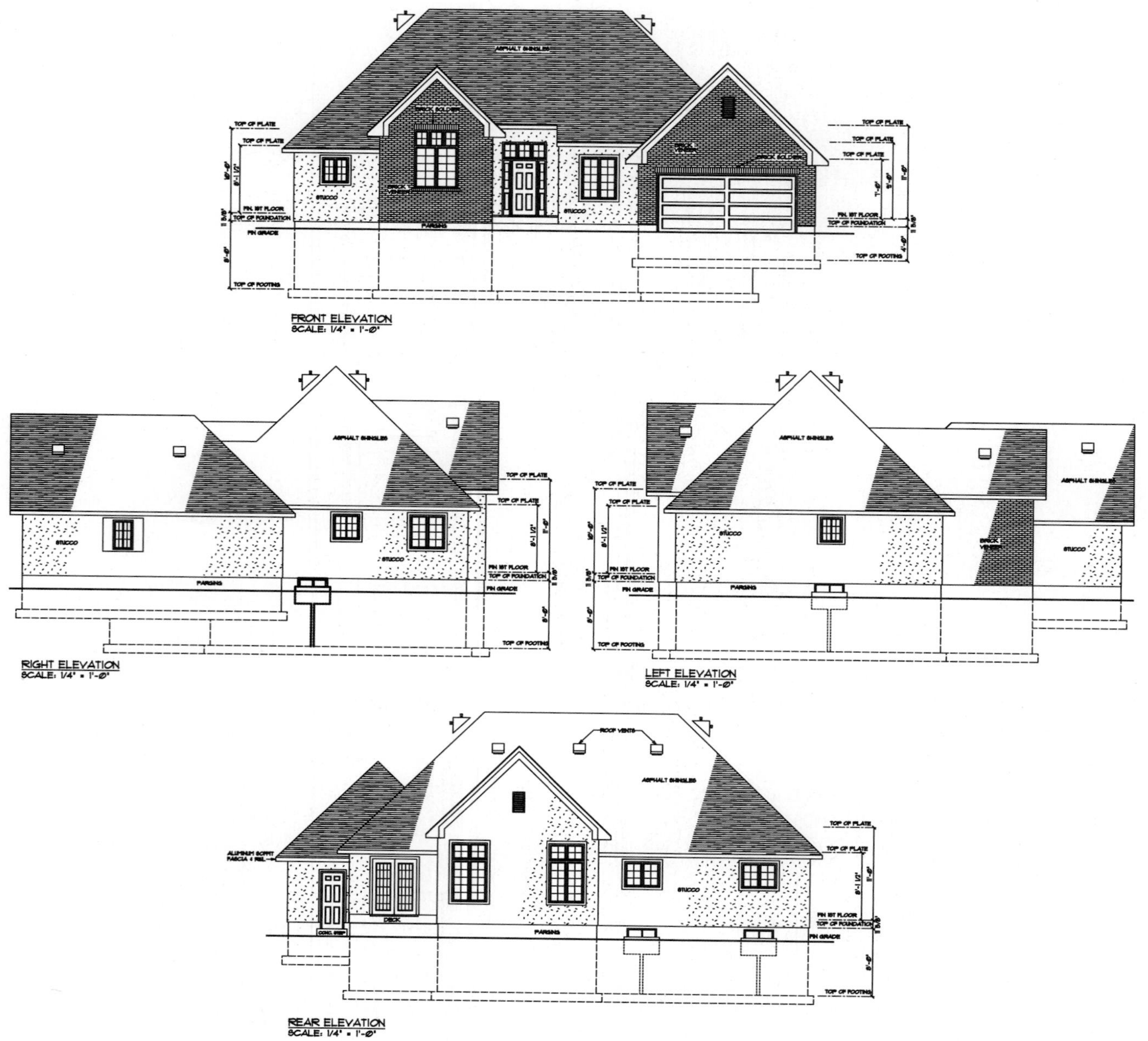

Goodheart-Willcox Publisher

Figure 23-3. Elevations are typically created for all four sides of a house. Each elevation is clearly labeled to show which side it represents.

required to describe the structure. Each elevation must identify which wall or side of the house is represented. The two methods commonly used to identify the elevation are by structure side (front, rear, right side, and left side) and by compass points (north, south, east, and west). The first method is preferred by most designers because there is a possibility of confusion when compass points are specified. The right and left sides of the structure are determined by facing the front of the building. The right-side elevation is then on the right side. Identify each elevation immediately below the drawing to avoid confusion.

Grade Line, Floors, and Ceilings

The reference point for most elevations is the ***grade line***. See **Figure 23-4**. Study the site or plot plan to determine the existing grade along each

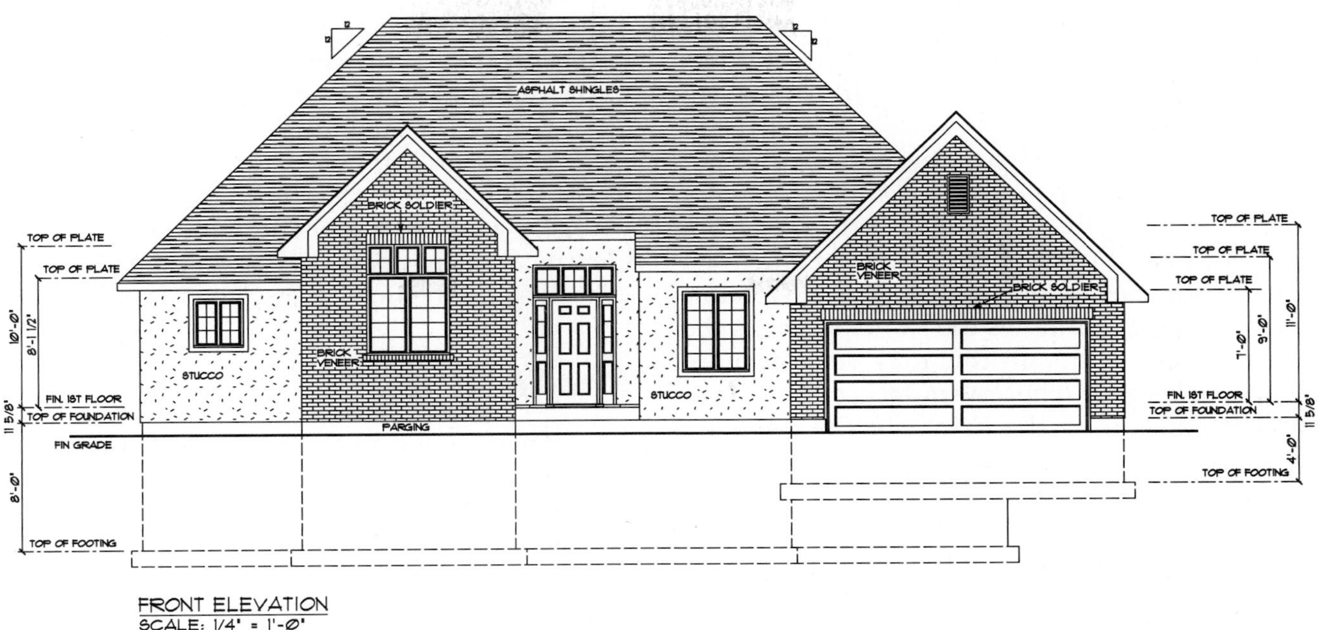

Goodheart-Willcox Publisher

Figure 23-4. In this enlargement of the front elevation from Figure 23-3, you can see the finished grade line and other important features given on an elevation.

exterior wall of the house. If the existing grade is not acceptable, a final grade line should also be indicated on each elevation that requires grading. It is often helpful to designate the desired elevation height of the grade at each corner of the house. This information is recorded on the site plan, as well as the elevation drawing, if the site is not comparatively level.

All features that are below grade should be drawn as hidden lines, as shown in **Figure 23-4**. Examples of below-grade features include foundation walls, footings, and window wells.

Two methods of representing floor-to-ceiling height are commonly used. The first is to indicate the distance from the finished floor to the finished ceiling. The floor and ceiling are represented using a centerline. The usual distance from the finished floor to the finished ceiling is 8′-0″ for the first floor and 7′-6″ or 8′-0″ for the second floor.

The second method is to show the construction dimension. This is measured from the top of the subfloor to the top of the wall plate. In this case, the construction dimension for the first floor is 8′-1 1/2″; the second floor dimension is 7′-7 1/2″ or 8′-1 1/2″. Carpenters usually prefer the latter method because it does not require them to do any calculation.

The minimum recommended height for garage ceilings is 8′-0″. Basements must have a clear headroom space of at least 6′-4″. All beams and heating ducts must be above this height. A full-height basement ceiling is more desirable and should be specified where practical.

Most building codes require that the top of the foundation wall be at least 8″ above the grade to protect the framing members from moisture. This requirement should be kept in mind when drawing elevations. The garage floor may be slightly higher than the grade, but should be at least 4″ lower than an interior floor when the garage is attached to the house.

Walls, Windows, and Doors

All visible wall corners are shown on the elevation using object lines. In rare instances, it may be desirable to show hidden walls. The exact wall height should be determined by drawing a wall section through the wall and locating the grade, sill, floor joists, and top plate. The section is helpful because the overhang will extend below the top of the wall in most instances. In other words, the exact wall height will be located above the line of the overhang in an elevation. Section drawings are discussed in Chapter 22, *Building Sections*. The basic steps for drawing a wall section are illustrated in **Figure 23-5**.

Windows and doors that are located on an exterior wall must be included on the elevation. Placement along the wall may be projected from the floor plan, but the vertical height is shown only on the elevation drawing. It is customary to place tops of windows the same height as the tops of doors, although this may vary in more complex designs. The lower face of the head jamb is considered the height of the opening. This dimension is usually 6′-10″ from the top of the subfloor.

Show sufficient detail on windows and doors to accurately indicate the window or door. If windows are hinged, show the swing using the proper symbol. See Chapter 21, *Doors and Windows*. If the windows or doors have brick mold or other trim, then show this on the elevation. The glass material symbol (hatch pattern) for an elevation may be used if desired. In some cases, you may want to show the window and door identification symbols or codes on the elevation, as well as on the floor plan. See **Figure 23-6**.

Roof Features

Showing roof features on an elevation drawing is important. It is here that the roof style and pitch are shown, as well as the chimney height and size. The roof pitch may be indicated using

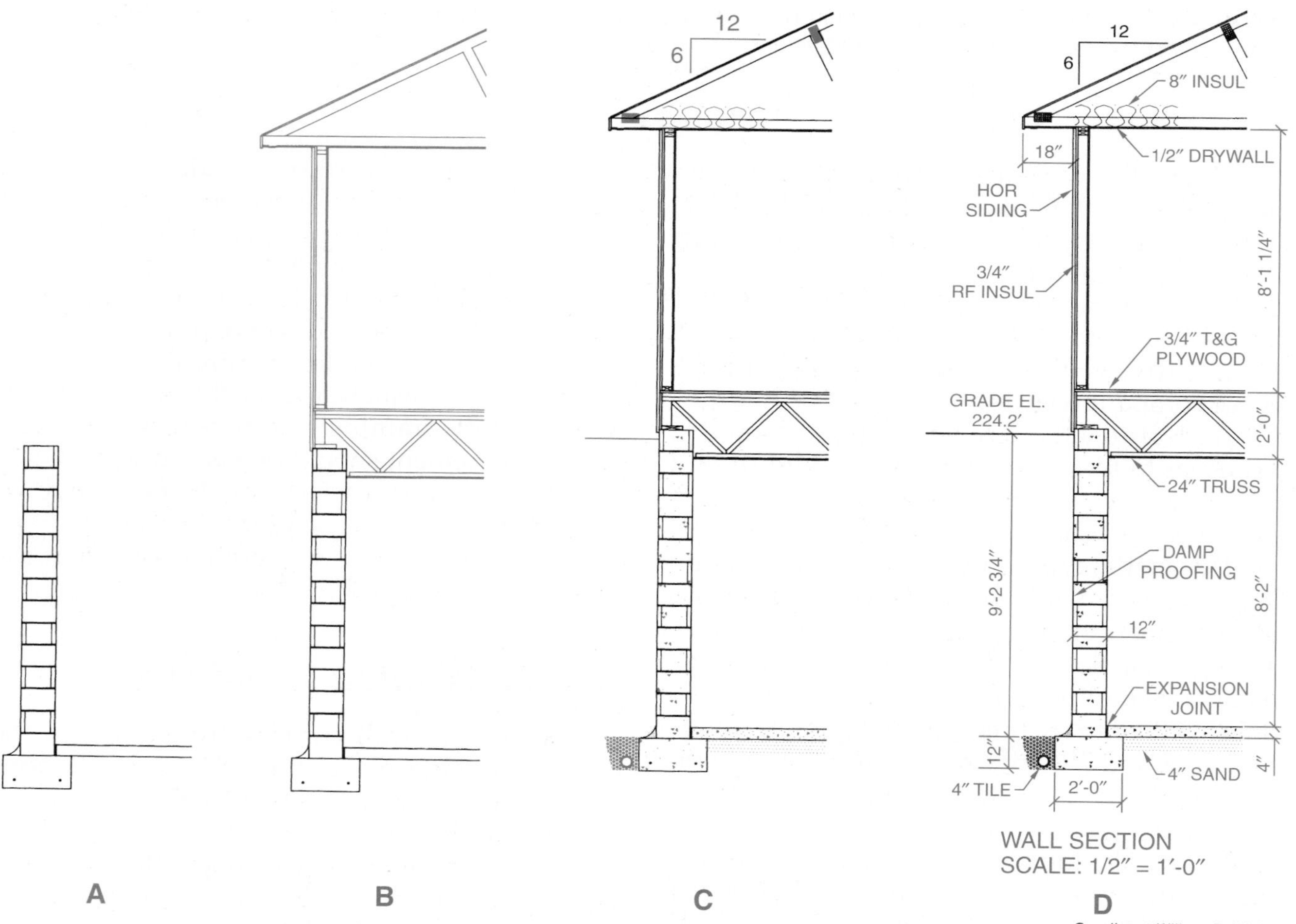

Goodheart-Willcox Publisher

Figure 23-5. The basic process for drawing a typical wall section. A—The footing, basement floor, and basement wall are first constructed. B—The first floor joists, first floor wall, and roof features are added. C—The grade line, drain tile, and material symbols (hatch patterns) are added. D—Notes and dimensions are added to complete the wall section.

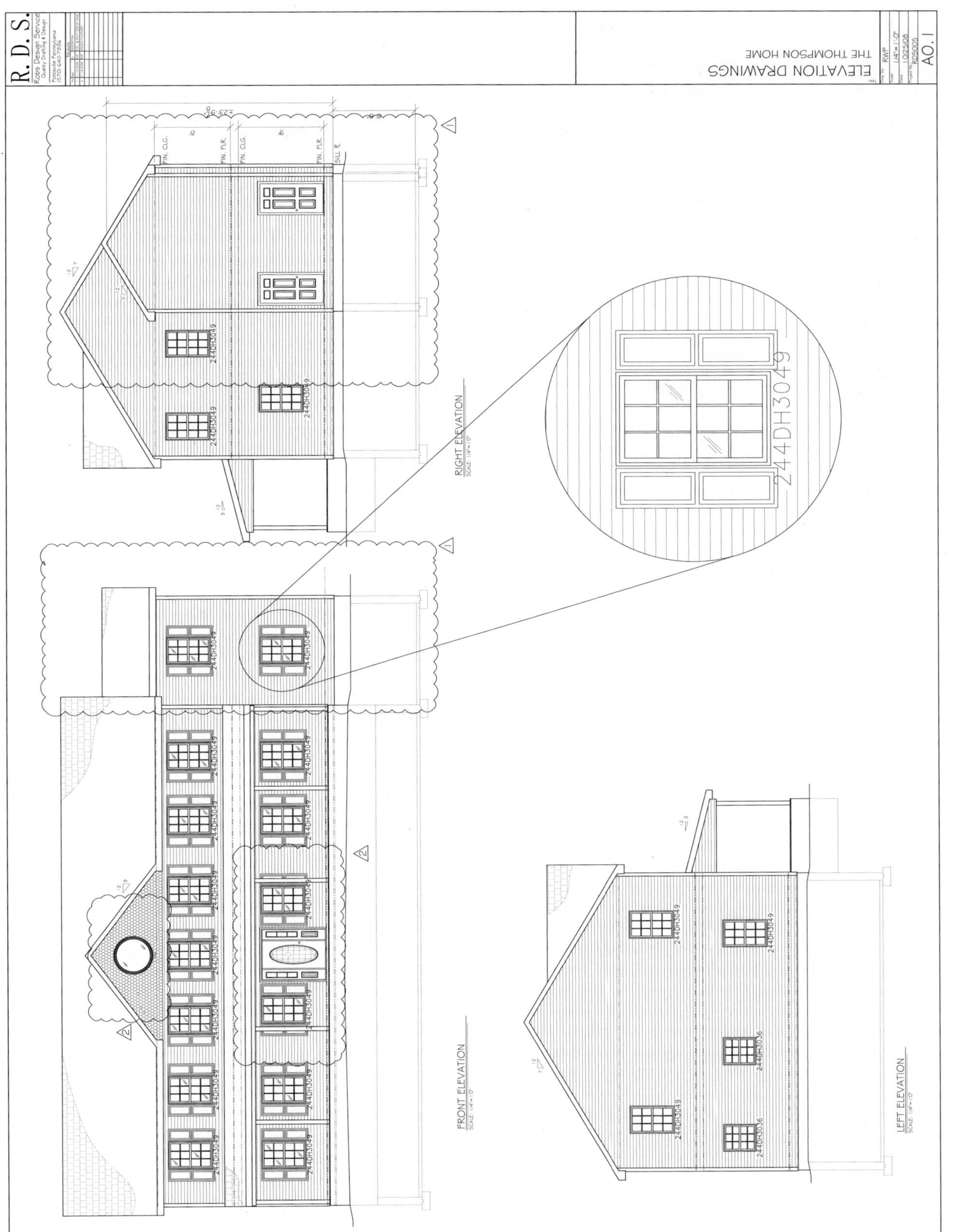

Rob Potts

Figure 23-6. In this home remodeling project, all of the windows will be replaced. Since the windows are an important part of the project, the part number for each window is given with the window in the elevations.

Green Architecture
Sustainable Exteriors

Exterior finishes for residential use are being developed with sustainability in mind. For example, one manufacturer has developed an eco-friendly stucco. Made entirely from natural limestone, it provides a green alternative to cements and even wood products that are highly processed. It can be used as is or colored with natural mineral pigments. It never needs painting, and it lasts for decades. This cuts down on maintenance, but more importantly, it eliminates the need for potentially harmful paints and other non-green materials.

Not all paint is toxic, however. New processes and technologies have enabled the manufacture of paint that is completely nontoxic and not petroleum-based, yet durable. Some of these paints are also biodegradable.

Many sustainable alternatives for exterior finishes seem expensive. In the long run, however, they can not only save money, but also help preserve the environment.

the fractional pitch or slope triangle. The slope triangle is usually preferred and it is placed on an elevation that shows the angle of the roof.

Gable ends must be drawn first to determine roof height. If more than one roof height is expected, the highest section should be drawn first. When a roof is complex, an elevation drawing cannot be completed without first constructing several details to determine various heights and termination points. The procedure for drawing a gable end is:

1. Locate the top of the upper wall plate and the centerline of the proposed ridge location. The ridge is usually in the center between the exterior walls.
2. Lay out the desired slope starting from the top-inside corner of the wall plate. A line from this point to the ridge will determine the underside. Note: A variation of this procedure is necessary for certain roof trusses.
3. Measure the width of the rafter perpendicular to the bottom edge and draw the top edge parallel to the bottom edge of the rafter.
4. Measure the amount of desired overhang. Do not forget to add the thickness of roof sheathing.
5. Repeat the procedure for the other side of the roof.

Chimneys that intersect the roof usually require more than one view to determine the points where they pass through the roof. First draw the view where the roof slope is shown. This view will indicate where the chimney passes through the roof. These points may then be projected to other views.

The chimney height above the highest roof point must be dimensioned. The International Residential Code requires that the chimney extend a minimum of 2′-0″ above any structure within 10′-0″ of the chimney and a minimum of 3′-0″ above the highest point where the chimney passes through the roof. Refer again to **Figure 23-2**.

Chimney flashing, roof covering material, and gable ventilators are also shown on the elevation. Use proper symbols and adequate dimensions and notes on the drawings to describe these features. Other features, such as roof ventilators, vent pipes, and gutters, may be shown if desired.

Dimensions, Notes, and Symbols

The dimensions that are located on the elevation are mainly height dimensions. Features that must be dimensioned include the thickness of the footing, distance from the footing to the grade, distances from finished floors to finished ceilings, overhang width, height of the top of windows and doors, and height of the chimney above the roof. Other dimensions may be required for features such as deck railings, retaining walls, and planters.

Notes should be included where additional information is needed or would be helpful to the builder. Some of the typical notes found on an elevation drawing provide grade information, exterior wall material notation, roof covering material identification, fascia material identification, and flashing material identification. Other notes may be required for specific situations.

Several symbols are frequently used on elevations. The roof pitch is always indicated and is normally shown using the slope triangle symbol. The exterior wall covering is usually a material symbol (hatch pattern). Many designers

Employability

Coping with Stress

Stress affects all of us at one point or another in our lives. Changes in family structure, getting married, having children, and deaths of loved ones all cause tremendous stress. All of these can affect your work performance. On the other hand, stress on the job can affect your family life. Therefore, one very important employability skill is the ability to handle stress.

The first step in handling stress—personal or professional—is to understand what triggers your stress. If you understand the cause, it is easier to deal with the result. For example, are you stressed at work because your workload seems too heavy? If you identify this as a stress trigger, you can then think about ways to handle it. For example, you could take a course or seminar to improve your work or time management skills. If your workload is completely unrealistic, you might want to talk with your manager about setting priorities that are agreeable to the company, yet remove some of the pressure from you. If you cannot find a way to reduce the stress at your job, you may even consider changing jobs.

Activity

Keep a log for one week. Every time you feel stressed, whether at school, work, or home, make an entry in your log. Describe what triggered the stress and how you handled the situation. At the end of the week, review your entries. What stress triggers can you identify? How might you avoid these triggers or reduce their impact in the future?

show material symbols extensively on the front elevation, but sparingly on the remaining views. Window swing symbols and cutting-plane lines are also drawn if needed.

Drawing Elevations

There are several accepted procedures for drawing elevations. The procedure presented in this chapter is a logical approach that yields fast and accurate results, if followed carefully.

Procedure
Manual Drafting

Drawing an Elevation

Follow these steps to construct a front elevation using manual drafting techniques.

1. Draw a section through the wall to be represented by the elevation. This section should be the same scale (1/4″ = 1′-0″) as the floor plan and the proposed elevation. The wall section drawing must be very accurate because it will be used to project the height of the wall and roof elements to the elevation. If all the exterior walls of the house are the same height and type of construction, then only one section is required. However, if some of the walls are different, a section for each type of wall will be needed. These section drawings may be discarded after the elevations are complete. Similar drawings will be made at a larger scale for the formal set of plans. Steps 1 and 2 are shown in **Figure 23-7**.
2. Place the floor plan directly above the space where the elevation is to be drawn. The exterior walls to be represented by the elevation should be facing down toward the elevation. Some drafters prefer to draw the elevation on top of the floor plan rather than below it. Either method is acceptable.
3. Project the height of the grade line, depth and thickness of footings, window and door heights, height of the eaves line, and roof height across from the section drawing to the space reserved for the elevation. These horizontal lines should be very light construction lines. Steps 3 and 4 are shown in **Figure 23-8**.
4. Project the horizontal length of exterior walls, windows, doors, and other elements down from the floor plan. These vertical lines may be drawn dark since their proper length will already have been determined.

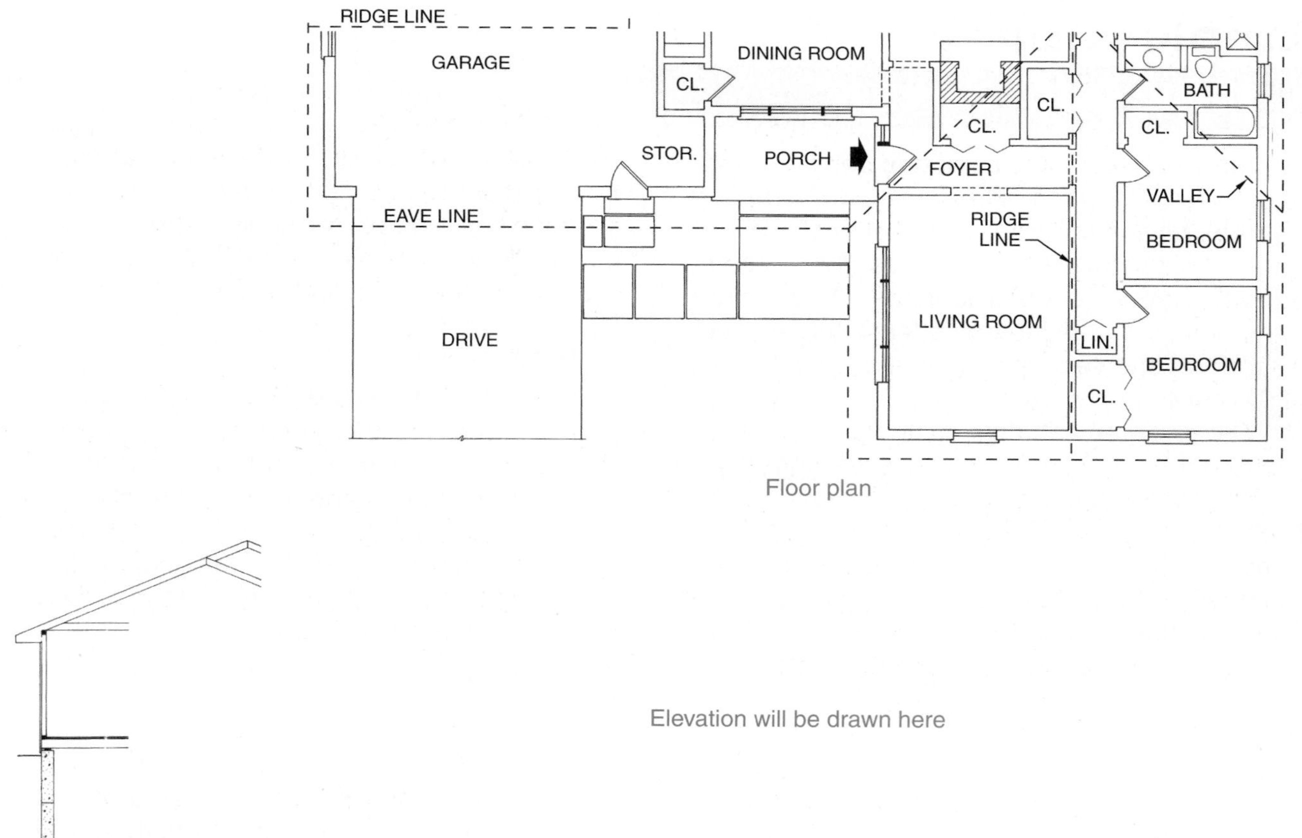

Goodheart-Willcox Publisher

Figure 23-7. Draw the floor plan and a wall section around the area in which the elevation is to be drawn.

5. Darken each feature and remove the construction lines. At this point, the elevation is complete enough to determine whether changes are desired in the overall design. Make any changes before proceeding. Steps 5 and 6 are shown in **Figure 23-9**.
6. Add features such as railings, window muntins, trim, window wells, and gable ventilators. Information on many of these features must be secured from reference sources such as Sweets™ product catalogs.
7. Add dimensions, notes, and material symbols. It is good practice to draw material symbols last since they may interfere with other information if drawn earlier.
8. Add the title and scale. Check the drawing to be sure that all features are shown as desired. **Figure 23-10** shows the finished elevation.

Repeat these steps for each elevation that needs to be drawn. It is customary to draw two elevations on a single sheet if space permits. For example, you may draw the front and rear elevations on the same sheet. See **Figure 23-11**.

Procedure
CADD

Drawing an Elevation

The procedure for drawing an elevation using CADD is essentially the same as for manual drafting, but there are some unique considerations. CADD packages vary in their ability to generate views automatically. With some

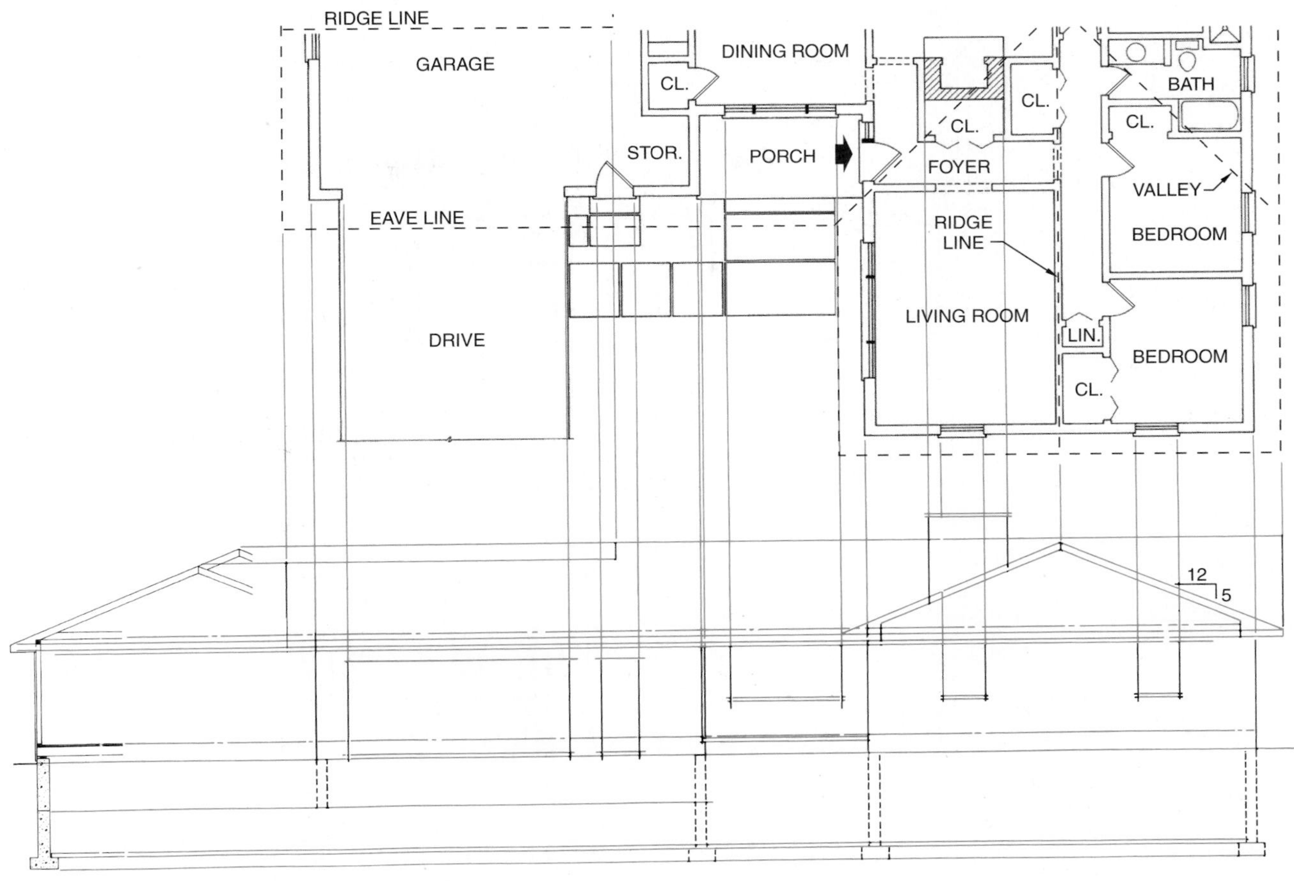

Goodheart-Willcox Publisher

Figure 23-8. Basic features of the house have been projected from the floor plan and wall section with light construction lines to the location where the elevation is to be drawn. Vertical lines can be darkened at this point.

CADD software programs, the drafter must draft every single line in an exterior elevation much in the same manner as when using a mechanical pencil. The following steps can be used to draw an elevation using a basic CADD program.

1. Draw a typical wall section to provide height measurements. **Figure 23-12** shows a typical wall section with sufficient information to construct a front elevation. Remember to draw all objects for the section at their actual size.
2. Place a copy of the floor plan above the space where the elevation is to be drawn. Place the side of the floor plan that will be shown in the elevation facing the area where the elevation will be drawn. Note: Only the information needed to draw the elevation is included on the floor plan copy.
3. Project features to be drawn on the elevation from the floor plan. See **Figure 23-13**. Use the software's construction line command, such as **RAY** or **XLINE**. You can project each line as it is needed, but it is usually more efficient to project them all at once. Projection lines should be placed on a separate layer to facilitate their removal when you are finished with them.
4. Locate the height of the grade line, depth and thickness of footings, and foundation wall from the section drawing on the elevation. All of these lines will be dashed (hidden) lines except the grade line. You may want to place these lines on two separate layers, because the hidden lines and grade line will be plotted at different widths than the projection lines. **Figure 23-14** shows the foundation completed up to the grade line.

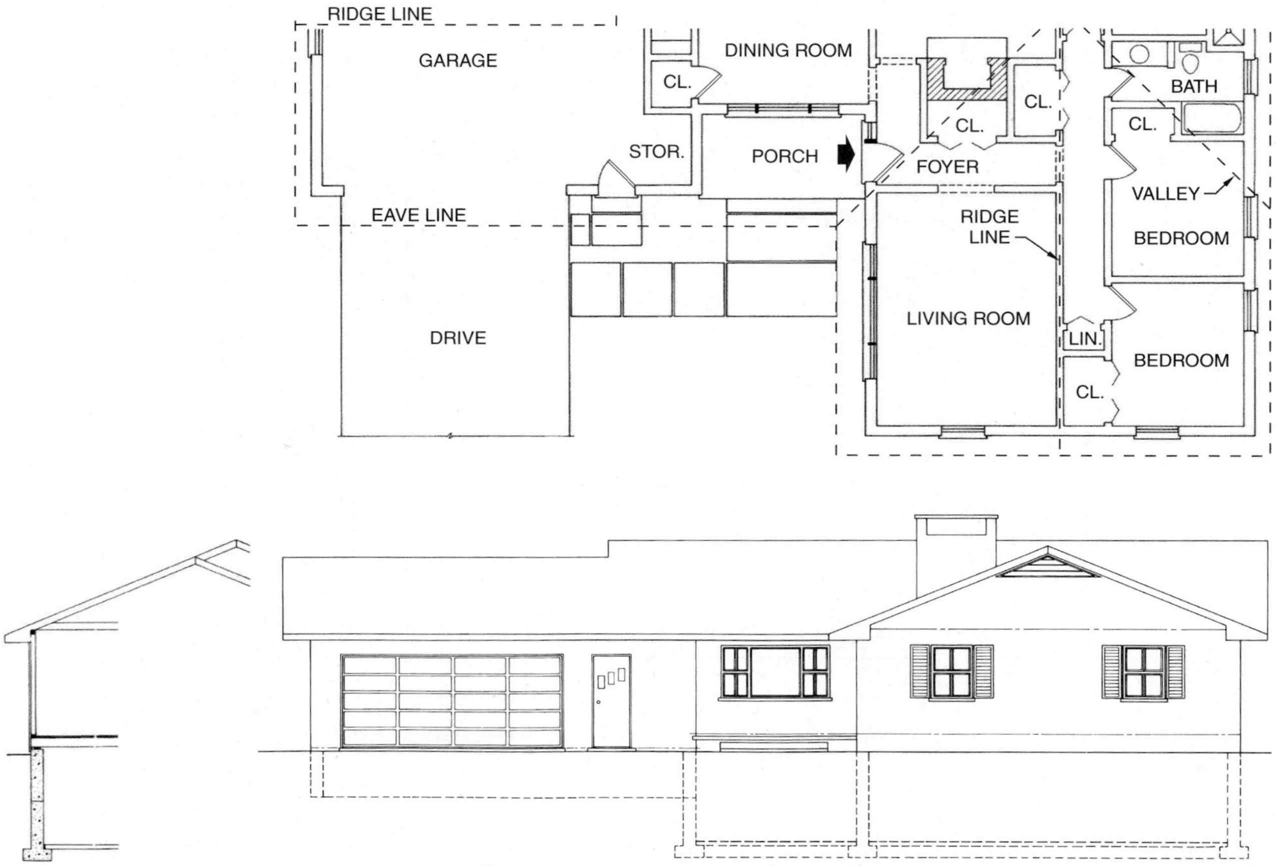

Goodheart-Willcox Publisher

Figure 23-9. Each feature has been darkened and construction lines removed. Note that some of the required dimensions could not be projected from the floor plan or the section. These must be secured from other sources.

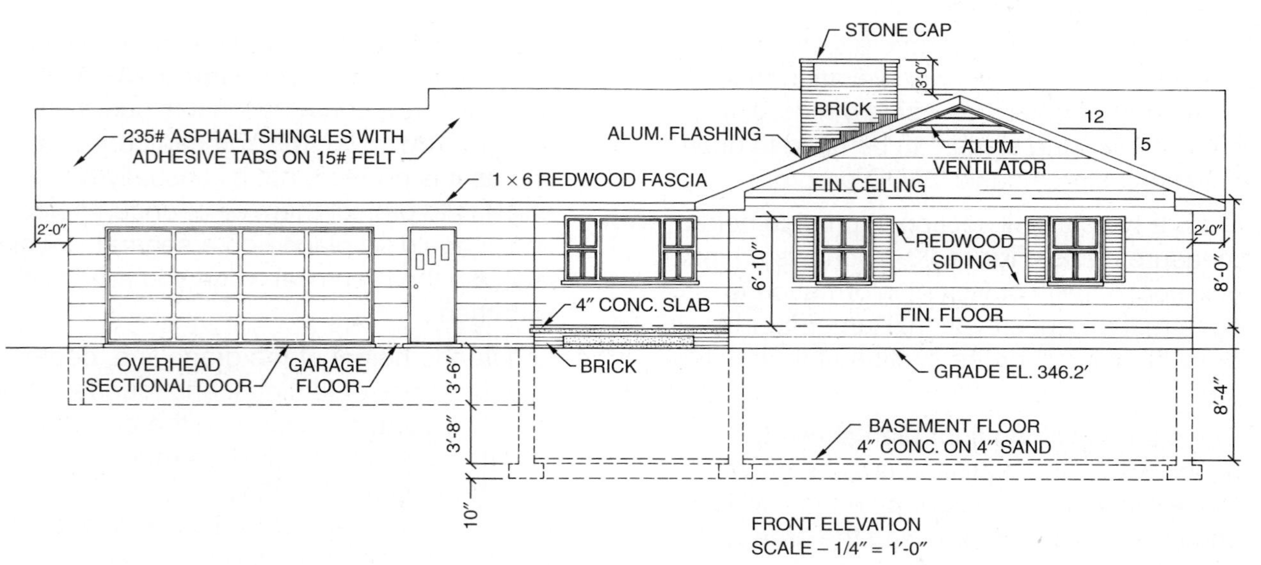

Goodheart-Willcox Publisher

Figure 23-10. Add dimensions, notes, and material symbols to complete the elevation.

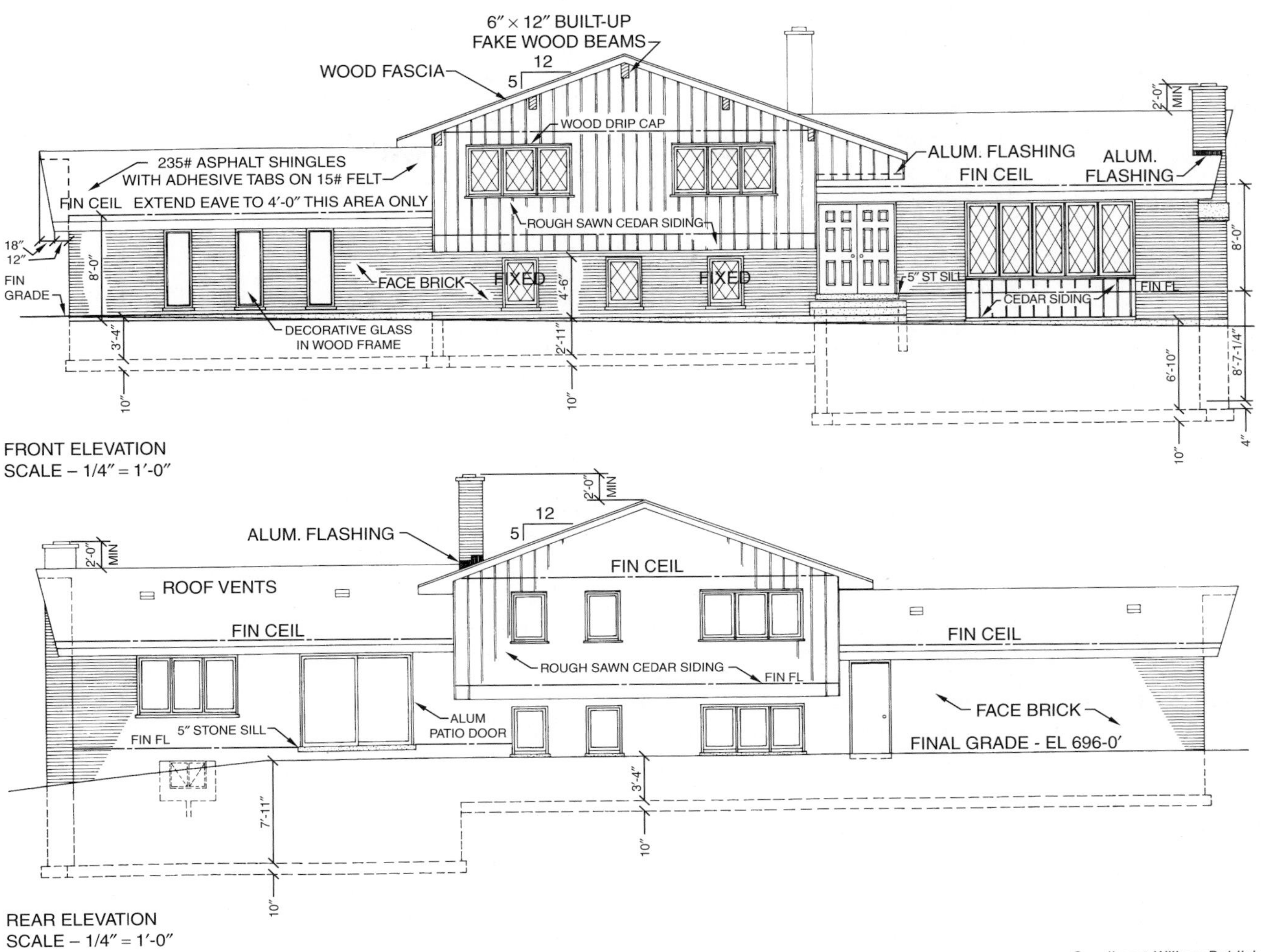

Figure 23-11. Two elevations may be placed on a single sheet when space permits. Notice that material symbols are used less extensively on the rear elevation.

5. Locate the wall height and roof lines on the elevation. The exterior walls above the grade can now be drawn, as well as the roof. The exterior wall lines should have a layer of their own because they will be a different width than any of the previous lines. See **Figure 23-15**.
6. Locate the height of windows, doors, and any other features. Windows are time-consuming to draw one at a time, so they should be developed and stored in the symbol library for use when needed. Remember, some CADD packages include manufacturers' door and window elevations and details. You can also get elevations from some of the major window manufacturers. **Figure 23-16** shows the windows completed.
7. Add dimensions and notes.
8. Add the material symbols (hatch patterns). Avoid hatching areas that contain text.
9. Add the scale and title last.
10. Hide or turn off the layer(s) containing the floor plan copy and wall section. **Figure 23-17** shows the completed front elevation.
11. Follow the same procedure to create elevations for the remaining sides of the house. Generally, material hatch patterns are used less on the other elevations, especially if the same material is used on all sides.

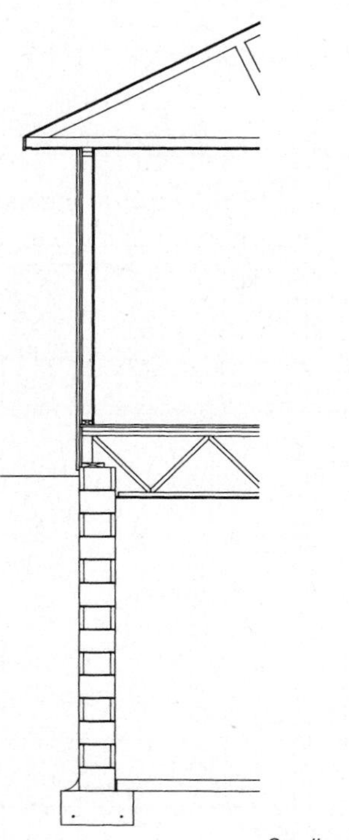

Goodheart-Willcox Publisher

Figure 23-12. This typical wall section was drawn with CADD and will be used to construct the front elevation.

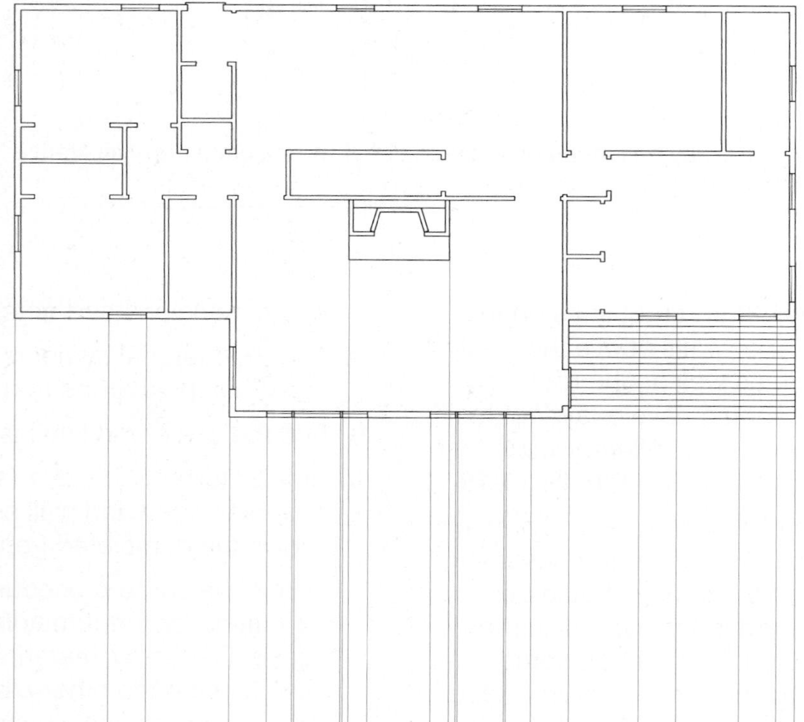

Goodheart-Willcox Publisher

Figure 23-13. The floor plan has been properly positioned to draw the front elevation, and projection lines have been drawn. Note: The typical wall section is off the screen at this point because of the zoom factor used to show details of the floor plan more clearly.

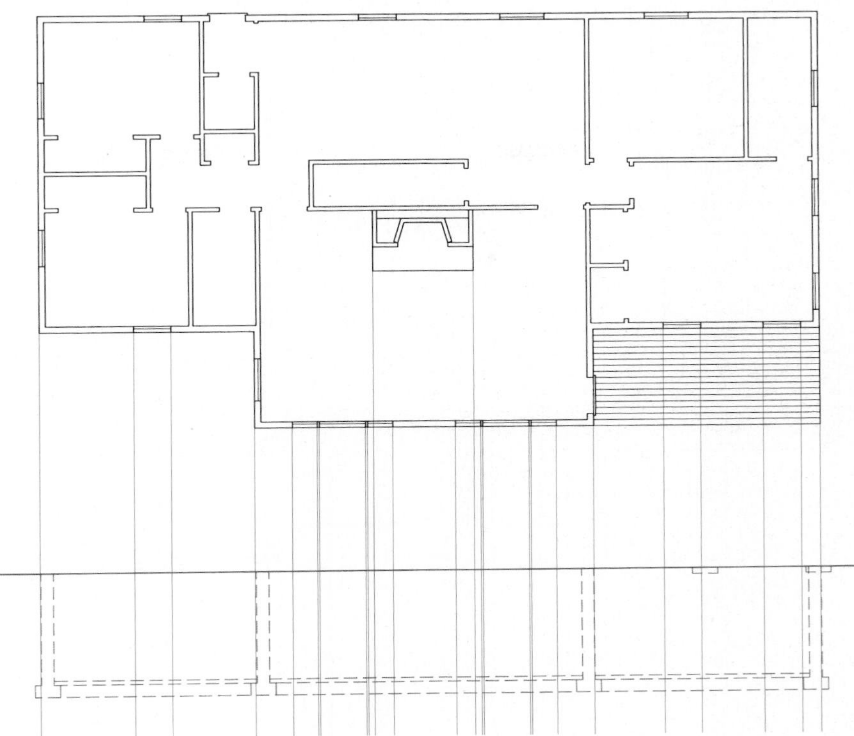

Goodheart-Willcox Publisher

Figure 23-14. The footings, basement floor, and basement walls have been added to the elevation.

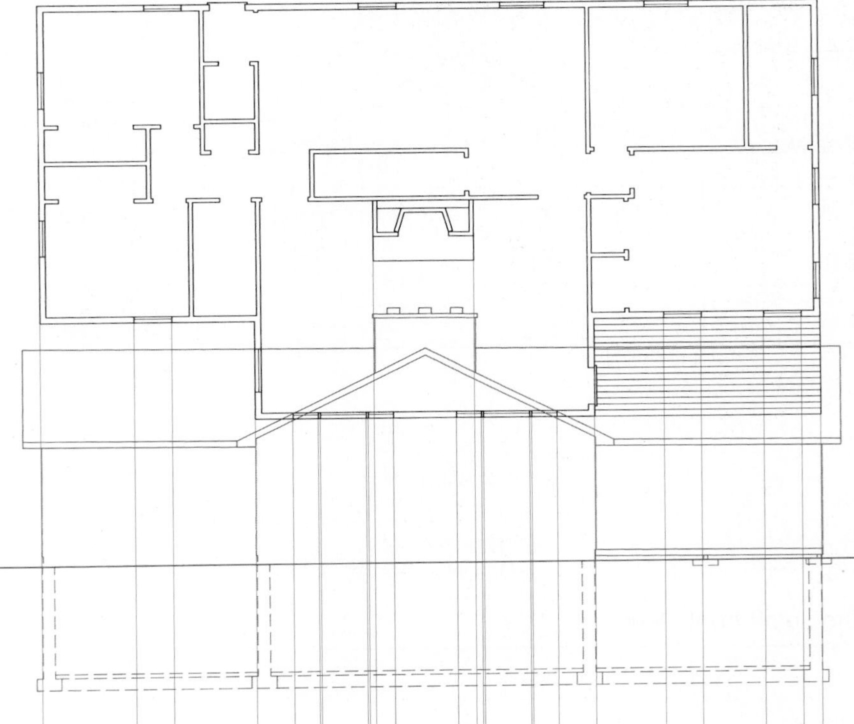

Goodheart-Willcox Publisher

Figure 23-15. The above-grade walls are added next. Notice how the floor plan overlaps the elevation. This is not a problem because the layer on which the floor plan copy resides will be turned off for plotting.

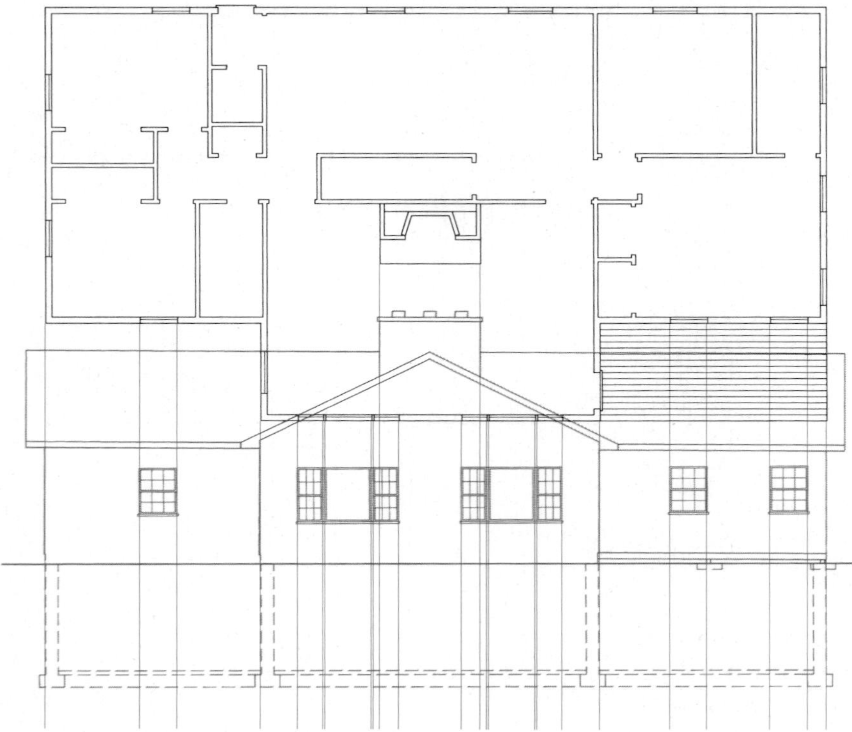

Goodheart-Willcox Publisher

Figure 23-16. All of the exterior features have now been added.

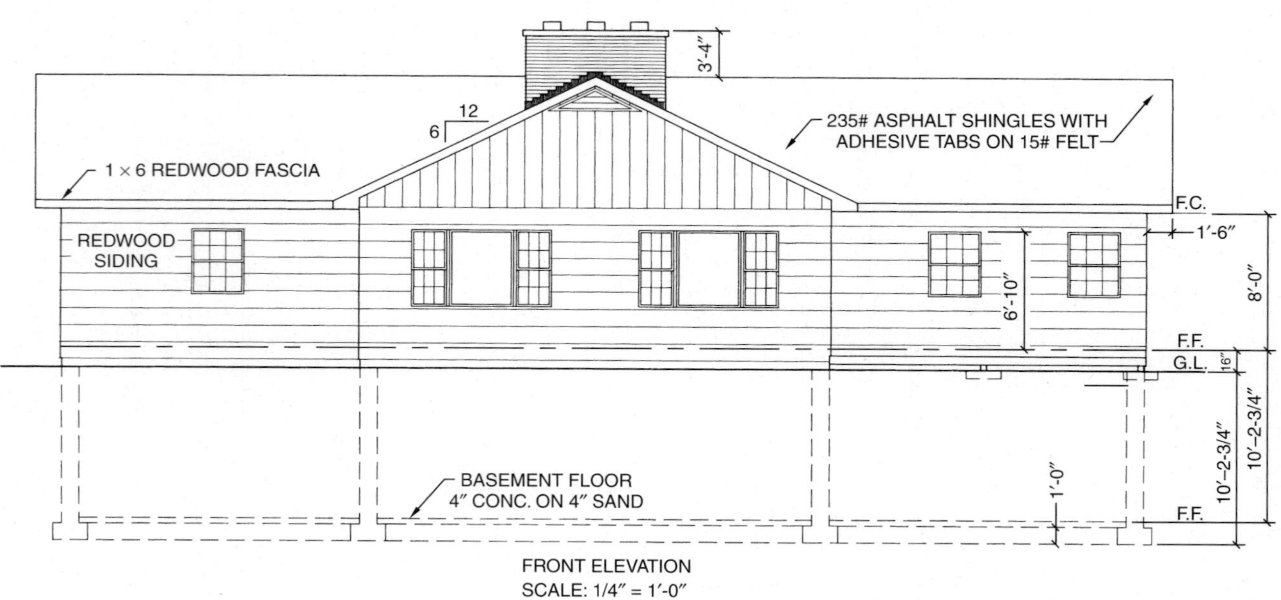

Goodheart-Willcox Publisher

Figure 23-17. The completed front elevation.

Parametric Modeling | Creating an Elevation View

Parametric modeling programs designed for use in architecture have the ability to generate elevation views automatically. See **Figure 23-18**. This speeds the process of preparing elevation views for a set of drawings. In some programs, four default elevation views are provided in the model file when a project is started using a default template. These are typically exterior elevations identified as north, south, east, and west. Additional elevation views, including interior elevations, can be created as needed. Creating elevation views in parametric modeling is similar to creating section views. Elevation views are typically created in a plan view, such as the first floor plan view. Once created, elevation views can be adjusted as needed to prepare them for the drawing documentation.

Elevation views are typically used to create the levels used in the project. ***Levels*** are assigned elevations that define key heights of the building. For each level that is created, you have the option to create a plan view associated with the level. Usually, levels are shown on the elevation views in a set of drawings to indicate important heights of the building. Elevation views are also useful for modeling certain features that are difficult to model in other views, such as light fixtures on an exterior wall.

The following procedure describes the steps for creating an elevation view. This is a typical sequence, but specific steps will vary depending on the program used.

1. Access the **ELEVATION** command in the floor plan view and select the appropriate view type to create an exterior or interior elevation. Once a view type is selected, an elevation tag symbol appears and is connected to the cursor. To create an exterior elevation, align the elevation tag symbol with an exterior feature, such as a wall. To create an interior elevation, align the elevation tag symbol with an interior feature, such as an arrangement of kitchen cabinets. The alignment direction of the elevation tag symbol changes automatically as the cursor is moved near different locations. Once the elevation tag symbol is aligned properly, pick to place the symbol. The default symbol used to represent the elevation tag can be changed by editing the tag properties.

Anthony J. Panozzo

Figure 23-18. This front elevation was generated automatically from a floor plan and rendered for presentation purposes.

Parametric Modeling | Creating an Elevation View *(Continued)*

2. Adjust the boundary establishing the extents of the elevation view. Typically, this can be done using grips. Adjusting the boundary is appropriate when the boundary extends further into the model than needed.
3. Change the default name of the elevation view. Use a descriptive name that reflects the contents of the view.
4. Open the elevation view and change the view scale to the appropriate scale. Make any adjustments needed to modify the display. For example, it may be necessary to adjust the lineweights of certain lines to display different thicknesses. In addition, it may be necessary to change the appearance of a hatch pattern used for a specific component. For example, you may need to turn off the visibility of the pattern or apply a different pattern. Typically, this can be done by adjusting the visibility settings of the view or using a painting or hatching tool.
5. If necessary, adjust the display of lines below grade. Adjust the visibility and thickness of the grade line if needed. If the site plan has been completed in the project, the grade line is generated from the topographical surface. To create the proper display, it may be necessary to access the visibility settings of the hatch pattern applied to the topographical surface.
6. Adjust the display of levels as needed. In some views, it may be necessary to turn the display of certain levels on or off. In addition, adjust the placement of levels to reduce crowding with other features. Typically, this can be done using grips. Elbow bends can be added to the levels to reduce crowding in areas where the levels are closely spaced.
7. Add dimensions and notes. Add material tags to identify materials.
8. Create a new sheet for the elevation view. Insert the elevation view onto the sheet. If needed, adjust the placement of text for the view title and scale.
9. Look over your work to be sure that you are finished. When you are sure the plan is complete, print or plot the sheet.
10. Follow the same procedure to create elevations for the remaining sides of the house.

Summary

- In the context of a set of construction drawings, an elevation is an orthographic projection drawing that shows one side of the structure to be built.
- The two methods commonly used to identify an elevation are by structure side (front, rear, right side, and left side) and by compass points (north, south, east, and west).
- The reference point for most elevations is the grade line.
- All features that are below grade should be drawn as hidden lines.
- The dimensions placed on an elevation are mainly height dimensions.
- Elevations can be drawn manually using traditional techniques; they can also be drawn using one of several CADD methods, depending on the software.

Internet Resources

Andersen Windows and Doors
Manufacturer of windows and doors

Autodesk, Inc.
General and architectural CADD software

CAD Forum
Architectural CADD symbols and blocks

Chief Architect
Architectural CADD software

eco stucco™
All-natural stucco exterior finishes

Marvin Windows and Doors
Manufacturer of windows and doors

Pella Corporation
Manufacturer of windows and doors

SoftPlan Systems
Architectural CADD software

Review Questions

Answer the following questions using the information in this chapter.

1. What is the primary purpose of an elevation drawing?
2. List five features that should be included on an elevation.
3. How many exterior elevations are usually required for a home? Name them.
4. What is the reference point for most elevations?
5. What type of line is used to represent features below grade in an elevation drawing?
6. The usual distance from the finished floor to the finished ceiling in a house is _____ for the first floor.
7. Why do most building codes require that the top of the foundation wall be at least 8″ above grade?
8. How is a typical wall section helpful for constructing the elevation?
9. Where is the slope triangle located on an elevation drawing?
10. What should you do before adding the roof features to an elevation drawing?
11. The minimum height that a chimney must extend above any structure within 10′-0″ of the chimney is _____.
12. From what two views can you obtain the horizontal and vertical measurements or line placements for an elevation?

Suggested Activities

1. Draw four elevations (front, rear, right side, and left side) for one of the floor plans you created in Chapter 13. Follow the procedure presented in this chapter. Add all necessary dimensions and notes. Submit the elevations with the floor plan.
2. Select a home from a newspaper or magazine that shows a photo and the floor plan. Using CADD, draft a front elevation of the home using a different style roof and exterior materials. Do not change the floor plan. Present your revision along with the originals.

3. Visit your local Habitat for Humanity location and request a copy of a floor plan the organization used to construct a home. Draft four new exterior elevations for the home illustrated on this floor plan. Give copies of your work to Habitat for Humanity and make an oral presentation to your class with your work.
4. Make a design sketch of a floor plan for a ranch-style home that has three bedrooms, two bathrooms, and a living room, kitchen, and dining room. Using CADD, create a bubble diagram from the sketch. Create circles, rectangles, or polylines to represent the bubble shapes. Label and dimension the rooms and spaces. Then, use the bubble diagram to draw and dimension a floor plan using a scale of 1/4″ = 1′-0″. Draw four elevations (front, rear, right side, and left side) from the floor plan. Create a wall section to provide height measurements following the procedure presented in this chapter.
5. Using CADD, draw a front elevation of the house shown in the photo below. The width of the house is 26′-0″. The windows and door are 3′-0″ wide. The ceiling height on the first floor is 12′-0″ and the ceiling height on the second floor is 8′-0″. Dimension the appropriate features.

Goodheart-Willcox Publisher

Problem Solving Case Study

A client has come to your office because, although she loves her house on the inside, she is tired of the outside look. She says her house looks “old and tired” next to her neighbors’ newer houses. She wants a complete exterior renovation that does not affect the inside spaces of the home. She has provided the photograph shown below. She will come back in one week to see your ideas for making her home look more up-to-date. Her only requirement is that it look nothing like it does right now.

Because you are only generating initial ideas, you do not yet need precise measurements. Estimate the necessary dimensions and create a front elevation to show an entirely new “look” for the client’s home. Use your imagination to create an entirely different look. Use CADD software so that you can easily adjust the dimensions later, after the client approves the initial elevation.

Robert Crum/Shutterstock.com

ADDA Certification Prep

The following questions are presented in the style used in the American Design Drafting Association (ADDA) Drafter Certification Test. Answer the questions using the information in this chapter.

1. Which of the following statements are true about elevations?
   A. The minimum recommended height for garage ceilings is 8′-0″.
   B. Elevations provide height information about basic features of the house that cannot be shown very well on other drawings.
   C. The roof pitch can be indicated using the fractional pitch or slope triangle.
   D. Windows and doors located on an exterior wall are typically not included on the elevation.
2. Which of the following statements are *false*?
   A. The purpose of an elevation is to show the finished appearance of a given side of the building and to furnish vertical height dimensions.
   B. The left and right side of a house are identified by standing inside the house and looking out.
   C. Most building codes require that the top of the foundation wall be at least 20″ above grade to protect the framing members from moisture.
   D. Chimneys that intersect the roof usually require more than one view to determine the points where they pass through the roof.
3. Which of the following statements are true about drawing architectural elevations?
   A. You should show sufficient detail on windows and doors to accurately indicate the window or door.
   B. The garage floor should be lower than the finished grade.
   C. The chimney height above the highest roof point must be dimensioned.
   D. Elevations drawn using manual techniques should be at the same scale as the floor plan.

Curricular Connections

1. **Social Science.** The external appearance of a home can say a lot about the people who live there. Preferred exterior materials vary from culture to culture, however. Conduct research to find out more about the preferred exterior finish materials (brick veneer, siding, stucco, etc.) in at least three countries, or at least three different areas of the United States. Determine whether the preferred materials can be obtained locally or must be imported. Write a summary of any correlation you find between the preferred materials and their costs.
2. **Language Arts.** Creative writing can help exercise your creativity, which in turn can help you think of creative solutions to architectural design problems. Look around your neighborhood or town to find a house that interests you. It could be an old or historic house, an abandoned property, or a brand-new house—whatever catches your interest, as long as you do not know the people who live there (or lived there). Write a fictional story about the house and its occupants. Be sure to include a plot, and develop the characters in the story using descriptive details.

STEM Connections

1. **Technology.** Investigate the features of the various architectural CADD programs that are now available. Create a table that shows each program and the features it has that could be used to create elevations and other plans for a set of architectural working drawings. Include a column for the price of each program.

Communicating about Architecture

1. **Listening and Speaking.** Obtain a set of architectural drawings that show the exterior elevations and floor plan for a home. Show the drawings in class and explain to your classmates the types of features that elevations are used to show.
2. **Speaking.** Pick a figure in this chapter, such as Figure 23-2. Working with a partner, describe and then redescribe the important information being conveyed by that figure. Through your collaboration, develop what you and your partner believe is the most interesting verbal description. Present your narration to the class.

Chapter 24

Stair Details

Objectives

After completing this chapter, you will be able to:

- Identify the basic types and shapes of stairways.
- Describe the basic parts of a stairway.
- Design a stairway for a residential structure.
- Perform stair calculations for a residential stairway.
- Draw a structural detail for a stairway.

Key Terms

baluster
circular stairs
double-L stairs
guardrail
handrail
headroom
housed stringer
landing
L stairs
main stairs
newel
nosing
plain stringer
rise
riser
run
service stairs
spiral stairs
stairway
straight run stairs
stringer
total rise
total run
tread
U stairs
well hole
winder stairs

A ***stairway*** is a series of steps installed between two or more floors of a building. A stairway may or may not have landings or platforms within the flight of stairs. Stairways provide easy access to various levels of the home. All styles of homes have stairs, except a ranch with no basement. The prime considerations in stair design should be safety and easy ascent and descent.

Types of Stairs

A house may have a ***main stairs*** from the first floor to the second floor or from a split foyer to the first floor. The main stairs are usually assembled with prefabricated parts of good quality, as shown in **Figure 24-1**. The treads are generally made of hardwoods such as oak, maple, or birch. They may or may not be carpeted as well. Some houses may also have ***service stairs*** intended for frequent, heavy use. These are typically constructed on location and made of Douglas fir or pine construction lumber. Service stairs are generally of a lesser quality than main stairs.

Stairways can be either open or closed. *Enclosed stairs* have a wall on both sides. They are also known as closed, housed, or box stairs. In contrast, *open stairs* have no wall on one or both sides. The stairway in **Figure 24-1** is an example of open stairs.

pics721/Shutterstock.com

Figure 24-1. This beautiful main stairway is visible from the entrance and was constructed with quality materials.

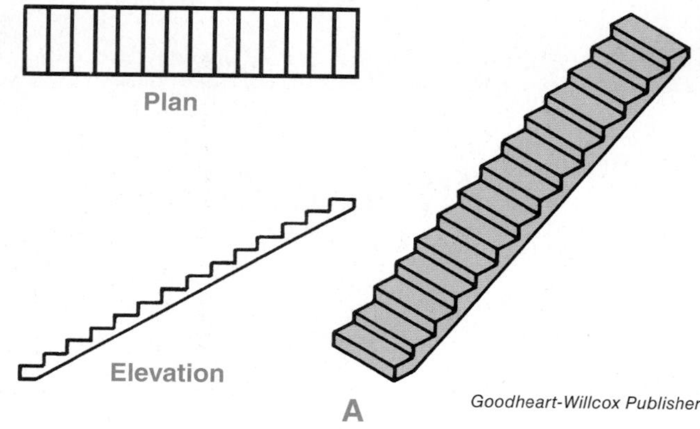

Figure 24-2. A—Straight run stairs. B—These straight run stairs are an example of enclosed stairs.

Stairway Configurations

Seven general shapes or configurations are commonly used in residential stairway construction. These include straight run, L, double-L, U, winder, spiral, and circular. The configuration of a stairway depends on the design of the home as well as available space.

Straight run stairs, as the name implies, have no turns. See **Figure 24-2**. These are the stairs used most in home construction. They are not as expensive to construct as other types of stairs. However, straight run stairs require a long, open space that may be difficult to accommodate in a floor plan.

L stairs have a landing at some point along the flight of stairs at which the stairway makes a 90° turn, as shown in **Figure 24-3**. A ***landing*** is a flat floor area at some point between the top and bottom of the stairway. If the landing is near the top or bottom of the stairs, the term *long L* is used to describe the stairs. L stairs are used when the space required for straight run stairs is not available.

Double-L stairs have two 90° turns and two landings along the flight, but are not U-shaped. See **Figure 24-4**. They may be used when space is not available for either straight or L stairs. Double-L stairs are not frequently used in residential construction. They are more expensive to build and may cause design challenges in the floor plan.

U stairs have two flights of steps parallel to each other with a landing between them, as shown in **Figure 24-5**. This type of stairs may be constructed as either wide U stairs or narrow U stairs. The difference between the two is the

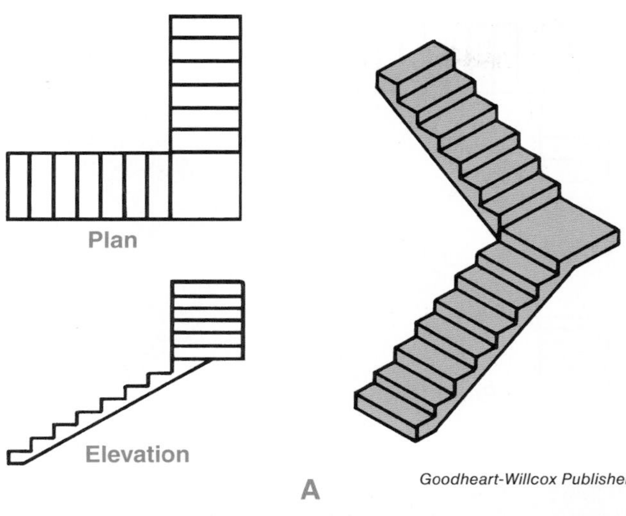

Figure 24-3. A—L stairs. B—These are long L stairs. Notice that the landing and turn are toward the top of the stairs.

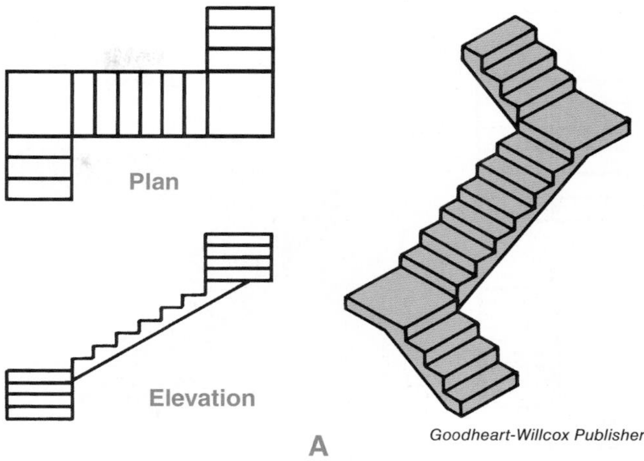

Figure 24-4. A—Double-L stairs. B—This homeowner incorporated double-L stairs into the back yard to blend with the natural setting.

horizontal space between the flights. Narrow U stairs have little or no space between the flights, as shown in **Figure 24-5**. Wide U stairs have a space between each flight. This space is called a ***well hole***.

Winder stairs have pie-shaped steps that are substituted for a landing. See **Figure 24-6**. This type of stairs is used when the space is not sufficient for the L, double-L, or U stairs. The midpoint width of the triangular steps in winder stairs should be equal to the tread width of the regular steps. For instance, if the regular tread width is 10″, then each triangular step should also be 10″ at the midpoint. Winder stairs are not as safe as other types and should be avoided whenever possible.

Spiral stairs are steps that rise like a corkscrew about a center point, as shown in **Figure 24-7**.

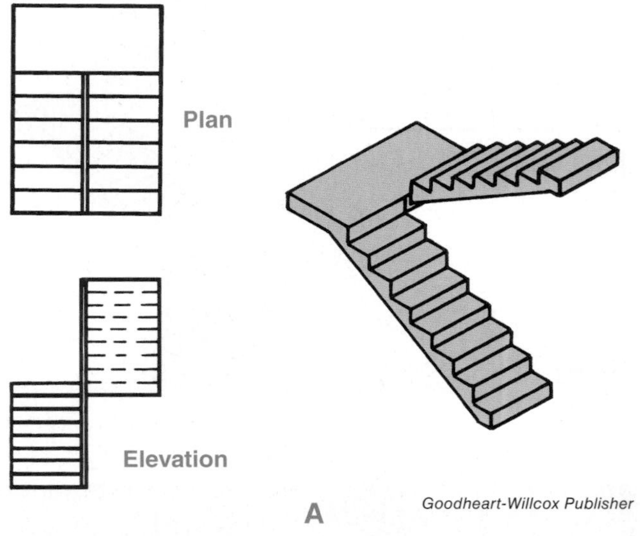

Figure 24-5. A—U stairs. B—These stairs are narrow U stairs. Notice the lack of a well hole.

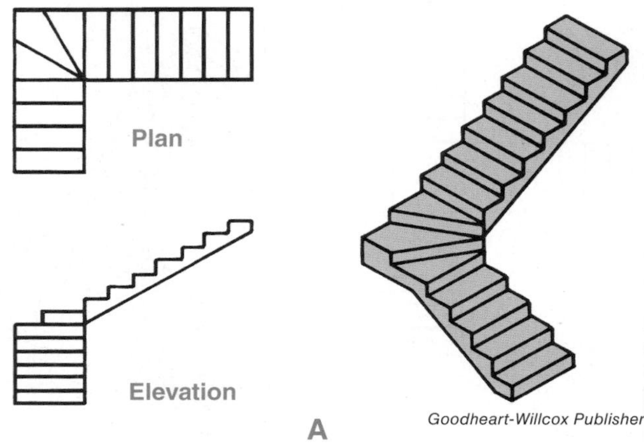

Figure 24-6. A—Winder stairs. B—Notice how narrow the inside of the triangular stairs can be. Because this constitutes a hazard for falls, avoid winder stairs whenever possible.

Spiral stairs can be used even when little space is available. Most spiral stairs are made from welded steel. However, they can be constructed from modular wood components. Several manufacturers supply components and finished stairs. Spiral stairs are not very safe because they generally have triangular steps similar to winder stairs. They can add an interesting design touch, however.

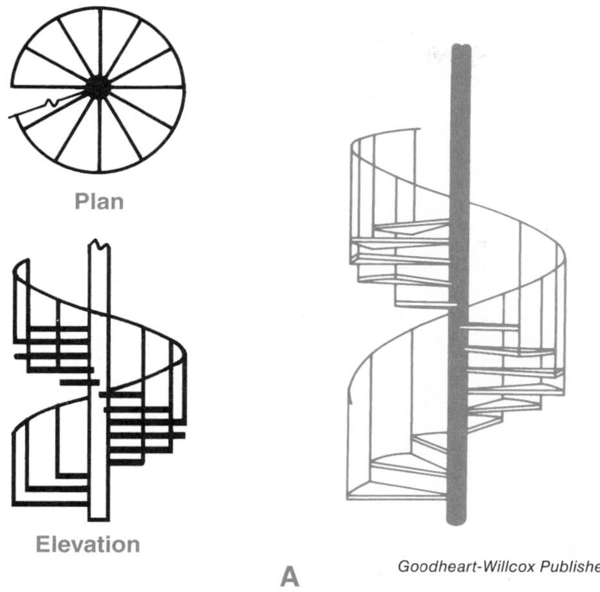

Figure 24-7. A—Spiral stairs. B—These decorative spiral stairs are made from prefabricated parts.

Circular stairs are trapezoidal steps that rise along an irregular curve or arc. These stairs are custom made. Many fine, large homes utilize these stairs, **Figure 24-8**. Circular stairs require a lot of space and are expensive to build.

Parts of a Stairway

To design stairways effectively, you need to understand the basic parts that make up a stairway and how to specify them. The three main structural parts of a stairway are the treads, risers, and stringers. ***Treads*** are the horizontal members of each step in a stairway. They are the part of the step on which a person walks. ***Risers*** are the vertical faces that run from one tread to the next. ***Stringers*** are structural members that support the treads and risers. They are also called the *carriage* of the stairway. The following sections describe each of these parts in more detail.

Stringers

The stringers are the main supporting members of the stairway. Several types of stringers are used, but plain stringers and housed stringers are the most common. ***Plain stringers*** are stringers that have been cut or notched to fit the profile of the stairs. ***Housed stringers*** have been routed or grooved to receive the treads and risers. See **Figure 24-9**.

Two stringers are usually sufficient. However, a main stairway should not be less than 3′-0″ wide. If the width of the stairs exceeds 3′-0″, a third stringer is required. The extra stringer is placed midway between the outside stringers and under the treads and risers.

Plain stringers are generally cut from 2 × 12 straight-grain fir. The treads and risers are nailed directly to the stringers. This type of construction is used for service stairs and occasionally for main stairs if they are to be carpeted. Stairs with plain stringers are sturdy, but they tend to squeak and may not have a finished appearance.

Housed stringers are made from finished lumber and are generally purchased precut or preassembled. Alternatively, the stringers may be cut from 1 × 12 or 2 × 12 lumber. Grooves 1/2″ deep are usually routed in the stringers to

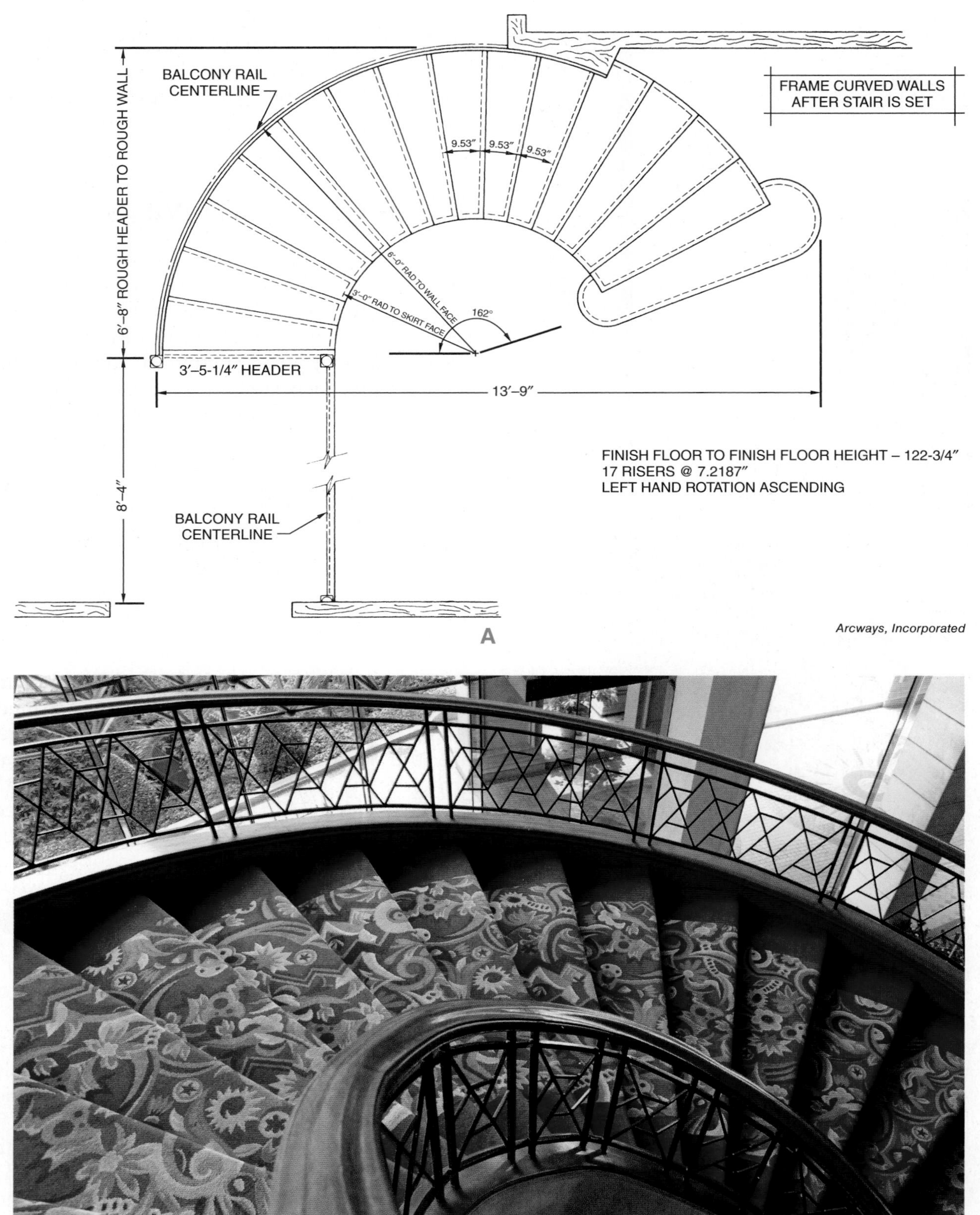

Figure 24-8. A—Plan view of typical circular stairs. B—Notice the trapezoidal shape of each stair in this stairway. Circular stairs are safer than spiral or winder stairs because their narrowest horizontal surface is wider.

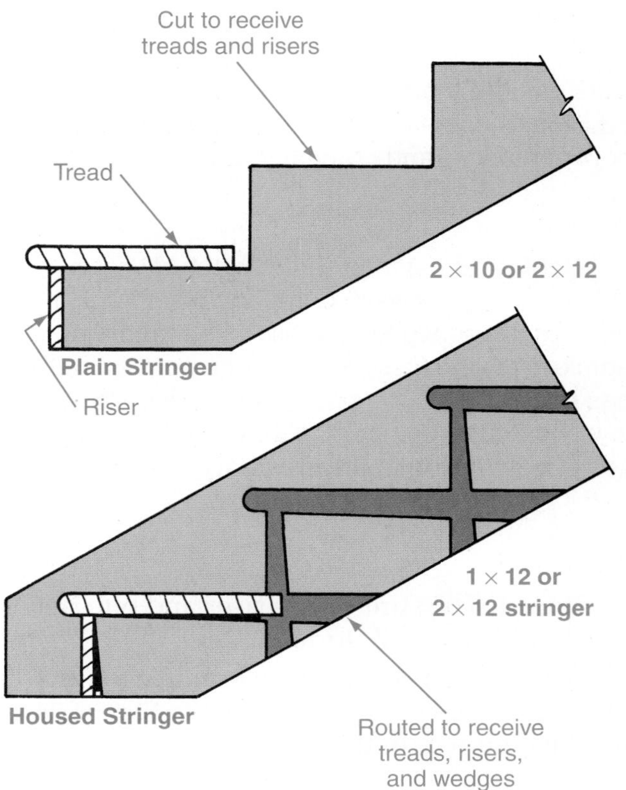

Figure 24-9. Details of plain and housed stringers.

hold the treads and risers. The bottom and back sides of the grooves are wider than the thickness of the treads and risers so that wedges may be driven in to hold them in place. **Figure 24-10** illustrates how the wedges are inserted into the grooves. The treads, risers, and wedges are glued and nailed in place.

Treads and Risers

The two other primary parts of a set of stairs are the treads and risers. Standard treads are available in 1-1/4″ oak in 10-1/2″ and 11-1/2″ widths. Both widths are 1-1/16″ thick actual size. The ***nosing***—the rounded projection of the tread that extends past the face of the riser—is not included in calculations. See **Figure 24-11**. A tread depth of 10-1/2″ is a popular choice for residential construction. The minimum tread depth required by the International Residential Code is 10″. Risers are 3/4″ thick actual size and vary in width depending on the slope of the stairs. The ideal riser height for residential construction is between 7″ and 7-5/8″. The maximum riser height permitted by the International Residential Code is 7-3/4″. Clear white pine is the customary riser material.

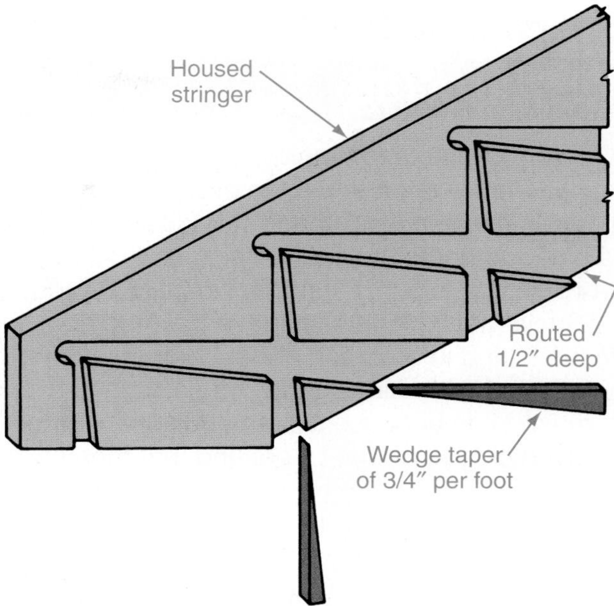

Figure 24-10. Wedges are used in a housed stringer to help hold the treads and risers in place. Treads, risers, and wedges are glued and nailed to the stringer.

Stair Design

Properly designed and constructed stairs must support the weight required by the application. They will also be wide enough to provide easy

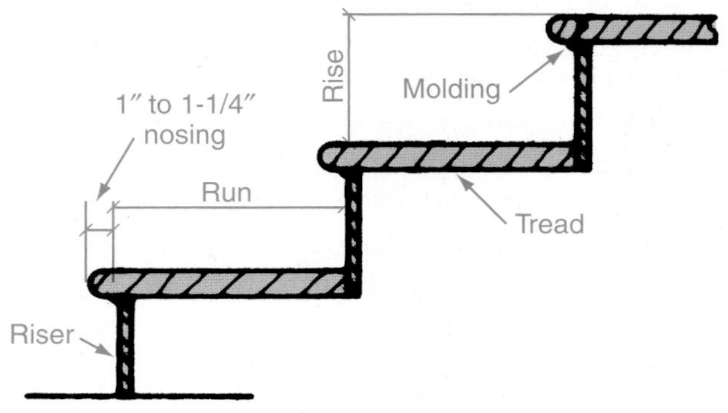

Figure 24-11. Tread and riser terms.

Employability

Networking

Many people find employment through networking. *Networking* is the exchange of information or services among individuals or groups. As a newcomer to the career field, the goal of your networking is to learn about possible job leads.

Social networking sites have become popular places to find information about companies and their available positions. Many companies network on these sites because it is an additional source of advertising for them. Users find that these sites expand their job search possibilities. In addition, these sites allow a personal exchange between users and company representatives.

Activity

Contact at least three architectural firms in your area. Ask each company whether it uses social networking sites to find potential employees and if so, how successful this method has been. If you use social networking sites, investigate the companies that say they use social networking to advertise available positions.

passage of people and furniture. The proper slope for stairs is between 30° and 35°.

Many AEC CADD programs have features to aid the drafter in creating stairs that are safe and have a structurally sound design. These features may come with the software or may need to be purchased as a special add-on. See **Figure 24-12**. In addition, some large manufacturers provide software to aid in specifying their products.

Slope of a Stairway

The slope of a stairway depends on not only the sizes of the treads and risers, but also on the rise and run. ***Rise*** is the distance from the top surface of one tread to the same position on the next tread. ***Run*** is the distance from the face of one riser to the face of the next. The ***total rise*** is the total floor-to-floor height of the stairway, and the ***total run*** is the total horizontal length of the stairway. See **Figure 24-13**.

The slope of stairs may be specified in degrees or as a ratio of the rise to run or riser to tread. Several rules have been devised for calculating the slope of stairs. Four of these rules are:

- **Rule 1.** The slope of the stairs should be between 30° and 35°. Many older stairs are too steep and, therefore, not as safe as modern stairs.
- **Rule 2.** The sum of two risers and one tread should equal 24″ to 25″.
- **Rule 3.** The product of the riser height multiplied by the tread width should equal approximately 75″.
- **Rule 4.** The sum of one riser and one tread should equal 17″ to 18″.

If a 10″ tread is used in an example for each of the rules, the riser heights shown in **Figure 24-14** will be required. In these examples, a riser height

Antoha713/Shutterstock.com

Figure 24-12. The spiral stairway in this CADD rendering was calculated automatically using CADD software. For complex stairs such as these, stairway calculation software can save a great deal of time.

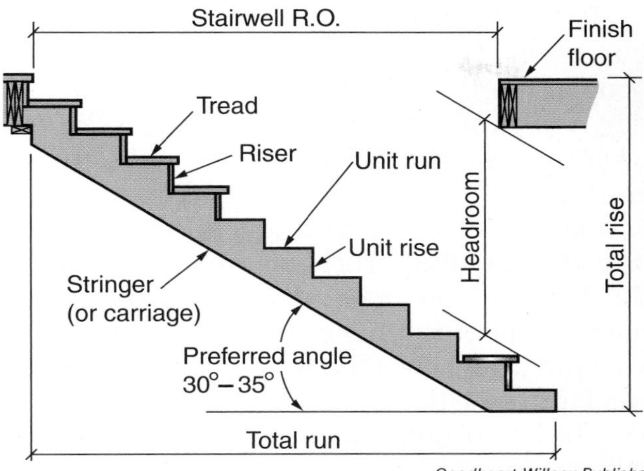

Goodheart-Willcox Publisher

Figure 24-13. Total run, total rise, and other critical stair dimensions.

of 7″ is the only one that creates stairs that fall within the proper slope angle. However, the slope angle can be reduced by increasing the tread width. For example, if the tread width is 10-1/2″, then the riser height would be 7-1/4″. This combination is based on using Rule 2 and a calculation of 25″ for the sum of two risers and one tread. This calculation would result in an angle slightly less than 35°. A ratio of 7-1/4″ to 10-1/2″ is considered ideal.

The first rule generally is not applied to service stairs; they are normally steeper than main stairs. However, a similar calculation can be used to determine the slope of service stairs. For example, if the treads are 10″ wide, a riser height between 5-3/4″ and 7″ would produce a 30° to 35° slope. A riser height of less than 7″ is considered too short. A 7:10 ratio and 35° slope are acceptable for service stairs.

	Tread Width	Riser Height	Approximate Slope
Rule 1	10″	7″	35°
Rule 2	10″	7″ to 7-1/2″	35° to 37°
Rule 3	10″	7-1/2″	37°
Rule 4	10″	7″ to 8″	35° to 38°

Goodheart-Willcox Publisher

Figure 24-14. Application of the rules for stairway slope. A 10″ tread is used in this example. The 7″ riser height is the only one that produces stairs that fall within the proper slope angle.

Green Architecture

Bamboo Stairs

Bamboo is generally considered a highly sustainable building product because it grows so rapidly and can be replaced easily within a few years. Many people have installed bamboo floors in their homes, both because they are sustainable and because of their natural beauty. However, relatively few people have considered bamboo for stairways. Bamboo can be "strand woven" to make it durable enough to be used as a structural material—meaning it can be used in stairways. Bamboo stairways are a good choice, especially if the floor above or below the stairway is also bamboo.

However, not all bamboo is sustainable. Some manufacturing methods introduce volatile organic compounds (VOCs). Also, since most bamboo products are imported from Asia, halfway around the world, transportation is an environmental concern. Furthermore, some bamboo farmers use inorganic pesticides and fertilizers. Bamboo stairs can be a beautiful addition to a home. However, if you decide to incorporate a bamboo stairway into a home design, be sure to choose a reputable supplier that can guarantee the sustainability of the product.

Headroom

Another critical aspect of stair design is headroom. ***Headroom*** is the shortest clear vertical distance measured between the nosing of the treads and the ceiling. See **Figure 24-15**. In most building codes, the minimum acceptable headroom is 6′-8″. It is important to keep this in mind when designing the upper floor of a building.

Handrails and Guardrails

All building codes require railings on stairs and ramps. In a residence, the International Residential Code requires railings whenever four or more risers are present.

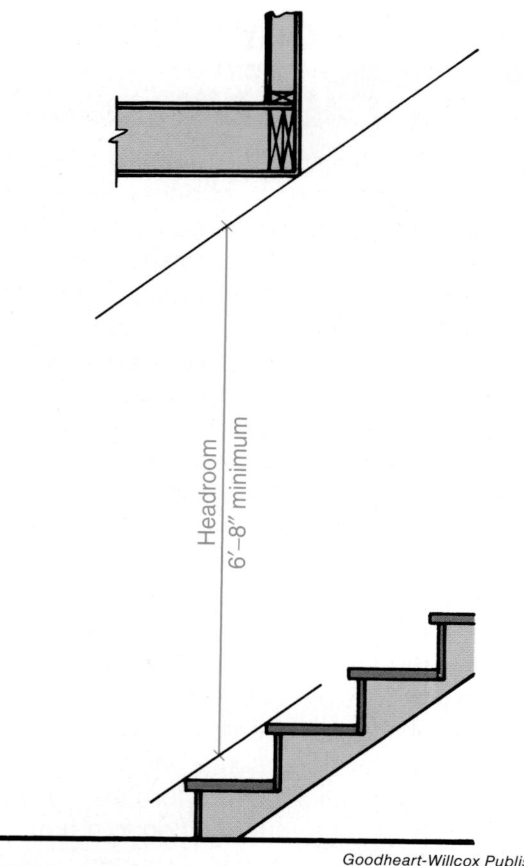

Goodheart-Willcox Publisher

Figure 24-15. Sufficient headroom is an important consideration in the design of stairs. Most building codes require a minimum of 6′-8″.

Railings come in two varieties: handrails and guardrails. The purpose of a ***handrail*** is to help people steady themselves as they travel up and down steps or ramps where they might slip, trip, or fall. Unless the stairs are very wide, one rail is sufficient. The handrail is usually a single rail and is supported by balusters and newels. The ***balusters*** are the vertical members that support the handrail on open stairs. ***Newels*** are the main posts of the handrail at the top, bottom, and points where the stairs change direction. See **Figure 24-16**.

The International Residential Code requires the following for handrails in residential structures:

- Handrail height: 34″ to 38″ above the tread nosing (see **Figure 24-17**).
- Handrail clearance (between the handrail and wall): At least 1-1/2″.
- Handrail length: Must begin at the bottom riser and end at the top riser.

The only allowable interruptions in a handrail are newels placed for support as necessary.

Guardrails are formed by closely spaced balusters or a grid below the handrail. They are designed to keep people from falling over the edge of a balcony or off the side or top of a staircase. See **Figure 24-18**. Guardrails must extend from the code-mandated height down to a specified

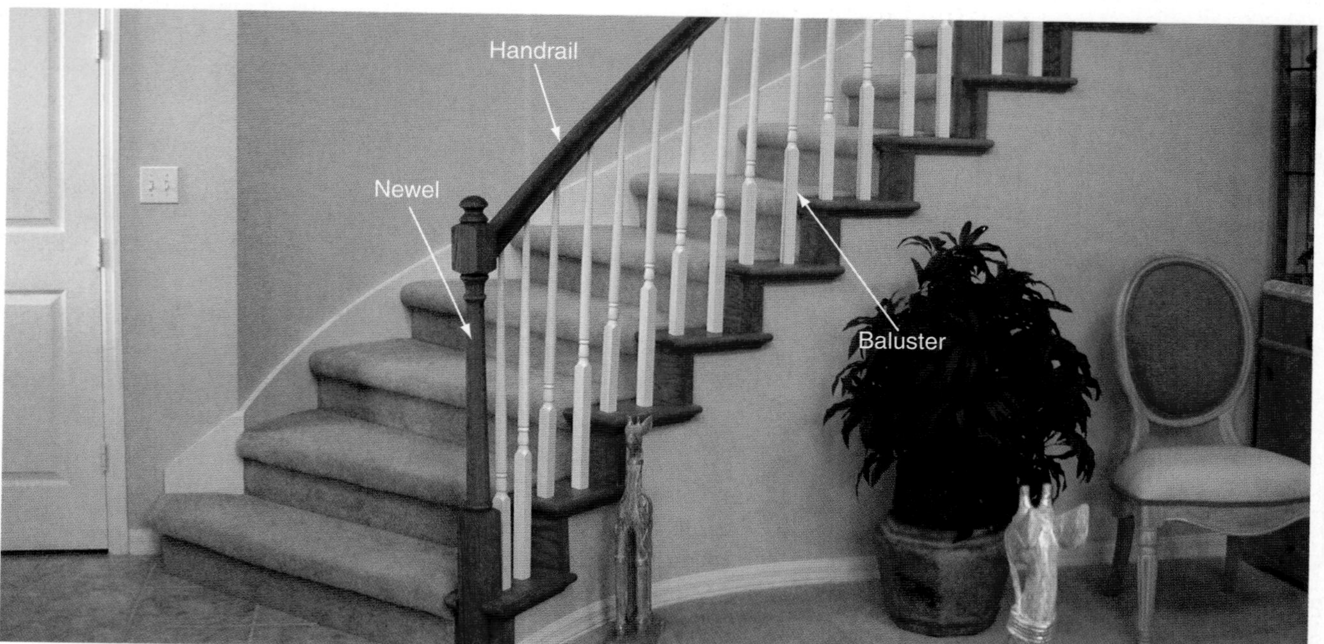

Goodheart-Willcox Publisher

Figure 24-16. The newel, handrail, and balusters are identified on this stairway. These are open stairs.

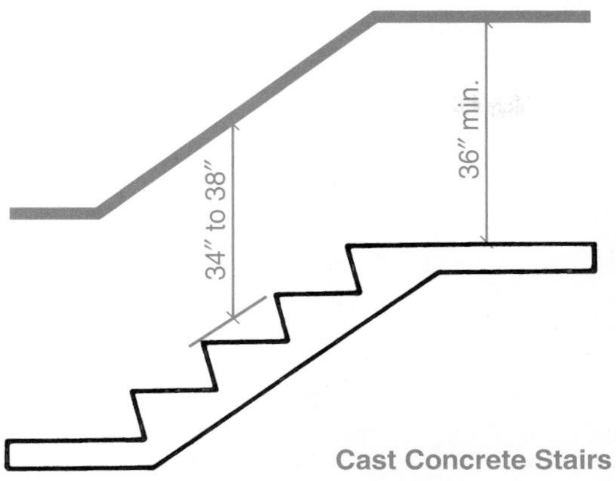

Goodheart-Willcox Publisher

Figure 24-17. Recommended handrail heights for all stairs.

pics721/Shutterstock.com

Figure 24-18. Guardrails can be decorative, but they must prevent people, including small children, from falling off the side or top of a staircase. The spacing of these balusters meets International Residential Code requirements.

distance above the floor. International Residential Code requirements for residential structures include:

- Guardrail height: 36″ minimum on stairs and landings that are 30″ above grade.
- Baluster spacing: Spaced so that a 4″ sphere cannot pass through any opening up to the required height.

The railing as a system must meet several minimum code requirements for loading and impact. For example, the railing must be able to resist a uniform load of 50 pounds per linear foot applied in any direction at the top and transfer the load to the building structure. In another test, the railing must be able to resist a concentrated load of 200 pounds per linear foot applied in any direction at the top and transfer the load to the building structure. Concentrated and uniform loads are not applied simultaneously.

In response to these requirements, manufacturers limit the length of their railing assemblies according to each material's capacity for loading. Therefore, lengths generally range from 3′ to 12′. As a general rule, polyvinyl chloride (PVC) has less than 18% of the longitudinal tensile strength of a similar aluminum or fiber-reinforced plastic (FRP) section. Tensile strength in the transverse direction (across the railing) presents a different picture. FRP has one-third the tensile strength of aluminum, but more than 1.6 times that of PVC. Be sure to consult the building code that applies in your area when specifying handrails and guardrails.

Structural Details

Procedures for building stairs vary widely from one part of the country to another. Local building codes often specify restrictions. Also, carpenters have their own preferences that add to the variations. Regardless of the procedure followed, the construction techniques must produce stairs that are sound. **Figure 24-19** shows the rough framing for open, straight run stairs with plain stringers. Ordinarily, this rough framing is not shown in a set of construction drawings. However, a plan view and elevation with various section details are shown. **Figure 24-20** illustrates a stair detail drawing. **Figure 24-21** illustrates typical railing details for stairs.

Adaptations for Special Needs

Stairs can be a significant obstacle for a person with physical challenges. If a person has difficulty walking but can still use stairs, the stairway may be adapted by simply installing sturdy handrails on both sides of the stairway. In addition, the treads should be covered with a nonskid surface, and risers should be closed, not open. Ideally, risers should be lower and the treads wider than normal, which would require rebuilding an existing stairway. These features can easily be incorporated into stairs in new construction.

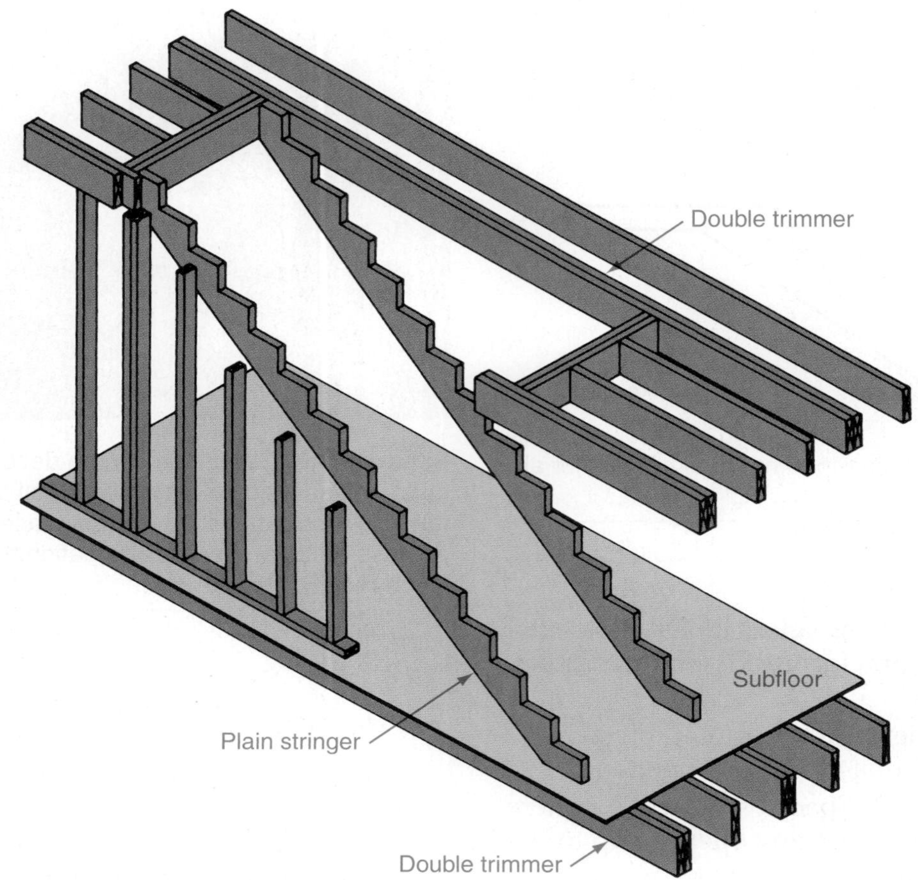

Goodheart-Willcox Publisher

Figure 24-19. This pictorial drawing shows the rough framing for open, straight run stairs with plain stringers.

Some physical challenges prevent a person from using stairs at all. In these cases, other adaptations must be implemented. For example, an existing stairway may need to be retrofitted with a stairlift. The installation of an elevator or ramp may also be required.

Stairlifts and Elevators

Installing a stairlift is a consideration for people who cannot climb stairs. A stairlift carries a person up and down an existing stairway on a special seat built into a fixture installed on the wall. Some stairlifts are constructed to lift a person seated in a wheelchair.

Installing an elevator is another alternative. In an existing home, a large closet may be converted into an elevator. In new construction, this feature can easily be incorporated into the design in the most efficient location. See **Figure 24-22**.

Ramps

Ramps may be installed at entries to enable physically challenged people to enter a structure. Ramps should have nonslip surfaces and, if possible, protection from rain, snow, and ice.

The recommended slope for a ramp is 1′ rise for every 12′ of distance, or a ratio of 1:12. In other words, to access a height of 3′, the minimum ramp length is 36′. If a more gradual slope is required, a longer ramp should be planned.

The maximum length of a ramp section is 30′. Ramps longer than 30′ should be built in two or more sections. Each section must be separated by a landing at least 5′ square. Landings are necessary rest stops for individuals who have difficulty moving uphill. An entry platform should extend 18″ beyond the handle side of the door to allow a wheelchair user to open the door easily.

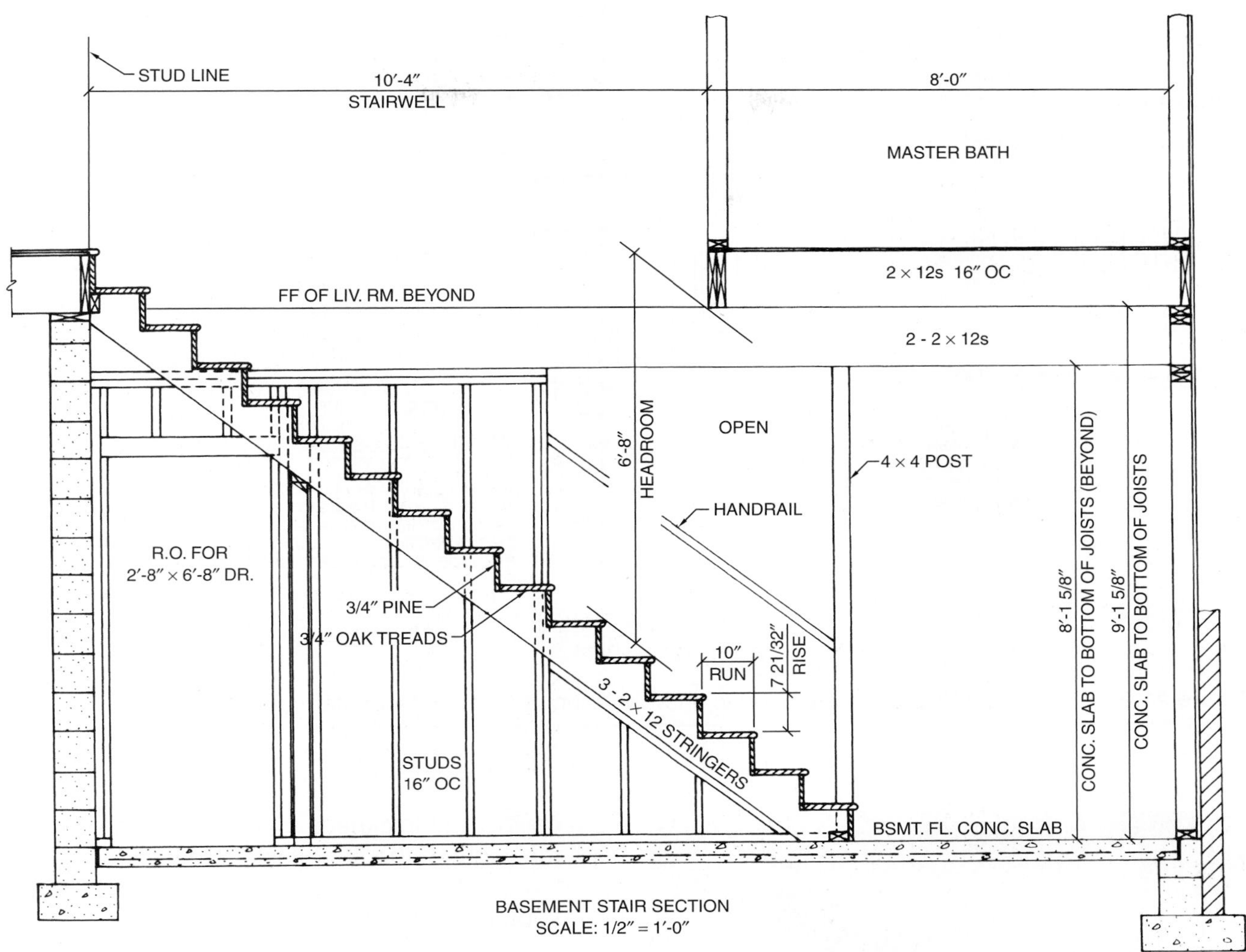

Goodheart-Willcox Publisher

Figure 24-20. A stair section detail drawing for a set of basement stairs.

The recommended width of a ramp is 48". The minimum width is 36" for wheelchair use.

Handrails should be placed on both sides of the ramp for safety. See **Figure 24-23**. A handrail height of 3' is commonly used. Wheelchair users, however, can pull themselves up the ramp more easily when handrails are 30" high. If curbs are used, they should be placed on both sides of the ramp at least 4" high.

Procedure Drafting

Calculating and Drawing Stairs

The following procedure may be used to determine the number and size of treads and risers for a set of stairs. This procedure can be used with manual drafting or CADD.

1. Determine the total rise of the stairs. Calculate the total rise by adding the distance from the finished lower floor to the finished

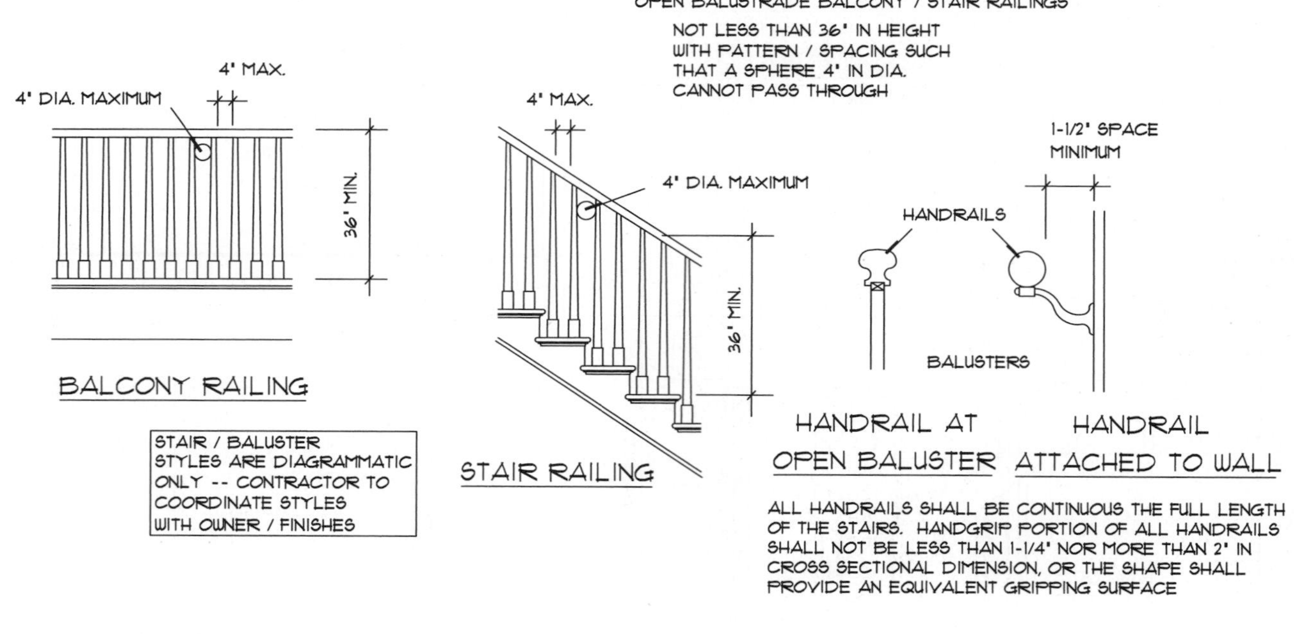

Lizz Layman

Figure 24-21. These detail drawings are used to show building requirements for stair railings.

pics721/Shutterstock.com

Figure 24-22. In some cases, a large closet can become an elevator, if enough space is available on the other floor to accommodate it.

ceiling, the thickness of the ceiling material, the width of the floor joists, the thickness of the subfloor, and the thickness of the finished floor, as shown below.

Finished lower floor to finished ceiling	8′-0″
Thickness of ceiling material (drywall)	1/2″
Width of the floor joists (2 × 10 lumber)	9-1/4″
Thickness of the subfloor (1/2″ plywood)	1/2″
Thickness of the finished floor and underlayment	1″
Total rise =	8′-11 1/4″

Since the size of each step is in inches, the total rise is converted to inches: total rise = (8 × 12″) + 11 1/4″ = 107-1/4″. **Figure 24-24** shows the first step in drawing stairs.

2. Determine how many risers will be required by first dividing the total rise by seven. Seven inches is an ideal riser height and, therefore, a logical place to start. When

Les Palenik/Shutterstock.com

Figure 24-23. A ramp for access to a private home. Notice the sturdy handrails and guardrails.

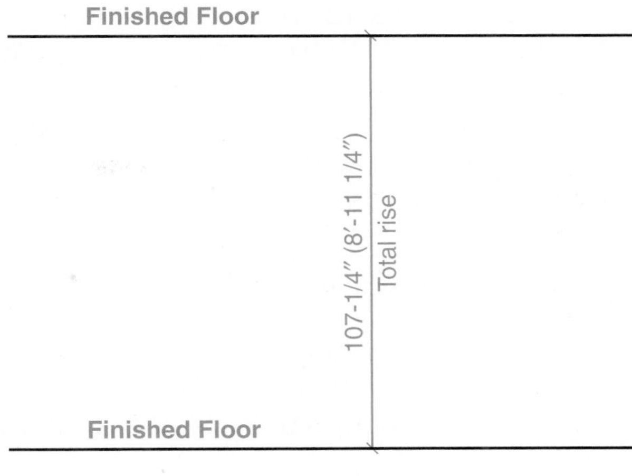

Goodheart-Willcox Publisher

Figure 24-24. The first step in drawing stairs is to determine the total rise and lay out the finished floor lines.

107-1/4″ is divided by seven, the result is 15.32 risers. The number of risers must be a whole number, so either 15 or 16 risers will be required. When 107-1/4″ is divided by 15, a riser height of 7.15″ is produced. This figure is acceptable, so further calculations will be based on 15 risers, each 7.15″ high. **Figure 24-25** shows how the total rise is divided into 15 equal parts. In CADD, you can use the **DIVIDE** command or a similar command, or you can place points every 7.15″ vertically. *Each riser must be exactly the same height*.

3. Determine the tread size and total run that will yield a stair slope between 30° and 35°. Start with the tread size. A 10-1/2″ tread width is common and will be used for a trial calculation. *There is always one less tread than the number of risers*. This is because the second floor serves as the top tread. The sum of two risers (7.15″ + 7.15″) and one tread (10-1/2″) equals 24.80″. Rule 2 states that this sum should equal 24″ to 25″, so this combination will be acceptable.

   For comparison, Rule 3 and Rule 4 will be applied. Rule 3 says that the product of the riser height and tread width should be approximately 75″. If 7.15″ is multiplied by 10.5″ the product is 75.1″, which is acceptable. Rule 4 says that the sum of one riser and one tread should equal 17″ to 18″. If 7.15″ is added to 10-1/2″, the result is 17.65″. This is within the required range. Because the requirements of all of these rules can be met with a tread width of 10-1/2″, you can use this tread width.

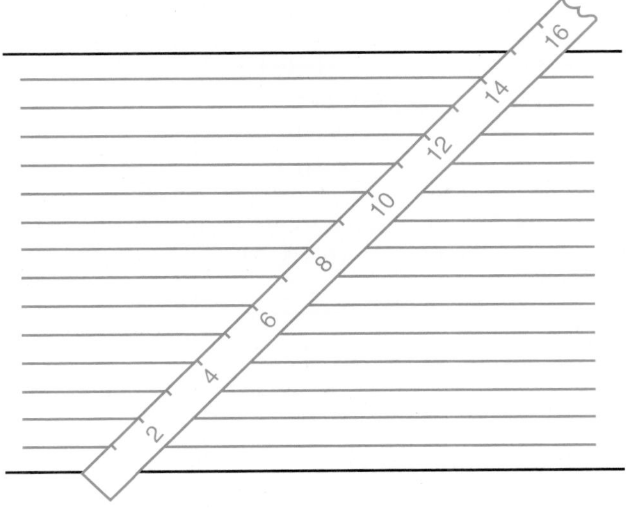

Goodheart-Willcox Publisher

Figure 24-25. Divide the total rise into the specified number of risers. The number of risers in this example is 15.

4. Calculate the total run by multiplying the tread width (10-1/2″) by the number of treads: 10-1/2″ × 14 treads = 147″.
5. Lay out the total run and tread widths, as shown in **Figure 24-26**. In CADD, use the **DIVIDE** command to determine the locations of the 14 treads.
6. Darken the tread and riser lines, draw the bottom edge of the stringer, and locate the stairwell rough opening size. This dimension is a function of the headroom dimension. Minimum headroom is 6′-8″. Step 4 is shown in **Figure 24-27**.
7. Remove all construction lines. Add dimensions and notes, as shown in **Figure 24-28**.

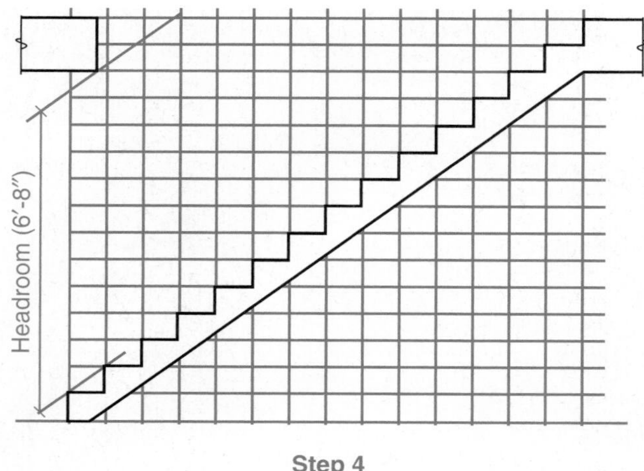

Goodheart-Willcox Publisher

Figure 24-27. Darken the tread and riser object lines. If you are using CADD, trim the construction lines to create the final object lines. Also, draw the stairwell rough opening.

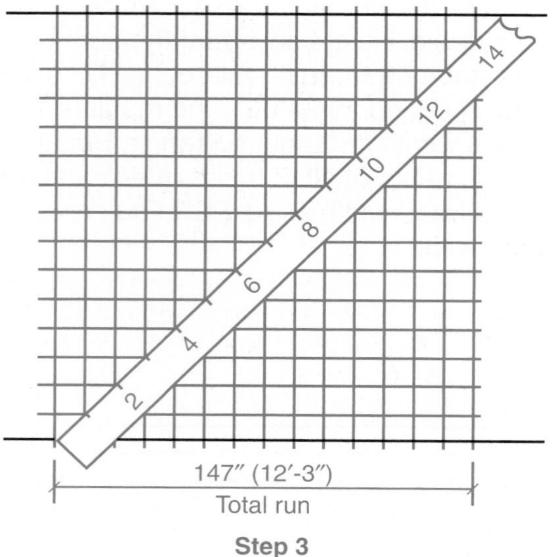

Goodheart-Willcox Publisher

Figure 24-26. Lay out the total run and divide it into the required number of treads. The number of treads in this example is 14.

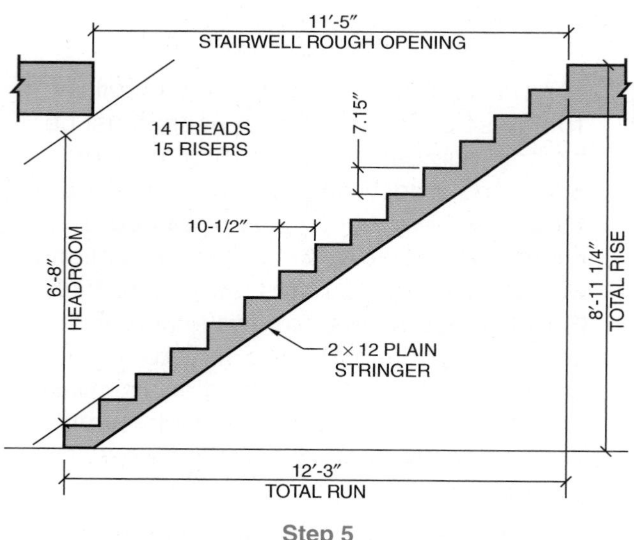

Goodheart-Willcox Publisher

Figure 24-28. Erase all construction lines. In CADD, you can erase the lines or turn off their layer. Also, add dimensions and notes.

Parametric Modeling | Creating Stairs

Parametric modeling programs used in architectural design provide special tools for designing stairs. Often, powerful tools are available in these programs to automatically generate a flight of stairs based on user-defined parameters. The user typically specifies the type of stair configuration and construction materials. The base and top floor levels are then specified and a sketch is made to create the stairs. The number of risers and treads is calculated automatically based on the distance between the floors, maximum riser height, and minimum tread depth. Common stair configurations, such as straight run stairs, L stairs, U stairs, and spiral stairs, can usually be created by using the appropriate stair type. Typically, the program provides default stair types that can be adjusted to create a flight of stairs with the required parameters.

Stairs in parametric modeling are special 3D components made up of an assembly of individual elements. The individual elements include the *run* (a unit made up of the risers and treads), side supports (the members commonly called stringers), landings, and railings. The individual elements can be modified separately, but any changes affect the entire stair system. In addition, stairs update automatically if the base or top floor level changes. These features provide significant design flexibility and greatly simplify the process of drawing stairs on a floor plan.

Stairs can be created when the initial floor plan is created, or they can be added after modeling other components. Stairs that pass through a floor above require a floor opening, which is usually modeled separately from the stairs. One way to create a floor opening is to modify an existing floor. This is done by editing the sketch for the floor and sketching a "cutout" boundary that forms the opening. Another method is to create a special type of component called an *opening* that establishes the required floor opening for the stairs. The opening extends from a base level and "cuts" through the specified top level.

The following procedure is designed for creating a straight run of stairs from the basement level to the first floor level in a one-story home. This procedure builds on the parametric modeling procedure presented in Chapter 14, *Floor Plans*. The following is presented as a typical sequence, but specific steps will vary depending on the program used and type of stair construction.

1. Open the Basement Floor plan view. Access the **STAIR** command. Select a default stair type or make a duplicate and edit it to create a stair system with the required materials and dimensions. A typical default stair type uses a 7″ maximum riser height and 11″ tread depth. If needed, change the default material used for the risers, treads, and supports to an appropriate material, such as wood. Set the base constraint to the Basement Floor level. Set the top constraint to the First Floor level. The base and top offsets should be 0′-0″.
2. Access the appropriate option of the **STAIR** command to draw a straight run of component-based stairs. Specify the run width, which is typically the width of the stairs. Specify the appropriate run justification. For example, set center justification to locate the cursor at the center of the run when sketching the stairs. Right or left justification can be used to align the run with a wall. This example is intended for a single run of stairs without a landing within the flight. When more than one run is created in a flight of stairs, the **STAIR** command typically generates a landing between runs automatically.
3. Pick the first point of the run and move the cursor in the direction of travel for the stairs. As you move the cursor, the on-screen display indicates the number of risers created and the number of risers remaining. The number of risers remaining is based on the total number of risers calculated by the program. Move the cursor past the final remaining riser when it appears and pick to place the end of the stairs.

Parametric Modeling | Creating Stairs *(Continued)*

4. Create the floor opening for the stairs on the first floor. Switch to a 3D view to verify that the stairs pass through the first floor. Open the First Floor plan view and edit the floor sketch to create a boundary for the opening. To assist in creating the sketch, pick the lines forming the outer perimeter of the stairs. As an alternative, switch to the Basement Floor plan view and create an opening that extends to the First Floor level. The lines forming the perimeter of the stairs can be picked to help create the sketch for the opening. Ensure that the minimum headroom requirements are met by the floor opening.
5. Depending on the type of stairs created, the program typically generates railings by default. However, additional railings may need to be created at the top of the stairs along the floor opening. Access the **RAILING** command to place additional railings. Select the desired type of railing and make a sketch for each railing in the appropriate plan view. Draw lines that connect to the existing railing lines along the stairs so that the railing is continuous throughout its length.
6. Add the appropriate dimensions and notes to the plan view drawings. If required, create a section through the stairs and prepare section and detail views for the set of drawings.

Summary

- Main stairs are the primary stairway to the second floor and are often of higher quality than service stairs, which are intended for frequent, heavy use.
- Several different shapes or configurations are used for residential stairways, depending on the house design and available space.
- The three main structural parts of a stairway are the treads, risers, and stringers.
- Many AEC CADD programs have features to calculate acceptable stair designs automatically.
- Model building codes such as the International Residential Code have specific requirements for handrails and guardrails in residential structures.

Internet Resources

Acorn Stairlifts
Manufacturer of stairlifts

Arcways
Manufacturer of custom stairways

International Code Council
International Residential Code

LP Building Products
Manufacturer of building materials

National Hardwood Lumber Association
Information about the hardwood lumber industry

Review Questions

Answer the following questions using the information in this chapter.

1. Identify the seven stairway configurations used in residential construction.
2. Stairs connecting the first floor to the second floor or a split foyer to the first floor are known as _____ stairs.
3. Stairs with walls on both sides are known as _____ stairs.
4. A stair without a wall on one or both sides is known as a(n) _____ stair.
5. Which type of stairs has two landings along the flight of steps?
6. Which type of stairs has two parallel flights of steps?
7. Pie-shaped steps are generally associated with _____ stairs.
8. List the three main structural parts of a stairway.
9. The rounded part of the tread that extends past the face of the riser is the _____.
10. What type of stringer is cut or notched to match the profile of the stairs?
11. What is the difference between rise and run?
12. The total horizontal length of the stairway is the total _____.
13. The total floor-to-floor vertical height of the stairway is the total _____.
14. What should the slope of a stairway be?
15. In most building codes, what is the minimum acceptable headroom for a stairway?
16. What is the difference between a handrail and a guardrail?
17. Vertical members that support the handrail on open stairs are called _____.
18. List the types of stairway drawings that are typically provided in a set of residential plans.
19. Name three structures that can be added to a home, or built into a new home, to increase accessibility for people with special needs.
20. Explain how to calculate the total rise of a stairway.

Suggested Activities

1. Visit a local lumber company that sells precut stairs. Collect information and literature about these stairs. Bring this literature to class to help build a catalog file on stairs.
2. Using CADD, design an enclosed, straight run stairs with housed stringers. The distance from the finished floor to the finished floor is 9′-1 1/4″. The distance between the finished walls is 3′-4″. Provide the necessary drawings, dimensions, and notes.

3. Select a basic type of stairs. Using CADD, create the necessary construction drawings. Then, build a scale model as accurately as possible. Display this model along with the construction drawings.
4. Locate at least two different stairways in residences in your community. The stairways may be in a private home or in a historic home that is open to the public. With permission, measure the tread width and riser height of each stairway. Using CADD, draw a profile of the tread and riser. Measure the slope using the appropriate CADD function. Rate the stairways on ease of travel and safety.

Problem Solving Case Study

You are an entry-level drafter for a large design drafting firm. Your supervisor has asked you to do the stair calculations for straight run stairs in a new custom home project. The finished floor to finished floor height from the first floor to the second floor is 10′-0″.

Given this information, design the stairs and answer the following questions.

1. How many treads are required?
2. How many risers are required?
3. What is the tread size?
4. What is the run of the stairs?

Certification Prep

The following questions are presented in the style used in the American Design Drafting Association (ADDA) Drafter Certification Test. Answer the questions using the information in this chapter.

1. Match each stairway configuration with its description.

   Stairway configurations: 1. L stairs, 2. U stairs, 3. Winder stairs, 4. Spiral stairs, 5. Circular stairs

   A. Have trapezoidal steps along an irregular curve or arc.
   B. Have a landing at which the stairway turns 90°.
   C. Have two flights of stairs parallel to each other.
   D. Steps rise like a corkscrew around a center point.
   E. Pie-shaped treads take the place of a landing.
2. Which of the following statements are true about stairways?
   A. The main supporting members of a stairway are the stringers.
   B. Eight general types of stairs are commonly used in residential construction.
   C. All building codes require railings on stairs and ramps.
   D. The two basic types of railings are handrails and guardrails.
3. Which of the following statements about stairways are *false*?
   A. Handrails usually consist of a single rail installed at a specified height.
   B. The slope of a stairway should be between 35° and 40°.
   C. Plain stringers contain grooves to hold the treads and risers in place.
   D. Total run is the total floor-to-floor height of a stairway.

Curricular Connections

1. **Social Science.** The owner of a Queen Anne Victorian home built in 1898 is in his early 60s and is considering making changes to improve accessibility as he grows older. The house is in excellent shape structurally. It currently has winder stairs from the first to the second floor, and the owner is afraid that sooner or later, he will fall. Consider all of the social, historical, and safety implications of various changes that could be made. What accessibility changes might you suggest to the homeowner? Explain why you decided on these changes.

STEM Connections

1. **Math.** A series of stairs is required for a four-story residential structure. The finished floor dimensions are as follows:

   First floor to second floor: 14′-0″

   Second floor to third floor: 12′-0″

   Third floor to fourth floor: 11′-0″

   How many risers and treads will be needed for each stairway?

2. **Science.** The Americans with Disabilities Act recommends that a walking surface have a static friction coefficient of 0.6 to help keep people and wheelchairs from slipping. Find out more about friction coefficients and how they apply in the ADA guidelines. Write a paragraph explaining why the ADA makes this recommendation.

Communicating about Architecture

1. **Reading.** With a partner, make flash cards of the key terms in this chapter. On the front of the card, write the term. On the back of the card, write the pronunciation and a brief definition. Use this chapter and a dictionary for guidance. Then take turns quizzing one another on the pronunciations and definitions of the key terms.

2. **Speaking.** Select five of the key terms in this chapter and imagine them being used by architects in a real-life context. With a partner, role-play a situation in which an architectural firm is asked to design a stairway with circular stairs for a new two-story home.

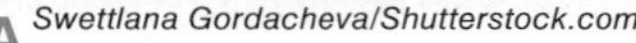

Swettlana Gordacheva/Shutterstock.com

A

Rade Kovac/Shutterstock.com

B

Wilm Ihlenfeld/Shutterstock.com

C

Fireplaces are available in many designs and styles. A—Traditional. B—Contemporary. C—This fireplace is visible from two different rooms.

Chapter 25

Fireplace, Chimney, and Stove Details

Objectives

After completing this chapter, you will be able to:

- Identify the parts of a standard masonry fireplace and chimney.
- Compare various types of fireplaces that are appropriate for a residence.
- Apply the appropriate principles to design a typical fireplace.
- Explain the difference between a radiant and circulating stove.

Key Terms

ash dump
catalytic stove
chimney
circulating stove
cleanout
damper
firebrick
fire chamber
fireclay
flue
hearth
inner hearth
prefabricated metal fireplace
radiant heat
radiant stove
saddle
single-face fireplace
smoke chamber
smoke shelf
three-face fireplace
two-face adjacent fireplace
two-face opposite fireplace

Almost everyone enjoys the sound and warmth of a roaring fire in the fireplace. The fireplace is often a focal point in the living room or family room. See **Figure 25-1**. Frank Lloyd Wright called a fireplace "the heart" of the house and typically located the fireplace in the center of the floor plan. Including a fireplace in a home plan is an important design consideration. However, many homes have fireplaces that are pleasing to the eye, yet fail to function properly. Care must be taken in the design and construction of a fireplace and chimney to make sure the fireplace will perform safely and according to local building codes.

Several different types of fireplaces are included in designs for today's homes. Some

Breadmaker/Shutterstock.com

Figure 25-1. An attractive fireplace may be the focal point of a living room.

are traditional in design, while others are contemporary. Metal fireplaces are commonplace. Some of these are wood-burning, but many are gas-fired and designed to give the impression of a wood fire. Often, the design of the fireplace depends on the building materials for its charm. See **Figure 25-2**.

Parts of a Fireplace

The basic parts of a fireplace include the fire chamber, hearth, damper, smoke shelf, and flue. The chimney and the framing around the fireplace are also considered parts of a fireplace. See **Figure 25-3**.

MaxFX/Shutterstock.com

Figure 25-2. Natural stone was dressed and used to create an interesting effect in this custom fireplace.

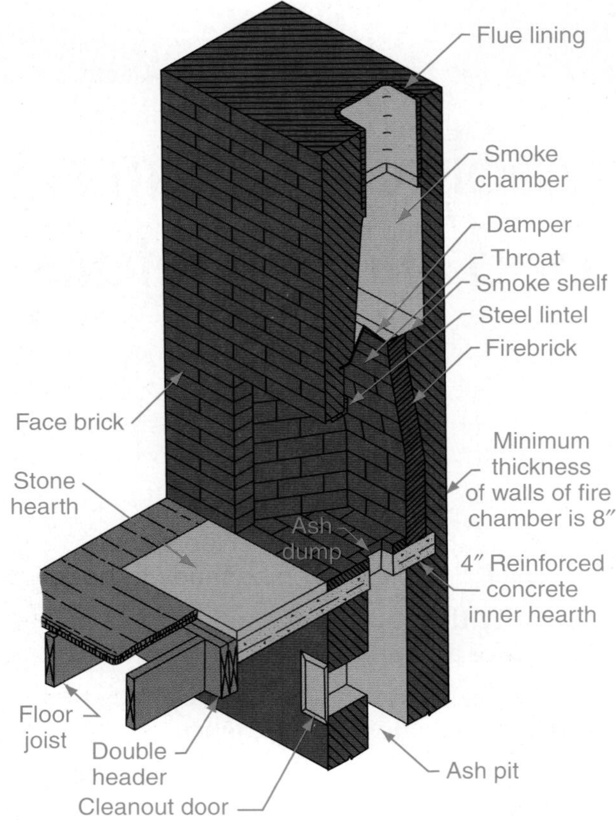

Goodheart-Willcox Publisher

Figure 25-3. This three-dimensional section drawing of a fireplace shows the various parts.

Fire Chamber

The ***fire chamber*** is the heart of the fireplace. This is where the fire is contained and controlled for safety and comfort. The fire chamber is usually lined with ***firebrick***, a type of brick that can withstand intense heat. ***Fireclay***—a fire-resistant, mortar-like material—is used as a bonding material between the firebricks.

The shape of the fire chamber is critical and must be designed to direct hot gases and smoke up the chimney. If the chamber is too deep, little heat will be reflected out into the room. On the other hand, if it is too shallow, the fireplace is likely to smoke into the room. The wall thickness on the back and sides of the fire chamber should be a minimum of 8″, as noted in **Figure 25-3**.

When space is available below the fireplace and finished floor, a cavity where ashes can collect and be removed is an excellent feature. This cavity, called an ***ash dump***, consists of a metal trap door in the middle of the fireplace floor that connects to the ash chamber below. A ***cleanout*** or door is provided in the ash chamber for the removal of ashes. See **Figure 25-4**.

Hearth

The ***hearth*** is an area around a wood-burning fireplace that protects the floor from sparks. It must be constructed of a noncombustible material and should extend at least 16″ in front of the fireplace to protect the floor from sparks. See **Figure 25-5**. In conventional construction, the hearth extends into the fireplace to form an ***inner hearth***. This part of the hearth makes up the floor of the firebox.

The inner hearth is covered with firebrick, whereas the outer hearth is usually covered with stone, slate, or ceramic tile. The hearth may be even with the floor level or raised to a pleasing height.

In many areas, building codes do not require gas fireplaces to have a hearth. However, especially when a gas fireplace is designed to look like a traditional fireplace, a hearth can be a pleasing and "authentic" touch.

Iriana Shiyan/Shutterstock.com

Figure 25-5. The black slate tile of this hearth extends into the room to protect the wood floor from sparks.

Damper

Every fireplace should have a ***damper*** to regulate the flow of air and stop downdrafts of cold air when the fireplace is not in operation. The damper is located in the throat of the fireplace, where the firebox meets the flue. Refer again to **Figure 25-3**. The damper opens toward the back of the throat.

Nejron Photo/Shutterstock.com

Figure 25-4. The cleanout in this fireplace is a drawer under the firebox that opens from inside the house. In other designs, the cleanout opens to the outside of the house.

The damper opening should be larger than the area of the flue lining and as long as the width dimension of the fireplace. It should be placed 8″ above the top of the fireplace opening. Common damper sizes are shown in **Figure 25-6**. Dampers are produced in both steel and cast iron.

Because the damper is the part of the fireplace that closes to keep outside air from entering the house, it is a good idea to install a high-quality damper. Ill-fitting dampers can be responsible for a great deal of heat loss and energy waste.

Smoke Shelf and Smoke Chamber

The damper alone cannot keep all of the cold air from entering a home, because the damper

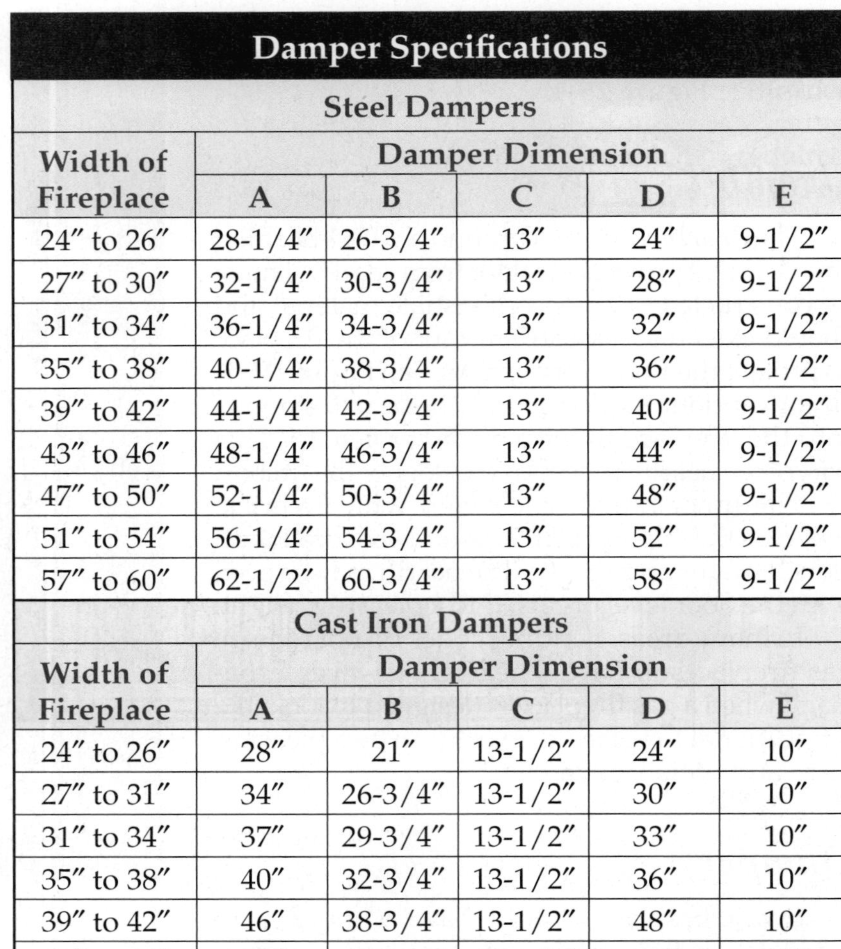

Damper Specifications					
Steel Dampers					
Width of Fireplace	Damper Dimension				
	A	B	C	D	E
24″ to 26″	28-1/4″	26-3/4″	13″	24″	9-1/2″
27″ to 30″	32-1/4″	30-3/4″	13″	28″	9-1/2″
31″ to 34″	36-1/4″	34-3/4″	13″	32″	9-1/2″
35″ to 38″	40-1/4″	38-3/4″	13″	36″	9-1/2″
39″ to 42″	44-1/4″	42-3/4″	13″	40″	9-1/2″
43″ to 46″	48-1/4″	46-3/4″	13″	44″	9-1/2″
47″ to 50″	52-1/4″	50-3/4″	13″	48″	9-1/2″
51″ to 54″	56-1/4″	54-3/4″	13″	52″	9-1/2″
57″ to 60″	62-1/2″	60-3/4″	13″	58″	9-1/2″
Cast Iron Dampers					
Width of Fireplace	Damper Dimension				
	A	B	C	D	E
24″ to 26″	28″	21″	13-1/2″	24″	10″
27″ to 31″	34″	26-3/4″	13-1/2″	30″	10″
31″ to 34″	37″	29-3/4″	13-1/2″	33″	10″
35″ to 38″	40″	32-3/4″	13-1/2″	36″	10″
39″ to 42″	46″	38-3/4″	13-1/2″	48″	10″
43″ to 46″	52″	44-3/4″	13-1/2″	48″	10″
47″ to 50″	57-1/2″	50-1/2″	13-1/2″	54″	10″
51″ to 54″	64″	56-1/2″	14-1/2″	60″	11-1/2″
57″ to 60″	76″	58″	14-1/2″	72″	11-1/2″

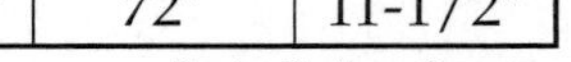

Donley Brothers Company

Figure 25-6. Typical design specifications for steel and cast iron dampers.

must be open while a fire is burning in the fireplace. A ***smoke shelf*** causes cold air flowing down the chimney to be deflected upward into the rising warm air from the fire. This action prevents the down-rushing cold air from forcing smoke into the room. The smoke shelf height is determined by the location of the damper.

The ***smoke chamber*** is the area just above the smoke shelf and damper. It is basically pyramidal in shape and directs smoke up and away from the firebox and into the flue. The back side of the smoke chamber is usually vertical. The chamber is normally constructed from brick or other heat-resistant masonry. A typical smoke shelf and smoke chamber are shown in the section drawing in **Figure 25-3**.

Chimney and Flue

A ***chimney*** is a freestanding, vertical structure that allows smoke from a fire to leave the home. The chimney houses the ***flue***, which is the actual path that conducts the smoke safely to the top of the chimney and into the outside air. The flue begins at the top of the smoke chamber and extends to the top of the chimney. The flue usually has a clay lining. Flue linings are available in round, square, and rectangular shapes and can be rigid or flexible. Refer to local building codes for flue lining requirements and installation guidelines.

Each flue requires at least 4″ of masonry on all sides. Each fireplace in a structure must have its own flue. Ideally, the flue will be centered directly above the fireplace and installed in a straight vertical line. A small amount of offset is permissible; however, efficiency is reduced when the flue is not straight. When an offset is required, use a flexible flue lining for maximum efficiency.

The flue must be large enough to provide the necessary updraft. A rule of thumb to follow in determining the proper flue size is that the cross-sectional area of the flue should be at least 1/10th the size of the fireplace opening. This is the minimum size specified by the International Residential Code for square flues. For round flues, the cross-sectional area should be at least 1/12 the size of the fireplace opening. For rectangular flues, the minimum size is based on the aspect ratio of the flue. When the aspect ratio is less than 2 to 1, the cross-sectional area should be at least 1/10 the size of the fireplace opening. When the aspect ratio is 2 to 1 or more, the cross-sectional area should be at least 1/8 the size of the fireplace opening. It is better to have a flue that is slightly too large than one that is too small; however, a flue that is significantly oversize will not function properly. You can find a list of standard flue lining sizes on the websites of most chimney and flue manufacturers.

Proper flue size is also related to several other factors. If the height of the flue is less than 14′, the size should be increased to provide the necessary updraft. The updraft is increased by making the flue higher. Prevailing winds and surrounding trees and buildings also affect the draft. If the flue is sheltered, the size should be increased. In addition, the height that the chimney extends above the roof must meet building code

Employability

E-Mail Etiquette

In everyday life and in business, there is a proper way to behave. This is known as *etiquette*. Rules of etiquette have been adapted to today's business needs, including proper conduct when writing e-mail. In many architectural firms, employees may write e-mail messages daily to coworkers, vendors, and customers. It is important to follow the proper etiquette when you write messages that represent your company. The rules of e-mail etiquette include:

- Use a tone that is appropriate to your relationship and to the writing situation.
- Do not use emoticons or slang in a business e-mail message.
- Let the reader know if you are sending an attachment by mentioning it in the message.
- Do not send or forward personal messages, jokes, chain letters, or spams.
- Never use profanity or any other type of derogatory language.
- Never respond in anger to an e-mail message. Wait until you are calm enough to respond in a professional manner.
- Avoid overuse of e-mail. Stop to think whether a phone call or personal visit would be more productive.
- Use the "blind carbon copy" window for large external mailings to protect recipients' privacy.
- Avoid using all capital letters in your message, because this implies shouting.

Activity

Imagine that you have received an e-mail message from a client at your architectural design firm. In the message, the client notes that he has received your latest design proposal and writes several paragraphs about how ugly your design is. Many of the items the client objects to are things that he originally wanted to be included in the design. He also threatens to speak to your supervisor about your work. You know that you based the design on the client's original wishes and that the design is as good as possible given the client's directions. Write an e-mail message back to the client. Maintain a professional manner and try to keep the client from seeking a different architectural firm.

requirements. The International Residential Code requires that the chimney extend a minimum of 2′-0″ above any structure within 10′-0″ of the chimney and a minimum of 3′-0″ above the highest point where the chimney passes through the roof. See **Figure 25-7**. This is a safety factor, since sparks may fly out of the top and cause a roof fire.

A single chimney may have several flues. A flue is required for a gas furnace, a gas water heater, an incinerator, and each fireplace. The efficiency of a chimney may be increased if it is placed within the house, rather than on an outside wall. However, future updates or repairs to the flue are more difficult when the fireplace and chimney are not on an outside wall.

Framing

The chimney is a freestanding structure. It does not support any part of the house. In fact, fire codes prohibit direct contact of framing with surfaces of the fireplace or chimney. The International Residential Code specifies a minimum of 2″ of clearance between the fireplace and framing at the front and sides of the fireplace. At the back side of the fireplace, a minimum of 4″ of clearance is required. A minimum of 2″ of clearance is required between the chimney and framing. Refer to local building codes for specific requirements. The openings in the floor, ceiling, and roof through which the chimney passes must have double headers and trimmers to give the necessary support. See **Figure 25-8**.

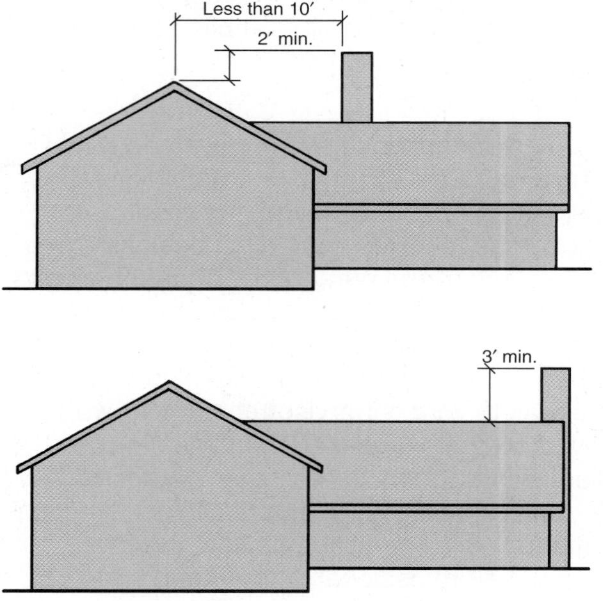

Goodheart-Willcox Publisher

Figure 25-7. Recommended chimney heights above the roof.

If a chimney is located along the ridge line (the peak or highest point) of a roof, the chance of water problems is minimized. However, if the chimney must be located along a single slope of the roof, special precautions must be taken to prevent leaking. Water can back up along the chimney and roof intersections and seep under the shingles. To prevent this, a ***saddle*** or *cricket* is built on the high side of the chimney to shed water. A saddle is particularly necessary if the roof slope is low or the chimney is wide. **Figure 25-9** shows the framing for a saddle.

The masonry above the fireplace opening on the interior of the house must be supported by a lintel, just as over a door or window. An angle steel lintel is the most common type. The required angle size varies with the width of the fireplace opening. A 3″ × 3″ × 1/4″ angle is sufficient for a 60″ opening.

Fireplace Design

The design of a fireplace depends on many factors. The homeowner's preferences and budget play a large role. The general style of the house should also be considered. A well-designed fireplace is functional and attractive, and it fits well with the style of the room and house.

Designing with CADD

Some CADD packages include an option or function that automates the process of specifying fireplaces. All the drafter has to specify is the width of the opening and the desired style of fireplace. The plan view, elevations, and details are generated automatically. If you are using a CADD package that does not have this option, you will need to draw the plan view, elevations, and details using the available CADD commands.

Fireplace Specifications

The first decisions to be made in designing a fireplace are the type of fireplace and the size of the opening. Generally, fireplaces can be

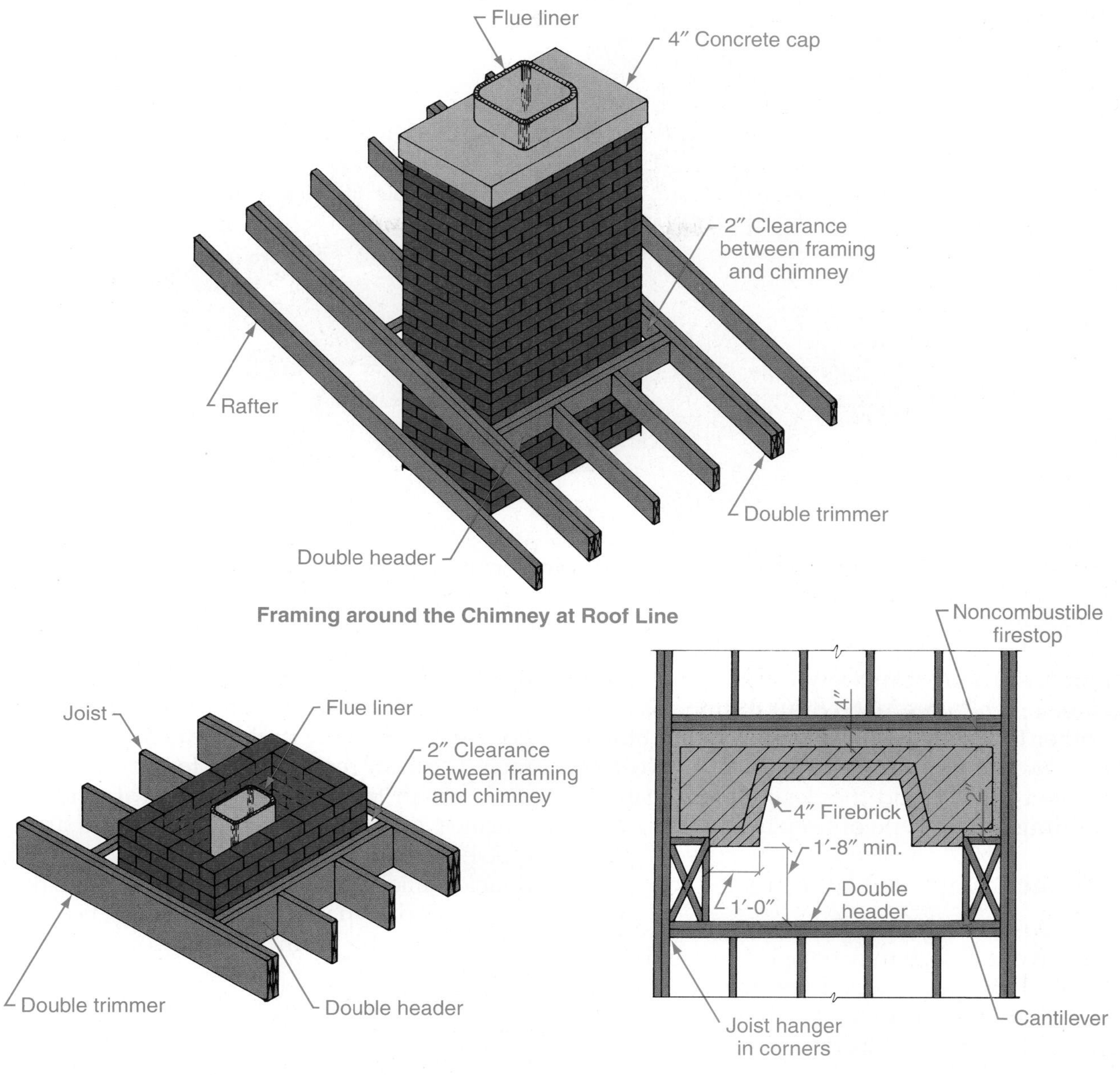

Figure 25-8. Typical framing for chimneys and fireplaces.

classified as single-face, two-face opposite, two-face adjacent, three-face, or prefabricated metal. See **Figure 25-10**. Each type has specific design requirements that must be met if the fireplace is to be safe and perform properly.

Single-Face Fireplace

A ***single-face fireplace*** has a single opening on one face and is the most common type. A single-face fireplace is shown in **Figure 25-1**. Single-face fireplaces are the least difficult to construct and usually function better than the other types of fireplaces. **Figure 25-11** provides specifications for several single-face fireplaces. The proper damper size can be determined from the table in **Figure 25-6**.

Two-Face Opposite Fireplace

A ***two-face opposite fireplace*** is open on both the front and back sides. Its primary advantage

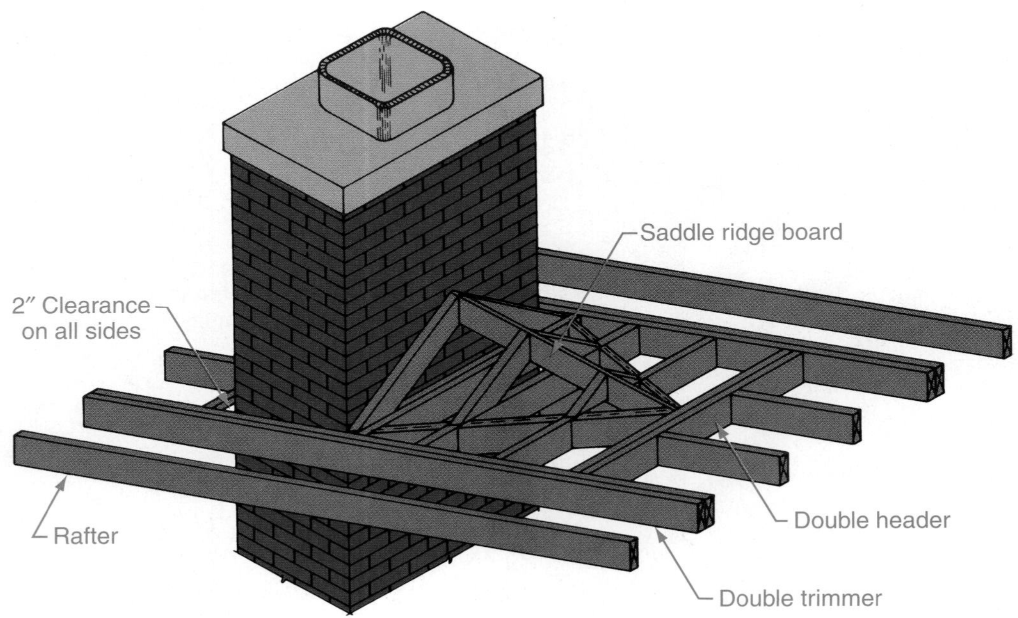

Figure 25-9. The framing for a saddle to shed water away from the chimney.

is that two rooms can view the fireplace. Care must be taken to prevent a draft from one side to the other that may result in smoke being blown into a room. **Figure 25-12** shows a two-face opposite fireplace and the design specifications pertaining to this type of fireplace.

Two-Face Adjacent Fireplace

A ***two-face adjacent fireplace*** is open on the front and one side. It may be open on the right or left side. This type is also known as a *projecting corner fireplace*. **Figure 25-13** shows a two-face adjacent fireplace and its design specifications.

Three-Face Fireplace

A ***three-face fireplace*** is open on three sides. Ordinarily, two long sides and one short side are open. This is also known as a *three-way fireplace*. This type is something of a novelty; however, it can add interest if the interior room layout is properly designed and arranged. **Figure 25-14** shows a three-face fireplace and typical design specifications.

Prefabricated Metal Fireplaces

Most fireplaces in new residential construction today are ***prefabricated metal fireplaces***. These units, made of steel, include not only the inner hearth and fire chamber, but also the throat, damper, smoke shelf, and smoke chamber. See **Figure 25-15**. Many prefabricated fireplaces also include a heat recirculation feature designed to draw air in from the room, heat it, and return warmed air to the room. These units are very efficient because the sides and back consist of a double-walled passageway where the air is heated. Cool air is drawn into the passageway, heated, and returned to the room through registers located at a higher level.

Some prefabricated fireplaces are wall-mounted, some are enclosed in masonry, and others are freestanding models. See **Figure 25-16**. Those that are enclosed in masonry can be incorporated into almost any fireplace and home style. Prefabricated fireplaces are generally purchased complete with all the necessary parts required to install them. **Figure 25-17** shows installation details for a typical prefabricated metal fireplace. Consult local building codes prior to installation.

Stoves

Wood- or coal-burning stoves generally produce more usable heat than fireplaces. They are frequently located in such a manner that heat is radiated from all sides. See **Figure 25-18**. They

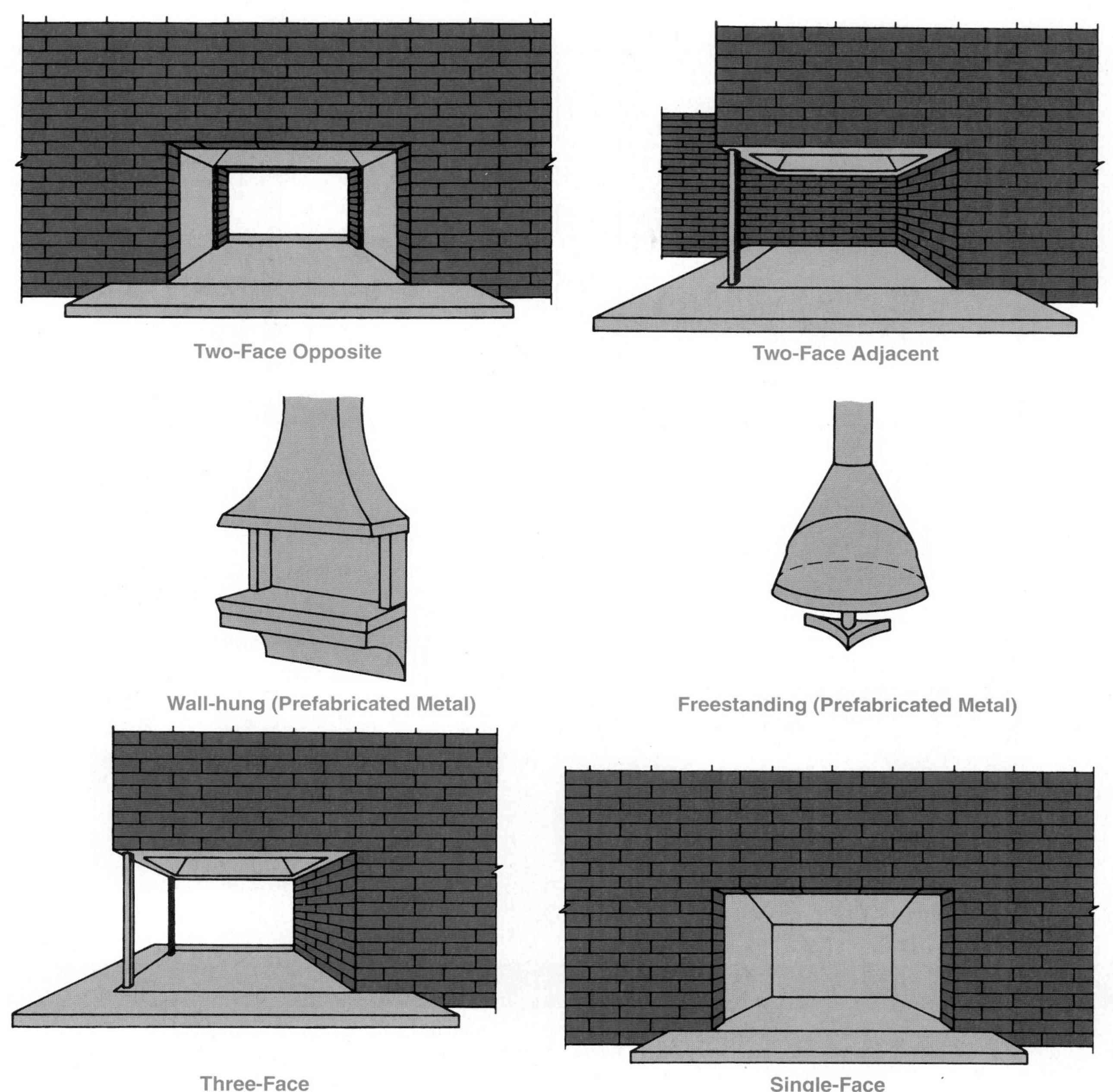

Figure 25-10. Types of fireplaces include single-face, two-face opposite, two-face adjacent, three-face, and prefabricated metal. Prefabricated fireplaces may be wall-hung or freestanding.

are typically used as local sources of heat, rather than a total heating system. The heating effectiveness of stoves varies greatly among manufacturers and models.

Types of Stoves

There are two main types of stoves: radiant stoves and circulating stoves. Both types produce ***radiant heat***, which is heat that passes through the air with no assistance from air flow. A ***radiant stove*** warms a room only through radiant heat. See **Figure 25-19**. A ***circulating stove*** uses air flow, as well as radiant heat, to distribute warmth throughout a room.

A circulating stove has an outer jacket to facilitate air movement. The jacket is designed to draw cold air in, warm it, and return warmed

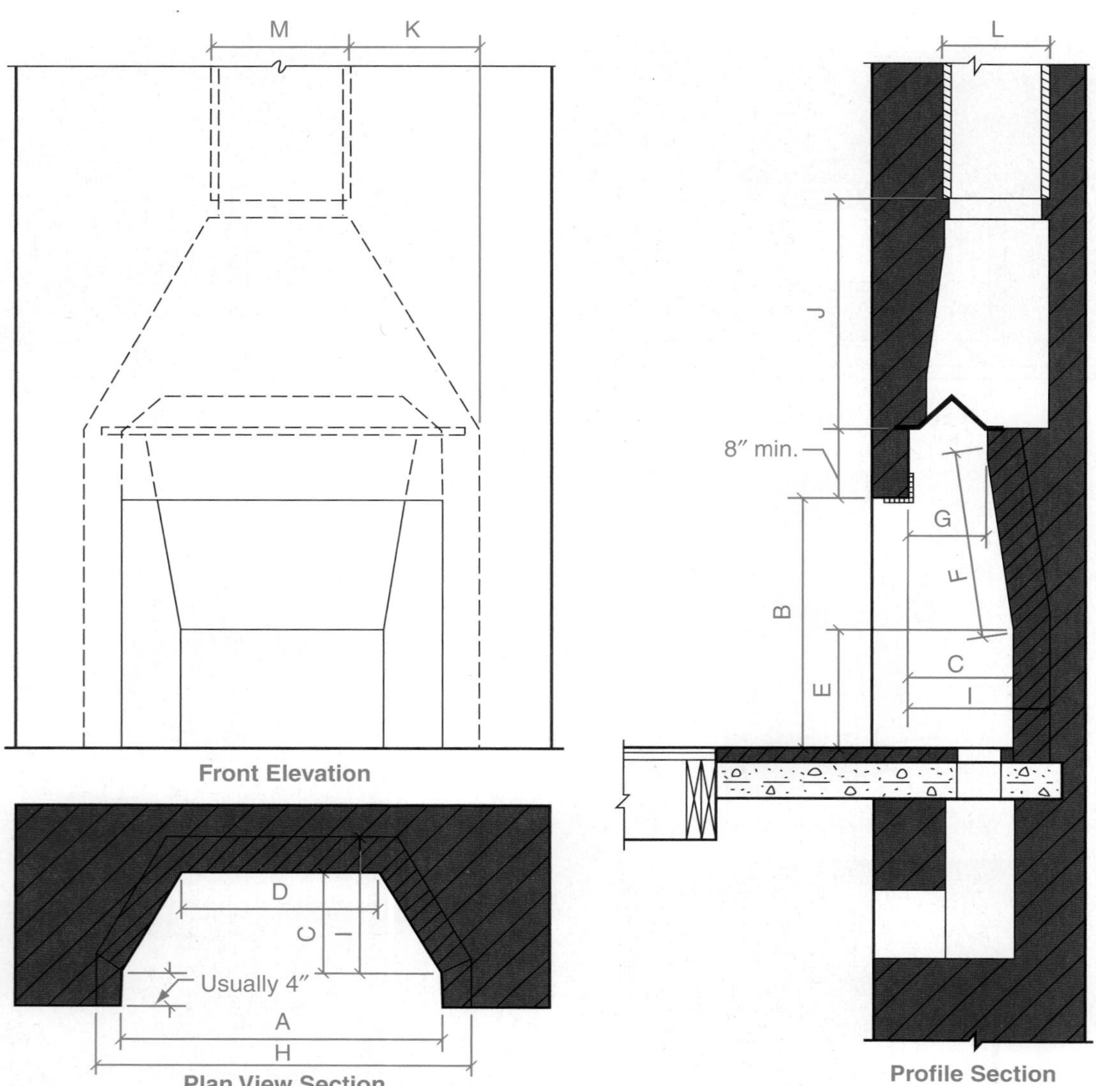

Design Data for Single-Face Fireplaces

Width	Height	Depth	Back	Verti-back	Slope Back	Throat	Width	Depth	Smoke Chamb	Flue Lining Sizes				
										Rectangular		Round	Modular	
A	B	C	D	E	F	G	H	I	J	K	L × M		K	L × M
24	24	16	11	14	15	8-3/4	32	20	19	11-3/4	8-1/2 × 8-1/2	8	10	8 × 12
26	24	16	13	14	15	8-3/4	34	20	21	12-3/4	8-1/2 × 8-1/2	8	11	8 × 12
28	24	16	15	14	15	8-3/4	36	20	21	11-1/2	8-1/2 × 13	10	12	8 × 12
30	29	16	17	14	18	8-3/4	38	20	24	12-1/2	8-1/2 × 13	10	13	12 × 12
32	29	16	19	14	21	8-3/4	40	20	24	13-1/2	8-1/2 × 13	10	14	12 × 12
36	29	16	23	14	21	8-3/4	44	20	27	15-1/2	13 × 13	12	16	12 × 12
40	29	16	27	14	21	8-3/4	48	20	29	17-1/2	13 × 13	12	16	12 × 12
42	32	16	29	14	23	8-3/4	50	20	32	18-1/2	13 × 13	12	17	16 × 16
48	32	18	33	14	23	8-3/4	56	22	37	21-1/2	13 × 13	15	20	16 × 16
54	37	20	37	16	27	13	68	24	45	25	13 × 18	15	26	16 × 20
60	37	22	42	16	27	13	72	27	45	27	13 × 18	15	26	16 × 20
60	40	22	42	16	29	13	72	27	45	27	18 × 18	18	26	16 × 20
72	40	22	54	16	29	13	84	27	56	33	18 × 18	18	32	20 × 20
84	40	24	64	20	26	13	96	29	67	36	20 × 20	20	36	20 × 20
96	40	24	76	20	26	13	108	29	75	42	24 × 24	22	42	20 × 20

Dimensions are in inches. Flue sizes are for a chimney height of at least 14′-0″.

Goodheart-Willcox Publisher

Figure 25-11. Design specifications for single-face fireplaces.

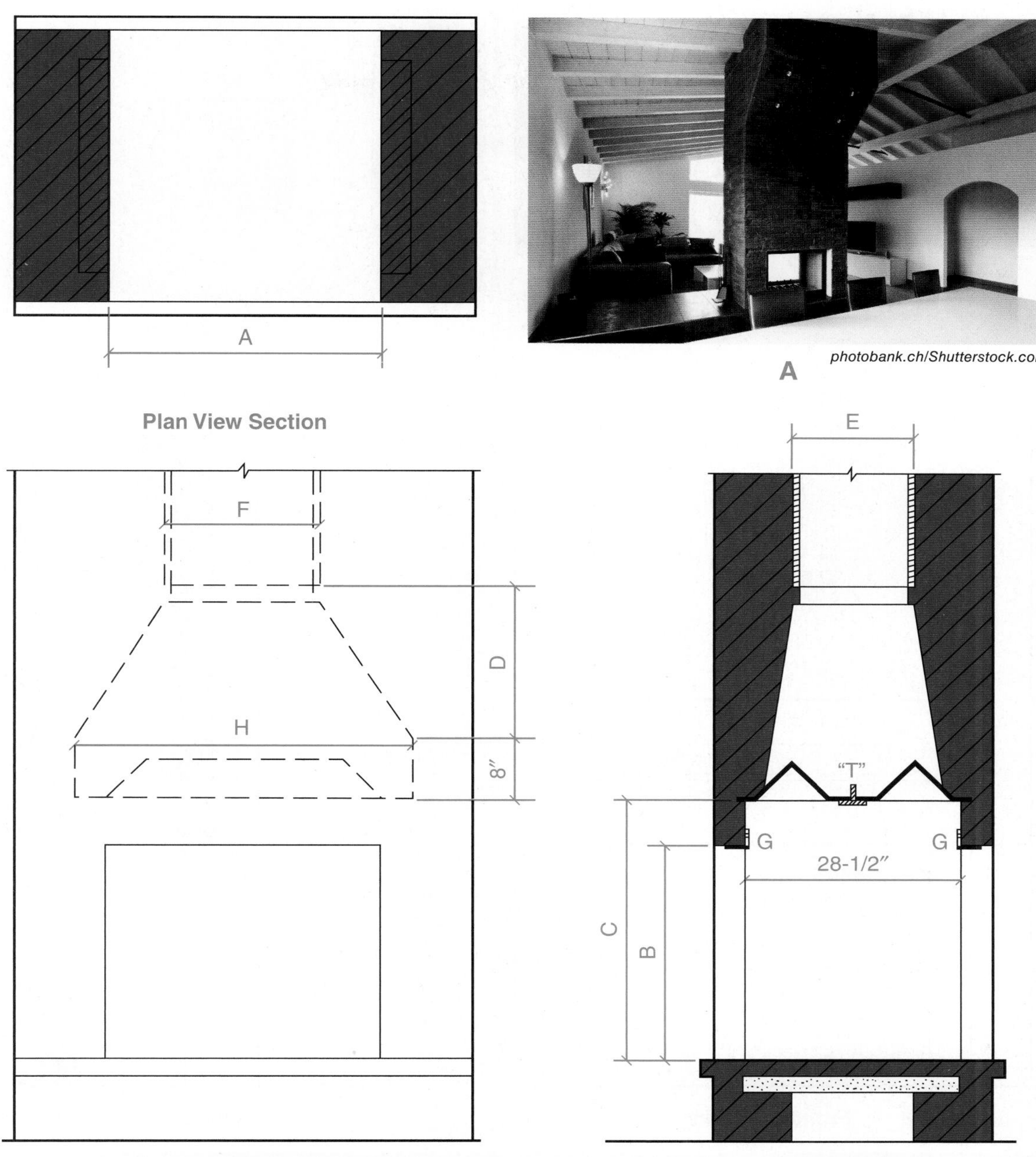

Design Data for Two-Face Opposite Fireplaces

A	B	C	D	Old Flue Size E	Old Flue Size F	Round	New Mod. Size E	New Mod. Size F	Angle G 2 Req'd.	H	Tee Length
28	24	35	19	13	13	12	12	16	36	36	35
32	29	35	21	13	18	15	16	16	40	40	39
36	29	35	21	13	18	15	16	20	42	44	43
40	29	35	27	18	18	18	16	20	48	48	47
48	32	37	32	18	18	18	20	20	54	56	55

Dimensions are in inches. Flue sizes are for a chimney height of at least 14′-0″. Angle G is 3″ × 3″ × 1/4″.

B

Goodheart-Willcox Publisher

Figure 25-12. A—Two rooms can benefit from a two-face opposite fireplace. B—Design specifications for two-face opposite fireplaces.

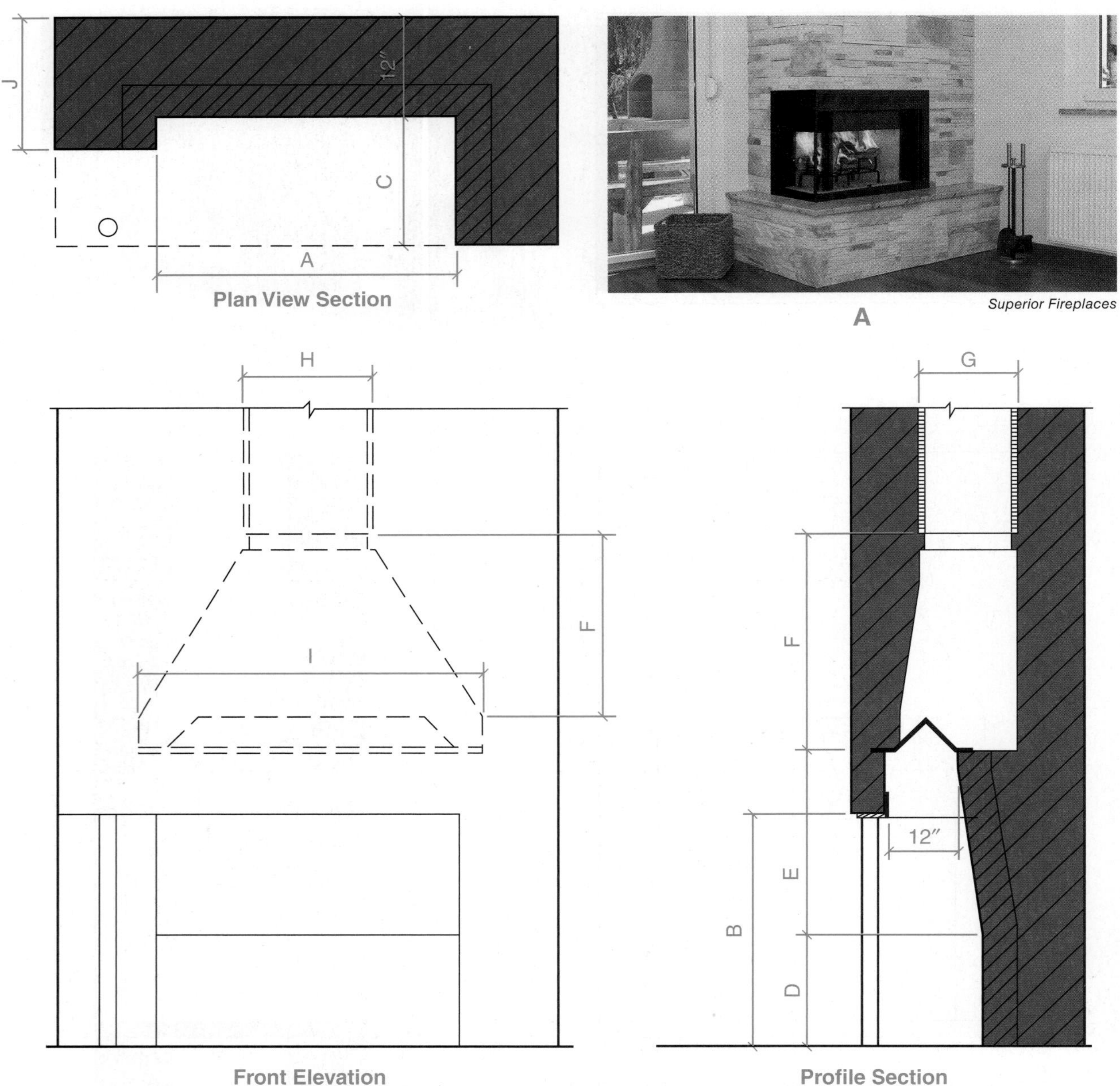

Design Data for Two-Face Adjacent Fireplaces

A	B	C	D	E	F	Old Flue G	Old Flue H	Round	Mod. Flue G	Mod. Flue H	I	J	Corner Post Height
28	26-1/2	16	14	20	29-1/4	13	13	12	12	12	36	16	26-1/2
32	26-1/2	16	14	20	32	13	13	12	12	16	40	16	26-1/2
36	26-1/2	16	14	20	35	13	13	12	12	16	44	16	26-1/2
40	29	16	14	20	35	13	18	15	16	16	48	16	29
48	29	20	14	24	43	13	18	15	16	16	56	20	29
54	29	20	14	23	45	13	18	15	16	16	62	20	29
60	29	20	14	23	51	13	18	15	16	20	68	20	29

Dimensions are in inches. Flue sizes are for a chimney height of at least 14′-0″.

B

Goodheart-Willcox Publisher

Figure 25-13. A—A two-face adjacent fireplace can provide a focal point for a corner location in a room. This fireplace is available in left-corner and right-corner versions. B—Design specifications for two-face adjacent fireplaces.

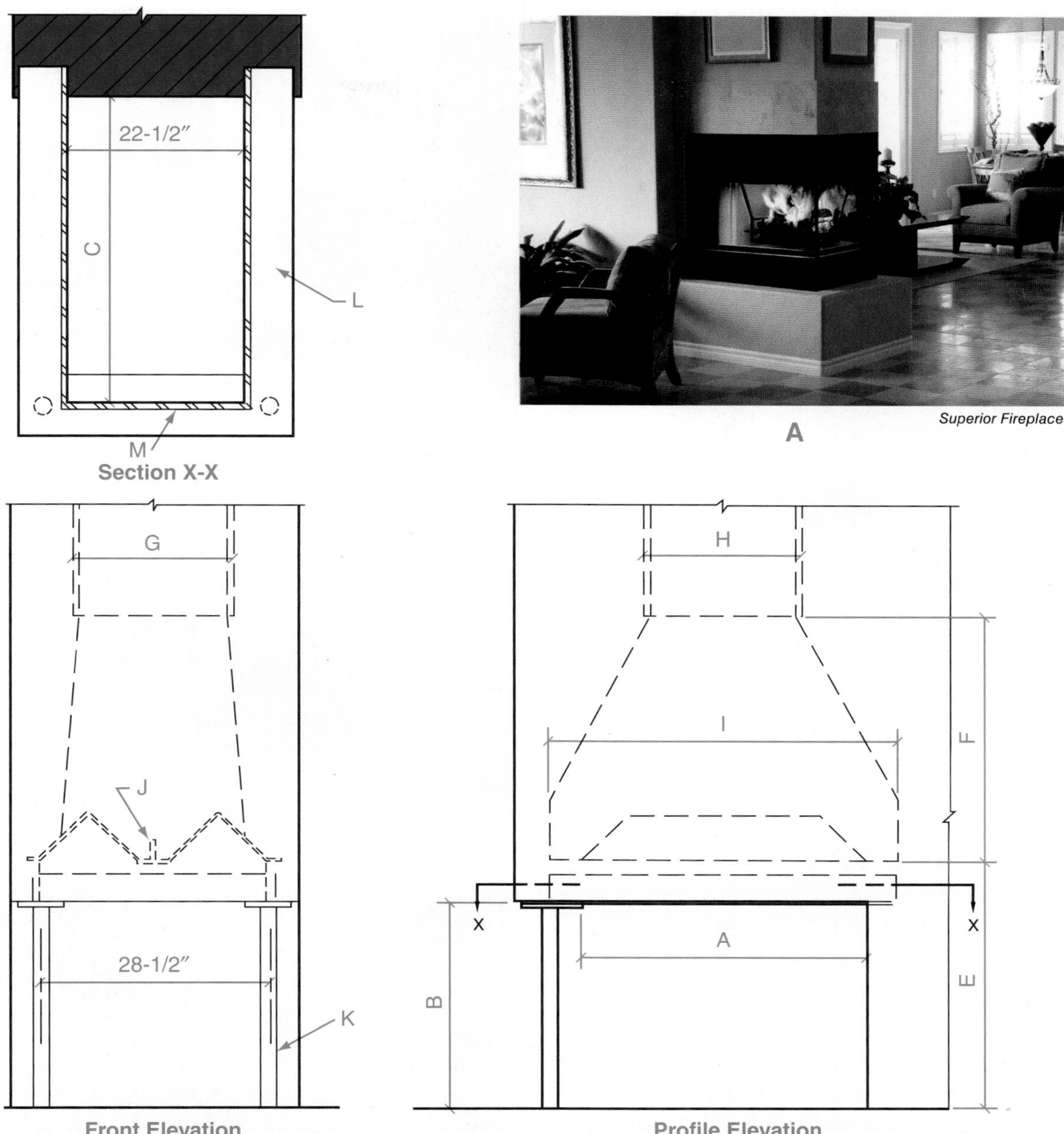

Design Data for Three-Face Fireplaces														
					Old Flue Size			New Modular Flue Size			Steel Tee	Post Height	Angle 2 Req'd.	Special Welding Tee
A	B	C	E	F	G	H	Round	G	H	I	J	K	L	M
28	26-1/2	32	32	24	18	18	18	16	20	36	35	26-1/2	36	34
32	26-1/2	36	32	27	18	18	18	20	20	40	39	26-1/2	40	34
36	26-1/2	40	32	32	18	18	18	20	20	44	43	26-1/2	44	34
40	26-1/2	44	32	35	18	18	18	20	20	48	47	26-1/2	48	34
48	26-1/2	52	32	35	20	20	20	20	24	56	55	26-1/2	56	34
Dimensions are in inches. Flue sizes are for a chimney height of at least 14′-0″.														

B

Goodheart-Willcox Publisher

Figure 25-14. A—The three-face fireplace in this home can be viewed from the dining area and an adjacent room. Notice that the hearth extends all the way around the three open sides. B—Design specifications for three-face fireplaces.

Heatilator, Inc.

Figure 25-15. This is a cutaway view of a prefabricated steel, heat-circulating fireplace.

A photobank.ch/Shutterstock.com

B tab62/Shutterstock.com

C Werner Stoffberg/Shutterstock.com

Figure 25-16. A—This prefabricated fireplace was mounted directly into the wall. Note the heating vents built into the wall below the unit. B—In this case, the homeowner decided to surround the prefabricated gas fireplace with tile and a mantel for a more traditional look. C—This small prefabricated gas fireplace is perfect for smaller homes.

Green Architecture

Pellet Stoves

Several manufacturers of wood-burning stoves now offer *pellet stoves*. These stoves burn pellets that are made from wood byproducts, such as sawdust, and wastes generated by the lumber and agricultural industries. The pellets are considered a carbon-neutral fuel because they neither reduce nor increase the amount of carbon dioxide in the surrounding air. They leave very little residue—as little as 1% if a high-quality pellet fuel is used. Pellet fuel can also be made from corn and some types of grain. Many pellet stoves are designed to use these alternative pellet sources as well as wood pellets.

Unlike traditional wood-burning stoves, pellet stoves do not always need a vertical flue. They do, however, require a sealed, double-walled vent system to channel exhaust gases out of the home. Many pellet stoves also require an outside air intake.

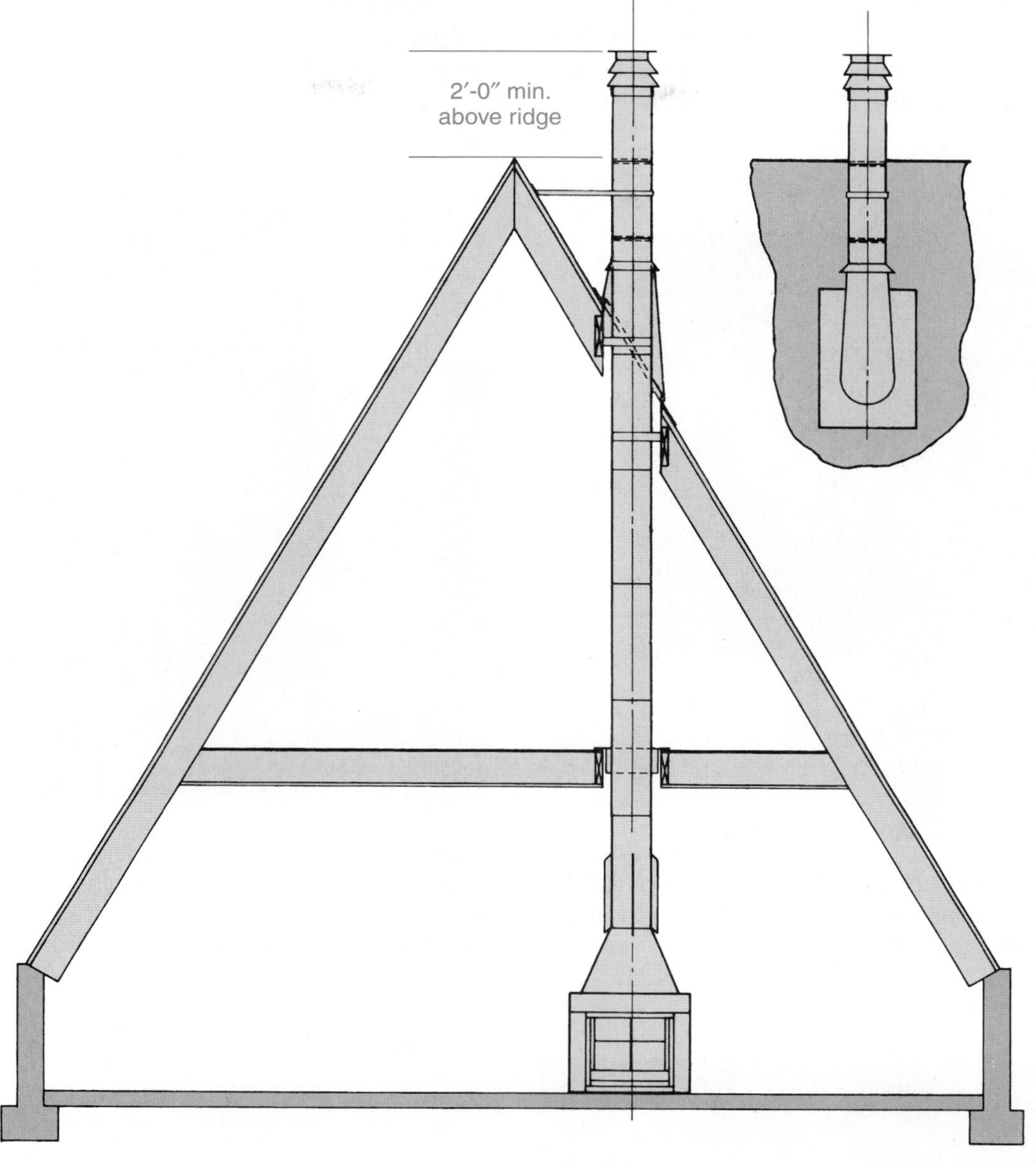

Goodheart-Willcox Publisher

Figure 25-17. A typical installation of a prefabricated metal fireplace in a cottage.

air to the room. Some stoves have a small blower to assist the air movement; others produce air flow without mechanical assistance. Circulated air flow provides more even heat than is possible with a radiant stove. Because of their lower surface temperature, circulating stoves are safer and can be placed closer to combustible material than radiant stoves.

Some wood-burning stoves use a ceramic catalyst. These ***catalytic stoves*** have a metal-coated ceramic chamber with a honeycomb design. This increases the efficiency of the stove by increasing combustion and lowering the temperature at which the wood burns. See **Figure 25-20**.

Stove Efficiency

Stoves are commonly classified according to their heating efficiency. Low-efficiency stoves range from 20% to 30% efficient. Examples of low-efficiency stoves include simple box stoves, Franklin stoves, pot belly stoves, and some parlor stoves. Medium-efficiency stoves range from 35% to 50% efficient. They provide better combustion and have less air leakage into the stove. Most include a device to ensure a constant burning rate. High-efficiency stoves are over 50% efficient. They include all of the features of the medium-efficiency stoves, but also use baffles, long smoke paths, and heat exchange devices to increase heat output.

Buslik/Shutterstock.com

Figure 25-18. This wood-burning stove has multiple windows and is designed to be viewed from the sides as well as from the front.

Paul Maguire/Shutterstock.com

Figure 25-19. A radiant stove radiates heat energy from all of its surfaces. Notice the floor protection provided around this stove. All wood- and coal-burning stoves must be vented to the outside, just like a fireplace.

A

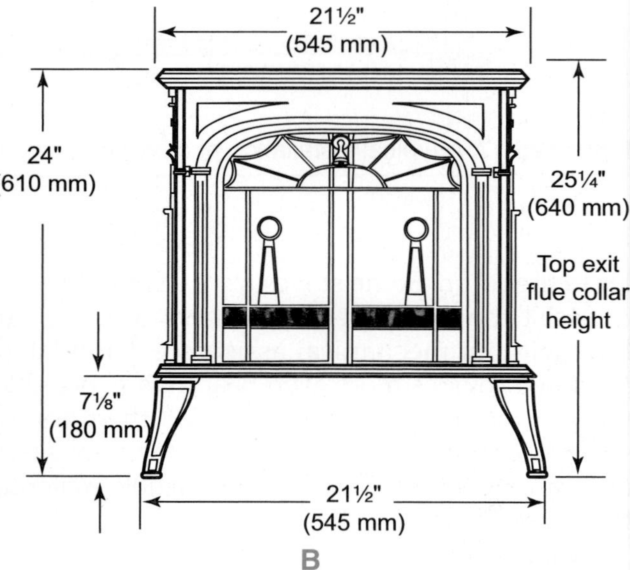

B

Vermont Castings

Figure 25-20. Catalytic stoves are among the most energy-efficient wood-burning stoves available today. A—This catalytic stove has an efficiency rating of 85%. B—Design specifications for the unit shown in A.

Summary

- Care must be taken in the design and construction of a fireplace and chimney to make sure the fireplace will perform safely and according to local building codes.
- The basic parts of a fireplace include the fire chamber, hearth, damper, smoke shelf, and flue.
- The hearth should be constructed of noncombustible material and should extend at least 16″ in front of the fireplace to protect the floor from sparks.
- Every fireplace should have a damper to regulate the flow of air and stop downdrafts of cold air when the fireplace is not in operation.
- The five general types of fireplaces are single-face, two-face opposite, two-face adjacent, three-face, and prefabricated metal.
- Wood- and coal-burning stoves generally produce more usable heat than fireplaces.

Internet Resources

Napoleon
Manufacturer of fireplaces, stoves, and inserts

Superior Clay Corporation
Manufacturer of clay flue liners

US Environmental Protection Agency (EPA)
Information about efficiency ratings for fireplaces and stoves

Vermont Castings
Manufacturer of fireplaces, stoves, and grills

Review Questions

Answer the following questions using the information in this chapter.

1. What might happen if the fire chamber in a fireplace is too shallow?
2. How far should the hearth of a wood-burning fireplace project into a room?
3. Why is a damper alone not sufficient to keep cold air from coming down through the chimney and entering a home?
4. What is a *smoke chamber*?
5. What is the difference between a chimney and a flue?
6. Increasing the flue height will _____ the draft.
7. How far must the chimney extend above the roof to meet building code requirements?
8. How do designers prevent water from backing up along a chimney at the roof line and seeping under the shingles?
9. The masonry above the fireplace opening on the interior of the house must be supported by a _____.
10. List the five general types of fireplaces that are commonly used in residential construction.
11. What is another name for a projecting corner fireplace?
12. What items are included with prefabricated metal fireplaces?
13. Wood- or coal-burning stoves are ordinarily used as _____ sources of heat.
14. Explain the difference between a radiant stove and a circulating stove.
15. What is a *catalytic stove*?
16. Name three features that are unique to a high-efficiency stove.

Suggested Activities

1. Select a residential plan that has a fireplace. Draw the fireplace details and dimension the drawings.
2. Design a fireplace following the principles outlined in this chapter. Draw the plan view and front elevation of the fireplace. Build a scale model of the fireplace. Describe the materials to be used in the actual fireplace.
3. Locate a residence under construction that has a fireplace. Obtain permission to enter the construction site. Measure the opening and depth of the fireplace. Sketch the fireplace. Bring the sketch to class and be prepared to discuss the construction techniques used.

4. Visit your local building department and obtain the local code restrictions for installing wood-burning stoves. Summarize the main points in class.
5. Using CADD, draw the plan view and profile in section of a single-face fireplace that has an opening of 28″.

Problem Solving Case Study

You are designing a custom home for the Ringsmuth family. The family has two teenage children and does a lot of informal entertaining. Mr. Ringsmuth wants one fireplace that can be seen from both the family room and the living room. He wants another fireplace in the master bedroom.

Design a home for the Ringsmuths. Sketch a floor plan that would accommodate the family and include the proposed fireplaces. Provide technical sketches showing the cross-section of each fireplace design. Also include elevation views of each fireplace.

ADDA Certification Prep

The following questions are presented in the style used in the American Design Drafting Association (ADDA) Drafter Certification Test. Answer the questions using the information in this chapter.

1. Which of the following statements about fireplaces are true?
   A. The smoke chamber is the area just below the smoke shelf and damper of a fireplace.
   B. Some CADD packages include an option or function for automating the design process of fireplaces.
   C. The wall thickness on the back and sides of the fire chamber should be a minimum of 10″.
   D. The smoke shelf causes cold air flowing down the chimney to be deflected upward into the rising warm air.
2. Which of the following statements about fireplaces and stoves are *false*?
   A. The hearth should extend at least 10″ in front of the fireplace or stove to protect the floor from sparks.
   B. If the height of the flue is less than 14′, the size should be decreased to provide the necessary updraft.
   C. The masonry above the fireplace opening must be supported by a lintel, just as over a door or window.
   D. Wood- or coal-burning stoves generally produce more usable heat than fireplaces.
3. Match each part of a fireplace with its definition.

   Parts of a fireplace: 1. Hearth, 2. Fire chamber, 3. Chimney, 4. Flue, 5. Damper
   A. Regulates the flow of air and stops downdrafts.
   B. Protects the floor near the fireplace from sparks.
   C. The path through which smoke moves from the fireplace to the outside air.
   D. The freestanding structure that allows smoke from a fire to leave the home safely.
   E. The "heart" of a fireplace, which contains and controls the fire.

Curricular Connections

1. **Social Science.** Historically, culture has played an important part in fireplace design. For example, one type of ancient Native American architecture reflects the cultural belief that fire is an integral part of nature. Research cultural influences on fireplace design and uses in each of the following types of cultures. Collect illustrations of each, and assemble them into a presentation. In your presentation, include a summary section that compares and contrasts these styles of fireplace design. Show your presentation to the class.
   - Native American
   - Chinese
   - European
   - African

2. **Language Arts.** Conduct research to find out more about the energy efficiency of today's wood-burning stoves. Write an essay on whether wood-burning stoves can be considered a "green" alternative to central heating systems.

STEM Connections

1. **Engineering.** This chapter describes a two-face opposite fireplace, which is open on two sides. In some homes, the fireplaces in adjoining rooms are completely separate but share the same chimney. How would the technical drawings for this design differ from drawings for a two-face opposite fireplace? Sketch your answer.

Communicating about Architecture

1. **Reading.** With a partner, make flash cards of the key terms in this chapter. On the front of the card, write the term. On the back of the card, write the pronunciation and a brief definition. Use this chapter and a dictionary for guidance. Then take turns quizzing one another on the pronunciations and definitions of the key terms.
2. **Speaking.** Working with a partner, create a poster that illustrates the different types of fireplaces you read about in this chapter. Label the features of each fireplace. Display the poster in the classroom as a reference aid for discussions and assignments.

Section 5

Presentation Methods

Koksharov Dmitry/Shutterstock.com

Chapter 26

Perspective Drawings

Objectives

After completing this chapter, you will be able to:

- Explain the purpose of a perspective drawing.
- Explain the difference between one-, two-, and three-point perspectives.
- Prepare a two-point perspective drawing using the office method.
- Prepare a one-point perspective drawing using the office method.
- Describe how to create a perspective using CADD.
- Explain how to draw complex shapes in perspective.

Key Terms

cone of vision
ground line (GL)
horizon line (HL)
office method
one-point perspective drawing
perspective drawing
pictorial drawing
picture plane (PP)
station point (SP)
true height line (THL)
two-point perspective drawing
vanishing points

Although orthographic drawings such as plan views and elevations provide much information about a proposed new home, the average person may have difficulty "seeing" the intended design from these views. Other views are often needed for communication with clients, potential clients, and sometimes supervisors or coworkers.

To communicate design ideas to customers, architectural companies may use perspective drawings or presentation drawings. These types of drawings are ***pictorial drawings***—they present a picture of the home design as it would look if the viewer were standing near the house and looking at it. See **Figure 26-1**. Some companies also use scale models for this purpose. Models are described in more detail in Chapter 28, *Architectural Models*.

Types of Pictorial Drawings

One type of pictorial drawing commonly used to communicate design ideas is the ***perspective drawing***. Two other types of pictorial drawings are also used to present design ideas. These are isometric and oblique drawings. **Figure 26-2** shows perspective, isometric, and oblique drawings of the same object to illustrate the differences among the three methods.

A perspective drawing is drawn from the perspective of a person standing near the home or object being drawn, as shown in **Figure 26-1**. Objects appear smaller when they are farther away, just as they would if you were standing

Sater Design Collection, Inc.

Figure 26-1. This is a perspective that has been hand-rendered. It is a true representation of the actual home.

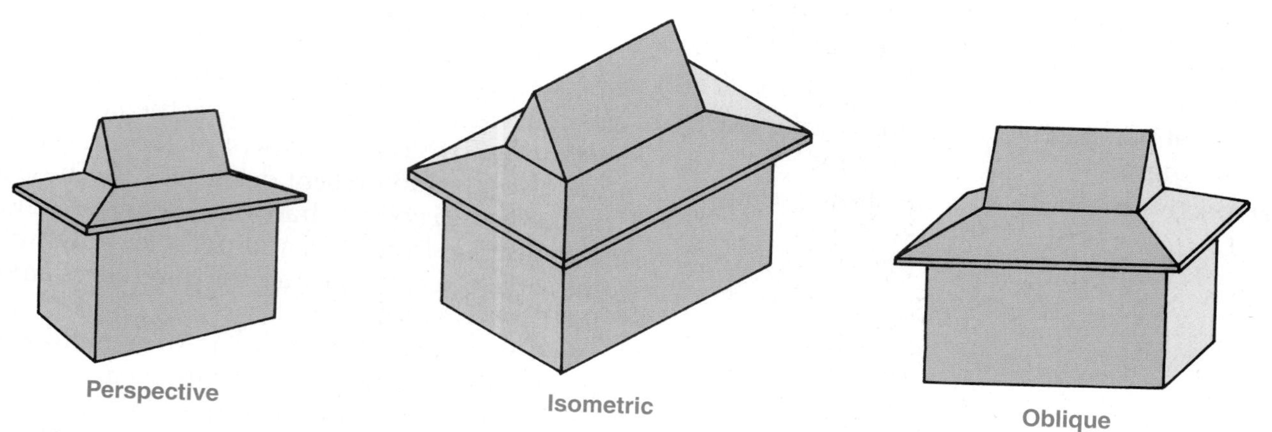

Goodheart-Willcox Publisher

Figure 26-2. Any of these pictorial methods may be used for presentation drawings. However, a perspective is the most realistic representation.

in front of the home looking at it. A perspective drawing applies this and other principles to achieve a three-dimensional representation showing more than one side of the object.

Isometric and oblique drawings do not show a building as realistically as a perspective. However, both are useful for some types of presentations and are generally much easier to draw than a perspective. This chapter concentrates on perspective drawings.

Types of Perspective Drawings

There are three basic types of perspective drawings:

- One-point (parallel) perspective
- Two-point (angular) perspective
- Three-point (oblique) perspective

Each type of perspective drawing is named for the number of vanishing points used to create it. See **Figure 26-3**. Vanishing points and other elements of perspective drawings are discussed in the next section.

One-point and two-point perspectives are commonly used for residential structures. Three-point perspectives are generally used for tall commercial buildings. Therefore, they are of little interest to residential architects and residential building designers and are not included in this chapter.

Elements of a Perspective Drawing

Information from the plan and elevation views is needed to develop a perspective drawing of a home design. This information is transferred to the perspective drawing and used to establish

Employability
Celliquette

With the increased use of cell phones both by individuals and by businesses, proper behavior when using a cell phone has become important. Proper behavior related to cell phone use is sometimes called *celliquette*. Here are a few basics of celliquette to remember:

- **At a meal or in a meeting, silence the cell phone and place it in your pocket or purse.** Do not set it on the table beside you. Placing the phone on the table indicates to others that the phone is more important to you than they are. This is considered very rude.
- **When at a meal or in a meeting, do not answer the phone or text unless it is an emergency.** If it is an emergency, excuse yourself from the meal or meeting before answering. If you are expecting a call or text that is pertinent to the current meeting, you may place the phone on the table, but explain to those around you that you are expecting the call or text.
- **When in a public place such as a movie theater or grocery store, talk quietly.** Talking loudly is annoying to people around you. Remember that no one else in the area needs or wants to hear the conversation.

Activity

With two or three classmates, role-play scenarios in which cell phones are used. Take turns being the person calling, the person answering, and other people in a meeting or at a meal. Use the following scenarios:

- You are in a weekly status meeting with your supervisor and coworkers when a client calls to discuss the preliminary design you sent her.
- You are having an informal lunch with business associates. A friend calls to ask if you want to go to the movies tonight.
- You are having dinner with an important client and are hoping to get the client to accept your latest design proposal. Your brother sends you an urgent text that your mother has been taken to the hospital.

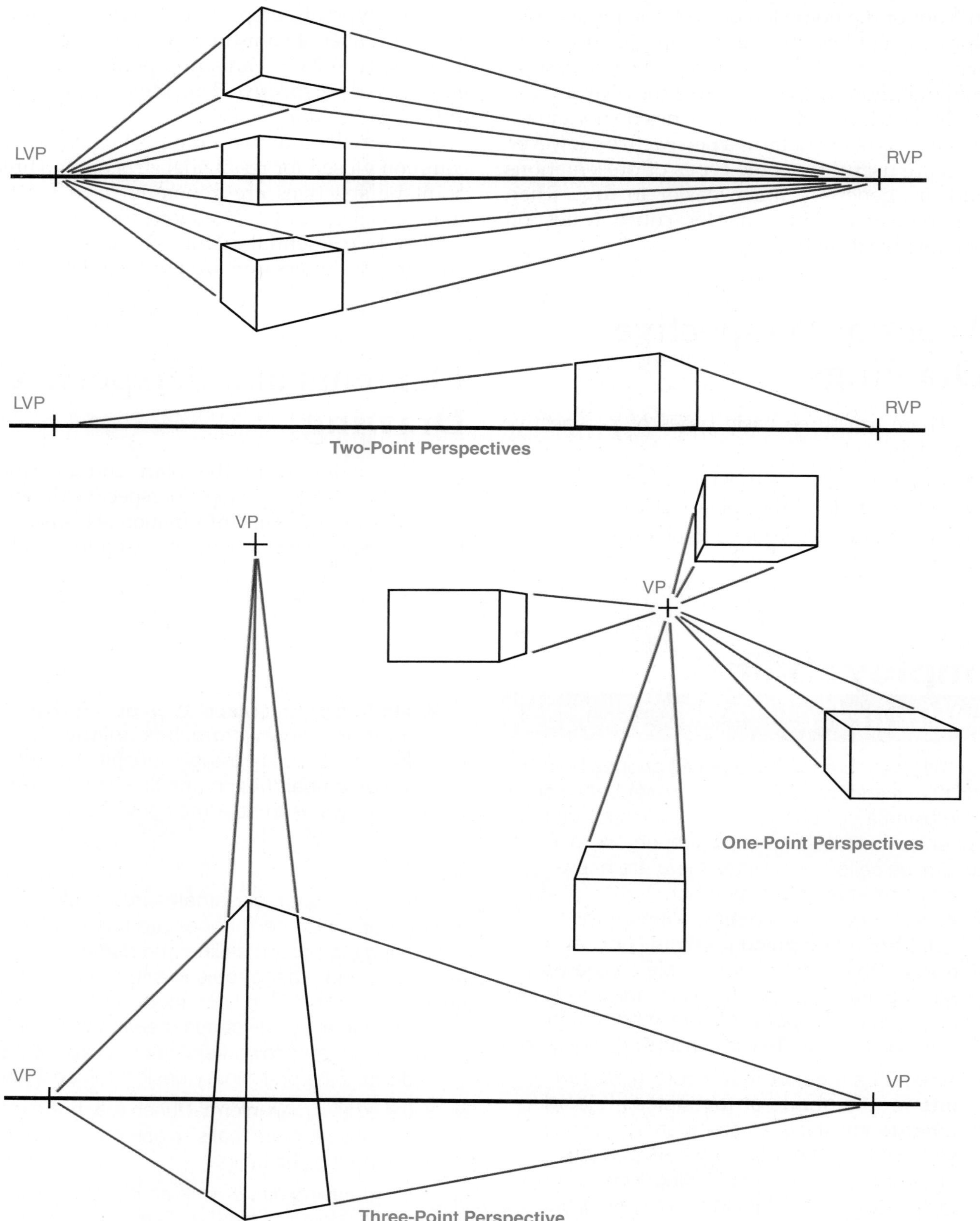

Goodheart-Willcox Publisher

Figure 26-3. The three basic types of perspective drawings are named for the number of vanishing points used to create the drawing. Notice how the object lines converge at the vanishing points.

its key elements. Each element of a typical perspective drawing is described in the following sections. Refer to **Figure 26-4** as you read about the parts of a perspective drawing.

Ground Line

The ***ground line (GL)*** represents the horizontal ground plane, the plane on which the object rests. In the least complex situation, the object to be drawn is positioned so that the foremost corner touches the picture plane that is perpendicular to the ground plane. The ground line is established by the elevation drawing. When the object touches the picture plane in the plan view, it must also touch the ground line in the perspective drawing. If the object is placed behind the picture plane in the plan view, then the object will appear to be above the ground line. Objects that pass through the picture plane will extend below the ground line.

Horizon Line

The ***horizon line (HL)*** represents the place where the ground and sky meet. The distance between the ground line and the horizon line represents the height of the observer's eye above the ground. This can be measured at the same scale as the plan view and elevation.

Picture Plane

In all types of drawing, objects are shown as they would materialize on an imaginary, transparent ***picture plane (PP)***. The picture plane may be in front of or behind the object, or may even pass through the object. On most perspective drawings, the picture plane is a vertical plane that is perpendicular to the ground plane. In the plan view, the picture plane is represented by a horizontal line called the *picture plane line*. It is normally located between the object and the station point (observer's eye).

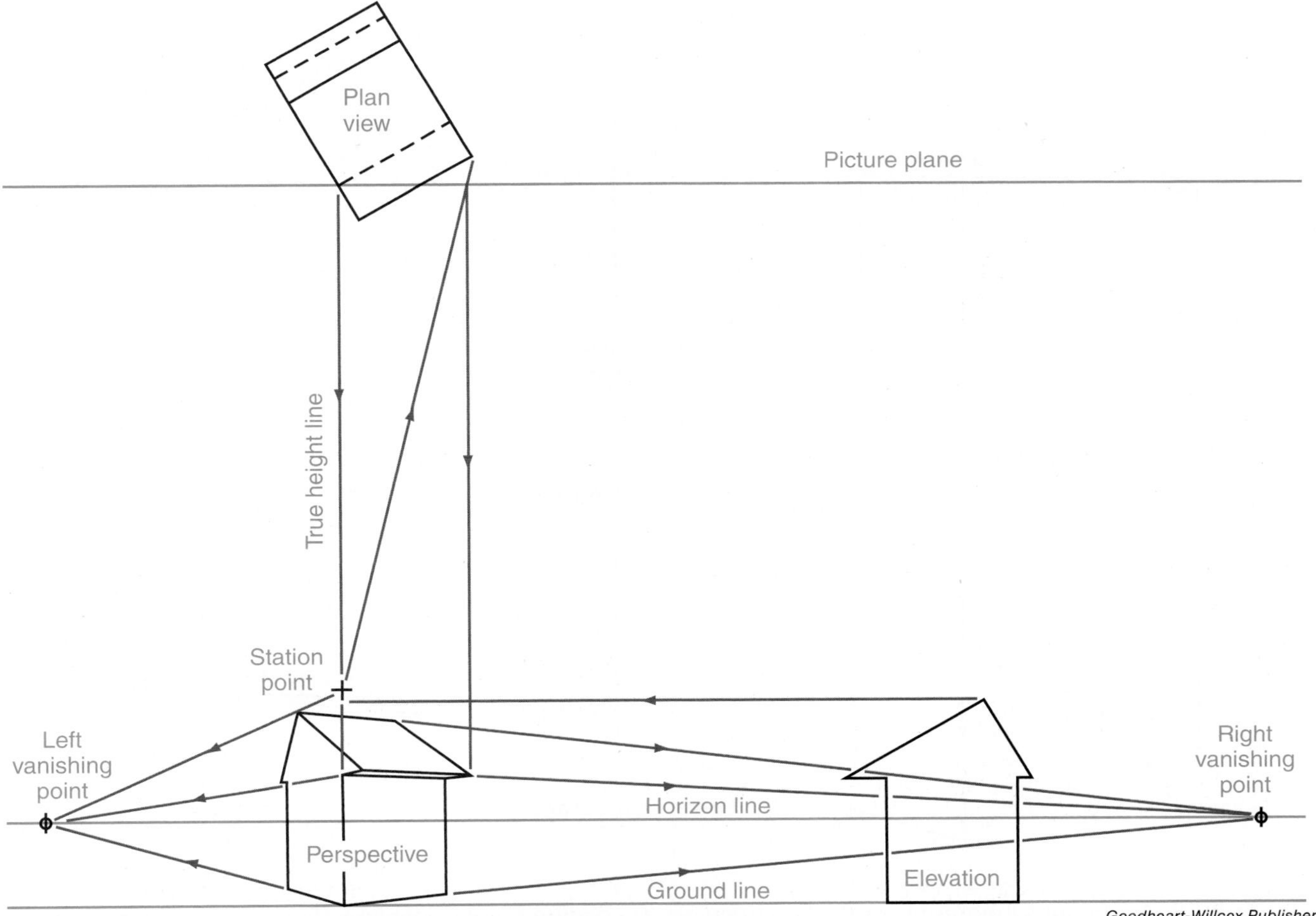

Figure 26-4. A typical two-point perspective drawing with the major elements identified.

Any portion of the object that touches the picture plane line is shown at true size in the perspective drawing. Any portion of the object that is behind the picture plane line appears smaller than its true size on the perspective drawing. Parts of the object that are in front of the picture plane (between the plane and the station point) appear larger than their true size in the perspective drawing.

Station Point

The ***station point (SP)*** is the location of the observer's eye. This point therefore marks the beginning point of the visual rays or sight lines in the perspective view. The rays radiate out from the station point to the object that is represented in the plan view. They pass through the picture plane line and position the various points of the object on the picture plane line. The distance from the station point to the picture plane line can be measured using the same scale as the plan and elevation drawings.

A perspective drawing differs from an orthographic drawing in the position of the station point. Remember, the station point is the location of the observer's eye. In orthographic projection, the station point is infinitely far away from the picture plane. Therefore, all visual rays or projection lines are parallel to one another. In a perspective drawing, however, the station point is a measurable distance from the object or picture plane, as shown in **Figure 26-5**. The object lines converge at a vanishing point.

Vanishing Points

Vanishing points are the points at which all lines on the object will converge if extended. Vanishing points are located on the horizon line in most perspective drawings. The sides of the object recede and become smaller as they approach the vanishing points.

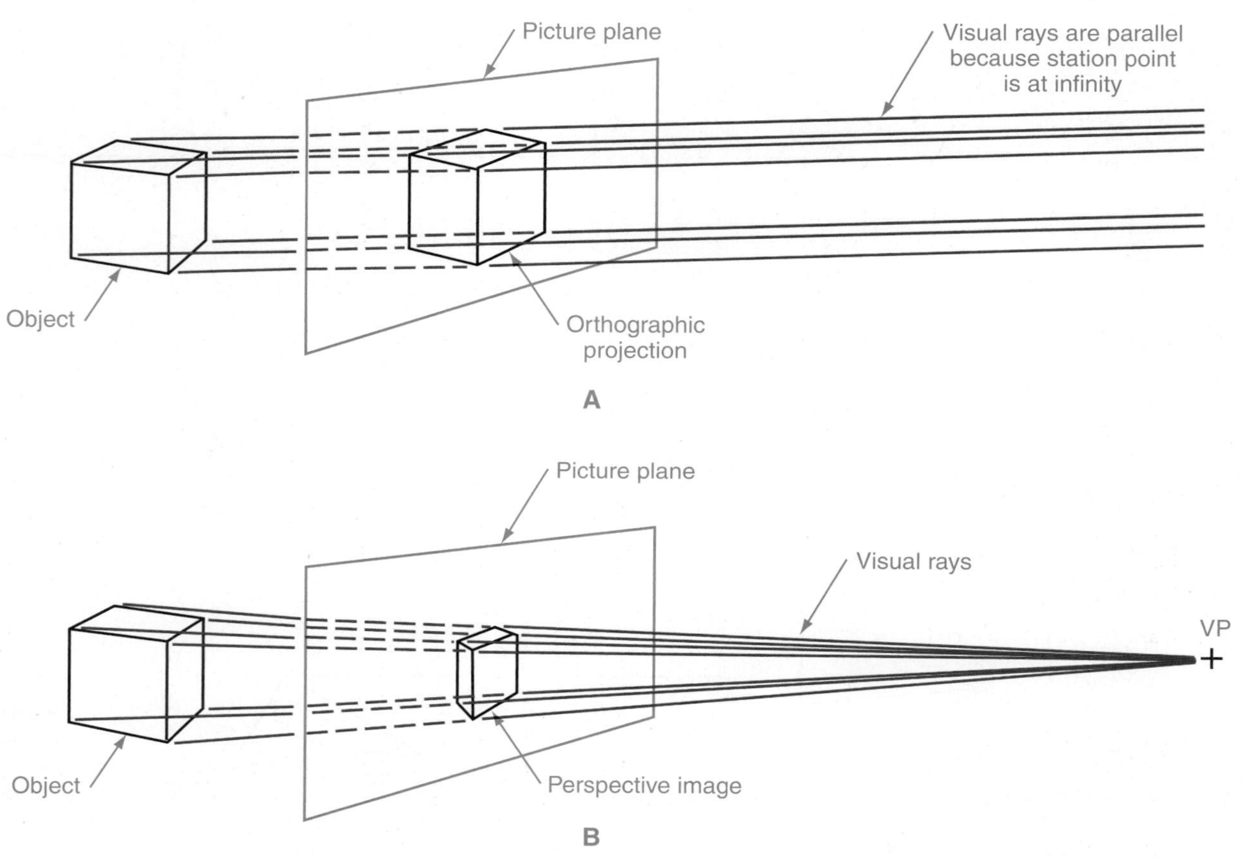

Figure 26-5. A—In an orthographic projection drawing, the station point is infinitely far from the picture plane. B—In a perspective drawing, the station point is a measurable distance from the picture plane.

True Height Line

A ***true height line (THL)***, or *true length line (TL)*, is established where the object touches the picture plane. This true height line is used to project heights to the perspective drawing. It is always essential to find at least one true height line in the perspective drawing so that height measurements can be made. If the object does not touch the picture plane, then a side may be extended until it touches the picture plane, thus establishing a true height corner.

Two-Point Perspectives

A ***two-point perspective drawing*** has a right vanishing point (RVP) and a left vanishing point (LVP). Two-point perspective drawings appear fairly realistic and are especially appropriate for exterior views. They produce a photo-like result that is quite accurate in detail. See **Figure 26-6**. Two-point perspective drawings provide an effective way to communicate with prospective clients and other interested parties.

Factors That Affect the Drawing

Before beginning to draw a perspective, you should understand the factors that influence the final perspective drawing. Keep the relationships among the elements of a perspective drawing in mind. In starting out, try to control all of these elements and change only one factor at a time to see the effect on the final outcome. If you change several things at once, you may never know the effect of each individual factor.

Station Point and Picture Plane

The first relationship to note is the distance the station point is from the picture plane. **Figure 26-7** shows how the perspective on the picture plane increases in size as the station

AOMARCH/Shutterstock.com

Figure 26-6. A two-point perspective generated using CADD software.

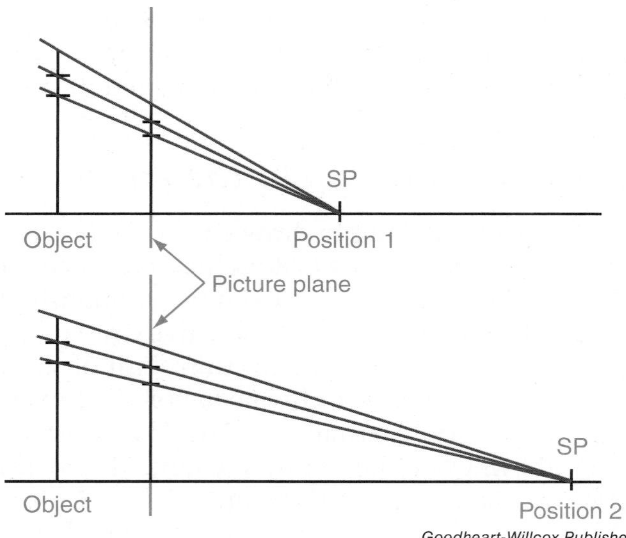

Goodheart-Willcox Publisher

Figure 26-7. The image on the picture plane is larger when the station point is moved from Position 1 to Position 2, which is farther away.

point is moved farther away from the picture plane. Appropriate location of the station point is vital to the final perspective. If it is too close, the drawing will be imprecise and unrealistic.

Cone of Vision

The ***cone of vision*** is the angle between opposite sides of the object with its vertex at the station point. In most instances, position the station point so that it forms a cone of vision of between 30° and 45°. To locate the station point with a proper cone of vision, draw a vertical line down from the corner of the object that touches the picture plane. Then, place a 30° or 45° triangle over the line so that half of the angle falls on either side of the line. In CADD, two intersecting lines that form a 30° or 45° angle can be used in place of the triangle. Next, move the triangle or intersecting lines along the vertical line. When the entire object is within the cone of vision represented by the triangle, the minimum distance has been established for the station point. **Figure 26-8** illustrates this process.

Vanishing Points and Station Point

Moving the station point in relation to the picture plane line also affects the position of the vanishing points. As the station point moves closer to the picture plane, the vanishing points come closer together. As the station point moves away, the vanishing points move farther apart.

The station point may also be moved from side to side to improve the viewing location. However, it should not be moved too far either way because distortion will result. The same effect can be accomplished by altering the angle of the plan view with respect to the picture plane line, rather than moving the station point.

Object and Picture Plane

Two factors affect the relationship between the position of the object and the picture plane line. First, the angle that the object forms with the picture plane line determines which portions of the object are emphasized in the final drawing. See **Figure 26-9**. The most common position is with an angle of 30° on one side and 60° on the other. This may be varied to suit the particular object.

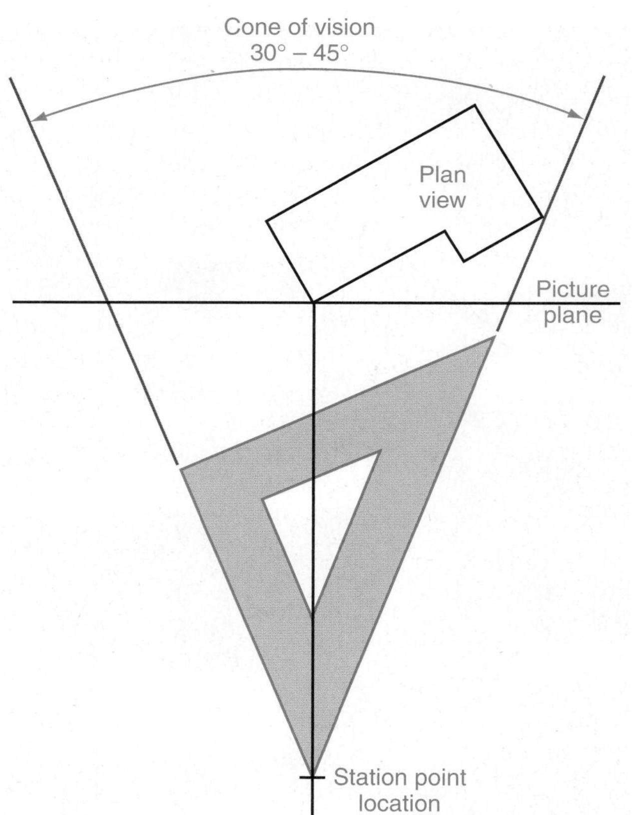

Goodheart-Willcox Publisher

Figure 26-8. Using a triangle to locate the station point at the minimum distance from the picture plane. The entire object must be within the cone of vision.

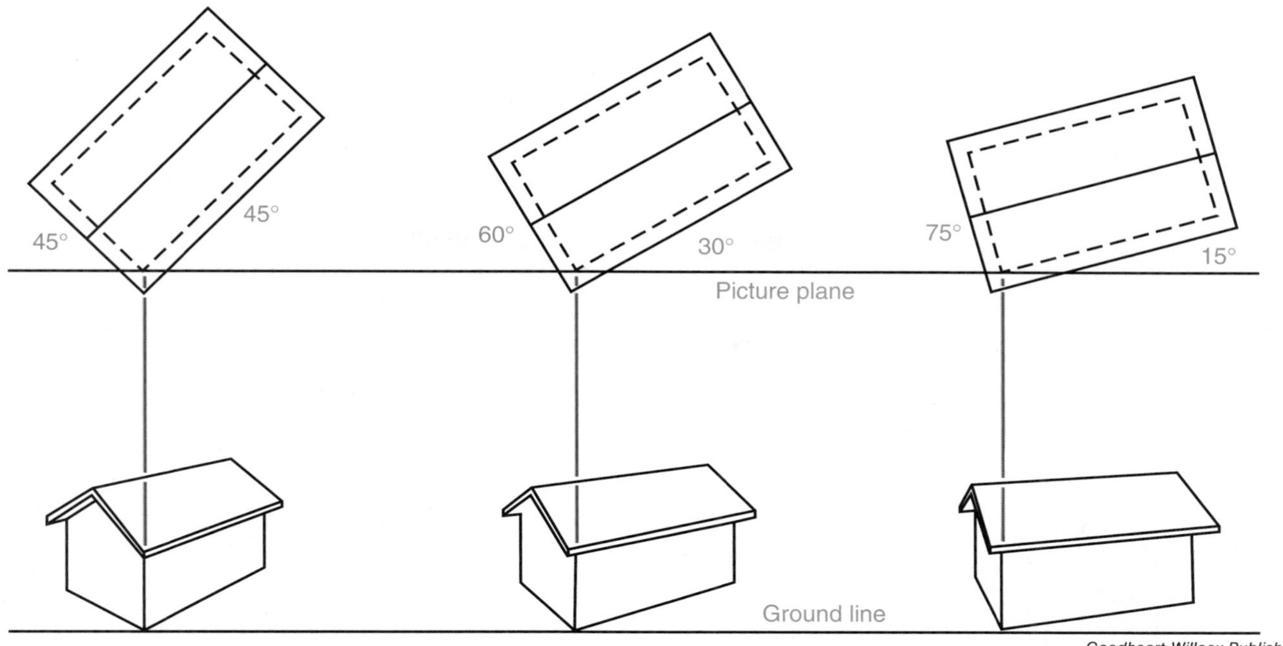

Goodheart-Willcox Publisher

Figure 26-9. The angle that the object makes with the picture plane can be varied to place emphasis on a certain part of the object.

The second factor is whether the object is behind, in front of, or passing through the picture plane line. See **Figure 26-10**. An object behind the picture plane line appears smaller than one in front of the picture plane line. As a result, size is dependent on this placement. Also, if the station point is not suitably far away when the object is in front of the picture plane line, distortion is significantly increased.

Height of Station Point

The appearance of the final perspective will vary greatly depending on the height of the station point. In a two-point perspective, this height is the distance from the ground line to the horizon line. The horizon line may be located well above the ground line (20′ to 30′), at a conventional height of 5′ or 6′, on the ground line, or below the ground line. See **Figure 26-11**. Names have been given to some of these relative positions, such as *bird's-eye view* and *worm's-eye view*. The proper placement depends on the particular object and which features are to be emphasized. In residential perspectives, the station point is commonly located at ground level, at 5′ or 6′ (an average person's height), or at about 30′ high.

Procedure Drafting

Drawing a Two-Point Perspective

Drafters use several methods for drawing two-point perspectives. The method most frequently used is known as the ***office method*** or *common method*. The following procedure is used to draw a two-point perspective using the common method.

1. Draw the plan view or roof plan of the object on a sheet of drawing paper. Draw an elevation view on a separate sheet of paper. Both need to be the same scale. See **Figure 26-12**. In CADD, you may want to draw each of these as blocks to be inserted later.
2. Secure a large sheet of paper to the drawing table. In CADD, you may want to set the drawing limits appropriately. Draw the picture plane line near the top of the sheet, the ground line near the bottom of the sheet, and the horizon line the desired distance above the ground line. These lines must be parallel. See **Figure 26-13**.

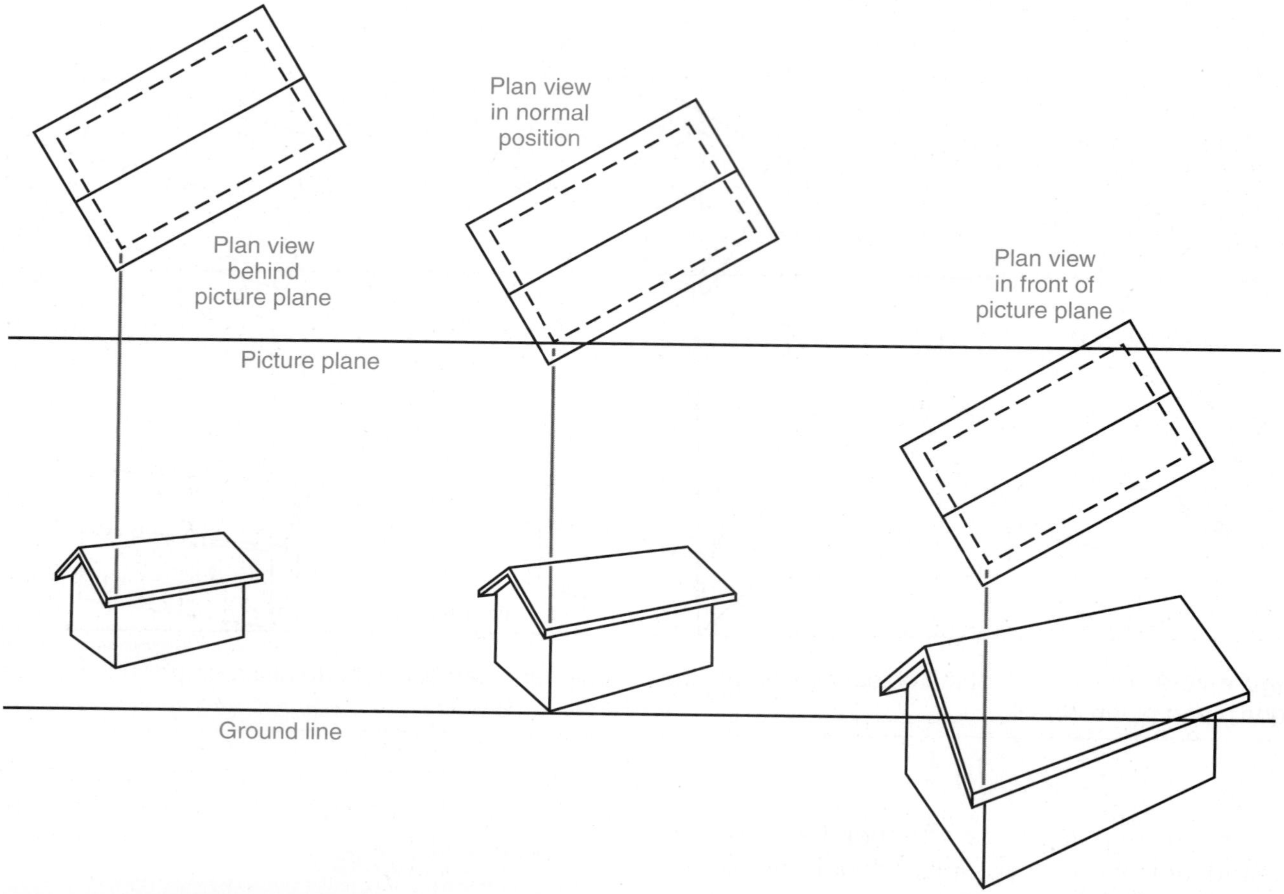

Plan view
in normal
position

Plan view
behind
picture plane

Plan view
in front of
picture plane

Picture plane

Ground line

Goodheart-Willcox Publisher

Figure 26-10. As an object is moved from behind to in front of the picture plane, it increases in size. Also, notice the distortion in the right-hand perspective.

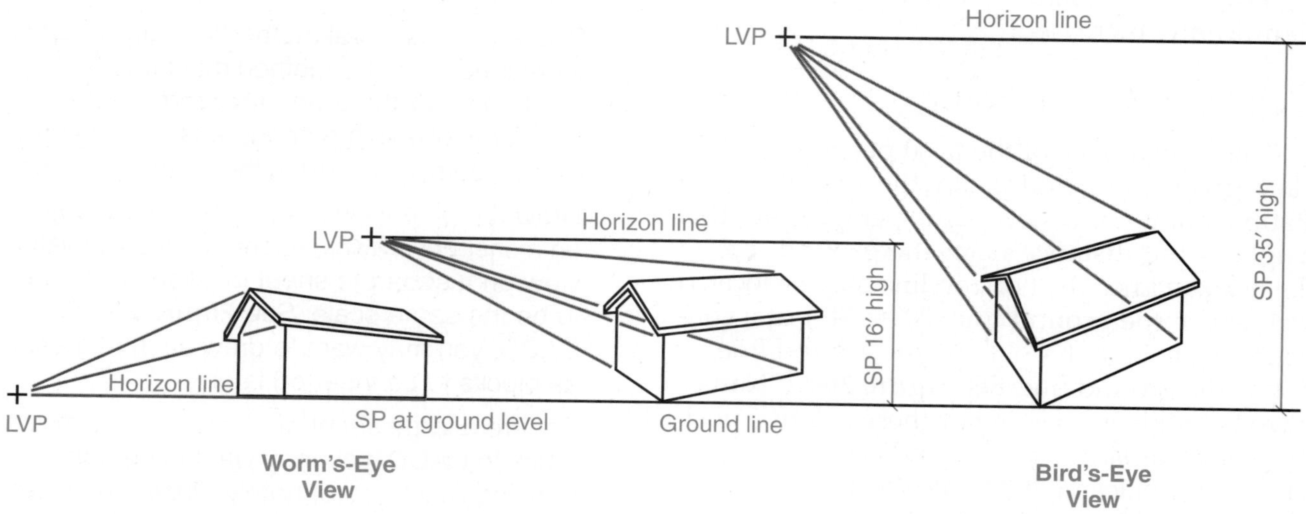

Goodheart-Willcox Publisher

Figure 26-11. Changing the height of the station point alters the final perspective view.

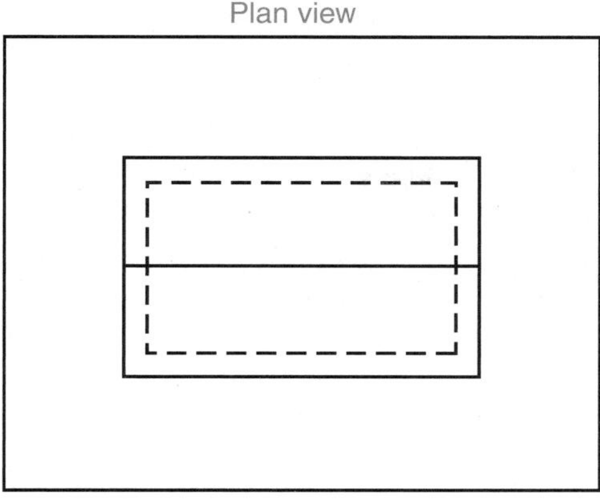

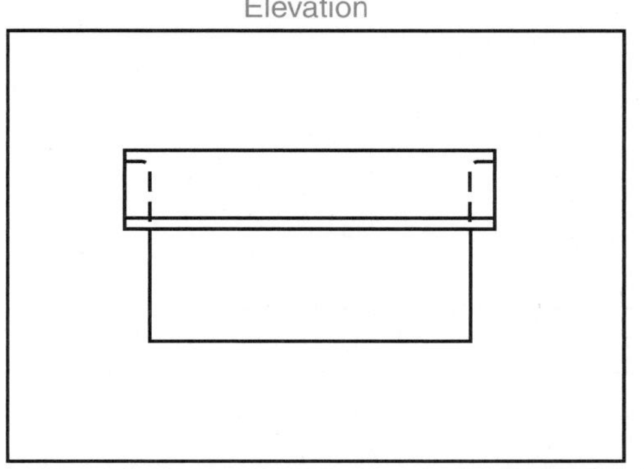

Goodheart-Willcox Publisher

Figure 26-12. Procedure for drawing a two-point perspective—Step 1.

3. Place the plan view or roof plan at a 30° angle with the picture plane so that the front corner touches the picture plane, as shown in **Figure 26-14**. Locate the elevation on the ground line to the extreme right or left side of the drawing.
4. Draw a vertical line down from the point where the object touches the picture plane line. Locate the station point using the cone of vision procedure described earlier. See **Figure 26-8** and **Figure 26-15**.
5. Determine the location of the right and left vanishing points by drawing two construction lines from the station point to the picture plane line. These construction lines must be parallel to the sides of the object in the plan view. See **Figure 26-16**. Draw a vertical line from the point where each of these lines intersects the picture plane down to the horizon line. This is the location of the right and left vanishing points.
6. Draw a true height line from the corner of the object that touches the picture plane down to the ground line. Project the object height of that corner from the elevation view to the true height line. The distance from the ground line to this point is the true height and the location of the object corner in the perspective drawing. See **Figure 26-17**.
7. Determine the location of the other corners of the object by drawing sight lines from the station point to each corner in the plan view. The point where the sight line crosses the picture plane is projected down to the perspective, as shown in **Figure 26-18**. Each corner of the object will be on one of these lines.
8. Find the length and vertical location of these corners by projecting the vertical true length from the true height corner to the vanishing points, **Figure 26-19**. Sides of the object that extend away to the right are projected to the right vanishing point; sides that extend to the left are projected to the left vanishing point. Inclined or oblique lines cannot be projected to either vanishing point. Their endpoints must be located and simply connected.
9. Complete the back two sides of the object by projecting the corners to the vanishing points. The location where the projection lines cross is the fourth corner. Check the accuracy of your work by drawing a vertical line down from the point where the sight line for the remaining corner crosses the picture plane line. It should pass through the point where the two projection lines cross, as shown in **Figure 26-20**. This corner will not be visible in the finished drawing.
10. To draw the ridge of the object, first extend the ridge line in the plan view until it touches the picture plane line. Then, draw a vertical line from the point at which the ridge intersects the picture plane line down to the ground line. This establishes a new true height line, as shown in **Figure 26-21**. Project the height of the ridge over to the true height line and project this point to the right vanishing point. The right vanishing point is used because the ridge extends away to the right.

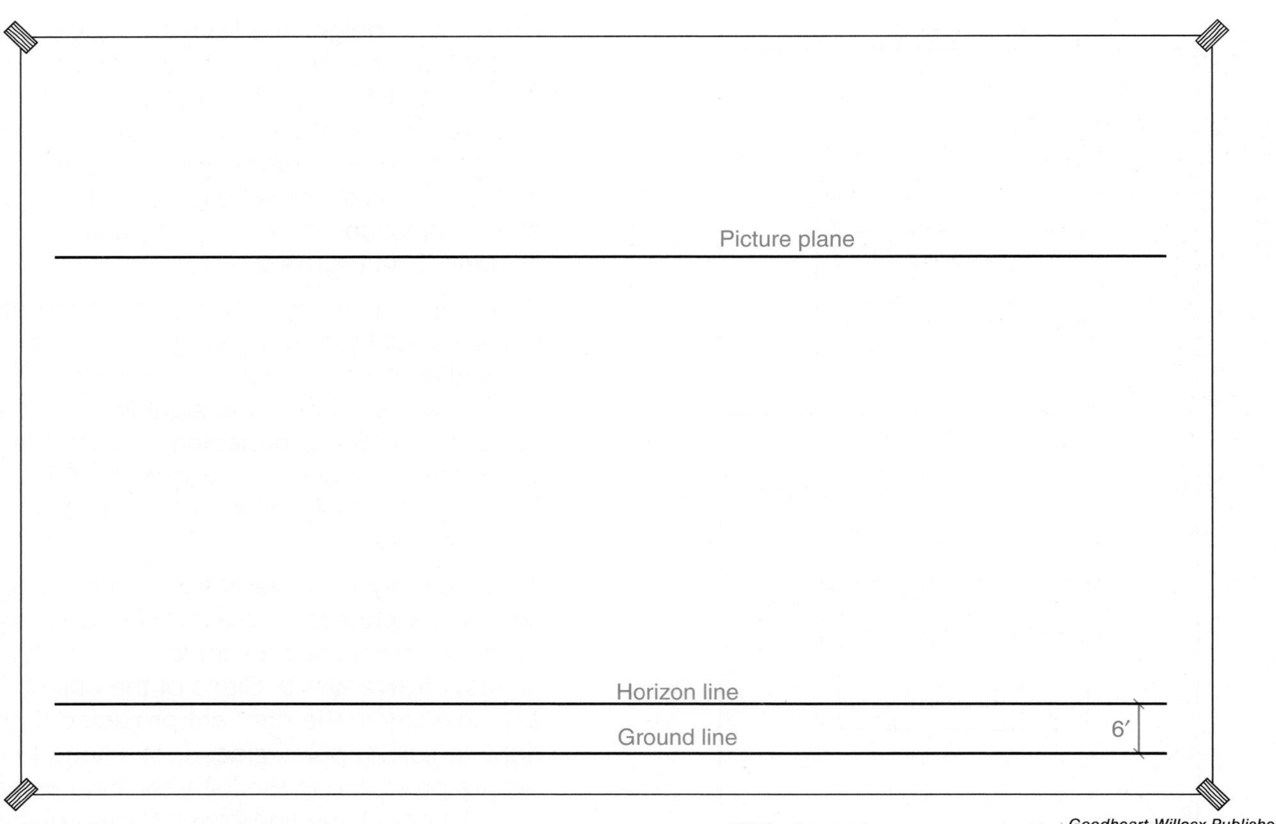

Goodheart-Willcox Publisher

Figure 26-13. Procedure for drawing a two-point perspective—Step 2.

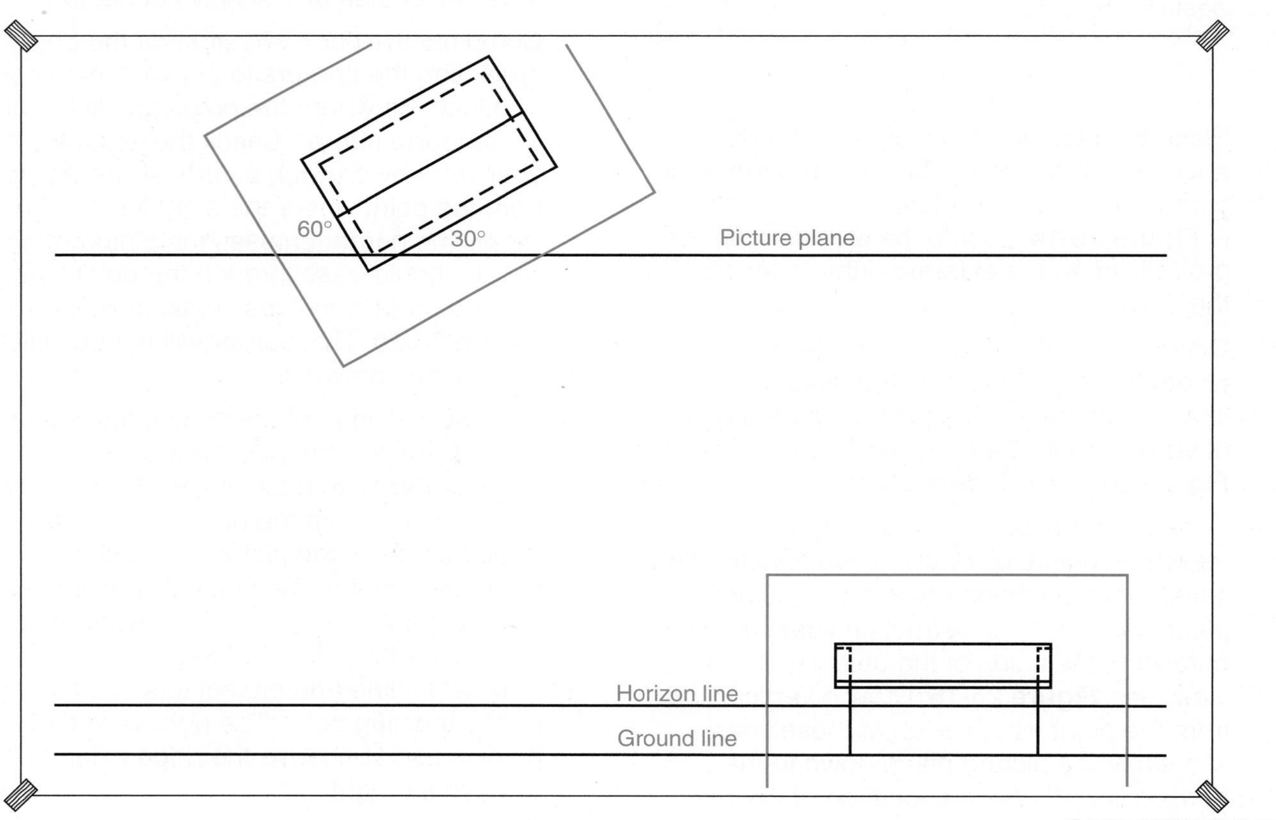

Goodheart-Willcox Publisher

Figure 26-14. Procedure for drawing a two-point perspective—Step 3.

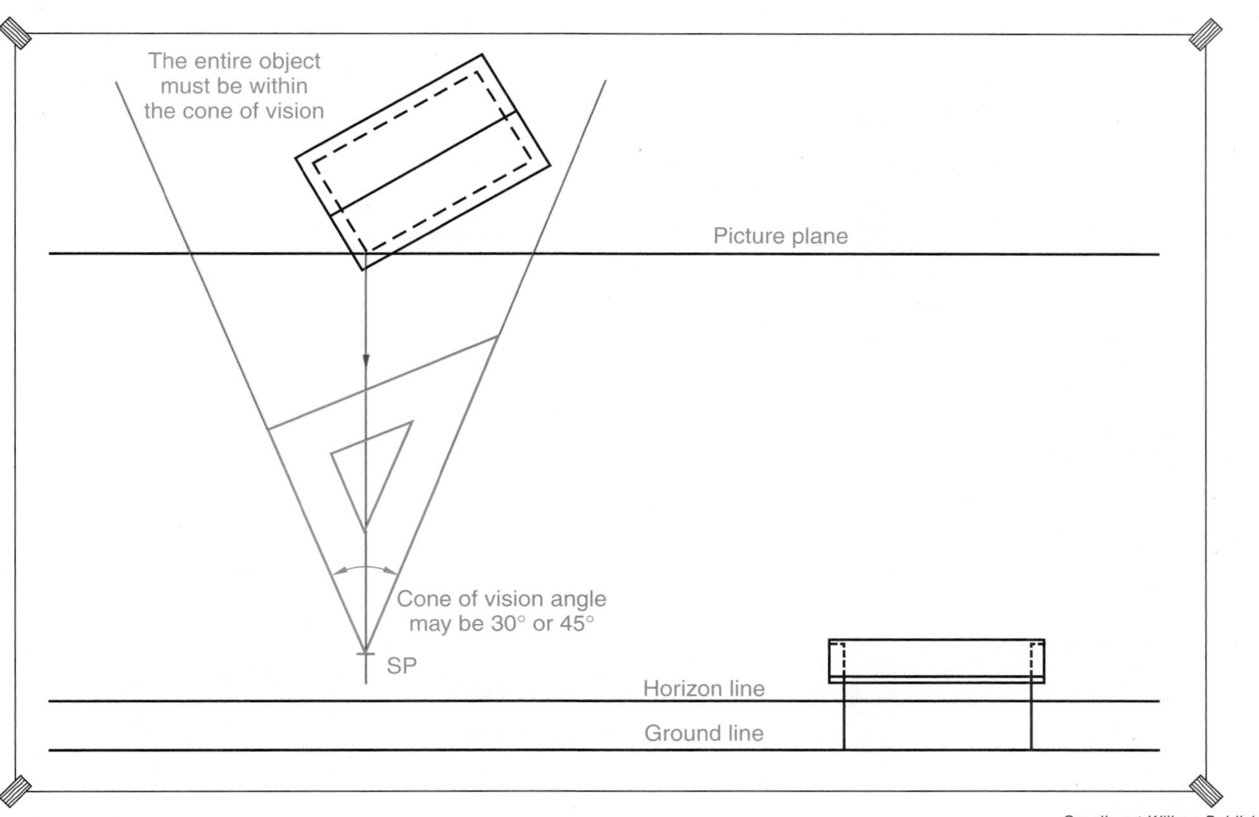

Goodheart-Willcox Publisher

Figure 26-15. Procedure for drawing a two-point perspective—Step 4.

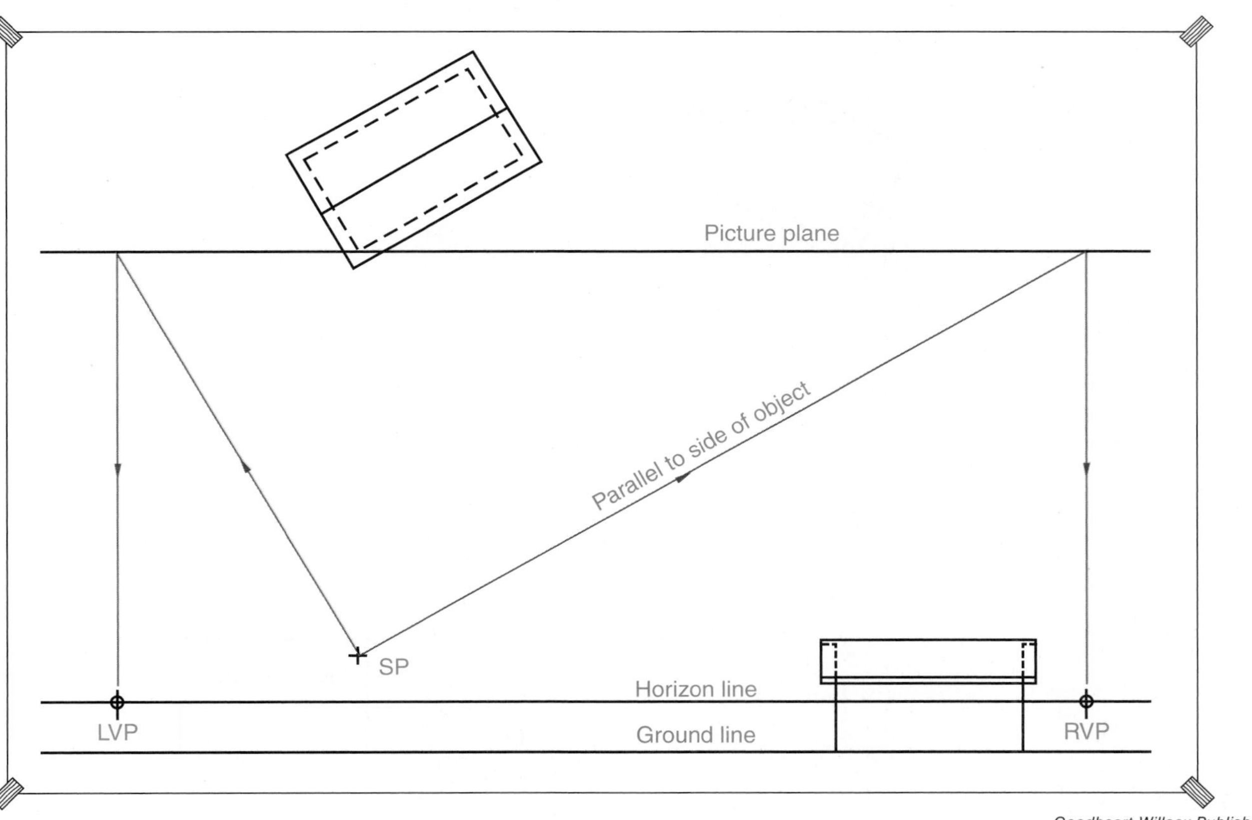

Goodheart-Willcox Publisher

Figure 26-16. Procedure for drawing a two-point perspective—Step 5.

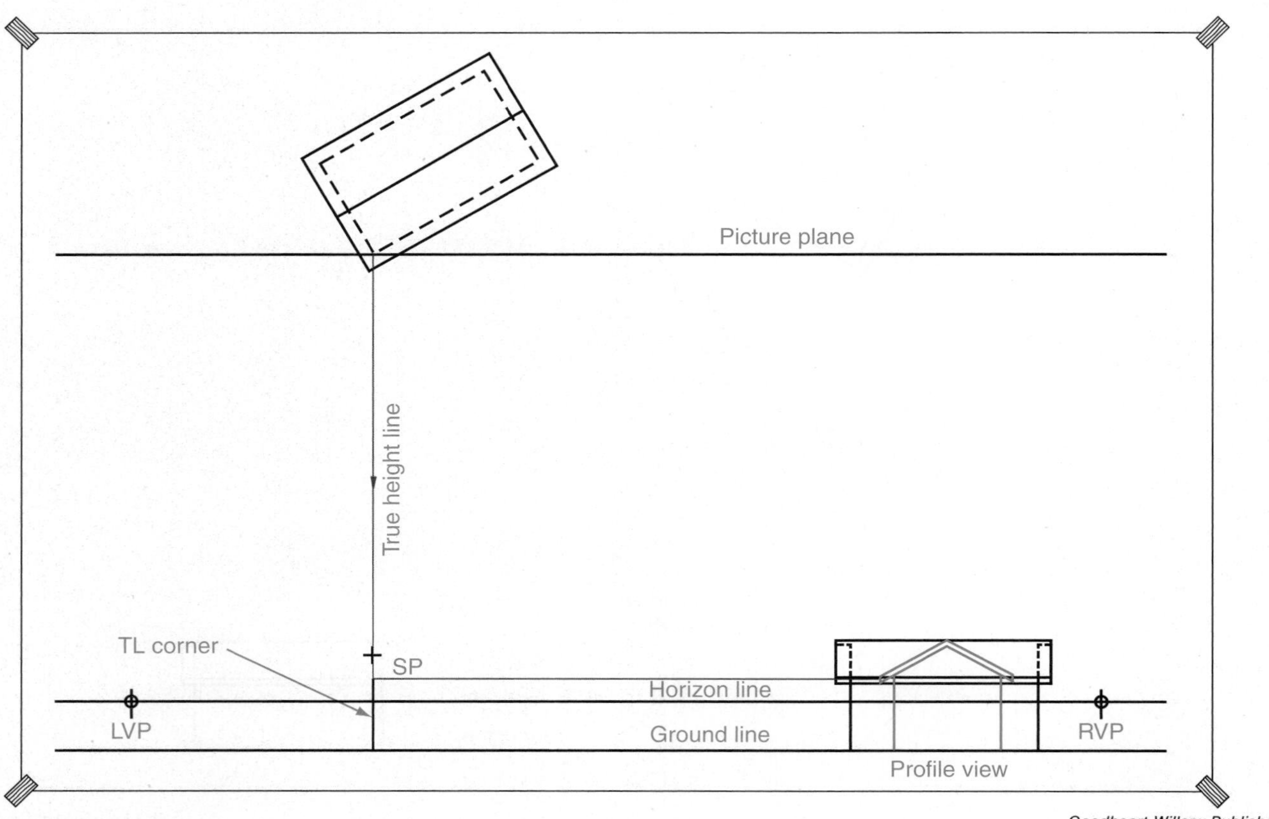

Goodheart-Willcox Publisher

Figure 26-17. Procedure for drawing a two-point perspective—Step 6.

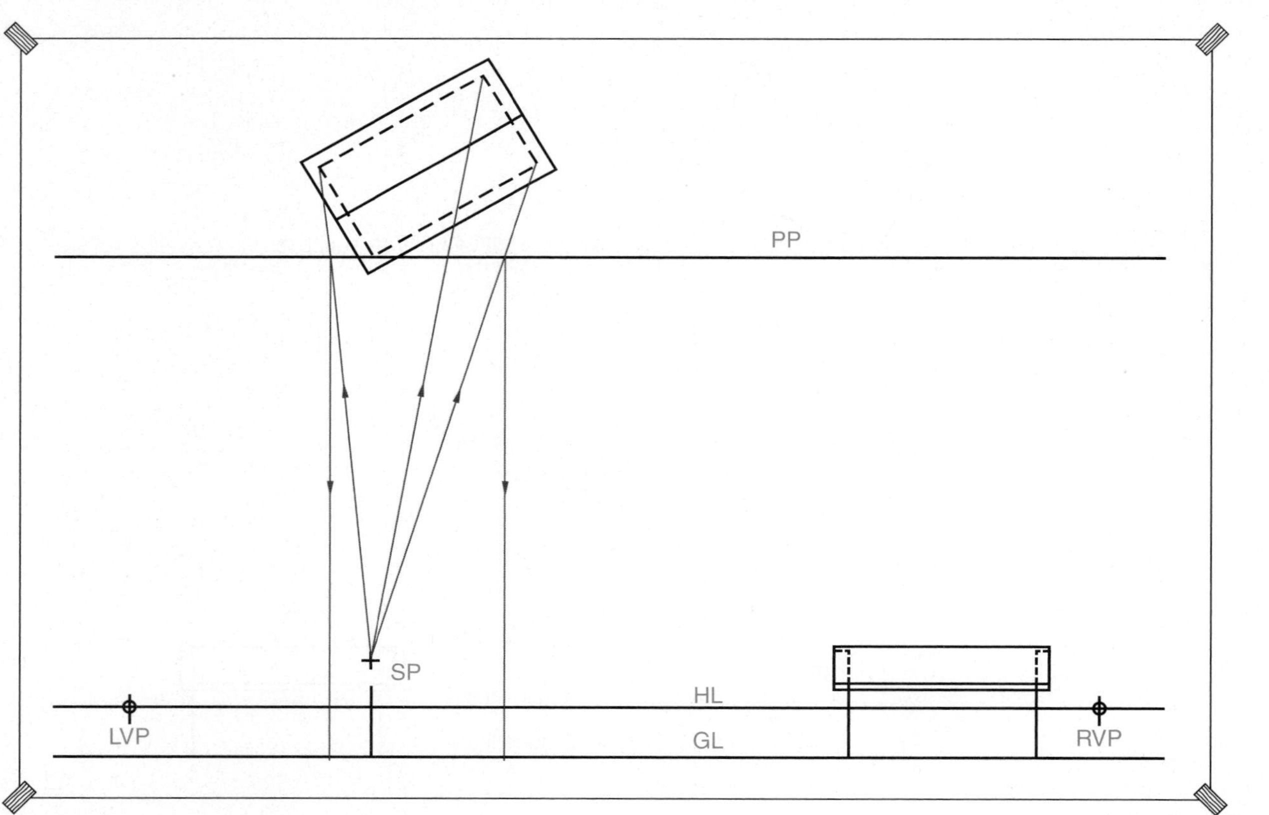

Goodheart-Willcox Publisher

Figure 26-18. Procedure for drawing a two-point perspective—Step 7.

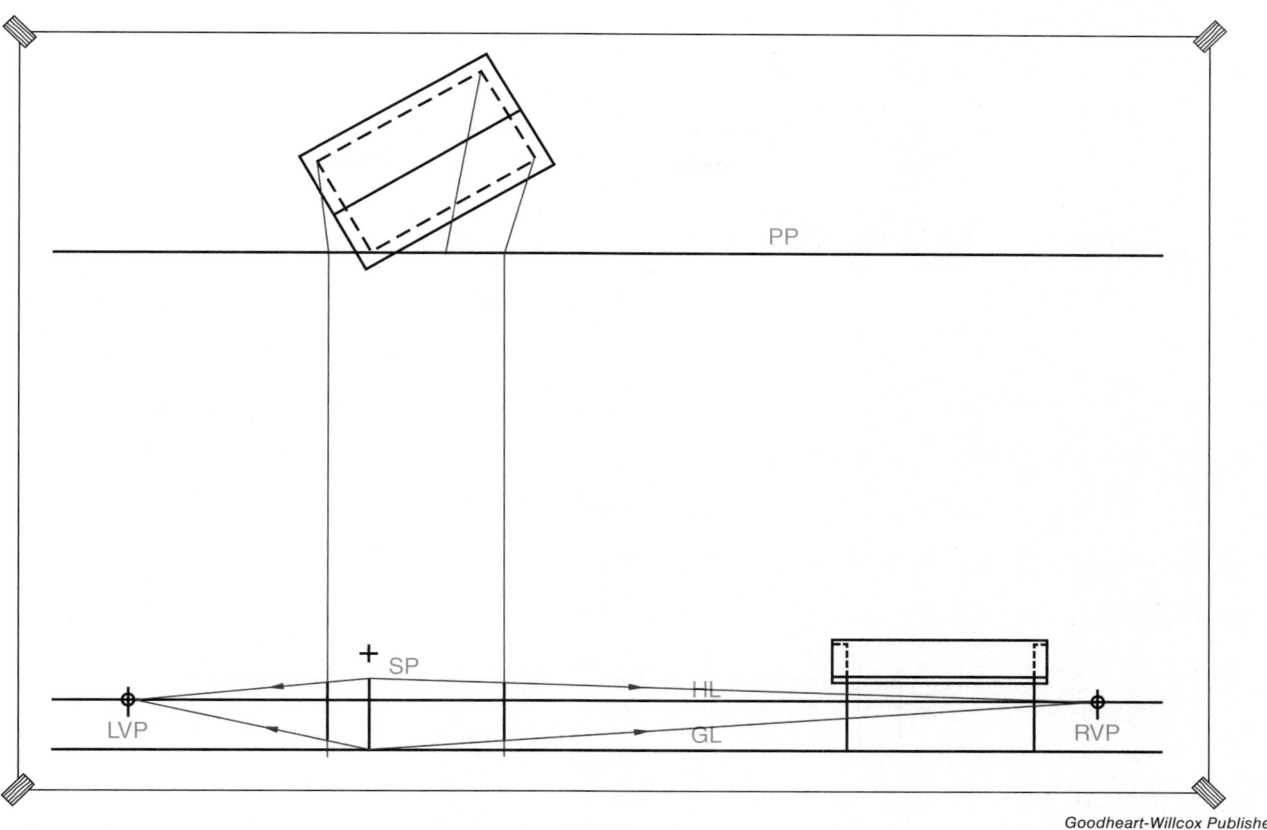

Goodheart-Willcox Publisher

Figure 26-19. Procedure for drawing a two-point perspective—Step 8.

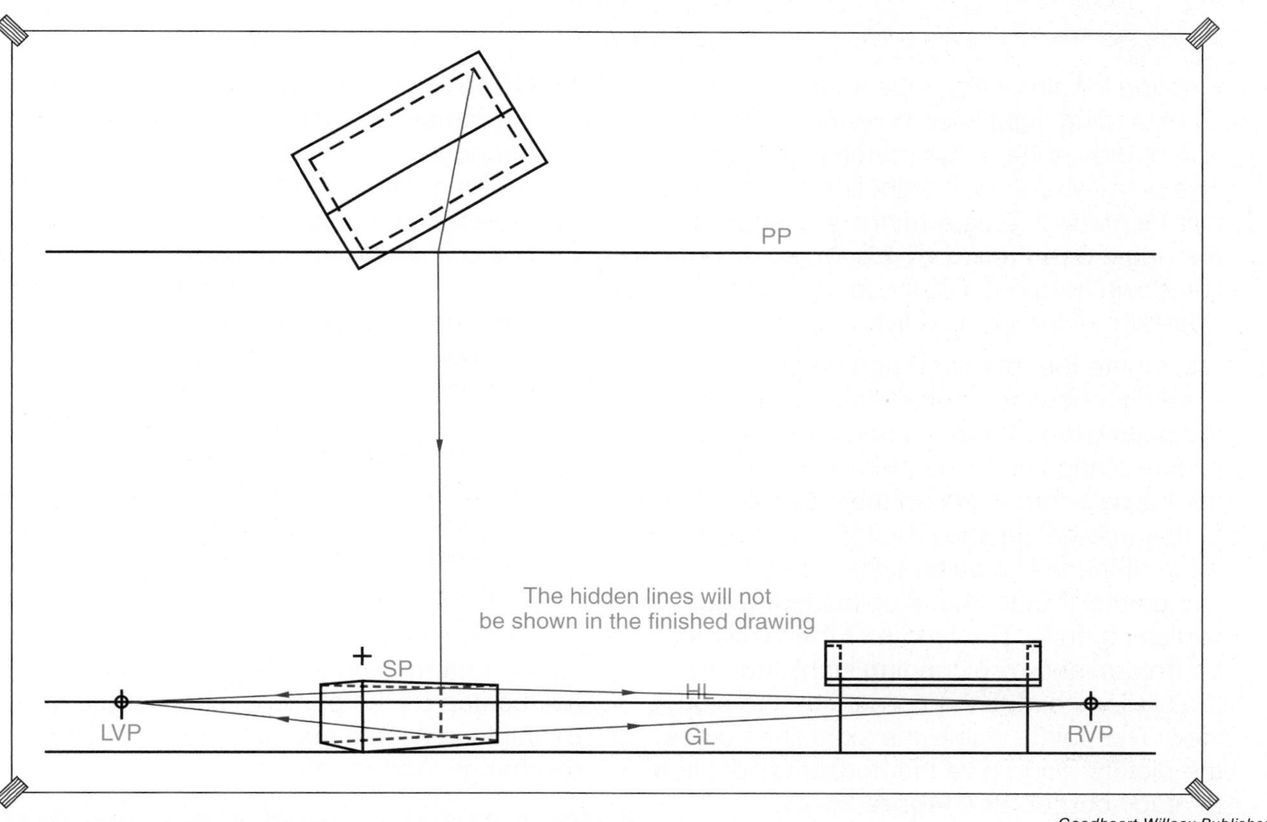

Goodheart-Willcox Publisher

Figure 26-20. Procedure for drawing a two-point perspective—Step 9.

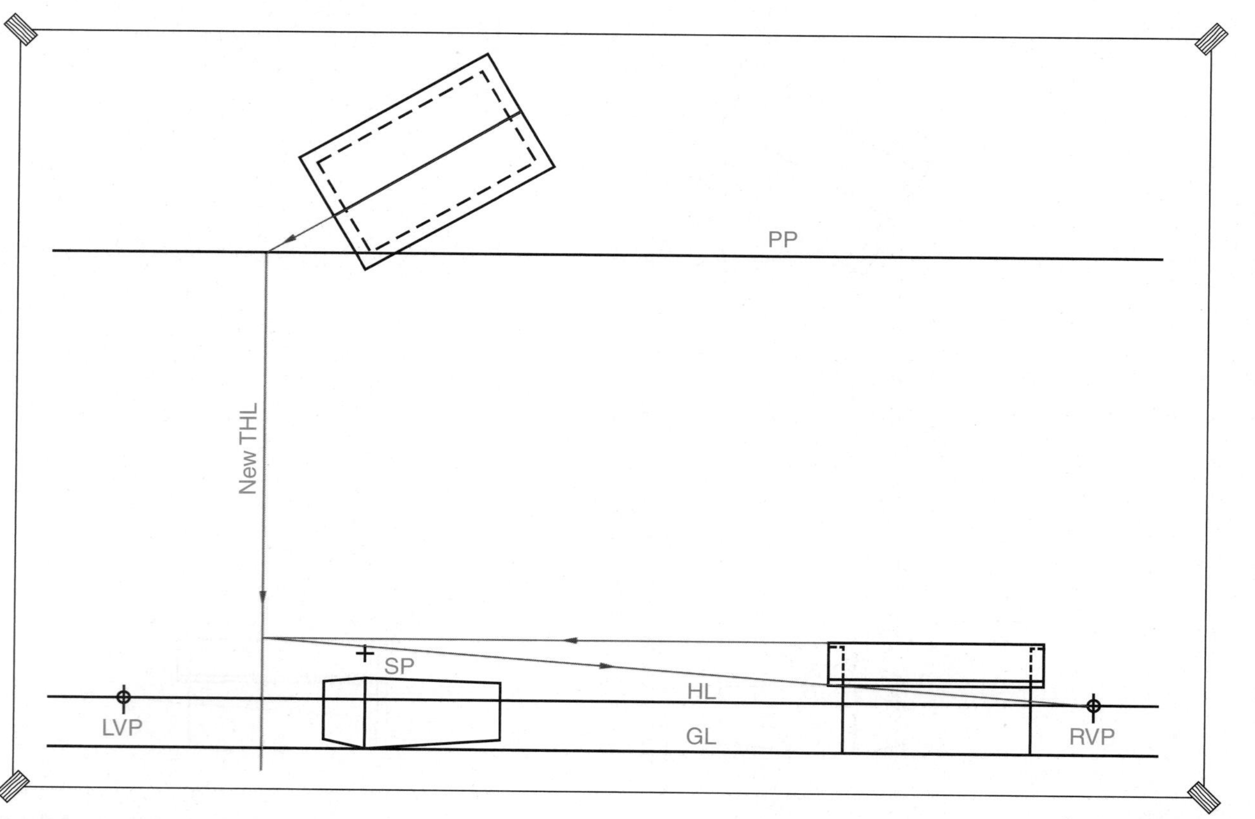

Goodheart-Willcox Publisher

Figure 26-21. Procedure for drawing a two-point perspective—Step 10.

11. Find the length of the ridge in the perspective by extending sight lines from the station point to the ends of the ridge on the plan view. The point where each sight line crosses the picture plane line determines the length of the ridge. See **Figure 26-22**. Project a vertical line down from each of these points to the ridge line in the perspective.
12. Determine the roof overhang height by drawing a new true height line down from the point where the overhang crosses the picture plane line in the plan view. Project the fascia board width on the elevation over to this true height line. The top and bottom edge of the fascia passes through these two points. Project these points to the right vanishing point. The length of the fascia may be determined by extending sight lines from the station point to the corners on the plan view. The points where the sight lines cross the picture plane give the horizontal location for each corner. See **Figure 26-23**.
13. Complete the perspective view by locating the remaining roof corner and connecting the ridge to the three visible corners. The extreme-left-corner height is drawn by projecting the top and bottom of the fascia board at the front corner to the left vanishing point and dropping the sight line location from the plan view. Where they cross is the roof corner. Connect the roof corner to the roof ridge. Draw the gable trim boards as shown in Step 6 of this procedure. The peak point of the gable under the roof may be located by finding the point on the plan view and dropping a line down to the perspective. Connect the top of the left corner to this peak point, as shown in **Figure 26-24**.

Establishing a new true height line is useful in rapidly determining the height of features that are not located on the principal sides of the object. Examples of these features are roof ridges, overhangs, and chimneys.

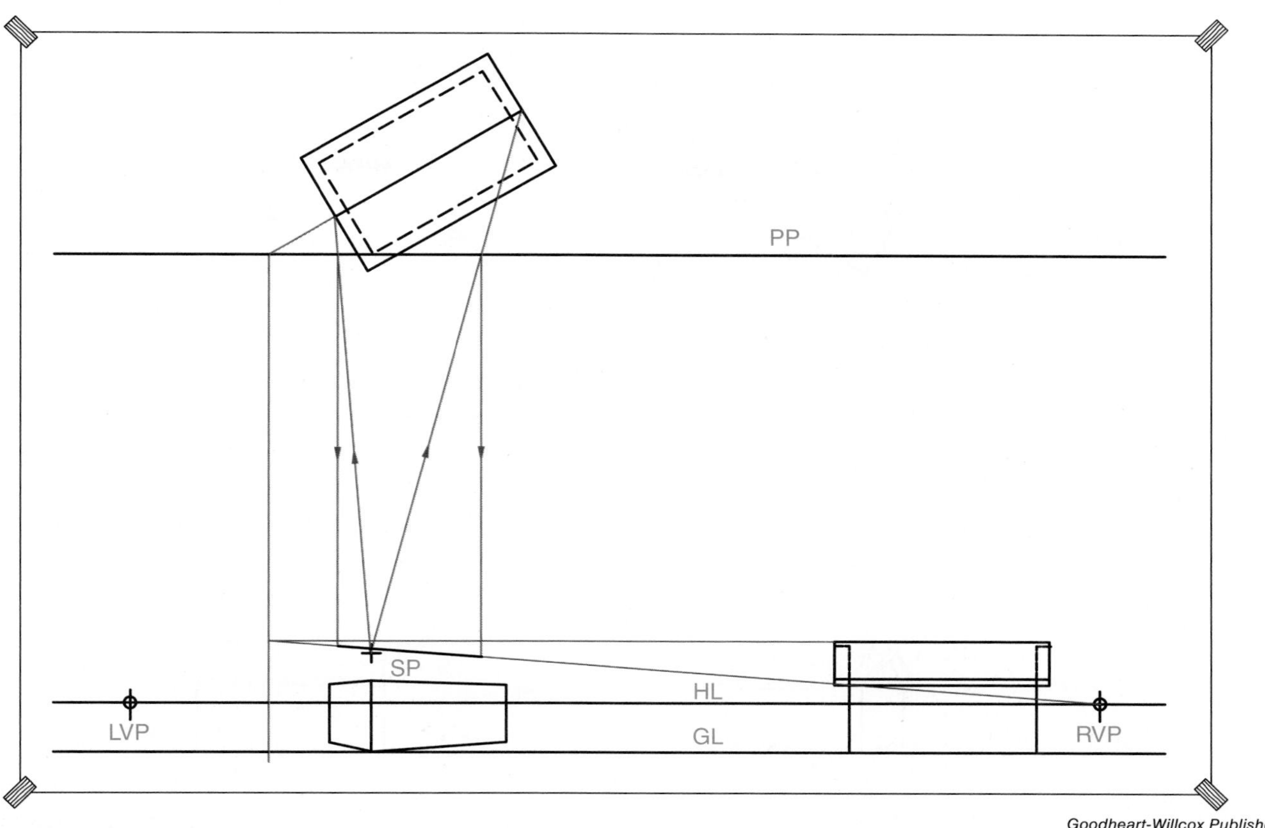

Goodheart-Willcox Publisher

Figure 26-22. Procedure for drawing a two-point perspective—Step 11.

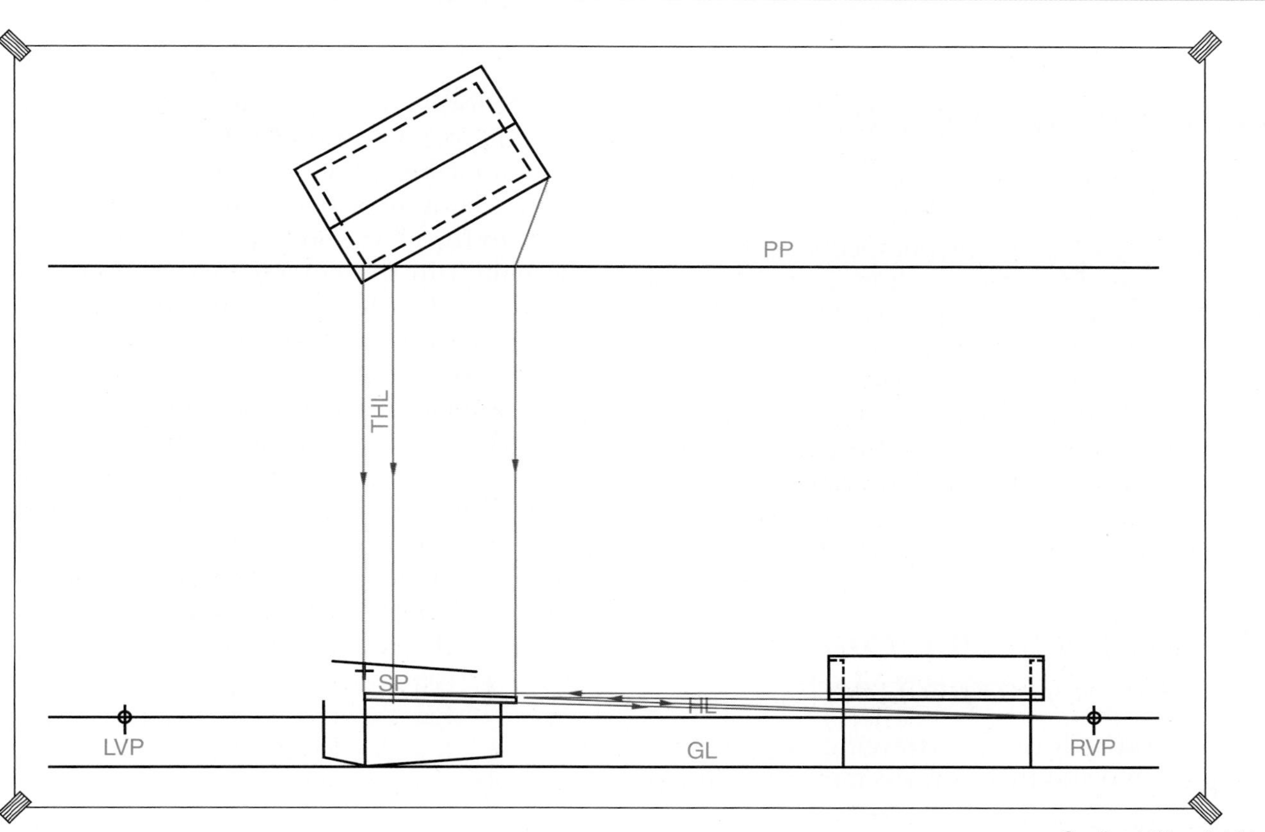

Goodheart-Willcox Publisher

Figure 26-23. Procedure for drawing a two-point perspective—Step 12.

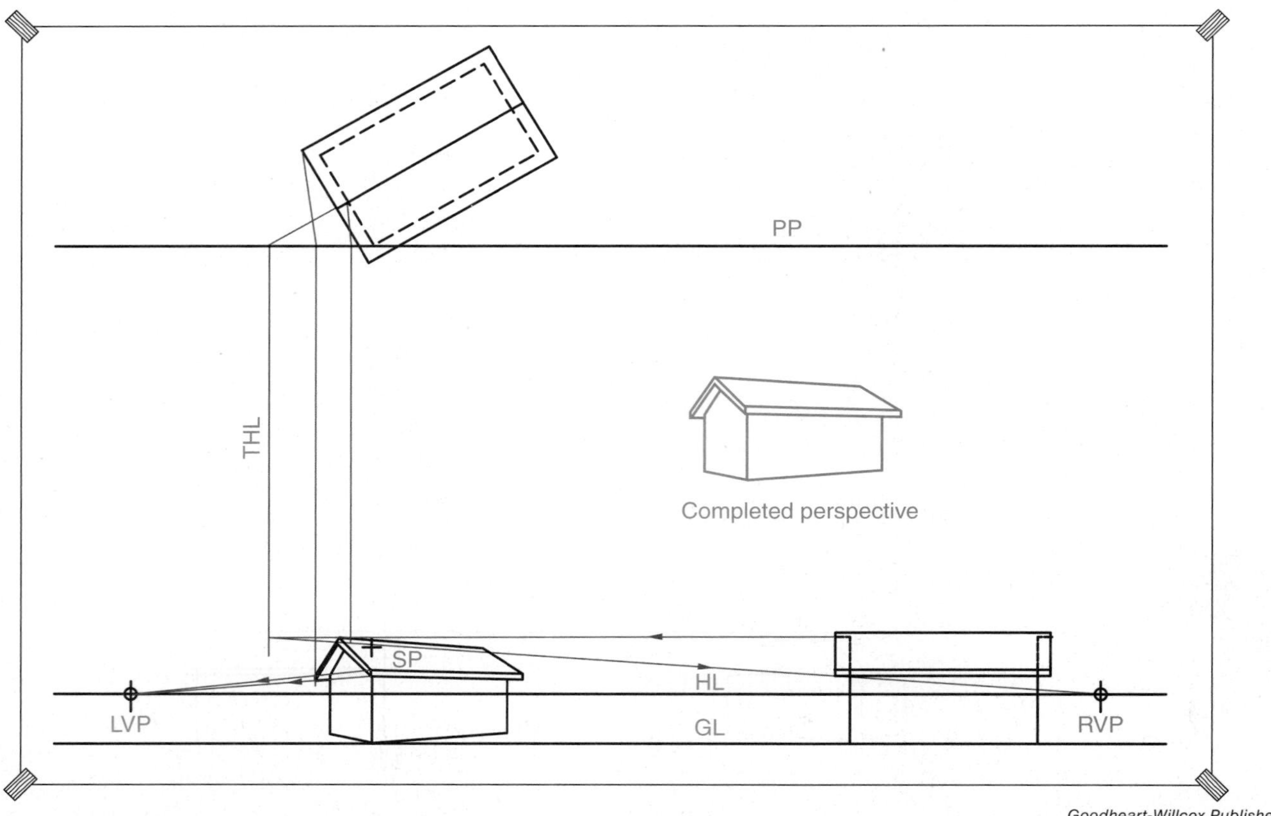

Goodheart-Willcox Publisher

Figure 26-24. Procedure for drawing a two-point perspective—Step 13.

One-Point Perspectives

One-point perspective drawings have only one vanishing point. They are not used as frequently as two-point perspectives, but they are well suited for interior drawings. Room and furniture layouts, kitchen cabinet pictorial details, and interior space studies are all candidates for one-point perspective techniques. See **Figure 26-25**. One-point perspectives may also be used in some situations for exterior views. Entries, courts, porches, and exterior architectural details may sometimes be best shown in one-point perspective. See **Figure 26-26**.

Differences in One-Point and Two-Point Perspectives

The procedure for drawing a one-point perspective using the common method is similar to that for a two-point perspective. One of the most important differences is the selection of an elevation from which to project height measurements. Sight lines are projected from the station point in the elevation to the object to determine the height in the perspective. Any elevation is acceptable for the two-point perspective, but a specific elevation is necessary for the one-point perspective.

Another difference in drawing a one-point perspective is that the vanishing point does not necessarily have to be located. However, the main difference is the most frequent position of the plan view. In one-point perspective, the plan view is usually placed parallel to the picture plane so that the horizontal and profile planes project to the vanishing point.

smena/Shutterstock.com

Figure 26-25. This living room layout is drawn as a one-point (parallel) perspective.

Procedure
Drafting

Drawing a One-Point Perspective

Figure 26-27 shows a typical one-point perspective of a kitchen. This perspective was developed using the following step-by-step drawing sequence. These steps can be used to draw any common one-point perspective.

1. Select a sheet of drawing paper about the size of a large drawing board. In CADD, you may need to set the drawing limits or extents. Draw the plan view near the top-left side. Draw the right-side elevation in the same orientation in the lower-right corner. Draw the picture plane line so that it touches the front of the plan view and the left side of the elevation. Draw the picture plane line in both the plan and elevation views. Study **Figure 26-28** carefully to be sure that you understand which elevation is to be drawn. The space between these drawings in the lower-left corner is where the perspective will be drawn.
2. Determine the location from which you wish to view the object. If one side should be emphasized more than the other, the station point should be slightly on the opposite side of the object. Locate the station point in relation to the plan view first. Label it SP^P. The station point in the plan view indicates from how far away and how much to the

AOMARCH/Shutterstock.com

Figure 26-26. This is a one-point perspective drawing of the same home design shown in Figure 26-6.

right or left you are viewing the object. Next, locate the station point in relation to the elevation view. This view shows the height of the viewing position. The height is measured from the ground line or floor line vertically. Label this station point SP^E, as shown in **Figure 26-29**. *The station point must be the same distance from the picture plane in both views.*

3. Any feature that touches the picture plane line is drawn at its true size. You can project these points down from the plan view and across from the elevation. Where the lines cross is the location of each feature. See **Figure 26-30**.
4. Features that are behind the picture plane line appear smaller than scale in the perspective. To draw them, project sight lines from the SP^P to each point of the detail in the plan view. The horizontal location of a feature is at the point where the sight line crosses the picture plane line. See **Figure 26-31**. The vertical location is determined by projecting sight lines from the SP^E to the elevation drawing. The height of the feature is at the point where the sight line crosses the profile view of the picture plane. Connect the points in the perspective to outline each detail.
5. The floor in this example is a tile floor that forms a grid. To locate the grid, first project those points that touch the picture plane line in the plan view down to the floor line. Then locate the grid line ends that touch the back wall in the perspective by drawing a sight line from the SP^P to each end. See **Figure 26-32**. The place where the sight line crosses the picture plane is the horizontal location of the point. The same procedure is followed in the elevation using SP^E to determine the vertical location of each point. Connect the points to complete the grid. **Figure 26-33** shows the completed perspective.

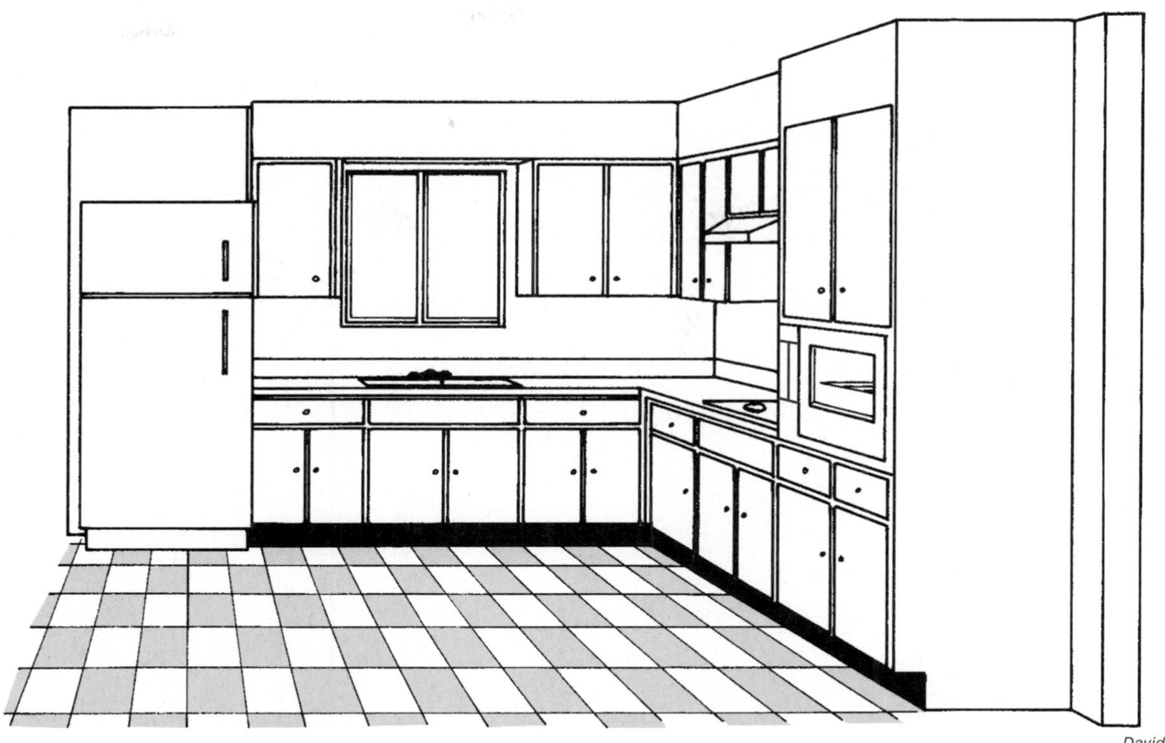

David Brownlee

Figure 26-27. This is a one-point perspective of a kitchen that was drawn using the procedure presented in the text.

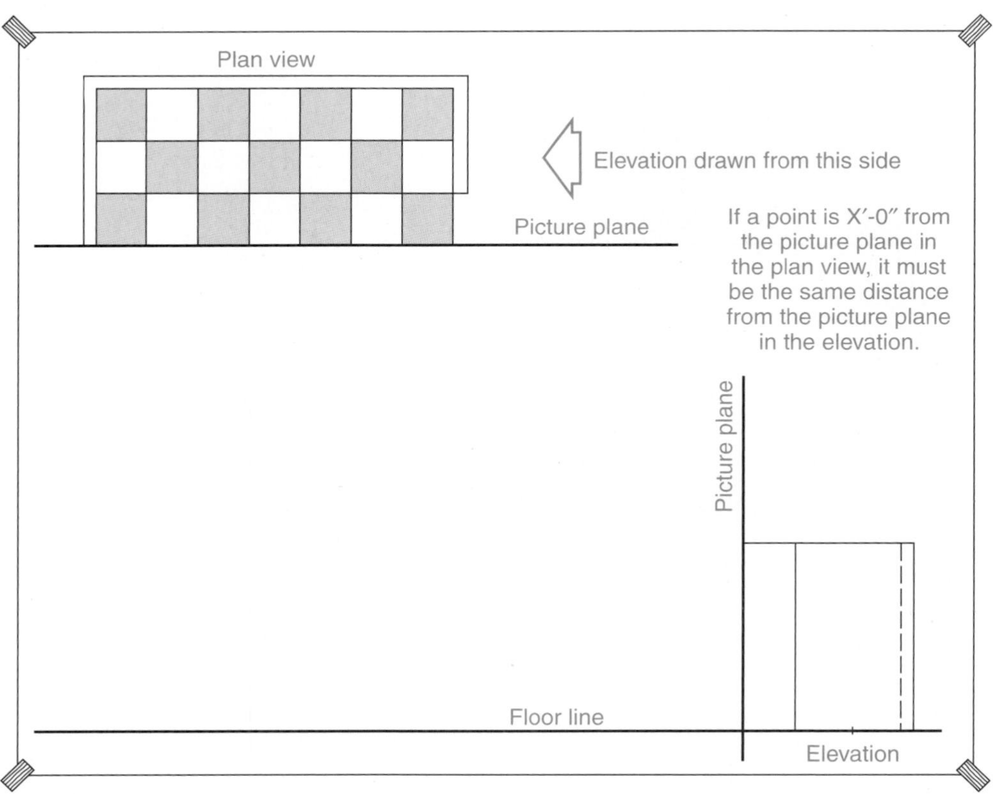

Goodheart-Willcox Publisher

Figure 26-28. Procedure for drawing a one-point perspective—Step 1.

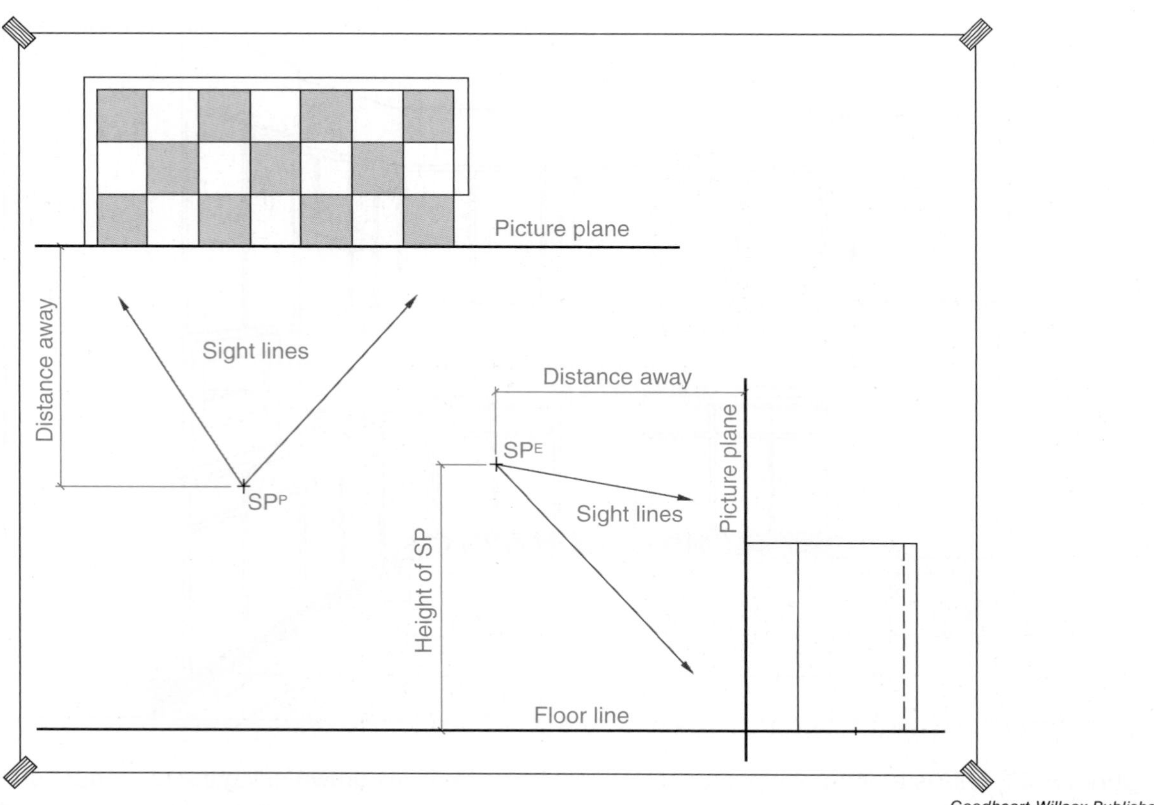

Goodheart-Willcox Publisher

Figure 26-29. Procedure for drawing a one-point perspective—Step 2.

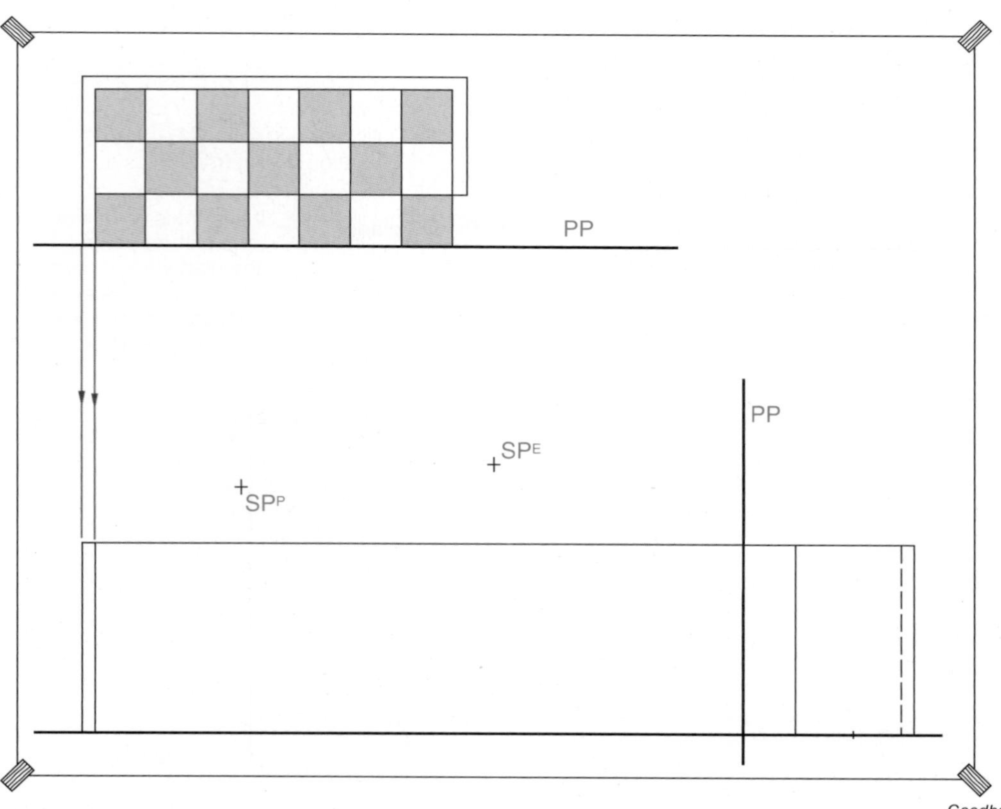

Goodheart-Willcox Publisher

Figure 26-30. Procedure for drawing a one-point perspective—Step 3.

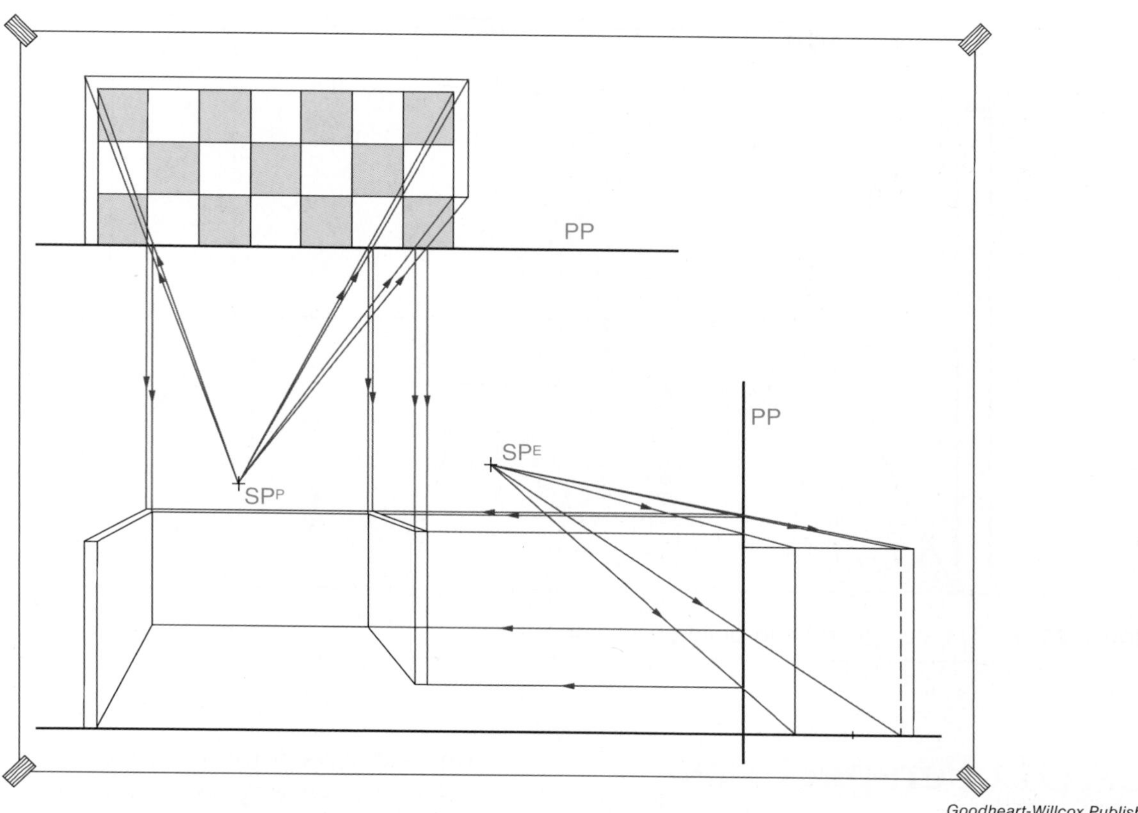

Goodheart-Willcox Publisher

Figure 26-31. Procedure for drawing a one-point perspective—Step 4.

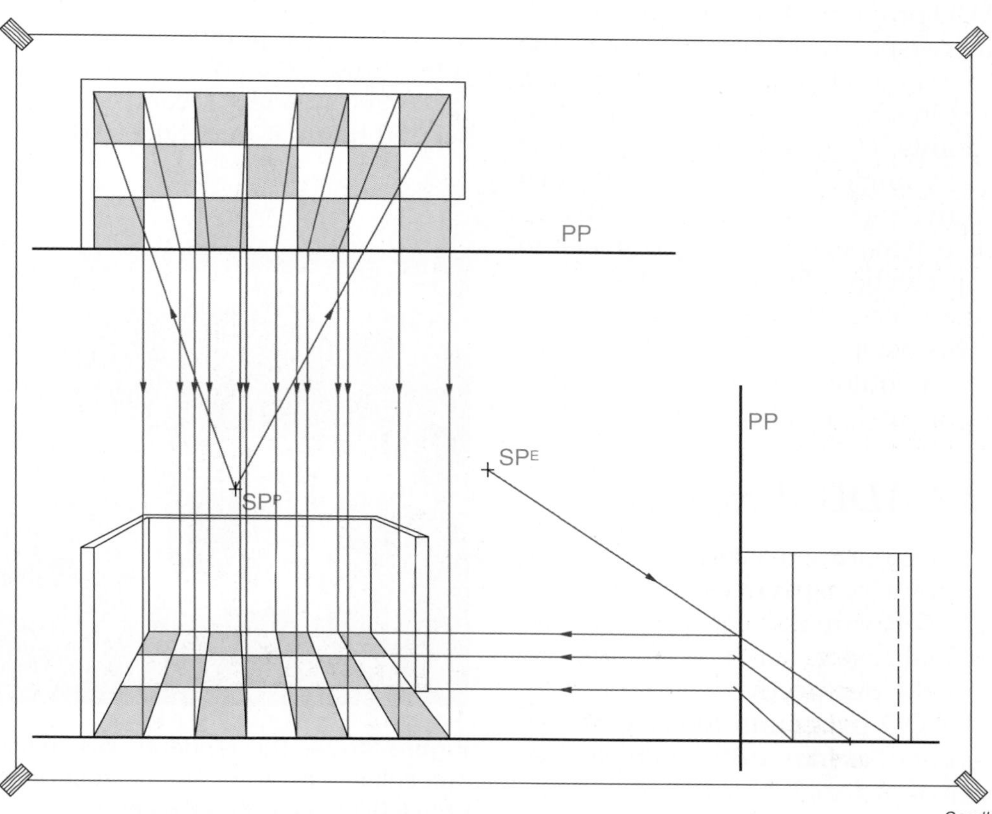

Goodheart-Willcox Publisher

Figure 26-32. Procedure for drawing a one-point perspective—Step 5.

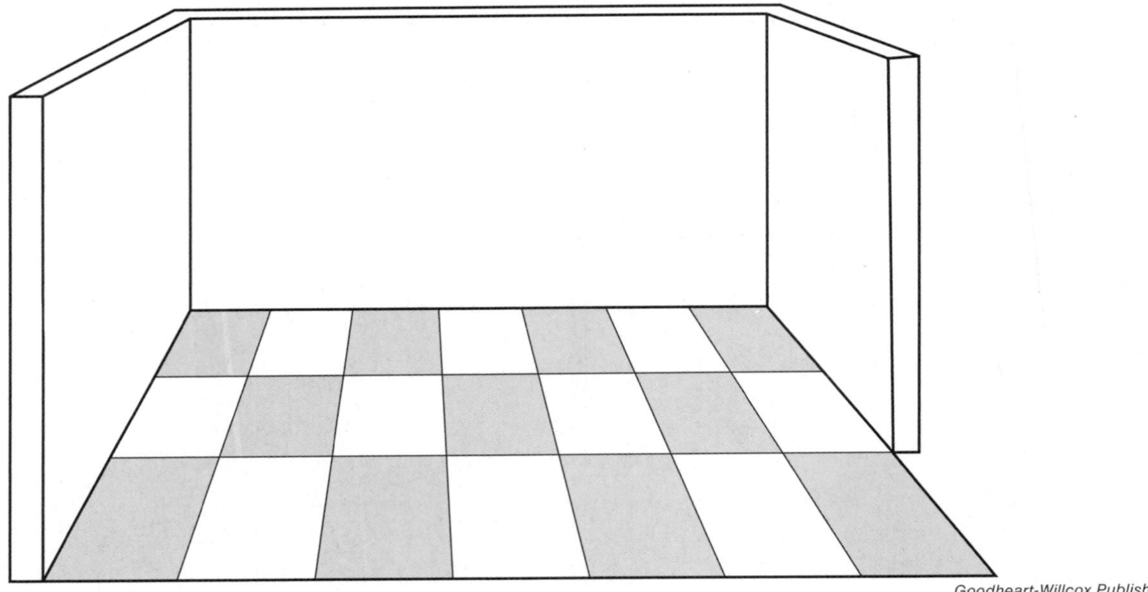

Goodheart-Willcox Publisher

Figure 26-33. The completed one-point perspective.

CADD Perspectives

Drawing perspectives using traditional construction methods is very time-consuming. However, CADD programs that have 3D capabilities can create perspectives in seconds, once the model is complete. As 3D models are constructed, the computer stores X, Y, and Z coordinate data for all object points. The resulting model can be viewed from any angle. You may need to turn on the perspective view or switch the software from parallel to perspective mode to generate a perspective projection. **Figure 26-34** shows a CADD-generated perspective of a residence with landscaping. This perspective closely approaches the accuracy that could be gained by taking a photograph of the real object.

Creating a CADD Perspective

The procedures outlined earlier for drawing one- and two-point perspectives can be used with any CADD software to create perspectives. However, the final result is a 2D drawing, just as it would be if the perspective were drawn by hand. Many CADD programs today offer 3D drawing tools or modes for creating perspectives and other types of pictorial drawings.

Most CADD programs can generate isometric, oblique, and perspective drawings from any defined viewpoint. However, depending on the software, you may not be able to select the type of perspective. Once the perspective is generated from a viewpoint, the drawing can be plotted as a wireframe or a hidden-line-removed plot.

Creating a perspective from a 3D model is quick and efficient. Often, the perspective is generated in a few seconds. Compare this to the several hours it may take to draw a perspective

SoftPlan Systems, Inc.

Figure 26-34. This rendering will be used as a presentation drawing. The perspective was generated from a 3D model. Materials and lights were added to the scene before it was rendered.

in 2D using traditional means. However, in order for the perspective to be correctly generated, the original 3D model must be properly created. Any errors in the model are often magnified in the computer-generated perspective.

Rendering a CADD Perspective

In addition to generating perspectives, most CADD software with 3D capabilities can *render* the model. To render the model is to color or shade the objects, giving them "mass" and "depth." Renderings are often used as presentation drawings. The rendering shown in **Figure 26-34** is an example of the realism that can be achieved by coloring and shading a CADD perspective. Models that are rendered for presentation purposes generally have materials or textures and colors applied to the objects, and one or more light sources added to the scene. Landscaping, vehicles, and people are often added as well.

Perspective Grids

One of the problems in constructing a two-point perspective using manual drafting techniques is the large size of the layout. It is not uncommon for the vanishing points for a residential perspective to be five feet apart or more. The use of a perspective grid reduces the size of work space needed and the time required to draw a large perspective. See **Figure 26-35**. The

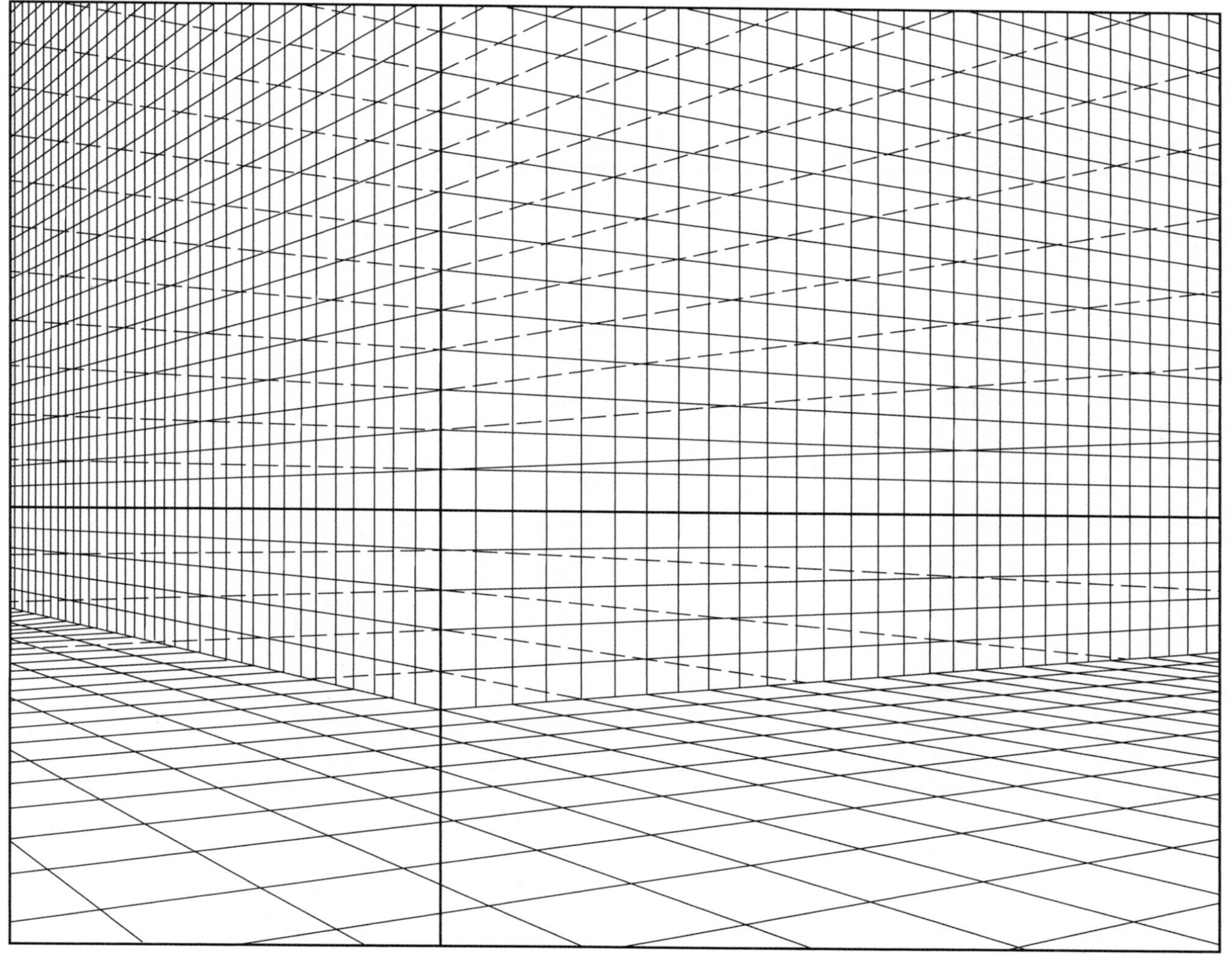

Goodheart-Willcox Publisher

Figure 26-35. A perspective grid used for drawing two-point perspectives.

chief disadvantage of using a perspective grid is the limited freedom in choosing the position of the station point and placement of the picture plane. Many grid variations are available, but each is for a specific layout. A supply of several variations from which to choose is needed to achieve the best position in each drawing.

A thorough understanding of perspectives is necessary before grids can be used effectively. A grid will not ensure a successful drawing if the person using it is not skilled in drawing perspectives.

Complex Features in Perspective

Frequently, objects to be drawn in perspective contain elements that are circular, curved, or not parallel to any of the principal reference planes. Such features may appear to be difficult to draw. However, the following techniques can make drawing complex features a little easier.

To draw circular objects, such as a round-top table or an oval area rug, superimpose a series of points or a grid over the surface, as shown in **Figure 26-36**. Locate several points on the curve that define the details of the surface. Then draw

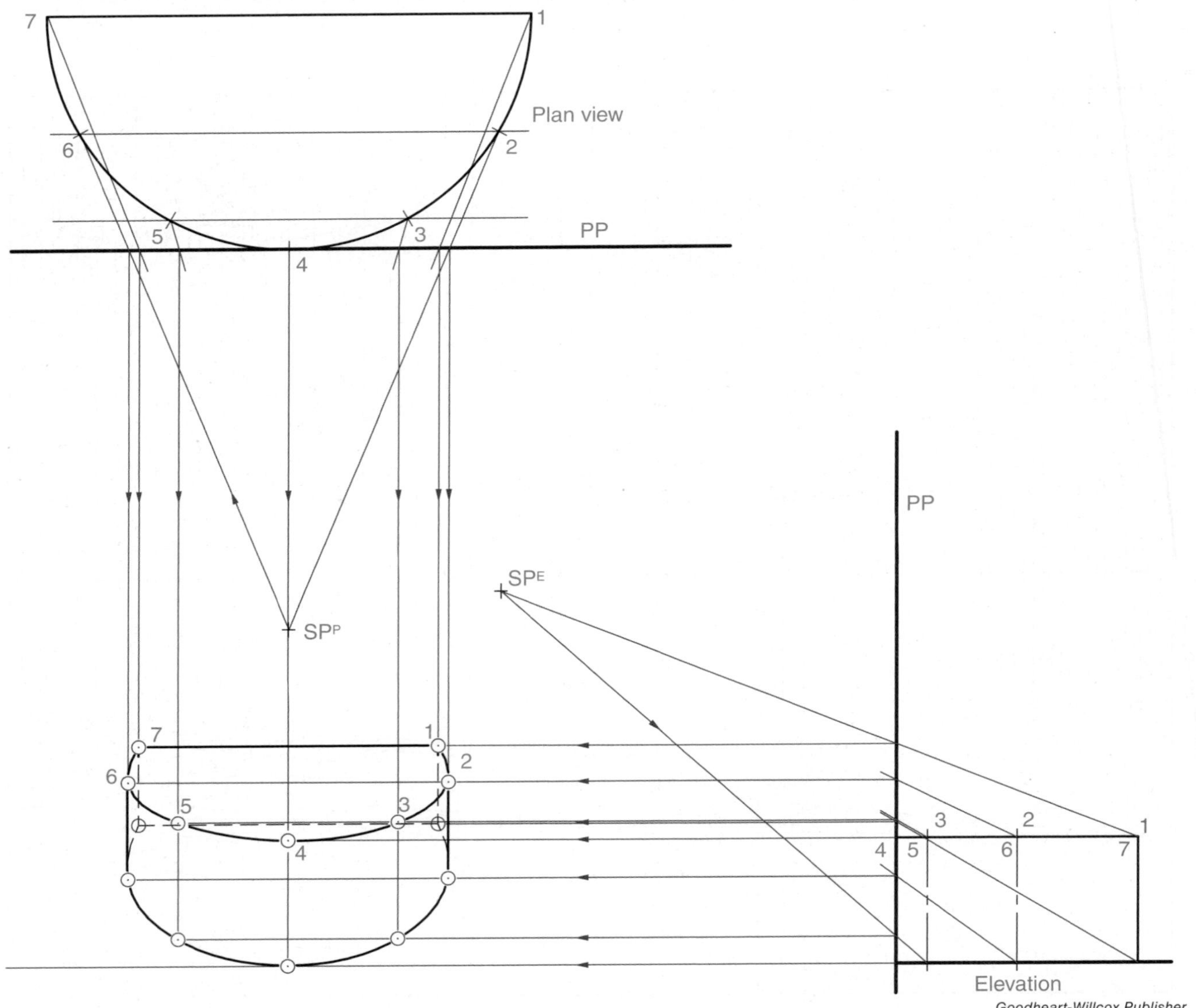

Goodheart-Willcox Publisher

Figure 26-36. This illustrates one method of drawing curved or circular objects in a one-point perspective.

the curve by connecting the points with a French curve (irregular curve).

Other objects that have a series of soft curves, such as a sofa or chair, can be drawn as though they have hard, sharp edges. Then the lines can be softened freehand, as shown in **Figure 26-37**.

Objects that involve a great deal of free form must be boxed in and then drawn freehand within the designated space. **Figure 26-38** is an example of a hand-rendered living room in which many objects had to be boxed in and finished using freehand techniques.

Remember, to draw any object, you are only connecting a series of points. If a sufficient number of points are located and connected accurately, the result will be true to form. Reduce complex objects to simpler parts and construct them one part at a time, rather than trying to locate all points and then connect them.

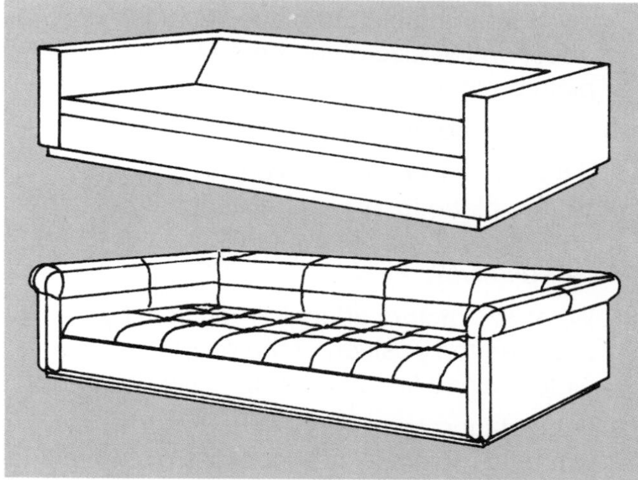

Goodheart-Willcox Publisher

Figure 26-37. An object with soft curves, such as this sofa, can be drawn first with hard edges (top) and then softened freehand (bottom).

Darlana Fowler

Figure 26-38. The details of this sofa and chair were drawn freehand after the basic shapes were boxed in perspective.

Green Architecture

To Print or Not to Print

The traditional method of presenting a custom home plan to a potential client is to create an attractive perspective drawing of the home. Techniques used today range from hand-rendered watercolors to illustrations carefully prepared using a computer. Computerized drawings may be generated directly within the CADD software or by using illustration software, such as Adobe® Illustrator. Regardless of how the drawing is prepared, it is generally transferred to paper at some point.

But why? Most architectural firms have computers with monitors large enough to create architectural working drawings without causing eyestrain. Consider using one of these systems to present your perspective drawings to potential clients. This is easy to accomplish if the drawing was created electronically. Even if it was done as a traditional watercolor, it can be scanned into the computer and displayed electronically. This type of presentation can greatly reduce the use of paper in the architectural office, especially for clients who tend to change their minds.

Summary

- Pictorial drawings present a picture of an object or home design as it would look if the viewer were standing nearby and looking at it.
- The three basic types of perspective drawings are one-point perspective, two-point perspective, and three-point perspective.
- In a perspective drawing, objects appear larger when they are close to the viewer and smaller when they are farther away.
- The most common type of perspective used in residential architectural work is the two-point perspective.
- Some CADD programs can create perspectives easily from any viewpoint.
- Complex features can be drawn in perspective by superimposing a series of points or a grid over the surface, then connecting the points with a smooth line.

Internet Resources

Arty Factory
Art and design information and lessons

Autodesk, Inc.
Revit® software publisher

Chief Architect
Chief Architect® software publisher

Draw 23
Videos on perspective and other types of drawing

Sater Design Collection
House plans and customizations

SoftPlan Systems
SoftPlan® software publisher

Studer Residential Designs
Custom home designs

Review Questions

Answer the following questions using the information in this chapter.

1. Name three types of pictorial drawings that are used as presentation drawings.
2. Identify the three basic types of perspectives.
3. Explain the difference between the ground line and the horizon line in a perspective drawing.
4. Parts of the object that are in front of the picture plane appear _____ than their true size in the perspective drawing.
5. What is the location of the observer's eye called in a perspective drawing?
6. What are vanishing points?
7. How many vanishing points does a two-point perspective have?
8. Vanishing points are located on the _____ line in most perspective drawings.
9. If a station point is moved from 20′ to 30′ away from the picture plane, what is the effect on the size of the perspective on the picture plane?
10. Define *cone of vision*.
11. If the station point is moved closer to the picture plane, how will this affect the distance between the vanishing points in a two-point perspective?
12. What two factors affect the relationship between the position of the object and the picture plane line in a perspective drawing?
13. If the station point is not suitably far away when the object is in front of the picture plane line, _____ is significantly increased.
14. What is the height of the station point in a worm's-eye view?
15. Name three differences in drawing one-point and two-point perspectives.
16. Briefly describe the procedure for drawing circular objects in perspective.

Suggested Activities

1. Using a simple, straight-line object supplied by your instructor, draw several two-point perspectives from different distances and positions. Identify how far away and how high the station point is in each drawing. Draw these representations using traditional methods.

2. Select a floor plan and elevation view from a newspaper or magazine. Using CADD, draw a two-point perspective of the residence. Use the procedure for drawing a two-point perspective described in this chapter. Display your work in class.
3. Select a large photograph (not a drawing) of a home or building from a magazine. Mount the photo on a piece of illustration board or stiff paper. Locate the horizon line and vanishing points and label each.
4. If your CADD system has 3D capabilities, draw a house of your own design using 3D techniques. Do not draw any interior features. Create a perspective display of the house and print a hidden-line-removed hard copy.

Problem Solving Case Study

Mr. and Mrs. Swenson have come to your office for help designing their dream home. Mrs. Swenson studied architecture for a few years, and she has definite ideas about how the house should look. She created the elevation sketches shown below to communicate her ideas. However, Mr. Swenson cannot visualize the appearance of the house from the elevations. Using the elevations provided by Mrs. Swenson, create a two-point perspective drawing to show Mr. Swenson. Add details such as landscaping to show the full potential of the house.

amalia19/Shutterstock.com

ADDA Certification Prep

The following questions are presented in the style used in the American Design Drafting Association (ADDA) Drafter Certification Test. Answer the questions using the information in this chapter.

1. Which of the following statements about perspective drawings are true?
   A. Perspectives are the most commonly used pictorial drawings for presentation drawings.
   B. A perspective drawing differs from an orthographic drawing in the position of the station point.
   C. As you create a 2D drawing using CADD, the computer stores X, Y, and Z coordinate data for each object.
   D. In orthographic projection, the station point is very close to the picture plane.
2. Match each element of a perspective drawing with its definition.

   Elements: 1. Ground line, 2. Horizon line, 3. Cone of vision, 4. Station point, 5. Vanishing point
   A. The line that represents the horizontal plane on which the object rests.
   B. The location of the observer's eye.
   C. The point at which all lines on the object will converge if extended.
   D. The angle between opposite sides of the object with its vertex at the station point.
   E. The line that represents the point at which the sky meets the ground.
3. Which of the following statements are *false*?
   A. The ground line is established using the elevation drawing.
   B. The distance between the ground line and the horizon line represents the height of the observer's eye above the ground.
   C. In a perspective drawing, the station point is infinitely far away from the picture plane line.
   D. The height of the station point has little effect on the appearance of the final perspective drawing.

Curricular Connections

1. **Social Science.** Go to the library or search online to view at least three paintings by one of the following artists: Sandro Botticelli, Leonardo da Vinci, Michelangelo Buonarroti, Edouard Manet, Winslow Homer, Oscar Claude Monet, Henri Matisse, Georgia O'Keefe, or Salvador Dali. Write a short essay on the extent to which the artist used perspective in his or her paintings. Include information about the life and times of the artist and how they may have affected the artist's work.
2. **Language Arts.** The elevation views of a house design show the house from every side and are sometimes made to look quite realistic. Elevations also convey important information about the house design, such as height information. Why are perspective drawings considered necessary in many architectural projects? Develop a two-minute oral presentation to explain your answer. Deliver your presentation to the class.

STEM Connections

1. **Math.** Find out more information about isometric and oblique drawings. From a mathematical perspective, in what ways might these drawings be more useful than a perspective drawing?

Communicating about Architecture

1. **Speaking.** Pick a figure in this chapter, such as Figure 26-6. Working with a partner, describe and then redescribe the important information being conveyed by that figure. Through your collaboration, develop what you and your partner believe is the most interesting verbal description. Present your narration to the class.
2. **Speaking.** Working in a group, brainstorm ideas for creating classroom tools (posters, flash cards, and/or games, for example) that will help the class learn and remember the different perspective drawing terms discussed in this chapter. Have the group members present their ideas to the class.

Chapter 27

Presentation Drawings

Objectives

After completing this chapter, you will be able to:

- Explain the purpose of a presentation drawing.
- Render presentation drawings using a variety of methods.
- List methods commonly used to increase the degree of realism in a presentation plan.
- Describe the different types of presentation plans.

Key Terms

backlight	key light
entourage	presentation drawing
fill light	rendering

The purpose of a ***presentation drawing*** is to show the finished structure. Presentation drawings are shown to people who are interested in the structure, such as the owner. They are generally rendered to enhance their appearance. Presentation drawings are usually pictorial views, but elevations are occasionally used for presentation as well.

Presentation drawings require a degree of realism that is accomplished through rendering. ***Rendering*** is the process of representing or depicting an object or scene in an artistic form by adding colors and shading. See **Figure 27-1**. Shades, shadows, and textures provide much more realism than just clear sharp lines. Creating presentation plans requires talents and skills that are not required to create technical drawings. Still, presentation plans are definitely an integral part of architectural drafting and should be mastered.

Rendering Methods

Today, most rendering is done on a computer, either within a CADD program or using an illustration program such as Adobe® Illustrator. However, several traditional methods are still used for special purposes or to create specific effects. These include:

- Pencil
- Colored Pencil
- Ink
- Watercolor
- Felt-tipped pen
- Airbrush

Rendering by Goodys Home Design; built by Costello Builders Inc., Lancaster, PA

Figure 27-1. This photorealistic rendering captures the essence of this home.

Each of these methods has advantages that should be considered before beginning the project. Each requires a certain amount of artistic ability and skill to produce a satisfactory rendering. The ability to prepare renderings is well worth developing.

Pencil Rendering

Pencil rendering is the easiest form of hand rendering for beginners. No special materials are needed and the product is acceptable if well done. Several common exterior materials are shown rendered in pencil in **Figure 27-2**. A perspective drawing rendered in pencil is shown in **Figure 27-3**.

The pencils used for rendering are generally softer than those used for orthographic drawings. One of the problems encountered in pencil rendering is the difficulty in keeping the drawing clean. A good practice is to cover the surrounding area to prevent smudges and smears.

Colored Pencil Rendering

Colored pencils can also be used to obtain a satisfactory rendering. Light shades or strong strokes are easily accomplished. Even the beginning student can achieve success with this technique. See **Figure 27-4**. Either regular colored pencils or watercolor pencils may be used. Drawings rendered in watercolor pencil can be transformed into a watercolor rendering by applying water to the drawing with a brush.

Ink Rendering

Renderings to be done by hand that will be used for reproduction are best done in ink. Ink lines are sharper than pencil lines, and fine detail is possible. Shading can be accomplished using several methods. The artist or drafter uses a series of parallel lines, a dot pattern, or solid shading. Drawing inks are also available in a broad spectrum of colors that can be used to add realism. See **Figure 27-5**.

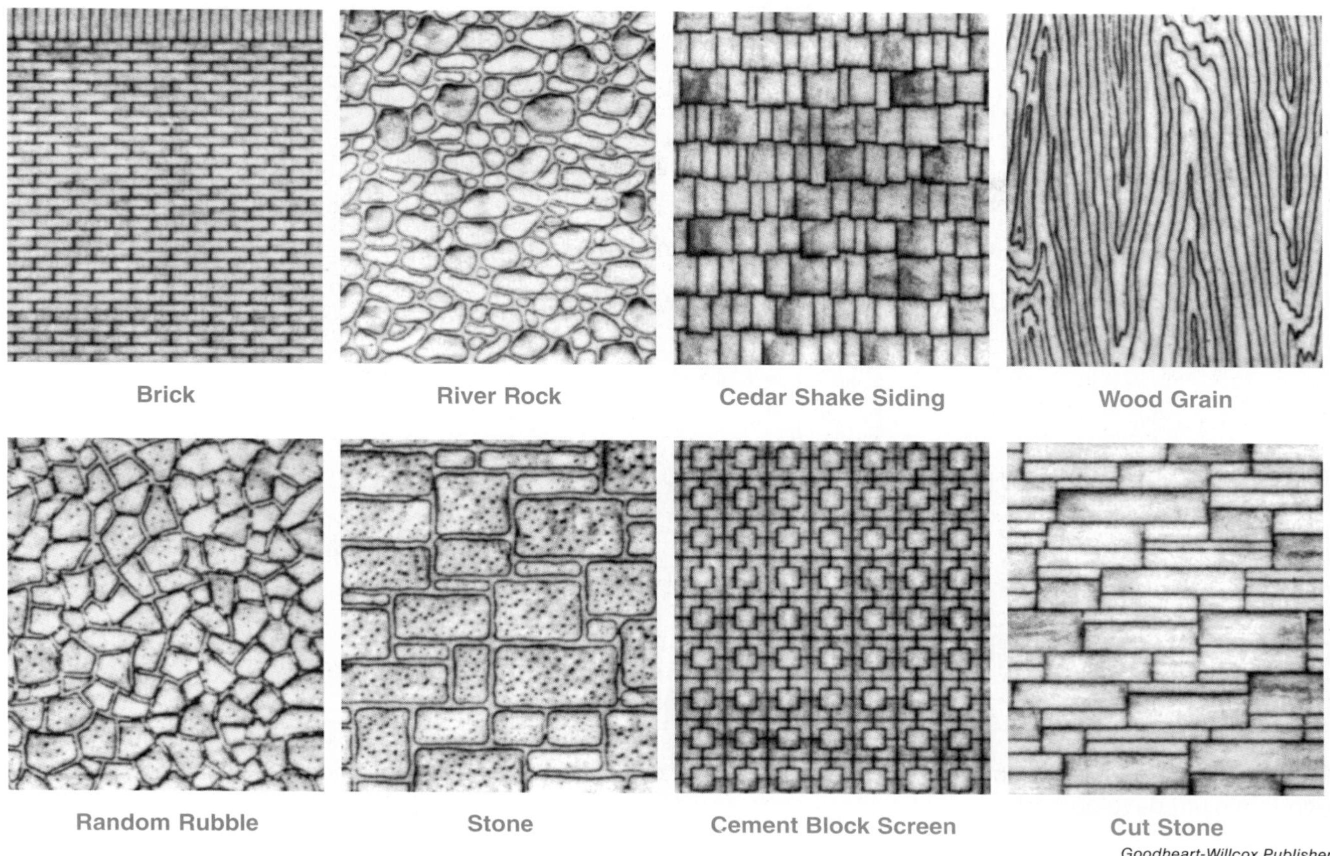

Goodheart-Willcox Publisher

Figure 27-2. Common exterior materials rendered in pencil.

Employability

Decision Making and Problem Solving

Employers value workers who have the ability to make sound decisions and solve any problems that arise. The processes for making decisions and solving problems are similar:

1. Identify the problem or issue to be decided.
2. Brainstorm possible solutions.
3. Decide which solution to implement.
4. Implement the solution.
5. Evaluate the results.

Having the ability to solve problems on the job shows an employer that you are able to handle more responsibility. Solving problems as a group can strengthen the team and help employees feel more pride in their work.

Making decisions and solving problems both require *critical thinking skills*. These are higher-level skills that enable you to think beyond the obvious. You learn to interpret information and make judgments. Supervisors appreciate employees who can analyze problems and think of workable solutions.

Activity

Think of a current school- or work-related problem you are having, or a process that you believe can be improved. Use the steps of the problem-solving process to propose a solution to the problem or an improvement to the process. If possible, implement your solution and evaluate the results.

K.Taylor Architectural Renderings/www.KTaylorRenderings.com; Appel Design Group Architects/www.ADGarchitects.com

Figure 27-3. A pencil drawing can show a large amount of detail. This is a pencil rendering of a large condominium development.

Shots Studio/Shutterstock.com

Figure 27-4. Colored pencils add depth and detail to a pencil drawing.

Genesis Studios, Inc.

Figure 27-5. An example of a colored ink rendering with realistic detail and depth.

Watercolor Rendering

Watercolor rendering is one of the most effective forms of rendering. See **Figure 27-6**. Vivid colors or broad expanses of light wash are possible with watercolor. A light wash is achieved by using very little paint with lots of water. While a watercolor rendering is one of the most effective types, it is also one of the most difficult to execute. Practice and patience are necessary to develop this technique.

Felt-Tipped Pen Rendering

Certain types of presentation drawings may be effectively rendered using felt-tipped pens or markers. Presentation site plans are frequently rendered using this technique. The result is distinct and differs greatly from other techniques. Fine detail may be accomplished by mixing other techniques with the pen or marker. **Figure 27-7** shows a perspective rendered in pen and marker.

Airbrush Rendering

Airbrush renderings are frequently produced by professional illustrators. A great deal

Sater Design Collection, Inc.

Figure 27-6. Watercolor rendering produces a very realistic effect.

of practice is required to produce a high-quality rendering using this technique. An airbrush is simply an air nozzle that sprays paint or colored ink. If examined closely, you will find the surface of the rendering is covered with many small dots of color that form subtle shades and shadows. See **Figure 27-8**. Areas not being sprayed should be blocked out with paper or rubber cement to prevent the accidental spraying of these areas.

Computer-Generated Rendering

Computer-generated renderings are used for presentation drawings as well as images in product literature, sales promotions, and client reports. These renderings are both professional and photorealistic. Full-color, three-dimensional representations complete with materials, lighting, and shadows are typical.

Many CADD packages are available that can produce sophisticated renderings such as the one shown in **Figure 27-1**. However, these programs are generally expensive and require large amounts of memory. Some lower-cost CADD software can produce adequate renderings. In general, however, the best renderings are produced with high-end software on high-end machines.

Realistic Detailing

Most presentation drawings include much more than just a basic perspective drawing. The drafter or artist adds various effects to make the drawing look more realistic. The most important of these are lighting, shading, and entourage.

Lighting

The most basic lighting for a rendered drawing is a light source behind and to one side of the observer. However, the best method for lighting a scene is the triangle lighting method used in traditional photography. This method of lighting uses a ***key light*** in front of the scene, a ***fill light*** to one side of the scene, and a ***backlight*** toward the rear of the scene. The key light provides most of the illumination. The fill light is used to remove shadows. The backlight is used to bring the object out of the background.

Genesis Studios, Inc.

Figure 27-7. This highly detailed, effective presentation plan was rendered in pen and marker.

K.Taylor Architectural Renderings/www.KTaylorRenderings.com

Figure 27-8. Airbrush renderings can provide vivid color as well as detail. They are often used for special effects, as shown in this highly realistic example.

CADD programs with advanced rendering functions typically allow you to place and adjust light sources. See **Figure 27-9**. Lights can be moved and their properties adjusted to produce the most pleasing or realistic effect. When the scene is rendered, shadows are generated automatically. A high-end CADD program with a full range of rendering and lighting capabilities can be used to render any scene realistically. The complex lighting in **Figure 27-10** includes indoor task lighting, light from a chandelier and lighted tray ceiling, and natural light from the outdoors.

Shading and Shadows

Exposing an object to a light source produces areas on the object that are lighter than those areas that are not exposed to the light. The areas on the object that are not exposed to the light should be shaded or darkened. In CADD, this task is usually automatic once the proper lighting is set up. However, in traditional renderings, you must determine which areas of which objects should be shaded.

To determine the areas of an object that should be shaded, you must first determine the angle of the sun or other light source. Once you have established the sun's angle, draw all shading from that angle. In a traditional rendering, 30°, 45°, or 60° is used as the angle of light. See **Figure 27-11**. As the angle is increased, more shadow is cast on the object. Choose a light source and direction that will produce a pleasing and realistic appearance. Also, select a shadow depth that does not cover important information. See **Figure 27-12**.

MaxFX/Shutterstock.com

Figure 27-9. Several lights were added to this rendering: interior and exterior building lights, as well as landscaping accent lights and a general backlight.

tangyan/Shutterstock.com

Figure 27-10. This rendered kitchen scene includes both indoor lights and natural light from the windows.

The shape of an object influences how the shading appears on the surface of the object. See **Figure 27-13**. For example, when an object has sharp edges, there is a sharp transition from light (no shading) to dark (shaded). Objects that are curved have a gradual transition from light to dark as the surface moves from no shade to full shade.

Shading can be hand-drawn using several patterns. **Figure 27-14** shows three common patterns that can be rendered with pencil or ink. Experiment with different methods before selecting the one to be used on a specific project. Begin by laying out the areas to be shaded. Then draw the shadows created by changes in the object surface. Do not make the shading too dark. Doing so will produce an unrealistic rendering. Be sure to use a consistent angle and shading technique. Practice will improve your technique.

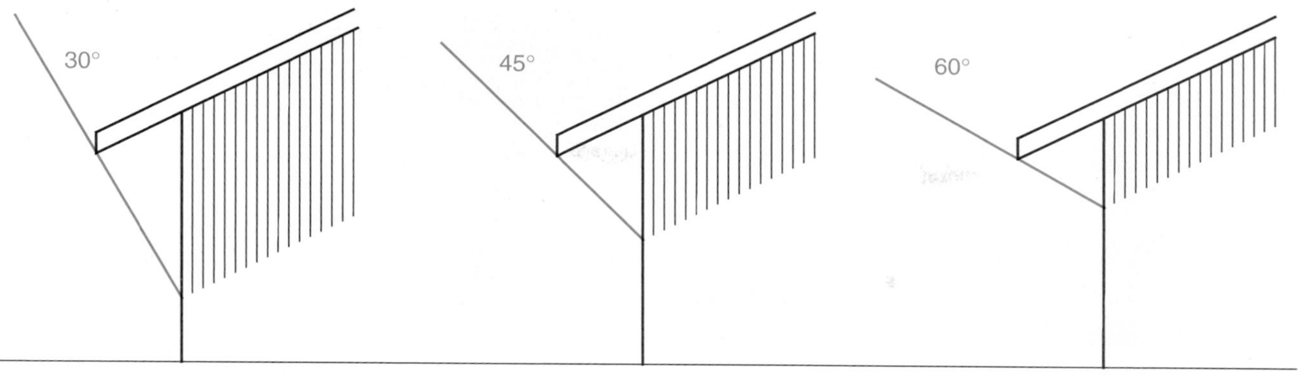

Goodheart-Willcox Publisher

Figure 27-11. The angle of the sun makes a significant amount of difference in the shading on a surface.

AOMARCH/Shutterstock.com

Figure 27-12. In this CADD rendering, the angle of the sun is at about 60°. The trees are between the light source (sun) and the building and pool areas, so the software automatically generates the shadows of the trees on these objects. Notice that the shading does not hide the important features of the drawing.

Goodheart-Willcox Publisher

Figure 27-13. Shadows should accurately represent the shape of the object casting them.

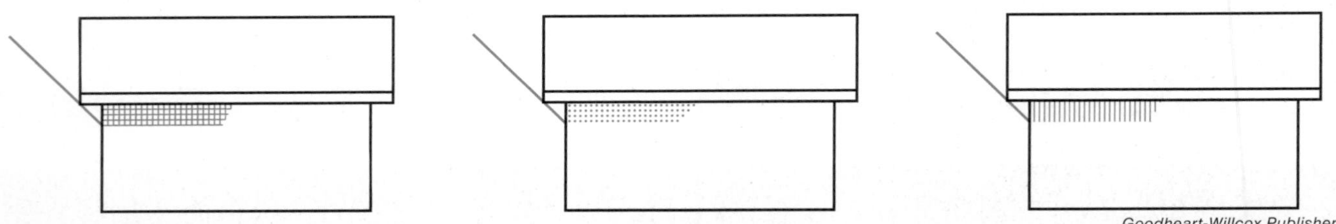
Goodheart-Willcox Publisher

Figure 27-14. These are three different techniques that can be used to shade areas.

Entourage

Entourage (pronounced "ahn-tu-razh") refers to surroundings such as trees, shrubs, cars, people, and terrain. These features add to the realism of a drawing and show an architectural structure in its proper setting. In presentation drawings created using traditional methods, entourage often represents objects in simplified form, rather than trying to make them look exactly as they would appear. Always draw entourage to the proper scale.

Architects usually develop a personal style of drawing entourage. For those who do not feel comfortable drawing these features, appliqués, rub-on symbols, and rubber stamps are available that can be used to add a professional appearance to drawings. **Figure 27-15** shows some types of entourage symbols that are representative of those commonly used by architects.

Some CADD programs include a large library of materials (textures) and entourage. Materials and entourage are important in presenting a realistic result. Most CADD programs that support materials and entourage symbols include a feature that allows you to develop your own and save them for future use. This is an important feature, especially if you frequently use symbols that are not readily available for purchase.

There are several suppliers of entourage for CADD drawings. Symbols or blocks are available for traditional 2D layouts in elevation, plan, and pictorial views. In addition, entourage is available for use with 3D models. Many suppliers offer various trees, cars, trucks, people, and animals. In addition, some suppliers offer animated entourage for use with 3D animations. Entourage for 3D models is generally available in several resolutions, from low to high. High-resolution 3D entourage can be very realistic.

An alternative to using entourage is to use digital images or photographs. Most CADD programs that support rendering allow you to use a digital image as a drawing background or material texture. This can be useful in showing a proposed building as it would appear on a site. See **Figure 27-16**.

Types of Presentation Plans

People understand architectural ideas better if they are presented in a manner in which they are accustomed. Presentation plans address this

Green Architecture

Green Presentations

When you think of a "green" architectural firm, you may think of one that minimizes the use of paper, uses resources wisely, and recycles as much as possible. All of these things are part of having a green office. To present your company to clients as a green company, you may want to go a step further by incorporating green ideas not only into your designs but also into your presentation drawings.

The most obvious items to include are solar panels if you are designing a home with a solar heating system. You would include those as a matter of course. However, what about the landscaping? Rather than inserting random trees and foliage into a presentation drawing to showcase a home, research and use trees, plants, and other items that are native to the area in which the home will be built. You may even want to create a CADD library of these items. By including native landscaping, you are showing potential clients that your concern about the environment is more than just an advertising ploy. You can also use the presentation drawing to educate potential clients about earth-friendly options for landscaping their new home.

objective and are, therefore, very useful. These drawings are designed to present the structure to the layperson, who may not understand a set of construction drawings, in an accurate and honest manner. They may also be used for advertising and other purposes. See **Figure 27-17**.

Several types of presentation drawings or plans are used to represent a structure. Exterior and interior perspectives, rendered elevations, presentation site plans, presentation floor plans, and rendered sections are commonly prepared to help sell the plan to a prospective client.

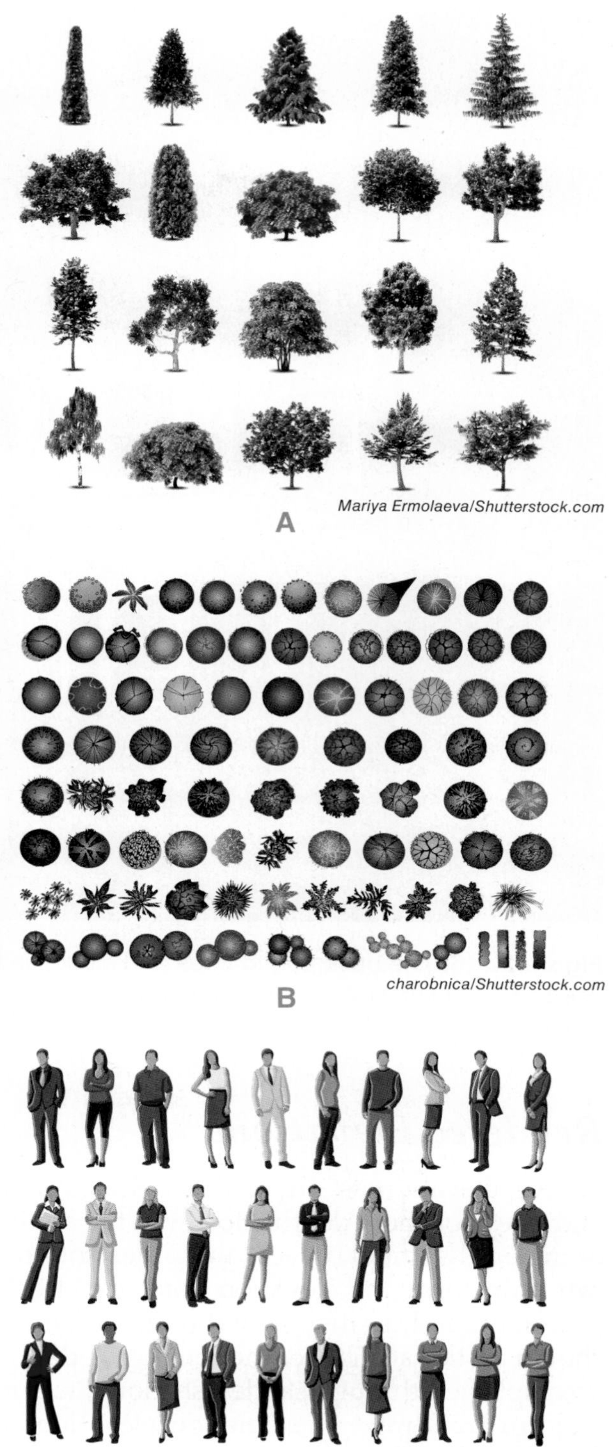

Figure 27-15. Typical entourage symbols. A—Elevation view symbols of trees. B—Plan view symbols of trees and bushes. C—Elevation view symbols of people.

Exterior Perspectives

The exterior perspective should present the structure as accurately as possible. Any distortion present in the drawing may misrepresent the appearance and create a false impression. Most of the presentation drawings shown so far in this chapter are exterior perspectives.

Rendering by Goodys Home Design; built by Hans Construction, Lancaster, PA

Figure 27-16. The background trees and clouds in this computer-generated drawing are a digital image that was used as a background for the rendering.

Rendered Elevations

An elevation is an orthographic drawing and does not show depth. However, the addition of material symbols, trees, and other entourage can transform an elevation into an effective presentation drawing. Even though no depth is shown in the structure, the feeling of depth is accomplished through shades, shadows, textures, and surroundings. Presentation elevations are frequently used instead of exterior perspectives because they are faster to draw and, if presented well, usually quite satisfactory. See **Figure 27-18**.

Presentation Site Plans

Presentation site plans are used to show the relationship between the site and structure. This is essentially a plan view of the site showing important topographical features, the house location, and property boundaries. The presentation site plan gives a bird's-eye view of the layout and provides an opportunity to show off the type of living afforded by the surroundings. Several styles of presentation site plans are possible. **Figure 27-19** shows two different treatments.

Presentation Floor Plans

Presentation floor plans may be used to emphasize features such as furniture arrangement, space utilization, and conveniences, as shown in **Figure 27-20**. Color may be used to call attention to similar features or to separate areas. The color should be functional, if possible, rather than used just to "color" the drawings.

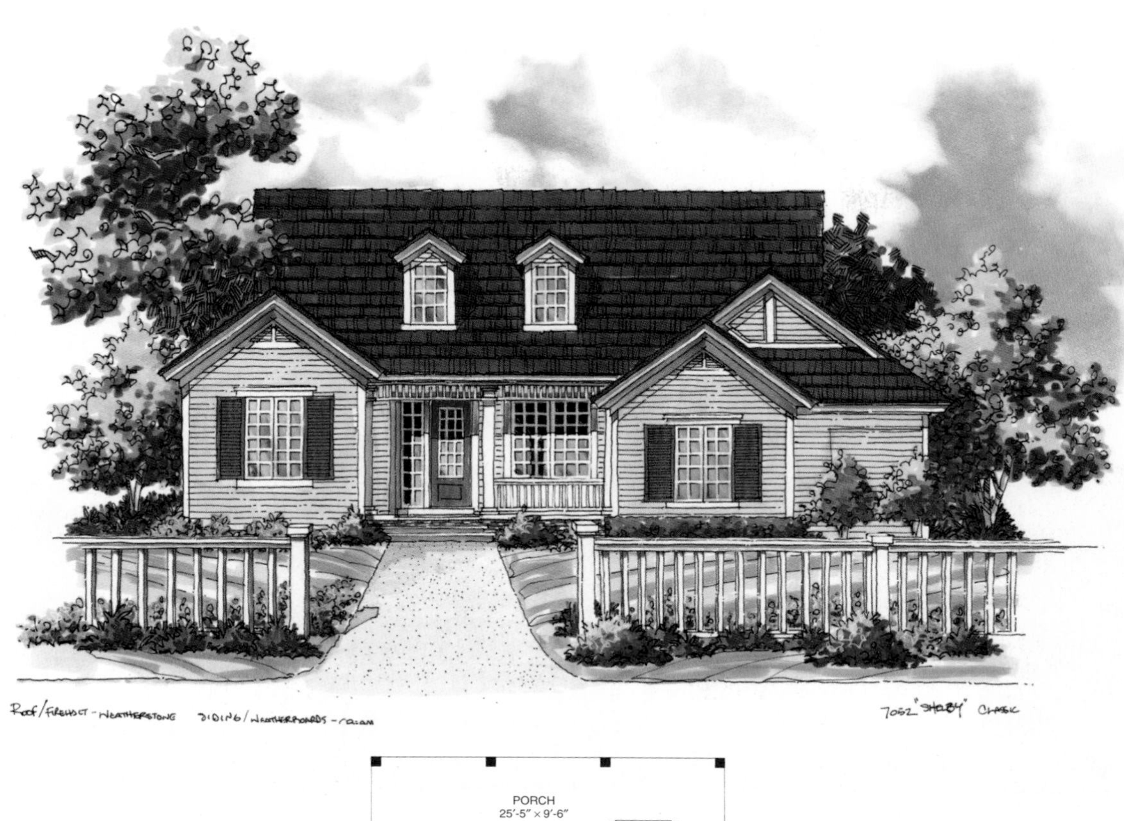

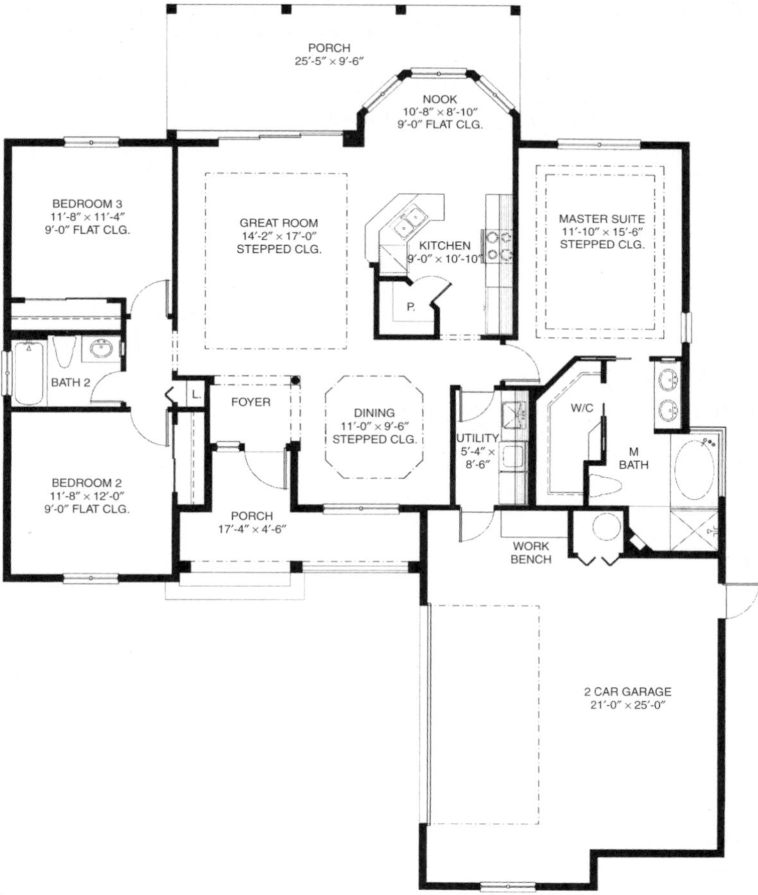

Sater Design Collection, Inc.

Figure 27-17. This presentation floor plan and perspective are used in marketing literature to sell the construction plans for this house.

Genesis Studios, Inc.

Figure 27-18. A presentation elevation can be just as effective as a perspective drawing, but it costs less because it takes less time to create. This presentation elevation provides an accurate representation of the landscaping surrounding the structure.

Rendered Sections

Frequently, a complex structure requires a rendered longitudinal section to emphasize the various levels. See **Figure 27-21**. Such a plan is effective in communicating the internal layout of the house and the relationships among the spaces and levels of the house. The realistic way in which information is presented helps clarify the plan.

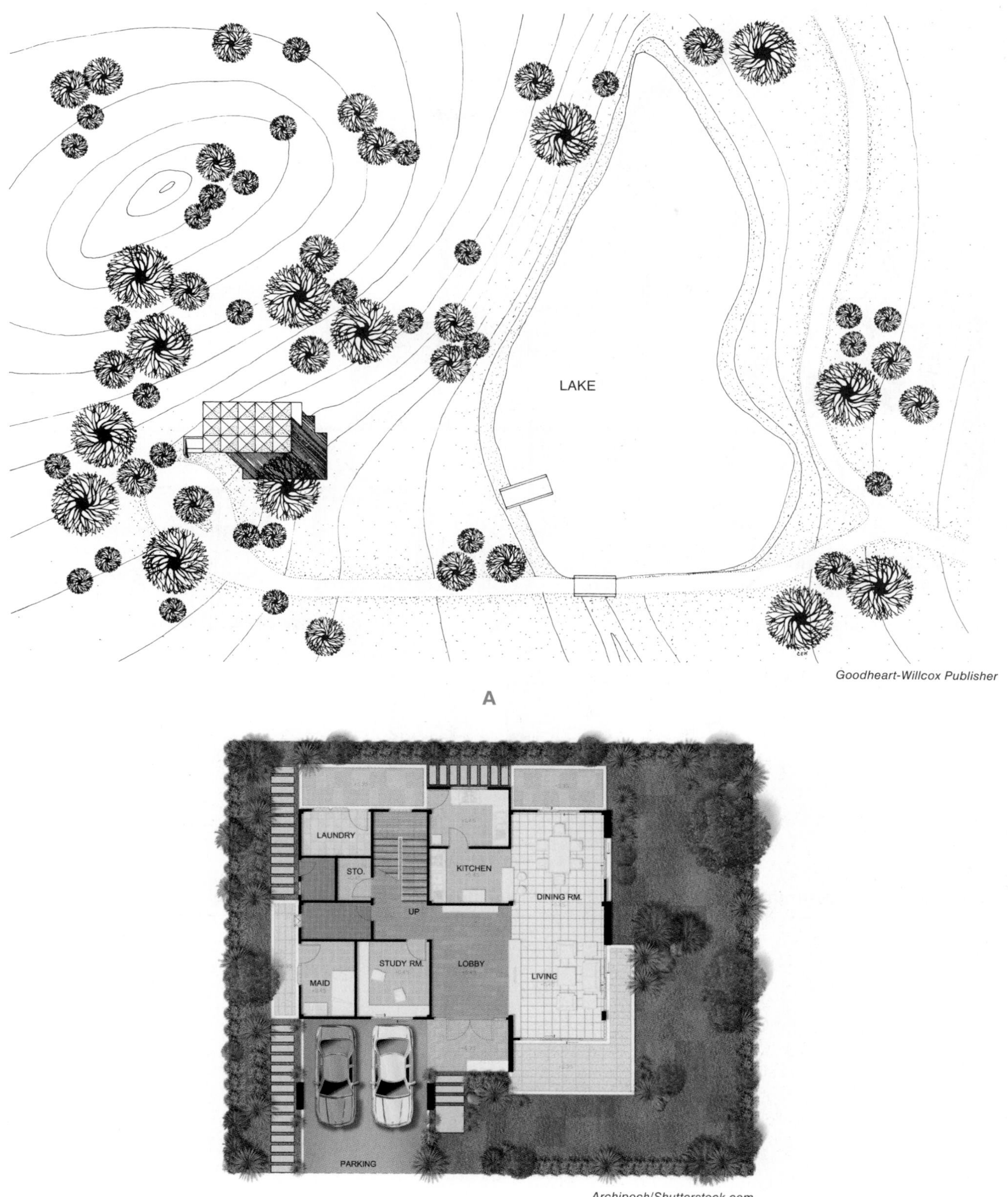

Goodheart-Willcox Publisher

Archipoch/Shutterstock.com

Figure 27-19. A—An ink rendering of a presentation site plan. B—A computer-generated presentation site plan.

WCI Communities, Inc.

Figure 27-20. A presentation floor plan that emphasizes the use of space and furniture.

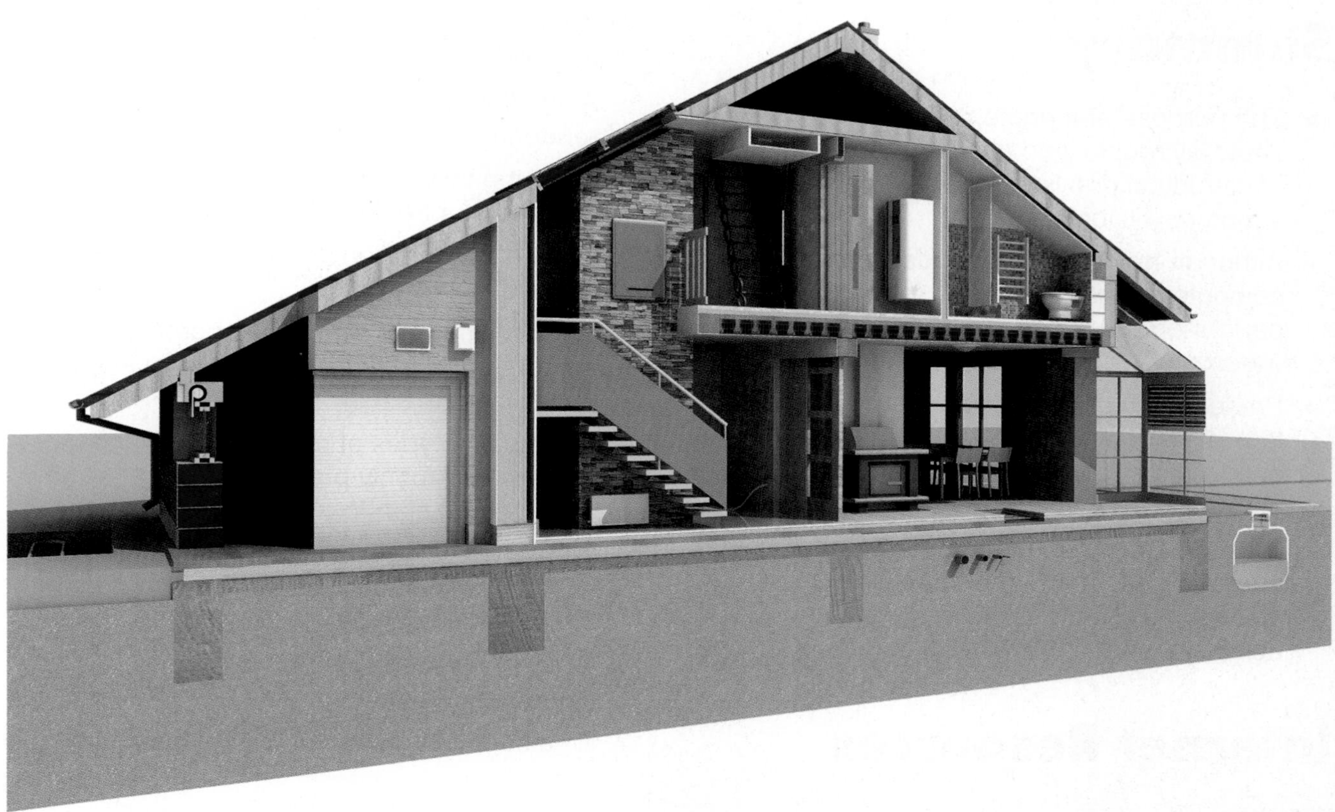

psynovec/Shutterstock.com

Figure 27-21. A rendered section helps a potential client understand the relationships between the spaces and levels in the home.

Summary

- The purpose of a presentation drawing is to show laypeople who may not understand construction drawings what the finished structure will look like.
- Although most rendering today is done on computers, traditional hand rendering is still performed using pencil, colored pencil, ink, watercolor, and airbrush techniques.
- Presentation drawings can be made to look more realistic through the careful use of lighting, shading and shadows, and entourage.
- Presentation drawings may be exterior perspectives, interior perspectives, elevations, site plans, floor plans, or sections, depending on their intended use.

Internet Resources

Adobe
Illustration software

Builder Online
Online magazine for builders and designers

CAD Depot
Landscaping symbols and other CADD information

CAD Forum
Architectural CADD symbols and blocks

Review Questions

Answer the following questions using the information in this chapter.

1. Define *rendering*.
2. Identify six traditional methods of rendering a presentation drawing.
3. Which method should be used for renderings to be done by hand that will be reproduced?
4. What three types of lights are used in the triangle lighting method?
5. At what angle is the sun shown in traditional renderings?
6. Describe three methods of shading that can be used in a traditional rendering.
7. What is the function of entourage on a presentation drawing?
8. What options are available for creating entourage on a hand-rendered presentation drawing?
9. Identify five types of presentation plans that are commonly prepared to help sell an architectural plan to a potential client.
10. Why might an architect choose to use a rendered elevation instead of a pictorial for a presentation drawing?
11. Name three features that may be emphasized on a presentation floor plan.
12. What is the purpose of a rendered section?

Suggested Activities

1. Select a simple construction floor plan. Develop a presentation floor plan that emphasizes the furniture layout.
2. Draw a one-point perspective of a furnished living room. Render the perspective and mount it on illustration board. Display your drawing in class.
3. Choose one of the elevations you drew in the activities for Chapter 22. Render the elevation.
4. Develop a presentation site plan showing the following features:
   - Property boundaries
   - House location
   - Driveway
   - Walks
   - Topographical features

   Present the plan in color.

Problem Solving Case Study

Your company has been hired by a developer to create the construction drawings and presentation drawings for the homes in a planned subdivision. The developer wants to include three basic floor plans in the subdivision. One of the plans should have two bedrooms and the other two plans should have three bedrooms. All of the plans should have two bathrooms.

Create suitable floor plans for this project or search for suitable floor plans online. Develop exterior presentation drawings for each floor plan to show the developer. To save time and expense, use rendered elevations to show the appearance of the homes.

Certification Prep

The following questions are presented in the style used in the American Design Drafting Association (ADDA) Drafter Certification Test. Answer the questions using the information in this chapter.

1. Which of the following statements about presentation drawings are true?
   A. The purpose of a presentation drawing is to show the finished structure.
   B. Renderings to be used for reproduction are best done in pencil, when completed by hand.
   C. Presentation drawings are being used less and less to communicate ideas.
   D. Architects usually develop a personal style of drawing entourage.
2. Which of the following statements are *false*?
   A. Airbrush renderings of presentation drawings are frequently produced by amateur illustrators.
   B. To determine the areas of an object that should be shaded, you must first determine the angle of the sun or light source.
   C. Watercolor rendering is one of the least effective forms of rendering.
   D. The shape of an object influences how the shading appears on the surface of the object.
3. Match each type of presentation plan with its description.

   Plans: 1. Exterior perspective, 2. Rendered elevation, 3. Presentation site plan, 4. Presentation floor plan, 5. Rendered section
   A. Shows the relationship between the site and the proposed structure.
   B. Communicates the internal layout of the house.
   C. Used to emphasize features such as furniture arrangement.
   D. Shows the outside of a house in a pictorial view.
   E. A rendered orthographic view.

Curricular Connections

1. **Language Arts.** Communicating with potential clients is one of the most important nontechnical skills an architect needs. In an architectural company, you will need to be able to communicate in writing and through your drawings. In many cases, you will also need to communicate verbally. Conduct research to find out what is and what is not appropriate when communicating verbally with a client. Then, with a classmate, take turns pretending to be an architect and a client talking in the office about a presentation drawing the architect has created for the client. Use proper grammar, avoid slang, and always be polite!

STEM Connections

1. **Technology.** Some of the illustration software programs used to render presentation drawings, such as Adobe® Illustrator, have special features that allow the artist to achieve a "hand-drawn" look. Investigate the various "hand-drawn" styles that are offered by computer illustration programs. Write a short report summarizing the available styles and explaining why they might be useful for presentation drawings.

2. **Science.** In a presentation rendering, the angle of the light source is an important consideration. However, the color of the light should also be considered. For example, natural sunlight has a yellowish cast. Conduct research to find out more about the effects of different types of light sources on the colors—including the color of shaded areas—in a photorealistic rendering. Write a summary of your findings.

Communicating about Architecture

1. **Speaking.** Make a pencil rendering of the home you live in or another home of your choice. Use the figures in this chapter as a guide. Present your drawing to the class. Make sure to point out any details and special features in your drawing.
2. **Speaking.** Pick a figure in this chapter, such as Figure 27-8. Working with a partner, describe and then redescribe the important information being conveyed by that figure. Through your collaboration, develop what you and your partner believe is the most interesting verbal description. Present your narration to the class.

Chapter 28

Architectural Models

Objectives

After completing this chapter, you will be able to:

- Explain the various types of physical architectural models used to represent residential structures.
- Summarize the steps for constructing a physical architectural model using balsa.
- Identify typical uses for computer-generated models.
- Explain walkthrough animation and cutaway views.

Key Terms

3D printing
architectural model
balsa
clipping path
cutaway view
foam board
physical model
presentation model
small-scale solid model
structural model
walkthrough animation

An ***architectural model*** is a scaled representation of a house and a portion of the site. It provides a way to show how the finished home will look in all three dimensions. The model may be viewed from any position, which greatly increases the amount of information communicated. Models are useful for checking the finished appearance of an architectural design and selling a design to a client. Architectural models can be either physical or virtual (computer-generated).

Physical Models

Models that are made from modeling materials such as wood, sandpaper, or scaled lumber or bricks are ***physical models***. Some physical models are very basic; others show minute detail. Although building an accurate physical model can be time-consuming, the result is worth the effort if it helps clients see your designs more clearly.

Types of Physical Models

Several types of physical models are used to represent architectural structures. One type is the ***small-scale solid model***, which shows only the exterior shape of the building. See **Figure 28-1**. This type of model is not hollow and contains no interior. It is frequently used to show space relationships and how a building will fit in with surrounding buildings. Scales used range from 1/32″ = 1′-0″ to 1/8″ = 1′-0″. Very little exterior detail is shown on solid models.

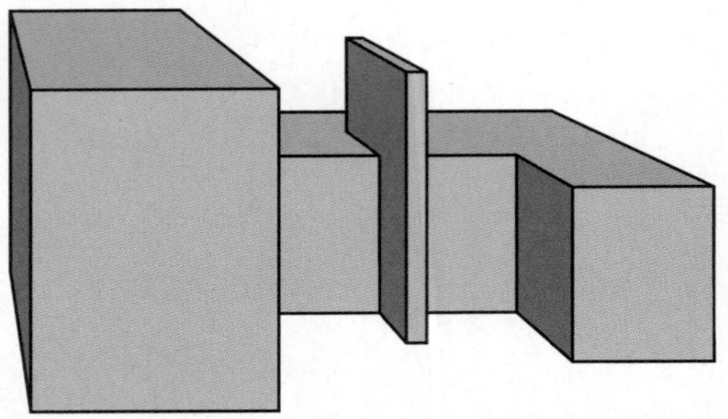

Goodheart-Willcox Publisher

Figure 28-1. A small-scale solid model is frequently used to study the mass of a building or show its relation to surrounding buildings.

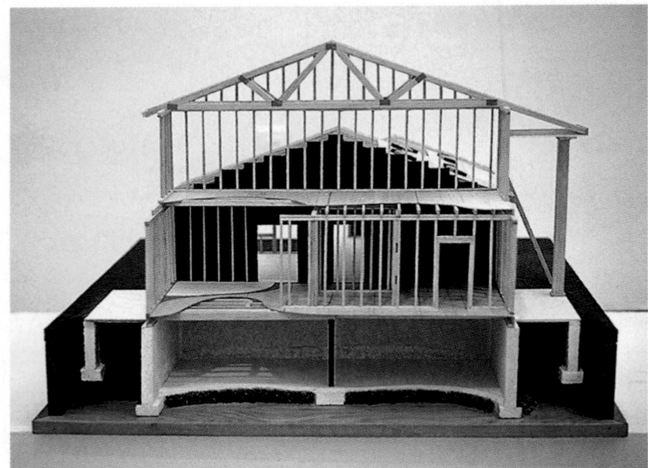

Goodheart-Willcox Publisher

Figure 28-3. This structural model shows the framing of the building.

Structural models are frequently used to show construction features of a residence. All structural materials used should be cut to scale, and proper building methods should be represented. See **Figure 28-2**. Structural models are usually 1/2″ = 1′-0″ or 1″ = 1′-0″ scale. If the scale is too small, the materials will be difficult to work with. Since the purpose of a structural model is to show the basic construction, most siding and roofing materials are left off to expose the structural aspects. See **Figure 28-3**. This type of model is useful when unusual construction procedures are to be used.

Most architectural models for residential use are ***presentation models***. The purpose of a presentation model is to show the appearance of the finished building as realistically as possible. A primary concern is to select materials that will closely resemble materials used in construction. Presentation models are usually 1/4″ = 1′-0″ scale. They may be larger or smaller, depending on the amount of detail desired, size of the structure, and funds for model construction. See **Figure 28-4**.

Brad L. Kicklighter

Figure 28-2. A structural model under construction using materials cut to the proper scale.

Brad L. Kicklighter

Figure 28-4. This presentation model is 1/2″ = 1′-0″ scale and accurately represents the materials to be used on the house.

Materials Used in Physical Models

Several basic materials are commonly used for architectural model construction. Some model builders prefer sheets of Styrofoam® called ***foam board***. This material is easy to cut and can be made to resemble many different types of exterior building materials. It is easy to glue and can be painted with various kinds of paint. However, Styrofoam® is soft and may be scratched or easily broken.

Another popular material for architectural models is cardboard or illustration board. **Figure 28-5** shows a residential model made from foam board and illustration board. Cardboard is easy to obtain, glues well, and can be painted with almost any type of paint. Two disadvantages are that cardboard warps easily, and it must be cut with a knife or razor-type blade, rather than by sawing. Pin holes are also more visible than in other materials.

Balsa wood is another popular material for building models of homes. ***Balsa*** is a softwood available in a wide variety of sizes. It is easy to cut with a sharp knife, can be sawed, is easy to finish, and can be sanded and scored to represent exterior materials. In addition, a balsa wood model is stronger than cardboard and does not warp as much. See **Figure 28-6**.

EML/Shutterstock.com

Figure 28-6. This presentation model was built using balsa wood.

Commercial Model Parts

Supplies for creating a physical model are also generally available at hobby stores and model train shops and can be very realistic in appearance. Accurately scaled windows, doors, bricks, and even roofing tiles and lumber can be purchased. Using commercial parts speeds up the modeling process and, unless you have a high degree of skill, may result in a more accurate model. See **Figure 28-7**. Scale building materials are available in several scale sizes. If you buy commercial model parts, be sure the items are the correct scale for the model you are building.

Laser-Cut Model Parts

If you use CADD software to create 2D drawings and prefer to use model parts specific to your models, you can use a laser cutting machine. This machine uses CADD drawing data

Goodheart-Willcox Publisher

Figure 28-5. The roof and interior walls of this model are made from illustration board. The exterior walls are made from Styrofoam® sheets.

Stephen Mahar/Shutterstock.com

Figure 28-7. A model of a vacation cabin built using commercially available parts. This model was built at a scale of 1″ = 1′-0″.

to guide the cutter. The principle of the machine is similar to that of a plotter, but instead of putting lines on paper, a laser cutting machine cuts or scores the material where the lines would have been. Materials such as Plexiglas®, plastics, wood, cardboard, paper, fabrics, rubber, and composites can be cut or scored with high precision and accuracy.

Constructing a Balsa Model

The following procedure is presented as an aid to building a presentation-type model from balsa wood. This is a typical procedure that can be applied to many different models. The model in this example has a removable roof. Many presentation models are built with removable roofs so the interior detail can be viewed more easily.

1. Obtain a set of plans drawn at a scale of 1/4″ = 1′-0″ for the home you want to model. In some cases, it may be desirable to build a model to another scale, but the majority of residential models are 1/4″ = 1′-0″ scale. Typically, only the floor plan and elevations are needed to build the model. See **Figure 28-8**. The procedure presented here is for a house on a flat site. If the building site is not flat, a site plan should be drawn using the same scale as the other plans. It is usually not necessary to draw the entire site at 1/4″ = 1′-0″ scale. Draw only the segment represented by the model. If the roof is multifaceted, it may be advantageous to develop a second floor or roof plan to aid in building the upper portion of the model, as shown in **Figure 28-9**.
2. Decide on the size of the base for the model. Storage and handling are major considerations. If the base is large, it may be hard to store and transport. A good-size base for an average residence is 30″ × 30″ or 30″ × 36″. The base should be 3/4″ plywood if the site is relatively flat. If the site is rolling, it must be accurately represented by building up the high spots with plaster of paris, Styrofoam®, or cardboard. See **Figure 28-10**. A lighter base should be used to reduce weight. Note that if the site is flat, the model can be completed on a workbench and placed on the base. If the site is rolling, it may be easier to build the model on the base.
3. After studying the floor plan and elevations, select a piece of balsa that approximates the thickness for the exterior walls of the model. Usually 3/16″ or 1/4″ thick material

Green Architecture
Sustainable Models

If your architectural firm is working toward sustainability, perhaps you should consider the materials used in your architectural models. First, consider what happens to the models when they are no longer needed. Are they given to clients as mementos, or are they discarded? If they are discarded, can you reuse any of the materials? Are those you cannot reuse recyclable? Choosing your modeling materials with reuse and recycling in mind will make your office greener.

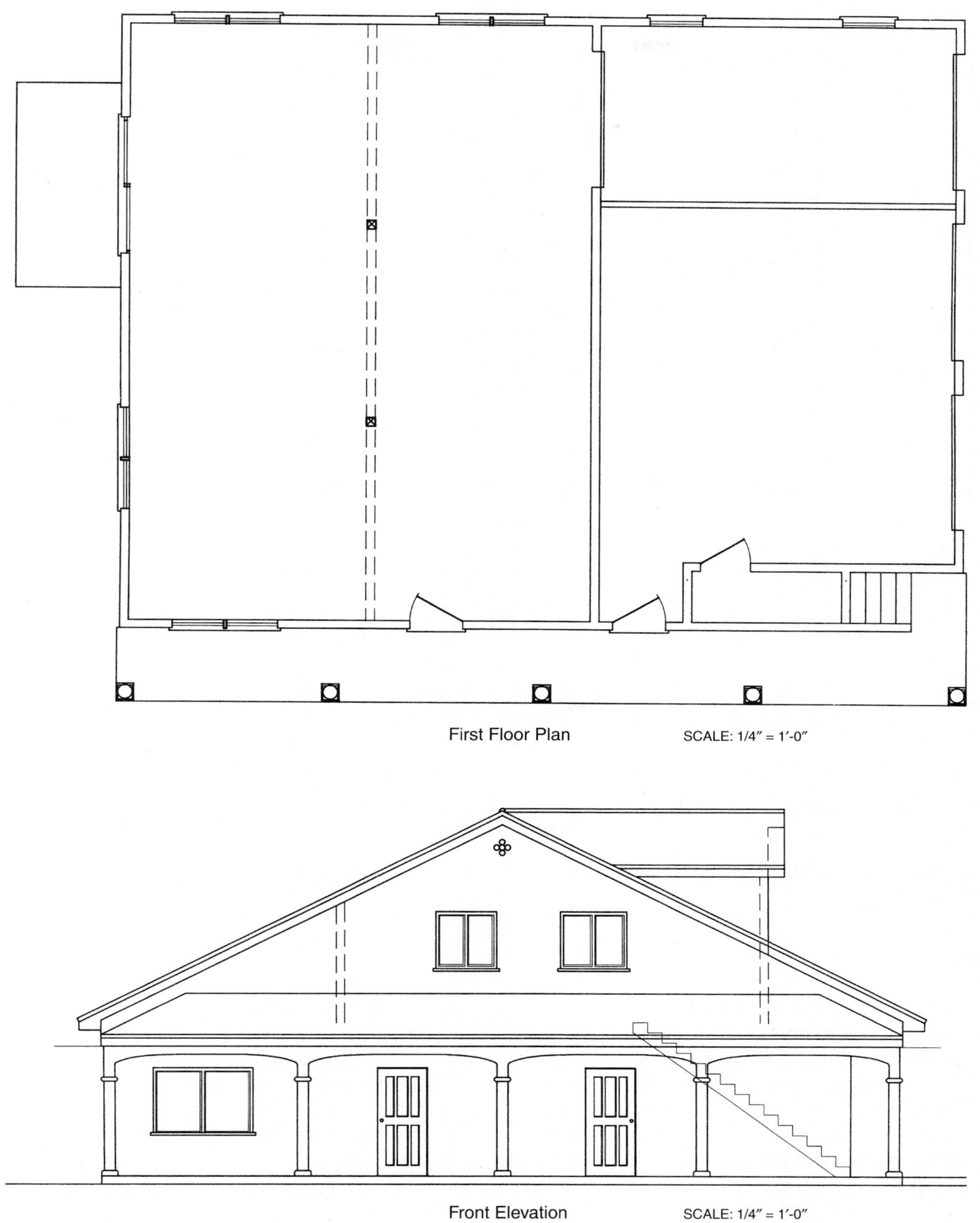

Goodheart-Willcox Publisher

Figure 28-8. Typically, only a floor plan and elevations are needed to construct a presentation model.

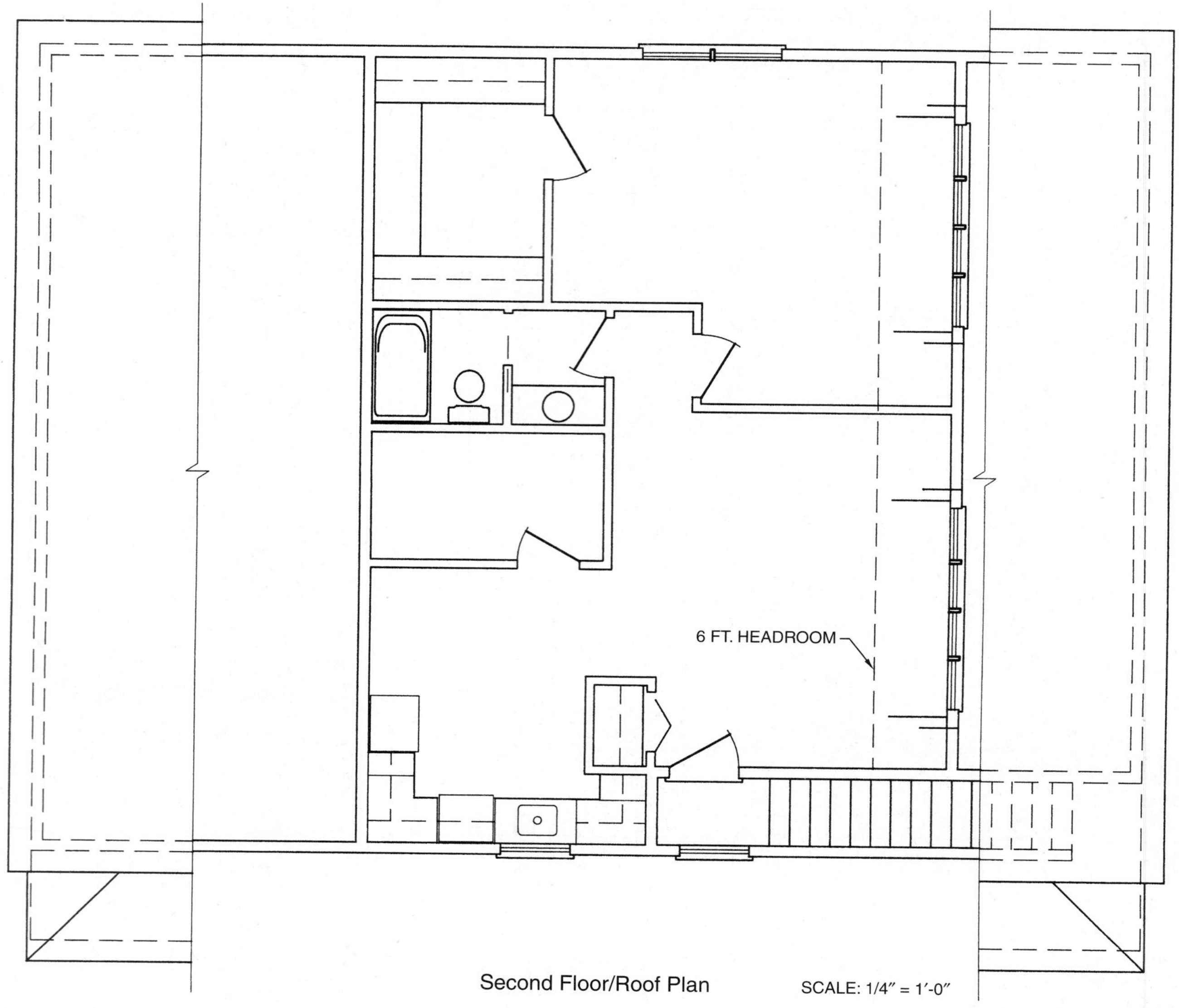

Goodheart-Willcox Publisher

Figure 28-9. If the house has a complex roof, a second floor plan or roof plan may be needed to construct the model.

is used. Lay out the length of one exterior wall and any openings in the wall, such as windows and doors. Cut this piece precisely, paying close attention to details. The corners may be mitered or butt jointed. A mitered corner is frequently cleaner and sharper. Proceed with the next exterior wall by cutting it to length and locating the windows and doors. Construct all the exterior walls in the same manner. Glue the walls together. Place them on the floor plan to ensure accuracy. See **Figure 28-11**.

4. Lay out each section of interior wall on a piece of 1/8″ thick balsa. This thickness closely approximates the thickness of an interior wall drawn to scale. Cut out each interior wall segment and glue the pieces together in their correct locations on the plan.
5. Apply the trim around windows and doors and insert exterior doors. This is usually 1/8″ thick material. The window glass may also be installed now or after the interior is painted. For best results, 1/16″ thick Plexiglas® may be used for window glass.

Melvin Denny Ako

A

Goodheart-Willcox Publisher

B

Figure 28-10. A—The base of this model was built up to accurately reflect the terrain on which the house is to be constructed. B—A rolling site may be modeled by building a support frame cut to the proper contour covered with screen and plaster of paris.

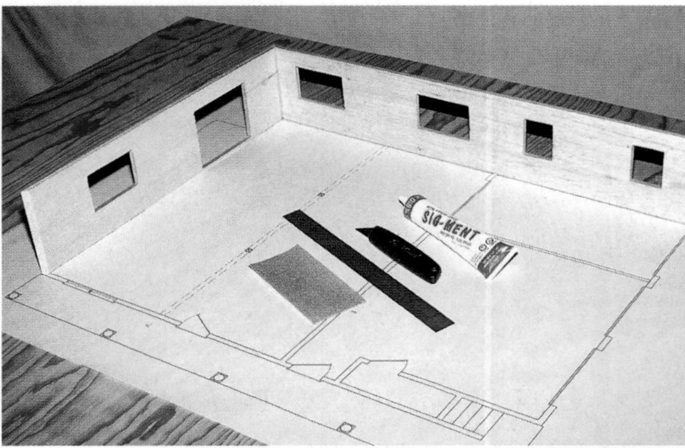

Brad L. Kicklighter

Figure 28-11. Two exterior walls have been completed and glued together. The floor plan is used as a template to ensure accuracy.

6. Apply exterior siding, brick, or other material to the walls. You may wish to make your own siding or represent other materials by scoring the board or gluing on thin strips. If you cut your own strips of siding, be sure to make them to scale. Commercial materials are available at hobby and model train shops. Again, opt for materials that are to scale. If you use sheet materials, use rubber cement to apply them to the walls. If you use individual strips, model cement or other fast-drying cement is recommended. Exterior materials are also available on plastic sheets that are embossed to provide a three-dimensional effect. These should be finished with enamel. The mortar joints should be painted with a water-based paint and wiped. This technique produces a realistic appearance. Any wood siding or three-dimensional brick, stone, or shingles should also be painted or stained.
7. Paint the interior walls with tempera paint. Paint the walls in soft pastels or white. Dark colors generally do not look realistic and should be avoided. **Figure 28-12** shows the completed first and second floor.
8. Roof construction comes next. You can assemble the roof on the roof plan or on the model. Experience has shown that the most acceptable results are frequently obtained by assembling the roof directly on the model. Since the roof framing will not be seen in a presentation model, it is not necessary to cut each rafter and ceiling joist. Lay out the gables on 1/4″ thick balsa and cut them out. Cut ridge boards from similar stock and glue them in place at the peaks of the gables. Use straight pins to hold the pieces in place until the glue dries. The roof sheathing can be 1/4″ balsa glued to the gables and ridge board. This thickness approximates the scaled thickness of the rafters and sheathing on the house. Use a strip of 1/16″ thick balsa to represent a fascia board. If the home has a chimney, construct a chimney to scale and accurately locate it on the roof. Finish the roof by gluing strips of sandpaper or other realistic roofing material to the sheathing. Be sure to represent flashing. This may be aluminum or copper foil. **Figure 28-13** shows the completed roof.
9. After the floor area has been painted or covered with an appropriate material, locate the model on the base and glue it in place.
10. Paint the area surrounding the house bright green. For best results, apply two coats and sprinkle grass flock before the second coat dries.
11. Add trees, shrubs, the drive, and the walk. The plants may be purchased or fabricated from a sponge and twigs. See **Figure 28-14**. Use your imagination to develop a landscape that looks realistic. Do not add so many plants that the landscape appears cluttered. The walk and drive can be painted balsa or sandpaper glued in place.
12. Check the model to be sure all details are complete. **Figure 28-15** shows a completed model. Notice the landscaping details. Furniture and major fixtures can be carved out of soap or wood and glued in place for added attraction, or scale furniture can be purchased. Again, the main consideration is scale.

There is no limit to the number of realistic details that can be added to a model. Use your imagination. Be creative, and develop a truly realistic presentation model.

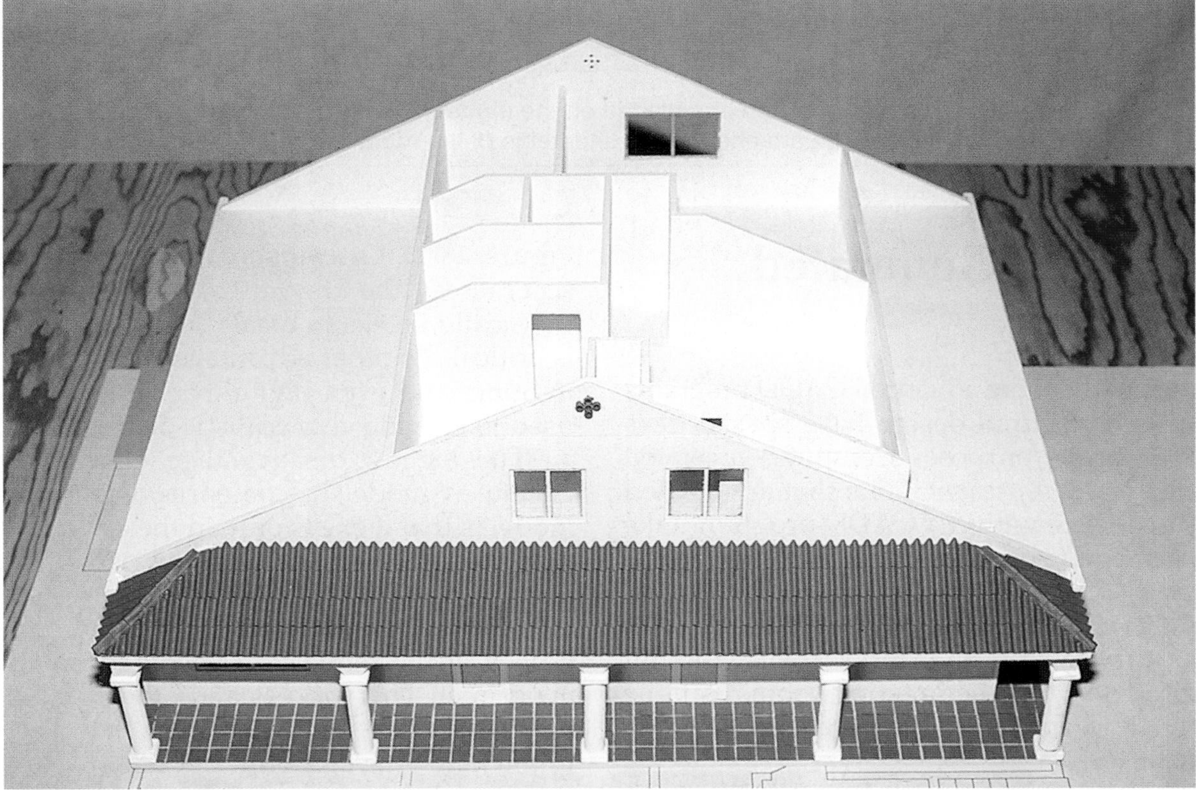

Brad L. Kicklighter

Figure 28-12. The first and second floor are complete. The second floor can be removed to show the first floor layout. Tempera colors were used to paint the walls and floor. The paving was made from individual squares of 1/32″ balsa. Columns were made from 1/2″ diameter dowel rods.

Brad L. Kicklighter

Figure 28-13. The roof has been completed and placed on the model. The terra cotta tile was made from corrugated cardboard. Small pegs are attached to the underside of the roof to ensure proper placement.

Computer-Generated Models

Some of the more advanced CADD programs used in architectural design have special tools for 3D modeling purposes. Computer-generated models are 3D representations that are created at their full size within a CADD program. Like physical models, some computer-generated models are very basic, and others contain complex details. Computer-generated models used for presentation purposes can be exterior shells, without interior detail, or the interior rooms can be finished and furnished very realistically. See **Figure 28-16**.

Computer-generated models have both advantages and disadvantages compared to physical models. One major advantage of computer-generated models is that they can represent sizes more exactly than physical models. See **Figure 28-17**. Of course, any model is only as accurate as the drafter who builds it, either physically or electronically. Attention to detail is critical. Another advantage is that materials, lighting, and even digital backgrounds can be used to provide very realistic details.

The biggest disadvantage of a computer-generated model in comparison to a physical model is that it exists only in the computer. The model can be printed from any viewing angle using a printer or plotter, but this results in a 2D representation only. However, a physical replica of the model can be produced using a 3D printer. This process and other applications for computer-generated models are discussed in the following sections.

3D Printing

For designers using CADD, the ability to show computer-generated renderings of a building

Brad L. Kicklighter

Figure 28-14. Landscaping materials may be purchased or may consist of twigs, dried flowers, sponges, and other inexpensive items.

Brad L. Kicklighter

Figure 28-15. A completed model with landscaping, drive, and walk. The model was mounted on a piece of 3/4″ × 30″ × 36″ plywood. The trees and plants were made from dried flowers. The grass is bright green flock made especially for models. Paving was made from balsa strips.

model to a client is a powerful tool. In cases where the design is created as a 3D model, there are additional processes available for conveying information about the project. Depending on the scope of the project, a 3D printer can be used to produce an architectural model of a structure. In basic terms, ***3D printing*** is a process that uses CADD data to produce a solid, physical model. This process takes considerably less time than building architectural models by hand, which can be labor-intensive and costly. Architectural models built using 3D printers are typically made of a durable plastic material. They can be produced at the desired scale with high precision.

CADD model file data supplies the necessary information to guide the operation of a 3D printer. There are different types of 3D printers available, and they are distinguished by the type of operating process used. Two common processes are stereolithography (SLA) and fused deposition

Zastolskiy Victor/Shutterstock.com

Figure 28-16. This CADD model interior has been rendered to show how the room could be furnished. If the client does not like the wall design or the placement of the window, the model can be updated to the client's preferences before construction begins.

Employability

Balancing Family and Work

Your success in a career will affect your satisfaction with your personal and family life. Likewise, your roles and responsibilities related to home life will affect your career. Balancing career and home life is important in any lifestyle.

Belonging to a family involves roles and responsibilities. As a son or daughter, your responsibilities at home may involve watching younger siblings, helping with family meals, and keeping your clothes and room clean. Usually these tasks do not interfere with your responsibilities to attend school and perform well. Adding a part-time job can complicate matters, however, and force you to manage your time more carefully.

The roles of spouse, parent, homemaker, and employee are much more demanding and may conflict at times. People with multiple roles must balance their responsibilities to fully meet them all. Sometimes family responsibilities will dictate the career decisions you make.

Activity

Consider your daily schedule during the school year. For one week, keep a daily log of your activities. Record your entries according to whether you are working, studying, spending time with friends, or spending time with family. Include time spent at school, study times, and any chores you have at home. At the end of the week, analyze your log to find the percentage of time you spent at school (and work, if applicable) and what percentage you spent with family. If you find that you are spending too much time at one or the other, think about ways to change the balance.

Martin Drafting and Design, Inc.

Figure 28-17. A CADD model can be built to very exact specifications and can be viewed from any angle to show detail.

modeling (FDM). In stereolithography, the operation of the machine is similar to that of a CNC machine tool. A laser beam is used to harden a liquid photocurable polymer plastic in the shape defined by the computer data. This is accomplished by curing thin layers of the polymer to form the desired shape. Construction begins at the bottom of the object and progresses layer by layer until the object is completed. In fused deposition modeling, a plastic filament or metal wire is extruded through a heated nozzle to build the object layer by layer. Another type of 3D printer uses print heads to deposit material in droplets to build the object, similar to inkjet printing. These processes are referred to as *additive manufacturing* processes.

The 3D printing process can be used for purposes other than creating models. Higher-end 3D printers can be used to build prototypes and production items in different colors and materials, such as metal. Today, manufacturers are using 3D printing to produce items such as medical implants and prosthetics. In the construction industry, 3D printers can be used to manufacture building products and even entire buildings.

Using a 3D printer can be an excellent way to produce high-quality architectural models. However, before purchasing a 3D printer, make certain that your CADD software can export compatible files for use with 3D printing.

Walkthrough Animations

CADD models lend themselves to a type of computer animation called a ***walkthrough animation***. The purpose of a walkthrough animation is to show a client, inspector, or review board a realistic representation of a building before construction begins, just as a traditional presentation drawing does. However, the viewer has the opportunity to move around inside the

3D model and view the rooms from various viewpoints. The design can be altered, different materials selected, and lighting added or adjusted based on client feedback. Then, a new walk-through animation can be created and presented for approval. See **Figure 28-18**.

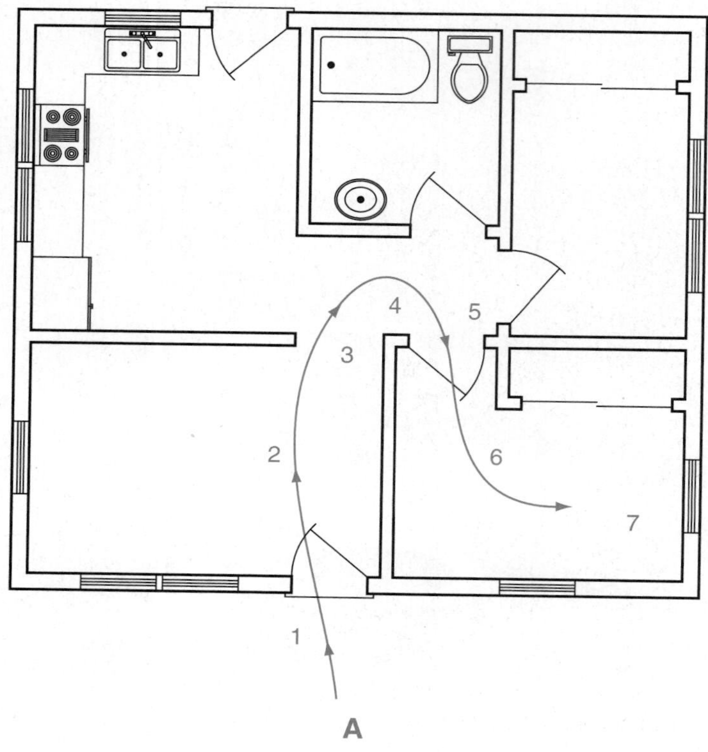

A

Action Number	Keyframe	Action
1	90	Pause at front door and open door.
2	330	Turn and look at living room.
3	420	Turn and move to doorway to hall.
4	510	Move to center of hall.
5	600	Pause at doorway and open door.
6	690	Enter bedroom.
7	840	Pause in front of window and view exterior.
Note: Based on a typical computer playback rate of 30 frames per second, there are 900 total frames in the animation resulting in 30 seconds of playback.		

B

Goodheart-Willcox Publisher

Figure 28-18. A—A floor plan diagram for a walkthrough animation. The path that the viewer will follow is shown in color. The numbers refer to keyframes at which specific actions will take place. B—The keyframes for the walkthrough animation shown in A with the actions identified by number.

Cutaway Views

In some ways, CADD models are more flexible than physical models. An alternative to creating a walkthrough animation is using a series of ***cutaway views***. A CADD model that has interior and exterior detail can be "cut away" along a ***clipping path*** to provide a simultaneous view of the interior and exterior. See **Figure 28-19**. The advantage of clipping a CADD model is that the model itself remains undamaged. Removing or hiding the clipping path restores the complete model. In addition, multiple clipping paths can be created to show various parts of the interior.

Nikonaft/Shutterstock.com

Figure 28-19. A clipping path has been used to cut away some of the exterior walls of this complex model, exposing interior detail.

Summary

- Physical models are constructed to show space relationships with other buildings, to show structural details, or to show how the finished building will look.
- Physical models can be constructed from materials such as foam board, cardboard, or wood; supplies that are purchased commercially; or parts laser-cut to specification.
- Most physical models are built at a scale of 1/4″ = 1′-0″.
- Computer-generated models are built at their full size using CADD software.
- A 3D printer can be used to produce an architectural model of a structure.
- Walkthrough animations and cutaway views can be used to show the interior of a CADD model.

Internet Resources

Kern Laser Systems
Supplier of laser cutting equipment

Micro-Mark
Model building supplies and tools for working with models

Oakridge Hobbies
Architectural scale model building supplies

Testors
Tools for working with models

Utrecht Art Supplies
Architectural model building supplies

Review Questions

Answer the following questions using the information in this chapter.

1. What is the purpose of an architectural model?
2. Name three types of physical architectural models that may be used for homes.
3. Explain the purpose of a small-scale solid model.
4. Why are most of the roofing and siding materials left off a structural model?
5. At what scale are most presentation models built?
6. Identify three types of materials that are commonly used in the construction of a model house. (Do not include finishing materials.)
7. What should you verify before using commercial model parts in a model?
8. Which architectural plans are typically needed for building an architectural model?
9. Exterior walls are usually thicker than interior walls. What is the material thickness of most exterior walls on house models that are constructed at 1/4″ = 1′-0″ scale?
10. What is the purpose of a walkthrough animation?

Suggested Activities

1. Obtain a floor plan of a freestanding (detached) two-car garage. Construct a balsa model to scale. A scale of 1/4″ = 1′-0″ is suggested. Mount the model on a 12″ square base. Record the time required to build the model and the total cost of the model. Display the model and your data for the class.
2. Obtain the plans for a one-story home. Build a presentation model of the home. Mount it on a suitable base and landscape the site. Display the model along with the plans.
3. Carve a permanent fixture, such as a bathtub or vanity, from soap. Check the dimensions of the carving for accuracy.
4. Design a storage or garden shed using CADD. Plot the floor plan and elevations. Build a structural model of your design. Present your design and model to the class.
5. Using CADD, design a small cottage that uses a solar power system to collect and store energy. Plot the floor plan and elevations. Build a 1/4″ = 1′-0″ presentation model of your design.
6. Design a walkthrough animation for the floor plan shown in Figure 28-18. Recreate the floor plan; then show the path of the animation through the home. Create a table to show keyframes and the actions that will happen at the keyframes. If you have software with animation capabilities, animate and render the scene.

Problem Solving Case Study

A client has just inherited a vacant lot in downtown Milwaukee. The area is undergoing urban renewal, and he wants to build a single-family home on the property. He has already checked with the zoning authorities and can get a variance to build the home. The only problem is that the lot is very long and narrow. The front of the property is only 40′ wide, although it extends back 150′. The setbacks are 10′ across the front of the property, 3′ on each side, and 10′ across the back of the property. The building on the right side of the lot is three stories tall and the one on the left is four stories. A 12′ alley runs behind the lot, and on the other side of the alley, the entire block is occupied by a three-story factory.

Design a two-bedroom home that does not violate the setbacks. Draw a floor plan. If the home has multiple stories, be sure to create a floor plan for each. Then create a small-scale solid model to show the client how the house will look in relation to the surrounding buildings.

Certification Prep

The following questions are presented in the style used in the American Design Drafting Association (ADDA) Drafter Certification Test. Answer the questions using the information in this chapter.

1. Match each type of model with its description.

   Models: 1. Presentation model, 2. Structural model, 3. Computer-generated model, 4. Small-scale solid model

   A. Is not hollow and has no interior.
   B. Shows the finished exterior as realistically as possible.
   C. Rarely includes roofing or siding materials.
   D. Exists only within a computer.

2. Which of the following statements about architectural models are true?
   A. The scale of structural models is usually 1/8″ = 1′-0″ or 3/32″ = 1′-0″.
   B. Models are useful in checking the finished appearance of an architectural design and selling a design to a client.
   C. The purpose of a presentation model is to show the appearance of the finished building as realistically as possible.
   D. If the scale for a model is too small, the materials will be difficult to work with.

3. Which of the following statements are *false*?
   A. Since the purpose of a presentation model is to show the basic construction, most siding and roofing materials are left off to expose the structural aspects.
   B. Structural models are not frequently used to show construction features of a residence.
   C. Balsa wood does not warp as much as cardboard and is stronger.
   D. Architectural models are commonly constructed of cardboard or illustration board.

Curricular Connections

1. **Language Arts.** Throughout history, models have been used to foresee design problems, problems with construction, and problems with materials. Some people with architectural backgrounds specialize in building architectural models for analysis. Conduct research to find at least three companies that specialize in building architectural models. Write a formal report about the companies. Compare and contrast the services they offer and the clients to whom they market their services.

STEM Connections

1. **Math.** Models can be built from inexpensive, everyday materials, but architectural firms need to create more elaborate models to showcase their designs. These models are expensive to create, both because they require many materials and because they require a considerable amount of time to build. Analyze the model shown in Figures 28-11 through 28-13. Make a list of all the materials that would be needed to build this model. List additional materials that would be needed to landscape the finished model. Using the Internet, find several companies that sell modeling materials. Record the prices of all the materials on your list. Add them up to find the total cost of materials. Then estimate the number of hours that would be required to build the model and calculate the cost of building at $38 per hour. What is the total cost to build the model?
2. **Engineering.** Both physical and computer-generated models are sometimes used to test the structural integrity of a building design. One of the advantages of computer-generated models is that they can be tested "to destruction" without destroying the model. Find out more about the types of structural analysis that can be performed on physical and computer-generated architectural models. Write a summary of your findings, including which type of model (physical or computer-generated) may be best suited for each type of testing.

Communicating about Architecture

1. **Reading and Speaking.** With a partner, make flash cards for the different types of architectural models discussed in this chapter. On the front of each flash card, write the name of the model. On the back, write a description of the model. Take turns quizzing one another on the models and descriptions.
2. **Speaking and Listening.** Working in small groups, prepare an oral presentation to describe the advantages of using different architectural models in various situations. Create posters or other visual aids to use in the presentation. Include illustrations of architectural drawings and computer renderings.

Melvin Denny Ako

This is an excellent example of a finely detailed architectural presentation model.

Section 6

Electrical, Plumbing, and Climate Control

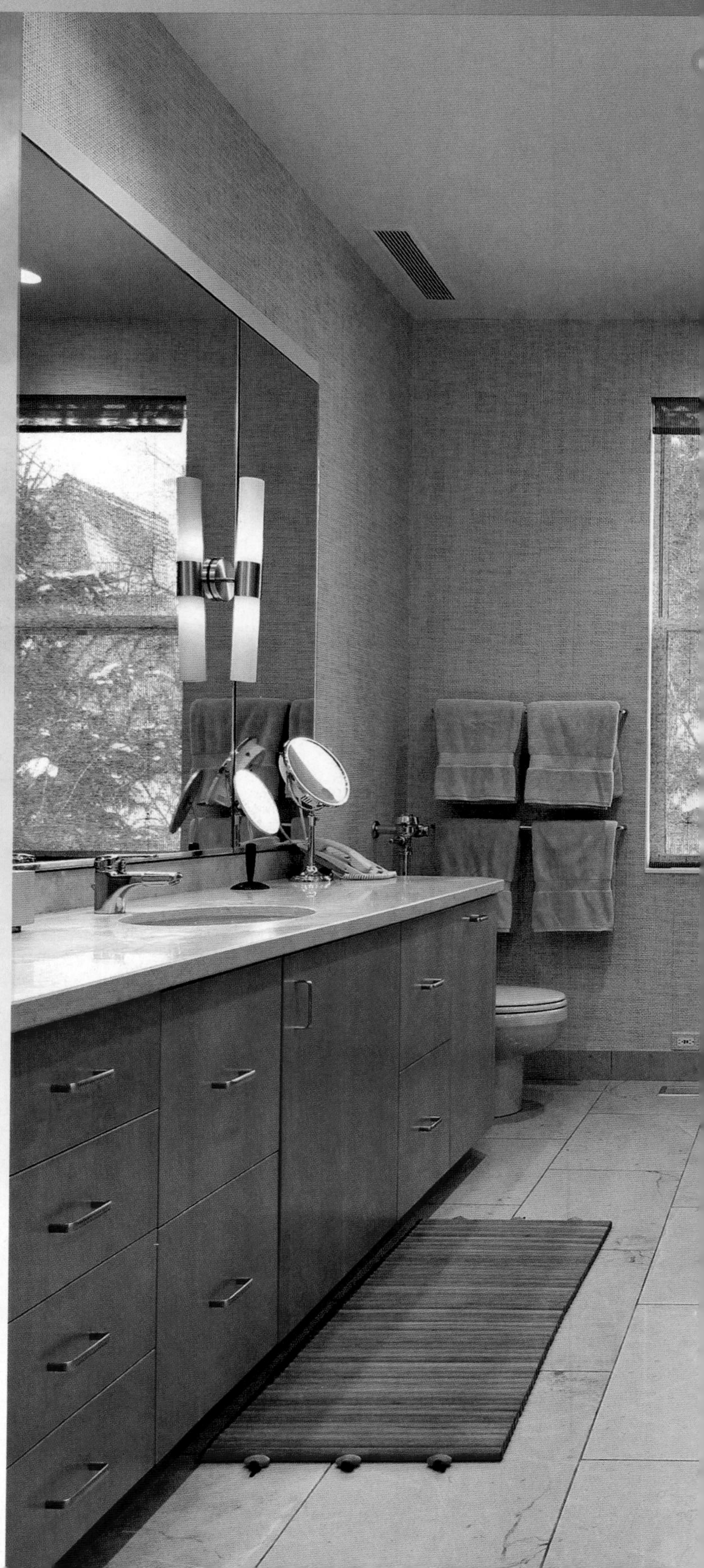

pics721/Shutterstock.com

Chapter 29

Residential Electrical

Objectives

After completing this chapter, you will be able to:

- Explain the characteristics of electricity in terms of amperes, volts, resistance, and watts.
- Describe how electricity is delivered to and distributed through residential structures.
- Identify the three types of branch circuits used in a residential structure.
- Calculate circuit requirements for a residence.
- Describe the types of outlets and switches used in a residence and their typical locations.
- Explain the advantages of low-voltage exterior lighting.

Key Terms

ampere (amp)
branch circuit
circuit
circuit breaker
conductor
conduit
dimmer switch
distribution panel
fuse
ground fault circuit interrupter (GFCI)
individual circuit
lighting circuit
lighting outlet
ohm
receptacle outlet
service drop
service entrance
single-pole switch
small-appliance circuit
special-purpose outlet
three-way switch
volt
voltage
watt

Planning for the electrical requirements of a home requires an understanding of several factors. These factors include the electrical requirements for lighting and appliances, code restrictions, and safety considerations. This chapter provides an overview of the electrical needs of a home.

Characteristics of Electric Current

To understand electric current and how it is supplied to a residential building, you will need to understand a few basic terms. An ***ampere (amp)*** is the unit used to measure the amount of electricity (current) flowing through a wire conductor per unit of time. Resistance to the flow of electricity is measured in ***ohms***. The pressure that forces the current through the wire is ***voltage***, which is measured in volts. One ***volt*** is the force that causes one ampere of current to flow through a wire that has one ohm of resistance.

Most electrical appliances are rated in ***watts***. One watt is equal to one ampere under one volt of pressure (amperes × volts = watts). You will need to consider the wattage of various household appliances to calculate the circuit requirements for a residence.

Service Entrance and Distribution Panel

The service entrance and distribution panel provide the foundation of a residential electrical system. The ***service entrance*** includes the fittings and conductors that bring electricity into the building. The ***distribution panel,*** also called a *service panel,* is the main distribution box that receives the electricity and distributes it to various points in the house through individual circuits. See **Figure 29-1**. Each ***circuit*** provides a path through which electricity flows from a source to one or more devices and then returns to the source. The circuits consist of ***conductors*** (typically copper wires) that permit the flow of electricity. The distribution panel also contains the main disconnect switch fuse or breaker that supplies the total electrical system of the house. This switch disconnects all current to the house and should be located as close to the incoming service as possible.

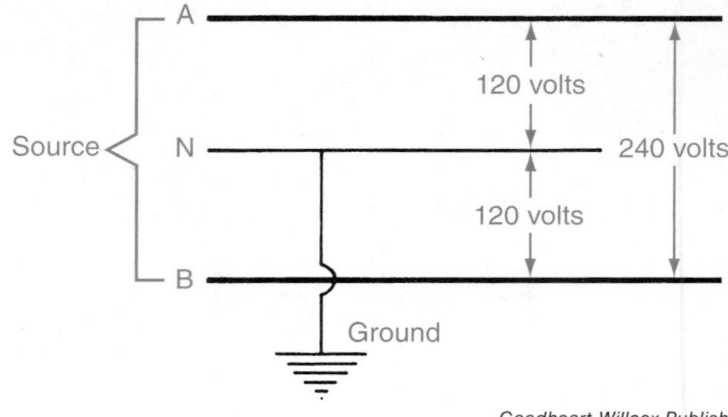

Goodheart-Willcox Publisher

Figure 29-2. Two voltages are available from this 240-volt, three-wire service drop. Half of the 120-volt circuits are connected to A and N; the other half are connected to B and N. All 240-volt circuits are connected to A and B.

Types of Service Entrance Equipment

A residence may have 120- or 240-volt service. Only two conductors are required for 120-volt service, but three are necessary for 240-volt service. Even if no 240-volt appliances are to be installed when the home is built, 240-volt service entrance equipment is recommended and is standard procedure. **Figure 29-2** illustrates how 120 volts can be derived from 240-volt service.

Incoming electrical service usually enters a house through a meter. The incoming service may be overhead or underground. **Figure 29-3A** shows an underground service layout. **Figure 29-3B** shows an overhead service layout and a common method of securing the service drop to the house. The ***service drop*** consists of the overhead service conductors between the last utility pole and the first point of attachment to the house. The conductors are generally run from the service drop or from the underground cable through a run of heavy ***conduit,*** which is a pipe or tube that protects the conductors from the environment and from accidental damage.

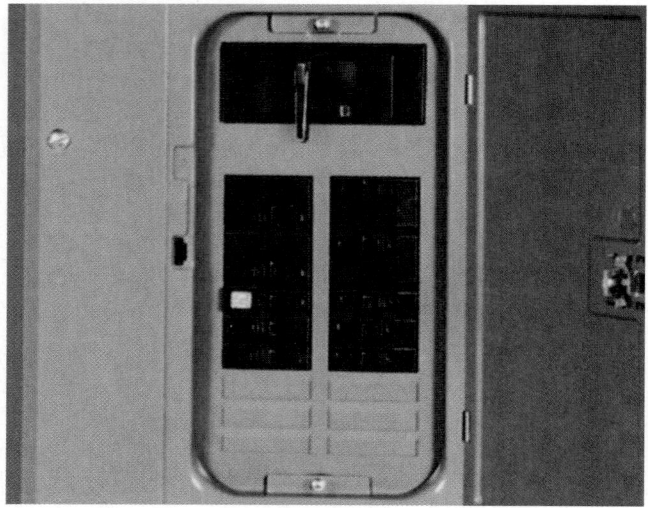

Square D Company

Figure 29-1. A distribution (service) panel.

Several service entrance designs are possible. However, a service head must be used if the service entrance is located along the eaves line of a single-story home. In addition, the service drop must be at least 10′ above grade at the service entrance to buildings and 12′ above residential property and driveways. No conductor may be closer than 3′ to windows, doors, porches, or similar structures where they may be touched.

Conductor Sizing

Copper or aluminum conductors are used to bring the current from the service head or underground cable to the meter and then the distribution panel. The size of the conductors depends on the size of service entrance equipment to be used in the home and the amount of amperage (current) supplied by the electric company. The table in **Figure 29-4** shows service conductor sizes recommended for various

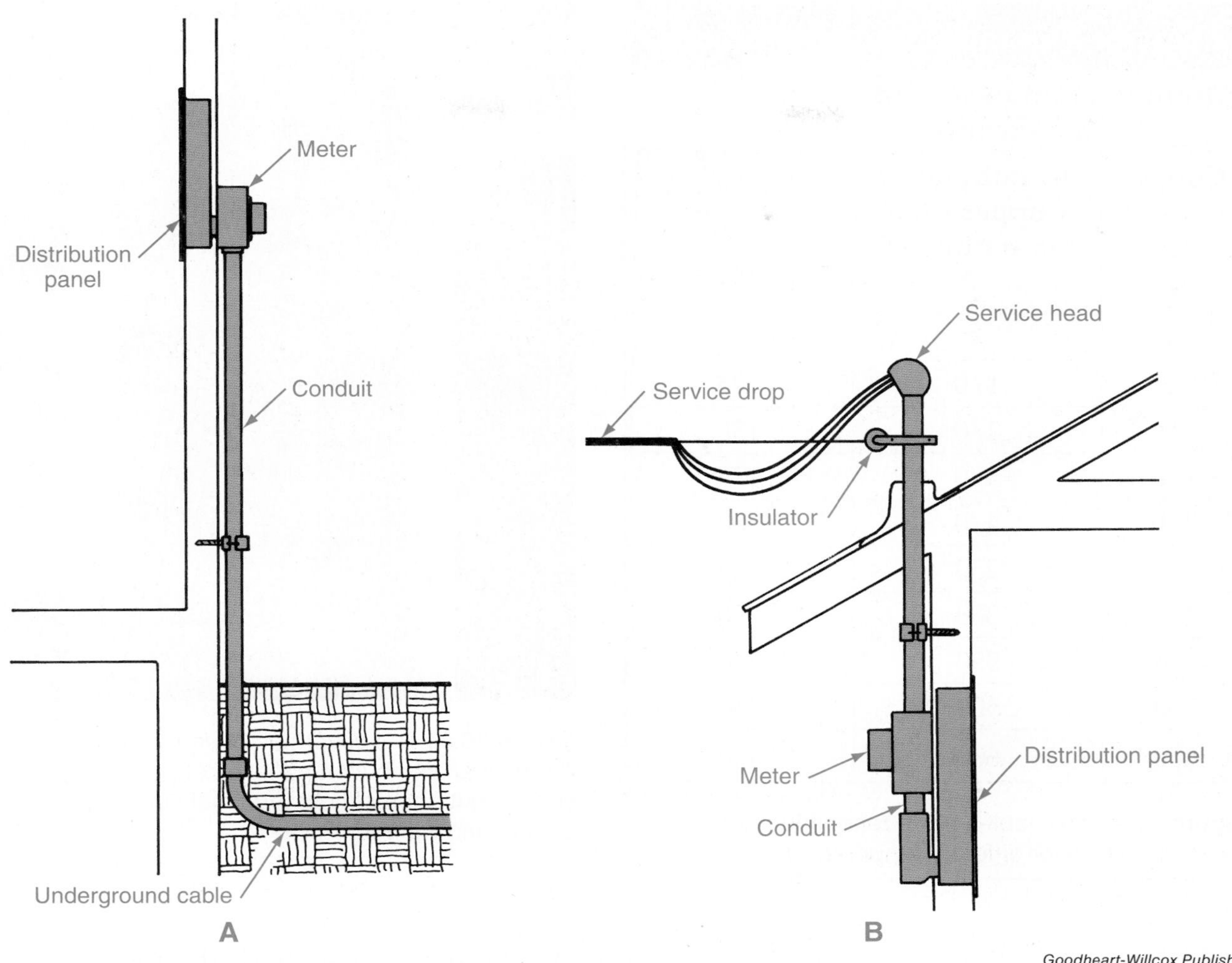

Figure 29-3. Electrical service to a house can be overhead or underground. A—Underground service. B—Overhead service.

amperage ratings. The National Electrical Code (NEC) provides specifications for determining allowable ampacities for different service ratings.

Figure 29-5 shows typical conductor sizes and designations. Notice that the conductor diameter increases as the designation number decreases. In most residential installations, 12 AWG (American Wire Gage) wire is generally recommended for branch lighting circuits. The smallest circuit conductor permitted by the National Electrical Code is 14 AWG.

Conductor size is important in a residential electrical system because current flowing through the wire produces heat. If the wire is too small for the amount of current, it may cause a fire. Even if a fire does not result, the heat increases resistance in the wire and electricity is wasted.

The Distribution Panel

From the meter, the conductors run to the distribution panel. See **Figure 29-6**. This is where the electricity is received from the meter and distributed to various points in the house through branch circuits. The distribution conductors are usually color-coded as follows:

- "Hot" (ungrounded) conductor: black or red insulation
- Grounded conductor: white insulation
- Grounding conductor: bare copper or green insulation

The capacity of the service entrance equipment should be sufficient to supply both present and future demands. The National Electrical Code recommends that a minimum of 100-amp

Service Entrance Conductor Sizing		
Minimum Conductor Size (AWG or kcmil)		Service Rating (Amperes)
Copper	Aluminum or Copper-Clad Aluminum	
4	2	100
3	1	110
2	1/0	125
1	2/0	150
1/0	3/0	175
2/0	4/0	200
3/0	250	225
4/0	300	250
250	350	300
350	500	350
400	600	400

Goodheart-Willcox Publisher

Figure 29-4. This table shows recommended service conductor sizes for different amperage ratings.

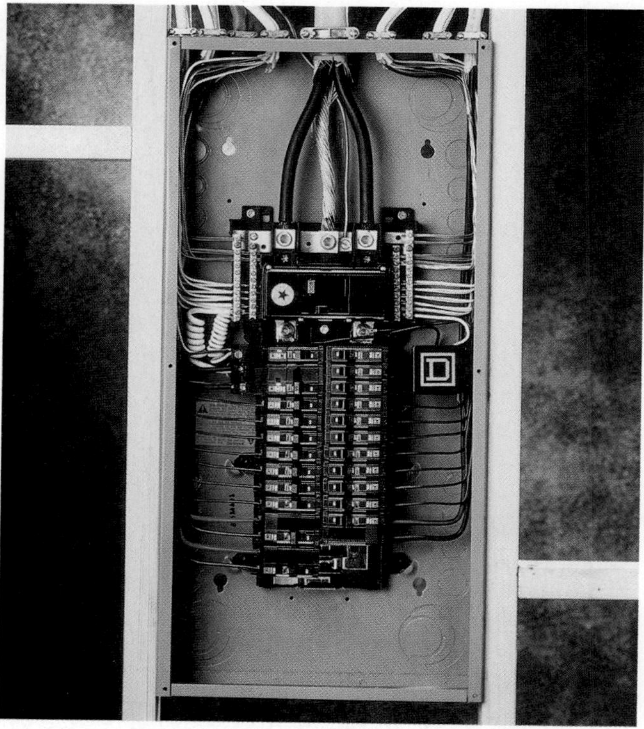

Square D Company

Figure 29-6. The cover has been removed from this typical distribution panel box to show the service entrance conductors, main disconnect switch, and wiring.

service be provided for all residences. However, many homes will require 150-amp, 200-amp, or higher service.

Overcurrent Protection

Residential electrical systems are protected either by fuses or by circuit breakers. Both devices provide overcurrent protection by opening the circuit if the current draw (load) is too high. A ***fuse*** is a device that has a fusible link that melts when the circuit becomes overloaded. When the link melts, the circuit becomes open and electricity can no longer flow. Once the fuse link melts, the fuse cannot be reused; it must be replaced. A ***circuit breaker*** is also a device designed to open the circuit automatically when the circuit becomes overloaded. Unlike a fuse, however, a circuit breaker can be reset after the overload problem is solved. Most new homes built today have circuit breakers, as shown in **Figure 29-7**.

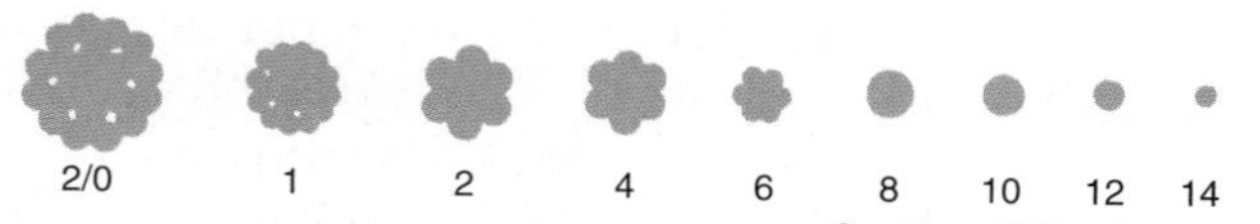

Goodheart-Willcox Publisher

Figure 29-5. Relative conductor sizes and gage number designations.

Branch Circuits

If a house had only one giant circuit to supply 100 amps of current, the wire would be very large, costly, and impossible to handle. Also, if the fuse were to blow or breaker were to trip, the total structure would be without power. Just as important, it would not be possible to install the proper circuit protection for various appliances that require far smaller amounts of current. Therefore, ***branch circuits*** are used to carry electricity from the distribution panel throughout the home. Each branch circuit supplies

Square D Company

Figure 29-7. Circuit breakers come in a variety of sizes and capacities.

electricity to devices that use a similar amount of current. For example, appliances and outlets are grouped together so that smaller breakers or fuses and smaller conductors (wires) may be used. Switches and outlets are not designed for large conductors.

There are three types of branch circuits that should be used in a residential structure: lighting circuits, small-appliance circuits, and individual circuits. The following sections describe these circuits in more detail.

Lighting Circuits

Permanently installed lighting fixtures, as well as outlets for lamps, radios, televisions, and similar 120-volt devices, are connected to ***lighting circuits***. Lighting circuits are frequently 12 AWG copper wire conductor with 20-amp overcurrent protection. This combination provides 2400 watts of lighting capacity (120 × 20 = 2400).

Building codes require a minimum of three watts of lighting power for each square foot of floor space. One lighting circuit would be sufficient for 800 square feet of floor space if this minimum were applied. This is a minimum, however, and is not satisfactory for most homeowners. One lighting circuit for each 400 square feet is a better rule of thumb.

To calculate the number of lighting circuits recommended for a typical 48′ × 60′ residence:

1. Figure the total area included in the house: 48′ × 60′ = 2880 square feet
2. Divide the total area in the house by 400 square feet: 2880/400 = 7.2 lighting circuits

The number of lighting circuits required for a house with 2880 square feet is seven. The table in **Figure 29-8** shows the minimum and recommended number of lighting circuits for various size houses.

Small-Appliance Circuits

Small-appliance circuits are located in the kitchen, usually above the countertop. These are designed for electric skillets, mixers, blenders, toasters, and similar appliances that require large amounts of current.

Small-appliance circuits also generally require 12 AWG copper wire conductor with 20-amp overcurrent protection. Like lighting circuits, each of these circuits is capable of supplying 2400 watts (20 × 120 = 2400). However, no lighting outlets may be operated from these circuits. The National Electrical Code specifies a minimum of two small-appliance circuits in the kitchen. However, two small-appliance circuits may not be sufficient for today's large kitchens and expanded work areas. Other appliance circuits

Residential Lighting Circuits

Number of Square Feet	Number of Lighting Circuits	
	Minimum	Recommended
1000	2	3
1200	2	3
1600	2	4
2000	3	5
2400	3	6
2800	4	7

Goodheart-Willcox Publisher

Figure 29-8. Minimum and recommended number of lighting circuits in residential buildings.

may also be appropriate in other areas of the house, such as a garage or workshop.

Individual Circuits

Some appliances require such a large amount of electricity that they must have their own circuit. Such circuits are called ***individual circuits***. These circuits serve single, permanently installed appliances such as a range, water heater, washer, dryer, water pump, and table saw. Each appliance has its own circuit. The following appliances are usually operated on individual circuits:

- Air conditioner
- Attic fan
- Clothes dryer
- Clothes washer
- Countertop oven
- Dishwasher
- Furnace
- Garbage disposal
- Range
- Table saw
- Water heater
- Water pump

In addition to these, any 120-volt, permanently connected appliance that is rated at over 1400 watts or has an automatically starting electric motor should have its own circuit.

Individual circuits may be 120 or 240 volts, depending on the requirements of the appliance on the circuit. Always check the rating of the appliance. The table in **Figure 29-9** shows the approximate requirements of several appliances.

Circuit Requirement Calculations

The size of service entrance equipment and number and type of branch circuits depend on a number of factors. These include the size of the house, size and number of appliances, and lighting to be installed. The increased load from planned future expansions should also be considered. The following example shows the circuit requirement calculations for a home that has 2400 square feet.

Size of residence = 2400 square feet

Lighting Circuits:
2400 square feet @ 3 watts per square foot = 7200 watts

Small-Appliance Circuits:
2 circuits for kitchen = 4800 watts
(120 volts × 20 amp × 2 = 4800 watts)

Appliance Circuits:
1 circuit for garage = 2400 watts

Individual Circuits:

1 circuit (240 volts) for self-contained range	=	12,000 watts
1 circuit (240 volts) for dryer	=	5000 watts
1 circuit for water heater	=	4000 watts
1 circuit for clothes washer	=	700 watts
1 circuit for garbage disposal	=	300 watts
1 circuit for solar attic fan	=	250 watts
1 circuit for dishwasher	=	1200 watts
1 circuit for air conditioner	=	2500 watts
Total	=	40,350 watts

For 120/240-volt 3-wire system feeders:
40,350 watts / 240 volts = 168.1 amps

This house will require 175-amp service. Main circuit breakers are produced in ratings of 30, 40, 50, 60, 70, 100, 125, 150, 175, and 200 amps. Since 168.1 is between 150 and 175, the logical choice is 175-amp service. This will also provide a spare circuit for future use.

Outlets and Switches

All outlets, switches, and joints where conductors are spliced must be housed in an electrical box. Also, all lighting fixtures must be mounted on a box. There are several types of boxes for various uses. See **Figure 29-10**. Boxes are made from plastic, metal with a galvanized coating, or other insulating materials.

Outlets

The three basic types of outlets are lighting outlets, receptacle outlets, and special-purpose outlets. A ***lighting outlet*** is a contact device that allows electricity to be drawn off a circuit specifically

Typical Appliance Requirements				
Appliance or Equipment	**Typical Wattage**	**Usual Voltage**	**Wire Size**	**Recommended Overcurrent Protection**
20,000 Btu Air Conditioner	2500	120/240	12	20 amp
Band Saw	300	120	12	20 amp
Bathroom Heater	2000	120/240	12	20 amp
Blender	300	120	12	20 amp
Coffee Maker	900	120	12	20 amp
Dehumidifier	350	120	12	20 amp
Dishwasher	1200	120/240	12	20 amp
Dryer (electric)	5000	120/240	10	30 amp
DVD Player	24	120	12	20 amp
Electric Fry Pan	1200	120	12	20 amp
Electric Range with Oven	12000	240	6	50–60 amp
Furnace	800	120	12	20 amp
Garage Door Opener	750	120	12	20 amp
Garbage Disposal	300	120	12	20 amp
Hand Iron	1100	120	12	20 amp
Home Computer	145	120	12	20 amp
Home Freezer	350	120	12	20 amp
Ironer	1500	120	12	20 amp
Microwave Oven	1450	120	12	20 amp
Range Oven (separate)	5000	120/240	10	30 amp
Range Top (separate)	5000	120/240	10	30 amp
Refrigerator	300	120	12	20 amp
Roaster	1400	120	12	20 amp
Rotisserie	1400	120	12	20 amp
Table Saw	1000	120/240	12	20 amp
Television	300	120	12	20 amp
Toaster	1000	120	12	20 amp
Trash Compactor	400	120	12	20 amp
Waffle Iron	1000	120	12	20 amp
Washer	700	120	12	20 amp
Water Heater	2000–5000	120	10	20 amp

Goodheart-Willcox Publisher

Figure 29-9. This table shows the typical requirements for common appliances. Refer to the manufacturer's specifications for actual usage.

Goodheart-Willcox Publisher

Figure 29-10. Typical metal and plastic electrical boxes used in residential construction.

Goodheart-Willcox Publisher

Figure 29-12. This is a typical weatherproof outlet, which is required for damp locations. The hinged cover protects the outlet from rain and other environmental hazards.

for lighting. A ***receptacle outlet***, also called a *receptacle* or a *convenience outlet*, is a general-purpose device that allows electricity to be drawn off the circuit for various purposes, such as radios, hair dryers, and chargers for cell phones. **Figure 29-11** shows examples of receptacle outlets.

Frequently, home designers forget to include weatherproof outlets and ample exterior lighting. Weatherproof outlets have a cover to protect them from dampness or water, as shown in **Figure 29-12**. These outlets provide a source of electricity for outside work or play. Placing at least one outlet on each side of the exterior is recommended. Exterior lighting enhances the appearance of the house and improves safety. Lighting fixtures and receptacle outlets should also be located in the attic and crawl spaces of the house.

The most common ***special-purpose outlets*** are telephone jacks and television outlets (cable, satellite, or standard antenna). See **Figure 29-13**. Other types of special-purpose outlets include built-in outlets for home entertainment or theater speakers, entrance signals, burglar alarm systems, and automatic fire alarm systems.

Entrance signals, such as doorbells and chimes, can be wired to signaling devices for disabled people. For example, a doorbell can be wired to lights or fans in a number of rooms. When the doorbell is activated, the light or fan comes on to alert deaf or deaf-blind occupants that

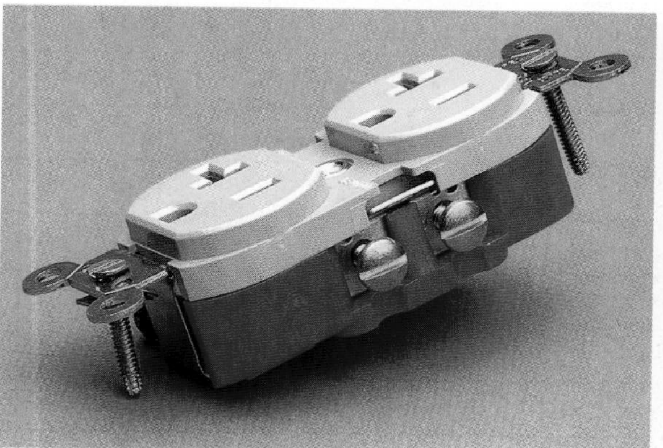

Leviton Manufacturing Co., Inc.

Figure 29-11. Several types of receptacle outlets are used in residential electrical systems.

djgis/Shutterstock.com

Figure 29-13. This outlet contains a convenient assortment of special-purpose outlets for telephone and cable connections.

somebody is at the door. These are specialized installations. Information is usually supplied by the manufacturer or the systems are professionally installed.

Ground Fault Circuit Interrupters

A ***ground fault circuit interrupter (GFCI)*** is a safety device that continually monitors the amount of current going to the load and compares it to that coming back. As long as the two are equal, the electricity continues to flow. However, if the amount of current returning is less than it should be, the GFCI trips (opens) the circuit. The logic of GFCI design is that if the current is not coming back via the wire, it must be going somewhere else. Potentially, the alternate path could be through a person to the earth. A GFCI receptacle is shown in **Figure 29-14**.

A GFCI could save your life. If you are ever unlucky enough to receive an electrical shock, but fortunate enough to have a GFCI in the circuit, it will feel like you are being stuck with a needle. Then, the GFCI will trip and open the circuit, stopping the current.

GFCIs are designed to open a circuit within approximately 25 milliseconds. The amount of current imbalance that the GFCI must detect before it trips is four to six milliamps (thousandths of an amp). Higher currents or longer exposure may cause the heart to go into fibrillation, which means that the heart goes out of synchronization and stops beating, which can result in death.

GFCIs can be placed as any receptacle. A type of GFCI can also be placed as a breaker in the distribution panel to protect an entire branch circuit. The preferred location is generally at the receptacle for convenience and lower cost. The National Electrical Code defines when and how GFCIs should be used. Some of the more common regulations are:

- **Kitchen.** All receptacles serving countertop surfaces must have GFCI protection.
- **Bathroom.** All receptacles installed in bathrooms must have GFCI protection.
- **Garage.** All receptacles installed in a garage must have GFCI protection.

Employability
Professional Language

Using professional language in the workplace is just as important as having the technical skills necessary to do the job. In school, you may be in the habit of joking with your friends, using slang and possibly even profanity. When you accept a job, or even an apprenticeship, this type of behavior is no longer appropriate. In fact, in many companies, it can be a cause for termination. If you have a habit of using slang or profanity in regular conversations…stop! In the workplace, your spoken communications should be polite, grammatically correct, and respectful of your employer, coworkers, and customers. This is one employability and workplace skill that is essential to your continued success in your career, no matter what career you choose.

Activity

With two or three classmates, develop a skit that demonstrates the use of professional language in the workplace or the likely result of using improper language. Do not use profanity in the skit. Perform your skit for the rest of the class.

- **Outdoors.** All receptacles installed outdoors that are readily accessible must have GFCI protection.
- **Crawl space.** All receptacles installed in crawl spaces at or below grade level must have GFCI protection.
- **Unfinished basement.** All receptacles installed in unfinished basements must have GFCI protection except for a receptacle supplying a permanently installed fire alarm or burglar alarm system.

Switches

Switches are devices that allow you to turn lights or appliances on and off. Doorbells are also a type of switch. **Figure 29-15** shows a variety of switch types.

Most switches in a house operate one fixture and are the single-pole type. A ***single-pole switch*** simply opens and closes the circuit. In some instances, three-way switches are used for extra convenience. A ***three-way switch*** allows a fixture to be turned on and off from two different locations, as shown in **Figure 29-16A**. Common locations for three-way switches are entrances, garages, stairs, and rooms that have more than one entrance. Fixtures can also be switched from three locations using two three-way switches and one four-way switch. See **Figure 29-16B**.

Goodheart-Willcox Publisher

Figure 29-14. A self-testing duplex GFCI receptacle. The buttons near the center of the receptacle are used to manually test the device and to reset the GFCI after it has been tripped.

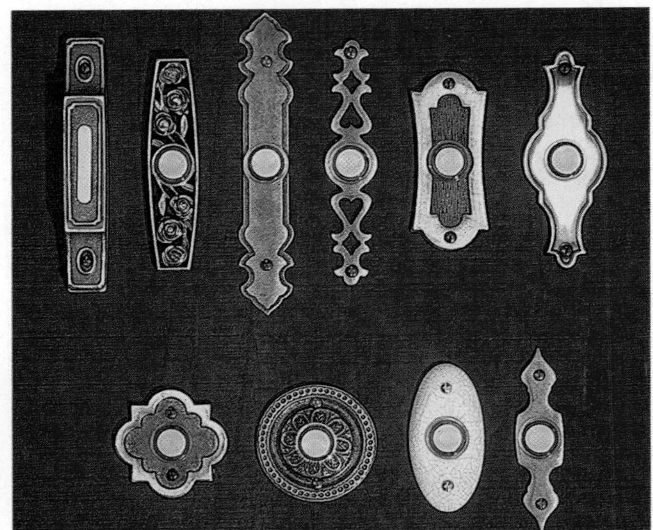

Broan-NuTone LLC

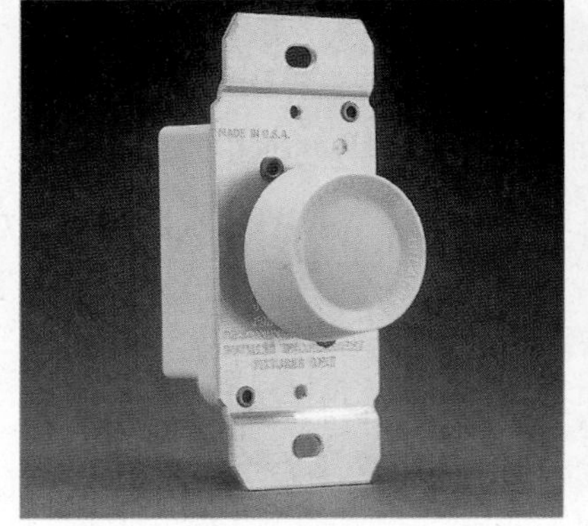

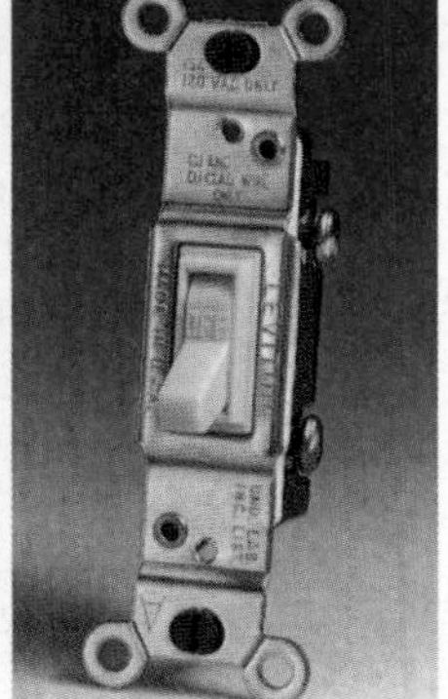

Leviton Manufacturing Co., Inc.

Figure 29-15. Various types of residential switches.

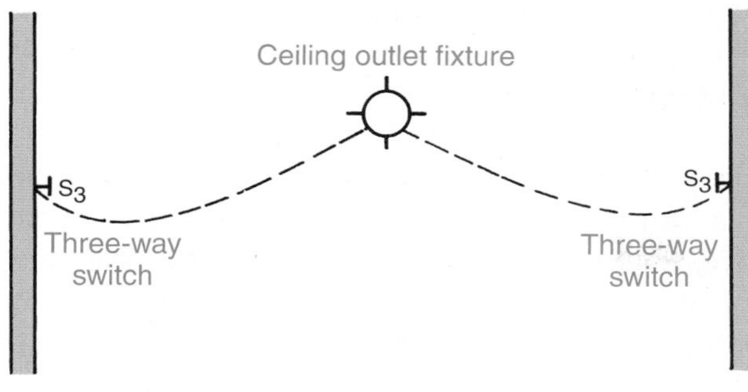

A

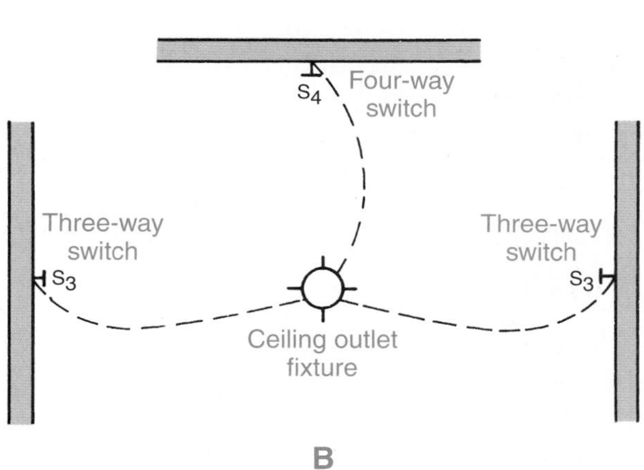

B

Goodheart-Willcox Publisher

Figure 29-16. A—A fixture or outlet can be switched from two locations using two three-way switches. B—One or more fixtures or outlets can be operated from three locations using two three-way switches and one four-way switch.

A ***dimmer switch*** is a switch that allows the light from a light fixture to be adjusted to the desired brightness. See **Figure 29-17**. It is commonly used for a main dining room ceiling fixture. The dimmer switch fits into a regular electrical box.

Locating Outlets and Switches

Placement of receptacle outlets, switches, and lighting fixtures requires some thought. Code requirements, furniture arrangements, and personal preference all play a role in their location. The National Electrical Code states that in living areas, no point along a wall should be more than 6′ from a receptacle outlet. However, placement of receptacle outlets about 8′ apart is more satisfactory and is recommended. This results in no point along a wall being more than 4′ from a receptacle outlet. As a general guideline, each room should have a minimum of three receptacle outlets.

The height of most receptacle outlets is 12″ or 18″ above the floor. The kitchen is an exception; small-appliance outlets are usually placed above the countertop. It is common practice to connect a switch to one or more receptacle outlets in each room where lamps are to be located. This allows the lamps to be turned on and off from a switch on the wall, which is often more convenient than using the switch on the lamp.

Leviton Manufacturing Co., Inc.

A

Goodheart-Willcox Publisher

B

Figure 29-17. A—Some dimmer switches are knobs that can be turned to increase or decrease brightness. B—Others are sliders, with or without a separate on-off switch.

Switches should be located in a logical place 48″ above the floor. For people seated in wheelchairs, a height of 30″ to 40″ may be more convenient. Care must be taken not to mount switches behind doors or in other hard-to-get-to places.

Switches in a bathroom should not be located within reach of the bathtub or shower. The primary objective when designing the placement of switches in the bathroom is to avoid this situation, which can result in electrocution.

Low-Voltage Exterior Lighting

Good outdoor lighting is both functional and aesthetic. It is functional because it provides light when and where you need it for outdoor activities, such as entertaining, cooking out, and yard games, or safety and security. Outdoor lighting is aesthetic because it increases the beauty of the yard, garden, or exterior of the home at night. See **Figure 29-18**.

Low-voltage (12-volt) lighting systems are a popular way to add lighting to the exterior of a house. The system consists of the lights, wire, one or more controllers, and transformers. These systems are generally more expensive to install than standard 120-volt lighting, but they are considered safer for outdoor use and easier to install. They also use less energy. As always, check with your local building department to secure permits and determine specific code requirements in your area before installing a low-voltage lighting system.

Green Architecture
Passive Energy Sources

When designing a new home or remodeling an existing one, consider using passive energy sources instead of the traditional "power grid" for at least some of the home's energy requirements. Solar, wind, or geothermal options are available in many locations. These options, known as *passive energy sources*, are often quite practical. Find out what types of systems are available in your area. For wind and geothermal options, you may need to check with the city or county to find out about any code restrictions. Some areas, for example, restrict the location and height of wind turbines for generating electricity from wind.

Although these alternative energy sources cost more than traditional utility-based electricity, if chosen and implemented carefully, they can be much more sustainable. In most cases, you can recover the additional cost within 5 to 10 years. After that, you can save money by generating your own electricity for some or all of your electricity needs. Even if you should find it necessary to relocate before you have fully recovered the installation costs, these systems will add to the value of your home.

Planning Low-Voltage Exterior Lighting

Planning is necessary for effective outdoor lighting. Begin by deciding where you will need light at night for safety, security, and outdoor activities. Then you can plan for the decorative lighting. The following are some things to keep in mind when planning for low-voltage exterior lighting:

- **Try to avoid glare.** Glare is the reason for the discomfort we feel when looking at a light that is too bright or aimed directly at us. Good lighting design avoids glare.
- **Outdoor light fixtures are either decorative or hidden.** Decorative fixtures, such as carriage lamps, are meant to be seen. See **Figure 29-19**. Only the effect of a

Anna Marynenko/Shutterstock.com

Figure 29-18. Well-designed exterior lighting provides safety and security while showcasing the beauty of a home.

Colman Lerner Gerardo/Shutterstock.com

Figure 29-19. This decorative, low-voltage garden light is powered by solar energy.

hidden lamp, not the fixture itself, is meant to be seen.

- **Use shielded fixtures to hide the light source.** Shielded fixtures let you see a lighted object, rather than the light itself. Shielding can be a diffusing panel or frosted globe.
- **Use more, smaller lights.** Several smaller sources of light are better than a few bright lights. For example, a design consisting of several low-voltage light sources along a drive or sidewalk is pleasing to look at and does not produce glare, **Figure 29-20**.
- **Remember safety when planning lighting.** Consider adding lights to improve safety along the driveway, front walk, and steps; around the front and back entries; on the deck or patio; around the swimming pool; and in planted areas. **Figure 29-21** shows a house with lighting added for safety and beauty.
- **Use light to shape an outdoor space.** For example, uplighting sharpens shapes. Notice the trees in the background of **Figure 29-21**. Backlighting shows the form of an object more clearly. Shadowing can make a plant seem larger and more prominent. Downlighting provides general lighting or focused lighting.

Low-Voltage Wiring Considerations

Low-voltage lighting systems are generally easy for most homeowners to install. Many types and sizes of prepackaged sets are readily available from home centers. Also, individual components—lights, wire, controllers, and transformers—can be purchased separately for a custom layout. Low-voltage solar systems are even easier to install, because there is no wiring involved. Consider the following points when planning and/or installing low-voltage exterior lighting:

- When lights are a great distance from the transformer, they provide less light due to a voltage drop. To avoid this condition, use a tee design with half the lights on each side of the tee. You might use 10 AWG wire for the main lines and 12 AWG wire between the lights to further reduce the voltage drop.
- Put no more than 100 watts of lighting on one line or leg of the tee. If you were to put 10 lights each of 20 watts on a circuit, half of them would be attached to each leg of the tee. Each leg of the tee would have 100 watts of lighting (5 lights × 20 watts = 100 watts). See **Figure 29-22**.
- Select the proper size transformer for your planned layout. Purchase a transformer with a built-in photocell and timer. You may need more than one transformer for a large layout with several circuits. Also, the gage of the low-voltage wire is related to the length of the run and the number and size of lights used. Each fixture should receive between 10.5 and 12 volts of power for a uniform appearance.
- Use a GFCI receptacle as a power source. Remember, the transformer in a low-voltage system will be connected to a 120-volt power source. The transformer should be housed in a watertight box, if located outside.
- Consider an indoor switch and timer combination. This will enable you to bypass the automatic controller so the lights can be turned on and off as desired.
- Prevent corrosion before it starts. Corrosion in lines and connectors reduces the brightness of lights in a low-voltage system. Many manufacturers provide metal clip-on connectors to attach the light fixtures to

SeanPavonePhoto/Shutterstock.com

Figure 29-20. Using several low-voltage lights to light a pathway at night provides sufficient light without glare.

the branch line. This is one common source of corrosion. A better idea is to splice the wires together and use waterproof wire nuts. Adding silicone gel inside the nut will add more protection.

Tomasz Markowski/Shutterstock.com

Figure 29-21. Sufficient lighting is critical around pool areas. Also, notice the uplighting that details the trees in this backyard.

- Call the utility company before you dig. Ask the utility to locate underground wires and pipes. The service is generally free and it might save you lots of time and money.
- Leave a little extra wire as you hook up the lights in case you decide to move a light after you test the effect.
- After checking out the entire setup, bury the wires at least 6″ deep.

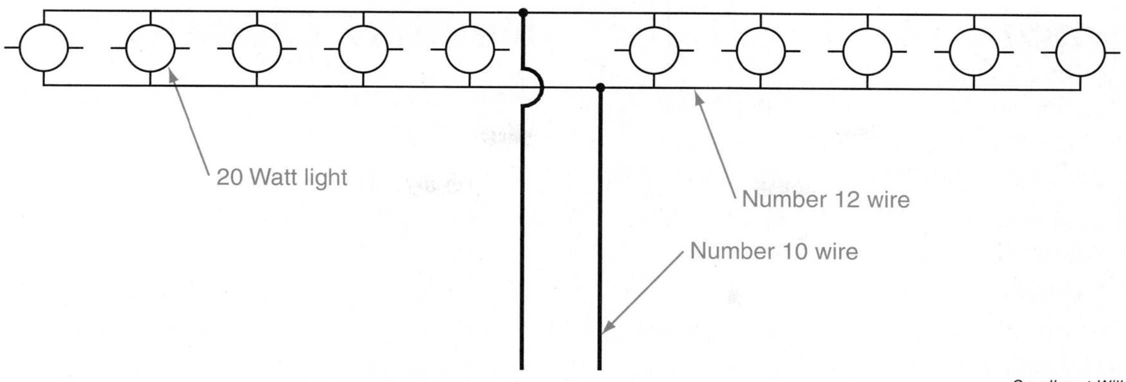

Goodheart-Willcox Publisher

Figure 29-22. Recommended wiring layout for low-voltage lights on one circuit. Each leg of the tee has 100 watts of lighting.

Summary

- The foundation of a residential electrical system is the service entrance and distribution panel, also called a service panel.
- Individual circuits may be 120 or 240 volts, depending on the requirements of the appliance(s) on the circuit.
- In most homes built today, circuit breakers are used for overcurrent protection.
- The size of service entrance equipment and number and types of branch circuits depend on the size of the house, size and number of appliances, and lighting to be installed.
- Lighting and small-appliance circuits generally require 12 AWG copper wire conductor with 20-amp overcurrent protection.
- A ground fault circuit interrupter (GFCI) is designed to open a circuit within approximately 25 milliseconds.
- Most switches in a house operate one fixture and are the single-pole type.
- Low-voltage (12-volt) lighting systems provide safety and security and can enhance the landscaping around a house.

Internet Resources

Eaton Wiring Devices
Manufacturer of electric switches, timers, and chargers

General Electric
Interior and exterior home lighting products

Home Controls, Inc.
Supplier of home automation equipment

Leviton
Manufacturer of electrical and electronics products

Lutron
Manufacturer of lighting control products

West Penn Wire
Manufacturer of electronic cable

Review Questions

Answer the following questions using the information in this chapter.

1. What is the unit used to measure the amount of electrical current flowing through a wire conductor per unit of time?
2. The term given to the pressure that forces current through a conductor is _____.
3. The result of multiplying amps by volts is _____.
4. Define *circuit*.
5. A material, such as copper wire, that carries the flow of electricity is called a(n) _____.
6. What is the purpose of the main disconnect switch?
7. How many service entrance conductors are required for 240-volt service?
8. The service drop must be at least _____ feet above grade at the service entrance to buildings and _____ feet above driveways.
9. Which conductor is larger in diameter: 12 AWG or 14 AWG?
10. What is the smallest conductor that may be used in a residential lighting circuit?
11. If the wiring in a circuit is too small for the load, what is likely to happen?
12. What color is generally used for the insulation on the "hot" conductor in a circuit?
13. What is the minimum service rating specified by the National Electrical Code for all residences?
14. What is the biggest practical difference between a fuse and a circuit breaker?
15. List three types of branch circuits found in a home.
16. Building codes require a minimum of _____ watts of lighting power for each square foot of floor space.
17. How many watts of lighting capacity are provided in a 120-volt circuit with 20-amp overcurrent protection?
18. What is the minimum number of small-appliance circuits required for a kitchen?

19. What is the purpose of a GFCI?
20. The National Electrical Code specifies that in living areas, no point along a wall should be more than _____ feet from a receptacle outlet.
21. Name three major components of a low-voltage lighting system.
22. List five general guidelines for planning low-voltage exterior lighting for a home.

Suggested Activities

1. Determine the service entrance rating for your home or apartment. Count the number of 120-volt and 240-volt circuits. Calculate the amperage required for all the appliances, equipment, and lighting. Determine if the incoming service is sufficient to operate all existing lights and appliances. Show your work.
2. Write to, or search online for, manufacturers that produce residential electrical supplies. Obtain literature and specifications for electrical boxes, wire, service entrance equipment, switches, and fixtures. Display the material and add it to the class collection for future use.
3. Open one of the site plans you created using CADD in Chapter 16. Plan a low-voltage exterior lighting plan that applies the principles discussed in this chapter.

Problem Solving Case Study

You are considering the purchase of a pre-owned home. You found a three-bedroom, two-bath home for sale that you really like, and you have hired a home inspector to check it for you. The inspector says the house, which was built in 1972, is generally in good shape, but the wiring should be updated to include GFCIs in the kitchen, bathrooms, and garage. Conduct research to find out how much this update would cost. Be sure to include the cost of the components and the electrician's labor.

ADDA Certification Prep

The following questions are presented in the style used in the American Design Drafting Association (ADDA) Drafter Certification Test. Answer the questions using the information in this chapter.

1. Which of the following statements are true?
   A. The foundation of a residential electrical system is the service entrance and distribution panel.
   B. Small-appliance circuits generally require 14 AWG copper wire conductor with 50-amp overcurrent protection.
   C. Incoming electrical service usually enters a house through a meter.
   D. A branch circuit is one of several individual circuits from the distribution panel that is routed to devices that use a similar amount of current.
2. Which of the following statements are *false*?
   A. The increased load from planned future expansions should be considered when planning the electrical system for a new home.
   B. You should call the utility company before you dig and ask the utility to locate underground wires and pipes.
   C. Low-voltage lighting systems are generally difficult for most homeowners to install.
   D. Overcurrent protection for most new homes today is provided by fuses.
3. Match each electrical term with its definition.

   Terms: 1. Ampere, 2. Watt, 3. Ohm, 4. Volt
   A. Unit used to measure the resistance in an electric circuit.
   B. Unit of force that causes current to move through a circuit.
   C. One ampere under one volt of pressure.
   D. Unit used to measure the amount of current flowing through a wire.

Curricular Connections

1. **Social Science.** Housing and electrical requirements tend to change over time. Consider a middle-class family with two adults and three children in the 1960s. List their daily activities and estimate the amount of electricity the family would use on a daily basis. You may need to do research to find out what appliances were commonly used at that time. Then make a second list of the daily activities of the same family today. Write an essay comparing their electrical needs. In your essay, explain why it is necessary for building codes, architects, and designers to keep up with current trends in society.

STEM Connections

1. **Science.** Research Ohm's law and compose a two-page written report on the relationships among voltage, current, and resistance.
2. **Math.** A planned residence will have 3200 square feet. It will include a 20,000 Btu air conditioner, two bathrooms with dedicated heaters, a clothes washer and electric dryer, a range and range top, a garbage disposal, a dishwasher, and a 3000-watt water heater. The kitchen will have three small-appliance circuits, and the two-car garage will have one appliance circuit. Use the table in Figure 29-9 to calculate the circuit requirement for this home. Assume that the home has a 120/240-volt 3-wire system feeder.

Communicating about Architecture

1. **Speaking and Listening.** With a partner, make flash cards of the key terms in this chapter. On the front of the card, write the term. On the back of the card, write the pronunciation and a brief definition. Use this chapter and a dictionary for guidance. Then take turns quizzing one another on the pronunciations and definitions of the key terms.
2. **Speaking.** While working with a partner, look at Figure 29-6 and describe the important information being conveyed by that figure. Through your collaboration, develop what you and your partner believe is the most interesting verbal description of the importance of the figure. Present your findings to the class.

Chapter 30

Electrical Plans

Objectives

After completing this chapter, you will be able to:

- Describe an electrical plan and identify its features.
- Identify typical electrical symbols found on a residential electrical plan.
- Draw an electrical plan for a residential structure using manual drafting techniques.
- Draw an electrical plan for a residential structure using CADD.

Key Terms

compact fluorescent lightbulb (CFL)
electrical plan
electron-stimulated luminescence (ESL) light
fluorescent light
incandescent light
light-emitting diode (LED) light
lighting fixture schedule
smart meter

The purpose of the ***electrical plan*** is to show the location and type of electrical equipment to be used. It is a plan view section drawing, similar to the floor and foundation plans. In fact, in manual drafting, it is usually traced from the floor plan. In CADD, a copy of the floor plan is used as a starting point, or layers are added to the floor plan for the electrical information. A well-planned and suitably connected electrical system results in convenience and trouble-free operation for the homeowner.

Required Information

The electrical plan displays the meter, distribution panel box, receptacle outlets, switches, and special electrical features. It identifies the number and types of circuits in the home. Information that should be on the plan includes the service entrance capacity, meter and distribution panel location, placement and type of switches, location and type of lighting fixtures, special electrical equipment, number and types of circuits, and lighting fixture schedule.

Symbols and a legend and notes that help to describe the system must also be included. Electrical symbols commonly used on an electrical plan are shown in **Figure 30-1**. The amperage rating of the service required should be designated beside the symbol representing the distribution panel.

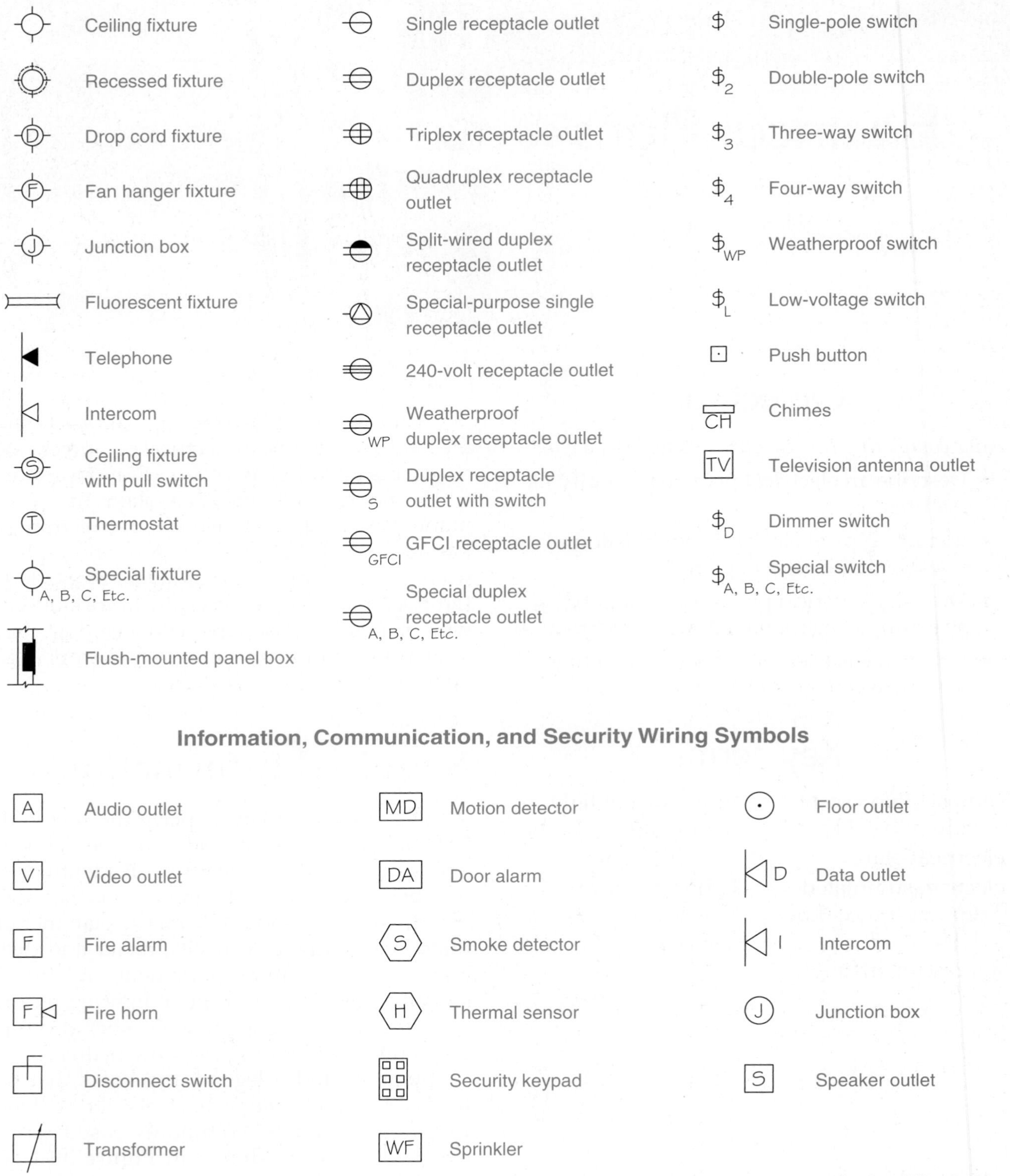

Ceiling fixture

Recessed fixture

Drop cord fixture

Fan hanger fixture

Junction box

Fluorescent fixture

Telephone

Intercom

Ceiling fixture with pull switch

Thermostat

Special fixture
A, B, C, Etc.

Flush-mounted panel box

Single receptacle outlet

Duplex receptacle outlet

Triplex receptacle outlet

Quadruplex receptacle outlet

Split-wired duplex receptacle outlet

Special-purpose single receptacle outlet

240-volt receptacle outlet

WP
Weatherproof duplex receptacle outlet

S
Duplex receptacle outlet with switch

GFCI
GFCI receptacle outlet

Special duplex receptacle outlet
A, B, C, Etc.

$ Single-pole switch

$_2 Double-pole switch

$_3 Three-way switch

$_4 Four-way switch

$_WP Weatherproof switch

$_L Low-voltage switch

Push button

CH Chimes

TV Television antenna outlet

$_D Dimmer switch

$_A, B, C, Etc. Special switch

Information, Communication, and Security Wiring Symbols

A Audio outlet

V Video outlet

F Fire alarm

F Fire horn

Disconnect switch

Transformer

MD Motion detector

DA Door alarm

S Smoke detector

H Thermal sensor

Security keypad

WF Sprinkler

Floor outlet

D Data outlet

I Intercom

J Junction box

S Speaker outlet

Goodheart-Willcox Publisher

Figure 30-1. These electrical symbols are commonly found on electrical plans.

Service Entrance

The National Electrical Code (NEC) requires that the service entrance equipment be located as close as practical to the point where the wires attach to the house. For example, the service conductors should not run for 15′ or 20′ inside the house before they reach the main disconnect switch. The closer the main breaker is to the meter, the better.

Another factor to be considered in locating the service entrance is where the largest amounts of electricity will be used. In most houses, this is the kitchen. Try to locate the meter and distribution panel close to the area of highest usage. Larger loads require larger conductors. Therefore, it is less expensive to have the distribution panel close to the large loads. Also, voltage drops are reduced with shorter runs, creating a more efficient system.

Electric meters are weatherproof and are designed for exterior installation. An outside location is usually preferred to allow for easier meter readings. However, the meter may be located inside or outside the house. In some areas of the country, ***smart meters*** have been installed. These meters can be read remotely by the utility company, eliminating the need for frequent access to the meter.

Switches

The number and placement of switches throughout the house is related to the number of lighting fixtures, switched outlets, and other equipment, such as whole-house fans. Take into consideration the traffic patterns and try to select the most logical location for each switch. The electrical plan must show whether the switches are single-pole, three-way, four-way, or another type. Use the proper symbol to show the type.

A home usually requires several types of switches. The least expensive type of switch is a simple on-off toggle switch. Other types include push button, dimmer, and delayed-action switches.

Switches are shown on the electrical plan connected to the fixtures, appliances, and outlets that they operate. A thin hidden line or centerline is generally used to show the connection. These lines *do not* represent the actual wiring, but merely indicate which switch operates a given outlet or fixture.

Do not use straight lines to connect the switches and outlets. Straight lines tend to be confused with other lines on the drawing. Instead, draw the lines using an irregular curve, rather than using a straightedge or drawing the lines freehand. In CADD, the **SPLINE** command or the **Spline** polyline editing option can be used. See **Figure 30-2**.

Employability

Negotiation

You will not always agree with your coworkers—or even your employer—regarding the best way to accomplish a task. When disagreement occurs, you will need to negotiate to decide how to perform the task. *Negotiation* is the process of coming to an agreement on an issue that requires all parties to give and take a little to achieve the intended result. The goal is a "win-win" solution in which everyone gets some or all of what they are seeking.

Negotiation begins with trying to understand the other person's interests. Together, try to reach possible solutions that meet your mutual concerns. Often the best solution becomes clear when everyone has ample time to explain what they are trying to accomplish.

Activity

Work with a classmate to develop your negotiation skills. Find a topic on which you do not agree. Examples might include the best types of replacements for incandescent lightbulbs or the best way to set up layers in a CADD drawing for an electrical plan. Negotiate with your classmate to come up with one best solution to your difference of opinion. What did each of you "give up" to achieve the solution? What did each of you gain?

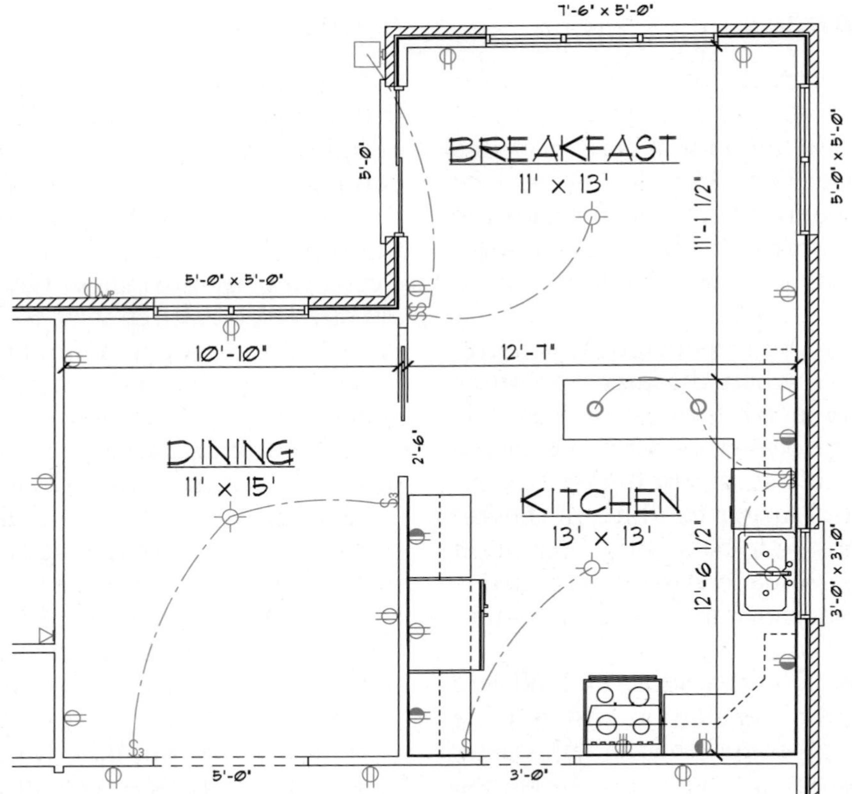

Goodheart-Willcox Publisher

Figure 30-2. Use curved hidden lines or centerlines to show the relationship of outlets and light fixtures to switches. Notice that the dining room has a three-way switch for the light fixture.

Receptacle Outlets

Receptacle outlets should be placed about 8′ apart along the wall of all rooms. Most receptacle outlets are the 120-volt, duplex type that have two receptacles. However, some may be split-wired to provide two different circuits at one receptacle outlet or to switch one of the two receptacles. All receptacle outlets should be grounded or GFCI to prevent severe shock.

Special-purpose receptacle outlets may have only one or several receptacles, depending on their use. They may be 120-volt or 240-volt outlets. Each of these should have a unique symbol and be identified in a legend.

Receptacle outlets can be switched or always "hot." Most rooms require at least one switched outlet for a lamp. It is wise to think about possible furniture arrangements before drawing the electrical plan to determine the most convenient locations.

Special-Purpose Outlets

Several kinds of special-purpose outlets may be installed. Each of these should have a unique symbol and be identified in a legend. Use the proper symbol for each outlet. Refer to **Figure 30-1**.

Lighting

It is difficult to determine what level of brightness will be desirable for everyone. Some people prefer more light than others. In all cases, sufficient light should be provided for the activity to be pursued in a given area.

Two types of lights have commonly been used in residences over the last decades—incandescent and fluorescent. An ***incandescent light*** is the traditional screw-in lightbulb. A ***fluorescent light*** generally has a tube, not a bulb, and is often used in schools and businesses. Fluorescent lights are popular in kitchens and workshops because of the bright illumination they provide.

Green Architecture

Phasing Out the Incandescent Lightbulb

For several years now, countries around the world have been phasing out the use of incandescent lightbulbs. For example, in Australia, a law was passed in 2007 resulting in the phasing out of incandescent bulbs beginning in 2009. In the European Union, incandescent bulbs were phased out over a period of several years, with the last phase enacted in 2012.

In the United States, restrictions affect traditional incandescent bulbs of 40 to 100 watts. The 100-watt incandescent bulbs were phased out in 2012. However, many types of lightbulbs are exempt from these restrictions. Exempted bulbs include appliance lamps (such as those in an oven or microwave), plant lights, and colored lights, among others.

Even though the United States currently exempts some types of lightbulbs from its restrictions, designers and architects can help homeowners be more energy-efficient by including the more energy-efficient lightbulb choices in their designs. New products are continually being developed that make this goal easier to achieve. Keep up-to-date with these new technologies and incorporate them in your designs when possible. This will help reduce our "energy footprint" and use of fossil fuels and will help increase energy efficiency.

The traditional incandescent lightbulb is not very energy-efficient. Countries around the world, including the United States, are phasing out the manufacture of these bulbs. Unfortunately, many people do not like the harsh brightness of the traditional fluorescent tubes. New types of bulbs are therefore being developed to replace the incandescent bulbs.

Currently, three main alternatives are ***compact fluorescent lightbulbs (CFLs), light-emitting diode (LED) lights,*** and ***electron-stimulated luminescence (ESL) lights***. See **Figure 30-3**. All of these are more energy-efficient than incandescent bulbs. However, CFLs contain mercury, which is a serious environmental and safety concern. If a CFL bulb breaks in your home,

Slaven/Shutterstock.com
A

gillmar/Shutterstock.com
B

ppart/Shutterstock.com
C

Figure 30-3. A—The incandescent lightbulb, invented by Thomas Edison more than 100 years ago, is inefficient by today's standards and is being phased out. B—CFL bulbs are more energy-efficient, but are not considered "green" because they contain mercury. C—LED bulbs are a good choice for most uses.

you will need to follow guidelines for removal of hazardous materials to avoid exposure to the mercury. Also, if you choose to use CFLs, be sure to recycle them when they burn out to keep the mercury from entering landfills. Most home improvement stores collect CFLs for recycling.

LED lights are a good alternative to CFLs. They contain no mercury, and they are acceptable for many uses. They also come in multiple colors.

ESL bulbs are very efficient—up to 70% more energy-efficient than incandescent bulbs. They use a technology similar to the cathode ray technology that was used in older computer monitors and televisions.

All lightbulbs and tubes should be shielded in a way that minimizes glare. Allowable exceptions are in closets and storage areas. Diffusing bowls and shades are commonly used to reduce glare.

Lighting fixtures may be permanently attached to the ceiling or wall. They can also be freestanding lamps that are plugged into receptacle outlets, either switched or unswitched. The trend seems to be using more freestanding lamps and fewer ceiling-mounted fixtures. However, a ceiling fixture should be planned in the dining room, centered over the table.

Recessed lighting fixtures are suitable for certain areas of the home, such as hallways, foyers, and special emphasis areas. See **Figure 30-4**. Many varieties of recessed fixtures are available. Each should be evaluated carefully before making a selection. Another type of lighting fixture that is popular in some areas is *track lighting*. This is a system in which several fixtures are mounted on a metal or plastic track and can be adjusted to different locations.

Mikhail Olykainen/Shutterstock.com

Figure 30-4. Recessed lighting can be used for general-purpose lighting or to highlight specific parts of a room, such as a wall niche or display. In this home, it is used for both.

Lighting fixtures that are to be located outside the house must be rated for exterior applications. Plan adequate lighting for walks, drives, porches, patios, and other outside areas. Exterior lighting should be used to enhance the appearance of the home, as well as make it more functional.

Each lighting fixture should be shown on the electrical plan with the proper symbol. The symbol should be placed in the actual location where the fixture is to be connected. If the placement must be exact, dimension the location. A ***lighting fixture schedule*** is often incorporated into the electrical plan. This schedule identifies the fixtures to be used, as shown in **Figure 30-5**.

Other Devices

Several other electrical devices should be shown on the electrical plan. The location of all telephone jacks should be designated. Other devices that should be shown on the plan include items such as an intercom system; home security devices; TV antenna, cable, or satellite TV jacks; door chimes; and audio outlets.

Branch Circuits

A well-designed electrical plan indicates the number and type of branch circuits required for the house. These are usually specified in note or diagram form on the same sheet as the electrical plan. It is not necessary to specify the exact circuit for each outlet, but the number of lighting, small-appliance, and individual circuits should be

Lighting Fixture Schedule						
Type	Manufacturer	Catalog No.	No. Req'd	Mounting Height	Watts	Remarks
A	Lightolier	4107	1	Ceiling	150	
B	Lightolier	4233	2	Ceiling	75	
C	Moldcast	MP 232	4	Gable Peak	150	Twin Floods
D	Progress	P-180	7	Ceiling	100	Recessed 10" Square
E	Lightolier	6349	2	6" Above Mirror	60	
F	Alkco	330-RS	1	Under Cabinet	40	
G	Emerson	220	2	Ceiling	60	Fan and Light Combination
H	Progress	P-138	2	18" Below Ceiling	100	Exterior-Hanging

Goodheart-Willcox Publisher

Figure 30-5. This is a typical lighting fixture schedule that includes the necessary information about each fixture.

listed. This information must be determined before the size of the service equipment can be specified.

Procedures for Drawing an Electrical Plan

After you have performed the calculations and understand a home's electrical requirements, the process of creating the electrical plan is relatively easy. Whether you are using manual drafting techniques or CADD, you can base the electrical plan on the floor plan. This provides a good head start on the development of the electrical plan. **Figure 30-6** and **Figure 30-7** show the electrical plans for the basement and first floor levels of a residence.

Procedure Manual Drafting

Drawing an Electrical Plan

Follow these steps to create an electrical plan using manual drafting techniques.

1. Trace all exterior walls, interior walls, and major appliances from the floor plan.
2. Locate the meter and distribution panel. Indicate the voltage and amperage rating. Also, locate the telephone junction box and home security or automation wiring enclosure. Double-check local building code requirements to be sure these items meet local codes.
3. Show all receptacle outlets using the proper symbols. Be sure to indicate those that are 240-volt, split-wired, weatherproof, or other receptacle types.
4. Locate all ceiling and wall lighting outlets. Use only standard lighting symbols.
5. Show all special-purpose outlets and fixtures, such as telephone jacks, chimes, intercom devices, home security sensors, smoke alarms, and data jacks.
6. Locate the switches and connect them to the outlets and lighting fixtures that they operate.
7. Add the lighting fixture schedule and symbol legend if necessary.
8. Note the number and type of circuits required.
9. Letter all other notes and the title, scale, and sheet number.
10. Check the drawing carefully to be sure that all information is accurate and complete.

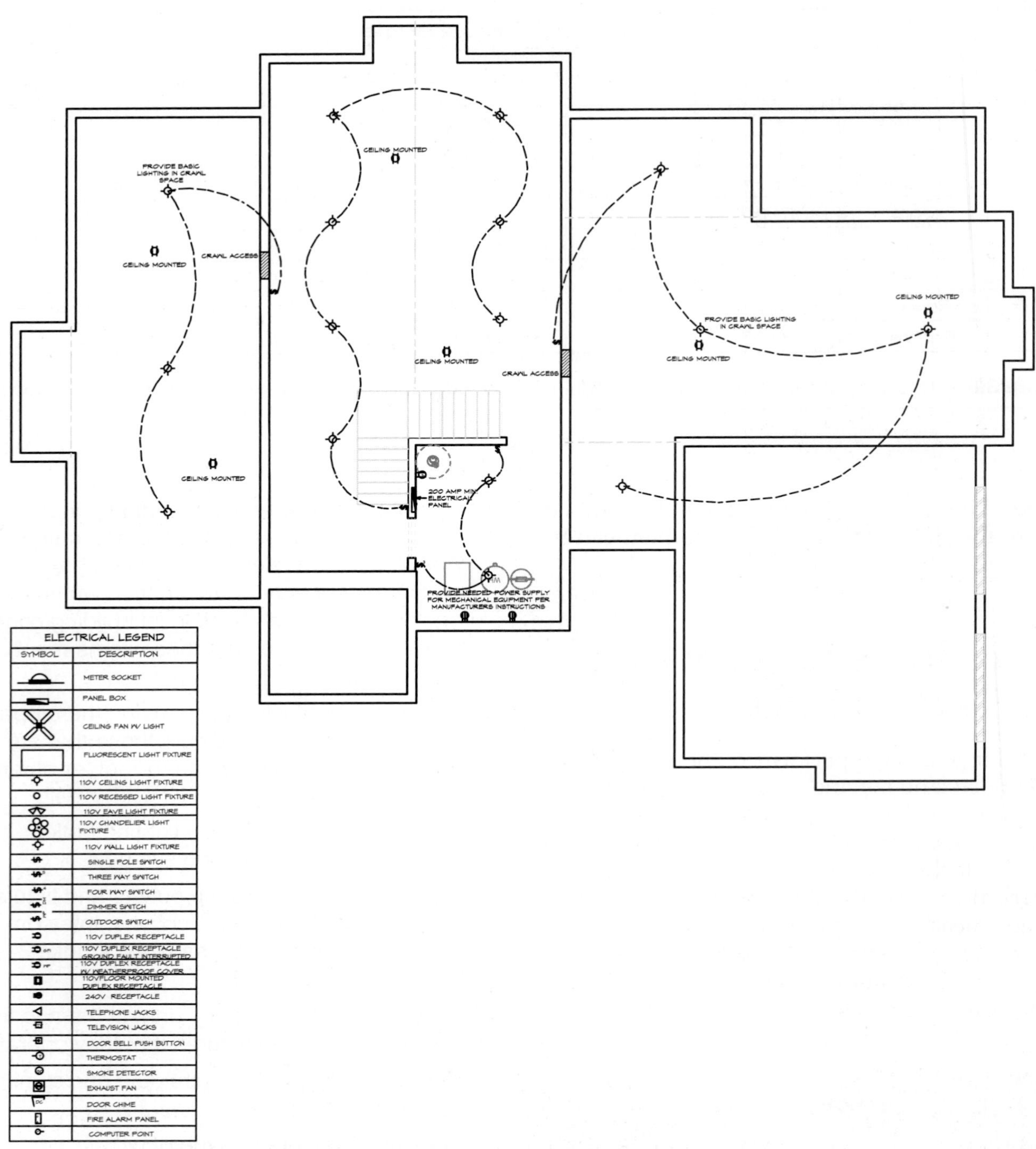

Martin Drafting and Design, Inc.

Figure 30-6. This basement electrical plan shows the necessary electrical features. The first floor electrical plan for this home is shown in Figure 30-7.

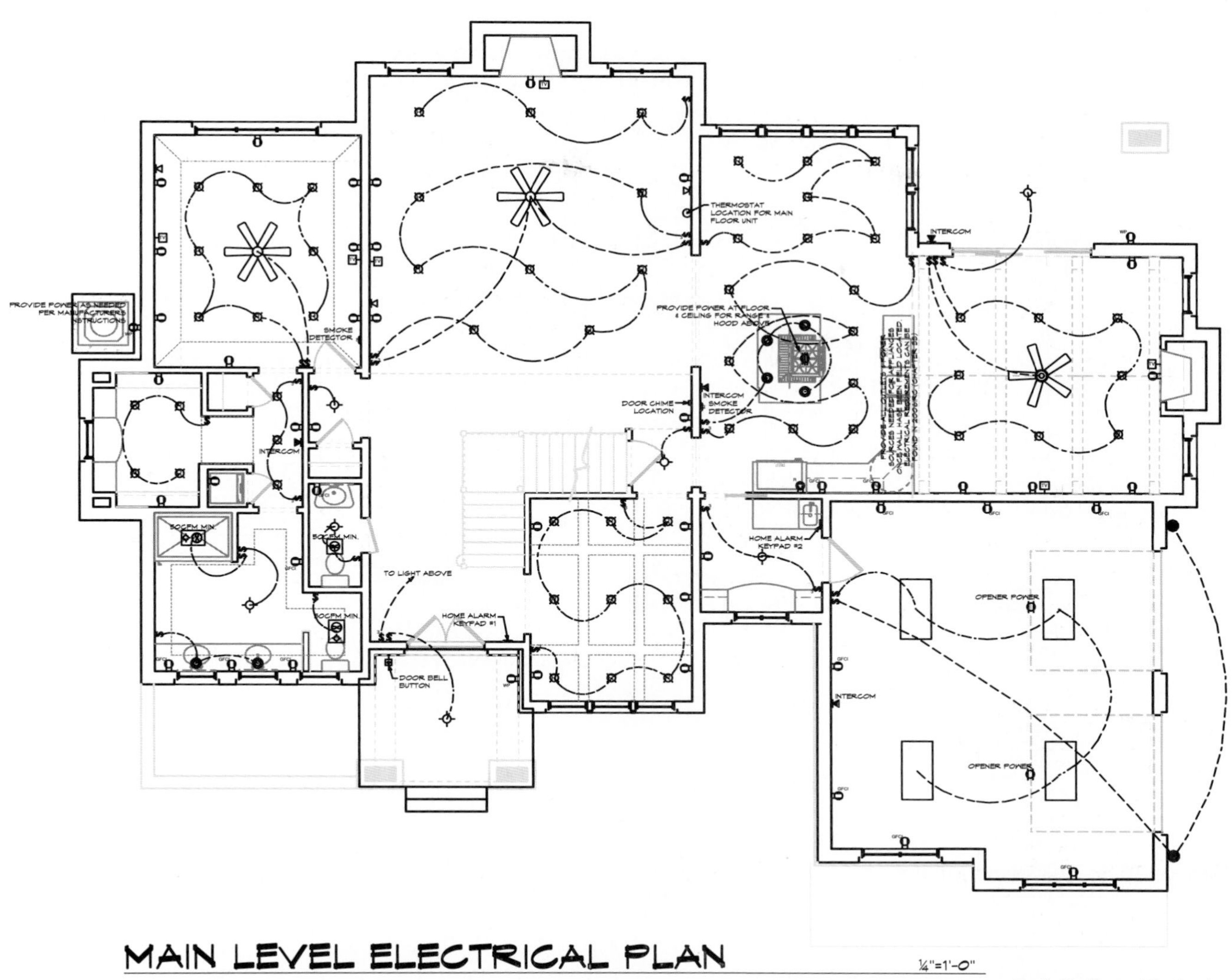

Martin Drafting and Design, Inc.

Figure 30-7. This first floor electrical plan shows the necessary electrical features. The basement electrical plan for this home is shown in Figure 30-6.

Procedure CADD

Drawing an Electrical Plan

An electrical plan can be drawn with a CADD system using the same basic steps explained for manual drafting. **Figure 30-8** shows an electrical plan that was drawn using CADD and the following step-by-step sequence. This procedure is for use with general-purpose CADD software.

1. If the electrical plan is to be a separate file, open the floor plan drawing and save it with a new name. This file will become the electrical plan. If you are combining the electrical plan with the floor plan, create a set of layers specifically for the electrical plan. Lock or freeze all other layers.
2. Locate the meter and distribution panel. Indicate the voltage and amperage rating. Also, locate the telephone junction box and home security or automation wiring enclosure. Double-check local building code requirements to be sure these items meet local codes.

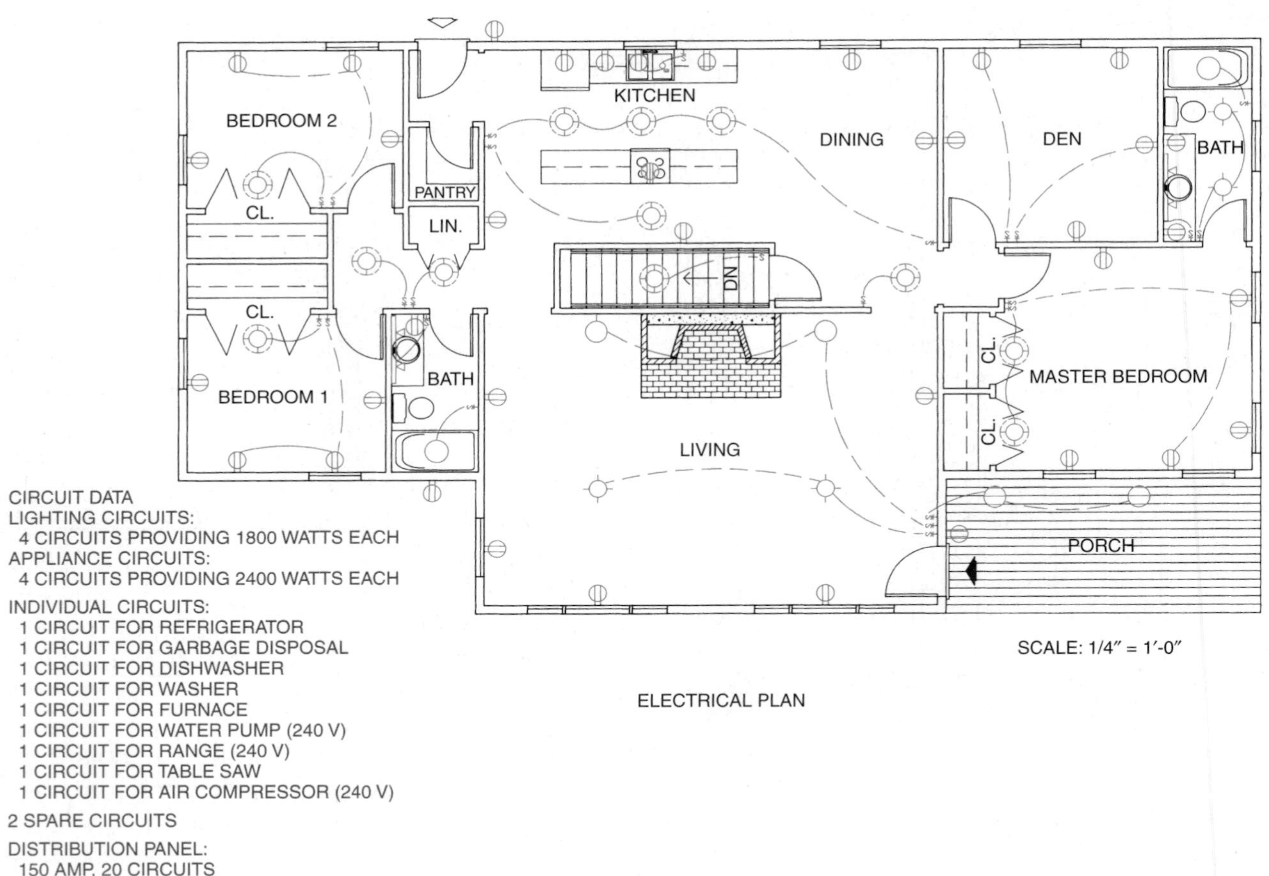

Goodheart-Willcox Publisher

Figure 30-8. This residential electrical plan was drawn using CADD.

3. Insert the proper symbols for all receptacle outlets, placing them on the electrical symbols layer. Be sure to indicate those that are 240-volt, split-wired, weatherproof, or other receptacle types.
4. Insert the proper symbols for all ceiling and wall lighting outlets on the electrical symbols layer.
5. Insert symbols for all special-purpose outlets and fixtures, including telephone jacks, chimes, intercom devices, home security sensors, smoke alarms, and data jacks. Insert the symbols on the electrical symbols layer.
6. Insert the proper symbols for all switches on the electrical symbols layer.
7. Connect switches to the outlets and lighting fixtures that they operate. Use a hidden or centerline linetype. Draw splines with the **SPLINE** command or draw polylines and use the **Spline** polyline editing option. Place these lines on a separate layer to achieve proper line width when plotting.
8. Add the lighting fixture schedule and symbol legend, if necessary.
9. Add a note indicating the number and type of circuits required. Create all other notes and add the title, scale, and sheet number. Specific notes should be placed on their own layer for ease of manipulation.
10. Check the drawing carefully to be sure that all information is accurate and complete.

Parametric Modeling | Creating an Electrical Plan

A residential electrical plan is created in parametric modeling by placing 3D components representing the required electrical features in the home. Different steps and techniques are involved, depending on the software and the amount of modeling required. For example, it is possible to place all of the electrical outlets, switches, light fixtures, and conduit runs into a model using 3D parametric components. However, for residential applications, it is common to show certain electrical features using view-specific 2D detail lines rather than components. For example, the outlets, switches, and light fixtures can be created as components. Then, connecting lines representing wiring from switches to outlets and fixtures on the plan are created using 2D detail lines.

The electrical plan is based on the floor plan. Typically, the program provides a component library for placing the required features. Components that are placed require a host component. For example, outlets and switches are hosted by walls and light fixtures are hosted by ceilings or walls.

The following procedure describes the steps for creating an electrical plan. This is a typical sequence, but specific steps will vary depending on the program used.

1. Open the first floor plan view. Make a duplicate of the view and change the name of the view to First Floor Electrical Plan. Adjust the visibility of components in the view to remove floor plan items that should not appear in the electrical plan.
2. Insert components for the electrical meter, distribution panel, and any other electrical equipment required. Load families containing the appropriate components into the project and insert each item on the plan. To change the orientation of a component, press the space bar while the component is selected. Make sure that you place items at the correct elevation.
3. Insert components for switches and outlets. Select the appropriate switch types and select the appropriate rating for each outlet. Locate these items on walls at the correct elevation.
4. Ceiling-mounted light fixtures are typically created in a ceiling plan. This is because each light fixture placed in the model requires a host (typically a ceiling). To place ceiling-mounted light fixtures, switch to the first floor ceiling plan. If ceilings have not yet been created in the project, place them using the **CEILING** command. Select the appropriate ceiling type, such as gypsum board, and place a ceiling in each room on the plan. Pick the internal areas on the plan representing the rooms. If needed, use sketch tools to create a sketch for the ceiling boundary. Specify the appropriate base level and offset height for each ceiling. For example, set the base level to the First Floor level and set the offset height to 8′-0″ to represent the ceiling height. Once the ceilings are created, you can place the light fixtures. Insert the appropriate component for each light fixture.
5. Open the electrical plan. Adjust the view range of the plan to display the light fixtures placed in the previous step. If needed, turn off the display of ceilings in the view to make the light fixtures visible. Another technique to display the light fixtures in the electrical plan is to edit the component type and add an invisible model line to the component. Switch to an appropriate view in edit mode, such as an elevation view, and sketch a vertical line along the centerline of the component. The line should extend to the appropriate elevation height so that the component is "cut" at the cutting plane elevation associated with the electrical plan view.
6. Add 2D detail lines in the electrical plan to connect the switches to the outlets and lighting fixtures. Set the line type to hidden and use the **Spline** option to draw detail splines connecting the devices.

Parametric Modeling | Creating an Electrical Plan *(Continued)*

7. Create a lighting fixture schedule. If needed, adjust the schedule format to display the number required for each type of fixture.
8. Add notes indicating the number and type of circuits required. Add room tags to identify each room on the electrical plan. Add any other information that is pertinent for your drawing.
9. Create a new sheet for the electrical plan. Insert the electrical plan view onto the sheet. If needed, adjust the placement of text for the view title and scale. Insert the lighting fixture schedule onto the sheet.
10. Look over your work to be sure that you are finished. When you are sure the plan is complete, print or plot the sheet.

Summary

- The purpose of an electrical plan is to show the location and type of electrical equipment to be used in a residence.
- The National Electrical Code (NEC) requires that the service entrance equipment be located as close as practical to the point where the wires attach to the house.
- Switches are shown on the electrical plan connected to the fixtures, appliances, and outlets that they operate.
- Most rooms require at least one switched outlet for a lamp.
- Lighting for a home can be accomplished with incandescent, fluorescent, CFL, LED, or ESL lightbulbs; incandescent bulbs are being phased out, however.
- Lighting fixtures that are to be located outside the house must be rated for exterior applications.
- The number and type of branch circuits planned for a residence should be indicated on the electrical plan.

Internet Resources

Eaton Wiring Devices
Manufacturer of electric switches, timers, and chargers

General Electric
Interior and exterior home lighting products

Home Controls, Inc.
Supplier of home automation equipment

Leviton
Manufacturer of electrical and electronics products

Lutron
Manufacturer of lighting control products

West Penn Wire
Manufacturer of electronic cable

Review Questions

Answer the following questions using the information in this chapter.

1. List the information required on an electrical plan.
2. Identify two factors to consider when locating the service entrance equipment.
3. What is a smart meter?
4. Name at least four types of switches that may be used in a residence.
5. Identify the following electrical symbols.

   A. 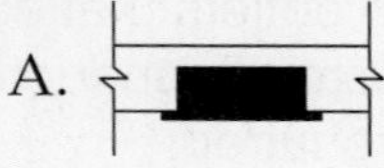

   B. S_3

   C.

   D.

   E.

6. What is the purpose of the hidden lines or centerlines between switches and outlets or fixtures on an electrical plan?
7. Why are many countries around the world phasing out the use of incandescent lightbulbs?
8. What is the purpose of a lighting fixture schedule?
9. In addition to switches and receptacle outlets, what other electrical devices should be shown on an electrical plan?
10. Why would you need to use more than one layer in a CADD program to show the switches, outlets, and connections on an electrical plan?

Suggested Activities

1. Select a floor plan of a small house or cottage and draw an electrical plan using CADD techniques. Show all outlets, all switches, the distribution panel, the meter, and other required electrical features. Identify the number of lighting, small-appliance, and individual circuits. Follow the procedure presented in this chapter and use appropriate layers.
2. Using the same plan as in Activity 1, develop a schematic of the circuits in the house and the appliances, fixtures, and outlets that each circuit serves. Indicate the size of conductors and overcurrent protection required.
3. Search online for information about house wiring, code requirements, and materials used in residential electrical systems in your area. Bring this information to class and pool it with information from other students to form a class reference.
4. Using CADD, draw the electrical plan shown in Figure 30-8. Be sure to use proper layers and linetypes in your drawing.
5. Develop electrical symbols and add them to your CADD symbol library. Refer to Figure 30-1 for examples.

Problem Solving Case Study

The custom home design firm at which you are employed has taken on a new client, the Robinsons. The family includes a mother, a stepfather, and a teenage son who is physically challenged and is confined to a wheelchair. They want you to design a home with three bedrooms, keeping in mind their son's disability.

Complete a floor plan for the Robinsons. Research the Americans with Disability Act requirements for residential electrical needs, and create an electrical plan showing all electrical outlets per ADA requirements. Present your finished floor plan with electrical outlet information and an electrical schedule to the class.

ADDA Certification Prep

The following questions are presented in the style used in the American Design Drafting Association (ADDA) Drafter Certification Test. Answer the questions using the information in this chapter.

1. Which of the following statements about electrical plans are true?
   A. The meter and distribution panel should be placed close to the bedrooms of a house.
   B. The purpose of an electrical plan is to show the location and type of electrical equipment to be used.
   C. Symbols and a legend and notes that help to describe the system should be included on an electrical plan.
   D. Lighting fixtures that are to be located outside the house must be rated for interior applications.
2. Which of the following statements about electrical plans are *false*?
   A. CFL lightbulbs are a truly sustainable option to replace incandescent lightbulbs.
   B. Incandescent lightbulbs are being phased out because they contain mercury.
   C. The least expensive type of switch is a simple on-off toggle switch.
   D. Each lighting fixture in a residence should be shown on the electrical plan with the proper symbol.
3. Match each type of light with the statement that best describes it.

   Lights: 1. CFL, 2. LED, 3. Incandescent, 4. ESL, 5. Fluorescent
   A. Comes in multiple colors.
   B. The least efficient type of light commonly used in homes today.
   C. Uses technology similar to that of a cathode ray tube.
   D. Consists of a tube rather than a bulb and gives off a very bright light.
   E. Can fit into a traditional lighting fixture, but contains mercury.

Curricular Connections

1. **Social Science.** Electric lights are not the only way to provide sufficient light to residences. Research and evaluate alternative lighting methods. Write a short essay describing your favorite nonelectric lighting method and explaining why it is your favorite.
2. **Technology.** Conduct research to find out more about smart meters. Find at least two areas in which they have already been implemented, and find out whether or when your local utility company plans to install them, if the company has not already. Prepare a 1-minute oral report and give it to the class.

STEM Connections

1. **Science.** Most of us associate the brightness of lightbulbs with their wattage. For example, we know that a 100-watt incandescent bulb is brighter than a 60-watt bulb. With the arrival of new types of lighting, such as CFL and LED, it has become more difficult to relate wattage to brightness. For example, a 23-watt CFL can give off the brightness equivalent to a 100-watt incandescent bulb. Therefore, lightbulb manufacturers have started to list the brightness of lightbulbs using lumens. Conduct research to find out what a lumen is and how it is related to wattage. What is the reason for the difference in brightness among incandescent, CFL, and LED lightbulbs? Write a scientific report on your findings.

Communicating about Architecture

1. **Reading and Speaking.** With a partner, make flash cards of the key terms in this chapter. On the front of the card, write the term. On the back of the card, write the pronunciation and a brief definition. Use this chapter and a dictionary for guidance. Then take turns quizzing one another on the pronunciations and definitions of the key terms.
2. **Speaking and Listening.** Working in small groups, prepare an oral presentation to describe the advantages of using alternative lights. Create posters or other visual aids to use in the presentation.

pics721/Shutterstock.com

The selection of plumbing fixtures is important in residential plumbing design. The oversize tub and shower in this large bathroom provide ample room for bathing and enhance the overall design.

Chapter 31

Residential Plumbing

Objectives

After completing this chapter, you will be able to:

- Identify the elements contained in a residential water supply system.
- Identify the elements of a residential water and waste removal system.
- Explain the layout of a septic system.
- Describe the development of water-conserving plumbing fixtures.

Key Terms

acrylonitrile butadiene styrene (ABS)
activated carbon system
branch main
building main
chlorinated polyvinyl chloride (CPVC)
cleanout
cold water branch lines
cold water main
cross-linked polyethylene (PEX)
disposal field
distillation system
distribution box
hot water branch lines
hot water main
house drain
house sewer
ion exchange
main stack
percolation test
plumbing fixture
polyvinyl chloride (PVC)
reverse osmosis system
secondary stack
septic system
septic tank
soil stack
stack vent
stack wall
trap
vent stack
water hammer
water softener

The residential plumbing system is taken for granted and is rarely a concern of homeowners. Nevertheless, it is a very important part of the house. A residential plumbing system provides an acceptable supply of water for household use in desired locations and removes the waste through a sanitary sewer or private septic system. Residential plumbing installations have three principal parts: the water supply, water and waste removal, and plumbing fixtures that facilitate the use of water.

Water Supply System

A residential water supply system begins at the city water main or a private source, such as a well, lake, or stream. The supply pipe that enters the house is known as the ***building main***. See **Figure 31-1**. It may be necessary to include a water softener, filter, or other treatment device at the building main. After any treatment device, the building main branches into two lines—the cold water and the hot water mains. Since the water supply system is under pressure, pipes can follow any path that is convenient and cost effective. *Note:* It is customary to provide a branch line to hose bibs before any water treating device. Hose bibs, which are exterior faucets, do not generally supply soft or filtered water.

The ***cold water main*** extends to various parts of the house to provide unheated water to the fixtures. ***Cold water branch lines*** run from the cold water main to each of the fixtures. Branch lines are smaller than mains. If a branch line is to supply more than one fixture, the

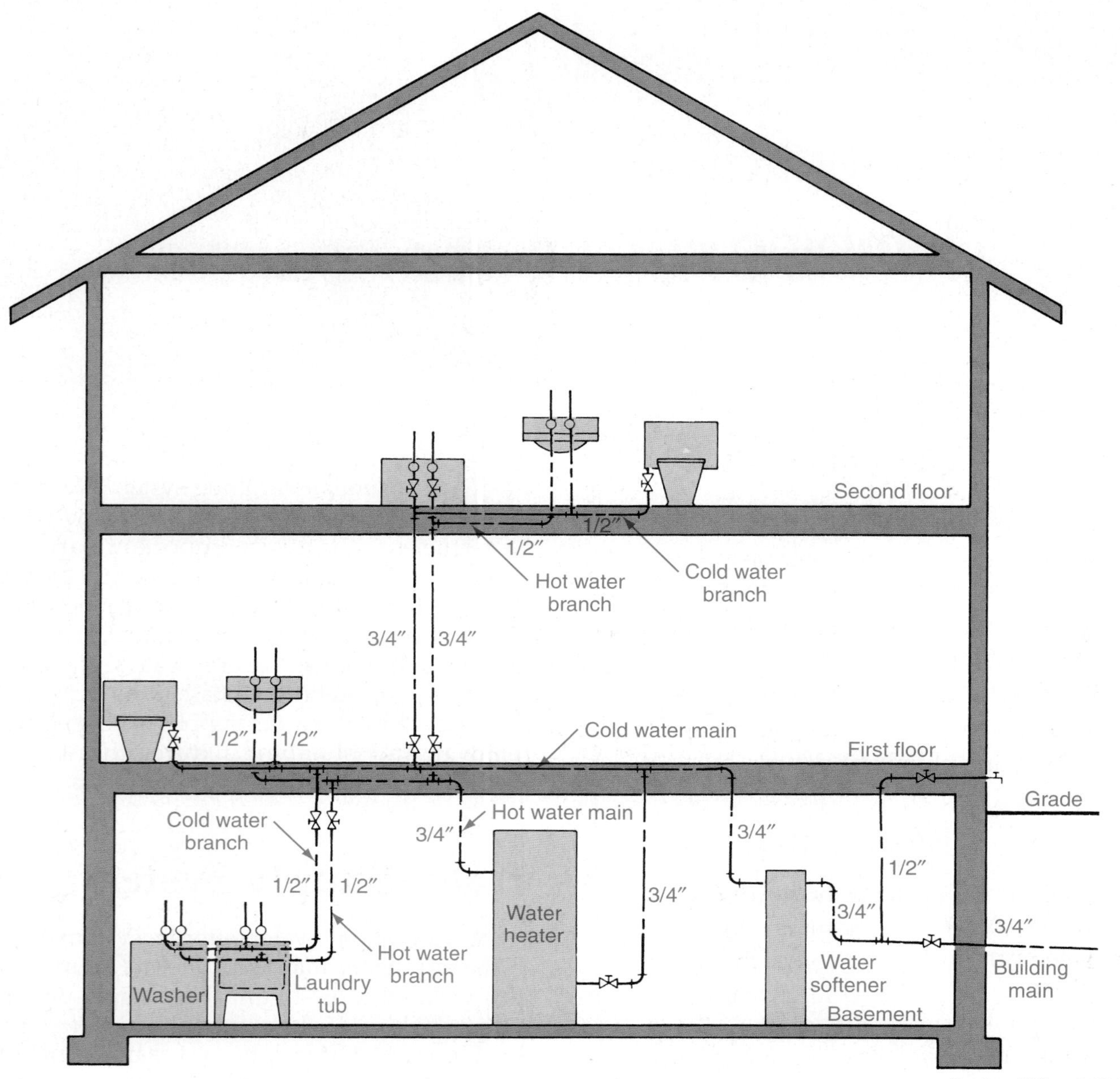

Goodheart-Willcox Publisher

Figure 31-1. The components of a residential water supply system.

diameter of the pipe must be increased to provide an ample amount of water.

The ***hot water main*** supplies heated water to the fixtures that require it. The hot water main runs from the building main to the water heater. See **Figure 31-2**. From the water heater, it usually travels parallel to the cold water main to where both hot and cold water are required, such as sinks. ***Hot water branch lines*** run from the hot water main to each fixture.

The location of the pipes may depend on several factors. In cold climates, care should be taken to locate pipes along interior walls to keep them from freezing. If this is not possible, the pipes should be insulated. Frost-free hose bibs are also available. Large, heavy pipes present a problem when they must pass through a joist. The customary solution is to place the pipe near the top of the joist and block the space above, as shown in **Figure 31-3**.

Green Architecture

On-Demand Water Heaters

One alternative to the traditional water heater with a large storage tank is one or more "on-demand" water heaters. See **Figure A**. These units, also called *tankless* water heaters, produce instant hot water and require only that a cold water line be piped to the unit. The water is heated by an electric heating element or a gas burner, depending on the model.

Although on-demand water heaters are more expensive to install than ordinary water heaters, they last longer, and they require less energy to use. The biggest advantage of using an on-demand water heater is that you do not waste energy keeping a large storage tank of water hot at all times. Water is heated only as it is needed. However, the amount of hot water that can be produced by an on-demand heater is limited. In larger homes or homes that use a lot of hot water, more than one unit may be needed.

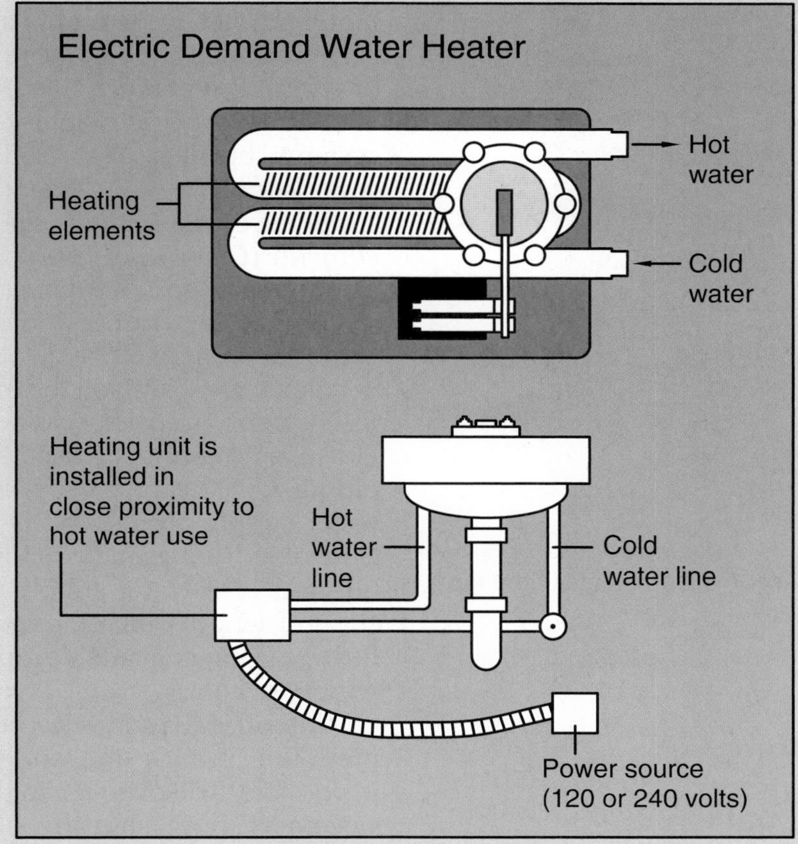

US Department of Energy

Figure A. An on-demand water heating system located under the sink provides instant hot water. A cold water line is all the plumbing needed. An on-demand water heating system is either electrically operated, as shown here, or gas-fired.

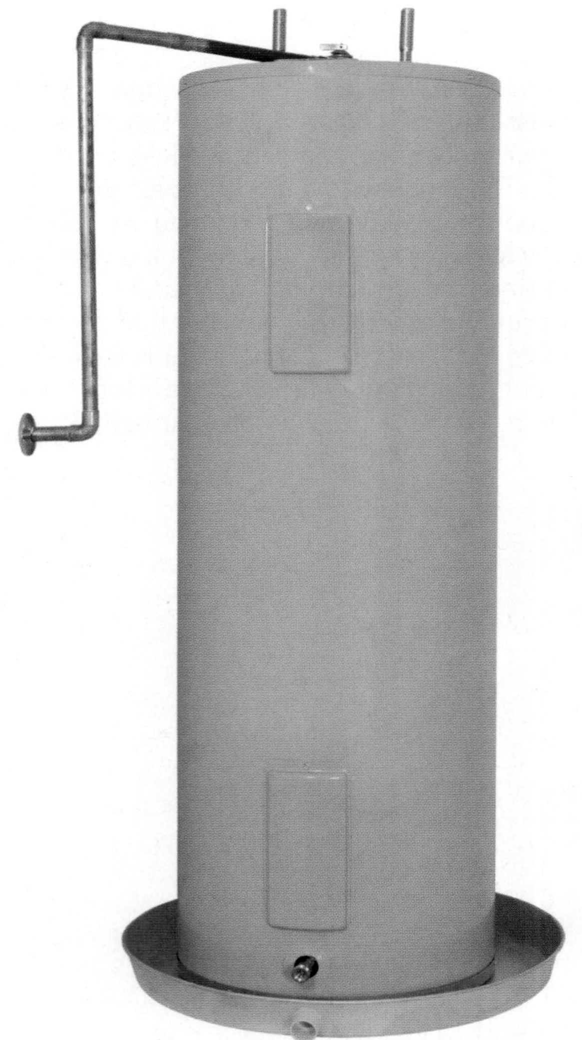

You Touch Pix of EuToch/Shutterstock.com

Figure 31-2. The hot water main connects to the top of this electric water heater.

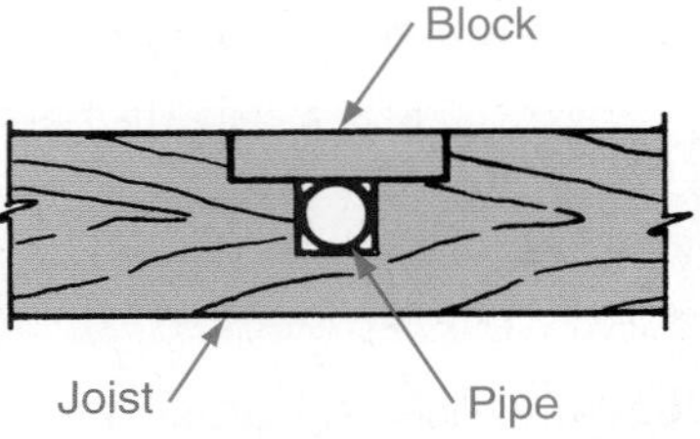

Goodheart-Willcox Publisher

Figure 31-3. When a large pipe, such as a drain, must pass through a joist, the joist should be blocked to prevent severe weakening of the member.

Pipes and Fittings

Indoor pipes and fittings may be copper tubing with soldered joints, plastic, or threaded galvanized steel. See **Figure 31-4**. Building codes specify material and connection requirements for water supply and drainage systems. Check the local code requirements before planning the system.

Copper tubing is used extensively in many areas for water supply systems. Rigid copper tubing (type L), copper fittings, and copper valves are typically used for interior installations. Copper pipe used for water supply pipes underground or in concrete is typically heavy-duty copper tubing (type K) with flare-type joints. Copper pipe is available in 1/2″, 3/4″, 1″, and larger diameters. Main lines are usually at least 3/4″ in diameter and branch lines are a minimum of 1/2″ in diameter.

Plastic pipe is widely used for drainage systems, but it is also used in many areas for water supply systems. Plastic materials used for supply systems include ***chlorinated polyvinyl chloride (CPVC)***, ***polyvinyl chloride (PVC)***, and ***cross-linked polyethylene (PEX)***. CPVC comes in straight 10′ lengths and is tan in color. PVC comes in straight 10′ or 20′ lengths and is white in color. Depending on local code requirements, PVC can be used for cold water supply piping. However, it cannot be used for hot water supply piping. CPVC can be used for both cold and hot water supply piping and is rated at 180°F. PEX is flexible tubing that can also be used for both hot and cold water supply piping. It comes in straight lengths or rolls and uses compression fittings. PEX is available in clear tubing and a variety of colors.

Shutoff valves should be supplied for each main line, branch line, and fixture. This makes it possible to isolate a single fixture from the system without shutting off the entire water supply. See **Figure 31-5**.

Plumbing codes require the installation of water hammer arrestors near quick-closing valves, such as a clothes washer valve or dishwasher valve. ***Water hammer*** is a condition that occurs when a valve suddenly closes and the increased pressure is absorbed by the supply piping, resulting in a loud noise. A water hammer arrestor cushions the water flow and reduces pipe noise during use. Depending on local code requirements, some plumbers install an air chamber at each faucet to reduce the possibility of water hammer. Most air chambers are simply short risers constructed from pipe with the end closed.

A

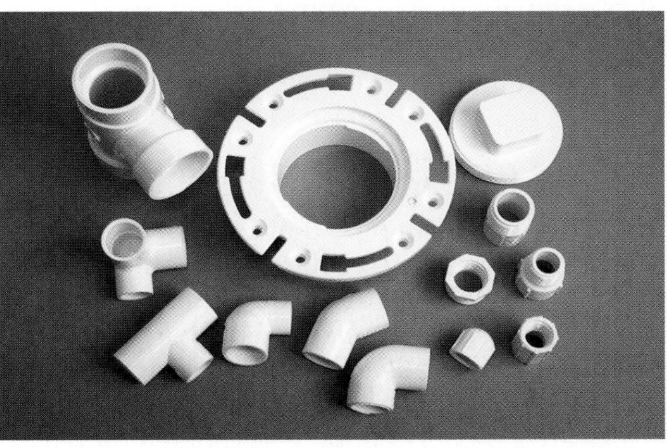

B

C

Goodheart-Willcox Publisher

Figure 31-4. Fittings for residential plumbing systems: A—copper; B—PVC; C—galvanized steel.

Cold and hot water branch lines are usually placed about 6″ apart. If they must be placed closer than this, some type of insulating material should be used to prevent the transfer of heat from one pipe to the other. Efficiency may be improved in any system if the hot water lines are insulated. In high-humidity areas, the cold water lines may need to be insulated as well to prevent additional condensation.

Water Treatment Devices

A homeowner might want an in-house water treatment device for any of several reasons. Some water sources, such as a lake, may provide safe drinking water, but the water may also have an odor that is less than pleasant. Some water sources, such as water from a well, may have high iron content or be too "hard" for household use. Water treatment devices can help reduce these unwanted conditions.

Four common types of in-house water treatment systems are reverse osmosis, distillation, water softener, and activated carbon. The proper system for a given situation depends on the impurities to be removed, amount of water needed, and cost. Local professionals can help in the decision of which system to purchase.

In a ***reverse osmosis system***, the line pressure forces water through a thin, semipermeable membrane. The purified water is collected in a

Goodheart-Willcox Publisher

Figure 31-5. This bathroom sink has two shutoff valves—one for the hot water and one for the cold water.

small storage tank, while the contaminants that were unable to pass through the membrane are drained away. This process can remove from 90% to 99% of the impurities in water, including lead and other toxic metals, arsenic, nitrates, and organic contaminants. However, it is not effective against high levels of minerals. This wastes three to five gallons of water for each gallon produced.

A ***distillation system*** works by heating water to make steam, which is then condensed in a coil to produce distilled water. This process removes most dissolved solids, including salts and heavy metals, but is not effective against volatile organic compounds. Distillation is slow, requiring up to two hours to produce one quart of distilled water. The heat produced by the process is a negative factor in the summer.

A ***water softener*** uses the line pressure to push hard water through a canister filled with a synthetic resin containing sodium ions. As the water runs through the canister, an ***ion exchange*** is performed. In this process, the sodium ions in the resin are exchanged for the calcium and magnesium ions in the hard water. When all of the sodium ions have been exchanged, the resin can be recharged with sodium and reused.

Water produced by sodium-based water softeners has a small amount of sodium added and, therefore, may not be suitable for people on low sodium diets. Nonsodium-based water softeners are also available, in which the sodium ions are replaced by another ion, usually potassium.

In an ***activated carbon system***, the line pressure forces water through one or more canisters filled with activated carbon granules. These granules trap contaminants such as chlorine, organic chemicals, and pesticides. These contaminants can produce bad odors and tastes. Some activated carbon systems also effectively remove lead. Filters must be replaced regularly to prevent bacteria buildup.

Water and Waste Removal

Used water and the waste carried within it is carried to the sanitary sewer or septic system through the waste removal or drainage system. See **Figure 31-6**. These pipes are isolated from the water supply system and must be sized for sufficient capacity, have the proper slope and venting, and have provisions for cleanout.

In planning a residential plumbing system, careful consideration should be given to the drainage network. It is practical to drain as many of the fixtures as possible into a single main drain. Unlike the water supply system, the drainage system is not under pressure. It depends on gravity to carry the waste to the sewer. All drain pipes must be pitched and large enough (usually 4″) to prevent solids from accumulating at any point within the system. Drain pipes are generally smooth inside with a minimum of projections and sharp turns.

Several types of pipe may be used for waste removal. Cast iron pipe is used extensively. Plastic materials used for waste piping include PVC and ***acrylonitrile butadiene styrene (ABS)***. ABS is available in straight 10′ or 20′ lengths and is black in color. Copper and brass alloy pipes, which will not rust and are easy to install, are also used for waste piping. Many local codes specify the type of pipe and connections to use, so check the code.

Stacks and Drainage

A vertical drain pipe that collects waste from one or more fixtures is called a ***soil stack***. Stacks that have toilets draining into them are called ***main stacks***. Every house must have at least one main stack. There may be several main stacks if the house has more than one bathroom. Main stacks are generally about 3″ in diameter if plastic or copper is used, or 4″ if cast iron is used.

Stacks that do not drain toilets are called ***secondary stacks***. These stacks may be smaller in diameter than main stacks; usually 2″. Each fixture is connected to the stack using a ***branch main***. These pipes must slope toward the stack to facilitate drainage.

All stacks (main and secondary) extend down into or below the basement or crawl space and empty into the house drain. The ***house drain*** is mostly horizontal with a slight slope and must be large enough to handle the anticipated load. All houses have at least one house drain, but larger houses may have several. Once the house drain passes to the outside of the house, it is called a ***house sewer***. The house sewer empties into the city sanitary sewer or a private septic system.

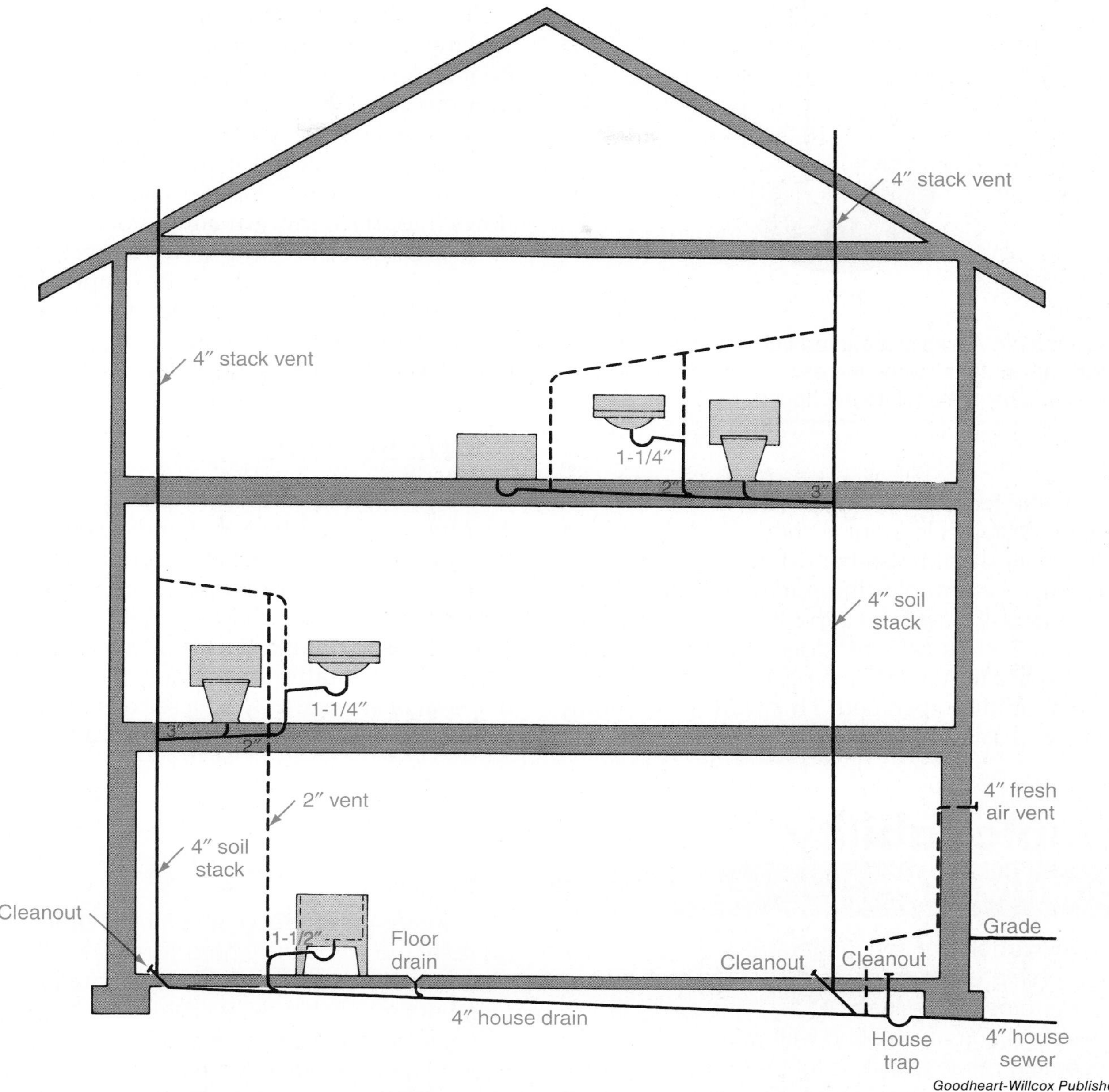

Goodheart-Willcox Publisher

Figure 31-6. The components of a residential drainage system.

Waste in the drainage system creates gases that have an unpleasant odor and may be harmful. These gases are dissipated into the air through vents in the system. A ***vent stack*** is a vertical soil pipe connected to the drainage system to allow ventilation and pressure equalization. In addition to providing an escape for gases, the vent stack provides an air inlet to the drainage system. Drains must be exposed to atmospheric pressure to operate properly. Another type of vent is a stack vent. A ***stack vent*** is a vertical extension of the soil stack above the highest horizontal fixture drain connected to the stack and protrudes about 12″ above the roof.

A ***trap*** is installed below each fixture to prevent gases from escaping through the fixture drain into the house. The trap is always filled with water to block the reverse flow of gases. See **Figure 31-7**. Toilets do not require a trap because they are manufactured with an internal trap.

Each stack requires a cleanout located at the base of the stack. The ***cleanout*** permits the use

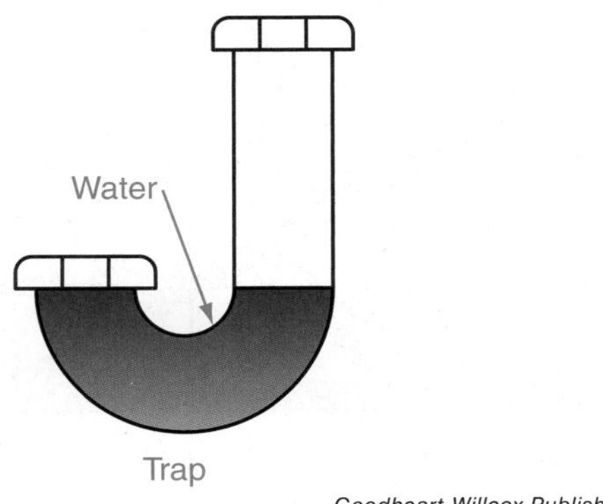

Goodheart-Willcox Publisher

Figure 31-7. A trap is a curved fitting that is always filled with water to block the escape of gases from the drainage system into the house.

of a cable to free waste from the house drain or sewer. A stack cleanout is shown in **Figure 31-8**. Cleanouts should also be installed anywhere the drainage system plumbing makes a sharp bend.

When 4″ cast iron pipe is used for the soil stack, a 2 × 4 stud wall does not provide sufficient space to house the pipe. In this case, a 2 × 6 stud should be specified. This wall is commonly referred to as a ***stack wall*** or *plumbing wall*.

House sewers are frequently not as deep as basement floors. Since a drain in the basement floor is desirable, and water will not flow uphill, a pump must be used to drain the basement. A concrete or tile pit, or sump, is located in an inconspicuous place in the basement, and the floor is usually sloped toward a drain that flows into the sump. An automatic sump pump is installed in the sump and connected to the house drain or storm drain, depending on local code requirements. When water reaches a predetermined level in the sump, the pump operates and removes the water. See **Figure 31-9**.

Septic Systems

Private sewage disposal systems, called ***septic systems***, are used for rural and isolated homes that cannot be connected to public sewers. A septic system has two basic components—the septic tank and the disposal field. Proper construction and maintenance of a private septic system are vitally important. The improper disposal of sewage may be a serious threat to the health and well-being of those in the surrounding

Employability
Leadership

All careers require leadership skills. *Leadership* is the ability to guide and motivate others to complete tasks or achieve goals. It involves communicating well with others, accepting responsibility, and making decisions with confidence. Employees with leadership skills are likely to be promoted to higher levels.

The most important role of leaders is to keep the team advancing toward its goal. This may require settling disputes among members as well as encouraging unproductive members to participate. Leaders inspire their groups and provide the motivation to keep everyone working together.

Good leaders encourage teamwork, because a team that works well together is more likely to reach its goals. Leaders listen to the opinions of others and make sure all team members are included in projects. Leaders also try to set a good example by doing a fair share of the work. In these ways, leaders cultivate a sense of harmony in the group.

Activity

You are the leader of an architectural design group at the company where you work. You are fortunate because all five of your team members are highly skilled designers. However, you sense increasing conflict within the group. Several group members are grumbling about Janine Watkins. Janine is one of the most vocal members of the group, but she is always 15 to 20 minutes late for the weekly group meetings. The other members are tired of having to go back over information she has missed. Since she also has an opinion on everything after she is brought up-to-date, her lack of punctuality generally prolongs the meeting by half an hour to an hour. Her ideas are excellent, but the other members believe her tardiness is reducing the productivity of the whole group. As the group leader, how would you handle this situation?

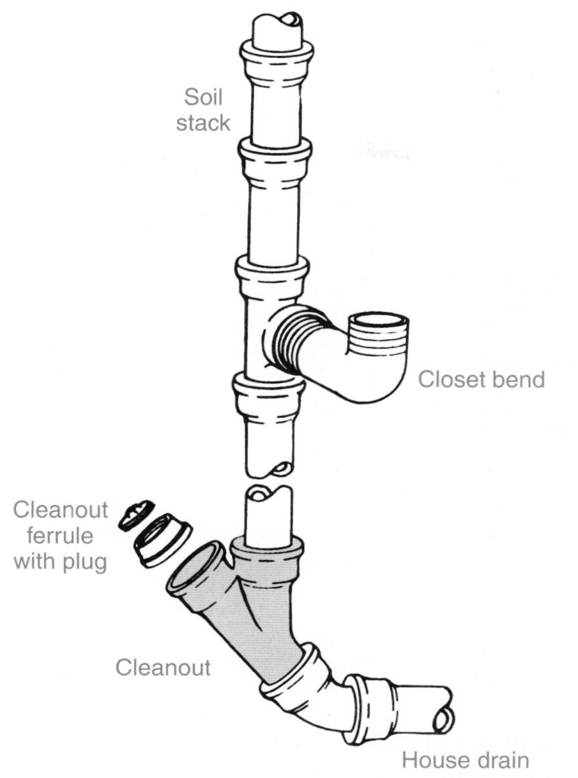

Figure 31-8. Cleanouts are required at the base of all stacks.

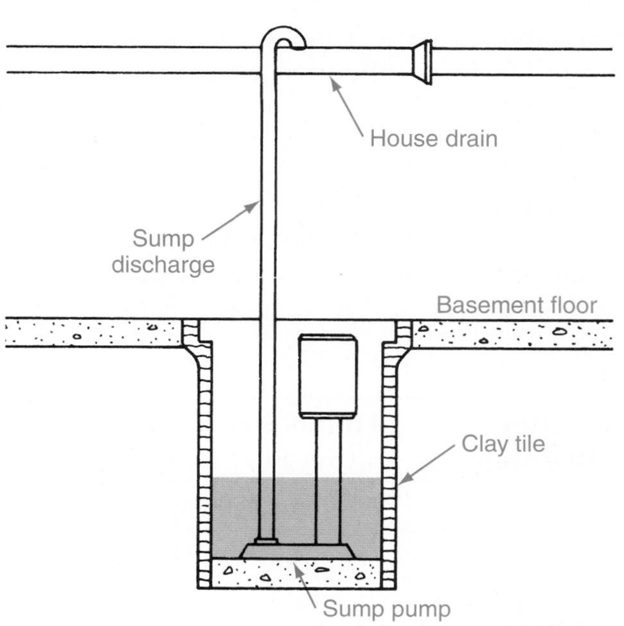

Figure 31-9. A sump pump removes water from the basement and discharges it into the house drain or to the outside of the house.

area. A large number of disease-producing organisms thrive in sewage.

Before a building permit is issued for construction of a septic system, the site is usually examined by a health department sanitarian to determine if the site is suitable for a septic system. The site must have an adequate area and the proper soil. The suggested minimum dimensions for placement of the well, septic tank, and disposal field on a one acre site are shown in **Figure 31-10**. Generally, the minimum lot size is one acre. A large land area and suitable soil conditions are necessary to isolate the disposal system from all wells, lakes, and streams to prevent contamination. Septic systems should also be isolated from property lines and buildings. Check with your local health department for minimum distances required.

Septic Tank

In a septic system, sewage from the house sewer first enters the septic tank. The ***septic tank*** performs two basic functions. It removes about 75% of the solids from the sewage by bacterial action before discharging the sewage into the disposal field. It also provides storage space for the settled solids while they undergo digestive action.

A septic tank should be watertight. It is usually constructed of reinforced concrete or concrete blocks with mortared joints. The interior surface is coated with cement and sand plaster. **Figure 31-11** shows the construction of a typical septic tank.

The liquid capacity of the septic tank should be about 1-1/2 times the average sewage flow from the house over a 30-hour period. In no case should the capacity be less than 750 gallons. Frequently, the number of bedrooms in a home is used as an indication of the size septic tank required. The size should take into consideration clothes washers, dishwashers, garbage disposals, and other devices that discharge into the sewer. In general, the liquid capacity should be doubled when a garbage disposal is used. **Figure 31-12** shows suggested septic tank sizes for typical residential use. However, always check with the local authorities before selecting a septic tank. Local health departments, building codes, and soil conditions can affect the required tank size.

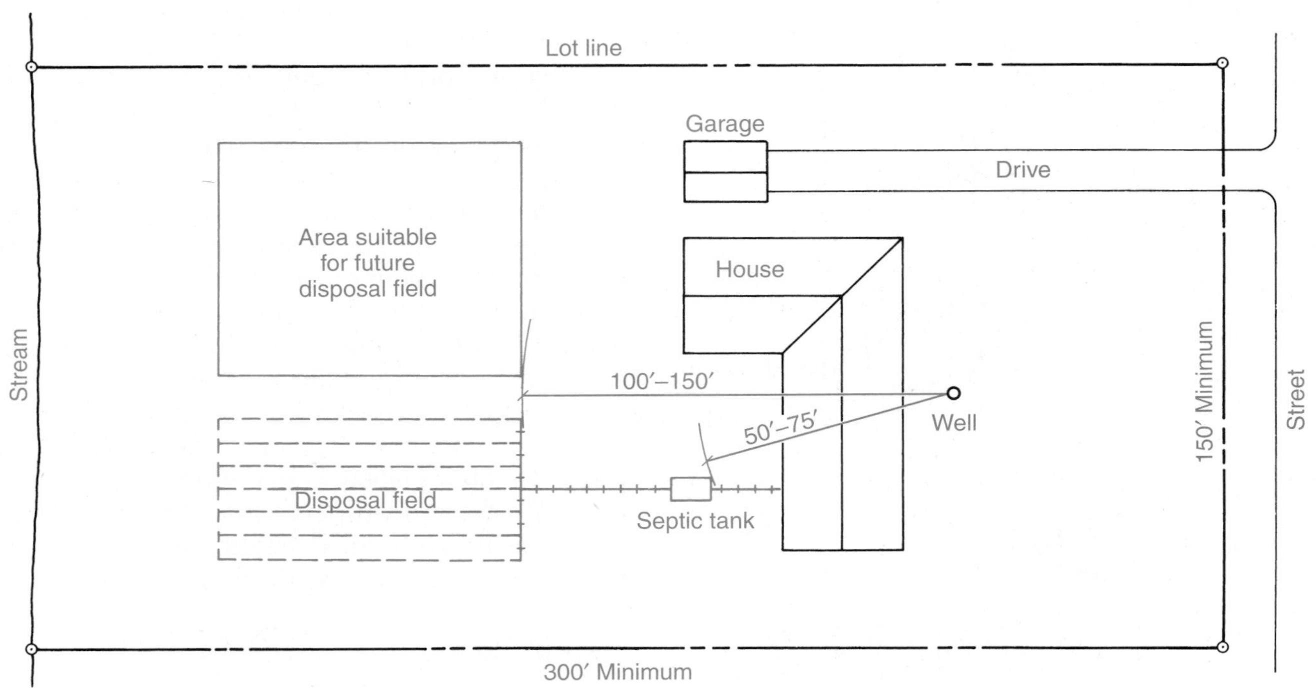

Goodheart-Willcox Publisher

Figure 31-10. Recommended minimum dimensions for placement of a private septic system and water well with respect to the house and property lines.

Disposal Field

The function of the ***disposal field*** is to receive sewage in liquid form from the septic tank and allow it to seep into the soil. The disposal field is also called a *drain field* or *leach field*. Dry, porous soil containing sand or gravel is ideal for a disposal field.

Goodheart-Willcox Publisher

Figure 31-11. Construction of a typical cast concrete septic tank.

The disposal field may be constructed using clay tile, perforated fiber pipe, or perforated plastic pipe. The drain field lines are laid nearly level about two feet below the surface of the ground or below the frost line. A slope of 1″ in 50′ is typical. The drain lines are positioned in a bed of pebbles usually covered with straw. **Figure 31-13** shows some of the important construction features of a disposal field.

The disposal field should be located in such a manner that surface water drainage is diverted away from it. If the disposal field becomes

Number of Bedrooms	Home Size (Sq. Ft.)	Tank Size
1	Less than 1500	750
2	1500	750
3	2500	1000
4	3500	1200
5	4500	1500

Goodheart-Willcox Publisher

Figure 31-12. Suggested septic tank sizes.

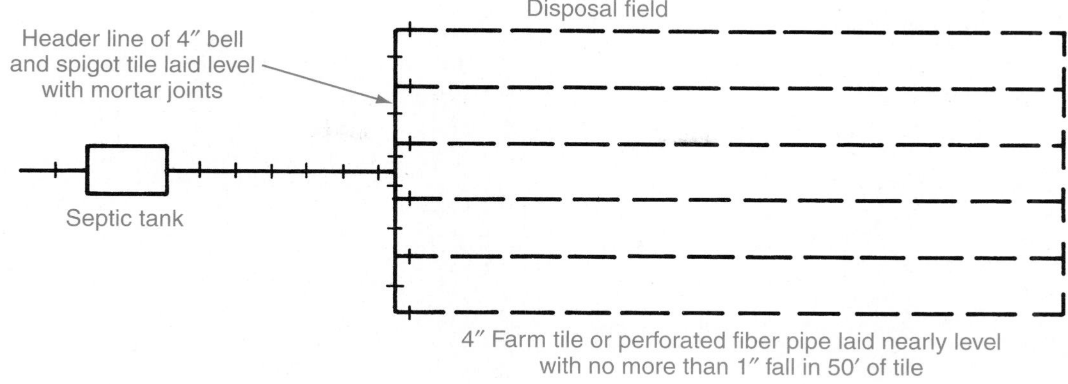

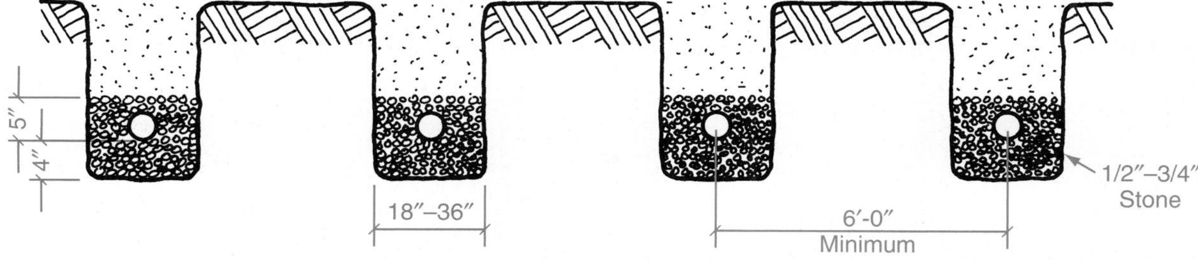

Tile in Individual Trenches

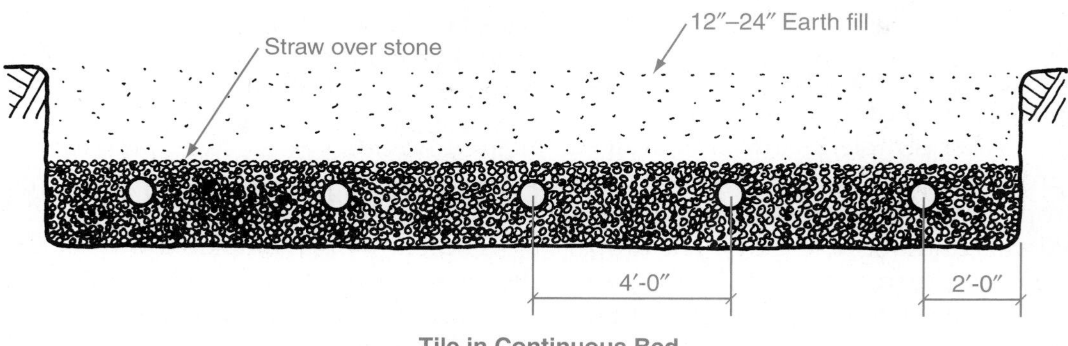

Tile in Continuous Bed

Goodheart-Willcox Publisher

Figure 31-13. A disposal field can be constructed using tile in individual trenches or in a continuous bed. A continuous bed requires less space than the individual trenches.

flooded, it will cease to function. The disposal field should also be located downhill from any water well. It should never be placed under a driveway, parking lot, or paved area, or in a place where heavy vehicles may drive over it.

Distribution Box

Some septic systems are equipped with a ***distribution box***. See **Figure 31-14**. In this design, liquid sewage flows from the septic tank to the distribution box. Drain pipes connected to the distribution box distribute the sewage evenly throughout the disposal field. Some of the newer systems allow the homeowner to control which parts of the disposal field are used. This allows one part of the disposal field to dry up while another part receives the sewage.

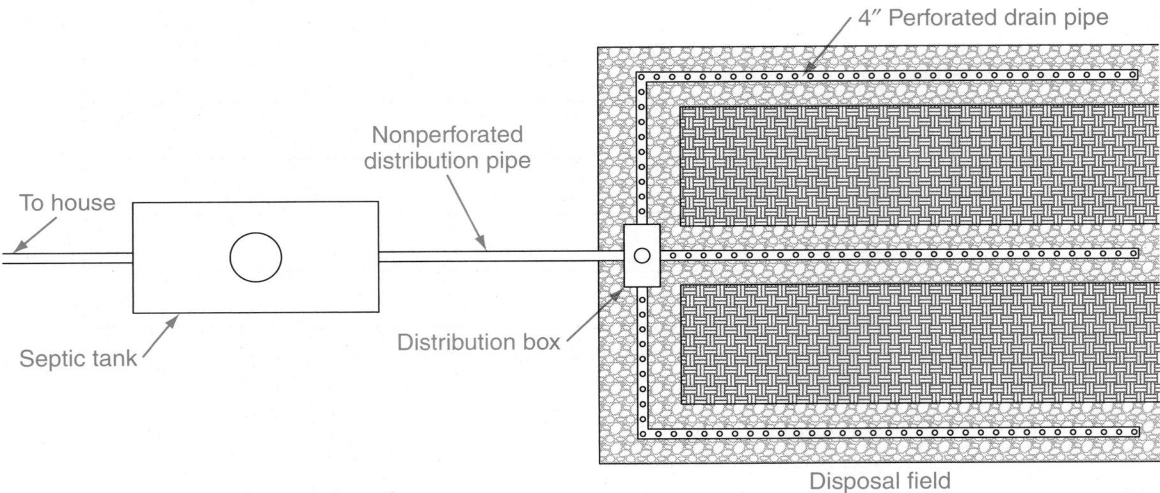

Goodheart-Willcox Publisher

Figure 31-14. A septic system equipped with a distribution box provides for even distribution of sewage to the disposal field.

Disposal Field Soil Tests

The suitability of the soil for a disposal field must be determined by soil tests. These tests are known as ***percolation tests***. They determine how readily the soil will absorb water and provide a guide for the required design and size of the disposal field.

The percolation rate is determined by filling a test hole with water to completely saturate the immediate area. After complete saturation, water is added to provide 4″ to 8″ of water in the test hole. The drop in water level is measured at 30-minute intervals until the hole is dry. The drop in level that occurs during the final 30-minute period is used to calculate the percolation rate for that test hole.

The standard percolation rate must be no greater than 45 minutes per inch. One test hole five feet deep or deeper is generally required to determine groundwater level and consistency of subsoil. The table in **Figure 31-15** shows the recommended seepage area required for various percolation rates. These requirements are general guidelines and are based on square footage per bedroom. Check local codes for specific design requirements.

Calculation of Disposal Field Size

The following example shows how to calculate the correct size of a disposal field. The example is for a three-bedroom home with a percolation rate of 25 minutes per inch.

Disposal Field Design		
Standard Percolation Rate (Minutes Per Inch)	Soil Drainage	Required Seepage Area (Square Feet Per Bedroom)
15 or less	Good	275
16–30	Fair	375
31–45	Poor	500
Over 45	Not Suitable	—

Goodheart-Willcox Publisher

Figure 31-15. Recommended seepage area for various percolation rates.

1. If the tile is placed in individual trenches, the seepage area required would be 3 × 375 square feet or 1125 square feet. See the table in **Figure 31-15**. Using 2′ wide trenches, 562 linear feet of trench would be required (1125 square feet/2 square feet per linear foot = 562 linear feet). Therefore, 8 trenches each 70′ long will provide the required field (562′/70′ = 8.03).
2. If the tile is placed in a continuous bed, the seepage area required would be 3 × 375 square feet or 1125 square feet. See the table in **Figure 31-15**. A 28.5′ × 40′ bed will provide the required field (28.5′ × 40′ = 1140 square feet).
3. The minimum necessary gross area available to install the disposal field and provide space for future expansion and replacement is:

   2-1/2 × 1125 square feet = 2812 square feet

Plumbing Fixtures

The third part of the residential plumbing system consists of the fixtures. A ***plumbing fixture*** is any device, such as a bathtub, shower, toilet, sink, or dishwasher, that requires water. The choice of fixtures is important. They are expensive to install and replace, so choose them wisely.

Plumbing codes specify minimum clearance and location dimensions that must be used when installing various fixtures. Be sure ample space is allowed for the fixture. Manufacturers specify roughing-in measurements for each of their fixtures. **Figure 31-16** illustrates some of the information supplied by one manufacturer.

Water Conservation

In the past, almost all residential toilets used gravity and 5 to 6 gallons of water to rinse the bowl clean and wash the waste down the drain. In 1975, pressurized toilet tanks were introduced, which slightly reduced the amount of water required. During the 1980s, however, the limitations of our water supply again became a concern. Demand for fresh water increased significantly and, in some areas of the country, water conservation laws were passed.

Toilet manufacturers responded by developing low-flow, water-saving models. The new models used 3.5 gallons per flush (gpf) instead of the old 5 or 6 gallons. Later, severe water shortages in California prompted that state's legislature to make 1.6 gpf toilets mandatory in all new residential construction.

In 1992, the US Congress passed a national standard that addressed water conservation—the National Energy Policy Act. This act stipulates that all new toilets manufactured in, or imported into, the United States for residential use must consume no more than 1.6 gpf. See **Figure 31-17**. Although the National Energy Policy Act permits

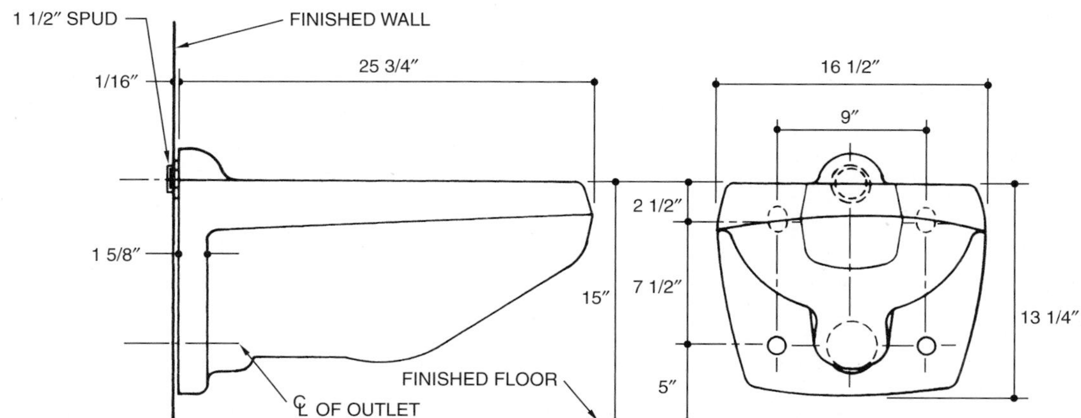

Courtesy of Kohler Co.

Figure 31-16. Rough-in specifications for a wall-mounted residential bathroom fixture. These specifications must be considered during the planning stage of new home design.

manufacturers to continue making 3.5 gpf toilets for commercial installations, some states, including California, New York, Massachusetts, and Texas, require 1.6 gpf designs for commercial use as well. Also, the National Energy Policy Act sets the maximum flow rates for showerheads and faucets. The maximum flow rates are 2.5 gallons per minute (gpm) at 80 psi of line pressure for showerheads and 2.2 gpm at 60 psi of line pressure for bath and kitchen faucets.

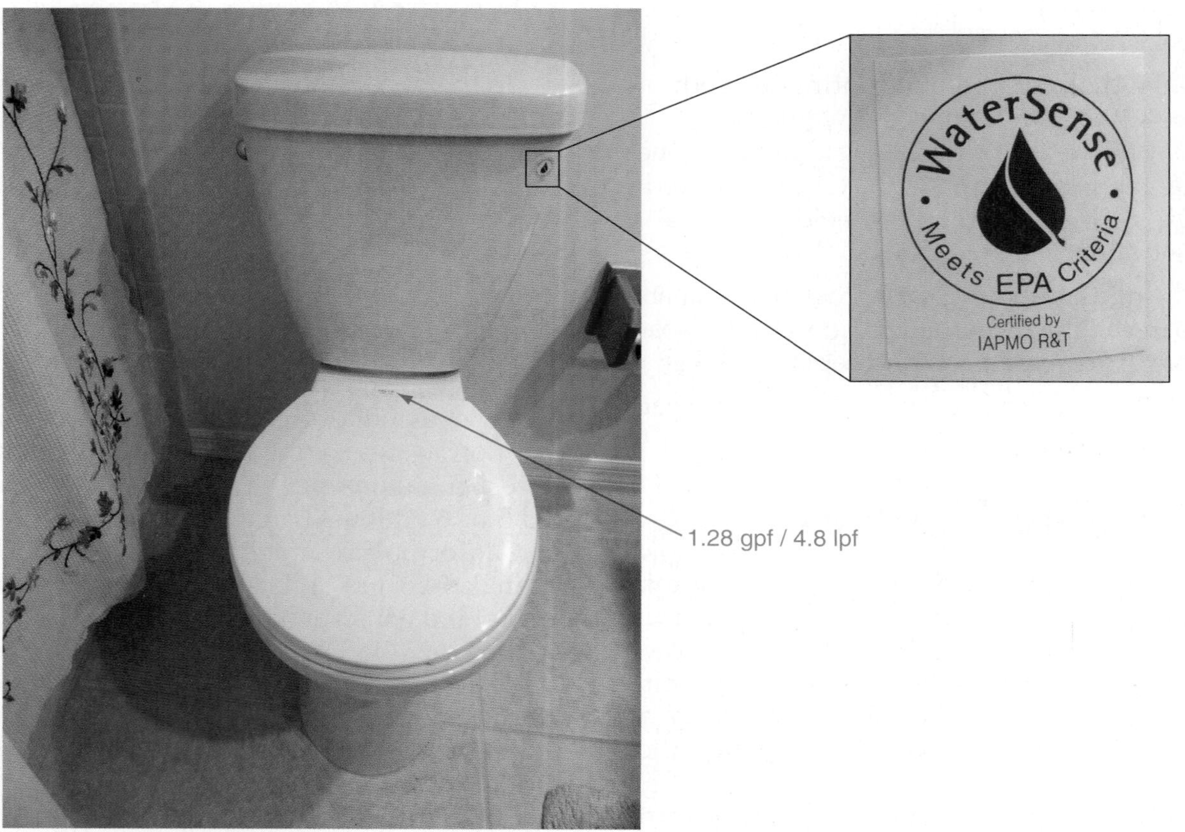

Goodheart-Willcox Publisher

Figure 31-17. This EPA-rated toilet uses a maximum of 1.28 gallons per flush.

Summary

- A residential water supply system begins at the city water main or a private source, such as a well, lake, or stream.
- Since the water supply system is under pressure, pipes may follow any path that is convenient and cost effective.
- Pipes used in the water supply system may be copper tubing with soldered joints, plastic, or threaded galvanized steel.
- Used water and other waste is carried to the sanitary sewer or septic system through the waste removal or drainage system.
- A private septic system has two basic components: the septic tank and the disposal field.
- Plumbing fixtures are all the devices in a home that require water.
- The National Energy Policy Act limits the water consumption of all new toilets manufactured in or imported into the United States.

Internet Resources

Environmental Protection Agency/Septic (Onsite/Decentralized) Systems
EPA discussion of septic systems

InspectAPedia
Encyclopedia of building and environmental inspection and testing

Jacuzzi
Manufacturer of bath fixtures

Kinetico Home Water Systems
Whole-house residential water treatment systems

Kohler
Plumbing fixtures

Moen
Plumbing fixtures

RainSoft Water Treatment Systems
Residential water treatment systems

Review Questions

Answer the following questions using the information in this chapter.

1. Identify the three parts of any residential plumbing system.
2. Briefly describe the flow of cold and hot water from the supply pipe that enters the house to the fixtures within the house.
3. List three types of pipe that are commonly used in the indoor water supply system.
4. Main water lines are usually at least _____ in diameter and branch lines are a minimum of _____ in diameter.
5. Where should shutoff valves be located in a water supply system?
6. What is *water hammer*?
7. Name four common types of water treatment systems.
8. The force that a drainage system depends on to carry waste to the sewer is _____.
9. What is the usual size for wastewater drain pipes?
10. List four types of pipe that are commonly used for drain pipes.
11. What is the difference between a main stack and a secondary stack in a water and waste removal system?
12. All stacks extend down into or below the basement or crawl space and empty into the _____ drain.
13. A(n) _____ is installed below each fixture to prevent gases from escaping through the fixture drain into the house.
14. Each stack requires a(n) _____ located at the base of the stack.
15. What type of wall is specified to provide sufficient space for a 4″ soil stack?
16. List the two main parts of a private sewage disposal system.

17. What is the purpose of a disposal field?
18. Soil tests used to determine the suitability of the soil for a disposal field are known as _____ tests.
19. A plumbing _____ is any device, such as a bathtub, shower, toilet, sink, or dishwasher, that requires water.
20. What is the maximum allowable water consumption, per flush, of new toilets in the United States?

Suggested Activities

1. Visit a house under construction that has the rough plumbing installed. Obtain permission to enter the site. Identify the hot and cold water supply systems and the drainage system. Make notes about the size and type of pipes used. Check to see where the shutoff valves are located and determine whether the house sewer is to be connected to a public sanitary sewer or a private septic system. Make a sketch of the supply and drainage systems.
2. Visit your local building or plumbing inspector. Ask for specifications and requirements for residential plumbing in your area. Invite the inspector to speak to the class.
3. Visit a local plumbing supply store and examine materials used in residential plumbing. Make a chart or table showing the relative costs of plastic, steel, and copper pipe and fittings.
4. Using a sandbox, build a scale model of a private sewage disposal system for a three-bedroom house with a soil percolation rate of 25 minutes per inch. Display the model.

Problem Solving Case Study

The Foster family recently bought a historic home in rural Alabama. The home was built in 1894 and was last updated in 1959. Structurally, the house is sound. The Fosters know they need to bring the wiring up to code, but they are not certain what will need to be done with the plumbing. From the stains in the sinks, they know the water has a high iron content. They had a water sample analyzed and discovered the water also has high levels of calcium, magnesium, and nitrates. The plumbing inspector they hired recommends re-plumbing the entire house. Mr. Foster thinks they can get by with just adding a whole-house water treatment system. Re-plumbing the entire house would be very expensive, and he is not sure the family can afford it. What would you recommend to the Fosters, and why?

ADDA Certification Prep

The following questions are presented in the style used in the American Design Drafting Association (ADDA) Drafter Certification Test. Answer the questions using the information in this chapter.

1. Which of the following statements about residential plumbing are true?
   A. A residential water supply system begins at the city water main or a private source, such as a well, lake, or stream.
   B. Water supply pipes underground or in concrete are usually made of Type L copper.
   C. Improper disposal of sewage may be a serious threat to the health and well-being of people in the surrounding area.
   D. Septic tanks should be porous to allow liquid sewage to flow from the tank into the surrounding ground.

2. Which of the following statements are *false*?
   A. Drains must be exposed to atmospheric pressure to operate properly.
   B. In a septic system, sewage from the house sewer first enters the distribution box.
   C. A house may have several main stacks if the house has more than one bathroom.
   D. Main water supply lines usually have pipes at least 8″ in diameter.
3. Match each type of water treatment system with its description.

   Water Treatment Systems: 1. activated carbon, 2. distillation, 3. reverse osmosis, 4. water softener
   A. Water flows through a semipermeable membrane to remove 90% to 99% of impurities.
   B. Water is heated to make steam, which then condenses.
   C. A resin is used to exchange sodium ions for calcium and magnesium ions.
   D. Granules in one or more canisters trap contaminants such as chlorine, organic chemicals, and pesticides.

Curricular Connections

1. **Social Science.** Personal and public sanitation systems have existed for thousands of years and on every continent. Conduct research to find out more about the history of plumbing and sanitation from the early Roman Period through today. Address the needs of personal and public sanitation systems, the development of plumbing fixtures, and environmental concerns related to plumbing and sanitation. Report your findings to the class.
2. **Language Arts.** Conduct research to find out more about on-demand water heaters. Compare models from three different manufacturers based on cost, energy efficiency, and flow rate. Write a report comparing the three models.

STEM Connections

1. **Math.** Based on the information in this chapter, calculate the total required seepage area for each of the following homes.

   A. Three-bedroom home on land with a percolation rate of 34 minutes per inch.

   B. Four-bedroom home on land with a percolation rate of 12 minutes per inch.

   C. Five-bedroom home on land with a percolation rate of 19 minutes per inch.

Communicating about Architecture

1. **Reading and Speaking.** With a partner, make flash cards of the key terms in this chapter. On the front of the card, write the term. On the back of the card, write the pronunciation and a brief definition. Use this chapter and a dictionary for guidance. Then take turns quizzing one another on the pronunciations and definitions of the key terms.
2. **Reading and Writing.** While working with a partner, look at Figure 31-1 and describe the important information being conveyed by that figure. Through your collaboration, develop what you and your partner believe is the most interesting verbal description of the importance of the figure. Present your findings to the class.

pics721/Shutterstock

Special design considerations are required for a kitchen in which plumbing fixtures are used in multiple locations.

Chapter 32

Plumbing Plans

Objectives

After completing this chapter, you will be able to:

- Identify the components of a residential plumbing plan.
- Identify typical plumbing symbols and fixtures found on a residential plumbing plan.
- Draw a residential plumbing plan using manual drafting techniques.
- Draw a residential plumbing plan using CADD techniques.

Key Terms

central vacuum system
plumbing fixture schedule
plumbing plan

The ***plumbing plan*** shows the location, size, and type of all plumbing equipment to be used in a residence. It is a plan view drawing that shows the complete plumbing system, including water supply lines, waste disposal lines, and plumbing fixtures. Gas lines and central vacuum systems are also included on the plumbing plan.

The plumbing system should be coordinated with the electrical and climate control systems. Homeowner convenience, health, and safety depend to a considerable extent on a well-planned plumbing system that operates efficiently.

Required Information

The plumbing plan includes the waste lines, soil stacks, and vent stacks, water supply lines, drain and plumbing fixture locations, and size and type of pipe to be used. Proper plumbing symbols should be used and identified in a legend. A plumbing fixture schedule is required, as well as any notes needed to fully describe the plumbing system.

Residential plumbing codes require that plumbing fixtures be located to provide sufficient access for servicing. See **Figure 32-1**. Check the local code to determine clearance dimensions and minimum space requirements for plumbing fixtures.

Usually, a single plumbing plan is adequate for a single-level house with or without a basement. A split-level or two-story house may require two or more plans, one for each level.

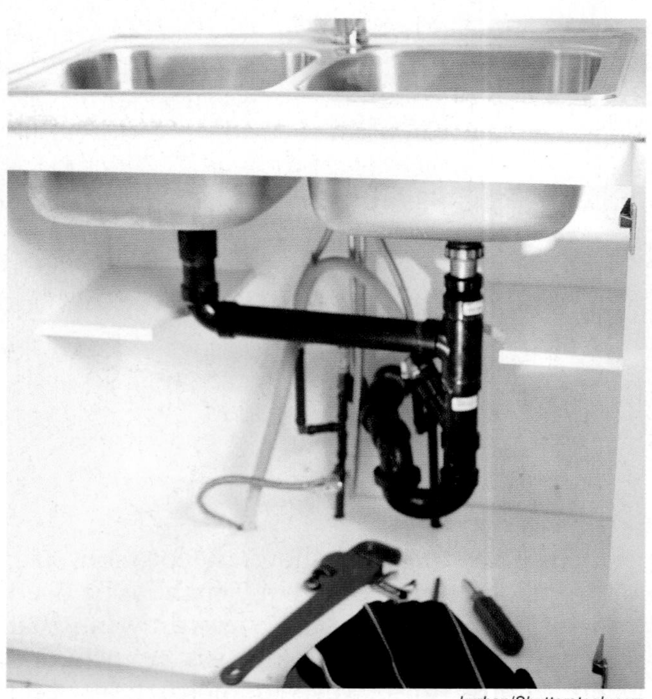

kurhan/Shutterstock.com

Figure 32-1. Plan plumbing fixtures with enough space to provide access for servicing.

Waste Lines, Stacks, and Vents

Proper location and appropriate size are the major considerations in planning the waste lines. The waste line network is usually designed first and then the rest of the plumbing system is planned around it.

Each toilet must have a main stack. A sufficient number of secondary stacks must also be included to properly vent the other plumbing fixtures. Waste lines and vent lines are larger in diameter than water supply lines. The table in **Figure 32-2** shows typical minimum sizes for residential waste and vent lines.

Since waste lines and vent lines are larger than supply lines, they are usually drawn using a wider line than that used for supply lines, as shown in **Figure 32-3**. Attempt to maintain a proper size relationship among all elements of the drawing.

Waste lines are not under pressure and depend on gravity to move the waste. The lines must be sloped slightly, usually 1/4″ per foot, to facilitate even flow. The required slope should be shown on the plumbing plan in either a general or specific note.

Minimum Waste, Vent, and Supply Pipe Sizes				
Plumbing Fixture	**Waste**	**Vent**	**Supply—Cold**	**Supply—Hot**
Bathtub	1-1/2″	1-1/4″	1/2″	1/2″
Bidet	1-1/2″	1-1/2″	1/2″	1/2″
Toilet	3″	2″	3/8″	—
Lavatory	1-1/2″	1-1/4″	3/8″	3/8″
Service Sink	2″	1-1/4″	1/2″	1/2″
Shower	2″	1-1/4″	1/2″	1/2″
Laundry Tub	1-1/2″	1-1/4″	1/2″	1/2″
Floor Drain	2″	1-1/4″	—	—
Building Main	4″ (House Drain)	—	3/4″	—
Cold Water Main	—	—	3/4″	—
Hot Water Main	—	—	—	3/4″
Cold Water Branch	—	—	1/2″	—
Hot Water Branch	—	—	—	1/2″

Goodheart-Willcox Publisher

Figure 32-2. This table shows typical minimum sizes for waste, vent, and supply pipes.

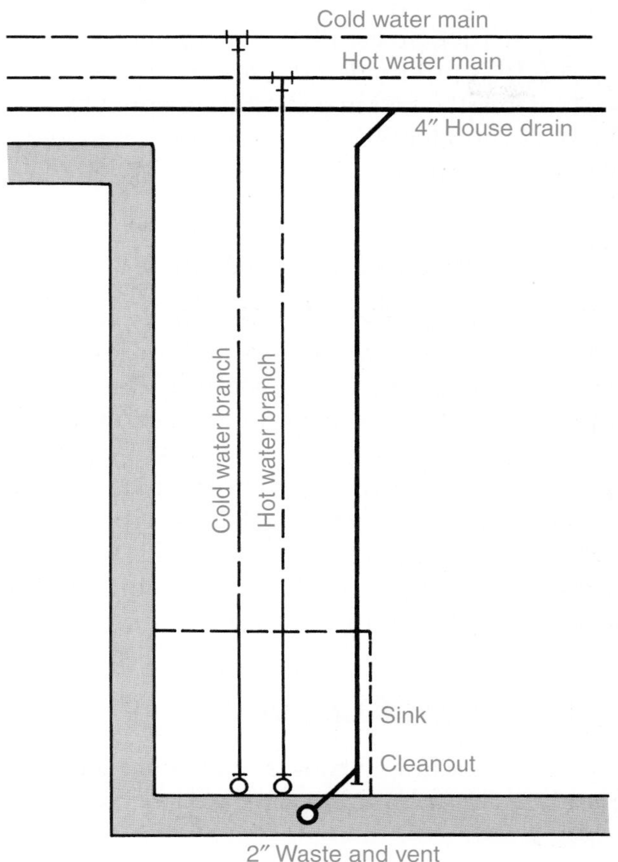

Goodheart-Willcox Publisher

Figure 32-3. Draw the lines for waste lines thicker than those for water supply lines to indicate the larger diameter of the waste pipes.

Care should be taken in locating the house drain and sewer so they are the correct height to connect properly with the public sewer or private septic system. The house drain should be no longer than necessary. Study all facets of the layout before deciding on the final location of the house drain and sewer.

Floor Drain Locations

Floor drains are usually located in basements. They are usually connected to the storm sewer or a dry well, not to the sanitary sewer system. Indicate drains with the proper symbol and show the location of the pipe leading to the storm sewer or dry well.

Water Supply Lines

The water supply begins at the city water main or private water source. Show the building main on the plumbing plan with the proper shutoff valves, meter, and size of pipe. Use the proper symbols. Also, show any required water softener, filter, water storage tank, or other treatment devices positioned along the building main. See **Figure 32-4**. Show the location of the water heater and identify it. Hose bibs and other plumbing fixtures that do not require softened or filtered water should be connected to the building main before it reaches the softener.

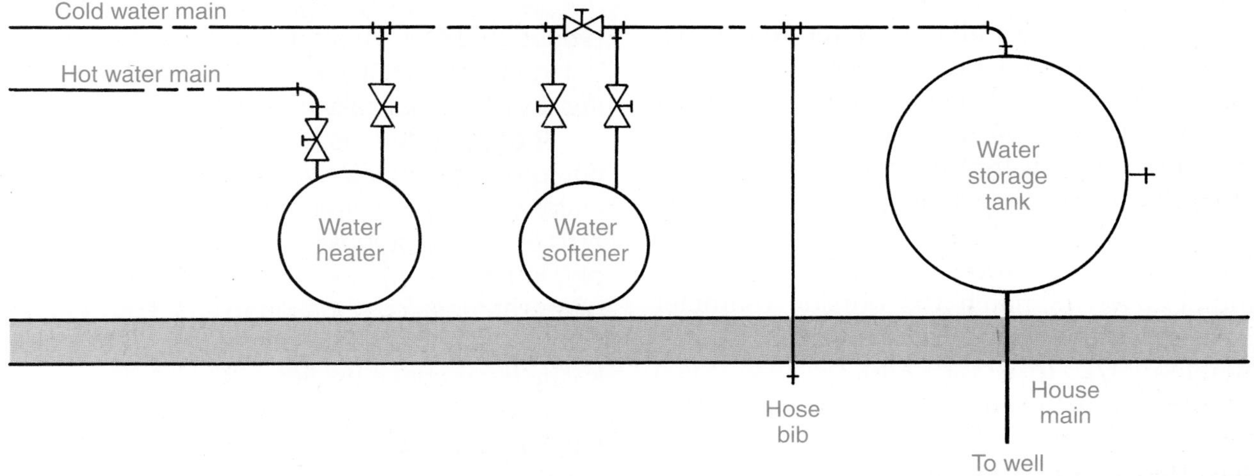

Goodheart-Willcox Publisher

Figure 32-4. This is typical supply piping for a home that requires a water storage tank, water softener, and water heater.

Shutoff valves should be provided for each plumbing fixture in the water supply system.

Identify the plumbing fixtures that require a water supply and determine the size of pipe needed for each. Each hot and cold water branch line should be sized so it will have the proper water-carrying capacity. Indicate the size of each line in the water supply system and specify the type of pipe to be installed.

Size and Type of Pipe

The proper pipe size for a given installation depends on the average amount of water used, peak loads, water pressure on the line, and length of the pipe run. Friction reduces the flow of water; therefore, larger pipe should be used for long runs. Rather than try to calculate the pipe size for each plumbing fixture and branch line in the house, refer to recommended minimum pipe sizes established by residential plumbing codes. Typical minimum sizes are shown in the table in **Figure 32-2**.

The plumbing plan should specify the type of pipe to be used throughout the system. Several types are available. It is advisable to check the local code to be sure that the type you wish to use is acceptable.

Copper pipe is a frequent choice for the water supply system. The pipe size is a nominal diameter that refers to the approximate inside diameter of the pipe. For example, a 1″ copper pipe, Type L, has a 1.025″ inside diameter (ID) and 1.125″ outside diameter (OD). Type L is a medium weight copper pipe; Type K is heavier and Type M is lighter. Type L is usually used for inside hot and cold water lines. Copper tubing with a designation of DWV is also available. It is thinner than Type M and is used in the sewage disposal system. DWV stands for "drain, waste, and vent."

In some areas, copper pipe has been largely replaced by chlorinated polyvinyl chloride (CPVC) or cross-linked polyethylene (PEX). CPVC is manufactured to match the outside diameter of corresponding copper tube sizes (CTS). It is available in 1/2″ to 2″ CTS and, because it is a thermoplastic material, it can be used for both hot and cold water. All of the model plumbing codes now accept CPVC for hot and cold water installations because it is resistant to corrosion, long-lasting, and cost-effective.

Like CPVC, PEX is sized to the outer diameter of copper tube sizes. PEX is available in 1/4″ to 3″ CTS. PEX pipe is flexible, and it comes both in straight lengths and in coils. It is accepted by all of the major model plumbing codes for residential water distribution.

Plumbing Fixture Schedule

A ***plumbing fixture schedule*** is useful in planning the plumbing system, ordering the plumbing fixtures, and installing the system. Information that is customarily shown on a plumbing fixture schedule includes the names of all plumbing fixtures for the residence, number required, identifying symbols, and pipe connection sizes. Also shown are remarks related to each item. A typical residential plumbing fixture schedule is shown in **Figure 32-5**.

Symbols and Legend

Use standard symbols whenever possible. Standard symbols are recognized and accepted

Green Architecture

Waterless Toilets

Waterless toilets have been used around the world for many years. In fact, you may have seen them in parks and other public facilities. Many people associate waterless toilets with pits in the ground and foul smells. However, the technology behind waterless toilets has changed and improved dramatically in recent years.

Today's waterless toilets are based on composting technology. In addition to using no water—a major environmental benefit—they also produce compost usable for flower gardens and landscaping. Several manufacturers now offer waterless/composting toilets. They employ various technologies to prevent foul odors and to safely decompose wastes.

To be safe and effective, waterless toilets have to be installed and maintained correctly. In addition, some local codes may restrict or forbid their use, so check with local authorities before installing them.

PLUMBING FIXTURE SCHEDULE										
IDENT. SYMBOL	TYPE OF FIXTURE	NO. REQ'D.	MANUFACTURER AND CATALOG NO.	PIPE CONNECTION SIZES						REMARKS
				C W	H W	S & W	VENT	TRAP	GAS	
WC_1	WATER CLOSET	1	ELJER "SILETTE" NO. E 5000 ONE-PIECE	3/8″	–	3″	2″	–	–	VITREOUS CHINA TWILIGHT BLUE
WC_2	WATER CLOSET	1	ELJER "SILETTE" NO. E 5000 ONE-PIECE	3/8″	–	3″	2″	–	–	VITREOUS CHINA TUSCAN TAN
T	BATHTUB	1	ELJER "RIVIERA" NO. E 1120	1/2″	1/2″	2″	1-1/2″	2″	–	ENAMELED CAST IRON TUSCAN TAN
L_1	LAVATORY	2	ELJER "BRENDA" NO. E 3328	1/2″	1/2″	2″	1-1/2″	1-1/2″	–	VITREOUS CHINA TUSCAN TAN
L_2	LAVATORY	1	ELJER "BARROW" NO. E 3471	1/2″	1/2″	2″	1-1/2″	1-1/2″	–	VITREOUS CHINA TWILIGHT BLUE
S	SINK	1	ELJER "KENTON" NO. E 2325	1/2″	1/2″	2″	1-1/2″	1-1/2″	–	ENAMELED CAST IRON WHITE 32″ × 20″
WS	WATER SOFTENER	1	SEARS "SERIES 60" NO. W 42 K 3482N	3/4″	–	–	–	–	–	17-1/2″ DIA. × 42″ HIGH DRAIN REQUIRED
WH	WATER HEATER	1	SEARS "MODEL 75" NO. 42 K 33741N	3/4″	3/4″	–	4″	–	1/2″	40 GAL. CAPACITY NATURAL GAS
CW	CLOTHES WASHER	1	WHIRLPOOL "SUPREME 80"	1/2″	1/2″	2″	1-1/2″	1-1/2″	–	WHITE
DW	DISH WASHER	1	WHIRLPOOL SSU 80	1/2″	1/2″	2″	1-1/2″	1-1/2″	–	WHITE
HB	HOSE BIB	3	CRANE B-106	3/4″	–	–	–	–	–	

Goodheart-Willcox Publisher

Figure 32-5. A typical residential plumbing fixture schedule.

by drafters, designers, contractors, and tradeworkers. If there is a chance that a symbol may not be standard or commonly used, explain the symbol in a legend. The legend should appear on the plan where the symbols are used. **Figure 32-6** shows some standard plumbing symbols. It is important to note that symbols are not usually drawn to the exact size of the feature that they represent. Take care to choose an appropriate symbol size and use the same size throughout the drawing.

Notes

Frequently, information other than that represented by symbols, dimensions, and specifications is needed to describe a plumbing installation. This information is recorded in general notes on the plumbing plan. The notes are located above the title block or in another prominent place. Notes may refer to materials, installation procedures, or any other facet of the plumbing system. When more than one drawing is needed for the plumbing plan, notes must appear on the drawing to which they refer.

Procedures for Drawing a Plumbing Plan

Several decisions and calculations must be made before the plumbing plan can be drawn. The exact plumbing fixtures to be used should be determined. Manufacturer catalogs are good sources of this information. The exact placement of each plumbing fixture must be decided. The location of public utilities, such as the public sewer, water, storm drains, and gas, must be established. The site plan usually provides this information. After initial information has been gathered, the drawing may proceed.

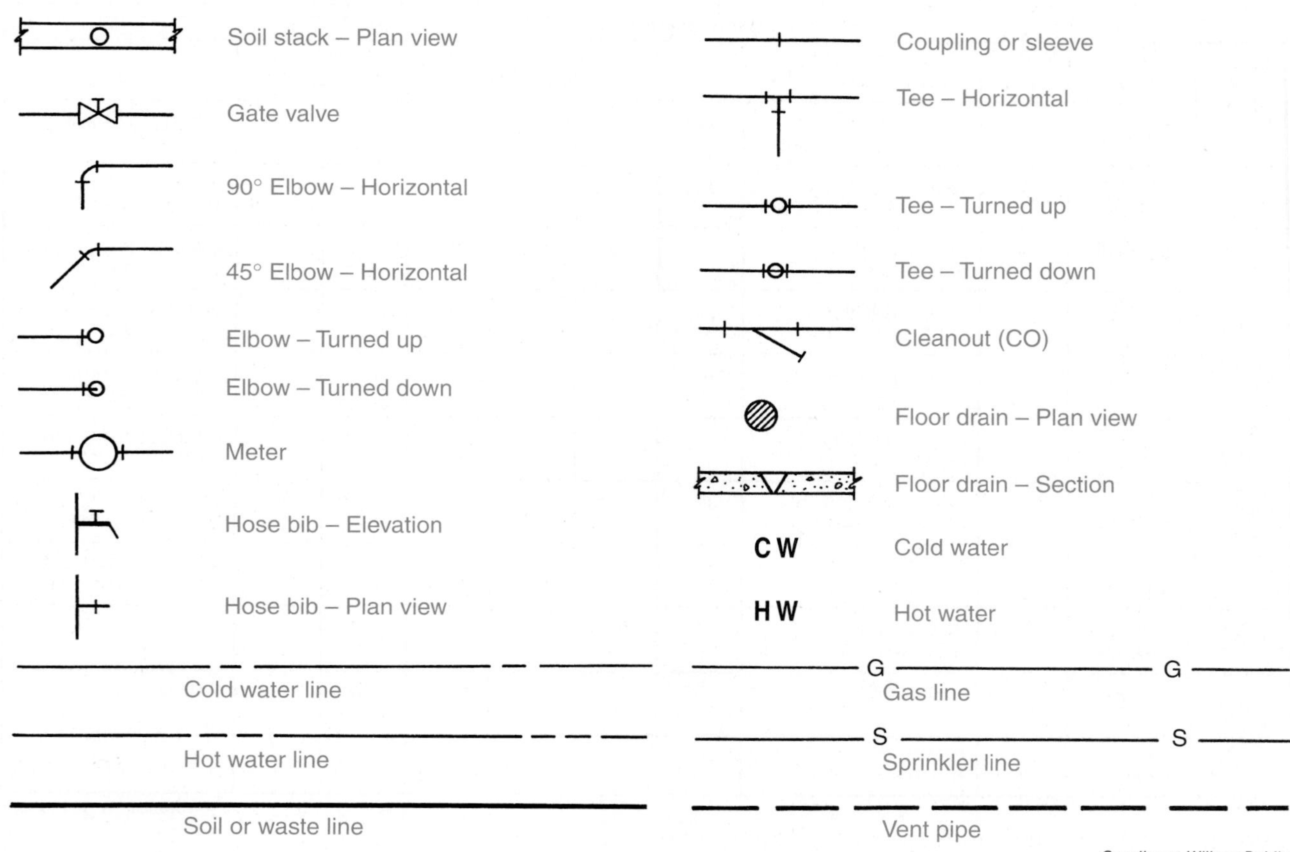

Figure 32-6. Standard plumbing symbols.

Procedure Manual Drafting

Drawing a Plumbing Plan

The following general steps are suggested for drawing a plumbing plan using manual drafting techniques. However, remember to follow office practice in your company to determine exactly which steps to use and in what order.

1. Trace the floor plan, showing only the exterior and interior walls, doors and windows, and features that relate to the plumbing plan. Be sure to indicate plumbing (stack) walls as necessary. On the plumbing plan, plumbing walls are drawn as 2×6 walls. Steps 1 and 2 are shown in **Figure 32-7**.
2. Draw the symbols for all plumbing fixtures that are to be connected to the house plumbing system. Plumbing fixtures may be drawn using a hidden line to draw attention to them.
3. Locate and draw the house drain, soil stacks, and vent stacks. Be sure to include cleanouts. Steps 3 and 4 are shown in **Figure 32-8**.
4. Connect all plumbing fixtures to the house drain. Show all fittings and secondary vents that are used.
5. Locate and draw the building main for the water supply system. Connect the water supply piping to the water heater, water softener, and hose bibs. Steps 5 through 8 are shown in **Figure 32-9**.
6. Draw the cold and hot water mains. Include shutoff valves where they are required. Draw the cold and hot water lines parallel where possible.
7. Locate and draw all cold water and hot water branch lines. Include shutoff valves. Use the proper symbols.

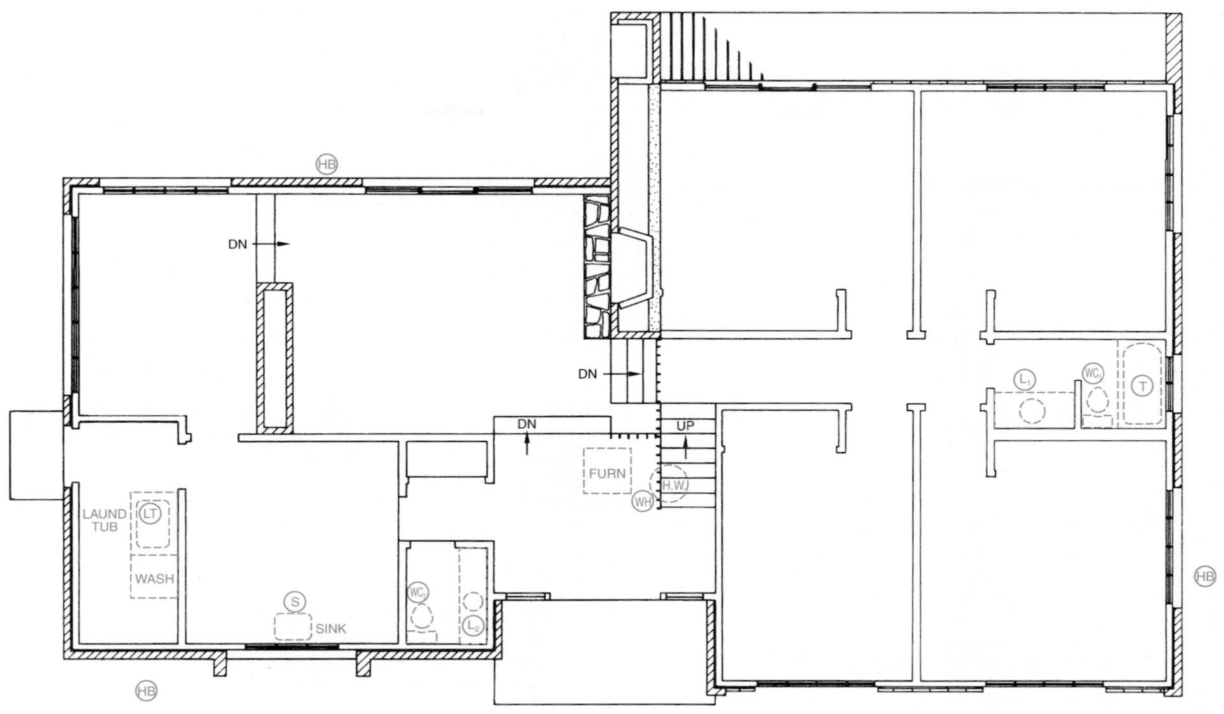

Goodheart-Willcox Publisher

Figure 32-7. The floor plan has been traced and the plumbing fixtures that are to be connected to the plumbing system are drawn as hidden lines.

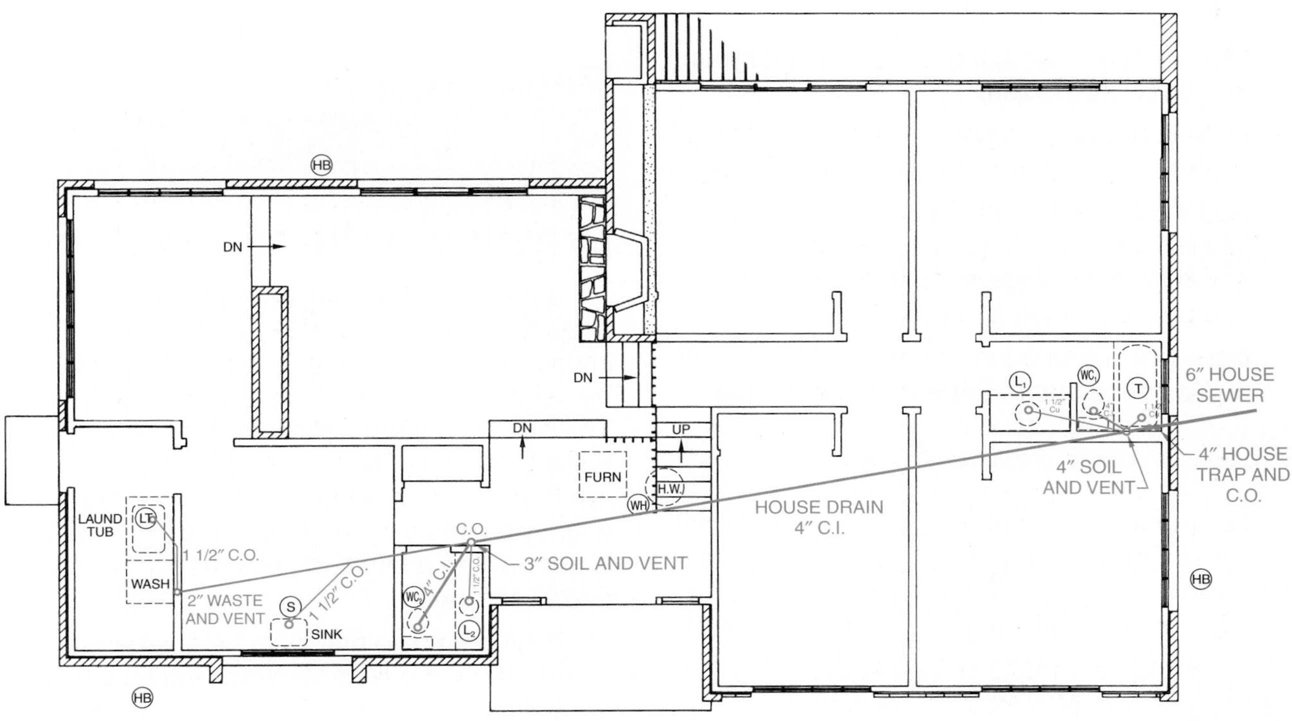

Goodheart-Willcox Publisher

Figure 32-8. The waste pipes, including drains, soil stacks, vent stacks, and cleanouts, have been added to the drawing. Notice how the pipe material, such as copper (Cu) and cast iron (CI), is indicated.

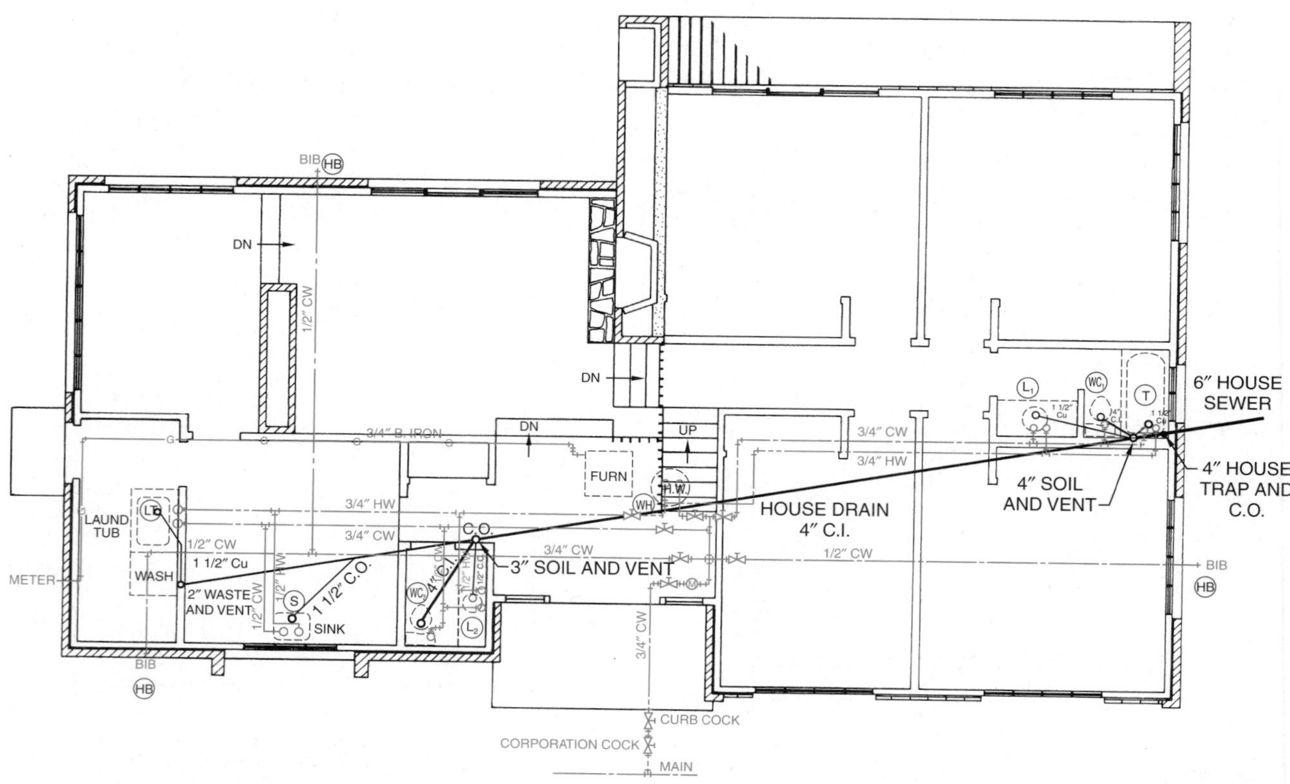

Goodheart-Willcox Publisher

Figure 32-9. The water supply system is added to the drawing. Shutoff valves are included, and labels are added as necessary.

8. Identify each element of the plumbing system and show pipe sizes.
9. Include a plumbing fixture schedule, symbol legend, and any required general notes.
10. Add the scale and title block to the drawing. Check the entire drawing for accuracy and omissions. **Figure 32-10** shows the completed plumbing plan.

Repeat this procedure for each floor or level of the house that requires a plumbing plan.

Be sure to include any other appropriate piping on the plumbing plan. This may vary from one house to the next. For example, piping for a ***central vacuum system*** should be shown on the plumbing plan. **Figure 32-11** shows the power unit for such a system and a pictorial view of the inlets around a house.

Procedure
CADD

Drawing a Plumbing Plan

Standard CADD software can be used to develop the plumbing plan. CADD programs intended specifically for piping drafting can also be used to design residential plumbing systems. The main advantage of specialized software is the inclusion of a symbol library with piping symbols, which eliminates the need to design your own symbols. The procedure provided here is for drawing a plumbing plan using standard CADD software.

1. If the plumbing plan is to be a separate file, open the floor plan drawing and save it with a new name. This file will become the plumbing plan. If you are combining the plumbing plan with the floor plan, create a set of layers specifically for the plumbing plan.

Lock or freeze all other layers. Check to be sure plumbing (stack) walls are drawn at their correct width.

2. Insert symbols for all plumbing fixtures that are to be connected to the house plumbing system. Symbols should be placed on their own layer. Plumbing fixtures may be drawn using a hidden line to draw attention to them.
3. Locate and draw the house drain, soil stacks, and vent stacks. Be sure to include cleanouts. Waste lines are wide lines (0.7 mm) and should be placed on a separate layer to facilitate correct plotting.
4. Connect all plumbing fixtures to the house drain. Show all fittings and secondary vents.
5. Locate and draw the building main for the water supply system. Connect the water supply piping to the water heater, water softener, and hose bibs. Water supply lines are thin lines (0.35 mm) and should be placed on a separate layer to facilitate correct plotting.
6. Draw the cold and hot water mains. Include shutoff valves where they are required. Draw the cold and hot water lines parallel where possible.
7. Locate and draw all cold water and hot water branch lines. Include shutoff valves. Use the proper symbols and place the symbols on their own layer.

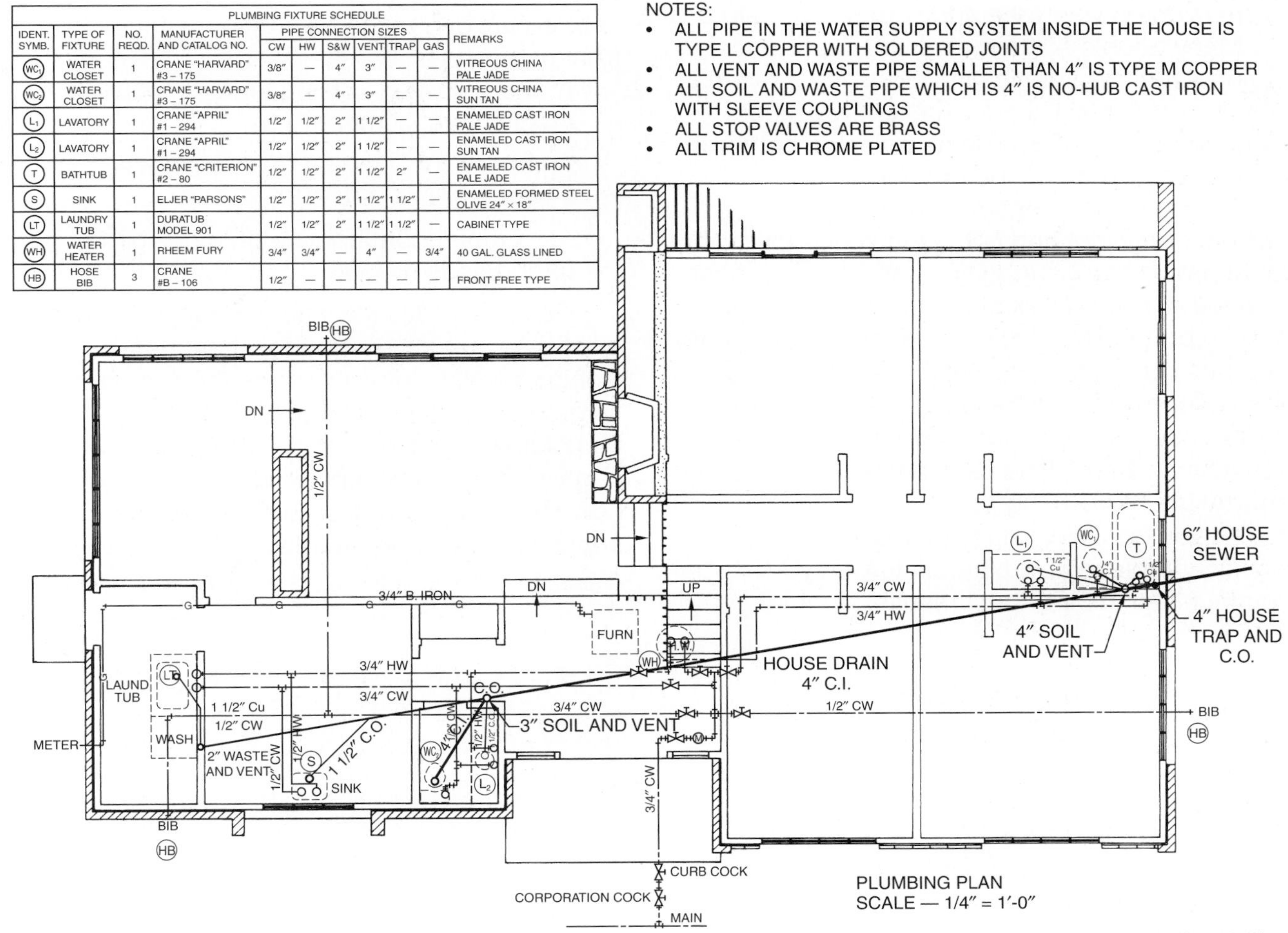

PLUMBING FIXTURE SCHEDULE										
IDENT. SYMB.	TYPE OF FIXTURE	NO. REQD.	MANUFACTURER AND CATALOG NO.	PIPE CONNECTION SIZES						REMARKS
				CW	HW	S&W	VENT	TRAP	GAS	
WC_1	WATER CLOSET	1	CRANE "HARVARD" #3 – 175	3/8″	—	4″	3″	—	—	VITREOUS CHINA PALE JADE
WC_2	WATER CLOSET	1	CRANE "HARVARD" #3 – 175	3/8″	—	4″	3″	—	—	VITREOUS CHINA SUN TAN
L_1	LAVATORY	1	CRANE "APRIL" #1 – 294	1/2″	1/2″	2″	1 1/2″	—	—	ENAMELED CAST IRON PALE JADE
L_2	LAVATORY	1	CRANE "APRIL" #1 – 294	1/2″	1/2″	2″	1 1/2″	—	—	ENAMELED CAST IRON SUN TAN
T	BATHTUB	1	CRANE "CRITERION" #2 – 80	1/2″	1/2″	2″	1 1/2″	2″	—	ENAMELED CAST IRON PALE JADE
S	SINK	1	ELJER "PARSONS"	1/2″	1/2″	2″	1 1/2″	1 1/2″	—	ENAMELED FORMED STEEL OLIVE 24″ × 18″
LT	LAUNDRY TUB	1	DURATUB MODEL 901	1/2″	1/2″	2″	1 1/2″	1 1/2″	—	CABINET TYPE
WH	WATER HEATER	1	RHEEM FURY	3/4″	3/4″	—	4″	—	3/4″	40 GAL. GLASS LINED
HB	HOSE BIB	3	CRANE #B – 106	1/2″	—	—	—	—	—	FRONT FREE TYPE

Goodheart-Willcox Publisher

Figure 32-10. The plumbing plan is complete.

8. Identify each element of the plumbing system and show pipe sizes.
9. Include a plumbing fixture schedule, symbol legend, and any required labels and general notes.
10. Add the scale and title block to the drawing. Check the entire drawing for accuracy and omissions.

Repeat this procedure for each floor or level of the house that requires a plumbing plan.

Employability

Nonverbal Communication

The primary forms of communication are verbal and nonverbal. *Verbal communication* involves speaking, listening, and writing. *Nonverbal communication* is sending and receiving messages without the use of words. It involves body language, which includes the expression on your face and your body posture.

Many people fail to realize the importance of nonverbal communication. Even if your verbal communication skills are excellent, your body language can confuse clients or leave them with a negative opinion of you or your work.

For example, suppose you create a new design for a client and bring it to your supervisor for approval. Your supervisor says, "This is good; I think the client will like it." If the supervisor is smiling or nodding, it is easy to tell that she really approves of the design. But if she is frowning, she is sending you a "mixed signal." Does the design need improvement? Are there errors that you haven't seen? She said the work was good, so why is she frowning?

As you can see, body language can play a significant role in how others interpret your verbal communications. For best results, whether you are communicating with coworkers, a supervisor, or clients, always be sure your nonverbal message agrees with your verbal message.

Activity

Conduct research online to find out more about positive and negative nonverbal communication. Then work with a classmate to role-play one of the following scenarios in front of the class:

- A designer interviewing for a job at an architectural company
- A supervisor listening to an employee present a new product idea
- A coworker commenting on a design that he or she does not like

Decide in advance whether you will depict positive or negative nonverbal communication. Conduct a class discussion on the scenario. If you employed positive communication techniques, what were they? If you employed negative communication techniques, discuss how the person could have improved the impression he or she made.

Photo courtesy of Broan-NuTone, LLC

A

Illustration courtesy of Broan-NuTone, LLC

B

Figure 32-11. A—The power unit for the central vacuum system in this home is located in the garage. B—Typical locations for inlets in a house. The piping for this system, shown here in color (purple), should be shown on the plumbing plan.

Parametric Modeling Creating a Plumbing Plan

A residential plumbing plan is created in parametric modeling by placing 3D components representing the required plumbing equipment in the home. The plumbing system must be carefully planned so that the piping does not interfere with the components of other systems, such as electrical conduit and the supply and return ducts in a heating and cooling system.

The plumbing plan is based on the floor plan and shows the layout of waste lines, supply lines, and plumbing fixtures. Typically, plumbing fixtures are added by the architectural drafter to the floor plan when it is created. Depending on the project, the existing plumbing fixtures may be used when creating the plumbing plan in a new project. For example, if the plumbing engineer is responsible for creating the plumbing plan, a new project can be started using a mechanical or plumbing template. The architectural model is then imported and a special copying function is used to copy the plumbing fixtures from the imported model into the project. A link between the files is established so that the status of the plumbing fixtures in the architectural model is monitored. If a change is made in the architectural project, an alert is issued in the plumbing project. The plumbing engineer can then review the change to determine the effects on the plumbing system. This facilitates collaboration between different disciplines involved in the design project. In some cases, the plumbing engineer may decide to insert different plumbing fixtures or modify the existing fixtures to meet the specific requirements for the plumbing system.

The following procedure describes the steps for creating a plumbing plan. This is a typical sequence, but specific steps will vary depending on the program used.

1. Use the appropriate project template to start a new mechanical or plumbing project. Establish the view that will be used to create the plumbing plan. Use the floor plan from the architectural model as an underlay to create the plumbing plan. If appropriate, copy the plumbing fixtures from the architectural model into the project. Otherwise, insert the appropriate components to locate the plumbing fixtures. Ensure that the fixtures include the required sanitary and supply connectors for connecting waste and supply piping. If needed, create the connectors or modify existing fixtures to provide the proper size connectors.
2. Adjust the visibility in the plumbing plan view to remove any items that should not appear in the plumbing plan. In addition, adjust the view range to display portions of the system that are below the elevation associated with the view.
3. Create systems in the project to organize the different groups of components in the plumbing system. Examples of typical systems are a cold water system, hot water system, and sanitary system. Assign the appropriate display color to each system. Typically, a number of default systems are available for use when a project is started with a mechanical or plumbing template.

4. Create the pipe runs used for the house drain, stacks, and vents. Use the **PIPE** command. Specify the appropriate pipe size and material for each run. Set the appropriate elevation and slope for the house drain. Create the vertical stacks and vents used for fixtures. For each vertical vent, specify the base level and height. Pipe fittings, such as tee and elbow fittings, are usually generated automatically by the program when creating offsets or turns in pipe runs. If needed, modify the default pipe fittings or place new fittings after creating the pipe runs.
5. Create the piping to connect each plumbing fixture to the house drain. Specify the appropriate pipe size and material. Ensure that the sanitary connectors for plumbing fixtures are properly sized. If needed, adjust pipe fittings in the sanitary piping after creating the connections.
6. Create the pipe run used for the building main. Specify the appropriate pipe size and material. Connect the supply piping to the water heater. Create the pipe runs for the cold water and hot water branch lines. For each run of pipe, set the appropriate elevation and specify vertical offsets as needed. If needed, adjust pipe fittings after creating the pipe runs.
7. Connect each plumbing fixture to the appropriate branch supply lines. Create the required supply piping to make the cold water and hot water connections. Switch to a 3D view to verify that the piping has been created correctly.
8. If necessary, insert shutoff valves and fixture traps. These can typically be placed as components. These items can also be shown on section drawings or details using view-specific 2D detail lines. This is an alternative to modeling each item.
9. Insert tags to identify pipe sizes and fixtures. Adjust the position of tags and add leaders to tags where needed.
10. Create a plumbing fixture schedule. If needed, adjust the schedule format to display the number required for each type of fixture. If required, create additional schedules for pipes and pipe fittings.
11. Create a new sheet for the plumbing plan. Insert the plumbing plan view onto the sheet. If needed, adjust the placement of text for the view title and scale. Insert the plumbing fixture schedule onto the sheet.
12. Look over your work to be sure that you are finished. When you are sure the plan is complete, print or plot the sheet.

Summary

- The plumbing system should be coordinated with the electrical and climate control systems.
- The plumbing plan includes the waste lines, soil stacks, and vent stacks, water supply lines, drain and plumbing fixture locations, and size and type of pipe to be used.
- Proper location and sufficient size are the major considerations in planning the waste lines.
- The proper pipe size for a given installation depends on the average amount of water used, peak loads, water pressure on the line, and length of the pipe run.
- A plumbing fixture schedule is useful in planning the plumbing system, ordering the plumbing fixtures, and installing the system.

Internet Resources

Jacuzzi
Manufacturer of bath fixtures

Kinetico Home Water Systems
Whole-house residential water treatment systems

Kohler
Plumbing fixtures

Moen
Plumbing fixtures

RainSoft Water Treatment Systems
Residential water treatment systems

Review Questions

Answer the following questions using the information in this chapter.

1. Explain the purpose of a plumbing plan.
2. Name two features that may be found on a plumbing plan that are not related to the water and waste removal system, water supply system, or plumbing fixtures.
3. Proper plumbing symbols should be used on a plumbing plan and identified in a _____.
4. How many plumbing plans are needed for a typical residential home?
5. Name two major considerations in planning the waste lines.
6. What part of the plumbing system is usually designed first?
7. How many main stacks must a residential home have?
8. Waste lines are not under pressure and depend on _____ to move the waste.
9. Why is larger diameter pipe needed for long runs?
10. List four types of copper pipe that are commonly used in residential plumbing systems.
11. To what does DWV refer?
12. What information is included on a plumbing fixture schedule?

Suggested Activities

1. Select a floor plan from a magazine or newspaper. Draw the floor plan using CADD. Then, design the water and waste removal systems. Determine the pipe size required for each drain and plumbing fixture. Specify the type of material to be used. Draw the plan to 1/4″ = 1′-0″ scale. Use the proper linetype and weight. Add necessary notes.
2. Using the same floor plan as in Activity 1, design the water supply system. Determine the pipe size for each branch and main line. Draw the plan in CADD using the proper symbols, linetype, and line weight.
3. Sometimes an isometric drawing is made of the entire plumbing system to further illustrate the layout. If your CADD system has isometric capabilities, create an isometric drawing of the plumbing system you designed in Activity 1 and Activity 2. Do not include the walls and floors of the house, but identify the important features of the system.
4. Visit a local plumbing shop or home improvement center and obtain samples of typical plumbing materials used in residential construction. Identify each item and explain where it might be used in the plumbing system.

5. Study Figure 32-7 and list the plumbing fixtures and appliances connected to the plumbing system. Using manufacturer catalogs or websites, select appliances and fixtures for the house. Create a plumbing fixture schedule.
6. Using CADD, draw standard plumbing symbols. See Figure 32-6 for examples. Add these symbols to your symbol library.

Problem Solving Case Study

A family of six has come to your architectural office in Springerville, Arizona, to discuss ideas for their new two-story residence. They want to build the house on four acres of flat land in a rural area 25 miles north of Springerville. They want the house to have at least five bedrooms, with room for expansion. Design a home for this family and create a floor plan. Remember to allow for stack walls where needed. Then create a plumbing plan for the residence. Print and display your floor plan and plumbing plan.

ADDA Certification Prep

The following questions are presented in the style used in the American Design Drafting Association (ADDA) Drafter Certification Test. Answer the questions using the information in this chapter.

1. Which of the following statements about plumbing plans are true?
   A. The water supply for a residence begins at the house shutoff valve.
   B. The plumbing plan includes the waste lines, soil stacks, and vent stacks, water supply lines, drain and plumbing fixture locations, and size and type of pipe to be used.
   C. The waste line network is usually designed first and then the rest of the plumbing system is planned around it.
   D. The plumbing plan should specify the type of pipe to be used throughout the system.
2. Which of the following statements are *false*?
   A. The exact placement of each plumbing fixture does not matter, as long as each fixture is shown on the plumbing plan.
   B. Gas lines are not included on a plumbing plan.
   C. Type K copper pipe is heavier than Type M copper pipe.
   D. Notes are used on a plumbing plan to convey information not provided by symbols, dimensions, and specifications.
3. Match each type of pipe with its description.

   Types of Pipe: 1. Copper, 2. CPVC, 3. PEX
   A. A metal pipe that uses soldered joints.
   B. A flexible plastic pipe used for residential distribution lines.
   C. A thermoplastic pipe used for cold and hot water lines in residential applications.

Curricular Connections

1. **Language Arts.** Conduct research online to find CADD programs designed specifically for plumbing system design. Write a report comparing and contrasting the features of two of these programs.
2. **Social Science.** The history of the flush toilet fixture is an interesting subject. Research the invention of the flush toilet and compose a three-page written report on the history and development of different flush toilet designs. Address the impact of different designs on the environment.

STEM Connections

1. **Technology.** A residential water and waste removal system is just one part of a larger system in most urban and suburban areas. Conduct research to find out where wastewater goes when it leaves homes in your community via the public sewer system. How is the water treated? What steps are taken to ensure public safety?

Communicating about Architecture

1. **Reading and Speaking.** With a partner, make flash cards for the different types of plumbing symbols shown in this chapter. Use symbols from a CADD symbol library. For each symbol, make a printout and mount it on the front of the card. On the back of the card, write the symbol name. Take turns quizzing one another on the names of the symbols.
2. **Reading and Writing.** While working with a partner, look at Figure 32-3 and describe the important information being conveyed by that figure. Through your collaboration, develop what you and your partner believe is the most interesting verbal description of the importance of the figure. Present your findings to the class.

Chapter 33

Residential Climate Control

Objectives

After completing this chapter, you will be able to:

- Discuss the components of a complete climate control system.
- List the advantages and disadvantages of various types of residential heating systems and cooling systems.
- Explain the need for humidifiers, dehumidifiers, and filters in residential climate control systems.
- Perform heat loss calculations for a typical residential structure.

Key Terms

British thermal unit (Btu)
climate control system
counterflow furnace
design temperature difference
electric radiant system
forced-air system
geothermal energy
geothermal heat pump
heat loss
heat pump
horizontal furnace
hydronic radiant system
hydronic system
infiltration
insulation
one-pipe system
plenum
relative humidity
resistivity
R-factor
solar orientation
thermostat
U-factor
upflow furnace
ventilation
weather stripping

Keeping our homes warm in the winter and cool in the summer is an important aspect of life in today's society. New homes are being built with complete ***climate control systems*** that include not only temperature control, but also humidity control, air circulation, and air cleaning.

Temperature Control

Temperature control includes both heating and cooling. Although many homes have heating and cooling systems to maintain the temperature of the home, proper planning at the home design stage can help improve the efficiency with which temperature control is accomplished.

Design Considerations

A well-designed home includes several features that help reduce the need for mechanical heating and cooling. These features include insulation, ventilation, and orientation of the house, among others.

Insulation

Adequate insulation that is properly installed is of prime importance. ***Insulation*** prevents heat or cold from transferring from one location to another. It helps to keep the house warm in winter and cool in summer.

Insulation should be placed in the ceiling, in the exterior walls, and under the floor when the house has a crawl space, as shown in **Figure 33-1**. Houses that are built on slab foundations should

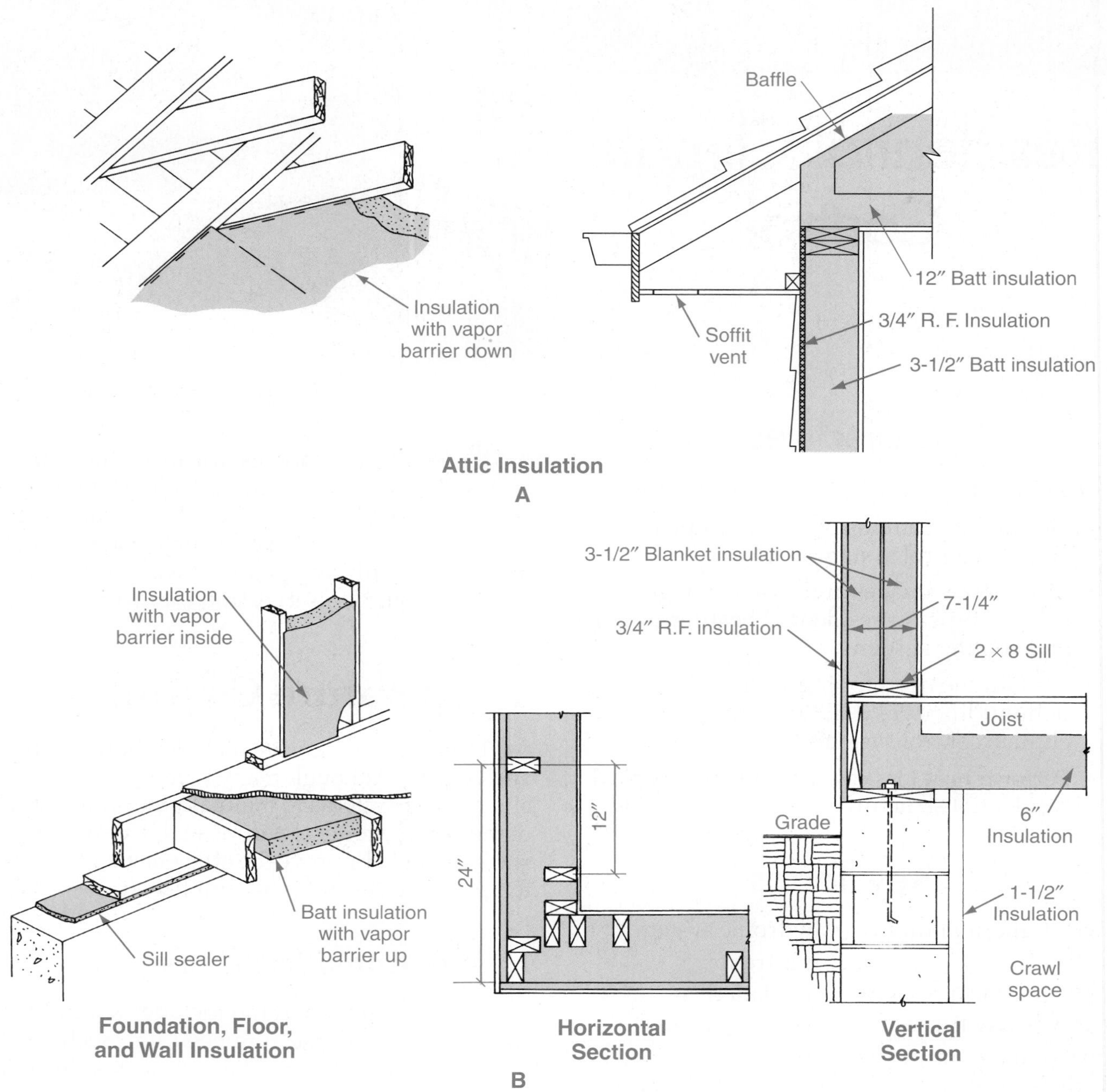

Figure 33-1. Adequate insulation must be installed in several locations. A—In the ceiling and soffit areas. B—In foundations, floors, and walls.

have rigid foam insulation along the inside of the foundation wall and horizontally along the perimeter of the floor. See **Figure 33-2**.

Ventilation

Ventilation is another important factor in temperature control. ***Ventilation*** reduces the temperature and moisture content in the house, crawl space, and attic by replacing the air in a space with fresh outside air. See **Figure 33-3**. If the attic and crawl space do not have the proper amount of ventilation, moisture is likely to condense and cause damage. If the attic is hot and moist, the house will be more difficult to cool. **Figure 33-4** shows an attic fan and how it can be used to ventilate the attic space.

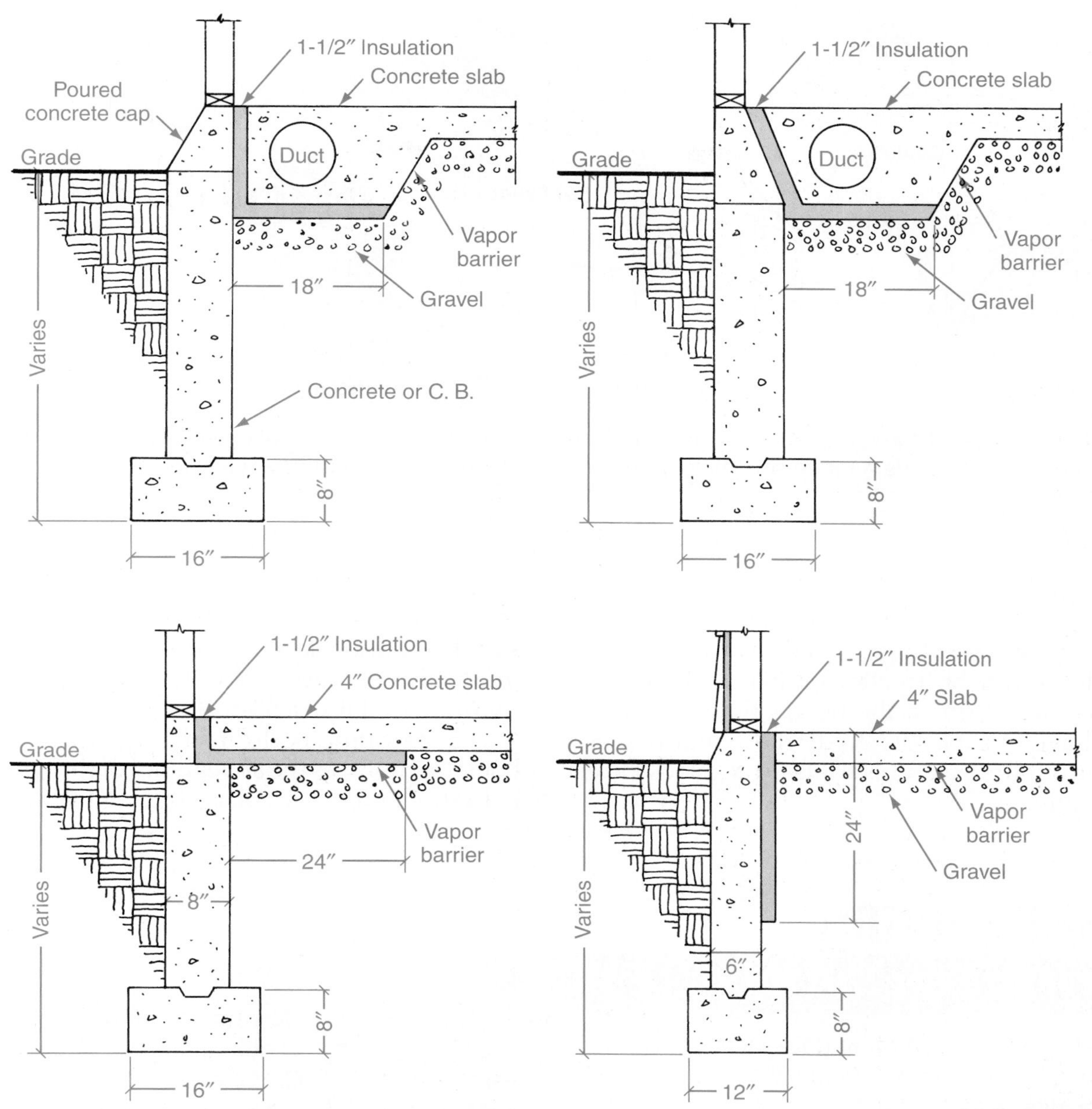

Goodheart-Willcox Publisher

Figure 33-2. Slab foundations should be insulated and have vapor barriers to reduce heat loss and moisture condensation.

Solar Orientation

A third factor that affects the temperature of a home is the ***solar orientation*** of the house. This is how the house is located on the lot in relation to the sun. The west walls of the house should be protected from the sun in the summer. This may be accomplished with trees or a garage to shade the west wall. In cold climates, an effort should be made to place all large areas of glass on the south side of the house away from the cold winter north winds and in position to take advantage of the winter sun.

Other Factors

Other factors also have a bearing on the efficiency of the temperature control system. For example, ***weather stripping*** seals small cracks around doors and movable windows to reduce heat loss. For non-movable windows, caulk is used for the same purpose.

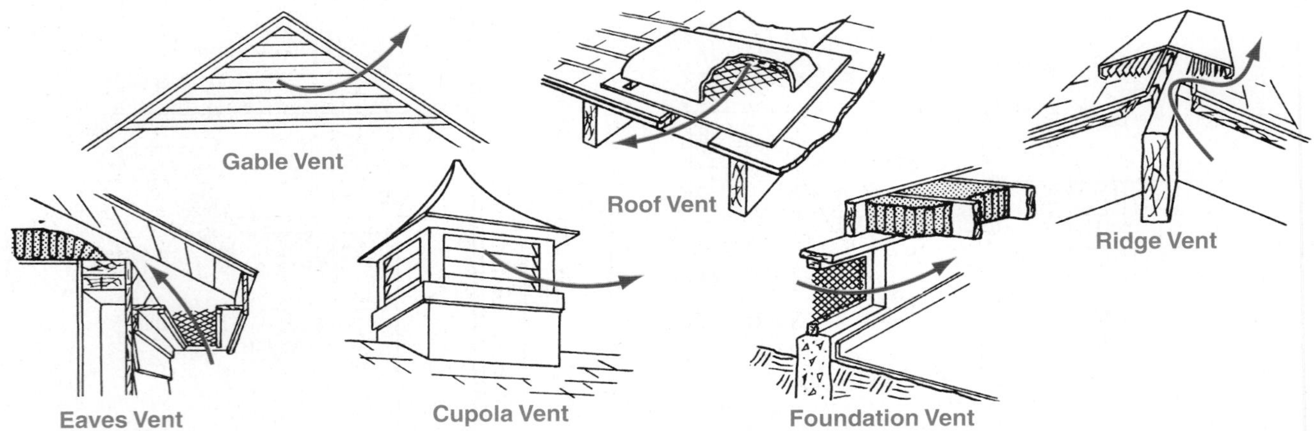

Figure 33-3. The attic and crawl space should be ventilated for more efficient heating and cooling. Insufficient ventilation may cause damage to sheathing and other structural members due to excess moisture.

Insulated window glass reduces heat loss or gain and lowers the cost of heating and cooling. See **Figure 33-5**. In extremely warm climates, windows can be treated or glazed to further reduce heat gain in the house. Some windows also have miniblinds inside the window glass. The miniblinds can be adjusted to block direct sunlight.

Roof color also makes a difference. Light-colored roofing materials absorb less heat from the sun than dark-colored materials. Houses located in a warm climate generally have light-colored roofing. See **Figure 33-6**.

Landscaping performs many functions for a home. It improves the appearance of the home and helps hold the soil in place and controls erosion.

Employability
Attitude on the Job

Your attitude can often determine your success in your job. Your *attitude* is your outlook on life. It is reflected by how you react to the events and people around you. A smile and courteous behavior can make customers and fellow employees feel good about themselves and you. Customers prefer to do business in friendly environments. Being friendly may take some effort on your part, but it does pay off.

Enthusiasm spreads easily from one person to another. Usually, *enthusiasm* means a person enjoys what he or she is doing. In an architectural office, enthusiasm builds a team spirit for working together.

People who do a good job feel pride in their work. They feel a sense of accomplishment and a desire to achieve more. This attitude can inspire others as well.

Activity

Consider the following scenario. Explain what effect each person's attitude had on the other person. Then rewrite the scenario so that both people have attitudes that contribute to a quality product and a good office environment.

Scenario: Jayme is working on a final set of plans for a client. Her supervisor, Clarissa, walks up and says, "Aren't those plans finished yet? The client will be here in 30 minutes!" Jayme replies, "I didn't know until after lunch that this client would be here today. I thought his appointment was for tomorrow. I'll try to have it done today, but I doubt it will be finished within 30 minutes." Clarissa says, "I sent you an e-mail about this 20 minutes ago, and those plans must be finished in time. Please have the plans ready in the conference room within 30 minutes."

Green Architecture

Solar Attic Fans

Attic fans have been used for decades to reduce the heat buildup in a home's attic space. Typically, the fan is placed on the roof. It draws air in through existing vents and forces it through the fan to the outside of the home. This air exchange helps cool the attic space, which in turn reduces air conditioning costs in the summer. In humid climates, attic fans can also reduce mold- and rot-producing moisture buildup in the attic.

In the past, attic fans have been electrically powered. Although homeowners saw a net decrease in their electricity bills during the hot summer months, they were still using electricity to power the fan. Today, solar attic fans are available that require no electricity to run. This makes solar attic fans a very Earth-friendly alternative for reducing heat buildup while also reducing dependence on nonrenewable energy sources.

Broan-NuTone, A Nortek Company

Figure 33-4. Proper attic ventilation is needed to reduce moisture and aid cooling in warm weather. An attic fan can improve attic ventilation.

If planned carefully, landscaping can also be used to block cold winds and provide shade, as shown in **Figure 33-7**.

Cooling Systems

Cooling systems remove heat from a building and provide cool, clean, dehumidified air. This allows a home to be comfortable in warm, humid weather. Also, since windows are closed while the cooling system is on, infiltration of dirt, pollen, and dust is reduced.

Central Air Conditioners

A central air conditioner is the most efficient type of residential cooling system. Heat pumps are frequently used to cool homes as well.

As room air is cooled, moisture condenses on the evaporator coil. The water is then drained away. This process dehumidifies the air and increases the comfort level inside the house.

The cooled and dried air is moved to various parts of the living space through a system of ducts. If a forced-air furnace is present, the ducts of the heating system may be used. The furnace blower is then used to move the air through the ducts. Otherwise, an independent blower and ductwork are required.

The most common residential cooling system is the compressor-cycle system. This system uses the heating and cooling of a compressed chemical refrigerant to cool air. See **Figure 33-8**. Low-pressure, high-temperature refrigerant vapor passes through the compressor, where it is pressurized. The high-pressure, high-temperature gas then travels through the condenser, where it cools to a liquid state. The high-pressure, low-temperature liquid then travels through an orifice. This changes the refrigerant to a low-pressure, low-temperature liquid. The refrigerant then passes through the evaporator coil, where it

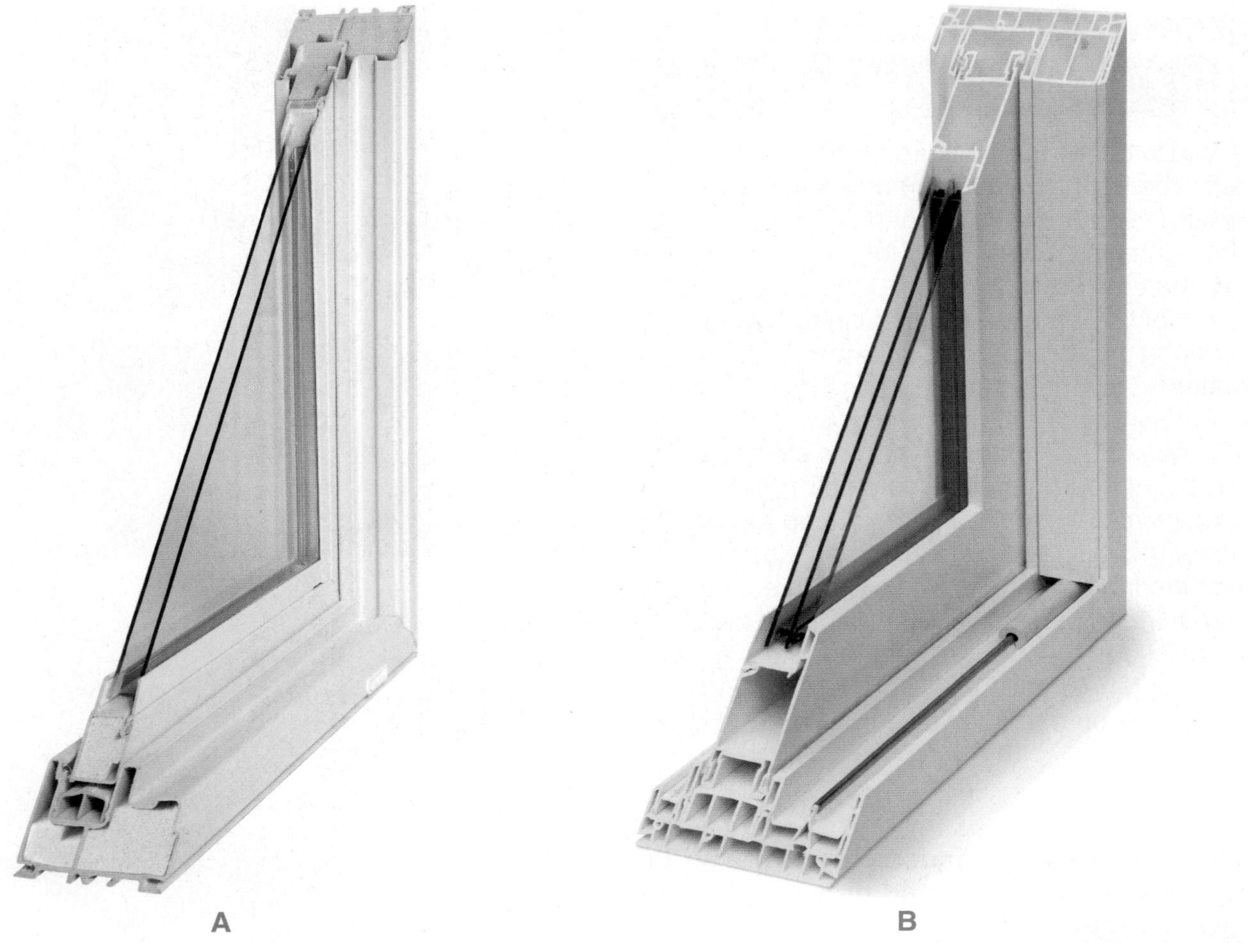

Pella® Windows and Doors

Figure 33-5. Cutaway views of insulated glass windows. A—Double-pane insulated window. B—Triple-pane insulated window.

removes heat from the air in the home as it changes into a gas again. This low-pressure, high-temperature gas returns to the compressor and the cycle begins again.

Compressor-cycle units normally have two separate components. The compressor and condenser are in a separate unit that is located outside the home. See **Figure 33-9**. These are the "hot" parts of the unit, so they are placed outside the house. The cooling coils are mounted in the ductwork of the house.

Room Air Conditioners

Room air conditioners contain a compressor, condenser, evaporator coil, and fan all in one unit. They can be installed in a window or in a wall opening designed for the unit. The condenser and compressor are located in the unit in a way such that they are outside the living space. See **Figure 33-10**. Room air conditioners should be well covered during cool weather because cold air can enter the room through the unit.

Heating Systems

Heating systems are usually one of four basic types: forced-air, hydronic, electric radiant, and heat pumps. To choose the right system for a particular home, you will need to consider:

- Availability of fuels
- Temperature variations
- Cost of installation and maintenance
- Type of house
- Owner's personal preference

FloridaStock/Shutterstock.com

Figure 33-6. The light-colored roofing on the homes in this south Florida community helps reflect heat, keeping the homes cooler in hot weather.

ARENA Creative/Shutterstock.com

Figure 33-7. Well-placed landscaping can help protect a home from winter winds as well as from the hot summer sun.

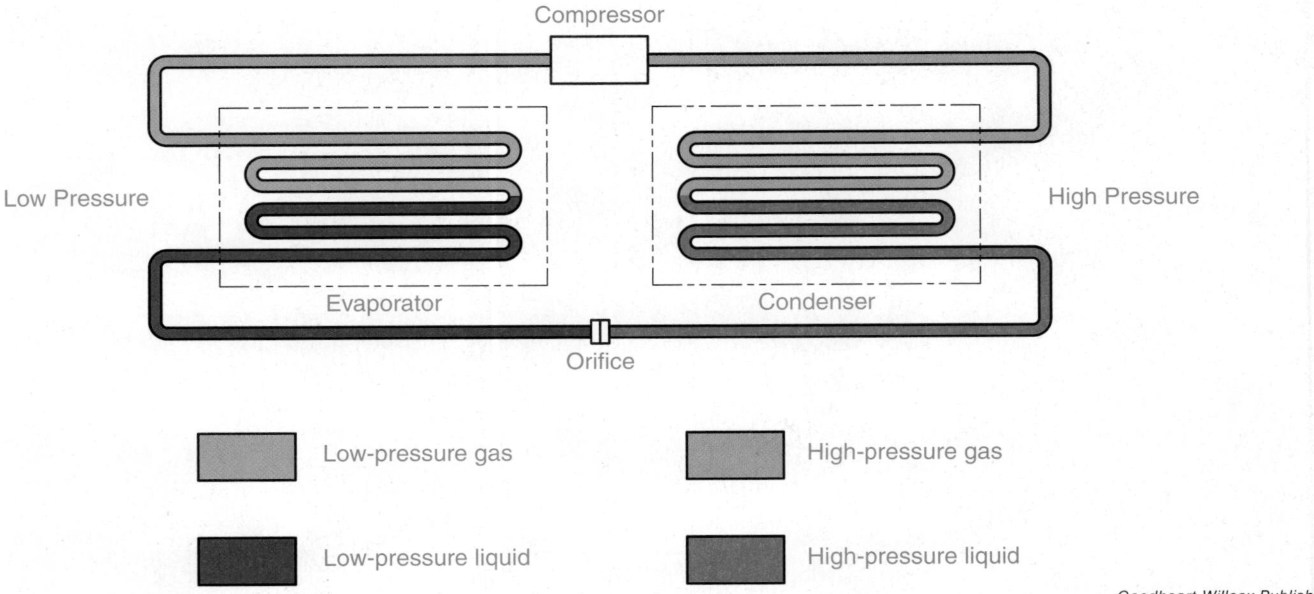

Goodheart-Willcox Publisher

Figure 33-8. This is a representation of the refrigerant and pressure states inside a compressor-cycle air conditioning system.

Forced-Air Systems

A ***forced-air system*** heats air in a furnace and forces it through pipes or ducts to all parts of the house. See **Figure 33-11**. A fan or blower is used to push the warm air. Cool air is drawn through cold air return ducts to the furnace. Before the cool air enters the heating chamber, it passes through a filter that removes dust and other particles. Some forced-air systems have built-in humidifiers, dehumidifiers, and air cleaners.

The forced-air system is popular because it is relatively inexpensive to purchase and install and quickly provides adequate amounts of heat. Humidification is simple, and the ductwork may also be used for central air conditioning. Furnaces may be located in the attic, in the basement, in the crawl space, or on the main level. Three basic types of forced-air furnaces are available for residential installations: upflow, counterflow, and horizontal. See **Figure 33-12**.

Copyright Carrier Corporation

Figure 33-9. This is a compressor-condenser unit for a central air conditioning system. These units are placed outside the home because they generate a significant amount of heat.

General Electric Company

Figure 33-10. Room air conditioners are designed as a single unit in which the heat-generating components remain outside the house.

Goodheart-Willcox Publisher

Figure 33-11. A forced-air system uses ductwork and a blower to deliver air to various parts of the home. This forced-air system is used for both heating and cooling.

The ***upflow furnace*** is designed for basement installation, so the plenum is on top of the furnace. The ***plenum*** is the chamber where warmed air is collected for distribution. When the furnace is to be located on the main floor with ducts below the floor, a ***counterflow furnace*** is required. On this type of furnace, the plenum is on the bottom and the warm air is forced downward. If the furnace is to be installed in the attic or crawl space, a ***horizontal furnace*** is a logical choice. This type of furnace requires minimum clearance. It can be suspended from ceilings and floor joists or installed on a concrete slab.

A typical forced-air system for a small home uses one thermostat that controls the temperature for the entire home. Large homes may require zones, which are areas that each have a thermostat to control temperature in that area. Systems that have zones usually require a separate furnace for each zone.

Forced-air systems do have some disadvantages. They create rapid movement of air that can cause drafts, which is disagreeable to some people. Also, noise is often transmitted through the ducts. The noise level is generally higher than with other systems due to the blower. In addition, ductwork is designed to fit between the joists and wall studs, as shown in **Figure 33-13.** The ducts are large and sometimes difficult to route to all parts of the dwelling. Furniture can also interfere with air movement, thus reducing the effectiveness of a forced-air system.

It is important to note that any home that has a combustion appliance, such as a gas stove or furnace, should also have a carbon monoxide (CO) detector. A CO detector is inexpensive insurance against health risks. A properly functioning detector can provide an early warning to occupants before carbon monoxide concentrations reach a dangerous level. For more information on CO and CO detectors, refer to Chapter 10, *Designing for Health and Safety.*

Hydronic Systems

A ***hydronic system***, or hot water system, consists of a boiler, water pipes, and radiators or radiant panels. The boiler heats the water in the system. The hot water is then pumped to the radiators, which are located throughout the house. Heat is transferred from the water to the air at the radiator. The cooled water is then returned from the radiator to the boiler for reheating.

The type of hydronic system used in most homes is known as the ***one-pipe system***. The one-pipe system uses radiators, also called *convectors,*

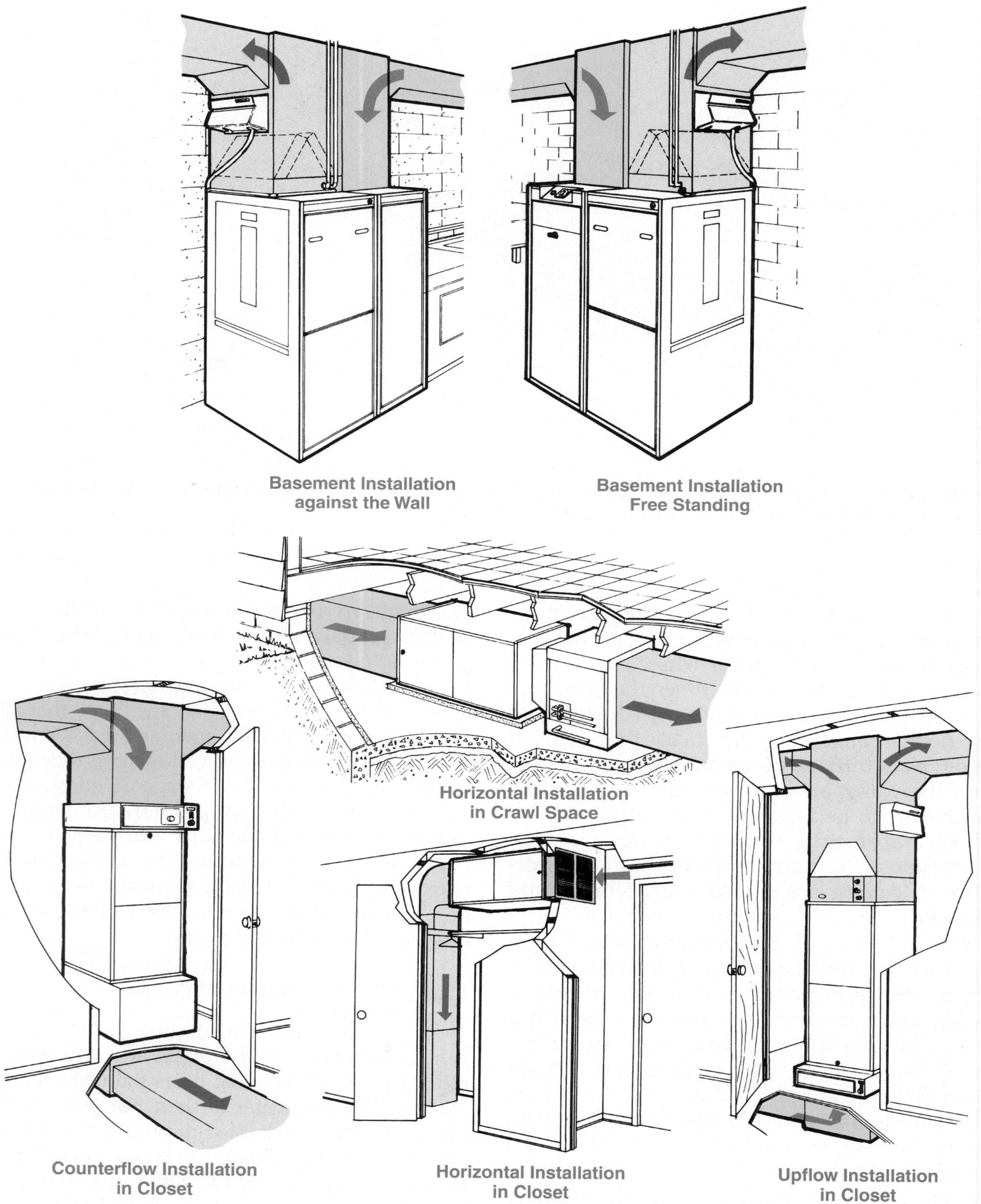

Lennox Industries, Inc.

Figure 33-12. Forced-air furnaces can be installed in a basement, crawl space, or first-floor closet.

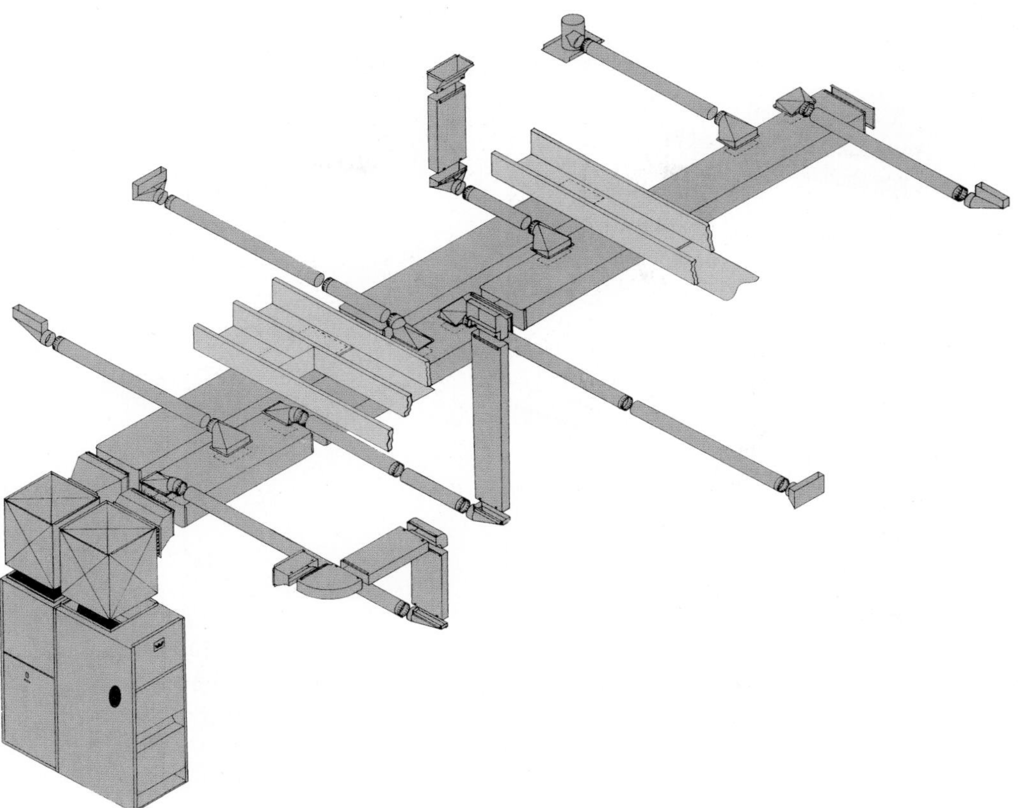

The Williamson Company

Figure 33-13. The plenum and ductwork of a forced-air system are designed to fit within the joists and studs of a frame structure.

connected in series. Heated water carried in the main pipe is diverted to the radiators and is then returned to the boiler, as shown in **Figure 33-14**. Special connectors allow small amounts of hot water to enter each radiator, equalizing the heat in the radiators throughout the home. Baseboard convectors are the most commonly used type of radiator in new homes. See **Figure 33-15**.

Another type of hydronic heating system utilizes copper pipes or other type of tubing embedded in a concrete floor or plastered ceiling. This system is often referred to as a ***hydronic radiant system***. See **Figure 33-16**. It is popular in mild climates and locations where the temperature is not likely to drop rapidly. A radiant heating system is silent and is completely hidden from sight.

One of the major advantages of a hydronic heating system is that each room can be controlled individually. Frequently the home is zoned into two or three areas that require about the same temperature. Each zone is then controlled by a separate thermostat. This adds to the heating comfort and energy efficiency of the home.

Other advantages of a hydronic heating system include the absence of noise transmitted from room to room and the lack of drafts. Hydronic heat is clean, quiet, and efficient. However, it has no provision for cooling, air filtration, or humidification. Also, its reaction time is slow compared to other systems. These may be considered serious deficiencies in some areas of the country.

Electric Radiant Systems

An ***electric radiant system*** uses resistance wiring to produce heat. The wire is embedded in the ceiling, floor, or baseboards. This system is clean, quiet, and produces a constant level of heat. The entire system is hidden if the wires are in the ceiling or floor. Individual heat control for each room or area is practical. Unlike most gas- or oil-fired systems, electric radiant systems do

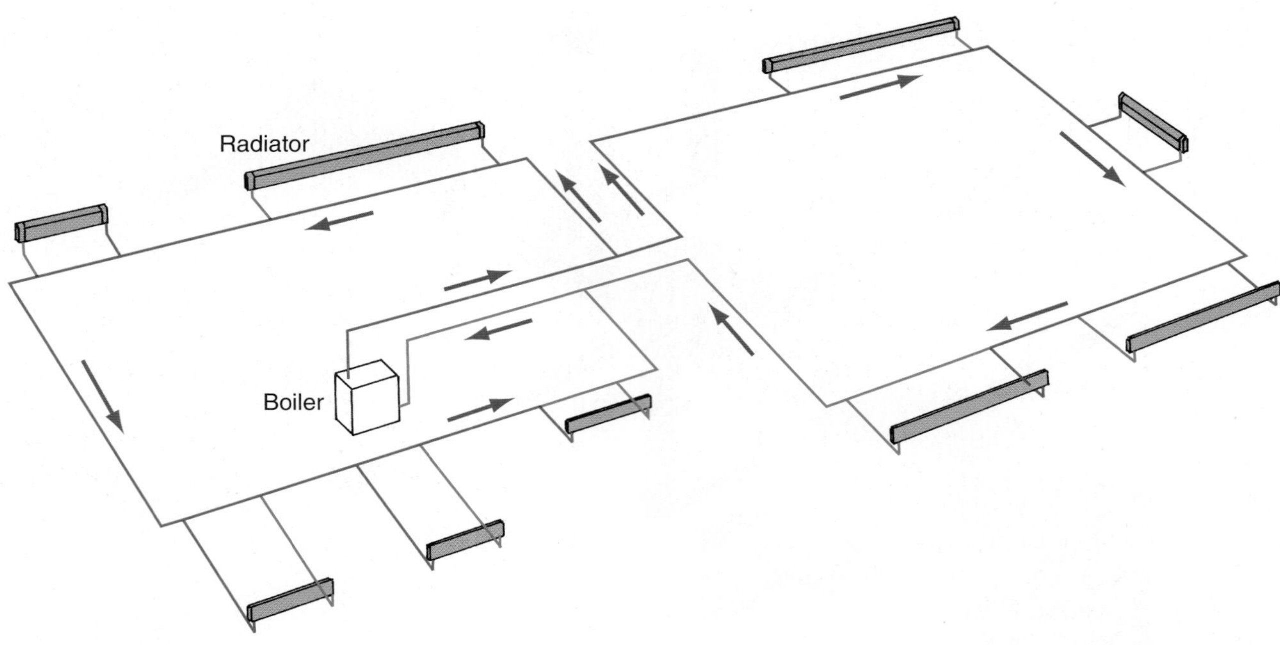

Goodheart-Willcox Publisher

Figure 33-14. This is a one-pipe hydronic system. This system has two heating zones.

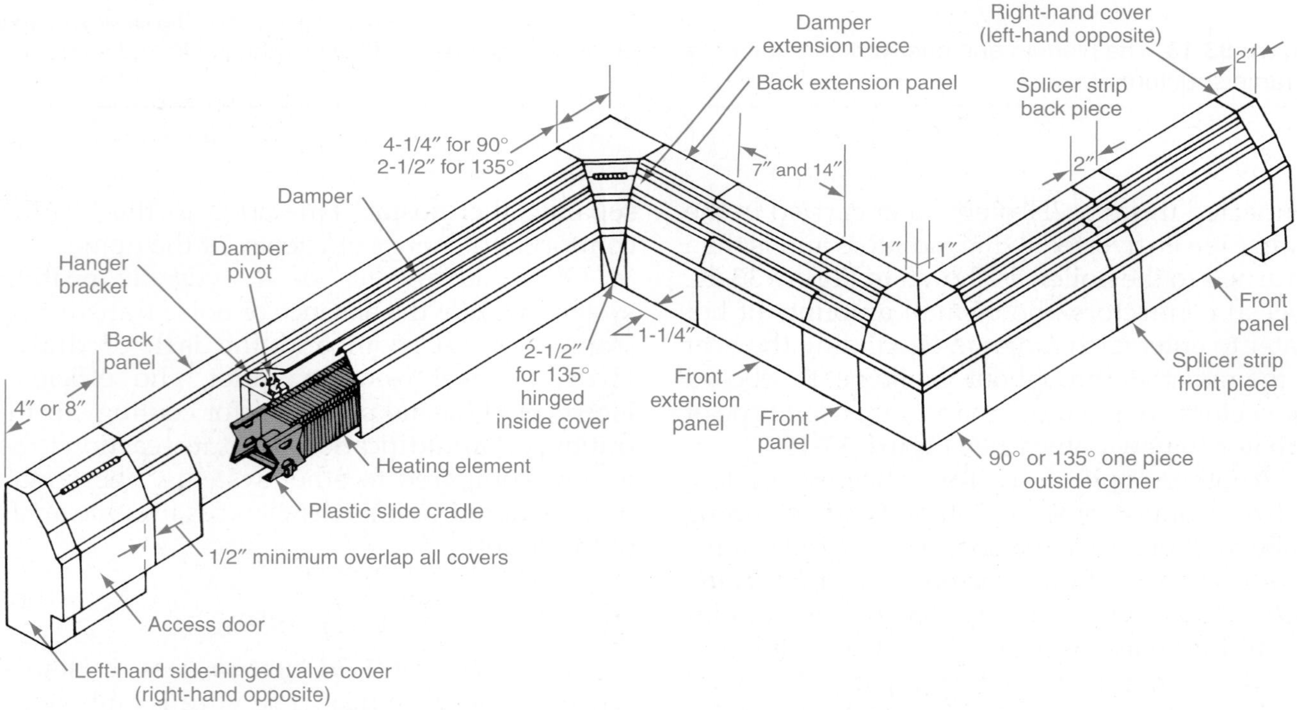

Damper extension piece
Back extension panel
Right-hand cover (left-hand opposite)
2″
Splicer strip back piece
2″
4-1/4″ for 90°
2-1/2″ for 135°
7″ and 14″
Damper
1″ 1″
Hanger bracket
Damper pivot
Front panel
Back panel
2-1/2″ for 135° hinged inside cover
1-1/4″
Front extension panel
Front panel
Splicer strip front piece
4″ or 8″
Heating element
90° or 135° one piece outside corner
Plastic slide cradle
1/2″ minimum overlap all covers
Access door
Left-hand side-hinged valve cover (right-hand opposite)

Crane Co.

Figure 33-15. Baseboard convectors are the most common type of radiator for new hydronic heating systems.

Goodheart-Willcox Publisher

A

Vanguard Plastics Inc.

B

Figure 33-16. A—These are the main controls of a hydronic radiant system. B—These flexible cross-linked polyethylene (PEX) pipes for a hydronic radiant system will be embedded in a concrete floor.

not require a chimney. The electric radiant system is reliable and free from maintenance difficulties. **Figure 33-17** shows a typical installation.

Disadvantages of electric radiant systems include no provision for humidification, air filtration, or cooling. Also, as with a hydronic system, the system is slow to recover if the temperature drops suddenly. Finally, in some areas of the country, electric radiant systems are expensive to operate due to the cost of electricity.

Heat Pumps

A ***heat pump*** serves the dual purpose of heating and cooling. It is essentially a refrigeration unit that "pumps" or transfers natural heat from air or water to heat or cool the house. Heat pumps operate on the principle that there is some heat in all air and water, and that this heat can be removed. Heat that has been removed is pumped into the house to heat it or pumped away from the house to cool it.

A heat pump requires electricity to operate a compressor. It is clean and requires no chimney. Since the main unit is located outside the house, limited interior space is required. Heat pumps are highly efficient in mild climates. In addition, air cleaning and humidification are easy.

A disadvantage of heat pumps is that efficiency drops considerably when the temperature is below 30°F. For this reason, heat pumps are not practical for cold climates.

Geothermal Heat Pumps

Geothermal heat pumps, also known as *ground-source heat pumps,* improve overall efficiency by using ***geothermal energy.*** Geothermal heat pumps use the Earth both as an inexpensive source of heat and as a place to deposit heat. See **Figure 33-18**.

A geothermal heat pump uses an antifreeze solution, instead of air, for the heat source and heat sink. The antifreeze is circulated through a long loop of plastic pipe buried in the ground in a deep trench. Wells are also used for this purpose.

The temperature of the subsoil is between 40°F and 50°F year-round. This temperature is much warmer than cold air in the winter and much cooler than hot air in the summer. Tests by the Environmental Protection Agency (EPA) have shown that geothermal heat pumps produce from three to five times as much energy (in heat) as is required from the consumer (in electricity) to run the system. However, the initial installation cost of the system is high.

Programmable Thermostats

A furnace or air conditioner is controlled by a thermostat. A ***thermostat*** is an automatic sensing device that sends a signal to activate a furnace or air conditioner at a temperature set by the homeowner. The thermostat is usually

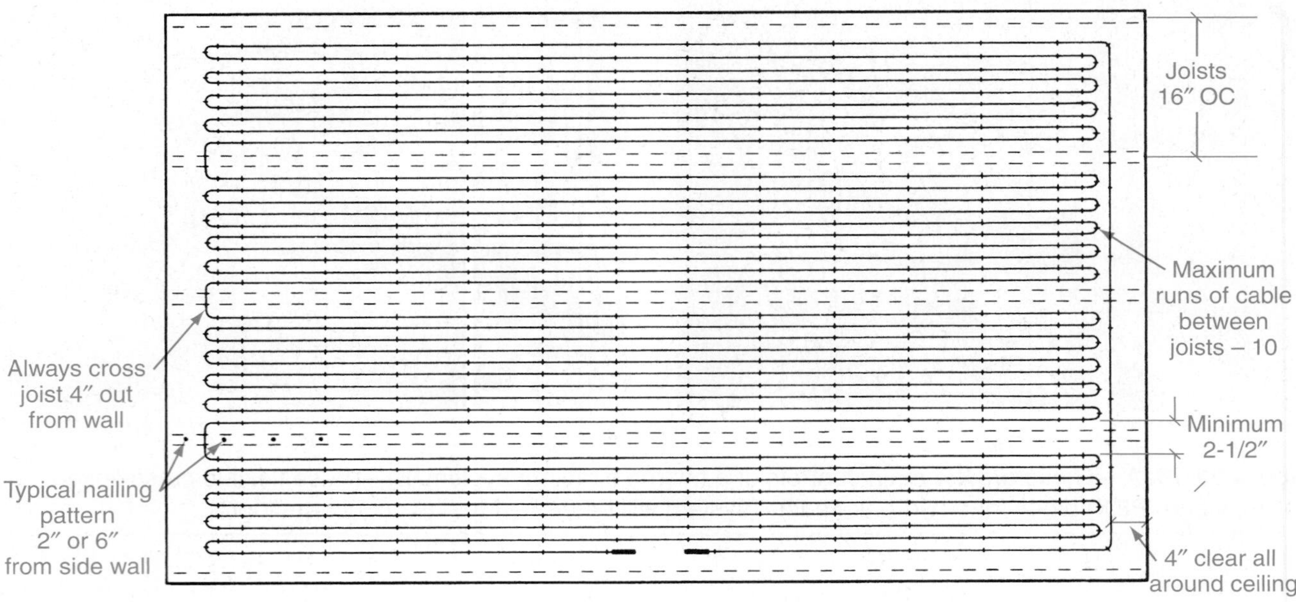

Typical Ceiling Layout Pattern

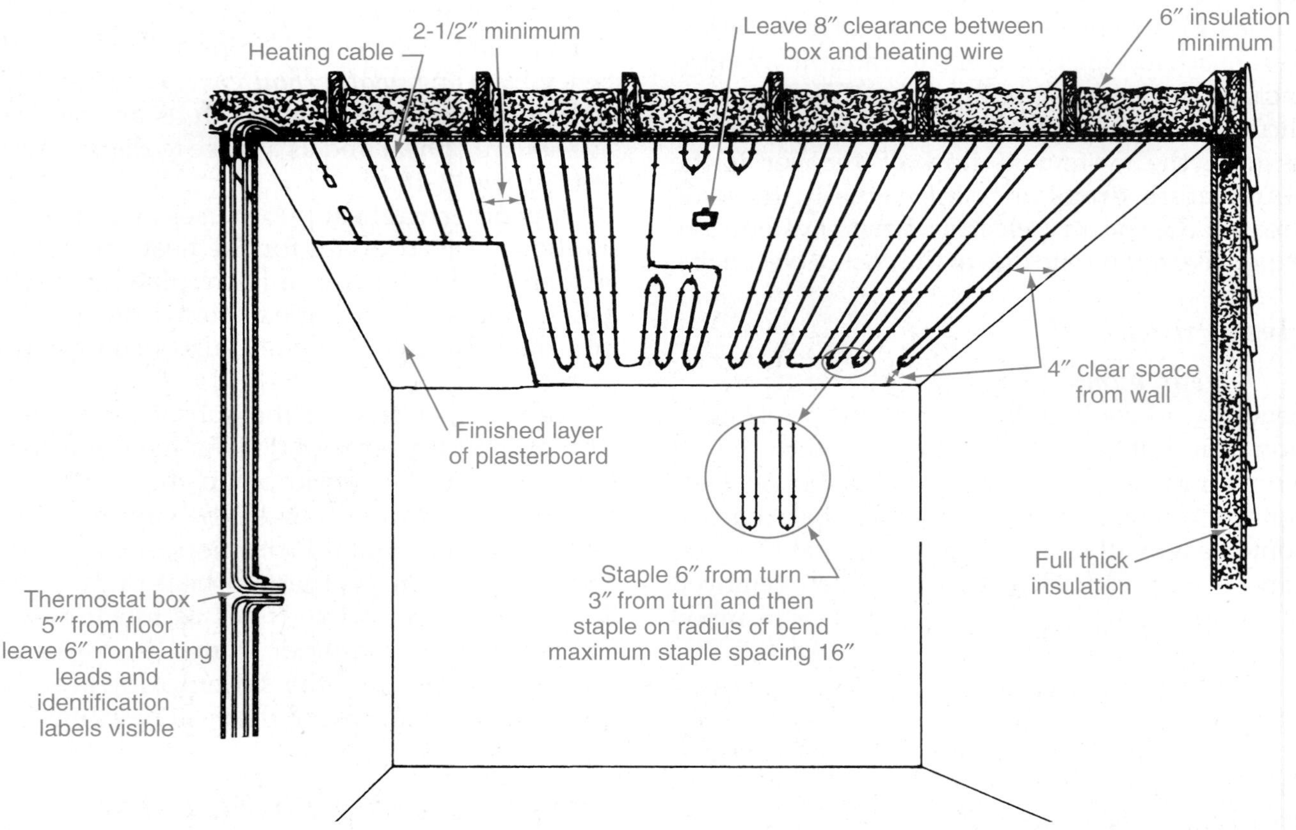

Goodheart-Willcox Publisher

Figure 33-17. A typical layout for resistance wiring used in radiant electrical heating systems. One watt of electricity provides 3.415 Btus of heat.

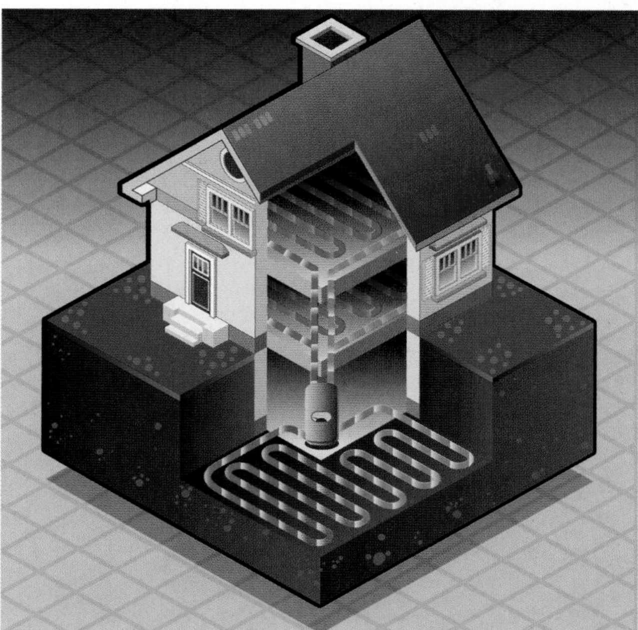

aurin/Shutterstock.com

Figure 33-18. A geothermal heat pump uses the Earth's heat energy to heat and cool a residence.

located on an inside wall of the house because the outside temperature may affect its accuracy if it is located on an exterior wall. The thermostat should also be located where it will be free from cold air drafts and heat from lamps.

Many new homes today have programmable thermostats with a microprocessor that can automatically control the home's heating and cooling systems. See **Figure 33-19**. Programmable thermostats can reduce heating and cooling costs up to 33%. These devices have a liquid crystal display and a small keypad for programming.

A typical heating and cooling program for the thermostat may partition the day into several periods, each set for a specific temperature. For example, during a northern winter heating season, the thermostat might be programmed as follows. Remember that this is only a guide. Depending on the region of the country you reside in, this example may not be the best for your particular climate.

- At 11:00 pm, the temperature is set to 60°F for the nighttime hours.
- At 6:00 am, the temperature is set to 75°F so the house is warm when you get up.
- When you leave for work or school, the temperature is set to a lower temperature, such as 65°F, to save energy during the day.
- Half an hour before you return in the evening, the temperature is set to 75°F so the house is warm when you return.

At any time during the program, you can manually adjust the temperature setting if you need to for any reason. The program can then be returned to its regular program with the touch of a button. Most programmable digital thermostats also include a "vacation" or "hold" mode that will maintain a set temperature for almost any period of time.

The programmable thermostat can control air conditioning during the cooling season in a fashion similar to that used during the heating season. Or, you may choose to have a single cooling cycle per day to reduce the temperature in the house only when it is the warmest outside. Some thermostats automatically adjust for seasonal changes using an internal calendar programmed into the thermostat. Most models contain battery backup so reprogramming is not required if the power fails. Batteries should be changed every year to prevent system failure as a result of a dead battery and a power failure.

Some programmable thermostats allow the home air conditioner or furnace to be controlled away from the home remotely by the homeowner

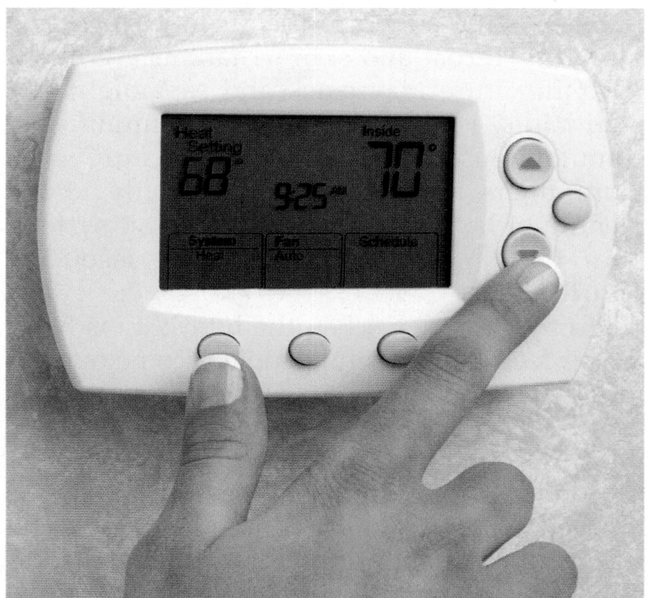

Steve Cukrov/Shutterstock.com

Figure 33-19. Programmable digital thermostats can be used to maximize energy savings.

using a mobile device or computer. This allows users to control their heating, ventilation, and air conditioning systems from virtually anywhere in the world. In some areas of the country, utility companies are working with homeowners to reduce power consumption by offering programmable thermostats that can be controlled remotely by the company. This provides a way to control use and lower costs during peak times. However, homeowners retain ultimate control and can override the temperature changes if desired.

Humidity Control

The air in our homes contains a certain amount of moisture in the form of water vapor. ***Relative humidity*** is the ratio of water vapor in the air to the amount required to saturate the air at a given temperature. Humidity control is important for total comfort and should be considered when planning a climate control system. A comfortable humidity level is around 50% when the temperature is about 75°F.

Air holds more water when the temperature is high than when it is low. During the winter months, especially in northern areas, the amount of moisture in the indoor air drops to a low level because of the expanding of the air during heating and the low relative humidity outside the house. If water is not added to the air to increase the humidity, throat and skin irritations are likely. Also, furniture may crack and separate at the glue joints. For these reasons, a humidifier is commonly used to increase the moisture level. Humidifiers may be attached directly to the plenum or heating ducts of a forced-air system, or a freestanding model may be used. See **Figure 33-20**.

In the summer, when the humidity is high, the air feels "sticky" and people become uncomfortable. Wood doors, windows, and drawers can swell and not operate smoothly. When the moisture content is too high, water is likely to condense on windows. This condition, if allowed to persist, may cause damage to the woodwork. A dehumidifier may be installed to remove water from the air. This device condenses water on cold coils and thus removes it from the air, reducing the relative humidity.

Photo Copyright Carrier Corporation

Figure 33-20. This power humidifier may be mounted on the plenum or a supply duct of a forced-air heating system.

Air Circulation and Cleaning

Circulation helps reduce localized areas of high or low humidity. High concentrations of moist air in the kitchen, laundry room, and bath are distributed throughout the house when the air is circulated. However, continuous recirculation of the same air in a house results in stale, unhealthy air. Provisions must be made to add fresh air into the house.

The air in most homes contains dust and other particles. Some type of air cleaning device is generally used to help reduce these potential allergens. Most furnaces have built-in filters. Others include electronic air cleaning grids. See **Figure 33-21**. Electronic air cleaners can remove up to about 95% of the dust particles in the air.

Heat Loss

Before you can determine the proper size of heating or cooling unit for a specific home, you will need to find out the heat loss for exposed surfaces of the home. ***Heat loss*** is the amount of

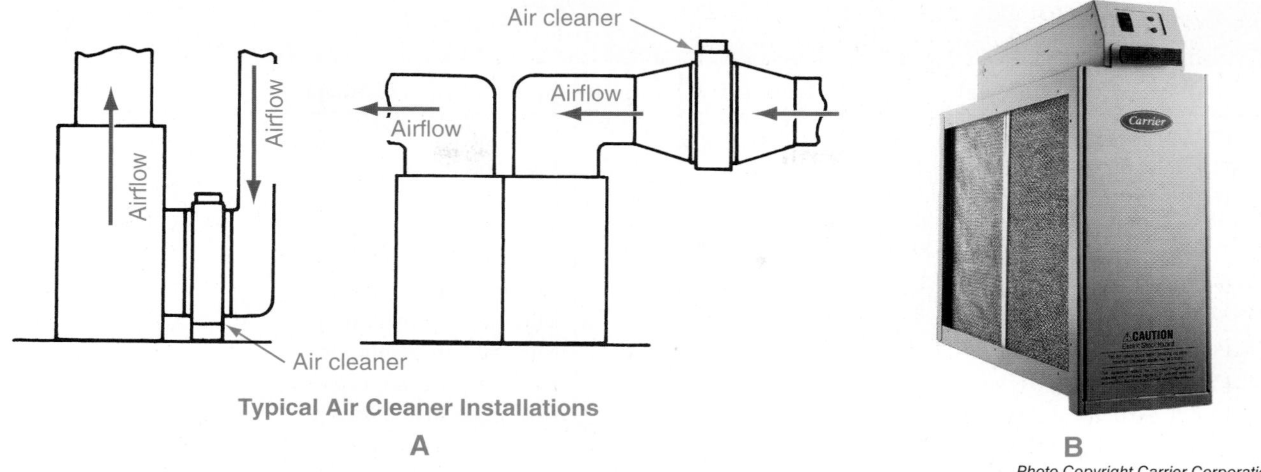

Figure 33-21. Electronic air cleaners can be installed with most forced-air heating, cooling, or ventilation systems.

heat that passes through the exposed surfaces of the house.

Factors That Affect Heat Loss

Heat loss can be calculated, but before you perform the calculations, you should understand the factors that affect heat loss. These factors include infiltration and the resistivity (R-factor) and U-factor of the building materials.

Infiltration

Infiltration is the amount of heat lost through spaces around windows and doors. For calculation purposes, it has been estimated that infiltration is equal to one air exchange per hour. For example, if a room is 10′ × 18′ and has an 8′ ceiling, the total volume is 1440 cubic feet. This figure, 1440 cubic feet, is the amount of air infiltration.

R-Factor

Resistivity, also called the ***R-factor*** or *R-value,* is the ability of a material to resist the transfer of heat or cold. Materials that transmit heat readily are called *conductors,* and those that do not are called *insulators.* **Figure 33-22** lists the R-factors for common building materials.

U-Factor

Furnaces and air conditioners are rated in ***British thermal units (Btus).*** One Btu is the quantity of heat required to increase the temperature of 1 pound of water 1°F. Your final heat loss calculations will be in Btus.

The number of Btus transmitted in one hour through one square foot of a building material for each degree of temperature difference is the ***U-factor.*** U-factors for common building materials can be determined by taking the reciprocal of the R-factor of the material. This is done by dividing 1.00 by the R-factor.

Figure 33-23 shows an energy-conserving exterior wall assembly with R-factors identified for each material. The net effective R-factor and total U-factor are also shown for the assembly.

Calculation Procedure

The following sections show calculations for determining a heating unit size. The procedure for calculating the size of cooling unit is the same, except that the design temperature difference must reflect summer temperatures rather than winter.

The ***design temperature difference*** is the difference between the inside design temperature and the outside design temperature. The desired temperature of a house is its inside design temperature. The inside design temperature used in calculations is typically 70°F. The outside design temperature is the average outdoor temperature during the winter (for heating units) or summer (for air conditioners).

Also, an allowance should be made for very humid locations. A larger unit is required in areas that have high humidity levels.

Resistivity to Heat Loss of Common Building Materials					
	Material	Resistivity		Material	Resistivity
4″	Concrete or stone	.32	1/2″	Plywood	.65
6″	Concrete or stone	.48	5/8″	Plywood	.80
8″	Concrete or stone	.64	3/4″	Plywood	.95
12″	Concrete or stone	.96	3/4″	Softwood sheathing or siding	.85
4″	Concrete block	.70		Composition floor covering	.08
8″	Concrete block	1.10	1″	Mineral batt insulation	3.50
12″	Concrete block	1.25	2″	Mineral batt insulation	7.00
4″	Common brick	.82	4″	Mineral batt insulation	14.00
4″	Face brick	.45	2″	Fiberglass insulation	7.00
4″	Structural clay tile	1.10	4″	Fiberglass insulation	14.00
8″	Structural clay tile	1.90	1″	Loose fill insulation	3.00
12″	Structural clay tile	3.00	1/2″	Gypsum wallboard	.45
1″	Stucco	.20	1″	Expanding polystyrene, extruded	4.00
15 lb	Building paper	.06	1″	Expanding polystyrene, molded beads	3.85
3/8″	Sheet rock or plasterboard	.33		Single thickness glass	.88
1/2″	Sand plaster	.15		Glassweld insulating glass	1.89
1/2″	Insulation plaster	.75		Single glass with storm window	1.66
1/2″	Fiberboard ceiling tile	1.20		Metal edge glass	1.85
1/2″	Fiberboard sheathing	1.45	4″	Glass block	2.13
3/4″	Fiberboard sheathing	2.18	1-3/8″	Wood door	1.82
	Roll roofing	.15		Same with storm door	2.94
	Asphalt shingles	.16	1-3/4″	Wood door	1.82
	Wood shingles	.86		Same with storm door	3.12
	Tile or slate	.08			

Goodheart-Willcox Publisher

Figure 33-22. This table shows resistivity of common building materials. The U-factor can be calculated by taking the reciprocal of the resistivity.

Walls

1. Find the total exterior wall area by multiplying the length by the height. This is the *gross wall area.*
2. Subtract the area filled by windows and doors in the exterior walls. The resulting area is called the *net wall area.*
3. Add the R-factors for each of the materials used in the construction of each wall. Each wall that is constructed differently must be calculated separately.
4. Take the reciprocal of the sum of the R-factors for each wall calculation. This figure is the U-factor for the net wall area.
5. Determine the U-factor for each door and window in the exterior wall by taking the reciprocal of its resistivity.
6. Calculate the design temperature difference by subtracting the outside design temperature from the inside design temperature. Example: IDT = 70°F, ODT = –10°F; therefore, 70°F minus –10°F = 80°F. The design temperature difference for this example is 80°F.
7. Determine the Btu loss per hour (Btu/H) for the net wall area by multiplying the net wall area by the net wall U-factor by the design temperature difference. Record this figure.
8. Determine the Btu/H for the windows by multiplying the window area by the glass U-factor by the design temperature difference. Record this figure.
9. Determine the Btu/H for the doors by multiplying the door area by the door U-factor by the design temperature difference. Record this figure.

In order to offset the performance of lower-cost R19 compressed fiberglass batts (equivalent to R18) as cavity insulation, this 2x6 wall assembly incorporates advanced framing techniques. The assembly includes conventional headers and double top plates. The framing factor is assumed to be no greater than 20 percent.[a]

2x6 with R19 Batt Insulation, Advanced Framing

COMPONENTS		R-VALUES
Wood/Vinyl Siding		0.59
Min. 7/16 Performance Category Wood Structural Panels		0.62
Cavity Insulation (R19 compressed fiberglass batts)		18
5-1/2" Framing	16% framing + 4% headers = 20% framing factor	6.88
5-1/2" Headers – Conventional		6.88
Air films and 1/2" Drywall		1.38
Net Effective R-Value of the Total Solid Wall		16.67
Total Wall U-Factor		0.060

(a) 20% framing factor is calculated using studs at 24" o.c. (framing factor = 22%) with a combination of insulated corners, insulated interior-exterior wall intersections and limited cripple supports at door and window openings (4% maximum reduction in framing percentage, 2% assumed).

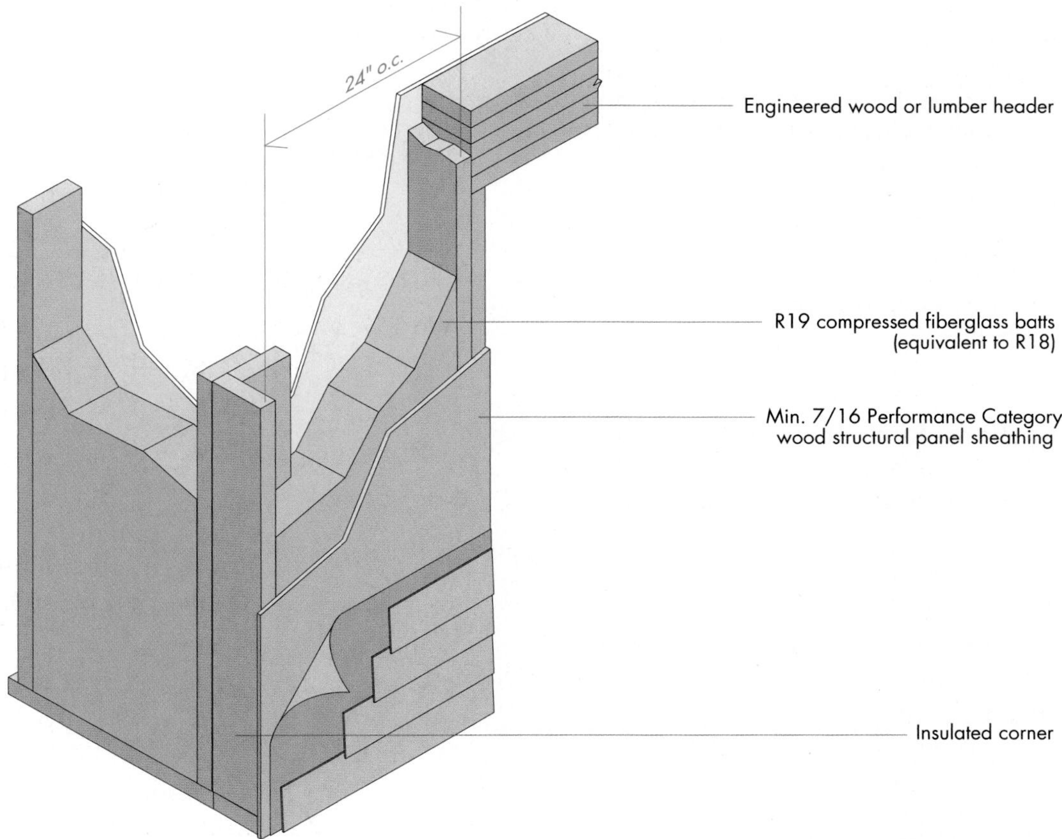

International Code Council & APA—The Engineered Wood Association

Figure 33-23. Exterior wall assembly showing R-factors for each material and the net effective R-factor and total U-factor for the assembly.

Ceiling

1. Find the total ceiling area by multiplying the length by the width.
2. Determine the U-factor for the ceiling by adding the R-factors for each material used in the ceiling and taking the reciprocal.
3. Calculate the Btu/H by multiplying the ceiling area by the total ceiling U-factor by the design temperature difference. Record this figure.

Floor

1. Find the total area of the floor by multiplying the length by the width. Heat loss is calculated only for floors over unheated areas, such as slab-type floors or floors over a crawl space.
2. Determine the U-factor for the floor by adding the resistivity for each material used and taking the reciprocal.
3. Calculate the Btu/H by multiplying the floor area by the total floor U-factor by the design temperature difference. Note that the design temperature difference may not be the same here as for walls and ceiling with heating ducts and hot water pipes that are not insulated. If the area is properly vented and pipes and ducts are insulated, then the same design temperature difference may be used. Record this figure.

Infiltration

1. Determine the volume of air in the room or home under consideration by multiplying the length by the width by the height. For an entire home, you will need to find the total volume of air in all of the rooms. This volume is equal to the air infiltration.
2. Calculate the air infiltration Btu/H heat loss by multiplying the volume of air infiltration by the U-factor (0.018) by the design temperature difference. Note that 0.018 Btu/H is required to warm one cubic foot of air 1°F. This is a constant and may be used in every calculation. Record this figure.

Final Calculation

Add the Btu/H for the walls, windows, doors, ceiling, floor, and air infiltration. The sum of these values is the total heat loss in Btu/H. This figure represents the heating (or cooling) unit size required for the room or house being calculated.

Example of Heat Loss Calculation

The following example applies the above calculation procedures to the room shown in **Figure 33-24**. This is a conventional calculation of heat loss. When using CADD software, some programs provide special features for calculating heating and cooling loads and preparing data reports. Residential building codes, including the International Residential Code, specify requirements for sizing heating and cooling units in accordance with established calculation methods. Refer to the local code for specific requirements. As you work through the following example, refer to **Figure 33-24** for the necessary construction details and R-factors.

Calculations for Walls

1. Total exterior area.

   12′-0″ × 8′-0″ = 96 square feet
   18′-0″ × 8′-0″ = 144 square feet
   Gross exterior wall area = 240 square feet

2. Window area.

   6′-0″ × 5′-0″ = 30 square feet
   6′-0″ × 5′-0″ = 30 square feet
   Total window area = 60 square feet

   Door area.
   3′-0″ × 6′-8″ = 21 square feet (approximate, includes the rough opening space)

   Net wall area.
   Net wall area = Gross wall area – door and window area
   = 240 square feet – 81 square feet
   = 159 square feet

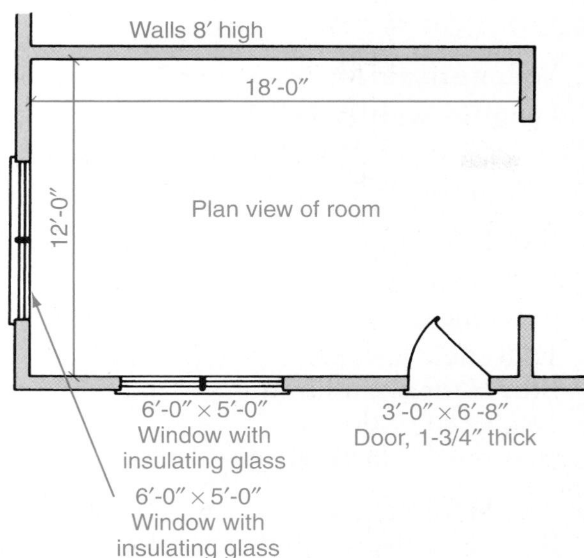

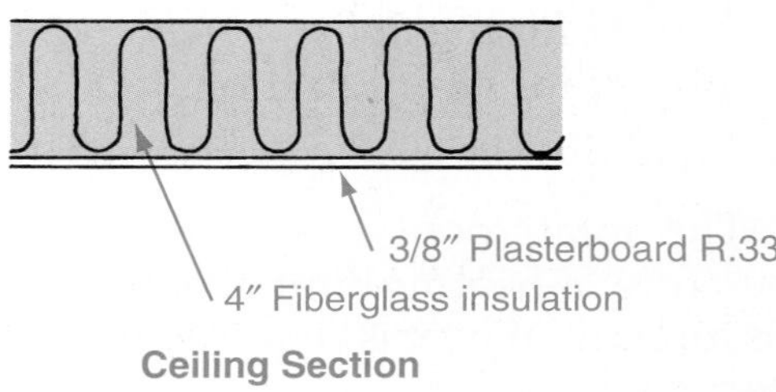

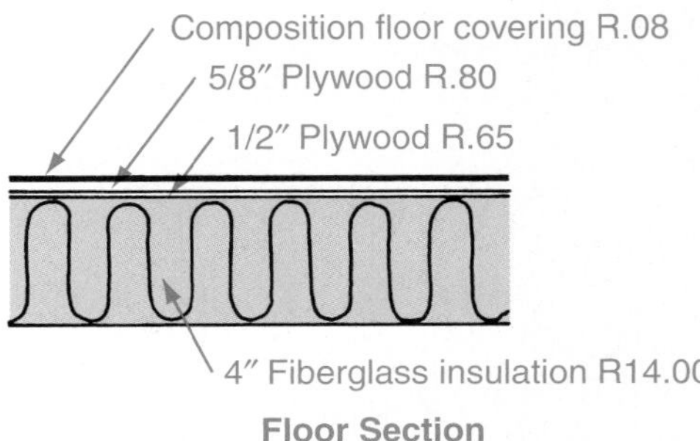

Goodheart-Willcox Publisher

Figure 33-24. This room is used for the heat loss calculations in the text.

3. R-factor of wall materials.

3/4″ softwood siding R-factor	=	.85
1/2″ fiberboard sheathing R-factor	=	1.45
4″ fiberglass insulation R-factor	=	14.00
3/8″ plasterboard R-factor	=	.33
Total R-factor	=	16.63
U-factor for net wall = 1.00 ÷ 16.63	=	.060

4. U-factor for doors and windows.

   1-3/4″ wood door = .55

   Insulating glass window = .54 for each

5. Design temperature difference.

Inside design temperature	=	70°F
Outside design temperature	=	–5°F
Design temperature difference	=	75°F

6. Btu/H for net wall.

   Net wall area × U-factor × temperature difference

   159 square feet × .060 × 75°F = 715.50
   Btu/H for the net walls = 715.50

7. Btu/H for the windows.

   Window area × U-factor × temperature difference

   60 square feet × .54 × 75°F = 2430.00
   Btu/H for the windows = 2430.00

8. Btu/H for the door.

   Door area × U-factor × temperature difference

   21 square feet × .55 × 75°F = 866.25
   Btu/H for the door = 866.25

Calculation for Ceiling

1. Total ceiling area.

   12′-0″ × 18′-0″ = 216 square feet

2. U-factor for ceiling.

3/8″ plasterboard R-factor	=	.33
4″ fiberglass insulation R-factor	=	14.00
Total R-factor	=	14.33
U-factor for ceiling = 1.00 ÷ 14.33	=	.070

3. Btu/H for the ceiling.

   Ceiling area × U-factor × temperature difference

   216 square feet × .070 × 75°F = 1134.00
   Btu/H for the ceiling = 1134.00

Calculation for Floor

1. Total floor area.

   12′-0″ × 18′-0″ = 216 square feet

2. U-factor for floor.

Composition floor covering R-factor	=	.08
5/8″ plywood R-factor	=	.80
1/2″ plywood R-factor	=	.65
4″ fiberglass insulation R-factor	=	14.00
Total R-factor	=	15.53
U-factor for floor = 1.00 ÷ 15.53	=	.064

3. Btu/H for the floor.

   Floor area × U-factor × temperature difference

   216 square feet × .064 × 75°F = 1036.80
   Btu/H for the floor = 1036.80

Calculation for Air Infiltration

1. Volume of air.

   Length × width × height

   18′-0″ × 12′-0″ × 8′-0″ = 1728 cubic feet
   Volume of air = air infiltration

2. Btu/H for air infiltration.

   Volume of air × .018 × temperature difference

   1728 cubic feet × .018 × 75°F = 2332.80
   Btu/H for air infiltration = 2332.80

Summary Calculations

Btu/H for net walls	=	715.50
Btu/H for the windows	=	2430.00
Btu/H for the door	=	866.25
Btu/H for the ceiling	=	1134.00
Btu/H for the floor	=	1036.80
Btu/H for air infiltration	=	2332.80
Total Btu/H	=	8515.35

The total room heat loss is 8,515 Btu/H. Therefore, a heating unit capable of producing this amount of heat is required to heat the room effectively.

Summary

- A complete climate control system controls temperature, humidity, air circulation, and air cleaning.
- Design features such as insulation, ventilation, and the solar orientation of the home affect the efficiency with which temperature control is accomplished.
- The most common residential cooling system is the compressor-cycle system.
- Common heating systems include forced-air, hydronic, hydronic radiant, electric radiant, heat pump, and geothermal heat pump systems.
- Programmable thermostats can help reduce heating and cooling costs by automatically adjusting the temperature to different settings at different times of the day and night.
- Both humidifiers and dehumidifiers may be needed to control humidity in a home.
- Most heating and cooling systems include some type of air cleaning device to reduce dust and other particles in the home.
- Heat loss can be calculated to determine the appropriate size of heating and cooling systems for a specific house.

Internet Resources

Carrier
Residential heating and cooling systems

Honeywell
Manufacturer of thermostats, humidifiers, and dehumidifiers

Lennox
Residential heating and cooling systems

Trane
Residential heating and cooling systems

Review Questions

Answer the following questions using the information in this chapter.

1. Identify the four features of a complete climate control system.
2. Name five design features that help increase the efficiency of climate control systems.
3. List four basic types of heating systems.
4. How does a forced-air system operate?
5. Identify three types of furnaces that are used in forced-air systems.
6. List the three main parts in a hydronic system.
7. Name two advantages of a hydronic system.
8. What type of heating system uses resistance wiring to produce heat?
9. A heat pump is essentially a(n) _____ unit.
10. What is a *thermostat*?
11. What is *relative humidity*?
12. Identify two possible outcomes from having too little moisture in the air.
13. What problems may occur if the humidity in a house is too high?
14. A(n) _____ is a device that removes moisture from the air in a house, reducing the relative humidity.

Suggested Activities

1. Select a plan of a medium-size home and get an estimate from a local utility company as to the cost of heating this home. Also ask for recommendations for insulation and ventilation. Report your findings.
2. Using a plan supplied by your instructor, calculate the total heat loss and specify the size heating unit required. Show your calculations.
3. Contact people in your community who have forced-air, hydronic, and electric radiant heating systems. Ask their opinion regarding dependability, advantages, disadvantages, economy, and serviceability of the systems. Report your findings.
4. Visit a local heating and air conditioning equipment supplier. Ask for catalogs and other literature showing heating and cooling equipment. Add the material to the classroom collection. Search online for manufacturers' literature and add the additional material to the collection.

5. Prepare a chart for each heating system discussed in the text showing advantages and disadvantages of each system. Display your chart.

Problem Solving Case Study

The Clements have come to your architectural design company because you advertise "custom designs with the Earth in mind." The family wants to build a new three-bedroom home in Palm Springs, California, where interior climate control is important during the hot California desert summer months. The Clements are interested in using the latest in "green" climate control equipment in their new home.

Conduct research to find the latest green technology for residential climate control. Prepare a written recommendation for the Clements for a system that meets their requirement for a green climate control system. In your recommendation, explain the top two or three choices and recommend the one you think would work best for a home in Palm Springs.

ADDA Certification Prep

The following questions are presented in the style used in the American Design Drafting Association (ADDA) Drafter Certification Test. Answer the questions using the information in this chapter.

1. Which of the following statements about residential climate control are true?
   A. Temperature control includes both heating and cooling.
   B. Weather stripping seals small cracks around doors and movable windows to reduce heat loss.
   C. The most common residential cooling system is the heat pump system.
   D. The upflow furnace is designed for basement installation, so the plenum is on top of the furnace.
2. Match each type of heating system with its description.

   Heating systems: 1. Forced-air, 2. Hydronic, 3. Hydronic radiant, 4. Electric radiant, 5. Heat pump
   A. Transfers natural heat from air or water to heat or cool the house.
   B. Utilizes copper pipes or other tubing embedded in the floor or ceiling.
   C. Heats air in a furnace and pushes it through ducts throughout the house.
   D. Uses resistance wiring embedded in the floor, ceiling, or baseboards to produce heat.
   E. Consists of a boiler, water pipes, and radiators or radiant panels.
3. Which of the following statements are *false*?
   A. An advantage of electric radiant systems is that the system is quick to recover if the temperature drops suddenly.
   B. A typical forced-air system for a small home uses one thermostat that controls the temperature for the entire home.
   C. Any residence that has a combustion appliance, such as a gas stove or furnace, should have a carbon monoxide (CO) detector.
   D. The type of hydronic system used in most homes is known as the three-pipe system.

Curricular Connections

1. **Social Science.** The use of heating and cooling systems to maintain the temperature of a residence is a fairly new concept. Early cultures had to be rather clever when it came to providing comfort from hot and cold weather. Conduct research to find out how other civilizations handled interior climate control. Research climate control techniques used by the ancient Chinese, ancient Greek, ancient Roman, and early Native American cultures. Collect illustrations of each, and assemble them into a presentation.
2. **Language Arts.** Conduct research to find out the causes of and remedies for "sick building syndrome." Write a five-page formal report on your findings.

STEM Connections

1. **Science.** Explore the concept of geothermal energy. How is it generated within the Earth? Are there any potential environmental problems associated with the use of geothermal energy? Prepare a 2-minute oral report on this subject and deliver it to the class.

Communicating about Architecture

1. **Reading.** With a partner, make flash cards of the key terms in this chapter. On the front of the card, write the term. On the back of the card, write the pronunciation and a brief definition. Use this chapter and a dictionary for guidance. Then take turns quizzing one another on the pronunciations and definitions of the key terms.
2. **Speaking.** Working in small groups, prepare an oral presentation to describe the advantages and disadvantages of each type of heating system discussed in this chapter. Create posters or other visual aids to use in the presentation.

Radiant Heat Inc.; Uecker, E.

The heat in this indoor pool room is provided by electric radiant heat. The units are located near the ceiling. All heating and cooling units must be indicated on the climate control plan.

Chapter 34

Climate Control Plans

Objectives

After completing this chapter, you will be able to:

- Plan the outlet and inlet locations for the distribution system of a residential climate control plan.
- Design the ductwork for a typical forced-air system.
- Draw a climate control plan using proper conventions and symbols.

Key Terms

climate control equipment schedule
climate control plan
diffuser
distribution system
ducts
ductwork
extended plenum system
grille
inlet
outlet
radial system
register
wall stack

A ***climate control plan*** shows the location, size, and type of heating, cooling, ventilating, humidifying, and air cleaning equipment and the required piping or ducts. The climate control system should be closely coordinated with the structural, plumbing, and electrical aspects of the house to avoid conflict with this other equipment. Like the electrical and plumbing plans, the climate control plan is a plan view section drawing of the home.

The climate control plan should include information about the size and location of the ***distribution system*** through which conditioned air is delivered throughout the house. It should also include the location of thermostats and registers or baseboard convectors, climate control equipment location and type, and an equipment schedule. Heat loss calculations and any general or specific notes needed to fully describe the system must also be included with the plan.

Distribution System

The distribution system, which delivers conditioned air to all parts of the home, usually consists of ducts or pipes. ***Ducts*** can be round or rectangular and are used in a forced-air system to move large quantities of air for heating or cooling. The network of ducts is called ***ductwork***. Pipes are used in hydronic systems to distribute hot water or steam from the boiler to radiators, baseboard units, or radiant panels. The distribution system should be represented on the climate control plan using the proper symbols. See **Figure 34-1**. The ducts should be

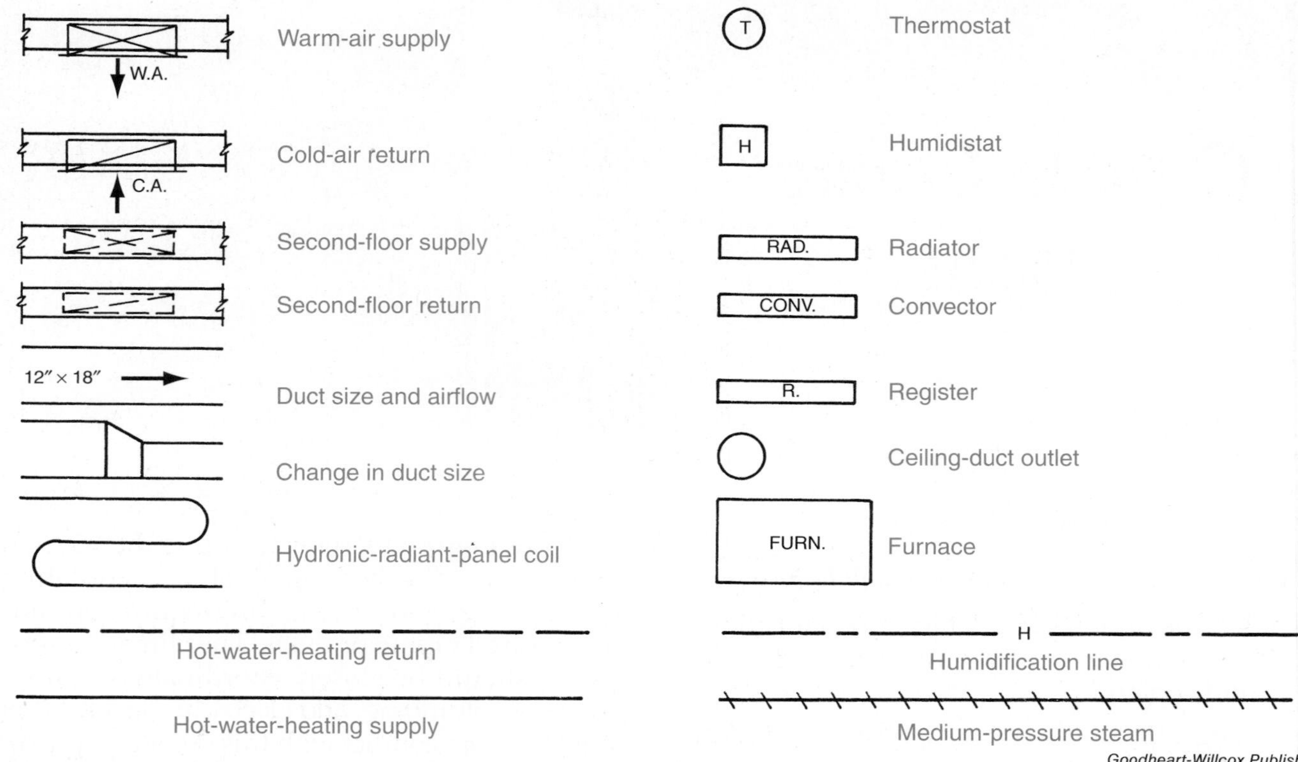

Figure 34-1. Symbols commonly used on a climate control plan.

drawn as close to scale as possible. The climate control plan is generally drawn at a scale of 1/4″ = 1′-0″ or the same scale as the floor plan. Sizes should be shown on the plan. Pipes are indicated by single lines and are not drawn to scale.

Planning Outlet and Inlet Locations

Outlets are the holes or surfaces through which air or heat from the climate control system enters each room of a home. A perimeter system of outlets is commonly specified. This provides uniform heating or cooling by concentrating the conditioned air where it is needed most—along the outside walls. See **Figure 34-2**.

Technically, the outlet in a forced-air system may be covered by a grille, register, or diffuser. A ***grille*** is a basic covering for an outlet and can be used for both supply air and return air. A ***register*** includes a damper that can be used to regulate air flow and is used only for supply air. A ***diffuser*** is similar to a register, but directs the air flow in a specific direction. However, these terms are often used interchangeably. For convenience, all outlet coverings are referred to as registers in this chapter unless the difference is important.

In a hydronic or electric radiant heat system, the outlet is generally a baseboard unit. There should be at least one outlet in each large area to be conditioned. This includes rooms, halls, stairwells, and any other areas that are to be heated or cooled. An average room has up to 180 square feet of floor space. Larger rooms or areas usually should be counted as two or more rooms. If a room has more than 15′ of exterior wall, then two or more outlets should be used.

Inlets, or cold air returns, are required for forced-air systems. They receive air to be returned to the furnace or air conditioner coil. If the house is a compact, one-story structure, one inlet is usually sufficient. If the house is L- or U-shaped or has several levels, then two or more inlets should be planned. Remember that closed doors and dead-end corridors block air circulation. Common sizes for outlets and inlets are listed in **Figure 34-3**. Inlets are not needed for hydronic or electric radiant systems.

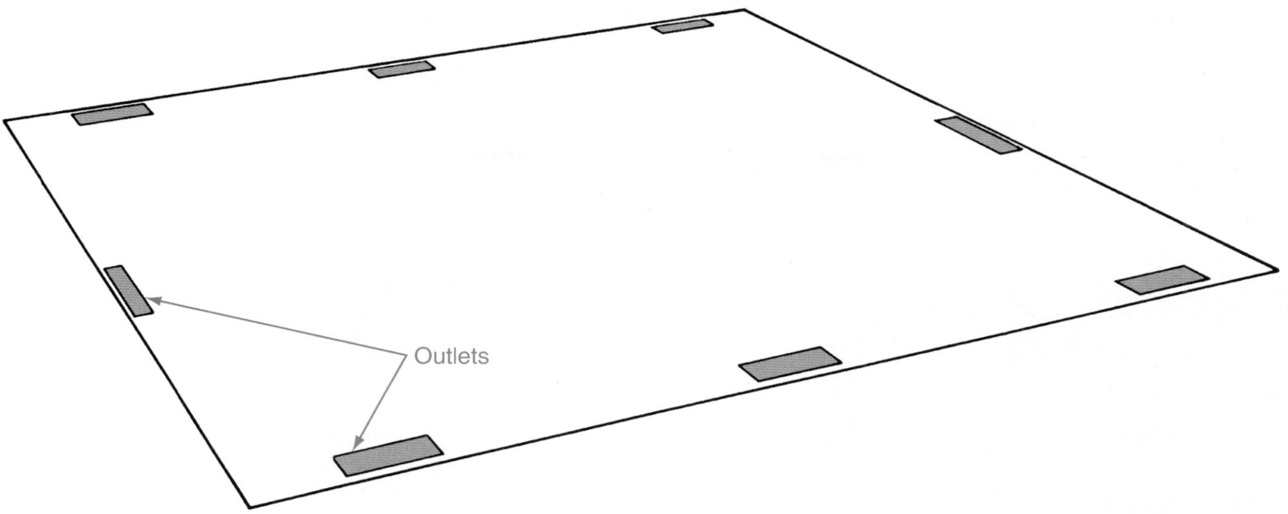

Goodheart-Willcox Publisher

Figure 34-2. A perimeter system of outlets provides uniform heat or cooling.

Planning Ductwork

The two basic types of ductwork for forced-air systems are the radial system and the extended plenum system. See **Figure 34-4**. In the ***radial system***, round ducts radiate out in all directions from the furnace. The ***extended plenum system*** has a large rectangular duct (plenum) for the main supply. Round ducts extend from the main supply to each register, as shown in **Figure 34-5**. The extended plenum system is usually preferred.

The round duct used to supply registers in the extended plenum system may be 6″ or 8″ in diameter. An 8″ duct is commonly recommended when the system is to be used for cooling as well as heating. The larger size is necessary when the same blower is used because cool air moves more slowly than warm air.

Traditional round ducts are rigid and are generally made of metal. In many areas of the country, however, flexible ducts may be used instead. They are similar to the traditional ducts, but are less expensive and easier to install. One of the disadvantages of flexible ducts is that they are less durable than rigid ducts. They can become pinched or punctured, resulting in reduced efficiency.

Another type of duct is a vertical duct designed to fit between the studs. This type of duct is called a ***wall stack*** and is usually 12″ × 3-1/4″.

Rectangular ducts used for extended plenums are 8″ deep and vary in width from 10″ to 28″.

Outlet Sizes		
Type	**Size**	**Supply**
Floor Diffuser	6″ × 12″	8″ Duct
Floor Diffuser	4″ × 12″	6″ Duct
Floor Diffuser	2-1/4″ × 12″	6″ Duct
Baseboard Diffuser	2-1/4″ × 15″	6″ Duct
Baseboard Diffuser	2-1/4″ × 24″	6″ Duct
Inlet Sizes		
Type	**Size**	**Furnace Size**
Baseboard Grille	6″ × 14″	—
Baseboard Grille	6″ × 30″	40,000 BTU
Ceiling or Wall Grille	16″ × 20″	75,000 BTU
High Side-Wall Grille	6″ × 14″	—
Floor Grille	8″ × 30″	60,000 BTU
Floor Grille	12″ × 30″	80,000 BTU
Floor Grille	18″ × 24″	90,000 BTU

Goodheart-Willcox Publisher

Figure 34-3. This table shows common sizes for outlets and inlets, according to the type of registers to be used.

The sectional area of the supply duct should equal the total area of all round register ducts. The size of the rectangular extended plenum is

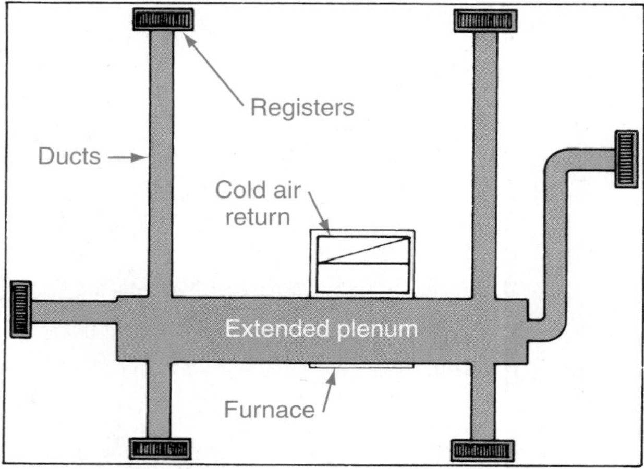

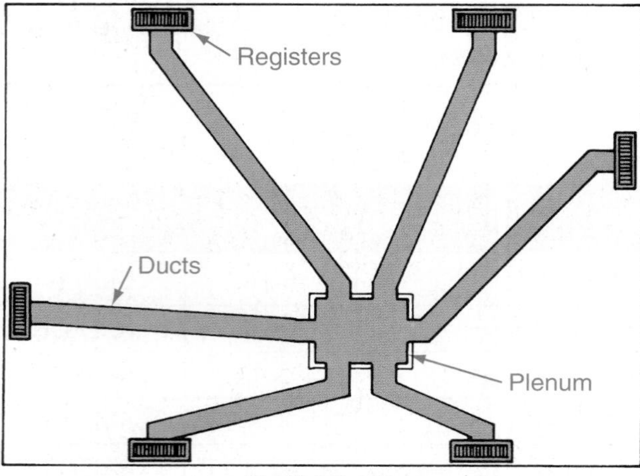

Goodheart-Willcox Publisher

Figure 34-4. The extended plenum and radial ductwork systems are commonly used for residential climate control.

based on the number and size of round ducts it serves. The extended plenum may remain the same size throughout its entire length or may be reduced in size as fewer registers remain to be supplied.

As a rule of thumb, the rectangular extended plenum size may be determined by using the following procedure. Remember, it is 8″ deep.

- For 6″ ducts, multiply the number of round ducts by 2 and add 2 to the product. The result is the required width of the plenum duct. Example: A rectangular plenum is to serve six 6″ round ducts. Therefore, 6 × 2 = 12 + 2 = 14″; the plenum duct will be 14″ × 8″.

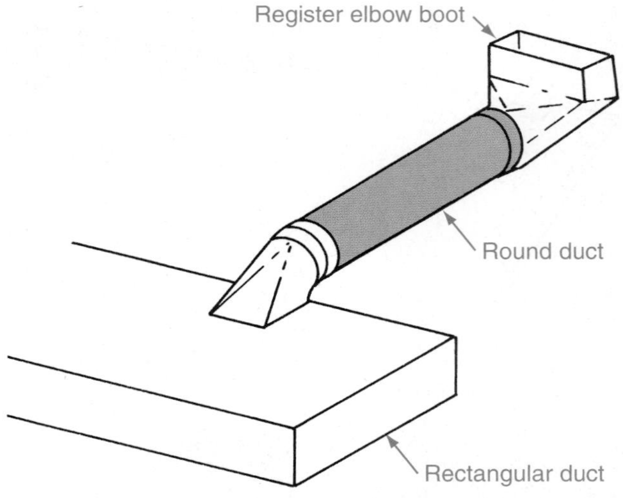

Goodheart-Willcox Publisher

Figure 34-5. Round duct, either 6″ or 8″ in diameter, is frequently used to connect registers to the main supply duct.

- For 8″ ducts, multiply the number of round ducts by 3 and add 2 to the product. The result is the required width of the plenum duct. Example: A rectangular plenum is to serve six 8″ round ducts. Therefore, 6 × 3 = 18 + 2 = 20″; the plenum duct will be 20″ × 8″.

Planning Piping for a Hydronic System

In a hydronic system, the main hot water supply from the boiler must be large enough to provide for adequate heating. The size of copper pipe usually considered to be adequate for most installations is:

- 1″ main for up to 71,000 Btu
- 1-1/2″ main for 72,000 to 160,000 Btu
- 2″ main for 161,000 to 240,000 Btu

The required size of baseboard unit or convector cabinet depends on the heat loss for a given area. It is best to calculate the heat loss for each room and then plan the number and size of outlets to match this value. The table in **Figure 34-6** shows the output rating for several common convector cabinets and fin-tube baseboard units. Locate outlets below windows for the most efficient heating. Any room that is over 15′ long should have at least two outlets.

Convector Cabinets		
Length	**Thickness**	**Btu/H output**
24″	6-3/8″	3,400
32″	6-3/8″	4,800
36″	8-3/8″	6,900
40″	8-3/8″	7,800
48″	8-3/8″	9,600
56″	8-3/8″	11,400
60″	10-3/8″	19,400
Fin-Tube Baseboard Units		
	Btu/H output	
Length	**Single**	**Double**
2′	—	2,280
4′	2,870	4,560
6′	4,260	6,840
8′	5,680	—

Goodheart-Willcox Publisher

Figure 34-6. This table shows several common convector cabinet and fin-tube baseboard unit sizes and output ratings.

Thermostat Placement

Every automatic climate control system requires at least one thermostat. A forced-air system needs only one thermostat if one furnace is used. Sometimes two furnaces are installed if the house is large or if more than one zone is required. Each zone needs a thermostat to provide accurate control. As many zones as desired may be used with electric radiant or hydronic systems, each with its own thermostat.

The placement of the thermostat is essential because it measures the temperature and activates the furnace. If it is placed where the sun may shine on it, in a draft, or near a lamp, the performance may not be satisfactory. Locate the thermostat on an inside partition in a place where the temperature will be representative of the room(s) as a whole. Show the location on the climate control plan using the proper symbol.

Green Architecture

Smart Climate Control Devices

Many responsible homeowners set their thermostats to a reasonable level before they leave on vacation. This is a "green" practice that can help conserve energy while no one is in the home. Programmable thermostats take this a step further by allowing people to program the climate control system to make the house comfortable only when they are at home, such as on nights and weekends. At other times, the thermostat is programmed to conserve energy.

Now, however, "smart" thermostats are available that can be controlled by voice, telephone, computer, and mobile device. Suppose you live in Michigan and leave for a two-week vacation in October. You leave the air conditioner on and set to 82°, and the furnace is off. Three days before you are scheduled to return, a major snowstorm occurs. Temperatures drop into the 20s and remain there. With a smart thermostat, you can contact your climate control system and change the settings so that the pipes do not freeze before you return.

Other devices can be programmed to contact you by telephone if a predetermined unsafe condition occurs in the home. These devices typically have sensors for temperature, water, and smoke detection. If a fire occurs or a water pipe breaks in the home while you are at school or work, you are notified immediately and can take steps to avoid disaster. Fire, smoke, and water damage are difficult to manage and may cause environmental problems such as mold or the release of volatile chemicals. Preventing such disasters from happening is a cost-effective way to secure your home and potentially help the environment.

Schedules, Calculations, and Notes

Various schedules may be useful on the climate control plan. A ***climate control equipment schedule*** provides an orderly means of specifying

Employability
Constructive Criticism

Part of behaving professionally on the job is responding appropriately to constructive criticism. *Constructive criticism* is feedback from an employer or coworker about how you can do your job better. Every employee, no matter how knowledgeable or experienced, can improve his or her performance. If you receive criticism from a supervisor or coworker, do not be offended. Instead, use the feedback to improve yourself. The more you improve, the more successful you will be in your work.

You may sometimes need to give constructive criticism to others, as well. The key to constructive criticism is courtesy. Instead of saying, "That is a dumb way to…", you could say something like, "I know how difficult that is; sometimes I have more success doing it this way. May I show you what I mean?" Put yourself in the other person's place and imagine how you would feel. Choose your wording carefully to avoid hurting or upsetting the other person.

Activity

Team up with a classmate to practice giving and receiving constructive criticism. Use the following scenarios as a basis for your practice:

- Your coworker plays music in her cubicle that is loud enough to distract you from your work.
- You are the supervisor of an employee who consistently arrives for work 10 minutes late.
- Your coworker's cubicle is consistently messy, which makes the company look sloppy when you walk by with potential clients on the way to the conference room.

equipment to be used in the system. Including a register schedule can reduce the amount of information placed on the drawing, helping to avoid crowding and making it easier to read the plan.

A complete climate control plan also shows a summary of the heat loss calculations. These calculations are important and form the basis for equipment selection. If space permits, the summary should be located on the climate control plan.

Add any other information on the plan that you feel will be helpful to the builder or subcontractors. Notes should be short and to the point.

Procedures for Drawing a Climate Control Plan

Many decisions and calculations must be made before completing the climate control plan. The type of heating and cooling system(s) must be determined and heat loss calculated for each room. Other drawings of the structure should be studied to determine the most practical layout before starting to draw. After all these preliminary details are addressed, then you may proceed with the drawing of the plan.

Procedure
Manual Drafting

Drawing a Climate Control Plan

A climate control plan is based on the floor plan for the residence. Therefore, when using manual drafting techniques, the best way to begin the drawing is to trace the relevant features from the floor plan. The following procedure is suggested, but office practice will dictate the procedure you will follow.

1. Trace the floor plan showing exterior and interior walls, doors and windows, and other features that relate to the climate control system. Steps 1, 2, and 3 are shown in **Figure 34-7**.
2. Locate the equipment to be used for heating, cooling, humidification, and air cleaning.

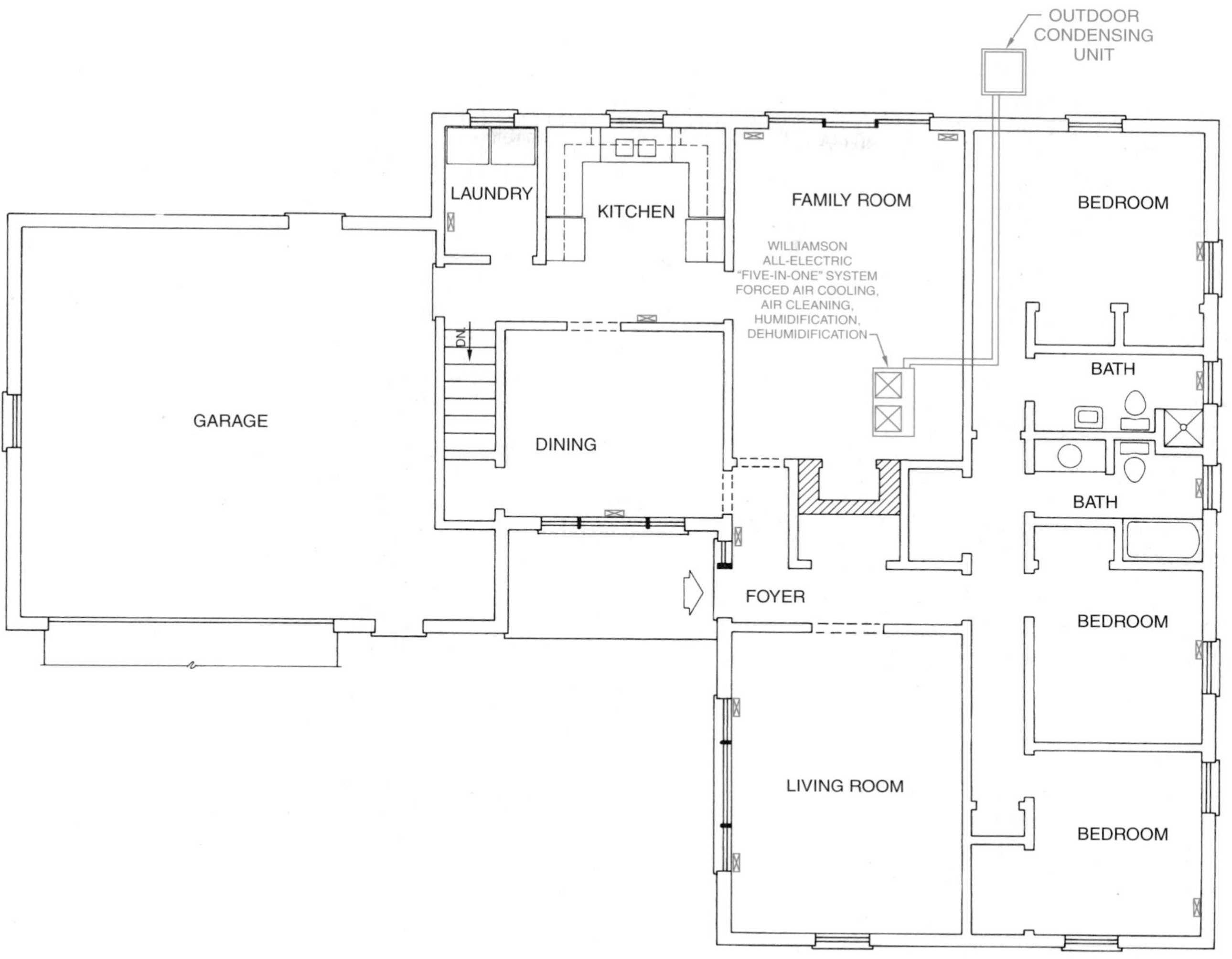

Goodheart-Willcox Publisher

Figure 34-7. The furnace, outdoor condensing unit, and registers are added to the climate control plan. The furnace is in the basement below the main floor level.

3. Locate registers, coils, baseboard units, or other means of temperature exchange on the plan. Use the proper symbols.
4. Draw the air return ducts using a hidden line. Also, draw the cold air return inlets. This step is for forced-air systems only. Steps 4, 5, 6, and 7 are shown in **Figure 34-8**.
5. Draw the supply duct or hot water main and connect it to the registers or convectors.
6. Locate thermostats and any other required controls.
7. Identify the size of ducts or pipe and other equipment.
8. Create schedules as required. Steps 8, 9, and 10 are shown in **Figure 34-9**.
9. Add the title block, scale, necessary notes, and dimensions.
10. Check the drawing for accuracy and to be sure that it is complete.

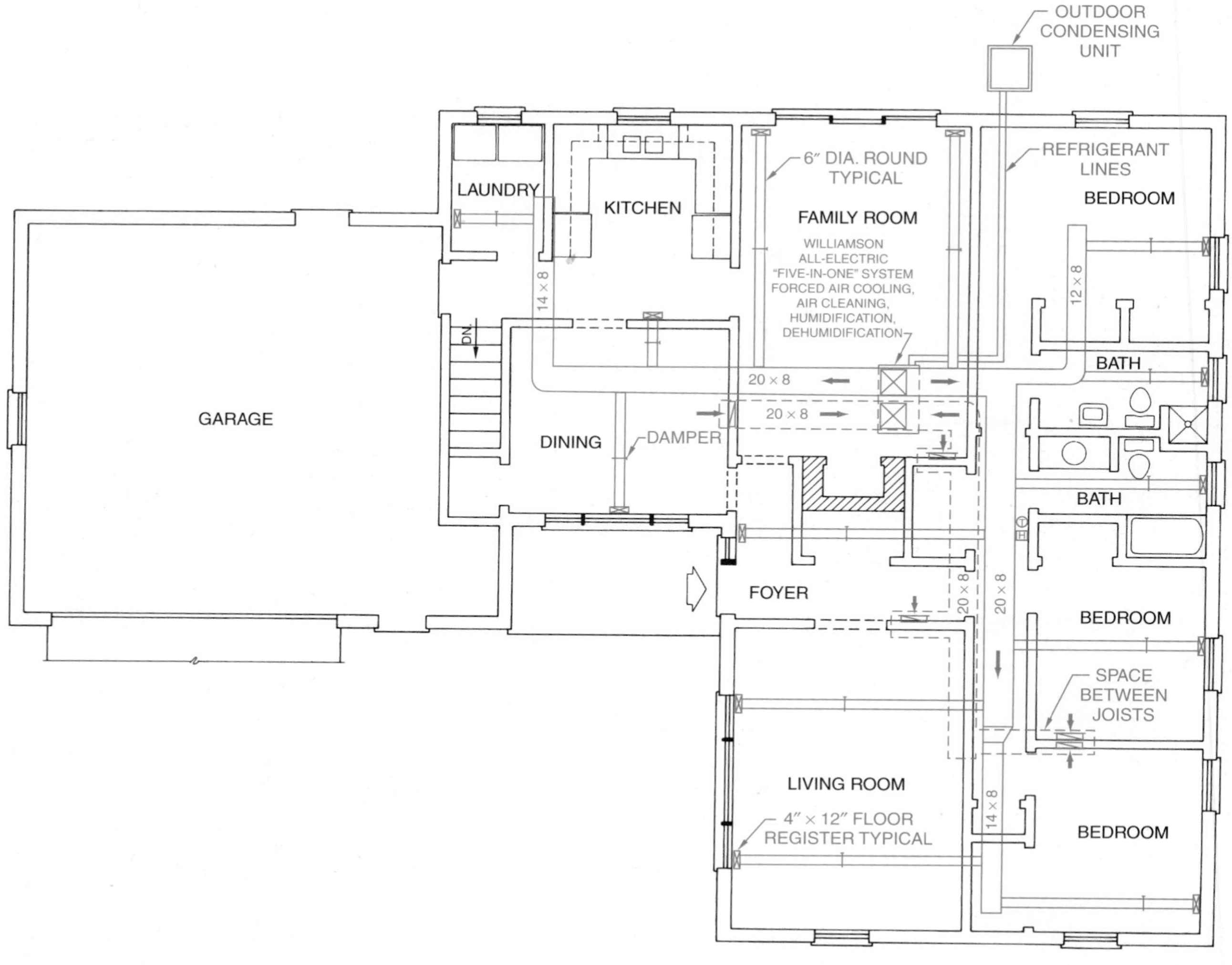

Goodheart-Willcox Publisher

Figure 34-8. The supply and cold air return ducts and cold air inlets are added to the climate control plan.

Procedure CADD

Drawing a Climate Control Plan

The step-by-step procedure for drawing a climate control plan with CADD is similar to that described for manual drafting. The only significant difference is in step 1. Instead of tracing the floor plan, you can copy the floor plan to a new file and use it directly as a basis for the climate control plan. This helps ensure consistency within the set of architectural plans.

Remember that layers are useful in specifying line widths, linetypes, colors, and other relationships. For example, the cold air return in a forced-air system is shown as a hidden line. This line is usually drawn as a medium width line (0.35 mm). It should be drawn on a dedicated layer set up to use a hidden line of the proper width. Only those features that use this particular linetype should be drawn on that layer.

If this approach is followed consistently, modifications and additions can easily be made to the drawing and specific layers can be turned off to see other details more clearly.

By setting up and using layers carefully, you can even combine the floor plan and climate control plan. Just turn off the floor plan layers that you do not want to appear on the climate control plan. This approach saves the work of copying or redrawing the needed items from the floor plan. Layers are, therefore, very important design tools that the drafter or designer can use to produce drawings more efficiently.

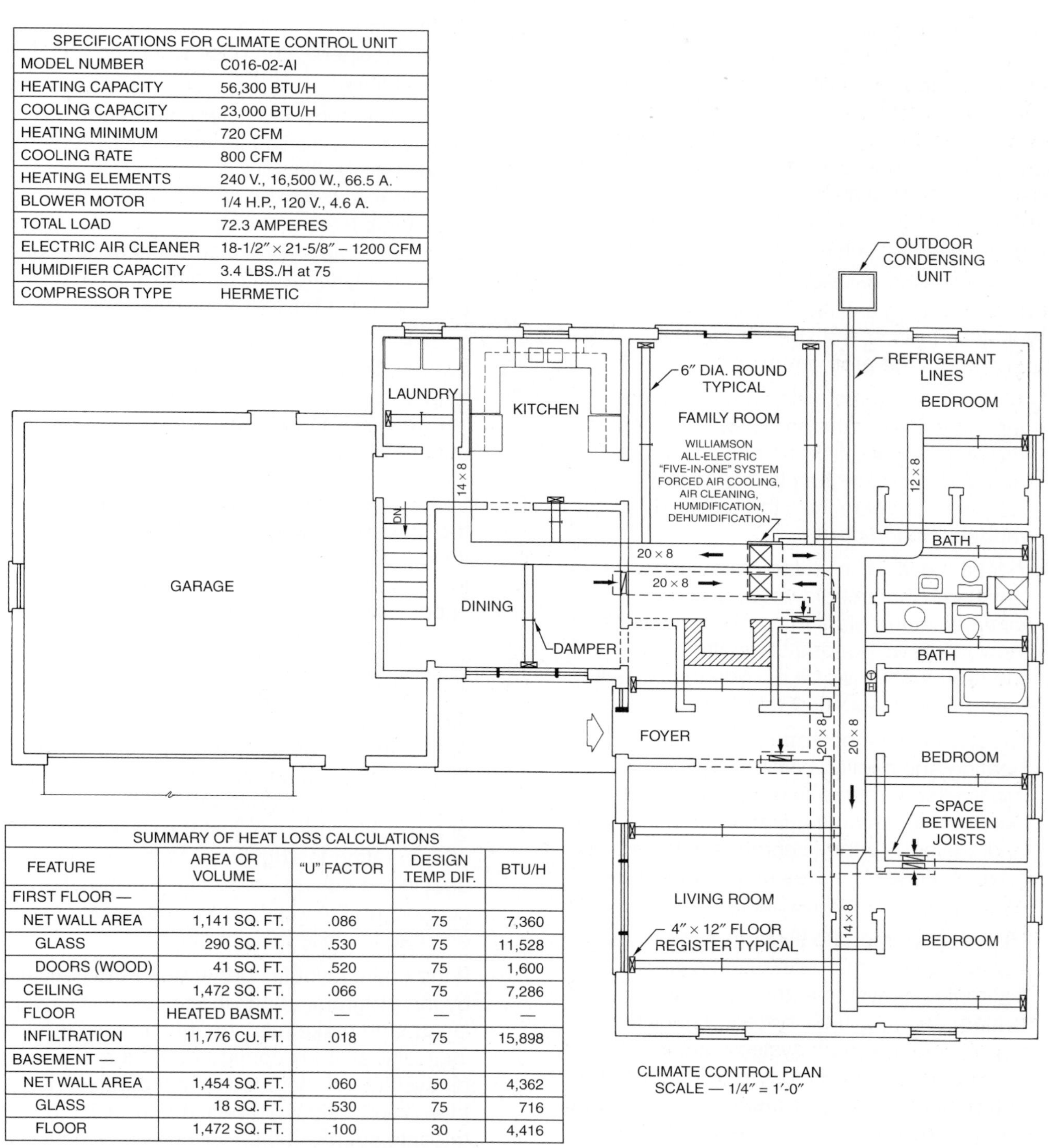

SPECIFICATIONS FOR CLIMATE CONTROL UNIT	
MODEL NUMBER	C016-02-AI
HEATING CAPACITY	56,300 BTU/H
COOLING CAPACITY	23,000 BTU/H
HEATING MINIMUM	720 CFM
COOLING RATE	800 CFM
HEATING ELEMENTS	240 V., 16,500 W., 66.5 A.
BLOWER MOTOR	1/4 H.P., 120 V., 4.6 A.
TOTAL LOAD	72.3 AMPERES
ELECTRIC AIR CLEANER	18-1/2″ × 21-5/8″ – 1200 CFM
HUMIDIFIER CAPACITY	3.4 LBS./H at 75
COMPRESSOR TYPE	HERMETIC

SUMMARY OF HEAT LOSS CALCULATIONS				
FEATURE	AREA OR VOLUME	"U" FACTOR	DESIGN TEMP. DIF.	BTU/H
FIRST FLOOR —				
NET WALL AREA	1,141 SQ. FT.	.086	75	7,360
GLASS	290 SQ. FT.	.530	75	11,528
DOORS (WOOD)	41 SQ. FT.	.520	75	1,600
CEILING	1,472 SQ. FT.	.066	75	7,286
FLOOR	HEATED BASMT.	—	—	—
INFILTRATION	11,776 CU. FT.	.018	75	15,898
BASEMENT —				
NET WALL AREA	1,454 SQ. FT.	.060	50	4,362
GLASS	18 SQ. FT.	.530	75	716
FLOOR	1,472 SQ. FT.	.100	30	4,416

TOTAL HEAT LOSS = 53,166 BTU/H

Goodheart-Willcox Publisher

Figure 34-9. A complete climate control plan showing basement and first floor installations. The furnace and ductwork can be drawn on the foundation or basement plan and the registers shown on the floor plan, if desired.

Parametric Modeling

Creating a Climate Control Plan

A residential climate control plan shows the layout of heating and cooling equipment, ductwork, supply registers, and cold air returns. In parametric modeling, the required items in the heating and cooling system are created by placing 3D components. The distribution system must be carefully planned so that it does not interfere with the components of other systems, such as electrical conduit and plumbing lines.

The following procedure describes the steps for creating a climate control plan. This is a typical sequence, but specific steps will vary depending on the program used.

1. Start a new project using a mechanical template. Import the architectural model into the project. Establish the plan view that will be used to create the climate control plan. Use the floor plan from the architectural model as an underlay.
2. Adjust the visibility in the plan view to remove any items that should not appear in the climate control plan. In addition, adjust the view range as needed to display portions of the system that will be outside the default view range associated with the view.
3. Create spaces and zones to be used in heating and cooling calculations. Spaces are similar to rooms and are used to identify bounded areas on the plan to be heated and cooled. A zone is composed of several spaces. Zones are created by selecting existing spaces on the plan.
4. Plan the appropriate systems to organize components in the distribution system. Examples of systems are a supply air system and return air system. Typically, supply and return air systems are identified by different display colors to distinguish the components of each system. As components are connected, they are assigned to the appropriate systems.
5. Locate the equipment to be used for heating and cooling. Insert an air handling unit to locate the furnace. Select the appropriate size unit. Specify the base level and an offset, if necessary.
6. Locate the supply registers, also known as supply diffusers. Depending on the program used, supply diffusers and return diffusers may be referred to as *air terminals*. Locate the supply diffusers at the appropriate elevation. Specify the appropriate size and airflow for each supply diffuser. The airflow is typically specified in cubic feet per minute (cfm).
7. Create the supply ducts for the distribution system. This can be done by placing ducts individually or using a special tool in the software to generate the system layout automatically. If you are placing ducts individually, create the main supply duct from the air handling unit first. Then create the branch ducts extending from the main supply duct and connect the supply diffusers to the branch ducts. Air handling units and supply diffusers typically have connectors for establishing connections with the ducts. For each duct, specify the appropriate elevation, size, and shape (the shape is typically rectangular or round). Specify vertical height offsets in the ductwork routing as needed. Fittings, such as tee or elbow fittings, are usually generated automatically at offsets or turns. If needed, adjust the default fittings after creating the ductwork. If the main supply duct in the design is open at the end after connecting the supply diffusers, create an end cap to close the opening.

   If the entire layout is generated automatically by the program, check the resulting ductwork layout and make adjustments as needed. Typically, settings configured for the supply air system can be used to make adjustments. In addition, grips can be used to resize or relocate supply ducts. Switch to a 3D view to verify that the ductwork has been created correctly. Make sure that none of the supply ductwork interferes with other building systems.

8. Locate the return diffusers. Locate these at the appropriate elevation. Specify the appropriate size and airflow for each return diffuser.
9. Create the air return ducts. These are created in the same manner as the supply ducts. If you are placing ducts individually, create the main return duct from the air handling unit first. Then create the branch ducts extending from the main return duct and connect the return diffusers to the branch ducts. For each duct, specify the appropriate elevation, size, and shape. If the layout is generated automatically by the program, check the resulting ductwork layout and make adjustments as needed. Switch to a 3D view to verify that the ductwork has been created correctly. Make sure that none of the return ductwork interferes with other building components.
10. Insert tags to identify ductwork sizes, diffusers, and air handling equipment. Adjust the position of tags and add leaders to tags where needed.
11. Create schedules to document the equipment and data associated with the heating and cooling system. If needed, adjust the schedule format to display the number and types of diffusers and other equipment in the distribution system.
12. Create a heating and cooling report for the entire system. This can usually be generated automatically based on the zones and spaces created in the project.
13. Create a new sheet for the climate control plan. Insert the climate control plan view onto the sheet. If needed, adjust the placement of text for the view title and scale. Insert the appropriate schedules and reports onto the sheet.
14. Look over your work to be sure that you are finished. When you are sure the plan is complete, print or plot the sheet.

Summary

- A climate control plan shows the location, size, and type of heating, cooling, ventilating, humidifying, and air cleaning equipment and the required piping or ducts.
- The climate control plan is generally drawn to a scale of 1/4″ = 1′-0″.
- Outlets and inlets are required for forced-air systems.
- Ducts can be round or rectangular and are used in a forced-air system to move large quantities of air for heating or cooling.
- Every automatic climate control system requires at least one thermostat.
- A climate control equipment schedule provides an orderly means of specifying equipment to be used in the system.

Internet Resources

Carrier
Residential heating and cooling systems

Honeywell
Manufacturer of thermostats, humidifiers, and dehumidifiers

Lennox
Residential heating and cooling systems

Trane
Residential heating and cooling systems

Review Questions

Answer the following questions using the information in this chapter.

1. What is the purpose of the climate control plan?
2. Identify four features that should be included on a climate control plan.
3. Why is a perimeter system of outlets generally specified?
4. What is the difference between a register and a diffuser?
5. When should a room have more than one outlet?
6. Name the two basic types of ductwork systems.
7. What size is required for round ducts that are used for both heating and cooling?
8. What is a wall stack?
9. A rectangular plenum duct that will supply four 6″ ducts should be what size?
10. Where should the thermostat be placed for a residential climate control system?
11. If a house has three heating zones, it will normally require ______ thermostats.
12. Why are heat loss calculations usually included on a climate control plan?

Suggested Activities

1. Using a simple plan provided by your instructor or one you designed yourself, plan a complete climate control system. Create a climate control plan based on your design.
2. Create an isometric drawing that represents the essential elements of a heating system. You may choose a forced-air, hydronic, hydronic radiant, electric radiant, heat pump, or geothermal heat pump system. Label the parts and prepare a display.
3. Using CADD, draw standard climate control symbols. Add the symbols to your symbol library.
4. Using CADD, design a climate control plan for the house shown in Figure 14-15. Place features of the climate control plan on separate layers as appropriate. Assign linetypes and colors as appropriate.

Problem Solving Case Study

A client has come to your residential climate control design service in Rocky Mount, North Carolina, to discuss ideas for the remodeling of the client's two-story residence. The residence has 3500 square feet of total livable area. The client wants to retrofit the home with a new, sustainable air conditioning unit, dehumidifier, and heating unit.

Conduct research if necessary to find suitable climate control components for this client. Determine the required sizes and make specific recommendations regarding the brands and features that will best meet the client's needs.

ADDA Certification Prep

The following questions are presented in the style used in the American Design Drafting Association (ADDA) Drafter Certification Test. Answer the questions using the information in this chapter.

1. Which of the following statements about climate control plans are true?
   A. The inlet in a forced-air system is called a register.
   B. The climate control plan includes information on size and location of the distribution system.
   C. The round duct used to supply registers in the extended plenum system may be 6″ or 8″ in diameter.
   D. The climate control plan is generally drawn at the same scale as the site plan.
2. Which of the following statements are *false*?
   A. Location of the thermostat is important because it measures the temperature and activates the furnace.
   B. The extended plenum system has a large circular duct (plenum) for the main supply.
   C. Every automatic climate control system requires at least two thermostats.
   D. The required size of baseboard unit or convector cabinet depends on the heat loss for a given area.
3. Match each item with its definition.

   Items: 1. Outlet, 2. Inlet, 3. Grille, 4. Register, 5. Diffuser
   A. A hole through which cold air is returned to the furnace for reheating.
   B. A basic outlet cover that can also be used for inlets.
   C. An outlet cover that directs air flow in a specific direction.
   D. A hole or surface through which warm air is delivered to a room.
   E. An outlet cover that contains a damper and is used only for supply air.

Curricular Connections

1. **Social Science.** Calculate the total annual cooling and heating costs for a one-story, 1800-square-foot concrete block structure (CBS) home and for a comparable wood frame home in your area. Check with the utility company that services your area for the latest and most accurate cost figures. Then choose another part of the country where the climate is different from yours and repeat the calculations. Compare the two sets of numbers. Write a report, based on your calculations, explaining how climate does or does not influence the building materials used in different parts of the country.

STEM Connections

1. **Math.** Calculate the plenum size for each of the following installations.
   A. A rectangular plenum that will serve nine 6″ round ducts.
   B. A rectangular plenum that will serve four 6″ round ducts.
   C. A rectangular plenum that will serve eight 8″ round ducts.
   D. A rectangular plenum that will serve five 8″ round ducts.
2. **Technology.** Conduct research into evaporative cooling systems. Write a report explaining how these systems work and why they are considered a sustainable technology.

Communicating about Architecture

1. **Listening.** In small groups, discuss your knowledge of climate control systems with your classmates. Take notes on the observations expressed by others. Then review the points discussed. Develop a summary of what you have learned and present it to the class.
2. **Listening and Speaking.** Listen closely as your classmates present their findings on climate control systems. Take notes on anything you find particularly interesting, and write down any questions you think of during the presentations. Once your classmates are finished presenting, share with the class one thought or question you had regarding their research.

Section 7

Specifications and Estimating Costs

alexmisu/Shutterstock.com

Chapter 35

Specifications

Objectives

After completing this chapter, you will be able to:

- Explain the purpose of specifications.
- List the sources of specification standards.
- Use a Description of Materials form.

Key Terms

MasterSpec®	specifications
master specifications	VHA Master Specifications

Although the working drawings in a set of architectural plans are very detailed, they do not include all of the details needed to build a home. ***Specifications*** are written documents that supplement the drawings in a set of architectural plans. The specifications provide additional written information about the types of construction materials, products, work to be completed, and quality of construction involved in building the home.

When the home is to be constructed for sale, the architect generally supplies the specifications. When the home is being designed and constructed for a specific client, the architect and client usually develop the specifications together. In either case, the architect is responsible for the preparation of specifications for residential structures.

Both the working drawings and the specifications (specs) become part of the total contract between the builder and client. They are legal and binding on both parties. For this reason, the specifications should be prepared very carefully, leaving little or no chance for misunderstandings between the contractor and client. See **Figure 35-1**.

Purpose of Specifications

Construction details that are found on the working drawings do not need to be repeated in the specifications. The purpose of the specifications is to provide important information about construction materials and processes that either will not fit on the drawings or that cannot be communicated on a drawing.

Marcin Balcerzak

Figure 35-1. The architect carefully reviews the working drawings and specifications for the new residence with the clients before construction begins.

For example, suppose a client wants the living room and bedrooms to have hardwood floors. The floor plan may show the wood floors and may even include a note about the type of wood to be used. Suppose the client wants oak floors. Even if the floor plan contains a note saying that the flooring will be oak, there are several different grades of oak flooring, as well as different widths and finishes. See **Figure 35-2**. If this information were not included in the specifications, the building contractor could use any grade and finish available and still be within the contract requirements. The contractor's choices may well not be what the client had in mind. In this case, the specifications should detail the grade of oak flooring to be used, the thickness of the flooring, the width of each board, the underlayment or surface preparation, and the finish to be used on the flooring. Even the brand or manufacturer of the flooring may be specified. Providing these detailed specifications helps ensure that the home will be built using acceptable materials of good quality.

It is the client's responsibility to carefully explain to the architect exactly what he or she wants, including the overall appearance and any specific details the client wants to include. The architect should carefully listen to the client's wishes for details such as floor coverings, paint colors, type and style of hardware, plumbing fixtures, wallpaper, and other items involving individual taste. These items allow the clients to express their own personal tastes and

Frank Anusewicz Gallery/Shutterstock.com

A

Anthro/Shutterstock.com

B

Lukiyanova Natalia/frenta/Shutterstock.com

C

Figure 35-2. All three of these flooring examples are oak, but their appearances vary significantly. A—Red oak finished naturally. B—White oak with a dark finish. C—White oak finished naturally.

Employability
Professional Behavior

No matter what career you choose, you will be expected to behave professionally on the job. Professional behavior can help the office run more smoothly. It can also help you advance in your career. Keep the following tips in mind for behaving professionally in the workplace:

- Show respect for your boss and coworkers.
- Limit personal conversations and phone calls to break times or lunch.
- Act courteously; remember that others are focusing on their work. Interruptions can cause them to lose concentration.
- Arrive at work on time and do not leave work early.
- Never raise your voice for any reason. Shouted arguments and loud laughter are equally inappropriate in the workplace.

Activity

Conduct research online to find out more about expected behavior in the workplace. Try to find information specific to the architectural field. Report your findings to the class.

preferences. For structural materials, however, the client should normally rely on the architect's judgment and suggestions.

While specifications for materials can be exact definitions, the question of tradework and quality of construction can be more difficult to define. What may appear to be a quality job of cabinet construction to one person may appear unsatisfactory to another. It is the purpose of the specifications to include what both the contractor and client agree on as an acceptable degree of tradework quality. The contractor should employ or subcontract only to qualified, skilled tradeworkers.

Master Specifications

Traditionally, there have been many types and styles of specifications in both long and short form. Specification guides or outlines can be purchased locally or supplied by the architect. However, most architects and home designers today use standard forms called ***master specifications*** that have been developed by reputable organizations. These documents are complete sets of specifications for use and adaptation by individual architectural companies. They contain suggested wording for almost every potential specification for a building project. Architectural firms choose the specifications that apply to their particular projects and delete or ignore the remaining items.

American Institute of Architects

The American Institute of Architects (AIA) *MasterSpec®* system is a set of master specifications widely used in the construction industry. ***MasterSpec***, published by Architectural Computer Services (ARCOM) for the AIA, is a master list of specifications on which architectural firms can build their own standards. It contains numbered divisions that address every part of building construction. The numbered divisions are based on the divisions in the MasterFormat® system published by the Construction Specifications Institute (CSI). The divisions addressed in the MasterSpec system and a brief description of their contents are shown in **Figure 35-3**.

Department of Veterans Affairs

Another set of master specifications is the ***VHA Master Specifications***, published by the Department of Veterans Affairs (VA). This set of specifications includes numbered divisions based on the MasterFormat standard and is similar to the AIA MasterSpec system, but it is not quite as extensive.

In addition, the VA provides other forms, such as the much shorter *Description of Materials* form shown in **Figure 35-4**. Although this form

American Institute of Architects (AIA) MasterSpec Divisions		
Division	**Name**	**Brief Summary of Contents**
00	Procurement and Contracting Requirements	Lists of drawing sheets and schedules, bid materials, schedule information, permit application, information about existing conditions and hazardous materials
01	General Requirements	Summary of the project, provisions for allowances, prices, alternate materials and substitutions, payment procedures, documentation of work, LEED requirements
02	Existing Conditions	Demolition
03	Concrete	Mixtures, reinforcing, forms, finishing, curing of concrete for various applications
04	Masonry	Brick masonry repair and repointing, stone repair and repointing, concrete masonry, glass masonry, stone cladding and veneers, cast stone
05	Metals	Structural steel framing, joists, decking, trusses, fabrications, stairs, gratings, railings
06	Wood, Plastics, and Composites	Rough carpentry, heavy timber construction, patio decking, sheathing, trusses, finish carpentry, paneling, laminate, wood stairs and railings, ornamental woodwork, wood trim
07	Thermal and Moisture Protection	Waterproofing, insulation, weather barriers, roofing materials, aluminum siding, fireproofing
08	Openings	All types of doors and windows and their frames (including skylights), all associated glass, mirrors, wall vents
09	Finishes	Drywall, plaster, tiles (including ceramic, glass, and stone), flooring materials, interior and exterior painting, staining and finishing
10	Specialties	Public signs, telephone enclosures, toilet enclosures, commercial laundries, flagpoles; not normally needed for residential construction
11	Equipment	Parking control equipment, loading dock equipment, food service equipment, stage equipment; not normally needed for residential construction
12	Furnishings	Horizontal and vertical blinds, curtains, drapes, shades, countertops
13	Special Construction	Saunas, metal buildings, control booths

(continued)

Goodheart-Willcox Publisher

Figure 35-3. Divisions addressed by the MasterSpec set of master specifications. The division numbers and names are based on the divisions in the Construction Specifications Institute (CSI) MasterFormat standard.

American Institute of Architects (AIA) MasterSpec Divisions *(Continued)*		
Division	**Name**	**Brief Summary of Contents**
14	Conveying Equipment	Elevators, dumbwaiters, escalators, trash and laundry chutes; not normally needed for residential construction
21	Fire Suppression	Fire suppression equipment, fire sprinkler systems; not normally needed for residential construction
22	Plumbing	Fittings, piping, valves, pipe insulation, pumps, septic tanks, sump pumps, water heaters, residential plumbing fixtures (toilets, sinks, tubs, showers), commercial plumbing, drinking fountains, water coolers
23	Heating, Ventilating, and Air Conditioning	HVAC piping, hangers and supports, insulation, control equipment, all components for all types of heating and cooling systems
26	Electrical	Equipment and cables for electrical systems, lighting controls, fuses and circuit breakers, lightning protection, surge protection, interior and exterior lighting
27	Communications	Equipment and cables for communications systems, antennas, public address systems, educational program systems
28	Electronic Safety and Security	Digital fire alarm systems, refrigerant alarms, grounding for electronic systems and equipment
31	Earthwork	Site clearing, excavating, grading, ground-water control, soil-based termite control, piles (concrete, steel, timber, composite, and cast grout), piers, shafts
32	Exterior Improvements	Paving and curbs
33	Utilities	Water wells, storm drains, pond and reservoir liners

Goodheart-Willcox Publisher

Figure 35-3. *(Continued)*

is not as detailed as the master specifications, it covers the most common material requirements. Instead of listing all of the possible specifications, it contains blanks and check boxes to be filled in by the architect to specify common materials.

Many people believe that specifications are needed only for the materials to be used in a project. However, a complete set of specifications also includes the equipment and processes to be used, as well as standards for work quality and environmental protection. For example, *Division 01—General Requirements* in the VHA Master Specifications includes provisions for temporary environmental controls to protect the environment during construction, as well as provisions for sustainable design processes. These provisions are also addressed in *Division 01—General Requirements* in the MasterSpec master specifications.

Department of Veterans Affairs | **DESCRIPTION OF MATERIALS**

PRIVACY ACT NOTICE: VA will not disclose information collected on this form to any source other than what has been authorized under the Privacy Act of 1974 or Title 38, CFR 1.576 for routine uses (for example: Authorizing release of information to Congress when requested for statistical purposes) as identified in the VA system of records, 55VA26, Loan Guaranty Home, Condominium and Manufactured Home Loan Applicant Records, Specially Adapted Housing Applicant Records, and Vendee Loan Applicant Records - VA, 17VA26, Loan Guaranty Fee Personnel and Program Participant Records - VA, and published in the Federal Register. Your obligation to respond is required to obtain or retain benefits.

RESPONDENT BURDEN: We need this information to establish the value and or cost of adaptations or new construction before work begins. Title 38, U.S.C. authorizes collections of this information. We estimate that you will need an average of 30 minutes to review the instructions, find the information, and complete this form. VA cannot conduct or sponsor a collection of information unless a valid OMB control number is displayed. You are not required to respond to a collection of information if this number is not displayed. Valid OMB control numbers can be located on the OMB Internet Page at www.reginfo.gov/public/do/PRAMain. If desired, you can call 1-800-827-1000 to get information on where to send comments or suggestions about this form.

☐ PROPOSED CONSTRUCTION ☐ UNDER CONSTRUCTION CASE NO. ______

PROPERTY ADDRESS *(Include City and State)*

NAME AND ADDRESS OF LENDER OR SPONSOR

NAME AND ADDRESS OF CONTRACTOR OR BUILDER

INSTRUCTIONS

1. For additional information on how this form is to be submitted, number of copies, etc., see the instructions in the VA Lender's Handbook.
2. Describe all materials and equipment to be used, whether or not shown on the drawings, by marking an X in each appropriate check-box and entering the information called for each space. If space is inadequate, enter "See misc." and describe under item 27 or on an attached sheet. **The use of paint containing more than the percentage of lead by weight permitted by law is prohibited.**
3. Work not specifically described or shown will not be considered unless required, then the minimum acceptable will be assumed. Work exceeding minimum requirements cannot be considered unless specifically described.
4. Include no alternates, "or equal" phrases, or contradictory items. (Consideration of a request for acceptance of substitute materials or equipment is not thereby precluded.)
5. Include signatures required at the end of this form.
6. The construction shall be completed in compliance with the related drawings and specifications, as amended during processing. The specifications include this Description of Materials and the applicable Minimum Property Requirements.

1. EXCAVATION

Bearing soil, type ______

2. FOUNDATIONS

Footings concrete mix ______ strength psi ______ Reinforcing ______

Foundation wall material ______ Reinforcing ______

Interior foundation wall material ______ Party foundation wall ______

Columns material and sizes ______ Piers material and reinforcing ______

Girders material and sizes ______ Sills material ______

Basement entrance areaway ______ Window areaways ______

Waterproofing ______ Footing drains ______

Termite protection ______

Basement space ground cover ______ insulation ______ foundation vents ______

Special foundations ______

Additional information ______

3. CHIMNEYS

Material ______ Prefabricated *(make and size)* ______

Flue lining material ______ Heater flue size ______ Fireplace flue size ______

Vents *(material and size)* gas or oil heater ______ water heater ______

Additional information ______

4. FIREPLACES

Type ☐ solid fuel ☐ gas-burning ☐ circulator *(make and size)* ______ Ash dump and clean-out ______

Fireplace facing ______ lining ______ hearth ______ mantel ______

Additional information

VA FORM JUL 2012 **26-1852** SUPERSEDES VA FORM 26-1852, OCT 1984, WHICH WILL NOT BE USED. Retain this record for three years Page 1 of 6

(continued)

Department of Veterans Affairs

Figure 35-4. This standard Department of Veterans Affairs form lends itself well to all types of specifications for residential construction.

5. EXTERIOR WALLS

Wood frame wood grade, and species ______ ☐ Corner bracing Building paper or felt ______

Sheathing ______ thickness ______ width ______ ☐ solid ☐ spaced ______ o.c. ☐ diagonal ______

Siding ______ grade ______ type ______ size ______ exposure ______ fastening ______

Shingles ______ grade ______ type ______ size ______ exposure ______ fastening ______

Stucco ______ thickness ______ Lath ______ weight ______ lb.

Masonry veneer ______ Sills ______ Lintels ______ Base flashing ______

Masonry ☐ solid ☐ faced ☐ stuccoed total wall thickness ______ facing thickness ______ facing material ______

Backup material ______ thickness ______ bonding ______

Door sills ______ Window sills ______ Lintels ______ Base flashing ______

Interior surfaces dampproofing, ______ coats of ______ furring ______

Additional information ______

Exterior painting material ______ number of coats ______

Gable wall construction ☐ same as main walls ☐ other construction ______

6. FLOOR FRAMING

Joists wood, grade, and species ______ other ______ bridging ______ anchors ______

Concrete slab ☐ basement floor ☐ first floor ☐ ground supported ☐ self-supporting mix ______ thickness ______

reinforcing ______ insulation ______ membrane ______

Fill under slab material ______ thickness ______

Additional information

7. SUBFLOORING *(Describe underflooring for special floors under item 21)*

Material grade and species ______ size ______ type ______

Laid ☐ first floor ☐ second floor ☐ attic ______ sq. ft. ☐ diagonal ☐ right angles

Additional information ______

8. FINISH FLOORING *(Wood only. Describe other finish flooring under item 21)*

Location	Rooms	Grade	Species	Thickness	Width	Bldg. Paper	Finish
First floor							
Second floor							
Attic floor	sq. ft.						

Additional information

9. PARTITION FRAMING

Studs wood, grade, and species ______ size and spacing ______ Other ______

Additional information

10. CEILING FRAMING

Joists wood, grade, and species ______ Other ______ Bridging ______

Additional information

11. ROOF FRAMING

Rafters wood, grade and species ______ Roof trusses *(see detail)* grade and species ______

Additional information

12. ROOFING

Sheathing wood, grade, and species ______ ☐ solid ☐ spaced ______ o.c.

Roofing ______ grade ______ size ______ type ______

Underlay ______ weight or thickness ______ size ______ fastening ______

Built-up roofing ______ number of piles ______ surfacing material ______

Flashing material ______ gauge or weight ______ ☐ gravel stops ☐ snow guards

Additional information

VA FORM 26-1852, JUL 2012 Retain this record for three years Page 2 of 6

(continued)

13. GUTTERS AND DOWNSPOUTS

Gutters material ____________ gauge or weight ________ size ________ shape ____________

Downspouts material ____________ gauge or weight ________ size ________ shape ________ number ______

Downspouts connected to ☐ Storm sewer ☐ sanitary sewer ☐ dry well ☐ Splash blocks material and size ____________

Additional information

14. LATH AND PLASTER

Lath ☐ walls ☐ ceilings material ____________ weight or thickness ________ Plaster coats ________ finish ________

Dry-wall ☐ walls ☐ ceilings material ____________ thickness ________ finish ________

Joint treatment ____________

15. DECORATING *(Paint, wallpaper, etc.)*

Rooms	Wall Finish Material and Application	Ceiling Finish Material and Application
Kitchen		
Bath		
Other		

Additional Information

16. INTERIOR DOORS AND TRIM

Doors type ____________ material ____________ thickness ________

Door trim type ________ material ________ Base type ________ material ________ size ________

Finish doors ____________ trim ____________

Other trim *(item, type and location)* ____________

Additional Information

17. WINDOWS

Windows type ____________ make ________ material ____________ sash thickness ________

Glass grade ____________ ☐ sash weights ☐ balances, type ____________ head flashing ________

Trim type ____________ material ________ Paint ____________ number coats ______

Weatherstripping type ____________ material ____________ Storm sash, number ______

Screens ☐ full ☐ half type ____________ number ______ screen cloth material ____________

Basement windows type ____________ material ____________ screens, number ______ Storm sash, number ______

Special windows ____________

Additional Information

18. ENTRANCES AND EXTERIOR DETAIL

Main entrance door material ____________ width ________ thickness ________ Frame material ________ thickness ________

Other entrance doors material ____________ width ________ thickness ________ Frame material ________ thickness ________

Head flashing ____________ Weatherstripping type ____________ saddles ________

Screen doors thickness ________ number ______ screen cloth material ____________ Storm doors thickness ________ number ______

Combination storm and screen doors thickness ________ number ______ screen cloth material ____________

Shutters ☐ hinged ☐ fixed Railings ____________ Attic louvers ____________

Exterior millwork grade and species ____________ Paint ____________ number coats ______

Additional Information

19. CABINETS AND INTERIOR DETAIL

Kitchen cabinets, wall units material ____________ lineal feet of shelves ________ shelf width ________

Base units material ____________ counter top ____________ edging ____________

Back and end splash ____________ Finish of cabinets ____________ number coats ______

Medicine cabinets make ____________ model ____________

Other cabinets and built-in furniture ____________

Additional Information

VA FORM 26-1852, JUL 2012 Retain this record for three years Page 3 of 6

(continued)

20. STAIRS

Stair	Treads		Risers		Stringers		Handrail		Balusters	
	Material	Thickness	Material	Thickness	Material	Size	Material	Size	Material	Size
Basement										
Main										
Attic										

Disappearing make and model number ______

Additional Information

21. SPECIAL FLOORS AND WAINSCOT *(Describe Carpet as listed in Certified Products Directory)*

Floors	Location	Material, Color, Border, Sizes, Gauge, Etc.	Threshold Material	Wall Base Material	Underfloor Material
	Kitchen				
	Bath				

Wainscot	Location	Material, Color, Border, Cap, Sizes, Gauge, Etc.	Height	Height Over Tub	Height in Showers (From Floor)
	Bath				

Additional Information

22. PLUMBING

Fixture	Number	Location	Make	MFR's Fixture Identification No.	Size	Color
Sink						
Lavatory						
Water closet						
Bathtub						
Shower over tub						
Stall shower						
Laundry trays						

Bathroom accessories ☐ Recessed material ______ number ______ ☐ Attached material ______ number ______

Additional Information

☐ Curtain rod ☐ Door ☐ Shower pan material ______

**(Show and describe individual system in complete detail in separate drawings and specifications according to requirements.)*

Water supply ☐ public ☐ community system ☐ individual *(private)*system*

Sewage disposal ☐ public ☐ community system ☐ individual *(private)*system*

House drain *(inside)* ☐ cast iron ☐ tile ☐ other ______ House sewer *(outside)* ☐ cast iron ☐ tile ☐ other ______

Water piping ☐ galvanized steel ☐ copper tubing ☐ other ______ Sill cocks, number ______

Domestic water heater type ______ make and model ______ heating capacity ______ gph. 100° rise.

Storage tank material ______ capacity ______ gallons

Gas service ☐ utility company ☐ liq. pet. gas ☐ other ______ ☐ Gas piping ☐ cooking ☐ house heating

Footing drains connected to ☐ Storm sewer ☐ sanitary sewer ☐ dry well ☐ Sump pump make and model ______

capacity ______ discharges into ______

Additional Information

VA FORM 26-1852, JUL 2012 Retain this record for three years Page 4 of 6

(continued)

23. HEATING

☐ Hot water ☐ Steam ☐ Vapor ☐ One-pipe system ☐ Two-pipe system
☐ Radiators ☐ Convectors ☐ Baseboard radiation Make and model ____________
☐ Radiant panel ☐ floor ☐ wall ☐ ceiling Panel coil material ____________
☐ Circulator ☐ Return pump make and model ____________ capacity ______ gpm.
Boiler make and model ____________ Output ______ Btuh. net rating ______ Btuh.
Additional Information ____________

Warm air ☐ Gravity ☐ Forced Type of system ____________
Duct material supply ______ return ______ insulation ______ thickness ______ ☐ Outside air intake
Furnace make and model ____________ Input ______ Btuh. Output ______ Btuh.
Additional Information ____________

☐ Space heater ☐ floor furnace ☐ wall heater Input ______ Btuh. Output ______ Btuh. number units ______
Make and model ____________
Additional Information ____________

Controls make and types ____________
Additional Information ____________

Fuel ☐ Coal ☐ oil ☐ gas ☐ liq. pet. gas ☐ electric ☐ other ______ storage capacity ______
Additional Information ____________

Firing equipment furnished separately ☐ Gas burner, conversion type ☐ Stoker hopper feed ☐ bin feed
Oil burner ☐ pressure atomizing ☐ vaporizing ____________
Make and model ____________

Control ____________
Additional Information ____________

Electric heating system type ____________ Input ______ watts @ ______ volts output ______ Btuh.
Additional Information ____________

Ventilating equipment ☐ attic fan, make and model ____________ capacity ______ cfm.
☐ kitchen exhaust fan, make and model ____________

Other heating, ventilating, or cooling equipment ____________
Additional Information

24. ELECTRICAL WIRING

Service ☐ overhead ☐ underground Panel ☐ fuse box ☐ circuit-breaker make ______ AMP's ______ No. circuits ______
Wiring ☐ conduit ☐ armored cable ☐ nonmetallic cable ☐ knob and tube ☐ other ______
Special outlets ☐ range ☐ water heater ☐ other ______
☐ Doorbell ☐ Chimes ☐ Push-button locations ______
Additional Information

25. LIGHTING FIXTURES

Total number of fixtures ______ Total allowance for fixtures, typical installation, $ ______
Nontypical installation ____________
Additional Information

VA FORM 26-1852, JUL 2012 Retain this record for three years Page 5 of 6

(continued)

26. INSULATION

Location	Thickness	Material, Type, and Method of Installation	Vapor Barrier
Roof			
Ceiling			
Wall			
Floor			

27. MISCELLANEOUS: *(Describe any main dwelling materials, equipment, or construction items not shown elsewhere; or use to provide additional information where the space provided was inadequate. Always reference by item number to correspond to numbering used on this form.)*

HARDWARE *(make, material, and finish)*

SPECIAL EQUIPMENT *(State material or make, model and quantity. Include only equipment and appliances which are acceptable by local and Federal law. Do not include items which, by established custom, are supplied by occupant and removed when he vacates premises or chattels prohibited by law from becoming realty.)*

PORCHES

TERRACES

GARAGES

WALKS AND DRIVEWAYS

Driveway width ________ base material ________ thickness ________ surfacing material ________ thickness ________
Front walk width ________ material ________ thickness ________ Service walk width ________ material ________ thickness ________
Steps material ________ treads ________ risers ________ Cheek walls ________

OTHER ONSITE IMPROVEMENTS

(Specify all exterior onsite improvements not described elsewhere, including items such as unusual grading, drainage structures, retaining walls, fence, railings, and accessory structures.)

LANDSCAPING, PLANTING, AND FINISH GRADING

Topsoil ________ thick ☐ front yard ☐ side yards ☐ rear yard to ________ feet behind main building
Lawns (seeded, sodded, or sprigged) ☐ front yard ________ ☐ side yards ________ ☐ rear yard ________
Planting ☐ as specified and shown on drawings ☐ as follows:

________ Shade trees deciduous ________ caliper ________ Evergreen trees ________ to ________ B & B
________ Low flowering trees deciduous ________ to ________ ________ Evergreen shrubs ________ to ________ B & B
________ High-growing shrubs deciduous ________ to ________ ________ Vines, 2-year ________
________ Medium-growing shrubs deciduous ________ to ________ Other
________ Low-growing shrubs deciduous ________ to ________

IDENTIFICATION –This exhibit shall be identified by the signature of the builder and/or the proposed purchaser if the latter is known at the time of application.

SIGNATURE OF BUILDER	DATE *(MM/DD/YYYY)*
SIGNATURE OF PURCHASER	DATE *(MM/DD/YYYY)*

VA FORM 26-1852, JUL 2012 Retain this record for three years Page 6 of 6

Green Architecture

Specifications for Green Homes

The leading master specifications incorporate LEED building standards in an effort to encourage architects, designers, and contractors to specify buildings that are more sustainable than those in the past. However, the final decisions are up to the architect and the client.

There is no "one size fits all" solution for sustainability. Choices depend on the region of the country, as well as the preferences and lifestyle of the client. The architect is responsible for staying up-to-date with the newest sustainable materials and practices. A knowledgeable architect can offer clients a variety of green alternatives, any of which can be specified for a new home. Understanding which green technologies and materials will suit a given client is both an art and a skill to be learned over time. However, even a beginning architect can stay current with new technologies and explain them to potential clients.

Completeness and Accuracy

The more specific and detailed the specifications are, the more accurately the building contractor can build the house. Therefore, for many projects, the specifications may consist of booklets more than an inch thick. Using a standard form template such as MasterSpec can greatly decrease the amount of time needed to prepare the specifications. When standard specification forms are used, each section may be filled in or left blank, as agreed by the architect and client. Each topic on the form should be carefully discussed with the architect, and in some cases the builder, so that everyone understands and agrees to its content.

Regardless of the specification forms used, all specifications should include the following items:

- A description of the materials to be used. This includes sizes, quality, brand names, style, and specification numbers.
- List of required building operations. These are usually described under major headings such as excavation, masonry, carpentry, millwork, plumbing, electrical, insulation, etc.
- Notes relative to cash allowances for such items as lighting fixtures and hardware that are to be selected by the client. Expenditures over the cash allowance must be paid by the client.
- Any environmental standards or requirements that must be met.
- An indication that all of the specifications refer to the detailed plans of the working drawings.
- A statement or agreement on the quality of the tradeworker's skill. This statement or agreement may be drawn up as a separate part of the contract. This is important to provide a definition of quality.
- Liability covered by the contractor during construction.

Figure 35-5 shows a portion of a set of specifications prepared by an architect. The portion shown provides an outline of materials and details of the responsibilities of the contractor. Note the major headings used for materials and required building operations.

CONTRACT SPECIFICATIONS

Mr. and Mrs. Frank E. Smith Residence
1103 Douglas Street
Glendale, GA

Date____________________

EXCAVATION: House to be excavated to depths shown on drawings, backfilled and graded with existing soil. Excavation overcut in garage and lower level to be filled with sand. Twelve inches of sand to be furnished under garage floor. Tree removal is included only within building or drive area.

CONCRETE: All concrete to be 5 bag mix. Included is all foundation work, front sidewalk, garage floor, lower level floor, basement floor, and front stoop. Garage floor to have 6/6 wire mesh. All tie rods in lower level and basement are to be broken off on the inside and outside of foundation and inside of walls to have brushed cement finished coat. Furnish and install Andersen basement windows complete with area wells and grates.

WATERPROOFING: Exterior of lower level and basement to receive two coats of Portland cement plaster and one spray coat of bituminous waterproofing.

STEEL: All steel beams, angles, plates, columns, and lintels are a part of this contract.

LUMBER: All floor joists are to be 2 × 10 kiln-dried southern yellow pine. All studs to be 2 × 4 white fir precuts. Ceiling joists and roof rafters to be 2 × 6 white fir. Roof sheathing and subfloor to be 4 × 8 × 1/2 C-D plywood. Exterior siding to be channel type prestained rough sawn cedar. Fascia and soffit to be 1 × 8 prestained rough sawn cedar. Basement and lower level stairs to have 2 × 10 oak treads, pine risers, and stringers. Two rows of 1 × 3 cross bridging to be installed.

MASONRY: Residence to have face brick four sides with an allowance of $500/3000. Fireplace to be face brick at $500/3000 allowance with slate hearth, colonial damper, cast iron ash drop and cleanout, 13/13 tile flue. Color mortar or raked joints will be extra.

CARPENTRY: All carpentry labor is included for all rough and trim work, including installation of all cabinets, tops, appliances, and hardware. Front door, garage service door, and door from garage to lower level to be weather stripped and to have aluminum thresholds.

STAIRWAY: Stairway from first to second floor to be mill-made with oak treads and pine or white wood risers and stringers. Furnish railings for foyer and dining room.

MILLWORK: All trim to be Colonial white pine; all interior doors to be Colonial pine panel (first and second floor) 1-3/8″ flush white birch on lower level; front and garage service doors to be 1-3/4″ pine panel; door from garage to lower level to be 1-3/4″ solid core pine panel; door from garage to lower level to be 1-3/4″ solid core birch. All windows to be Andersen casements in insulating glass with screens on operating windows and muntin bars where indicated on drawings. All windows to have birch stools.

CABINETS: All kitchen and vanity cabinets to be birch or oak, prefinished, with ranch or provincial grooves and lap type doors with flush surface. Purchaser to select from standard finishes.

FLOORING: Floors for living room, dining room, upper hall, and bedrooms to be 5/8″ plywood. Floors under ceramic tile in second floor baths and foyer to be 1/2″ plywood. Floors in kitchen to be 5/8″ underlayment plywood screwed in place. All floors to be laid directly on top of subfloors.

DRYWALL: All drywall to be 1/2″ adhesive applied before nailing (three coat finish) garage ceiling and firewall to be 5/8″ fire code with three exterior walls to be 1/2″ regular drywall.

INSULATION: Ceiling of house to have 12″ fiberglass insulation except cathedral ceiling in living and dining room to have 4″ fiberglass batt insulation. Walls of house to have 3-1/2″ fiberglass batts and 3/4″ rigid foam weatherboard. Garage ceiling and garage exterior walls are insulated similar to house.

GLAZING: Obscure DS glass to be installed in basement sash. A 54″ × 48″ plate glass mirror to be installed in upper hall bath. Decorative glass panels to be installed in garage.

SHINGLES: All shingles to be 235 lb. asphalt with adhesive tabs laid over 15 lb. roofing felt.

HEATING AND SHEET METAL: A Carrier or Bryant gas forced-air furnace and electric air conditioner to be installed with deluxe high wall returns on the second floor. A power humidifier, copper gutters and downspouts and flashing, exhaust ducts for fans are part of this contract.

PLUMBING: All plumbing fixtures to be Kohler in almond except blue in bath No. 2. Two water closets to be Willworth model. Two lavatories to be Castelle, one tub to be Caribbean, two prefab shower bases, one 32″ × 21″ stainless steel kitchen sink, one single compartment standard laundry tub. Water heater to be Rheem Fury 40 gal. glass lined. All faucets to be Moen mixing valve type. Shutoff valves are included at all sinks, lavatories, and water closets. Three hose bibs to be installed (front free type). Floor drain to be installed in basement, laundry room, and garage. Drawing tile to be installed around lower level and deep basement leading into a submersible sump pump for grade discharge. Gas lines to be run to furnace and water heater. Install dishwasher and disposal. All water lines to be copper and all sewer lines to be PVC. Install bypass for future softener by owner. Rough in only for powder room lavatory and water closet.

ELECTRICAL: 200 amp underground electrical service with circuit breakers, one recessed chime with front and rear button. Install 240 volt outlet for range and oven. Provide electrical installation of furnace, power humidifier, dishwasher, and disposal. Light fixture allowance is $1250.00.

HARDWARE: Interior and exterior door locks to be Schlage A Series. Kitchen cabinet and vanity hardware to be America. Allowance for all finish hardware is $800.00 which includes closet rods, hinges, locks, latches, pulls, door bumpers, etc.

PAINTING: First floor and lower level trim to be stained, sealed, an varnished. Walls and ceilings of house to receive a prime and finish coat. Exterior trim on windows and doors to receive two coats. Walltex is included at $16.00 per roll for baths No. 1 and 2. Second floor trim and doors to be painted (bedroom level).

PERMIT: All permits and inspection fees are included in this contract.

SURVEY: Topography, survey, and building site are a part of this contract.

INSURANCE: Contractor to carry builders risk, covering fire theft, liability, and property damage. Purchaser to insure building upon final closing.

QUALITY: Contractor to provide all material necessary to build on real estate in a good, substantial, and quality tradeworker manner.

Goodheart-Willcox Publisher

Figure 35-5. A portion of a set of specifications for a home designed specifically for the owner.

Summary

- Specifications provide additional information that is not shown in the set of working drawings.
- The architect is generally responsible for the preparation of specifications for residential structures.
- Both the specifications and the working drawings become part of the contract for a building project.
- Two common sets of master specifications are the AIA's MasterSpec system and the VA's VHA Master Specifications.
- The more specific and detailed the specifications are, the more accurately the building contractor can build the house.

Internet Resources

American Institute of Architects (AIA)
Information about specifications and contract documents

Architectural Computer Services (ARCOM)
Construction and building specifications, including MasterSpec

Construction Specifications Institute (CSI)
MasterFormat standard and resources for developing master specifications

Department of Veterans Affairs Office of Construction & Facilities Management
Technical Information Library—Master Construction Specifications 2004

Review Questions

Answer the following questions using the information in this chapter.

1. What are specifications?
2. What is the relationship of specifications to the building contract?
3. Why are construction details found on the working drawings not included in the specifications?
4. Why is it important that the architect listen carefully to the client's wishes when writing specifications?
5. Which organization publishes the MasterSpec master specifications?
6. The divisions in the MasterSpec master specifications are based on the divisions in what standard?
7. How are master specifications used?
8. How does the VA's Description of Materials form relate to the VHA Master Specifications?
9. Which division in the VHA Master Specifications addresses environmental protection during a construction project?
10. Briefly list the seven major types of information that should be included in any set of specifications for a residential structure.

Suggested Activities

1. Prepare a set of specifications for one of the homes you have designed using this text. Or, use a set of working drawings supplied by your instructor. Prepare a sheet similar to the one shown in Figure 35-5. Have another student be the client. Use this person's suggestions for appliances, floor coverings, and other items.
2. Write to manufacturers of appliances and plumbing fixtures or visit their websites. Prepare a presentation of the latest fixtures from which a client can select when planning a new home.
3. Visit a brick supplier and obtain information on the types of face brick available for residential construction and present prices. Write a short report on how you would present the selection of face brick and cost allowance to a client when planning specifications. Give an oral presentation in which you present the information to the class as you would to a client.

4. Secure a set of working drawings for a residence. Download the *Description of Materials* form from the Department of Veterans Affairs website and fill in all necessary information for the project. Plan the specifications as if you were an architect planning your own private residence. Using the information obtained in Activity 2, make selections based on your preferences.
5. If your CADD system has schedule-generation functions, create an automated schedule for use in specifying materials and building processes for a construction project.

Problem Solving Case Study

Your architectural firm designed a home for Ms. Cooper. You were responsible for creating the specifications for the project, so you sat down with Ms. Cooper and carefully went over all of the details. Together, you agreed on the following cash allowances:

- $1800 for appliances, including refrigerator, range with hood, dishwasher, and built-in microwave
- $1100 for lighting fixtures and ceiling fans

These items were written into the specifications and included in the contract. Today, Ms. Cooper comes to your office, enraged that she was told she would have to pay "extra" for both her appliances and the lighting fixtures. "We have a contract!" she exclaims. "You can't charge me more!" When you review Ms. Cooper's selections, you discover that she has chosen an expensive "French door" refrigerator and a top-of-the-line convection range, as well as a beautiful—but expensive—chandelier for the dining room. Her total appliance expenditures are $3695, and her total lighting costs are $2093.

Ms. Cooper is a good client, and this is a big contract for your office. What should you tell Ms. Cooper?

ADDA Certification Prep

The following questions are presented in the style used in the American Design Drafting Association (ADDA) Drafter Certification Test. Answer the questions using the information in this chapter.

1. Which of the following statements about specifications are true?
   A. The architect is generally responsible for the preparation of specifications for residential structures.
   B. The specifications become part of the complete set of building plans.
   C. Working drawings and specifications become part of the total contract between the builder and client.
   D. Construction details are found both on the working drawings and on the specifications.
2. Which of the following statements are *false*?
   A. The more detailed the specifications are, the more accurately the house can be built.
   B. The client should, in most cases, rely on the architect's judgment and suggestions for structural materials.
   C. When a home is being designed and constructed for a specific client, the architect and client usually develop the specifications together.
   D. Specifications include materials needed to build the house, but rarely include processes.
3. Which of the following statements are true?
   A. Many of the details of the actual building construction do not show up in the specifications.
   B. The architect should carefully listen to the client's wishes in such details as floor coverings and paint colors.
   C. The MasterSpec master specifications are available from the Department of Veterans Affairs.
   D. Providing detailed specifications helps ensure that a home will be built using acceptable materials of good quality.

Curricular Connections

1. **Language Arts.** Go to the Department of Veterans Affairs website and review the various parts of the VHA Master Specifications. Each division has numbered sections available as separate downloadable document files. Choose one division that is applicable to residential construction. Write a report describing how the specifications in this division help control the materials and quality in a residential building project.

STEM Connections

1. **Math.** Conduct research online or in local stores to find current prices for the basic appliances and light fixtures that might be included in a typical three-bedroom home. Use your findings to calculate a reasonable cash allowance to be included in specifications for such a home.
2. **Technology.** Conduct research to find various types of underlayments for wood flooring. Create a chart to compare the advantages and disadvantages of each type. What type would you specify for your clients? Would cost be a factor?

Communicating about Architecture

1. **Speaking.** With a partner, make flash cards of the key terms in this chapter. On the front of the card, write the term. On the back of the card, write the pronunciation and a brief definition. Use this chapter and a dictionary for guidance. Then take turns quizzing one another on the pronunciations and definitions of the key terms.
2. **Reading.** Working in small groups, create a poster that illustrates items to be included in a set of specifications. Display your poster in the classroom as a convenient reference aid for discussions and assignments.

Chapter 36

Estimating Building Costs

Objectives

After completing this chapter, you will be able to:

- Explain the process of estimating the building cost for a residence.
- Prepare a preliminary estimate of the cost of a residential structure using the square foot or cubic foot method.
- Generate a final estimate for a simple structure.

Key Terms

cubic foot method
design contingency
estimating
final estimate
material takeoff
preliminary estimate
square foot method
work breakdown structure (WBS)

After the house has been designed, construction drawings completed, and specifications prepared, an estimate should be made of the cost to build the house. ***Estimating*** is an organized effort to determine the total cost of materials, labor, and other services required to build a house.

Preliminary Estimates

A ***preliminary estimate***, or rough estimate, of the cost to build a home is usually generated at the design stage of the home building process, just after the initial floor plan is created. See **Figure 36-1**. The purpose of a preliminary estimate is to provide the client with a general "ballpark" idea of the cost of the project. It is often presented to the client to obtain project approval. This estimate reveals probable costs to determine whether the project is within the client's budget. It may also be used to place limits on the construction budget.

Because the design is not yet finalized, the preliminary estimate cannot be exact. In some cases, a ***design contingency*** of 10% to 15% is included to allow for design changes. The design contingency gives the client an idea of how much cost overrun there may be on the project. Preliminary estimates are usually created by the architect or builder.

The two most common manual methods of estimating the cost of building a home are the square foot method and the cubic foot method. A rough estimate of the building cost can be determined by using either method.

OtnaYdur/Shutterstock.com

Figure 36-1. The preliminary estimate is based on the initial working drawings.

Square Foot Method

The ***square foot method*** produces an estimate of the building cost based on the total area in the house. The first step is to compute the number of square feet in the house. This number is multiplied by a constant that is determined by local conditions. Garages, porches, and basements are figured separately since they are not as expensive to construct as the living part of the house. These are usually figured at one half of the cost per square foot of the living area.

A constant value of $100 per square foot is used in the following example for comparative purposes. This figure is reasonable for some areas, but may vary substantially in different locations, for different styles of homes, and by materials specified. For example, a single-level home is usually more expensive to build than a two-story home that provides the same area of living space. Most builders use a different constant for each house style and adjust it for special features, such as an extra bath or fireplace. Before trying to calculate the cost of a home, check with local builders to determine the constant for your area.

The number of square feet is determined by multiplying the length of the house by the width. All wall thicknesses are included in the total. For example, a 24′ × 60′ house with a 20′ × 20′ garage has 1440 square feet of living space plus 400 square feet of garage space. If the building cost per square foot is $100, then the building cost of the living area is 1440 × $100 = $144,000. The building cost of the garage is 400 × $50 = $20,000. The estimated building cost of the complete home is $144,000 + $20,000 = $164,000. This price does not include the land.

Cubic Foot Method

The ***cubic foot method*** produces an estimate of the building cost based on the volume of the house, rather than area. The volume of a house is determined by finding the area and then multiplying the area by the height. The height is figured from the floor to the ceiling for each level of the house, including the basement. The attic volume is also included, which is calculated by finding the area (length by the width) and multiplying this figure by 1/2 of the rise. The rise of the roof is the distance from the ceiling to the ridge. This procedure takes into account the volume lost due to the sloping roof.

Using the same 24′ × 60′ house for the cubic foot method, the area is 1440 square feet and the height is 8′. The living space is 1440 × 8 = 11,520 cubic feet, not including the attic. The area of the attic is 1440 square feet. The rise of the roof is 4′, so 1/2 of the rise is 2′. The volume of the attic is 1440 × 2 = 2880 cubic feet. The total cubic feet for the house is 11,520 + 2880 = 14,400 cubic feet. If the cost for a cubic foot is $10, the estimated building cost for the living space is 14,400 × $10 = $144,000.

The volume of the garage must also be computed and added to this figure. The volume is 400 × 8 = 3200 cubic feet. The garage attic with a rise of 3′ is 400 × 1-1/2′ = 600 cubic feet. The total volume of the garage is 3200 + 600 = 3800 cubic feet. The cost per cubic foot of garage space is figured at 1/2 of the cost per cubic foot of the living space. Therefore, the estimated building cost of the garage is 3800 × $5 = $19,000. The total estimated building cost of the house using the cubic foot method is $144,000 + $19,000 = $163,000, not including land cost.

Compare the estimates calculated by the square foot method and the cubic foot method. The difference in estimated building cost is $1000 in this case. Remember, in order to achieve an accurate estimate with either method, you must use an accurate constant.

Final Estimates

There are so many variables involved in the cost of a home that preliminary estimates may vary considerably from the actual cost. After the design has been finalized, a more accurate cost estimate is required. This estimate, called a ***final estimate*** or ***material takeoff***, is obtained by determining the quantity, quality, and cost of materials to be used and the cost of labor required for installation. An allowance for material waste, supervision, and overhead is also included in this estimate.

Unlike the preliminary estimate, which is frequently done by the architect, the final estimate is often created by an outside company that specializes in estimation. The first step in compiling an accurate estimate is to study the final working drawings and specifications very carefully to become fully acquainted with the various elements of the structure. The specifications provide important details that affect the final cost. See **Figure 36-2**.

Materials Estimate

After becoming familiar with the plans, the estimator compiles a list of the materials required to construct the house. Most estimates follow the headings as listed on a good set of specifications. The order of the headings usually coincides with the construction sequence. When all of the materials have been listed and priced, a total cost for materials can be calculated. Prices should be secured from sources where the materials will be purchased to get an accurate figure. A typical materials list is shown in **Figure 36-3**.

Photo courtesy of James Hardie® Siding Products

Figure 36-2. The nonstandard sizes and unique styles found on this house considerably increased the building cost.

Article and Description	Price	Amount
General Information		
Area of Basement, 1240 Square Feet		
Area of First Floor, 2250 Square Feet		
Height of Basement Floor to First Floor, 9′-1 5/8″ and 10′-1 5/8″		
First Floor Ceiling Height, 8′-0″, 7′-0″ and Slopes		
Ceiling to Roof, 4′-6″ and 3′-1″		
Size of Garage and/or Carport, 24′-1″ × 22′-10″		
Excavating and Grading (will vary with local site conditions)		
Rough Excavating, depends on site		
Trench Excavating (wall footings), 19 Cubic Yards		
Backfill, depends on site and soil		
Finished Grading, depends on site		
Hand Excavating (column footings), 1/2 Cubic Yard		
Material Sub Total		
Labor Sub Total		
Masonry		
Concrete Footings, 19.5 Cubic Yards		
Concrete Walls		
4″ Block, 40 Square Feet		
8″ Block, 1600 Square Feet		
10″ Block, 40 Square Feet		
12″ Block, 420 Square Feet		
Exposed Concrete above Grade (block), 60 Square Feet		
Reinforcing Rods		
2 - #4×4′-0″		
18 - #3×30′-0″		
Wire Mesh Reinforcing, 2100 Square Feet		
Concrete Basement Floor 4″ Thick ×1200 Square Feet		
Patio Floor 4″ Thick × 225 Square Feet		
Concrete Platforms on Ground (@ garbage cans), 4″ Thick × 15 Square Feet		
Concrete Sidewalks (under flagstone walk), 4″ Thick × 15 Square Feet		
Garage Floor, 4″ Thick × 600 Square Feet		
Concrete Steps (under flagstone), 7 Square Feet		
Concrete Hearth setting bed for flagstone for fireplace, 3″ Thick × 6 Square Feet		
Flue Lining		
12″ × 16″ T.C., 21′		
8″ × 8″ T.C., 19′		
220 Firebrick		
2400 Common Brick and Chimney		
Mortar, 8.2 Cubic Yards		
Drain Tile (depends on site), as required		
Chimney Cap, 15 Square Feet		
Supported Concrete Slabs, 1″ setting bed × 185 Square Feet		
Supported Concrete Slabs, 4″ Thick × 175 Square Feet		
Stone Veneer, 8″ Thick × 34′-0″×10′-0″		
Pea Gravel Patio and Walk, 3 Cubic Yards		
19,000 Exterior Face Brick		
Flagstones, 250 Square Feet		
6 Vents in Foundation Walls		
Cement Block Quoins		
160, 8″ Blocks		
15, 10″ Blocks		
45, 12″ Blocks		
Water Proofing Foundation Walls, 850 Square Feet		
Material Sub Total		
Labor Sub Total		
Carpenter's Lumber List		
Joists		
42 Pcs., 2 × 12 × 20′-0″		
38 Pcs., 2 × 12 × 18′-0″		
23 Pcs., 2 × 12 × 16′-0″		
3 Pcs., 2 × 12 × 8′-0″		
Bridging 1 × 4, 340 Square Feet		
Sub Flooring, 2010 Square Feet		
Ceiling Joists		
13 Pcs., 2 × 8 × 20′-0″		
27 Pcs., 2 × 16 × 18′-0″		
8 Pcs., 2 × 6 × 16′-0″		
50 Pcs., 2 × 6 × 12′-0″		
23 Pcs., 2 × 6 × 8′-0″		
8 Pcs., 2 × 6 × 14′-0″		

Article and Description	Price	Amount
Carpenter's Lumber List (continued)		
Deck Beams		
2 Pcs., 2 × 10 × 14′-0″		
2 Pcs., 2 × 10 × 12′-0″		
4 Pcs., 2 × 10 × 8′-0″		
2 Pcs., 2 × 8 × 18′-0″		
12 Pcs., 2 × 8 × 14′-0″		
10 Pcs., 2 × 8 × 10′-0″		
4 Pcs., 2 × 8 × 6′-0″		
Deck Flooring		
21 Pcs., 2 × 6 (redwood) × 14′-0″		
18 Pcs., 2 × 6 (redwood) × 12′-0″		
18 Pcs., 2 × 6 (redwood) × 10′-0″		
18 Pcs., 2 × 6 (redwood) × 8′-0″		
Lintels		
2 Pcs., 2 × 12 × 15′-0″ (Flitch beams)		
8 Pcs., 2 × 12 × 18′-0″ (Flitch beams)		
6 Pcs., 2 × 12 × 3′-4″		
2 Pcs., 2 × 12 × 3′-8″		
2 Pcs., 2 × 12 × 5′-0″		
2 Pcs., 2 × 12 × 7′-0″		
8 Pcs., 2 × 12 × 9′-0″		
2 Pcs., 2 × 12 × 10′-0″		
Stair Stringers		
3 Pcs., 2 × 12 × 16′-0″		
Exterior Wall Plates, 2 × 4 × 1260′		
Exterior Wall Plates, 2 × 6 × 150′		
Exterior Studs		
180 Pcs., 2 × 4 × 8′-0″		
93 Pcs., 2 × 4 × 9′-0″		
7 Pcs., 2 × 4 × 10′-0″		
9 Pcs., 2 × 4 × 11′-0″		
6 Pcs., 2 × 4 × 12′-0″		
Interior Plates		
2 × 4, 800′		
2 × 6, 30′		
2 × 8, 105′		
Interior Studs		
55 Pcs., 2 × 4 × 9′-0″		
7 Pcs., 2 × 6 × 9′-0″		
10 Pcs., 2 × 8 × 9′-0″		
210 Pcs., 2 × 4 × 8′-0″		
11 Pcs., 2 × 6 × 8′-0″		
25 Pcs., 2 × 8 × 8′-0″		
Headers		
2 Pcs., 2 × 12 × 4′-0″		
18 Pcs., 2 × 4 × 3′-0″		
16 Pcs., 2 × 4 × 2′-8″		
6 Pcs., 2 × 6 × 4′-4″		
4 Pcs., 2 × 8 × 6′-4″		
Roof Sheathing 1/2″ Plywood, 3850 Board Feet		
Ridge Boards, 2 × 10, 110′		
Rafters		
60 Pcs., 2 × 8 × 22′-0″		
97 Pcs., 2 × 8 × 16′-0″		
14 Pcs., 2 × 8 × 12′-0″		
4 Pcs., 2 × 8 × 10′-0″		
Fascia Cornice 1 × 10, 340′		
Porch Steps		
2 Pcs., 2 × 12 × 10′-0″		
Waterproof Roofing Paper, 38-1/2 Squares		
Building Paper under Wood Floor, 21-1/2 Squares		
Posts		
1 Pc., 4 × 4 × 8′-0″		
Girders Laminated Beams		
1 Pc., 5-1/4″ × 14-1/2″ × 24′-0″		
Porch Posts		
8 Pcs., 4 × 4 × 8′-0″		
Porch Railing 2 × 4, 128 Linear Feet		
Porch Cap 2 × 6, 64 Linear Feet		
Exterior Sheathing 1/2″ Insulating Board, 2400 Square Feet		
Siding, 1250 Square Feet		
Basement Stair Posts		
1 Pc., 4 × 4 × 8′-0″		
Basement Stair Railings		
1 Pc., 2 × 4 × 6′-0″		

(Continued on next page)

Goodheart-Willcox Publisher

Figure 36-3. Typical list for materials, fixtures, and finishes.

Article and Description	Price	Amount
Carpenter's Lumber List (continued)		
Soffits or Roof Overhang		
1/2″ Plywood, 3′-4″ × 205′		
1/2″ Plywood, 2′-0″ × 145′		
Scaffolding and Extra Joists (approx.), as required		
Plastic Ceiling at Kitchen and Master Bath		
3 Pcs., 1 × 12 × 14′-0″		
Valance		
1 × 6, 126′		
1 × 10, 132′		
Furring Strips, as required		
Wind Stops at Eaves, 300′		
Battens 1 × 2, 1100′		
Shelving		
10 Pcs., 1 × 10 × 10′-0″		
8 Pcs., 1 × 10 × 8′-0″		
Rafter Ties		
2 × 4, 70′		
24 Pcs., 2 × 4 × 10′-0″		
Material Sub Total		
Labor Sub Total		
MILLWORK		
Windows and Screens (as selected)		
Window Frames		
4 4′-0″ × 6′-0″ Vertical Sliding Steel Windows		
3 Double 4′-0″ × 6′-0″ Vertical Sliding Steel Windows		
4 4′-0″ × 5′-0″ Vertical Sliding Steel Windows		
1 3′-0″ × 3′-0″ Horizontal Sliding Steel Windows		
Fixed Plastic Screen (weather resistant)		
Note: Provide frames for above plastic screens.		
Storm Sash and Window screens or Rolling Metal Screens, as required		
Doors and Trim		
Exterior Door Frames		
4 Frames for 2′-8″ × 6′-8″ × 1-3/4″ Solid Core Wood Doors		
1 Frame for 2-2′-8″ × 6′8″×1-3/4″ Solid Core Wood Doors		
1 Frame for 2′-8″ × 6′-8″ × 1-3/8″ Hollow Core Wood Doors		
1 Frame for 16′-0″ × 8′-0″ Sliding Glass Door		
3 Frames for 8′-0″ × 6′-8″ Sliding Glass Door		
Interior Door Frames		
8 Frames 2′-8″ × 6′-8″ × 1-3/8″ Hollow Core Wood Doors		
7 Frames 2′-4″ × 6′-8″ × 1-3/8″ Hollow Core Wood Doors		
3 Frames 4′-0″ × 6′-8″ × 1-3/8″ Hollow Core Wood Doors (folding)		
2 Frames for 6′-0″ × 6′-8″ × 1-3/8″ Hollow Core Wood Doors (folding)		
Special Door Frames		
1 Frame for 2′-0″ × 6′-8″ Shower Door (master bath)		
Exterior Doors		
6 2′-8″ × 6′-8″ × 1-3/4″ Solid Core Doors		
1 2′-8″ × 6′-8″ × 1-3/8″ Hollow Core Door		
1 16′-0″ × 8′-0″ Sliding Glass Door		
3 8′-0″ × 6′-8″ Sliding Glass Doors		
Interior Doors		
8 2′-8″ × 6′-8″ × 1-3/8″ Hollow Core Doors		
7 2′-4″ × 6′-8″ × 1-3/8″ Hollow Core Doors		
6 2′-0″ × 6′-8″ × 1-3/8″ Hollow Core Folding Doors (louvered)		
4 3′-0″ × 6′-8″ × 1-3/8″ Hollow Core Folding Doors (louvered)		
Interior Door Trim, 330 Linear Feet		
Screen Doors, as required		
Cabinets and Miscellaneous Millwork		
Room Base, 375′		
Clothes Closet Hook Strips, 75′		
(Including Storage Closet but not Kitchen)		
At other shelving, 125′		
Closet Shelving, 1′-6″ × 115′		
Closet Shelving, 1′-8″ × 12′-6″		
Closet Poles, 50′		
Outside Door Thresholds, Entry – Bronze Thresholds, × 5′-4″		
Ceiling Mold around Chimney, 30′-0″		
Kitchen Broom Closet and Pantry		
5 Shelves 1′-8″ × 3/4″ × 2′-6″		
2 Sides 1′-8″ × 3/4″ × 8′-0″		
10 Cleats, 1′-2″ × 1′-8″		

Article and Description	Price	Amount
Cabinets and Miscellaneous Millwork (continued)		
Kitchen Cupboards		
Doors and Exposed Faces, 180 Square Feet		
Sides and Partitions, 100 Square Feet		
Shelves, 115 Square Feet		
Backs, Sides, and Bottom, 90 Square Feet		
Tops (Plastic Laminated), 65 Square Feet		
1 × 2 Framing, 220′		
Wood Legs at Island, 7		
Drawer Track, 20 Ft.		
Basement Stairs		
16 Pine Risers 7-1/2″ × 3/4″ × 3′4″		
15 Oak Treads 10-1/2″ × 1-1/4″ × 3′4″		
Decorative Screen-In Foyer, 7′-0 × 11′-0″		
Clothes Chute Door 3/4″ Plywood, 1′-0″ × 2′-6″		
Bathroom Cabinets (1st Floor)		
1 × 2 Frame, 53′		
1 × 4 Kickboard, 12′-4″		
Doors, etc., 31 Square Feet		
Shelves, etc., 67 Square Feet		
Special Beams (false)		
2 Pcs., 2 × 4 × 18′-0″		
5 Pcs., 4 × 4 × 18′-0″		
Window Valances		
1 × 10, 130′.		
1 × 6, 130′.		
China Closets		
3 16″ × 28″ × 1/4″ Plate Glass Shelves		
2 54″ Adjustable Shelf Standards		
6 16″ Adjustable Shelf Brackets		
3″ × 1-1/8″ × 2′-4″ Plate Glass Shelves		
2-1/4″ × 1-1/8″ × 4′-8″ Plate Glass Shelves		
3/4″ × 3/4″ × 9′-0″ Plate Glass Shelves		
15″ × 24″ × 1/4″ Frosted Plastic Top		
3/4″ Plywood, 40 Square Feet		
2 × 6 – 4′-8″		
1 × 3 – 5′-0″		
2 × 3 – 2′-4″		
Breakfast Room Cabinets		
Kickboard 1 × 4, 8′.		
Doors and Sides, 56 Square Feet		
Shelves, 53 Square Feet		
Frame 1 × 2, 53′		
Full Length Mirror		
Baths		
1 80 × 50		
1 68 × 50		
Basement		
1 68 × 50		
Material Sub Total		
Labor Sub Total		
Insulation		
Batt Type Ceilings, 2230 Square Feet		
Batt Type Walls, 1650 Square Feet		
Material Sub Total		
Labor Sub Total		
Weatherstripping and Caulking		
Windows, 275′		
Exterior Doors, 205′		
Material Sub Total		
Labor Sub Total		
Plastering or Drywall		
Living Room Walls, 340 Square Feet		
Living Room Ceiling, 530 Square Feet		
Dining Room Walls, 290 Square Feet		
Dining Room Ceiling, 215 Square Feet		
Foyer Walls, 31 Square Feet		
Foyer Ceiling, 102 Square Feet		
Hall Walls, 250 Square Feet		
Hall Ceiling, 80 Square Feet		
Basement Stairway Walls, 300 Square Feet		
Basement Stairway Ceiling, 35 Square Feet		
Kitchen Walls, 490 Square Feet		
Kitchen Ceiling, 290 Square Feet		

(Continued on next page)

Goodheart-Willcox Publisher

Figure 36-3. *(Continued)*

Article and Description	Price	Amount
Plastering or Drywall (continued)		
Bathroom Walls		
Basement, 65 Square Feet		
1st Floor, 230 Square Feet		
Bathroom Ceiling		
Basement, 50 Square Feet		
1st Floor, 85 Square Feet		
Bedroom Walls		
Basement, 410 Square Feet		
1st Floor, 780 Square Feet		
Bedroom Ceilings		
Basement, 245 Square Feet		
1st Floor, 480 Square Feet		
Closet Walls		
Basement, 120 Square Feet		
1st Floor, 610 Square Feet		
Closet Ceilings		
Basement, 16 Square Feet		
1st Floor, 105 Square Feet		
Garage Walls, 600 Square Feet		
Garage Ceiling, 515 Square Feet		
Laundry Walls Basement, 195 Square Feet		
Laundry Ceiling Basement, 65 Square Feet		
Storage Room Walls, 120 Square Feet		
Storage Room Ceiling, 21 Square Feet		
Study Walls, 350 Square Feet		
Study Ceiling, 170 Square Feet		
Material Sub Total		
Labor Sub Total		
Finish Flooring		
Living Room, 408 Square Feet		
Dining Room, 201 Square Feet		
Foyer, 102 Square Feet		
Halls, 80 Square Feet		
Basement Stairway, 50 Square Feet		
Kitchen, 290 Square Feet		
Bathrooms, 115 Square Feet		
Bedrooms, 450 Square Feet		
Closets, 100 Square Feet		
Storage Room, 22 Square Feet		
Study, 155 Square Feet		
Material Sub Total		
Labor Sub Total		
Painting and Finishing		
Exterior Siding, 1250 Square Feet		
Exterior Cornice, 360′		
Exterior Doors (both sides), 230 Square Feet		
Basement Doors (both sides), 270 Square Feet		
Basement Stairs (top sides), 94 Square Feet		
Interior Doors (both sides), 720 Square Feet		
Interior Door Trims, 330′.		
Sheet Metal Items		
Chimney Flashing, 16′		
Wall Flashing @ Decks, 41′		
Ridge Vent, 116′		
Kitchen Cupboards (including Shelves and Interior), 650 Square Feet		
Linen Closets (including Shelves), 145 Square Feet		
Broom Closet and Pantry (including Shelves), 200 Square Feet		
Closet Shelving (both sides), 150 Square Feet		
Closet Poles, 50′		
Closet Hook Strip (clothes closets), 75′		
Wood Base, 375′		
Porch Posts (pipe columns), 35′		
Garage Doors (both sides), 225 Square Feet		
Exposed Bricks		
Interior, 200 Square Feet		
Exterior, 1250 Square Feet		
Interior Beams		
4 × 4 False Beams, 112′		
5-1/4 × 14-1/2 Laminated Beams, 48′		
Exterior Cinder Block Walls, 60 Square Feet		
Living Room Walls, 340 Square Feet		
Living Room Ceiling (including top side of Valance), 615 Square Feet		

Article and Description	Price	Amount
Painting and Finishing (continued)		
Living Room Floor		
Flagstone, 38 Square Feet		
Carpeted, 408 Square Feet		
Dining Room Walls, 290 Square Feet		
Dining Room Ceiling, 215 Square Feet		
Dining Room Floor		
Flagstone Passage, 14 Square Feet		
Carpeted, 201 Square Feet		
Foyer Walls, 31 Square Feet		
Foyer Ceiling, 102 Square Feet		
Foyer Floor Flagstone, 102 Square Feet		
Hall Walls, 250 Square Feet		
Hall Ceiling, 80 Square Feet		
Hall Floor, 80 Square Feet		
Basement Stairway Walls, 300 Square Feet		
Basement Stairway Ceiling, 35 Square Feet		
Kitchen Walls, 325 Square Feet		
Kitchen Plastic Ceiling, 48 Square Feet		
Kitchen Ceiling, 240 Square Feet		
Kitchen Floor, 290 Square Feet		
Bathroom Walls		
Basement, 60 Square Feet		
1st Floor, 230 Square Feet		
Bathroom Ceilings		
Plastic Ceiling, 51 Square Feet		
Basement, 50 Square Feet		
1st Floor, 105 Square Feet		
Bathroom Floors		
Basement, 20 Square Feet		
1st Floor, 115 Square Feet		
Bedroom Walls		
Basement, 410 Square Feet		
1st Floor, 780 Square Feet		
Bedroom Ceilings (including valances)		
Basement, 245 Square Feet		
1st Floor, 480 Square Feet		
Bedroom Floors		
Basement, 245 Square Feet		
1st Floor, 450 Square Feet		
Closet Walls		
Basement, 120 Square Feet		
1st Floor, 520 Square Feet		
Closet Ceilings		
Basement, 16 Square Feet		
1st Floor, 90 Square Feet		
Closet Floors		
Basement, 18 Square Feet		
1st Floor, 90 Square Feet		
Garage Walls, 600 Square Feet		
Garage Ceiling, 515 Square Feet		
Laundry Walls		
Concrete Block, 80 Square Feet		
Other, 195 Square Feet		
Laundry Ceiling, 65 Square Feet		
Laundry Floor, 65 Square Feet		
Breakfast Room Walls, see Kitchen		
Breakfast Room Ceiling, see Kitchen		
Breakfast Room Floor, see Kitchen		
Storage Room Walls, 120 Square Feet		
Storage Room Ceiling, 21 Square Feet		
Storage Room Floor, 21 Square Feet		
Study Walls, 350 Square Feet		
Study Ceiling (including Valance), 170 Square Feet		
Study Floor, 155 Square Feet		
Special Mold Quarter Round, 500′		
Bathroom Cabinets (including shelves and interior)		
Basement, 105 Square Feet		
1st Floor, 210 Square Feet		
China Cabinet (including shelves and interior), 35 Square Feet		
Deck Steps (one side), 20 Square Feet		
Full Length Mirrors		
Baths		
1 80 × 50		
1 68 × 50		
Basement		
1 68 × 50		

(Continued on next page)

Goodheart-Willcox Publisher

Figure 36-3. *(Continued)*

Article and Description	Price	Amount
Painting and Finishing (continued)		
Square Edge Trim 3/4 × 3/4, 10′		
Battens 1 × 2, 1100′		
Wood Decks		
2 × 6 Flat 3/16″ Spacers, 365 Square Feet		
2 2 × 10 Beams, 42′		
2 2 × 8 Beams, 132′		
1 2 × 8 Beams, 14′		
Guard Rail, 190′		
Material Sub Total		
Labor Sub Total		
Miscellaneous Hardware		
40 Foundation Anchor Bolts 1/2″ Diam. ABs to Sill		
1 Clean out Door Frame Unit		
1 Ash Dump Unit		
1 Fireplace Damper Unit		
2 Angle Iron Fireplace Lintels 3-1/2″ × 3-1/2″ × 1/2″ × 5′-4″		
1 Angle Iron Fireplace Lintel 3-1/2″ × 3-1/2″ × 1/2″ × 6′-0″		
Nails approximately 400 Lbs.		
1 Dowel for Wood Post Anchors and Footings		
Lally Columns 3″ Diam. Pipe Columns		
1 2′-0″		
1 7′-0″		
3 8′-6″		
Miscellaneous Builders Hardware, as required		
250 Wall Ties		
Roof Beams Flitch Plates		
4 11″ × 3/8″ × 18′-0″		
1 11″ × 3/8″ × 15′-0″		
1 Angle 3-1/2″ × 3-1/2″ × 3/8″ × 3′-0″		
1 Angle 3-1/2″ × 3-1/2″ × 1/2″ × 4′-4″		
5 Column Caps for 3″ Diam. Pipe Column Units		
5 Column Bases for 3″ Diam. Pipe Column Units		
Wire Mesh Reinforcement, (see Masonry Section)		
Steps down to Living Room Floor		
4 Angles 1-1/2″ × 1-1/2″ × 3′-0″		
2 Junior Channels 12″ × 1-1/2″ × 5′-0″		
Miscellaneous Bolts at Deck Rail 32 Machine Bolts 3/4″ Diam. × 6″		
Extra Heavy Corrugated Sheets Metal Forming, 180 Square Feet		
Reinforcement Bars, see Masonry Section		
Material Sub Total		
Labor Sub Total		
Finish Hardware		
2 Basement Doors		
2 Pr. 3-1/2 × 3-1/2 Butts		
2 Latch Sets		
1 Pr. Front Entrance Doors		
3 Pr. 4 × 4 Butts		
1 Lockset		
1 Rear Entrance Door		
1-1/2 Pr. 4 × 4 Butts		
1 Lockset		
4 Side Doors (including Doors from Garage)		
6 Pr. 4 × 4 Butts		
4 Locksets		
Screen Doors (as required)		
4 Bathroom Doors		
4 Pr. 3-1/2 × 3-1/2 Butts		
4 Locksets (Bath)		
3 - 8′-0″ × 6′-8″ Glass Sliding Door Unit		
1 – 16′-0″ × 8′-0″ Glass Sliding Door Unit		
Double Acting Doors		
1 2′-8″ × 6′-8″		
1 Pr. 3-1/2 × 3-1/2 Double Acting		
1 Push Plate each Side		
9 Interior Doors		
9 Pr. 3-1/2 × 3-1/2 Butts		
9 Latch Sets		
Storm Sashes, as required		
Kitchen Cabinets (Storage and Bathroom included)		
41 Pr. Cabinet Hinges		
95 Knobs or Pulls		
42 Friction Catches		
Closets Folding Wood (4 panel)		
3 4′-0″ × 6′-8″		
2 6′-0″ × 6′-8″		

Article and Description	Price	Amount
Finish Hardware (continued)		
20 Pr. 3-1/2 × 3-1/2 Butts		
10 Pulls		
10 Catches		
Miscellaneous Cabinets - Dining Room		
2 Pr. Cabinet Hinges		
2 Pulls		
2 Catches		
1 Mail Box Unit		
5 Floor Door Stops		
16 Regular Door Stops		
1 Doz. Coat and Hat Hooks		
Miscellaneous Small Hardware, as required		
1 Overhead Garage Door Unit 16′-0″ × 7′-0″		
Shower Door (Master Bath)		
1 Pr. Metal Hinges		
1 Knob Set Unit		
1 Friction Catch		
Material Sub Total		
Labor Sub Total		
Sheet Metal Work		
Flashing around Chimney, 16 Linear Feet		
Flashing at Vertical Walls at Exterior Decks, 41′		
Exhaust Fan Grills		
3 Bathroom required		
1 Kitchen required		
4 – 8″ Diam. Ducts to Roof Vents		
Valleys, 40′		
Ridge Vent, 116′		
1 Metal Clothes Chute Unit 12″ × 16″		
Metal Lined Bread Drawer, 12 Square Feet		
Material Sub Total		
Labor Sub Total		
Floor Finishing Material		
Resilient		
Tile		
Wood		
Carpet		
Tile Fireplace Hearth		
Cove Base		
Miscellaneous		
Material Sub Total		
Labor Sub Total		
Wall Finishing Material		
Work Tabletops and Backs Plastic Laminated, 90 Square Feet		
Tile Base in Bathroom, 80′		
Tile or Chrome inserts in Bathroom		
3 Toilet Paper Holders		
3 Soap Dishes and Grab Bars		
10 Towel Bars		
3 Robe Hooks		
Bathroom Tile Wainscot, 270 Square Feet		
Material Sub Total		
Labor Sub Total		
Roofing		
38-1/2 Sqs. Owner's Choice		
Material Sub Total		
Labor Sub Total		
Plumbing		
Note: This survey does not list the quantities of each item required for the mechanical equipment, as there is a variation in any system chosen. However, the form given will be of assistance to your dealer in arriving at an accurate estimate.		
1 Double Kitchen Sink		
3 Water Closet Units		
2 Bath Tubs		
3 Shower Head Units		
3 Floor Drain Units		
4 Top Mounted Lavatories		
Automatic Washer Outlet		
4 Hose Bib Units		

(Continued on next page)

Goodheart-Willcox Publisher

Figure 36-3. *(Continued)*

Article and Description	Price	Amount	Article and Description	Price	Amount
Plumbing (continued) Hot Water Heater 40 Gallons Gas fired Unit (50 Gallons Electric) 1 Garbage Disposer Unit ____ Miscellaneous Gas Range, Grill with Cover and Rotisserie, Hood with 2 Dual Blowers (1200 CFM), Built-In Refr.-Freezer ____ Material Sub Total ____ Labor Sub Total ____			Electric Wiring (continued) 2 23′-0″ Single Tube Units (Living Room) ____ 1 14′-0″ Single Tube Unit (Bedroom) ____ 1 13′-0″ Single Tube Unit (Bedroom) ____ 1 12′-6″ Single Tube Unit (Bedroom) ____ Material Sub Total ____ Labor Sub Total ____		
Electric Wiring 21 Ceiling Outlets (6 Spots) ____ 4 Bracket Outlets, Outside Fixtures ____ 57 Duplex Receptacles ____ 10 Waterproof Receptacles ____ 32 Wall Switches ____ 1 Dimmer Switch Dining Room Spots ____ 10 Three-way Switches ____ 1 Set Entrance Chime ____ 1 Ceiling Outlet (vapor-proof) over Master Bath Shower ____ 2 Push Buttons ____ 7 Porch Lights Twin Floods @ each Unit ____ 7 Hall and Entrance Lights 150 W Ceiling Flush Mounted Units 1 Kitchen Fan – Hood-Fan Combination Unit ____ 1 Bathroom Exhaust Fan ____ 1 Bathroom Combination Heater and Ventilator ____ 1 Bathroom Combination Heater, Ventilator and Light ____ 2 – 240V Receptacles (Dryer and Range) ____ Special Tubular Light Installations 2 2′-0″ Single Tube Units (20W) ____ 11 4′-0″ Single Tube Units (40W) ____			Telephone Wiring Note: Call the nearest telephone company business office for assistance in planning adequate built-in telephone facilities. These will include: 1. Entrance pipe or underground entrance conduit ____ 2. Galvanized iron protector cabinet ____ 3. Interior thin-wall conduit to all outlets ____ 4. Standard outlet boxes with telephone cover ____ 5. Telephone or jack locations ____ 6. Miscellaneous or special items ____ Material Sub Total ____ Labor Sub Total ____ Heating A heating unit will be required of sufficient size for a house with 3490 square feet and/or 30,250 cubic feet. Material Sub Total ____ Labor Sub Total ____		

Goodheart-Willcox Publisher

Figure 36-3. *(Continued)*

Employability

Entrepreneurship

Entrepreneurs are people who start and run their own business. Many people decide to become entrepreneurs because they enjoy working for themselves. Starting a business may also provide a sense of accomplishment. If the business does well, the entrepreneur can make a sizable profit.

The architectural field is ideal for people who want to work for themselves. Many architects become entrepreneurs and hire a small support staff. Some architects even work out of their own homes. Architectural drafters can also be entrepreneurs. Opening a design and drafting service that specializes in architectural drawing may provide a good income without the constraints of having to report to work at an office every day.

Entrepreneurship has some disadvantages, too. Working for yourself is hard work. In addition to the actual work you receive from clients, you must also manage advertising, accounting, and all of the other areas associated with a business. Of course, you can hire a marketing agent and an accountant, but you are ultimately responsible for all areas of the business, so you will need at least some knowledge in all of these areas. Entrepreneurship can increase your stress levels, and if the business fails, you might lose everything. Therefore, as tempting as the thought of working for yourself may be, you should look into it carefully before deciding to become an entrepreneur.

Activity

Investigate the requirements for opening a small business in your area. Choose a business related to architecture or another subject that interests you. What licenses would you need? How much capital (money) would you need to invest to get the business off the ground? Share your answers with the class.

Labor Estimate

After the cost of materials has been determined, the labor cost must be calculated. In the past, labor cost was less than half of the total building cost for a house. Today, the labor cost in most sections of the country ranges from 60% to 80% of the total building cost. The labor cost for building a house has steadily increased year after year. It would be wise to research this area carefully before trying to estimate labor cost. Publications such as the latest edition of the *Building Construction Cost Data* book give detailed information on labor cost for various areas of the country. General contractors and subcontractors can also provide help in arriving at the projected cost. Their experience will enable them to make an accurate estimate of labor cost for a given job.

Other Costs

Other costs that must be included in the total building cost include insurance, fees for permits, environmental impact fees, and any other applicable fees. Most areas require a building permit, plumbing permit, electrical permit, and health permit. Also, there may be fees for hookup of electrical, gas, sewer, telephone, and water services. The cost of these permits and fees may be as small as a few dollars or as much as several hundred dollars. In addition, many builders add the cost of insurance to protect materials and workers in the event of an accident or damage. This cost should also be added to the cost of construction. Investigate these areas to determine their exact costs.

Once all of these elements are evaluated, the total building cost of the house can be calculated. This estimate will most likely be more accurate than one calculated with the approximate methods presented earlier, but it may still be a few hundred dollars off. It is impossible to exactly calculate the building cost of a house. The final building cost may vary from the estimate for several reasons, such as material price fluctuations and labor overruns. Even builders who have been in the business for years sometimes fail to accurately estimate the cost of a job. Therefore, it is extremely important that you learn to prepare drawings and specifications accurately to help eliminate unexpected costs. Be sure all specifications are complete and easy to understand.

Green Architecture

Costs of Green Building Design

Most architects and building designers will tell you that the initial costs of building a "green" residence are significantly higher than costs for traditional construction. While this is true in most cases, an experienced estimator can help a client achieve a more sustainable home for little more than traditional building costs. More and more people are beginning to request green features in their homes. By keeping up-to-date with available products, processes, and guidelines, an estimator can offer the home buyer a range of green solutions. Some of these solutions, such as reducing water use through the installation of low-flow toilets and faucets, may not increase the cost of the home at all.

Computer Estimates

Several software programs are available for performing construction estimates and preparing various reports, such as a materials list or bill of materials. These programs can greatly reduce the amount of time needed for project estimation. They allow the architect or estimator to import the floor plan for the proposed home. The software analyzes the floor plan and calculates the costs automatically. In addition, the user can input changes and make selections to improve the accuracy of the resulting estimates. See **Figure 36-4**.

Organizing Estimates

Estimates are generally organized according to a work breakdown structure. The ***work breakdown structure (WBS)*** is a formal listing of construction information by category, which makes the estimate easier to understand. Two common systems used in WBS development are

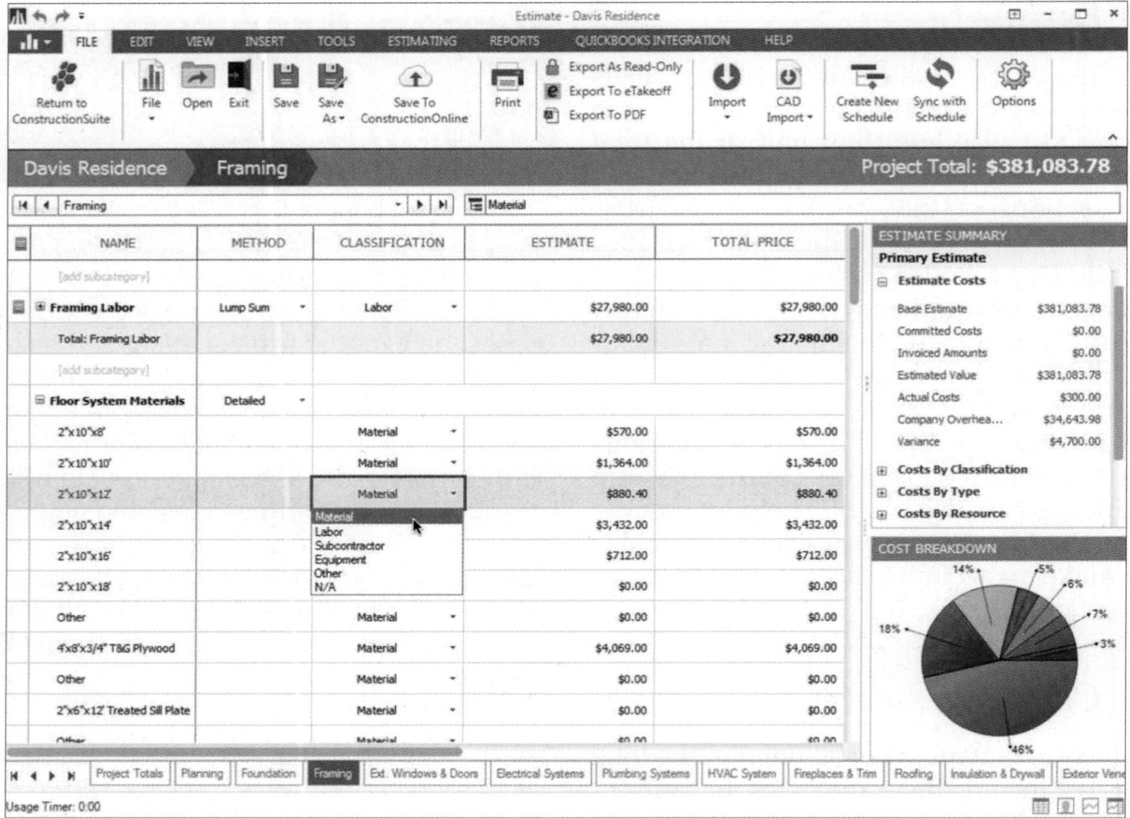

UDA Technologies

Figure 36-4. Construction estimating software programs base detailed estimates on drawing data that you import. This example shows an estimate for the framing required for a residential construction project.

MasterFormat® and UniFormat™. Both of these systems have been developed by the Construction Specifications Institute (CSI).

The UniFormat system is more commonly used in making preliminary estimates. UniFormat uses coded levels and titles to identify the major functions or systems of the building. The MasterFormat system is typically used for final estimates and is more widely used. MasterFormat uses numbered divisions and titles to identify construction requirements, products, and activities. There are 50 divisions in the current MasterFormat edition. See **Figure 36-5**. Note that this is a complete list of the MasterFormat divisions and some divisions are not applicable to residential construction. In addition, as shown in **Figure 36-5**, some of the divisions are reserved for future use. The MasterFormat divisions are organized under groups and subgroups. Content within the divisions is organized into specific sections and titles.

As previously discussed, the organization of information in most estimates mirrors the specifications and coincides with the construction sequence. The arrangement of divisions in the MasterFormat system aligns with the construction sequence and provides a standard order for specifying detailed information in residential construction projects.

MasterFormat® Division Numbers and Titles

Procurement and Contracting Requirements Group

Division 00—Procurement and Contracting Requirements

Specifications Group

General Requirements Subgroup

Division 01—General Requirements

Facility Construction Subgroup

Division 02—Existing Conditions
Division 03—Concrete
Division 04—Masonry
Division 05—Metals
Division 06—Wood, Plastics, and Composites
Division 07—Thermal and Moisture Protection
Division 08—Openings
Division 09—Finishes
Division 10—Specialties
Division 11—Equipment
Division 12—Furnishings
Division 13—Special Construction
Division 14—Conveying Equipment
Division 15—Reserved for future expansion
Division 16—Reserved for future expansion
Division 17—Reserved for future expansion
Division 18—Reserved for future expansion
Division 19—Reserved for future expansion

Facility Services Subgroup

Division 20—Reserved for future expansion
Division 21—Fire Suppression
Division 22—Plumbing
Division 23—Heating, Ventilating, and Air Conditioning (HVAC)
Division 24—Reserved for future expansion
Division 25—Integrated Automation
Division 26—Electrical
Division 27—Communications
Division 28—Electronic Safety and Security
Division 29—Reserved for future expansion

Site and Infrastructure Subgroup

Division 30—Reserved for future expansion
Division 31—Earthwork
Division 32—Exterior Improvements
Division 33—Utilities
Division 34—Transportation
Division 35—Waterway and Marine Construction
Division 36—Reserved for future expansion
Division 37—Reserved for future expansion
Division 38—Reserved for future expansion
Division 39—Reserved for future expansion

Process Equipment Subgroup

Division 40—Process Integration
Division 41—Material Processing and Handling Equipment
Division 42—Process Heating, Cooling, and Drying Equipment
Division 43—Process Gas and Liquid Handling, Purification, and Storage Equipment
Division 44—Pollution and Waste Control Equipment
Division 45—Industry-Specific Manufacturing Equipment
Division 46—Water and Wastewater Equipment
Division 47—Reserved for future expansion
Division 48—Electrical Power Generation
Division 49—Reserved for future expansion

Goodheart-Willcox Publisher

Figure 36-5. The MasterFormat system is used to identify requirements, products, and activities in construction projects. The current edition of MasterFormat contains 50 divisions. The divisions are organized under groups and subgroups.

Summary

- Estimating is an organized effort to determine the total cost of materials, labor, and other services required to build a house.
- Two methods of creating an initial estimate of building costs are the square foot method and the cubic foot method.
- Final estimates include accurate costs for materials, labor, and all other costs of building the home.
- Estimation software can speed the process of estimation and uses drawing data from the floor plan of the proposed home.

Internet Resources

American Institute of Architects (AIA)
Information about estimating and contract documents

Construction Specifications Institute (CSI)
Master specifications and estimation guidelines

CSI UniFormat
Estimation format for preliminary building estimates

MasterFormat
Estimation format for final building estimates

UniFormat II
ASTM UniFormat II estimating spreadsheet in Microsoft Excel format

Review Questions

Answer the following questions using the information in this chapter.

1. What is the purpose of a preliminary estimate?
2. What is the purpose of a design contingency?
3. List two methods commonly used to calculate preliminary building cost estimates.
4. Explain the relationship between the constant used for estimating living space in a house and the constant used for estimating garage space.
5. If the building cost of a house with 1500 square feet is estimated, using the square foot method, to be $170,000, what is the cost per square foot constant? (Assume that the home does not have a garage.)
6. What is a material takeoff, and how does it differ from a preliminary estimate?
7. Where should the estimator get the prices used in a final estimate?
8. What percentage of the total cost of building a home is generally labor cost?
9. List the permits and fees usually required for building a new home.
10. What are two common systems used in WBS development? What type of estimate is commonly produced with each system?

Suggested Activities

1. Using a house plan that you have designed, calculate the building cost using the square foot method.
2. Using the same plan as in Activity 1, calculate a more accurate estimate for materials only by listing the materials to be used and pricing them in detail. Research and use price data from a local lumber company and other material suppliers.
3. If your CADD system has functions for generating a materials list or bill of materials, create an automated list that specifies materials and pricing for a house plan that you have designed. Research and use price data from a local lumber company and other material suppliers.
4. Establish current salary rates for carpenters, plumbers, electricians, masons, and other skilled construction workers in your area, such as framers, flooring experts, and glazers, who work together to build a house. Record rates and sources used. Prepare a report and present it to your class.

Problem Solving Case Study

The Albertsons were referred to your architectural design office by the Kendalls, for whom you designed a beautiful 1800-square-foot home with a two-car garage. The home has a concrete block stucco (CBS) exterior, with three standard bedrooms, a great room, a kitchen, and two bathrooms. The Kendalls are very happy with their home and its preliminary cost estimate, which was $200,000. You calculated the price of the home using the $100 per square foot constant that is normal in your area.

The Albertsons explain that they do not want their home to look like "everybody else's." They want a unique look with lots of glass, including a two-story octagonal sunroom with glass walls. They want the house to have 1500 to 1600 square feet, plus a two-car garage. You design a 1600-square-foot house according to their general specifications and price using a constant of $160 per square foot, resulting in a price of $276,000. When you present the design to the Albertsons, they love the design, but are appalled at the price. "This house is smaller than the one you designed for the Kendalls," they exclaim. "How can it possibly cost more than theirs?"

Prepare an answer to give to the Albertsons, explaining the difference in cost. Give specific examples to show why their home will cost more to build than the home you designed for the endalls.

Certification Prep

The following questions are presented in the style used in the American Design Drafting Association (ADDA) Drafter Certification Test. Answer the questions using the information in this chapter.

1. Which of the following statements about estimating building costs are true?
   A. The square foot method produces an estimate of the building cost based on the total cubic area in the house.
   B. Estimating is an organized effort to determine the total cost of materials, labor, and other services required to build a house.
   C. The volume of a house is determined by multiplying the length of the house by the width.
   D. There are so many variables involved in the cost of a home that estimates obtained by the square foot or cubic foot method may vary considerably from the actual cost.
2. Which of the following statements are true?
   A. The first step in compiling a material takeoff is to study the final working drawings and specifications.
   B. The purpose of the design contingency on a preliminary estimate is to give the client a firm, final figure for construction.
   C. Most builders use a different constant for each house style and adjust it for special features, such as an extra bath or fireplace.
   D. Permits and environmental impact fees are not included in the final estimate of building costs.

3. Which of the following statements are *false*?
   A. Most estimates do not follow the headings as listed on a good set of specifications.
   B. Garages, porches, and basements are figured using the same constant used for the living room and bedrooms, since all of these are part of the living area of the house.
   C. A single-level home is often more expensive to build than a two-story home that provides the same area of living space.
   D. Two common systems used in developing a work breakdown structure are MasterFormat and UniFormat.

Curricular Connections

1. **Social Science.** Conduct research to find the standard labor rates for residential carpenters, plumbers, and electricians in the following cities: Chicago, IL; Hot Springs, AR; Cheyenne, WY; Mobile, AL; Philadelphia, PA; and your local area. If you live in one of the cities mentioned, choose a sixth city in another area of the country. Create a chart using your findings. How do the rates compare? Why are they different?

STEM Connections

1. **Math.** Calculate a preliminary estimate for a home that has 2450 square feet and a 30′ × 20′ three-car garage using both the square foot method and the cubic foot method. The home has 10′ ceilings, and the rise of the roof is 8′ for both the house and the garage. The attic is 1225 square feet. Use the following constants for the living areas: $140 per square foot and $14 per cubic foot. Compare the estimates. Why are they different?
2. **Technology.** Conduct research to find out more about estimation software programs. Select one that interests you and find out more details about how the program works. Prepare an oral report to share your findings with the class.

Communicating about Architecture

1. **Speaking.** With a partner, make flash cards of the key terms in this chapter. On the front of the card, write the term. On the back of the card, write the pronunciation and a brief definition. Use this chapter and a dictionary for guidance. Then take turns quizzing one another on the pronunciations and definitions of the key terms.
2. **Reading.** Working in small groups, create a poster that illustrates information and costs to be included in a final estimate. Display your poster in the classroom as a convenient reference aid for discussions and assignments.

Reference Section

David Papazian/Shutterstock.com

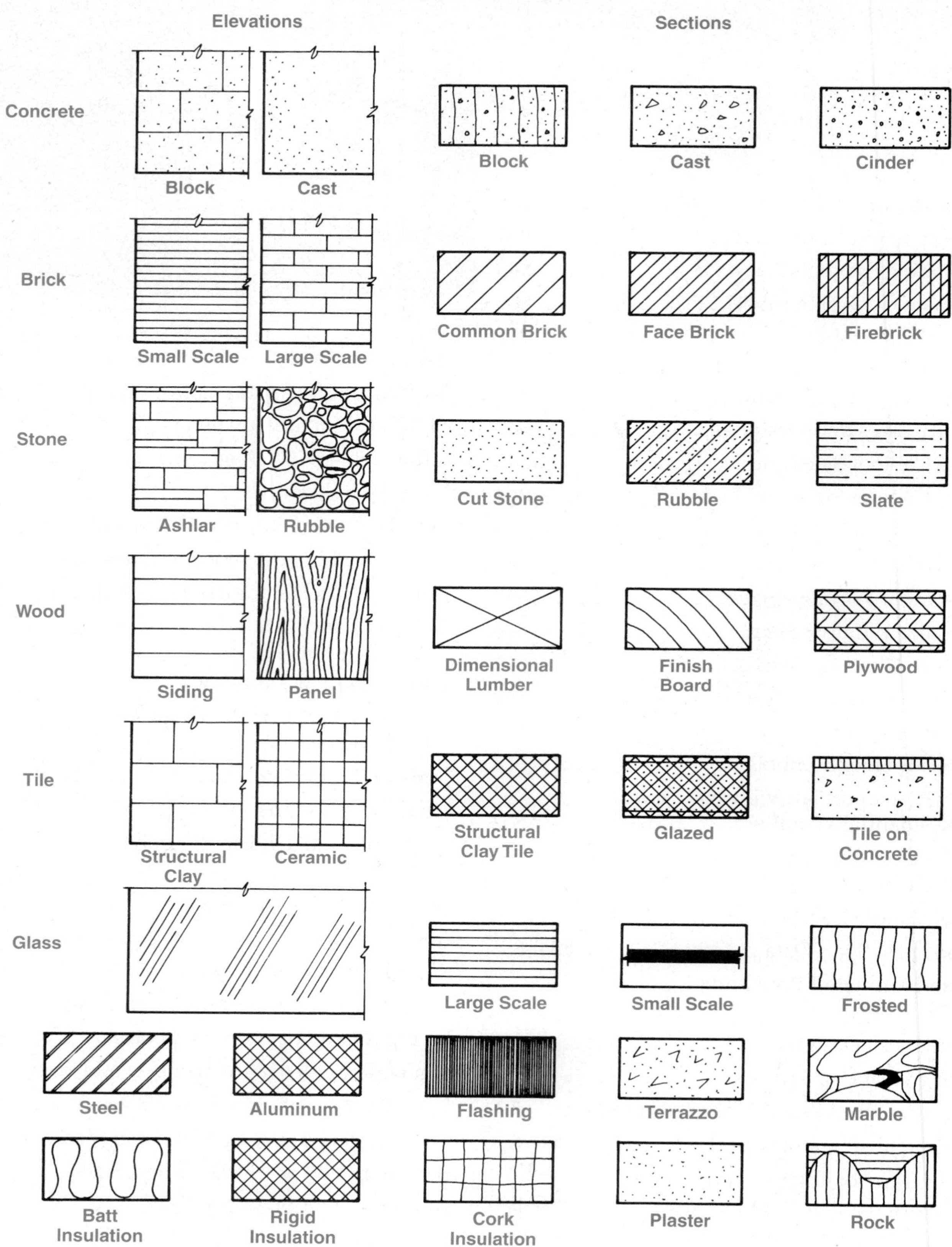
Building Material Symbols
Elevations
Sections
Concrete
Block
Cast
Block
Cast
Cinder
Brick
Small Scale
Large Scale
Common Brick
Face Brick
Firebrick
Stone
Ashlar
Rubble
Cut Stone
Rubble
Slate
Wood
Siding
Panel
Dimensional Lumber
Finish Board
Plywood
Tile
Structural Clay
Ceramic
Structural Clay Tile
Glazed
Tile on Concrete
Glass
Large Scale
Small Scale
Frosted
Steel
Aluminum
Flashing
Terrazzo
Marble
Batt Insulation
Rigid Insulation
Cork Insulation
Plaster
Rock

Topographical Symbols

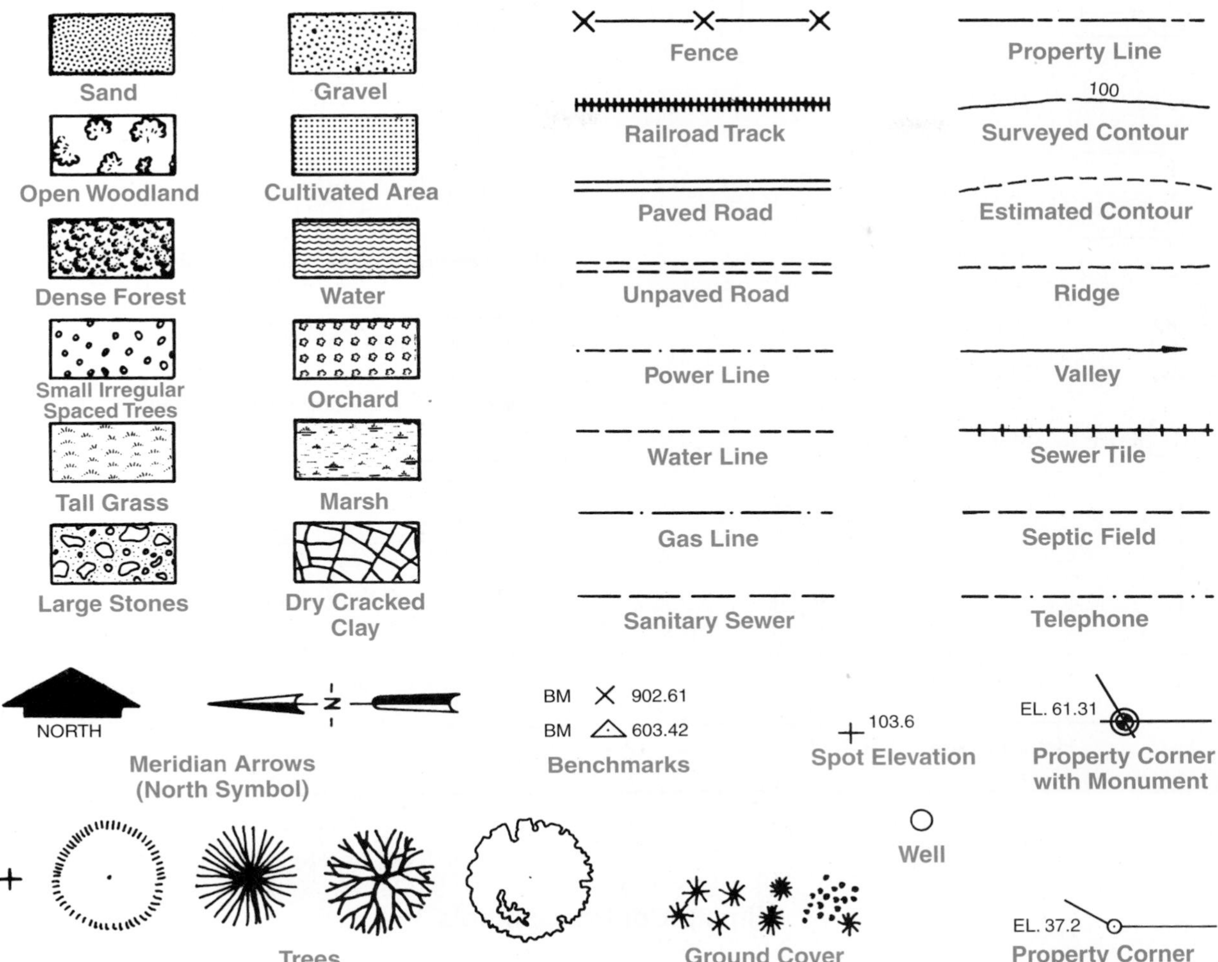

Plumbing Symbols

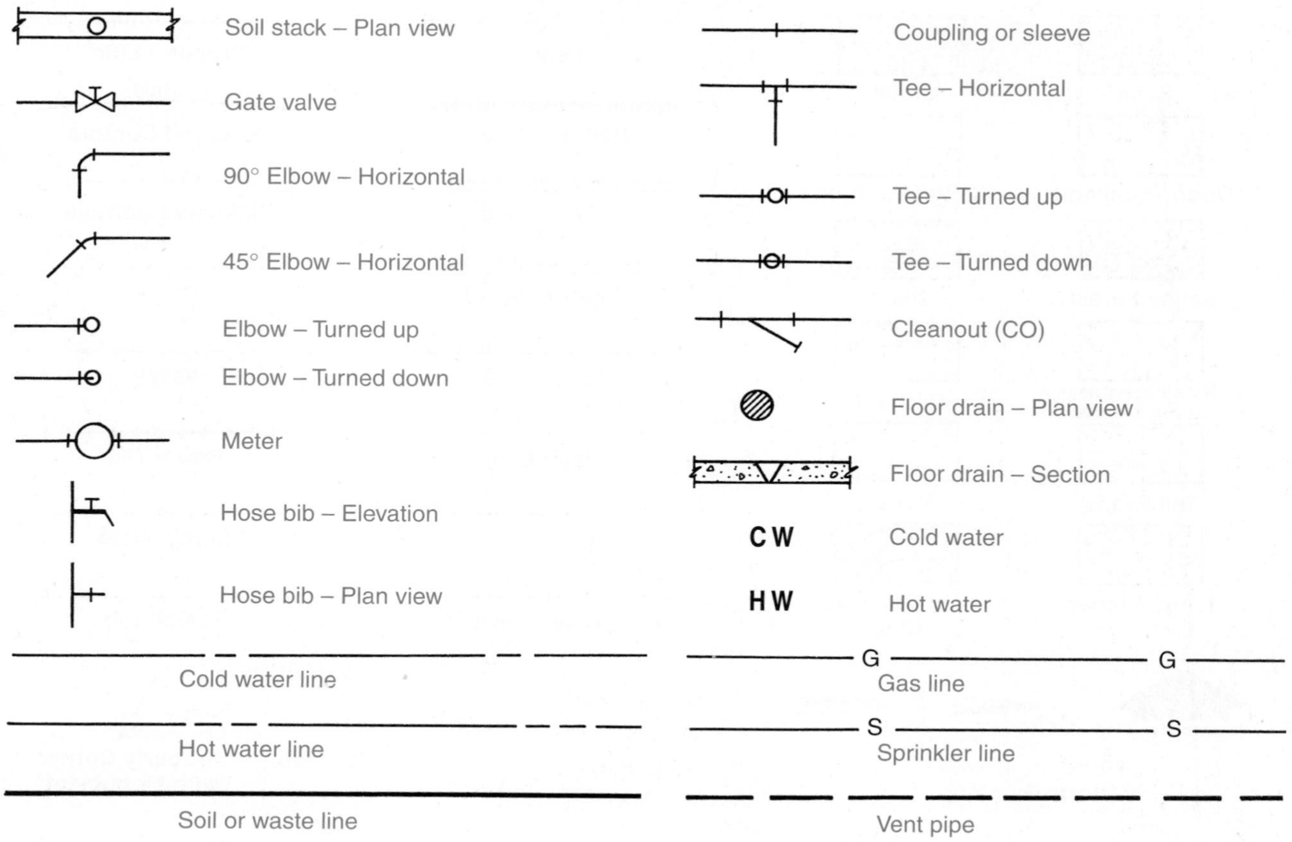

Soil stack – Plan view
Gate valve
90° Elbow – Horizontal
45° Elbow – Horizontal
Elbow – Turned up
Elbow – Turned down
Meter
Hose bib – Elevation
Hose bib – Plan view
Coupling or sleeve
Tee – Horizontal
Tee – Turned up
Tee – Turned down
Cleanout (CO)
Floor drain – Plan view
Floor drain – Section
CW
Cold water
HW
Hot water
Cold water line
Hot water line
Soil or waste line
G
G
Gas line
S
S
Sprinkler line
Vent pipe

Climate Control Symbols

W.A.
Warm-air supply
C.A.
Cold-air return
Second-floor supply
Second-floor return
12″ × 18″
Duct size and airflow
Change in duct size
Hydronic-radiant-panel coil
Hot-water-heating return
Hot-water-heating supply
T
Thermostat
H
Humidistat
RAD.
Radiator
CONV.
Convector
R.
Register
Ceiling-duct outlet
FURN.
Furnace
H
Humidification line
Medium-pressure steam

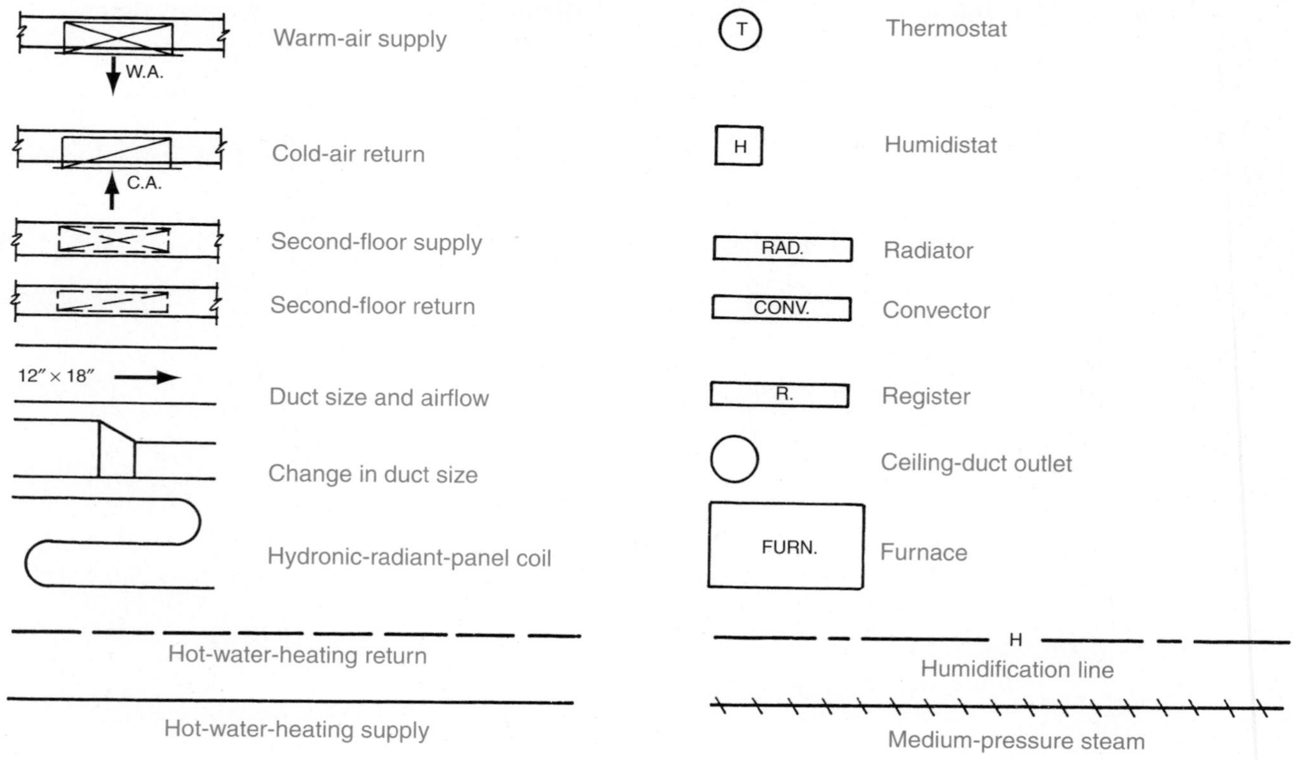

Electrical Symbols

Ceiling fixture

 Recessed fixture

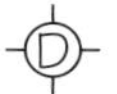 Drop cord fixture

 Fan hanger fixture

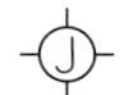 Junction box

 Fluorescent fixture

 Telephone

 Intercom

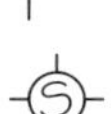 Ceiling fixture with pull switch

 Thermostat

Special fixture

Flush-mounted panel box

Single receptacle outlet

Duplex receptacle outlet

Triplex receptacle outlet

Quadruplex receptacle outlet

Split-wired duplex receptacle outlet

Special-purpose single receptacle outlet

240-volt receptacle outlet

WP — Weatherproof duplex receptacle outlet

S — Duplex receptacle outlet with switch

GFCI — GFCI receptacle outlet

A, B, C, Etc. — Special duplex receptacle outlet

\$ — Single-pole switch

$\$_2$ — Double-pole switch

$\$_3$ — Three-way switch

$\$_4$ — Four-way switch

$\$_{WP}$ — Weatherproof switch

$\$_L$ — Low-voltage switch

Push button

CH — Chimes

TV — Television antenna outlet

$\$_D$ — Dimmer switch

$\$_{A, B, C, Etc.}$ — Special switch

Information, Communication, and Security Wiring Symbols

A — Audio outlet

V — Video outlet

F — Fire alarm

F — Fire horn

Disconnect switch

Transformer

MD — Motion detector

DA — Door alarm

S — Smoke detector

H — Thermal sensor

Security keypad

WF — Sprinkler

Floor outlet

D — Data outlet

I — Intercom

J — Junction box

S — Speaker outlet

Vanity Sizes and Designs

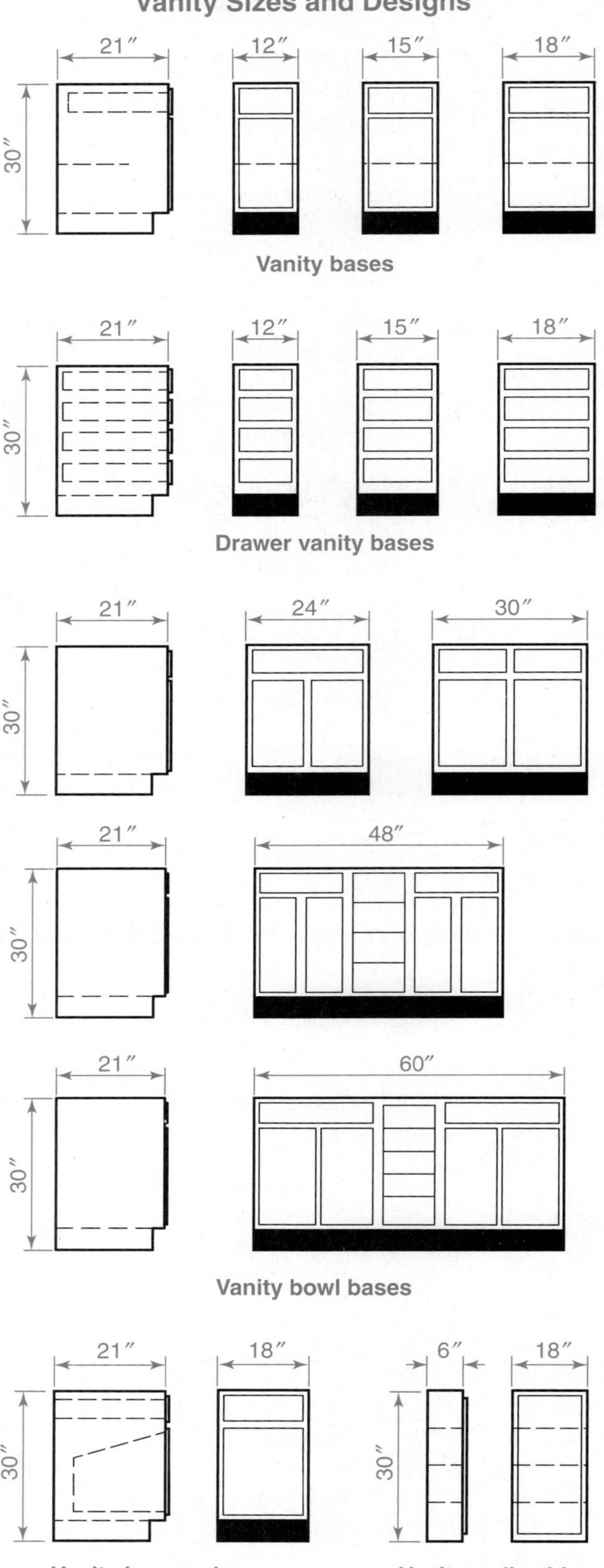

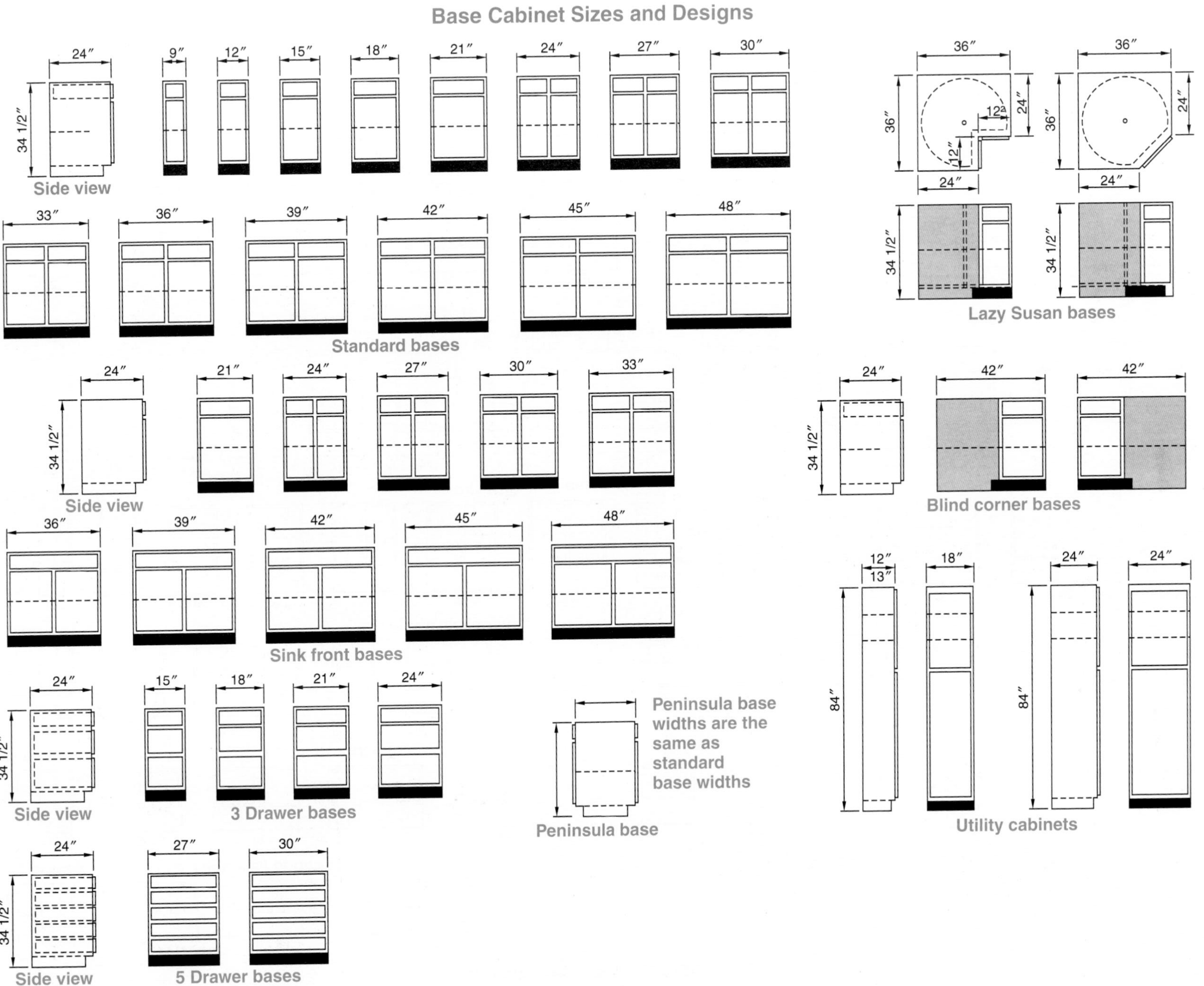
Base Cabinet Sizes and Designs
Side view
Standard bases
Side view
Sink front bases
Side view
3 Drawer bases
Side view
5 Drawer bases
Lazy Susan bases
Blind corner bases
Peninsula base widths are the same as standard base widths
Peninsula base
Utility cabinets

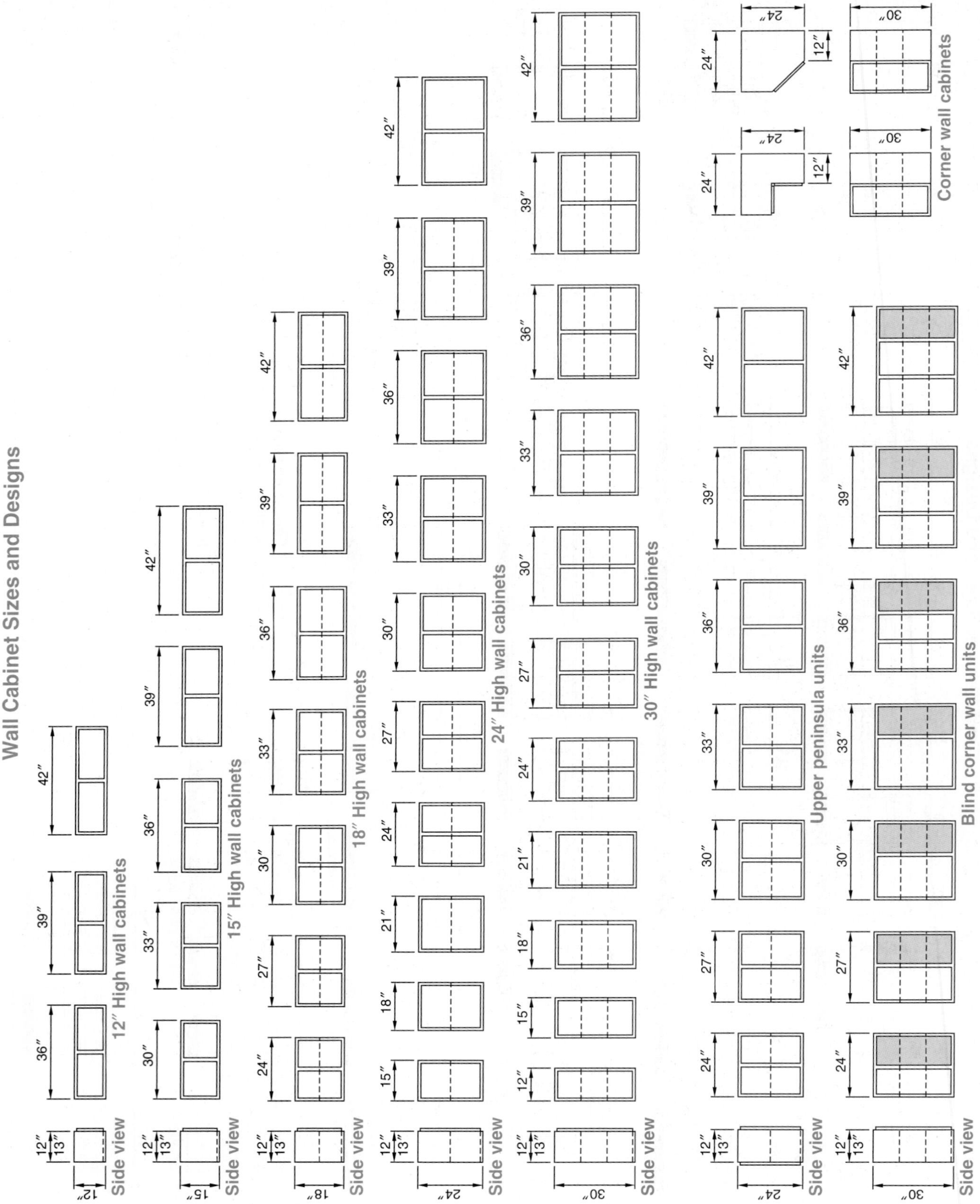
Wall Cabinet Sizes and Designs
12″ High wall cabinets
15″ High wall cabinets
18″ High wall cabinets
24″ High wall cabinets
30″ High wall cabinets
Upper peninsula units
Blind corner wall units
Corner wall cabinets
Side view
12″
13″
15″
18″
21″
24″
27″
30″
33″
36″
39″
42″

Double-Hung Window Sizes

Unit Size Chart

Unit Dimension (height)	Minimum Rough Opening (height)	Unobstructed Glass* (height)	1'-9 5/8" (549)	2'-1 5/8" (651)	2'-5 5/8" (752)	2'-7 5/8" (803)	2'-9 5/8" (854)	2'-11 5/8" (905)	3'-1 5/8" (956)	3'-5 5/8" (1057)	3'-9 5/8" (1159)
Minimum Rough Opening			1'-10 1/8" (562)	2'-2 1/8" (664)	2'-6 1/8" (765)	2'-8 1/8" (816)	2'-10 1/8" (867)	3'-0 1/8" (917)	3'-2 1/8" (968)	3'-6 1/8" (1070)	3'-10 1/8" (1172)
Unobstructed Glass*			15" (381)	19" (483)	23" (584)	25" (635)	27" (686)	29" (737)	31" (787)	35" (889)	39" (991)
3'-0 7/8" (937)	3'-0 7/8" (937)	13 15/16" (354)	TW18210	TW20210	TW24210	TW26210	TW28210	TW210210	TW30210	TW34210	TW38210
3'-4 7/8" (1038)	3'-4 7/8" (1038)	15 15/16" (405)	TW1832	TW2032	TW2432	TW2632	TW2832	TW21032	TW3032	TW3432	TW3832
3'-8 7/8" (1140)	3'-8 7/8" (1140)	17 15/16" (456)	TW1836	TW2036	TW2436	TW2636	TW2836	TW21036	TW3036	TW3436	TW3836
4'-0 7/8" (1241)	4'-0 7/8" (1241)	19 15/16" (506)	TW18310	TW20310	TW24310	TW26310	TW28310	TW210310	TW30310	TW34310	TW38310
4'-4 7/8" (1343)	4'-4 7/8" (1343)	21 15/16" (557)	TW1842	TW2042	TW2442	TW2642	TW2842	TW21042	TW3042	TW3442	TW3842
4'-8 7/8" (1445)	4'-8 7/8" (1445)	23 15/16" (608)	TW1846	TW2046	TW2446	TW2646	TW2846	TW21046	TW3046♦	TW3446♦	TW3846♦
5'-0 7/8" (1546)	5'-0 7/8" (1546)	25 15/16" (659)	TW18410	TW20410	TW24410	TW26410	TW28410	TW210410♦	TW30410♦	TW34410♦	TW38410♦
5'-4 7/8" (1648)	5'-4 7/8" (1648)	27 15/16" (710)	TW1852	TW2052	TW2452	TW2652	TW2852♦	TW21052♦	TW3052♦	TW3452♦	TW3852♦
5'-8 7/8" (1749)	5'-8 7/8" (1749)	35 15/16" (913) / 23 15/16" (608)	TW1856	TW2056	TW2456	TW2656	TW2856	TW21056	TW3056♦	TW3456♦	TW3856♦
6'-0 7/8" (1851)	6'-0 7/8" (1851)	31 15/16" (811)	TW18510	TW20510	TW24510♦	TW26510♦	TW28510♦	TW210510♦	TW30510♦	TW34510♦	TW38510♦
6'-4 7/8" (1953)	6'-4 7/8" (1953)	33 15/16" (862)	TW1862	TW2062	TW2462♦	TW2662♦	TW2862♦	TW21062♦	TW3062♦	TW3462♦	TW3862♦

These 5'-9" height units are "cottage style" units, and have unequal sash. The top sash is shorter than the bottom sash.

♦ Units with equal sash heights are ordered by description. Contact dealer for lead times.

Tilt-Wash (DC) and Tilt-Wash II (TW) Standard Sizes

Courtesy Andersen Windows Inc.

Horizontal Sliding Window Sizes

Unit Size Chart

Note:
Unit Dimension refers to overall outside-to-outside frame. Unobstructed Glass refers to visible glass dimensions. Numbers in parentheses are metric measurements.

Unit Dimension	Rough Opening	Unobstructed Glass*	2'-11¼" (895) / 3'-0" (914) / 12 9/16" (319)	3'-11¼" (1200) / 4'-0" (1219) / 18 9/16" (472)	4'-11¼" (1505) / 5'-0" (1524) / 24 9/16" (624)	5'-11¼" (1810) / 6'-0" (1829) / 30 9/16" (776)
1'-10¼" (565)	1'-11" (584)	14 1/8" (359)	G32	G42		
2'-11¼" (895)	3'-0" (914)	27 1/8" (689)	G33	G43	G53	G63
3'-5 1/4" (1048)	3'-6" (1067)	33 1/8" (841)	G336	G436	G536	G636
3'-11¼" (1200)	4'-0" (1219)	39 1/8" (994)	G34	G44	G54	G64
4'-11¼" (1505)	5'-0" (1524)	51 1/8" (1299)	G35	G45	G55	G65

G32 G42
G33 G43 G53 G63
G336 G436 G536 G636
G34 G44 G54 G64
G35 G45 G55 G65

Active sash Passive sash

Note:
Venting indicated as viewed from the exterior.

Dimension to top of operator handle in open position

Top of subfloor to top of window unit 6' 10-1/8" (2086)

	G2 sizes	G3 sizes	G36 sizes	G4 sizes	G5 sizes
Dimension to top of operator handle in open position	10-1/16" (256)	1' 9-3/8" (543)	2' 1-3/8" (645)	2' 5-1/16" (738)	2' 4-9/16" (725)
Floor line to handle	6' 0-1/16" (1830)	5' 0-3/4" (1543)	4' 8-3/4" (1441)	4' 5-1/16" (1348)	4' 5-9/16" (1360)

Floor line

Gliding Window Handle Locations

Gliding Window Basic Unit Sizes

Courtesy Andersen Windows Inc.

Casement Window Sizes

Unit Sizes - Standard Windows

Note:
Handing is viewed from exterior. Unit Dimension refers to overall outside-to-outside frame. Unobstructed Glass refers to visible glass dimensions. Numbers in parentheses are metric measurements.

Unit Dimension / Minimum Rough Opening / Unobstructed Glass	1'-7 1/4" (489) / 1'-8" (508) / 12 5/8" (321)	1'-11 1/4" (591) / 2'-0" (610) / 16 5/8" (422)	2'-3 1/4" (692) / 2'-4" (711) / 20 5/8" (524)	2'-5 1/4" (743) / 2'-6" (762) / 22 5/8" (575)	2'-7 1/4" (794) / 2'-8" (813) / 24 5/8" (625)	2'-9 1/4" (845) / 2'-10" (864) / 26 5/8" (676)	2'-11 1/4" (895) / 3'-0" (914) / 28 5/8" (727)
1'-11 1/4" (591) / 2'-0" (610) / 16 3/4" (425)	ACW1820	ACW2020	ACW2420				
2'-3 1/4" (692) / 2'-4" (711) / 20 3/4" (527)	ACW1824	ACW2024	ACW2424	ACW2624	ACW2824		
2'-7 1/4" (794) / 2'-8" (813) / 24 3/4" (629)	ACW1828	ACW2028	ACW2428	ACW2628	ACW2828	ACW21028	ACW3028
2'-11 1/4" (895) / 3'-0" (914) / 28 3/4" (770)	ACW1830	ACW2030	ACW2430	ACW2630	ACW2830	ACW21030	ACW3030
3'-3 1/4" (997) / 3'-4" (1016) / 32 3/4" (832)	ACW1834	ACW2034	ACW2434	ACW2634	ACW2834	ACW21034	ACW3034
3'-7 1/4" (1099) / 3'-8" (1118) / 36 3/4" (933)	ACW1838	ACW2038	ACW2438	ACW2638*♦	ACW2838*♦	ACW21038♦	ACW3038♦
3'-11 1/4" (1200) / 4'-0" (1219) / 40 3/4" (1035)	ACW1840	ACW2040	ACW2440*♦	ACW2640*♦	ACW2840♦	ACW21040♦	ACW3040♦
4'-3 1/4" (1302) / 4'-4" (1321) / 44 3/4" (1137)	ACW1844	ACW2044	ACW2444*♦	ACW2644*♦	ACW2844♦	ACW21044♦	ACW3044♦
4'-7 1/4" (1403) / 4'-8" (1422) / 48 3/4" (1238)	ACW1848	ACW2048	ACW2448*♦	ACW2648*♦	ACW2848♦	ACW21048♦	ACW3048♦
4'-11 1/4" (1505) / 5'-0" (1524) / 52 3/4" (1340)	ACW1850	ACW2050	ACW2450*♦	ACW2650*♦	ACW2850♦	ACW21050♦	ACW3050♦
5'-3 1/4" (1607) / 5'-4" (1626) / 56 3/4" (1441)	ACW1854	ACW2054	ACW2454*♦	ACW2654*♦	ACW2854♦	ACW21054♦	ACW3054♦
5'-7 1/4" (1708) / 5'-8" (1727) / 60 3/4" (1543)	ACW1858	ACW2058	ACW2458*♦	ACW2658*♦	ACW2858♦	ACW21058♦	ACW3058♦
5'-11 1/4" (1810) / 6'-0" (1829) / 64 3/4" (1645)	ACW1860	ACW2060	ACW2460*♦	ACW2660*♦	ACW2860♦	ACW21060♦	ACW3060♦

Venting Configuration

Left | Right | Stationary

All sizes available left, right and stationary unless noted.

A-Series Casement Standard Window Unit Sizes

Courtesy Andersen Windows Inc.

Awning Window Sizes

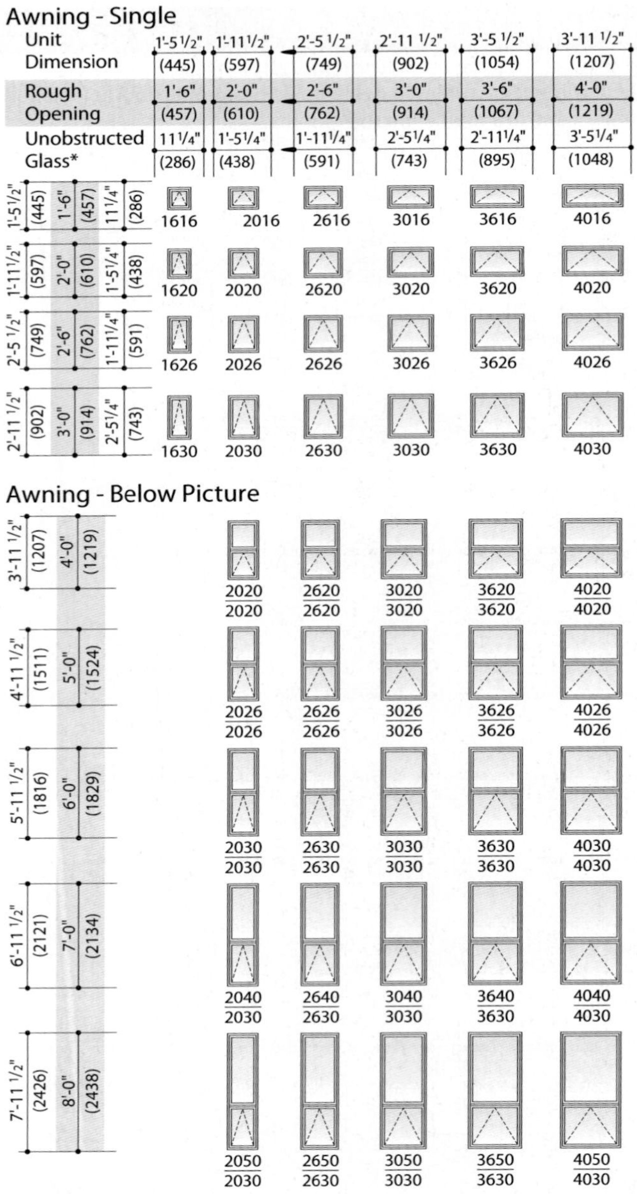

Awning - Single

Unit Dimension / Rough Opening / Unobstructed Glass* (height)	1'-5 1/2" (445) / 1'-6" (457) / 11 1/4" (286)	1'-11 1/2" (597) / 2'-0" (610) / 1'-5 1/4" (438)	2'-5 1/2" (749) / 2'-6" (762) / 1'-11 1/4" (591)	2'-11 1/2" (902) / 3'-0" (914) / 2'-5 1/4" (743)	3'-5 1/2" (1054) / 3'-6" (1067) / 2'-11 1/4" (895)	3'-11 1/2" (1207) / 4'-0" (1219) / 3'-5 1/4" (1048)
1'-5 1/2" (445) / 1'-6" (457) / 11 1/4" (286)	1616	2016	2616	3016	3616	4016
1'-11 1/2" (597) / 2'-0" (610) / 1'-5 1/4" (438)	1620	2020	2620	3020	3620	4020
2'-5 1/2" (749) / 2'-6" (762) / 1'-11 1/4" (591)	1626	2026	2626	3026	3626	4026
2'-11 1/2" (902) / 3'-0" (914) / 2'-5 1/4" (743)	1630	2030	2630	3030	3630	4030

Awning - Below Picture

Unit Dimension / Rough Opening (height)					
3'-11 1/2" (1207) / 4'-0" (1219)	2020 / 2020	2620 / 2620	3020 / 3020	3620 / 3620	4020 / 4020
4'-11 1/2" (1511) / 5'-0" (1524)	2026 / 2026	2626 / 2626	3026 / 3026	3626 / 3626	4026 / 4026
5'-11 1/2" (1816) / 6'-0" (1829)	2030 / 2030	2630 / 2630	3030 / 3030	3630 / 3630	4030 / 4030
6'-11 1/2" (2121) / 7'-0" (2134)	2040 / 2030	2640 / 2630	3040 / 3030	3640 / 3630	4040 / 4030
7'-11 1/2" (2426) / 8'-0" (2438)	2050 / 2030	2650 / 2630	3050 / 3030	3650 / 3630	4050 / 4030

Note:

Unit Dimension refers to overall outside-to-outside frame.
Unobstructed Glass refers to visible glass dimensions.

Courtesy Andersen Windows Inc.

Picture Window Sizes

Unit Dimension / Minimum Rough Opening / Unobstructed Glass	2'-11 1/2" (902) / 3'-0" (914) / 29 1/2" (749)	3'-11 1/2" (1207) / 4'-0" (1219) / 41 1/2" (1054)	4'-5 1/2" (1359) / 4'-6" (1372) / 47 1/2" (1207)	4'-8 1/2" (1435) / 4'-9" (1448) / 50 1/2" (1283)	4'-11 1/2" (1511) / 5'-0" (1524) / 53 1/2" (1359)	5'-5 1/2" (1664) / 5'-6" (1676) / 59 1/2" (1511)	5'-11 1/2" (1816) / 6'-0" (1829) / 65 1/2" (1664)
2'-11 1/2" (902) / 3'-0" (914) / 29 1/2" (749)	244FX3030	244FX4030	244FX4630	244FX4930	244FX5030	244FX5630	244FX6030
3'-11 1/2" (1207) / 4'-0" (1219) / 41 1/2" (1054)	244FX3040	244FX4040	244FX4640	244FX4940	244FX5040	244FX5640	244FX6040
4'-5 1/2" (1359) / 4'-6" (1372) / 47 1/2" (1207)	244FX3046	244FX4046	244FX4646	244FX4946	244FX5046	244FX5646	244FX6046
4'-8 1/2" (1435) / 4'-9" (1448) / 50 1/2" (1283)	244FX3049	244FX4049	244FX4649	244FX4949	244FX5049	244FX5649	244FX6049
4'-11 1/2" (1511) / 5'-0" (1524) / 53 1/2" (1359)	244FX3050	244FX4050	244FX4650	244FX4950	244FX5050	244FX5650	244FX6050
5'-5 1/2" (1664) / 5'-6" (1676) / 59 1/2" (1511)	244FX3056	244FX4056	244FX4656	244FX4956	244FX5056		
5'-11 1/2" (1816) / 6'-0" (1829) / 65 1/2" (1664)	244FX3060	244FX4060	244FX4660	244FX4960	244FX5060		

Note:

Unit Dimension refers to overall outside-to-outside frame. Unobstructed Glass refers to visible glass dimensions.

Courtesy Andersen Windows Inc.

Glass Sliding Door Sizes

Unit Size Chart - 6′ 8″ Height

Note:
Unit Dimension refers to overall outside-to-outside frame. Unobstructed Glass refers to visible glass dimensions. Numbers in parentheses are metric measurements.

	FWG 2668	FWG 2968S	FWG 5068 L	FWG 5068R	FWG 10068-4*
Unit Dimension		2'-8" (813)	4'-11 1/4" (1505)	4'-11 1/4" (1505)	9'-9" (2972)
Rough Opening		2'-8 3/4" (832)	5'-0" (1524)	5'-0" (1524)	9'-9 3/4" (2991)
Center Line Meeting Stiles			2'-5 5/8" (752), 2'-5 5/8" (752)	2'-5 5/8" (752), 2'-5 5/8" (752)	2'-5 11/16" (754), 2'-4 13/16" (732), 2'-4 13/16" (732), 2'-5 11/16" (754)
Unobstructed Glass Dimension	21 1/8" (537) × 63 1/8" (1603)				
Height		6'-7 1/2" (2019); 6'-8" (2032)			

	FWG 3068	FWG 3368S	FWG 6068L	FWG 6068R	FWG 12068-4*
Unit Dimension		3'-2" (965)	5'-11 1/4" (1810)	5'-11 1/4" (1810)	11'-9" (3581)
Rough Opening		3'-2 3/4" (984)	6'-0" (1829)	6'-0" (1829)	11'-9 3/4" (3600)
Center Line Meeting Stiles			2'-11 5/8" (905), 2'-11 5/8" (905)	2'-11 5/8" (905), 2'-11 5/8" (905)	2'-11 11/16" (906), 2'-10 13/16" (884), 2'-10 13/16" (884), 2'-11 11/16" (906)
Unobstructed Glass Dimension	27 1/8" (689) × 63 1/8" (1603)				
Height		6'-7 1/2" (2019); 6'-8" (2032)			

	FWG 4068	FWG 4368S	FWG 8068 L	FWG 8068R	FWG 16068-4*
Unit Dimension		4'-2" (1270)	7'-11 1/4" (2419)	7'-11 1/4" (2419)	15'-9" (4801)
Rough Opening		4'-2 3/4" (1289)	8'-0" (2438)	8'- 0" (2438)	15'-9 3/4" (4820)
Center Line Meeting Stiles			3'-11 5/8" (1210), 3'-11 5/8" (1210)	3'-11 5/8" (1210), 3'-11 5/8" (1210)	3'-11 11/16" (1211), 3'-10 13/16" (1189), 3'-10 13/16" (1189), 3'-11 11/16" (1211)
Unobstructed Glass Dimension	39 1/8" (994) × 63 1/8" (1603)				
Height		6'-7 1/2" (2019); 6'-8" (2032)			6'-8 1/4" (2038)

Frenchwood® Gliding Unit Sizes - 6′ 8″ Height

Courtesy Andersen Windows Inc.

Window and Door Symbols

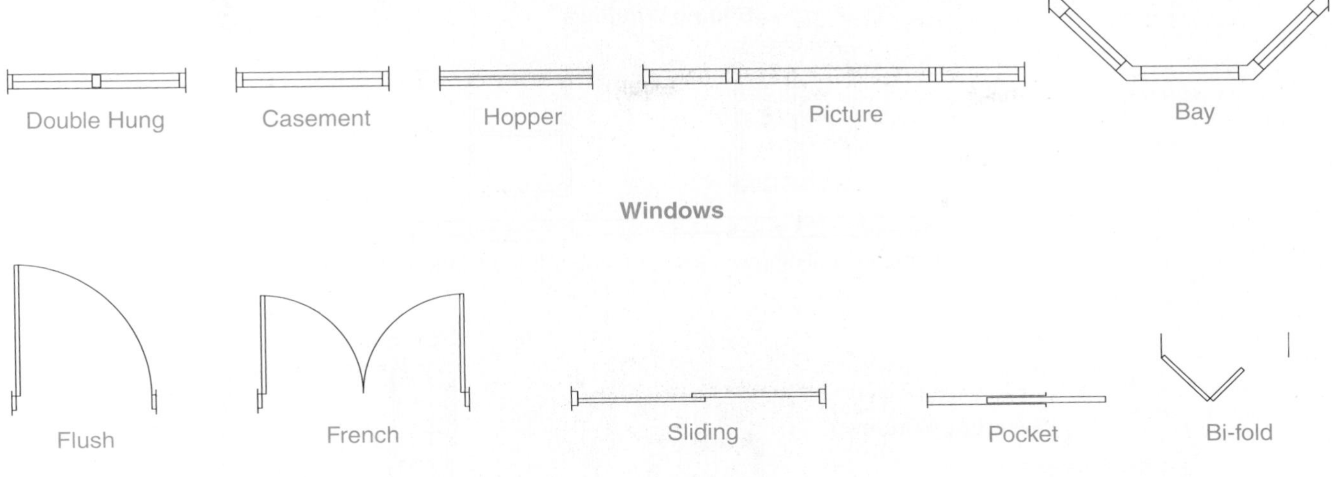

Exterior Door Symbols

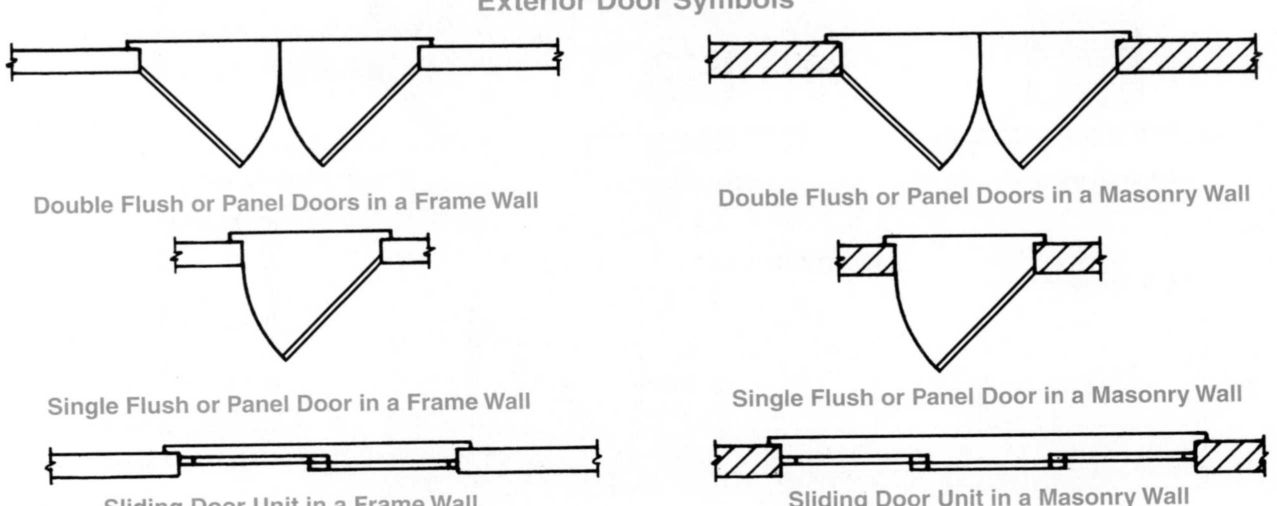

Elevation and Plan Views of Typical Residential Windows

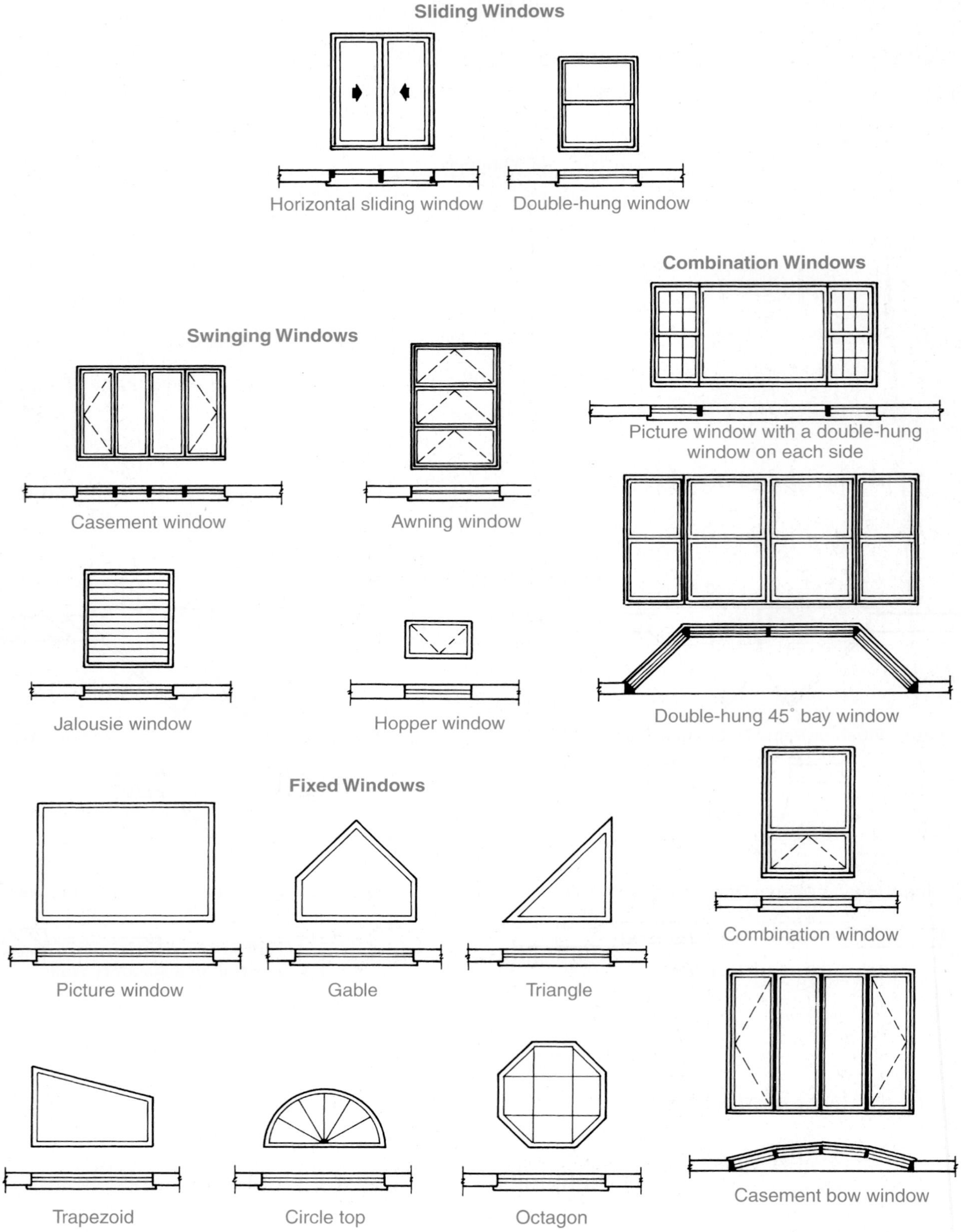

Sliding Windows

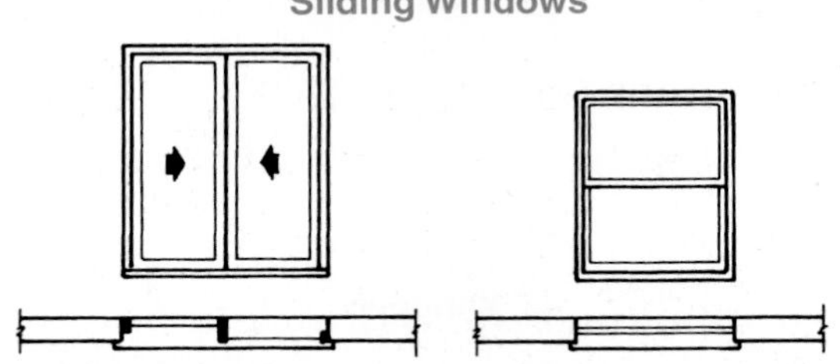

Horizontal sliding window

Double-hung window

Combination Windows

Picture window with a double-hung window on each side

Double-hung 45° bay window

Combination window

Casement bow window

Swinging Windows

Casement window

Awning window

Jalousie window

Hopper window

Fixed Windows

Picture window

Gable

Triangle

Trapezoid

Circle top

Octagon

Resistivity to Heat Loss of Common Building Materials

	Material	Resistivity		Material	Resistivity
4″	Concrete or stone	.32	1/2″	Plywood	.65
6″	Concrete or stone	.48	5/8″	Plywood	.80
8″	Concrete or stone	.64	3/4″	Plywood	.95
12″	Concrete or stone	.96	3/4″	Softwood sheathing or siding	.85
4″	Concrete block	.70		Composition floor covering	.08
8″	Concrete block	1.10	1″	Mineral batt insulation	3.50
12″	Concrete block	1.25	2″	Mineral batt insulation	7.00
4″	Common brick	.82	4″	Mineral batt insulation	14.00
4″	Face brick	.45	2″	Fiberglass insulation	7.00
4″	Structural clay tile	1.10	4″	Fiberglass insulation	14.00
8″	Structural clay tile	1.90	1″	Loose fill insulation	3.00
12″	Structural clay tile	3.00	1/2″	Gypsum wallboard	.45
1″	Stucco	.20	1″	Expanding polystyrene, extruded	4.00
15 lb	Building paper	.06	1″	Expanding polystyrene, molded beads	3.85
3/8″	Sheet rock or plasterboard	.33		Single thickness glass	.88
1/2″	Sand plaster	.15		Glassweld insulating glass	1.89
1/2″	Insulation plaster	.75		Single glass with storm window	1.66
1/2″	Fiberboard ceiling tile	1.20		Metal edge glass	1.85
1/2″	Fiberboard sheathing	1.45	4″	Glass block	2.13
3/4″	Fiberboard sheathing	2.18	1-3/8″	Wood door	1.82
	Roll roofing	.15		Same with storm door	2.94
	Asphalt shingles	.16	1-3/4″	Wood door	1.82
	Wood shingles	.86		Same with storm door	3.12
	Tile or slate	.08			

Recommended Foot Candle Levels

Area	Level
TV Viewing	5 FC
Storage	10 FC
Stairway	20 FC
Dining	20 FC
Bedroom	20 FC
Bath	30 FC
Living	30 FC
Den	30 FC
Reading	50 FC
Sewing	50 FC
Kitchen	50 FC
Shop	70 FC
Drawing	100 FC

Floor Joist Span Data

FLOOR JOIST SPANS FOR COMMON LUMBER SPECIES
(Residential sleeping areas, live load = 30 psf, L/Δ = 360)[a]

JOIST SPACING (inches)	SPECIES AND GRADE		DEAD LOAD = 10 psf				DEAD LOAD = 20 psf			
			2 x 6	2 x 8	2 x 10	2 x 12	2 x 6	2 x 8	2 x 10	2 x 12
			Maximum floor joist spans							
			(ft - in.)	(ft - in.)	(ft - in.)	(ft - in.)	(ft - in.)	(ft - in.)	(ft - in.)	(ft - in.)
12	Douglas fir-larch	SS	12-6	16-6	21-0	25-7	12-6	16-6	21-0	25-7
	Douglas fir-larch	#1	12-0	15-10	20-3	24-8	12-0	15-7	19-0	22-0
	Douglas fir-larch	#2	11-10	15-7	19-10	23-4	11-8	14-9	18-0	20-11
	Douglas fir-larch	#3	9-11	12-7	15-5	17-10	8-11	11-3	13-9	16-0
	Hem-fir	SS	11-10	15-7	19-10	24-2	11-10	15-7	19-10	24-2
	Hem-fir	#1	11-7	15-3	19-5	23-7	11-7	15-3	18-9	21-9
	Hem-fir	#2	11-0	14-6	18-6	22-6	11-0	14-4	17-6	20-4
	Hem-fir	#3	9-8	12-4	15-0	17-5	8-8	11-0	13-5	15-7
	Southern pine	SS	12-3	16-2	20-8	25-1	12-3	16-2	20-8	25-1
	Southern pine	#1	11-10	15-7	19-10	24-2	11-10	15-7	18-7	22-0
	Southern pine	#2	11-3	14-11	18-1	21-4	10-9	13-8	16-2	19-1
	Southern pine	#3	9-2	11-6	14-0	16-6	8-2	10-3	12-6	14-9
	Spruce-pine-fir	SS	11-7	15-3	19-5	23-7	11-7	15-3	19-5	23-7
	Spruce-pine-fir	#1	11-3	14-11	19-0	23-0	11-3	14-7	17-9	20-7
	Spruce-pine-fir	#2	11-3	14-11	19-0	23-0	11-3	14-7	17-9	20-7
	Spruce-pine-fir	#3	9-8	12-4	15-0	17-5	8-8	11-0	13-5	15-7
16	Douglas fir-larch	SS	11-4	15-0	19-1	23-3	11-4	15-0	19-1	23-3
	Douglas fir-larch	#1	10-11	14-5	18-5	21-4	10-8	13-6	16-5	19-1
	Douglas fir-larch	#2	10-9	14-2	17-5	20-3	10-1	12-9	15-7	18-1
	Douglas fir-larch	#3	8-7	10-11	13-4	15-5	7-8	9-9	11-11	13-10
	Hem-fir	SS	10-9	14-2	18-0	21-11	10-9	14-2	18-0	21-11
	Hem-fir	#1	10-6	13-10	17-8	21-1	10-6	13-4	16-3	18-10
	Hem-fir	#2	10-0	13-2	16-10	19-8	9-10	12-5	15-2	17-7
	Hem-fir	#3	8-5	10-8	13-0	15-1	7-6	9-6	11-8	13-6
	Southern pine	SS	11-2	14-8	18-9	22-10	11-2	14-8	18-9	22-10
	Southern pine	#1	10-9	14-2	18-0	21-4	10-9	13-9	16-1	19-1
	Southern pine	#2	10-3	13-3	15-8	18-6	9-4	11-10	14-0	16-6
	Southern pine	#3	7-11	10-0	11-1	14-4	7-1	8-11	10-10	12-10
	Spruce-pine-fir	SS	10-6	13-10	17-8	21-6	10-6	13-10	17-8	21-4
	Spruce-pine-fir	#1	10-3	13-6	17-2	19-11	9-11	12-7	15-5	17-10
	Spruce-pine-fir	#2	10-3	13-6	17-2	19-11	9-11	12-7	15-5	17-10
	Spruce-pine-fir	#3	8-5	10-8	13-0	15-1	7-6	9-6	11-8	13-6

(continued)

FLOOR JOIST SPANS FOR COMMON LUMBER SPECIES *(continued)*
(Residential sleeping areas, live load = 30 psf, L/Δ = 360)[a]

JOIST SPACING (inches)	SPECIES AND GRADE		DEAD LOAD = 10 psf				DEAD LOAD = 20 psf			
			2 x 6	2 x 8	2 x 10	2 x 12	2 x 6	2 x 8	2 x 10	2 x 12
			Maximum floor joist spans							
			(ft - in.)	(ft - in.)	(ft - in.)	(ft - in.)	(ft - in.)	(ft - in.)	(ft - in.)	(ft - in.)
19.2	Douglas fir-larch	SS	10-8	14-1	18-0	21-10	10-8	14-1	18-0	21-4
	Douglas fir-larch	#1	10-4	13-7	16-9	19-6	9-8	12-4	15-0	17-5
	Douglas fir-larch	#2	10-1	13-0	15-11	18-6	9-3	11-8	14-3	16-6
	Douglas fir-larch	#3	7-10	10-0	12-2	14-1	7-0	8-11	10-11	12-7
	Hem-fir	SS	10-1	13-4	17-0	20-8	10-1	13-4	17-0	20-7
	Hem-fir	#1	9-10	13-0	16-7	19-3	9-7	12-2	14-10	17-2
	Hem-fir	#2	9-5	12-5	15-6	17-1	8-11	11-4	13-10	16-1
	Hem-fir	#3	7-8	9-9	11-10	13-9	6-10	8-8	10-7	12-4
	Southern pine	SS	10-6	13-10	17-8	21-6	10-6	13-10	17-8	21-6
	Southern pine	#1	10-1	13-4	16-5	19-6	9-11	12-7	14-8	17-5
	Southern pine	#2	9-6	12-1	14-4	16-10	8-6	10-10	12-10	15-1
	Southern pine	#3	7-3	9-1	11-0	13-1	6-5	8-2	9-10	11-8
	Spruce-pine-fir	SS	9-10	13-0	16-7	20-2	9-10	13-0	16-7	19-6
	Spruce-pine-fir	#1	9-8	12-9	15-8	18-3	9-1	11-6	14-1	16-3
	Spruce-pine-fir	#2	9-8	12-9	15-8	18-3	9-1	11-6	14-1	16-3
	Spruce-pine-fir	#3	7-8	9-9	11-10	13-9	6-10	8-8	10-7	12-4
24	Douglas fir-larch	SS	9-11	13-1	16-8	20-3	9-11	13-1	16-5	19-1
	Douglas fir-larch	#1	9-7	12-4	15-0	17-5	8-8	11-0	13-5	15-7
	Douglas fir-larch	#2	9-3	11-8	14-3	16-6	8-3	10-5	12-9	14-9
	Douglas fir-larch	#3	7-0	8-11	10-11	12-7	6-3	8-0	9-9	11-3
	Hem-fir	SS	9-4	12-4	15-9	19-2	9-4	12-4	15-9	18-5
	Hem-fir	#1	9-2	12-1	14-10	17-2	8-7	10-10	13-3	15-5
	Hem-fir	#2	8-9	11-4	13-10	16-1	8-0	10-2	12-5	14-4
	Hem-fir	#3	6-10	8-8	10-7	12-4	6-2	7-9	9-6	11-0
	Southern pine	SS	9-9	12-10	16-5	19-11	9-9	12-10	16-5	19-8
	Southern pine	#1	9-4	12-4	14-8	17-5	8-10	11-3	13-1	15-7
	Southern pine	#2	8-6	10-10	12-10	15-1	7-7	9-8	11-5	13-6
	Southern pine	#3	6-5	8-2	9-10	11-8	5-9	7-3	8-10	10-5
	Spruce-pine-fir	SS	9-2	12-1	15-5	18-9	9-2	12-1	15-0	17-5
	Spruce-pine-fir	#1	8-11	11-6	14-1	16-3	8-1	10-3	12-7	14-7
	Spruce-pine-fir	#2	8-11	11-6	14-1	16-3	8-1	10-3	12-7	14-7
	Spruce-pine-fir	#3	6-10	8-8	10-7	12-4	6-2	7-9	9-6	11-0

For SI: 1 inch = 25.4 mm, 1 foot = 304.8 mm, 1 pound per square foot = 0.0479 kPa.

Note: Check sources for availability of lumber in lengths greater than 20 feet.

a. Dead load limits for townhouses in Seismic Design Category C and all structures in Seismic Design Categories D_0, D_1 and D_2 shall be determined in accordance with Section R301.2.2.2.1.

Glue-Laminated Roof and Floor Beam Data

Span Data for Glued Laminated Roof Beams*
Maximum Deflection 1/240th of the Span

Beam Size (Actual)	Wgt. of Beam Per Lin. Ft. in Pounds	Span in Feet											
		10	12	14	16	18	20	22	24	26	28	30	32
		Pounds Per Lin. Ft. Load Bearing Capacity											
3″ × 5-1/4″	3.7	151	85										
3″ × 7-1/4″	4.9	362	206	128	84								
3″ × 9-1/4″	6.7	566	448	300	199	137	99						
3″ × 11-1/4″	8.0	680	566	483	363	252	182	135	102				
4-1/2″ × 9-1/4″	9.8	850	673	451	299	207	148	109					
4-1/2″ × 11-1/4″	12.0	1,036	860	731	544	378	273	202	153				
3-1/4″ × 13-1/2″	10.4	1,100	916	784	685	479	347	258	197	152	120		
3-1/4″ × 15″	11.5	1,145	1,015	870	759	650	473	352	267	206	163	128	104
5-1/4″ × 13-1/2″	16.7	1,778	1,478	1,266	1,105	773	559	415	316	245	193	154	124
5-1/4″ × 15″	18.6	1,976	1,647	1,406	1,229	1,064	771	574	438	342	269	215	174
5-1/4″ × 16-1/2″	20.5	2,180	1,810	1,550	1,352	1,155	933	768	586	457	362	290	236
5-1/4″ × 18″	22.3	2,378	1,978	1,688	1,478	1,308	1,113	918	766	598	478	382	311

Example: Clear span = 20′-0″
Beam spacing = 10′-0″
Dead load = 8 lbs./sq. ft. (roofing and decking)
Live load = 20 lbs./sq. ft. (snow)
Total load = Live load + dead load × beam spacing
= (20 + 8) × 10 = 280 lbs./lin. ft.

The beam size required is 3-1/4″ × 13-1/2″, which supports 347 lbs./lin. ft. over a span of 20′-0″.

*Beams may be Douglas fir, larch or southern yellow pine.

Span Data for Glued Laminated Floor Beams*
Maximum Deflection 1/360th of the Span

Beam Size (Actual)	Wgt. of Beam Per Lin. Ft. in Pounds	Span in Feet											
		10	12	14	16	18	20	22	24	26	28	30	32
		Pounds Per Lin. Ft. Load Bearing Capacity											
3″ × 5-1/4″	3.7	114	64										
3″ × 7-1/4″	4.9	275	156	84	55								
3″ × 9-1/4″	6.7	492	319	198	130	89							
3″ × 11-1/4″	8.0	590	491	361	239	165	119						
4-1/2″ × 9-1/4″	9.8	738	479	298	196	134	96						
4-1/2″ × 11-1/4″	12.0	900	748	541	359	248	178	131	92				
3-1/4″ × 13-1/2″	10.4	956	795	683	454	316	228	169	128	98			
3-1/4″ × 15″	11.5	997	884	756	626	436	315	234	178	137	108		
5-1/4″ × 13-1/2″	16.7	1,541	1,283	1,095	732	509	367	271	205	158	123	96	
5-1/4″ × 15″	18.6	1,713	1,423	1,219	1,009	703	508	376	286	221	173	137	109
5-1/4″ × 16-1/2″	20.5	1,885	1,568	1,340	1,170	939	678	505	384	298	235	187	151
5-1/4″ × 18″	22.3	2,058	1,710	1,464	1,278	1,133	886	660	503	391	309	247	200

Example: Clear span = 20′-0″
Beam spacing = 10′-0″
Dead load = 7 lbs./sq. ft. (decking and carpet)
Live load = 40 lbs./sq. ft. (furniture and occupants)
Total load = Live load + dead load × beam spacing
= (40 + 7) × 10 = 470 lbs./lin. ft.

The beam size required is 5-1/4″ × 15″, which supports 508 lbs./lin. ft. over a span of 20′-0″.

*Beams may be Douglas fir, larch or southern yellow pine.

Potlatch Forests, Inc.

Roof Truss Designs

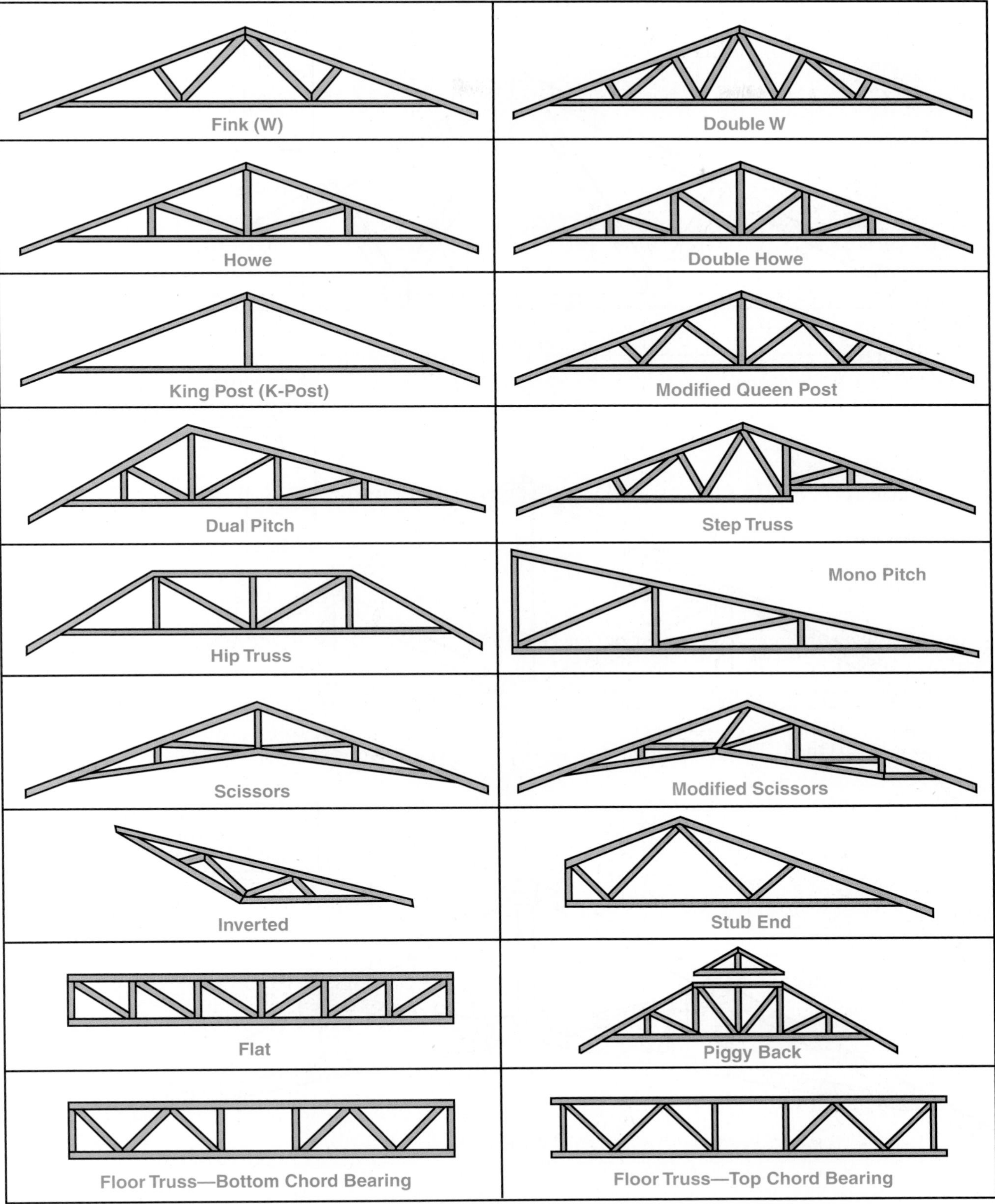

Design Data for W-Type, K-Post, and Scissor Trusses

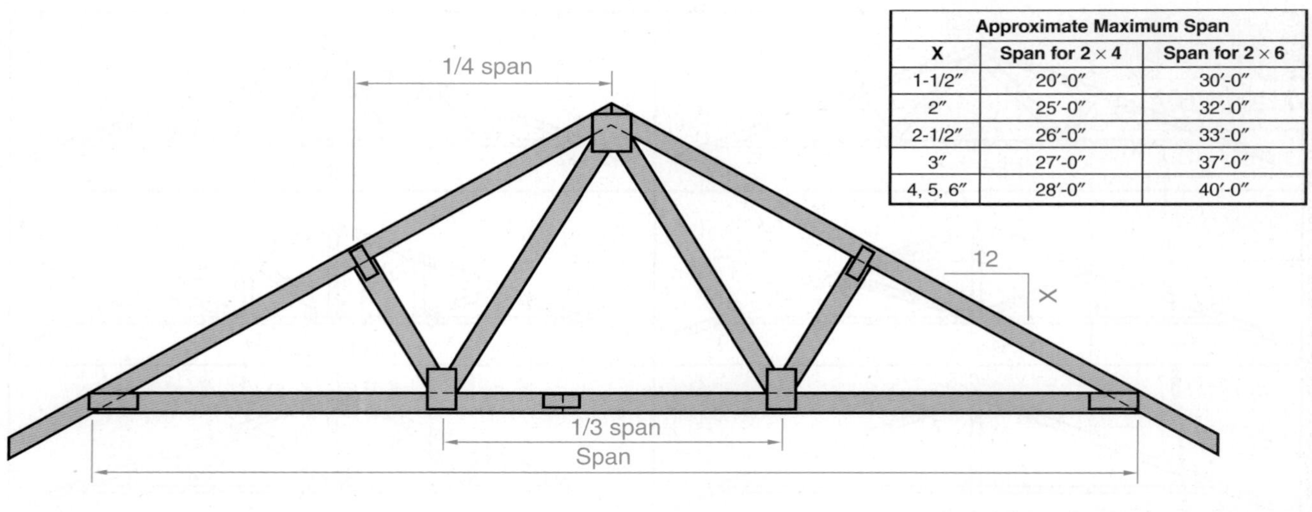

Approximate Maximum Span		
X	Span for 2 × 4	Span for 2 × 6
1-1/2″	20′-0″	30′-0″
2″	25′-0″	32′-0″
2-1/2″	26′-0″	33′-0″
3″	27′-0″	37′-0″
4, 5, 6″	28′-0″	40′-0″

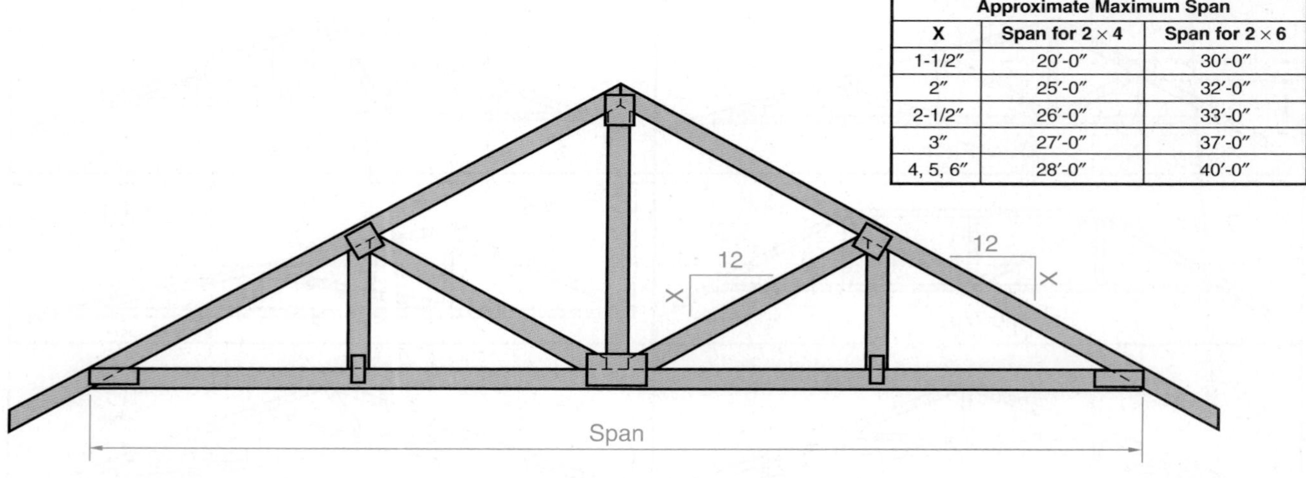

Approximate Maximum Span		
X	Span for 2 × 4	Span for 2 × 6
1-1/2″	20′-0″	30′-0″
2″	25′-0″	32′-0″
2-1/2″	26′-0″	33′-0″
3″	27′-0″	37′-0″
4, 5, 6″	28′-0″	40′-0″

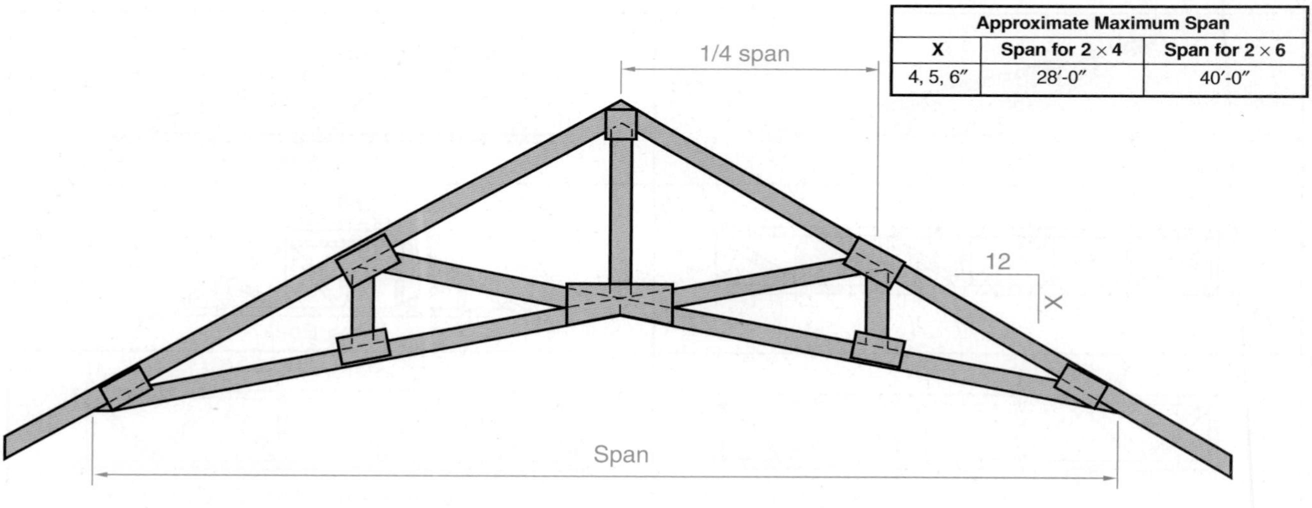

Approximate Maximum Span		
X	Span for 2 × 4	Span for 2 × 6
4, 5, 6″	28′-0″	40′-0″

Manufactured Wood Floor Truss Data

Span Data for Manufactured Wood Floor Trusses

Maximum Spans: 40-10-5 320 Series

Depth	Deflection	24″ O.C.	19.2″ O.C.	16″ O.C.	12″ O.C.
9-1/4″	L/480	**12′9″**	**13′10″**	**14′8″**	**16′1″**
	L/360	**14′1″**	**15′3″**	**16′1″**	**17′11″**
11-1/4″	L/480	**15′3″**	**16′7″**	**17′8″**	**19′6″**
	L/360	**16′0″**	**18′4″**	**19′7″**	**21′6″**
11-7/8″	L/480	**16′0″**	**17′4″**	**18′6″**	**20′4″**
	L/360	**16′0″**	**19′2″**	**20′5″**	**22′6″**
14″	L/480	**18′3″**	**19′9″**	**20′11″**	**23′3″**
	L/360	**18′6″**	**20′8″**	**23′3″**	**25′7″**
16″	L/480	**18′6″**	**22′2″**	**23′8″**	**26′2″**
	L/360	**18′6″**	**22′11″**	**26′2″**	**28′9″**

Maximum Spans: 40-10-5 420 Series

Depth	Deflection	24″ O.C.	19.2″ O.C.	16″ O.C.	12″ O.C.
9-1/4″	L/480	**14′4″**	**15′6″**	**16′6″**	**18′2″**
	L/360	**15′10″**	**17′1″**	**18′2″**	**19′11″**
11-1/4″	L/480	**16′0″**	**18′8″**	**19′10″**	**21′10″**
	L/360	**16′0″**	**20′0″**	**21′10″**	**24′1″**
11-7/8″	L/480	**16′0″**	**19′6″**	**20′8″**	**22′10″**
	L/360	**16′0″**	**20′0″**	**22′10″**	**25′3″**
14″	L/480	**20′3″**	**22′1″**	**23′8″**	**26′0″**
	L/360	**20′3″**	**24′0″**	**26′0″**	**28′0″**
16″	L/480	**22′0″**	**24′11″**	**26′7″**	**29′3″**
	L/360	**22′0″**	**26′0″**	**29′3″**	**32′0″**

- Up to 12" may be field-trimmed from each end of the SpaceJoist TE truss. Contact your SpaceJoist representative or Engineering Department prior to any additional trimming.
- Span charts reflect the benefit of composite action afforded by a glued-nailed or glued-screwed connection of the sheathing to the top chord of the truss. Consult SpaceJoist for appropriate spans if a nailed-only or screwed-only connection is to be utilized.
- Span dimensions are out-to-out at bearing supports.
  Minimum required bearing length is 1-3/4".
- Span charts are for the uniformly loaded conditions specified in the heading of each chart.
- For SpaceJoist trusses supporting concentrated (point) loads, cantilevered end conditions, or other special loading conditions, contact your SpaceJoist representative.
- Some spans may require top chord supports and/or web stiffeners. Contact SpaceJoist engineering for required reinforcements.

  *** Span Charts for additional loadings are available from your SpaceJoist representative.**

SpaceJoist/Alpine

Ceiling Joist Span Data

CEILING JOIST SPANS FOR COMMON LUMBER SPECIES
(Uninhabitable attics without storage, live load = 10 psf, L/Δ = 240)

CEILING JOIST SPACING (inches)	SPECIES AND GRADE		DEAD LOAD = 5 psf			
			2 × 4	2 × 6	2 × 8	2 × 10
			Maximum ceiling joist spans			
			(feet - inches)	(feet - inches)	(feet - inches)	(feet - inches)
12	Douglas fir-larch	SS	13-2	20-8	Note a	Note a
	Douglas fir-larch	#1	12-8	19-11	Note a	Note a
	Douglas fir-larch	#2	12-5	19-6	25-8	Note a
	Douglas fir-larch	#3	11-1	16-3	20-7	25-2
	Hem-fir	SS	12-5	19-6	25-8	Note a
	Hem-fir	#1	12-2	19-1	25-2	Note a
	Hem-fir	#2	11-7	18-2	24-0	Note a
	Hem-fir	#3	10-10	15-10	20-1	24-6
	Southern pine	SS	12-11	20-3	Note a	Note a
	Southern pine	#1	12-5	19-6	25-8	Note a
	Southern pine	#2	11-10	18-8	24-7	Note a
	Southern pine	#3	10-1	14-11	18-9	22-9
	Spruce-pine-fir	SS	12-2	19-1	25-2	Note a
	Spruce-pine-fir	#1	11-10	18-8	24-7	Note a
	Spruce-pine-fir	#2	11-10	18-8	24-7	Note a
	Spruce-pine-fir	#3	10-10	15-10	20-1	24-6
16	Douglas fir-larch	SS	11-11	18-9	24-8	Note a
	Douglas fir-larch	#1	11-6	18-1	23-10	Note a
	Douglas fir-larch	#2	11-3	17-8	23-4	Note a
	Douglas fir-larch	#3	9-7	14-1	17-10	21-9
	Hem-fir	SS	11-3	17-8	23-4	Note a
	Hem-fir	#1	11-0	17-4	22-10	Note a
	Hem-fir	#2	10-6	16-6	21-9	Note a
	Hem-fir	#3	9-5	13-9	17-5	21-3
	Southern pine	SS	11-9	18-5	24-3	Note a
	Southern pine	#1	11-3	17-8	23-10	Note a
	Southern pine	#2	10-9	16-11	21-7	25-7
	Southern pine	#3	8-9	12-11	16-3	19-9
	Spruce-pine-fir	SS	11-0	17-4	22-10	Note a
	Spruce-pine-fir	#1	10-9	16-11	22-4	Note a
	Spruce-pine-fir	#2	10-9	16-11	22-4	Note a
	Spruce-pine-fir	#3	9-5	13-9	17-5	21-3

(continued)

CEILING JOIST SPANS FOR COMMON LUMBER SPECIES *(continued)*

(Uninhabitable attics without storage, live load = 10 psf, L/Δ = 240)

CEILING JOIST SPACING (inches)	SPECIES AND GRADE		DEAD LOAD = 5 psf			
			2 × 4	2 × 6	2 × 8	2 × 10
			Maximum ceiling joist spans			
			(feet - inches)	(feet - inches)	(feet - inches)	(feet - inches)
19.2	Douglas fir-larch	SS	11-3	17-8	23-3	Note a
	Douglas fir-larch	#1	10-10	17-0	22-5	Note a
	Douglas fir-larch	#2	10-7	16-8	21-4	26-0
	Douglas fir-larch	#3	8-9	12-10	16-3	19-10
	Hem-fir	SS	10-7	16-8	21-11	Note a
	Hem-fir	#1	10-4	16-4	21-6	Note a
	Hem-fir	#2	9-11	15-7	20-6	25-3
	Hem-fir	#3	8-7	12-6	15-10	19-5
	Southern pine	SS	11-0	17-4	22-10	Note a
	Southern pine	#1	10-7	16-8	22-0	Note a
	Southern pine	#2	10-2	15-7	19-8	23-5
	Southern pine	#3	8-0	11-9	14-10	18-0
	Spruce-pine-fir	SS	10-4	16-4	21-6	Note a
	Spruce-pine-fir	#1	10-2	15-11	21-0	25-8
	Spruce-pine-fir	#2	10-2	15-11	21-0	25-8
	Spruce-pine-fir	#3	8-7	12-6	15-10	19-5
24	Douglas fir-larch	SS	10-5	16-4	21-7	Note a
	Douglas fir-larch	#1	10-0	15-9	20-1	24-6
	Douglas fir-larch	#2	9-10	15-0	19-1	23-3
	Douglas fir-larch	#3	7-10	11-6	14-7	17-9
	Hem-fir	SS	9-10	15-6	20-5	Note a
	Hem-fir	#1	9-8	15-2	19-10	24-3
	Hem-fir	#2	9-2	14-5	18-6	22-7
	Hem-fir	#3	7-8	11-2	14-2	17-4
	Southern pine	SS	10-3	16-1	21-2	Note a
	Southern pine	#1	9-10	15-6	20-5	24-0
	Southern pine	#2	9-3	13-11	17-7	20-11
	Southern pine	#3	7-2	10-6	13-3	16-1
	Spruce-pine-fir	SS	9-8	15-2	19-11	25-5
	Spruce-pine-fir	#1	9-5	14-9	18-9	22-11
	Spruce-pine-fir	#2	9-5	14-9	18-9	22-11
	Spruce-pine-fir	#3	7-8	11-2	14-2	17-4

Check sources for availability of lumber in lengths greater than 20 feet.

For SI: 1 inch = 25.4 mm, 1 foot = 304.8 mm, 1 pound per square foot = 0.0479 kPa.

a. Span exceeds 26 feet in length.

Span Data for Tongue-and-Groove Heavy Timber Roof Decking

Two Inch Nominal Thickness[a] Allowable Roof Load Limited By Bending														
Bending Stress, psi	Allowable Uniformly Distributed Total Roof Load[b,c,d,e], psf													
	Simple Span, ft							Controlled Random Layup Span, ft						
	6	7	8	9	10	11	12	6	7	8	9	10	11	12
875	73	54	41	32	26	22	18	61	45	34	27	22	18	15
950	79	58	44	35	28	24	20	66	48	37	29	24	20	16
1000	83	61	47	37	30	25	21	69	51	39	31	25	21	17
1050	88	64	49	39	32	26	22	73	54	41	32	26	22	18
1100	92	67	52	41	33	27	23	76	56	43	34	28	23	19
1150	96	70	54	42	34	28	24	80	59	45	35	29	24	20
1200	100	73	56	44	36	30	25	83	61	47	37	30	25	21
1250	104	76	58	46	38	31	26	87	64	49	39	31	26	22
1300	108	80	61	48	39	32	27	90	66	51	40	32	27	22
1350	112	83	63	50	40	33	28	94	69	53	42	34	28	23
1400	117	86	66	52	42	35	29	97	71	55	43	35	29	24
1450	121	89	68	54	44	36	30	101	74	57	45	36	30	25
1500	125	92	70	56	45	37	31	104	76	58	46	38	31	26
1550	129	95	73	57	46	38	32	108	79	60	48	39	32	27
1600	133	98	75	59	48	40	33	111	82	62	49	40	33	28
1650	138	101	77	61	50	41	34	114	84	64	51	41	34	29
1700	142	104	80	63	51	42	35	118	87	66	52	42	35	30
1750	146	107	82	65	52	43	36	122	89	68	54	44	36	30
1900	158	116	89	70	57	47	40	132	97	74	59	48	39	33
2000	167	122	94	74	60	50	42	139	102	78	62	50	41	35

[a] Based on 1-1/2 in. net thickness. To determine allowable loads for 1-7/16 in. net thickness, multiply tabulated values by 0.918.
[b] To determine allowable uniformly distributed total roof loads for other span conditions, use simple span load values for combination simple span and two-span continuous, and two-span continuous layups; and use controlled random layup road values for cantilevered pieces intermixed layup.
[c] Duration of load, $C_D = 1.0$ used in this table. For other durations of load, adjust by the appropriate factor.
[d] No increase for size effect has been applied ($C_F = 1.00$). F_b values have been previously adjusted.
[e] Dry conditions of use.

(continued)

American Institute of Timber Construction

Three and Four Inch Nominal Thickness
Allowable Roof Load Limited by Bending
Simple Span And Controlled Random Layups (3 or more spans)

Bending Stress, psi	Allowable Uniformly Distributed Total Roof Load[a,c,e,f,g], psf																									
	3 Inch Nominal Thickness[b] Span, ft													4 Inch Nominal Thickness[d] Span, ft												
	8	9	10	11	12	13	14	15	16	17	18	19	20	8	9	10	11	12	13	14	15	16	17	18	19	20
875	114	90	73	60	51	43	37	32	28	25	22	20	18	223	176	143	118	99	84	73	64	56	49	44	40	36
950	124	98	79	65	55	47	40	35	31	27	24	22	20	242	192	155	128	108	92	79	69	61	54	48	43	39
1000	130	103	83	69	58	49	42	37	32	29	26	23	21	255	202	163	135	113	97	83	72	64	56	50	45	41
1050	137	108	88	72	61	52	45	39	34	30	27	24	22	268	212	172	142	119	101	88	76	67	59	53	48	43
1100	143	113	92	76	64	54	47	41	36	32	28	25	23	281	222	180	148	125	106	92	80	70	62	55	50	45
1150	150	118	96	79	66	57	49	42	37	33	30	26	24	293	232	188	155	130	111	96	83	73	65	58	52	47
1200	156	123	100	83	69	59	51	44	39	35	31	28	25	306	242	196	162	136	116	100	87	76	68	60	54	49
1250	163	129	104	86	72	62	53	46	41	36	32	29	26	319	252	204	169	142	121	104	91	80	71	63	56	51
1300	169	134	108	90	75	64	55	48	42	37	33	30	27	332	262	212	175	147	126	108	94	83	73	66	59	53
1350	176	139	112	93	78	66	57	50	44	39	35	31	28	344	272	220	182	153	130	112	98	86	76	68	61	55
1400	182	144	117	96	81	69	60	52	46	40	36	32	29	357	282	229	189	159	135	117	102	89	79	70	63	57
1450	189	149	121	100	84	71	62	64	47	42	37	33	30	370	292	237	196	164	140	121	105	92	82	73	66	59
1500	195	164	125	103	87	74	64	56	49	43	38	35	31	383	302	245	202	170	145	125	109	96	85	76	68	61
1550	202	159	129	107	90	76	66	57	50	45	40	36	32	396	312	253	209	176	150	129	112	99	88	78	70	63
1600	208	165	133	110	92	79	68	59	52	46	41	37	33	408	323	261	216	181	155	133	115	102	90	81	72	65
1650	215	170	138	114	95	81	70	61	54	48	42	38	34	421	333	270	223	187	159	138	120	105	93	83	75	67
1700	221	175	142	117	98	84	72	63	55	49	44	39	35	434	343	278	229	193	164	142	123	108	96	86	77	69
1750	228	180	146	120	101	86	74	65	57	50	45	40	36	447	353	286	236	198	169	146	127	112	99	88	79	71
1900	247	195	158	131	110	94	81	70	62	55	49	44	40	485	383	310	256	216	184	158	138	121	107	96	86	78
2000	260	206	167	138	116	99	85	74	65	58	51	46	42	510	403	327	270	227	193	167	145	128	113	101	90	82

[a] These load values may also be used for cantilevered pieces intermixed, combination simple span and two-span continuous, and two-span continuous layups.

[b] 2-1/2 in. net thickness. To determine allowable loads for 2-5/8 in. net thickness, multiply tabulated loads by 1.10.

[c] All spans to the right of the double line require special ordering of additional long lengths to assure that at least 20% of the decking is equal to the span length or longer.

[d] 3-1/2 in. net thickness.

[e] Duration of load, C_D = 1.0 used in this table. For other durations of load, adjust by the appropriate factor.

[f] No increase for size effect has been applied (C_F = 1.00). F_b values have been previously adjusted.

[g] Dry conditions of use.

Span and Load Tables for American Standard S-Beams and W-Beams

Maximum Allowable Uniform Loads for American Standard S-Beams with Lateral Support

Span in Feet

Size of Beam	Weight of Beam Per Foot	4	6	8	10	12	14	16	18	20	22	24	26	28	30	32	34	36	38	40
4 x 2-5/8	7.7	12.6	8.4	6.3	5.0															
4 x 2-3/4	9.5	14.5	9.7	7.3	5.8															
5 x 3	10.0	20.3	13.6	10.2	8.1	6.8														
6 x 3-3/8	12.5	30.4	20.2	15.2	12.1	10.1	8.7													
6 x 3-5/8	17.2	37.7	25.1	18.9	15.1	12.6	10.8													
8 x 4	18.4	59.3	39.5	29.6	23.7	19.8	16.9	14.8	13.2	11.9										
8 x 4-1/8	23.0	69.0	46.0	34.5	27.6	23.0	19.7	17.2	15.3	13.8										
10 x 4-5/8	25.4	89.6	67.8	50.8	40.7	33.9	29.1	25.4	22.6	20.3	18.5	16.9								
10 x 5	35.0	127	84.8	63.6	50.9	42.4	36.3	31.8	28.3	25.4	23.1	21.2								
12 x 5	31.8	121	100	75.1	60.1	50.1	42.9	37.5	33.4	30.0	27.3	25.0	23.1	21.5	20.0					
12 x 5-1/8	35.0	148	107	80.1	64.1	53.4	45.8	40.1	35.6	32.0	29.1	26.7	24.7	22.9	21.4					
12 x 5-1/4	40.8	160	126	94.7	75.7	63.1	54.1	47.3	42.1	37.9	34.4	31.6	29.1	27.0	25.2					
12 x 5-1/2	50.0	219	146	109	87.5	72.9	62.5	54.7	48.6	43.8	39.8	36.5	33.7	31.3	29.2					
15 x 5-1/2	42.9		166	124	99.4	82.9	71.0	62.2	55.2	49.7	45.2	41.4	38.2	35.5	33.1	31.1	29.2	27.6		
15 x 5-5/8	50.0	238	184	138	111	92.2	79.0	69.2	61.5	55.3	50.3	46.1	42.6	39.5	36.9	34.6	32.5	30.7		
18 x 6	54.7		239	187	149	125	107	93.4	83.0	74.7	67.9	62.3	57.5	53.4	49.8	46.7	44.0	41.5	39.3	37.4
18 x 6-1/4	70.0	369	297	223	178	149	127	111	99.0	89.1	81.0	74.3	68.5	63.6	59.4	55.7	52.4	49.5	46.9	44.6
20 x 6-1/4	66		291	250	200	166	143	125	111	99.9	90.8	83.2	76.8	71.3	66.6	62.4	58.8	55.5	52.6	49.9
20 x 6-3/8	75.0		364	273	218	182	156	137	121	109	99.3	91.0	84.0	78.0	72.8	68.3	64.2	60.7	57.5	54.6

Loads are in kips. 1 kip = 1000 pounds

Maximum Allowable Uniform Loads for Wide Flange W-Beams with Lateral Support

Span in Feet

Size of Beam	Weight of Beam Per Foot	4	6	8	10	12	14	16	18	20	22	24	26	28	30	32	34	36	38	40
8 x 4	13	56.9	37.9	28.4	22.8	19.0	16.3	14.2	12.6											
8 x 5-1/4	18	74.9	56.6	42.4	33.9	28.3	24.2	21.2	18.9	17.0										
8 x 5-1/4	21	82.8	67.9	50.9	40.7	33.9	29.1	25.4	22.6	20.4										
8 x 6-1/2	24		76.8	57.6	46.1	38.4	32.9	28.8	25.6											
8 x 8	31		91.2	75.8	60.6	50.5	43.3	37.9	33.7	30.3										
10 x 5-3/4	22		86.5	64.9	51.9	43.2	37.1	32.4	28.8	25.9	23.6	21.6								
10 x 8	33		113	96.8	77.4	64.5	55.3	48.4	43.0	38.7	35.2	32.3								
10 x 10	49			136	121	100	86.1	75.3	67.0	60.3	54.8	50.2								
12 x 6-1/2	26		112	92.8	74.3	61.9	53.0	46.4	41.3	37.1	33.8	30.9	28.6	26.5	24.8					
12 x 8	40			141	114	94.8	81.3	71.1	63.2	56.9	51.7	47.4	43.8	40.6						
12 x 10	53				155	130	111	97.2	86.4	77.7	70.7	64.8	59.8	55.5	51.8					
12 x 12	65				189	158	135	119	105	94.8	86.2	79.0	72.9	67.7	63.2					
14 x 6-3/4	30		149	118	94.4	78.7	67.4	59.0	52.5	47.2	42.9	39.3	36.3	33.7	31.5	29.5	27.8			
14 x 8	43			167	139	116	99.2	86.8	77.2	69.5	63.1	57.9	53.4	49.6	46.3	43.4	40.9			
14 x 10	61				204	170	145	127	113	102	92.5	84.8	78.3	72.7	67.9	63.6	59.9			
14 x 10-1/8	74				251	210	180	157	140	126	114	105	96.7	89.8	83.8	78.6	74.0			
14 x 14-1/2	90					247	218	191	170	153	139	127	117	109	102	95.4	89.8			
16 x 7	36		187	160	128	106	91.2	79.8	71.0	63.9	58.1	53.2	49.1	45.6	42.6	39.9	37.6	35.5	33.6	
16 x 7-1/8	57			262	210	175	150	131	116	105	95.3	87.3	80.6	74.9	69.9	65.5	61.6	58.2	55.2	52.4
16 x 10-1/4	77				299	250	214	187	166	150	136	125	115	107	99.8	93.6	88.1	83.2	78.8	74.9
18 x 7-1/2	50			252	202	168	144	126	112	101	91.6	84.0	77.5	72.0	67.2	63.0	59.3	56.0	53.1	50.4
18 x 7-5/8	65			330	265	221	190	166	147	133	121	111	102	94.8	88.5	83.0	78.1	73.7	69.9	66.4
18 x 7-5/8	71			364	291	243	208	182	162	146	132	121	112	104	97.1	91.1	85.7	80.9	76.7	72.9
21 x 8-1/4	62			336	287	240	205	180	160	144	131	120	111	103	95.8	89.8	84.5	79.8	75.6	71.9

Loads are in kips. 1 kip = 1000 pounds

American Institute of Steel Construction

The Metric System		
Linear Measure		
10 millimeters	=	1 centimeter
10 centimeters	=	1 decimeter
10 decimeters	=	1 meter
10 meters	=	1 decameter
10 decameters	=	1 hectometer
10 hectometers	=	1 kilometer
Square Measure		
100 square millimeters	=	1 square centimeter
100 square centimeters	=	1 square decimeter
100 square decimeters	=	1 square meter
100 square meters	=	1 square decameter
100 square decameters	=	1 square hectometer
100 square hectometers	=	1 square kilometer
Cubic Measure		
1000 cubic millimeters	=	1 cubic centimeter
1000 cubic centimeters	=	1 cubic decimeter
1000 cubic decimeters	=	1 cubic meter
Liquid Measure		
10 milliliters	=	1 centiliter
10 centiliters	=	1 deciliter
10 deciliters	=	1 liter
10 liters	=	1 decaliter
10 decaliters	=	1 hectoliter
10 hectoliters	=	1 kiloliter
Weights		
10 milligrams	=	1 centigram
10 centigrams	=	1 decigram
10 decigrams	=	1 gram
10 grams	=	1 decagram
10 decagrams	=	1 hectogram
10 hectograms	=	1 kilogram
100 kilograms	=	1 quintal
10 quintals	=	1 metric ton

Weights and Measures Conversion Table

Linear Measure				
1 inch	=		=	2.54 centimeters
1 foot	=	12 inches	=	0.3048 meters
1 yard	=	3 feet	=	0.9144 meters
1 rod	=	5-1/2 yards	=	5.029 meters
1 rod	=	16-1/2 feet	=	5.029 meters
1 furlong	=	40 rods	=	201.17 meters
1 mile (statute)	=	5280 feet	=	1609.3 meters
1 mile (statute)	=	1760 yards	=	1609.3 meters
1 league (land)	=	3 miles	=	4.83 kilometers
Square Measure				
1 square inch	=		=	6.452 square centimeters
1 square foot	=	144 square inches	=	929 square centimeters
1 square yard	=	9 square feet	=	0.8361 square meters
1 square rod	=	30-1/4 square yards	=	25.29 square meters
1 acre	=	43,560 square feet	=	0.4047 hectare
1 acre	=	160 square yards	=	0.4047 hectare
1 square mile	=	640 acres	=	259 hectares
1 square mile	=	640 acres	=	2.59 square kilometers
Cubic Measure				
1 cubic inch	=		=	16.387 cubic centimeters
1 cubic foot	=	1728 cubic inches	=	0.0283 cubic meters
1 cubic yard	=	27 cubic feet	=	0.7646 cubic meters
Chain Linear Measure (For Surveyor's Chain)				
1 link	=	7.92 inches	=	20.12 centimeters
1 chain	=	100 links	=	20.12 meters
1 chain	=	66 feet	=	20.12 meters
1 furlong	=	10 chains	=	201.17 meters
1 mile	=	80 chains	=	1609.3 meters
Chain Square Measure				
1 square pole	=	625 square links	=	25.29 square meters
1 square chain	=	16 square poles	=	404.7 square meters
1 acre	=	10 square chains	=	0.4047 hectare
1 square mile	=	640 acres	=	259 hectares
1 section	=	640 acres	=	259 hectares
1 township	=	36 square miles	=	9324.0 hectares
Angular and Circular Measure				
1 minute	=	60 seconds		
1 degree	=	60 minutes		
1 right angle	=	90 degrees		
1 straight angle	=	180 degrees		
1 circle	=	360 degrees		

Millimeter-Inch Equivalents

Inches		Millimeters	Inches		Millimeters
Fractions	Decimals		Fractions	Decimals	
	.00394	.1	15/32	.46875	11.9063
	.00787	.2		.47244	12.00
	.01181	.3	31/64	.484375	12.3031
1/64	.015625	.3969	1/2	.5000	12.70
	.01575	.4		.51181	13.00
	.01969	.5	33/64	.515625	13.0969
	.02362	.6	17/32	.53125	13.4938
	.02756	.7	35/64	.546875	13.8907
1/32	.03125	.7938		.55118	14.00
	.0315	.8	9/16	.5625	14.2875
	.03543	.9	37/64	.578125	14.6844
	.03937	1.00		.59055	15.00
3/64	.046875	1.1906	19/32	.59375	15.0813
1/16	.0625	1.5875	39/64	.609375	15.4782
5/64	.078125	1.9844	5/8	.625	15.875
	.07874	2.00		.62992	16.00
3/32	.09375	2.3813	41/64	.640625	16.2719
7/64	.109375	2.7781	21/32	.65625	16.6688
	.11811	3.00		.66929	17.00
1/8	.125	3.175	43/64	.671875	17.0657
9/64	.140625	3.5719	11/16	.6875	17.4625
5/32	.15625	3.9688	45/64	.703125	17.8594
	.15748	4.00		.70866	18.00
11/64	.171875	4.3656	23/32	.71875	18.2563
3/16	.1875	4.7625	47/64	.734375	18.6532
	.19685	5.00		.74803	19.00
13/64	.203125	5.1594	3/4	.7500	19.05
7/32	.21875	5.5563	49/64	.765625	19.4469
15/64	.234375	5.9531	25/32	.78125	19.8438
	.23622	6.00		.7874	20.00
1/4	.2500	6.35	51/64	.796875	20.2407
17/64	.265625	6.7469	13/16	.8125	20.6375
	.27559	7.00		.82677	21.00
9/32	.28125	7.1438	53/64	.828125	21.0344
19/64	.296875	7.5406	27/32	.84375	21.4313
5/16	.3125	7.9375	55/64	.859375	21.8282
	.31496	8.00		.86614	22.00
21/64	.328125	8.3344	7/8	.875	22.225
11/32	.34375	8.7313	57/64	.890625	22.6219
	.35433	9.00		.90551	23.00
23/64	.359375	9.1281	29/32	.90625	23.0188
3/8	.375	9.525	59/64	.921875	23.4157
25/64	.390625	9.9219	15/16	.9375	23.8125
	.3937	10.00		.94488	24.00
13/32	.40625	10.3188	61/64	.953125	24.2094
27/64	.421875	10.7156	31/32	.96875	24.6063
	.43307	11.00		.98425	25.00
7/16	.4375	11.1125	63/64	.984375	25.0032
29/64	.453125	11.5094	1	1.0000	25.4000

Conversion Diagram for Rafters

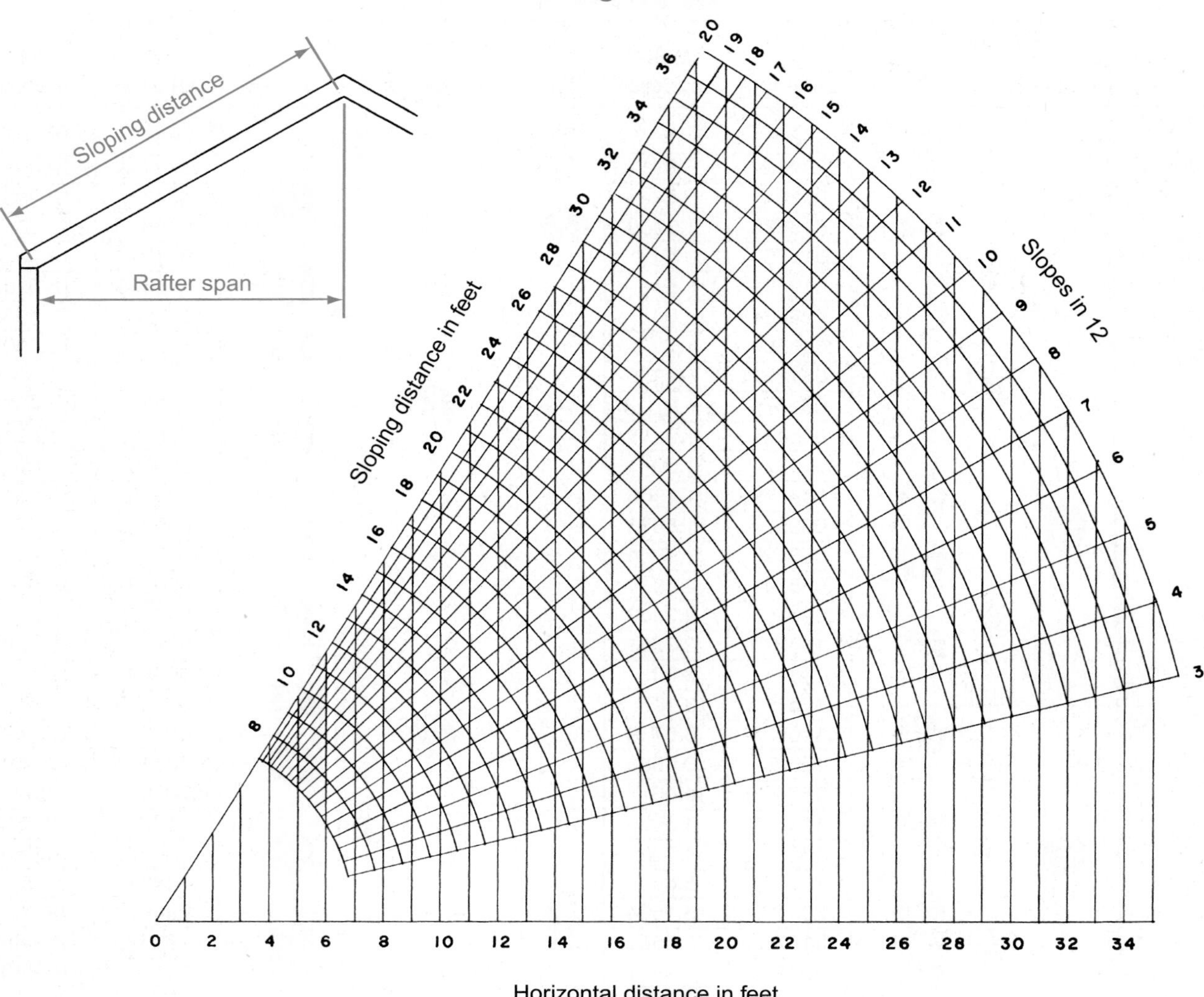

To use the diagram, select the known horizontal distance and follow the vertical line to its intersection with the radial line of the specified slope, then proceed along the arc to read the sloping distance. In some cases it may be desirable to interpolate between the one foot separations. The diagram also may be used to find the horizontal distance corresponding to a given sloping distance or to find the slope when the horizontal and sloping distances are known.

Example: With a roof slope of 8/12 and a horizontal distance of 20′, the sloping distance may be read as 24′.

Rafter Span Data

RAFTER SPANS FOR COMMON LUMBER SPECIES
(Roof live load = 20 psf, ceiling not attached to rafters, L/Δ = 180)

RAFTER SPACING (inches)	SPECIES AND GRADE		DEAD LOAD = 10 psf					DEAD LOAD = 20 psf				
			2 x 4	2 x 6	2 x 8	2 x 10	2 x 12	2 x 4	2 x 6	2 x 8	2 x 10	2 x 12
			Maximum rafter spans[a]									
			(feet - inches)	(feet - inches)	(feet - inches)	(feet - inches)	(feet - inches)	(feet - inches)	(feet - inches)	(feet - inches)	(feet - inches)	(feet - inches)
12	Douglas fir-larch	SS	11-6	18-0	23-9	Note b	Note b	11-6	18-0	23-9	Note b	Note b
	Douglas fir-larch	#1	11-1	17-4	22-5	Note b	Note b	10-6	15-4	19-5	23-9	Note b
	Douglas fir-larch	#2	10-10	16-10	21-4	26-0	Note b	10-0	14-7	18-5	22-6	26-0
	Douglas fir-larch	#3	8-9	12-10	16-3	19-10	23-0	7-7	11-1	14-1	17-2	19-11
	Hem-fir	SS	10-10	17-0	22-5	Note b	Note b	10-10	17-0	22-5	Note b	Note b
	Hem-fir	#1	10-7	16-8	22-0	Note b	Note b	10-4	15-2	19-2	23-5	Note b
	Hem-fir	#2	10-1	15-11	20-8	25-3	Note b	9-8	14-2	17-11	21-11	25-5
	Hem-fir	#3	8-7	12-6	15-10	19-5	22-6	7-5	10-10	13-9	16-9	19-6
	Southern pine	SS	11-3	17-8	23-4	Note b	Note b	11-3	17-8	23-4	Note b	Note b
	Southern pine	#1	10-10	17-0	22-5	Note b	Note b	10-6	15-8	19-10	23-2	Note b
	Southern pine	#2	10-4	15-7	19-8	23-5	Note b	9-0	13-6	17-1	20-3	23-10
	Southern pine	#3	8-0	11-9	14-10	18-0	21-4	6-11	10-2	12-10	15-7	18-6
	Spruce-pine-fir	SS	10-7	16-8	21-11	Note b	Note b	10-7	16-8	21-9	Note b	Note b
	Spruce-pine-fir	#1	10-4	16-3	21-0	25-8	Note b	9-10	14-4	18-2	22-3	25-9
	Spruce-pine-fir	#2	10-4	16-3	21-0	25-8	Note b	9-10	14-4	18-2	22-3	25-9
	Spruce-pine-fir	#3	8-7	12-6	15-10	19-5	22-6	7-5	10-10	13-9	16-9	19-6
16	Douglas fir-larch	SS	10-5	16-4	21-7	Note b	Note b	10-5	16-3	20-7	25-2	Note b
	Douglas fir-larch	#1	10-0	15-4	19-5	23-9	Note b	9-1	13-3	16-10	20-7	23-10
	Douglas fir-larch	#2	9-10	14-7	18-5	22-6	26-0	8-7	12-7	16-0	19-6	22-7
	Douglas fir-larch	#3	7-7	11-1	14-1	17-2	19-11	6-7	9-8	12-12	14-11	17-3
	Hem-fir	SS	9-10	15-6	20-5	Note b	Note b	9-10	15-6	19-11	24-4	Note b
	Hem-fir	#1	9-8	15-2	19-2	23-5	Note b	9-0	13-1	16-7	20-4	23-7
	Hem-fir	#2	9-2	14-2	17-11	21-11	25-5	8-5	12-3	15-6	18-11	22-0
	Hem-fir	#3	7-5	10-10	13-9	16-9	19-6	6-5	9-5	11-11	14-6	16-10
	Southern pine	SS	10-3	16-1	21-2	Note b	Note b	10-3	16-1	21-2	25-7	Note b
	Southern pine	#1	9-10	15-6	19-10	23-2	Note b	9-1	13-7	17-2	20-1	23-10
	Southern pine	#2	9-0	13-6	17-1	20-3	23-10	7-9	11-8	14-9	17-6	20-8
	Southern pine	#3	6-11	10-2	12-10	15-7	18-6	6-0	8-10	11-2	13-6	16-0
	Spruce-pine-fir	SS	9-8	15-2	19-11	25-5	Note b	9-8	14-10	18-10	23-0	Note b
	Spruce-pine-fir	#1	9-5	14-4	18-2	22-3	25-9	8-6	12-5	15-9	19-3	22-4
	Spruce-pine-fir	#2	9-5	14-4	18-2	22-3	25-9	8-6	12-5	15-9	19-3	22-4
	Spruce-pine-fir	#3	7-5	10-10	13-9	16-9	19-6	6-5	9-5	11-11	14-6	16-10
19.2	Douglas fir-larch	SS	9-10	15-5	20-4	25-11	Note b	9-10	14-10	18-10	23-0	Note b
	Douglas fir-larch	#1	9-5	14-0	17-9	21-8	25-2	8-4	12-2	15-4	18-9	21-9
	Douglas fir-larch	#2	9-1	13-3	16-10	20-7	23-10	7-10	11-6	14-7	17-10	20-8
	Douglas fir-larch	#3	6-11	10-2	12-10	15-8	18-3	6-0	8-9	11-2	12-7	15-9
	Hem-fir	SS	9-3	14-7	19-2	24-6	Note b	9-3	14-4	18-2	22-3	25-9
	Hem-fir	#1	9-1	13-10	17-6	21-5	24-10	8-2	12-0	15-2	18-6	21-6
	Hem-fir	#2	8-8	12-11	16-4	20-0	23-2	7-8	11-2	14-2	17-4	20-1
	Hem-fir	#3	6-9	9-11	12-7	15-4	17-9	5-10	8-7	10-10	13-3	15-5
	Southern pine	SS	9-8	15-2	19-11	25-5	Note b	9-8	15-2	19-7	23-4	Note b
	Southern pine	#1	9-3	14-3	18-1	21-2	25-2	8-4	12-4	15-8	18-4	21-9
	Southern pine	#2	8-2	12-3	15-7	18-6	21-9	7-1	10-8	13-6	16-0	18-10
	Southern pine	#3	6-4	9-4	11-9	14-3	16-10	5-6	8-1	10-2	12-4	14-7
	Spruce-pine-fir	SS	9-1	14-3	18-9	23-11	Note b	9-1	13-7	17-2	21-0	24-4
	Spruce-pine-fir	#1	8-10	13-1	16-7	20-3	23-6	7-9	11-4	14-4	17-7	20-4
	Spruce-pine-fir	#2	8-10	13-1	16-7	20-3	23-6	7-9	11-4	14-4	17-7	20-4
	Spruce-pine-fir	#3	6-9	9-11	12-7	15-4	17-9	5-10	8-7	10-10	13-3	15-5

(continued)

RAFTER SPANS FOR COMMON LUMBER SPECIES *(continued)*
(Roof live load = 20 psf, ceiling not attached to rafters, L/Δ = 180)

RAFTER SPACING (inches)	SPECIES AND GRADE		DEAD LOAD = 10 psf					DEAD LOAD = 20 psf				
			2 x 4	2 x 6	2 x 8	2 x 10	2 x 12	2 x 4	2 x 6	2 x 8	2 x 10	2 x 12
			Maximum rafter spans[a]									
			(feet - inches)	(feet - inches)	(feet - inches)	(feet - inches)	(feet - inches)	(feet - inches)	(feet - inches)	(feet - inches)	(feet - inches)	(feet - inches)
24	Douglas fir-larch	SS	9-1	14-4	18-10	23-9	Note b	9-1	13-3	16-10	20-7	23-10
	Douglas fir-larch	#1	8-7	12-6	15-10	19-5	22-6	7-5	10-10	13-9	16-9	19-6
	Douglas fir-larch	#2	8-2	11-11	15-1	18-5	21-4	7-0	10-4	13-0	15-11	18-6
	Douglas fir-larch	#3	6-2	9-1	11-6	14-1	16-3	5-4	7-10	10-0	12-2	14-1
	Hem-fir	SS	8-7	13-6	17-10	22-9	Note b	8-7	12-10	16-3	19-10	23-0
	Hem-fir	#1	8-5	12-4	15-8	19-2	22-2	7-4	10-9	13-7	16-7	19-3
	Hem-fir	#2	7-11	11-7	14-8	17-10	20-9	6-10	10-0	12-8	15-6	17-11
	Hem-fir	#3	6-1	8-10	11-3	13-8	15-11	5-3	7-8	9-9	11-10	13-9
	Southern pine	SS	8-11	14-1	18-6	23-8	Note b	8-11	13-10	17-6	20-10	24-8
	Southern pine	#1	8-7	12-9	16-2	18-11	22-6	7-5	11-1	14-0	16-5	19-6
	Southern pine	#2	7-4	11-0	10-11	16-6	19-6	6-4	9-6	12-1	14-4	16-10
	Southern pine	#3	5-8	8-4	10-6	12-9	15-1	4-11	7-3	9-1	11-0	13-1
	Spruce-pine-fir	SS	8-5	13-3	17-5	21-8	25-2	8-4	12-2	15-4	18-9	21-9
	Spruce-pine-fir	#1	8-0	11-9	14-10	18-2	21-0	6-11	10-2	12-10	15-8	18-3
	Spruce-pine-fir	#2	8-0	11-9	14-10	18-2	21-0	6-11	10-2	12-10	15-8	18-3
	Spruce-pine-fir	#3	6-1	8-10	11-3	13-8	15-11	5-3	7-8	9-9	11-10	13-9

Check sources for availability of lumber in lengths greater than 20 feet.

For SI: 1 inch = 25.4 mm, 1 foot = 304.8 mm, 1 pound per square foot = 0.0479 kPa.

a. The tabulated rafter spans assume that ceiling joists are located at the bottom of the attic space or that some other method of resisting the outward push of the rafters on the bearing walls, such as rafter ties, is provided at that location. Where ceiling joists or rafter ties are located higher in the attic space, the rafter spans shall be multiplied by the following factors:

H_C/H_R	Rafter Span Adjustment Factor
1/3	0.67
1/4	0.76
1/5	0.83
1/6	0.90
1/7.5 or less	1.00

where:

H_C = Height of ceiling joists or rafter ties measured vertically above the top of the rafter support walls.

H_R = Height of roof ridge measured vertically above the top of the rafter support walls.

b. Span exceeds 26 feet in length.

Classification of Softwood Plywood

Group 1	Group 2	Group 3	Group 4	Group 5
Apitong	Cedar, Port	Alder, Red	Aspen	Basswood
Beech,	Orford	Birch, Paper	Bigtooth	Poplar,
American	Cypress	Cedar, Alaska	Quaking	Balsam
Birch	Douglas	Fir,	Cativo	
Sweet	Fir 2[a]	Subalpine	Cedar	
Yellow	Fir	Hemlock,	Incense	
Douglas	Balsam	Eastern	Western	
Fir 1[a]	California	Maple,	Red	
Kapur	Red	Bigleaf	Cottonwood	
Keruing	Grand	Pine	Eastern	
Larch,	Noble	Jack	Black	
Western	Pacific	Lodgepole	(Western	
Maple, Sugar	Silver	Ponderosa	Poplar)	
Pine	White	Spruce	Pine	
Caribbean	Hemlock,	Redwood	Eastern	
Ocote	Western	Spruce	White	
Pine, Southern	Lauan	Englemann	Sugar	
Loblolly	Almon	White		
Longleaf	Bagtikan			
Shortleaf	Mayapis			
Slash	Red Lauan			
Tanoak	Tangile			
	White Lauan			
	Maple, Black			
	Mengkulang			
	Meranti, Red[b]			
	Mersawa			
	Pine			
	Pond			
	Red			
	Virginia			
	Western			
	White			
	Spruce			
	Red			
	Sitka			
	Sweetgum			
	Tamarack			
	Yellow poplar			

(a) Refers to Douglas fir from the states of Washington, Oregon, California, Idaho, Montana, and Wyoming, as well as from Alberta and British Columbia shall be classified as Douglas Fir No. 1. Those grown in Nevada, Utah, Colorado, Arizona, and New Mexico shall be classified as Douglas Fir No. 2. (b) Red Meranti shall be limited to species with a specific gravity of 0.41 or more, based on green volume and oven-dry weight.

APA-The Engineered Wood Association

Softwood Plywood Veneer Grades

Grade	Description
A	Smooth paintable. Not more than 18 neatly made repairs, boat, sled, or router type, and parallel to grain, permitted. May be used for natural finish in less demanding application. Synthetic or wood repairs permitted.
B	Solid surface. Shims, sled, or router repairs, and tight knots to 1" across grain permitted. Wood or synthetic repairs permitted. Some minor splits permitted.
C	Tight knots to 1 1/2". Knotholes to 1" across grain and some to 1 1/2" if total width of knots and knotholes is within specified limits. Synthetic or wood repairs. Discoloration and sanding defects that do not impair strength permitted. Limited splits allowed. Stitching permitted.
C Plugged	Improved C veneer with splits limited to 1/8" width and knotholes or other open defects limited to 1/4" by 1/2". Wood or synthetic repairs permitted. Some broken grain permitted.
D	Knots and knotholes to 2 1/2" width across grain and 1/2" larger within specified limits. Limited splits are permitted. Stitching permitted. Limited to Exposure 1 or Interior panels.

APA-The Engineered Wood Association

Plywood Panel Grade-Trademark Stamp

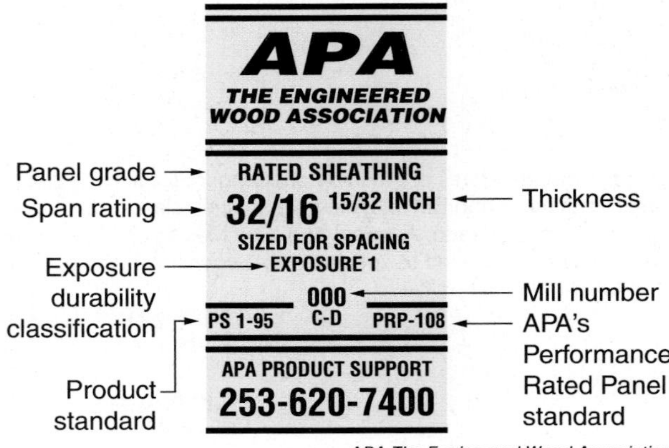

APA-The Engineered Wood Association

Plywood Panels Manufactured to APA Standards

Panel name	Typical trademarks	Descriptions/sizes/uses
APA RATED SHEATHING Typical Trademark	 RATED SHEATHING 40/20 19/32 INCH SIZED FOR SPACING EXPOSURE 1 000 PS-2-92 SHEATHING PRP-108 HUD-UM-40C APA THE ENGINEERED WOOD ASSOCIATION RATED SHEATHING 24/16 7/16 INCH SIZED FOR SPACING EXPOSURE 1 000 PRP-108 HUD-UM-40C	Specially designed for subflooring and wall and roof sheathing. Also good for a broad range of other construction and industrial applications. Can be manufactured as plywood, as a composite, or as OSB. EXPOSURE DURABILITY CLASSIFICATION: Exterior, Expose 1, Exposure 2. COMMON THICKNESSES: 5/16, 3/8, 7/16, 15/32, 1/2, 19/32, 5/8, 23/32, 3/4.
APA STRUCTURAL I RATED SHEATHING(a) Typical Trademark	 RATED SHEATHING STRUCTURAL I 32/16 15/32 INCH SIZED FOR SPACING EXPOSURE 1 000 PS 1-95 C-D PRP-108 APA THE ENGINEERED WOOD ASSOCIATION RATED SHEATHING 32/16 15/32 INCH SIZED FOR SPACING EXPOSURE 1 000 STRUCTURAL I RATED DIAPHRAGMS-SHEAR WALLS PANELIZED ROOFS PRP-108 HUD-UM-40C	Unsanded grade for use where shear and cross-panel strength properties are of maximum importance, such as panelized roofs and diaphragms. Can be manufactured as plywood, as a composite, or as OSB. EXPOSURE DURABILITY CLASSIFICATION: Exterior, Expose 1, COMMON THICKNESSES: 5/16, 3/8, 7/16, 15/32, 1/2, 19/32, 5/8, 23/32, 3/4.
APA RATED STURD-I-FLOOR Typical Trademark	 RATED SHEATHING 24 OC 23/32 INCH SIZED FOR SPACING T&G NET WIDTH 47-1/2 EXPOSURE 1 000 PS-2-92 SINGLE FLOOR PRP-108 HUD-UM-40C APA THE ENGINEERED WOOD ASSOCIATION RATED SHEATHING 20 OC 19/32 INCH SIZED FOR SPACING T&G NET WIDTH 47-1/2 EXPOSURE 1 000 PRP-108 HUD-UM-40C	Specially designed as combination subfloor-underlayment. Provides smooth surface for application of carpet and pad and possesses high concentrated and impact load resistance. Can be manufactured as plywood, as a composite, or as OSB. EXPOSURE DURABILITY CLASSIFICATION: Exterior, Expose 1, Exposure 2. COMMON THICKNESSES: 19/32, 5/8, 23/32, 3/4, 1, 1-1/8.
APA RATED SIDING Typical Trademark	 RATED SIDING 24 OC 19/32 INCH SIZED FOR SPACING EXPOSURE 1 000 PRP-108 HUD-UM-40C APA THE ENGINEERED WOOD ASSOCIATION RATED SIDING 303-18-S/W 16 OC 11/32 INCH GROUP 1 SIZED FOR SPACING EXTERIOR 000 PS 1-95 PRP-108 FHA-UM-64	For exterior siding, fencing, etc. Can be manufactured as plywood, as a composite or as an overlaid OSB. Both panel and lap siding available. Special surface treatment such as V-groove, channel groove, deep groove (such as APA Texture 1-11), brushed, rough sawn and overlaid (MDO) with smooth- or texture-embossed face. Span Rating (stud spacing for siding qualified for APA Sturd-I-Wall applications) and face grade classification (for veneer-faced siding) indicated in trademark. EXPOSURE DURABILITY CLASSIFICATION: Exterior, COMMON THICKNESSES: 11/32, 3/8, 7/16, 15/32, 1/2, 19/32, 5/8.

Specific grades, thickness and exposure durability classifications may be in limited supply in some areas. Check with your supplier before specifying.

Specify Performance Rated Panels by thickness and Span Rating. Span Ratings are based on panel strength and stiffness. Since these properties are a function of panel composition and configuration as well as thickness, the same Span Rating may appear on panels of different thickness. Conversely, panels of the same thickness may be marked with different Span Ratings.

(a) All plies in Structural I plywood panels are special improved grades and panels marked PS I are limited to Group I species. Other panels marked Structural I Rated qualify through special performance testing. Structural II plywood panels are also provided for, but rarely manufactured. Application recommendations for Structural II plywood are identical to those for APA RATED SHEATHING plywood.

APA-The Engineered Wood Association

Sizes and Dimensions for Reinforcing Bars					
Weight	Nominal Dia	Size	Number	Nominal Cross Section Area	Nominal Perimeter
.376 lb/ft	.375″	3/8	3	.11 in^2	1.178
.668 lb/ft	.500″	1/2	4	.20 in^2	1.571
1.043 lb/ft	.625″	5/8	5	.31 in^2	1.963
1.502 lb/ft	.750″	3/4	6	.44 in^2	2.356
2.044 lb/ft	.875″	7/8	7	.60 in^2	2.749
2.670 lb/ft	1.000″	1	8	.79 in^2	3.142
3.400 lb/ft	1.128″	1*	9	1.00 in^2	3.544
4.303 lb/ft	1.270″	1-1/8*	10	1.27 in^2	3.990
5.313 lb/ft	1.410″	1-1/4*	11	1.56 in^2	4.430
7.650 lb/ft	1.693″	1-1/2*	14	2.25 in^2	5.320
13.600 lb/ft	2.257″	2*	18	4.00 in^2	7.090

These sizes rolled in rounds equivalent to square cross section area.

Recommended Styles of Welded Wire Fabric Reinforcement for Concrete		
Type of Construction	**Recommended Style**	**Remarks**
Barbecue Foundation Slab	6×6-W2.0×W2.0 to 4×4-W2.9×W2.9	Use heavier style fabric for heavy, massive fireplaces or barbecue pits.
Basement Floors	6×6-W1.4×W1.4, 6×6-W2.0×W2.0, or 6×6-W2.9×W2.9	For small areas (15′ maximum side dimension), use 6×6-W1.4×W1.4. As a rule of thumb, the larger the area or the poorer the subsoil, the heavier the gauge.
Driveways	6×6-W2.9×W2.9	Continuous reinforcement between 25′ to 30′ contraction joints.
Residential Foundation Slabs	6×6-W1.4×W1.4	Use heavier gauge over poorly drained subsoil or when maximum dimension is greater than 15′.
Garage Floors	6×6-W2.9×W2.9	Position at midpoint of 5″ or 6″ thick slab.
Patios and Terraces	6×6-W1.4×W1.4	Use 6×6-W2.0×W2.0 if subsoil is poorly drained.
Porch Floor A) 6″ thick slab up to 6′ span B) 6″ thick slab up to 8′ span	 6×6-W2.9×W2.9 4×4-W4.0×W4.0	Position 1″ from bottom form to resist tensile stresses.
Sidewalks	6×6-W1.4×W1.4 or 6×6-W2.0×W2.0	Use heavier gauge over poorly drained subsoil. Construct 25′ to 30′ slabs as for driveways.
Steps (free span)	6×6-W2.9×W2.9	Use heavier style if more than five risers. Position fabric 1″ from bottom form.
Steps (on ground)	6×6-W2.0×W2.0	Use 6×6-W2.9×W2.9 for unstable subsoil.

Gypsum Wallboard Application Data					
Thickness	Approx. Weight lbs/ft^2	Size	Location	Application Method	Max. Spacing of Framing Members
1/4″	1.1	4′ × 8′ to 12′	Over existing walls & ceilings	Horizontal or vertical	
3/8″	1.5	4′ × 8′ to 14′	Ceilings	Horizontal	16″
3/8″	1.5	4′ × 8′ to 14′	Sidewalls	Horizontal or vertical	16″
1/2″	2.0	4′ × 8′ to 14′	Ceilings	Vertical Horizontal	16″ 24″
1/2″	2.0	4′ × 8′ to 14′	Sidewalls	Horizontal or vertical	24″
5/8″	2.5	4′ × 8′ to 14′	Ceilings	Vertical Horizontal	16″ 24″
5/8″	2.5	4′ × 8′ to 14′	Sidewalls	Horizontal or vertical	24″
1″	4.0	2′ × 8′ to 12′		For laminated partitions	

Wood Foundations

Typical Wood Foundation

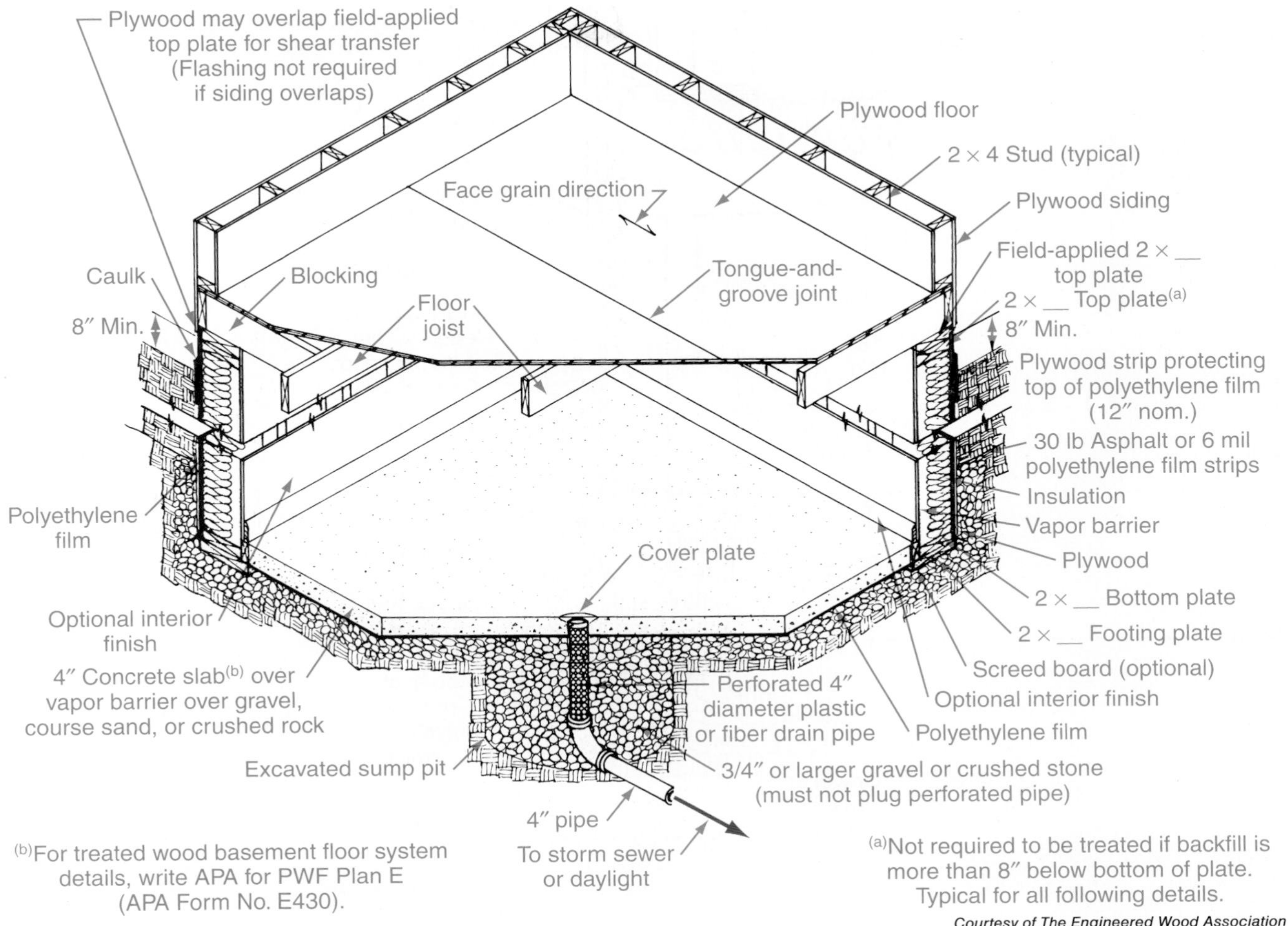

Courtesy of The Engineered Wood Association

Wood Foundations

Crawl Space

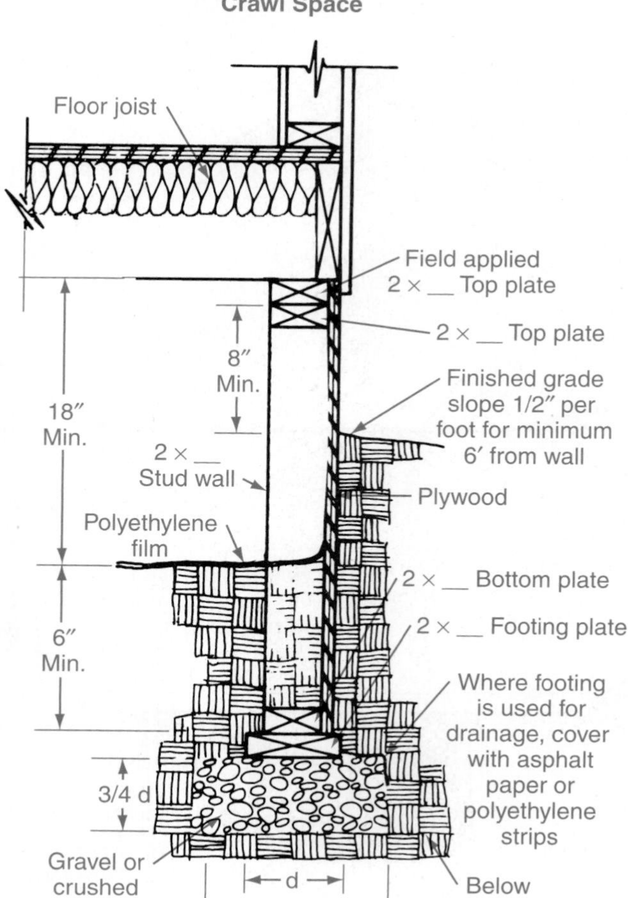

Courtesy of The Engineered Wood Association

Wood Foundations

Crawl Space PWF on Concrete Footing

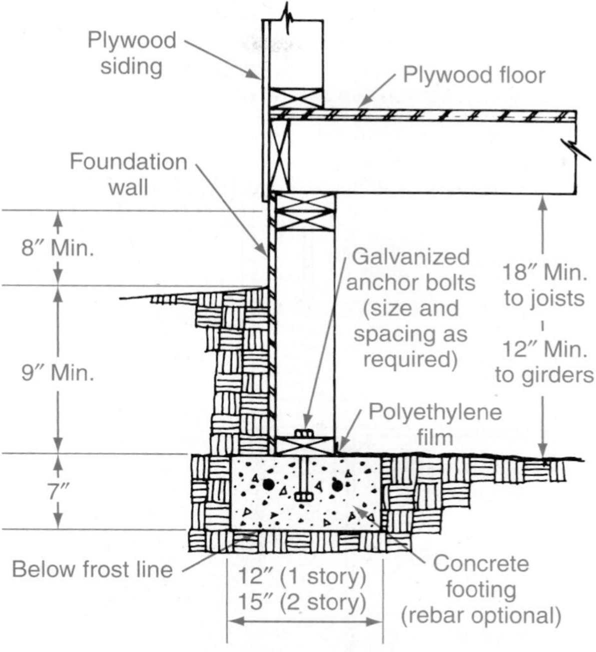

Courtesy of The Engineered Wood Association

Wood Foundations

Basement Wall

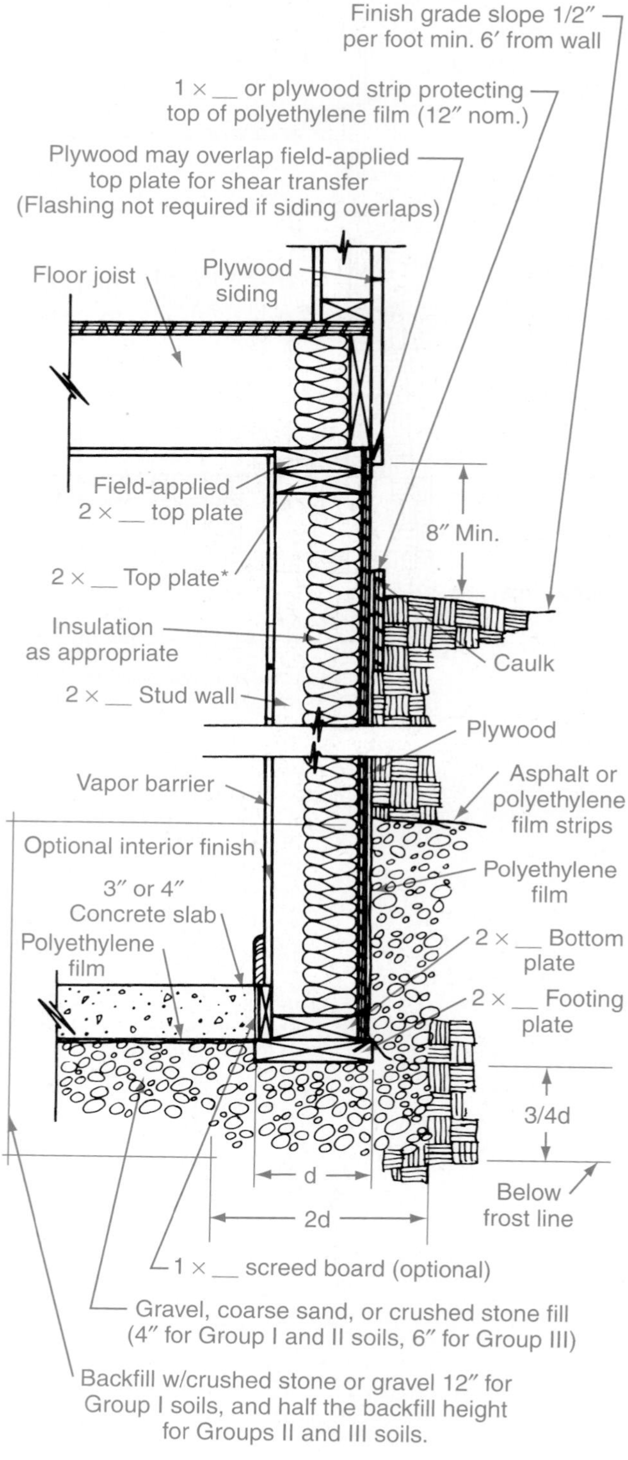

*Not required to be treated if backfill is more than 8″ below bottom of plate. Typical for all following details.

Courtesy of The Engineered Wood Association

Wood Foundations
Knee Wall with Brick Veneer

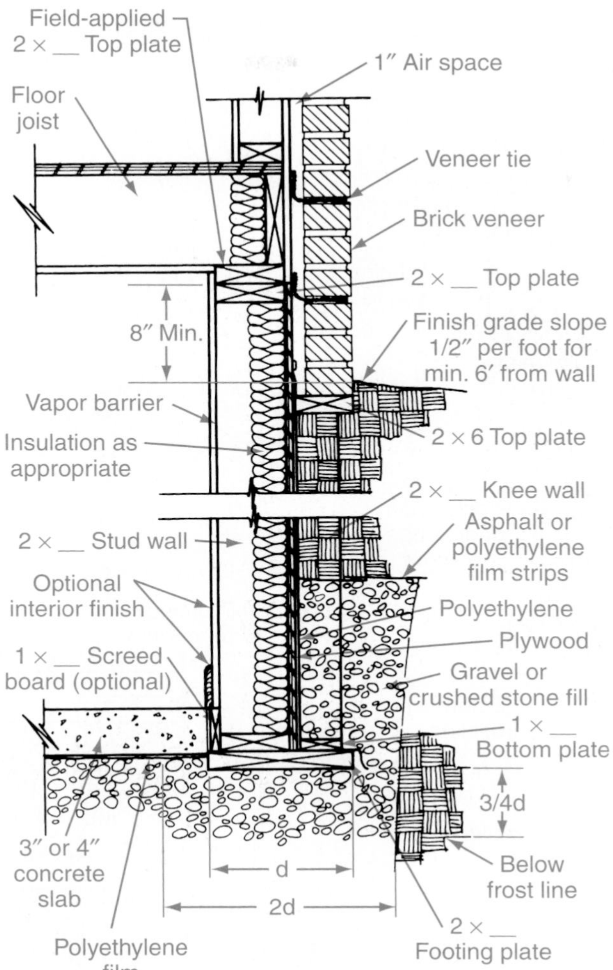

Courtesy of The Engineered Wood Association

Wood Foundations

Garage PWF Details—Exterior Walls

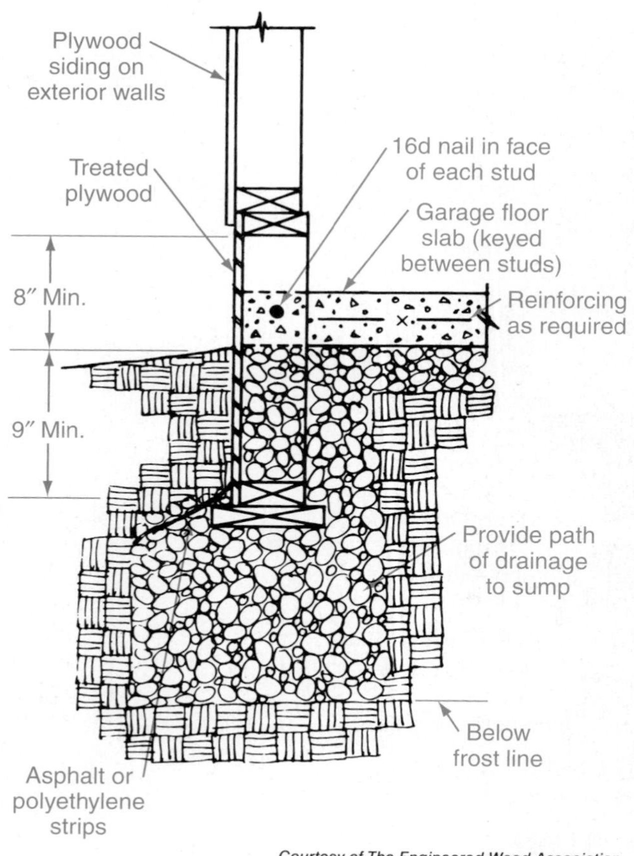

Courtesy of The Engineered Wood Association

Garage PWF Details—Interior Walls (Between House and Garage)

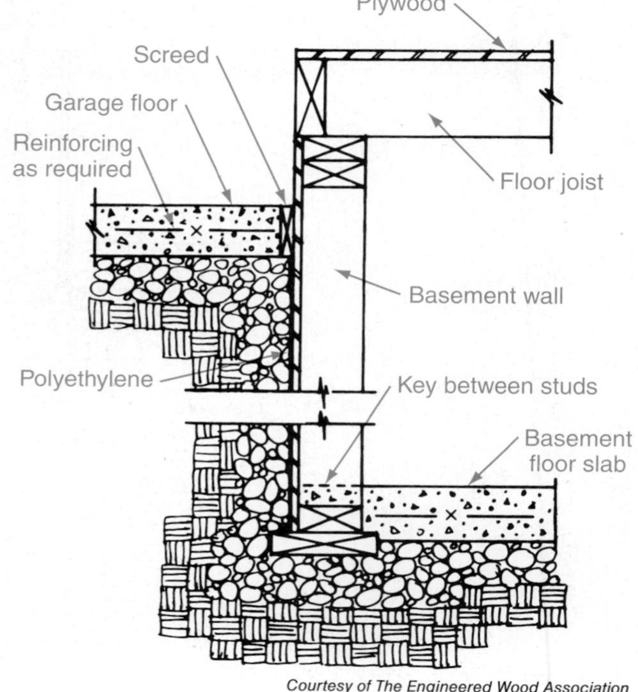

Courtesy of The Engineered Wood Association

Garage PWF Details—Garage Door

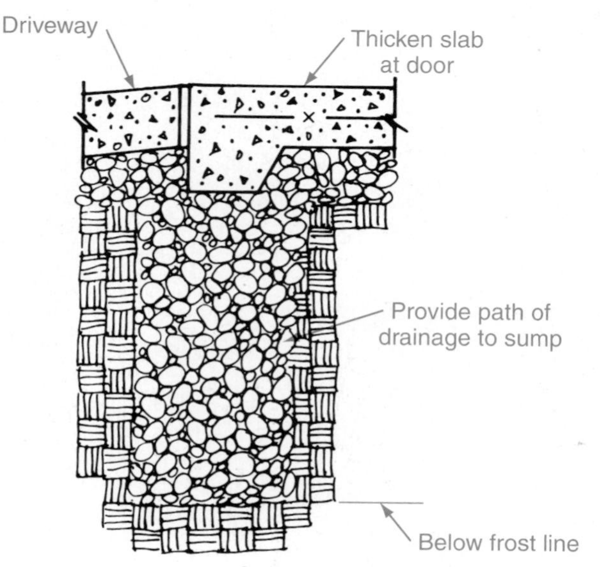

Courtesy of The Engineered Wood Association

MasterFormat® Division Numbers and Titles

Procurement and Contracting Requirements Group

Division 00—Procurement and Contracting Requirements

Specifications Group

General Requirements Subgroup

Division 01—General Requirements

Facility Construction Subgroup

Division 02—Existing Conditions
Division 03—Concrete
Division 04—Masonry
Division 05—Metals
Division 06—Wood, Plastics, and Composites
Division 07—Thermal and Moisture Protection
Division 08—Openings
Division 09—Finishes
Division 10—Specialties
Division 11—Equipment
Division 12—Furnishings
Division 13—Special Construction
Division 14—Conveying Equipment
Division 15—Reserved for future expansion
Division 16—Reserved for future expansion
Division 17—Reserved for future expansion
Division 18—Reserved for future expansion
Division 19—Reserved for future expansion

Facility Services Subgroup

Division 20—Reserved for future expansion
Division 21—Fire Suppression
Division 22—Plumbing
Division 23—Heating, Ventilating, and Air Conditioning (HVAC)
Division 24—Reserved for future expansion
Division 25—Integrated Automation
Division 26—Electrical
Division 27—Communications
Division 28—Electronic Safety and Security
Division 29—Reserved for future expansion

Site and Infrastructure Subgroup

Division 30—Reserved for future expansion
Division 31—Earthwork
Division 32—Exterior Improvements
Division 33—Utilities
Division 34—Transportation
Division 35—Waterway and Marine Construction
Division 36—Reserved for future expansion
Division 37—Reserved for future expansion
Division 38—Reserved for future expansion
Division 39—Reserved for future expansion

Process Equipment Subgroup

Division 40—Process Integration
Division 41—Material Processing and Handling Equipment
Division 42—Process Heating, Cooling, and Drying Equipment
Division 43—Process Gas and Liquid Handling, Purification, and Storage Equipment
Division 44—Pollution and Waste Control Equipment
Division 45—Industry-Specific Manufacturing Equipment
Division 46—Water and Wastewater Equipment
Division 47—Reserved for future expansion
Division 48—Electrical Power Generation
Division 49—Reserved for future expansion

Clearance Requirements

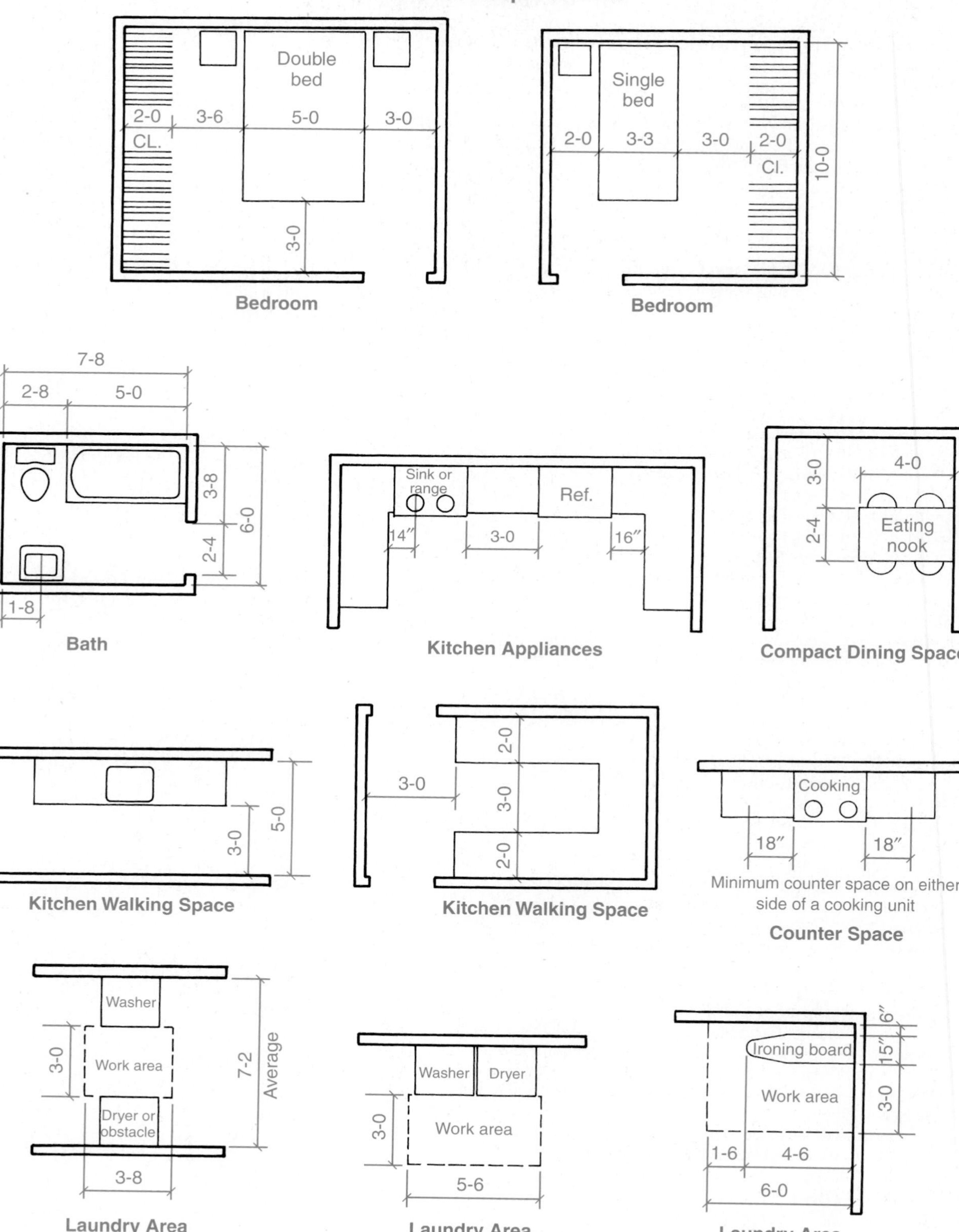

Abbreviations

Term	Abbreviation
Acoustic	ACST
Acrylonitrile butadiene styrene	ABS
Actual	ACT
Addition	ADD
Adhesive	ADH
Aggregate	AGGR
Air conditioning	AIR COND
Alternate	ALT
Aluminum	AL
American Association of Registered Architects	ARA
American Institute of Architects	AIA
American Society for Testing and Materials	ASTM
American wire gage	AWG
Amount	AMT
Ampere	AMP
Anchor bolt	AB
Approximate	APPROX
Architectural	ARCH
Area	A
Asbestos	ASB
Asphalt	ASPH
Assembly	ASSY
Automatic	AUTO
Average	AVG
Balcony	BALC
Basement	BSMT
Bathroom	B
Beam	BM *or* BMS
Bedroom	BR
Benchmark	B M
Between	BET
Bits per inch	bpi
Blocking	BLKG
Board feet	BD FT
Bottom	BOT
Bracket	BRKT
British thermal unit	Btu
Broom closet	BC
Building	BLDG
Buzzer	BUZ
Cabinet	CAB
Casing	CSG
Cast iron	CI
Cathode ray tube	CRT
Caulking	CLKG
Ceiling	CL
Cement	CEM
Centerline	CL *or* ℄
Center to center	C to C
Central processing unit	CPU
Ceramic	CER
Circuit	CKT
Circuit breaker	CIR BKR
Cleanout	CL *or* CO
Closet	CLOS *or* CL
Clothes dryer	CLD
Column	COL
Composition	COMP
Concrete	CONC
Concrete block	CONC B
Construction	CONST
Copper	COP *or* CU
Counter	CTR
Courses	C
Cross section	X-SECT
Cubic feet	CU FT
Cubic yard	CU YD
Damper	DMPR
Decorative	DEC
Detail	DET
Diagram	DIA
Dimension	DIM
Dining room	DR
Dishwasher	DW
Door	DR
Double hung	DH
Down	DN
Downspout	DS
Drain	D *or* DR
Drawing	DWG
Drywall	DW
Elbow	ELL
Electric	ELEC
Elevation	EL *or* ELEV
Entrance	ENT
Estimate	EST
Excavate	EXC
Exterior	EXT
Fabricate	FAB
Family room	FAM R
Federal Housing Authority	FHA
Finish	FIN
Firebrick	FBRK
Fireproof	FP
Fitting	FTG
Fixture	FIX
Flange	FLG
Flashing	FLSHG
Floor	FL
Floor drain	FD
Flooring	FLG
Footing	FTG
Foundation	FDN
Frame	FR
Full size	FS
Gallon	GAL
Galvanized	GALV
Glass	GL
Grade	GR
Gypsum	GYP
Hall	H
Hardware	HDW
Header	HDR
Heater	HTR
Horizontal	HORIZ
Hose bibb	HB
Inside diameter	ID
Insulation	INS
Interior	INT
International Standards Organization	ISO
Joint	JT
Joist	JST
Kiln dried	KD
Kitchen	K
Kitchen cabinets	KC
Kitchen sink	KS
Laminated	LAM
Landing	LDG
Laundry	LAU
Lavatory	LAV
Leader	LDR
Level	LEV
Light	LT
Linen closet	LCL
Linoleum	LINO
Living room	LR
Lumber	LBR
Manufacturer	MFR
Material	MATL
Maximum	MAX
Medicine cabinet	MC
Metal	MET
Minimum	MIN
Modular	MOD
Molding	MLDG
National Electric Code	NEC
Plate glass	PL GL
Plates	PLTS
Platform	PLATF
Plumbing	PLMB
Plywood	PLY
Polyvinyl chloride	PVC
Prefabricated	PREFAB
Property	PROP
Push button	PB
Radiator	RAD
Random length	RL & W
Range	R
Receptacle	RECP
Recessed	REC
Reference	REF
Refrigerator	REF
Register	REG
Reinforce	REINF
Return	RET
Riser	R
Roof	RF
Roofing	RFG
Rough	RGH
Round	RD
Schedule	SCH
Section	SECT
Self-closing	SC
Service	SERV
Sewer	SEW
Sheet metal	SM
Shelves	SHLV's
Shower	SH
Siding	SDG
Sill cock	SC
Socket	SOC
Soil pipe	SP
Specification	SPEC
Square	SQ
Stairs	ST
Standpipe	ST P
Station point	SP
Steel	STL
Structural	STR
Surface	SUR
Surface four sides	S4S
Surface two sides	S2S
Suspended ceiling	SUSP CLG
Switch	S *or* SW
Symbol	SYM
Tee	T
Telephone	TEL
Television	TV
Temperature	TEMP
Terra cotta	TC
Thermostat	THERMO
Thickness	THK
Tongue and groove	T & G
Tread	TR
Unfinished	UNFIN
Vanishing point	VP
Vanity	VAN
Ventilation	VENT
Ventilator	V
Vertical	VERT
Wall cabinet	W CAB
Wall vent	WV
Water	W
Water closet	WC
Water heater	WH
Waterproof	WP
Weep hole	WH
Wide flange	WF
Window	WDW
With	W/
Wood	WD
Wrought iron	WI
Zinc	Z *or* ZN

Rigid Foam Comparison			
	Expanded Polystyrene (EPS)	Extruded Polystyrene (XPS)	Polyisocyanurate (PIR)
Insulating Value	R-4 per inch	R-5 per inch	R-7 per inch
Density	0.9 pcf to 1.8 pcf	2 pcf	Varies
Compressive Strength	10 psi to 25 psi	30 psi	16 psi to 25 psi
Perm-Rating	5.0 per inch	1.2 per inch	0.4 to 1.6 per inch
Foil Face	Yes	Yes	Yes
Polyethylene Face	Yes	Yes	Yes
Kraft Paper Face	Yes	Yes	Yes
Fiberglass Mat Face	No	No	Yes
Fire Resistance	Softens at 165°F Melts at 200°F	Softens at 165°F Melts at 200°F	Maximum service temperature is 250°F
Common Applications	Exterior Stucco Below Grade Under Slab Wall Frames	Exterior Stucco Below Grade Under Slab Wall Frames	Exterior Stucco Roof Applications Under Slab Wall Frames
Gases Produced When Burned	Carbon Monoxide Carbon Dioxide	Carbon Monoxide Carbon Dioxide	Hydrogen Cyanide* Nitrogen Oxide*

*Chemical asphyxiants

Design Temperatures and Degree Days (Heating Season)

State	City	Outside Design Temperature (°F)	Degree Days (°F-Days)
Alabama	Birmingham	17	2,600
Alaska	Anchorage	–23	10,900
Arizona	Phoenix	31	1,800
Arkansas	Little Rock	15	3,200
California	Los Angeles	37	2,000
California	San Francisco	35	3,000
Colorado	Denver	–5	6,200
Connecticut	Hartford	3	6,200
Florida	Tampa	36	600
Georgia	Atlanta	17	3,000
Idaho	Boise	3	5,800
Illinois	Chicago	–8	6,600
Indiana	Indianapolis	–2	5,600
Iowa	Des Moines	–10	6,600
Kansas	Wichita	3	4,600
Kentucky	Louisville	5	4,600
Louisiana	New Orleans	29	1,400
Maryland	Baltimore	10	4,600
Massachusetts	Boston	6	5,600
Michigan	Detroit	3	6,200
Minnesota	Minneapolis	–19	8,400
Mississippi	Jackson	21	2,200
Missouri	St. Louis	2	5,000
Montana	Helena	–17	8,200
Nebraska	Lincoln	–5	5,800
Nevada	Reno	5	6,400
New Hampshire	Concord	–8	7,400
New Mexico	Albuquerque	12	4,400
New York	Buffalo	3	7,000
New York	New York City	11	5,000
North Carolina	Raleigh	16	3,400
North Dakota	Bismarck	–23	8,800
Ohio	Columbus	0	5,600
Oklahoma	Tulsa	8	3,800
Oregon	Portland	17	4,600
Pennsylvania	Philadelphia	10	5,100
Pennsylvania	Pittsburgh	1	6,000
Rhode Island	Providence	5	6,000
South Carolina	Charleston	24	2,000
South Dakota	Sioux Falls	–15	7,800
Tennessee	Chattanooga	13	3,200
Texas	Dallas	17	2,400
Texas	San Antonio	18	1,600
Utah	Salt Lake City	3	6,000
Vermont	Burlington	–12	8,200
Virginia	Richmond	14	3,800
Washington	Seattle	21	5,200
West Virginia	Charleston	7	4,400
Wisconsin	Madison	–11	7,800
Wyoming	Cheyenne	–9	7,400

A more complete listing of monthly and yearly degree days and outside design temperatures can be found in the ASHRAE Handbook of Fundamentals published by the American Society of Heating, Refrigerating and Air-Conditioning Engineers, Inc.

Living Room Furniture Symbols and Sizes

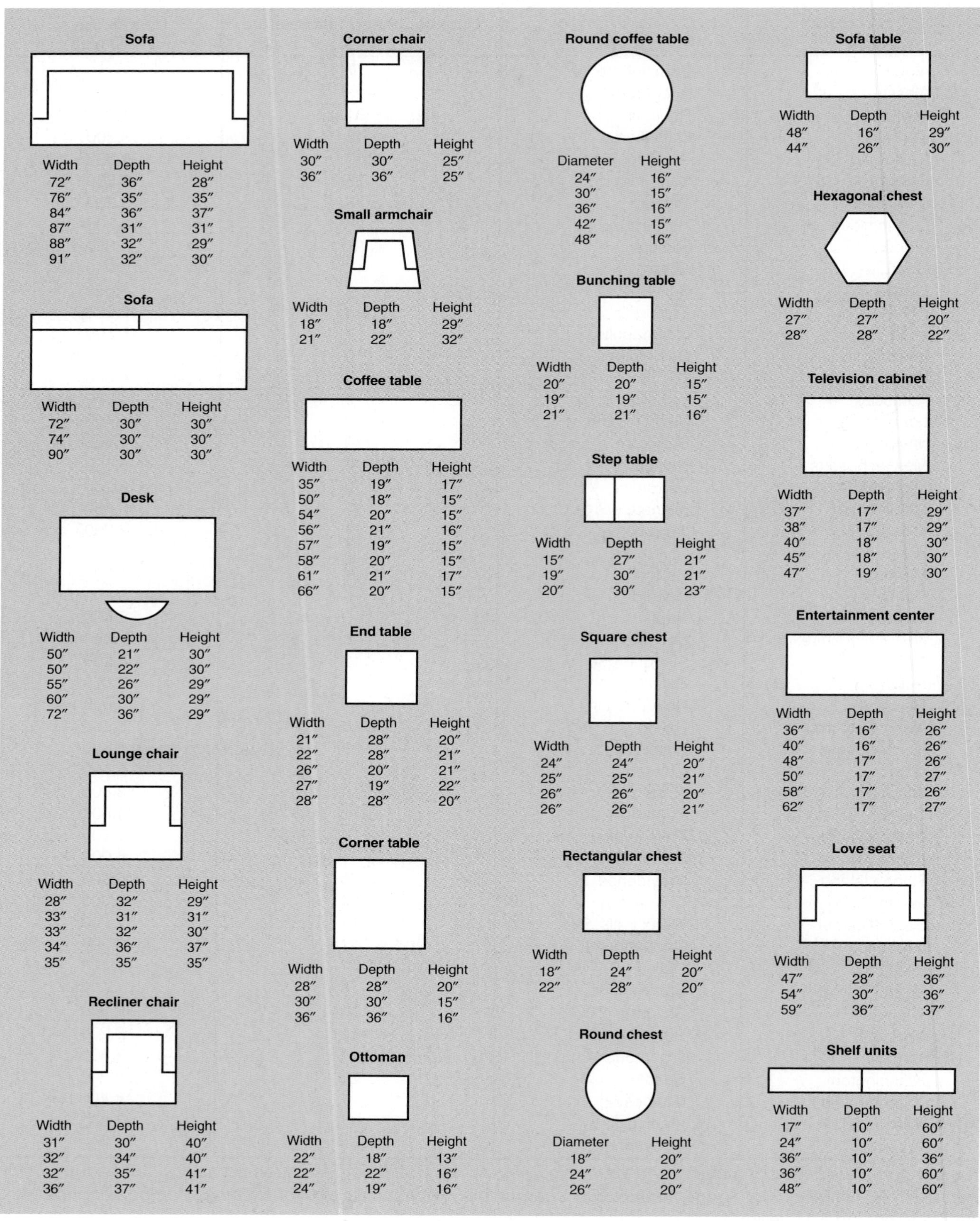

Sofa

Width	Depth	Height
72″	36″	28″
76″	35″	35″
84″	36″	37″
87″	31″	31″
88″	32″	29″
91″	32″	30″

Sofa

Width	Depth	Height
72″	30″	30″
74″	30″	30″
90″	30″	30″

Desk

Width	Depth	Height
50″	21″	30″
50″	22″	30″
55″	26″	29″
60″	30″	29″
72″	36″	29″

Lounge chair

Width	Depth	Height
28″	32″	29″
33″	31″	31″
33″	32″	30″
34″	36″	37″
35″	35″	35″

Recliner chair

Width	Depth	Height
31″	30″	40″
32″	34″	40″
32″	35″	41″
36″	37″	41″

Corner chair

Width	Depth	Height
30″	30″	25″
36″	36″	25″

Small armchair

Width	Depth	Height
18″	18″	29″
21″	22″	32″

Coffee table

Width	Depth	Height
35″	19″	17″
50″	18″	15″
54″	20″	15″
56″	21″	16″
57″	19″	15″
58″	20″	15″
61″	21″	17″
66″	20″	15″

End table

Width	Depth	Height
21″	28″	20″
22″	28″	21″
26″	20″	21″
27″	19″	22″
28″	28″	20″

Corner table

Width	Depth	Height
28″	28″	20″
30″	30″	15″
36″	36″	16″

Ottoman

Width	Depth	Height
22″	18″	13″
22″	22″	16″
24″	19″	16″

Round coffee table

Diameter	Height
24″	16″
30″	15″
36″	16″
42″	15″
48″	16″

Bunching table

Width	Depth	Height
20″	20″	15″
19″	19″	15″
21″	21″	16″

Step table

Width	Depth	Height
15″	27″	21″
19″	30″	21″
20″	30″	23″

Square chest

Width	Depth	Height
24″	24″	20″
25″	25″	21″
26″	26″	20″
26″	26″	21″

Rectangular chest

Width	Depth	Height
18″	24″	20″
22″	28″	20″

Round chest

Diameter	Height
18″	20″
24″	20″
26″	20″

Sofa table

Width	Depth	Height
48″	16″	29″
44″	26″	30″

Hexagonal chest

Width	Depth	Height
27″	27″	20″
28″	28″	22″

Television cabinet

Width	Depth	Height
37″	17″	29″
38″	17″	29″
40″	18″	30″
45″	18″	30″
47″	19″	30″

Entertainment center

Width	Depth	Height
36″	16″	26″
40″	16″	26″
48″	17″	26″
50″	17″	27″
58″	17″	26″
62″	17″	27″

Love seat

Width	Depth	Height
47″	28″	36″
54″	30″	36″
59″	36″	37″

Shelf units

Width	Depth	Height
17″	10″	60″
24″	10″	60″
36″	10″	36″
36″	10″	60″
48″	10″	60″

Dining Room Furniture Symbols and Sizes

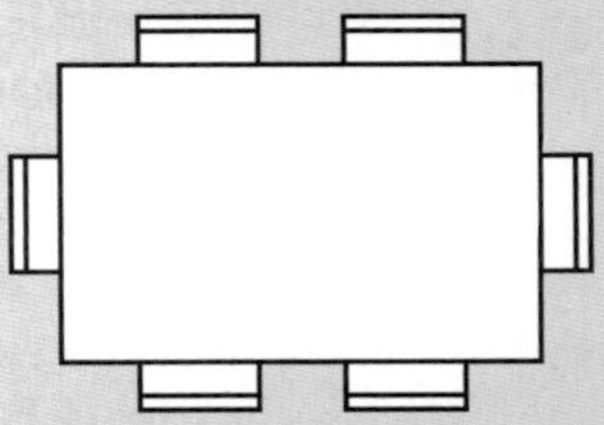

Rectangular dining table

Length	Width	Height
42″	30″	29″
48″	30″	29″
48″	42″	29″
60″	40″	28″
60″	42″	29″
72″	36″	28″

Oval dining table

Length	Width	Height
54″	42″	28″
60″	42″	28″
72″	40″	28″
72″	48″	28″
84″	42″	28″

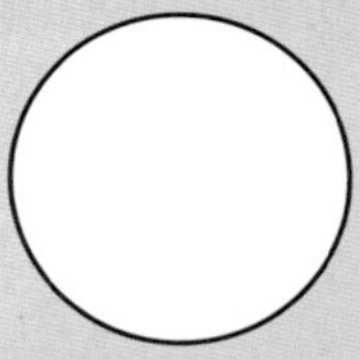

Round dining table

Diameter	Height
32″	28″
36″	28″
42″	28″
48″	28″

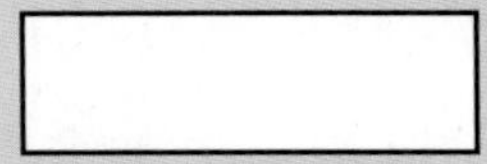

China cabinet or hutch

Length	Width	Height
48″	16″	65″
50″	20″	60″
62″	16″	66″

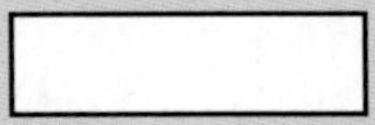

Buffet

Length	Width	Height
36″	16″	31″
48″	16″	31″
52″	18″	31″

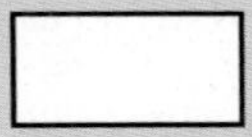

Server or cart

Length	Width	Height
36″	16″	30″
52″	18″	33″
64″	16″	30″

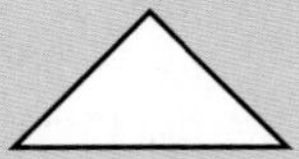

Corner cabinet

Width	Depth	Height
36″	15″	80″
38″	16″	80″

Dining chairs

Width	Depth	Height
17″	19″	29″
20″	17″	36″
22″	19″	29″
24″	21″	31″

Seat height 16″

Laundry Room Symbols and Sizes

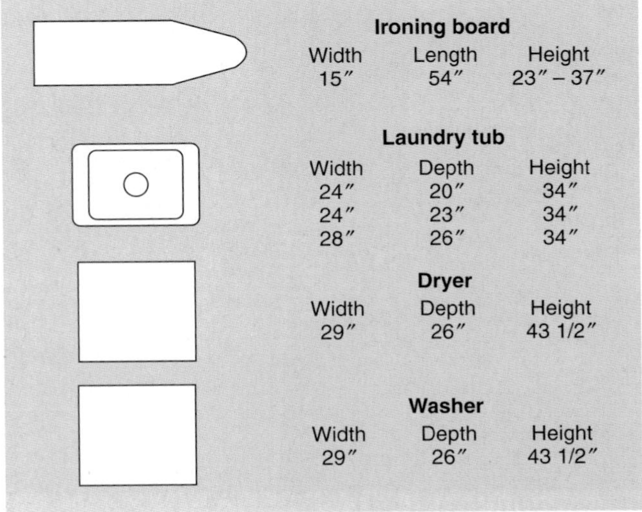

Ironing board

Width	Length	Height
15″	54″	23″ – 37″

Laundry tub

Width	Depth	Height
24″	20″	34″
24″	23″	34″
28″	26″	34″

Dryer

Width	Depth	Height
29″	26″	43 1/2″

Washer

Width	Depth	Height
29″	26″	43 1/2″

Bedroom Furniture Symbols and Sizes

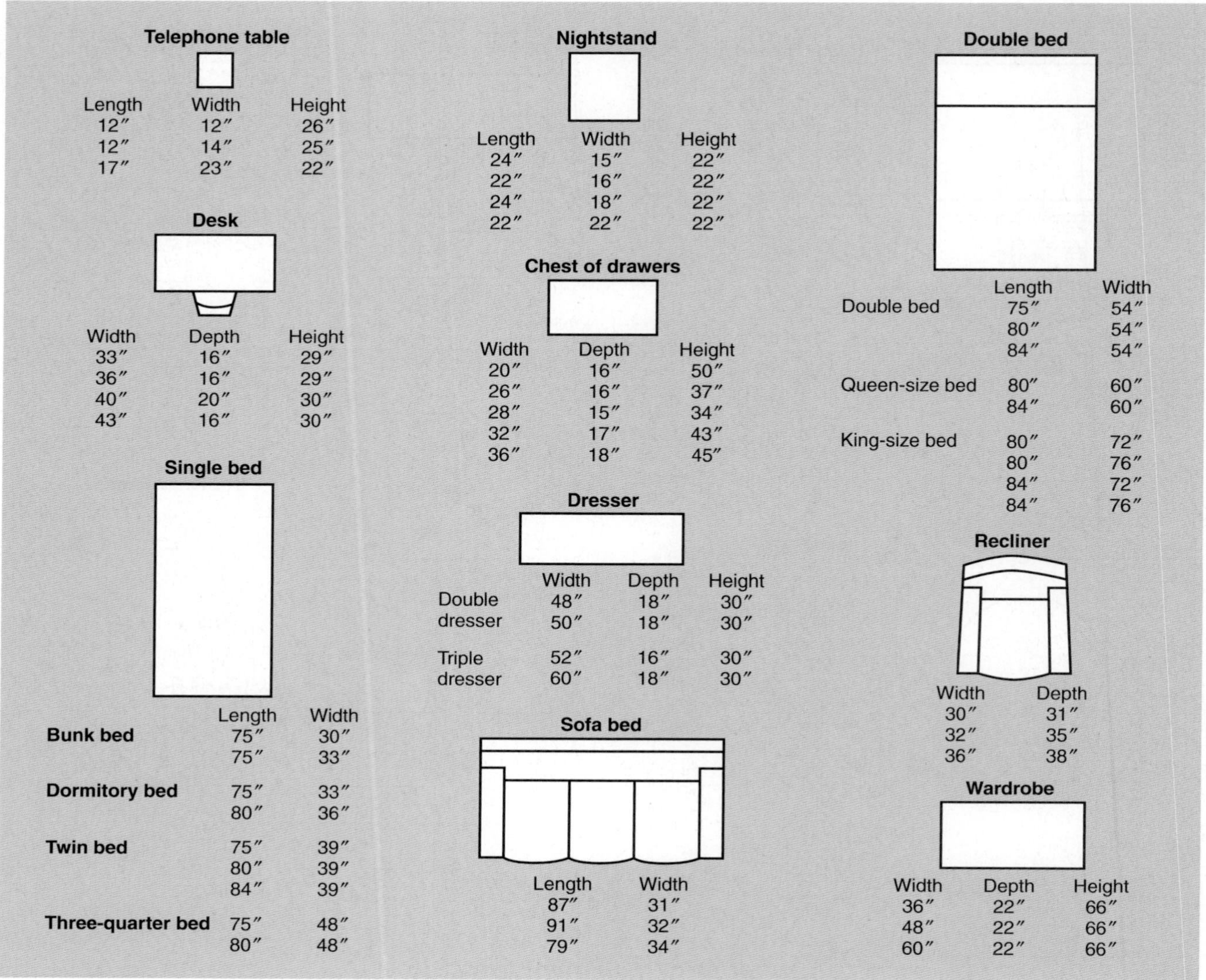

Telephone table

Length	Width	Height
12″	12″	26″
12″	14″	25″
17″	23″	22″

Desk

Width	Depth	Height
33″	16″	29″
36″	16″	29″
40″	20″	30″
43″	16″	30″

Single bed

	Length	Width
Bunk bed	75″	30″
	75″	33″
Dormitory bed	75″	33″
	80″	36″
Twin bed	75″	39″
	80″	39″
	84″	39″
Three-quarter bed	75″	48″
	80″	48″

Nightstand

Length	Width	Height
24″	15″	22″
22″	16″	22″
24″	18″	22″
22″	22″	22″

Chest of drawers

Width	Depth	Height
20″	16″	50″
26″	16″	37″
28″	15″	34″
32″	17″	43″
36″	18″	45″

Dresser

	Width	Depth	Height
Double dresser	48″	18″	30″
	50″	18″	30″
Triple dresser	52″	16″	30″
	60″	18″	30″

Sofa bed

Length	Width
87″	31″
91″	32″
79″	34″

Double bed

	Length	Width
Double bed	75″	54″
	80″	54″
	84″	54″
Queen-size bed	80″	60″
	84″	60″
King-size bed	80″	72″
	80″	76″
	84″	72″
	84″	76″

Recliner

Width	Depth
30″	31″
32″	35″
36″	38″

Wardrobe

Width	Depth	Height
36″	22″	66″
48″	22″	66″
60″	22″	66″

Bathroom Fixture Symbols and Sizes

Standard tub

Width	Length	Height
30-3/4″	54″	16″
30″	60″	14″
30″	60″	16-1/2″
31″	60″	15-1/2″
31-1/2″	60″	16″
31-1/2″	66″	18″
30-3/4″	72″	16″

Square tub

Width	Length	Height
37″	42″	12″
42″	48″	14″

Water closet

	Width	Depth	Height
Floor mounted two-piece	17″	25-1/2″	29-1/2″
	21″	26-3/4″	28″
	21″	28-3/4″	28″
Floor mounted one-piece	20-3/8″	27-3/4″	20″
	20-3/8″	29-3/4″	20″
Wall hung two-piece	22-1/2″	26″	31″
Floor hung one-piece	14″	24-1/4″	15″

Bidet

Width	Depth	Height
15″	22″	15″

Wall hung sink

Width	Depth
19″	17″
20″	18″
22″	19″
24″	20″

Circular lavatory

18″ Diameter

Appliance Symbols and Sizes

Refrigerator

Cu. Ft.	Width	Height	Depth
9	24″	56″	29″
12	30″	68″	30″
14	31″	63″	24″
19	34″	70″	29″
21	36″	66″	29″

Standard free-standing range

Width	Height	Depth
20″	30″	24″
21″	36″	25″
30″	36″	26″
40″	36″	27″

Double-oven range

Width	Height	Depth
30″	61″	26″
30″	64″	26″
30″	67″	27″
30″	71″	27″

Drop-in range

Width	Height	Depth
23″	23″	22″
24″	23″	22″
30″	24″	25″

Built-in cooktop

Width	Height	Depth
12″	2″	18″
24″	3″	22″
48″	3″	22″

Built-in microwave

Width	Height	Depth
24″	19″	15″
27″	22″	20″
30″	22″	24″

Over-the-range microwave

Width	Height	Depth
30″	15″ to 17″	15″ to 16″
36″	15″ to 17″	15″ to 16″

Range hood

Width	Height	Depth
24″	5″	12″
30″	6″	17″
66″	7″	26″
72″	8″	28″

Single-compartment sink

Width	Depth
24″	21″
30″	20″

Double-compartment sink

Width	Depth
32″	21″
36″	20″
42″	21″

Brick Names and Sizes		
Name	Nominal Size	Actual Size
Roman	2 × 4 × 12	1-5/8 × 3-5/8 × 11-5/8″
Modular	2-2/3 × 4 × 8	2-1/4 × 3-5/8 × 7-5/8″
SCR Brick	2-2/3 × 6 × 12	2-1/8 × 5-1/2 × 11-1/2″
Standard	Nonmodular	2-1/4 × 3-5/8 × 8″
Norman	2-2/3 × 4 × 12	2-1/4 × 3-5/8 × 11-5/8″
Firebrick*	2-2/3 × 4 × 9	2-1/2 × 3-5/8 × 9″

*Firebrick is not used for exterior wall construction, but is included because it is used in fireplaces.

Common Brick Bonds

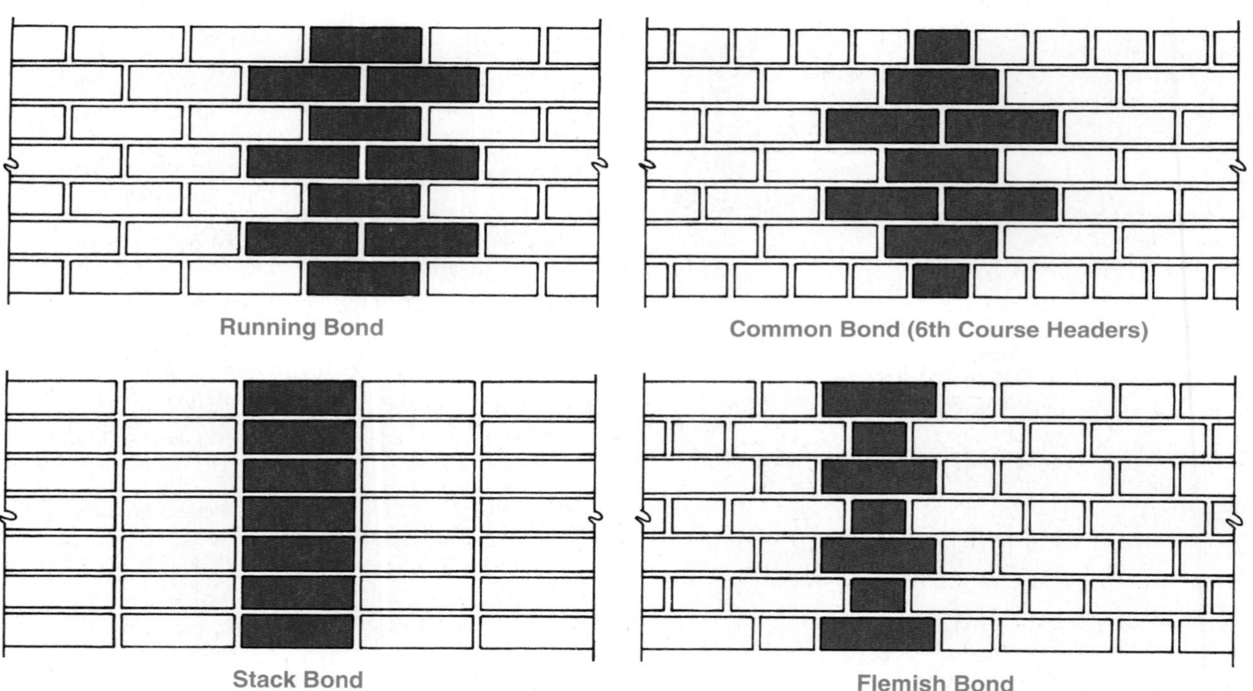

Glossary

alexmisu/Shutterstock.com

1/2 bath: A bathroom that contains only a sink and a toilet, with no tub or shower. (8)
3/4 bath: A bathroom that contains a sink, toilet, and shower, but no tub. (8)
3D printing: A process that uses computer data to produce a solid, physical model. (28)
9-12-15 unit method: A method of laying out square corners by staking out a right angle with legs that are 9 units along one leg and 12 units along the other. The corner is square when the third leg of the triangle measures exactly 15 units. (18)

A

absolute coordinates: Point locations measured from the coordinate system origin. (5)
access hole: An opening that allows entry into the attic of a home. (20)
accessibility: A measure of how easily all people, including those who are physically handicapped or have limited mobility, can use something. (7)
accordion door: Door constructed of multiple panels that are hinged along their vertical edges so that they can be folded out of the way when not in use; frequently used to close large openings. (21)
acre: A plot of land comprising a total area of 43,560 square feet.
acrylonitrile butadiene styrene (ABS): A thermoplastic plumbing pipe used in waste piping. (31)
activated carbon system: A water treatment device in which one or more canisters are filled with activated carbon granules that trap contaminants such as chlorine, organic chemicals, and pesticides. (31)
active listening: Giving your full attention to the speaker and asking questions if necessary to understand, rather than just "hear," the speaker's message. (3)
active solar space heating: Involves collecting heat from solar radiation and then using pumps, fans, or other devices to distribute the heat to desired locations.
adaptive reuse: The process of changing the purpose of a building. (13)
addition: New space or square footage added onto a home. (13)
adhesive: A natural or synthetic material, generally in paste or liquid form, used to fasten, glue, or fabricate materials together.
adobe: A natural building material, dating back 4000 years to Egyptian civilization. It is made of water, sand, clay, and straw mixed together and then formed into desired shapes that are dried in the sun. (1)
AEC-specific CADD package: CADD software designed specifically for use in the architectural, engineering, and construction (AEC) industries. (5)
aging-in-place: The ability of people to live comfortably and remain in their home as they become older. (7)
air-dried lumber: Lumber that has been piled in yards or sheds for a length of time; the minimum moisture content is usually 12% to 15%.
alcove: A recessed opening off a wall of a larger room; often used as a sitting area, coat room, or storage area.
alphabet of lines: The collection of line types used in drafting. (4)

Americans with Disabilities Act (ADA): A law that makes it illegal to discriminate against disabled persons in the areas of employment, public and private transportation, and access to public and commercial buildings.

ampere (amp): The unit used to measure the amount of electricity (current) flowing through a wire conductor per unit of time. (29)

analog data: Always received with noise added into the content.

anchor: Usually any metal fastener used to attach parts, such as joists, trusses, or posts, to masonry or masonry materials.

anchor bolt: A threaded rod inserted in masonry construction to anchor the sill plate to the foundation.

animation: A sequence of frames displayed quickly in succession to give the impression of motion. (5)

animation key: Stores data related to animated movement in an animation; each keyframe has at least one animation key.

annotative objects: Drawing objects that are automatically scaled to the correct size by the software when the drawing is plotted. (5)

ANSI: Abbreviation for the American National Standards Institute.

apartment: A multifamily housing unit available for rent and occupancy as specified by the terms of a lease. (1)

apron: Trim used under the stool on interior windows. Also, the concrete area in front of a garage door opening.

arcade: A series of arches supported by columns or piers to provide an open passageway.

arch: A curved structure that will support itself and the weight above its curved opening by mutual pressure.

architect: A person who works closely with clients to design structures by making preliminary drawings, sketches, and suggestions for materials to be used. (3)

architectural drafter: A person who creates detailed working drawings based on the original drawings prepared by the architect or designer. (3)

architectural engineer: A person who works with all of the systems of a building to integrate the design, construction, and operation of the building. (3)

architectural illustrator: An artist who prepares drawings, sketches, renderings, and other types of illustrations to present ideas to potential clients and create advertisement materials for commercial catalogs and publications. (3)

architectural model: A scaled representation of a house and a portion of the site on which it will be built. (28)

architectural style: A classification of a structure based on its appearance, the materials used, structural and decorative details, building techniques, and artistic expression. (1)

areaway: Below-grade recessed area around the foundation to allow light and ventilation into a basement window.

aromatic red cedar: A wood primarily used in construction for chests and closet linings for its moth-proof value; has similar characteristics to Western red cedar.

arris: A sharp edge formed when two planes or surfaces meet; found on edges of moldings, doors, and shelves, and in cabinet construction.

ASCII: American Standard Code for Information Interchange; an industry standard used in transmitting information between computers, printers, and peripheral devices.

ash dump: A cavity below a fireplace where ashes can collect and be removed. (25)

ashlar stonework: Stonework that uses dressed, cut, or squared stones to provide a regular pattern or finished appearance. (20)

asphalt shingles: Composition roof shingles made from asphalt-impregnated felt covered with mineral granules.

assessment: The levy of a tax or charge on property, usually according to established rates.

assessor: A public official responsible for the evaluation of property for the purposes of taxation.

assignee: A person to whom a transfer of interest is made in connection with a mortgage or contract for a home or piece of property.

assignor: A person who makes an assignment for a mortgage or contract for a home or piece of property.

ASTM: Abbreviation for the American Society of Testing and Materials.

atrium: A central hall or open court within a structure.

atrium design: An earth-sheltered house that places living areas around a central courtyard with all windows opening into the courtyard.

attached greenhouse: A type of isolated gain system; also called a *sun space*.

attachment: The legal seizure of property to require payment of a debt.

attic: The space between the ceiling and the roof of a structure. (2, 13)

attic ventilators: Screened openings provided to ventilate an attic space; can also consist of power-driven fans used as an exhaust system.

attribute: Text information saved with a block when the block is inserted into a drawing. (5)

autoclave: A device that can treat a product in a vessel under high temperature and pressure.

awning window: A window with sashes that are hinged at the top and open outward, like an awning. (21)

B

bachelor's degree: A college or university degree that generally requires four years of full-time study.

backfill: The replacement of excavated earth into a trench around and against a basement foundation.

backlight: A general, diffused light source used to bring the object out of the background in a rendered presentation drawing. (27)

balcony: A narrow porch extending from an upper floor of a residence. (7)

balloon framing: Framing in which the wall studs rest directly on the sill plate and each floor "hangs" from the studs. (19)

balsa: A softwood that is used for many modeling purposes because it is easy to cut and accepts a variety of finishes. (28)

baluster: A vertical member of a stairway that supports the handrail on open stairs. (24)

balustrade: A series of balusters connected by a rail; generally used for porches and balconies.

band joist: A framing member resting on the sill, placed perpendicular to the floor joists and to which the floor joists are attached. Another term for *rim joist*. (19)

banister: A handrail with supporting posts used alongside a stairway.

baseboard: The finish board covering the interior wall where the wall and floor meet.

basement: A full-height area located fully or partially below the ground level of the main floor; used for utilities, storage, and additional livable space. (2)

basement plan: A combination foundation and floor plan; includes the information commonly shown on the foundation plan as well as interior walls, stairs, windows, and doors in the basement. (15)

base shoe: A molding used next to the floor in interior baseboards.

basic unit size: The overall dimensions of a window or door unit.

batt: A roll or sheet of insulation designed to be installed between the members of frame construction.

batten: Narrow strips of wood used to cover joints or as decorative vertical members over plywood or wide boards.

batter boards: A layout of 2 × 4 stakes with 1 × 6 horizontal boards nailed to the stakes, located about 4′ outside of where the footing will be; used to retain the location of the foundation during excavation and construction. (18)

bay window: A unit with a large center window and a narrower window on each side. The side windows are set at an angle to the exterior wall, normally 45°, so that the unit forms a "bay" with extra square footage inside the house. (21)

beam: A structural member that supports the joists when the joists must span a long distance. (19)

beam ceiling: A ceiling in which the ceiling beams are exposed to view.

bearing: The direction from one object or position to another. (16)

bearing partition: A partition that supports any vertical load in addition to its own weight.

bearing wall: A wall that runs perpendicular to the direction of the floor joists and is designed to support part of the load of the structure. (18)

beech: A whitish- to reddish-brown hardwood used especially in construction for interior and exterior cabinet parts; blends well with birch for stained kitchen cabinets and vanities.

benchmark: A permanent object used by surveyors to establish a point of reference. (16)

bidet: A device that looks something like a toilet and is used for personal cleaning. (8)

bifold door: A door made of two vertical sections hinged so they will fold out of the way when they are opened; often used for closet doors. (21)

BIM model: The virtual building model in a BIM project. (12)

birch: Hard and heavy, light-reddish-brown hardwood; widely used hardwood veneer for flush doors, cabinetwork, and paneling; mill products include interior trim, flooring, sash, and trim.

blind nailing: A method of nailing so that the nail is not visible.

block: A symbol or set of objects that has been saved for later re-use. (5)

board foot: A method of lumber measurement using nominal dimensions of 1″ thick, 12″ wide, and 12″ long, or the equivalent.

border line: Very heavy line used to form a boundary for an architectural drawing. (4)

bow window: A set of windows placed to form an arc that extends out from the wall of a house. (21)

box bay: A window design that combines a picture window parallel to the wall with two casement windows placed at 90° to the wall.

box cornice: A cornice in which the space between the end of a projecting rafter and the wall is enclosed with a soffit board. (17)

box sill: The method of sill construction used in platform framing; consists of a 2 × 6 mudsill and a header joist the same size as the floor joists. (19)

branch circuit: A circuit used to carry electricity from the distribution panel throughout the home. (29)

branch main: Pipe that connects a fixture to the stack in a water and waste removal system. (31)

brick: A fired clay masonry product. (20)

brick ledge: The portion of the foundation wall on which the brick veneer rests. (15)

brick mold: The trim that covers the space between a door jamb and the door opening in a masonry wall. (21)

brick veneer: A facing of brick laid against and fastened to sheathing of a frame wall or tile wall construction.

bridging: Small wood or metal members that are inserted in a diagonal position between the floor joists at midspan to act both as tension and compression members for the purpose of bracing the joists and spreading the action of loads.

British thermal unit (Btu): A unit of measurement for heat. One Btu is the quantity of heat required to increase the temperature of 1 pound of water 1°F. (33)

brown coat: The second stucco layer in the three-coat process; covers any lath not covered by the scratch coat, adds strength to the shell, trues up the surface, and provides an appropriate surface for the final coat. (20)

building code: Written code that specifies requirements for construction methods and materials for plumbing, electrical, and general building construction. (6)

building information modeling (BIM): A design, coordination, construction, and building management process in which a virtual building model physically and functionally replicates the actual building. (12)

building main: The water supply pipe that enters the house in a residential water supply system. (31)

building section: A vertical cut or slice through a structure that illustrates the type of foundation, wall, and roof construction to be used. (6, 22)

built-up roof: A roofing composed of three to five layers of asphalt felt laminated with coal tar, pitch, or asphalt; top is finished with crushed slag or gravel; generally used on flat or low-pitched roofs.

bundled cable: A cable that has several types of conductors inside one PVC jacket.

Bureau of Land Management: The branch of government in charge of surveying public lands.

business etiquette: Rules for conducting yourself professionally and courteously, in a polite and businesslike manner, at all times. (3)

C

cable pair: The two wires of a telephone line.

CAD: The acronym for computer-aided (or computer-assisted) drawing. (5)

CADD: The acronym for computer-aided drafting and design. (5)

CADD workstation: A computer "system" that generally consists of a computer or processor, monitor, graphics adapter, input and pointing device, and hard copy device.

cantilevered joists: Joists that overhang the lower level of a structure; used when a design calls for a cantilevered area parallel to the joists. (19)

Cape Ann: An early Colonial house with a central chimney, gambrel roof, and attic rooms.

Cape Cod: One of the earliest and best known of the traditional Colonial styles.

carbon monoxide (CO): An odorless, tasteless, invisible gas that is potentially deadly when inhaled in high concentrations. (10)

carbon monoxide (CO) detector: A device that detects dangerous concentrations of carbon monoxide.

carport: A garage not fully enclosed.

Cartesian coordinates: X,Y,Z absolute coordinates used to locate position in space.

casement window: A window in which the sash is hinged at the side and swings outward when opened. (21)

casing: The trim that covers the space between a door jamb and the rough framing. (21)

catalytic stove: A stove that uses a ceramic catalyst to increase combustion, which results in an increase in efficiency. (25)

caulk: A waterproof material used to seal cracks.

cavity wall: A wall constructed of concrete blocks; units are arranged to provide a continuous air space 2″ to 3″ thick. (20)

cement: A mixture of lime, silica, alumina, iron components, and gypsum. (18)

cement mortar mix: A type of concrete used as a base for tile or stone flooring; a mixture of one part Portland cement and six parts sand. (19)

centerline: Line that indicates the center of symmetrical objects, such as windows and doors, and the center point of holes. (4)

central processing unit (CPU): A unit containing the processor, RAM, and input/output interfaces; the "box" found on most PCs.

central vacuum system: A vacuum cleaning system that is built into the walls of a home, with inlets throughout the house to which a vacuum hose can be attached. (32)

chain: A unit of land measurement 66′ in length.

chamfer: A beveled edge on a board formed by removing the sharp corner; generally used on moldings, edges of drawer fronts, and cabinet doors.

chase: A slot or continuous groove built in a masonry wall to accommodate ducts, pipes, or conduits.

chimney: A freestanding, vertical structure that houses the fireplace flue and allows smoke from a fire to leave the home safely. (25)

chipped grain: Wood surface that has been roughened by the action of cutting tools; considered a defect when surfaces are to be smoothly finished.

chlorinated polyvinyl chloride (CPVC): A thermoplastic plumbing pipe used in water supply and drainage piping. (31)

chords: Horizontal flanges at the top and bottom of a floor truss. (19)

circle top window: Circular window typically installed above another window; available in quarter circles, half circles, ellipses, or full circles.

circuit: A continuous path through which electricity flows from a source to one or more devices and then returns to the source. (29)

circuit breaker: A device designed to open a circuit automatically when the circuit becomes overloaded. Unlike fuses, circuit breakers can be reset and reused after they have been tripped. (29)

circular stairs: A custom-made stairway with trapezoidal steps that rise along an irregular curve or arc. (24)

circulating stove: A stove that uses air flow, as well as radiant heat, to distribute warmth throughout a room. (25)

clash detection: A process used for checking for interference between components in a building design. (12)

cleanout: In plumbing, an access pipe that allows the plumbing lines to be cleaned out or unplugged. In a fireplace, a door to allow access for removal of ashes from an ash dump. (25, 31)

clear span: The horizontal distance from the inside of one exterior stud wall to the inside of the opposite exterior stud wall. (17)

clear title: A title to property that is free of any defects.

cleat: A piece of wood fastened to another member to serve as a brace or support; normally used in frame construction.

clerestory window: Window that is placed high on a wall to allow light into a room. Some clerestory windows can be opened to provide ventilation, as well. (21)

climate control equipment schedule: An orderly means of specifying equipment to be used in a climate control system; similar to a door or window schedule. (34)

climate control plan: A plan view section drawing that shows the location, size, and type of heating, cooling, ventilating, humidifying, and air cleaning equipment and the required piping or ducts. (34)

climate control system: A system that controls not only temperature, but also humidity, air circulation, and air cleaning. (33)

clipping path: The path along which a model is "cut" to show a section view of the interior. (28)

close cornice: A cornice in which the rafter does not project beyond the wall. (17)

closed plan: A residential floor plan that has separate rooms for living and dining. *See also* open plan. (7)

clothes care center: Provides an area for washing, drying, pressing, folding, storing, and mending clothes; intended to be more than a "utility" room.

cold water branch lines: Pipes that run from the cold water main to each of the fixtures in a residential water supply system. (31)

cold water main: The pipe in a residential water supply system that branches off the house main and extends to various parts of the house to provide unheated water to the branch lines. (31)

collar beam: Nominal 1″ or 2″ thick member connecting opposite roof rafters; serves to stiffen the roof structure.

combination window: A window that is a mixture of two or more types of windows.

comfort-height toilet: A toilet that has a seat 17″ to 19″ from the floor. Comfort-height toilets make access easier for elderly people, disabled people, and other people who have limited mobility. (8)

command: Instructions you provide to CADD software to produce the end result, such as drawing a line or creating a dimension. (5)

command line: Where a computer command can be typed to activate it.

common brick: Brick that is less uniform in size and color than face brick and may have a lip on one or more edges. (20)

common method: The most common of several methods for drawing two-point perspectives; also called the *office method*.

compact fluorescent lightbulb (CFL): A type of fluorescent lightbulb that fits into light fixtures traditionally used for incandescent lightbulbs. The fluorescent tube is curved to fit into the space occupied by an incandescent bulb, making it a more attractive alternative than standard fluorescent tubes for many applications. (30)

computer-aided drafting and design (CADD): The process of using computer software for drafting and design functions.

concrete: A structural material made by combining cement, sand, aggregate, and water. (18)

condensation: The physical change of a gas into a liquid. For example, water vapor condenses to become liquid water. (10)

conditions and restrictions: The phrase used to designate any conditions to which the use of land may not be put and the penalties for failure to comply.

condominium: A multifamily housing unit available for purchase in which ownership includes a share of common property and facilities. (1)

conduction: The flow of heat through an object by transferring heat from one molecule to another.

conductor: A material, such as copper, that permits the flow of electricity; usually refers to a wire. (29)

conduit: A pipe or tube through which wires and cables are run to protect them from the environment and from accidental damage. (29)

cone of vision: The angle between opposite sides of an object shown in perspective, with the vertex of the angle at the station point. (26)

contemporary*:* Modern house style not directly related to styles of the past.

contract: An agreement between a seller and purchaser; the title is withheld from the purchaser until all required payments to the seller have been completed.

contract specification sheet: A document prepared by the architect that contains details of the responsibilities of the parties involved in a construction project.

construction details: Enlarged detail views of wall, foundation, or roof construction. (6)

construction line: Very light line for the drafter's use in constructing a drawing. (4)

construction simulation: An animation that illustrates construction processes in sequential order. (12)

construction technologist: A person who specializes in areas of construction technology, such as managing construction, purchasing, expediting, specifications writing, estimating and bidding, quality control, and site supervision. (3)

contour interval: The vertical distance between two adjacent contour lines. (16)

contour line: A line that connects points having the same elevation on a site. Contour lines are used to show the shape and elevation of the land. (16)

contraction joints: Joints formed in freshly placed concrete with a jointing tool to prevent cracks from expansion and contraction due to changes in temperature and moisture content. (18)

convection: Refers to the transfer of heat by a moving fluid, such as liquids and gases.

convenience outlet: A contact device attached to a circuit to allow electricity to be drawn off for appliances or lighting.

cooperative: A type of ownership for multifamily housing in which each resident buys shares in a corporation. The corporation manages the property. (1)

coping: A cap or top course of a masonry wall used to protect areas beneath it from water penetration.

corbel: A ledge or shelf constructed by laying successive courses of masonry out from the face of the wall.

core: The inner layer(s) of plywood; may consist of veneer, solid lumber, or composition board.

corner bracing: Diagonal bracing at the corners of a frame structure to stiffen and strengthen the wall.

cornice: The overhang of the roof at the eave line that forms a connection between the roof and side walls. (17)

cornice return: The portion of the cornice that returns on the gable end of a house.

corridor kitchen: A kitchen in which the work centers are located on two walls opposite each other. (9)

counterflashing: A flashing used under the regular flashing.

counterflow furnace: A furnace in which the plenum is on the bottom and warm air is forced downward. This type of furnace is designed to be located on the main floor of a home with ducts beneath the floor. (33)

coursed rubble: Rubble stonework in which all of the stones are generally flat or rectangular, so that the result looks like courses (rows) of stone. (20)

courtyard: An outdoor space that is partially or fully enclosed by walls or a roof. (7)

cove: Molded trim of a concave shape used around cabinet construction and other built-ins.

Craftsman period: Social and cultural movement that lasted from 1860 to about 1930. Inspired by the English Arts and Crafts movement, its purpose was to renew the human spirit by reuniting art, labor, and the artist while promoting hand workmanship. (1)

crawl space: An area less than full height, located at or below the ground level of the main floor. The area is typically used for storage and maintenance. (2)

creep: Horizontal movement of pavers in a flexible paving system. (18)

cricket: A built-up area on the high side of a roof next to the chimney to shed water and prevent it from seeping under the shingles. Also called a *saddle*. (25)

cripple stud: A structural member, also called a *jack stud*, that is not full length due to a wall opening. (20)

cross bracing: Boards nailed diagonally across studs or other boards to make framework rigid.

cross bridging: 1 × 3 boards with the ends cut at an angle to fit snugly against joists; used to stiffen a floor and spread the load over a broader area. (19)

crosshatch lines: Used to show that the feature has been sectioned; also called *section lines*.

cross-linked polyethylene (PEX): A flexible plumbing pipe used in water supply piping. (31)

cross section: A building section that extends all the way across a building. Also called a *full building section*. (22)

crown molding: A decorative molding used at the top of cabinets, at ceiling corners, and under a roof overhang.

cubic foot method: A method of building cost estimation based on the volume of a proposed house design. (36)

cul-de-sac: A street or court with no outlet, which provides a circular turnaround for vehicles.

cull: Building material (especially boards) that is rejected because of defects or below usable grade.

cupola: A small, decorative structure built on the roof of a house; often placed over an attached garage and may also be used for ventilation purposes.

curtain wall: A wall that does not support much weight. (19)

cutaway view: A view of a virtual model in which some of the walls have been hidden or clipped so that the interior is visible. (28)

cutting-plane line: Heavy line used to show where an object or structure is to be sectioned. (22)

D

dado joint: A groove cut across the face of a piece of stock to receive the end of another board; often used in quality shelf and cabinet construction.

damper: A device that regulates the flow of air and stops downdrafts of cold air when a fireplace is not in operation. (25)

daylight basement: Similar to a regular basement except the slope of the land allows the placement of windows on an exterior wall to bring daylight into the area. (2)

daylighting: Using windows and skylights to provide natural sunlight for a home. (11)

dead load: The static or fixed weight of the structure itself. (18)

deck: An outdoor feature that is similar to a patio but is typically above grade. (7)

deed: A legal document that confers ownership of property. (6)

dehumidifying system: A system that removes moisture vapor from the air to reduce the relative humidity in the space. (13)

design contingency: An amount of cost variation that is included in a preliminary estimate to account for design changes as the design is finalized; usually 10% to 15%. (36)

design temperature difference: The difference between the inside design temperature (desired indoor temperature) and the outside design temperature (the average outdoor temperature for a season). (33)

detail components: View-specific symbols that appear only in the view in which they are created. (12)

detailing: The process of using 2D geometry to represent non-modeled features in views. (12)

detail lines: View-specific lines that appear only in the view in which they are created. (12)

diffuser: An outlet cover that is similar to a register, but directs the air flow in a specific direction. (34)

digital data: Refers to information that is converted to only a few specific values, commonly described as "1s and 0s."

dimension line: Thin line that shows the size or location of an object or feature. (4)

dimensional lumber: Lumber that is available in common nominal widths and thicknesses, such as 2 × 4, 1 × 6, and 2 × 12; available in various lengths.

dimmer switch: A switch that allows the amount of light from a light fixture to be adjusted to the desired brightness. (29)

dioxins: A family of chemicals that are environmental pollutants and are also among the most carcinogenic (cancer-causing) chemicals known. (11)

direct gain systems: Solar heating systems that incorporate large areas of south-facing glazing (glass or other material) that permit large amounts of sunlight to enter the interior space of the dwelling to directly heat the air inside.

discrimination: Treating someone unfairly, either personally or professionally, based upon the person's age, race, religion, or gender. (3)

display grid: A set of nonprinting visual guidelines in the drawing area, much like the lines on graph paper. (5)

disposal field: The area that receives liquid sewage from the septic tank and allows it to seep into the soil. Also called a *drain field* or *leach field*. (31)

distillation system: A water treatment system in which water is heated to make steam, which is then condensed to produce distilled water. (31)

distribution box: A box that receives liquid sewage from the septic tank and distributes it evenly throughout the disposal field. (31)

distribution panel: The main distribution box that receives the electricity from the external power line and distributes it to various points in the house through individual circuits. Also called a *service panel*. (29)

distribution system: The system of ducts or pipes that delivers heated or cooled air or water throughout a house. (34)

dome: A roof used over an entryway or a complete structure in the form of a hemisphere.

door jamb: The frame that fits inside the rough opening for a door. (21)

door schedule: A list of all of the doors to be installed in a building, including complete specifications. (21)

door stop: The strip on the door jamb against which the door closes.

dormer: A projecting structure on a roof that has walls, a front-facing window, and a roof. (2, 13)

double-action door: Door that is hinged so that it can swing either way (in or out) through an arc of 180°. (21)

double glazing: A pane of two pieces of glass sealed with an air space between to provide insulation.

double header: Two or more timbers joined for strength.

double-hung window: A window that has two sashes that slide up and down in grooves formed in the window frame. (21)

double-L stairs: A stairway that has two 90° turns and two landings along the flight, but is not U-shaped. (24)

Douglas fir: A yellow to pale reddish softwood; a veneer wood primarily converted into plywood and widely used in building and construction; lumber used in general construction; mill products used for sash, flooring, and doors.

downspout: A vertical pipe that receives the water from a gutter outlet and carries it to ground level, where an extension directs the water away from the house. (17)

drawing aids: CADD commands and functions that help you locate positions on screen and on existing objects; make the task of drawing easier, faster, and more accurate.

drawing commands: CADD commands that allow you to create objects.

dressed size: The actual size of lumber after jointing and surfacing.

drip cap: A piece placed over the top piece of casing to shed water. (21)

drywall: Interior covering material, such as gypsum board or plywood, that is applied in large sheets or panels.

dry well: A pit located on porous ground and walled up with rock that allows water to seep through; used for the disposal of rainwater or the effluent from a septic tank.

ducts: Round or rectangular passages in a forced-air heating or cooling system that transport conditioned air throughout the house. (34)

ductwork: The network or system of ducts in the distribution system of a forced-air climate control system. (34)

duplex outlet: Electrical wall outlet having two plug receptacles.

Dutch door: A door that has separate lower and upper sections that can be opened independently. (21)

E

earnest money: A partial payment made as part of the purchase price to bind a contract for property.

earthquake zone: An area that is known to be prone to earthquakes. Also called a *seismic area*. (10)

earth-sheltered dwelling: A structure that uses soil to reduce heat loss or gain.

easement: An area of a piece of property to which another has certain rights for the purpose of placing power lines, drains, and other specified uses.

eaves: The lower portion of the roof that overhangs the wall.

ecosystem: The interaction of plants and animals with each other and the environment. (11)

editing commands: CADD commands that allow you to modify drawings in several ways.

electric radiant system: A heating system in which resistance wiring embedded in the ceiling, floor, or baseboards is used to produce heat. (33)

electrical plan: A plan that locates switches, electrical outlets, ceiling fixtures, television and cable jacks, LAN connections, the service entrance location, and the panel box. (6, 30)

electron-stimulated luminescence (ESL) light: A lightbulb that produces light by accelerating electrons to hit a fluorescent surface, similar to the process used in cathode ray tubes. (30)

elevation: A drawing, typically made as an orthographic projection, that shows the exterior features of one side of a structure. (4, 6, 23)

ell: An extension or wing of a building at a right angle to the main section.

ellipse: A regular oval shape that has a major (longer) diameter and a minor (shorter) diameter. (4)

employability skills: Skills that help you get and keep a job. (3)

enclosed stairs: Stairs that have a wall on both sides; also known as closed, housed, or box stairs.

engineered wood products (EWPs): A class of structural wood members that combine wood veneers and fibers with adhesives to form beams, headers, joists, and panels that have uniformly high quality and strength. (19)

entourage: Surroundings such as trees, shrubs, cars, people, and terrain that add realism to a presentation drawing. (27)

entrepreneur: A person who starts, manages, and assumes the risks of a business. (3)

equity: The amount a house is worth minus the amount the homeowner owes on it. (6)

ergonomics: The science of adapting the workstation to fit the needs of the drafter. (5)

escutcheon: Door hardware that accommodates the knob and keyhole.

estimating: The organized effort to determine the total cost of materials, labor, and other services required to build a house. (36)

estimator: A person who calculates the costs of materials and labor for building a structure. (3)

excavate: Remove the top soil at a construction site. (18)

expansion floor plan: A floor plan that includes a proposed design for later expansion of the building or home. (14)

expansion joint: A bituminous fiber strip used to separate blocks or units of concrete to prevent cracking due to expansion as a result of temperature changes.

expansive clay: A type of soil that swells when wet and produces very high pressure against underground walls.

extended plenum system: A ductwork system that has a large, rectangular duct or plenum for the main supply. Round ducts extend from the main supply to the individual registers. (34)

extension line: Thin line that runs from the ends of a dimension line to the object or feature being dimensioned. (4)

exterior insulation finish system (EIFS): A wall covering system that provides thermal insulation and a durable external finish resembling stucco or stone. (20)

F

facade: The front elevation or the face of a structure.

face brick: Brick that is uniform in size and has sharp corners and lines. (20)

face size: The exposed width of a molded piece of lumber after installation.

face veneer: Veneer selected for exposed surfaces in plywood.

facing: Any material attached to the outer portion of a wall used as a finished surface.

family: A collection of components that represent variations of the same item in different sizes and orientations. (12)

fascia: A vertical board nailed onto the ends of the rafters.

fiberboard: A building board made with fibrous material and used as an insulating board.

file interoperability: The ability of electronic file data to be compatible across different platforms and software applications. (12)

fill: Sand, gravel, or loose earth used to bring a subgrade up to a desired level around a house.

filled insulation: A loose insulating material poured from bags or blown by machine into walls.

fillet: A smoothly fitted internal arc of a specified radius between two lines, arcs, or circles. (5)

fill light: A diffused light source used to provide general lighting in a rendered presentation drawing. (27)

final estimate: An accurate estimate of building costs based on the final working drawings and specifications; includes the quantity, quality, and cost of materials to be used and the cost of labor required for installation. (36)

finish coat: The third stucco layer in the three-coat process; a thin layer in which texture or design patterns are applied. (20)

firebrick: A type of brick that can withstand intense heat. (25)

fire chamber: The part of a fireplace where the fire is contained and controlled. (25)

fireclay: A fire-resistant, mortar-like material that is used as a bonding material between firebricks in a fireplace. (25)

firecut: An angled cut on a joist end in solid brick and stone walls to prevent toppling the wall if the house should catch fire. (20)

firestop: A solid, tight closure of a concealed space; placed to prevent the spread of fire and smoke through such a space.

firewall: Any wall designed to resist the spread of fire between sections of a house or other structure; commonly used between the main structure and an attached garage.

flagstone: Flat stone used for floors, steps, walks, or walls.

flash flood: A sudden flood usually caused by heavy rain, although not necessarily in the flooded areas. Heavy rains in the mountains many miles upstream of a town can cause unexpected flash flooding in the town if the rainfall rates are high enough. (10)

flashing: A strip of weather-resistant metal laid beneath the surface roofing material to shed water away from areas of potential leakage. (17)

flexible paving system: A paving system with a well-compacted subgrade beneath a layer of crushed stone, a sand setting bed, and fine sand between the pavers. (18)

float: A short board, about a foot long, with a handle attached to one of the wide sides. Floats are used to embed the large aggregate in concrete just beneath the surface, remove imperfections to produce a flat surface, and prepare for final steel-troweling. (18)

floodplain: A low-lying area near a river or other body of water that floods when the water level in the body of water rises. (10)

floor framing plan: A plan that shows the direction of floor joists and major supporting members. (6)

floor plan: A horizontal section view of a structure taken about 4′ from floor level. It shows all exterior and interior walls, doors, windows, patios, walks, decks, fireplaces, mechanical equipment, built-in cabinets, appliances, bathroom fixtures, and other fixed features of the structure. (4, 6, 14)

floor trusses: Trusses made of engineered wood, designed for light frame construction, that are used in place of floor joists in some residential structures. (19)

flue: The path or structure that conducts smoke from a fire safely to the top of the chimney. (25)

flue lining: Sleeve used for the inner lining of chimneys.

fluorescent light: A light that contains a glass tube coated with a material that fluoresces (glows) when an electric current is applied. (30)

flush door: A door that is smooth on both sides. (21)

fly ash: Ash that has been recovered as a byproduct of coal-burning energy plants. (11)

fly rafters: End rafters of the gable overhang supported by roof sheathing and lookouts.

foam board: A type of Styrofoam® that is available in sheets of various thicknesses. (28)

footing: A reinforced concrete structure that supports the foundation wall by spreading its weight over a larger area. (15, 18)

footprint: The area of land occupied by the floor plan of a building. (2)

forced-air system: A heating system in which air is heated in a furnace and then forced through pipes or ducts to all parts of a house. (33)

form, concrete: A temporary structure built to contain concrete during placement and initial hardening.

foundation: The supporting portion of a structure below the first-floor construction, or below grade, including the footings.

foundation plan: A plan that specifies the foundation size and the materials to be used in constructing the foundation or other structure. (6)

foundation walls: The part of a house that extends down from the first floor to the footing. (18)

foyer: A room or area just inside the main entry of a home that provides a place to greet guests and to remove overcoats and boots. (7)

franchise: A license to sell an established company's products or services. (3)

free-form roof: A roof that may take any shape, offering complete freedom of design; the design may include planar, curved, and warped surfaces. (17)

freehand sketching: A method of making a drawing without the use of instruments.

French doors: Panel doors in which all of the panels are glass. (21)

frieze: In house construction, a horizontal member connecting the top of the siding with the soffit of the cornice.

front elevation: In architectural drawing, the front view of an object.

front-loading: Involving as many stakeholders as possible in the early stages of a building project to gather input for design, construction, and building management. (12)

frost line: The depth of frost penetration in soil below which footings are placed to prevent movement; varies in different parts of the country.

full bath: A bathroom that contains a sink, toilet, and bathtub or tub/shower combination. (8)

full building section: A building section that extends all the way across a building. Also called a *cross section*. (22)

furniture plan: A plan that identifies the furniture to be used and its placement in each area of the house.

furring strips: Strips of 2 × 2 or 1 × 3 lumber affixed to a masonry wall to provide a nailing surface for drywall, plaster, or paneling. (20)

fuse: A device that has a fusible link that melts when a circuit becomes overloaded, opening the circuit and stopping the flow of electricity. (29)

G

gable end: The extension of a gable roof beyond the end wall of the house; also called a *rake*. (17)

gain: A—A recess or notch into which a door hinge fits flush with the surface. B—Refers to the way heat is extracted from solar radiation.

garrett: An attic or unfinished part of a house just under the roof.

Garrison: A house style that has a distinguishing overhanging second story and narrow siding.

gazebo: A roofed structure that is similar to a porch, but is detached from the house. (7)

geothermal energy: Energy from heat within the Earth. (11, 33)

geothermal heat pump: A heat pump designed to use geothermal energy as its heat source. Also called *ground-source heat pump*. (33)

girder: A large or principal beam of wood or steel used to support concentrated loads at isolated points along its length.

glass size: The dimension of unobstructed glass.

glazing: Placing of glass in windows or doors.

glue-laminated members: Members that consist of 1× or 2× lumber glued in stacks to the desired shape and size; used for beams, columns, and arches. (19)

grade: The surface of the ground around a building.

grade line: The line or level of the finished grade (earth) around the structure. (23)

grade, wood: A designation given to the quality of manufactured lumber.

gravel stop: A strip of metal with a vertical lip used to retain the gravel around the edge of a built-up roof.

gray water: Water that has been used in baths, showers, clothes washers, and bathroom sinks. (11)

great room: A general-purpose room that replaces the living room, family room, and dining room in houses designed with an open floor plan. The great room may also be open to the kitchen. (7)

green building: A building process that works toward sustainability by striving to use materials and processes more efficiently, while reducing pollution and causing as little damage to the environment as possible. (11)

greenwashing: The practice of making false claims that a product is green when in fact, it is not green and may actually be harmful to the environment. (11)

grid snap: An invisible grid feature that causes the cursor to "jump" or snap to the closest snap grid point. (5)

grids: Layouts for drawing available in a wide variety of sizes and forms. Some grids are designed to be used under a sheet of tracing paper while others are designed to be drawn on directly.

grille: A basic covering for an outlet that can be used for both supply air and return air. (34)

gross annual income: The amount of money earned before taxes and other deductions are taken out. (6)

ground fault circuit interrupter (GFCI): A safety device that continually monitors the amount of current going to the load and compares it to that coming back. If the amount of current returning to the device is less than that going to the load, the device trips (opens) the circuit to prevent electric shock. (8, 29)

ground line (GL): The line that represents the horizontal ground plane in a perspective drawing; the plane on which the object rests. (26)

grout: A plaster-like material used to seal between ceramic and other tile in kitchens, showers, and baths.

guardrail: A railing designed to keep people from falling over the edge of a balcony or off the side or top of a staircase. (24)

guideline: Very lightly drawn line for use in hand lettering; similar to a construction line. (4)

gusset: A piece of metal or plywood used to fasten the members of a wood truss together, adding strength to the truss assembly. (17)

gutter: A trough that collects water from the roof and directs it to a downspout. (17)

H

habitable space: The area in a house that is usable for living activities such as sleeping, eating, and recreation. (2)

half-timbering: Heavy, partly exposed wood timbers used as framing elements in a building; the spaces between the timbers are filled with masonry. (1)

handrail: A railing that helps people steady themselves as they travel up and down steps or ramps where they might slip, trip, or fall. (24)

hanger: A metal strap used to support piping or the ends of joists.

harassment: Tormenting, teasing, or intentionally bothering someone, especially if the person has asked you to stop. (3)

hardwood: Wood produced from broadleaved trees; examples include oak, maple, walnut, and birch.

hatching: A pattern of lines or other symbols used to show where material has been cut away in a section view or indicate a type of material, such as gravel or brick. (5)

hatch pattern: A graphic symbol that represents a building material. Most CADD packages contain several standard hatch patterns that can be used to describe building materials. (14)

header: A—A beam placed perpendicular to joists and to which joists are nailed in framing for a chimney, stairway, or other opening. B—A wood lintel.

header-and-stud framing: A method of constructing headers for window and door openings in which shorter studs and jack studs are firmly nailed to the sole and top plates of the opening. (20)

headroom: The shortest clear vertical distance in a stairway, measured between the nosing of the treads and the ceiling. (24)

hearth: A fire-resistant area around a wood-burning fireplace that protects the floor from sparks. (25)

heat exchanger: A device for removing heat from water or air and transferring the heat to another medium.

heating and cooling plan: A plan that illustrates components of the climate control system of the house.

heating, ventilation, and air conditioning (HVAC) plan: A plan that shows components of the climate control system of a house. (6)

heat loss: The amount of heat that passes through the exposed surfaces of a house. (33)

heat pump: A heating system that transfers natural heat from air or water to heat or cool a house. (33)

hickory: A hard and heavy brown to reddish-brown hardwood; used as face veneer for decorative interior plywood paneling and as solid lumber in special flooring applications. Pecan, a variety of the hickory family, has similar properties and construction applications.

hidden line: Thin, dashed line that represents an edge that is behind a visible surface in a given view. (4)

hip rafter: The diagonal rafter that extends from the plate to the ridge to form the hip.

hip roof: A roof that rises by inclined planes from all four sides of a building.

hopper window: A window that is hinged at the bottom and swings to the inside of the house. (21)

horizon line (HL): The line formed where the ground and sky meet in the background of a perspective drawing. (26)

horizontal furnace: A furnace that can be suspended from ceilings and floor joists or installed on a concrete slab because it requires minimum clearance. (33)

horizontal sliding window: A window that has two sashes; a track attached to the head jamb and sill provides for horizontal movement.

hose bib: A water faucet made for the threaded attachment of a hose.

hot water branch lines: Pipes that run from the hot water main to each of the fixtures in a residential water supply system. (31)

hot water main: The pipe in a residential water supply system that branches off the house main, runs through the water heater, and then runs throughout the house to supply hot water branch lines. (31)

house drain: The main drain pipe that receives water and waste from all of the stacks; becomes the house sewer after it passes to the exterior of the house. (31)

housed stringer: A stringer that has been routed or grooved to receive the treads and risers of a stairway. (24)

house sewer: The part of the house drain that runs from the house to the city sanitary sewer or a private septic system. (31)

humidifier: A device used to increase the moisture level (water vapor) in air.

humidistat: A controlling device to regulate or maintain the desired degree of humidity (water vapor) in a house.

hurricane: A tropical storm (cyclone) with winds that have reached a sustained speed of 74 miles per hour (64 knots) or more.

hurricane code: A building code designed to reduce property damage during a hurricane by requiring structures to be constructed to withstand hurricane-force winds. (10)

hurricane tie: A strap or clip that anchors roof components to a house. Hurricane ties help the roof withstand the high winds typical of hurricanes and tornadoes. (10)

hydronic radiant system: A type of hydronic heating system that has copper pipes or other type of tubing embedded in a concrete floor or plastered ceiling. (33)

hydronic system: A hot water heating system. (33)

I

improvements: Any additions to property that tend to increase its value, such as buildings, streets, or sewers.

incandescent light: The traditional screw-in lightbulb that relies on a glowing filament to provide light. (30)

indirect gain systems: Solar heating systems that heat the interior space by storing heat in a thermal mass, then releasing the heat into the interior space; a large thermal mass is placed between the sun and the living space.

individual circuit: A branch circuit dedicated to a single appliance that requires a large amount of electricity, such as an air conditioner or clothes dryer. (29)

Indoor Radon Abatement Act: A law passed in 1988 that set a goal for the Environmental Protection Agency to reduce indoor radon levels to those of outdoor air. (10)

industrialized housing: Houses built in a factory.

infiltration: The amount of heat lost through spaces around windows and doors. (33)

inlet: A cold air return for a forced-air climate control system. (34)

inner hearth: The part of a hearth that makes up the floor of the fireplace. (25)

inquiry commands: Commands designed to list the database records for selected objects; calculate distances, areas, and perimeters; and identify absolute coordinates of points.

inside design temperature: The desired room temperature level.

insulated concrete forms (ICFs): Concrete wall forms made of foam insulation that are filled with concrete and remain in place to become part of the exterior wall structure. (20)

insulating board: Any board suitable for insulating purposes; usually manufactured board, such as fiberboard.

insulation: A material that prevents heat or cold from transferring from one location to another. (33)

interior designer: A designer who specializes in the interior detailing of structures, including architectural highlights such as half-walls or recessed lighting. (3)

interior trim: General term for all the finish molding, casing, baseboard, and cornice applied within the building by finish carpenters.

intermediate level: The level located between the basement level and the living level of a split-level house. (2)

interpolation: A technique used to locate, by proportion, intermediate points between grid elevations developed from survey data. (16)

ion exchange: A process used in water softeners in which sodium ions in a resin are exchanged for calcium and magnesium ions, reducing the hardness of the water. (31)

island kitchen: A modification of a straight-line, L-shaped, or U-shaped kitchen that includes a freestanding island. The island may house the sink, cooking center, or food preparation center, and may also serve as an eating area. (9)

ISO: Abbreviation for the International Standards Organization.

isolated gain systems: Solar heating systems that collect and store solar energy in an area outside of the living space.

J

jack rafter: A rafter that spans the distance from the wall plate to a hip or from a valley to a ridge.

jack stud: A structural member positioned inside a wall opening to help support the header over the opening; also called a *trimmer*. (20)

jalousie window: A window that has a series of narrow, horizontal glass slats that are held in metal clips, which in turn are fastened to an aluminum frame. (21)

jamb: The side and head lining of a doorway, window, or other opening.

job site safety: The safety of all of those individuals involved at a construction site; the primary concern for every employer and employee.

job skills: Technical skills you need to perform a job correctly. (3)

joists: Structural members that provide support for the floor. (19)

K

keyframe: A frame in an animation on which an important action takes place.

key light: The main light that provides most of the illumination in a rendered presentation drawing, from which shadows are calculated and drawn. (27)

kiln-dried lumber: Lumber that has been kiln-dried, generally to a moisture content of 6% to 12%.

king post: The center upright piece in a roof truss.

king stud: A full-height structural member at the sides of a wall opening to which trimmers (also called *jack studs*) are nailed to provide additional support. (20)

kip: Unit of measurement for the load a beam will support; equal to 1000 pounds. (18)

knee wall: A low wall resulting from one-and-one-half-story construction.

L

lally column: A steel column used as a support for girders and beams.

laminated beam: A beam made of superimposed layers of similar materials by joining them with glue and pressure.

laminated veneer lumber (LVL): A product in which veneers of wood are stacked in parallel and glued under pressure; used for headers, beams, columns, joists, and as flanges for wood I-joists. (19)

landing: A flat floor area at some point between the top and bottom of the stairway. The areas at the top and bottom of the stairway may also be considered landings. (24)

landscaping plan: A plan that shows the type and placement of plants and other elements included in landscaping the site of a new structure. (6, 16)

land surveyor: A person who establishes areas and boundaries of real estate property. (3)

laser scanner: A device that captures point data from a building or site by recording XYZ coordinates of individual points in space. (5)

lath: A wire or ribbed material that provides support and attachment for the layers of stucco applied to a wall. (20)

lattice: A framework of crossed wood or metal strips.

lavatory: A bathroom sink. (8)

layer: A virtual piece of paper on which CADD objects are placed. (5)

leader: A vertical pipe or downspout that carries rainwater from the gutter to the ground or storm sewer.

lease: A contract for the use of land for a period of years with a designated payment of a monthly or annual rental.

ledger strip: A strip of lumber nailed along the bottom of the side of a girder on which joists rest.

left side elevation: In architectural drawing, the left side view of an object.

legal description: A written indication of the location and boundaries of a parcel of land; reference is generally made to a recorded plat of survey.

levels: Assigned elevations that define key heights of the building. (12)

lifelong learning: Willingness to learn new skills on a continual basis to keep your job skills current. (3)

light-emitting diode (LED) light: A lightbulb that relies on light-emitting diode technology. Most LED lightbulbs intended for residential use are supplied with standard bases so they will fit the same light fixtures traditionally used for incandescent bulbs. (30)

lighting circuit: A branch circuit used for permanently installed lighting fixtures, as well as outlets for lamps, radios, televisions, and similar 120-volt devices. (29)

lighting fixture schedule: A schedule of lighting fixtures that contains all of the fixtures, switches, and other materials and information needed to install the electrical system for a residence; similar to a door and window schedule. (30)

lighting outlet: A contact device that allows electricity to be drawn off a circuit specifically for lighting. (29)

lintel: A horizontal structural member that supports the load over an opening such as a door or window. (18)

live load: A fixed or moving load that is not a structural part of the house; examples include furniture, occupants, and snow on the roof. (18)

living area: The area of a home in which the family relaxes, entertains guests, dines, and meets together. (7)

living level: The habitable area in a split-level house where the family relaxes, entertains guests, dines, and spends time together. (2)

long break line: Thin, straight line used to show that part of a long feature has been omitted from a drawing. (4)

longitudinal building section: A full building section taken lengthwise across the longest overall dimension of a building. (22)

longitudinal method: A method of roof beam placement in post and beam construction in which the beams are placed at right angles to the roof slope; roof decking is laid from the ridge pole to the eaves line. (19)

lookout: A support member that fastens the soffit in a wide box cornice. (17)

lot: A measured amount of property (land) having fixed boundaries.

lot line: The line forming the legal boundary of a piece of property.

louver: An opening with a series of horizontal slats so arranged as to permit ventilation but to exclude rain, sunlight, or vision.

L-shaped kitchen: A kitchen in which the work centers are located on two adjacent walls. (9)

L stairs: A stairway that has a landing at some point along the flight of stairs at which the stairway turns. (24)

M

mail-order house: An inexpensive, mass-produced house that could be ordered from a mail-order catalog and was delivered unassembled to purchasers as a do-it-yourself kit. (1)

main entry: The front entry of a home, designed for use by guests and opening into the living area of the home. (7)

main stack: A soil stack in a residential water and waste removal system into which one or more toilets drain. (31)

main stairs: The primary set of stairs from the first floor to the second floor or from a split foyer to the first floor. (24)

major module: In modular construction, a 4′-0″ cube or 12 standard modules on each side.

mansard roof: A double-pitched hip roof, designed by Francois Mansart, a 17th-century French Renaissance architect, that allows the top level of a building to be used for additional living space. The lower slope of the roof is highly pitched and often has patterned shingles and dormer windows. (1)

mantel: The shelf above a fireplace; also used in referring to the decorative trim around a fireplace opening.

maple: A hardwood generally light tan in color and used in construction where hardness is a major factor; used for cabinetwork, flooring, doors, trim, interior railings, posts, and furniture.

masonry: Stone, brick, concrete, hollow tile, concrete block, gypsum block, or other similar building units or materials or a combination of the same, bonded together with mortar to form a wall, pier, buttress, or similar mass.

masonry wall: A wall constructed entirely of brick, concrete block, stone, clay tile, terra cotta, or a combination of these materials. (20)

MasterSpec®: A set of master specifications published by Architectural Computer Services (ARCOM) for the American Institute of Architects (AIA). (35)

master specifications: Complete sets of specifications developed by reputable organizations for use and adaptation by individual architectural companies. (35)

mastic: A flexible adhesive for joining building materials.

material specifications: Criteria governing the types of materials, fixtures, and other physical items.

material symbol: A graphic symbol or hatch pattern that represents building materials on a drawing. (14)

material takeoff: A list of quantities of materials used in constructing a building. (12, 36)

mean sea level: A standardized elevation that specifies sea level as the average level between high and low tides. (16)

metal wall ties: Strips of corrugated metal used to tie a brick veneer wall to a framework.

millwork: Lumber that is shaped to a given pattern or molded form; includes dressing, matching, and machining; examples include casing, base, panel door parts, and stair rails.

minor module: In modular construction, a 16″ cube or 24″ cube.

mirror line: The centerline about which a mirror operation takes place. (5)

miter joint: A joint made with the ends or edges of two pieces of lumber cut at a 45° angle and fitted together.

model building code: A set of rules developed by independent agencies that can be adopted or incorporated into law by state and local governments. (10)

model ethics code: List of objectives for ethical practices in the business environment.

Modernism: A 20th-century social movement that rejected the classical European constraints of the orderly past and the industrialization of the nation. It strove to bring back quality of life through craftsmanship. (1)

modular components: Building parts that have been preassembled either in a plant or on-site.

modular construction: Construction in which the size of all the building materials is based on a common unit of measure.

moisture barrier: A membrane that retards the flow of moisture vapor and reduces condensation. (13)

mold: The common term for several types of fungus that reproduce through spores. Mold can grow almost anywhere moisture is present. (10)

monitor: The display device or "screen" used on a computer system.

monolithic slab foundation: A thicker extension of a slab floor that forms the support for the structure. It is cast at the same time as the floor and is not a separate unit. (18)

mortar: A mixture of cement, sand, and water; used by a mason as a bonding agent for brick and stone.

mortgage: A document used to hold property as security for a debt.

mortise: A slot cut into a board, plank, or timber, usually edgewise, to receive the tenon of another board, plank, or timber to form a joint.

mudroom: A room directly connected to the service entry of a home that provides a place to remove and store muddy or snowy boots, overcoats, and other outdoor gear. (9)

mudsill: A 2 × 6 plate that forms the base of a box sill in platform framing. (19)

mullions: Horizontal and vertical members placed between window units; generally larger than muntins. (21)

multifamily housing: Housing that provides a home for more than one family. (1)

multiview drawing: A drawing that contains enough views of an object or structure to represent its true size and shape from all sides. (4)

muntins: Small vertical and horizontal bars that separate the total glass area of a window into smaller units. (21)

N

narrow box cornice: A cornice that is usually between 6″ and 12″ wide; the soffit board is nailed directly to the bottom side of the rafters.

narrow U stairs: A set of U stairs that have little or no space between the flights.

net zero energy building: A building that produces as much energy per year as it consumes, or one for which the net energy cost for the year is $0. (11)

newel: A main post that supports the handrail of a stairway at the top, bottom, and points in between where the stairs change directions. (24)

New England gambrel: Colonial style that includes a gambrel roof with pitch change between the ridge and eaves.

nominal size: The size of lumber before dressing, rather than its actual size.

nonbearing wall: A wall supporting no load other than its own weight.

nonrenewable energy source: An energy source that will someday be used up and cannot be reproduced. (11)

north arrow: A symbol on a plan or map that shows the direction of north. (16)

nosing: The rounded projection of a stair tread that extends past the face of the riser. (24)

O

oak, red: Hard and tough hardwood rich light to medium brown in color and used for flooring, interior trim, stair treads, and railings; popular as a face veneer plywood for paneling and cabinetwork; white oak has similar characteristics and applications.

object: An element used to create drawings. Common objects in CADD software include lines, points, circles, and arcs. (5)

object line: Heavy line that shows the outline of the features of an object or structure. (4)

object snap: A drawing aid that allows the cursor to "jump" to certain locations on existing objects, such as the endpoint or midpoint of a line or the center of a circle. (5)

office method: A commonly used method for creating perspective drawings; also called the *common method*. (26)

ohm: A unit of measure used to describe the amount of resistance to the flow of electricity. (29)

on-center (OC): The measurement of spacing for studs, rafters, joists, and other framing members from the center of one member to the center of the next.

one-and-one-half story: A one-story house with a tall, wide roof that allows for expansion of living space into the attic. (2)

one-pipe system: A hydronic system in which radiators are connected in series. Heated water carried in the main pipe is diverted to the radiators and then returned to the furnace. (33)

one-point perspective drawing: A perspective drawing that has only one vanishing point. (26)

one-story: A house design in which all of the living space is located on one level. (2)

open cornice: A cornice in which the rafter ends are exposed and the space between the projecting rafter and the wall is not enclosed. (17)

open plan: A residential design in which there are few walls in the living area of the home. Instead of having a separate dining room, an open plan often has a great room with areas, rather than rooms, dedicated to relaxing, dining, and entertaining. *See also* closed plan. (7)

open stairs: Stairs that have no wall on one or both sides.

oriented strand board (OSB): A panel product in which long strands of wood are mixed with resin, placed in layers, and pressed and cured. (19)

orthographic projection: A technique for representing the true height, width, and depth of a three-dimensional object on two-dimensional paper. Orthographic projection uses an infinite viewpoint to allow projection lines to be parallel. (4)

outlet: A hole or surface through which air or heat from the climate control system enters each room of a home. (34)

outside design temperature: The average outdoor temperature for the winter months.

overall dimension: The overall length of a wall or the entire side of a house from end to end. (14)

overhang: The projecting area of a roof or upper story beyond the wall of the lower part.

overhead doors: Another term for *garage doors*. (9)

P

pallet: An inexpensive wood skid used to stack and ship construction materials such as brick or concrete block.

panel: In residential construction, a thin flat piece of wood, plywood, or similar material, framed by stiles and rails, as in a door, or fitted into grooves of thicker material with molded edges for decorative wall treatment.

panel door: A door that has a heavy frame around the outside and at least one cross member that separates panels of wood, glass, metal, or other material. (21)

paper, building: A general term for paper, felt, or similar sheet materials used in buildings without reference to their properties or uses.

parallel strand lumber (PSL): A product in which thin strands of wood are glued together under pressure; used for beams, columns, and headers to provide high strength and span capacity. (19)

parametric: Term used to describe a type of modeling software program that lets you adjust the parameters of an object without using formal commands. For example, you can change the size of a parametric object without using the **SCALE** command. (5)

parametric model: A 3D model defined by parameters controlling object size and shape. (12)

parametric modeling: A type of 3D modeling in which parameters control object size and shape and may be altered by the user to change dimensional and spatial relationships. (14)

parapet: A low wall or railing around the edge of a roof.

parasol roof: A roof that looks like an upturned parasol (umbrella); usually constructed from concrete.

parge coat: A thin coat of plaster applied over the foundation wall for refinement of the surface or for damp-proofing. (18)

partial building section: A building section that cuts through half or more of the structure, but not its entire length. (22)

particleboard: A composition board made of wood chips or particles bonded together with an adhesive under high pressure.

passive solar space heating: Involves capturing, storing, and using solar radiation to heat a dwelling without the use of fans or pumps to circulate the heat.

patio: An outdoor feature at ground level that is usually near the residence but is not structurally connected to it. (7)

pattern books: Publications such as treatises, essays, and books of architectural design and construction that are used for inspiration and guidance. (1)

paving: The use of brick to cover exterior traffic areas such as driveways, patios, and sidewalks; may be installed either as a rigid or flexible system.

peninsula kitchen: A kitchen that includes base cabinets and counter areas extending into the room from one of the walls. Peninsulas are often used to separate the kitchen area from a dining or family room. (9)

percolation test: A soil test that determines how readily the soil will absorb water; this test provides a guide for the required design and size of the disposal field in a septic system. (31)

period home: A home designed to represent the past and traditional values. Period houses were common just after the Industrial Revolution. (1)

periphery: The boundary or the complete outside edge of a parcel of land or an object on a drawing.

persistent bioaccumulative toxicants (PBTs): Chemicals that are toxic to people and animals and do not break down quickly, so they accumulate in the body. (11)

personal management skills: Personal skills that allow you to perform your job well, such as social skills, productivity, and responsibility. (3)

perspective drawing: A type of pictorial drawing that shows objects in the foreground larger than those in the background, just as they would appear if a person were viewing the actual objects. (26)

physical model: A model made of modeling materials such as wood, sandpaper, or scaled lumber or bricks. (28)

pictorial drawing: A drawing that presents a three-dimensional image of an object in two dimensions. (26)

pictorial presentation: A rendering that is sometimes included in a set of working drawings to show how the structure will appear when finished. (6)

picture plane (PP): A transparent plane onto which a drawing is projected. (26)

picture window: A fixed-glass unit that is usually rather large; the term "picture window" is used because the view is framed, like a picture.

pier: A masonry pillar that supports the floor framing. (15)

pier foundation: A type of foundation that consists of piers resting on a footing, usually below the house. (18)

pilaster: A rectangular column that projects from a basement wall to strengthen it; also used for additional girder or beam support. (15, 18)

pine, white: Softwood of light tan color used for doors, sash, interior and exterior trim, siding, and panels; lower grades are used for sheathing subflooring and roofing.

pine, yellow: Softwood of medium texture, moderately hard, and yellow to reddish-brown in color; used for joists, rafters, studs, and general construction where extra strength and stiffness are required.

plain stringer: A stringer that has been cut or notched to fit the profile of a stairway. (24)

plan view: A top view of a structure. Types of plan views include floor plans, site plans, roof plans, and foundation plans, among others. (4)

plaster: A mortar-like composition used for covering walls and ceilings; usually made of Portland cement mixed with sand and water.

plat: A drawing of surveyed land indicating the location, boundaries, and dimensions of the parcel; also contains information as to easements, restrictions, and lot number.

platform framing: Framing in which the floor joists form a platform on which the walls rest; another platform, formed by either the ceiling joists or the floor joists of the upper floor, rests on the walls. (19)

plenum: The chamber in a heating system where warmed air is collected for distribution. (33)

plot plan: A type of plan view drawing that shows the contours of the building site and the location and orientation of proposed new construction on the property. A *plot* can be described as an empty piece of land. (16)

plumb cut: Any cut in a rafter that is vertical or perpendicular to the ground. (17)

plumbing fixture: Any device, such as a bathtub, shower, toilet, sink, or dishwasher, that requires water. (31)

plumbing fixture schedule: A schedule that specifies names of all plumbing fixtures to be used in the residence, number required, identifying symbols, pipe connection sizes, and a space for remarks. (32)

plumbing plan: A plan view drawing that shows the complete plumbing system, including the location, size, and type of all plumbing equipment and fixtures to be used in a residence. (6, 32)

plywood: A piece of wood made of three or more layers of veneer joined with glue and usually laid with the grain of adjoining plies at right angles.

pocket door: A type of sliding door that slides into a wall pocket when opened. (21)

point cloud: A three-dimensional digital representation of an existing building or construction site consisting of millions of points. (5)

polar coordinates: Point locations measured by entering a given distance and angle from a fixed point, most commonly a previous point. (5)

polygonal rubble: Rubble stonework in which the stones are dressed with relatively straight edges to fit a particular place in the pattern, but still give a rubble, not ashlar, appearance; also called *uncoursed cobweb.* (20)
polyvinyl chloride (PVC): A thermoplastic plumbing pipe used in distribution and drainage piping. (31)
porch: An outdoor space that is structurally connected to the residence. (7)
portfolio: A collection of your best professional design drafting work that you can show to potential employers. (3)
portico: A covered entryway attached to a house, usually open on three sides and supported by posts or columns.
post and beam construction: A construction method that uses posts, beams, and planks as framing members to carry the majority of the live and dead loads to the foundation; the structural members are larger and spaced farther apart than conventional framing members. (19)
post (column) foundation: A type of foundation that consists of columns or posts resting on a footing. Columns are often located within the house rather than under it and support a beam that in turn supports joists. (18)
Postmodernism: An architectural movement of the mid- to late-20th century that marked the return of embellishment and injected wit and character into architecture. (1)
precast: Term describing concrete shapes that are made before being placed into a structure.
prefabricated houses: Houses that are built in sections or component parts in a plant and then assembled at the site.
prefabricated metal fireplace: A steel fireplace unit that includes the inner hearth and fire chamber, throat, damper, smoke shelf, and smoke chamber. (25)
preframed panels: Fabricated panels consisting of precut lumber and plywood manufactured to standard dimensions ready for structural use.
prehung units: Jambs assembled with the door hung and ready for installation.
preliminary estimate: A rough estimate of building costs based on the preliminary design documents. (36)
presentation drawing: A pictorial or elevation drawing used to show laypeople what a finished structure will look like. (27)
presentation model: A model constructed to show the appearance of the finished building as realistically as possible. (28)
preservation: A type of renovation that concentrates on stabilizing and preserving the original materials and structures of a building. (13)
preservative: Any substance that, for a reasonable length of time, will prevent the action of wood-destroying fungi, various kinds of borers, and similar destructive agents when the wood has been properly coated or impregnated with it.
primitives: 3D objects such as boxes, cones, and spheres that can be placed together to construct 3D models. (5)
project: In parametric modeling software, a file that stores all of the model geometry and views associated with the model. (12)
project template: In parametric modeling software, a file configured with predefined settings, model content and views that can be applied to a new project. (12)
property lines: The lines that define the boundaries of a building site or plot of land. (16)
proportion: Size relationship of one part to another, or to the whole object. (4)
purlins: Horizontal roof members laid over trusses to support rafters.

Q

quarter round: A small molding that has the cross section of a quarter circle.
quarter-sawed lumber: Lumber that has been sawed so that the medullary rays showing on the end grain are nearly perpendicular to the face of the lumber.
quoins: Stone or other building materials set in the corners of masonry sections of a house for appearance.

R

rabbet: A groove cut along the edge of a board producing an L-shaped strip; used as trim and for jointery in cabinet construction.

radial system: A ductwork system in which round ducts radiate in all directions from the furnace. (34)

radiant heat: Heat that passes through the air with no assistance from air flow. (25)

radiant heating: A method of heating usually consisting of a forced hot water system with pipes placed in the floor, wall, or ceiling; electrically heated panels may also be used.

radiant stove: A stove that warms a room using radiant heat only. (25)

radiant system: A hydronic heating system that utilizes copper pipes or other type of tubing embedded in a concrete floor or plastered ceiling.

radon: An invisible, odorless, tasteless, radioactive gas produced by the decay of uranium. (10)

radon mitigation: The process of reducing radon levels in a building. (10)

rafter: A roof framing member that is perpendicular to the top wall plate and extends from the ridge of the roof to the plate or beyond. (17)

rails: The horizontal members that separate panels in a panel door. (21)

rake: The extension of a gable roof beyond the end wall of the house; also called a *gable end*. (17)

ranch: A long, low, one-story house that developed from the homes built by ranchers in the southwestern United States.

random rubble: Stonework having irregular shaped units and no indication of systematic courses.

rear elevation: In architectural drawing, the rear view of an object.

receptacle outlet: A general-purpose device that allows electricity to be drawn off an electric circuit for various purposes, such as radios, hair dryers, and chargers for cell phones. Also called a *receptacle*. (29)

reclaiming: Salvaging materials instead of throwing them away when they have fulfilled their purpose. (11)

recycling: Processing or reprocessing used materials or waste to make them usable again, either for the same purpose or a different purpose. (11)

redwood: Light to deep reddish-brown softwood; mill products include sash, doors, blinds, siding, and trim; commonly used for garden furniture and exterior decking.

register: An outlet cover that includes a damper that can be used to regulate air flow; used only for supply air. (34)

regular polygon: An object with sides of equal length and equal interior angles.

reinforcement bars (rebar): Steel bars used to reinforce concrete. (18)

relative coordinates: Point locations measured from a previous point. (5)

relative humidity: The ratio of water vapor in the air to the amount required to saturate the air at a given temperature. (33)

relays: Electrically operated switches.

remodeling: Changing an existing space into a new form. (13)

rendering: A full-color presentation drawing created by adding materials, surface textures, and lights to a 3D model. (5, 27)

renewable energy source: A source of energy that can supply electricity or other forms of energy from continually replenished sources. (11)

renovation: The process of returning a run-down home or structure to a desirable condition. (13)

residential building designer: A specialist who is familiar with the complex process of planning and designing a residential structure while complying with local ordinances and building codes. (3)

resistivity: The ability of a material to resist the transfer of heat or cold. Also called the *R-factor* or *R-value*. (33)

resolution: Term referring to the sharpness of the display on a computer monitor.

restoration: A type of renovation that involves returning a home to the "look and feel" of its original state, often by employing new or improved materials. (13)

résumé: A document that summarizes your job qualifications, experience, and education. (3)

retaining wall: A wall that holds back an earth embankment.

reverse osmosis system: A water treatment system in which line pressure forces water through a thin, semipermeable membrane that removes contaminants; the purified water is collected in a small storage tank, while the contaminants that were unable to pass through the membrane are drained away. (31)

R-factor: A common term for resistivity, the ability of a material to resist the transfer of heat or cold. (33)

rheostat: An instrument used for regulating electric current.

ribbon: A horizontal member notched into the studs to support the joists on the second floor level in balloon framing with solid sill construction. (19)

ribbon windows: Wide, short windows often used on the first-floor level to provide added privacy.

ridge: The top edge of the roof where two slopes meet.

ridge board: The board placed on edge at the ridge of the roof into which the upper ends of the rafters are fastened.

right side elevation: In architectural drawing, the right side view of an object.

rigid paving system: A paving system with a well-compacted subgrade, a properly prepared base, a reinforced concrete slab, a mortar setting bed, and pavers with mortar joints between them. (18)

rim joist: A framing member resting on the sill, placed perpendicular to the floor joists and to which the floor joists are attached. Another term for *band joist*. (19)

riprap: A sustaining wall or foundation of random stone that is used to prevent erosion on an embankment.

rise: The distance from the top surface of one stair tread to the same position on the next tread. Also, the vertical distance measured from the top of the wall plate to the underside of the rafters. (17, 24)

riser: A vertical face that runs from one tread to the next in a stairway. Not all stairways have risers. (24)

Romanticism: A social movement in the early 1800s that focused on nature, antiquity, emotion, individuality, democracy, and art. (1)

roof framing plan: A drawing that shows the exterior roof lines and the size and location of all roof framing members; included to clarify construction information associated with the roof. (6, 17)

roof pitch: The relationship between the rise and clear span of the roof. (17)

roof plan: A separate plan that may be needed in a set of working drawings if the roof of the structure is intricate and not clearly shown by the standard drawings. (6, 17)

roof sheathing: Material such as plywood or boards placed over the rafters to support the roofing material. (17)

roof slope: The slant of the roof. (17)

roof truss: An assembly of members that form a rigid framework of triangular shapes to support a roof. (17)

rough opening: The rough framed space in a wall required to install the window or door.

round: A smoothly fitted external arc of a specified radius between two lines, arcs, or circles. (5)

rubble stonework: Stonework made up of undressed stones of irregular shapes. (20)

run: One-half the distance of the clear span. Also, the distance from the face of one riser in a stairway to the face of the next riser. (17, 24)

R-value: A unit of measure that indicates the effectiveness of an insulating material used in a building. (13)

S

saddle: A built-up area on the high side of a roof next to the chimney to shed water and prevent it from seeping under the shingles. Also called a *cricket*. (25)

safe room: A room within a house that is constructed to withstand tornado-force winds. (10)

salt box: Colonial style house patterned after early cracker, coffee, tea, and salt boxes.

sash: Part of a window that slides up and down in grooves formed in the window frame; holds one or more panes of glass. (21)

sash opening: The size of the opening inside the frame or the outside dimensions of the sash.

schedule: A list of all items of a specific type that are needed for construction. (12)

scratch coat: The first stucco layer in the three-coat stucco system, which covers the lath and provides support for the second coat; also called the *foundation coat*. (20)

screed: A long straightedge, usually a board, that is worked back and forth across the surface of newly poured concrete to bring excess water to the surface and settle the aggregate. (18)

screed board: A board attached to the inside of the foundation wall to serve as an elevation guide for the basement floor slab. (18)

scuttle: A small opening in a ceiling that provides access to an attic or roof.

secondary stack: A soil stack in a residential water and waste removal system that does not drain toilets. (31)

section: A rectangular area of land used in the survey system that is approximately one mile square.

section lines: A pattern of lines used to show that a feature has been sectioned. (4)

section view: A view that shows an object or structure as if part of it had been cut away to expose the features inside. (4)

seismic area: An area that is known to be prone to earthquakes. Also called an *earthquake zone*. (10)

semi-volatile organic compounds (SVOCs): Chemicals that contain carbon compounds that vaporize slowly at room temperature, so they are released over a longer period than VOCs. (11)

septic system: A private sewage disposal system used at rural or isolated home sites that cannot be connected to public sewers. (31)

septic tank: The tank in a septic system that receives sewage from the house sewer, removes solids, and discharges liquid sewage into the disposal field. (31)

service area: The part of the house where food is prepared, clothes are laundered, goods are stored, the car is parked, and equipment for upkeep of the house is stored. (7)

service drop: The overhead service conductors between the last utility pole and the first point of attachment to a house. (29)

service entrance: The fittings and conductors that bring electricity into a building. (29)

service entry: An entry that is usually connected to the kitchen; it is designed to be convenient, rather than beautiful. (7)

service panel: The main distribution box that receives the electricity from the external power line and distributes it to various points in the house through individual circuits. Also called a *distribution panel*. (29)

service stairs: A set of stairs intended for heavy and frequent use. (24)

setbacks: Boundaries that establish minimum distances from the property lines where structures cannot be located. (16)

sheathing: The structural covering, usually wood boards or plywood, used over studs or rafters of a structure.

shed roof: A flat roof, slanting in only one direction.

sheet: A layout that contains a title block and a view for printing. (12)

shiplap: Wood sheathing that is rabbeted so that the edges of the boards make a flush joint.

shoe mold: A small mold (trim) used against the baseboard at the floor.

short break line: Thick line used to show where part of an object or structure has been removed to reveal an underlying feature. (4)

shotgun house: A traditional one-story house style from the south that is one room wide, with front and back entrances. Each room opens directly into the next. In today's modified shotgun house, the rooms may open onto a common hallway that has entrances at the front and back of the house. (2)

siding: The finish covering of the outside wall of a frame building, whether made of horizontal weatherboards, vertical boards with battens, shingles, or other material.

sill: For an exterior door, the part of the door jamb at the bottom of the door opening between the two side jambs; designed to drain water away from the door and provide support for the side jambs. In framing, the lowest member of the frame of a structure, which rests on the foundation and supports the floor joists or the studs of the wall. Also called a *sill plate*. (19, 21)

single-face fireplace: A fireplace that has a single opening or can be viewed from one side only. (25)

single-pole switch: A switch that has only two positions (on and off) and serves to open and close the circuit. (29)

site: The parcel of land on which a structure will be built. (6)

site plan: A plan that shows the contours of the building site and the location and orientation of proposed new construction on the property. (16)

skylight: A window located on the roof of a building. (21)

slab construction: A building system in which the walls rest on a foundation with a concrete floor at ground level. (2)

slab foundation: A floor and foundation system constructed with a concrete slab floor. (18)

sleeper: Usually a wood member embedded in concrete, as in a floor, that serves to support and to fasten subfloor or flooring.

sleeping area: The area where the family sleeps, rests, and bathes. (7)

sleeping level: The highest level in a split-level house; contains the bedrooms and bathrooms. (2)

sliding doors: Doors that slide next to each other when opened; often used for large openings. Also called *bypass doors*. (21)

small-appliance circuit: A type of branch circuit used in kitchens where appliances requiring large amounts of current may be used. (29)

small-scale solid model: A model that shows only the exterior shape of a building; used to show space relationships and how a building will fit in with surrounding buildings. (28)

smart meter: An electric meter that can be read remotely by the utility company, eliminating the need to send a utility worker to read the meter once a month. (30)

smoke chamber: The area just above the smoke shelf and damper that directs smoke up and away from the firebox. (25)

smoke detector: A small appliance that gives a loud warning signal or displays a bright strobe light when it detects smoke in the house. (10)

smoke shelf: A horizontal shelf-like structure that deflects cold air flowing down the chimney upward into the rising warm air from the fire. (25)

snap: A function that allows the cursor to "grab onto" certain locations on the screen. (5)

soffit: Usually the underside of an overhanging cornice.

software: A program used to instruct a computer to perform intended tasks.

softwood: Wood produced from coniferous trees; examples include fir, pine, spruce, redwood, and cedar.

soil stack: A vertical drain pipe that collects waste from one or more fixtures in a residential water and waste removal system. (31)

solar collector: Device for trapping the sun's energy.

solar energy: Energy harvested from the sun. (11)

solar harvesting: Collecting solar energy (sunlight) and converting it to electrical power or thermal energy. (11)

solar orientation: The placement of the house on the lot in relation to the sun. (33)

solar radiation: Energy from the sun.

sole plate: The bottom horizontal member of a frame wall, on which the studs rest. (20)

solid blocking: A method of constructing headers for window and door openings in which the header size is increased to completely fill the space from the top of the rough opening to the top plate. (20)

solid modeling: Creating 3D models that have volume, mass, and material characteristics. (5)

space diagram: A drawing or sketch showing the location and arrangement of rooms and areas in a building. (14)

special-purpose entry: An entry that provides access to a patio, deck, or courtyard. (7)

special-purpose outlet: An outlet used for telephone and cable connections, burglar or fire alarm systems, or other electrical needs. (29)

special-purpose room: A room that is dedicated to a special interest, such as music, art, or hobbies. Home offices are also considered special-purpose rooms. (7)

special-shape window: A fixed window that is in a made-to-order shape and size.

specific section: A building section that shows a feature, method, or technique that is specific to one location or instance in the building. (22)

specifications: Written documents that supplement the drawings in a set of architectural plans by providing additional written information about the types of construction materials, products, work to be completed, and quality of construction involved in building the home. (6)

specifications writer: A person who prepares all the written information needed to describe materials, methods, and fixtures to be used in a structure. (3)

spiral stairs: A stairway with steps that rise like a corkscrew about a center point. (24)

split bedroom plan: A house plan in which the master bedroom is separated from the remaining bedrooms. (8)

split-entry: A type of split-level house that has two livable levels separated by the entrance's foyer stairway. (2)

split-level: A house design developed to solve the problem of a sloping site by shifting floor level areas to accommodate the site. (2)

spruce: Pale yellowish softwood used for general building purposes as planks, dimension stock, and joists; millwork products include doors, sash, casing, and trim.

square: A unit of measurement of 100 square feet; usually applied to roofing material.

square foot: The US architectural standard of measurement of a 1′ × 1′ area; abbreviated ft^2 or sq. ft. (2)

square foot method: A method of building cost estimation based on the number of square feet in a proposed house design. (36)

stack vent: A vertical extension of the soil stack above the highest horizontal fixture drain connected to the stack; protrudes about 12″ above the roof. (31)

stack wall: A wall that is constructed thick enough to contain 4″ pipes and vents in a residential plumbing system. Also called a *plumbing wall.* (31)

stairway: A series of steps installed between two or more floors of a building. (24)

standard module: In modular construction, a 4″ cube.

station point (SP): The location of the observer's eye in a perspective drawing. (26)

steel framing: The use of steel instead of wood for the complete framework of a residential structure.

stem wall: A type of foundation wall typically used in a crawl space foundation or slab foundation to support the above-grade walls. (18)

stepped footing: A footing that follows the slope on a hilly terrain in a stair-step pattern of horizontal and vertical portions. (18)

stick-built: Term used to describe residential structures that have been built by fastening together thousands of small pieces, such as boards and bricks, on the job site.

stiles: The vertical members that separate panels in a panel door. (21)

stool: The horizontal ledge or strip used as part of the frame below an interior window.

storage devices: A device that saves computer data for later use by placing the data on storage media; the computer hard drive in a PC is a storage device with self-contained media.

storm surge: A dome of ocean water fueled by a hurricane that can be 20′ at its highest point and up to 100 miles wide. When a storm surge sweeps ashore, it can demolish entire communities. (10)

straight run stairs: A stairway that has no turns. (24)

straight-line kitchen: A kitchen in which all of the work centers are located on a single wall. (9)

stretcher course: A row of masonry in a wall with the long side of the units exposed to the exterior.

stringer: A structural member that supports the treads and risers on a stairway. (24)

structural C: The predominant steel component used for floor joists, wall studs, roof rafters, and ceiling joists in residential construction. (20)

structural insulated panels: Structural members that combine two outer "skins" and an insulating foam core into a single unit for framing applications. (20)

structural model: A model that shows the construction features of a residence. (28)

stucco: A coating applied to the outside of a structure that forms a protective, low-maintenance, yet decorative shell around the structure; consists of Portland cement, lime, sand, and water. (20)

stud: A vertical wall framing member.

subfloor: The surface, affixed to the floor joists, on which the underlayment for the final finished floor will rest; consists of a panel product such as plywood, tongue-and-groove boards, or common boards. (19)

subgrade: A fill or earth surface on which concrete is placed.

sump: A pit in a basement floor that collects water and into which a sump pump is placed to remove the water.

sump pump: A pump that removes water that has collected in a sump pit. (13)

sun space: A type of isolated gain system; also called an *attached greenhouse*.

surface modeling: Creating 3D models by drawing a skin or covering over a wireframe model. (5)

survey: A description of the measure and marking of land, including maps and field notes that describe the property.

suspended ceiling: A ceiling system supported by hanging from the overhead structural framing.

sustainability: Meeting the needs of humans for food, housing, and other needs and wants, while having no negative effects on the environment. (11)

sustainable building: A building that can be built, used for a long time, and then reused or recycled without having any negative effects on the environment. (11)

symbol library: A drawing file that contains a collection of blocks or symbols that are typically related, such as plumbing, bathroom, or electrical symbols. (5)

T

tail beam: A relatively short beam or joist supported in a wall on one end and by a header at the other.

take-home pay: Earnings after taxes and other deductions have been subtracted.

teamwork: Working closely with others toward a common goal. (3)

template: A guide used to draw standard symbols and features. (4)

termite shield: A shield, usually of noncorrosive metal, placed in or on a foundation wall or other mass of masonry or around pipes to prevent passage of termites.

terrazzo flooring: Wear-resistant flooring made of marble chips or small stones embedded in concrete and polished smooth.

T-foundation: A foundation wall and footing combination, constructed as two separate parts or cast as a single unit. (18)

thermal lag: The principle in which structures with a large thermal mass, such as concrete structures, are able to delay the transfer of heat due to the heat storage capacity of the building mass; the basis for passive solar systems.

thermal mass: A material that can store large amounts of heat, such as stone, masonry, or concrete.

thermostat: An automatic sensing device that sends a signal to activate a furnace or air conditioner at a temperature set by the homeowner. (33)

three-coat stucco system: The traditional method of applying stucco that consists of a scratch coat, brown coat, and finish coat of stucco. (20)

three-face fireplace: A fireplace that is open on three sides. (25)

three-way switch: A switch that allows a fixture to be turned on and off from two different locations. (29)

threshold: A strip of wood or metal with beveled edges used over the finish floor and the sill of exterior doors.

title: A legal document that provides evidence of property ownership. (6)

title search: An examination of the title to a property to determine whether there are any legal claims against the property. (6)

topographical features: All existing natural and human-made structures on a property, including trees, shrubs, streams, ponds, roads, utilities, and fences. (16)

topographical surface: The site component in a parametric model. (16)

topography: The physical characteristics of the land on a site. (6)

tornado: A swirling column of air extending from a thunderstorm cloud down to the ground.

total rise: The total floor-to-floor height of a stairway. (24)

total run: The total horizontal length of a stairway. (24)

townhouse: A two- to four-story house connected to one or more similar houses by a common wall. Townhouses are also known as rowhouses. (1)

tracking: An alignment feature that allows you to align new geometry with objects that already exist in the drawing. (5)

tract: A specified area of land.

tradework specifications: Criteria governing the work to be completed and its quality.

traffic circulation: The movement of people from one area or room to another. (7)

transom: A window placed above a door or permanent window that is hinged for ventilation purposes.

transom bar: A horizontal divider in an awning window.

transverse building section: A building section taken crosswise across the shorter overall dimension of a building. (22)

transverse method: A method of roof beam placement in post and beam construction in which the beams follow the roof slope and decking runs parallel to the roof ridge. (19)

trap: A pipe fitting installed below each fixture and filled with water to block the reverse flow of gases into the house. (31)

tread: A horizontal member of a stairway that constitutes the step (surface) on which a person walks. (24)

trim: The finish materials in a building, such as moldings, applied around openings (window trim, door trim) or at the floor and ceiling of rooms (baseboard, cornice).

trimmer: A structural member positioned inside a wall opening to help support the header over the opening; also called a *jack stud*. (20)

trowel: A rectangular instrument that is used in a circular motion after concrete is floated to further harden the surface and develop a smooth finish. (18)

troweling: The finishing operation that produces a smooth, hard surface on a concrete slab.

true height line (THL): The line established where the object touches the picture plane in a perspective drawing. The THL is used to project heights to the perspective drawing. Also called a *true length line (TL)*. (26)

truss: A system of structural members arranged and fastened in triangular units to form a rigid framework for support of loads over a long span.

two-face adjacent fireplace: A fireplace that is open on the front and one side. Also called a *projecting corner fireplace*. (25)

two-face opposite fireplace: A fireplace that is open on both the front and back sides. (25)

two-point perspective drawing: A perspective drawing that has two vanishing points: a right vanishing point (RVP) and a left vanishing point (LVP). (26)

two-story: A house design that has living space on two full levels. (2)

typical section: A building section that shows features or sizes that are used in many different places in the structure. (22)

U

U stairs: A stairway that has two flights of steps parallel to each other with a landing between them. (24)

U-factor: The number of Btus transmitted in one hour through one square foot of a building material for each degree of temperature difference; calculated by taking the reciprocal of the material's resistivity (R-factor). (33)

uncoursed cobweb: Rubble stonework in which the stones are dressed with relatively straight edges to fit a particular place in the pattern, but still give a rubble, not ashlar, appearance; also called *polygonal rubble*. (20)

underlayment: A material placed under finish coverings, such as flooring or shingles, to provide a smooth, even surface for applying the finish.

universal design: A design approach concerned with meeting the needs of all people regardless of age, health, or ability. (7)

upflow furnace: A furnace designed for basement installation, with the plenum on top of the furnace. (33)

U-shaped kitchen: A kitchen in which the work centers are located on three adjoining walls, in a U shape. (9)

V

valley: The internal angle formed by the junction of two sloping sides of a roof.

valley rafter: The diagonal rafter at the intersection of two intersecting sloping roofs.

vanishing points: The points at which all lines on an object in a perspective drawing will converge if they are extended. (26)

vanity: A cabinet that encloses a sink. (8)

veneer: Extremely thin sheets of wood produced by slicing or rotary cutting a log.

veneer construction: Type of wall construction in which frame or masonry walls are faced with other exterior surfacing materials.

vent stack: A vertical soil pipe connected to the drainage system to allow ventilation and pressure equalization. (31)

ventilation: The circulation of fresh air, especially within a closed space. (10, 33)

verandah: A large porch that typically extends along an entire wall of a residence. (7)

VHA Master Specifications: A set of master specifications provided by the Department of Veterans Affairs and accepted by major lenders for construction loans. (35)

Victorian period: The general name for an architectural period during the Industrial Revolution. In this period, architects made use of new technology by designing and constructing extremely ornate residences. (1)

video card: The device that transmits data from the central processing unit (CPU) to the monitor.

view range: In parametric modeling software, range of cutting planes that define the visibility range of objects in a plan view. (12)

view template: In parametric modeling software, a configuration of display, visibility, and graphics settings for a view. (12)

virtual model: A model constructed entirely within a computer.

volatile organic compounds (VOCs): Chemicals that contain carbon compounds that vaporize at room temperature. (11)

volt: A unit of measure defined as the force that causes one ampere of current to flow through a wire that has one ohm of resistance. (29)

voltage: The pressure that forces electric current to flow through a wire conductor. (29)

W

wainscot: Surfacing on the lower part of an interior wall when finished differently from the remainder of the wall.

walkout basement: A daylight basement with the addition of an entry that allows access to the outdoors. (2)

walkthrough animation: A computer animation that allows prospective clients to "walk through" a 3D model of a proposed house. (28)

wall section: A building section that shows details on one exterior wall. (22)

wall stack: A vertical duct designed to fit between the studs; usually measures 12″ × 3-1/4″. (34)

wall tie: A small metal strip or steel wire used to bind tiers of masonry in cavity wall and veneer construction.

warm air solar system: An active solar heating system that contains an array or group of collectors, called a bank; a heat storage box filled with stones or other thermal mass; and one or more blowers with controls for operating the system.

warm water solar system: An active solar heating system that is composed of a bank of collectors, a warm water storage tank, a pump to circulate the water, some form of heat exchange device in the living space, and controls for operating the system.

warped roof: A roof with complex curvature; the most common shape is a hyperbolic paraboloid. (17)

water closet: Another term for *toilet*; often abbreviated WC on floor plans. (8)

water conditioner: A device used to remove dissolved minerals from water to make it soft; generally used in houses supplied by well water, which may contain calcium, magnesium, and other minerals, to remove hardness that causes scale buildup in plumbing.

water hammer: A condition that occurs when a valve suddenly closes and the increased pressure is absorbed by the supply piping, resulting in a loud noise. (31)

water softener: A water treatment system that uses line pressure to push hard water through a canister filled with a synthetic resin, where ion exchange is performed to soften the water. (31)

water vapor: Water in its gaseous state. (10)

watt: A unit of measure used to describe the energy (electrical) needs of appliances. One watt is equal to one ampere under one volt of pressure (amperes × volts = watts). (29)

weather stripping: A material or device that seals small cracks around doors and movable windows to reduce heat loss. (33)

weatherization: Preventing air from leaking around the windows and doors in a building. (11)

web: The framework between the chords in a floor truss. (19)

weep hole: An opening at the bottom of a wall that allows the drainage of water.

well hole: The space between flights of stairs in wide U stairs. (24)

wide box cornice with lookouts: A cornice that normally requires additional support members, called lookouts, for fastening the soffit.

wide box cornice without lookouts: A cornice that has a sloped soffit; the soffit material is nailed to the underside of the rafters.

wide U stairs: A set of U stairs that have a well hole between each flight.

winder stairs: A stairway in which pie-shaped steps are substituted for a landing. (24)

window schedule: A list of all of the windows to be installed in a building, including complete specifications. (21)

wireframe: A group of lines in 3D space that represent the edges of a 3D model. Wireframe models have no thickness and no "skin" or covering. (5)

wood foundation: A foundation that consists of a below-grade, plywood-sheathed, pressure-treated stud wall. (18)

wood I-joist: A structural member made from 2 × 4 machine-stressed lumber or LVL flanges grooved to receive a 3/8″ OSB or plywood web that is glued in place. (19)

work breakdown structure (WBS): A formal listing of construction information by category; used to make building estimates more organized and easier to understand. (36)

work centers: The three main areas of activity in a kitchen: the food preparation center, cleanup center, and cooking center. (9)

work ethic: A practice of behavior that includes enthusiasm for the work, willingness to work late to meet deadlines, and preparedness to work at starting time.

work triangle: A measure of kitchen efficiency that is determined by drawing a line from the front-center of the range to the refrigerator, from the refrigerator to the sink, and then from the sink back to the range. The sum of the lengths of these three lines should not exceed 21′ in an efficient kitchen. (9)

working drawings: A set of architectural drawings that contain all of the drawings and related specifications required to bid on and construct a building. (4, 6)

workplace skills: Employability skills related to keeping a job and advancing in a career. (3)

wythe: A continuous vertical section of masonry one unit in thickness.

X

xeriscaping: Landscaping using only native plants or plants that are appropriate for the local climate and ecosystem. (11)

Z

zoning: A planning tool used by communities to restrict the kinds of structures built in various areas. (6)

Index

B

C

D

E

F

H

I

J

K

N

O

P

Q

R

S